ARCTIC OCEAN 266
pe 140-171
RUSSIA 168
SWEDEN
FINLAND
NORWAY
EST.
LATV.
LITH.
POLAND
BELARUS
EASTERN EUROPE 166
WEST CENTRAL EUROPE 156
EAST CENTRAL EUROPE 158
CZECH REP.
GER.
SLOVAKIA
UKRAINE
MOLDOVA
SWITZ.
AUST.
HUNG.
ROM.
SLOV.
CROATIA
BALKAN PENINSULA 162
BOSN. & HERZG.
SERB.
BULG.
MONT.
KOS.
MACED.
ALBAN.
ITALY 160
GREECE
GREECE AND THE AEGEAN 164
MALTA
TUNISIA
GEORGIA
ARM.
AZERB.
ASIA MINOR AND TRANSCAUCASIA 180
TURKEY
CYPRUS
SYRIA
IRAQ
LEB.
ISRAEL
EASTERN MEDITERRANEAN 182
JORDAN
IRAQ AND KUWAIT 186
KUWAIT
IRAN 188
KAZAKHSTAN
CENTRAL ASIA 192
UZBEKISTAN
TURKMENISTAN
KYRGYZSTAN
TAJIKISTAN
AFGHANISTAN
AFGHANISTAN AND PAKISTAN 190
PAKISTAN
MONGOLIA
CHINA AND MONGOLIA 196
CHINA
KOREAN PENINSULA 200
NORTH KOREA
SOUTH KOREA
JAPAN 202
EASTERN CHINA 198
Asia 172-207
NEPAL
BHUTAN
SOUTH ASIA 194
BANGLADESH
INDIA
SRI LANKA
MALDIVES
MYANMAR
LAOS
PENINSULAR SOUTHEAST ASIA 204
THAILAND
VIETNAM
CAMBODIA
PHILIPPINES
BRUNEI
MALAYSIA
SINGAPORE
INSULAR SOUTHEAST ASIA 206
INDONESIA
TIMOR-LESTE
PAPUA NEW GUINEA 240
PACIFIC OCEAN 262
Northern Mariana Islands
Guam
PALAU
FEDERATED STATES OF MICRONESIA
MARSHALL ISLANDS
OCEANIA 244-249
NAURU
KIRIBATI
SOLOMON ISLANDS
TUVALU
VANUATU
FIJI ISLANDS
New Caledonia
AUSTRALIA 234-243
NEW ZEALAND 240
Australia, New Zealand, Oceania 232-249
NORTHERN AFRICA 216
LIBYA
EGYPT
SAUDI ARABIA
BAHRAIN
QATAR
U.A.E.
OMAN
ARABIAN PENINSULA 184
YEMEN
NILE VALLEY 218
SUDAN
ERITREA
DJIBOUTI
ETHIOPIA
SOMALIA
THE HORN AND GREAT RIFT VALLEY 226
Africa 208-231
NIGER
CHAD
WEST CENTRAL AFRICA 222
NIGERIA
CENTRAL AFRICAN REPUBLIC
CAMEROON
CONGO
GABON
DEMOCRATIC REPUBLIC OF THE CONGO
CONGO BASIN 224
UGANDA
KENYA
RWANDA
BURUNDI
TANZANIA
SEYCHELLES
COMOROS
ANGOLA
ZAMBIA
MALAWI
MOZAMBIQUE
ZIMBABWE
MADAGASCAR
MAURITIUS
Réunion
NAMIBIA
BOTSWANA
SWAZILAND
SOUTH AFRICA
LESOTHO
SOUTHERN AFRICA 228
INDIAN OCEAN 264
tarctica 250-253

Selected Other Maps

Key to Atlas Maps

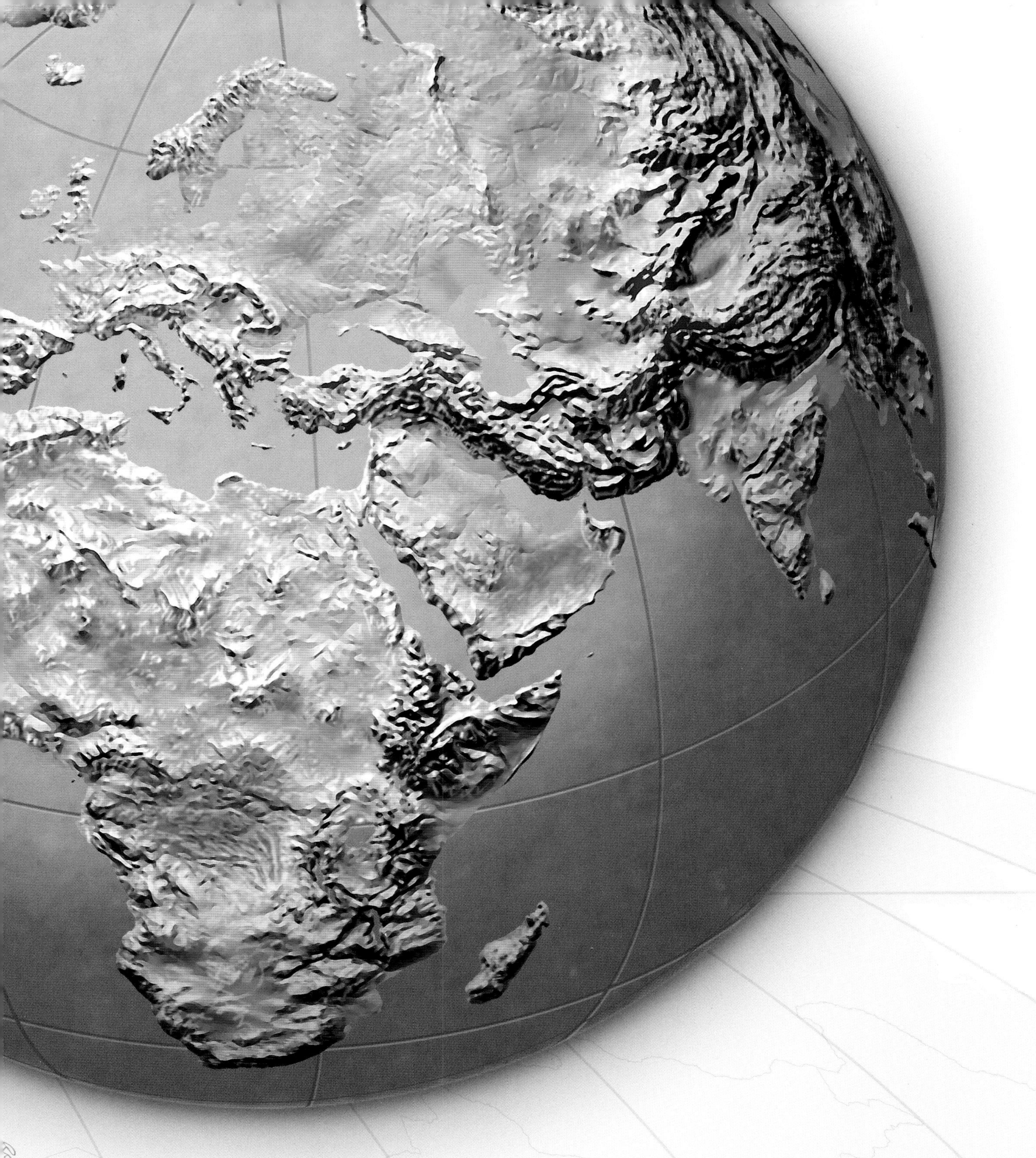

NATIONAL GEOGRAPHIC

VISUAL Atlas of the World

NATIONAL GEOGRAPHIC

VISUAL Atlas of the World

NATIONAL GEOGRAPHIC
WASHINGTON, D.C.

FOUNDED IN 1888, the National Geographic Society is one of the largest nonprofit scientific and educational organizations in the world. It reaches more than 285 million people worldwide each month through its official journal, *National Geographic,* and its four other magazines; the National Geographic Channel; television documentaries; radio programs; films; books; videos and DVDs; maps; and interactive media. National Geographic has funded more than 8,000 scientific research projects and supports an education program combating geographic illiteracy.

For more information, please call 1-800-NGS LINE (647-5463) or write to the following address:

National Geographic Society
1145 17th Street N.W.
Washington, D.C. 20036-4688 U.S.A.

Visit us online at www.nationalgeographic.com/books

NATIONAL GEOGRAPHIC SOCIETY
INCORPORATED A.D. 1888

For information about special discounts for bulk purchases, please contact National Geographic Books Special Sales: ngspecsales@ngs.org

For rights or permissions inquiries, please contact National Geographic Books Subsidiary Rights: ngbookrights@ngs.org

For more information about our award-winning National Geographic atlases, please visit: www.shopng.com/atlases

Library of Congress Cataloging-in-Publication Data

National Geographic Society (U.S.)
National Geographic visual atlas of the world.
p. cm.
Includes bibliographical references and index.
ISBN 978-1-4262-0332-9 (slipcover)
1. Atlases. 2. Physical geography--Maps. I. Title.
G1021.N3 2008
912--dc22
2008627044

Printed in Italy

This atlas was made possible by the contributions of numerous experts and organizations around the world, including the following:

Center for International Earth Science Information Network (CIESIN), Columbia University

Central Intelligence Agency (CIA)

Conservation International

Cooperative Association for Internet Data Analysis (CAIDA)

Global Land Cover Group, University of Maryland

Global Land Cover Project, Boston University

International Energy Agency (IEA)

International Union for Conservation of Nature (IUCN)

Lunar and Planetary Institute

National Aeronautics and Space Administration (NASA)
NASA Ames Research Center,
NASA Goddard Space Flight Center,
NASA Jet Propulsion Laboratory (JPL),
NASA Marshall Space Flight Center

National Geospatial Intelligence Agency (NGIA)

National Oceanic and Atmospheric Administration (NOAA)
National Climatic Data Center,
National Environmental Satellite, Data, and Information Service;
National Geophysical Data Center;
National Ocean Service

National Science Foundation

Population Reference Bureau

Scripps Institution of Oceanography

Sea Around Us Project

Smithsonian Institution

United Nations (UN)
UN Conference on Trade and Development,
UN Development Programme,
UN Educational, Scientific and Cultural Organization (UNESCO),
UN Environment Programme (UNEP),
UN Population Division,
Food and Agriculture Organization (FAO),
International Telecommunication Union (ITU),
World Conservation Monitoring Centre (WCMC)

U.S. Board on Geographic Names

U.S. Department of Agriculture

U.S. Department of Commerce: Bureau of the Census, National Oceanic and Atmospheric Administration

U.S. Department of Energy

U.S. Department of the Interior: Bureau of Land Management, National Park Service, U.S. Geological Survey

U.S. Department of State: Office of the Geographer

World Bank

World Health Organization/Pan American Health Organization (WHO/PAHO)

World Resources Institute (WRI)

World Trade Organization (WTO)

Worldwatch Institute

World Wildlife Fund (WWF)

For a complete listing of contributors, see page 412.

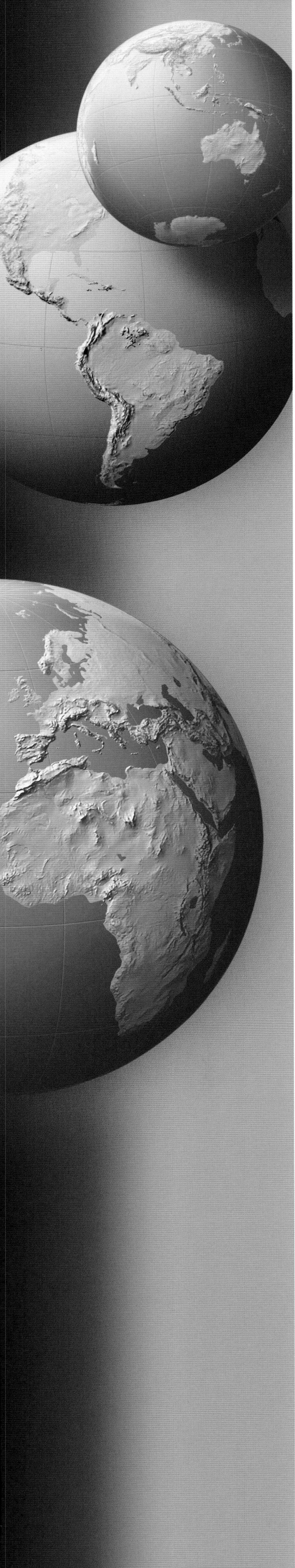

Introduction

"IN WILDNESS IS THE PRESERVATION OF THE WORLD," Henry David Thoreau famously wrote in the mid-1800s. A century later the United Nations took to heart Thoreau's message, but expanded it beyond the natural realm to include the wonders of this world made by human hands as well. The community of nations understood we have a planetary heritage that goes beyond country boundaries and the preoccupations of any given era. Preserving that heritage unites us as a world family. We now have places on Earth called World Heritage sites, places that represent our collective legacy — from the natural grandeur of the Great Barrier Reef to the ethereal beauty of the Taj Mahal, from the alluring antiquity of Moroccan medinas to the majesty of medieval cathedrals.

In the 30 years since the World Heritage designation was established by UNESCO — the United Nations Educational, Scientific and Cultural Organization — we've come to accept it as part of the fabric of international cooperation. But in fact it's a groundbreaking idea. For the first time in history, humanity has banded together to prevent the "deterioration or disappearance of any item of the cultural or natural heritage," knowing that such a loss "constitutes a harmful impoverishment of the heritage of all the nations of the world." Every country in the world has been invited to join in this effort, and as of today, 185 have done so. Scattered across the globe, from the remotest pockets to the largest cities, the number of World Heritage sites—more than 850—continues to grow. Nearly 150 different countries hold "properties" that are dedicated to preservation and recognized on the World Heritage List as cultural, natural, or mixed sites.

The *Visual Atlas of the World* celebrates these worldly treasures in compelling photographs and text, and of course National Geographic's signature cartography. In the following pages regions are covered in a detailed map surrounded by images of some of their most remarkable World Heritage sites. The sites are as surprising and varied as the countries themselves — an ancient walled city, a work of modern architecture, a valley, an island, a necropolis, even an ecosystem or wine-growing region. Smaller regional maps track protected areas, including all World Heritage sites, urbanization trends, and natural land cover. Every map reflects state-of-the-art advances in cartography and geographic data collection and information.

Based on the latest scientific imaging, a paleogeographic spread at the beginning of the atlas sets the stage for what is to come by tracing the long geologic time of Earth and the slow movement of plates across its face. What did Earth look like in the far past and what will it look like in the future? Geologic dynamism, after all, is one of the most distinctive elements of this ever changing planet of ours. But change can also wreak havoc, ruin, and loss, and it was the desire to combat this that inspired the World Heritage designation.

Ironically, the hand of man that created many of these marvels now threatens them through environmental degradation, overuse, and sometimes even willful destruction, as in the Taliban's 2001 demolition of the monumental Buddhas in the Bamiyan Valley of Afghanistan. UNESCO is now working to preserve the Bamiyan ruins and safeguard other sites in the valley, a place that "bears exceptional testimony to a cultural tradition in the Central Asian region, which has disappeared." So much that is now protected under the World Heritage umbrella "bears exceptional testimony" and so much could also disappear, without the continued cooperation and support among nations and peoples. Today, some 30 World Heritage sites are considered endangered.

National Geographic has long been committed to keeping these remarkable places at the forefront of global attention. In 1986 we published a book on World Heritage sites that began with a foreword by then Secretary-General of the UN, Javier Pérez de Cuéllar. Calling for "Earth-patriotism," he wrote, "We must develop a sense of belonging to this earth as a whole. What nature and human hands have wrought should enrich all of us." For more than a century, the National Geographic has advocated Earth-patriotism, and the *Visual Atlas of the World* continues our tradition of covering and celebrating the great cultural, natural, and human diversity of the planet we all call home.

John M. Fahey, Jr.
PRESIDENT AND CHIEF EXECUTIVE OFFICER

Contents

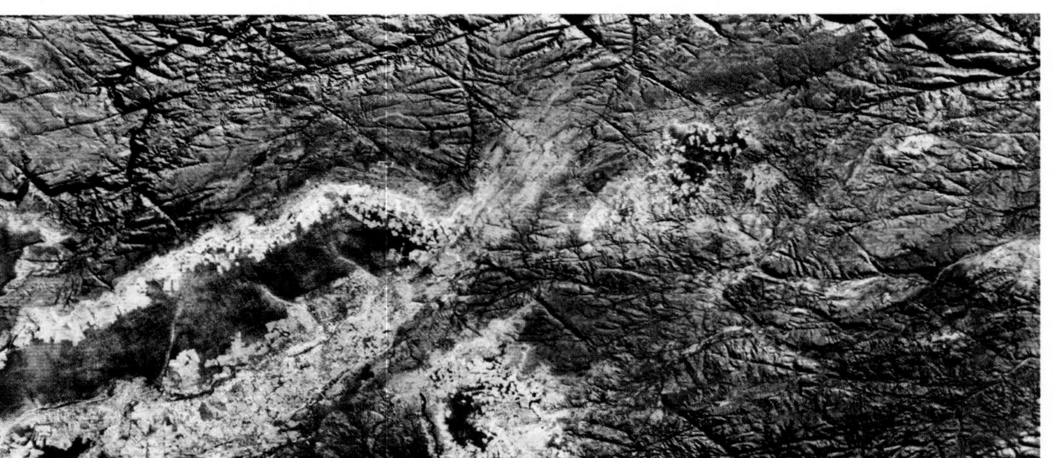

Satellite view of Victoria Falls, Zambezi River, Africa

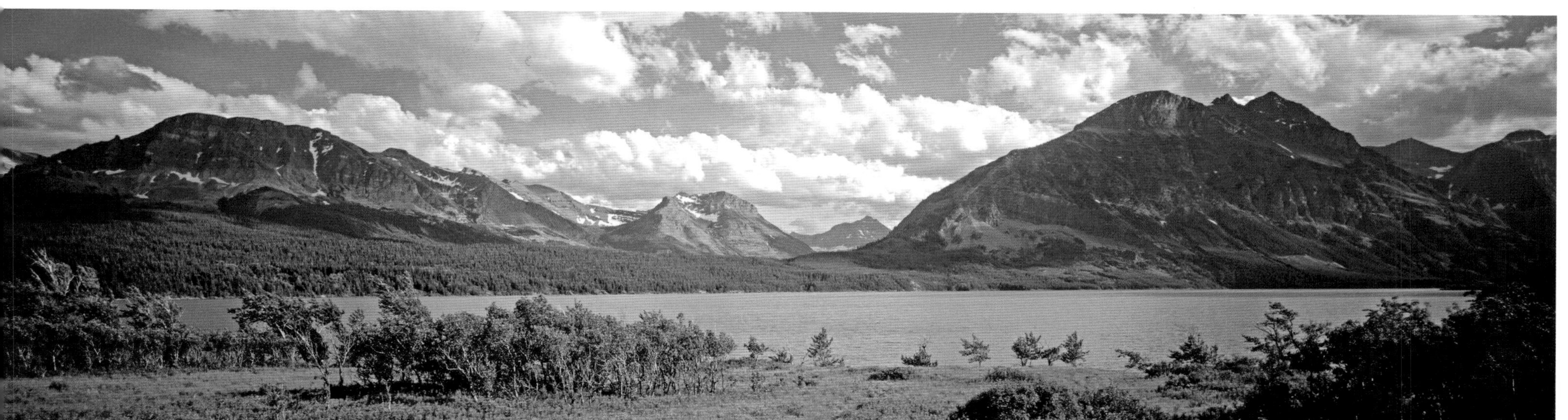
Glacier National Park, British Columbia, Canada

NORTH AMERICA 98

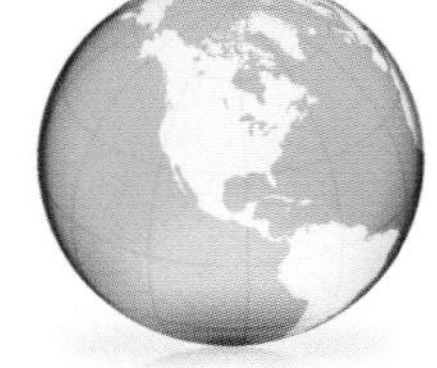

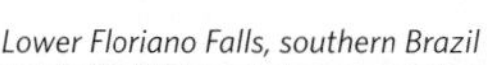
Lower Floriano Falls, southern Brazil

SOUTH AMERICA 124

EUROPE 140

Roman Forum and Colosseum, Rome, Italy

Rice terraces, Guangxi Zhuangzu, China

ASIA 172

AFRICA 208

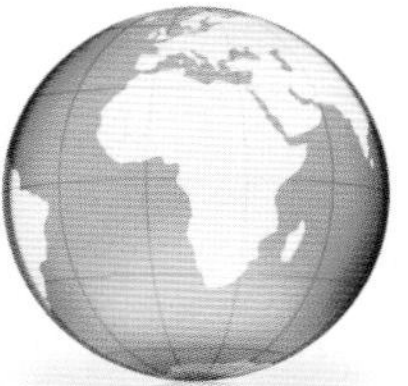

Baobab trees, western Madagascar

AUSTRALIA AND OCEANIA 232

OCEANS 254

Rocky coast of Hastings Point, New South Wales, Australia

ANTARCTICA 250

Signy Island, Antarctica

SPACE 270

FLAGS AND FACTS 284

APPENDIX 304

INDEX 312

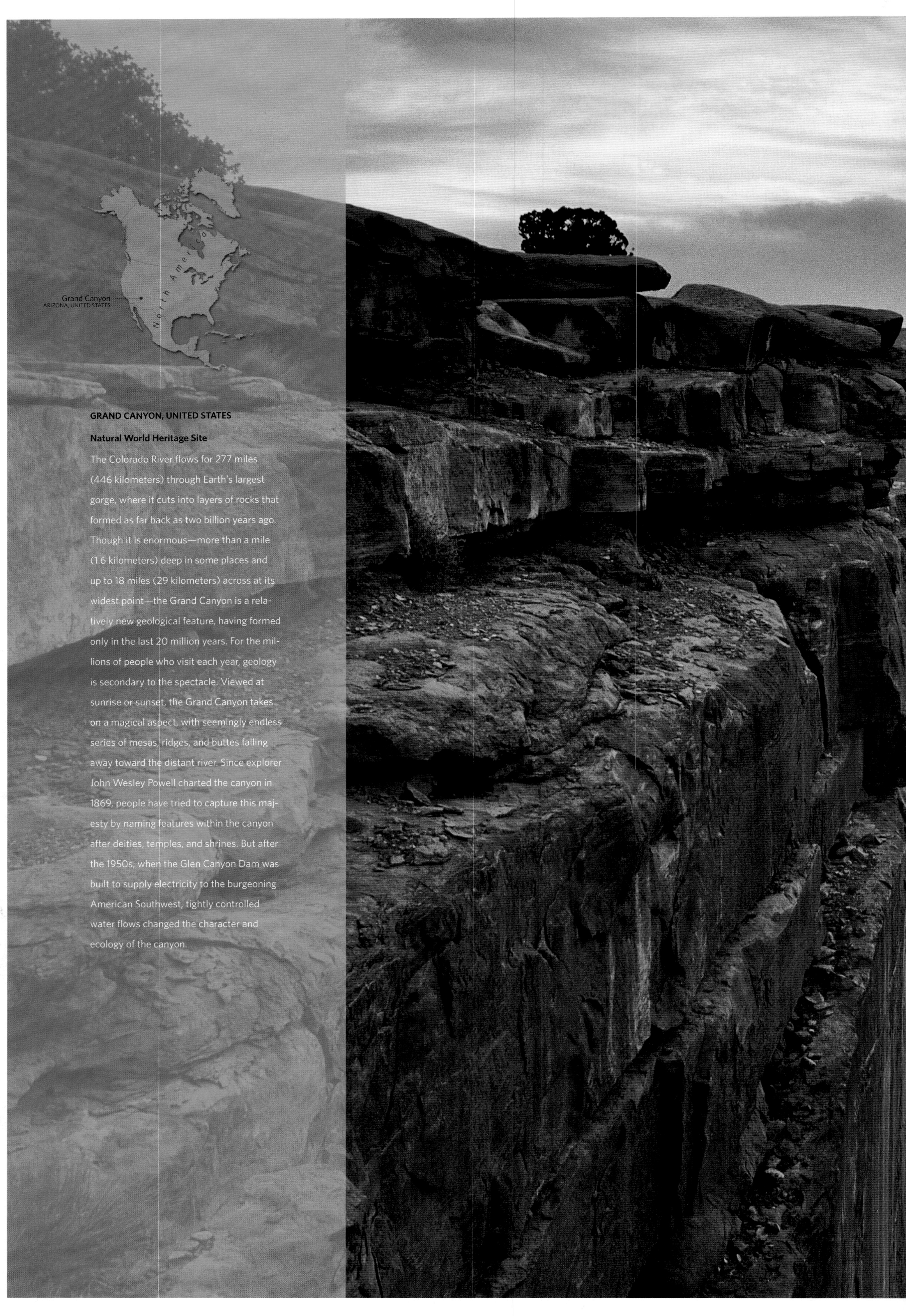
Grand Canyon
ARIZONA, UNITED STATES
North America

GRAND CANYON, UNITED STATES

Natural World Heritage Site

The Colorado River flows for 277 miles (446 kilometers) through Earth's largest gorge, where it cuts into layers of rocks that formed as far back as two billion years ago. Though it is enormous—more than a mile (1.6 kilometers) deep in some places and up to 18 miles (29 kilometers) across at its widest point—the Grand Canyon is a relatively new geological feature, having formed only in the last 20 million years. For the millions of people who visit each year, geology is secondary to the spectacle. Viewed at sunrise or sunset, the Grand Canyon takes on a magical aspect, with seemingly endless series of mesas, ridges, and buttes falling away toward the distant river. Since explorer John Wesley Powell charted the canyon in 1869, people have tried to capture this majesty by naming features within the canyon after deities, temples, and shrines. But after the 1950s, when the Glen Canyon Dam was built to supply electricity to the burgeoning American Southwest, tightly controlled water flows changed the character and ecology of the canyon.

Oceans

A sleek tiger shark, from a species second in size only to the great white among the ranks of predatory sharks, glides past giant kelp in Monterey Bay, California. The world's oceans are the site of a bewildering variety of life as well as dramatic geologic and climatic processes, including (top to bottom): Plunging breaker waves in Waimea Bay, on the north shore of O'ahu, Hawai'i—the often violent type favored by expert surfers—are indicative of steep underwater beach drop-off; Massive thunderstorms pile up over the Atlantic Ocean, gaining energy from warm water off the Florida coast; The slender coral ring of Moruroa, a French Polynesian atoll used for nuclear tests, surrounds a deep blue lagoon; A colorful cornucopia of sea life swarms across a coral reef in the Cayman Islands.

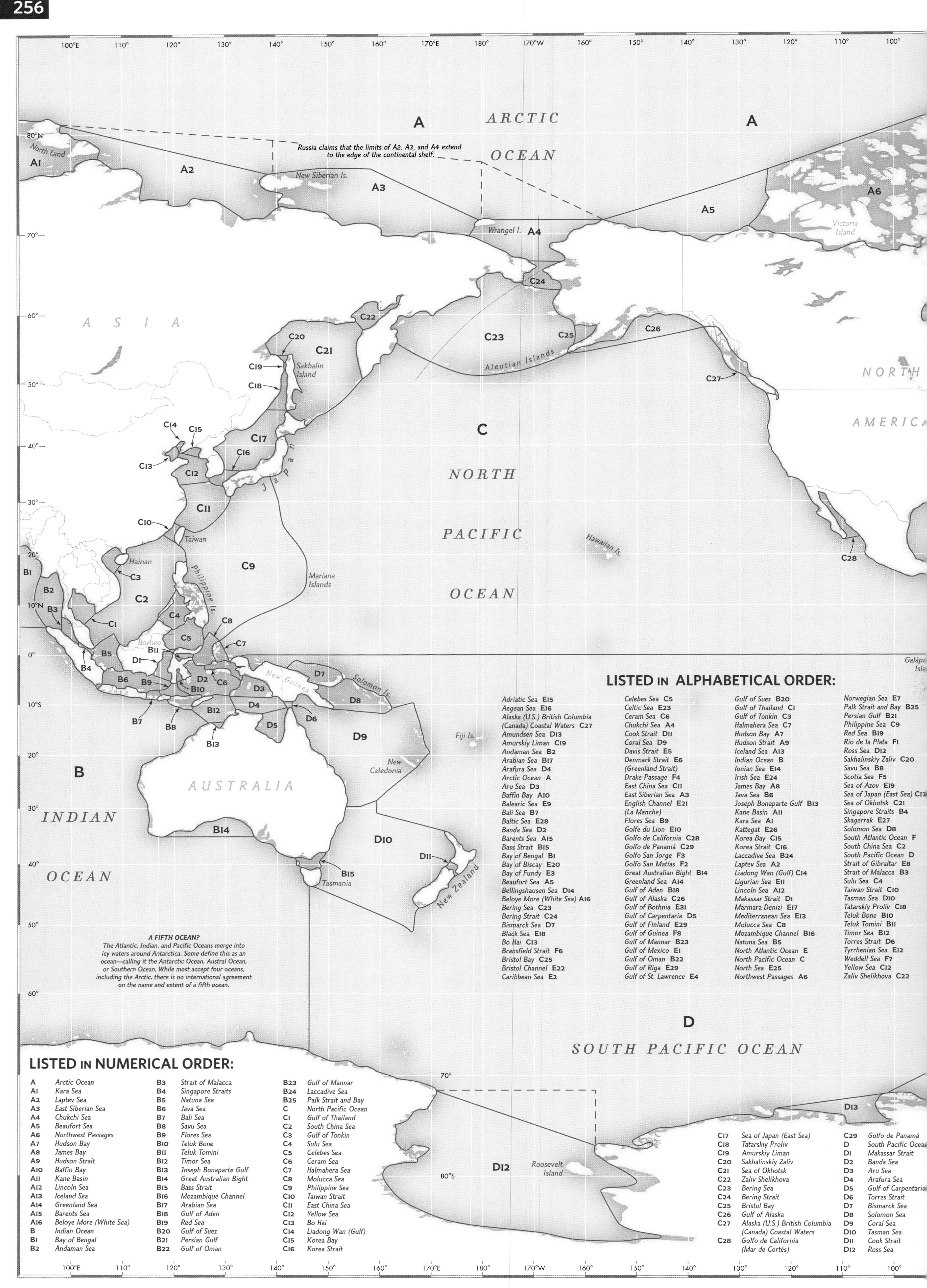

ARCTIC OCEAN
A
Russia claims that the limits of A2, A3, and A4 extend to the edge of the continental shelf.
North Land
A1
A2
New Siberian Is.
A3
Wrangel I.
A4
A5
A6
Victoria Island
ASIA
C24
C22
C20
C21
C23
C25
C26
Sakhalin Island
C19
C18
Aleutian Islands
C27
NORTH AMERICA
C14
C15
C13
C17
C16
C12
C
NORTH PACIFIC OCEAN
Japan
C11
C10
Taiwan
Hawaiian Is.
C28
Hainan
C3
B1
B2
B3
C9
Mariana Islands
C2
Philippine Is.
C1
C4
C8
C5
C7
Borneo
B11
D1
B5
B4
B6
B9
B10
D2
C6
Java
D7
D3
New Guinea
Solomon Is.
D8
D4
D6
B7
B8
B12
D5
B13
D9
Fiji Is.
New Caledonia
B
INDIAN OCEAN
AUSTRALIA
B14
D10
D11
B15
Tasmania
New Zealand
Galápagos Isl.
A FIFTH OCEAN?
The Atlantic, Indian, and Pacific Oceans merge into icy waters around Antarctica. Some define this as an ocean—calling it the Antarctic Ocean, Austral Ocean, or Southern Ocean. While most accept four oceans, including the Arctic, there is no international agreement on the name and extent of a fifth ocean.
D
SOUTH PACIFIC OCEAN
D13
D12
Roosevelt Island
80°N
70°
60°
50°
40°
30°
20°
10°N
0°
10°S
20°
30°
40°
50°
60°
70°
80°S
100°E
110°
120°
130°
140°
150°
160°
170°E
180°
170°W
160°
150°
140°
130°
120°
110°
100°
LISTED IN ALPHABETICAL ORDER:
Adriatic Sea E15
Aegean Sea E16
Alaska (U.S.) British Columbia (Canada) Coastal Waters C27
Amundsen Sea D13
Amurskiy Liman C19
Andaman Sea B2
Arabian Sea B17
Arafura Sea D4
Arctic Ocean A
Aru Sea D3
Baffin Bay A10
Balearic Sea E9
Bali Sea B7
Baltic Sea E28
Banda Sea D2
Barents Sea A15
Bass Strait B15
Bay of Bengal B1
Bay of Biscay E20
Bay of Fundy E3
Beaufort Sea A5
Bellingshausen Sea D14
Beloye More (White Sea) A16
Bering Sea C23
Bering Strait C24
Bismarck Sea D7
Black Sea E18
Bo Hai C13
Bransfield Strait F6
Bristol Bay C25
Bristol Channel E22
Caribbean Sea E2
Celebes Sea C5
Celtic Sea E23
Ceram Sea C6
Chukchi Sea A4
Cook Strait D11
Coral Sea D9
Davis Strait E5
Denmark Strait E6 (Greenland Strait)
Drake Passage F4
East China Sea C11
East Siberian Sea A3
English Channel E21 (La Manche)
Flores Sea B9
Golfe du Lion E10
Golfo de California C28
Golfo de Panamá C29
Golfo San Jorge F3
Golfo San Matías F2
Great Australian Bight B14
Greenland Sea A14
Gulf of Aden B18
Gulf of Alaska C26
Gulf of Bothnia E31
Gulf of Carpentaria D5
Gulf of Finland E29
Gulf of Guinea F8
Gulf of Mannar B23
Gulf of Mexico E1
Gulf of Oman B22
Gulf of Riga E29
Gulf of St. Lawrence E4
Gulf of Suez B20
Gulf of Thailand C1
Gulf of Tonkin C3
Halmahera Sea C7
Hudson Bay A7
Hudson Strait A9
Iceland Sea A13
Indian Ocean B
Ionian Sea E14
Irish Sea E24
James Bay A8
Java Sea B6
Joseph Bonaparte Gulf B13
Kane Basin A11
Kara Sea A1
Kattegat E26
Korea Bay C15
Korea Strait C16
Laccadive Sea B24
Laptev Sea A2
Liadong Wan (Gulf) C14
Ligurian Sea E11
Lincoln Sea A12
Makassar Strait D1
Marmara Denizi E17
Mediterranean Sea E13
Molucca Sea C8
Mozambique Channel B16
Natuna Sea B5
North Atlantic Ocean E
North Pacific Ocean C
North Sea E25
Northwest Passages A6
Norwegian Sea E7
Palk Strait and Bay B25
Persian Gulf B21
Philippine Sea C9
Red Sea B19
Río de la Plata F1
Ross Sea D12
Sakhalinskiy Zaliv C20
Savu Sea B8
Scotia Sea F5
Sea of Azov E19
Sea of Japan (East Sea) C1
Sea of Okhotsk C21
Singapore Straits B4
Skagerrak E27
Solomon Sea D8
South Atlantic Ocean F
South China Sea C2
South Pacific Ocean D
Strait of Gibraltar E8
Strait of Malacca B3
Sulu Sea C4
Taiwan Strait C10
Tasman Sea D10
Tatarskiy Proliv C18
Teluk Bone B10
Teluk Tomini B11
Timor Sea B12
Torres Strait D6
Tyrrhenian Sea E12
Weddell Sea F7
Yellow Sea C12
Zaliv Shelikhova C22
LISTED IN NUMERICAL ORDER:
A Arctic Ocean
A1 Kara Sea
A2 Laptev Sea
A3 East Siberian Sea
A4 Chukchi Sea
A5 Beaufort Sea
A6 Northwest Passages
A7 Hudson Bay
A8 James Bay
A9 Hudson Strait
A10 Baffin Bay
A11 Kane Basin
A12 Lincoln Sea
A13 Iceland Sea
A14 Greenland Sea
A15 Barents Sea
A16 Beloye More (White Sea)
B Indian Ocean
B1 Bay of Bengal
B2 Andaman Sea
B3 Strait of Malacca
B4 Singapore Straits
B5 Natuna Sea
B6 Java Sea
B7 Bali Sea
B8 Savu Sea
B9 Flores Sea
B10 Teluk Bone
B11 Teluk Tomini
B12 Timor Sea
B13 Joseph Bonaparte Gulf
B14 Great Australian Bight
B15 Bass Strait
B16 Mozambique Channel
B17 Arabian Sea
B18 Gulf of Aden
B19 Red Sea
B20 Gulf of Suez
B21 Persian Gulf
B22 Gulf of Oman
B23 Gulf of Mannar
B24 Laccadive Sea
B25 Palk Strait and Bay
C North Pacific Ocean
C1 Gulf of Thailand
C2 South China Sea
C3 Gulf of Tonkin
C4 Sulu Sea
C5 Celebes Sea
C6 Ceram Sea
C7 Halmahera Sea
C8 Molucca Sea
C9 Philippine Sea
C10 Taiwan Strait
C11 East China Sea
C12 Yellow Sea
C13 Bo Hai
C14 Liadong Wan (Gulf)
C15 Korea Bay
C16 Korea Strait
C17 Sea of Japan (East Sea)
C18 Tatarskiy Proliv
C19 Amurskiy Liman
C20 Sakhalinskiy Zaliv
C21 Sea of Okhotsk
C22 Zaliv Shelikhova
C23 Bering Sea
C24 Bering Strait
C25 Bristol Bay
C26 Gulf of Alaska
C27 Alaska (U.S.) British Columbia (Canada) Coastal Waters
C28 Golfo de California (Mar de Cortés)
C29 Golfo de Panamá
D South Pacific Ocea
D1 Makassar Strait
D2 Banda Sea
D3 Aru Sea
D4 Arafura Sea
D5 Gulf of Carpentaria
D6 Torres Strait
D7 Bismarck Sea
D8 Solomon Sea
D9 Coral Sea
D10 Tasman Sea
D11 Cook Strait
D12 Ross Sea

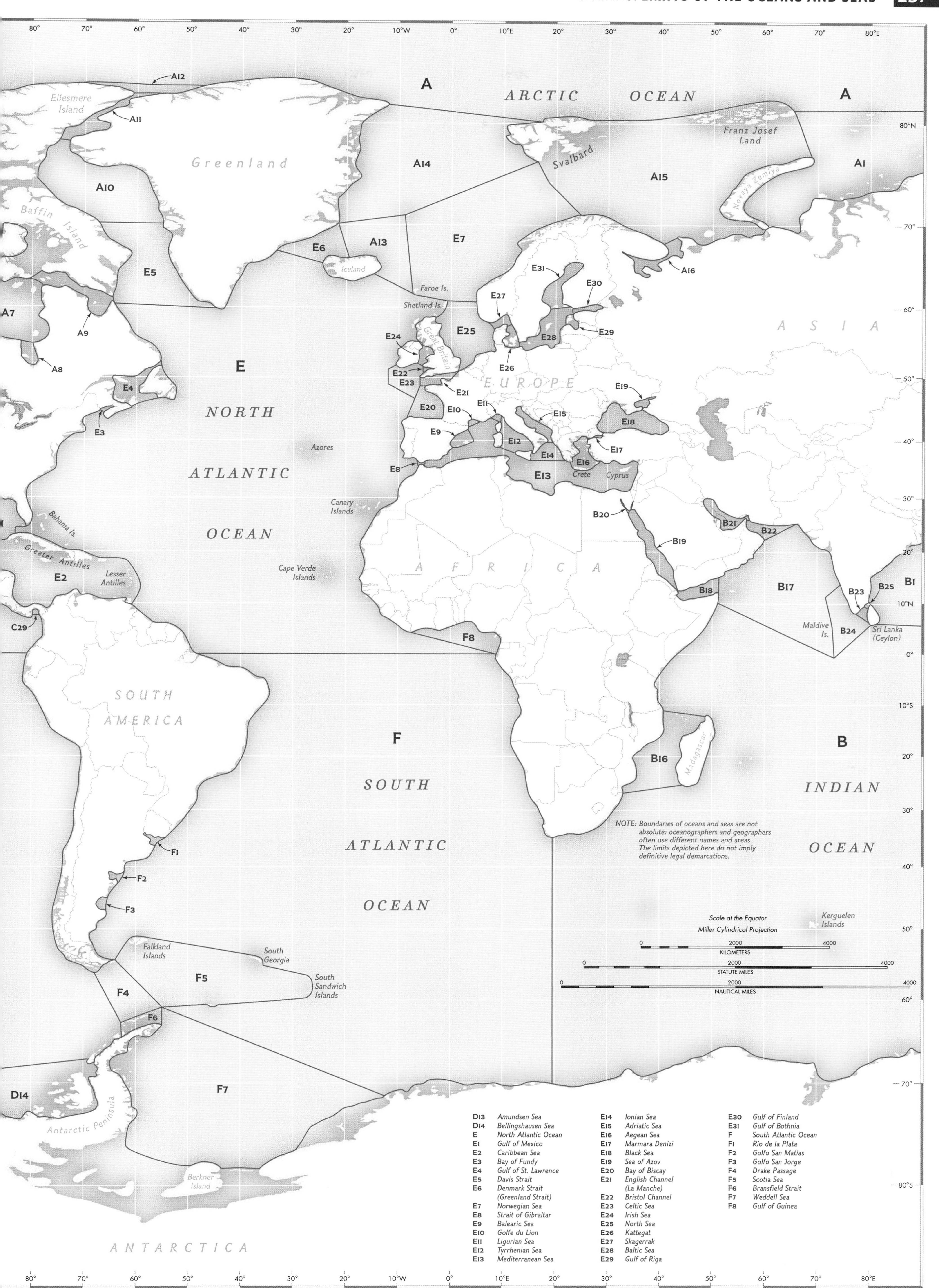
ARCTIC OCEAN
NORTH ATLANTIC OCEAN
SOUTH ATLANTIC OCEAN
INDIAN OCEAN
Greenland
Ellesmere Island
Baffin Island
Iceland
Faroe Is.
Shetland Is.
Great Britain
Svalbard
Franz Josef Land
Novaya Zemlya
EUROPE
ASIA
AFRICA
SOUTH AMERICA
ANTARCTICA
Antarctic Peninsula
Berkner Island
Azores
Canary Islands
Cape Verde Islands
Bahama Is.
Greater Antilles
Lesser Antilles
Crete
Cyprus
Madagascar
Maldive Is.
Sri Lanka (Ceylon)
Falkland Islands
South Georgia
South Sandwich Islands
Kerguelen Islands
NOTE: Boundaries of oceans and seas are not absolute; oceanographers and geographers often use different names and areas. The limits depicted here do not imply definitive legal demarcations.
Scale at the Equator
Miller Cylindrical Projection
0 2000 4000 KILOMETERS
0 2000 4000 STATUTE MILES
0 2000 4000 NAUTICAL MILES
D13 Amundsen Sea
D14 Bellingshausen Sea
E North Atlantic Ocean
E1 Gulf of Mexico
E2 Caribbean Sea
E3 Bay of Fundy
E4 Gulf of St. Lawrence
E5 Davis Strait
E6 Denmark Strait (Greenland Strait)
E7 Norwegian Sea
E8 Strait of Gibraltar
E9 Balearic Sea
E10 Golfe du Lion
E11 Ligurian Sea
E12 Tyrrhenian Sea
E13 Mediterranean Sea
E14 Ionian Sea
E15 Adriatic Sea
E16 Aegean Sea
E17 Marmara Denizi
E18 Black Sea
E19 Sea of Azov
E20 Bay of Biscay
E21 English Channel (La Manche)
E22 Bristol Channel
E23 Celtic Sea
E24 Irish Sea
E25 North Sea
E26 Kattegat
E27 Skagerrak
E28 Baltic Sea
E29 Gulf of Riga
E30 Gulf of Finland
E31 Gulf of Bothnia
F South Atlantic Ocean
F1 Río de la Plata
F2 Golfo San Matías
F3 Golfo San Jorge
F4 Drake Passage
F5 Scotia Sea
F6 Bransfield Strait
F7 Weddell Sea
F8 Gulf of Guinea

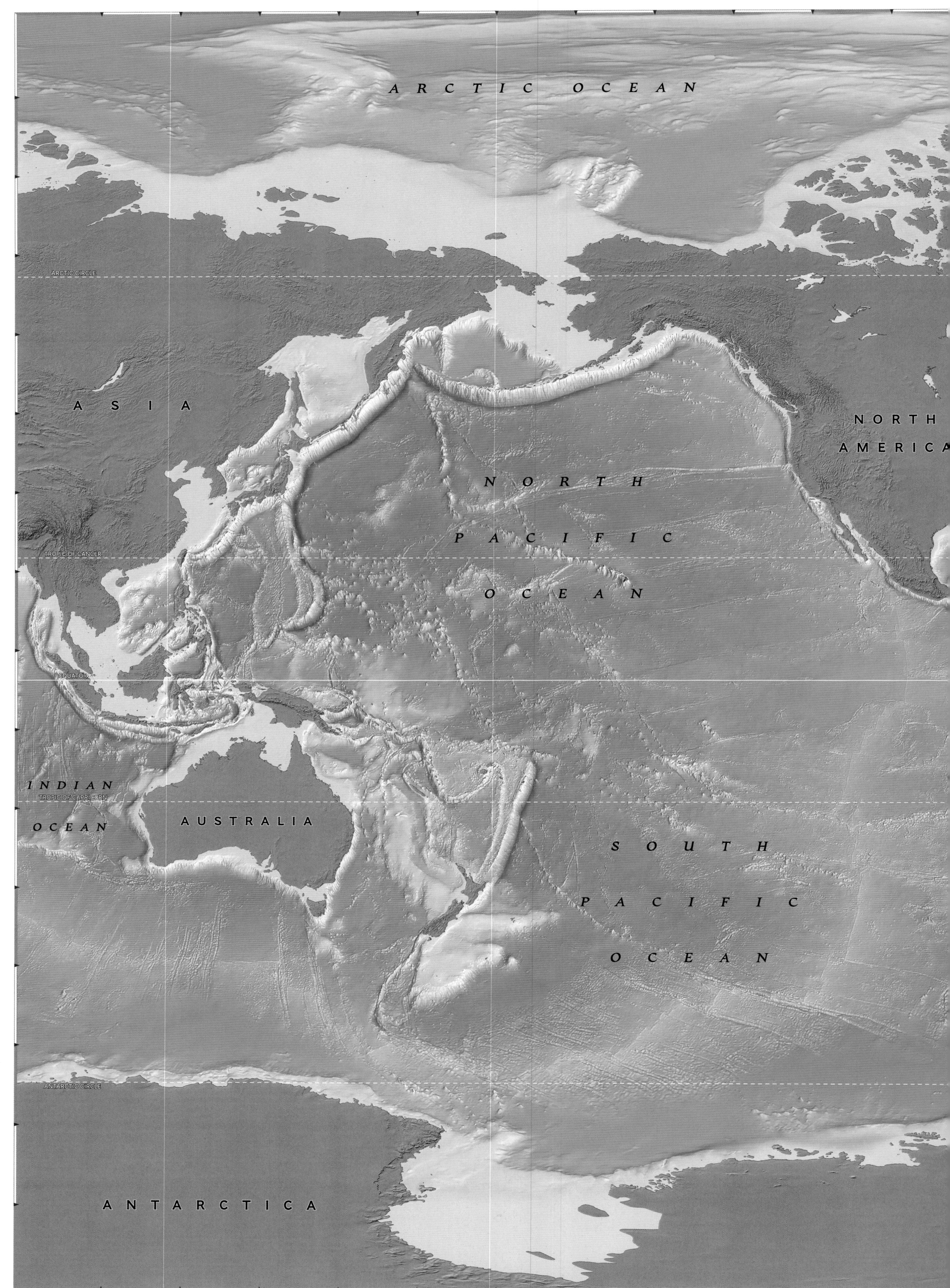
ARCTIC OCEAN
ARCTIC CIRCLE
ASIA
NORTH AMERICA
NORTH PACIFIC OCEAN
TROPIC OF CANCER
EQUATOR
INDIAN OCEAN
TROPIC OF CAPRICORN
AUSTRALIA
SOUTH PACIFIC OCEAN
ANTARCTIC CIRCLE
ANTARCTICA

ARCTIC OCEAN
ARCTIC CIRCLE
EUROPE
ASIA
NORTH ATLANTIC OCEAN
TROPIC OF CANCER
AFRICA
EQUATOR
SOUTH AMERICA
INDIAN OCEAN
TROPIC OF CAPRICORN
SOUTH ATLANTIC OCEAN
ANTARCTIC CIRCLE
Miller Cylindrical Projection
SCALE 1:72,080,330
1 CENTIMETER = 721 KILOMETERS; 1 INCH = 1138 STATUTE MILES
0 2000 4000
KILOMETERS
0 2000 4000
STATUTE MILES
0 2000 4000
NAUTICAL MILES
Scale at the Equator
ANTARCTICA

ARCTIC OCEAN
LINCOLN SEA
BARENTS PLAIN
BARENTS SEA
SVALBARD
Spitsbergen
YERMAK PLATEAU
KNIPOVICH RIDGE
SPITSBERGEN FRACTURE ZONE
Molloy Hole -5669 (-18599ft) Arctic Ocean's deepest point
BOREAS PLAIN
GREENLAND SEA
GREENLAND FRACTURE ZONE
GREENLAND PLAIN
MOHNS RIDGE
NORWEGIAN BASIN
NORWEGIAN SEA
JAN MAYEN FRACTURE ZONE
Jan Mayen
ICELAND PLATEAU
ICELAND SEA
KOLBEINSEY RIDGE
ICELAND
DENMARK STRAIT
FAROE-ICELAND RIDGE
FAROE ISLANDS
SHETLAND ISLANDS
NORTH SEA
SCANDINAVIA
GULF OF BOTHNIA
BALTIC SEA
Gulf of Finland
Kola Peninsula
EUROPE
BRITISH ISLES
Great Britain
Ireland
CELTIC SEA
ENGLISH CHANNEL
BAY OF BISCAY
BISCAY PLAIN
PORCUPINE PLAIN
WEST EUROPEAN BASIN
IBERIAN BASIN
Iberian Peninsula
Strait of Gibraltar
MEDITERRANEAN SEA
TYRRHENIAN SEA
ADRIATIC SEA
IONIAN SEA
AEGEAN SEA
Balkan Peninsula
Anatolia
BLACK SEA
Cyprus
Crete
Sicily
Sardinia
Corsica
BALEARIC IS.
RED SEA
TROPIC OF CANCER
ARCTIC CIRCLE
GREENLAND
Miller Cylindrical Projection
SCALE 1:41,200,000
1 CENTIMETER = 412 KILOMETERS; 1 INCH = 650 STATUTE MILES
KILOMETERS
STATUTE MILES
NAUTICAL MILES
Scale at the Equator
Soundings in meters below sea level
REYKJANES RIDGE
IMARSSUAK SEACHANNEL
MAURY SEACHANNEL
IRELAND TROUGH
Rockall
CHARLIE-GIBBS FRACTURE ZONE
LABRADOR BASIN
LABRADOR SEA
NORTHWEST ATLANTIC MID-OCEAN CANYON
DAVIS STRAIT
BAFFIN BAY
BAFFIN BASIN
BAFFIN ISLAND
KANE BASIN
QUEEN ELIZABETH ISLANDS
ELLESMERE ISLAND
Axel Heiberg Island
Devon Island
Jones Sound
Lancaster Sd.
PARRY CHANNEL
Gulf of Boothia
HUDSON STRAIT
Ungava Peninsula
Ungava Bay
FOXE BASIN
HUDSON BAY
NORTH AMERICA
Labrador
Island of Newfoundland
Grand Banks of Newfoundland
Gulf of St. Lawrence
Gulf of Maine
NEWFOUNDLAND BASIN
Flemish Cap
Orphan Knoll
NEWFOUNDLAND PLAIN
Newfoundland Ridge
SOHM PLAIN
New England Seamounts
HATTERAS PLAIN
Cape Hatteras
BERMUDA RISE
Bermuda
NORTH AMERICAN BASIN
NARES PLAIN
BAHAMA ISLANDS
Blake Plateau
Florida
GULF OF MEXICO
Cuba
YUCATAN BASIN
Yucatan Peninsula
NORTH ATLANTIC OCEAN
MID-ATLANTIC RIDGE
AZORES PLATEAU
AZORES
MADEIRA ISLANDS
CANARY ISLANDS
CANARY BASIN
CAPE VERDE PLAIN
KANE FRACTURE ZONE
ATLANTIS FRACTURE ZONE
HAYES FRACTURE ZONE
OCEANOGRAPHER FRACTURE ZONE
PICO FRACTURE ZONE
MAXWELL FRACTURE ZONE
BIGHT FRACTURE ZONE
Silver Plain -8605 (-28232ft) Atlantic Ocean's deepest point
PUERTO RICO TRENCH

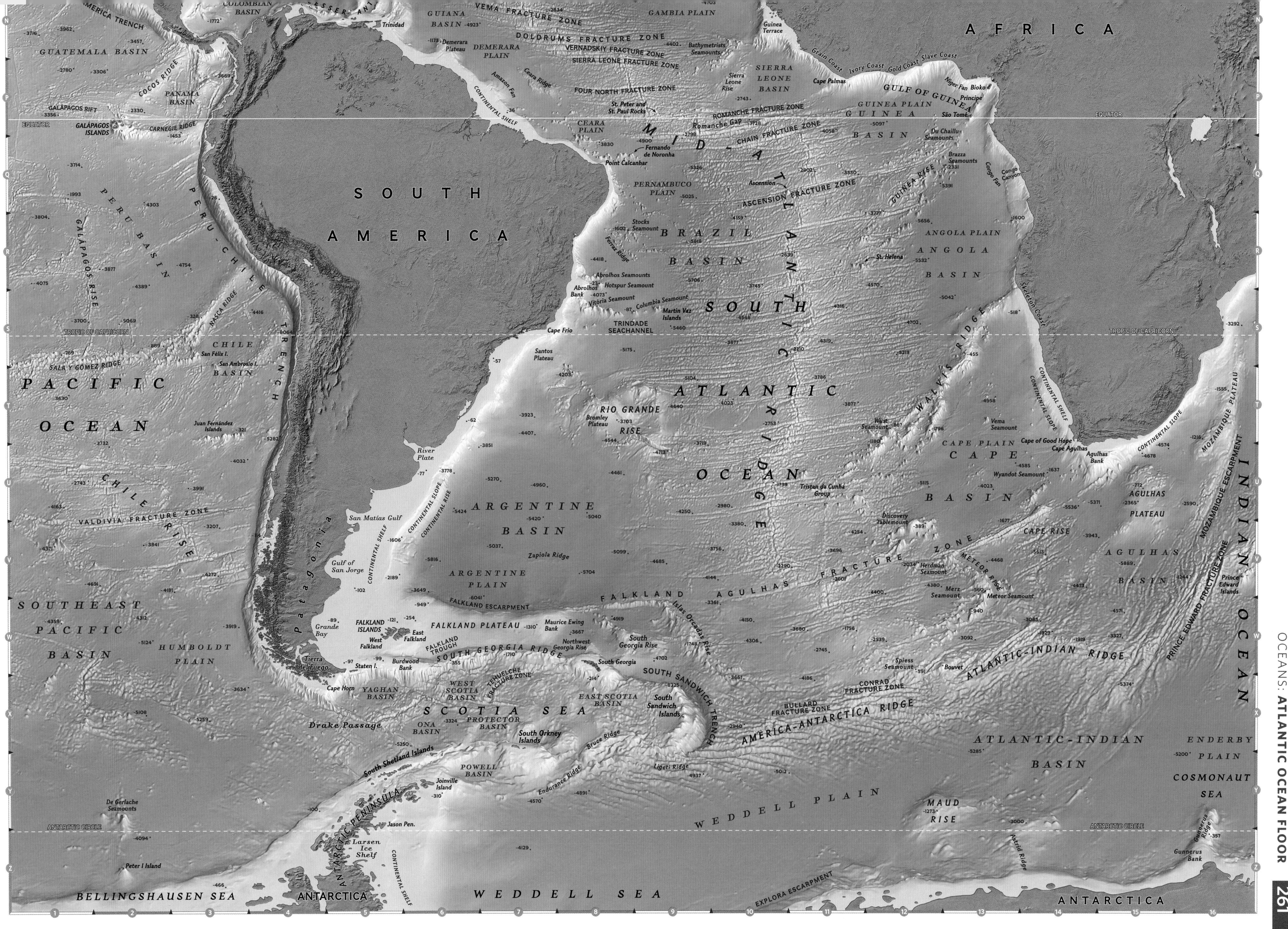
AFRICA
SOUTH AMERICA
PACIFIC OCEAN
INDIAN OCEAN
SOUTH ATLANTIC OCEAN
MID-ATLANTIC RIDGE
GAMBIA PLAIN
VEMA FRACTURE ZONE
DOLDRUMS FRACTURE ZONE
VERNADSKIY FRACTURE ZONE
SIERRA LEONE FRACTURE ZONE
FOUR NORTH FRACTURE ZONE
ROMANCHE FRACTURE ZONE
Romanche Gap
CHAIN FRACTURE ZONE
ASCENSION FRACTURE ZONE
Ascension
GUIANA BASIN
Demerara Plateau
DEMERARA PLAIN
Amazon Fan
Ceara Ridge
CEARA PLAIN
CONTINENTAL SHELF
Trinidad
Bathymetrists Seamounts
Guinea Terrace
SIERRA LEONE BASIN
Sierra Leone Rise
Grain Coast
Ivory Coast
Gold Coast
Slave Coast
Cape Palmas
GULF OF GUINEA
Niger Fan
Bioko
Príncipe
São Tomé
GUINEA PLAIN
GUINEA BASIN
GUINEA RISE
Du Chaillu Seamounts
Brazza Seamounts
Congo Fan
Congo Canyon
St. Peter and St. Paul Rocks
Fernando de Noronha
Point Calcanhar
PERNAMBUCO PLAIN
Stocks Seamount
Ferraz Ridge
BRAZIL BASIN
Abrolhos Seamounts
Hotspur Seamount
Abrolhos Bank
Vitória Seamount
Columbia Seamount
Martin Vaz Islands
TRINDADE SEACHANNEL
St. Helena
ANGOLA PLAIN
ANGOLA BASIN
Skeleton Coast
WALVIS RIDGE
CONTINENTAL SLOPE
Cape Frio
Santos Plateau
RIO GRANDE RISE
Bromley Plateau
Wüst Seamount
Vema Seamount
CAPE PLAIN
CAPE BASIN
Cape of Good Hope
Cape Agulhas
Agulhas Bank
Wyandot Seamount
Tristan da Cunha Group
Discovery Tablemount
CAPE RISE
AGULHAS PLATEAU
AGULHAS BASIN
MOZAMBIQUE PLATEAU
MOZAMBIQUE ESCARPMENT
PRINCE EDWARD FRACTURE ZONE
Prince Edward Islands
River Plate
San Matías Gulf
Gulf of San Jorge
Patagonia
ARGENTINE BASIN
ARGENTINE PLAIN
Zapiola Ridge
FALKLAND ESCARPMENT
FALKLAND AGULHAS FRACTURE ZONE
Herdman Seamount
METEOR RISE
Merz Seamount
Meteor Seamount
Islas Orcadas Rise
FALKLAND PLATEAU
Maurice Ewing Bank
Northwest Georgia Rise
South Georgia Rise
FALKLAND ISLANDS
East Falkland
West Falkland
Grande Bay
FALKLAND TROUGH
SOUTH GEORGIA RIDGE
Burdwood Bank
Staten I.
Tierra del Fuego
South Georgia
SOUTH SANDWICH TRENCH
ATLANTIC-INDIAN RIDGE
Spiess Seamount
Bouvet
CONRAD FRACTURE ZONE
BULLARD FRACTURE ZONE
AMERICA-ANTARCTICA RIDGE
Cape Horn
YAGHAN BASIN
WEST SCOTIA BASIN
TEHUELCHE FRACTURE ZONE
EAST SCOTIA BASIN
South Sandwich Islands
SCOTIA SEA
Drake Passage
ONA BASIN
PROTECTOR BASIN
South Orkney Islands
Bruce Ridge
South Shetland Islands
POWELL BASIN
Joinville Island
Endurance Ridge
Ligeti Ridge
ATLANTIC-INDIAN BASIN
ENDERBY PLAIN
COSMONAUT SEA
WEDDELL PLAIN
MAUD RISE
Astrid Ridge
Gunnerus Ridge
Gunnerus Bank
ANTARCTIC PENINSULA
Jason Pen.
Larsen Ice Shelf
De Gerlache Seamounts
ANTARCTIC CIRCLE
Peter I Island
BELLINGSHAUSEN SEA
ANTARCTICA
WEDDELL SEA
EXPLORA ESCARPMENT
TROPIC OF CAPRICORN
EQUATOR
COLOMBIAN BASIN
MIDDLE AMERICA TRENCH
GUATEMALA BASIN
COCOS RIDGE
PANAMA BASIN
GALÁPAGOS RIFT
GALÁPAGOS ISLANDS
CARNEGIE RIDGE
PERU BASIN
PERU-CHILE TRENCH
GALÁPAGOS RISE
NASCA RIDGE
CHILE BASIN
San Félix I.
San Ambrosio I.
SALA Y GÓMEZ RIDGE
Juan Fernández Islands
CHILE RISE
VALDIVIA FRACTURE ZONE
SOUTHEAST PACIFIC BASIN
HUMBOLDT PLAIN

Miller Cylindrical Projection
SCALE 1:44,200,000
1 CENTIMETER = 442 KILOMETERS; 1 INCH = 698 STATUTE MILES
KILOMETERS
STATUTE MILES
NAUTICAL MILES
Scale at the Equator
Soundings in meters below sea level
ARCTIC CIRCLE
TROPIC OF CANCER
EQUATOR
TROPIC OF CAPRICORN
EAST SIBERIAN SEA
CHUKCHI SEA
Chukchi Peninsula
Bering Strait
St. Lawrence Island
CONTINENTAL SHELF
BERING SEA
ALEUTIAN BASIN
BOWERS RIDGE
SHIRSHOV RIDGE
Pribilof Islands
ALEUTIAN ISLANDS
ALEUTIAN TRENCH
Detroit Tablemount
SEA OF OKHOTSK
Kamchatka Peninsula
Sakhalin
KURIL BASIN
KURIL TRENCH
Hokkaidō
ASIA
SEA OF JAPAN (EAST SEA)
Honshu
JAPAN
JAPAN TRENCH
IZU TRENCH
YELLOW SEA
EAST CHINA SEA
Kyūshū
RYUKYU ISLANDS
RYUKYU TRENCH
Taiwan
Daitō Is.
Bonin Islands
BONIN TRENCH
NORTHWEST PACIFIC BASIN
SHATSKY RISE
EMPEROR SEAMOUNTS
EMPEROR TROUGH
HESS RISE
CHINOOK TROUGH
NORTH PACIFIC
HAWAIIAN RIDGE
NORTHWEST HAWAIIAN RIDGE
Midway Islands
Lisianski I.
Isakov Seamount
Makarov Seamount
Grosvenor Seamount
Mapmaker Seamounts
MID-PACIFIC MOUNTAINS
Magellan Seamounts
Wake I.
Johnston Atoll
Hainan
INDOCHINA PENINSULA
BAY OF BENGAL
Andaman Islands
ANDAMAN BASIN
Nicobar Islands
SOUTH CHINA SEA
PALAWAN TROUGH
Luzon
PHILIPPINE ISLANDS
PHILIPPINE TRENCH
PHILIPPINE SEA
KYUSHU-PALAU RIDGE
WEST MARIANA BASIN
MARIANA TROUGH
Mariana Islands
MARIANA TRENCH
Guam
Challenger Deep -10920 (-35827ft) World's greatest ocean depth
YAP TRENCH
PALAU TRENCH
Palau
SULU BASIN
Mindanao
CELEBES BASIN
Malay Peninsula
Strait of Malacca
Sumatra
CONTINENTAL SHELF
Borneo
Celebes
INDONESIA
GREATER SUNDA ISLANDS
BANDA SEA
WEBER BASIN
Java
Bali
Lesser Sunda Islands
CAROLINE ISLANDS
WEST CAROLINE BASIN
EAURIPIK RISE
EAST CAROLINE BASIN
EAST MARIANA BASIN
Chuuk
Pohnpei (Ponape)
Enewetak Atoll
Bikini Atoll
Kwajalein Atoll
MARSHALL ISLANDS
Majuro Atoll
Taongi Atoll
CENTRAL PACIFIC BASIN
MAGELLAN RISE
Butaritari
Tarawa
Gilbert Islands
Howland I.
Baker I.
Nauru
Banaba
Beru
New Guinea
BISMARCK SEA
BISMARCK ARCHIPELAGO
SOLOMON ISLANDS
Nikumaroro
Phoenix Islands
Rawaki
Nanumea
Tuvalu
Funafuti
Atafu
Tokelau
Swains Is.
Samoa Islands
Wallis Is.
Savai'i
Upolu
VITYAZ TRENCH
NINETYEAST RIDGE
JAVA TRENCH
JAVA RIDGE
Christmas I.
-7125 (-23376ft) Indian Ocean's deepest point
Cocos Is.
INVESTIGATOR RIDGE
NORTH AUSTRALIAN BASIN
EXMOUTH PLATEAU
WHARTON BASIN
WALLABY PLATEAU
CUVIER PLATEAU
EAST INDIAMAN RIDGE
CONTINENTAL SHELF
Great Barrier Reef
CORAL SEA BASIN
CORAL SEA
NORTH NEW HEBRIDES TRENCH
VANUATU
New Caledonia
NORTH FIJI BASIN
FIJI PLATEAU
Fiji Islands
NEW HEBRIDES TRENCH
LAU BASIN
Tonga Islands
TONGA TRENCH
Ata
AUSTRALIA
INDIAN OCEAN
BROKEN RIDGE
PERTH BASIN
NATURALISTE PLATEAU
DIAMANTINA FRACTURE ZONE
CONTINENTAL SLOPE
SOUTH AUSTRALIAN BASIN
LORD HOWE RISE
NEW CALEDONIA BASIN
NORFOLK RIDGE
SOUTH FIJI BASIN
LAU RIDGE
KERMADEC TRENCH
Kermadec Islands
LOUISVILLE RIDGE
Lord Howe I.
Ball's Pyramid
Taupo Tablemount
TASMAN PLAIN
Gascoyne Tablemount
TASMAN SEA
Tasmania
EAST TASMAN PLATEAU
SOUTH TASMAN RISE
NEW ZEALAND
North Island
South Island
Chatham Is.
CHATHAM RISE
BOUNTY TROUGH
Bounty Is.
Antipodes Is.
Bollons Tablemount
CAMPBELL PLATEAU
Auckland Is.
Campbell I.
MACQUARIE RIDGE
EMERALD BASIN
SOUTHEAST INDIAN RIDGE

BEAUFORT SEA
BAFFIN BAY
ALASKA
HUDSON BAY
GULF OF ALASKA
NORTH AMERICA
TUFTS PLAIN
CASCADIA BASIN
JUAN DE FUCA RIDGE
MENDOCINO FRACTURE ZONE
PIONEER FRACTURE ZONE
MURRAY FRACTURE ZONE
MOLOKAI FRACTURE ZONE
CLARION FRACTURE ZONE
CLIPPERTON FRACTURE ZONE
NORTHEAST PACIFIC BASIN
GULF OF MEXICO
MEXICO BASIN
NORTH ATLANTIC OCEAN
BAHAMA ISLANDS
GREATER ANTILLES
CAYMAN TRENCH
CARIBBEAN SEA
LESSER ANTILLES
MIDDLE AMERICA TRENCH
GUATEMALA BASIN
PANAMA BASIN
COCOS RIDGE
CARNEGIE RIDGE
GALÁPAGOS ISLANDS
GALÁPAGOS RIFT
GALÁPAGOS FRACTURE ZONE
MARQUESAS ISLANDS
MARQUESAS FRACTURE ZONE
TUAMOTU ARCHIPELAGO
SOCIETY ISLANDS
SOUTH PACIFIC OCEAN
AUSTRAL ISLANDS
EAST PACIFIC RISE
EASTER FRACTURE ZONE
SALA Y GÓMEZ RIDGE
PERU BASIN
GALÁPAGOS RISE
NAZCA RIDGE
PERU-CHILE TRENCH
CHILE BASIN
SOUTH AMERICA
CHALLENGER FRACTURE ZONE
CHILE RISE
VALDIVIA FRACTURE ZONE
AGASSIZ FRACTURE ZONE
SOUTHWEST PACIFIC BASIN
SOUTHEAST PACIFIC BASIN
MENARD FRACTURE ZONE
ELTANIN FRACTURE ZONE
UDINTSEV FRACTURE ZONE
HUMBOLDT PLAIN
ARCTIC CIRCLE
TROPIC OF CANCER
EQUATOR
TROPIC OF CAPRICORN
Davis Strait
Gulf of Maine
Hudson Canyon
Cape Hatteras
Bermuda
Blake Plateau
CONTINENTAL SHELF
Campeche Bank
Yucatán Peninsula
Hispaniola
Puerto Rico
-8605 (-28232ft) Atlantic Ocean's deepest point
Alaska Peninsula
Kodiak Seamount
Pratt Seamount
Welker Seamount
Gilbert Seamount
Bowie Seamount
Comstock Seamount
Eickelberg Seamount
Harris Seamount
Fieberling Tablemount
Moonless Mountains
Isla de Guadalupe
Baja California
PATTON ESCARPMENT
CEDROS TRENCH
Henderson Seamount
Mendelssohn Seamount
Oahu
Hawai'i
Islas Revillagigedo
Mathematicians Seamounts
Palmyra Atoll
Kiritimati (Christmas)
Manihiki Atoll
Pukapuka
Manuae
Tahiti
Mangaia
Îles Maria
Morane
Îles Gambier
President Thiers Bank
Pitcairn I.
Ducie I.
Sala y Gómez
Easter Island
Neilson Reef
Marotiri
San Félix I.
San Ambrosio I.
Juan Fernández Islands
Falkland Islands
CONTINENTAL SHELF

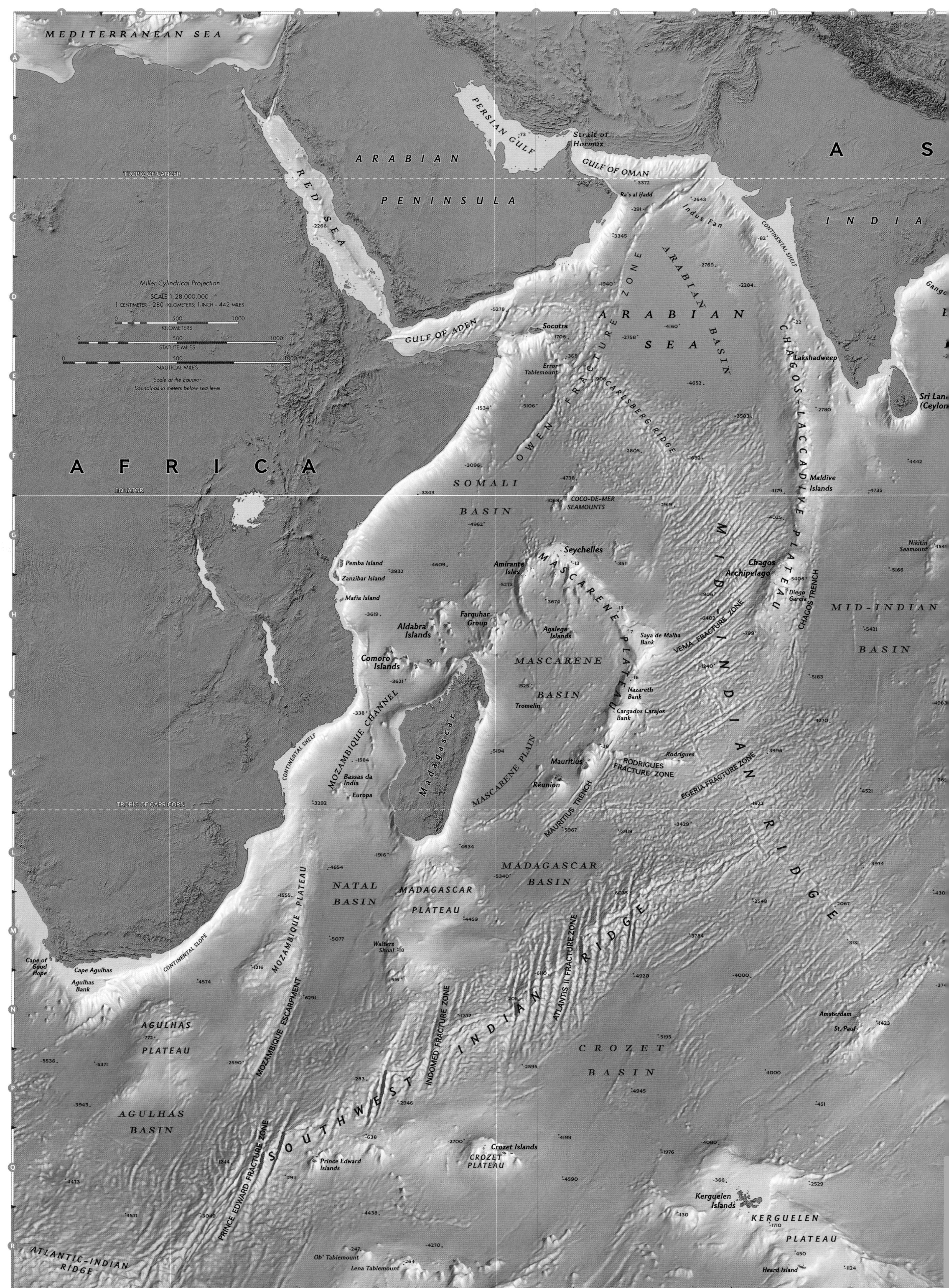
MEDITERRANEAN SEA
PERSIAN GULF
Strait of Hormuz
ARABIAN PENINSULA
RED SEA
GULF OF OMAN
Ra's al Ḥadd
Indus Fan
CONTINENTAL SHELF
INDIA
ASIA
Miller Cylindrical Projection
SCALE 1:28,000,000
1 CENTIMETER = 280 KILOMETERS; 1 INCH = 442 MILES
KILOMETERS
STATUTE MILES
NAUTICAL MILES
Scale at the Equator
Soundings in meters below sea level
TROPIC OF CANCER
GULF OF ADEN
Socotra
ARABIAN SEA
ARABIAN BASIN
OWEN FRACTURE ZONE
CARLSBERG RIDGE
Error Tablemount
CHAGOS-LACCADIVE PLATEAU
Lakshadweep
Sri Lanka (Ceylon)
Maldive Islands
AFRICA
EQUATOR
SOMALI BASIN
COCO-DE-MER SEAMOUNTS
Seychelles
Amirante Isles
MASCARENE PLATEAU
MID-INDIAN RIDGE
Chagos Archipelago
Diego Garcia
CHAGOS TRENCH
Nikitin Seamount
MID-INDIAN BASIN
Pemba Island
Zanzibar Island
Mafia Island
Aldabra Islands
Farquhar Group
Agalega Islands
Saya de Malha Bank
VEMA FRACTURE ZONE
Comoro Islands
MASCARENE BASIN
Tromelin
Nazareth Bank
Cargados Carajos Bank
MOZAMBIQUE CHANNEL
Madagascar
CONTINENTAL SHELF
Bassas da India
Europa
MASCARENE PLAIN
Mauritius
Réunion
Rodrigues
RODRIGUES FRACTURE ZONE
EGERIA FRACTURE ZONE
MAURITIUS TRENCH
TROPIC OF CAPRICORN
MADAGASCAR BASIN
NATAL BASIN
MADAGASCAR PLATEAU
MOZAMBIQUE PLATEAU
Walters Shoal
CONTINENTAL SLOPE
Cape of Good Hope
Cape Agulhas
Agulhas Bank
AGULHAS PLATEAU
MOZAMBIQUE ESCARPMENT
INDOMED FRACTURE ZONE
ATLANTIS II FRACTURE ZONE
SOUTHWEST INDIAN RIDGE
CROZET BASIN
Amsterdam
St. Paul
AGULHAS BASIN
PRINCE EDWARD FRACTURE ZONE
Prince Edward Islands
Crozet Islands
CROZET PLATEAU
Kerguelen Islands
KERGUELEN PLATEAU
Heard Island
ATLANTIC-INDIAN RIDGE
Ob' Tablemount
Lena Tablemount

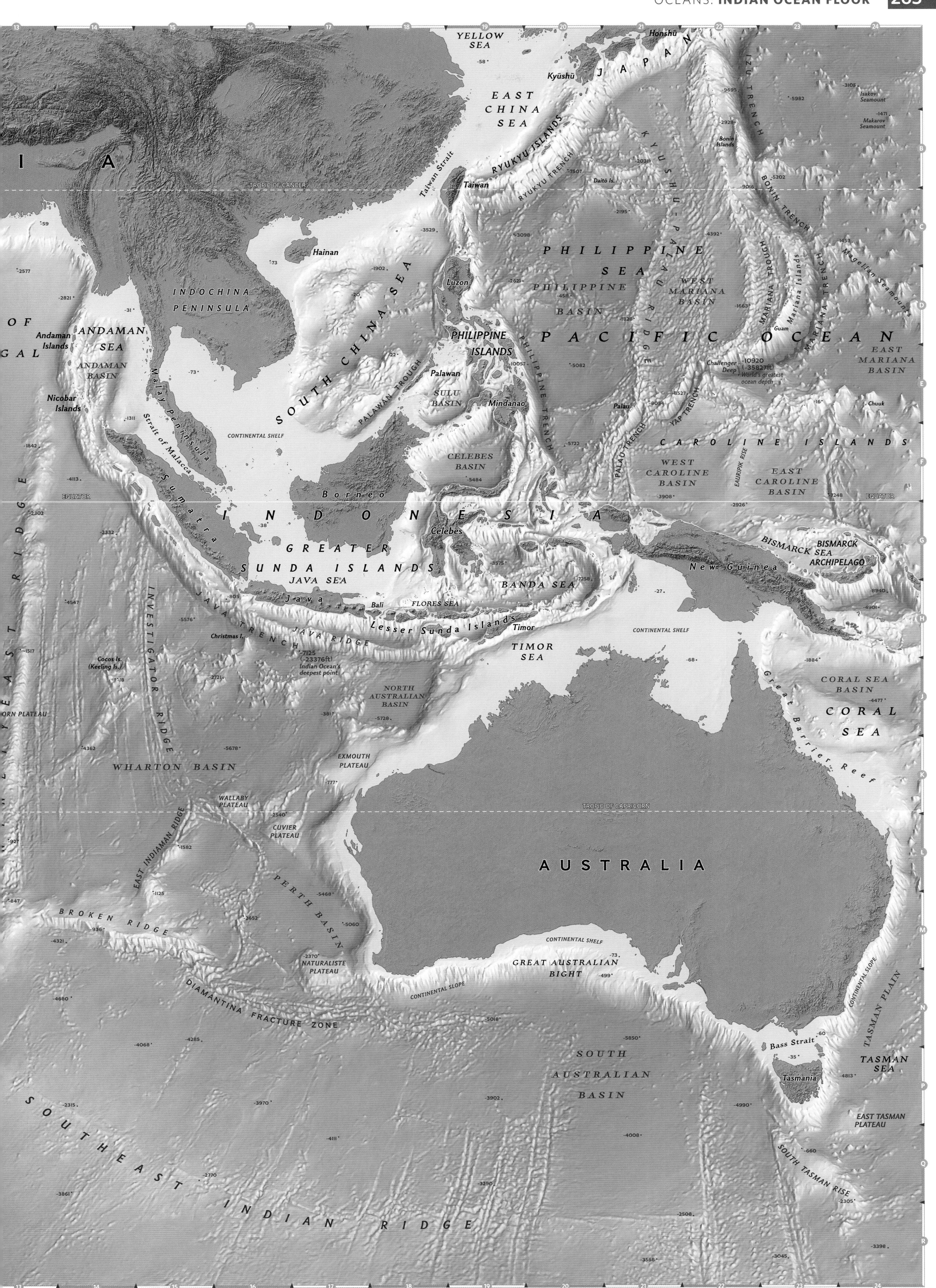
YELLOW SEA
EAST CHINA SEA
JAPAN
Honshū
Kyūshū
RYUKYU ISLANDS
RYUKYU TRENCH
Taiwan Strait
Taiwan
TROPIC OF CANCER
Daitō Is.
IZU TRENCH
Bonin Islands
BONIN TRENCH
KYUSHU-PALAU RIDGE
Isakov Seamount
Makarov Seamount
Magellan Seamounts
Hainan
INDOCHINA PENINSULA
SOUTH CHINA SEA
Luzon
PHILIPPINE SEA
PHILIPPINE BASIN
WEST MARIANA BASIN
MARIANA TROUGH
Mariana Islands
MARIANA TRENCH
Guam
PACIFIC OCEAN
EAST MARIANA BASIN
Challenger Deep
-10920 (-35827ft) World's greatest ocean depth
PHILIPPINE ISLANDS
PHILIPPINE TRENCH
Palawan
PALAWAN TROUGH
SULU BASIN
Mindanao
Palau
PALAU TRENCH
YAP TRENCH
Chuuk
ANDAMAN SEA
ANDAMAN BASIN
Andaman Islands
Nicobar Islands
Malay Peninsula
Strait of Malacca
CONTINENTAL SHELF
CELEBES BASIN
CAROLINE ISLANDS
WEST CAROLINE BASIN
EAURIPIK RISE
EAST CAROLINE BASIN
Sumatra
Borneo
EQUATOR
INDONESIA
Celebes
GREATER SUNDA ISLANDS
JAVA SEA
BANDA SEA
BISMARCK SEA
BISMARCK ARCHIPELAGO
New Guinea
Java
Bali
FLORES SEA
Lesser Sunda Islands
Timor
JAVA TRENCH
JAVA RIDGE
Christmas I.
-7125 (-23376ft) Indian Ocean's deepest point
Cocos Is. (Keeling Is.)
INVESTIGATOR RIDGE
TIMOR SEA
CONTINENTAL SHELF
NORTH AUSTRALIAN BASIN
Great Barrier Reef
CORAL SEA BASIN
CORAL SEA
WHARTON BASIN
EXMOUTH PLATEAU
WALLABY PLATEAU
CUVIER PLATEAU
EAST INDIAMAN RIDGE
TROPIC OF CAPRICORN
AUSTRALIA
PERTH BASIN
BROKEN RIDGE
NATURALISTE PLATEAU
CONTINENTAL SHELF
GREAT AUSTRALIAN BIGHT
CONTINENTAL SLOPE
CONTINENTAL SLOPE
TASMAN PLAIN
DIAMANTINA FRACTURE ZONE
Bass Strait
SOUTH AUSTRALIAN BASIN
Tasmania
TASMAN SEA
EAST TASMAN PLATEAU
SOUTH TASMAN RISE
SOUTHEAST INDIAN RIDGE

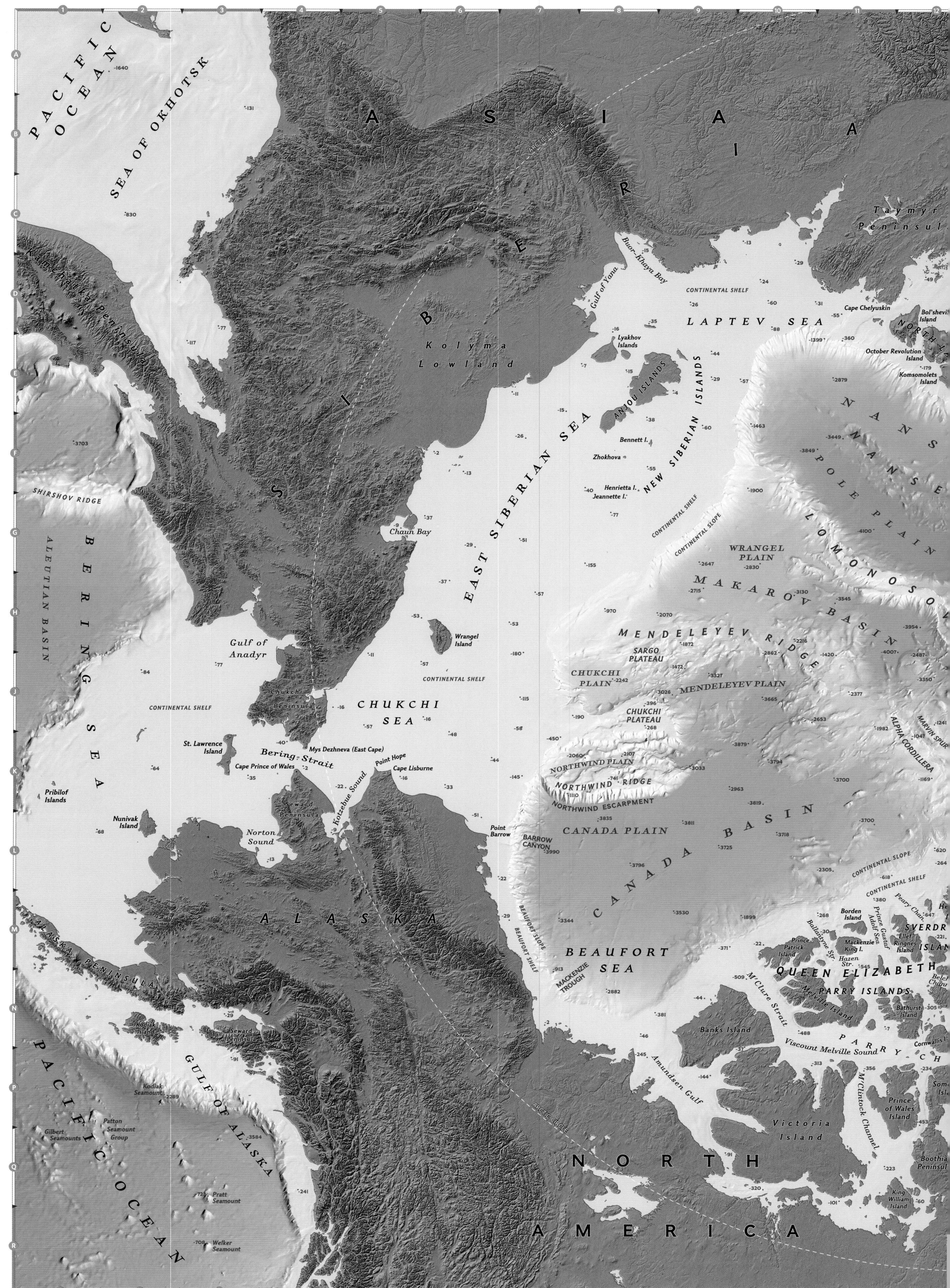
PACIFIC OCEAN
SEA OF OKHOTSK
A S I A
S I B E R I A
Kolyma Lowland
Taymyr Peninsula
Buor-Khaya Bay
Gulf of Yana
CONTINENTAL SHELF
LAPTEV SEA
Cape Chelyuskin
Bol'shevik Island
October Revolution Island
Komsomolets Island
Lyakhov Islands
ANJOU ISLANDS
NEW SIBERIAN ISLANDS
Bennett I.
Zhokhova
Henrietta I.
Jeannette I.
EAST SIBERIAN SEA
Kamchatka Peninsula
SHIRSHOV RIDGE
ALEUTIAN BASIN
BERING SEA
Chaun Bay
CONTINENTAL SLOPE
NANSEN BASIN
POLE PLAIN
LOMONOSOV
WRANGEL PLAIN
MAKAROV BASIN
MENDELEYEV RIDGE
SARGO PLATEAU
CHUKCHI PLAIN
MENDELEYEV PLAIN
CHUKCHI PLATEAU
Wrangel Island
Gulf of Anadyr
Chukchi Peninsula
CHUKCHI SEA
St. Lawrence Island
Bering Strait
Mys Dezhneva (East Cape)
Cape Prince of Wales
Point Hope
Cape Lisburne
Kotzebue Sound
Pribilof Islands
Nunivak Island
Seward Peninsula
Norton Sound
Point Barrow
BARROW CANYON
NORTHWIND PLAIN
NORTHWIND RIDGE
NORTHWIND ESCARPMENT
CANADA PLAIN
CANADA BASIN
ALPHA CORDILLERA
MARVIN SPUR
ALASKA
ALASKA PENINSULA
BEAUFORT SLOPE
BEAUFORT SHELF
BEAUFORT SEA
MACKENZIE TROUGH
Borden Island
Prince Patrick Island
Mackenzie King I.
Ellef Ringnes Island
SVERDRUP ISLANDS
QUEEN ELIZABETH
PARRY ISLANDS
Melville Island
M'Clure Strait
Banks Island
Viscount Melville Sound
Bathurst Island
Cornwallis I.
Amundsen Gulf
M'Clintock Channel
Prince of Wales Island
Victoria Island
Boothia Peninsula
King William Island
Kodiak Island
Kodiak Seamount
GULF OF ALASKA
Patton Seamount Group
Gilbert Seamounts
Pratt Seamount
Welker Seamount
PACIFIC OCEAN
NORTH AMERICA
ARCTIC CIRCLE

EUROPE
KARA SEA
BARENTS SEA
NORWEGIAN SEA
GREENLAND SEA
ICELAND SEA
BALTIC SEA
NORTH SEA
ATLANTIC OCEAN
BAFFIN BAY
SCANDINAVIA
GREENLAND
ICELAND
Gulf of Ob
Yamal Peninsula
Gyda Peninsula
Baydarata Bay
Pechora Bay
Chesha Bay
WHITE SEA
Kola Peninsula
GULF OF FINLAND
GULF OF BOTHNIA
KATTEGAT
SKAGERRAK
Novaya Zemlya
EAST NOVAYA ZEMLYA TROUGH
CONTINENTAL SHELF
Gusinaya Bank
MURMANSK RISE
North Cape
FRANZ JOSEF LAND
Graham Bell I.
George Land
Alexandra Land
OLGA BASIN
SVALBARD
Edgeøya
Bjørnøya
Spitsbergen Bank
North East Land
Spitsbergen
BARENTS PLAIN
SVYATAYA ANNA TROUGH
SVYATAYA ANNA FAN
VORONIN TROUGH
Molloy Hole
-5669 (-18599ft)
Arctic Ocean's deepest point
YERMAK PLATEAU
KNIPOVICH RIDGE
MOHNS RIDGE
BOREAS PLAIN
GREENLAND FRACTURE ZONE
SPITSBERGEN FRACTURE ZONE
GREENLAND PLAIN
DUMSHAF PLAIN
NORWEGIAN BASIN
VORING PLATEAU
Røst Bank
Halten Bank
AEGIR RIDGE
JAN MAYEN FRACTURE ZONE
Jan Mayen
JAN MAYEN RIDGE
ICELAND PLATEAU
KOLBEINSEY RIDGE
Ob' Bank
Belgica Bank
Morris Jesup Rise
CONTINENTAL SLOPE
FAROE-SHETLAND TROUGH
SHETLAND ISLANDS
FAROE ISLANDS
BRITISH ISLES
FAROE-ICELAND RIDGE
WYVILLE THOMSON RIDGE
Outer Bailey
George Bligh Bank
Rockall
ICELAND BASIN
Heimaey
Surtsey
DENMARK STRAIT
MAURY SEACHANNEL
Gardar Ridge
REYKJANES RIDGE
BIGHT FRACTURE ZONE
CHARLIE-GIBBS FRACTURE ZONE
IMARSSUAK SEACHANNEL
Eirik Ridge
Cape Farewell
LINCOLN SEA
Robeson Chan.
Hall Basin
Kennedy Chan.
KANE BASIN
Smith Snd.
Ellesmere Island
Jones Sd.
Lancaster Sd.
Bylot I.
Qimusseriarsuaq
Qeqertarsuaq (Disko)
BAFFIN BASIN
Baffin Island
DAVIS STRAIT
Melville Peninsula
Prince Charles Island
FOXE BASIN
ARCTIC CIRCLE
Azimuthal Equidistant Projection
SCALE 1:13,500,000
1 CENTIMETER = 135 KILOMETERS; 1 INCH = 213 STATUTE MILES
KILOMETERS
STATUTE MILES
NAUTICAL MILES
Soundings in meters below sea level

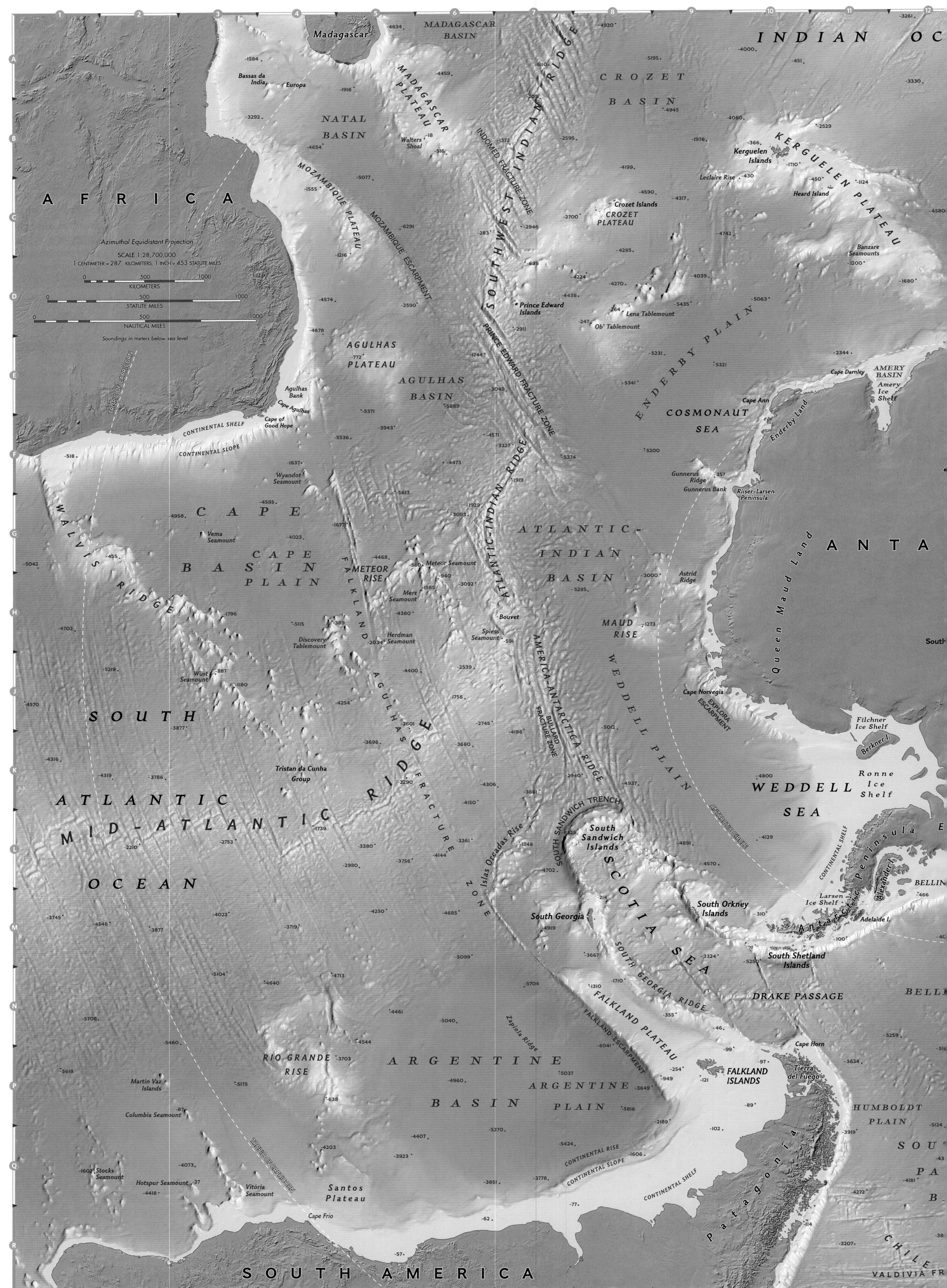
AFRICA
Madagascar
INDIAN OCEAN
MADAGASCAR BASIN
MADAGASCAR PLATEAU
NATAL BASIN
MOZAMBIQUE PLATEAU
MOZAMBIQUE ESCARPMENT
CROZET BASIN
SOUTHWEST INDIAN RIDGE
INDOMED FRACTURE ZONE
KERGUELEN PLATEAU
Kerguelen Islands
Heard Island
Crozet Islands
CROZET PLATEAU
Prince Edward Islands
PRINCE EDWARD FRACTURE ZONE
Lena Tablemount
Ob' Tablemount
ENDERBY PLAIN
COSMONAUT SEA
AMERY BASIN
Amery Ice Shelf
Cape Darnley
Cape Ann
Enderby Land
Azimuthal Equidistant Projection
SCALE 1:28,700,000
1 CENTIMETER = 287 KILOMETERS; 1 INCH = 453 STATUTE MILES
KILOMETERS
STATUTE MILES
NAUTICAL MILES
Soundings in meters below sea level
AGULHAS PLATEAU
AGULHAS BASIN
Agulhas Bank
Cape Agulhas
Cape of Good Hope
CONTINENTAL SHELF
CONTINENTAL SLOPE
Wyandot Seamount
CAPE BASIN
CAPE BASIN PLAIN
Vema Seamount
WALVIS RIDGE
METEOR RISE
Meteor Seamount
Merz Seamount
Herdman Seamount
Discovery Tablemount
FALKLAND AGULHAS FRACTURE ZONE
ATLANTIC-INDIAN RIDGE
ATLANTIC-INDIAN BASIN
Bouvet
Spiess Seamount
Gunnerus Ridge
Gunnerus Bank
Riiser-Larsen Peninsula
Astrid Ridge
MAUD RISE
Queen Maud Land
ANTA
AMERICA-ANTARCTICA RIDGE
BULLARD FRACTURE ZONE
WEDDELL PLAIN
Cape Norvegia
EXPLORA ESCARPMENT
Filchner Ice Shelf
Berkner I.
Ronne Ice Shelf
WEDDELL SEA
Wüst Seamount
SOUTH ATLANTIC OCEAN
MID-ATLANTIC RIDGE
Tristan da Cunha Group
SOUTH SANDWICH TRENCH
South Sandwich Islands
Islas Orcadas Rise
SCOTIA SEA
South Georgia
South Orkney Islands
Larsen Ice Shelf
Antarctic Peninsula
Alexander I.
Adelaide I.
South Shetland Islands
SOUTH GEORGIA RIDGE
DRAKE PASSAGE
FALKLAND PLATEAU
FALKLAND ESCARPMENT
Zapiola Ridge
RIO GRANDE RISE
ARGENTINE BASIN
ARGENTINE PLAIN
FALKLAND ISLANDS
Cape Horn
Tierra del Fuego
HUMBOLDT PLAIN
Martin Vaz Islands
Columbia Seamount
Stocks Seamount
Hotspur Seamount
Vitória Seamount
Santos Plateau
Cape Frio
CONTINENTAL RISE
Patagonia
SOUTH AMERICA
TROPIC OF CAPRICORN
ANTARCTIC CIRCLE
Leclaire Rise
Banzare Seamounts
Walters Shoal
Bassas da India
Europa
CHILE
VALDIVIA FR

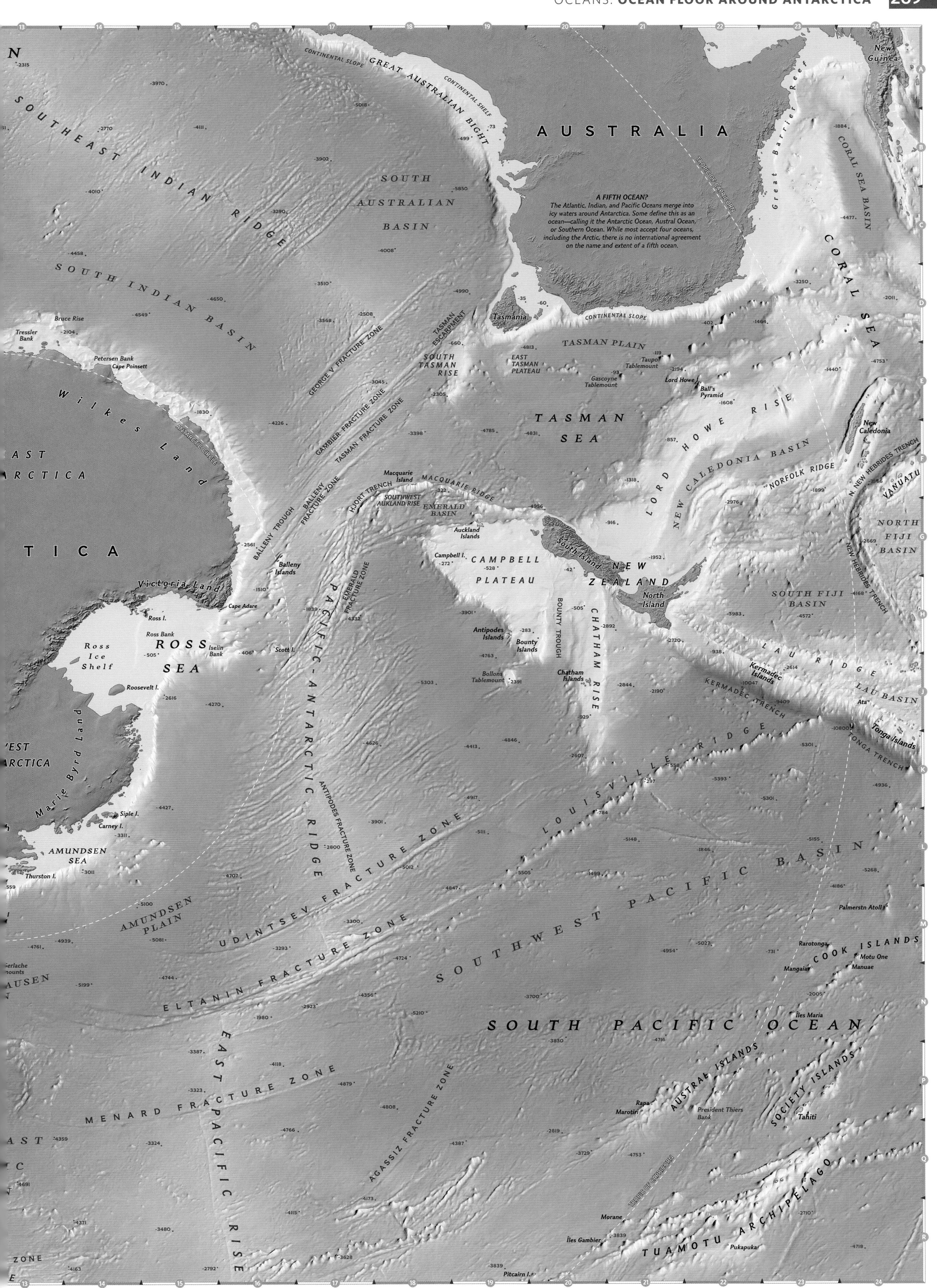
AUSTRALIA
A FIFTH OCEAN?
The Atlantic, Indian, and Pacific Oceans merge into icy waters around Antarctica. Some define this as an ocean—calling it the Antarctic Ocean, Austral Ocean, or Southern Ocean. While most accept four oceans, including the Arctic, there is no international agreement on the name and extent of a fifth ocean.
GREAT AUSTRALIAN BIGHT
SOUTHEAST INDIAN RIDGE
SOUTH INDIAN BASIN
SOUTH AUSTRALIAN BASIN
TASMAN SEA
CORAL SEA
CORAL SEA BASIN
Great Barrier Reef
New Guinea
Tasmania
TASMAN PLAIN
SOUTH TASMAN RISE
EAST TASMAN PLATEAU
LORD HOWE RISE
NEW CALEDONIA BASIN
NORFOLK RIDGE
New Caledonia
VANUATU
NORTH FIJI BASIN
SOUTH FIJI BASIN
LAU RIDGE
LAU BASIN
Tonga Islands
TONGA TRENCH
KERMADEC TRENCH
Kermadec Islands
NEW ZEALAND
South Island
North Island
CAMPBELL PLATEAU
CHATHAM RISE
BOUNTY TROUGH
Chatham Islands
Antipodes Islands
Bounty Islands
Campbell I.
Auckland Islands
EMERALD BASIN
MACQUARIE RIDGE
Macquarie Island
HJORT TRENCH
SOUTHWEST AUKLAND RISE
BALLENY TROUGH
BALLENY FRACTURE ZONE
Balleny Islands
Wilkes Land
Victoria Land
ROSS SEA
Ross Ice Shelf
Roosevelt I.
Ross I.
Cape Adare
Scott I.
Marie Byrd Land
AMUNDSEN SEA
AMUNDSEN PLAIN
Thurston I.
Siple I.
Carney I.
PACIFIC-ANTARCTIC RIDGE
LOUISVILLE RIDGE
UDINTSEV FRACTURE ZONE
ELTANIN FRACTURE ZONE
SOUTHWEST PACIFIC BASIN
SOUTH PACIFIC OCEAN
EAST PACIFIC RISE
MENARD FRACTURE ZONE
AGASSIZ FRACTURE ZONE
COOK ISLANDS
AUSTRAL ISLANDS
SOCIETY ISLANDS
Tahiti
TUAMOTU ARCHIPELAGO
Îles Gambier
Pitcairn I.
Morane
Pukapuka
Palmerstn Atoll
Rarotonga
Mangaia
Îles Maria
Rapa
Marotiri
TROPIC OF CAPRICORN
ANTARCTIC CIRCLE

IN THE FIRST DECADE OF THE NEW MILLENNIUM, astronomers are conducting extensive surveys of new frontiers in space, registering millions of galaxies, each composed of billions of stars. New orbiters and surface rovers have explored Mars, confirming the presence of liquid water in its distant past. Titan, a moon of Saturn cloaked in a thick, hazy nitrogen atmosphere, was imaged with radar from the Cassini spacecraft, revealing lakes that probably consist of liquid ethane. Other Cassini photographs showed water geysers erupting from cracks in Saturn's icy moon Enceladus, whetting the appetites of scientists who search for life elsewhere in our solar system. The New Horizons spacecraft is now en route to Pluto and the distant Kuiper belt, gathering clues to the origin of our solar system. Meanwhile, a copper "cannonball" deployed from a spacecraft created the first man-made impact crater on a comet, allowing the composition of the comet to be studied, while another returned interplanetary dust to Earth.

Wherever we look, we see evidence of cataclysmic events, indicating that we live in a 14-billion-year-old universe that is still evolving. Massive stars can literally explode at the end of their lives, ejecting heavy elements such as carbon, oxygen, calcium, and iron. Some of these titanic events produce bizarre neutron stars and black holes. We see galaxies in groups and clusters devouring each other, becoming ever larger; invisible "dark matter" of unknown composition dominates over their visible stars and gas. The universe began with a big bang and has been expanding ever since; indeed, the expansion is accelerating, propelled by a mysterious "dark energy" whose exact nature and origin is the deepest mystery of all. With the much anticipated James Webb Space Telescope, scheduled for launch in 2013, we should be able to witness the formation of the first stars and galaxies. We are also preparing to explore the next frontier of astronomical observation, looking for gravitational waves that disturb the very fabric of space and time.

Space

From top to bottom, at left: Backdropped by New Zealand and Cook Strait in the Pacific Ocean, NASA astronauts work on construction on the International Space Station during the 2006 *Discovery* shuttle mission's first spacewalk; a Hubble Space Telescope image of Saturn, its rings, and several of its moons during a rare occasion (once every 15 years) in which the planet's rings were tilted nearly edge-on to Earth and to the sun; an artist's rendering of the Phoenix Mission spacecraft, which landed on Mars in May 2008 as part of an effort to study the planet's water history and biological potential through an exploration of its northern circumpolar region; another Hubble image captures evidence of dark matter in the galaxy cluster Cl 0024+17, whose presence is indicated by a ringlike structure in the image below and to the left. Dark matter makes up the bulk of the universe's mass and is believed to form the underlying structure of the cosmos; images such as this provide some of the strongest evidence to date for its existence.

Whirlpool Galaxy

Above, a Hubble Space Telescope image of the Whirlpool Galaxy (M51, or NGC 5194) and its smaller companion galaxy (NGC 5195); both are about 31 million light-years away. The dark regions in this face-on spiral galaxy show where clouds of gas and dust are being compressed, leading to the formation of massive, powerful stars that cause the surrounding, lower-density gas to glow with a bright pink color. A black hole millions of times more massive than the sun resides in the center of the spiral galaxy.

The Moon: Near Side

THE YOUNG EARTH HAD NO MOON. At some point in Earth's early history (certainly within the first 100 million years), an object roughly the size of Mars struck Earth a great, glancing blow. Instantly, most of the rogue body and a sizable chunk of Earth were vaporized. The ensuing cloud rose to above 14,000 miles (22,500 km) altitude, where it condensed into innumerable solid particles that orbited Earth as they aggregated into ever larger moonlets, eventually combining to form the Moon. This "giant impact" hypothesis of the Moon's origin is based on computer simulations and on laboratory analyses of lunar rocks gathered by six teams of Apollo astronauts. It also fits with data on the lunar topography and environment recorded by the United States' Clementine and Lunar Prospector spacecraft.

The airless lunar surface bakes in the Sun at up to 243°F (117°C) for two weeks at a time. All the while, it is sprayed with the solar wind of subatomic particles. Then, for an equal period, the same spot is in the dark, cooling to about minus 272°F (-169°C) when the Sun sets. Day and night, the Moon is bombarded by micrometeoroids and larger space rocks. Orbiting at an average distance of 239,000 miles (385,000 km), the Moon's rotation is synchronized with its orbital period in such a way that it is gravitationally locked, meaning it always shows the same face, the near side, to Earth. The far side can never be seen from Earth and has been photographed only from spacecraft.

Recently, NASA scientists used Earth-based radio telescopes to produce very detailed radar maps of the southern polar region, revealing that the terrain is much more rugged than had previously been thought. The south pole, specifically the area near the Shackleton Crater, has been considered as a possible landing site for a future manned mission to the Moon. It remains attractive because the bottoms of deep craters in this region may contain water ice, deposited there by previous comet impacts. The ice is a potential source of liquid water for drinking, as well as hydrogen and oxygen for fuel. If future missions to the Moon and Mars are able to use local resources, they will not be as reliant on new supplies from Earth. *(Continued on page 274)*

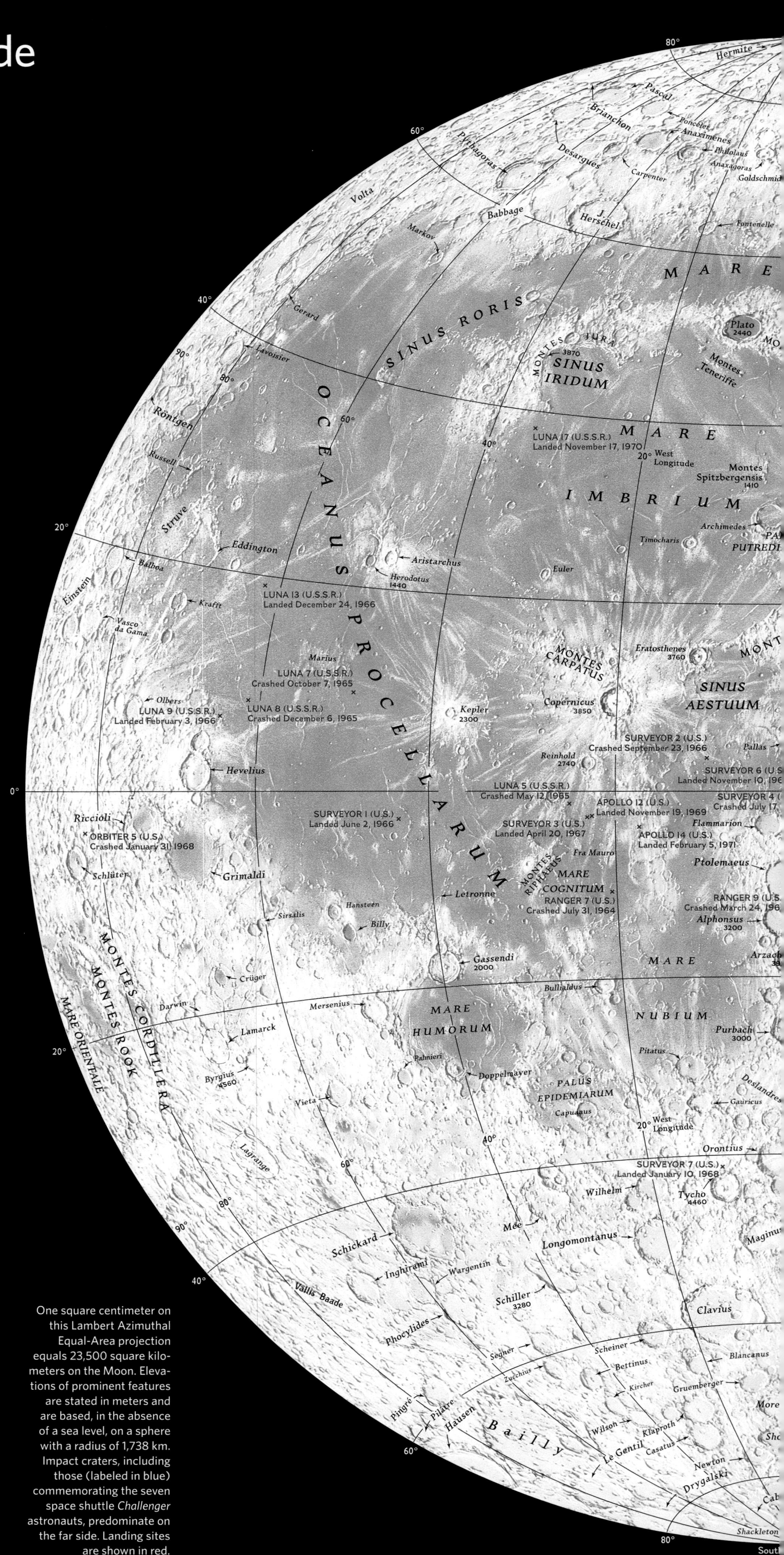

MARE
SINUS RORIS
SINUS IRIDUM
MONTES JURA
MARE IMBRIUM
OCEANUS PROCELLARUM
MONTES CARPATUS
SINUS AESTUUM
MARE COGNITUM
MONTES RIPHAEUS
MARE HUMORUM
MARE NUBIUM
PALUS EPIDEMIARUM
MONTES CORDILLERA
MONTES ROOK
MARE ORIENTALE
Vallis Baade
Plato 2440
Montes Teneriffe
Montes Spitzbergensis 1410
Archimedes
Timocharis
Eratosthenes 3760
Copernicus 3850
Kepler 2300
Reinhold 2740
Aristarchus
Herodotus 1440
Euler
Marius
Olbers
Hevelius
Riccioli
Grimaldi
Schlüter
Sirsalis
Hansteen
Billy
Letronne
Fra Mauro
Gassendi 2000
Bullialdus
Mersenius
Crüger
Darwin
Lamarck
Byrgius 4560
Vieta
Lagrange
Palmieri
Doppelmayer
Capuanus
Pitatus
Purbach 3000
Ptolemaeus
Alphonsus 3200
Flammarion
Orontius
Tycho 4460
Wilhelm
Longomontanus
Mee
Schickard
Inghirami
Wargentin
Schiller 3280
Phocylides
Segner
Zucchius
Scheiner
Bettinus
Kircher
Clavius
Blancanus
Gruemberger
Pingré
Pilâtre
Hausen
Bailly
Wilson
Le Gentil
Klaproth
Casatus
Newton
Drygalski
Shackleton
Hermite
Pascal
Brianchon
Poncelet
Anaximenes
Philolaus
Anaxagoras
Goldschmidt
Desargues
Carpenter
Pythagoras
Volta
Babbage
J. Herschel
Fontenelle
Markov
Gerard
Lavoisier
Röntgen
Russell
Struve
Eddington
Balboa
Einstein
Krafft
Vasco da Gama
Pallas
Gauricus
Deslandres
Maginus
Arzachel
LUNA 17 (U.S.S.R.) Landed November 17, 1970
LUNA 13 (U.S.S.R.) Landed December 24, 1966
LUNA 7 (U.S.S.R.) Crashed October 7, 1965
LUNA 8 (U.S.S.R.) Crashed December 6, 1965
LUNA 9 (U.S.S.R.) Landed February 3, 1966
LUNA 5 (U.S.S.R.) Crashed May 12, 1965
ORBITER 5 (U.S.) Crashed January 31, 1968
SURVEYOR 1 (U.S.) Landed June 2, 1966
SURVEYOR 2 (U.S.) Crashed September 23, 1966
SURVEYOR 3 (U.S.) Landed April 20, 1967
SURVEYOR 6 (U.S.) Landed November 10, 1967
SURVEYOR 7 (U.S.) Landed January 10, 1968
APOLLO 12 (U.S.) Landed November 19, 1969
APOLLO 14 (U.S.) Landed February 5, 1971
RANGER 7 (U.S.) Crashed July 31, 1964
RANGER 9 (U.S.) Crashed March 24, 1965
20° West Longitude

One square centimeter on this Lambert Azimuthal Equal-Area projection equals 23,500 square kilometers on the Moon. Elevations of prominent features are stated in meters and are based, in the absence of a sea level, on a sphere with a radius of 1,738 km. Impact craters, including those (labeled in blue) commemorating the seven space shuttle *Challenger* astronauts, predominate on the far side. Landing sites are shown in red.

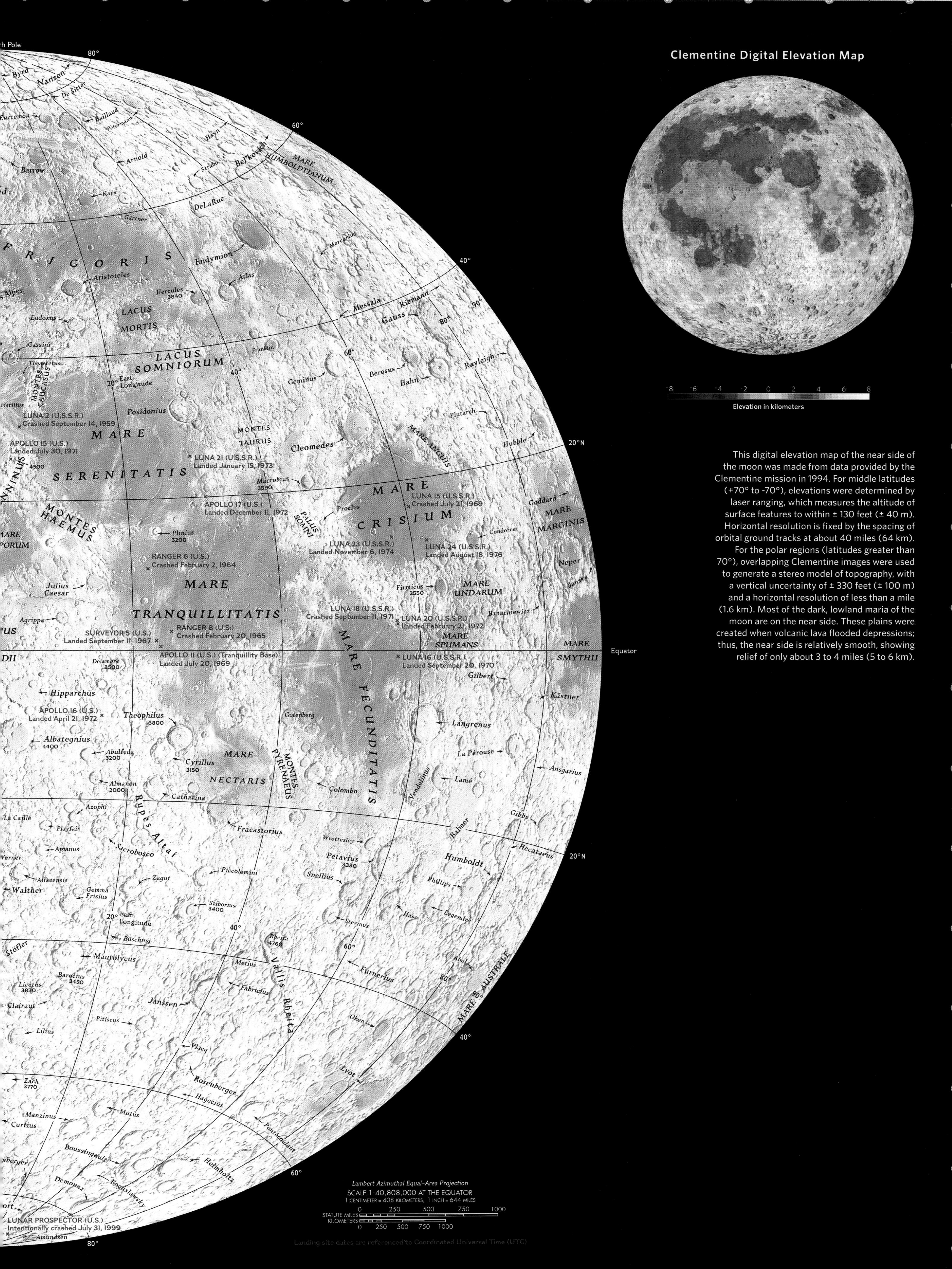

MARE FRIGORIS
MARE HUMBOLDTIANUM
LACUS MORTIS
LACUS SOMNIORUM
MARE SERENITATIS
MONTES TAURUS
MONTES HAEMUS
MARE TRANQUILLITATIS
MARE CRISIUM
MARE ANGUIS
PALUS SOMNI
MARE UNDARUM
MARE SPUMANS
MARE MARGINIS
MARE SMYTHII
MARE FECUNDITATIS
MARE NECTARIS
MONTES PYRENAEUS
Rupes Altai
Vallis Rheita
MARE AUSTRALE
LUNA 2 (U.S.S.R.) Crashed September 14, 1959
APOLLO 15 (U.S.) Landed July 30, 1971
LUNA 21 (U.S.S.R.) Landed January 15, 1973
APOLLO 17 (U.S.) Landed December 11, 1972
LUNA 15 (U.S.S.R.) Crashed July 21, 1969
LUNA 23 (U.S.S.R.) Landed November 6, 1974
LUNA 24 (U.S.S.R.) Landed August 18, 1976
RANGER 6 (U.S.) Crashed February 2, 1964
LUNA 18 (U.S.S.R.) Crashed September 11, 1971
LUNA 20 (U.S.S.R.) Landed February 21, 1972
SURVEYOR 5 (U.S.) Landed September 11, 1967
RANGER 8 (U.S.) Crashed February 20, 1965
APOLLO 11 (U.S.) (Tranquillity Base) Landed July 20, 1969
LUNA 16 (U.S.S.R.) Landed September 20, 1970
APOLLO 16 (U.S.) Landed April 21, 1972
LUNAR PROSPECTOR (U.S.) Intentionally crashed July 31, 1999
20° East Longitude
Equator
20°N
Lambert Azimuthal Equal-Area Projection
SCALE 1:40,808,000 AT THE EQUATOR
1 CENTIMETER = 408 KILOMETERS; 1 INCH = 644 MILES
STATUTE MILES 0 250 500 750 1000
KILOMETERS 0 250 500 750 1000
Landing site dates are referenced to Coordinated Universal Time (UTC)

Clementine Digital Elevation Map

-8 -6 -4 -2 0 2 4 6 8

Elevation in kilometers

This digital elevation map of the near side of the moon was made from data provided by the Clementine mission in 1994. For middle latitudes (+70° to -70°), elevations were determined by laser ranging, which measures the altitude of surface features to within ± 130 feet (± 40 m). Horizontal resolution is fixed by the spacing of orbital ground tracks at about 40 miles (64 km). For the polar regions (latitudes greater than 70°), overlapping Clementine images were used to generate a stereo model of topography, with a vertical uncertainty of ± 330 feet (± 100 m) and a horizontal resolution of less than a mile (1.6 km). Most of the dark, lowland maria of the moon are on the near side. These plains were created when volcanic lava flooded depressions; thus, the near side is relatively smooth, showing relief of only about 3 to 4 miles (5 to 6 km).

The Moon: Far Side

(Continued from page 272)

The rocks and materials brought back by the Apollo missions are extremely dry; the Moon has no indigenous water. However, it is bombarded by water-rich comets and meteoroids. Most of this water is lost to space, but some is trapped and frozen in permanently shadowed areas near the Moon's poles.

To the unaided eye, the bright lunar highlands and the dark maria (Latin for "seas") make up the "man in the Moon." A telescope shows that they consist of a great variety of round impact features, scars left by objects that struck the Moon long ago. In the highlands, craters are closely packed together. In the maria, they are fewer. The largest scars are the impact basins, ranging up to about 1,500 miles (2,400 km) across. The basin floors were flooded with lava some time after the titanic collisions that formed them. The dark lava flows are what the eye discerns as maria. Wrinkled ridges, domed hills, and fissures mark the maria, all familiar aspects of volcanic landscapes. Young craters are centers of radial patterns of bright ejecta, material thrown from the impacts that made them. Because the force of gravity is weaker on the Moon (only about one-sixth that on Earth), blocks of rock hurled from impacts travel farther than they would on Earth.

The Moon has no mountains like the Himalaya, produced by one tectonic plate bumping into another. There is no continental drift. Everywhere, the lunar surface is sheathed in regolith, a rocky rubble created by the constant bombardment by meteoroids, asteroids, and comets. Lunar mountains consist of volcanic domes, as well as the central peaks and rims of impact craters.

The Lunar Reconnaissance Orbiter, planned for a late-2008 launch, should provide exceptionally clear images of the lunar surface, including three-dimensional information and polar illumination observations. It will also perform detailed measurements of the temperature and radiation environment. These data will help scientists choose interesting, yet safe, locations for future manned missions to the Moon, planned to commence around 2020. Members of the general public were invited to submit their names for inclusion in an electronic roster that will travel aboard the Orbiter.

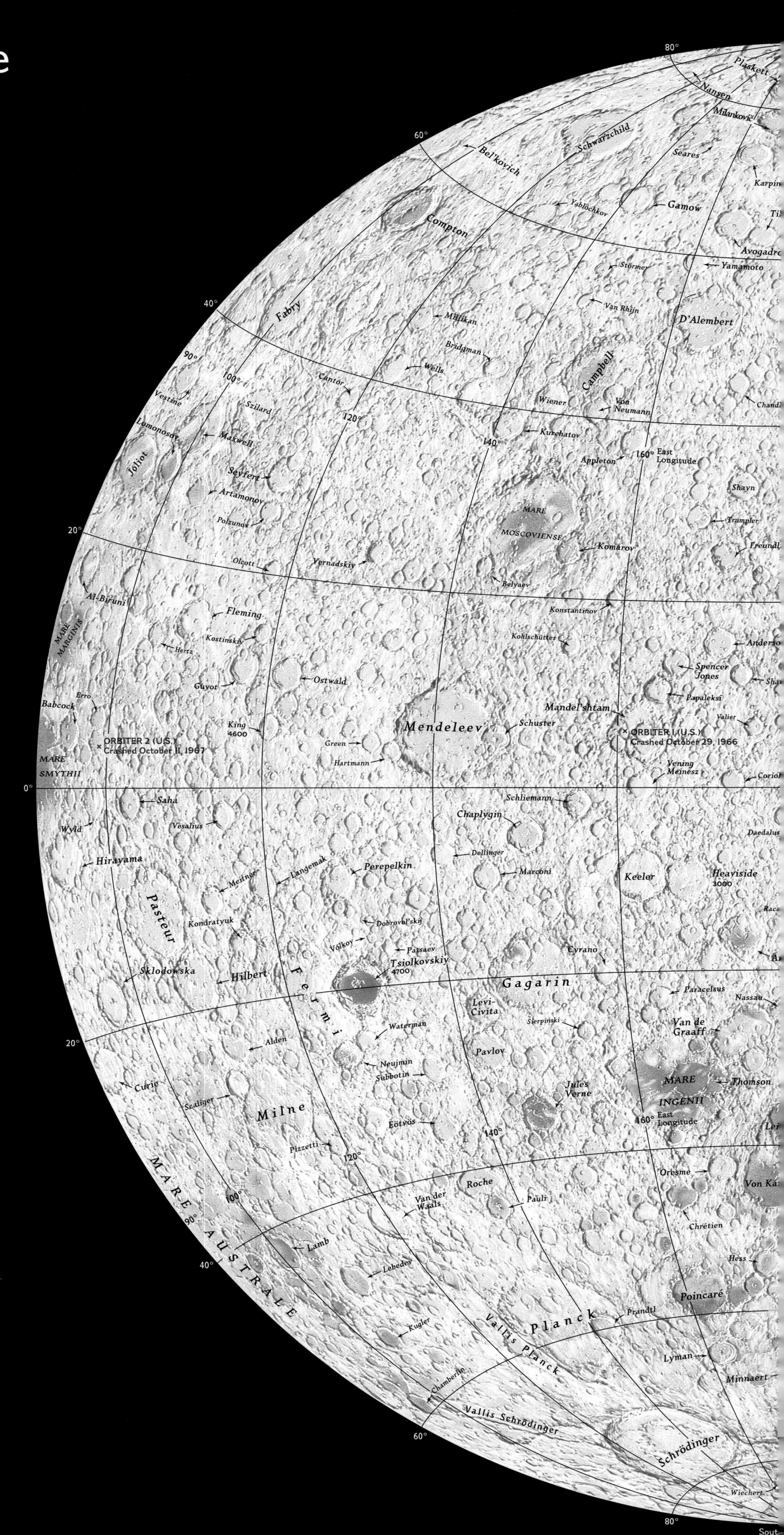
80°
60°
40°
20°
0°
20°
40°
60°
80°
90°
100°
120°
140°
160° East Longitude
Plaskett
Nansen
Milankovič
Bel'kovich
Schwarzschild
Seares
Karpinskiy
Compton
Yablochkov
Gamow
Avogadro
Stormer
Yamamoto
Fabry
Millikan
Van Rhijn
D'Alembert
Bridgman
Wells
Campbell
Cantor
Wiener
Von Neumann
Vestine
Szilard
Lomonosov
Maxwell
Kurchatov
Joliot
Appleton
Seyfert
Artamonov
Shayn
Polzunov
MARE MOSCOVIENSE
Trumpler
Komarov
Freundlich
Olcott
Vernadskiy
Belyaev
Al-Biruni
Konstantinov
Fleming
MARE MARGINIS
Kostinskiy
Kohlschütter
Anderson
Hertz
Spencer Jones
Ostwald
Guyot
Papaleksi
Erro
Babcock
Mandel'shtam
Valier
King 4600
Mendeleev
Schuster
ORBITER 2 (U.S.) Crashed October 11, 1967
ORBITER 1 (U.S.) Crashed October 29, 1966
Green
MARE SMYTHII
Hartmann
Vening Meinesz
Saha
Schliemann
Wyld
Vesalius
Chaplygin
Daedalus
Hirayama
Dellinger
Perepelkin
Marconi
Keeler
Heaviside 3000
Langemak
Meitner
Pasteur
Dobrovol'skiy
Kondratyuk
Volkov
Patsaev
Tsiolkovskiy 4700
Cyrano
Sklodowska
Hilbert
Fermi
Gagarin
Paracelsus
Nassau
Levi-Civita
Sierpinski
Van de Graaff
Waterman
Alden
Pavlov
Neujmin
Subbotin
MARE INGENII
Thomson
Curie
Jules Verne
Scaliger
Milne
Eötvös
Pizzetti
Oresme
Von Kármán
Roche
Van der Waals
Pauli
MARE AUSTRALE
Chrétien
Lamb
Lebedev
Hess
Poincaré
Kugler
Vallis Planck
Planck
Prandtl
Lyman
Chamberlin
Minnaert
Vallis Schrödinger
Schrödinger
Wiechert

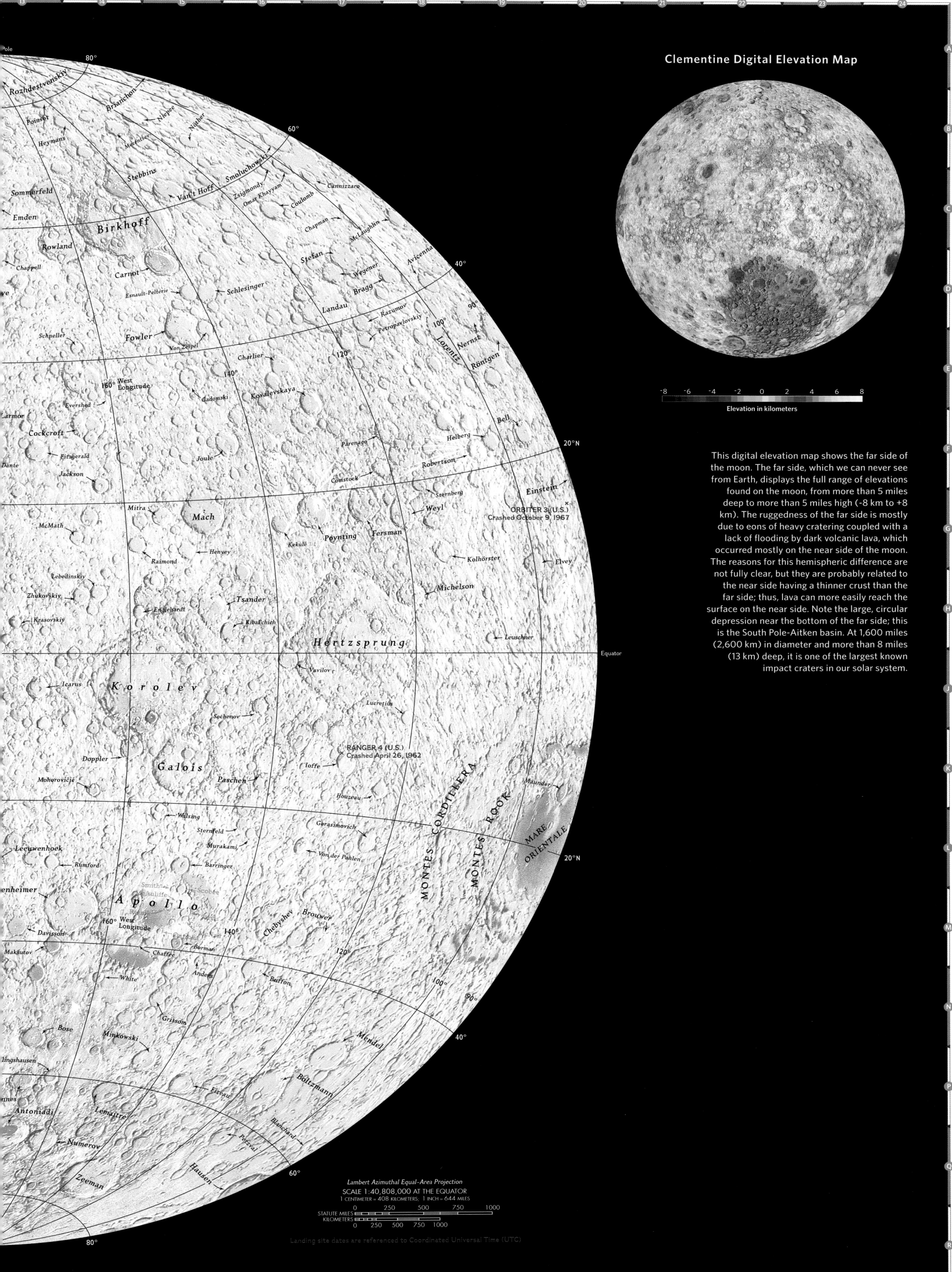

Clementine Digital Elevation Map
-8 -6 -4 -2 0 2 4 6 8
Elevation in kilometers
This digital elevation map shows the far side of the moon. The far side, which we can never see from Earth, displays the full range of elevations found on the moon, from more than 5 miles deep to more than 5 miles high (-8 km to +8 km). The ruggedness of the far side is mostly due to eons of heavy cratering coupled with a lack of flooding by dark volcanic lava, which occurred mostly on the near side of the moon. The reasons for this hemispheric difference are not fully clear, but they are probably related to the near side having a thinner crust than the far side; thus, lava can more easily reach the surface on the near side. Note the large, circular depression near the bottom of the far side; this is the South Pole-Aitken basin. At 1,600 miles (2,600 km) in diameter and more than 8 miles (13 km) deep, it is one of the largest known impact craters in our solar system.
80°
60°
40°
20°N
Equator
20°N
40°
60°
80°
160° West Longitude
140°
120°
100°
90°
Rozhdestvenskiy
Brianchon
Poinsot
Heymans
Niepce
Nöther
Merzenius
Stebbins
Smoluchowski
Van't Hoff
Sommerfeld
Emden
Birkhoff
Zsigmondy
Omar Khayyam
Coulomb
Cannizzaro
Rowland
Chapman
McLaughlin
Chappell
Carnot
Stefan
Wegener
Avicenna
Esnault-Pelterie
Schlesinger
Bragg
Landau
Razumov
Petropavlovskiy
Schjelerup
Fowler
Von Zeipel
Lorentz
Nernst
Röntgen
Charlier
Evershed
Gadomski
Kovalevskaya
Bell
Cockcroft
Parenago
Helberg
Fitzgerald
Joule
Robertson
Jackson
Comstock
Sternberg
Einstein
Mitra
Mach
Weyl
ORBITER 3 (U.S.)
Crashed October 9, 1967
McMath
Kekulé
Poynting
Fersman
Henyey
Raimond
Kolhörster
Elvey
Lebedinskiy
Michelson
Zhukovskiy
Tsander
Engelhardt
Krasovskiy
Kibal'chich
Hertzsprung
Leuschner
Vavilov
Icarus
Korolev
Lucretius
Sechenov
RANGER 4 (U.S.)
Crashed April 26, 1962
Doppler
Ioffe
Galois
Paschen
Mohorovičić
Maunder
Houzeau
Wilsing
Sternfeld
Gerasimovich
MONTES CORDILLERA
MONTES ROOK
MARE ORIENTALE
Murakami
Leeuwenhoek
Von der Pahlen
Rumford
Barringer
Apollo
Chebyshev
Brouwer
Davisson
Borman
Maksutov
Chaffee
Anders
Buffon
White
Grissom
Bose
Minkowski
Mendel
Boltzmann
Fizeau
Antoniadi
Lemaître
Blanchard
Numerov
Petzval
Zeeman
Hausen
Lambert Azimuthal Equal-Area Projection
SCALE 1:40,808,000 AT THE EQUATOR
1 CENTIMETER = 408 KILOMETERS; 1 INCH = 644 MILES
STATUTE MILES 0 250 500 750 1000
KILOMETERS 0 250 500 750 1000
Landing site dates are referenced to Coordinated Universal Time (UTC)

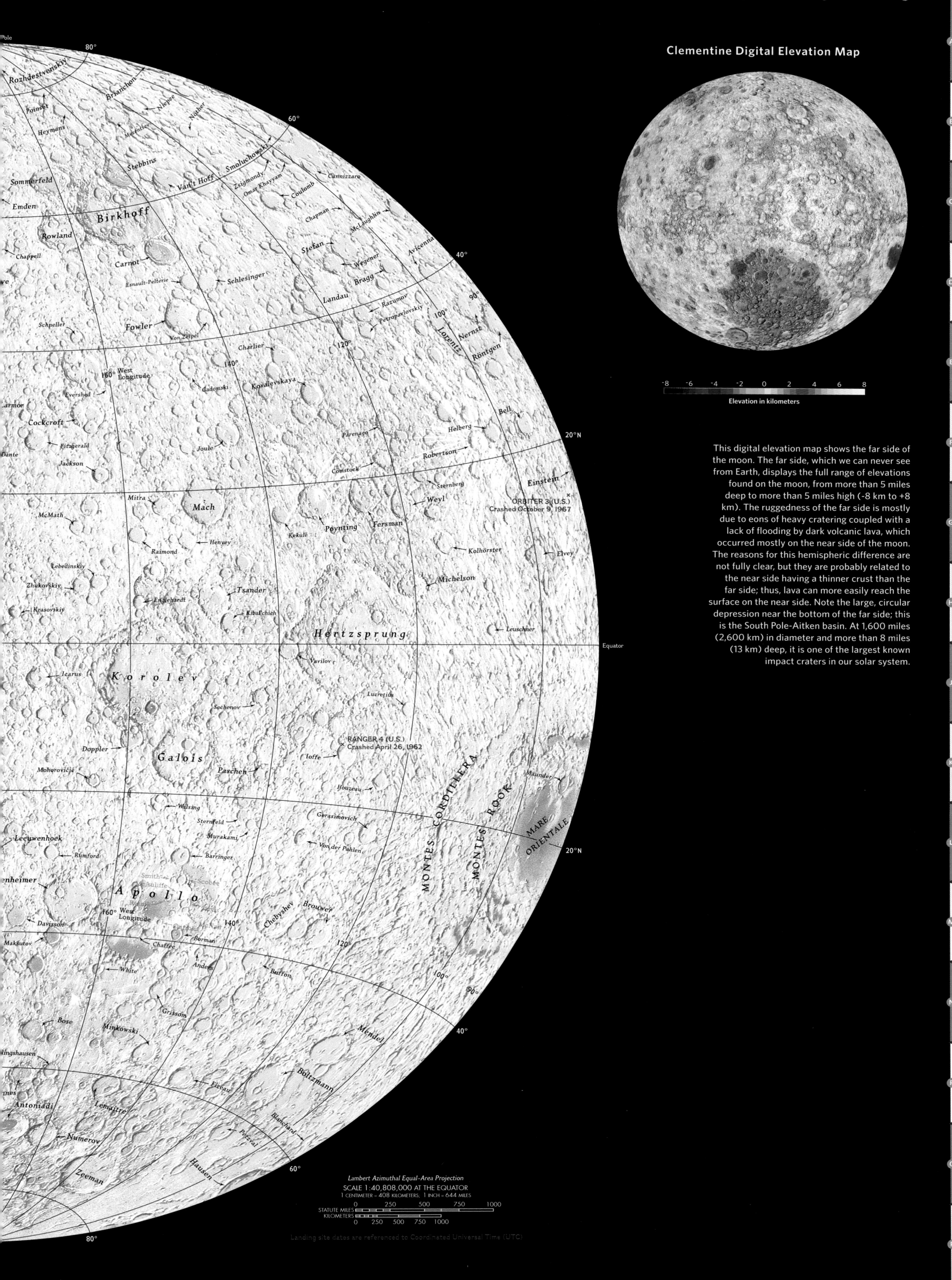
Clementine Digital Elevation Map
-8 -6 -4 -2 0 2 4 6 8
Elevation in kilometers
This digital elevation map shows the far side of the moon. The far side, which we can never see from Earth, displays the full range of elevations found on the moon, from more than 5 miles deep to more than 5 miles high (-8 km to +8 km). The ruggedness of the far side is mostly due to eons of heavy cratering coupled with a lack of flooding by dark volcanic lava, which occurred mostly on the near side of the moon. The reasons for this hemispheric difference are not fully clear, but they are probably related to the near side having a thinner crust than the far side; thus, lava can more easily reach the surface on the near side. Note the large, circular depression near the bottom of the far side; this is the South Pole-Aitken basin. At 1,600 miles (2,600 km) in diameter and more than 8 miles (13 km) deep, it is one of the largest known impact craters in our solar system.
ORBITER 3 (U.S.)
Crashed October 9, 1967
RANGER 4 (U.S.)
Crashed April 26, 1962
Hertzsprung
Korolev
Galois
Apollo
Birkhoff
Mach
MONTES CORDILLERA
MONTES ROOK
MARE ORIENTALE
Rozhdestvenskiy
Poinsot
Heymans
Brianchon
Niepce
Nöther
Sommerfeld
Stebbins
Van't Hoff
Smoluchowski
Zsigmondy
Omar Khayyam
Cannizzaro
Coulomb
Emden
Rowland
Chappell
Chapman
McLaughlin
Carnot
Stefan
Avicenna
Wegener
Esnault-Pelterie
Schlesinger
Bragg
Landau
Razumov
Petropavlovskiy
Schjeller
Fowler
Von Zeipel
Lorentz
Nernst
Röntgen
Charlier
160° West Longitude
140°
120°
100°
90°
Evershed
Gadomski
Kovalevskaya
Cockcroft
Bell
Fitzgerald
Joule
Parenago
Helberg
Robertson
Jackson
Comstock
Sternberg
Einstein
Mitra
Weyl
McMath
Poynting
Fersman
Kekulé
Henyey
Raimond
Kolhörster
Elvey
Lebedinskiy
Michelson
Zhukovskiy
Tsander
Engelhardt
Krasovskiy
Kibal'chich
Leuschner
Vavilov
Equator
Icarus
Lucretius
Sechenov
Doppler
Ioffe
Mohorovičić
Paschen
Houzeau
Maunder
Wilsing
Gerasimovich
Sternfeld
Murakami
Leeuwenhoek
Von der Pahlen
Rumford
Barringer
Chebyshev
Brouwer
Davisson
Berman
Maksutov
Chaffee
Anders
White
Buffon
Grissom
Bose
Minkowski
Mendel
Boltzmann
Fizeau
Antoniadi
Lemaître
Blanchard
Numerov
Petzval
Zeeman
Hausen
80°
60°
40°
20°N
Lambert Azimuthal Equal-Area Projection
SCALE 1:40,808,000 AT THE EQUATOR
1 CENTIMETER = 408 KILOMETERS; 1 INCH = 644 MILES
STATUTE MILES 0 250 500 750 1000
KILOMETERS 0 250 500 750 1000
Landing site dates are referenced to Coordinated Universal Time (UTC)

Solar System

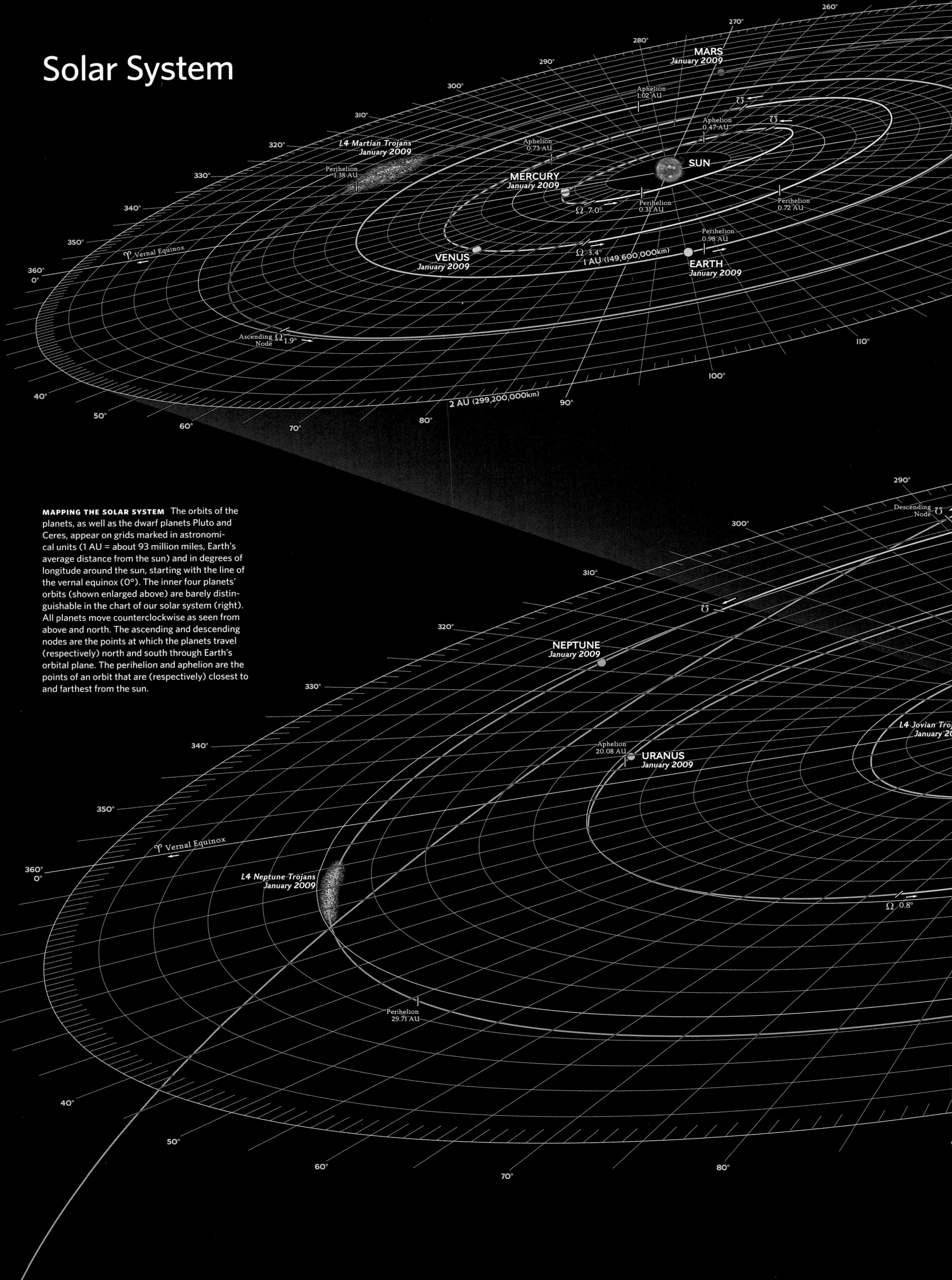

MARS
January 2009
SUN
MERCURY
January 2009
VENUS
January 2009
EARTH
January 2009
L4 Martian Trojans
January 2009
Aphelion 1.02 AU
Aphelion 0.47 AU
Aphelion 0.73 AU
Perihelion 1.38 AU
Perihelion 0.31 AU
Perihelion 0.72 AU
Perihelion 0.98 AU
Ω 7.0°
Ω 3.4°
Ascending Node Ω 1.9°
1 AU (149,600,000km)
2 AU (299,200,000km)
♈ Vernal Equinox
NEPTUNE
January 2009
URANUS
January 2009
Aphelion 20.08 AU
L4 Neptune Trojans
January 2009
Perihelion 29.71 AU
Descending Node
Ω 0.8°

MAPPING THE SOLAR SYSTEM The orbits of the planets, as well as the dwarf planets Pluto and Ceres, appear on grids marked in astronomical units (1 AU = about 93 million miles, Earth's average distance from the sun) and in degrees of longitude around the sun, starting with the line of the vernal equinox (0°). The inner four planets' orbits (shown enlarged above) are barely distinguishable in the chart of our solar system (right). All planets move counterclockwise as seen from above and north. The ascending and descending nodes are the points at which the planets travel (respectively) north and south through Earth's orbital plane. The perihelion and aphelion are the points of an orbit that are (respectively) closest to and farthest from the sun.

Africa

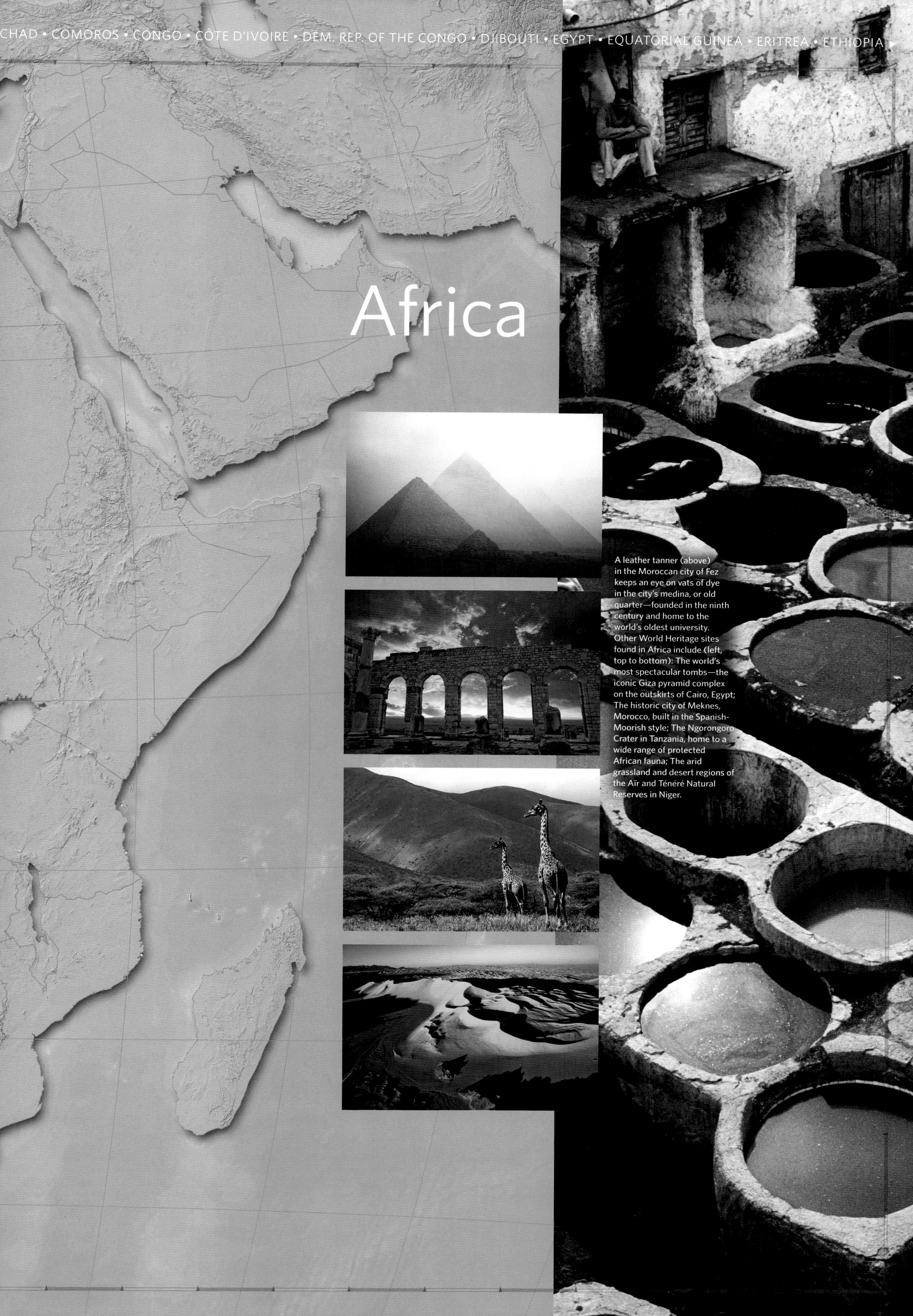

A leather tanner (above) in the Moroccan city of Fez keeps an eye on vats of dye in the city's medina, or old quarter—founded in the ninth century and home to the world's oldest university. Other World Heritage sites found in Africa include (left, top to bottom): The world's most spectacular tombs—the iconic Giza pyramid complex on the outskirts of Cairo, Egypt; The historic city of Meknes, Morocco, built in the Spanish-Moorish style; The Ngorongoro Crater in Tanzania, home to a wide range of protected African fauna; The arid grassland and desert regions of the Aïr and Ténéré Natural Reserves in Niger.

Longitude West 20° of Greenwich
Longitude East 20° of Greenwich
EUROPE
ASIA
IBERIAN PENINSULA
BALKAN PENINSULA
ANATOLIA (ASIA MINOR)
ARABIAN PENINSULA
BLACK SEA
CASPIAN SEA
MEDITERRANEAN SEA
RED SEA
GULF OF ADEN
PERSIAN GULF
Corsica
Sardinia
Balearic Is.
Sicily
Peloponnesus
Crete
Rhodes
Cyprus
Strait of Gibraltar
Cape Blanc
G. of Tunis
G. of Hamamet
G. of Gabes
Jerba I.
Chott Melrhir
Shott el Jerid
Madeira
MADEIRA ISLANDS
Salvage Islands
CANARY ISLANDS
La Palma
Tenerife
Gomera
Ferro
Gran Canaria
Lanzarote
Fuerteventura
C. Beddouza
Cape Rhir
C. Boujdour
TROPIC OF CANCER
C. Blanc
C. Timiris (Mirik)
C. Verde
Bissagos Is.
Er Rif 2456
Tell Atlas
2308
2326
ATLAS MOUNTAINS
High Atlas
Saharan Atlas
Jebel Toubkal 4165
Oued Drâa
Hamada du Drâa
Great Western Dunes
Great Eastern Dunes
Tademaït Plateau
Sebkha Mekerrhane
Sebkha Azzel Matti
Erg Iguidi
Erg Chech
Zednes 460
Tanezrouft
Hamada de Tinrhert
Şaḩrā' Awbārī
Tassili-n-Ajjer
Mount Tahat 3003
Ahaggar Mts.
Tassili Oua-n-Ahaggar
Adrar des Iforas
1000
Tarazit Massif
Aïr Massif
Mt. Bagzane 2022
Ténéré
Djado Plateau
Şaḩrā' Marzūq
Gefara
Jabal Nafūsah
Cape Misurata
Gulf of Sidra
Jabal as Sawdā'
Al Harūj al Aswad
1200
Rebiana Sand Sea
Ras al Hilāl
Jabal al Akhḑar
G. of Bomba
G. of Salûm
Arabs Gulf
Libyan Plateau
264
-133 Qattara Depression
Sand Sea of Calanscio
Sarīr Calanscio
Western Desert
Libyan Desert
Kufra Oasis
Gilf Kebîr Plateau
Abu Ballâs 467
Jebel 'Uweinat 1893
Gebel Siri 420
Toshka Lakes
Lake Nasser
L. Nubia
Nubian Desert
Jebel Abyad Plateau
Nile River Delta
Nile
SUEZ CANAL
SINAI
Mt. Sinai 2285
G. of Suez
Gulf of Aqaba
Râs Muhammad
Eastern Desert
Râs Banâs
Cape Elba (Ras Hadarba)
Suakin Archipelago
Ras Kasar
Jebel Sabidana 1907
Dahlak Archipelago
Lowest point in Africa
Bab el Mandeb
G. of Tadjoura
Cape Gwardafuy
2408
SOMALI PENINSULA
Ogadēn
Haud
SAHARA
Akchâr
Djouf
El Mreyyé
Tagant
Trarza
Lake Faguibine
Niger
Inland Niger Delta
Lake Débo
Bani
Sénégal
Gambia
Falémé
Fouta Djallon
1116
Loma Mts.
1948
Source of the Niger
Nimba Mts.
765
White Volta
Black Volta
Komoé
Lake Volta
Kainji Res.
UPPER GUINEA
Slave Coast
Grain Coast
Cavalla
Bafing
Benue
Jos Plateau
1781
Hadejia
Gana
Yobe
Manga
Lake Chad
Pic Touside 3315
Tibesti Mountains
Emi Koussi 3415
Bodele Depression
Ennedi
1310
Jebel Teljo 1954
3088
Marra Mts.
Guéra Massif 1613
Chari
Logone
Mbang Mts.
1213
Karre Mts.
Dar Rounga
1400
Chaîne des Bongos
Tondou Massif
Bahr el 'Arab
Sudd
Mountain Nile
SAHEL
Jebel ed Dair 1412
Nuba Mts.
1325
White Nile
El Gezira
Blue Nile
Atbara
Ras Dejen 4620
Lake Tana
ETHIOPIAN HIGHLANDS
Gurage 3719
Lake Abaya
Mendebo Mts.
Batu 4307
VALLEY
Danakil Desert
Lake Assal -156 (-512 ft)
-116
200

Azimuthal Equidistant Projection

SCALE 1:18,690,600

1 CENTIMETER = 187 KILOMETERS; 1 INCH = 295 MILES

KILOMETERS 0 200 400 600 800 1000

STATUTE MILES 0 200 400 600 800 1000

International boundary

Disputed or undefined boundary

Tristan da Cunha Group
Tristan da Cunha I.
Inaccessible I.
Nightingale I.

ATLANTIC OCEAN

INDIAN OCEAN

Mozambique Channel

MADAGASCAR

KALAHARI DESERT

CONGO BASIN

GREAT RIFT VALLEY

KENYA HIGHLANDS

KATANGA PLATEAU

LOWER GUINEA

EQUATOR

TROPIC OF CAPRICORN

Meridian of Greenwich (London)

Saint Helena 823

Ascension 875

Annobón

São Tomé

Príncipe

Cape Lopez

Kilimanjaro 5895 (19340 ft)
Highest point in Africa

Mt. Kenya 5199

Mt. Elgon 4321

Ruwenzori 5109

Lake Victoria 1133

Sources of the Nile

Serengeti Plain

Masai Steppe

Olduvai Gorge

Lake Tanganyika

Lake Malawi

Zambezi River Delta

Victoria Falls

Lake Kariba

Okavango Delta

Makgadikgadi Pans

Etosha Pan

Namib Desert

Skeleton Coast

Drakensberg

Thabana Ntlenyana 3482

Great Karroo

Cape of Good Hope

Cape Agulhas

Comoro Is.

Aldabra Is.

Cap d'Ambre

Maromokotro 2876

Boby Peak 2658

Bemaraha Plat.

Cape Ste. Marie

Zanzibar Island

Pemba Island

Mafia Island

Cape Delgado

Longitude West 20° of Greenwich
BELGIUM
LUX.
PARIS
FRANCE
GERMANY
SWITZERLAND
Bern
PRAHA (Prague)
CZECH REP.
POLAND
WIEN (Vienna)
AUSTRIA
SLOVAKIA
Bratislava
BUDAPEST
HUNGARY
Ljubljana
SLOVENIA
Zagreb
CROATIA
BOSNIA & HERZEGOVINA
Sarajevo
BEOGRAD (Belgrade)
SERBIA
MONTENEGRO
Podgorica
KOSOVO
Skopje
MACEDONIA
Tiranë (Tirana)
ALBANIA
SOFIYA (Sofia)
BULGARIA
ROMANIA
BUCUREŞTI (Bucharest)
MOLDOVA
Chişinău
KYIV (Kiev)
UKRAINE
RUSSIA
KAZAKHSTAN
UZBEKISTAN
TURKMENISTAN
CASPIAN SEA
BAKI (Baku)
AZERBAIJAN
ARMENIA
YEREVAN
GEORGIA
T'BILISI
ABKHAZIA
BLACK SEA
TURKEY (ANATOLIA)
ANKARA (Angora)
GREECE
Athína (Athens)
ITALY
ROMA (Rome)
ANDORRA
SPAIN
MADRID
PORTUGAL
Lisboa (Lisbon)
AZORES (AÇORES) Portugal
GIBRALTAR U.K.
Strait of Gibraltar
MEDITERRANEAN SEA
MALTA
TUNIS
TUNISIA
ALGER (Algiers)
Oran
Constantine
Annaba
MOROCCO
CASABLANCA
RABAT
FÈS (Fez)
Marrakech
Tanger (Tangier)
MADEIRA ISLANDS Portugal
CANARY ISLANDS (ISLAS CANARIAS) Spain
Las Palmas
Laayoune
WESTERN SAHARA
Morocco
ALGERIA
LIBYA
ṬARĀBULUS (Tripoli)
Banghāzī (Benghazi)
TRIPOLITANIA
CYRENAICA
FEZZAN
EGYPT
EL ISKANDARĪYA (Alexandria)
EL QĀHIRA (Cairo)
EL GÎZA
Bûr Sa'îd (Port Said)
El Suweis (Suez)
Luxor
Aswân
Boundary claimed by Sudan
Treaty boundary
CYPRUS
Lefkosia (Nicosia)
LEBANON
BEYROUTH (Beirut)
SYRIA
DIMASHQ (Damascus)
ISRAEL
Jerusalem
JORDAN
'AMMĀN
IRAQ
BAGHDĀD
IRAN
TEHRĀN
KUWAIT
Al Kuwayt (Kuwait)
PERSIAN GULF
BAHRAIN
Al Manāmah (Manama)
QATAR
Ad Dawhah (Doha)
U.A.E.
SAUDI ARABIA
AR RIYĀD (Riyadh)
TROPIC OF CANCER
RED SEA
YEMEN
Şan'ā' (Sanaa)
GULF OF ADEN
DJIBOUTI
Djibouti
SOMALILAND
Hargeysa
PUNTLAND
Garoowe
ERITREA
Asmara
ETHIOPIA
ĀDĪS ĀBEBA (Addis Ababa)
SUDAN
Port Sudan
KHARTOUM
KHARTOUM NORTH
OMDURMAN
Kassala
El Obeid
Kosti
El Fasher
Nyala
DARFUR
White Nile
Blue Nile
SAHARA
MAURITANIA
Nouakchott
MALI
BAMAKO
Tombouctou (Timbuktu)
NIGER
Niamey
AOZOU STRIP
CHAD
N'Djamena
Lake Chad
SENEGAL
DAKAR
GAMBIA
Banjul
GUINEA-BISSAU
Bissau
GUINEA
CONAKRY
SIERRA LEONE
Freetown
LIBERIA
Monrovia
CÔTE D'IVOIRE (IVORY COAST)
Yamoussoukro (legislative)
ABIDJAN (administrative)
BURKINA FASO
OUAGADOUGOU
GHANA
KUMASI
BENIN
NIGERIA
ABUJA
KANO
LAGOS
CENTRAL AFRICAN REPUBLIC

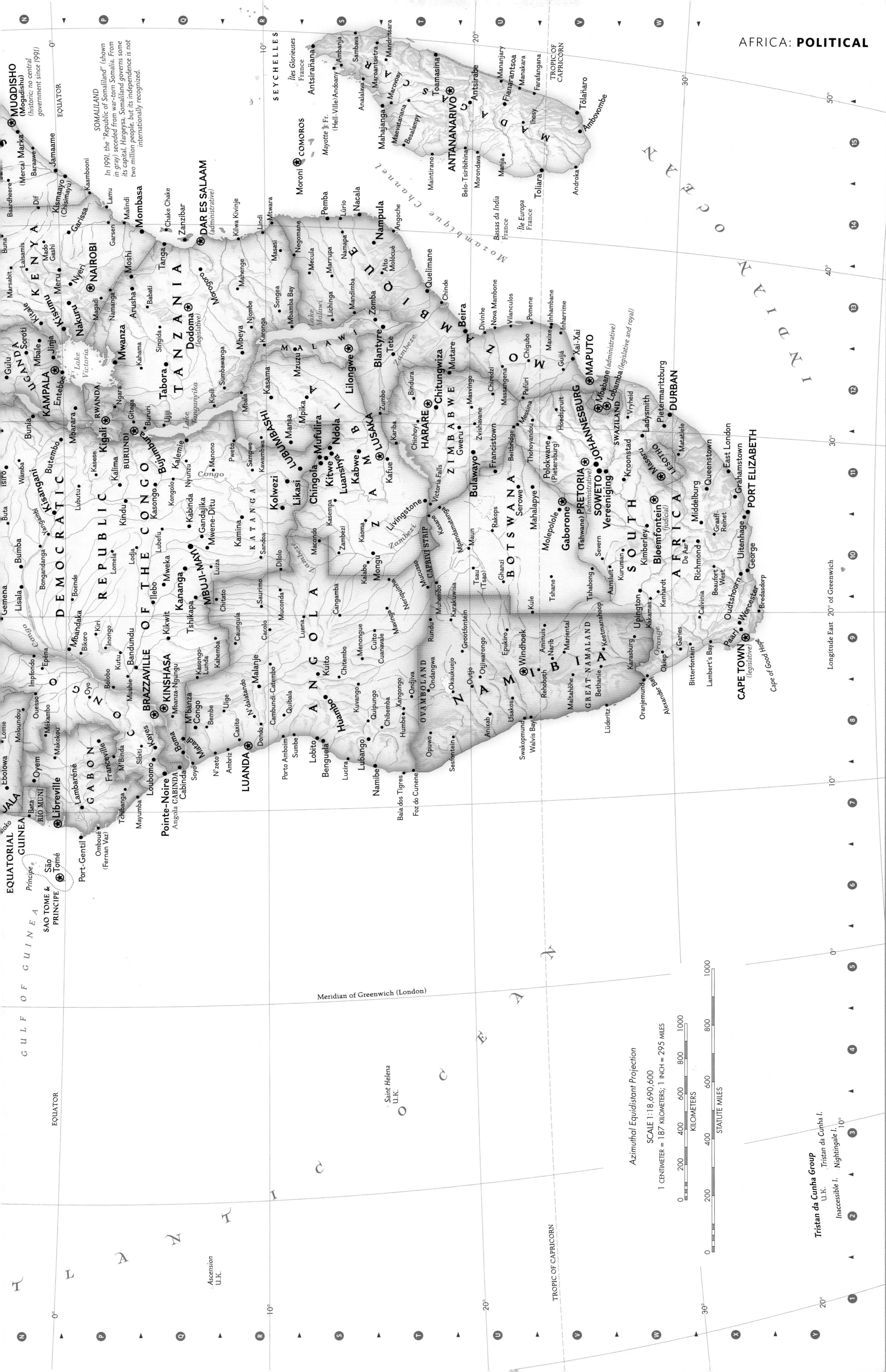

SOMALILAND
In 1991, the "Republic of Somaliland" (shown in gray) seceded from war-torn Somalia. From its capital, Hargeysa, Somaliland governs some two million people, but its independence is not internationally recognized.

MUQDISHO (Mogadishu) *(historic; no central government since 1991)*

Azimuthal Equidistant Projection
SCALE 1:18,690,600
1 CENTIMETER = 187 KILOMETERS; 1 INCH = 295 MILES

KILOMETERS 0 200 400 600 800 1000
STATUTE MILES 0 200 400 600 800 1000

Longitude East 20° of Greenwich

Meridian of Greenwich (London)

EQUATOR

TROPIC OF CAPRICORN

ATLANTIC OCEAN

INDIAN OCEAN

GULF OF GUINEA

Mozambique Channel

Africa: Themes

Continental Facts

TOTAL NUMBER OF COUNTRIES: 53

TOTAL AREA: 30,065,000 sq km (11,608,000 sq mi)

FIRST INDEPENDENT COUNTRY: Ethiopia, over 2,000 years old

"YOUNGEST" COUNTRY: Eritrea, May 24, 1993

MOST POPULOUS COUNTRY: Nigeria 144,430,000

LEAST POPULOUS COUNTRY: Seychelles 86,000

LARGEST COUNTRY BY AREA: Sudan 2,505,813 sq km (967,500 sq mi)

SMALLEST COUNTRY BY AREA: Seychelles 455 sq km (176 sq mi)

HIGHEST ELEVATION: Kilimanjaro, Tanzania 5,895 m (19,340 ft)

LOWEST ELEVATION: Lake Assal, Djibouti -156 m (-512 ft)

Climate Zones

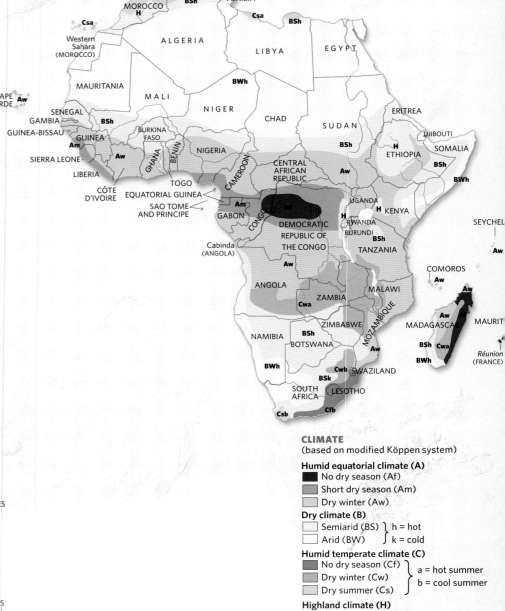

CLIMATE
(based on modified Köppen system)

Humid equatorial climate (A)
- No dry season (Af)
- Short dry season (Am)
- Dry winter (Aw)

Dry climate (B)
- Semiarid (BS)
- Arid (BW)

h = hot
k = cold

Humid temperate climate (C)
- No dry season (Cf)
- Dry winter (Cw)
- Dry summer (Cs)

a = hot summer
b = cool summer

Highland climate (H)
- Unclassified highlands

Water Availability

MOROCCO
TUNISIA
Western Sahara (MOROCCO)
ALGERIA
LIBYA
EGYPT
CAPE VERDE
MAURITANIA
MALI
NIGER
CHAD
SUDAN
ERITREA
SENEGAL
GAMBIA
GUINEA-BISSAU
GUINEA
BURKINA FASO
NIGERIA
DJIBOUTI
SOMALIA
ETHIOPIA
SIERRA LEONE
LIBERIA
CÔTE D'IVOIRE
GHANA
TOGO
BENIN
CAMEROON
CENTRAL AFRICAN REPUBLIC
EQUATORIAL GUINEA
SAO TOME AND PRINCIPE
GABON
CONGO
DEMOCRATIC REPUBLIC OF THE CONGO
UGANDA
KENYA
RWANDA
BURUNDI
SEYCHELLES
Cabinda (ANGOLA)
TANZANIA
COMOROS
ANGOLA
ZAMBIA
MALAWI
MOZAMBIQUE
ZIMBABWE
MADAGASCAR
MAURITIUS
NAMIBIA
BOTSWANA
Réunion (FRANCE)
SWAZILAND
SOUTH AFRICA
LESOTHO

WATER AVAILABILITY
(in millimeters per person per year)
- More than 750
- 251–750
- 26–250
- Less than 26

Natural Events

MOROCCO
TUNISIA
Western Sahara (MOROCCO)
ALGERIA
LIBYA
EGYPT
CAPE VERDE
MAURITANIA
MALI
NIGER
CHAD
SUDAN
ERITREA
DJIBOUTI
SENEGAL
GAMBIA
GUINEA-BISSAU
GUINEA
BURKINA FASO
NIGERIA
SOMALIA
ETHIOPIA
SIERRA LEONE
LIBERIA
GHANA
BENIN
TOGO
CAMEROON
CENTRAL AFRICAN REPUBLIC
CÔTE D'IVOIRE
EQUATORIAL GUINEA
SAO TOME AND PRINCIPE
GABON
CONGO
DEMOCRATIC REPUBLIC OF THE CONGO
UGANDA
RWANDA
BURUNDI
KENYA
SEYCHELLES
Cabinda (ANGOLA)
TANZANIA
COMOROS
ANGOLA
ZAMBIA
MALAWI
MOZAMBIQUE
MADAGASCAR
MAURITIUS
ZIMBABWE
NAMIBIA
BOTSWANA
Réunion (FRANCE)
Rodrigues (MAURITIUS)
SWAZILAND
SOUTH AFRICA
LESOTHO
RECORDED NATURAL EVENT
Earthquake
Richter scale magnitude
More than 7.0
6.0–7.0
Less than 6.0
Fire Intensity
(from gas burn-off, slash-and-burn agriculture, or natural causes)
High
Low
0 500 1,000
STATUTE MILES
0 500 1,000
KILOMETERS
Same scale for all six thematic maps
Tsunami
Run-up height
5–10 m 16–32 ft
Less than 5 m Less than 16 ft
Volcano
Major eruption

Population Density
POPULATION DENSITY
People per Square Km
People per Square Mile
More than 195 More than 500
60-195 150-500
10-59 25-149
1-9 1-24
Less than 1 Less than 1
Energy Consumption
PER CAPITA ENERGY CONSUMPTION (in metric tons of oil equivalent)
More than 5
3-5
1-2.9
Less than 1
No data
Major Energy Deposit
Coal
Natural gas
Oil
Oil pipeline
Oil transit chokepoint
Dominant Economy
DOMINANT ECONOMY (per GDP sector)
Agriculture Industry* Services
70%-100%
50%-69.9%
0%-49.9%
No data
*Includes the mining industry
Service 100%
Agricultural 100%
Industrial 100%
DJIBOUTI
LIBERIA
EQUATORIAL GUINEA
AFRICA'S ECONOMY
per Gross Domestic Product (GDP) sector
MOROCCO
TUNISIA
ALGERIA
LIBYA
EGYPT
Western Sahara (MOROCCO)
MAURITANIA
MALI
NIGER
CHAD
SUDAN
ERITREA
DJIBOUTI
SOMALIA
ETHIOPIA
CAPE VERDE
SENEGAL
GAMBIA
GUINEA-BISSAU
GUINEA
SIERRA LEONE
LIBERIA
CÔTE D'IVOIRE
BURKINA FASO
GHANA
TOGO
BENIN
NIGERIA
CAMEROON
CENTRAL AFRICAN REPUBLIC
EQUATORIAL GUINEA
SAO TOME AND PRINCIPE
GABON
CONGO
Cabinda (ANGOLA)
DEMOCRATIC REPUBLIC OF THE CONGO
UGANDA
KENYA
RWANDA
BURUNDI
TANZANIA
SEYCHELLES
COMOROS
ANGOLA
ZAMBIA
MALAWI
MOZAMBIQUE
ZIMBABWE
NAMIBIA
BOTSWANA
MADAGASCAR
MAURITIUS
Réunion (FRANCE)
SWAZILAND
SOUTH AFRICA
LESOTHO

Medina of Tunis, Tunisia ❶

Founded in the second millennium B.C., Tunis was occupied by the Phoenicians and Greeks, before being destroyed by the Romans in the first century B.C. It wasn't until the seventh century A.D., when Tunis came under Arab Muslim control, that the walled medina was constructed. The Almohad and Hafsid Berber dynasties ruled the old city from the 12th to 16th centuries, making Tunis one of the greatest and richest cities in the Islamic world. Some 700 palaces, mosques, mausoleums, Muslim schools, and fountains remain, including the Bey's Palace and the Aghlabid-era Ez-Zitouna (Olive Tree) Mosque.

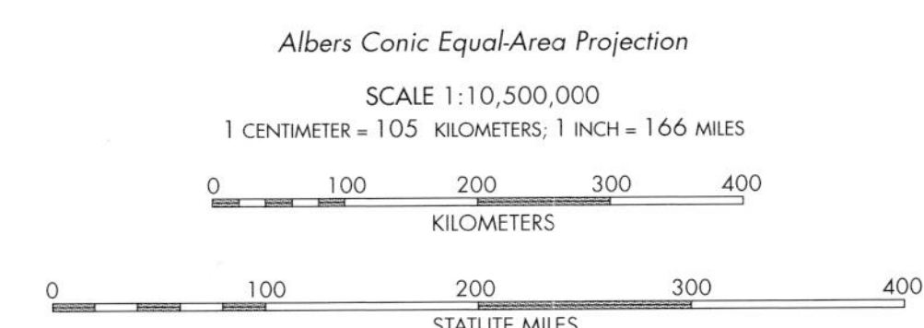

Albers Conic Equal-Area Projection
SCALE 1:10,500,000
1 CENTIMETER = 105 KILOMETERS; 1 INCH = 166 MILES
0 100 200 300 400
KILOMETERS
0 100 200 300 400
STATUTE MILES

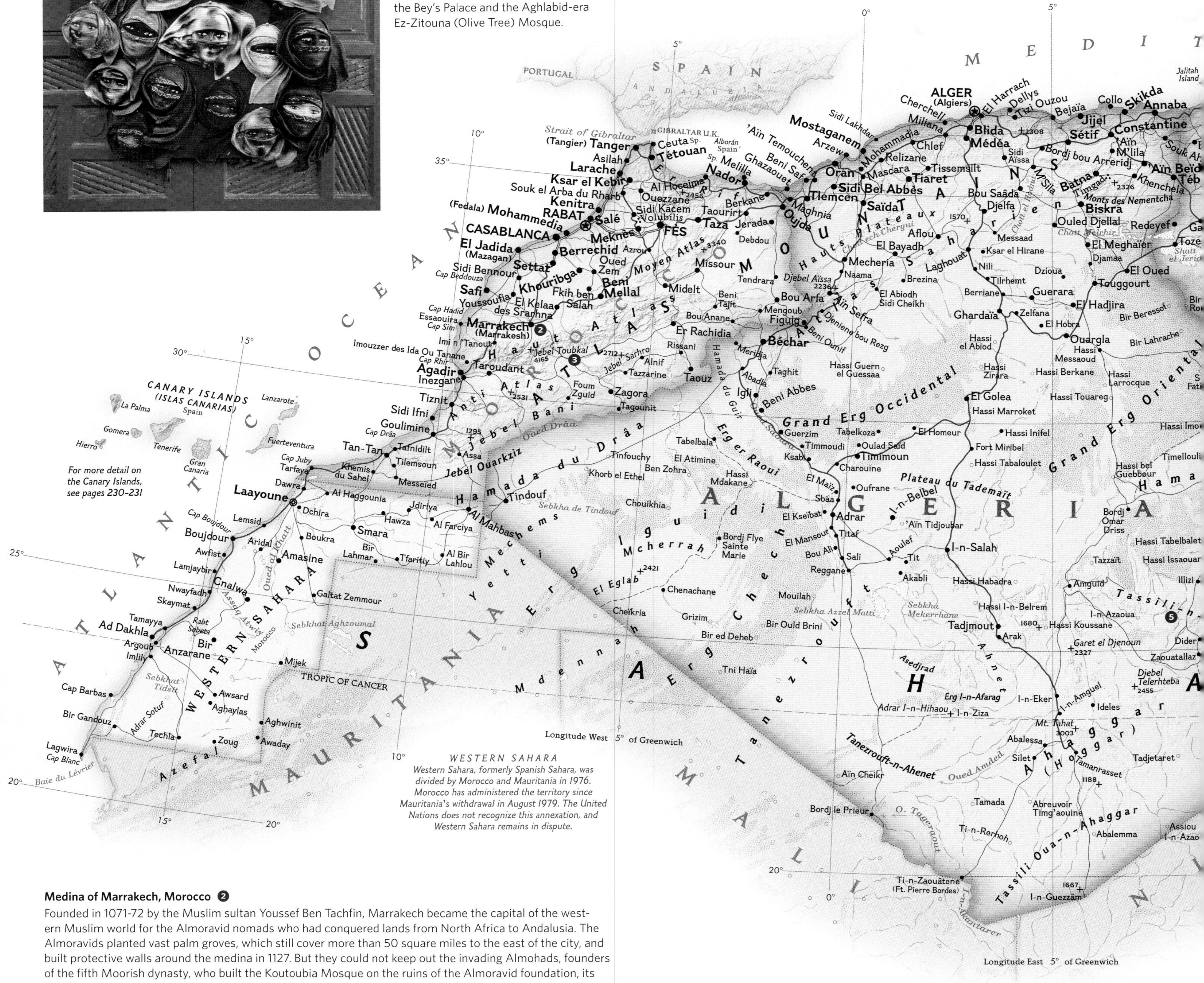

For more detail on the Canary Islands, see pages 230-231

WESTERN SAHARA

Western Sahara, formerly Spanish Sahara, was divided by Morocco and Mauritania in 1976. Morocco has administered the territory since Mauritania's withdrawal in August 1979. The United Nations does not recognize this annexation, and Western Sahara remains in dispute.

Medina of Marrakech, Morocco ❷

Founded in 1071-72 by the Muslim sultan Youssef Ben Tachfin, Marrakech became the capital of the western Muslim world for the Almoravid nomads who had conquered lands from North Africa to Andalusia. The Almoravids planted vast palm groves, which still cover more than 50 square miles to the east of the city, and built protective walls around the medina in 1127. But they could not keep out the invading Almohads, founders of the fifth Moorish dynasty, who built the Koutoubia Mosque on the ruins of the Almoravid foundation, its 250-foot-high minaret remaining a key to Muslim architecture and an imposing feature of the city's skyline.

Ksar of Ait-Ben-Haddou, Morocco ❸

A traditional pre-Saharan habitat, a *ksar* is a group of earthen buildings surrounded by high walls for protection from the elements and invaders, and then reinforced by corner towers. Ait-Ben-Haddou was located on the caravan route between the Sahara and Marrakech, and was intricately constructed of bricks molded by pounding earth into masonry units.

Archaeological Site of ❹ Leptis Magna, Libya
A natural harbor protected by Mediterranean islands, the ancient city of Leptis Magna was a trading port for the Phoenicians in the first millennium B.C., and, under the Roman Empire in the second century B.C., became one of the three powerful cities of the North African Tripolitania region. Birthplace of the Roman emperor Septimius Severus, it prospered as a trading center on the trans-Saharan caravan route for more than 600 years, becoming so prosperous in the olive trade that Julius Caesar imposed an annual tax of three million pounds of olive oil.

Sicilia (Sicily) Italy
Cap Bon
Pantelleria Italy
Nabeul
Gulf of Hammamet
Sousse
Mahdia
Linosa
Isole Pelagie Italy
Lampedusa
MALTA
TUNISIA
Shergui I.
Gharbi I.
Jerba I.
Medenine
Ben Gardane
Foum Tataouine
Remada
Kriti (Crete) Greece
MEDITERRANEAN SEA
Zuwārah
Az Zāwiyah
TARĀBULUS (Tripoli)
Al Khums
Leptis Magna
Mişrātah
Tāwurghā'
Gharyān
Jabal Nafūsah
Nālūt
Jādū
Banī Walīd
Bu'ayrāt al Ḩasūn
Mizdah
Qaryat al Qaddāḩīyah
Qaşr Bū Hādī
Surt (Sidra)
As Sulţān
Khalīj Surt (Gulf of Sidra)
Sīnāwin
Bi'r 'Allāq
Al Qaryah ash Sharqīyah
Qaryat abu Nujaym
Bi'r Nāşirah
Ash Shuwayrif
Al Ḩamrā'
Dirj
TRIPOLITANIA
Hūn
Waddān
Jabal as Sawdā'
Zillah
Ra's al Unūf
An Nawfalīyah
Ḩişn Tāqrifat
(Beida) Al Bayḑā'
Sūsah (Apollonia)
Darnah (Derna)
Ra's at Tīn
Marţūbah
Khalīj al Bumbah
Tubruq (Tobruk)
Al Bardī
Amsā'ad
Shaḩḩāt (Cyrene)
Al Marj (Barce)
Tulmaythah
Tūkrah
Ar Rajmah
(Benghazi) Banghāzī
Madīnat al Abyār
Zāwiyat al Mukhaylá
Al 'Adam
Qamīnis
Sulūq
Zāwiyat Masūs
Antalāt
Sāwinnū
Qaryat az Zuwaytīnah
Ajdābiyā
Marsá al Burayqah (Port Brega)
Al 'Uqaylah
Qaşr ash Shaqqah
Libyan Plateau (Ad Diffah)
Al Jaghbūb
Marādah
Abū Na'īm
Awjilah
Jālū
Bi'r Zalţan
Sarīr Kalanshiyū ar Ramlī al Kabīr (Sand Sea of Calanscio)
Sarīr Kalanshiyū
Tinrhert
Şaḩrā' Awbārī
Birāk
Al Fuqahā'
Umm al 'Abīd
Al Mahrūqah
Adīrī
Sabhā
Al Harūj al Aswad
Qaltat Bū as Su'ūd
Thamad Bū Hashīshah
LIBYA
Awbārī (Ubari)
Ghaddūwah
Tmassah
Wadi Irawen
Zawīlah
Tasāwah
Marzūq
Wāw al Kabīr
Jabal Bin Ghunaymah
Al 'Uwaynāt (Serdeles)
Ghāt
Al Birkah
Şaḩrā' Marzūq
Al Qaţrūn
Tajarhī
FEZZAN
Tāzirbū
Al Jazīrah
Bi'r Bū Zurayyiq
Bi'r adh Dhakar
Bi'r Bū Hawsh
Buzaymah
Al Kufrah
At Tāj
Al Jawf
(Kufra Oasis)
Qārat Kūdī
Şaḩrā' Rabyānah
Ma'ţan Bishrah
Jabal Arkanū
Jabal Bū Sunbul
As Sarfaia
TROPIC OF CANCER
Sarīr Tibastī
Jabal at Tarhūnī
'Ayn Zuwayyah
'Ayn al Ghazāl
Ma'ţan as Sarra
Bikkū Bittī 2266
Toummo
Jabal Ḩadīd
Libyan Desert
EGYPT
SUDAN
CHAD
NIGER

Tassili-n-Ajjer, Algeria ❺
Located on nearly 28,000 square miles of desert with eroded sandstones jutting up from dunes to form a "forest of rock," the site's prehistoric cave art totals more than 15,000 drawings and engravings depicting animal migrations, climatic changes, and Saharan life from 6000 B.C. to this era's early centuries. Paintings from the oldest, "naturalistic" period show animals typical of savanna, while the following "archaic" era corresponds to fauna of more humid climates. The Bovidian period (4000-1500 B.C.) has the largest number of paintings and shows bovine herds; the Equidian period catalogs species disappearing because of dryness and the appearance of the horse; and the Cameline period corresponds with the onset of the desert climate and the use of the Arabic camel.

Morocco
Tunisia
Canary Islands Spain
Algeria
Libya
Western Sahara Morocco
Africa

Protected Areas and World Heritage Sites

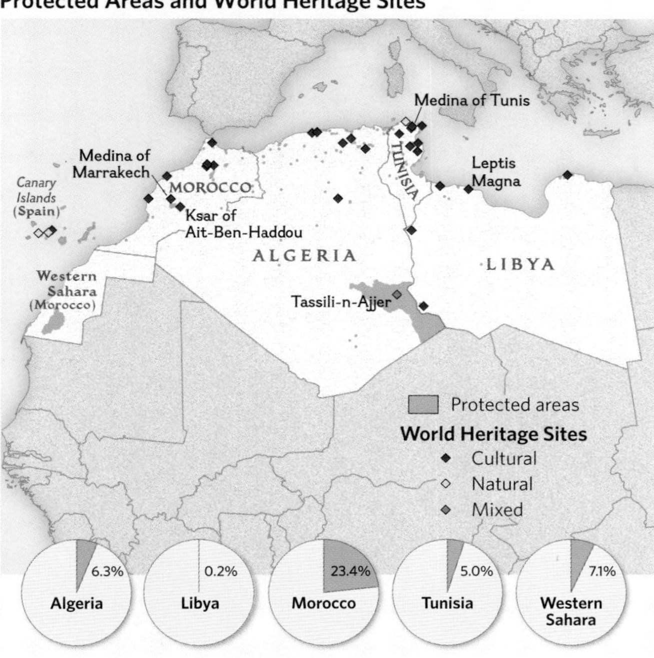
Medina of Tunis
Medina of Marrakech
Canary Islands (Spain)
MOROCCO
Ksar of Ait-Ben-Haddou
TUNISIA
Leptis Magna
ALGERIA
LIBYA
Western Sahara (Morocco)
Tassili-n-Ajjer
Protected areas
World Heritage Sites
Cultural
Natural
Mixed
6.3% Algeria
0.2% Libya
23.4% Morocco
5.0% Tunisia
7.1% Western Sahara
Percent of Land Area Protected

Urbanization and Largest Cities

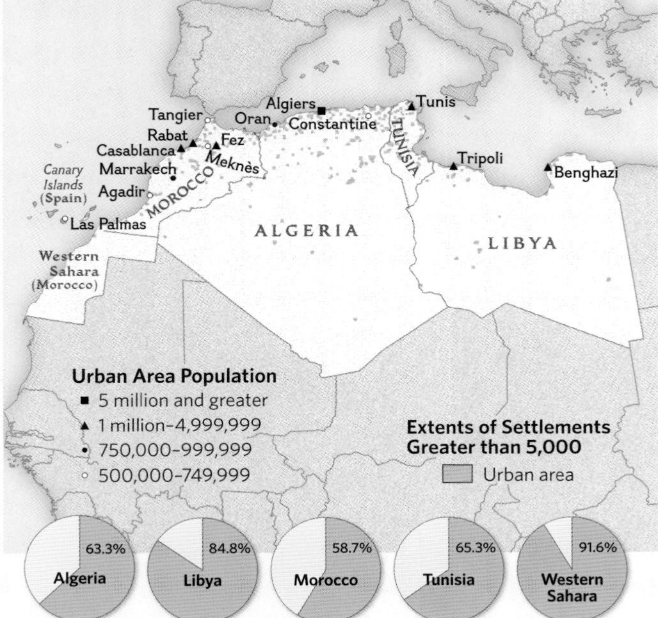
Algiers
Tunis
Tangier
Oran
Constantine
Rabat
Fez
Casablanca
Meknès
Marrakech
Agadir
Canary Islands (Spain)
Las Palmas
MOROCCO
TUNISIA
Tripoli
Benghazi
ALGERIA
LIBYA
Western Sahara (Morocco)
Urban Area Population
5 million and greater
1 million–4,999,999
750,000–999,999
500,000–749,999
Extents of Settlements Greater than 5,000
Urban area
63.3% Algeria
84.8% Libya
58.7% Morocco
65.3% Tunisia
91.6% Western Sahara
Percent of Population in Urban Areas

Natural Land Cover

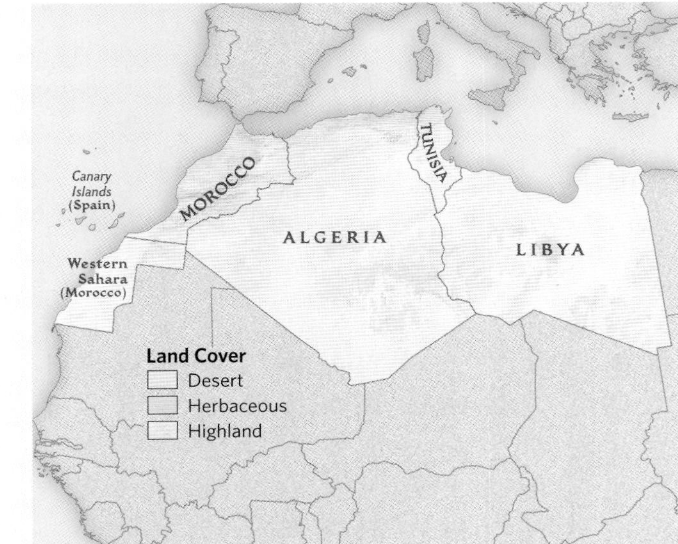
Canary Islands (Spain)
MOROCCO
TUNISIA
ALGERIA
LIBYA
Western Sahara (Morocco)
Land Cover
Desert
Herbaceous
Highland

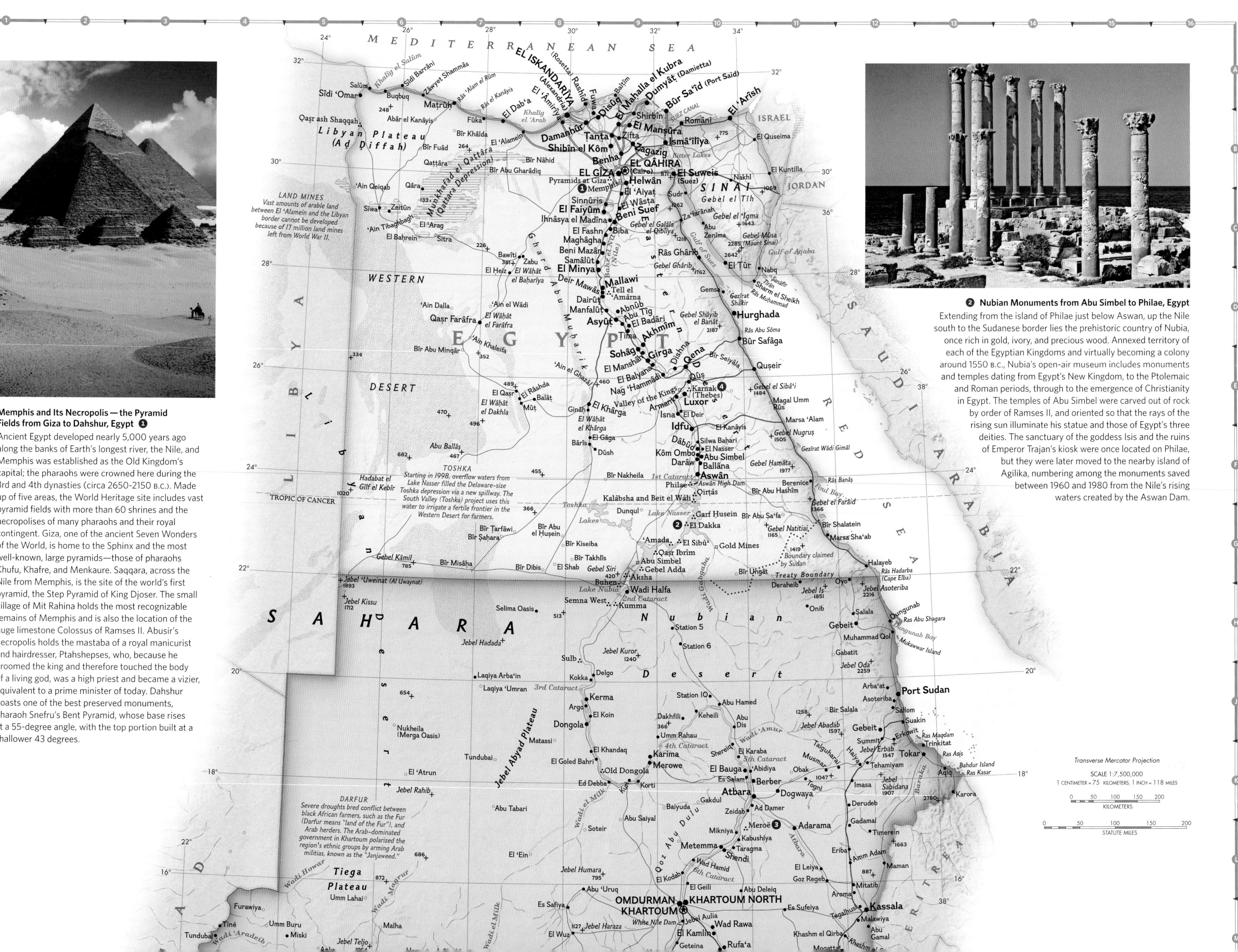
MEDITERRANEAN SEA
EL ISKANDARIYA (Alexandria)
EL QÂHIRA (Cairo)
EL GIZA
Bûr Sa'îd (Port Said)
El Suweis (Suez)
ISRAEL
JORDAN
SINAI
SAUDI ARABIA
RED SEA
EGYPT
LIBYA
ERITREA
WESTERN DESERT
Libyan Plateau (Ad Diffah)
Munkhafad el Qattâra (Qattara Depression)
SAHARA
Nubian Desert
Jebel Abyad Plateau
Tiega Plateau
Lake Nasser
Aswân
Luxor
Asyût
Wadi Halfa
Port Sudan
Atbara
Kassala
OMDURMAN
KHARTOUM
KHARTOUM NORTH
TROPIC OF CANCER
LAND MINES
Vast amounts of arable land between El 'Alamein and the Libyan border cannot be developed because of 17 million land mines left from World War II.
TOSHKA
Starting in 1998, overflow waters from Lake Nasser filled the Delaware-size Toshka depression via a new spillway. The South Valley (Toshka) project uses this water to irrigate a fertile frontier in the Western Desert for farmers.
DARFUR
Severe droughts bred conflict between black African farmers, such as the Fur (Darfur means "land of the Fur"), and Arab herders. The Arab-dominated government in Khartoum polarized the region's ethnic groups by arming Arab militias, known as the "Janjaweed."
Transverse Mercator Projection
SCALE 1:7,500,000
1 CENTIMETER = 75 KILOMETERS; 1 INCH = 118 MILES
KILOMETERS
STATUTE MILES

Memphis and Its Necropolis—the Pyramid Fields from Giza to Dahshur, Egypt ❶

Ancient Egypt developed nearly 5,000 years ago along the banks of Earth's longest river, the Nile, and Memphis was established as the Old Kingdom's capital; the pharaohs were crowned here during the 3rd and 4th dynasties (circa 2650-2150 B.C.). Made up of five areas, the World Heritage site includes vast pyramid fields with more than 60 shrines and the necropolises of many pharaohs and their royal contingent. Giza, one of the ancient Seven Wonders of the World, is home to the Sphinx and the most well-known, large pyramids—those of pharaohs Khufu, Khafre, and Menkaure. Saqqara, across the Nile from Memphis, is the site of the world's first pyramid, the Step Pyramid of King Djoser. The small village of Mit Rahina holds the most recognizable remains of Memphis and is also the location of the huge limestone Colossus of Ramses II. Abusir's necropolis holds the mastaba of a royal manicurist and hairdresser, Ptahshepses, who, because he groomed the king and therefore touched the body of a living god, was a high priest and became a vizier, equivalent to a prime minister of today. Dahshur boasts one of the best preserved monuments, Pharaoh Snefru's Bent Pyramid, whose base rises at a 55-degree angle, with the top portion built at a shallower 43 degrees.

❷ Nubian Monuments from Abu Simbel to Philae, Egypt

Extending from the island of Philae just below Aswan, up the Nile south to the Sudanese border lies the prehistoric country of Nubia, once rich in gold, ivory, and precious wood. Annexed territory of each of the Egyptian Kingdoms and virtually becoming a colony around 1550 B.C., Nubia's open-air museum includes monuments and temples dating from Egypt's New Kingdom, to the Ptolemaic and Roman periods, through to the emergence of Christianity in Egypt. The temples of Abu Simbel were carved out of rock by order of Ramses II, and oriented so that the rays of the rising sun illuminate his statue and those of Egypt's three deities. The sanctuary of the goddess Isis and the ruins of Emperor Trajan's kiosk were once located on Philae, but they were later moved to the nearby island of Agilika, numbering among the monuments saved between 1960 and 1980 from the Nile's rising waters created by the Aswan Dam.

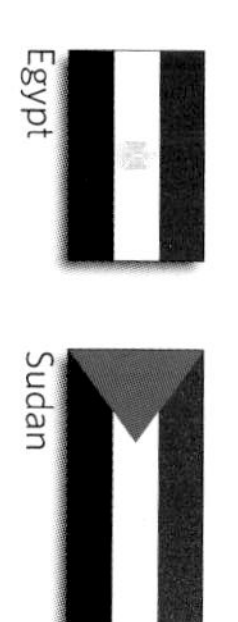
Egypt
Sudan

The Island of Meroe, Sudan (Tentative List) ❸

"Island of Meroe" was used by some writers in antiquity to identify the region surrounded on three sides by the waters of the Blue Nile, Nile, and Atbara Rivers. The site contains palaces, cemeteries, and temples of the Meroitic Kingdom at Meroe—the capital city from the fourth century B.C. to the fourth century A.D.—Musawwarat es-Sufra, and Naqa. Meroe is the location of the most extensive field of pyramids in Sudan. The lion temple at Musawwarat es-Sufra has inscriptions of King Natakamani standing before the lion god, Apedemek, lord of royal power, while Naqa's lion temple has reliefs at its entrance depicting the king and his queen, Amantorie, striking their enemies.

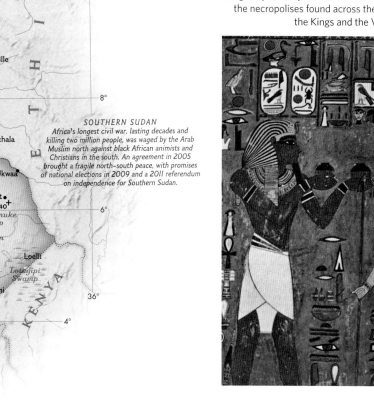

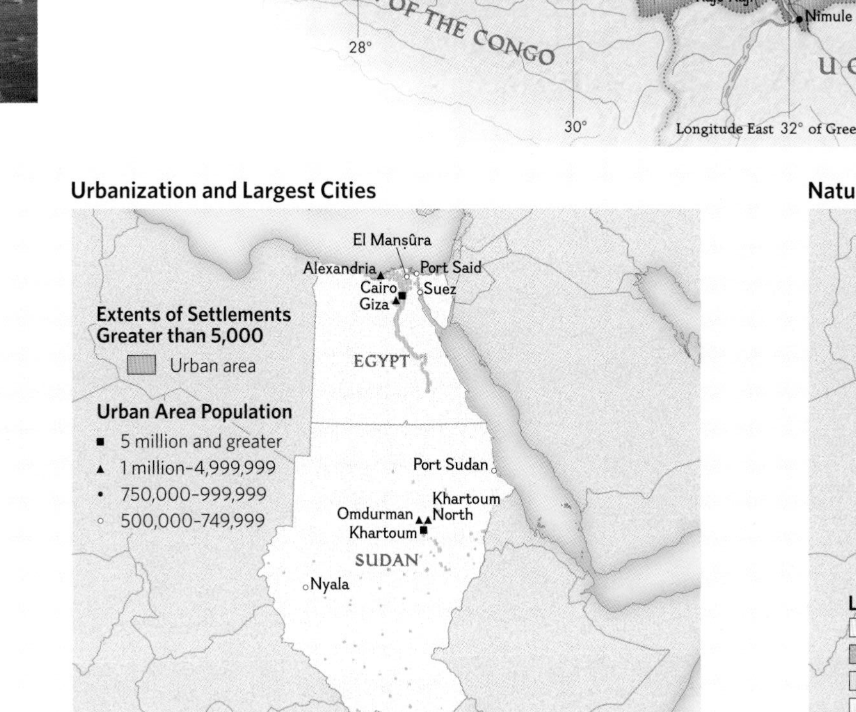

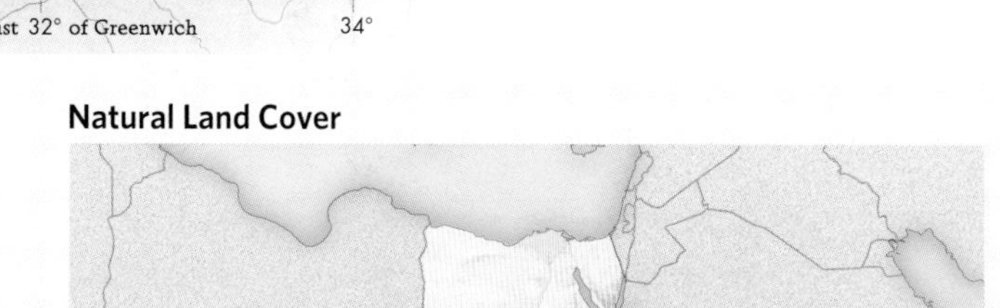
SOUTHERN SUDAN
Africa's longest civil war, lasting decades and killing two million people, was waged by the Arab Muslim north against black African animists and Christians in the south. An agreement in 2005 brought a fragile north-south peace, with promises of national elections in 2009 and a 2011 referendum on independence for Southern Sudan.
SUDAN
SOUTHERN SUDAN
CENTRAL AFRICAN REPUBLIC
DEM. REP. OF THE CONGO
UGANDA
KENYA
ETHIOPIA
Longitude East 32° of Greenwich

❹ Ancient Thebes with its Necropolis, Egypt

Thebes lies on the Nile in east-central Egypt and was the city of the father of all pharaohs, the god Amon, meaning "hidden" and typically depicted as a ram. Capital of Egypt during the Middle and New Kingdoms, it reached its most glorious period in the 18th dynasty (circa 1539–1075 B.C.) when the pharaohs departed to liberate Egypt from the Hyksos, and eventually established an empire extending from north of the Sudanese border to the Euphrates River. The site includes temples and palaces at Karnak, whose monuments were built by different pharaohs over a span of 1,500 years; Luxor, whose temple's entrance was originally lined by six colossal statues of Ramses II; and the necropolises found across the Nile in the Valley of the Kings and the Valley of the Queens.

Protected Areas and World Heritage Sites

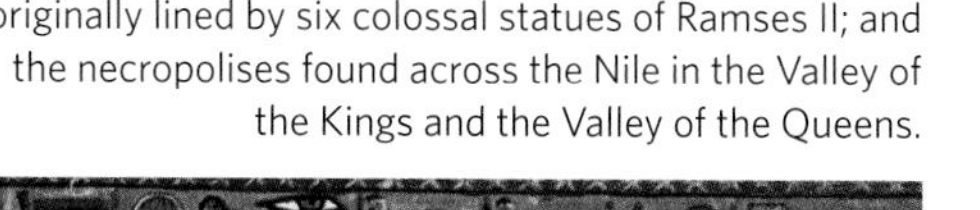
Protected areas
World Heritage Sites
Cultural
Natural
Memphis and its Necropolis
Ancient Thebes
EGYPT
Nubian Monuments from Abu Simbel to Philae
The Island of Meroë (Tentative)
SUDAN
12.5%
Egypt
7.8%
Sudan

Percent of Land Area Protected

Urbanization and Largest Cities

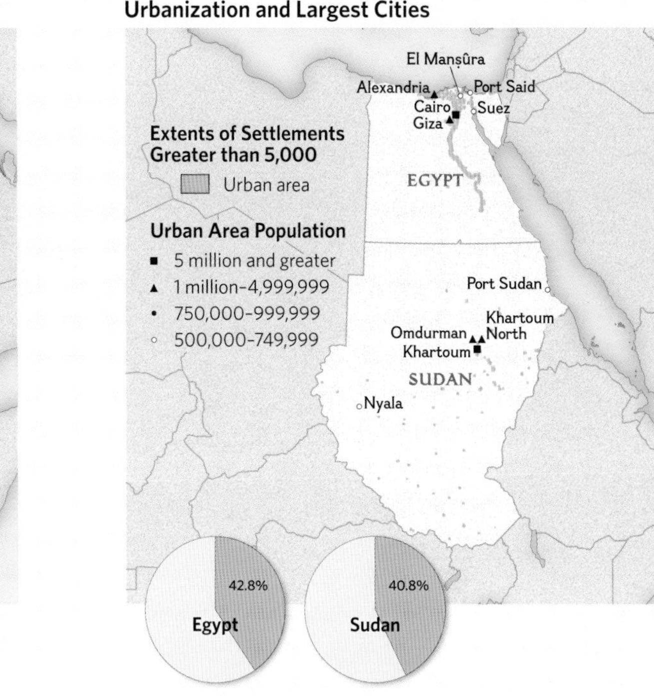
Extents of Settlements Greater than 5,000
Urban area
Urban Area Population
5 million and greater
1 million–4,999,999
750,000–999,999
500,000–749,999
El Mansûra
Alexandria
Port Said
Cairo
Suez
Giza
EGYPT
Port Sudan
Khartoum North
Omdurman
Khartoum
SUDAN
Nyala
42.8%
Egypt
40.8%
Sudan

Percent of Population in Urban Areas

Natural Land Cover

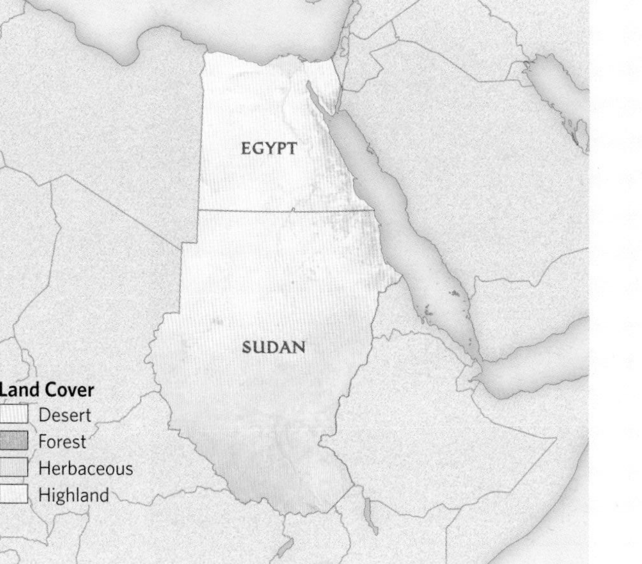
EGYPT
SUDAN
Land Cover
Desert
Forest
Herbaceous
Highland
Egypt
Sudan
Africa

Benin

Burkina Faso

Côte d'Ivoire

Gambia
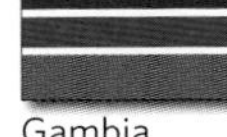
Ghana

Island of Saint-Louis, Senegal ❶
Located at the mouth of the Senegal River on an island with an extensive system of quays, Saint-Louis was colonized by the French in 1633 and developed into a trading post for rubber, leather, gold, ivory, and slaves. The entire settlement is in a magnificent lagoon formed by the two arms of the Senegal River. The town was urbanized only in 1854, and ten years later, the first museum of West African history, ethnography, and industry opened.

CANARY ISLANDS
Spain
MOROCCO
WESTERN SAHARA
Morocco
TROPIC OF CANCER
MAURITANIA
Nouadhibou
Nouakchott
Saint-Louis
SENEGAL
DAKAR
Thiès
Kaolack
GAMBIA
Banjul
Ziguinchor
GUINEA-BISSAU
Bissau
GUINEA
CONAKRY
SIERRA LEONE
Freetown
LIBERIA
MONROVIA
Grain Coast
ATLANTIC OCEAN
BAMAKO
Kayes
Atâr
Chinguetti
Ouadane
Tidjikdja

Ancient *Ksour* of Ouadane, Chinguetti, Tichitt, and Oualata, Mauritania ❷
Caravans crossing the Sahara desert in the 11th and 12th centuries established these four *ksour* (towns) as trading posts and religious centers. Located on the outskirts of either a fertile valley or an oasis, their original function was for religious instruction, and each settlement is situated around a mosque with a square minaret. They have original and decorative medieval stone houses densely packed along narrow, twisting streets that provide areas shaded from the sun. Due to the extreme climatic conditions, no public open spaces exist, and each dwelling has ventilation ducts or small windows at ground level, low doorways, and continuous walls to the street.

Old Towns of Djénné, Mali ❸
Inhabited since 250 B.C., Djénné was built on a series of *toguere* (hills) to avoid being flooded during the wet season, when the waters of the Niger River annually flood the inland delta and turn the riverside city into an island. The Niger later helped the town become an important link in the trans-Saharan gold trade, and a market center for trading leather crafts and rock salt. During the 15th and 16th centuries, Djénné became a focal point for the spread of Islam, and because wood and stone were scarce, villagers built the Great Mosque (below) in the city's center from bricks of mud mixed with rice husks and straw, which they dried in the sun for a month, making the bricks tough, thick, and rain resistant. During the dry season, Djénné hosts a major event in which the people come together and re-plaster the mosque walls, repairing cracks and other signs of erosion caused by the wind and rain.

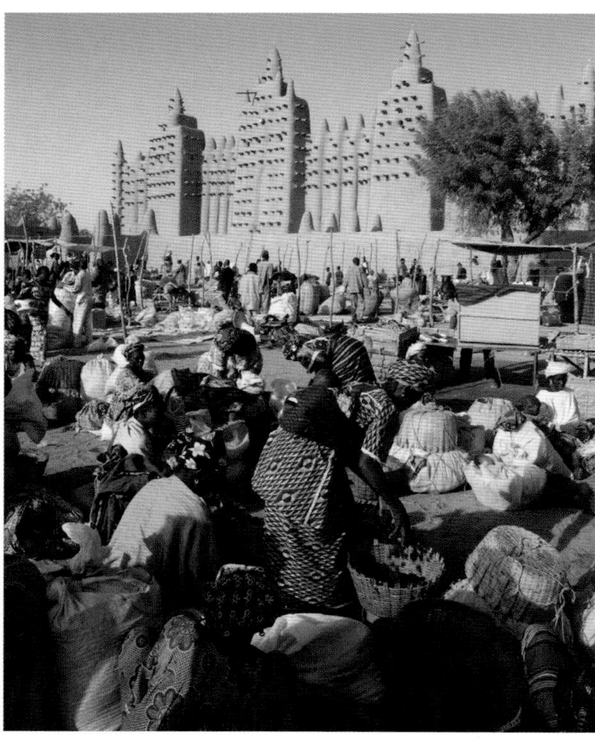

Forts and Castles, Volta, Greater Accra, Central and Western Regions, Ghana ❹
During their era of expansive maritime exploration, the Portuguese, Dutch, and British established trading posts to carry wealth from their sea odysseys back to the crown. Between 1482 and 1786, they landed on the central and western portions of the Gold Coast of Ghana and built fortifications and castles. Today, the remains of three castles and fifteen citadels are in good condition, ten forts are in ruins, seven sites have traces of former ramparts, and two fortresses are being used as prisons.

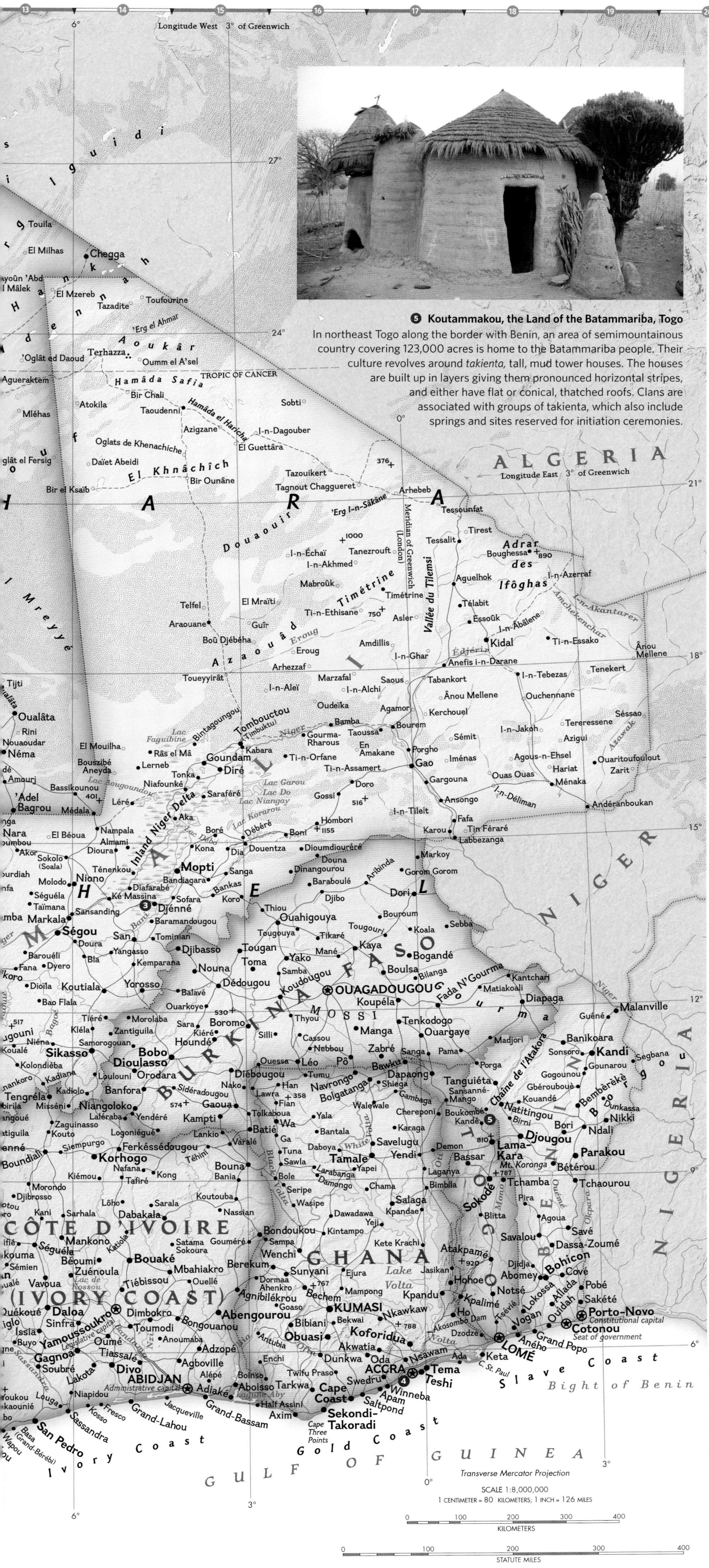

Guinea · Guinea-Bissau · Liberia · Mali · Mauritania · Senegal · Sierra Leone · Togo

5 Koutammakou, the Land of the Batammariba, Togo
In northeast Togo along the border with Benin, an area of semimountainous country covering 123,000 acres is home to the Batammariba people. Their culture revolves around *takienta,* tall, mud tower houses. The houses are built up in layers giving them pronounced horizontal stripes, and either have flat or conical, thatched roofs. Clans are associated with groups of takienta, which also include springs and sites reserved for initiation ceremonies.

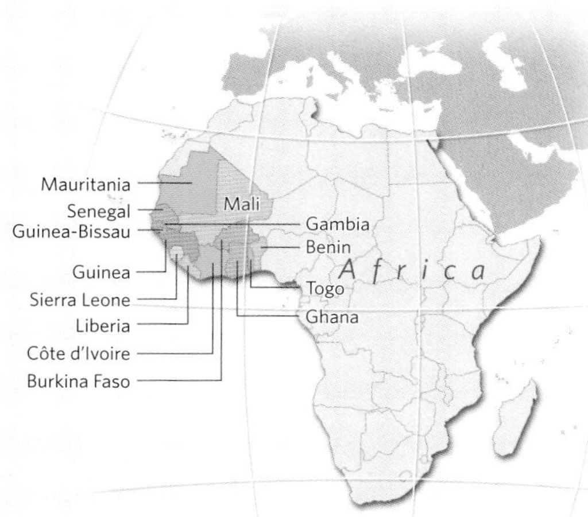

Transverse Mercator Projection
SCALE 1:8,000,000
1 CENTIMETER = 80 KILOMETERS; 1 INCH = 126 MILES

Mauritania · Senegal · Guinea-Bissau · Guinea · Sierra Leone · Liberia · Côte d'Ivoire · Burkina Faso · Mali · Gambia · Benin · Togo · Ghana · Africa

Protected Areas and World Heritage Sites

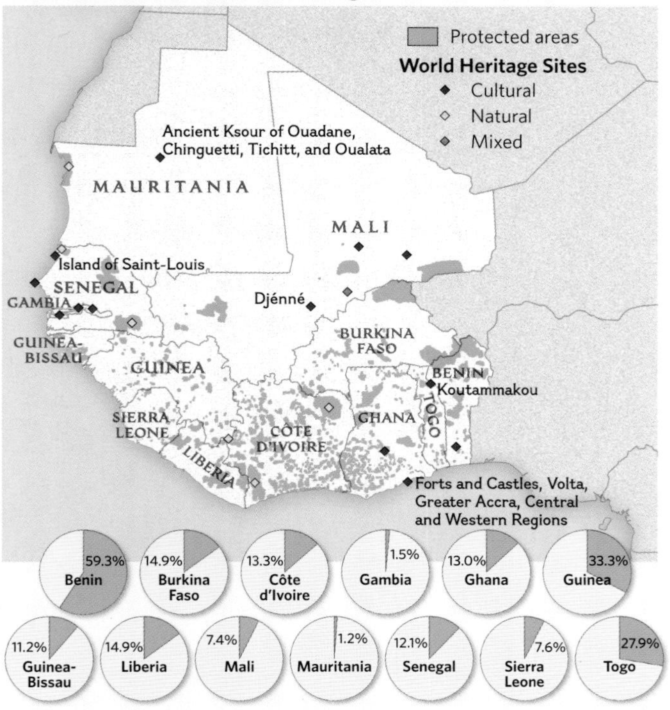

Protected areas
World Heritage Sites
◆ Cultural
◇ Natural
◈ Mixed

Ancient Ksour of Ouadane, Chinguetti, Tichitt, and Oualata
Island of Saint-Louis
Djénné
Koutammakou
Forts and Castles, Volta, Greater Accra, Central and Western Regions

Benin	Burkina Faso	Côte d'Ivoire	Gambia	Ghana	Guinea	Guinea-Bissau	Liberia	Mali	Mauritania	Senegal	Sierra Leone	Togo
59.3%	14.9%	13.3%	1.5%	13.0%	33.3%	11.2%	14.9%	7.4%	1.2%	12.1%	7.6%	27.9%

Percent of Land Area Protected

Urbanization and Largest Cities

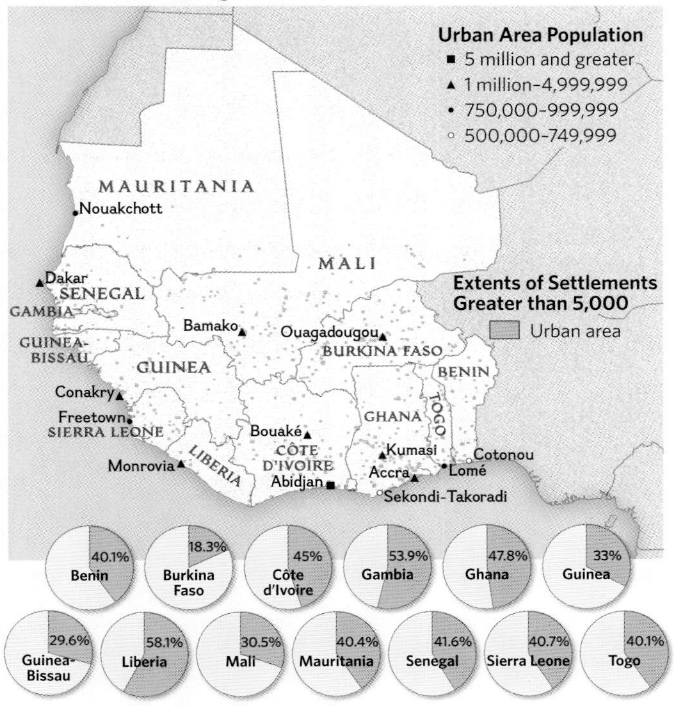

Urban Area Population
■ 5 million and greater
▲ 1 million–4,999,999
• 750,000–999,999
◦ 500,000–749,999

Extents of Settlements Greater than 5,000
Urban area

Nouakchott · Dakar · Bamako · Ouagadougou · Conakry · Freetown · Monrovia · Bouaké · Abidjan · Kumasi · Accra · Lomé · Cotonou · Sekondi-Takoradi

Benin	Burkina Faso	Côte d'Ivoire	Gambia	Ghana	Guinea	Guinea-Bissau	Liberia	Mali	Mauritania	Senegal	Sierra Leone	Togo
40.1%	18.3%	45%	53.9%	47.8%	33%	29.6%	58.1%	30.5%	40.4%	41.6%	40.7%	40.1%

Percent of Population in Urban Areas

Natural Land Cover

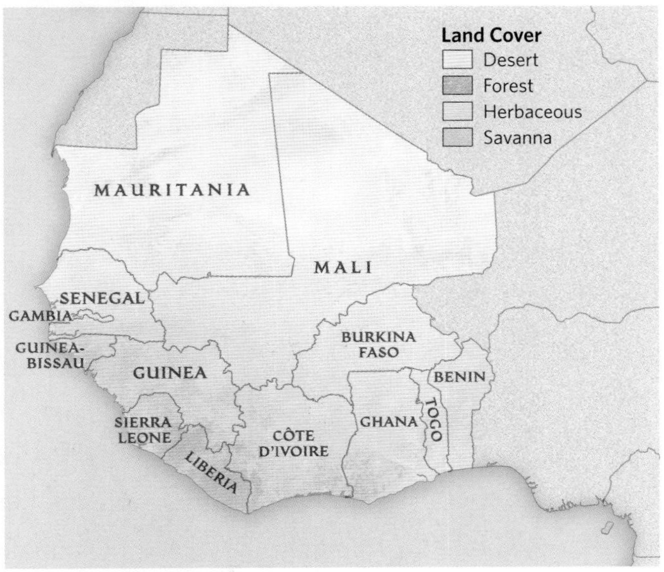

Land Cover
Desert
Forest
Herbaceous
Savanna

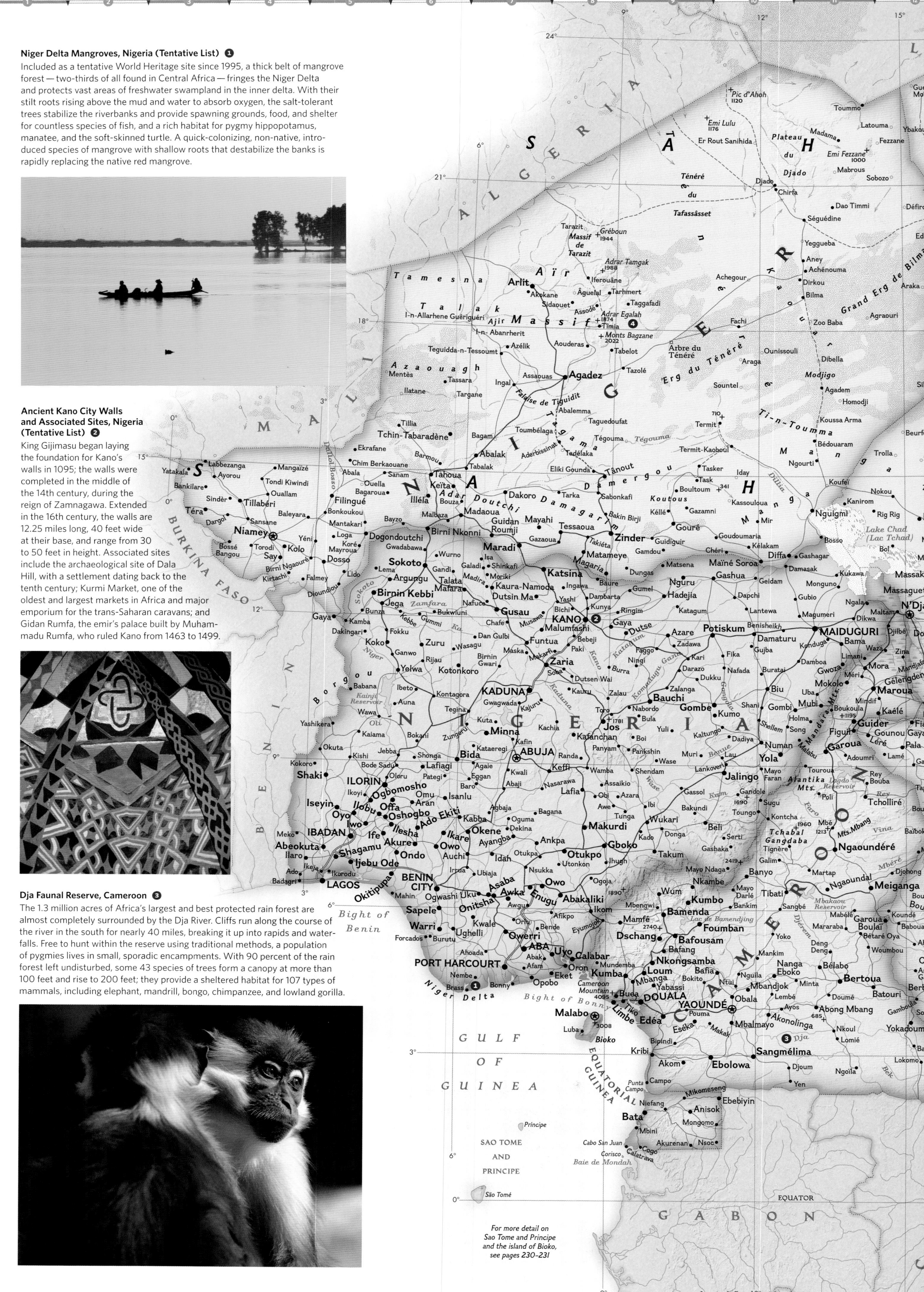
ALGERIA
MALI
NIGER
NIGERIA
BURKINA FASO
BENIN
CAMEROON
EQUATORIAL GUINEA
SAO TOME AND PRINCIPE
GABON
GULF OF GUINEA
Bight of Benin
Bight of Bonny
Niger Delta
Lake Chad (Lac Tchad)
Aïr Massif
Ténéré du Tafassâsset
Erg du Ténéré
Grand Erg de Bilma
Plateau du Djado
Niamey
Agadez
Zinder
Maradi
Sokoto
Kano
Katsina
Kaduna
Abuja
Ilorin
Ibadan
Lagos
Benin City
Port Harcourt
Calabar
Maiduguri
N'Djamena
Douala
Yaoundé
Malabo
Bata
Bioko
Ngaoundéré
Garoua
Sangmélima
EQUATOR
Longitude East 12° of Greenwich
For more detail on Sao Tome and Principe and the island of Bioko, see pages 230–231

Niger Delta Mangroves, Nigeria (Tentative List) 1

Included as a tentative World Heritage site since 1995, a thick belt of mangrove forest — two-thirds of all found in Central Africa — fringes the Niger Delta and protects vast areas of freshwater swampland in the inner delta. With their stilt roots rising above the mud and water to absorb oxygen, the salt-tolerant trees stabilize the riverbanks and provide spawning grounds, food, and shelter for countless species of fish, and a rich habitat for pygmy hippopotamus, manatee, and the soft-skinned turtle. A quick-colonizing, non-native, introduced species of mangrove with shallow roots that destabilize the banks is rapidly replacing the native red mangrove.

Ancient Kano City Walls and Associated Sites, Nigeria (Tentative List) 2

King Gijimasu began laying the foundation for Kano's walls in 1095; the walls were completed in the middle of the 14th century, during the reign of Zamnagawa. Extended in the 16th century, the walls are 12.25 miles long, 40 feet wide at their base, and range from 30 to 50 feet in height. Associated sites include the archaeological site of Dala Hill, with a settlement dating back to the tenth century; Kurmi Market, one of the oldest and largest markets in Africa and major emporium for the trans-Saharan caravans; and Gidan Rumfa, the emir's palace built by Muhammadu Rumfa, who ruled Kano from 1463 to 1499.

Dja Faunal Reserve, Cameroon 3

The 1.3 million acres of Africa's largest and best protected rain forest are almost completely surrounded by the Dja River. Cliffs run along the course of the river in the south for nearly 40 miles, breaking it up into rapids and waterfalls. Free to hunt within the reserve using traditional methods, a population of pygmies lives in small, sporadic encampments. With 90 percent of the rain forest left undisturbed, some 43 species of trees form a canopy at more than 100 feet and rise to 200 feet; they provide a sheltered habitat for 107 types of mammals, including elephant, mandrill, bongo, chimpanzee, and lowland gorilla.

Aïr and Ténéré Natural ❹ Reserves, Niger

The world's third largest reserve at more than 19 million acres, this arid desert ecosystem consists of the volcanic rock mass of the Aïr Massif, which rise up to more than 6,500 feet, and a vast flat plain of the Ténéré desert. In the sheltered, wetter areas of the mountains above 3,000 feet, wild olive, millet, and sorghum thrive next to *gueltas,* permanent rock pools that harbor aquatic communities. One-sixth of the reserve is managed as a sanctuary, protecting among other threatened species two kinds of gazelles, the dama and the slender-horned, and the addax, a large, light-colored antelope.

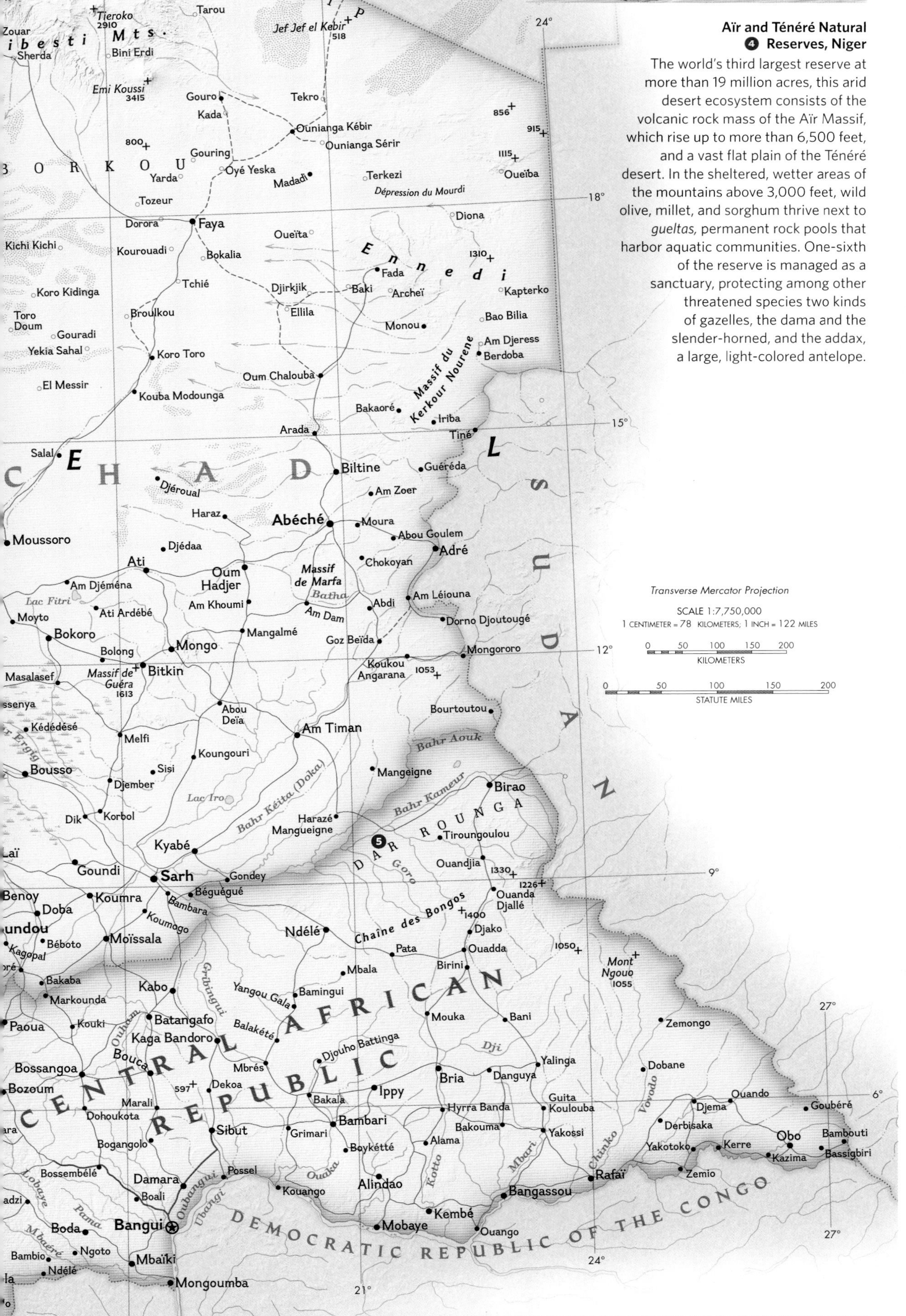

Transverse Mercator Projection

SCALE 1:7,750,000
1 CENTIMETER = 78 KILOMETERS; 1 INCH = 122 MILES

0 50 100 150 200
KILOMETERS
0 50 100 150 200
STATUTE MILES

Manovo-Gounda St. Floris National Park, ❺ Central African Republic

The park's more than four million acres divide three main zones. The grassy, seasonally flooded lowland plains of the Bahr Kameur and Bahr Aouk rivers to the north support large seasonal populations of pelicans, marabou storks, and a wide range of waterfowl and shorebirds. The sandstone plateau in the south rises 300 to 650 feet from the plain, and five rivers run from the massif, draining into the Bahr Aouk and Bahr Kameur. Vast woodland savannas cover most of the region, and are home to a variety of species, including black rhinoceros, elephant, cheetah, wild dog, red-fronted gazelle, and buffalo.

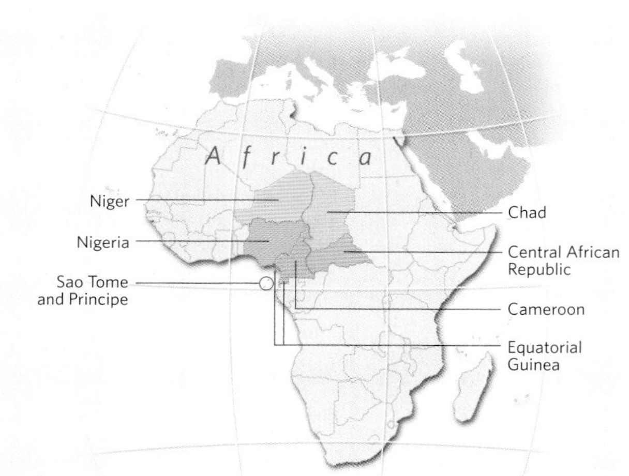
Africa
Niger
Nigeria
Sao Tome and Principe
Chad
Central African Republic
Cameroon
Equatorial Guinea

Protected Areas and World Heritage Sites

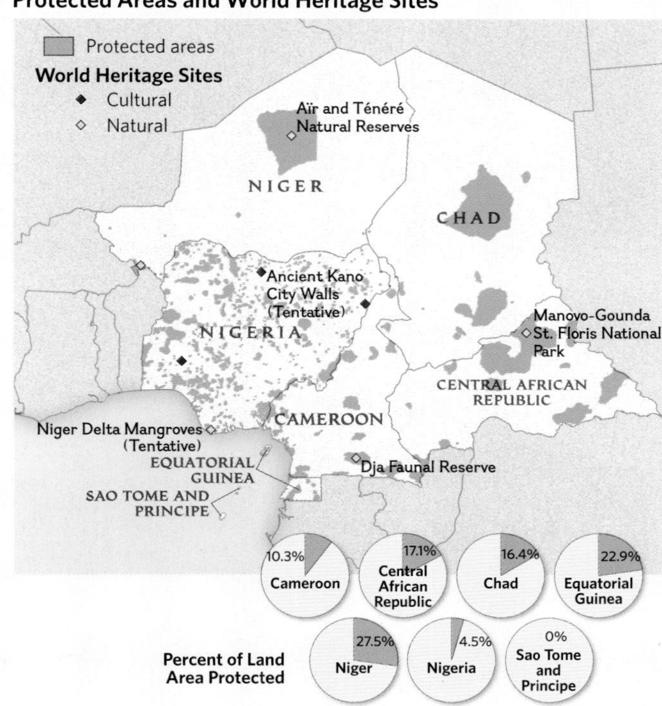
Protected areas
World Heritage Sites
Cultural
Natural
Aïr and Ténéré Natural Reserves
NIGER
CHAD
Ancient Kano City Walls (Tentative)
NIGERIA
Manovo-Gounda St. Floris National Park
CENTRAL AFRICAN REPUBLIC
CAMEROON
Niger Delta Mangroves (Tentative)
EQUATORIAL GUINEA
SAO TOME AND PRINCIPE
Dja Faunal Reserve
10.3% Cameroon
17.1% Central African Republic
16.4% Chad
22.9% Equatorial Guinea
Percent of Land Area Protected
27.5% Niger
4.5% Nigeria
0% Sao Tome and Principe

Urbanization and Largest Cities

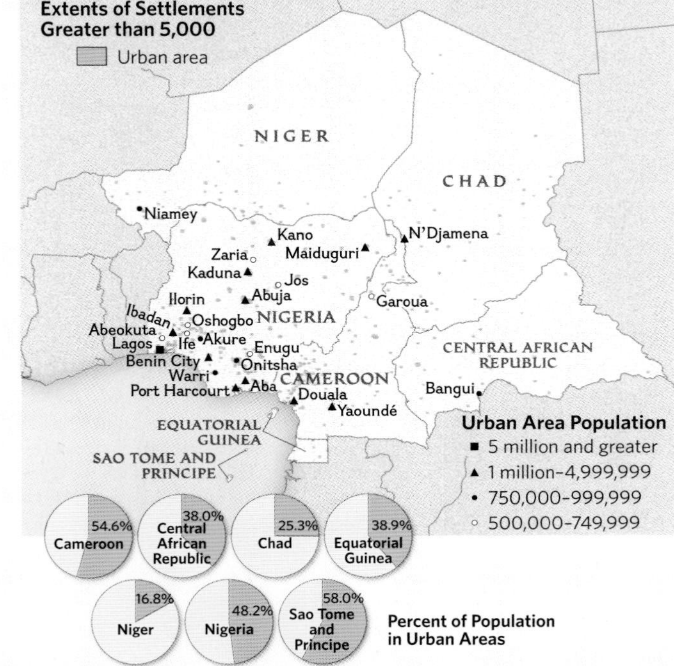
Extents of Settlements Greater than 5,000
Urban area
NIGER
CHAD
Niamey
Kano
N'Djamena
Zaria
Maiduguri
Kaduna
Jos
Ilorin
Abuja
Garoua
Ibadan
Oshogbo
NIGERIA
Abeokuta
Ife
Akure
Lagos
Enugu
Benin City
Onitsha
Warri
Aba
CAMEROON
Port Harcourt
Douala
Yaoundé
CENTRAL AFRICAN REPUBLIC
Bangui
EQUATORIAL GUINEA
SAO TOME AND PRINCIPE
Urban Area Population
5 million and greater
1 million–4,999,999
750,000–999,999
500,000–749,999
54.6% Cameroon
38.0% Central African Republic
25.3% Chad
38.9% Equatorial Guinea
16.8% Niger
48.2% Nigeria
58.0% Sao Tome and Principe
Percent of Population in Urban Areas

Natural Land Cover

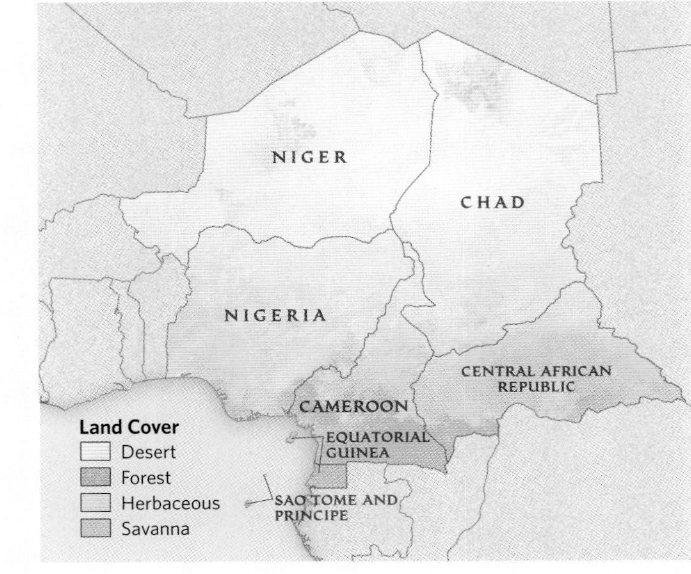
NIGER
CHAD
NIGERIA
CENTRAL AFRICAN REPUBLIC
CAMEROON
EQUATORIAL GUINEA
SAO TOME AND PRINCIPE
Land Cover
Desert
Forest
Herbaceous
Savanna

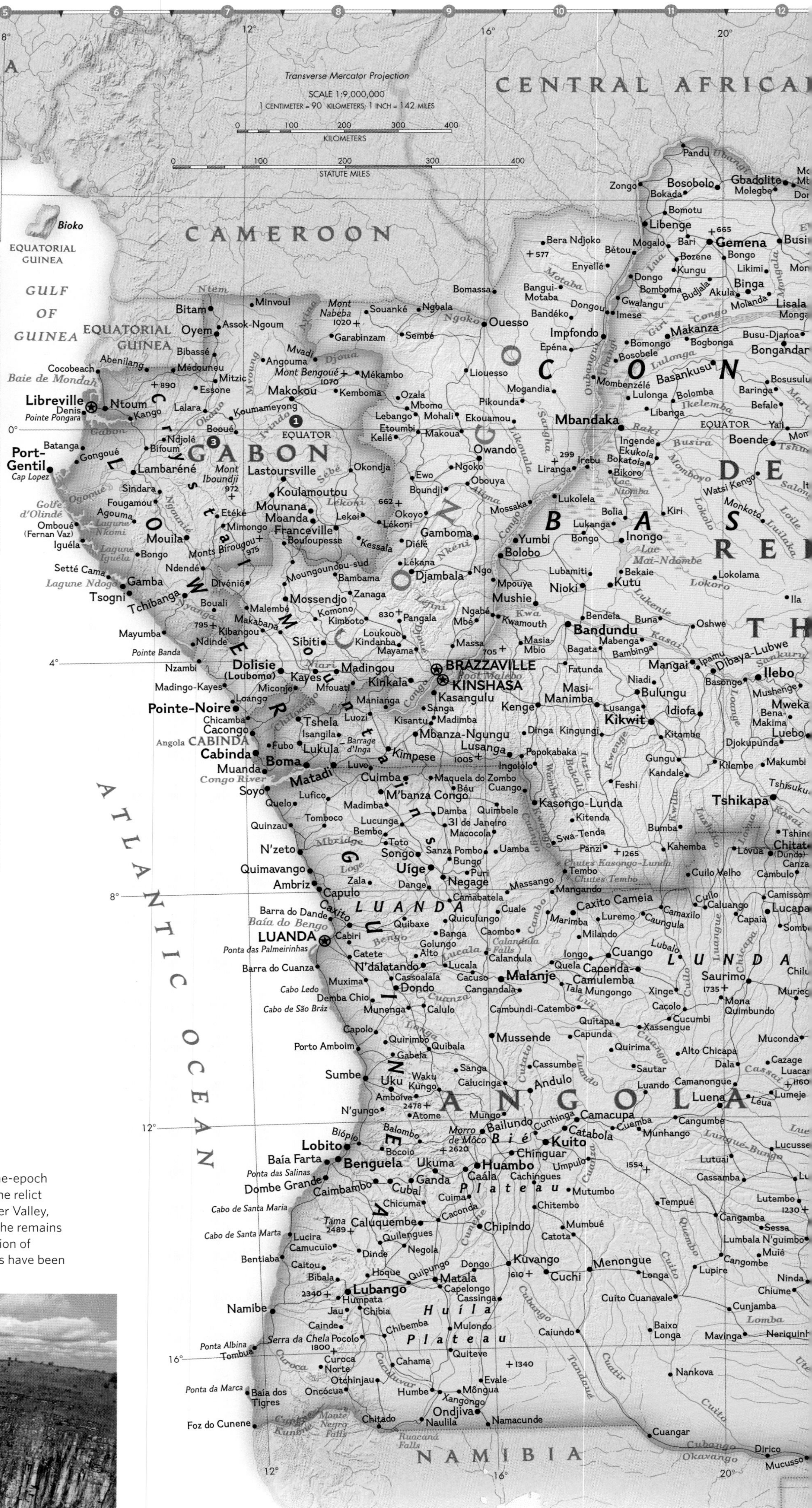

Transverse Mercator Projection
SCALE 1:9,000,000
1 CENTIMETER = 90 KILOMETERS; 1 INCH = 142 MILES

NIGERIA · CAMEROON · CENTRAL AFRICAN · EQUATORIAL GUINEA · GABON · CONGO · DEMOCRATIC REPUBLIC OF THE CONGO · ANGOLA · NAMIBIA · GULF OF GUINEA · ATLANTIC OCEAN

Ivindo National Park, Gabon (Tentative List) 1

More than a thousand square miles of nearly impassable lowland forest was designated a national park in 2002 after an extensive exploration by the Wildlife Conservation Society and the National Geographic Society. Draining almost all of northeastern Gabon, the slow, black waters of the Ivindo River feature spectacular waterfalls, including the two-mile-wide Kongou Falls that tops 185 feet at its tallest drop. The Langoué Bai, a swampy, mineral-rich water hole, is a virtual "forest elephant city," with ever widening tracks leading to the clearing. Buffalo, wild hogs, sitatungas (large forest antelopes), chimpanzees, parrots, and gorillas that have never seen humans come here to bathe and socialize.

Virunga National Park, Democratic Republic of the Congo 2

Covering nearly two million acres, the park's habitats range from marshes, lakes, and rivers — where the largest concentration of hippopotamuses in Africa live — to savannas, lowland forests, and lava plains of the active volcanoes Nyamuragira and Nyiragongo — which account for two-fifths of the volcanic eruptions on the African continent — to moist, rugged mountain slopes, where bamboo forests support a third of the world's endangered mountain gorillas.

Ecosystem and Relict Cultural Landscape of Lopé-Okanda, Gabon 3

Although similar to other areas of the Congo Basin, the dense rain forests of Lopé-Okanda have recolonized almost all the space once occupied by Pleistocene-epoch savanna. Due to relatively dry conditions, the rain forest could not take over all the relict savanna, resulting in an unusual combination. The park includes the Ogooué River Valley, one of the principle migration routes for Neolithic and Iron Age cultures, where the remains of substantial settlements with evidence of ironworking and an extensive collection of some 1,800 rock art petroglyphs have been found. More than 1,550 plant species have been recorded, with ongoing surveys predicting the number to possibly reach 3,500.

Kahuzi-Biega National Park, 4 Democratic Republic of the Congo

Named after the two extinct volcanoes of Kahuzi and Biega, the park was once home to thousands of elephants and endangered eastern lowland gorillas, but slash-and-burn farming destroyed much of the forests, and the Rwandan war brought millions of refugees, armed militia intent on selling the animals and ivory, and bushmeat hunters working to feed laborers of nearby mining camps. The number of all wildlife dwindled drastically, with gorillas and elephants near extinction. In 2001, UNESCO provided funding to help protect the park's animals, and now some 250 gorillas inhabit the bamboo and tropical forests of the mountains.

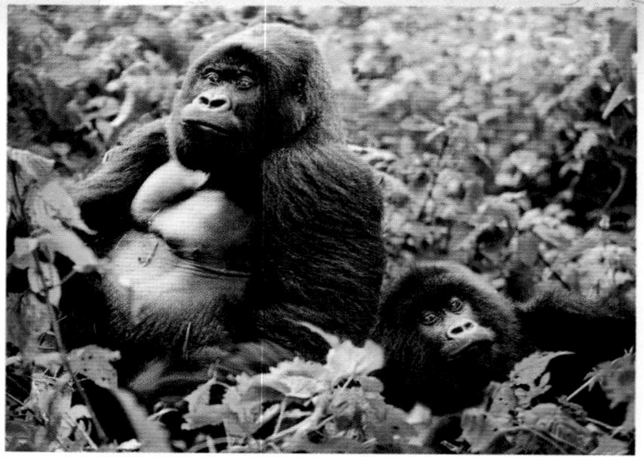

Angola  | Congo  | Democratic Republic of the Congo 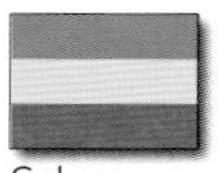 | Gabon 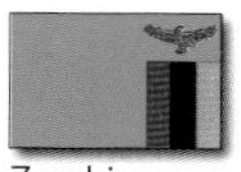 | Zambia

Okapi Wildlife Reserve, Democratic Republic of the Congo 5

The sanctuary encompasses nearly one-fifth of the Ituri Forest in northeast Democratic Republic of the Congo and is home to two traditional nomadic pygmy tribes, the Mbuti and the Efe. Initially set up as a captive-breeding center for the rare okapi, the reserve now holds more than 4,000 of the 30,000 okapi still surviving in the wild. In total, the reserve shelters 329 bird and 52 mammal species, including 13 primate species, more than found in any other African forest, one of the highest number of duiker species, elephant, water chevrotain (lesser mountain deer), African golden cat, and giant forest hog.

Mosi-oa-Tunya/Victoria Falls, Zambia and Zimbabwe 6

Nearly 180 million years ago, magma shot out of the earth and formed a basalt plateau that cooled and solidified into countless crevices. A lake submerged the plateau and mud and debris deposited in the cracks. When the plateau rose again, the deposits became soft rocks, and the Zambezi River later eroded the rocks downstream, creating a waterfall about 200,000 years ago. The sedimentary rocks continued to erode, moving the waterfall upstream and leaving gorges in the fall's former location. The current waterfall, more than 5,500 feet wide and dropping nearly 360 feet, is the eighth highest in the world and recedes nearly three inches a year.

Africa: Congo, Gabon, Cabinda (Angola), Angola, Democratic Republic of the Congo, Zambia

Protected Areas and World Heritage Sites

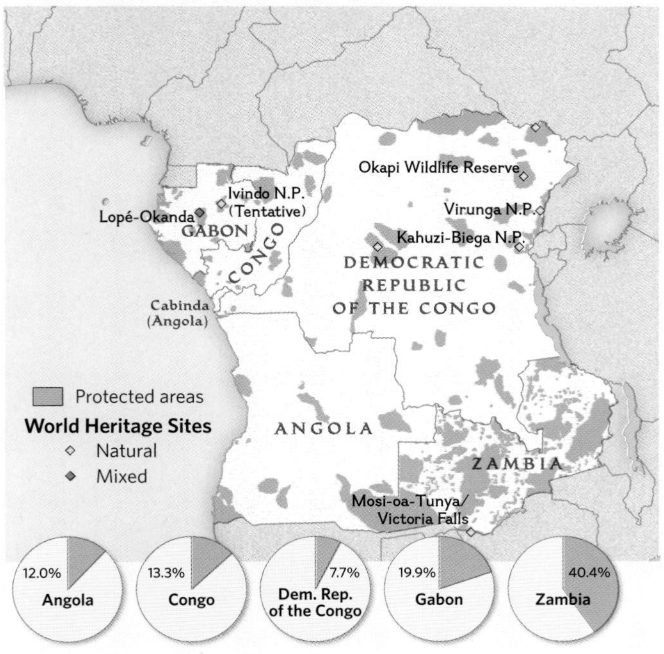

Protected areas

World Heritage Sites
- Natural
- Mixed

Angola	Congo	Dem. Rep. of the Congo	Gabon	Zambia
12.0%	13.3%	7.7%	19.9%	40.4%

Percent of Land Area Protected

Urbanization and Largest Cities

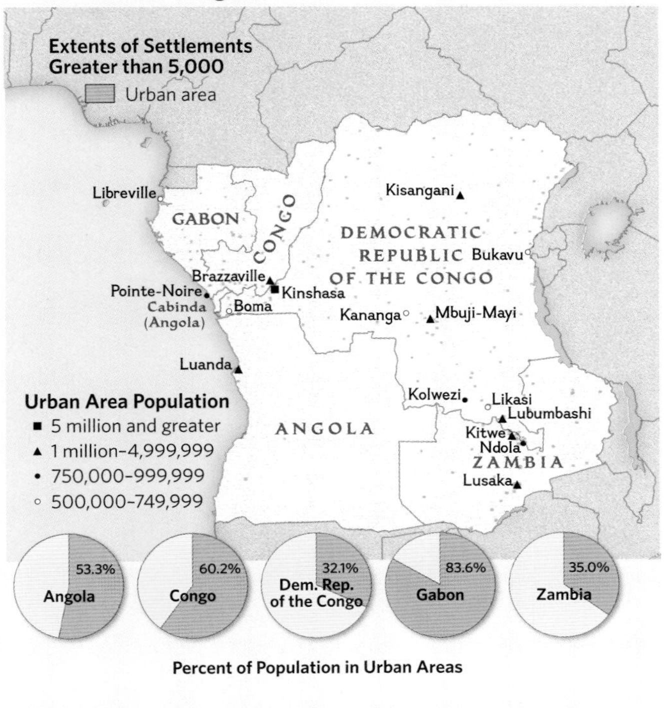

Extents of Settlements Greater than 5,000
- Urban area

Urban Area Population
- 5 million and greater
- 1 million–4,999,999
- 750,000–999,999
- 500,000–749,999

Angola	Congo	Dem. Rep. of the Congo	Gabon	Zambia
53.3%	60.2%	32.1%	83.6%	35.0%

Percent of Population in Urban Areas

Natural Land Cover

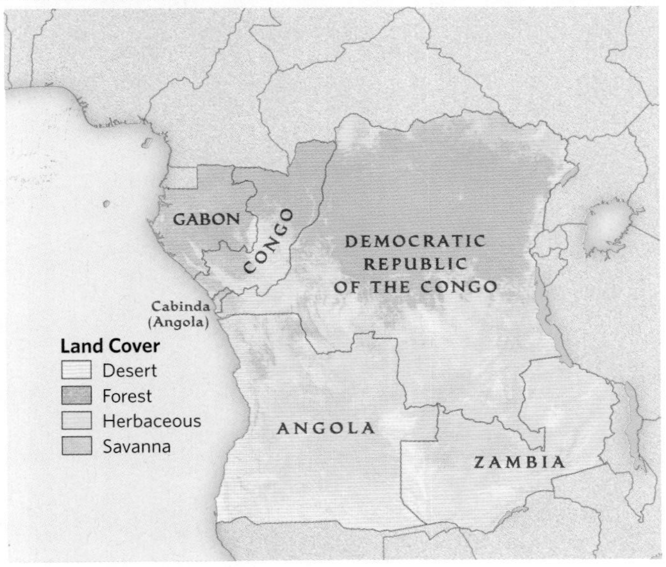

Land Cover
- Desert
- Forest
- Herbaceous
- Savanna

Fasil Ghebbi, Gondar Region, Ethiopia ❶

According to legend, the Ethopian emperor Fasilides was on a hunting trip and followed a buffalo to Gondar. He established the fortress-city of Fasil Ghebbi in 1635 as his residence and surrounded it with a 2,900-foot-long wall. Within the compound are baroque-style castles, palaces, churches, and monasteries built by Fasilides and his successors with Hindu and Arab influences. Fasilides' grandson, Iyasu the Great, built his castle in the center of the main compound, decorating the interior with ivory and mirrors and covering its ceilings with gold and precious stones.

Lamu Old Town, Kenya ❷

Once the most important trade center in East Africa, Lamu is East Africa's oldest and best preserved Swahili settlement; its architecture and urban layout reflect influences from its more than 700 years of contact with European, Arabian, and Indian cultures. Using Swahili techniques, the buildings are constructed from coral stone and mangrove timber and display simple designs enhanced by inner courtyards, verandas, and intricately carved wooden doors. Muslims from all over Africa have come to Lamu since the 19th century to take part in religious festivals led by descendants of the Prophet Muhammad.

❸ Aksum, Ethiopia

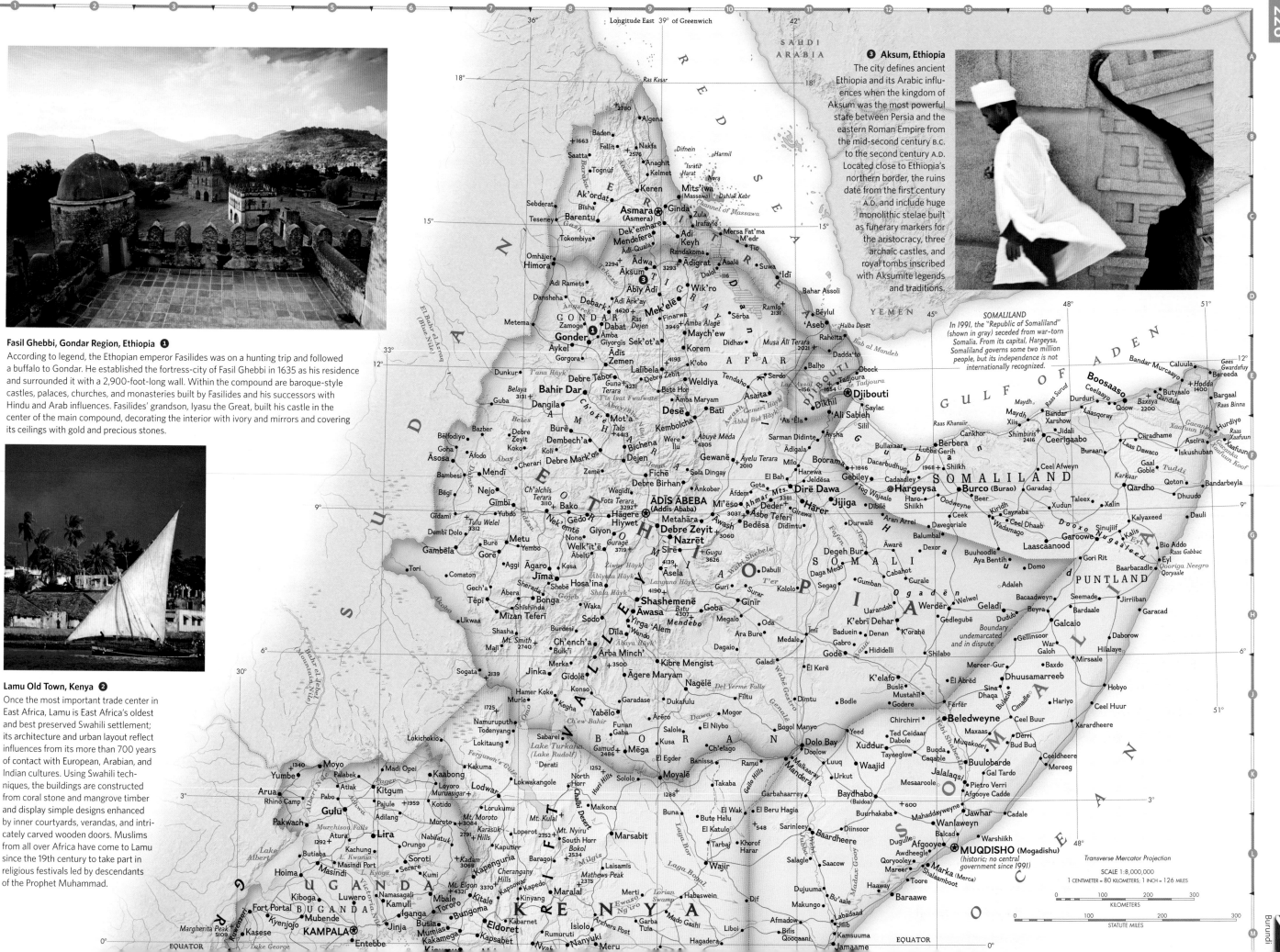

The city defines ancient Ethiopia and its Arabic influences when the kingdom of Aksum was the most powerful state between Persia and the eastern Roman Empire from the mid-second century B.C. to the second century A.D. Located close to Ethiopia's northern border, the ruins date from the first century A.D. and include huge monolithic stelae built as funerary markers for the aristocracy, three archaic castles, and royal tombs inscribed with Aksumite legends and traditions.

SOMALILAND

In 1991, the "Republic of Somaliland" (shown in gray) seceded from war-torn Somalia. From its capital, Hargeysa, Somaliland governs some two million people, but its independence is not internationally recognized.

Transverse Mercator Projection

SCALE 1:8,000,000

1 CENTIMETER = 80 KILOMETERS; 1 INCH = 126 MILES

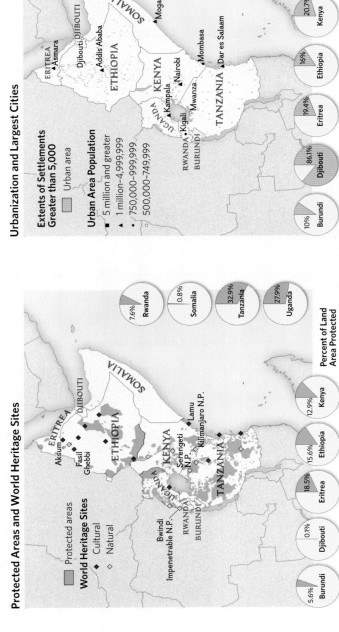

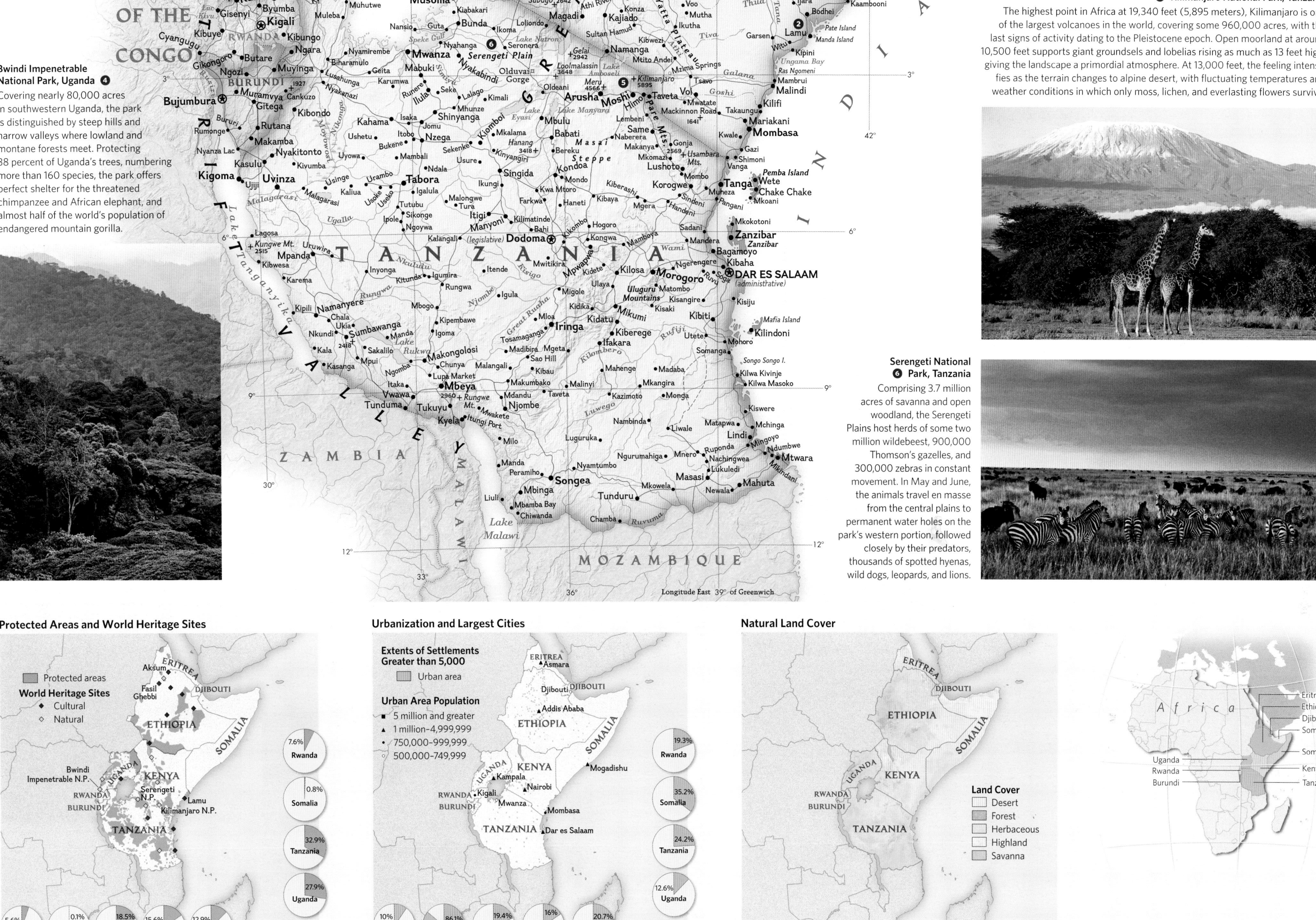
DEM. REP. OF THE CONGO
BURUNDI
RWANDA
TANZANIA
ZAMBIA
MALAWI
MOZAMBIQUE
INDIAN
GREAT RIFT VALLEY
Lake Victoria
Lake Tanganyika
Lake Malawi
NAIROBI
DODOMA (legislative)
DAR ES SALAAM (administrative)
Kigali
Bujumbura
Zanzibar
Mombasa
Arusha
Moshi
Kilimanjaro 5895
Serengeti Plain
Longitude East 39° of Greenwich
Protected Areas and World Heritage Sites
Protected areas
World Heritage Sites
Cultural
Natural
Aksum
Fasil Ghebbi
Bwindi Impenetrable N.P.
Serengeti N.P.
Kilimanjaro N.P.
Lamu
5.6% Burundi
0.1% Djibouti
18.5% Eritrea
15.6% Ethiopia
12.9% Kenya
7.6% Rwanda
0.8% Somalia
32.9% Tanzania
27.9% Uganda
Percent of Land Area Protected
Urbanization and Largest Cities
Extents of Settlements Greater than 5,000
Urban area
Urban Area Population
5 million and greater
1 million–4,999,999
750,000–999,999
500,000–749,999
Asmara
Djibouti
Addis Ababa
Mogadishu
Kampala
Nairobi
Kigali
Mwanza
Mombasa
Dar es Salaam
10% Burundi
86.1% Djibouti
19.4% Eritrea
16% Ethiopia
20.7% Kenya
19.3% Rwanda
35.2% Somalia
24.2% Tanzania
12.6% Uganda
Percent of Population in Urban Areas
Natural Land Cover
Land Cover
Desert
Forest
Herbaceous
Highland
Savanna
Africa
Eritrea
Ethiopia
Djibouti
Somaliland
Somalia
Kenya
Tanzania
Uganda
Rwanda
Burundi

Bwindi Impenetrable National Park, Uganda ❹
Covering nearly 80,000 acres in southwestern Uganda, the park is distinguished by steep hills and narrow valleys where lowland and montane forests meet. Protecting 38 percent of Uganda's trees, numbering more than 160 species, the park offers perfect shelter for the threatened chimpanzee and African elephant, and almost half of the world's population of endangered mountain gorilla.

❺ Kilimanjaro National Park, Tanzania
The highest point in Africa at 19,340 feet (5,895 meters), Kilimanjaro is one of the largest volcanoes in the world, covering some 960,000 acres, with the last signs of activity dating to the Pleistocene epoch. Open moorland at around 10,500 feet supports giant groundsels and lobelias rising as much as 13 feet high, giving the landscape a primordial atmosphere. At 13,000 feet, the feeling intensifies as the terrain changes to alpine desert, with fluctuating temperatures and weather conditions in which only moss, lichen, and everlasting flowers survive.

Serengeti National ❻ Park, Tanzania
Comprising 3.7 million acres of savanna and open woodland, the Serengeti Plains host herds of some two million wildebeest, 900,000 Thomson's gazelles, and 300,000 zebras in constant movement. In May and June, the animals travel en masse from the central plains to permanent water holes on the park's western portion, followed closely by their predators, thousands of spotted hyenas, wild dogs, leopards, and lions.

Botswana Comoros Lesotho

Twyfelfontein or /Ui-//aes, Namibia ❶
With one of the largest concentrations of rock petroglyphs in Africa, Twyfelfontein or /Ui-//aes includes six painted rock shelters with 2,075 identifiable drawings on 235 separate surfaces, and excavated objects dating to the late Stone Age, including ostrich eggshell beads and schist pendants. The majority of the engravings represent human and animal footprints along with depictions of rhinoceroses, elephants, ostriches, and giraffes, and were produced by either grinding and polishing or using a harder stone to etch outlines in the rock. The site forms a coherent record of South African hunter-gatherer rituals over some 2,000 years, linking the economic and ceremonial customs of the tribes.

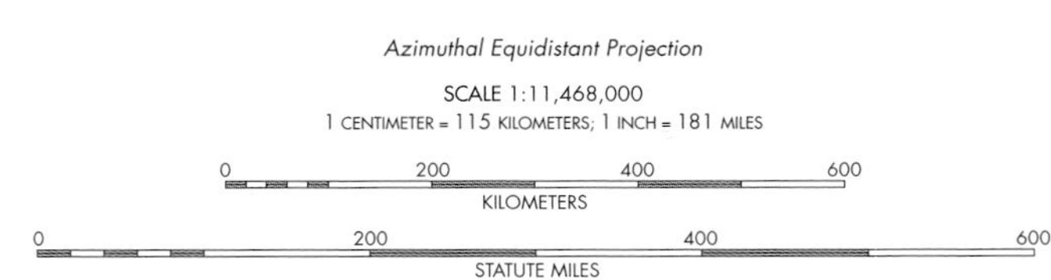
Azimuthal Equidistant Projection
SCALE 1:11,468,000
1 CENTIMETER = 115 KILOMETERS; 1 INCH = 181 MILES
0 200 400 600
KILOMETERS
0 200 400 600
STATUTE MILES

Richtersveld Cultural and Botanical Landscape, South Africa ❷
Covering more than 395,000 acres of the harsh, dry landscape of mountainous desert in northwestern South Africa, this region sustains an indigenous community of Nama, seminomadic pastoralists whose livelihood follows seasonal patterns that may have persisted for as much as two millennia in southern Africa. It is the only area where the Nama continue to build *|haru oms*—domed, portable houses covered with fine mats of braided rushes—and to move their herds of livestock between some 40 stockposts to optimize grazing, at higher levels in winter and on lower lying land in summer.

Robben Island, ❸ South Africa
In 1657, Jan van Riebeeck of the Dutch East India Company set the stage for the island's history of human suffering when he and other colonists enslaved the indigenous Africans; later, prisoners of war were sent to the island to cut stone for building Cape Town. Since then, the island has been used as a British hospital for lepers and the mentally ill, a military base in World War II, and a maximum-security prison for political prisoners of the apartheid regime.

Mana Pools National Park, Sapi and Chewore Safari Areas, Zimbabwe ❹
More than 2,600 square miles of woodland and savanna along the Zambezi River support numerous threatened animals, including one of the largest groups of black rhinos, more than 6,500 elephants, and an important concentration of Nile crocodiles. Numerous leopards, hippos, and buffalo join them on the floodplains during the dry season, when water elsewhere is scarce and when the Albida acacia trees emerge from their wet-season dormancy to shed their protein-rich pods.

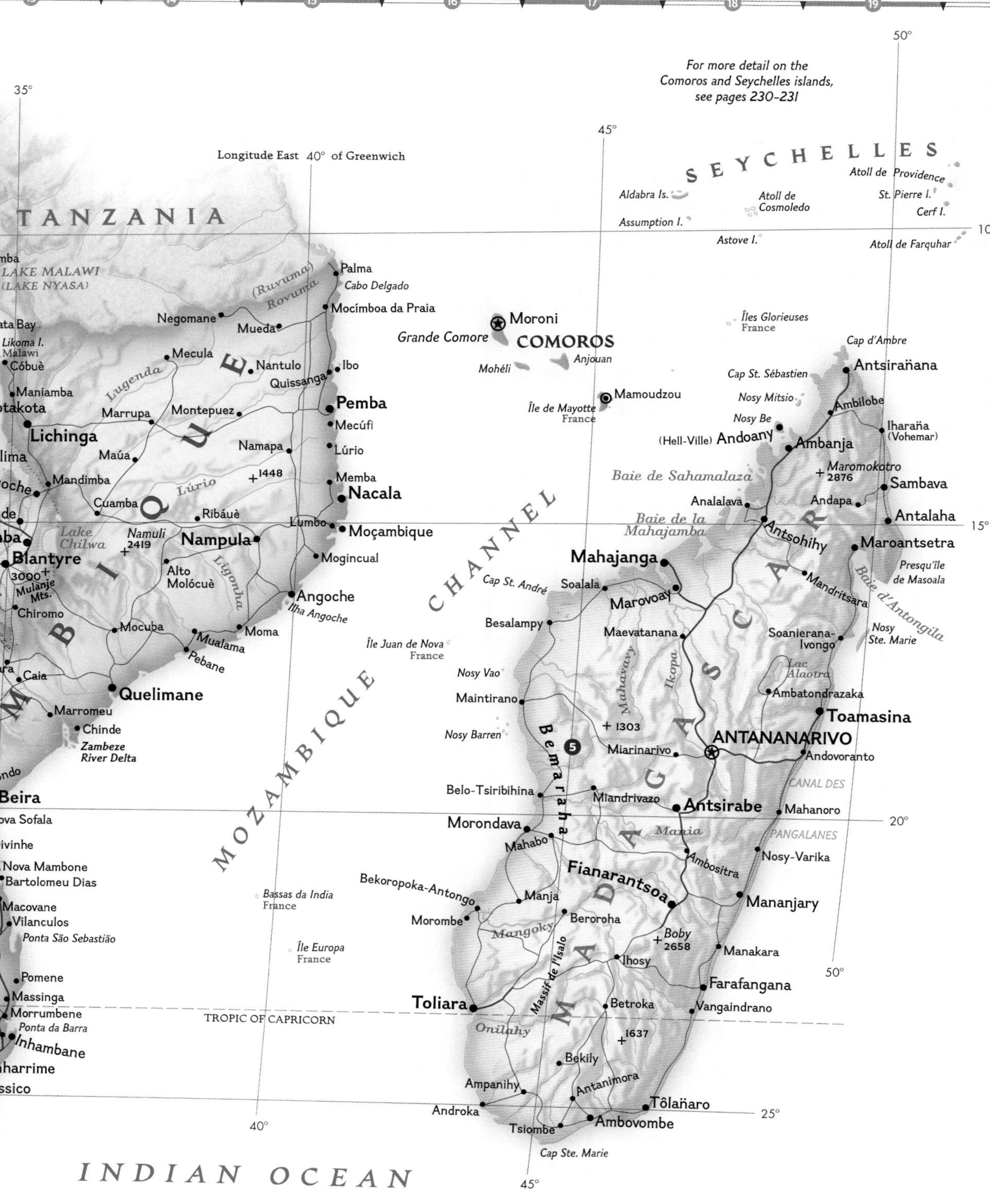
For more detail on the Comoros and Seychelles islands, see pages 230–231
Longitude East 40° of Greenwich
TANZANIA
SEYCHELLES
Aldabra Is.
Atoll de Cosmoledo
Atoll de Providence
St. Pierre I.
Cerf I.
Assumption I.
Astove I.
Atoll de Farquhar
LAKE MALAWI (LAKE NYASA)
Palma
Cabo Delgado
Mocímboa da Praia
Negomane
Mueda
Moroni
Grande Comore
COMOROS
Mohéli
Anjouan
Îles Glorieuses France
Cap d'Ambre
Antsirañana
Mecula
Nantulo
Quissanga
Ibo
Cóbuè
Maniamba
Lichinga
Marrupa
Montepuez
Pemba
Mecúfi
Mamoudzou
Île de Mayotte France
Cap St. Sébastien
Nosy Mitsio
Ambilobe
Nosy Be
(Hell-Ville) Andoany
Ambanja
Iharaña (Vohemar)
Namapa
Lúrio
Memba
Nacala
Maromokotro 2876
Sambava
Baie de Sahamalaza
Analalava
Andapa
Antalaha
Mandimba
Cuamba
Ribáuè
Lumbo
Moçambique
Nampula
Namuli 2419
Blantyre
Mulanje Mts.
Alto Molócuè
Mogincual
Baie de la Mahajamba
Antsohihy
Maroantsetra
Presqu'île de Masoala
Mahajanga
Soalala
Cap St. André
Marovoay
Mandritsara
Baie d'Antongila
Angoche
Ilha Angoche
Chiromo
Mocuba
Mualama
Pebane
Moma
Besalampy
Maevatanana
Soanierana-Ivongo
Nosy Ste. Marie
Île Juan de Nova France
Nosy Vao
Maintirano
Lac Alaotra
Ambatondrazaka
Toamasina
Quelimane
Marromeu
Chinde
Zambeze River Delta
1303
ANTANANARIVO
Miarinarivo
Andovoranto
Nosy Barren
Bemaraha
MOZAMBIQUE CHANNEL
Beira
Belo-Tsiribihina
Miandrivazo
Antsirabe
Mahanoro
Canal des Pangalanes
Morondava
Mahabo
Ambositra
Nosy-Varika
Nova Sofala
Nova Mambone
Bartolomeu Dias
Bekoropoka-Antongo
Fianarantsoa
Manja
Mananjary
Bassas da India France
Macovane
Vilanculos
Ponta São Sebastião
Morombe
Beroroha
Mangoky
Boby 2658
Manakara
Île Europa France
Ihosy
Massif de l'Isalo
Farafangana
Vangaindrano
Pomene
Massinga
Morrumbene
Ponta da Barra
Inhambane
TROPIC OF CAPRICORN
Toliara
Betroka
Onilahy
1637
Bekily
Ampanihy
Antanimora
Tôlañaro
Androka
Tsiombe
Ambovombe
Cap Ste. Marie
INDIAN OCEAN
MADAGASCAR
MOZAMBIQUE

Africa

Malawi
Zimbabwe
Botswana
Namibia
South Africa
Lesotho
Swaziland
Seychelles
Comoros
Madagascar
Mozambique

Protected Areas and World Heritage Sites

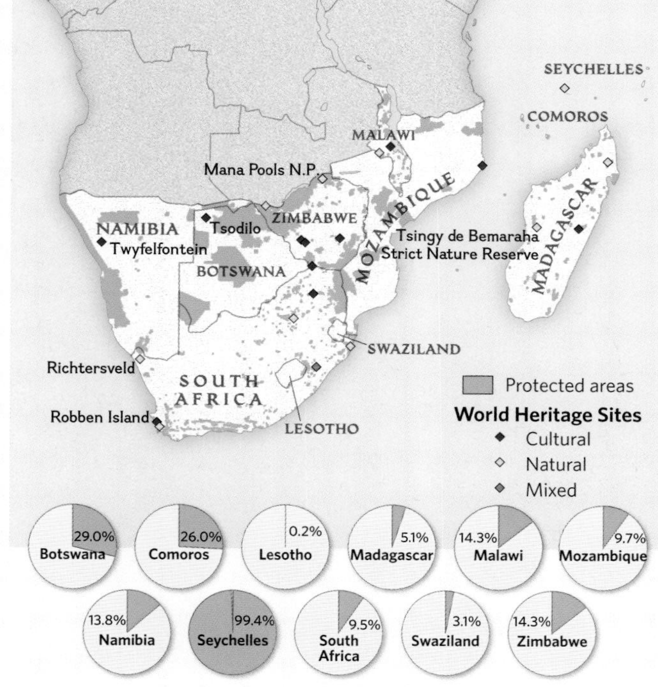
SEYCHELLES
COMOROS
MALAWI
Mana Pools N.P.
NAMIBIA
Twyfelfontein
Tsodilo
ZIMBABWE
MOZAMBIQUE
Tsingy de Bemaraha Strict Nature Reserve
MADAGASCAR
BOTSWANA
SWAZILAND
Richtersveld
SOUTH AFRICA
Robben Island
LESOTHO
Protected areas
World Heritage Sites
Cultural
Natural
Mixed
29.0% Botswana
26.0% Comoros
0.2% Lesotho
5.1% Madagascar
14.3% Malawi
9.7% Mozambique
13.8% Namibia
99.4% Seychelles
9.5% South Africa
3.1% Swaziland
14.3% Zimbabwe

Percent of Land Area Protected

Urbanization and Largest Cities

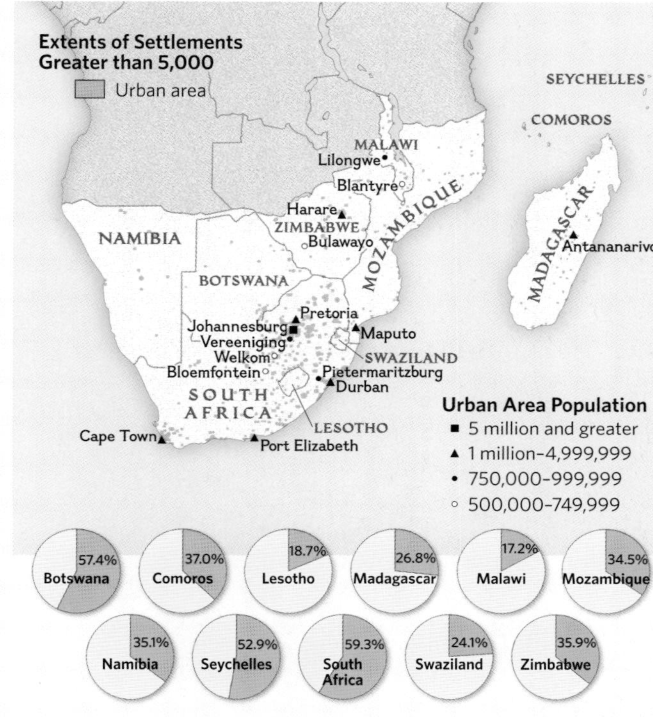
Extents of Settlements Greater than 5,000
Urban area
SEYCHELLES
COMOROS
MALAWI
Lilongwe
Blantyre
Harare
ZIMBABWE
Bulawayo
MOZAMBIQUE
MADAGASCAR
Antananarivo
NAMIBIA
BOTSWANA
Pretoria
Johannesburg
Vereeniging
Maputo
Welkom
SWAZILAND
Bloemfontein
Pietermaritzburg
Durban
SOUTH AFRICA
LESOTHO
Cape Town
Port Elizabeth
Urban Area Population
5 million and greater
1 million–4,999,999
750,000–999,999
500,000–749,999
57.4% Botswana
37.0% Comoros
18.7% Lesotho
26.8% Madagascar
17.2% Malawi
34.5% Mozambique
35.1% Namibia
52.9% Seychelles
59.3% South Africa
24.1% Swaziland
35.9% Zimbabwe

Percent of Population in Urban Areas

Natural Land Cover

SEYCHELLES
COMOROS
MALAWI
NAMIBIA
ZIMBABWE
MOZAMBIQUE
MADAGASCAR
BOTSWANA
SWAZILAND
SOUTH AFRICA
LESOTHO
Land Cover
Desert
Forest
Herbaceous
Savanna

Tsodilo, Botswana 6

More than 4,500 rock art paintings are preserved in the harsh Kalahari Desert in an area of only 3.8 square miles, inspiring archaeologists to refer to Tsodilo as the "Louvre of the desert." The site chronicles the changing traditions, cultures, and technologies of the Kalahari people over the course of nearly 100,000 years, and is said to be home to the spirits of each animal, bird, insect, and plant that has been created. Caves and rock shelters provide evidence of a relatively rare phenomenon in Botswana, evidence that small, mobile groups of humans repeatedly camped on brief seasonal visits, possibly to coincide with the ripening of the mongongo trees.

5 Tsingy de Bemaraha Strict Nature Reserve, Madagascar

Dubbed the "ark of evolution," the island nation of Madagascar lies off the southeast African coast in the Indian Ocean, and an estimated 80 percent of its plants and animals are found nowhere else on Earth. On the western side of the island, the limestone seabed rose to create a plateau nearly 200 million years ago. Heavy rains followed, eroding and sharpening the rocks into *tsingy*, pointed peaks, which tower more than 300 feet over 375,000 acres of savanna; undisturbed, dry deciduous forest; lakes; and mangrove swamps. Roots of trees growing at the foot of the pinnacles penetrate the rock's surface searching for water in the limestone caves, which provides nourishment to produce leaves throughout the year for 30 species of lemurs, including the endangered sifaka.

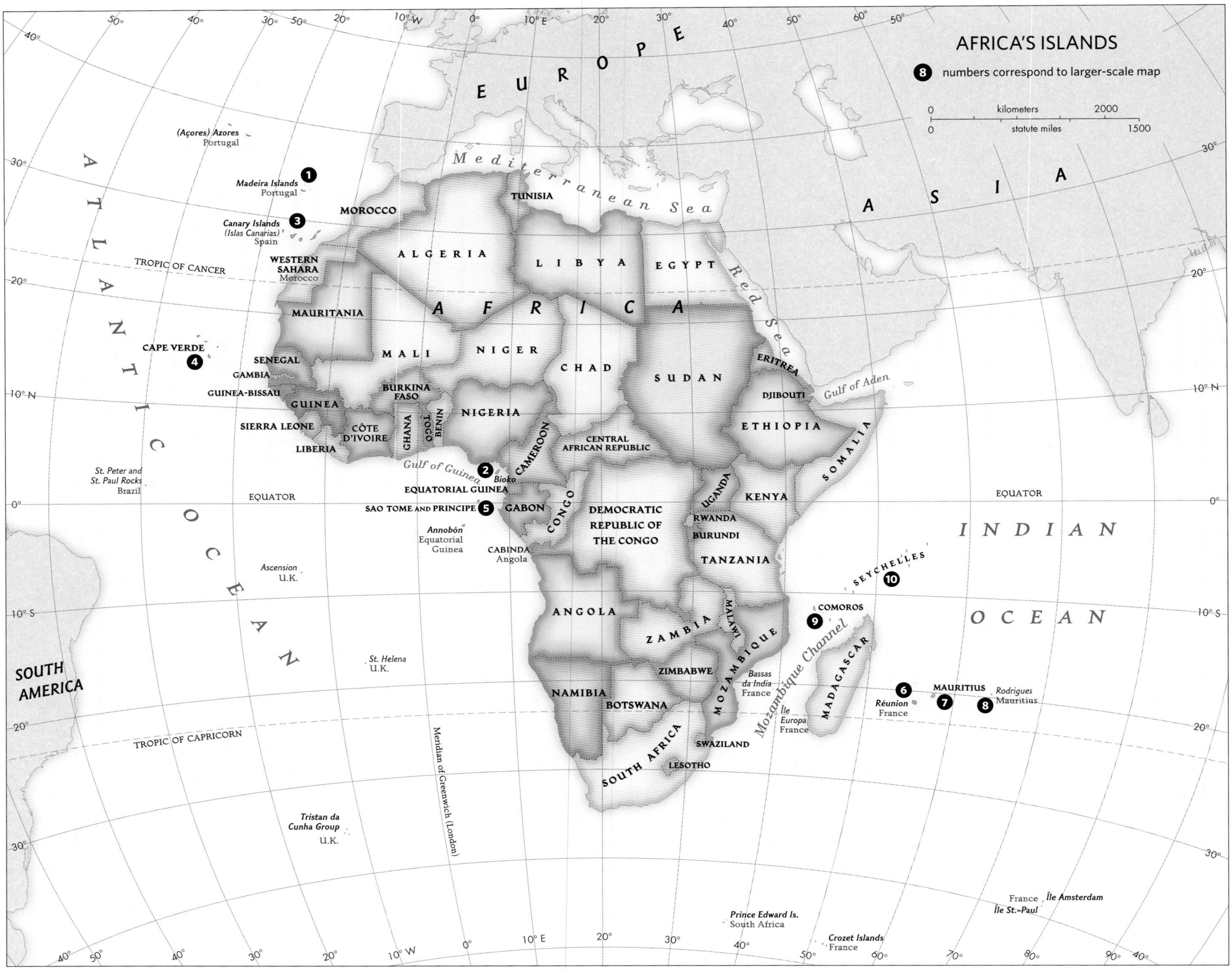

AFRICA'S ISLANDS

8 numbers correspond to larger-scale map

0 kilometers 2000
0 statute miles 1500

EUROPE
ASIA
AFRICA
ATLANTIC OCEAN
INDIAN OCEAN
Mediterranean Sea
Red Sea
Gulf of Aden
Gulf of Guinea
Mozambique Channel
TROPIC OF CANCER
TROPIC OF CAPRICORN
EQUATOR
Meridian of Greenwich (London)
SOUTH AMERICA

(Açores) Azores
Portugal
Madeira Islands 1
Portugal
Canary Islands 3
(Islas Canarias)
Spain
CAPE VERDE 4
St. Peter and St. Paul Rocks
Brazil
Ascension
U.K.
St. Helena
U.K.
Tristan da Cunha Group
U.K.
Bioko 2
EQUATORIAL GUINEA
SAO TOME AND PRINCIPE 5
Annobón
Equatorial Guinea
CABINDA
Angola
SEYCHELLES 10
COMOROS 9
Bassas da India
France
Île Europa
France
MADAGASCAR
Réunion 6
France
MAURITIUS 7
Rodrigues 8
Mauritius
France
Île Amsterdam
Île St.-Paul
Prince Edward Is.
South Africa
Crozet Islands
France

MOROCCO
ALGERIA
TUNISIA
LIBYA
EGYPT
WESTERN SAHARA
Morocco
MAURITANIA
MALI
NIGER
CHAD
SUDAN
ERITREA
DJIBOUTI
ETHIOPIA
SOMALIA
SENEGAL
GAMBIA
GUINEA-BISSAU
GUINEA
SIERRA LEONE
LIBERIA
CÔTE D'IVOIRE
BURKINA FASO
GHANA
TOGO
BENIN
NIGERIA
CAMEROON
CENTRAL AFRICAN REPUBLIC
GABON
CONGO
DEMOCRATIC REPUBLIC OF THE CONGO
UGANDA
KENYA
RWANDA
BURUNDI
TANZANIA
ANGOLA
ZAMBIA
MALAWI
MOZAMBIQUE
ZIMBABWE
NAMIBIA
BOTSWANA
SOUTH AFRICA
SWAZILAND
LESOTHO

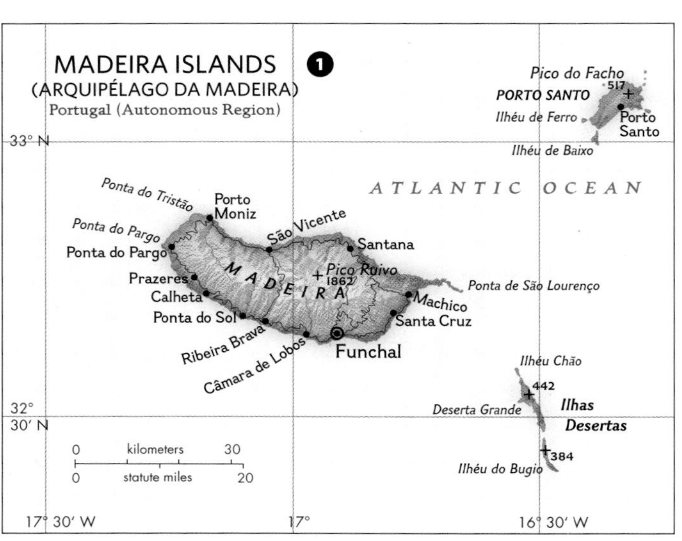
MADEIRA ISLANDS 1
(ARQUIPÉLAGO DA MADEIRA)
Portugal (Autonomous Region)
Pico do Facho
517
PORTO SANTO
Ilhéu de Ferro
Porto Santo
Ilhéu de Baixo
ATLANTIC OCEAN
Ponta do Tristão
Porto Moniz
São Vicente
Santana
Ponta do Pargo
MADEIRA
Pico Ruivo
1862
Ponta de São Lourenço
Prazeres
Calheta
Ponta do Sol
Machico
Santa Cruz
Ribeira Brava
Câmara de Lobos
Funchal
Ilhéu Chão
442
Ilhas Desertas
Deserta Grande
384
Ilhéu do Bugio
0 kilometers 30
0 statute miles 20
33° N
32° 30′ N
17° 30′ W
17°
16° 30′ W

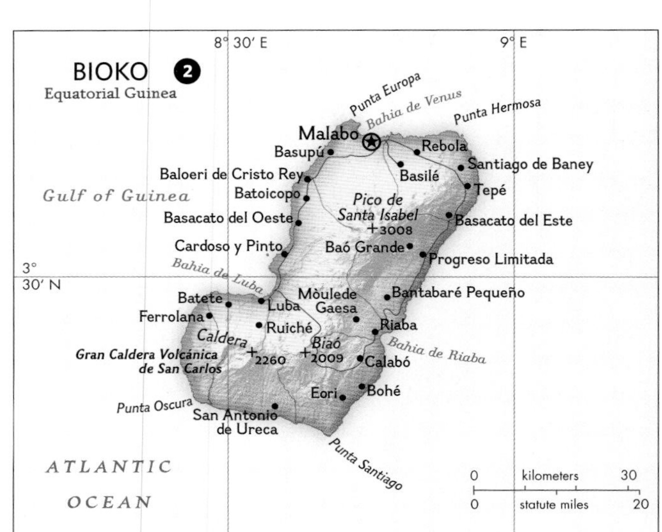
BIOKO 2
Equatorial Guinea
8° 30′ E
9° E
Punta Europa
Bahía de Venus
Punta Hermosa
Malabo
Basupú
Rebola
Basilé
Santiago de Baney
Baloeri de Cristo Rey
Batoicopo
Tepé
Gulf of Guinea
Pico de Santa Isabel
3008
Basacato del Oeste
Basacato del Este
Cardoso y Pinto
Baó Grande
Progreso Limitada
Bahía de Luba
Batete
Moulede Gaesa
Bantabaré Pequeño
Ferrolana
Luba
Ruiché
Riaba
Caldera
Gran Caldera Volcánica de San Carlos
2260
Biaó
2009
Bahía de Riaba
Calabó
Eori
Bohé
Punta Oscura
San Antonio de Ureca
Punta Santiago
ATLANTIC OCEAN
3° 30′ N
0 kilometers 30
0 statute miles 20

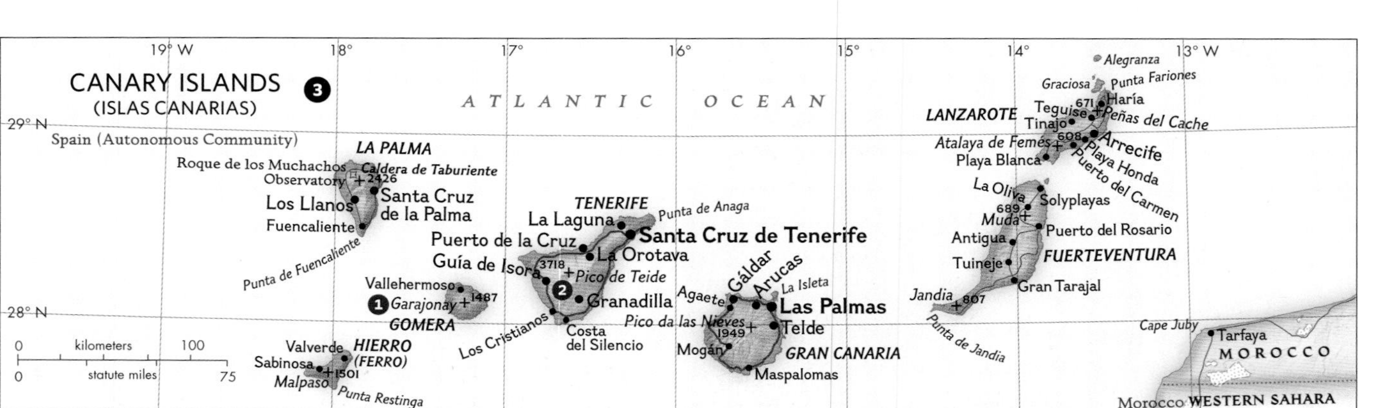
CANARY ISLANDS 3
(ISLAS CANARIAS)
Spain (Autonomous Community)
ATLANTIC OCEAN
19° W
18°
17°
16°
15°
14°
13° W
29° N
28° N
LA PALMA
Roque de los Muchachos
Observatory
Caldera de Taburiente
2426
Los Llanos
Santa Cruz de la Palma
Fuencaliente
Punta de Fuencaliente
TENERIFE
Punta de Anaga
La Laguna
Santa Cruz de Tenerife
Puerto de la Cruz
La Orotava
Guía de Isora
3718
Pico de Teide
Vallehermoso
Garajonay
1487
GOMERA
Granadilla
Los Cristianos
Costa del Silencio
Valverde
HIERRO (FERRO)
Sabinosa
1501
Malpaso
Punta Restinga
Gáldar
Arucas
Agaete
La Isleta
Las Palmas
Pico de las Nieves
1949
Telde
Mogán
GRAN CANARIA
Maspalomas
Alegranza
Graciosa
Punta Fariones
Haría
Peñas del Cache
LANZAROTE
Teguise
671
Tinajo
608
Arrecife
Atalaya de Femés
Playa Blanca
Playa Honda
Puerto del Carmen
La Oliva
Solyplayas
689
Muda
Antigua
Puerto del Rosario
Tuineje
FUERTEVENTURA
Gran Tarajal
Jandía
807
Punta de Jandía
Cape Juby
Tarfaya
MOROCCO
Morocco
WESTERN SAHARA
0 kilometers 100
0 statute miles 75

Garajonay National Park, Canary Islands, Spain 3

Established in 1981, the park covers more than 9,800 acres of the 145-square-mile island of Gomera in the Canary archipelago off the northwest coast of Africa. Mountain heights range between 1,968 and 4,878 feet (600 and 1,487 meters); springs and streams nourish the vegetation of the region, of which 34 plant species are endemic. Nearly 70 percent of the region is covered by laurel forest that, though altered, resembles the flora of the Tertiary period, which once blanketed the southern portion of the European continent, but which has largely disappeared because of climatic changes.

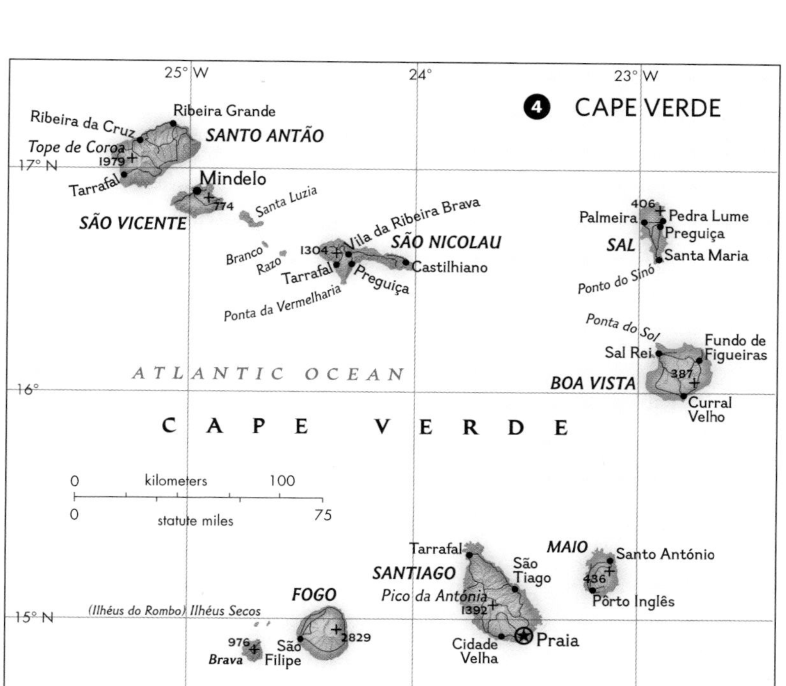
4 CAPE VERDE
25° W
24°
23° W
17° N
16°
15° N
Ribeira da Cruz
Ribeira Grande
SANTO ANTÃO
Tope de Coroa
1979
Tarrafal
Mindelo
774
Santa Luzia
SÃO VICENTE
Vila da Ribeira Brava
Branco
Raso
1304
SÃO NICOLAU
Tarrafal
Preguiça
Castilhiano
Ponta da Vermelharia
Palmeira
406
Pedra Lume
Preguiça
SAL
Santa Maria
Ponto do Sino
Ponta do Sol
Sal Rei
Fundo de Figueiras
387
BOA VISTA
Curral Velho
ATLANTIC OCEAN
CAPE VERDE
0 kilometers 100
0 statute miles 75
Tarrafal
São Tiago
SANTIAGO
Pico da Antónia
1392
MAIO
436
Santo António
Porto Inglês
FOGO
(Ilhéus do Rombo) Ilhéus Secos
976
Brava
São Filipe
2829
Cidade Velha
Praia

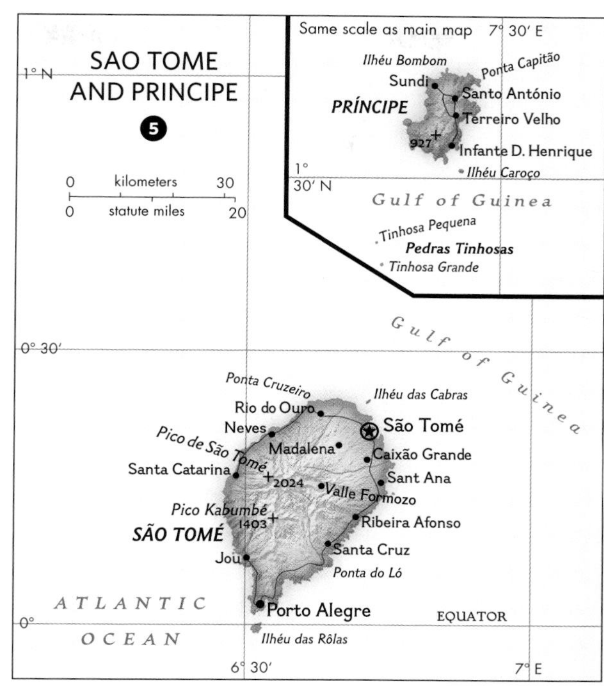
SAO TOME AND PRINCIPE 5
1° N
0 kilometers 30
0 statute miles 20
Same scale as main map 7° 30′ E
Ilhéu Bombom
Sundi
Ponta Capitão
Santo António
PRÍNCIPE
Terreiro Velho
927
Infante D. Henrique
Ilhéu Caroço
1° 30′ N
Gulf of Guinea
Tinhosa Pequena
Pedras Tinhosas
Tinhosa Grande
Gulf of Guinea
0° 30′
Ponta Cruzeiro
Rio do Ouro
Ilhéu das Cabras
Neves
São Tomé
Pico de São Tomé
Madalena
Caixão Grande
Santa Catarina
2024
Sant Ana
Valle Formozo
Pico Kabumbé
1403
Ribeira Afonso
SÃO TOMÉ
Santa Cruz
Jou
Ponta do Ló
ATLANTIC OCEAN
Porto Alegre
EQUATOR
0°
Ilhéu das Rôlas
6° 30′
7° E

Teide National Park, Canary Islands, Spain 2

The 46,925 acres of Teide National Park on the island of Tenerife encompass the highest peak on Spanish soil, the stratovolcano Pico de Teide, which last erupted in 1909 and rises 12,198 feet (3,718 meters) above sea level and 24,606 feet (7,500 meters) above the ocean floor. Volcanic features dominate the landscape and include ridges, cones, craters, domes, and fissures. Tenerife is the world third largest volcanic structure, and because of local atmospheric conditions, a "sea of clouds" frequently forms below the caldera, creating a unique backdrop to the mountain.

RÉUNION 6
France

55° 00′ E
55° 30′
56° 00′ E
21°
21° 30′ S
La Possession
Saint-Denis
Sainte-Marie
Sainte-Suzanna
Pointe des Galets
Le Port
Saint-André
Saint-Paul
Bras-Panon
2277
Salazie
Saint-Benoît
St.-Gilles-les-Bains
Hell-Bourg
Trois-Bassins
Piton des Neiges
3069
941
2896
Cilaos
1685
La Plaine
Sainte-Rose
Saint-Leu
Entre-Deux
La Plaine des Cafres
Piton de la Fournaise
2631
Les Avirons
Étang-Salé
La Rivière
Le Tampon
Saint-Louis
Saint-Pierre
Petite Ile
281
Pointe de la Table
Saint-Philippe
Saint-Joseph
INDIAN OCEAN
0 kilometers 30
0 statute miles 20

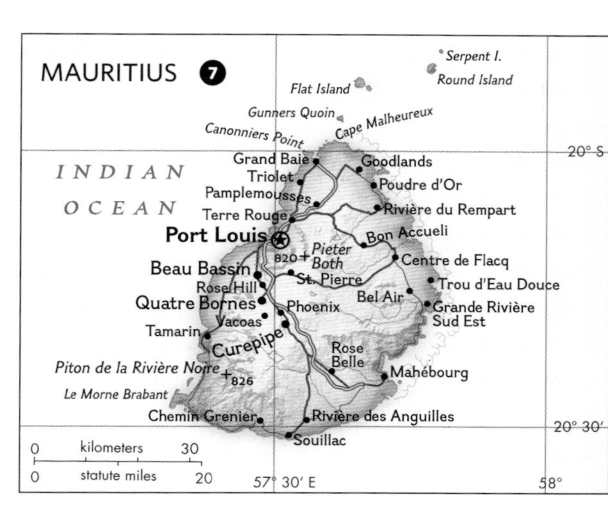
MAURITIUS 7
Serpent I.
Round Island
Flat Island
Gunners Quoin
Cape Malheureux
Canonniers Point
20° S
INDIAN OCEAN
Grand Baie
Triolet
Goodlands
Pamplemousses
Poudre d'Or
Terre Rouge
Rivière du Rempart
Port Louis
Bon Accueil
Pieter Both
820
Beau Bassin
Centre de Flacq
Rose Hill
St. Pierre
Trou d'Eau Douce
Quatre Bornes
Phoenix
Bel Air
Grande Rivière Sud Est
Tamarin
Vacoas
Curepipe
Rose Belle
Piton de la Rivière Noire
826
Mahébourg
Le Morne Brabant
Chemin Grenier
Rivière des Anguilles
Souillac
20° 30′
0 kilometers 30
0 statute miles 20
57° 30′ E
58°

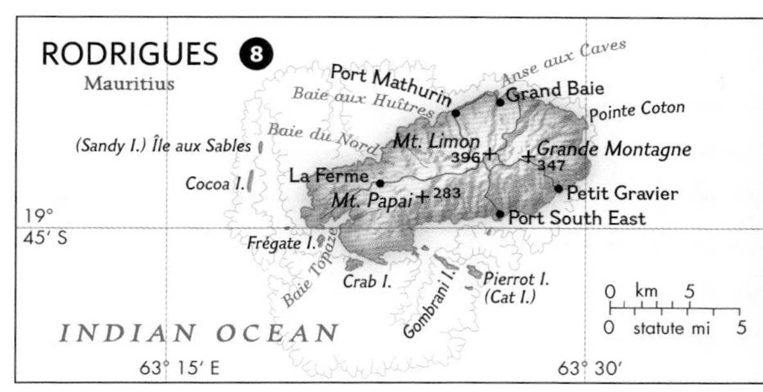
RODRIGUES 8
Mauritius
Port Mathurin
Anse aux Caves
Baie aux Huîtres
Grand Baie
Pointe Coton
Baie du Nord
Mt. Limon
396
Grande Montagne
347
(Sandy I.) Île aux Sables
Cocoa I.
La Ferme
Mt. Papai
283
Petit Gravier
Port South East
19° 45′ S
Frégate I.
Baie Topaze
Crab I.
Gombrani I.
Pierrot I. (Cat I.)
0 km 5
0 statute mi 5
INDIAN OCEAN
63° 15′ E
63° 30′

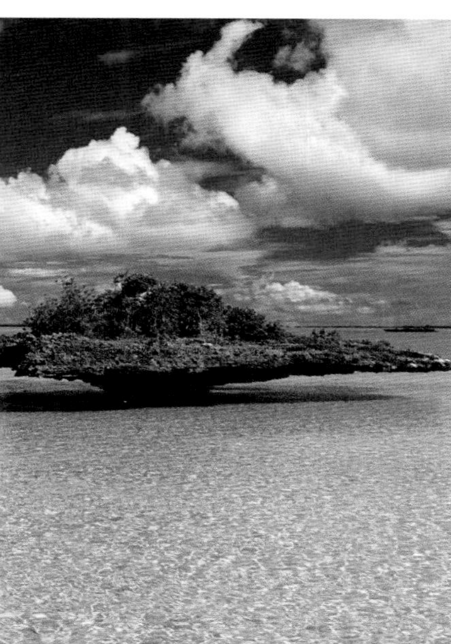

Aldabra Atoll, Seychelles 3

Located 260 miles northwest of Madagascar, the Aldabra atoll is composed of four islands of coral limestone separated by narrow passages enclosing a shallow lagoon. Surrounded by a 125,000-year-old coral reef, it is the only place in the world where a reptile—the 110-pound (on average) giant tortoise—is the dominant plant-eating animal. The reef, which makes access to the atoll difficult, and their isolation have together prevented substantial human impact on the atoll's environment; as a result, Aldabra supports some 150,000 giant tortoises, the world's largest population of this species.

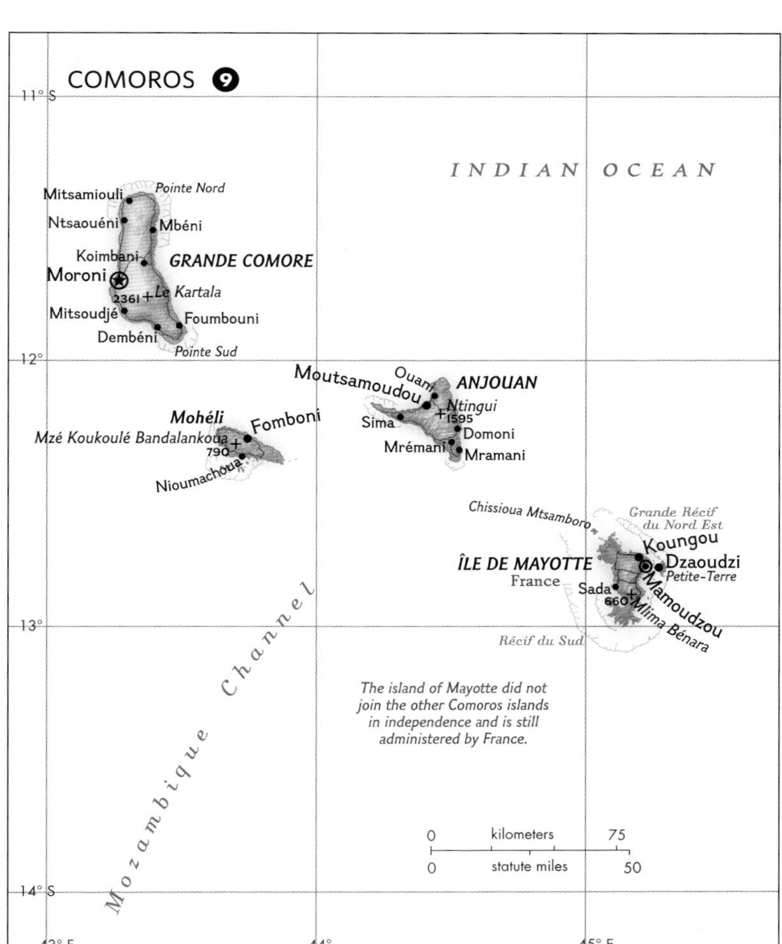
COMOROS 9
11° S
12°
13°
14° S
INDIAN OCEAN
Mitsamiouli
Pointe Nord
Ntsaouéni
Mbéni
Koimbani
GRANDE COMORE
Moroni
2361
Kartala
Mitsoudjé
Foumbouni
Dembéni
Pointe Sud
Moutsamoudou
Ouani
ANJOUAN
Ntingui
1595
Sima
Domoni
Mohéli
Fomboni
Mrémani
Mramani
Mzé Koukoulé Bandalankoua
790
Nioumachoua
Chissioua Mtsamboro
Grande Récif du Nord Est
Koungou
ÎLE DE MAYOTTE
France
Dzaoudzi
Petite-Terre
Sada
660
Mamoudzou
Mlima Bénara
Récif du Sud
Mozambique Channel
The island of Mayotte did not join the other Comoros islands in independence and is still administered by France.
0 kilometers 75
0 statute miles 50
43° E
44°
45° E

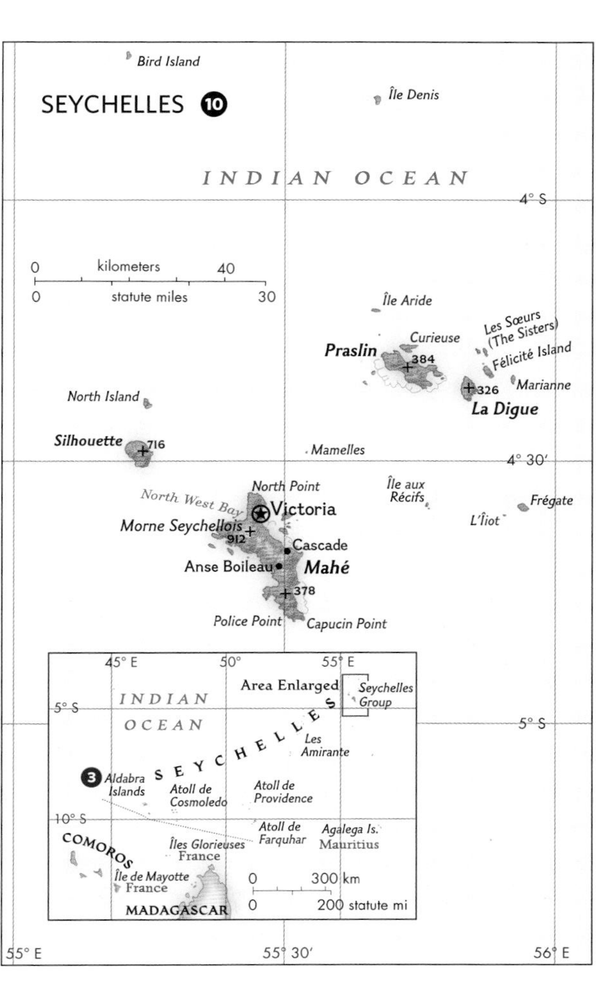
SEYCHELLES 10
Bird Island
Île Denis
INDIAN OCEAN
4° S
0 kilometers 40
0 statute miles 30
Île Aride
Les Sœurs (The Sisters)
Praslin
Curieuse
Félicité Island
384
326
Marianne
La Digue
North Island
Silhouette
716
Mamelles
4° 30′
North Point
Île aux Récifs
Frégate
North West Bay
Victoria
L'Îlot
Morne Seychellois
912
Cascade
Anse Boileau
Mahé
378
Police Point
Capucin Point
45° E
50°
55° E
Area Enlarged
Seychelles Group
INDIAN OCEAN
5° S
SEYCHELLES
Les Amirante
Aldabra Islands
Atoll de Cosmoledo
Atoll de Providence
10° S
Atoll de Farquhar
Agalega Is. Mauritius
COMOROS
Îles Glorieuses France
Île de Mayotte France
0 300 km
0 200 statute mi
MADAGASCAR
55° E
55° 30′
56° E

FROM THE PLATYPUS TO THE EUCALYPTUS, the flora and fauna of Australia followed unique evolutionary byways thanks to the island continent's geographic isolation. Its cultural development was defined as well by sequestration. Humans first reached its shores 40,000 or more years ago, and by the time Europeans arrived in the 17th century — making Australia the last continent except Antarctica they would explore — indigenous Australian cultures speaking hundreds of languages resided throughout the continent. Much of the country's fame today rests on its natural features, including the magnificent Great Barrier Reef, home to a bewildering array of marine life, and the continent's arid, iconic interior — the outback.

Thousands of islands that dot the Pacific to the north and east of Australia make up the scattered geographic region known as Oceania, which includes New Zealand, Papua New Guinea, and three traditional groupings of smaller islands: Polynesia ("many islands"), Melanesia ("black islands"), and Micronesia ("small islands"). Some of the islands and island chains of this highly diverse, culturally rich region are self-governing nations, while many others are territories of foreign countries.

KEY Cultural World Heritage Site Natural World Heritage Site Mixed World Heritage Site

Australia and Oceania

Palms sway on Australia's Lord Howe Islands (right), the remnants of an ancient volcano that rises out of the seafloor some 6,500 feet below the surface. Other World Heritage sites in Australia and Oceania include (left, top to bottom): the glaciated peaks of New Zealand's Fiordland National Park, reflected in Milford Sound; the soaring interlocking "shells" of Australia's renowned Sydney Opera House; the Great Barrier Reef, the world's largest coral reef system, covering 14,000 square miles off Australia's northeastern coast; and the vast bulk of Uluru, or Ayers Rock—the outback massif sacred to Aboriginal Australians.

Azimuthal Equidistant Projection
SCALE 1:8,128,200
1 CENTIMETER = 81 KILOMETERS; 1 INCH = 128 MILES
KILOMETERS
STATUTE MILES
State boundary
Sumba
SAVU SEA
Sawu
Roti
Timor
TIMOR SEA
Ashmore Islands
Cartier Island
Bonaparte Archipelago
Browse Island
Cape Van Diemen
Bathurst I.
Melville Island
Cape Fourcroy
Port Essington
Croker I.
Cobourg Pen.
Van Diemen Gulf
Clarence Str.
Charles Point
Point Blaze
Anson Bay
Cape Ford
Murrenja Hill
Cape Bougainville
Cape Talbot
Cape Londonderry
Cape Voltaire
Joseph Bonaparte Gulf
Endeavour Hill
Brunswick Bay
Buccaneer Archipelago
Cape Leveque
King Sd.
Dampier Land
Cape Bertholet
Kimberley Plateau
Mount Ord
King Leopold Ranges
Lake Argyle
Lake Woods
Roebuck Bay
Cape Latouche Treville
Cape Bossut
Eighty Mile Beach
GREAT SANDY DESERT
Tanami Desert
Mount Frederick
Mount Tanami
Lewis Range
Southesk Tablelands
Lake White
Dampier Archipelago
Barrow Island
Exmouth Gulf
North West Cape
Lake Waukarlycarly
Percival Lakes
Lake Mackay
Lake Dora
Lake Auld
Hamersley Range
Chichester Ra.
Mt. Meharry
WESTERN PLATEAU
Lake Disappointment
TROPIC OF CAPRICORN
Mount Zeil
Macdonnell Ranges
James Ra.
NORTH WEST BASIN
Point Cloates
Ophthalmia Ra.
Mount Augustus
Lofty Ra.
Lake Macleod
Cape Cuvier
Mt. Essendon
Mount Madley
Gibson Desert
Lake Neale
Lake Amadeus
Amadeus Depression
Petermann Ranges
Mt. Olga (Kata Tjuta)
Ayers Rock (Uluru)
Collier Range
Gascoyne
Robinson Range
Geographe Channel
Lake Burnside
Lake Carnegie
Mount Aloysius
Musgrave Ranges
Cape Inscription
Dirk Hartog I.
Shark Bay
Lake Gillen
Baker Lake
Mount Sir Thomas
Murchison
Lake Wells
Lake Annean
Lake Throssell
Point Lilian
Nicholson Range
Lake Austin
Lake Darlot
Lake Meramangye
Serpentine Lakes
Mt. Redcliffe
Rason Lake
Bluff Point
Canning Hill
Lake Carey
Great Victoria Desert
Lake Dey Dey
Lake Raeside
Lake Maurice
Houtman Abrolhos
Geelvink Channel
Mongers Lake
Lake Barlee
Lake Minigwal
Lake Ballard
Lake Moore
Lake Rebecca
Lake Goongarrie
Nullarbor Plain
Yarle Lakes
Lake Yindarlgooda
Green Head
Mt. Grey
Walyahmoning Rock
EUCLA BASIN
Lake Lefroy
Hampton Tableland
Lake Cowan
Cape Adieu
Red Rocks Point
Point Brown
Swan
Darling Range
Lake Johnston
Lake Dundas
Point Culver
Cape Peron
Lake Hope
C. Bouvard
Mt. Ragged
GREAT AUSTRALIAN BIGHT
Murray
Geographe Bay
Cape Pasley
Cape Arid
Cape Naturaliste
Archipelago of the Recherche
Bluff Knoll
Cape Leeuwin
Cape Knob
King George Sound
Point D'Entrecasteaux
West Cape Howe
INDIAN OCEAN
Longitude East 128° of Greenwich

Torres Strait
Prince of Wales I.
Cape York
Endeavour Strait
NEW GUINEA
Great Barrier Reef
Wessel Is.
Cape Wilberforce
Cape Arnhem
Gove Pen.
Cape Grenville
Temple Bay
Duifken Point
Albatross Bay
Cape York Peninsula
Cape Weymouth
Cape Sidmouth
Groote Eylandt
GULF OF CARPENTARIA
Cape Keer-weer
Princess Charlotte Bay
Limmen Bight
Mount Young 65
CORAL SEA
Cape Flattery
Cape Bedford
Mitchell
Cape Tribulation
Cape Kimberley
Mornington I.
Wellesley Is.
Gilbert
Atherton Tableland
Bartle Frere 1611
Double Point
Magdelaine Cays
Herald Cays
Tregrosse Islets
Rockingham Bay
Hinchinbrook Island
Barkly Tableland
Lake Sylvester
Gregory
Flinders
Cloncurry
Norman
Gregory Range
Gilbert Range
Herbert
GREAT DIVIDING RANGE
Great Barrier Reef
Georgina
Burdekin
Cumberland Is.
Clarke Range
Repulse Bay
Cloncurry Plateau
Diamantina
Connors Range
Northumberland Islands
Swain Reefs
Capricorn Channel
Cape Manifold
Landsborough Creek
Lake Galilee
Belyando
Marshall
Hay
CENTRAL LOWLANDS
GREAT ARTESIAN BASIN
Thomson
Drummond Range
Mackenzie
Fitzroy
TROPIC OF CAPRICORN
Cato I.
Capricorn Group
Simpson Desert
CHANNEL COUNTRY
Barcoo
Buckland Tableland
Callione Range
Hervey Bay
Sandy Cape
Lake Yamma Yamma
Dawson
Fraser Island (Great Sandy I.)
Sturt Stony Desert
Double Island Point
LAKE EYRE BASIN
Grey Range
Warrego
Cooper Cr.
L. Eyre North
Darling Downs
Nebine Cr.
Wallam Cr.
Moreton Island
Point Lookout
North Stradbroke I.
Lowest point in Australia -16 (-52 ft)
Lake Eyre
Lake Gregory
Caryapundy Swamp
Weir
L. Eyre South
Lake Blanche
Source of the Darling
Lake Callabonna
Barwon
Gwydir
Cape Byron
Narran Lake
Woody Head
Lake Frome
Lake Torrens
Peri Lake
Darling
Namoi
New England Range
Solitary Islands
Island Lagoon
Gairdner
Acraman
Ranges
Lake Gilles
Flinders Ranges
Macquarie
Castlereagh
Bogan
Neckarboo Range
Port Macquarie
Eyre Peninsula
Liverpool Range
Marobee Range
Burrendong Res.
TASMAN SEA
Spencer Gulf
MURRAY RIVER BASIN
Lachlan
Broughton Islands
Yorke Pen.
Mount Lofty Ranges
Lake Cowal
Murray
Murrumbidgee
Riverina
Cape Spencer
Investigator Str.
Gulf St. Vincent
Encounter Bay
Kangaroo I.
Lake Alexandrina
Lake Albert
Edward
Lake Tyrrell
Murrumbidgee
Botany Bay
Lake George
Lake Hindmarsh
Jervis Bay
Lake Eucumbene
Cape Jaffa
Waranga Basin
Source of the Murray
Mount Kosciuszko 2228 (7310 ft)
Highest point in Australia
Mt. William 1167
Lake Eildon
Australian Alps
Snowy
Cape Northumberland
Lake Corangamite
Gippsland
Discovery Bay
Cape Nelson
Port Phillip Bay
Lake Wellington
Ninety Mile Beach
Cape Howe
Cape Otway
Bass Str.
Wilsons Promontory
Wilsons Promontory
Bass Strait
King I.
Flinders I.
FURNEAUX GROUP
Hunter Is.
Cape Barren I.
Great Western Tiers
Mt. Ossa 1617
TASMANIA
L. Gordon
Mt. Hobbs 823
L. Pedder
South West Cape
Tasman Pen.
Same Scale as Main Map

INDONESIA
TIMOR SEA
Azimuthal Equidistant Projection
SCALE 1:8,128,200
1 CENTIMETER = 81 KILOMETERS; 1 INCH = 128 MILES
0 100 200 300 400
KILOMETERS
0 100 200 300 400
STATUTE MILES
Aboriginal Lands
Homesteads
Ashmore Islands Australia
Cartier Island Australia
Browse Island
Melville Island
Garden Point
Milikapiti
Bathurst Island
Nguiu
Minjilang
Van Diemen Gulf
Darwin
Delissaville
Humpty Doo
Maningrida
Oenpelli
Jabiru
Adelaide River
Burrundie
Goodparla
El Sharana
Tipperary
Pine Creek
Daly
Wadeye
Katherine
Mainoru
Bamyili-Beswick
Maranboy
Mataranka
Roper
Willeroo
Joseph Bonaparte Gulf
Kalumburu
Port Warrender
Forrest River
Wyndham
Ivanhoe
Kununurra
Legune
Bullo River
Timber Creek
Delamere
Larrimah
Newry
Victoria
Victoria River Downs
Daly Waters
Top Springs
Waterloo
Kuri Bay
Collier Bay
Karunjie
L. Argyle
Gibb River
Spring Creek
Mt. Barnett
Turkey Creek
Mt. House
Lombadina
King Sd.
KIMBERLEY
Glenroy
Ord
Ord River
Mt. Sanford
Newcastle Waters
Beetaloo
Elliott
Beagle Bay
Derby
Lansdowne
Alice Downs
Wave Hill
Inverway
NORTH
Broome
Roebuck Plains
Yeeda
Camballin
Fitzroy Crossing
Nicholson
Lajamanu
Helen Springs
Muckety
Halls Creek
Birrindudu
Nerrima
Fitzroy
Margaret River
Gordon Downs
Dampier Downs
Cherrabun
Christmas Creek
Tanami Desert
Lagrange
GREAT
Billiluna
Tennant Creek
Anna Plains
Tanami
SANDY DESERT
Balgo
TERRITORY
Wallal Downs
Wauchope
Pardoo
Warrabri
DeGrey
Goldsworthy
Port Hedland
Shay Gap
Warrawagine
Willowra
Barrow Creek
Point Samson
Mundabullangana
De Grey
Karratha
Roebourne
Whim Creek
Bamboo
Anningie
Barrow Island
Marble Bar
Lake Mackay
Tea Tree
Yuendumu
Pine Hill
Aileron
Fortescue
Hillside
Nullagine
Exmouth Gulf
Onslow
Pannawonica
Bonney Downs
WESTERN
Mt. Wedge
Bushy Park
Exmouth
Peedamulla
Wittenoom
Roy Hill
Papunya
Learmonth
Nanutarra
Mt. Stuart
Marillana
Balfour Downs
Haast Bluff
Wyloo
Tom Price
Alice Springs
Jigalong
Bullara
Uaroo
Rocklea
Parraburdoo
Newman
Hermannsburg
Ewaninga
Cardabia
Ashburton Downs
Ashburton
Lake Amadeus
Henbury
Mundiwindi
Gibson Desert
Wallara
TROPIC OF CAPRICORN
Lyndon
Docker River
Mount Ebenezer
Gnaraloo
Minilya
Mount Vernon
Bulloo Downs
Finke
Yulara
Erldunda
Curtin Springs
Quobba
Glenayle
PLATEAU
Kulgera
Mt. Cavenagh
Gascoyne Junction
Landor
Milgun
Gascoyne
Amata
Ernabella
Carnarvon
Dairy Creek
Peak Hill
New Springs
Lake Carnegie
Carnegie
Warburton
Agnes Creek
Wongawal
Carey Downs
Mooloogool
Cunyu
Everard Park
Wooramel
Paroo
Milly Milly
Lake Violet
Denham
Shark Bay
Belele
Wiluna
Murchison
Mileura
Meekatharra
AUSTRALIA
Hamelin
Curbur
Wellbourn Hill
Carrarang
Meadow
Mount Keith
Mount Willoughby
Big Bell
Murgoo
Daydawn
Melrose
Cosmo Newberry
Eurardy
Pinegrove
Sandstone
Agnew
Kalbarri
Galina Mine
Yalgoo
Edah
Mt. Magnet
Laverton
Great Victoria Desert
Coober Pedy
Lynton
Wurarga
Leonora
Murrin Murrin
Northampton
Mullewa
Fields Find
Narndee
Mt. Ida
Malcolm
Lake Maurice
Geraldton
Tardun
Lake Barlee
Kookynie
Yerilla
Walkaway
Narngulu
Pintharuka
Paynes Find
Diemal Find
Menzies
Maralinga
Dongara
Mingenew
Perenjori
Lake Moore
Riverina
Mouroubra
Davyhurst
Cook
Hughes
Deakin
Reid
Forrest
Fisher
Watson
Ooldea
Barton Siding
Wynbring
Tarcoola
Carnamah
Coorow
Bardoc
Yindi
Wubin
Kalannie
Wialki
Bonnie Rock
Kalgoorlie
Golden Ridge
Coonana
Kitchener
Rawlinna
Nurina
Loongana
Jurien
Pithara
Burakin
Mukinbudin
Coolgardie
Karonie
Zanthus
Naretha
Haig
Koonalda
Moora
Bullfinch
Eucla Motel
Koonibba
Wongan Hills
Trayning
Southern Cross
Mundrabilla
Bookabie
Chinta
Konnongorring
Goomalling
Marvel Loch
Madura
Fowlers Bay
Toodyay
Merredin
Lake Cowan
Cocklebiddy Motel
Fraser Range
John Eyre Motel
Smoky Bay
Muchea
Bruce Rock
Wundowie
Norseman
Balladonia
PERTH
Quairading
Narembeem
Streaky Bay
Fremantle
Kwinana
Corrigin
Hyden
Rockingham
Kondinin
Pingelly
Kulin
Mandurah
Wickepin
Lake King
Salmon Gums
GREAT AUSTRALIAN BIGHT
Pinjarra
Narrogin
Red Lake
Grass Patch
Waroona
Williams
Lake Grace
Newdegate
Wagin
Gibson
Bunbury
Collie
Ravensthorpe
Esperance
Capel
Katanning
Hopetoun
Dunsborough
Busselton
Cowaramup
Bridgetown
Borden
Jerramungup
Witchcliffe
Nannup
Karridale
Pemberton
Mt. Barker
Porongurup
Flinders Bay
Northcliffe
Albany
Nornalup
Denmark
Torbay
INDIAN OCEAN
Longitude East 124° of Greenwich

ARAFURA SEA
Torres Strait
Prince of Wales Island
PAPUA NEW GUINEA
Bamaga
Cape York Peninsula
Nhulunbuy
Yirrkala
Groote Eylandt
Numbulwar
GULF OF CARPENTARIA
Weipa
Moreton
Scrubby Creek
Lockhart River
Aurukun
Silver Plains
Princess Charlotte Bay
Coen
Ebagoola
Yarraden
Edward River
Munburra
Kowanyama
Koolburra
Fairview
Laura
Cooktown
Rossville
Butchers Hill
Mitchell
Palmerville
Mt. Mulgrave
Mornington Island
Mornington
Inkerman
Galbraith
Robinson River
McArthur River
Wollogorang
Borroloola
Bing Bong
Macaroni
Vanrook
Delta Downs
Gilbert
Port Douglas
Mt. Molloy
Trinity Beach
Cairns
Mungana
Almaden
Westmoreland
Karumba
Normanton
Burketown
Doomadgee
Abingden Downs
Gilbert River
Ravenshoe
Innisfail
Tully
Cardwell
Milgarra
Wallabadah
Croydon
Georgetown
Einasleigh
Forest Home
Forsayth
Augustus Downs
Gregory Downs
Donors Hill
Nardoo
Brunette Downs
Anthony Lagoon
Alroy Downs
Gallipoli
Riversleigh
Esmeralda
Macknade
Halifax
Bambaroo
The Lynd
Wurung
Kamileroi
Thorntonia
Camooweal
Canobie
Taldora
Woodstock
Townsville
Middle Park
Soudan
Avon Downs
Kajabbi
Millungera
Saxby Downs
Chudleigh Park
Ayr
Reid River
Burdekin
Quamby
Dalgonally
Cambridge Downs
Balfes Creek
Sellheim
Ravenswood
Bowen
Mount Isa
Cloncurry
Julia Creek
Richmond
Boonderoo
Harvest Home
Dalbeg
Proserpine
Collinsville
Lake Nash
Annitowa
Oban
Urandangi
Duchess
McKinlay
Flinders
Tarbrax
Hughenden
Longton
Mt. Elsie
Natal Downs
Selwyn
Dajarra
Kynuna
Whitewood
Netherdale
Mackay
Argadargada
Tobermorey
Chatsworth
Olio
Tangorin
Mt. Douglas
Mt. Coolon
Sarina
Georgina
Linda Downs
Lerida
Goonyella
Ilbilbie
Glenormiston
Boulia
Lucknow
QUEENSLAND
Chorregon
Muttaburra
Grosvenor Downs
Clairview
Old Cork
Morella
Aramac
Blair Athol
Clermont
Dysart
Marion Downs
Diamantina Lakes
Longreach
Ilfracombe
Barcaldine
Marlborough
Byfield
Breadalbane
Tocal
Alice
Pinehill
Emerald
Blackwater
The Caves
Yeppoon
Emu Park
Bedourie
Connemara
Yalleroi
Bogantungan
Dingo
Comet
Duaringa
Rockhampton
Cluny
Warbreccan
Stonehenge
Isisford
Blackall
Springsure
Gladstone
Glengyle
Monkira
Palparara
Thomson
Jundah
Benlidi
Castlevale
Rolleston
Woorabinda
Calliope
Simpson Desert
Moraberree
Welford
Yaraka
Lorne
Banana
Biloela
Thangool
Miriam Vale
Betoota
Listowel Downs
Tambo
Monto
Rosedale
Windorah
Coolabri
Theodore
Birdsville
Gilmore Hut
Hervey Bay
Pandie Pandie
Thylungra
Adavale
Oakwood
Taroom
Mulgildie
Childers
Bundaberg
Gilpeppee
Augathella
Eidsvold
Mundubbera
Maryborough
Gunnewin
Nickavilla
Charleville
Morven
Auburn
Tiaro
Cordillo Downs
Clifton Hills
Arrabury
Eromanga
Quilpie
Cheepie
Mitchell
Wandoan
Theebine
Gympie
Cooladdi
Sommariva
Roma
Yuleba
Durong
Wondai
Durham Downs
Innamincka
Tobermory
Toompine
Wyandra
Boatman
Miles
Chinchilla
Tewantin
Cowarie
Condamine
Nambour
Maroochydore
Warrego
Coongoola
Grassmere
Surat
Caloundra
Caboolture
Thargomindah
Tilboroo
Meandarra
Tara
Dalby
Bongaree
Lake Eyre North
Mulka
Cooper Cr.
Epsilon
Bransby
Bulloo Downs
Bingara
Cunnamulla
Bendena
Bindle
Toowoomba
BRISBANE
William Creek
Etadunna
Narylico
Bollon
St. George
Millmerran
Ipswich
Beenleigh
Kilcowera
Boorara
Tuen
Fernlee
Goondiwindi
Boonah
Gold Coast
Tinnenburra
Bundaleer
Dirranbandi
Warwick
Lake Stewart
Hungerford
Barringun
Goodooga
Tweed Heads
L. Eyre South
Marree
Tibooburra
Yantabulla
Enngonia
Mungindi
Boggabilla
Murwillumbah
Moolawatana
Milparinka
Wanaaring
Fords Bridge
Weilmoringle
Yetman
Lismore
Ballina
Lyndhurst
Mt. Arrowsmith
Collerina
Cumborah
Barwon
Coolatai
Woodburn
Andamooka
Leigh Creek
Lake Frome
Milpa
Yancannia
Brewarrina
Pokataroo
Warialda
Glen Innes
Yamba
Woomera
Lake Torrens
Westwood Downs
Tongo
Louth
Bourke
Gongolgon
Rowena
Burren Junction
Bingara
Grafton
Ulmarra
Pimba
Blinman
Parachilna
Frome Downs
White Cliffs
Tilpa
Byrock
Carinda
Pilliga
Narrabri
Guyra
Glenreagh
Mootwingee
Coolabah
Armidale
Coffs Harbour
Hawker
Wilcannia
Mount Murchison
Innesowen
Coonamble
Gunnedah
Uralla
Darling
Hermidale
Tamworth
Broken Hill
Cobar
Nyngan
Coonabarabran
Werris Creek
Kempsey
Port Augusta
Cockburn
Olary
Nymagee
Trangie
Gilgandra
Coolah
Quirindi
Port Macquarie
Iron Knob
Wilmington
Yunta
Kudgee
SOUTH WALES
Tullamore
Dubbo
Dunedoo
Gloucester
Comboyne
Kendall
Whyalla
Port Pirie
Gladstone
Oakvale
Tolarno
Yallock
Mount Hope
Mudgee
Gulgong
Taree
Coonbah
Ivanhoe
Condobolin
Parkes
Muswellbrook
Forster-Tuncurry
Cowell
Port Broughton
Poolcarie
Mossgiel
Roto
Orange
Bathurst
Singleton
Maitland
Brinkworth
Hillston
Lake Cargelligo
Cessnock
Raymond Terrace
Tumby Bay
Balaklava
Morgan
Renmark
Wentworth
Culpataro
Lachlan
Newcastle
Budgewoi
Spencer Gulf
Mildura
Booligal
Goolgowi
West Wyalong
Lithgow
Gosford
Gawler
Port Lincoln
ADELAIDE
Murray Bridge
Robinvale
Murrumbidgee
Griffith
Katoomba
Richmond
SYDNEY
Crafers
Tallem Bend
Balranald
Temora
Young
Victor Harbor
Strathalbyn
Ouyen
Narrandera
Cootamundra
Wollongong
Kiama
Nowra
Murrayville
Moulamein
Boorooorban
Gundagai
Kangaroo Island
Kingscote
Meningie
Lascelles
Sea Lake
Deniliquin
Urana
Wagga Wagga
Canberra
Queanbeyan
Tintinara
Keith
Jerilderie
Bordertown
Warracknabeal
Birchip
Echuca
Albury
AUSTRALIAN CAPITAL TERRITORY
JERVIS BAY TERRITORY
Kingston South East
Horsham
St. Arnaud
Shepparton
Wodonga
Naracoorte
Bendigo
Corryong
Wangaratta
Narooma
Robe
Dunolly
Stawell
Castlemaine
Seymour
Penola
Mansfield
Bega
Casterton
VICTORIA
Bombala
Merimbula
Mt. Gambier
Hamilton
Ballarat
Sunbury
Melton
MELBOURNE
Bonang
Orbost
Cann River
Portland
Mortlake
Geelong
Cranbourne
Sale
Nowa Nowa
Mallacoota
Port Fairy
Warrnambool
Colac
Moe
Traralgon
Bairnsdale
Leongatha
Apollo Bay
Wonthaggi
Welshpool
Port Albert
Wilsons Promontory
Bass Str.
Coral Sea Islands Territory
Willis Islets
Magdelaine Cays
Herald Cays
Coringa Islets
Tregrosse Islets
Great Barrier Reef
Australia
West Islet
Cato I.
TROPIC OF CAPRICORN
CORAL SEA
TASMAN SEA
GREAT DIVIDING RANGE
CHANNEL COUNTRY
GREAT ARTESIAN BASIN
NEW SOUTH WALES
Wilsons Promontory
Bass Strait
Egg Lagoon
King Island
Currie
Flinders I.
Emita
Cape Barren I.
Hunter Islands
Stanley
Burnie
Devonport
George Town
Marrawah
Waratah
Deloraine
Launceston
Corinna
Rosebery
Tullah
St. Marys
Conara Jct.
Queenstown
Strahan
Tarraleah
Triabunna
Ouse
Hamilton
TASMANIA
Same Scale as Main Map
Hobart
Kingston
Geeveston
136°
140°
144°
148°
152°
156°
12°
16°
20°
24°
28°
32°
36°
40°

Australia
New Zealand and Oceania: Themes

Continental Facts

TOTAL NUMBER OF COUNTRIES: 14

TOTAL AREA: 8,510,000 sq km (3,286,000 sq mi)

FIRST INDEPENDENT COUNTRY: Australia, Jan. 1, 1901

"YOUNGEST" COUNTRY: Palau, Oct. 1, 1994

MOST POPULOUS COUNTRY: Australia 21,000,000

LEAST POPULOUS COUNTRY: Nauru 14,000

LARGEST COUNTRY BY AREA: Australia 7,692,024 sq km (2,969,906 sq mi)

SMALLEST COUNTRY BY AREA: Nauru 21 sq km (8 sq mi)

HIGHEST ELEVATION: Mount Wilhelm, Papua New Guinea 4,509 m (14,793 ft)

LOWEST ELEVATION: Lake Eyre, Australia -16 m (-52 ft)

Climate Zones

FEDERATED STATES OF MICRONESIA
PALAU
MARSHALL ISLANDS
NAURU
KIRIBATI
Howland I.
Baker I.
(U.S.)
PAPUA NEW GUINEA
SOLOMON ISLANDS
TUVALU
VANUATU
Tokelau (N.Z.)
American Samoa (U.S.)
Wallis and Futuna Is. (FR.)
SAMOA
FIJI IS.
TONGA
Niue (N.Z.)
New Caledonia (FRANCE)
Norfolk I. (AUSTRALIA)
AUSTRALIA
Tasmania
NEW ZEALAND
H, Aw, Am, Cwa, BSh, BWh, Cfa, Cfb, Csa, Csb

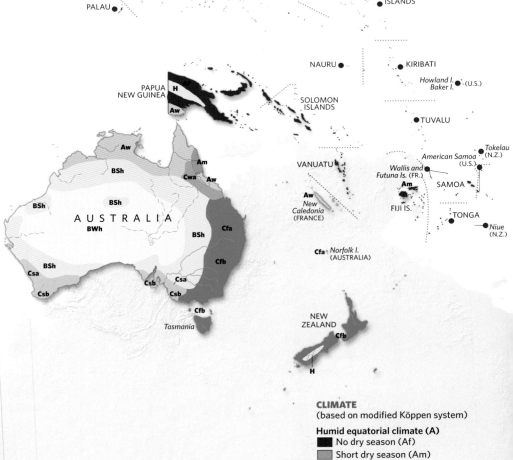

CLIMATE
(based on modified Köppen system)

Humid equatorial climate (A)
- No dry season (Af)
- Short dry season (Am)
- Dry winter (Aw)

Dry climate (B)
- Semiarid (BS)
- Arid (BW)

h = hot
k = cold

Humid temperate climate (C)
- No dry season (Cf)
- Dry summer (Cs)

a = hot summer
b = cool summer

Highland climate (H)
- Unclassified highlands

Water Availability

FEDERATED STATES OF MICRONESIA
PALAU
MARSHALL ISLANDS
NAURU
KIRIBATI
Howland I.
Baker I.
(U.S.)
PAPUA NEW GUINEA
SOLOMON ISLANDS
TUVALU
VANUATU
Tokelau (N.Z.)
Wallis and Futuna Is. (FR.)
American Samoa (U.S.)
SAMOA
FIJI IS.
TONGA
Niue (N.Z.)
New Caledonia (FRANCE)
Norfolk I. (AUSTRALIA)
AUSTRALIA
Tasmania
NEW ZEALAND

WATER AVAILABILITY
(in millimeters per person per year)
- More than 750
- 251–750
- 26–250
- Less than 26
- No data available

Natural Events

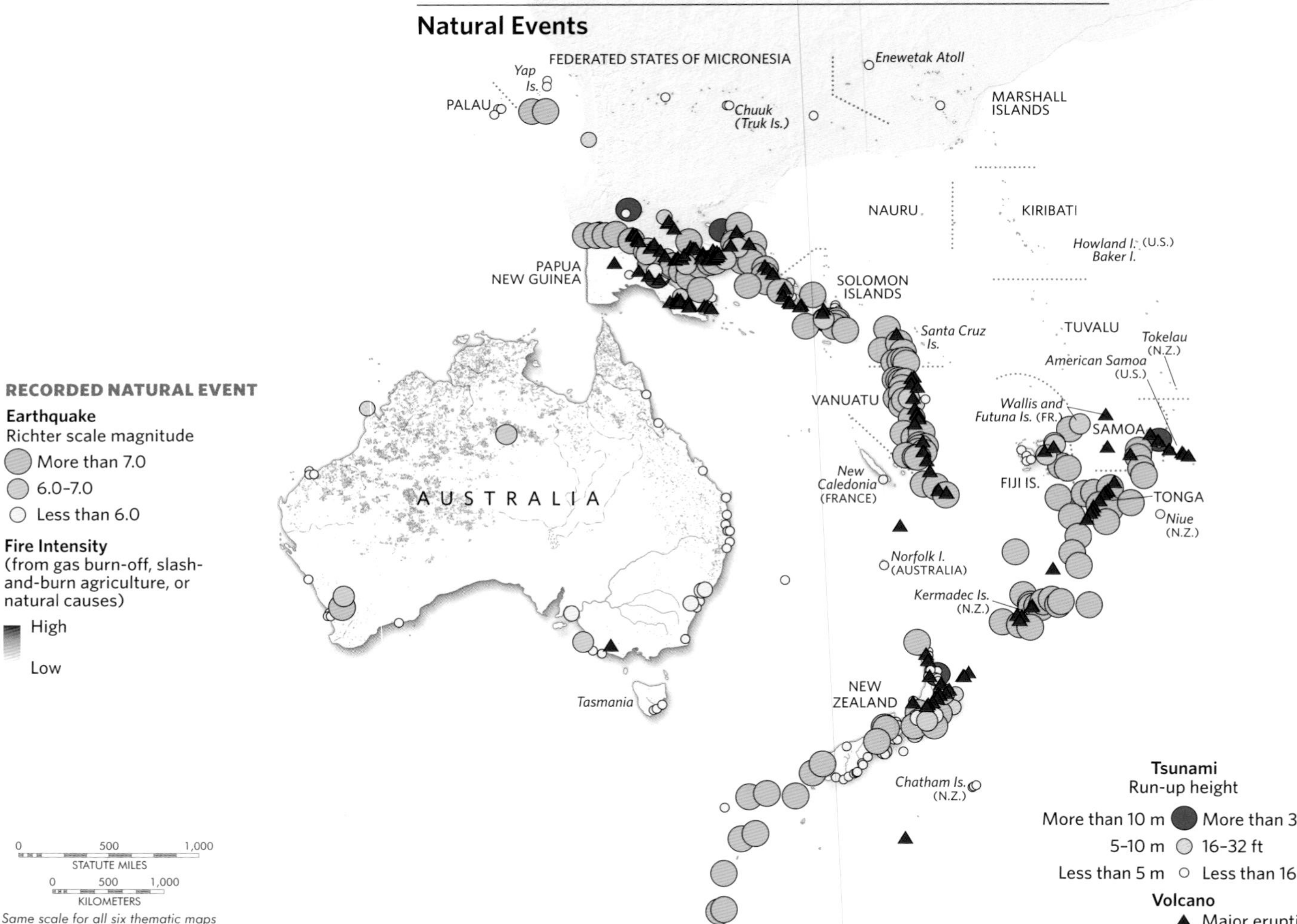
FEDERATED STATES OF MICRONESIA
Yap Is.
PALAU
Chuuk (Truk Is.)
Enewetak Atoll
MARSHALL ISLANDS
NAURU
KIRIBATI
Howland I.
Baker I.
(U.S.)
PAPUA NEW GUINEA
SOLOMON ISLANDS
Santa Cruz Is.
TUVALU
Tokelau (N.Z.)
American Samoa (U.S.)
Wallis and Futuna Is. (FR.)
SAMOA
VANUATU
New Caledonia (FRANCE)
FIJI IS.
TONGA
Niue (N.Z.)
AUSTRALIA
Norfolk I. (AUSTRALIA)
Kermadec Is. (N.Z.)
Tasmania
NEW ZEALAND
Chatham Is. (N.Z.)
0 500 1,000 STATUTE MILES
0 500 1,000 KILOMETERS

Same scale for all six thematic maps

RECORDED NATURAL EVENT

Earthquake
Richter scale magnitude
- More than 7.0
- 6.0–7.0
- Less than 6.0

Fire Intensity
(from gas burn-off, slash-and-burn agriculture, or natural causes)
- High
- Low

Tsunami
Run-up height
- More than 10 m / More than 32 ft
- 5–10 m / 16–32 ft
- Less than 5 m / Less than 16 ft

Volcano
- ▲ Major eruption

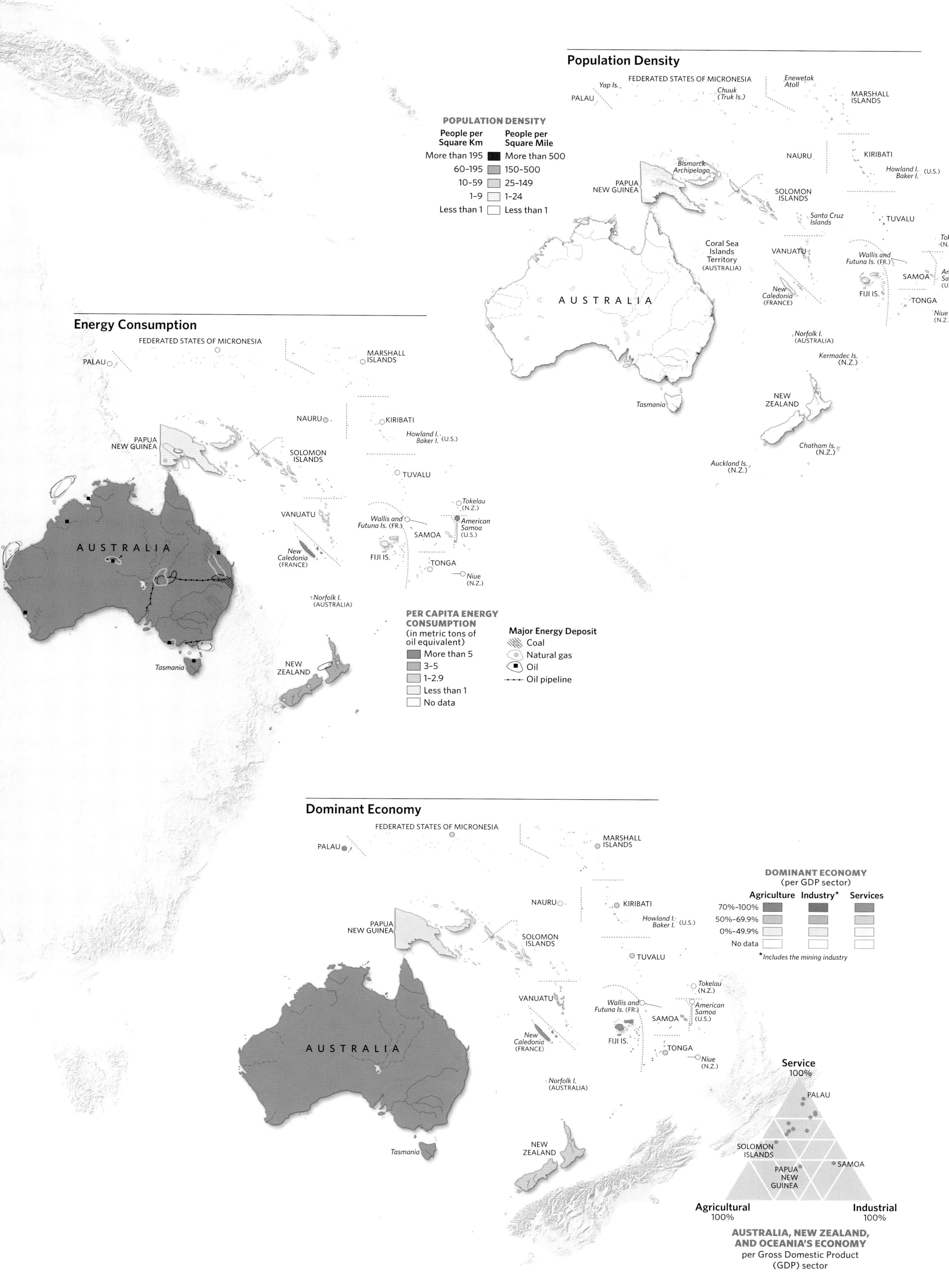
Population Density
FEDERATED STATES OF MICRONESIA
Yap Is.
PALAU
Chuuk (Truk Is.)
Enewetak Atoll
MARSHALL ISLANDS
POPULATION DENSITY
People per Square Km
People per Square Mile
More than 195
More than 500
60–195
150–500
10–59
25–149
1–9
1–24
Less than 1
Less than 1
NAURU
KIRIBATI
Howland I. Baker I. (U.S.)
Bismarck Archipelago
PAPUA NEW GUINEA
SOLOMON ISLANDS
Santa Cruz Islands
TUVALU
Tokelau (N.Z.)
Coral Sea Islands Territory (AUSTRALIA)
VANUATU
Wallis and Futuna Is. (FR.)
SAMOA
American Samoa (U.S.)
AUSTRALIA
New Caledonia (FRANCE)
FIJI IS.
TONGA
Niue (N.Z.)
Norfolk I. (AUSTRALIA)
Kermadec Is. (N.Z.)
Tasmania
NEW ZEALAND
Chatham Is. (N.Z.)
Auckland Is. (N.Z.)
Energy Consumption
FEDERATED STATES OF MICRONESIA
PALAU
MARSHALL ISLANDS
NAURU
KIRIBATI
Howland I. Baker I. (U.S.)
PAPUA NEW GUINEA
SOLOMON ISLANDS
TUVALU
Tokelau (N.Z.)
VANUATU
Wallis and Futuna Is. (FR.)
SAMOA
American Samoa (U.S.)
AUSTRALIA
New Caledonia (FRANCE)
FIJI IS.
TONGA
Niue (N.Z.)
Norfolk I. (AUSTRALIA)
PER CAPITA ENERGY CONSUMPTION (in metric tons of oil equivalent)
More than 5
3–5
1–2.9
Less than 1
No data
Major Energy Deposit
Coal
Natural gas
Oil
Oil pipeline
Tasmania
NEW ZEALAND
Dominant Economy
FEDERATED STATES OF MICRONESIA
PALAU
MARSHALL ISLANDS
NAURU
KIRIBATI
Howland I. Baker I. (U.S.)
PAPUA NEW GUINEA
SOLOMON ISLANDS
TUVALU
DOMINANT ECONOMY (per GDP sector)
Agriculture
Industry*
Services
70%–100%
50%–69.9%
0%–49.9%
No data
*Includes the mining industry
Tokelau (N.Z.)
VANUATU
Wallis and Futuna Is. (FR.)
SAMOA
American Samoa (U.S.)
New Caledonia (FRANCE)
FIJI IS.
TONGA
Niue (N.Z.)
AUSTRALIA
Norfolk I. (AUSTRALIA)
Tasmania
NEW ZEALAND
Service 100%
PALAU
SOLOMON ISLANDS
SAMOA
PAPUA NEW GUINEA
Agricultural 100%
Industrial 100%
AUSTRALIA, NEW ZEALAND, AND OCEANIA'S ECONOMY
per Gross Domestic Product (GDP) sector

NEW GUINEA AND BISMARCK ARCHIPELAGO
EQUATOR
Kepulauan Asia
Kepulauan Mapia (St. David Islands)
Waigeo
Selat Dampier
Kwoka 3000
Saukorem
Sorong
Manokwari
Supiori
Biak
Tanjung D'Urville
Numfoor
Mamberamo
Teminabuan
Konda
Ransiki
Irimi
Selat Yapen
Pom
Yapen
1496
Sarmi
Ceram Sea
Teluk Berau
Bebiram
Muturi
Teluk Cenderawasih
Dom 1340
Wonti
Ansudu
Demta
Jayapura
Vanimo
Kokas
Susunu
Wasado 1070
Tariku-Taritatu Plain
2272
2160
1617
Weri
Tel. Sebakor
Kaimana
Nabire
IRIAN JAYA
Yafi
Lumi
Aitape
Maprik
Wewak
Peg. Kumawa 1489
Kepulauan Watubela
Goreda
3749
Pegunungan Maoke
Puncak Jaya 4884
Pk. Trikora 4750
Peg. Jayawijaya
Teluk Kamrau
Umari
Amamapare
Yapero
Puncak Mandala 4760
Sepik
Angoram
Ambunti
INDONESIA
NEW GUINEA
KEP. KAI
Kai Kecil
Cut
Gumzai
Kola
Wokam
Maikoor
Wangal
Trangan
KEPULAUAN ARU
Sia
Teluk Flamingo
Agats
Telefomin
Tanahmerah
Kiunga
Tari
Mendi
Mt. Hagen
Goroka
Central Range
Maru
Molu
Fordate
Larat
Yamdena
Wuliaru 188
Meyanodas
KEPULAUAN TANIMBAR
Tanjung Ngabordamlu
Eliase
Pirimapun
Tanjung De Jongs
Kepi
Mapi
Lake Murray
Strickland
Kikori
Gurimatu
Muting
DOLAK (YOS SUDARSO)
Kimaam
Okaba
Merauke
Tanjung Vals
Komoran
Bensbach
Balimo
Fly
Iamara
Sibidiro
Daru
Gesoa
Gulf of Papua
Mercator Projection
SCALE 1:13,292,000
1 CENTIMETER = 133 KILOMETERS; 1 INCH = 210 MILES
KILOMETERS
STATUTE MILES
ARAFURA SEA
TORRES STRAIT
AUSTRALIA
Gulf of Carpentaria
CAPE YORK PENINSULA
Ninigo Group
Wuvulu Island
Hermit Is.
Sae Is.
ADMIRALTY ISLANDS
Manus
Kabuli
718
Lou
Momote
Mussau Is.
Mussau
Tabalo
651
Emirau
Rambutyo
Ysabel Channel
Umbukul
960
New Hanover
Kavieng
Tabar Is.
Lihir Group
Lihir
853
1481
Tanga Islands
Nuguria Is.
BISMARCK
Purdy Islands
Schouten Is.
BISMARCK SEA
NEW IRELAND
Namatanai
Samo
Feni Islands
Green Is.
Manam
Bogia
Ulingan
Karkar
ARCHIPELAGO
Rabaul
Witu Is.
Open Bay
Mt. Ulawun 2334
2438
2021
Cape St. George
Madang
1831
Long Island
1304
Mt. Wilhelm 4509
Saidor
Umboi
Kimbe Bay
Wide Bay
St. George's Chan.
Buka
Ramu
Bismarck Ra.
Aiyura
Huon Pen.
4121
1655
Gloucester
NEW BRITAIN
Jacquinot Bay
Kandrian
Uvol
Bougainville
2743
Wakunai
Torokina
2251
Buin
Empress Augusta Bay
Finschhafen
PAPUA NEW GUINEA
Lae
Huon Gulf
Wau
Menyamya
SOLOMON SEA
SOLOMON ISLANDS
Ihu
Kikori
Garaina
Tapini
3655
Ioma
Lusancay Is.
TROBRIAND ISLANDS
Losuia
Kiriwina
Kulumadau
Woodlark
Laughlan Islands
Bereina
Mt. Victoria 4035
Popondetta
Tufi
Goodenough I.
Fergusson I.
427
D'ENTRECASTEAUX IS.
2566
Port Moresby
Rigo
Wanigela
Owen Stanley Ra.
3676
Normanby I.
Bonvouloir Is.
Palli
Cape Rodney
Gurney
Samarai
Goschen Strait
Conflict Group
LOUISIADE ARCHIPELAGO
Misima
838
Rossel I.
806
Tagula
CORAL SEA
Longitude East 150° of Greenwich
135°
140°
145°
150°
155°
0°
5°
10°

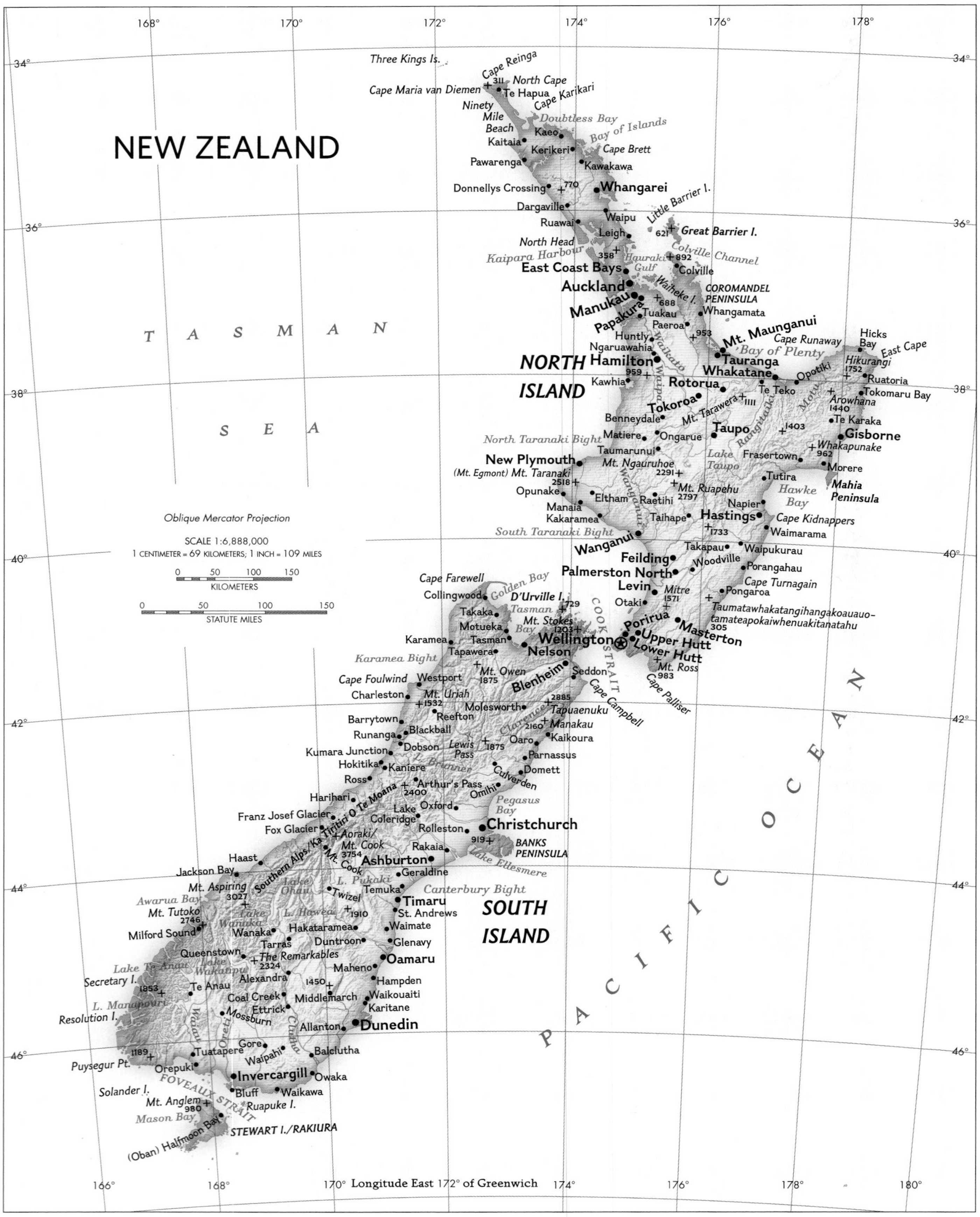

NEW ZEALAND

Three Kings Is.
Cape Reinga
311
North Cape
Te Hapua
Cape Karikari
Cape Maria van Diemen
Ninety Mile Beach
Doubtless Bay
Bay of Islands
Kaeo
Kaitaia
Kerikeri
Cape Brett
Pawarenga
Kawakawa
Donnellys Crossing
770
Whangarei
Dargaville
Little Barrier I.
Ruawai
Waipu
Leigh
621
Great Barrier I.
North Head
Kaipara Harbour
358
Hauraki Gulf
892
Colville Channel
Colville
East Coast Bays
Auckland
Waiheke I.
COROMANDEL PENINSULA
Manukau
688
Whangamata
Papakura
Tuakau
Paeroa
953
Huntly
Ngaruawahia
Mt. Maunganui
Cape Runaway
Hicks Bay
East Cape
Bay of Plenty
Tauranga
NORTH ISLAND
Hamilton
Whakatane
Hikurangi
1752
959
Kawhia
Rotorua
Te Teko
Ruatoria
Tokomaru Bay
Tokoroa
Mt. Tarawera
1111
Arowhana
1440
Te Karaka
Benneydale
Matiere
Ongarue
Taupo
1403
Gisborne
North Taranaki Bight
Taumarunui
Frasertown
Whakapunake
962
New Plymouth
Mt. Ngauruhoe
Lake Taupo
Morere
(Mt. Egmont) Mt. Taranaki
2518
2291
Tutira
Opunake
Mt. Ruapehu
2797
Hawke Bay
Mahia Peninsula
Eltham
Raetihi
Napier
Manaia
Kakaramea
Taihape
Hastings
Cape Kidnappers
South Taranaki Bight
1733
Waimarama
Wanganui
Takapau
Waipukurau
Feilding
Woodville
Porangahau
Palmerston North
Cape Turnagain
Levin
Mitre
1571
Pongaroa
Otaki
Taumatawhakatangihangakoauauotamateapokaiwhenuakitanatahu
305
Porirua
Masterton
Wellington
Upper Hutt
Lower Hutt
Mt. Ross
983
Cape Palliser
COOK STRAIT
Cape Farewell
Golden Bay
Collingwood
D'Urville I.
729
Takaka
Tasman Bay
Motueka
Mt. Stokes
1203
Tasman
Karamea
Nelson
Tapawera
Karamea Bight
Mt. Owen
1875
Blenheim
Seddon
Cape Foulwind
Westport
Charleston
Mt. Uriah
1532
Cape Campbell
2885
Molesworth
Tapuaenuku
Reefton
Barrytown
Blackball
2160
Manakau
Runanga
Clarence
Kaikoura
Dobson
Lewis Pass
Oaro
1875
Kumara Junction
Parnassus
Hokitika
Kaniere
Domett
Ross
Arthur's Pass
2400
Culverden
Harihari
Omihi
Pegasus Bay
Franz Josef Glacier
Lake Coleridge
Oxford
Fox Glacier
Rolleston
Christchurch
Aoraki/ Mt. Cook
3754
919
BANKS PENINSULA
Rakaia
Haast
Ashburton
Lake Ellesmere
Southern Alps/Kā Tiritiri O Te Moana
Jackson Bay
L. Pukaki
Geraldine
Mt. Aspiring
3027
Temuka
Canterbury Bight
Awarua Bay
Timaru
Mt. Tutoko
2746
L. Hawea
1910
St. Andrews
SOUTH ISLAND
Milford Sound
Wanaka
Hakataramea
Waimate
Tarras
Duntroon
Glenavy
Queenstown
The Remarkables
2324
Oamaru
Lake Te Anau
Maheno
Secretary I.
1853
Te Anau
Alexandra
1450
Hampden
L. Manapouri
Coal Creek
Middlemarch
Waikouaiti
Ettrick
Karitane
Resolution I.
Mossburn
Allanton
Dunedin
Gore
Balclutha
1189
Tuatapere
Waipahi
Puysegur Pt.
Orepuki
Invercargill
Owaka
FOVEAUX STRAIT
Solander I.
Bluff
Waikawa
Mt. Anglem
980
Ruapuke I.
Mason Bay
(Oban) Halfmoon Bay
STEWART I./RAKIURA
TASMAN SEA
PACIFIC OCEAN
Oblique Mercator Projection
SCALE 1:6,888,000
1 CENTIMETER = 69 KILOMETERS; 1 INCH = 109 MILES
KILOMETERS
STATUTE MILES
Longitude East 172° of Greenwich
166° 168° 170° 172° 174° 176° 178° 180°
34° 36° 38° 40° 42° 44° 46°

New Zealand

Papua New Guinea

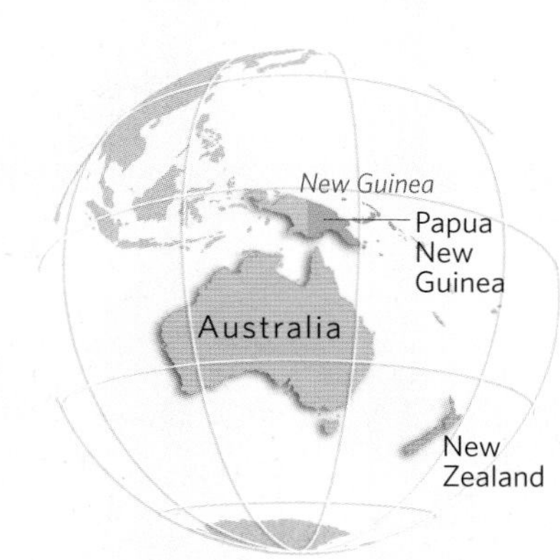
New Guinea
Papua
New
Guinea
Australia
New
Zealand

Protected Areas and World Heritage Sites

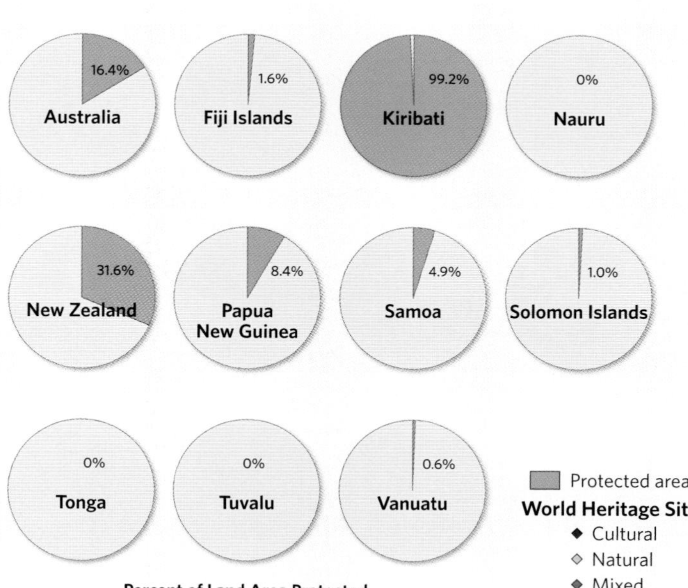
16.4%
Australia
1.6%
Fiji Islands
99.2%
Kiribati
0%
Nauru
31.6%
New Zealand
8.4%
Papua
New Guinea
4.9%
Samoa
1.0%
Solomon Islands
0%
Tonga
0%
Tuvalu
0.6%
Vanuatu

Percent of Land Area Protected

Protected areas

World Heritage Sites

- ◆ Cultural
- ◇ Natural
- ◆ Mixed

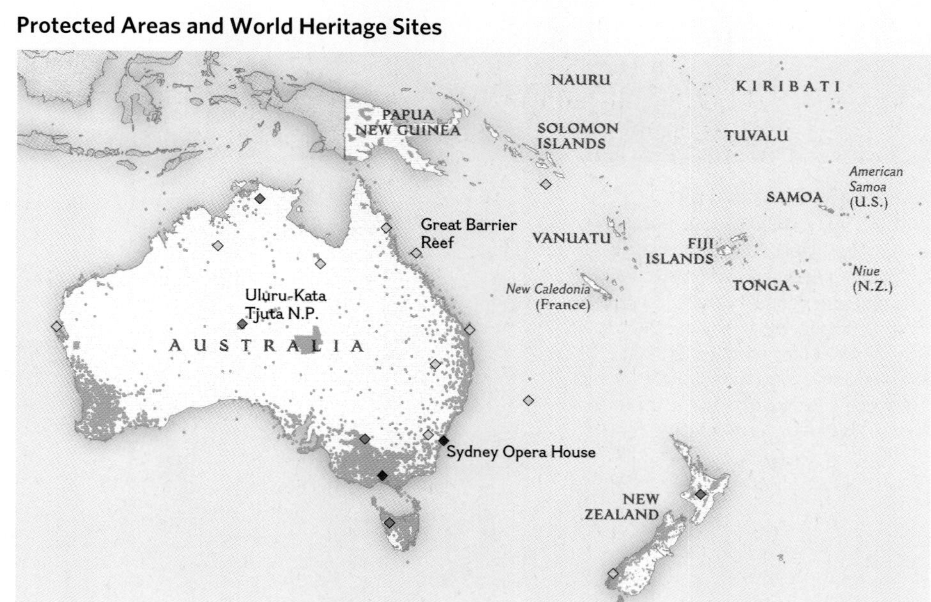
NAURU
KIRIBATI
PAPUA
NEW GUINEA
SOLOMON
ISLANDS
TUVALU
American
Samoa
(U.S.)
SAMOA
Great Barrier
Reef
VANUATU
FIJI
ISLANDS
Niue
(N.Z.)
TONGA
New Caledonia
(France)
Uluru-Kata
Tjuta N.P.
AUSTRALIA
Sydney Opera House
NEW
ZEALAND

Urbanization and Largest Cities

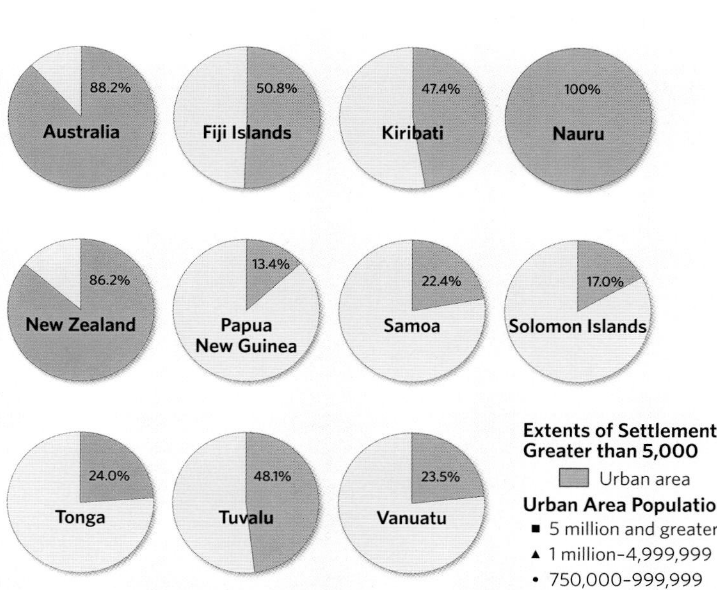
88.2%
Australia
50.8%
Fiji Islands
47.4%
Kiribati
100%
Nauru
86.2%
New Zealand
13.4%
Papua
New Guinea
22.4%
Samoa
17.0%
Solomon Islands
24.0%
Tonga
48.1%
Tuvalu
23.5%
Vanuatu

Percent of Population in Urban Areas

Extents of Settlements Greater than 5,000

Urban area

Urban Area Population

- ■ 5 million and greater
- ▲ 1 million–4,999,999
- • 750,000–999,999
- ◦ 500,000–749,999

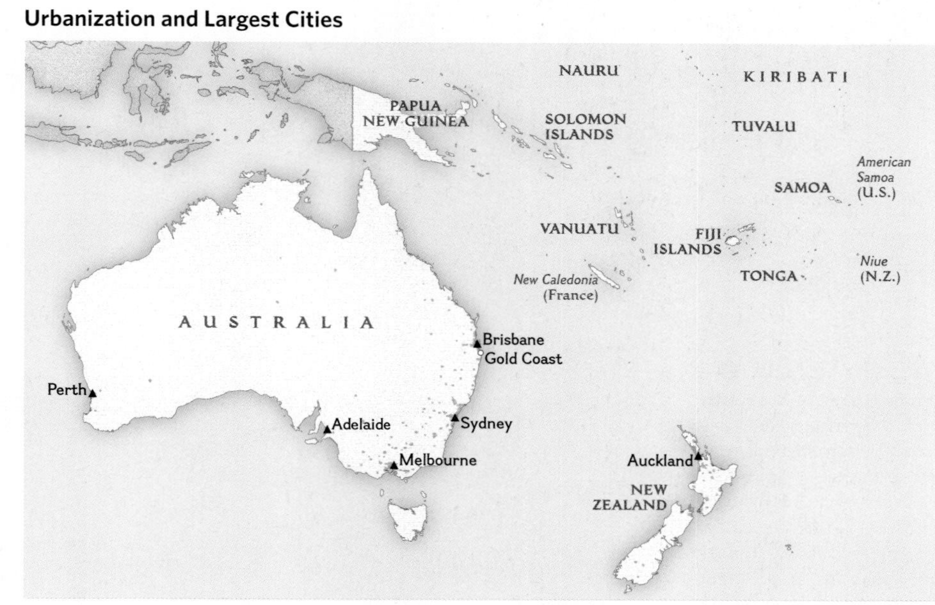
NAURU
KIRIBATI
PAPUA
NEW GUINEA
SOLOMON
ISLANDS
TUVALU
American
Samoa
(U.S.)
SAMOA
VANUATU
FIJI
ISLANDS
Niue
(N.Z.)
TONGA
New Caledonia
(France)
AUSTRALIA
Brisbane
Gold Coast
Perth
Adelaide
Sydney
Melbourne
Auckland
NEW
ZEALAND

Natural Land Cover

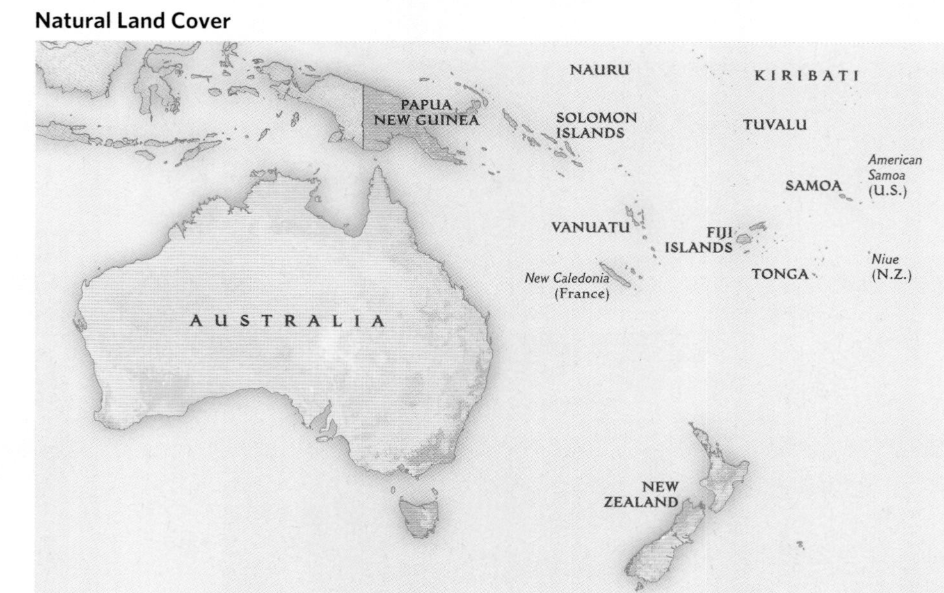
NAURU
KIRIBATI
PAPUA
NEW GUINEA
SOLOMON
ISLANDS
TUVALU
American
Samoa
(U.S.)
SAMOA
VANUATU
FIJI
ISLANDS
Niue
(N.Z.)
TONGA
New Caledonia
(France)
AUSTRALIA
NEW
ZEALAND

Land Cover

- Desert
- Forest
- Glacier
- Herbaceous
- Highland
- Savanna

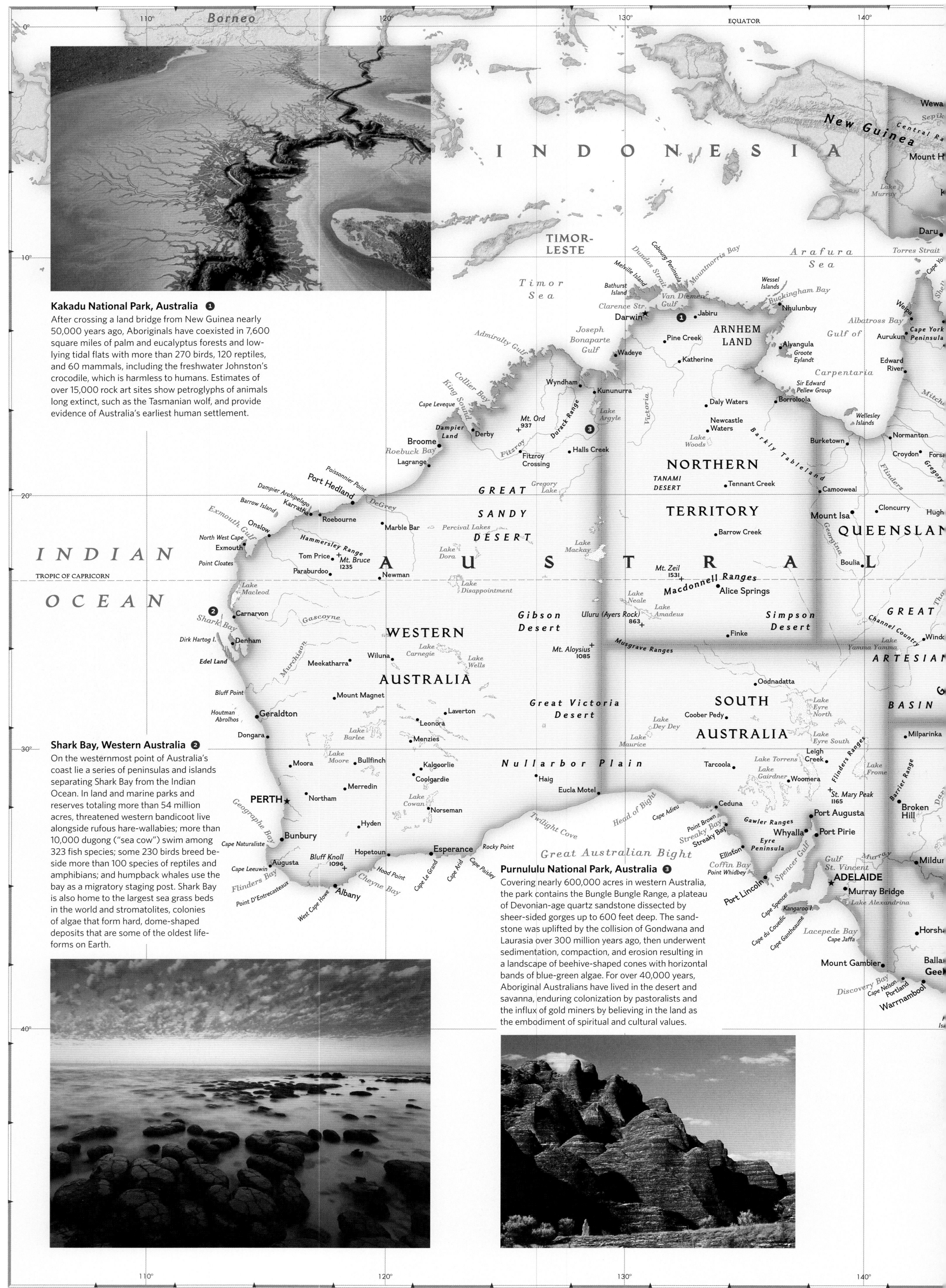

110°
120°
130°
140°
0°
10°
20°
30°
40°
Borneo
EQUATOR
I N D O N E S I A
New Guinea
TIMOR-LESTE
Timor Sea
Arafura Sea
Torres Strait
Gulf of Carpentaria
INDIAN OCEAN
TROPIC OF CAPRICORN
Darwin
Jabiru
ARNHEM LAND
Nhulunbuy
Pine Creek
Katherine
Wadeye
Wyndham
Kununurra
Lake Argyle
Derby
Broome
Lagrange
Port Hedland
Karratha
Roebourne
Onslow
Exmouth
Marble Bar
Tom Price
Mt. Bruce 1235
Paraburdoo
Newman
Carnarvon
Denham
Shark Bay
Geraldton
Dongara
Moora
PERTH
Northam
Bunbury
Augusta
Albany
Esperance
Hopetoun
Kalgoorlie
Coolgardie
Norseman
Meekatharra
Wiluna
Mount Magnet
Laverton
Leonora
Menzies
Merredin
Hyden
Bullfinch
GREAT SANDY DESERT
Gibson Desert
Great Victoria Desert
Nullarbor Plain
Great Australian Bight
Eucla Motel
Haig
WESTERN AUSTRALIA
A U S T R A L
NORTHERN TERRITORY
TANAMI DESERT
Tennant Creek
Barrow Creek
Daly Waters
Newcastle Waters
Halls Creek
Mt. Zeil 1531
Macdonnell Ranges
Alice Springs
Uluru (Ayers Rock) 863
Mt. Aloysius 1085
Musgrave Ranges
Finke
Simpson Desert
SOUTH AUSTRALIA
Oodnadatta
Coober Pedy
Tarcoola
Ceduna
Whyalla
Port Augusta
Port Pirie
Port Lincoln
ADELAIDE
Murray Bridge
Kangaroo I.
Mount Gambier
Portland
Warrnambool
Broken Hill
Milparinka
Leigh Creek
Woomera
St. Mary Peak 1165
QUEENSLAN
Mount Isa
Cloncurry
Camooweal
Burketown
Normanton
Croydon
Boulia
Barkly Tableland
GREAT ARTESIAN BASIN
Weipa
Aurukun
Cape York Peninsula
Edward River
Wellesley Islands
Groote Eylandt
Alyangula
Borroloola

Kakadu National Park, Australia ❶

After crossing a land bridge from New Guinea nearly 50,000 years ago, Aboriginals have coexisted in 7,600 square miles of palm and eucalyptus forests and low-lying tidal flats with more than 270 birds, 120 reptiles, and 60 mammals, including the freshwater Johnston's crocodile, which is harmless to humans. Estimates of over 15,000 rock art sites show petroglyphs of animals long extinct, such as the Tasmanian wolf, and provide evidence of Australia's earliest human settlement.

Shark Bay, Western Australia ❷

On the westernmost point of Australia's coast lie a series of peninsulas and islands separating Shark Bay from the Indian Ocean. In land and marine parks and reserves totaling more than 54 million acres, threatened western bandicoot live alongside rufous hare-wallabies; more than 10,000 dugong ("sea cow") swim among 323 fish species; some 230 birds breed beside more than 100 species of reptiles and amphibians; and humpback whales use the bay as a migratory staging post. Shark Bay is also home to the largest sea grass beds in the world and stromatolites, colonies of algae that form hard, dome-shaped deposits that are some of the oldest life-forms on Earth.

Purnululu National Park, Australia ❸

Covering nearly 600,000 acres in western Australia, the park contains the Bungle Bungle Range, a plateau of Devonian-age quartz sandstone dissected by sheer-sided gorges up to 600 feet deep. The sandstone was uplifted by the collision of Gondwana and Laurasia over 300 million years ago, then underwent sedimentation, compaction, and erosion resulting in a landscape of beehive-shaped cones with horizontal bands of blue-green algae. For over 40,000 years, Aboriginal Australians have lived in the desert and savanna, enduring colonization by pastoralists and the influx of gold miners by believing in the land as the embodiment of spiritual and cultural values.

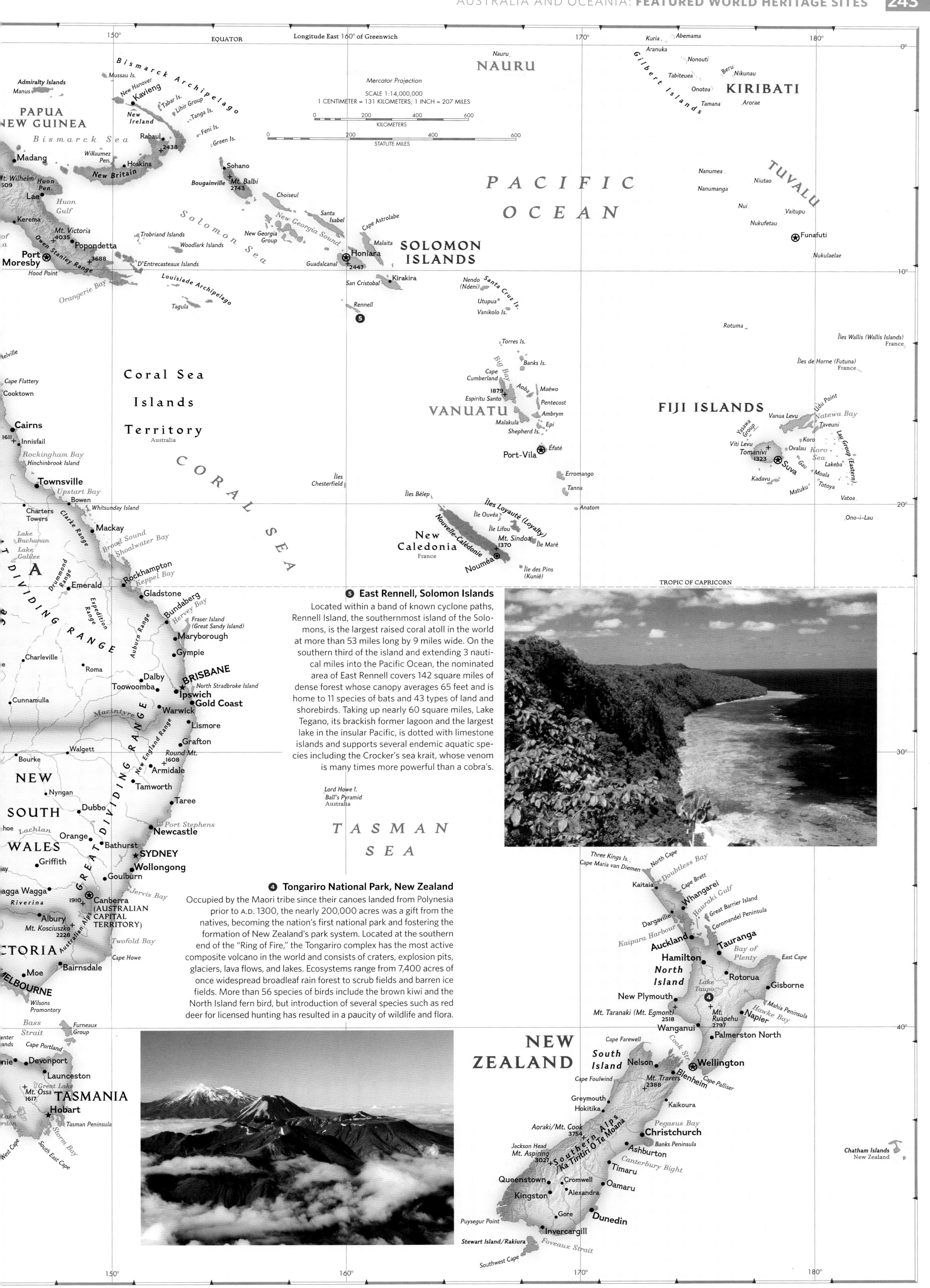
EQUATOR
Longitude East 160° of Greenwich
Mercator Projection
SCALE 1:14,000,000
1 CENTIMETER = 131 KILOMETERS; 1 INCH = 207 MILES
KILOMETERS
STATUTE MILES
PAPUA NEW GUINEA
Bismarck Archipelago
Bismarck Sea
Port Moresby
NAURU
KIRIBATI
Gilbert Islands
TUVALU
Funafuti
PACIFIC OCEAN
SOLOMON ISLANDS
Honiara
Solomon Sea
Coral Sea Islands Territory
Australia
CORAL SEA
VANUATU
Port-Vila
FIJI ISLANDS
Suva
New Caledonia
France
Nouméa
TROPIC OF CAPRICORN
TASMAN SEA
Lord Howe I.
Ball's Pyramid
Australia
NEW SOUTH WALES
GREAT DIVIDING RANGE
BRISBANE
SYDNEY
Canberra
(AUSTRALIAN CAPITAL TERRITORY)
VICTORIA
MELBOURNE
TASMANIA
Hobart
NEW ZEALAND
North Island
South Island
Auckland
Wellington
Christchurch
Dunedin
Chatham Islands
New Zealand

❺ East Rennell, Solomon Islands

Located within a band of known cyclone paths, Rennell Island, the southernmost island of the Solomons, is the largest raised coral atoll in the world at more than 53 miles long by 9 miles wide. On the southern third of the island and extending 3 nautical miles into the Pacific Ocean, the nominated area of East Rennell covers 142 square miles of dense forest whose canopy averages 65 feet and is home to 11 species of bats and 43 types of land and shorebirds. Taking up nearly 60 square miles, Lake Tegano, its brackish former lagoon and the largest lake in the insular Pacific, is dotted with limestone islands and supports several endemic aquatic species including the Crocker's sea krait, whose venom is many times more powerful than a cobra's.

❹ Tongariro National Park, New Zealand

Occupied by the Maori tribe since their canoes landed from Polynesia prior to A.D. 1300, the nearly 200,000 acres was a gift from the natives, becoming the nation's first national park and fostering the formation of New Zealand's park system. Located at the southern end of the "Ring of Fire," the Tongariro complex has the most active composite volcano in the world and consists of craters, explosion pits, glaciers, lava flows, and lakes. Ecosystems range from 7,400 acres of once widespread broadleaf rain forest to scrub fields and barren ice fields. More than 56 species of birds include the brown kiwi and the North Island fern bird, but introduction of several species such as red deer for licensed hunting has resulted in a paucity of wildlife and flora.

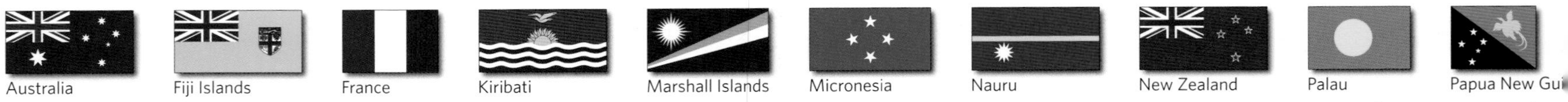

Australia · Fiji Islands · France · Kiribati · Marshall Islands · Micronesia · Nauru · New Zealand · Palau · Papua New Guinea

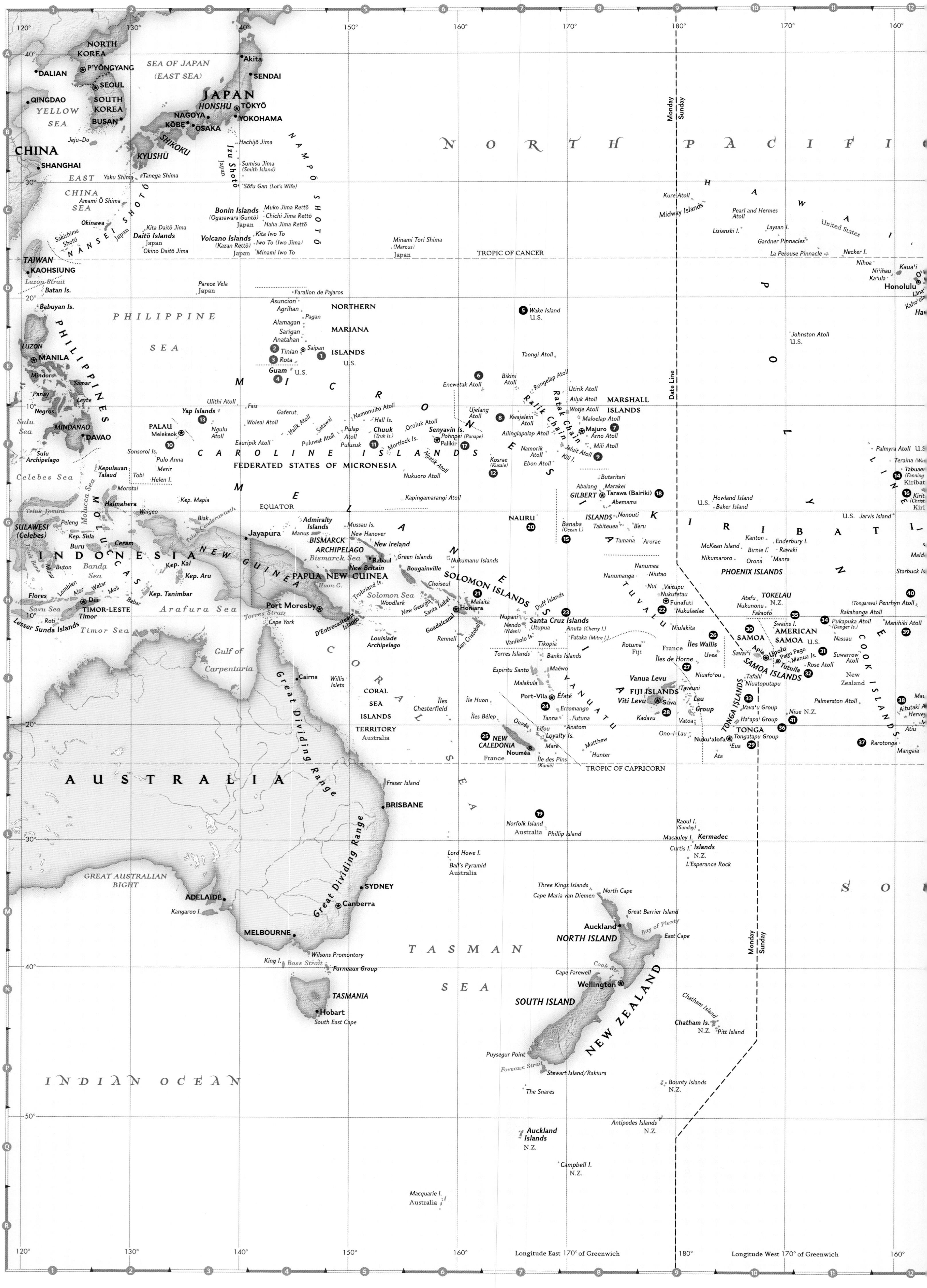

Samoa
Solomon Islands
Tonga
Tuvalu
United Kingdom
United States
Vanuatu
CANADA
Cape Mendocino
Sierra Nevada
San Francisco
UNITED STATES
Washington
OCEAN
LOS ANGELES
SAN DIEGO
TIJUANA
Baja California
Golfo de California
ATLANTIC OCEAN
Isla de Guadalupe Mexico
Isla Cedros
Punta Eugenia
MEXICO
GULF OF MEXICO
BAHAMAS
TROPIC OF CANCER
Rocas Alijos Mexico
Cabo Falso
Mazatlán
CUBA
Islas Revillagigedo Mexico
Isla San Benedicto
Isla Clarión
Isla Socorro
Isla Roca Partida
MEXICO CITY
HAITI
JAMAICA
DOMINICAN REPUBLIC
Acapulco
Belmopan
BELIZE
CARIBBEAN SEA
GUATEMALA
GUATEMALA CITY
HONDURAS
Tegucigalpa
San Salvador
EL SALVADOR
NICARAGUA
MANAGUA
Clipperton France
San José
COSTA RICA
Panamá
PANAMA
VENEZUELA
Golfo de Panamá
Isla del Coco Costa Rica
BOGOTÁ
COLOMBIA
Isla de Malpelo Colombia
Isla Darwin
Ecuador
Galápagos Islands (Archipiélago de Colón)
EQUATOR
Isla San Salvador
Isla Santa Cruz
Isla Fernandina
Isla Isabela
Isla San Cristóbal
Isla Santa María
QUITO
ECUADOR
GUAYAQUIL
ANDES
For more detail on the Galápagos Islands, see pages 134–135
MARQUESAS ISLANDS France
Eiao
Hatutu
Nuku Hiva
Ua Huka
Ua Pu
Hiva Oa
Tahuata
Mohotani (Motane)
Fatu Hiva
Caroline Island
Vostok Island
Flint Island
BRAZIL
Trujillo
PERU
LIMA
BOLIVIA
Bora-Bora
TUAMOTU ARCHIPELAGO
Huahine
Mataiva
Manihi
Takaroa
Napuka
Pukapuka
Makatea
Rangiroa
Tikei
Moorea
Makemo
Papeete
Anaa
Tatakoto
Tahiti
Hikueru
Hao
SOCIETY ISLANDS
FRENCH POLYNESIA France
Hereheretue
Îles Duc de Gloucester
Tureia
Rimatara
Rurutu
Tematagi
Moruroa
Marutea
Morane
Mangareva
United Kingdom
Tubuai
Îles Gambier
Temoe
TROPIC OF CAPRICORN
Raivavae (Vavitu)
AUSTRAL ISLANDS (TUBUAI IS.)
Oeno Island
Henderson Island
Ducie Island
Pitcairn Island
Sala-y-Gómez Chile
Isla San Félix
Isla San Ambrosio Chile
Isla de Pascua (Easter Island) Chile
Rapa
Marotiri (Îlots de Bass)
PACIFIC OCEAN
Valparaíso
SANTIAGO
Isla Santa Clara
Isla Robinson Crusoe
Isla Alejandro Selkirk
Islas Juan Fernández Chile
Concepción
CHILE
ARGENTINA
Mercator Projection
SCALE 1:34,544,000 AT THE EQUATOR
1 CENTIMETER = 345 KILOMETERS; 1 INCH = 545 MILES
0 500 1000 1500 2000 KILOMETERS
0 500 1000 1500 2000 STATUTE MILES
Isla Grande de Chiloé
Archipiélago de los Chonos
20 Numbered islands correspond to larger-scale maps on the following pages.
Major Pacific Island Groups
Mariana Islands
Marshall Islands
Caroline Islands
Society Islands and Tuamotu Archipelago
Other island
Golfo de Penas
Isla Campana
Isla Wellington
Isla Madre de Dios
Archipiélago Reina Adelaida
Isla Santa Inés
150° 140° 130° 120° 110° 100° 90° 80° 70°
40° 30° 20° 10° 0° 10° 20° 30° 40° 50°

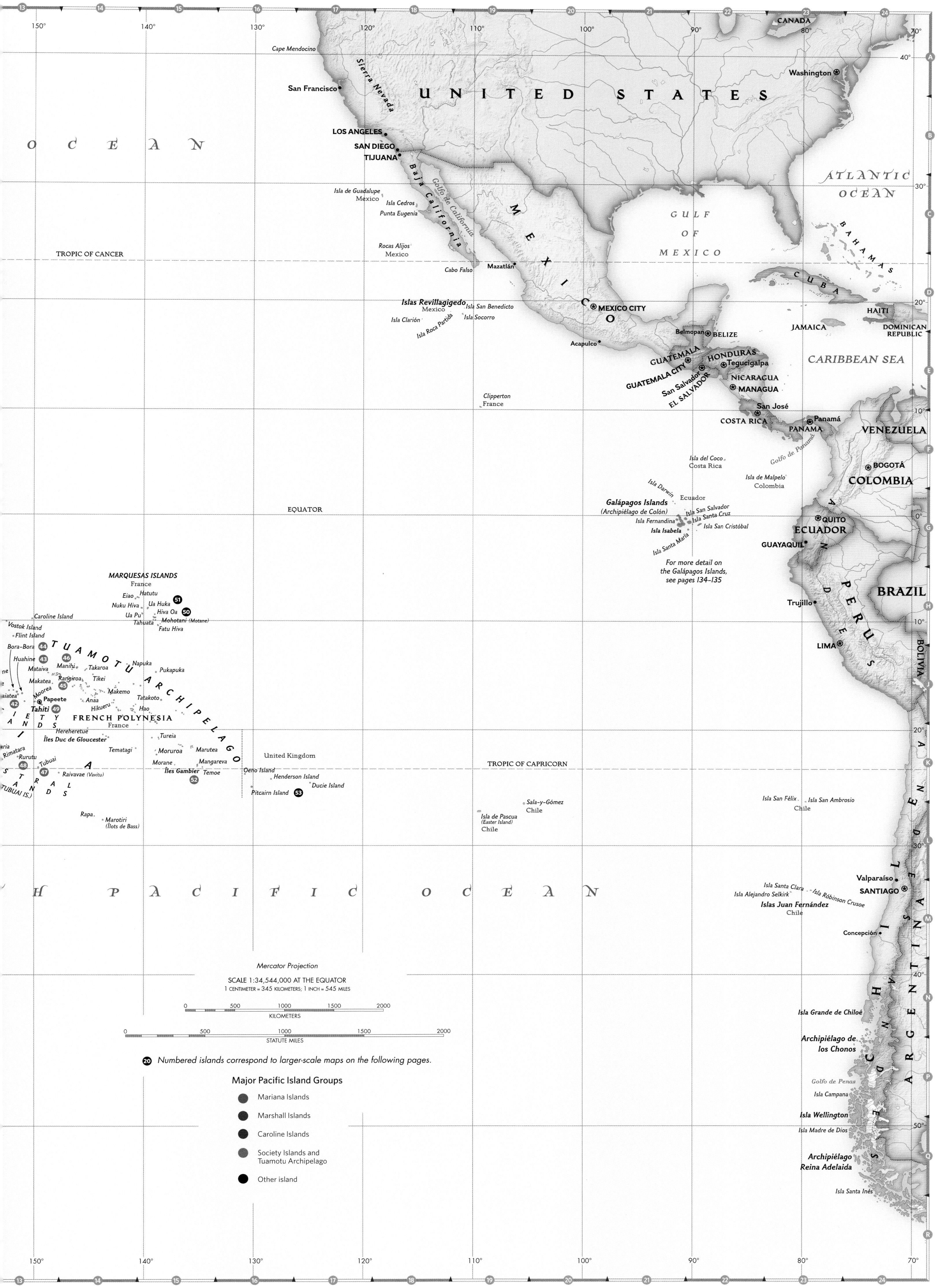

Australia Kiribati Marshall Islands

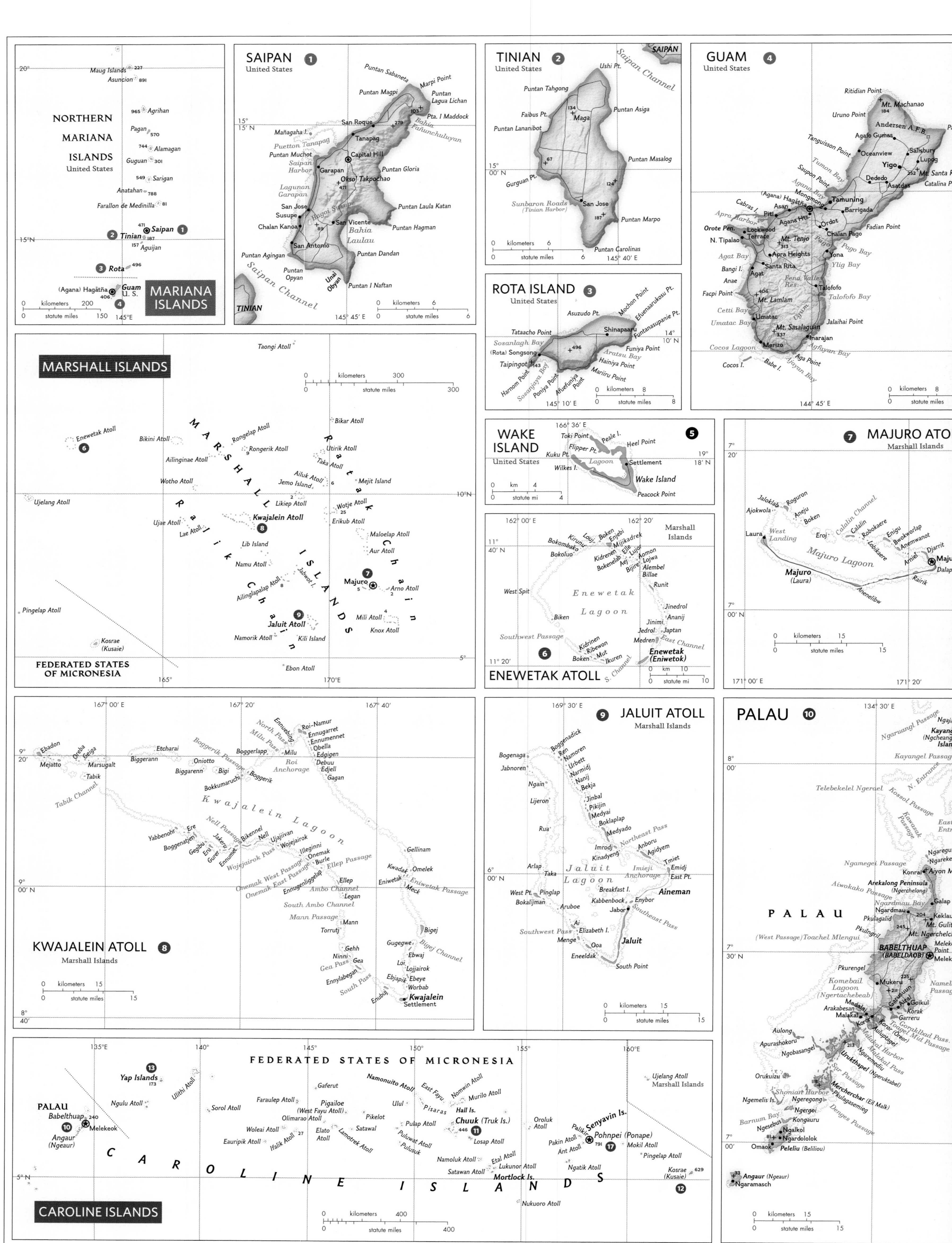
NORTHERN MARIANA ISLANDS
United States
Maug Islands 227
Asuncion 891
965 Agrihan
Pagan 570
744 Alamagan
Guguan 301
549 Sarigan
Anatahan 788
Farallon de Medinilla 81
471 Saipan
Tinian 187
157 Aguijan
Rota 496
(Agana) Hagåtña
406
Guam
U. S.
MARIANA ISLANDS
SAIPAN
United States
Puntan Sabaneta
Marpi Point
Puntan Magpi
Puntan Lagua Lichan
Pta. I Maddock
San Roque
Mañagaha I.
Tanapag
Puetton Tanapag
Puntan Muchot
Capital Hill
Saipan Harbor
Garapan
Puntan Gloria
Okso' Takpochao
Lagunan Garapan
San Jose
Susupe
Puntan Laula Katan
Chalan Kanoa
San Vicente
Puntan Hagman
Bahia Laulau
San Antonio
Puntan Dandan
Puntan Agingan
Puntan Opyan
Unai Obyan
Puntan I Naftan
Saipan Channel
TINIAN
TINIAN
United States
Ushi Pt.
Saipan Channel
Puntan Tahgong
Faibus Pt.
Maga
Puntan Asiga
Puntan Lananibot
Puntan Masalog
Gurguan Pt.
Sunharon Roads (Tinian Harbor)
San Jose
Puntan Marpo
Puntan Carolinas
ROTA ISLAND
United States
Asuzudo Pt.
Mochon Point
Shinapaaru
Tataacho Point
Sosanlagh Bay
(Rota) Songsong
Taipingot
Puntan Point
Hainiya Point
Mariiru Point
Aratsu Bay
GUAM
United States
Ritidian Point
Mt. Machanao
Uruno Point
Andersen A.F.B.
Tanguisson Point
Agafo Gumas
Oceanview
Salisbury
Lupog
Yigo
Mt. Santa Rosa
Catalina Pt.
Dededo
Asatdas
Tumon Bay
Saupon Point
Agana Bay
(Agana) Hagåtña
Mongmong
Tamuning
Barrigada
Cabras I.
Apra Harbor
Piti
Asan
Agana Hts.
Ordot
Orote Pen.
Lockwood Terrace
Chalan Pago
Fadian Point
N. Tipalao
Mt. Tenjo
Pago Bay
Agat Bay
Apra Heights
Yona
Bangi I.
Santa Rita
Ylig Bay
Anae
Agat
Facpi Point
Talofofo
Talofofo Bay
Mt. Lamlam
Cetti Bay
Umatac
Umatac Bay
Jalaihai Point
Mt. Sasalaguan
Inarajan
Cocos Lagoon
Merizo
Aga Point
Cocos I.
Babe I.
Ajayan Bay
MARSHALL ISLANDS
Taongi Atoll
Bikar Atoll
Enewetak Atoll
Bikini Atoll
Rongelap Atoll
Rongerik Atoll
Utirik Atoll
Taka Atoll
Ailinginae Atoll
Ailuk Atoll
Jemo Island
Mejit Island
Wotho Atoll
Likiep Atoll
Wotje Atoll
Ujelang Atoll
Ujae Atoll
Lae Atoll
Kwajalein Atoll
Erikub Atoll
Maloelap Atoll
Aur Atoll
Lib Island
Namu Atoll
Ailinglapalap Atoll
Jabwot I.
Majuro
Arno Atoll
Pingelap Atoll
Mili Atoll
Jaluit Atoll
Knox Atoll
Namorik Atoll
Kili Island
Kosrae (Kusaie)
Ebon Atoll
FEDERATED STATES OF MICRONESIA
MARSHALL ISLANDS
Ratak Chain
Ralik Chain
WAKE ISLAND
United States
Toki Point
Peale I.
Heel Point
Flipper Pt.
Kuku Pt.
Wilkes I.
Lagoon
Settlement
Wake Island
Peacock Point
MAJURO ATOLL
Marshall Islands
Jaloklab
Ajokwola
Rongrong
Aneju
Boken
Calalin Channel
Laura
West Landing
Eroj
Calalin
Enigu
Bokaetoktok
Robokaere
Bwokworlap
Anemwanot
Djarrit
Majuro Lagoon
Majuro (Laura)
Dalap
Rairik
Anenelibw
ENEWETAK ATOLL
Marshall Islands
Bokombako
Bokoluo
Kirunu
Louj
Boken
Enjebi
Mijikadrek
Kidrenen
Bokenelab
Elle
Aej
Lujor
Aomon
Bijire
Lojwa
Alembel
Billae
West Spit
Runit
Enewetak Lagoon
Jinedrol
Biken
Ananij
Jinimi
Japtan
Jedrol
Medren
Southwest Passage
East Channel
Kidrinen
Ribewon
Boken
Mut
Ikuren
Enewetak (Eniwetok)
KWAJALEIN ATOLL
Marshall Islands
Ebadon
Mejatto
Oreba
Geiga
Marsugalt
Tabik
Tabik Channel
Etcharai
Biggerann
Oniotto
Biggarenn
Bigi
Boggerik Passage
Boggerlapp
North Pass
Milu Pass
Ennubirr
Roi-Namur
Ennugarret
Ennumennet
Obella
Edgigen
Debuu
Edjell
Gagan
Roi Anchorage
Boggerik
Bokkumaruchi
Kwajalein Lagoon
Nell Passage
Yabbenohr
Ere
Boggenatjen
Bikennel
Nell
Ujae
Wojejairok
Illeginni
Onemak
Burle
Ellep Passage
Gellinam
Wojejairok Pass
Onemak West Passage
Onemak East Passage
Ennugenliggelap
Ellep
Ambo Channel
Legan
South Ambo Channel
Mann Passage
Mann
Torrutj
Kwadak
Omelek
Eniwetak
Meck
Eniwetak Passage
Bigej
Bigej Channel
Gehh
Ninni
Gea
Gea Pass
Enylabegan
South Pass
Gugegwe
Ebwaj
Loi
Lojjairok
Ebjapik
Ebeye
Enubuj
Worbab
Kwajalein
Settlement
JALUIT ATOLL
Marshall Islands
Bogenaga
Boggenadick
Ren
Namoren
Jabnoren
Urbett
Narmidj
Ngain
Nanij
Bekja
Lijeron
Jinbal
Pikijin
Medyai
Boklaplap
Rua
Medyado
Northeast Pass
Imrodj
Kinadyeng
Anboru
Agidyem
Jaluit Lagoon
Imieji Anchorage
Tmiet
Emidj
East Pt.
Arlap
Taka
Breakfast I.
Aineman
West Pt.
Pinglap
Bokalijman
Kabbenbock
Enybor
Jabor
Aruboe
Southeast Pass
Ai
Southwest Pass
Elizabeth I.
Menge
Jaluit
Ooa
Eneeldak
South Point
PALAU
Ngarruangl Passage
Ngajangel
Kayangel (Ngcheangel Islands)
Kayangel Passage
Telebekelel Ngerael
N. Entrance
Kossol Passage
Kossol Reef
East Entrance
Ngaregur
Ngarekeklau
Ngamegei Passage
Konrai
Aiyon Mt.
Arekalong Peninsula (Ngerchelong)
Aiwokako Passage
Galap
Ngardmau Bay
Ngardmau
Keklau
Pkulagalid
Mt. Gulitel
Mt. Ngerchelchuus
PALAU
(West Passage) Toachel Mlengui
BABELTHUAP (BABELDAOB)
Melekeok Point
Melekeok
Pkurengel
Mukeru
Namelakl Passage
Komebail Lagoon (Ngertachebeab)
Arakabesan
Malakal
Madalai
Koror
Korak
Garreru
Goikul
Aulong
Apurashokoru
Ngobasangel
Malakal Harbor
Orukuizu
Urukthapel (Ngeruktabel)
Mercherchar (Eil Malk)
Ngemelis Is.
Shonian Harbor
Ngeregong
Ngergoi
Barnum Bay
Ngesebus
Kongauru
Ngalkol
Ngardololok
Omaok
Peleliu (Beliliou)
Angaur (Ngeaur)
Ngaramasch
Denges Passage
FEDERATED STATES OF MICRONESIA
Yap Islands
Ulithi Atoll
Ngulu Atoll
PALAU
Babelthuap
Melekeok
Angaur (Ngeaur)
Sorol Atoll
Gaferut
Faraulep Atoll
Pigailoe (West Fayu Atoll)
Olimarao Atoll
Woleai Atoll
Eauripik Atoll
Ifalik Atoll
Elato Atoll
Lamotrek Atoll
Satawal
Pikelot
Namonuito Atoll
East Fayu
Nomwin Atoll
Murilo Atoll
Ulul
Pisaras
Hall Is.
Pulap Atoll
Chuuk (Truk Is.)
Losap Atoll
Puluwat Atoll
Pulusuk
Namoluk Atoll
Etal Atoll
Satawan Atoll
Lukunor Atoll
Mortlock Is.
Nukuoro Atoll
Oroluk Atoll
Senyavin Is.
Palikir
Pohnpei (Ponape)
Pakin Atoll
Ant Atoll
Mokil Atoll
Pingelap Atoll
Ngatik Atoll
Kosrae (Kusaie)
Ujelang Atoll
Marshall Islands
CAROLINE ISLANDS
CAROLINE ISLANDS
kilometers
statute miles

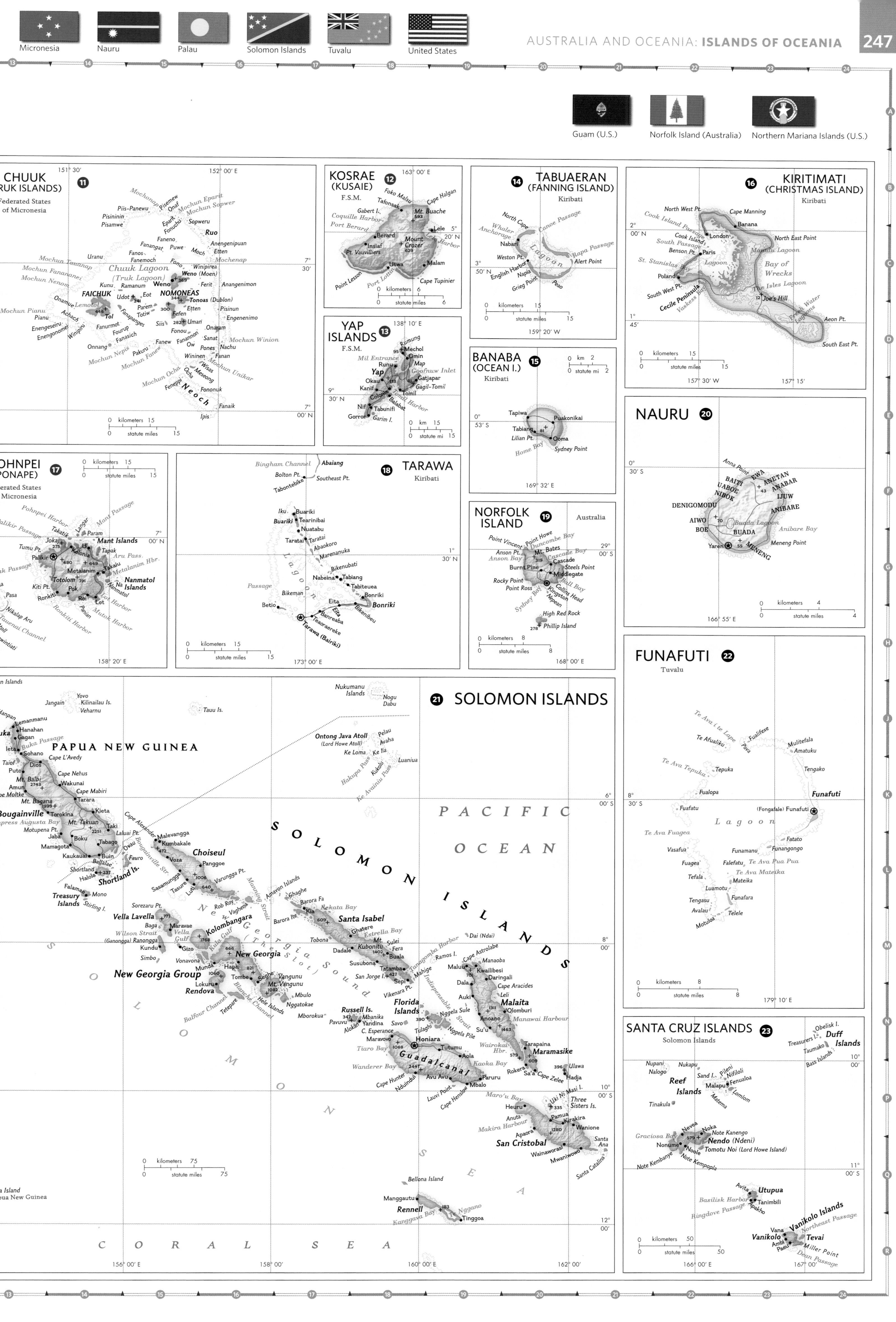
Micronesia
Nauru
Palau
Solomon Islands
Tuvalu
United States
Guam (U.S.)
Norfolk Island (Australia)
Northern Mariana Islands (U.S.)
CHUUK (TRUK ISLANDS) 11
Federated States of Micronesia
Chuuk Lagoon (Truk Lagoon)
Weno (Moen)
FAICHUK
NOMONEAS
Tonoas (Dublon)
Fefen
Uman
Udot
Tol
Piis-Panewu
Pisininin
Pisamwe
Ruo
Neoch
Ipis
KOSRAE (KUSAIE) 12
F.S.M.
Mt. Buache
Lele
Mount Crozer
Utwa
Malam
Cape Tupinier
Tafunsak
Coquille Harbor
Port Berard
Pt. Vauvilliers
Insiaf
Berard
Cape Halgan
Foko Malsu
Port Lottin
Point Lesson
Gabert I.
YAP ISLANDS 13
F.S.M.
Mil Entrance
Yap
Rumung
Map
Mechol
Omin
Gatjapar
Gagil-Tomil
Goofnuw Inlet
Tomil Harbor
Colonia
Okau
Kanif
Runu
Nif
Tabunifi
Balabat
Gorror
Garim I.
TABUAERAN (FANNING ISLAND) 14
Kiribati
North Cape
Whaler Anchorage
Canoe Passage
Lagoon
Napia
Nabari
Weston Pt.
English Harbor
Grieg Point
Rapa Passage
Alert Point
Peao
KIRITIMATI (CHRISTMAS ISLAND) 16
Kiribati
North West Pt.
Cape Manning
Banana
London
Paris
Poland
Cook Island Passage
Cook Island
South Passage
Benson Pt.
St. Stanislas Bay
South West Pt.
Cecile Peninsula
Vaskess Bay
Joe's Hill
North East Point
Manulu Lagoon
Bay of Wrecks
The Isles Lagoon
Fresh Water Lagoons
Aeon Pt.
South East Pt.
BANABA (OCEAN I.) 15
Kiribati
Tapiwa
Tabiang
Lilian Pt.
Home Bay
Buakonikai
Ooma
Sydney Point
NAURU 20
Anna Point
EWA
BAITI
ANETAN
ANABAR
UABOE
NIBOK
IJUW
ANIBARE
DENIGOMODU
AIWO
BOE
BUADA
Buada Lagoon
Anibare Bay
Yaren
MENENG
Meneng Point
POHNPEI (PONAPE) 17
Federated States of Micronesia
Pohnpei Harbor
Palikir Passage
Palikir
Kolonia
Sokehs
Mant Islands
Mant Passage
Takatik
Langar
Param
Tumu Pt.
Jokaj
Tapak
Aru Pass.
Metalanim Hbr.
Metalanim
Takaiu
Nanmatol Islands
Totolom
Kiti Pt.
Pok
Ronkiti
Rol
Lot
Pasa
Nikalap Aru
Tauenai Channel
Ronkiti Harbor
Mutok Harbor
TARAWA 18
Kiribati
Bingham Channel
Abaiang
Bolton Pt.
Southeast Pt.
Tabontebike
Iku
Buariki
Tearinibai
Nuatabu
Taratai
Abaokoro
Marenanuka
Bikenubati
Nabeina
Tabiang
Tabiteuea
Bonriki
Bikeman
Betio
Eita
Banreaba
Teaoraereke
Bikenibeu
Tarawa (Bairiki)
Lagoon
Passage
NORFOLK ISLAND 19
Australia
Point Vincent
Point Howe
Duncombe Bay
Anson Pt.
Anson Bay
Mt. Bates
Cascade Bay
Cascade
Steels Point
Middlegate
Burnt Pine
Rocky Point
Point Ross
Kingston
Collins Head
Ball Bay
Sydney Bay
Nepean
High Red Rock
Phillip Island
FUNAFUTI 22
Tuvalu
Te Ava i te Lape
Fualifeke
Te Afualiku
Pava
Mulitefala
Amatuku
Te Ava Tepuka
Tepuka
Tengako
Fualopa
Funafuti
Fuafatu
(Fongafale) Funafuti
Lagoon
Te Ava Fuagea
Fatato
Vasafua
Funamanu
Funangongo
Fuagea
Falefatu
Te Ava Pua Pua
Te Ava Mateika
Tefala
Mateika
Luamotu
Tengasu
Funafara
Avalau
Motuloa
Telele
SOLOMON ISLANDS 21
PAPUA NEW GUINEA
PACIFIC OCEAN
SOLOMON ISLANDS
SOLOMON SEA
CORAL SEA
Green Islands
Buka
Buka Passage
Bougainville
Empress Augusta Bay
Cape L'Avedy
Cape Nehus
Wakunai
Cape Mabiri
Cape Moltke
Mt. Balbi
Mt. Bagana
Torokina
Mt. Takuan
Kieta
Tarara
Boku
Tabago
Buin
Bougainville Str.
Shortland Is.
Treasury Islands
Mono
Stirling I.
Choiseul
Ontong Java Atoll (Lord Howe Atoll)
Nukumanu Islands
Tauu Is.
Vella Lavella
Kolombangara
New Georgia
New Georgia Group
Rendova
Gizo
Ranongga
Munda
Vangunu
Mt. Vangunu
Blanche Channel
Manning Strait
New Georgia Sound (The Slot)
Santa Isabel
Russell Is.
Florida Islands
Honiara
Guadalcanal
Malaita
Maramasike
Indispensable Strait
Auki
San Cristobal
Three Sisters Is.
Kirakira
Santa Ana
Santa Catalina
Bellona Island
Rennell
Kangava Bay
Tinggoa
Sikaiana
Yela Island
Papua New Guinea
SANTA CRUZ ISLANDS 23
Solomon Islands
Obelisk I.
Duff Islands
Treasurers I.
Taumako
Bass Islands
Nupani
Nalogo
Nukapu
Reef Islands
Pileni
Nifiloli
Fenualoa
Sand I.
Malapu
Lomlom
Matema
Tinakula
Graciosa Bay
Nevea
Noka
Note Kanengo
Nendo (Ndeni)
Tomotu Noi (Lord Howe Island)
Nonume
Noole
Note Kembanye
Note Kempopla
Utupua
Tanimbili
Basilisk Harbor
Hingdove Passage
Vanikolo Islands
Vanikolo
Tevai
Vana
Northeast Passage
Miller Point
Dean Passage

Fiji Islands

France

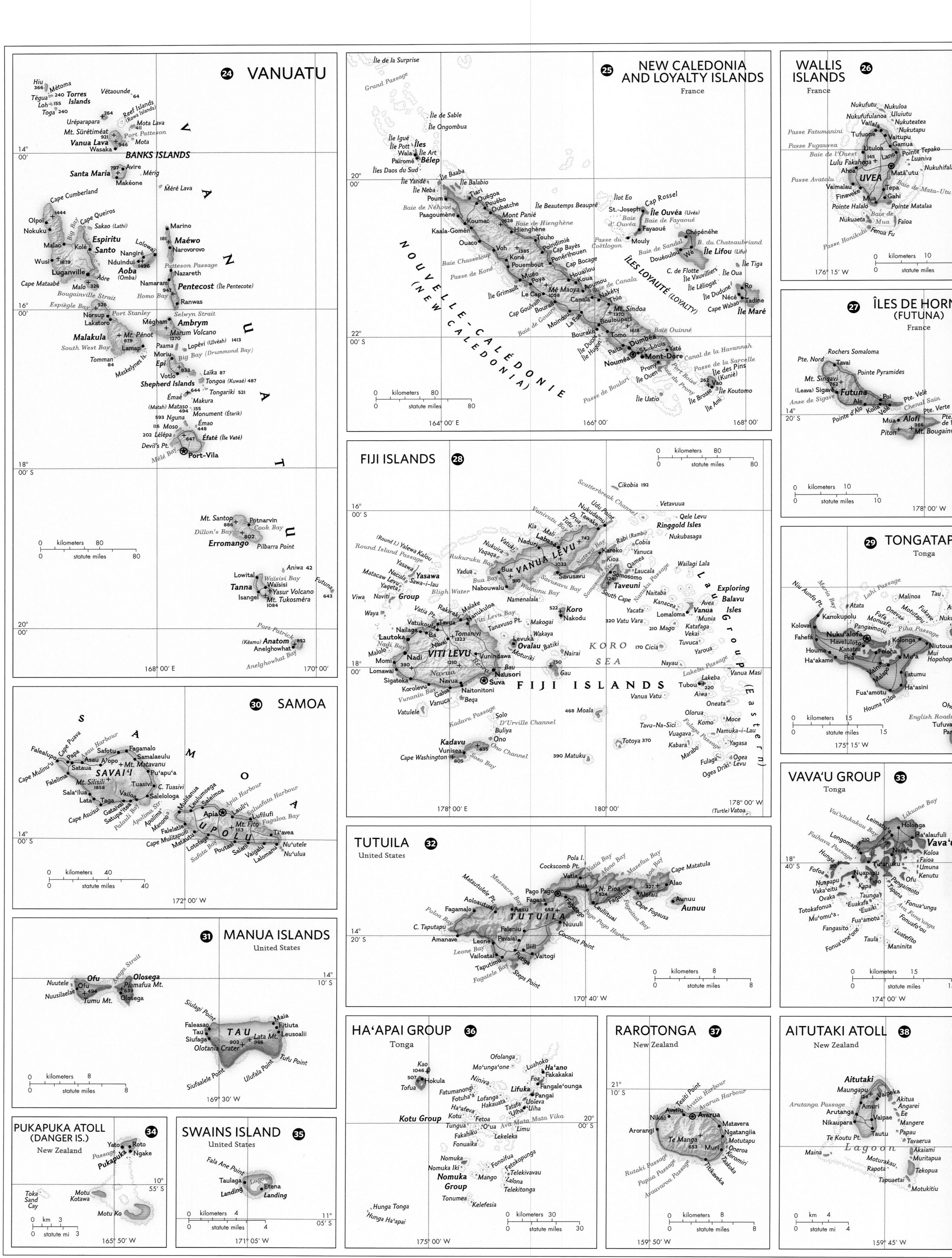

24 VANUATU
Hiu
Métoma
Tégua
Loh
Toga
Torres Islands
Vétaounde
Ureparapara
Reef Islands (Rowa Islands)
Mota Lava
Mt. Sürétiméat
Port Patteson
Vanua Lava
Mota
Wasaka
BANKS ISLANDS
Santa Maria
Avire
Mérig
Makéone
Méré Lava
Cape Cumberland
Olpoï
Nokuku
Cape Queiros
Sakao (Lathi)
Big Bay
Espiritu Santo
Malao
Kolé
Wusi
Nangiré
Nduindui
Luganville
Aoba (Omba)
Aöre
Cape Mataabé
Malo
Bougainville Strait
Espiègle Bay
Lolowai
Maéwo
Marino
Narovorovo
Patteson Passage
Nazareth
Namaram
Pentecost (Île Pentecote)
Homo Bay
Ranwas
Port Stanley
Norsup
Lakatoro
Selwyn Strait
Ambrym
Mégham
Marum Volcano
Malakula
Mt. Pénot
South West Bay
Lamap
Tomman
Maskelynes Is.
Paama
Lopévi (Ulvéah)
Big Bay (Drummond Bay)
Moriu
Epi
Votlo
Laïka
Tongoa (Kuwaé)
Shepherd Islands
Tongariki
Émaé
Makura
(Matah) Mataso
Monument (Étarik)
Nguna
Moso
Émao
Lélépa
Éfaté (Île Vaté)
Devil's Pt.
Mélé Bay
Port-Vila
V A N U A T U
Mt. Santop
Potnarvin
Dillon's Bay
Cook Bay
Erromango
Pilbarra Point
Aniwa
Lowital
Waïsisi Bay
Waïsisi
Tanna
Yasur Volcano
Isangel
Mt. Tukosméra
Futuna
Port Patrick
(Kéamu) Anatom
Anelghowhat
Anelghowhat Bay
14° 00'
16° 00'
18° 00' S
20° 00'
168° 00' E
170° 00'
0 kilometers 80
0 statute miles 80
25 NEW CALEDONIA AND LOYALTY ISLANDS
France
Île de la Surprise
Grand Passage
Île de Sable
Île Ongombua
Île Igué
Île Pott
Îles Belep
Île Art
Wala
Païromé
Bélep
Îles Daos du Sud
Île Baaba
Île Yandé
Île Neba
Île Balabio
Baie de Néhoué
Poum
Tiari
Ouégoa
Pouébo
Ouébatche
Paagoumène
Koumac
Mont Panié
Hienghène
Baie de Hienghène
Kaala-Gomén
Touho
Ouaco
Voh
Poindimié
Cap Bayes
Ponérihouen
Koné
Pouembout
Baie Chasseloup
Passe de Koné
Île Grimault
Muéo
Poya
Le Cap
Houaïlou
Kouaoua
Canala
Baie de Canala
Mé Maoya
Nakéty
Thio
Cap Goulvain
Bourail
Moindou
La Foa
Mt. Sindoa
Boulouparis
Bouraké
Tomo
Baie Ouinné
Dumbéa
Mont-Dore
Nouméa
St.-Louis
Yaté
Canal de la Havannah
Prony
Île Ouen
Passe de Boulari
Île Uatio
Passe de la Sarcelle
Île des Pins (Kunié)
Vao
Île Koutomo
Île Brosse
Île Ami
Îlot Eo
Cap Rossel
St.-Joseph
Île Ouvéa (Uvéa)
Baie d' Ouvéa
Baie de Fayaoué
Fayaoué
Mouly
Passe du Coëtlogon
Chépénéhé
B. du Chateaubriand
Baie de Sandal
Île Lifou (Lifu)
Douéoulou
Wé
Île Tiga
C. de Flotte
Île Vauvilliers
Île Oua
Île Léliogat
Île Dudune
Nécé
Tadine
Ro
Cape Wabao
Île Maré
ÎLES LOYAUTÉ (LOYALTY)
NOUVELLE-CALÉDONIE (NEW CALEDONIA)
20° 00'
22° 00' S
164° 00' E
166° 00'
168° 00'
0 kilometers 80
0 statute miles 80
26 WALLIS ISLANDS
France
Nukufutu
Nukuloa
Nukufufulanoa
Uluiutu
Nukuteatea
Vailala
Nukutapu
Passe Fatumanini
Tufuone
Vaitupu
Gamua
Passe Fugauvea
Utuloa
Baie de l'Ouest
Pointe Tepako
Lano
Luaniva
Lulu Fakahega
Ahoa
Matā'utu
Nukuhifala
Passe Avatolu
UVEA
Vaimalau
Baie de Mata-Utu
Finetoka
Tepa
Gahi
Mua
Pointe Halalo
Pointe Matalaa
Nukuaeta
Baie de Mua
Faïoa
Passe Honikulu
Fenua Fu
176° 15' W
0 kilometers 10
0 statute miles
27 ÎLES DE HORN (FUTUNA)
France
Rochers Somaloma
Pte. Nord
Tavai
Pointe Pyramides
Mt. Singavi
(Leava) Sigave
Futuna
Anse de Sigave
Poi
Ale
Pte. Velé
Chenal Sain
Pointe d'Alo
Kolia
Pte. Verte
Alofi
Mua
Piton
Mt. Bougainvil
Pte. de Vo
14° 20' S
178° 00' W
0 kilometers 10
0 statute miles 10
28 FIJI ISLANDS
Cikobia
Vetauvua
Scatterbreak Channel
Qele Levu
Ringgold Isles
Nukubasaga
Udu Point
Nukudamu
Tawake
Vanua Levu
Labasa
Naduri
Mali
Kia
Drua
Tutu
Rabi (Rambi)
Cobia
Yanuca
Karoko
Kioa
Qamea
Somosomo
Laucala
Taveuni
Nanuku Passage
Wailagi Lala
South Cape
Naitaba
Exploring Isles
Kanacea
Avea
Vanua Balavu
Munia
Lomaloma
Katafaga
Vekai
Tuvuca
Yacata
Vatu Vara
Mago
Cicia
Yaroua
Lau Group (Eastern)
(Round I.) Yalewa Kalou
Round Island Passage
Yasawa
Nukuira
Vatuki
Yaqaga
Bligh Water
Rukuruku Bay
Yasawa
Nacula
Sawa-i-lau
Matacaw Levu
Yaqeta
Naviti
Yasawa Group
Viwa
Waya
Yadua
Bua Bay
Bua
Nabouwalu
Savusavu
Savusavu Bay
Wainunu Bay
Namenalala
Koro
Nakodu
Makogai
Wakaya
Ovalau
Levuka
Batiki
Nairai
Koro Sea
Lautoka
Nadi Bay
Nadi
Nailaga
Vatukoula
Tavua
Rakiraki
Malake
Nanukuloa
Viti Levu Bay
Ba
Tomanivi
Viti Levu
Vunindawa
Tailevu Pt.
Motoriki
Malolo
Momi
Lomawai
Sigatoka
Korolevu
Navua
Galoa
Vunaniu Bay
Vanuca
Vatulele
Beqa
Naitonitoni
Bau
Nausori
Suva
Gau
Nayau
Lakeba Passage
Lakeba
Vanua Masi
Tubou
Aiwa
Vanua Vatu
Oneata
F I J I   I S L A N D S
Moala
Solo
D'Urville Channel
Buliya
Ono
Kadavu
Vunisea
Cape Washington
Kadavu Passage
Ono Channel
Soso Bay
Matuku
Totoya
Tavu-Na-Sici
Olorua
Moce
Komo
Namuka-i-Lau
Vuagava
Kabara
Yagasa
Marabo
Fulaga
Ogea Levu
Ogea Driki
16° 00' S
18° 00'
178° 00' E
180° 00'
178° 00' W
(Turtle) Vatoa
0 kilometers 80
0 statute miles 80
29 TONGATAPU
Tonga
Niu Aunofo Pt.
Malinoa
Lahi Passage
Tau
Atata
Onevai
Motutapu
Fukave
Nuku
Kanokupolu
Pangaimotu
Piha Passage
Kolovai
Fahefa
Nukuʻalofa
Havelulot
Kolonga
Niutoua
Houma
Folaha
Muʻa
Mui Hopohopo
Haʻakame
Fatumu
Fuaʻamotu
Haʻasini
Houma Toloa
English Roads
Tufuvai
175° 15' W
0 kilometers 15
0 statute miles 15
30 SAMOA
Falealupo
Papa
Safotu
Fagamalo
Samalaeulu
Asau Harbour
Asau
Aʻopo
Mt. Matavanu
Cape Mulinuʻu
Satupaitea
Fagamalo
Puʻapuʻa
Satuao
SAVAIʻI
Falelima
Mt. Silisili
Tuasivi
C. Tuasivi
Salailua
Taga
Salelologa
Vailoa
Cape Asuisui
Gataivai
Apolima Str.
Apolima
Manono
Mulifanua
Leulumoega
Saleimoa
Apia
Apia Harbour
Lauliʻi
Saluafata Harbour
Lufilufi
Fagaloa Bay
Mt. Fito
Faleolo
Tiʻavea
Cape Mulitapuili
Matautu
Lotofaga
Safata Bay
Poutasi
Salani
Vaigalu
Lalomanu
UPOLU
Nuʻutele
Nuʻulua
S A M O A
14° 00' S
172° 00' W
0 kilometers 40
0 statute miles 40
31 MANUA ISLANDS
United States
Asaga Strait
Ofu
Olosega
Nuutele
Piumafua Mt.
Nuusilaelae
Tumu Mt.
Olosega
Siulagi Point
Faleasao
Maia
Fitiuta
Tau
Leusoalii
Siufaga
TAU
Lata Mt.
Olotania Crater
Tufu Point
Siufaalele Point
Ulufala Point
14° 10' S
169° 30' W
0 kilometers 8
0 statute miles 8
32 TUTUILA
United States
Pola I.
Cockscomb Pt.
Vatia Bay
Afono Bay
Masefau Bay
Aoa Bay
Cape Matatula
Vatia
Aua
Tula
Alao
Matautuele Pt.
Massacre Bay
Pago Pago
N. Pioa
Alofau
Aunuu
Aunuu
Aoloautuai
Fagasa
Fagamalo
TUTUILA
Fagaitua
Cape Fogausa
Poloa Bay
Nuuuli
Pago Pago Harbor
C. Taputapu
Faleniu
Pavaiai
Amanave
Leone
Leone Bay
Iliili
Vailoatai
Coconut Point
Taputimu
Vaitogi
Fagatele Bay
Steps Point
14° 20' S
170° 40' W
0 kilometers 8
0 statute miles 8
33 VAVAʻU GROUP
Tonga
Vaiʻutukakau Bay
Likuone Bay
Leimatuʻa
Holonga
Faihava Passage
Longomapu
Vavaʻu
Neiafu
Koloa
Hunga
Faioa
Umuna
Kenutu
Ofu
Pangaimotu
Fofoa
Nuapapu
Vakaʻeitu
Ovaka
Kapa
Taunga
Totokafonua
Muʻomuʻa
Fonuaʻunga
Fangasito
Fuaʻamotu
Luatafito
Fonuaʻoneʻone
Taula
Maninita
18° 40' S
174° 00' W
0 kilometers 15
0 statute miles 15
34 PUKAPUKA ATOLL (DANGER IS.)
New Zealand
Yato
Roto
Pukapuka
Ngake
Toka Sand Cay
Motu Kotawa
Motu Ko
10° 55' S
165° 50' W
0 km 3
0 statute mi 3
35 SWAINS ISLAND
United States
Fala Ane Point
Taulaga
Etena
Landing
Landing
11° 05' S
171° 05' W
0 kilometers 4
0 statute miles 4
36 HAʻAPAI GROUP
Tonga
Ofolanga
Moʻungaʻone
Kao
Luahoko
Haʻano
Fakakakai
Hokula
Tofua
Niniva
Foa
Fangaleʻounga
Fotuhaʻa
Lifuka
Pangai
Lofanga
Hakauata
ʻUoleva
Haʻafeva
Tatafa
ʻUiha
Kotu Group
Kotu
Fetoa
Tungua
ʻOʻua
Limu
Fakahiku
Lekeleka
Fonuaika
Nomuka
Nomuka Iki
Nomuka Group
Mango
Fonoifua
Fetokopunga
Telekivavau
Lalona
Telekitonga
Tonumea
Kelefesia
Hunga Tonga
Hunga Haʻapai
20° 00' S
175° 00' W
0 kilometers 30
0 statute miles 30
37 RAROTONGA
New Zealand
Teaiti Point
Avatiu Harbour
Avarua Harbour
Avatiu
Avarua
Nikao
Matavera
Ngatangiia
Arorangi
Te Manga
Muri
Motutapu
Oneroa
Koromiri
Taakoka
Rutaki Passage
Papua Passage
Avaavaroa Passage
Titikaveka
21° 10' S
159° 50' W
0 kilometers 8
0 statute miles 8
38 AITUTAKI ATOLL
New Zealand
Aitutaki
Maungapu
Vaipeka
Akitua
Angarei
Arutanga Passage
Amuri
Ee
Arutanga
Vaipae
Mangere
Nikaupara
Papau
Te Koutu Pt.
Tautu
Tavaerua
Lagoon
Maina
Akaiami
Muritapua
Moturakau
Rapota
Tekopua
Tapuaetai
Motukitiu
159° 45' W
0 km 4
0 statute mi 4

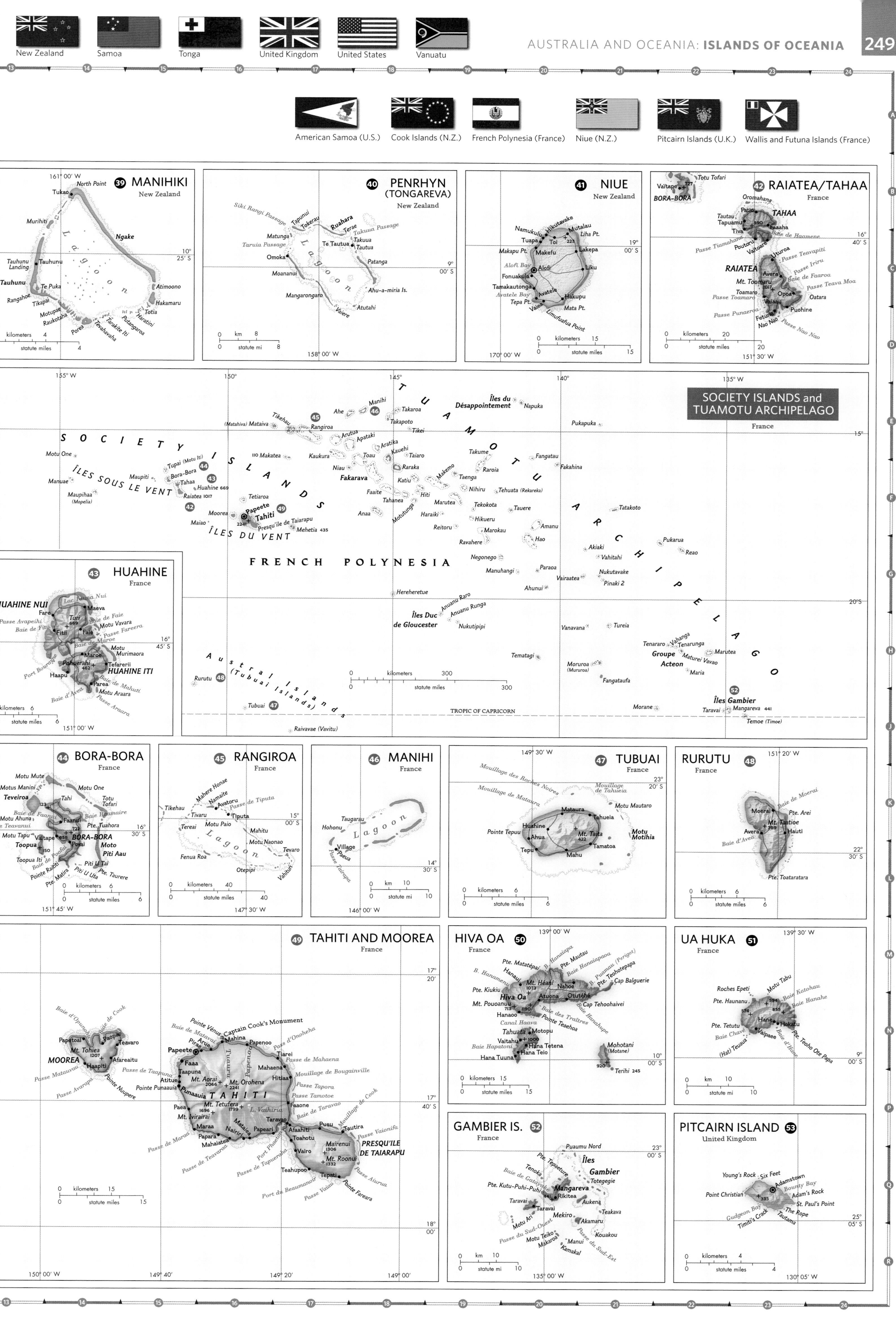
New Zealand
Samoa
Tonga
United Kingdom
United States
Vanuatu
American Samoa (U.S.)
Cook Islands (N.Z.)
French Polynesia (France)
Niue (N.Z.)
Pitcairn Islands (U.K.)
Wallis and Futuna Islands (France)
39 MANIHIKI
New Zealand
North Point
Tukao
Murihiti
Ngake
Lagoon
Tauhunu Landing
Tauhunu
Te Puka
Rangahoe
Tikapai
Motupae
Raukotaha
Porea
Atimoono
Hakamaru
Totia
Haratini
161° 00′ W
10° 25′ S
40 PENRHYN (TONGAREVA)
New Zealand
Siki Rangi Passage
Tapunui
Tokerau
Ruahara
Terae
Takuua Passage
Takuua
Tautua
Te Tautua
Matunga
Taruia Passage
Omoka
Moananui
Mangarongaro
Patanga
Ahu-a-miria Is.
Atutahi
Vaiere
Lagoon
158° 00′ W
9° 00′ S
41 NIUE
New Zealand
Namukulu
Hikutavake
Mutalau
Liha Pt.
Tuapa
Toi
Makapu Pt.
Makefu
Lakepa
Alofi Bay
Alofi
Liku
Fonuakula
Tamakautonga
Avatele Bay
Avatele
Tepa Pt.
Hakupu
Vaiea
Mata Pt.
Limufuafua Point
170° 00′ W
19° 00′ S
42 RAIATEA/TAHAA
France
Totu Tofari
Vaitape
BORA-BORA
Oromahana
Patio
TAHAA
Tautau
Tapuamu
Tiva
Faaaha
Baie de Haamene
Passe Tiamahana
Poutoru
Vaitoare
Uturoa
Passe Teavapiti
Passe Iriru
RAIATEA
Avera
Mt. Toomaru
Baie de Faaroa
Passe Teava Moa
Tomaro
Passe Toamaro
Opoa
Vaiaau
Oatara
Passe Punaeroa
Puohine
Fetuna
Nao Nao
Passe Nao Nao
151° 30′ W
16° 40′ S
SOCIETY ISLANDS and TUAMOTU ARCHIPELAGO
France
SOCIETY ISLANDS
ÎLES SOUS LE VENT
ÎLES DU VENT
TUAMOTU ARCHIPELAGO
FRENCH POLYNESIA
Îles du Désappointement
Napuka
Manihi
Ahe
Takaroa
Takapoto
Tikei
Rangiroa
Tikehau
(Matahiva) Mataiva
Pukapuka
Arutua
Apataki
Aratika
Kauehi
Taiaro
Kaukura
Toau
Makatea
Niau
Raraka
Fakarava
Katiu
Makemo
Taenga
Takume
Raroia
Fangatau
Fakahina
Nihiru
Tehuata (Rekareka)
Faaite
Tahanea
Hiti
Motutunga
Marutea
Tekokota
Tauere
Hikueru
Haraiki
Reitoru
Marokau
Amanu
Ravahere
Hao
Akiaki
Vahitahi
Nengonego
Manuhangi
Paraoa
Vairaatea
Nukutavake
Pinaki 2
Ahunui
Tatakoto
Pukarua
Reao
Motu One
Tupai (Motu Iti)
Bora-Bora
Tahaa
Maupiti
Manuae
Maupihaa (Mopelia)
Huahine
Raiatea
Tetiaroa
Moorea
Papeete
Tahiti
Presqu'île de Taiarapu
Mehetia
Maiao
Hereheretue
Îles Duc de Gloucester
Anuanu Raro
Anuanu Runga
Nukutipipi
Vanavana
Tureia
Tenararo
Vahanga
Tenarunga
Groupe Acteon
Maturei Vavao
Marutea
Maria
Tematagi
Moruroa (Mururoa)
Fangataufa
Austral Islands (Tubuai Islands)
Rurutu
Tubuai
Raivavae (Vavitu)
Morane
Îles Gambier
Taravai
Mangareva
Temoe (Timoe)
TROPIC OF CAPRICORN
155° W
150°
145°
140°
135° W
15°
20°S
43 HUAHINE
France
HUAHINE NUI
Passe Avapeihi
Baie de Fitii
Fare
Fitii
Maeva
Faie
Motu Vavava
Passe Fareera
Maroe
Motu Murimaora
Tefarerii
HUAHINE ITI
Port Bourayne
Haapu
Parea
Motu Araara
Baie d'Avea
Passe Araara
151° 00′ W
16° 45′ S
44 BORA-BORA
France
Motu Mute
Motus Manini
Teveiroa
Motu One
Tahi
Totu Tofari
Faanui
Motu Ahuna
Passe Teavanui
Pte. Tuahora
Motu Tapu
Vaitape
BORA-BORA
Toopua
Motu Piti Aau
Toopua Iti
Piti U Tai
Pointe Raititi
Pte. Taurere
Pte. Matira
151° 45′ W
16° 30′ S
45 RANGIROA
France
Tikehau
Mahere Honae
Avatoru
Passe de Tiputa
Tiputa
Tivaru
Tereai
Motu Paio
Mahitu
Motu Naonao
Tevaro
Fenua Roa
Otepipi
Vahituri
Lagoon
147° 30′ W
15° 00′ S
46 MANIHI
France
Taugarau
Hohonu
Village
Paeua
Passe Tairapa
Lagoon
146° 00′ W
14° 30′ S
47 TUBUAI
France
Mouillage des Roches Noires
Mouillage de Mataura
Mouillage de Tahueia
Motu Mautaro
Mataura
Tahueia
Huahine
Pointe Tepuu
Ahua
Mt. Taita
Motu Motihia
Tepu
Tamatoa
Mahu
149° 30′ W
23° 20′ S
RURUTU 48
France
Baie de Moerai
Moerai
Pte. Arei
Mt. Taatioe
Avera
Hauti
Baie d'Avera
Pte. Toataratara
151° 20′ W
22° 30′ S
49 TAHITI AND MOOREA
France
MOOREA
Baie d'Opunohu
Baie de Cook
Papetoai
Paopao
Teavaro
Mt. Tohiea
Afareaitu
Haapiti
Passe Matauvau
Passe Avarapa
Pointe Nuupere
Passe de Taapuna
Pointe Vénus
Baie de Matavai
Captain Cook's Monument
Mahina
Papenoo
Arue
Pirae
Papeete
Faaa
Passe d'Onohehu
Tiarei
Passe de Mahaena
Mahaena
Mouillage de Bougainville
Hitiaa
Passe Tapora
Passe Tamotoe
Punaauia
Taapuna
Atitue
Mt. Aorai
Mt. Orohena
Pointe Punaauia
TAHITI
Paea
Mt. Tetufera
Mt. Ivirairai
L. Vaihiria
Faaone
Baie de Taravao
Mouillage de Cook
Taravao
Maraa
Papara
Mahaiatea
Nairii
Papeari
Afaahiti
Pueu
Tautira
Passe Vaionifa
Toahotu
Vairo
Mt. Ronui
PRESQU'ILE DE TAIARAPU
Passe de Maraa
Passe de Teavaraa
Port Phaeton
Passe de Tapuaeraha
Teahupoo
Tepati
Passe Aiurua
Pointe Fareara
Port de Beaumanoir
Passe Vaiau
150° 00′ W
149° 40′
149° 20′
149° 00′
17° 20′
17° 40′ S
18° 00′
HIVA OA 50
France
Pte. Matatépai
B. Hanaiapa
Pte. Mautau
Baie Hanaiapaoa
Pte. Puamau (Perigot)
Cap Balguerie
Pte. Teohotepapa
B. Hanamenu
Hanaui
Mt. Heani
Nahoe
Pte. Kiukiu
Hiva Oa
Atuona
Otutoho
Cap Tehoohaivei
Mt. Pouoanuu
Hanaoo
Baie des Traitres
Pointe Teaehoa
Baie Hanatekuua
Canal Haava
Tahuata
Motopu
Vaitahu
Baie Hapatoni
Hana Tetena
Hana Teio
Hana Tuuna
Mohotani (Motane)
Terihi
139° 00′ W
10° 00′ S
UA HUKA 51
France
Roches Epeti
Motu Tabu
Baie Hanahe
Baie Hatohau
Pte. Haunanu
Hane
Hokatu
Pte. Tetutu
Baie Chave
Vaipaee
Baie d'Hane
Pte. Teoho Ote Papa
(Hat) Teuaua
139° 30′ W
9° 00′ S
GAMBIER IS. 52
France
Puaumu Nord
Îles Gambier
Pte. Tepaeture
Totegegie
Tenoko
Baie de Gatavake
Pte. Kutu-Puhi-Puhi
Mangareva
Rikitea
Aukena
Taravai
Mekiro
Teakava
Akamaru
Motu Ari
Kouakou
Passe du Sud-Ouest
Motu Teiko
Makaroa
Manui
Kamaka
Passe du Sud-Est
135° 00′ W
23° 00′ S
PITCAIRN ISLAND 53
United Kingdom
Young's Rock
Six Feet
Adamstown
Bounty Bay
Adam's Rock
Point Christian
St. Paul's Point
The Rope
Gudgeon Bay
Tautama
Timiti's Crack
130° 05′ W
25° 05′ S

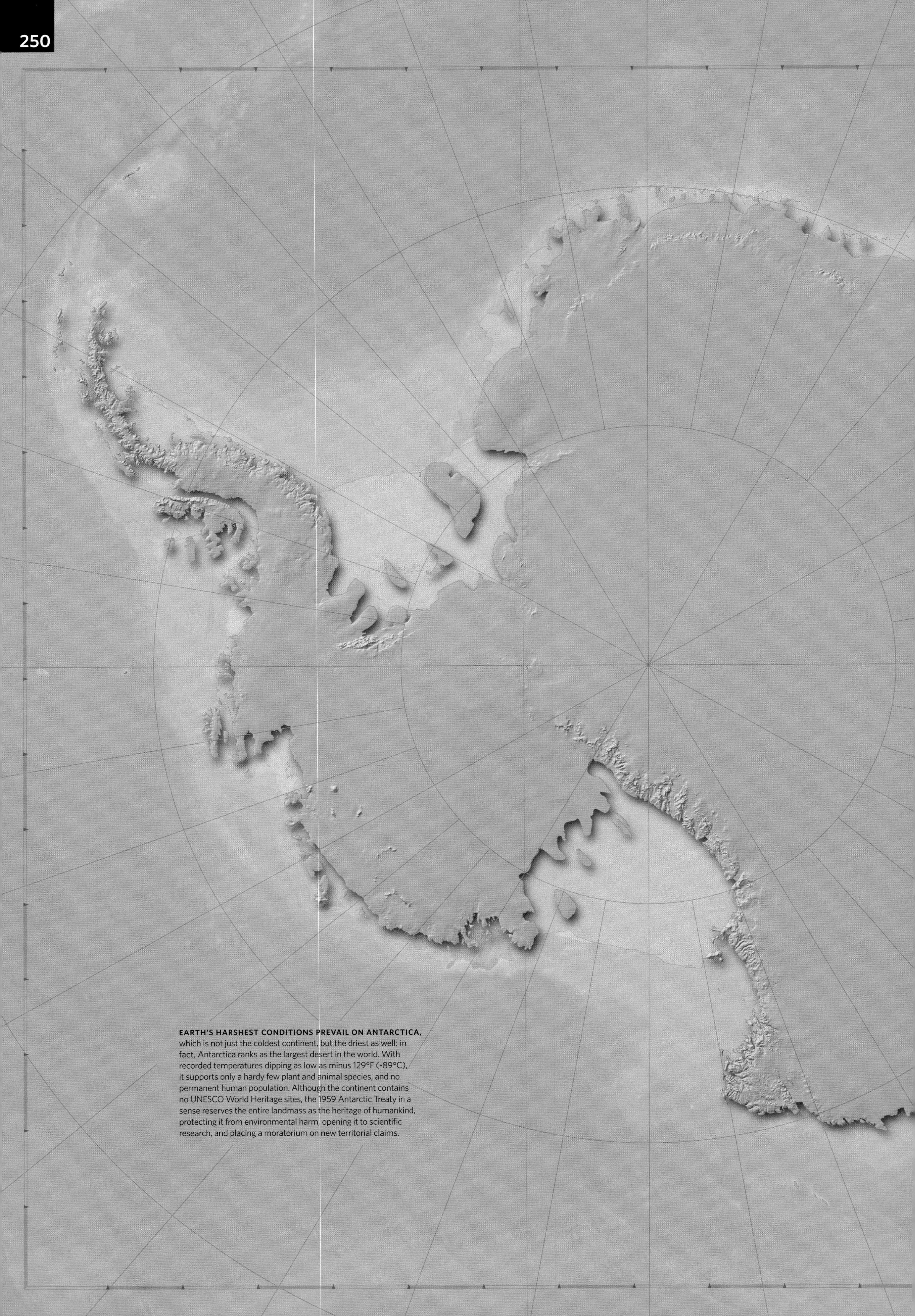

EARTH'S HARSHEST CONDITIONS PREVAIL ON ANTARCTICA, which is not just the coldest continent, but the driest as well; in fact, Antarctica ranks as the largest desert in the world. With recorded temperatures dipping as low as minus 129°F (-89°C), it supports only a hardy few plant and animal species, and no permanent human population. Although the continent contains no UNESCO World Heritage sites, the 1959 Antarctic Treaty in a sense reserves the entire landmass as the heritage of humankind, protecting it from environmental harm, opening it to scientific research, and placing a moratorium on new territorial claims.

Antarctica

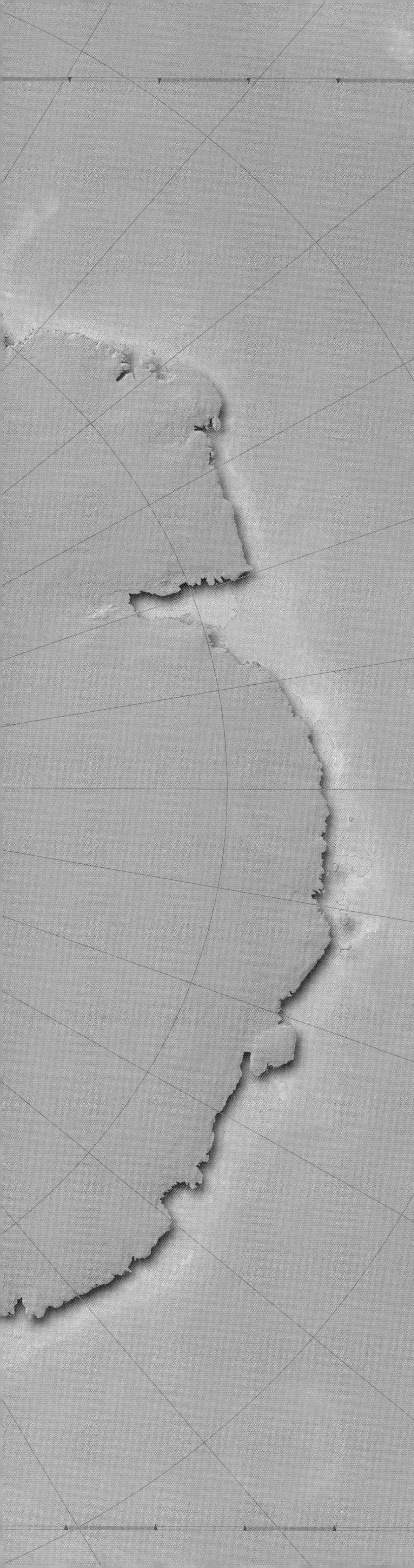

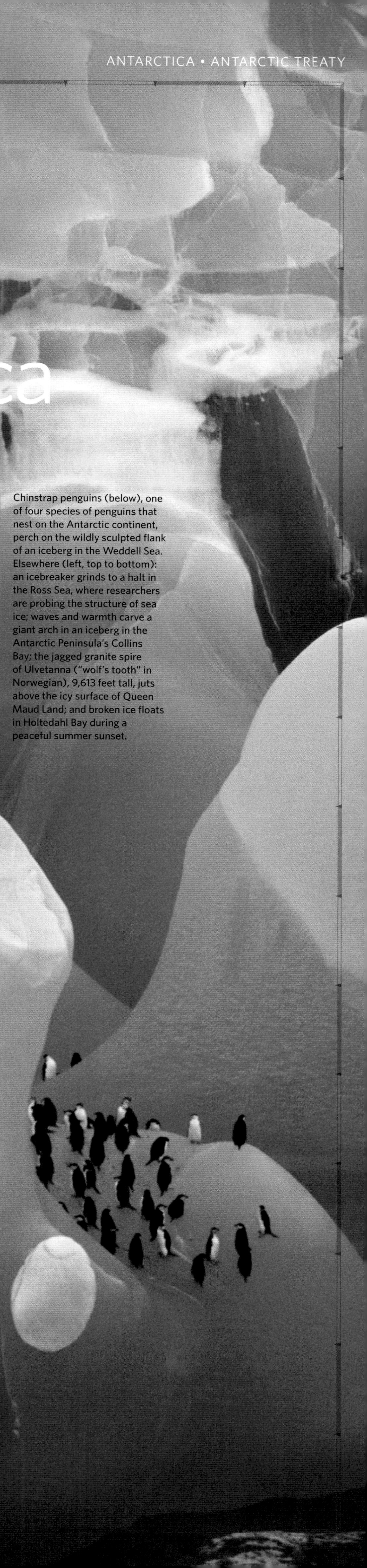

Chinstrap penguins (below), one of four species of penguins that nest on the Antarctic continent, perch on the wildly sculpted flank of an iceberg in the Weddell Sea. Elsewhere (left, top to bottom): an icebreaker grinds to a halt in the Ross Sea, where researchers are probing the structure of sea ice; waves and warmth carve a giant arch in an iceberg in the Antarctic Peninsula's Collins Bay; the jagged granite spire of Ulvetanna ("wolf's tooth" in Norwegian), 9,613 feet tall, juts above the icy surface of Queen Maud Land; and broken ice floats in Holtedahl Bay during a peaceful summer sunset.

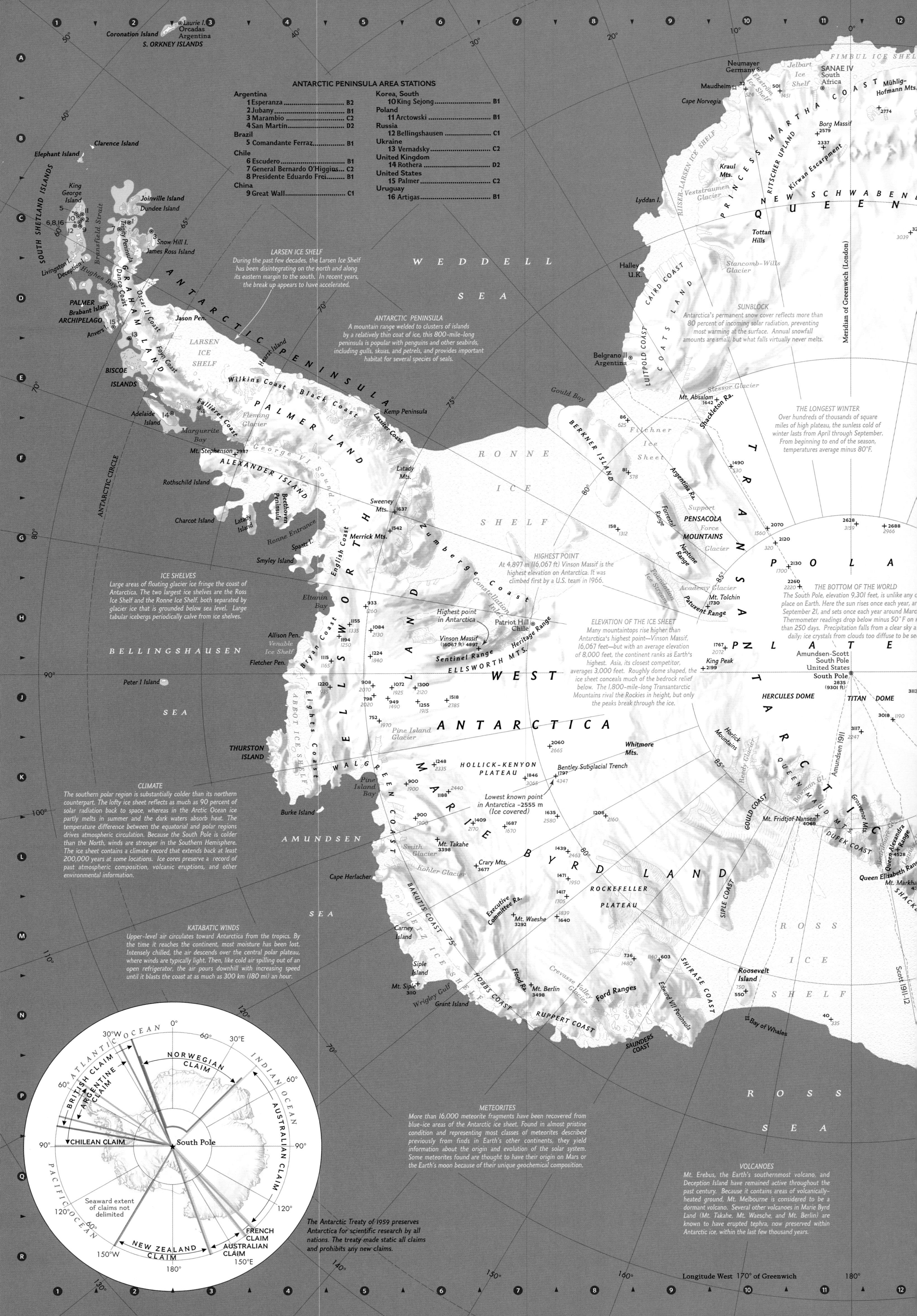

ANTARCTIC PENINSULA AREA STATIONS
Argentina
1 Esperanza B2
2 Jubany B1
3 Marambio C2
4 San Martin D2
Brazil
5 Comandante Ferraz B1
Chile
6 Escudero B1
7 General Bernardo O'Higgins C2
8 Presidente Eduardo Frei B1
China
9 Great Wall C1
Korea, South
10 King Sejong B1
Poland
11 Arctowski B1
Russia
12 Bellingshausen C1
Ukraine
13 Vernadsky C2
United Kingdom
14 Rothera D2
United States
15 Palmer C2
Uruguay
16 Artigas B1
LARSEN ICE SHELF
During the past few decades, the Larsen Ice Shelf has been disintegrating on the north and along its eastern margin to the south. In recent years, the break up appears to have accelerated.
ANTARCTIC PENINSULA
A mountain range welded to clusters of islands by a relatively thin coat of ice, this 800-mile-long peninsula is popular with penguins and other seabirds, including gulls, skuas, and petrels, and provides important habitat for several species of seals.
SUNBLOCK
Antarctica's permanent snow cover reflects more than 80 percent of incoming solar radiation, preventing most warming at the surface. Annual snowfall amounts are small, but what falls virtually never melts.
THE LONGEST WINTER
Over hundreds of thousands of square miles of high plateau, the sunless cold of winter lasts from April through September. From beginning to end of the season, temperatures average minus 80°F.
HIGHEST POINT
At 4,897 m (16,067 ft) Vinson Massif is the highest elevation on Antarctica. It was climbed first by a U.S. team in 1966.
THE BOTTOM OF THE WORLD
The South Pole, elevation 9,301 feet, is unlike any other place on Earth. Here the sun rises once each year, around September 21, and sets once each year around March 23. Thermometer readings drop below minus 50°F on more than 250 days. Precipitation falls from a clear sky as daily; ice crystals from clouds too diffuse to be seen.
ICE SHELVES
Large areas of floating glacier ice fringe the coast of Antarctica. The two largest ice shelves are the Ross Ice Shelf and the Ronne Ice Shelf, both separated by glacier ice that is grounded below sea level. Large tabular icebergs periodically calve from ice shelves.
ELEVATION OF THE ICE SHEET
Many mountaintops rise higher than Antarctica's highest point—Vinson Massif, 16,067 feet—but with an average elevation of 8,000 feet, the continent ranks as Earth's highest. Asia, its closest competitor, averages 3,000 feet. Roughly dome shaped, the ice sheet conceals much of the bedrock relief below. The 1,800-mile-long Transantarctic Mountains rival the Rockies in height, but only the peaks break through the ice.
CLIMATE
The southern polar region is substantially colder than its northern counterpart. The lofty ice sheet reflects as much as 90 percent of solar radiation back to space, whereas in the Arctic Ocean ice partly melts in summer and the dark waters absorb heat. The temperature difference between the equatorial and polar regions drives atmospheric circulation. Because the South Pole is colder than the North, winds are stronger in the Southern Hemisphere. The ice sheet contains a climate record that extends back at least 200,000 years at some locations. Ice cores preserve a record of past atmospheric composition, volcanic eruptions, and other environmental information.
KATABATIC WINDS
Upper-level air circulates toward Antarctica from the tropics. By the time it reaches the continent, most moisture has been lost. Intensely chilled, the air descends over the central polar plateau, where winds are typically light. Then, like cold air spilling out of an open refrigerator, the air pours downhill with increasing speed until it blasts the coast at as much as 300 km (180 mi) an hour.
METEORITES
More than 16,000 meteorite fragments have been recovered from blue-ice areas of the Antarctic ice sheet. Found in almost pristine condition and representing most classes of meteorites described previously from finds in Earth's other continents, they yield information about the origin and evolution of the solar system. Some meteorites found are thought to have their origin on Mars or the Earth's moon because of their unique geochemical composition.
VOLCANOES
Mt. Erebus, the Earth's southernmost volcano, and Deception Island have remained active throughout the past century. Because it contains areas of volcanically-heated ground, Mt. Melbourne is considered to be a dormant volcano. Several other volcanoes in Marie Byrd Land (Mt. Takahe, Mt. Waeshe, and Mt. Berlin) are known to have erupted tephra, now preserved within Antarctic ice, within the last few thousand years.
The Antarctic Treaty of 1959 preserves Antarctica for scientific research by all nations. The treaty made static all claims and prohibits any new claims.
NORWEGIAN CLAIM
BRITISH CLAIM
ARGENTINE CLAIM
CHILEAN CLAIM
AUSTRALIAN CLAIM
FRENCH CLAIM
NEW ZEALAND CLAIM
South Pole
Seaward extent of claims not delimited
ATLANTIC OCEAN
INDIAN OCEAN
PACIFIC OCEAN
WEDDELL SEA
BELLINGSHAUSEN SEA
AMUNDSEN SEA
ROSS SEA
RONNE ICE SHELF
ROSS ICE SHELF
ANTARCTIC PENINSULA
GRAHAM LAND
PALMER LAND
ALEXANDER ISLAND
ELLSWORTH LAND
WEST ANTARCTICA
MARIE BYRD LAND
QUEEN MAUD LAND
NEW SCHWABENLAND
TRANSANTARCTIC MOUNTAINS
POLAR PLATEAU
Highest point in Antarctica
Vinson Massif (16067 ft) 4897
Lowest known point in Antarctica -2555 m (Ice covered)
Bentley Subglacial Trench
Amundsen-Scott South Pole United States
South Pole 2835 (9301 ft)
ANTARCTIC CIRCLE
Meridian of Greenwich (London)
Longitude West 170° of Greenwich

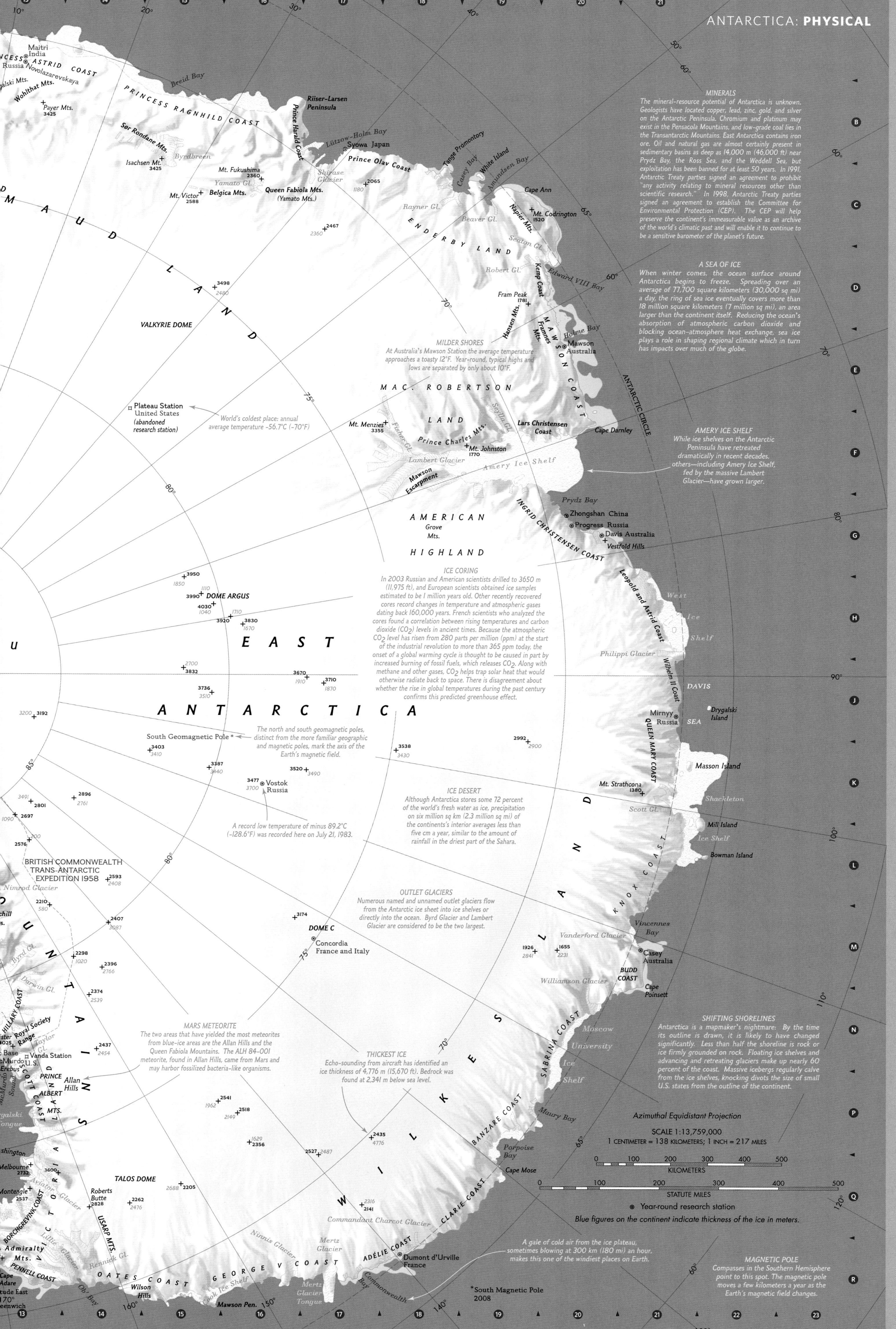
MINERALS
The mineral-resource potential of Antarctica is unknown. Geologists have located copper, lead, zinc, gold, and silver on the Antarctic Peninsula. Chromium and platinum may exist in the Pensacola Mountains, and low-grade coal lies in the Transantarctic Mountains. East Antarctica contains iron ore. Oil and natural gas are almost certainly present in sedimentary basins as deep as 14,000 m (46,000 ft) near Prydz Bay, the Ross Sea, and the Weddell Sea, but exploitation has been banned for at least 50 years. In 1991, Antarctic Treaty parties signed an agreement to prohibit "any activity relating to mineral resources other than scientific research." In 1998, Antarctic Treaty parties signed an agreement to establish the Committee for Environmental Protection (CEP). The CEP will help preserve the continent's immeasurable value as an archive of the world's climatic past and will enable it to continue to be a sensitive barometer of the planet's future.
A SEA OF ICE
When winter comes, the ocean surface around Antarctica begins to freeze. Spreading over an average of 77,700 square kilometers (30,000 sq mi) a day, the ring of sea ice eventually covers more than 18 million square kilometers (7 million sq mi), an area larger than the continent itself. Reducing the ocean's absorption of atmospheric carbon dioxide and blocking ocean-atmosphere heat exchange, sea ice plays a role in shaping regional climate which in turn has impacts over much of the globe.
MILDER SHORES
At Australia's Mawson Station the average temperature approaches a toasty 12°F. Year-round, typical highs and lows are separated by only about 10°F.
World's coldest place: annual average temperature -56.7°C (-70°F)
AMERY ICE SHELF
While ice shelves on the Antarctic Peninsula have retreated dramatically in recent decades, others—including Amery Ice Shelf, fed by the massive Lambert Glacier—have grown larger.
ICE CORING
In 2003 Russian and American scientists drilled to 3650 m (11,975 ft), and European scientists obtained ice samples estimated to be 1 million years old. Other recently recovered cores record changes in temperature and atmospheric gases dating back 160,000 years. French scientists who analyzed the cores found a correlation between rising temperatures and carbon dioxide (CO_2) levels in ancient times. Because the atmospheric CO_2 level has risen from 280 parts per million (ppm) at the start of the industrial revolution to more than 365 ppm today, the onset of a global warming cycle is thought to be caused in large part by increased burning of fossil fuels, which releases CO_2. Along with methane and other gases, CO_2 helps trap solar heat that would otherwise radiate back to space. There is disagreement about whether the rise in global temperatures during the past century confirms this predicted greenhouse effect.
The north and south geomagnetic poles, distinct from the more familiar geographic and magnetic poles, mark the axis of the Earth's magnetic field.
South Geomagnetic Pole
ICE DESERT
Although Antarctica stores some 72 percent of the world's fresh water as ice, precipitation on six million sq km (2.3 million sq mi) of the continents's interior averages less than five cm a year, similar to the amount of rainfall in the driest part of the Sahara.
A record low temperature of minus 89.2°C (-128.6°F) was recorded here on July 21, 1983.
Vostok Russia
OUTLET GLACIERS
Numerous named and unnamed outlet glaciers flow from the Antarctic ice sheet into ice shelves or directly into the ocean. Byrd Glacier and Lambert Glacier are considered to be the two largest.
DOME C
Concordia France and Italy
BRITISH COMMONWEALTH TRANS-ANTARCTIC EXPEDITION 1958
MARS METEORITE
The two areas that have yielded the most meteorites from blue-ice areas are the Allan Hills and the Queen Fabiola Mountains. The ALH 84-001 meteorite, found in Allan Hills, came from Mars and may harbor fossilized bacteria-like organisms.
THICKEST ICE
Echo-sounding from aircraft has identified an ice thickness of 4,776 m (15,670 ft). Bedrock was found at 2,341 m below sea level.
SHIFTING SHORELINES
Antarctica is a mapmaker's nightmare: By the time its outline is drawn, it is likely to have changed significantly. Less than half the shoreline is rock or ice firmly grounded on rock. Floating ice shelves and advancing and retreating glaciers make up nearly 60 percent of the coast. Massive icebergs regularly calve from the ice shelves, knocking divots the size of small U.S. states from the outline of the continent.
Azimuthal Equidistant Projection
SCALE 1:13,759,000
1 CENTIMETER = 138 KILOMETERS; 1 INCH = 217 MILES
KILOMETERS
STATUTE MILES
Year-round research station
Blue figures on the continent indicate thickness of the ice in meters.
A gale of cold air from the ice plateau, sometimes blowing at 300 km (180 mi) an hour, makes this one of the windiest places on Earth.
MAGNETIC POLE
Compasses in the Southern Hemisphere point to this spot. The magnetic pole moves a few kilometers a year as the Earth's magnetic field changes.
*South Magnetic Pole 2008
EAST ANTARCTICA
QUEEN MAUD LAND
WILKES LAND
AMERICAN HIGHLAND
ENDERBY LAND
MAC. ROBERTSON LAND
PRINCESS RAGNHILD COAST
PRINCESS ASTRID COAST
Prince Harald Coast
Prince Olav Coast
Kemp Coast
MAWSON COAST
Lars Christensen Coast
INGRID CHRISTENSEN COAST
Leopold and Astrid Coast
Wilhelm II Coast
QUEEN MARY COAST
KNOX COAST
BUDD COAST
SABRINA COAST
BANZARE COAST
CLARIE COAST
ADÉLIE COAST
GEORGE V COAST
OATES COAST
PENNELL COAST
BORCHGREVINK COAST
SCOTT COAST
HILLARY COAST
VALKYRIE DOME
DOME ARGUS
TALOS DOME
Plateau Station United States (abandoned research station)
Maitri India
Novolazarevskaya Russia
Syowa Japan
Mawson Australia
Zhongshan China
Progress Russia
Davis Australia
Mirnyy Russia
Casey Australia
Dumont d'Urville France
Vanda Station
McMurdo U.S.
Riiser-Larsen Peninsula
Lützow-Holm Bay
Breid Bay
Tange Promontory
Casey Bay
Amundsen Bay
White Island
Cape Ann
Mt. Codrington 1520
Napier Mts.
Edward VIII Bay
Fram Peak 1781
Hansen Mts.
Framnes Mts.
Holme Bay
Cape Darnley
ANTARCTIC CIRCLE
Amery Ice Shelf
Prydz Bay
Vestfold Hills
Lambert Glacier
Mawson Escarpment
Prince Charles Mts.
Mt. Johnston 1770
Mt. Menzies 3355
Grove Mts.
Payer Mts. 3425
Wohlthat Mts.
Sør Rondane Mts.
Isachsen Mt. 3425
Mt. Fukushima 2360
Yamato Gl.
Mt. Victor 2588
Belgica Mts.
Queen Fabiola Mts. (Yamato Mts.)
Shirase Glacier
Rayner Gl.
Beaver Gl.
Robert Gl.
West Ice Shelf
Philippi Glacier
DAVIS SEA
Drygalski Island
Masson Island
Shackleton Ice Shelf
Mt. Strathcona 1380
Scott Gl.
Mill Island
Bowman Island
Vincennes Bay
Vanderford Glacier
Williamson Glacier
Cape Poinsett
Moscow University Ice Shelf
Maury Bay
Porpoise Bay
Cape Mose
Commandant Charcot Glacier
Mertz Glacier
Mertz Glacier Tongue
Ninnis Glacier
Commonwealth Bay
Cook Ice Shelf
Mawson Pen.
Wilson Hills
Rennick Gl.
Lillie Glacier
Aviator Glacier
Roberts Butte 2828
USARP MTS.
PRINCE ALBERT MTS.
Allan Hills
Royal Society Range
Taylor Gl.
Darwin Gl.
Byrd Gl.
Nimrod Glacier
Admiralty Mts.
Cape Adare
Erebus
Ob' Bay

EARTH'S PREDOMINANT PHYSICAL FEATURE is the vast, continuous body of water that accounts for more than two-thirds of its surface, totaling some 139 million square miles. The global ocean is a dominant climate factor, with currents carrying heat from the equator toward the poles. It absorbs huge amounts of atmospheric carbon as well, mitigating the recent human-generated surge in greenhouse gases—thus moderating global warming. Oceans have always been a key resource, providing food to much of the world's population. To guard against overfishing—an increasing problem as Earth's population rises—governments have begun setting aside marine sanctuaries, like one the United States established in 2006 around the Northwestern Hawaiian Islands.

The global ocean is customarily divided into the Pacific, Atlantic, Indian, and Arctic Oceans. (A fifth, the Southern Ocean, is sometimes recognized.) Through most of history, oceans were the ultimate frontier, mysterious and impassable. One of humanity's great achievements was the conquering of oceans by explorers such as Vasco da Gama and Zheng He. Today, ocean exploration continues with great advances in undersea mapping and growing understanding of previously mysterious undersea ecosystems.

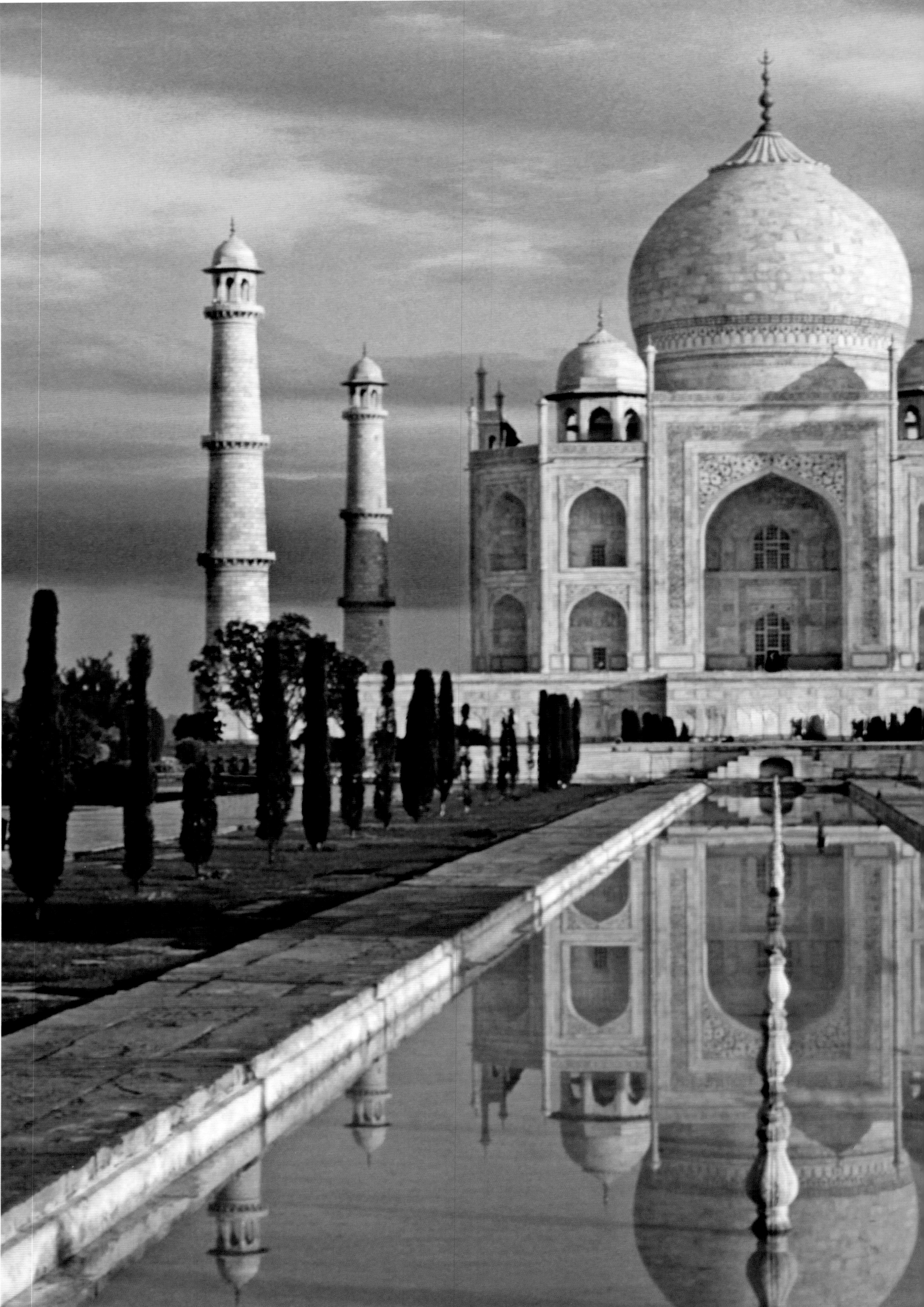

A
S
I
O
Taj Mahal
INDIA

TAJ MAHAL, INDIA

Cultural World Heritage Site

Its world-renowned beauty doubled in a reflecting pool, the Taj Mahal glows in the colors of a sunset over the city of Agra, India. The graceful marble mausoleum on the bank of the Yamuna River has been called a love poem in stone; it was built by the Mogul emperor Shah Jahan in memory of his favorite wife, Mumtaz Mahal, who died in childbirth. Completed around 1648 after close to 20 years of construction, the building displays an essentially Persian style typical of Mogul architecture, incorporating Indian elements as well as architectural traditions from central Asia and Turkey. The symmetry of the Taj Mahal—the building appears identical from each side—is a signature of Persian architecture. It's said that the only thing marring the scheme is the sarcophagus of Shah Jahan himself, placed off to one side of his beloved wife by the emperor's son, who had deposed and imprisoned his father years earlier.

South
America
Machu Picchu
PERU

MACHU PICCHU, PERU

Mixed World Heritage Site

So well hidden in the rugged Andes Mountains that Spanish conquistadores never found it, the 15th-century Inca city of Machu Picchu remained abandoned and overgrown by jungle for most of its existence. But in 1911, Yale University professor Hiram Bingham discovered the mountaintop redoubt that was quickly acclaimed as one of the most dramatic archaeological finds ever made. Despite its monumental architecture and huge system of terraces on surrounding mountainsides, Machu Picchu was not a metropolis like Cusco, the nearby Inca capital. Researchers have advanced various theories about its use, but many agree it had a sacred role in the Inca Empire, which dominated western South America prior to the European takeover of the continent. Today, with hundreds of thousands of tourists visiting the former lost city every year, physical preservation of the site has become a major concern.

Using This Atlas

MAP POLICIES Maps are a rich, useful, and—to the extent humanly possible—accurate means of depicting the world. Yet maps inevitably make the world seem a little simpler than it really is. A neatly drawn boundary may, in reality, be a hotly contested war zone. The government-sanctioned, "official" name of a provincial city in an ethnically diverse region may bear little resemblance to the name its citizens routinely use. These cartographic issues often seem obscure and academic. But maps arouse passions. Despite our carefully reasoned map policies, users of National Geographic maps write us strongly worded letters when our maps are at odds with their worldviews.

How do National Geographic cartographers deal with these realities? With constant scrutiny, considerable discussion, and help from many outside experts. Examples:

Countries: Issues of national sovereignty and contested borders often boil down to "de facto versus de jure" discussions. Governments and international agencies frequently make official rulings about contested regions. These de jure decisions, no matter how legitimate, are often at odds with the wishes of individuals and groups, and they often stand in stark contrast to real-world situations. The inevitable conclusion: It is simplest and best to show the world as it is—de facto—rather than as we or others wish it to be. Africa's Western Sahara, for example, was divided by Morocco and Mauritania after the Spanish government withdrew in 1976. Although Morocco now controls the entire territory, the United Nations does not recognize Morocco's sovereignty over this still disputed area. This atlas shows the de facto Moroccan rule but includes an explanatory note.

Place-names: Ride a barge down the Danube, and you'll hear the river called *Donau, Duna, Dunaj, Dunărea, Dunav, Dunay.* These are local names. This atlas uses the conventional name, "Danube," on physical maps. On political maps, local names are used, with the conventional name in parentheses where space permits. Usage conventions for both foreign and domestic place-names are generally established by the U.S. Board on Geographic Names, a group with representatives from several federal agencies.

World Thematic Maps

Thematic maps reveal the rich patchwork and infinite interrelationships of our changing planet. The thematic section at the beginning of the atlas focuses on ***physical*** and ***natural*** topics such as geology, landforms, land cover, and biodiversity. It also charts ***human*** patterns, with information on population, languages, religions, military strength, and the world economy. Two-page spreads on energy and minerals illustrate how people have learned to use Earth's resources, while spreads devoted to environmental stresses and protected areas focus on the far-reaching effects of human activities and the need for resource conservation. Also included are spreads illustrating the advancement of technology and the Internet. Throughout this section of the atlas, maps are coupled with satellite imagery, charts, diagrams, photographs, and tabular information; together, they create a very useful framework for studying geographic patterns.

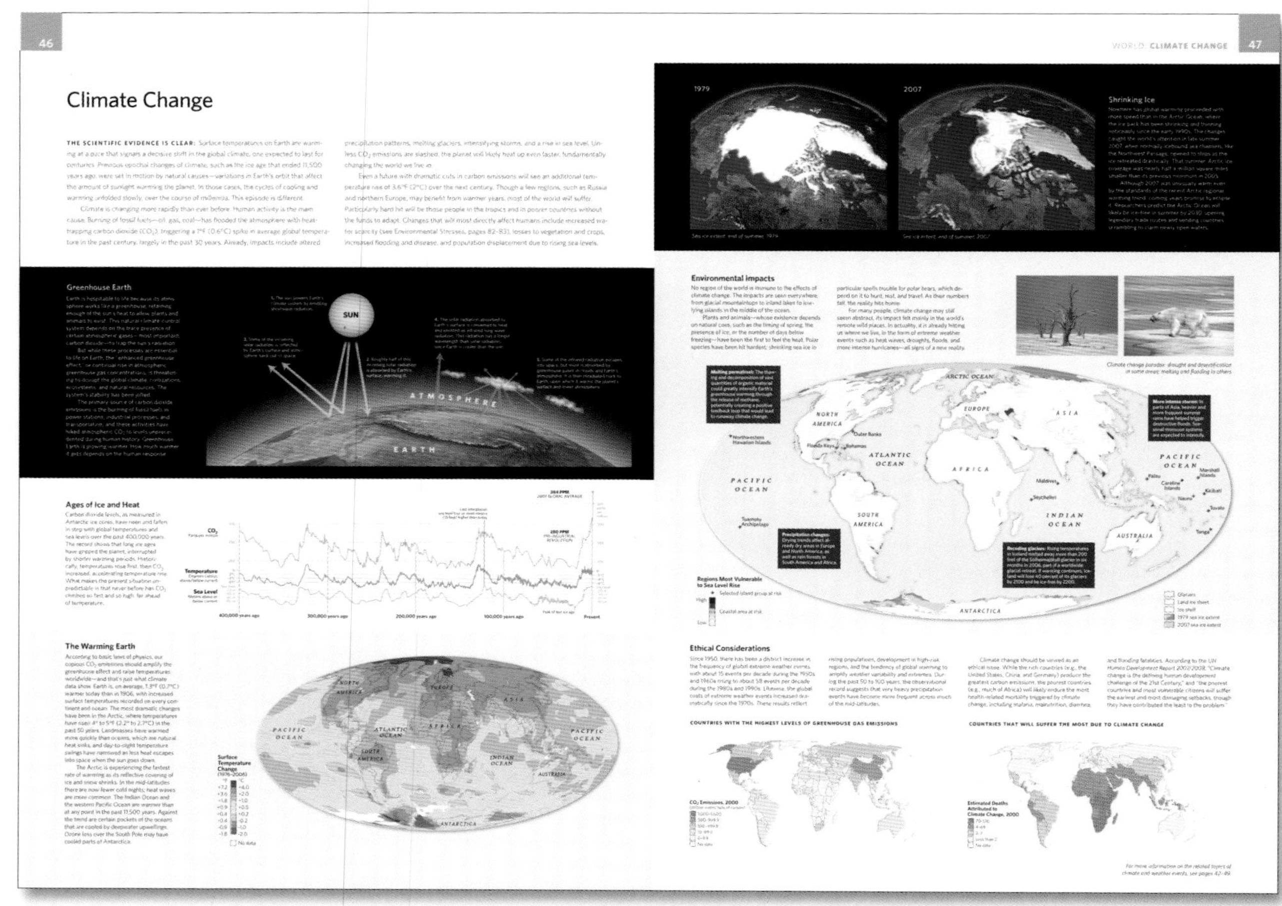
Climate Change

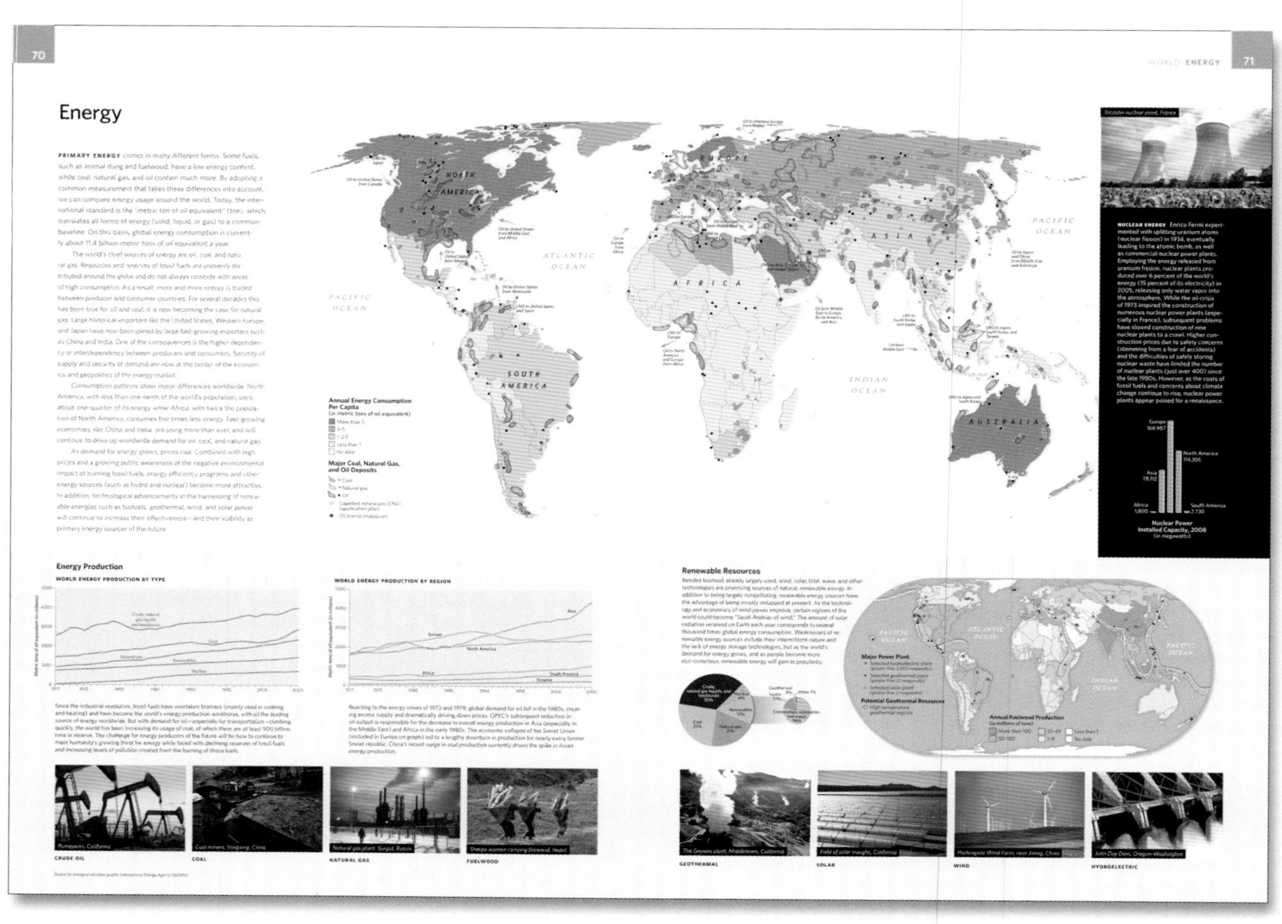
Energy

Physical Maps

Physical maps of the world, the continents, and the ocean floor reveal landforms and vegetation in stunning detail. Painted by relief artists John Bonner and Tibor Tóth, the maps have been edited for accuracy. Although painted maps are human interpretations, these depictions can emphasize subtle features that are sometimes invisible in satellite imagery.

Physical features: Colors and shading illustrate variations in elevation, landforms, and vegetation. Patterns indicate specific landscape features, such as sand, glaciers, and swamps.

Water features: Blue lines indicate rivers; other water bodies are shown as areas of blue. Lighter shading reflects the limits of the continental shelf.

Boundaries and political divisions are shown in red. Dotted lines indicate undefined or disputed boundaries.

Lake Turkana
(L. Rudolf)
Mt. Elgon
4321
GREAT RIFT
Lake
Victoria
Serengeti
Plain
Olduvai G.
Iwembere
Steppe

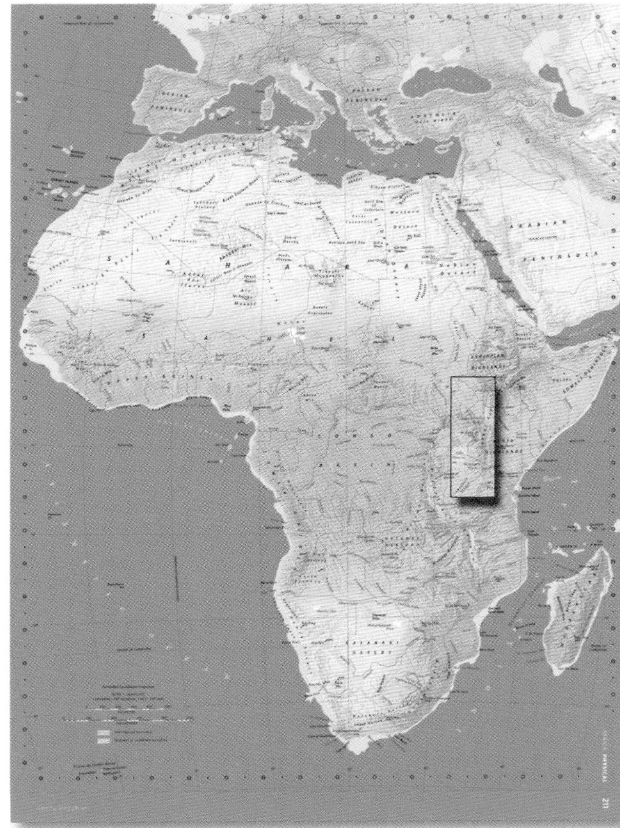

Political Maps

Political maps portray features such as international boundaries, the locations of cities, road networks, and other important elements of the world's human geography. Most index entries are keyed to the political maps, listing the page numbers and then the specific locations on the pages. (See page 312 for details on how to use the index.)

Physical features: Gray relief shading depicts surface features such as mountains, hills, and valleys.

Water features are shown in blue. Solid lines and filled-in areas indicate perennial water features; dashed lines and patterns indicate intermittent features.

Boundaries and political divisions are defined with both lines and colored bands; they vary according to whether a boundary is internal or international (for details, see map symbols key at right).

Cities: The regional political maps that form the bulk of this atlas depict four categories of cities or towns. The largest cities are shown in all capital letters (e.g., LAGOS).

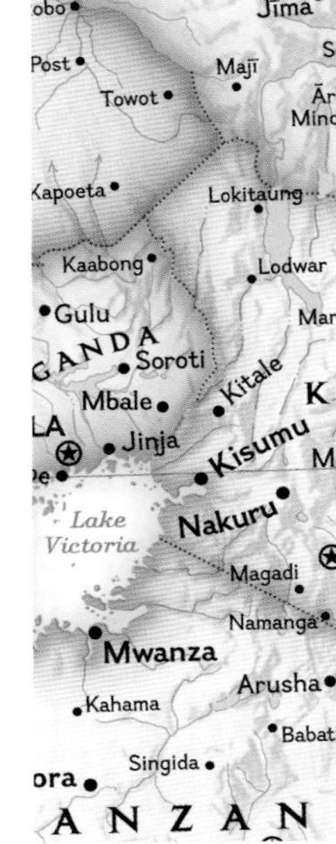
Jima
Towot
Maji
Kapoeta
Lokitaung
Kaabong
Lodwar
Gulu
Soroti
Mbale
Jinja
Kitale
Kisumu
Lake
Victoria
Nakuru
Magadi
Namanga
Mwanza
Arusha
Kahama
Babati
Singida
ANZAN

Regional Maps

This atlas divides the continents into several subregions, each displayed on a two-page spread. Large-scale maps capture the political divisions and major surface features, while accompanying regional thematic maps lend insight into natural and human factors that give character to a region. The maps are surrounded by eye-catching photos and explanatory captions for some of the region's more enchanting places, providing a closer look into the region.

Highway network: Superhighways are shown with a double red line, while other highways use a single red line. When shown, car ferries are depicted as a dashed red line.

World Heritage site photos: Numbered red dots show the locations of the corresponding UNESCO World Heritage Sites pictured on the spread.

Other features of note: Features found on the maps include smaller man-made objects, such as dams, canals, ruins, and other notable sites.

For more details on the regional map spreads, see pages 18–19.

Tarfside
Spittal
of Glenshee
Pitlochry
Forfar
Sidlaw Hills
Dundee
Perth
St. Andrews
Glenrothes
Kirkcaldy
Firth of Forth
Falkirk
Edinburgh
Musselburgh
Penicuik
Motherwell
Galashiels
Selkirk
Hawick
Wanlockhead
Beattock
Thornhill
Dumfries

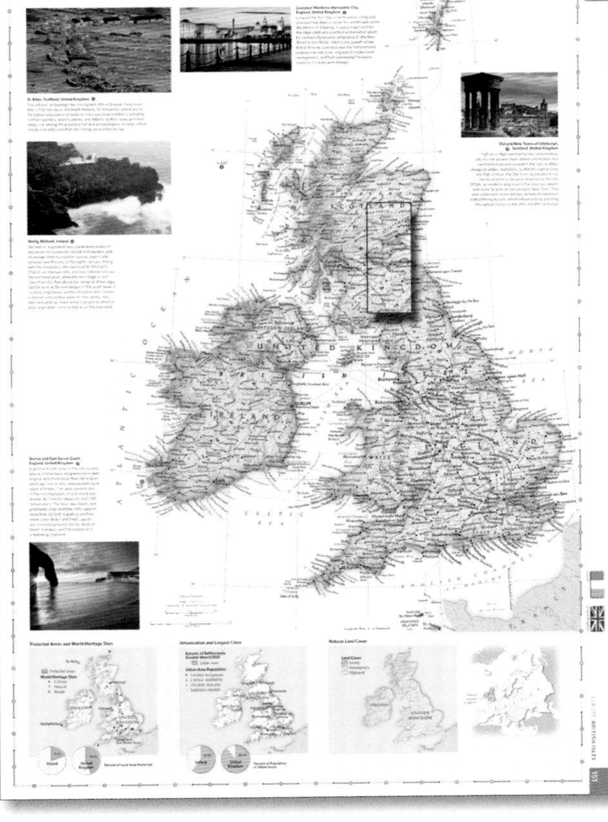

Map Symbols

BOUNDARIES

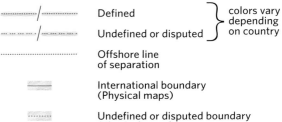

Defined
Undefined or disputed
(colors vary depending on country)
Offshore line of separation
International boundary (Physical maps)
Undefined or disputed boundary (Physical maps)

CITIES

Capitals
Towns

TRANSPORTATION

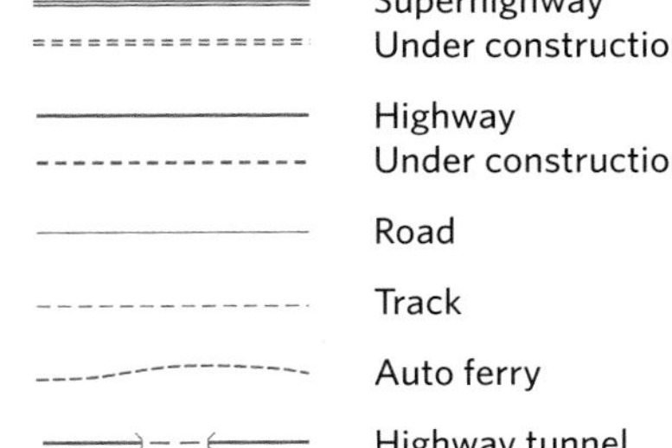
Superhighway
Under construction
Highway
Under construction
Road
Track
Auto ferry
Highway tunnel

WATER FEATURES

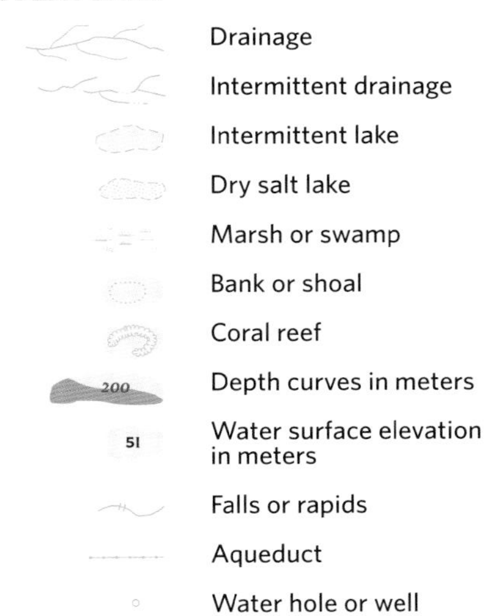
Drainage
Intermittent drainage
Intermittent lake
Dry salt lake
Marsh or swamp
Bank or shoal
Coral reef
200
Depth curves in meters
51
Water surface elevation in meters
Falls or rapids
Aqueduct
Water hole or well

PHYSICAL FEATURES

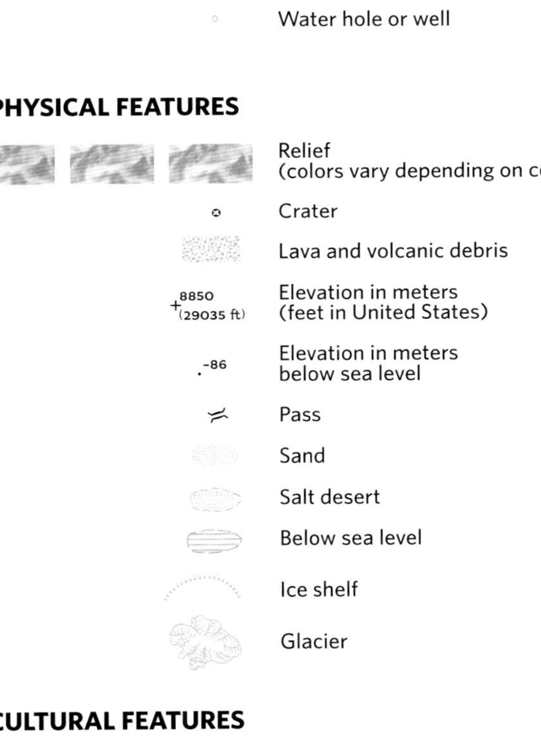
Relief
(colors vary depending on country)
Crater
Lava and volcanic debris
8850
(29035 ft)
Elevation in meters
(feet in United States)
-86
Elevation in meters below sea level
Pass
Sand
Salt desert
Below sea level
Ice shelf
Glacier

CULTURAL FEATURES

Canal
Dam
Wall
Site
Ruin
Antarctic year-round research station
Landing site (Moon and Mars)

"Using This Atlas" is continued on the next page.

Using This Atlas (continued)

THE REGIONAL SPREADS IN THIS ATLAS carve the surface of the planet into smaller areas to allow for more detailed treatment than is reflected in the continental physical and political maps. These regions maximize map scale for as many countries as possible. On many spreads, the map has been rotated 90 degrees, so that north is to the left, taking advantage of the shape of the region in order to enlarge the map and show more detail.

For ease of use, these spreads were designed so that each country is shown in its entirety on only one region. To highlight the places featured within a spread, the country or countries included in the region are illustrated in bright colors and full detail, while the adjacent areas are shown in gray and with less detail. The shape of the region is also repeated in the three thematic maps along the right side of the spread. A header giving the name of the continent, followed by the name of the region as defined for this atlas, is included at the top right of each spread, along with each featured country's national flag.

Priority is usually given to cities and towns on these maps, but other features are included in abundance. Each map has a shaded-relief background to provide a sense of the area's terrain, and many physical features are labeled. Rivers and lakes are shown in detail; highways and major roads are included as well. Other features seen in regional maps include spot elevations, passes, tunnels, ruins, and other notable sites. In addition to the somewhat subjective compilation of places, more-technical information is also included. Latitude and longitude grids are used for geographic reference, and the map's projection and scale are implicitly stated.

A special feature in regional spreads is the inclusion of photographs of certain UNESCO World Heritage sites. (For more information about these sites, including a world map and a complete listing, see pages 92–97.) In addition to being labeled on the Protected Areas and World Heritage Sites thematic maps, the locations of the photographed sites are indicated on the regional maps with corresponding numbered red dots.

By employing the technical aspects of map projections and GIS databases, the artistic coloring and design of the maps, and the visual elements of flags, photos, thematic maps, and pie charts, the regional spreads bring distant parts of Earth together in a compelling, highly visual way. These carefully crafted works of art are also useful references for understanding the world we live in, one region at a time.

Index and grid
Beginning on page 312 is a full index of the more than 40,000 place-names found in this atlas. The edge of each map is marked with letters (in rows) and numbers (in columns), to which the index entries are referenced. As an example, "**Sampit,** *Indonesia* **206 J8**" (see inset section, right) refers to the grid section on page 206 where row J and column 8 meet. More examples and additional details about the index are included on page 312.

Samothrace *see* Samothráki, island, *Gr.* **164 G10**
Samothráki, *Gr.* **164 F10**
Samothráki (Samothrace), island, *Gr.* **164 G10**
Sampa, *Ghana* **221 N15**
Sampacho, *Arg.* **138 H11**
Sampit, *Indonesia* **206 J8**
Sam'po, *N. Korea* **200 D14**
Samp'o, *N. Korea* **200 E11**
Sampwe, *Dem. Rep. of the Congo* **225 J15**
Sam Rayburn Reservoir, *Tex., U.S.* **109 L13**

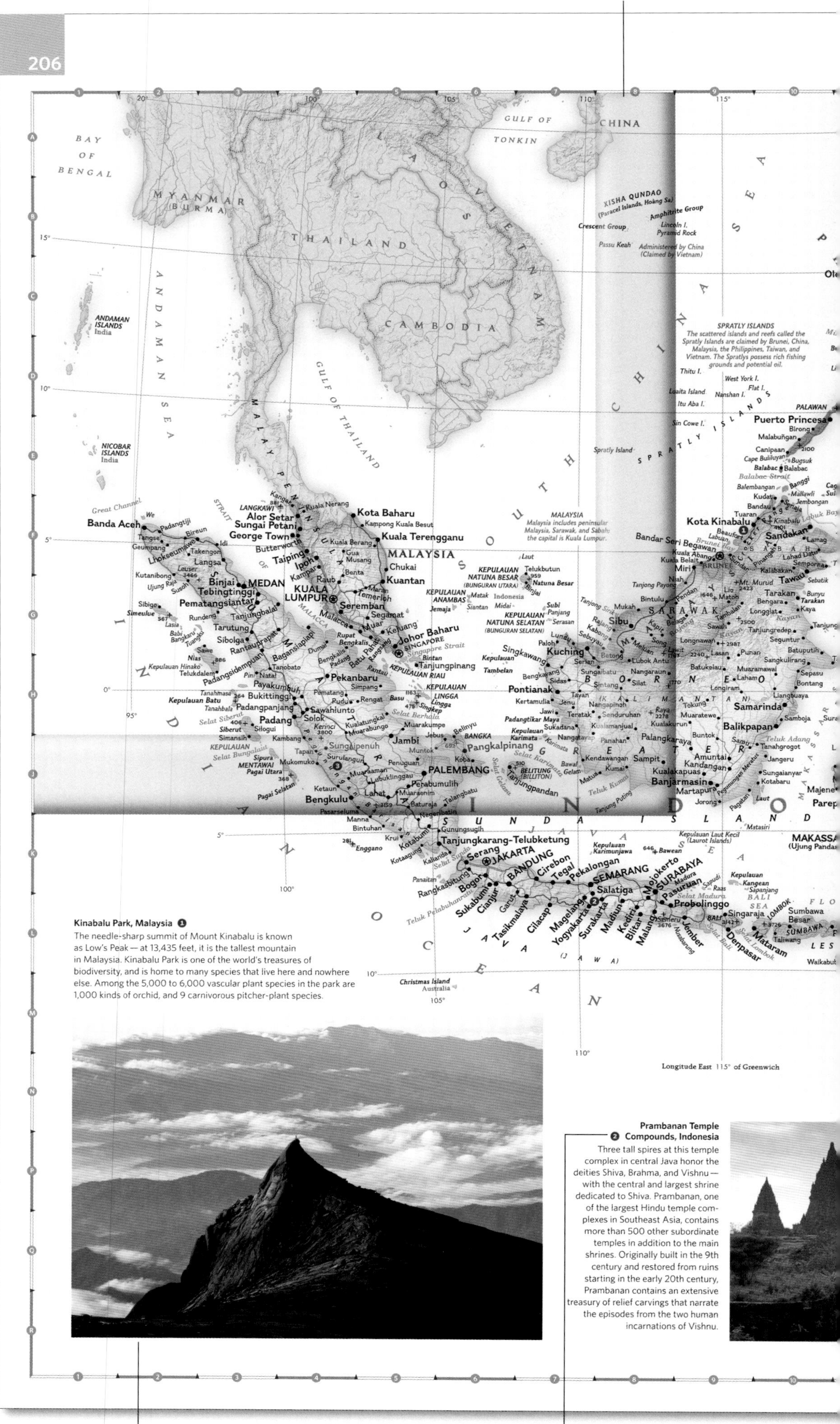

206
BAY OF BENGAL
GULF OF TONKIN
CHINA
MYANMAR (BURMA)
THAILAND
LAOS
VIETNAM
CAMBODIA
ANDAMAN SEA
GULF OF THAILAND
ANDAMAN ISLANDS India
NICOBAR ISLANDS India
SPRATLY ISLANDS
SOUTH CHINA SEA
MALAYSIA
Kota Baharu
Kuala Terengganu
Kuantan
KUALA LUMPUR
MEDAN
George Town
Banda Aceh
Johor Baharu
SINGAPORE
Pekanbaru
Padang
Jambi
PALEMBANG
Bengkulu
Pontianak
Kuching
Sibu
SARAWAK
Kota Kinabalu
Sandakan
Puerto Princesa
Balikpapan
Samarinda
Banjarmasin
Pangkalpinang
Tanjungkarang-Telukbetung
JAKARTA
BANDUNG
SEMARANG
SURABAYA
Denpasar
Mataram
BALI SEA
Christmas Island Australia
INDIAN OCEAN
Longitude East 115° of Greenwich
Kinabalu Park, Malaysia 1
The needle-sharp summit of Mount Kinabalu is known as Low's Peak—at 13,435 feet, it is the tallest mountain in Malaysia. Kinabalu Park is one of the world's treasures of biodiversity, and is home to many species that live here and nowhere else. Among the 5,000 to 6,000 vascular plant species in the park are 1,000 kinds of orchid, and 9 carnivorous pitcher-plant species.
Prambanan Temple Compounds, Indonesia 2
Three tall spires at this temple complex in central Java honor the deities Shiva, Brahma, and Vishnu—with the central and largest shrine dedicated to Shiva. Prambanan, one of the largest Hindu temple complexes in Southeast Asia, contains more than 500 other subordinate temples in addition to the main shrines. Originally built in the 9th century and restored from ruins starting in the early 20th century, Prambanan contains an extensive treasury of relief carvings that narrate the episodes from the two human incarnations of Vishnu.

UNESCO World Heritage site photos
Arranged around the main map on every regional spread in this atlas are several attention-grabbing photographs, depicting some of the UNESCO World Heritage sites within each region. The photos were chosen in order to illustrate the remarkable nature of the World Heritage List, and to highlight the stunning variety of cultural and natural places included within it.

Bullets
The photographed UNESCO World Heritage sites on the pages include numbered red dots next to their names. Each of these sites is plotted on the main map, linking the photos to thei corresponding locations.

Map projections and map scales
Map projections determine how land shapes are distorted when transferred from a sphere (Earth) to a flat piece of paper. Many different projections are used in this atlas—each carefully chosen for a map's particular coverage area and purpose. Scale information indicates the actual Earth distance represented by a given length on a map. Here, map scale is expressed in three ways: as a representative fraction, as a verbal statement, and as a bar scale.

Flags
Sovereign flags for the countries featured on each spread are included at the top of the page.

Page headers
The header on the right side of each spread contains the continent name, followed by the name of the region.

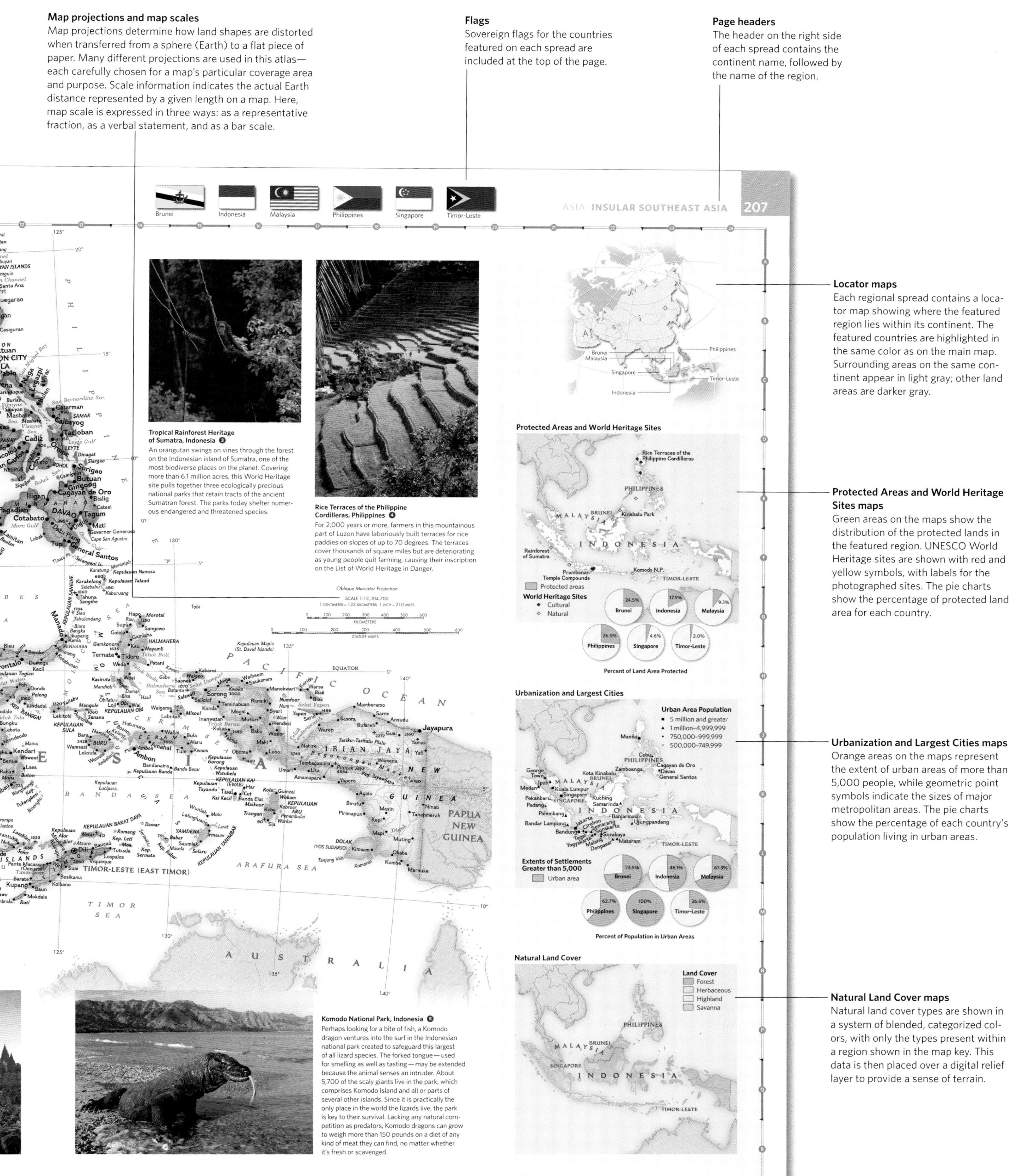

Brunei
Indonesia
Malaysia
Philippines
Singapore
Timor-Leste
ASIA INSULAR SOUTHEAST ASIA 207
Tropical Rainforest Heritage of Sumatra, Indonesia
An orangutan swings on vines through the forest on the Indonesian island of Sumatra, one of the most biodiverse places on the planet. Covering more than 6.1 million acres, this World Heritage site pulls together three ecologically precious national parks that retain tracts of the ancient Sumatran forest. The parks today shelter numerous endangered and threatened species.
Rice Terraces of the Philippine Cordilleras, Philippines
For 2,000 years or more, farmers in this mountainous part of Luzon have laboriously built terraces for rice paddies on slopes of up to 70 degrees. The terraces cover thousands of square miles but are deteriorating as young people quit farming, causing their inscription on the List of World Heritage in Danger.
Oblique Mercator Projection
Protected Areas and World Heritage Sites
Protected areas
World Heritage Sites
Cultural
Natural
Percent of Land Area Protected
Urbanization and Largest Cities
Urban Area Population
5 million and greater
1 million–4,999,999
750,000–999,999
500,000–749,999
Extents of Settlements Greater than 5,000
Urban area
Percent of Population in Urban Areas
Natural Land Cover
Land Cover
Forest
Herbaceous
Highland
Savanna
PACIFIC OCEAN
ARAFURA SEA
TIMOR SEA
AUSTRALIA
PAPUA NEW GUINEA
TIMOR-LESTE (EAST TIMOR)
Komodo National Park, Indonesia
Perhaps looking for a bite of fish, a Komodo dragon ventures into the surf in the Indonesian national park created to safeguard this largest of all lizard species. The forked tongue—used for smelling as well as tasting—may be extended because the animal senses an intruder. About 5,700 of the scaly giants live in the park, which comprises Komodo Island and all or parts of several other islands. Since it is practically the only place in the world the lizards live, the park is key to their survival. Lacking any natural competition as predators, Komodo dragons can grow to weigh more than 150 pounds on a diet of any kind of meat they can find, no matter whether it's fresh or scavenged.

Locator maps
Each regional spread contains a locator map showing where the featured region lies within its continent. The featured countries are highlighted in the same color as on the main map. Surrounding areas on the same continent appear in light gray; other land areas are darker gray.

Protected Areas and World Heritage Sites maps
Green areas on the maps show the distribution of the protected lands in the featured region. UNESCO World Heritage sites are shown with red and yellow symbols, with labels for the photographed sites. The pie charts show the percentage of protected land area for each country.

Urbanization and Largest Cities maps
Orange areas on the maps represent the extent of urban areas of more than 5,000 people, while geometric point symbols indicate the sizes of major metropolitan areas. The pie charts show the percentage of each country's population living in urban areas.

Natural Land Cover maps
Natural land cover types are shown in a system of blended, categorized colors, with only the types present within a region shown in the map key. This data is then placed over a digital relief layer to provide a sense of terrain.

Thematic maps
In combination, the three thematic maps on each regional spread—Protected Areas and World Heritage Sites, Urbanization and Largest Cities, and Natural Land Cover—provide a fascinating overview of the area's cultural and physical geography. Protected Areas and World Heritage Sites maps offer a quick glance at the protected land areas in the region, with pie charts that show which countries are protecting more, or less, of their territory. These maps also serve as locators for the region's UNESCO World Heritage sites. Urbanization and Largest Cities maps indicate where our larger cities and towns are located, and how they merge together, while the graphs indicate which countries' populations are more urban. Natural Land Cover maps highlight the sometimes subtle and sometimes abrupt changes in land cover across Earth's surface.

Like the other planets of the solar system, Earth formed about 4.5 billion years ago, coalescing out of a cloud of dust and gases left swirling in space after the birth of the sun. What sets this rocky planet apart from other known worlds, however, is what happened perhaps a billion years later: the advent life in the form of single-celled organisms. The biosphere that exists today—incredibly rich, amazingly complex, and in some ways quite fragile—is the heritage of this ancient common ancestor of all life.

Earth has been remarkably hospitable to humanity, and our recent rise to dominate the planet like no species before must rank as one of the most momentous chapters in its history. Today, a vast population—approaching seven billion people, with about 15,000 babies born hourly—magnifies the effects of our individual actions. Rising living standards and growing demands for oil, electricity, and automobiles strain finite resources, while reliance on fossil fuels is changing global climate in ways potentially catastrophic for societies and ecosystems. In the face of these challenges is a growing worldwide consensus that humanity must quickly find ways to reduce our impact—aiming not to dominate, but peacefully coexist with the natural world.

World

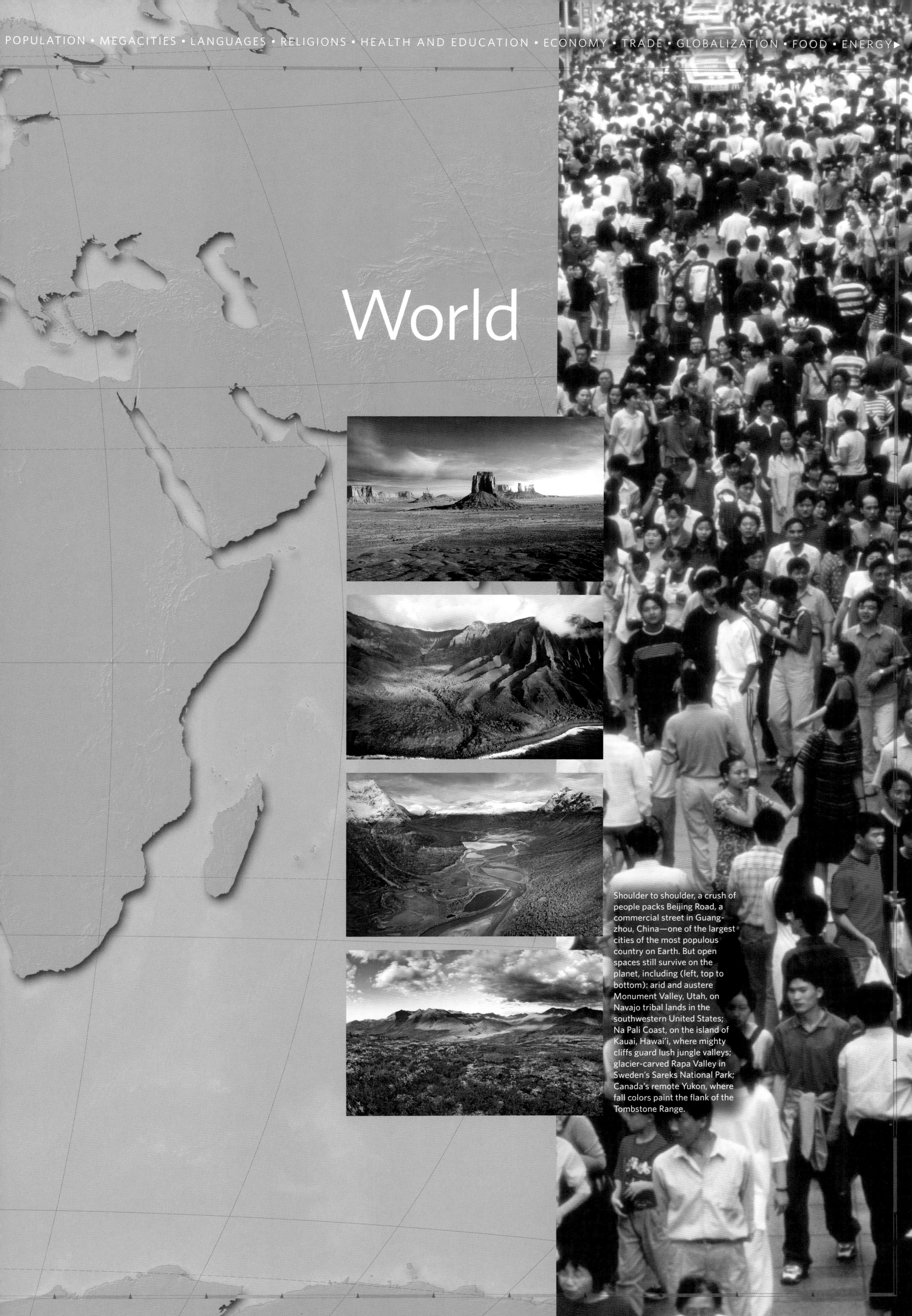

Shoulder to shoulder, a crush of people packs Beijing Road, a commercial street in Guangzhou, China—one of the largest cities of the most populous country on Earth. But open spaces still survive on the planet, including (left, top to bottom): arid and austere Monument Valley, Utah, on Navajo tribal lands in the southwestern United States; Na Pali Coast, on the island of Kauai, Hawai'i, where mighty cliffs guard lush jungle valleys; glacier-carved Rapa Valley in Sweden's Sareks National Park; Canada's remote Yukon, where fall colors paint the flank of the Tombstone Range.

ARCTIC
LOMONOSOV RIDGE
MAKAROV BASIN
MENDELEYEV PLAIN
CANADA BASIN
CHUKCHI PLAIN
CHUKCHI PLATEAU
NORTHWIND ESCARPMENT
CANADA PLAIN
QUEEN ELIZABETH ISLANDS
GREENLAND
Baffin Bay
Lincoln Sea
SIBERIA
ALASKA
ARCTIC CIRCLE
BERING SEA
Beaufort Sea
Brooks Range
North Slope
Aleutian Islands
ALEUTIAN TRENCH
Alexander Archipelago
Queen Charlotte Is.
Vancouver Island
ROCKY MOUNTAINS
Great Plains
Canadian Shield
Hudson Bay
LABRADOR SEA
NORTH AMERICA
NORTH ATLANTIC OCEAN
NORTH PACIFIC
NORTHEAST PACIFIC BASIN
MENDOCINO FRACTURE ZONE
PIONEER FRACTURE ZONE
MURRAY FRACTURE ZONE
MOLOKAI FRACTURE ZONE
CLARION FRACTURE ZONE
CLIPPERTON FRACTURE ZONE
GALÁPAGOS FRACTURE ZONE
MARQUESAS FRACTURE ZONE
Appalachian Mountains
Coastal Plain
GULF OF MEXICO
MEXICO BASIN
CARIBBEAN SEA
COLOMBIAN BASIN
Greater Antilles
Lesser Antilles
PUERTO RICO TRENCH
CAYMAN TRENCH
CENTRAL AMERICA
MIDDLE AMERICA TRENCH
NORTH AMERICAN BASIN
BERMUDA RISE
HATTERAS PLAIN
SOHM PLAIN
MID-ATLANTIC RIDGE
TROPIC OF CANCER
EQUATOR
TROPIC OF CAPRICORN
ANTARCTIC CIRCLE
OCEAN
CENTRAL PACIFIC BASIN
GUATEMALA BASIN
PANAMA BASIN
Galápagos Islands
Amazon Basin
SOUTH AMERICA
ANDES
Brazilian Highlands
PERU BASIN
PERU-CHILE TRENCH
CHILE BASIN
EAST PACIFIC RISE
SOUTH PACIFIC OCEAN
Tuamotu Archipelago
Society Islands
SOUTHWEST PACIFIC BASIN
TONGA TRENCH
KERMADEC TRENCH
LOUISVILLE RIDGE
CHATHAM RISE
CHALLENGER FRACTURE ZONE
VALDIVIA FRACTURE ZONE
MENARD FRACTURE ZONE
ELTANIN FRACTURE ZONE
HEEZEN FRACTURE ZONE
UDINTSEV FRACTURE ZONE
PACIFIC-ANTARCTIC RIDGE
SOUTHEAST PACIFIC BASIN
ARGENTINE PLAIN
BRAZIL BASIN
SOUTH ATLANTIC OCEAN
RIO GRANDE RISE
FALKLAND PLATEAU
Scotia Sea
Drake Passage
SOUTH SANDWICH TRENCH
BELLINGSHAUSEN PLAIN
AMUNDSEN PLAIN
WEDDELL SEA
WEDDELL PLAIN
ANTARCTIC PENINSULA
Ellsworth Land
Marie Byrd Land
Ross Sea
TRANSANTARCTIC MOUNTAINS
ANTAR
Longitude West of Greenwich

Winkel Tripel Projection, Central Meridian 0°
SCALE 1:71,849,000
1 CENTIMETER = 718 KILOMETERS; 1 INCH = 1,134 MILES AT THE EQUATOR
KILOMETERS
STATUTE MILES

ARCTIC
NORTH
PACIFIC
OCEAN
NORTH
ATLANTIC
OCEAN
SOUTH
PACIFIC
OCEAN
SOUTH
ATLANTIC
OCEAN
CANADA
UNITED STATES
MEXICO
BRAZIL
GREENLAND
(KALAALLIT NUNAAT)
Denmark
ALASKA
U.S.
RUSSIA
CUBA
HAITI
DOMINICAN REP.
JAMAICA
BAHAMAS
BELIZE
GUATEMALA
HONDURAS
EL SALVADOR
NICARAGUA
COSTA RICA
PANAMA
COLOMBIA
VENEZUELA
GUYANA
SURINAME
FRENCH GUIANA
France
ECUADOR
PERU
BOLIVIA
PARAGUAY
CHILE
ARGENTINA
URUGUAY
ICELAND
PORTUGAL
MOROCCO
WESTERN SAHARA
Morocco
MAURITANIA
SENEGAL
GAMBIA
GUINEA-BISSAU
GUINEA
SIERRA LEONE
LIBERIA
CAPE VERDE
IRELAND
UNITED KINGDOM
QUEEN ELIZABETH ISLANDS
ELLESMERE ISLAND
PARRY ISLANDS
VICTORIA ISLAND
BAFFIN ISLAND
BAFFIN BAY
DAVIS STRAIT
Denmark Strait
Knud Rasmussen Land
BEAUFORT SEA
BERING SEA
HUDSON BAY
LABRADOR SEA
LABRADOR
ISLAND OF NEWFOUNDLAND
GULF OF MEXICO
CARIBBEAN SEA
GREATER ANTILLES
LESSER ANTILLES
ST. KITTS AND NEVIS
ANTIGUA AND BARBUDA
DOMINICA
ST. LUCIA
BARBADOS
ST. VINCENT AND THE GRENADINES
GRENADA
TRINIDAD AND TOBAGO
SCOTIA SEA
WEDDELL SEA
ROSS SEA
ANTARCTIC PENINSULA
ELLSWORTH LAND
MARIE BYRD LAND
TRANSANTARCTIC MOUNTAINS
ANTARCTICA
Drake Passage
ROCKY MOUNTAINS
ANDES
Amazon
PAMPAS
PATAGONIA
KIRIBATI
POLYNESIA
LINE ISLANDS
HAWAI'I
United States
FRENCH POLYNESIA
France
TUAMOTU ARCHIPELAGO
SOCIETY IS.
AUSTRAL ISLANDS (TUBUAI ISLANDS)
COOK ISLANDS
New Zealand
MARQUESAS ISLANDS
France
PHOENIX ISLANDS
TOKELAU
N.Z.
AMERICAN SAMOA
U.S.
SAMOA
TONGA
Îles Wallis
France
Fiji Islands
Lau Group
Niue
N.Z.
Kermadec Islands
N.Z.
Chatham Is.
N.Z.
Pitcairn Islands
United Kingdom
Ducie Island
Rapa
Îles Gambier
Tubuai
Rarotonga
Nuku'alofa
Papeete
Tahiti
Rangiroa
Apia
Pago Pago
Midway Is.
U.S.
Johnston Atoll
U.S.
Palmyra Atoll
U.S.
Kiritimati (Christmas I.)
Howland Island
Baker Island
U.S.
Jarvis I.
U.S.
Kaua'i
Honolulu
Maui
Hilo
Hawai'i
Aleutian Islands
Alaska Peninsula
Cold Bay
Kodiak
Alexander Archipelago
Queen Charlotte Islands
Vancouver I.
Wrangel I.
Date Line
Monday
Sunday
ARCTIC CIRCLE
ANTARCTIC CIRCLE
TROPIC OF CANCER
TROPIC OF CAPRICORN
EQUATOR
North Magnetic Pole 2008
Longitude West of Greenwich
Brooks Range
Barrow
Nome
Bethel
Anchorage
Fairbanks
Mt. McKinley (Denali) 6194 (20320 ft)
Valdez
Whitehorse
Skagway
Juneau
Inuvik
Great Bear Lake
Déline
Great Slave Lake
Yellowknife
Hay River
Fort Smith
Fort St. John
Peace River
Fort McMurray
Prince Rupert
Prince George
Edmonton
Calgary
Saskatoon
Regina
Winnipeg
Lake Winnipeg
Vancouver
Victoria
Seattle
Portland
Eugene
Boise
Helena
Billings
Fargo
Minneapolis
Milwaukee
Chicago
Detroit
Toronto
Ottawa
Montréal
Québec
Timmins
Thunder Bay
Chibougamau
Fort Albany
Chisasibi
Fort Severn
Thompson
Sanikiluaq
Kuujjuaq
Nain
Labrador City
Sept-Îles
St. John's
St.-Pierre & Miquelon
France
Charlottetown
Halifax
Boston
New York
Philadelphia
Washington
Buffalo
Columbus
Indianapolis
Omaha
Kansas City
Denver
Salt Lake City
Reno
Sacramento
San Francisco
Las Vegas
Los Angeles
San Diego
Tijuana
Mexicali
Phoenix
Albuquerque
Santa Fe
Oklahoma City
Tulsa
Dallas
Austin
San Antonio
Houston
New Orleans
Memphis
Nashville
Atlanta
Birmingham
Charlotte
Jacksonville
Orlando
Tampa
Miami
El Paso
Ciudad Juárez
Chihuahua
Nuevo Laredo
Laredo
Monterrey
Mazatlán
Tampico
Guadalajara
Mexico City
Puebla
Veracruz
Mérida
Cancún
Acapulco
Tuxtla Gutiérrez
Baja California
Yucatán
Mississippi
Great Plains
Resolute
Cambridge Bay
Taloyoak
Bathurst Inlet
Pond Inlet
Igloolik
Qaanaaq (Thule)
Upernavik
Nuuk (Godthåb)
Narsarsuaq
Reykjavík
Iqaluit
Chesterfield Inlet
Whale Cove
Arviat
Faroe Is.
Denmark
Dublin
Lisbon
Madeira Islands
Portugal
Azores (Açores)
Portugal
Rabat
Casablanca
Marrakech
Canary Islands (Islas Canarias)
Spain
Santa Cruz
Laayoune
Fdérik
Atar
Cap Barbas
Nouakchott
Dakar
Banjul
Bissau
Conakry
Freetown
Monrovia
Praia
Bermuda Islands
U.K.
Turks and Caicos Is.
U.K.
Havana
Cayman Is.
U.K.
Kingston
Port-au-Prince
Santo Domingo
San Juan
PUERTO RICO
U.S.
Virgin Is.
U.S. & U.K.
Guadeloupe France
Martinique France
Neth. Curaçao
Neth. Aruba
Port-of-Spain
Belmopan
Guatemala City
San Salvador
Tegucigalpa
Managua
San José
Panama City
Barranquilla
Cartagena
Maracaibo
Caracas
Mérida
Medellín
Bogotá
Cali
Quito
Guayaquil
Cuenca
Puerto Ayacucho
Georgetown
Paramaribo
Cayenne
Isla del Coco
Costa Rica
Isla de Malpelo
Colombia
Clipperton
France
Isla Guadalupe
Mexico
Islas Revillagigedo
Mexico
Isla Clarión
GALÁPAGOS ISLANDS (ARCHIPIÉLAGO DE COLÓN)
Ecuador
Boa Vista
Macapá
Belém
São Luís
Fortaleza
Natal
Recife
Manaus
Santarém
Itaituba
Óbidos
Barcelos
Mitú
Leticia
Iquitos
Piura
Trujillo
Eirunepé
Manicoré
Marabá
Caxias
Juàzeiro do Norte
Carolina
Prainha
Cruzeiro do Sul
Rio Branco
Ji-Paraná (Rondônia)
Guajará Mirim
Vilhena
Porangatu
Feira de Santana
Aracaju
Salvador (Bahia)
Ilhéus
Peixe
Lima
Ayacucho
Ica
Cusco
Trinidad
La Paz
Cuiabá
Cáceres
Brasília
Goiânia
Montes Claros
Tacna
Arica
Cochabamba
Sucre
Santa Cruz
Corumbá
Campo Grande
Belo Horizonte
Vitória
Iquique
Antofagasta
San Salvador de Jujuy
Asunción
Bauru
São Paulo
Rio de Janeiro
Curitiba
Florianópolis
San Miguel de Tucumán
Salta
Posadas
Porto Alegre
La Rioja
Córdoba
Pelotas
Salto
Montevideo
Buenos Aires
Mar del Plata
Bahía Blanca
Mendoza
Rio Cuarto
Santa Rosa
Neuquén
Viedma
Peninsula Valdés
Puerto Madryn
Comodoro Rivadavia
Puerto Deseado
Cerro Aconcagua 6960 (22834 ft)
Santiago
Concepción
Valdivia
Puerto Montt
Balmaceda
Península de Taitao
Río Gallegos
Punta Arenas
Ushuaia
TIERRA DEL FUEGO
Stanley
FALKLAND ISLANDS (ISLAS MALVINAS)
U.K.
Islas Diego Ramírez
Chile
Archipiélago Juan Fernández
Chile
Isla San Félix
Chile
Isla San Ambrosio
Isla Sala y Gómez
Chile
Easter Island (Isla de Pascua)
Chile
St. Peter and St. Paul Rocks
Brazil
Arquipélago de Fernando de Noronha
Brazil
Ascension
U.K.
Ilha de Trindade
Ilhas Martin Vaz
Brazil
Tristan da Cunha Group
U.K.
Shag Rocks
U.K.
South Georgia
U.K.
South Sandwich Islands
U.K.
S. Orkney Is.
S. Shetland Is.
Scott I.
Berkner Island
Vinson Massif 4897 (16067 ft)
180°
160°
140°
120°
100°
80°
60°
40°
20°
90°
70°
60°
50°
40°
30°
20°
10°
0°
10°
20°
30°
40°
50°
60°
70°
80°
90°

Longitude East of Greenwich
O C E A N
FRANZ JOSEF LAND
Russia
SEVERNAYA ZEMLYA
NEW SIBERIAN IS.
LAPTEV SEA
EAST SIBERIAN SEA
BARENTS SEA
KARA SEA
NOVAYA ZEMLYA
Spitsbergen
SVALBARD
Norway
Nordaustlandet
ARCTIC CIRCLE
R U S S I A
Murmansk
Arkhangel'sk
FINLAND
Helsinki
St. Petersburg
Moscow
Nizhniy Novgorod
Kazan'
Perm'
Yekaterinburg
Omsk
Novosibirsk
Chelyabinsk
Ufa
Samara
Volgograd
Rostov
Noril'sk
Yakutsk
Magadan
Irkutsk
Chita
Ulan Ude
Krasnoyarsk
Surgut
Tomsk
Novokuznetsk
Barnaul
Khabarovsk
Vladivostok
BERING SEA
KAMCHATKA PENINSULA
Petropavlovsk Kamchatskiy
SEA OF OKHOTSK
SAKHALIN
Kuril Islands
Aleutian Islands U.S.
Date Line
Sunday Monday
Stockholm
Oslo
Tallinn
ESTONIA
LATVIA
Riga
LITHUANIA
Vilnius
Minsk
BELARUS
POLAND
Warsaw
Berlin
GERMANY
Hamburg
Amsterdam
Prague
CZECH REP.
Vienna
Munich
Budapest
SLOVAKIA
Bratislava
HUNG.
ROMANIA
Bucharest
MOLDOVA
Chişinău
UKRAINE
Kiev
Belgrade
Sofia
BULG.
ITALY
Rome
Istanbul
Ankara
T U R K E Y
Izmir
Adana
BLACK SEA
CASPIAN SEA
GEORGIA
T'bilisi
ARM.
Yerevan
AZERB.
Baku
Athens
GREECE
K A Z A K H S T A N
Astana
Almaty
Bishkek
KYRGYZSTAN
Tashkent
UZBEKISTAN
TURKMENISTAN
Ashgabat
TAJIKISTAN
Dushanbe
AFGHANISTAN
Kabul
Mashhad
Tehran
I R A N
Eşfahān
Shīrāz
IRAQ
Baghdad
SYRIA
Damascus
LEB.
Beirut
CYPRUS
Nicosia
ISRAEL
Jerusalem
Amman
JORDAN
KUWAIT
Kuwait City
BAHRAIN
QATAR
Doha
Riyadh
S A U D I A R A B I A
Mecca
Jeddah
UNITED ARAB EMIRATES
Abu Dhabi
Dubai
Muscat
OMAN
Y E M E N
Sanaa
Aden
Gulf of Aden
Socotra Yemen
PAKISTAN
Islamabad
Lahore
Faisalabad
Karachi
Quetta
I N D I A
New Delhi
Delhi
Jaipur
Kanpur
Ahmadabad
Bhopal
Vadodara
Surat
Indore
Nagpur
Kolkata (Calcutta)
Mumbai (Bombay)
Pune
Hyderabad
Bangalore
Chennai (Madras)
Mysore
Kochi
Madurai
Thiruvananthapuram
Visakhapatnam
NEPAL
Kathmandu
Mt. Everest
BHUTAN
Thimphu
BANGLADESH
Dhaka
Chittagong
SRI LANKA
Colombo
Kandy
Jaffna
MALDIVES
Male
Maldive Islands
LAKSHADWEEP India
ANDAMAN ISLANDS India
NICOBAR ISLANDS India
ARABIAN SEA
BAY OF BENGAL
MONGOLIA
Ulaanbaatar
GOBI
C H I N A
Beijing
Tianjin
Shanghai
Nanjing
Wuhan
Chongqing
Chengdu
Xi'an
Lanzhou
Hangzhou
Guangzhou
Hong Kong
Macau
Shenyang
Harbin
Changchun
Jilin
Qiqihar
Dalian
Qingdao
Jinan
Taiyuan
Zhengzhou
Changsha
Nanchang
Fuzhou
Xiamen
Kunming
Guiyang
Nanning
Ürümqi
Lhasa
TIBET
Taklimakan Desert
KUNLUN MOUNTAINS
TAIWAN
Taipei
Kaohsiung
NORTH KOREA
Pyongyang
SOUTH KOREA
Seoul
Busan
J A P A N
Tokyo
Yokohama
Osaka
Kyoto
Sapporo
Hiroshima
Fukuoka
HOKKAIDO
HONSHU
KYUSHU
SHIKOKU
SEA OF JAPAN (EAST SEA)
YELLOW SEA
EAST CHINA SEA
MYANMAR (BURMA)
Yangon (Rangoon)
Mandalay
Nay Pyi Taw
LAOS
Vientiane
THAILAND
Bangkok
CAMBODIA
Phnom Penh
VIETNAM
Hanoi
Haiphong
Ho Chi Minh City
HAINAN
Paracel Is.
Spratly Islands
SOUTH CHINA SEA
PHILIPPINES
Manila
Quezon City
Cebu
Davao
LUZON
MINDANAO
PHILIPPINE SEA
MALAYSIA
Kuala Lumpur
SINGAPORE
BRUNEI
Bandar Seri Begawan
SABAH
SARAWAK
BORNEO
Medan
Padang
I N D O N E S I A
Jakarta
Bandung
Semarang
Surabaya
Yogyakarta
Palembang
Makassar
Balikpapan
Pontianak
Manado
Ambon
Jayapura
Denpasar
TIMOR-LESTE (EAST TIMOR)
Dili
Kupang
GREATER SUNDA ISLANDS
LESSER SUNDA ISLANDS
Java Sea
PALAU
Melekeok
FEDERATED STATES OF MICRONESIA
CAROLINE ISLANDS
NORTHERN MARIANA ISLANDS U.S.
Saipan
Guam U.S.
MARSHALL ISLANDS
Majuro
KIRIBATI
Tarawa
NAURU
EQUATOR
PAPUA NEW GUINEA
Port Moresby
NEW GUINEA
BISMARCK ARCH.
New Britain
New Ireland
SOLOMON ISLANDS
Honiara
TUVALU
Funafuti
VANUATU
Port-Vila
FIJI ISLANDS
Suva
New Caledonia France
Nouméa
Wake Island U.S.
TROPIC OF CANCER
NORTH PACIFIC OCEAN
SOUTH PACIFIC OCEAN
TROPIC OF CAPRICORN
AUSTRALIA
Perth
Adelaide
Melbourne
Sydney
Canberra
Brisbane
Darwin
Alice Springs
Townsville
Cairns
Hobart
TASMANIA
Great Sandy Desert
Great Victoria Desert
Simpson Desert
Great Australian Bight
Arafura Sea
Coral Sea
TASMAN SEA
Lord Howe I. Ball's Pyramid Australia
Norfolk Island Australia
NEW ZEALAND
NORTH ISLAND
SOUTH ISLAND
Auckland
Hamilton
Wellington
Christchurch
Dunedin
I N D I A N O C E A N
Chagos Archipelago (Oil Islands)
Diego Garcia
British Indian Ocean Territory
Christmas I. Australia
Cocos (Keeling) Islands Australia
Île Amsterdam France
Prince Edward Islands South Africa
Crozet Islands France
Kerguelen Islands France
McDonald Is. Heard Island Australia
Shag I.
Auckland Is. N.Z.
Macquarie I. Australia
SEYCHELLES
Victoria
COMOROS
Moroni
MADAGASCAR
Antananarivo
MAURITIUS
Port Louis
Réunion France
St.-Denis
Rodrigues Mauritius
EGYPT
Cairo
Alexandria
Aswān
LIBYA
Tripoli
Benghazi
TUNISIA
Tunis
MALTA
SUDAN
Khartoum
Omdurman
Port Sudan
El Obeid
SOUTH SUDAN
Juba
ERITREA
Asmara
DJIBOUTI
Djibouti
ETHIOPIA
Addis Ababa
SOMALILAND
Hargeysa
SOMALIA
Mogadishu
KENYA
Nairobi
Mombasa
UGANDA
Kampala
RWANDA
Kigali
BURUNDI
Bujumbura
TANZANIA
Dodoma
Dar es Salaam
Zanzibar
Kilimanjaro 5895 (19340 ft)
CHAD
N'Djamena
NIGER
NIGERIA
Abuja
Kano
CAMEROON
Yaoundé
CENTRAL AFRICAN REPUBLIC
Bangui
GABON
Libreville
CONGO
Brazzaville
DEMOCRATIC REPUBLIC OF THE CONGO
Kinshasa
ANGOLA
Luanda
CABINDA
ZAMBIA
Lusaka
MALAWI
Lilongwe
MOZAMBIQUE
Maputo
Beira
ZIMBABWE
Harare
Bulawayo
BOTSWANA
Gaborone
NAMIBIA
Windhoek
SOUTH AFRICA
Pretoria
Johannesburg
Cape Town
Port Elizabeth
East London
Durban
SWAZILAND
Mbabane
LESOTHO
Maseru
Kalahari Desert
Mozambique Chan.
ANTARCTIC CIRCLE
ENDERBY LAND
QUEEN MAUD LAND
WILKES LAND
TRANSANTARCTIC MOUNTAINS
ROSS SEA
Ross Ice Shelf
Amery Ice Shelf
Shackleton Ice Shelf
West Ice Shelf
Riiser-Larsen Peninsula
South Magnetic Pole 2008
Balleny Islands
Winkel Tripel Projection, Central Meridian 0°
SCALE 1:71,849,000
1 CENTIMETER = 718 KILOMETERS; 1 INCH = 1,134 MILES AT THE EQUATOR
0 500 1000 1500 2000 2500
KILOMETERS
0 500 1000 1500 2000 2500
STATUTE MILES
International boundaries and disputed territories, where scale permits, reflect de facto status at the time of publication.

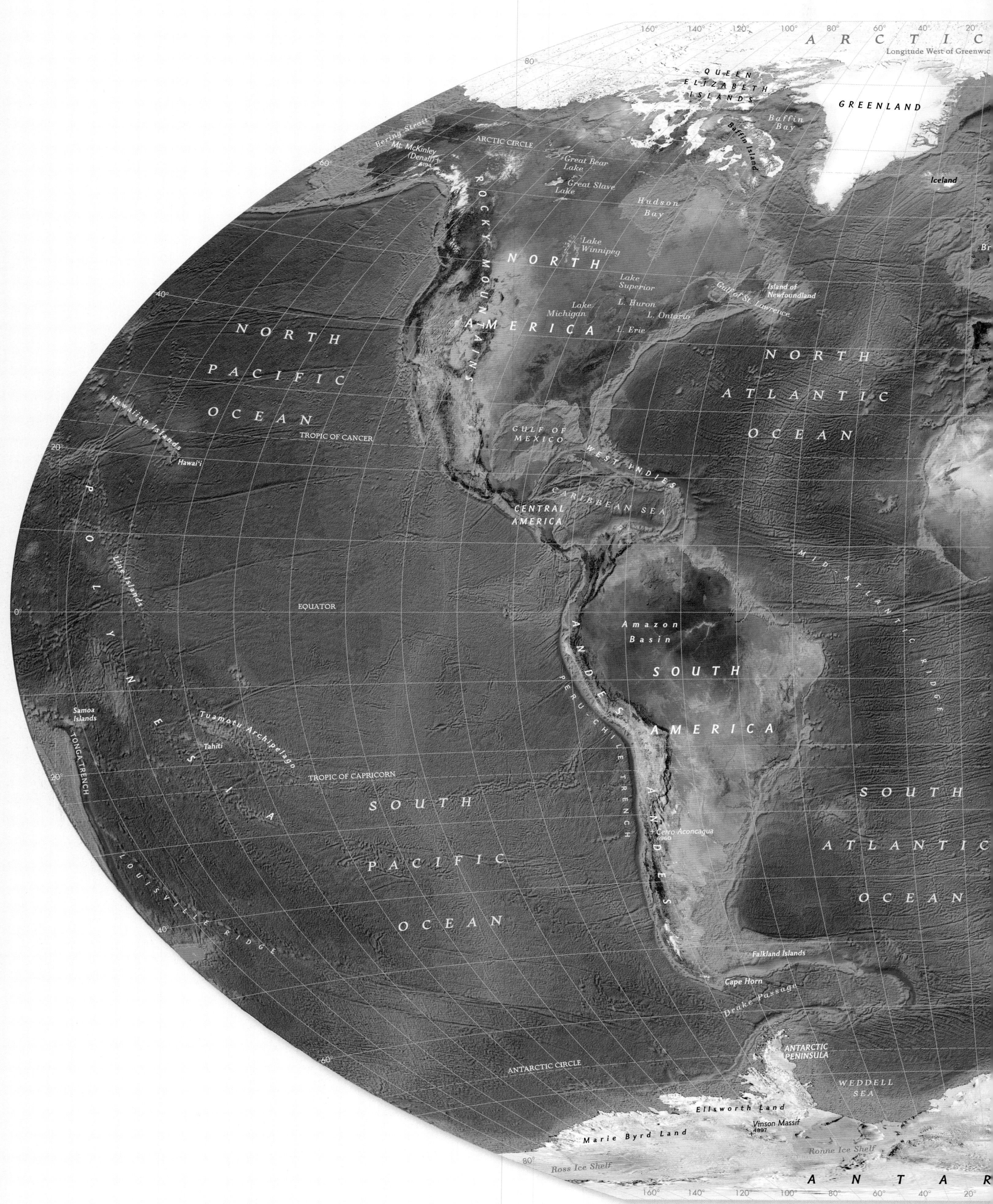
ARCTIC
Longitude West of Greenwich
QUEEN ELIZABETH ISLANDS
GREENLAND
Baffin Bay
Baffin Island
Iceland
Bering Strait
ARCTIC CIRCLE
Mt. McKinley (Denali)
6194
Great Bear Lake
Great Slave Lake
Hudson Bay
ROCKY MOUNTAINS
Lake Winnipeg
NORTH AMERICA
Lake Superior
Island of Newfoundland
Gulf of St. Lawrence
Lake Michigan
L. Huron
L. Ontario
L. Erie
NORTH PACIFIC OCEAN
NORTH ATLANTIC OCEAN
Hawaiian Islands
Hawai'i
TROPIC OF CANCER
GULF OF MEXICO
WEST INDIES
CARIBBEAN SEA
CENTRAL AMERICA
POLYNESIA
Line Islands
MID-ATLANTIC RIDGE
EQUATOR
Amazon Basin
ANDES
SOUTH AMERICA
PERU-CHILE TRENCH
Samoa Islands
TONGA TRENCH
Tuamotu Archipelago
Tahiti
TROPIC OF CAPRICORN
SOUTH PACIFIC OCEAN
SOUTH ATLANTIC OCEAN
Cerro Aconcagua
6960
LOUISVILLE RIDGE
Falkland Islands
Cape Horn
Drake Passage
ANTARCTIC PENINSULA
ANTARCTIC CIRCLE
WEDDELL SEA
Ellsworth Land
Vinson Massif
4897
Marie Byrd Land
Ronne Ice Shelf
Ross Ice Shelf
ANTAR

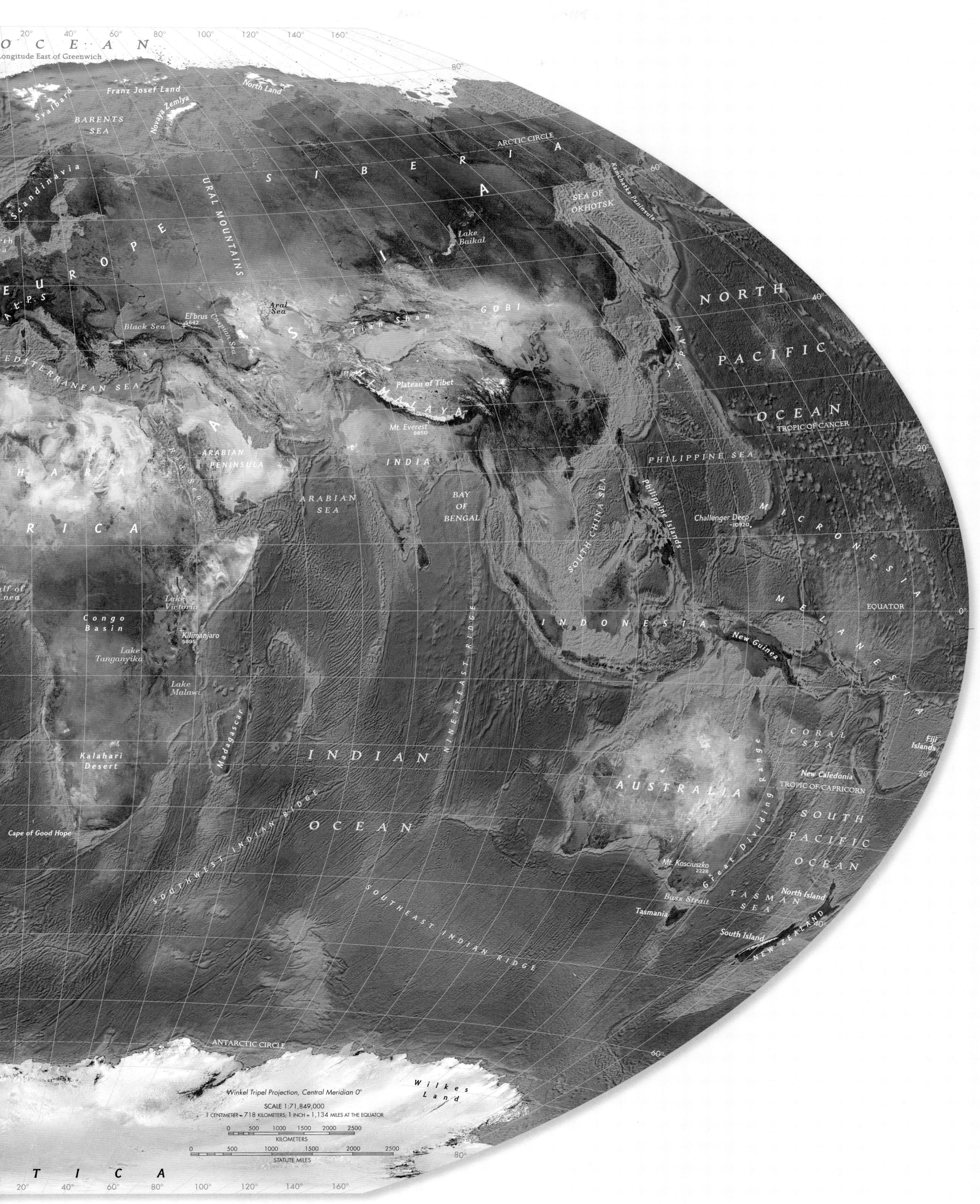
OCEAN
Longitude East of Greenwich
Franz Josef Land
North Land
Svalbard
BARENTS SEA
Novaya Zemlya
ARCTIC CIRCLE
SIBERIA
Scandinavia
URAL MOUNTAINS
SEA OF OKHOTSK
Kamchatka Peninsula
Lake Baikal
EUROPE
ASIA
ALPS
NORTH PACIFIC OCEAN
Aral Sea
El'brus 5642
Caspian Sea
Black Sea
GOBI
Tian Shan
JAPAN
MEDITERRANEAN SEA
HIMALAYA
Plateau of Tibet
Mt. Everest 8850
TROPIC OF CANCER
ARABIAN PENINSULA
Red Sea
INDIA
PHILIPPINE SEA
SAHARA
ARABIAN SEA
BAY OF BENGAL
SOUTH CHINA SEA
Philippine Islands
Challenger Deep -10920
MICRONESIA
AFRICA
Gulf of Guinea
Lake Victoria
Congo Basin
Kilimanjaro 5895
EQUATOR
INDONESIA
NINETYEAST RIDGE
New Guinea
MELANESIA
Lake Tanganyika
Lake Malawi
Madagascar
CORAL SEA
Fiji Islands
Kalahari Desert
INDIAN OCEAN
AUSTRALIA
Great Dividing Range
New Caledonia
TROPIC OF CAPRICORN
Cape of Good Hope
SOUTHWEST INDIAN RIDGE
SOUTH PACIFIC OCEAN
Mt. Kosciuszko 2228
Bass Strait
TASMAN SEA
North Island
Tasmania
SOUTHEAST INDIAN RIDGE
South Island
NEW ZEALAND
ANTARCTIC CIRCLE
Wilkes Land
Winkel Tripel Projection, Central Meridian 0°
SCALE 1:71,849,000
1 CENTIMETER = 718 KILOMETERS; 1 INCH = 1,134 MILES AT THE EQUATOR
0 500 1000 1500 2000 2500
KILOMETERS
0 500 1000 1500 2000 2500
STATUTE MILES
ANTARCTICA

North Pole

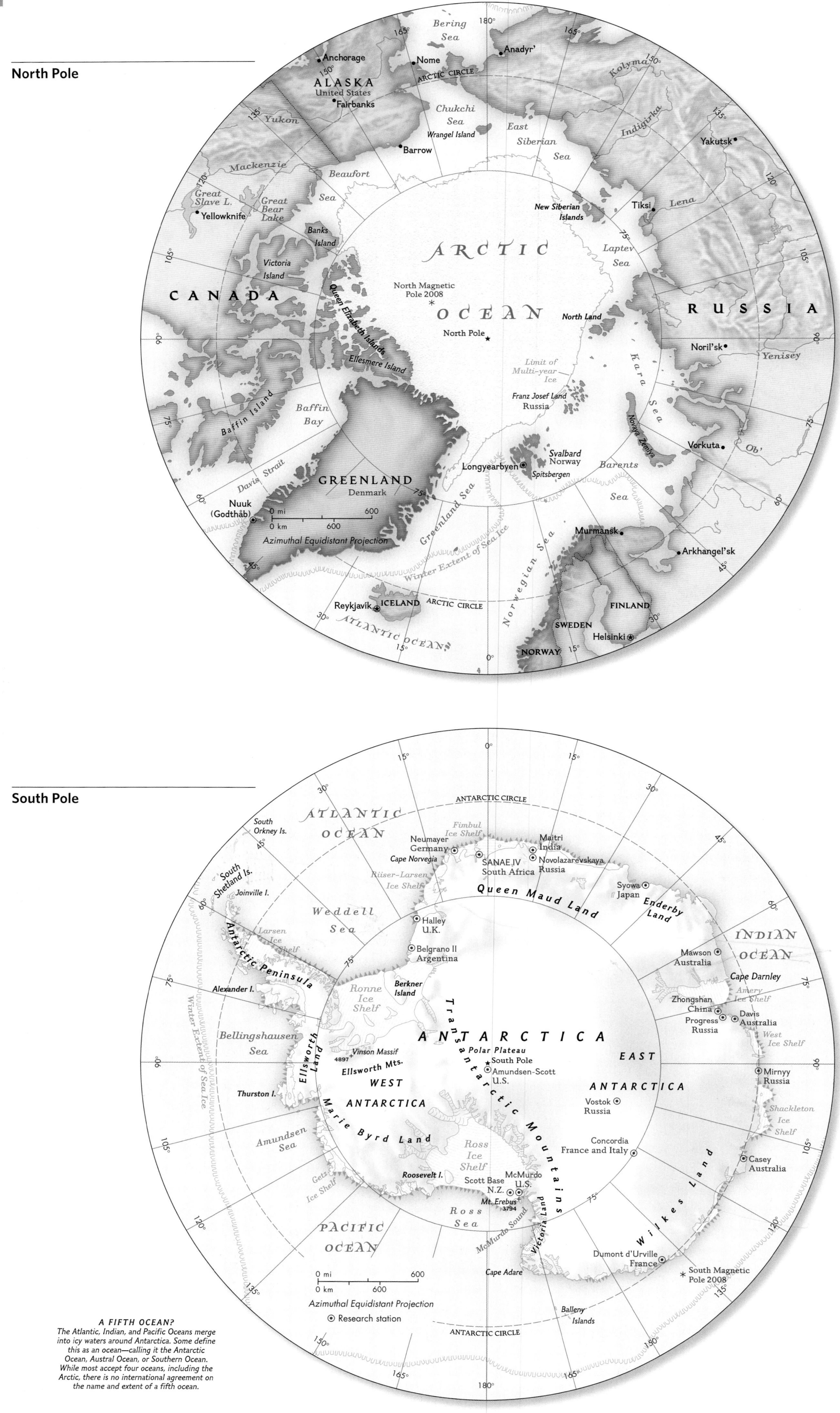
ARCTIC OCEAN
North Magnetic Pole 2008
North Pole
CANADA
RUSSIA
ALASKA
United States
GREENLAND
Denmark
Anchorage
Nome
Fairbanks
Anadyr'
Barrow
Bering Sea
Chukchi Sea
Wrangel Island
East Siberian Sea
Beaufort Sea
Yukon
Mackenzie
Great Slave L.
Yellowknife
Great Bear Lake
Banks Island
Victoria Island
Queen Elizabeth Islands
Ellesmere Island
Baffin Island
Baffin Bay
Davis Strait
Nuuk (Godthåb)
Kolyma
Indigirka
Yakutsk
Lena
Tiksi
New Siberian Islands
Laptev Sea
North Land
Noril'sk
Yenisey
Kara Sea
Limit of Multi-year Ice
Franz Josef Land
Russia
Novaya Zemlya
Vorkuta
Ob'
Svalbard
Norway
Longyearbyen
Spitsbergen
Barents Sea
Greenland Sea
Winter Extent of Sea Ice
Norwegian Sea
Murmansk
Arkhangel'sk
ICELAND
Reykjavík
ARCTIC CIRCLE
ATLANTIC OCEAN
FINLAND
SWEDEN
NORWAY
Helsinki
0 mi 600
0 km 600
Azimuthal Equidistant Projection

South Pole

ANTARCTICA
WEST ANTARCTICA
EAST ANTARCTICA
ATLANTIC OCEAN
INDIAN OCEAN
PACIFIC OCEAN
ANTARCTIC CIRCLE
South Orkney Is.
South Shetland Is.
Joinville I.
Antarctic Peninsula
Larsen Ice Shelf
Weddell Sea
Alexander I.
Bellingshausen Sea
Thurston I.
Amundsen Sea
Getz Ice Shelf
Winter Extent of Sea Ice
Neumayer Germany
Cape Norvegia
Fimbul Ice Shelf
Riiser-Larsen Ice Shelf
SANAE IV South Africa
Maitri India
Novolazarevskaya Russia
Queen Maud Land
Syowa Japan
Enderby Land
Halley U.K.
Belgrano II Argentina
Mawson Australia
Cape Darnley
Amery Ice Shelf
Zhongshan China
Progress Russia
Davis Australia
West Ice Shelf
Ronne Ice Shelf
Berkner Island
Ellsworth Land
Vinson Massif
4897
Ellsworth Mts.
Transantarctic Mountains
Polar Plateau
South Pole
Amundsen-Scott U.S.
Mirnyy Russia
Vostok Russia
Shackleton Ice Shelf
Marie Byrd Land
Ross Ice Shelf
Roosevelt I.
Concordia France and Italy
Casey Australia
Scott Base N.Z.
McMurdo U.S.
Mt. Erebus 3794
Ross Sea
McMurdo Sound
Victoria Land
Wilkes Land
Cape Adare
Dumont d'Urville France
South Magnetic Pole 2008
Balleny Islands
0 mi 600
0 km 600
Azimuthal Equidistant Projection
Research station

A FIFTH OCEAN?
The Atlantic, Indian, and Pacific Oceans merge into icy waters around Antarctica. Some define this as an ocean—calling it the Antarctic Ocean, Austral Ocean, or Southern Ocean. While most accept four oceans, including the Arctic, there is no international agreement on the name and extent of a fifth ocean.

Western Hemisphere

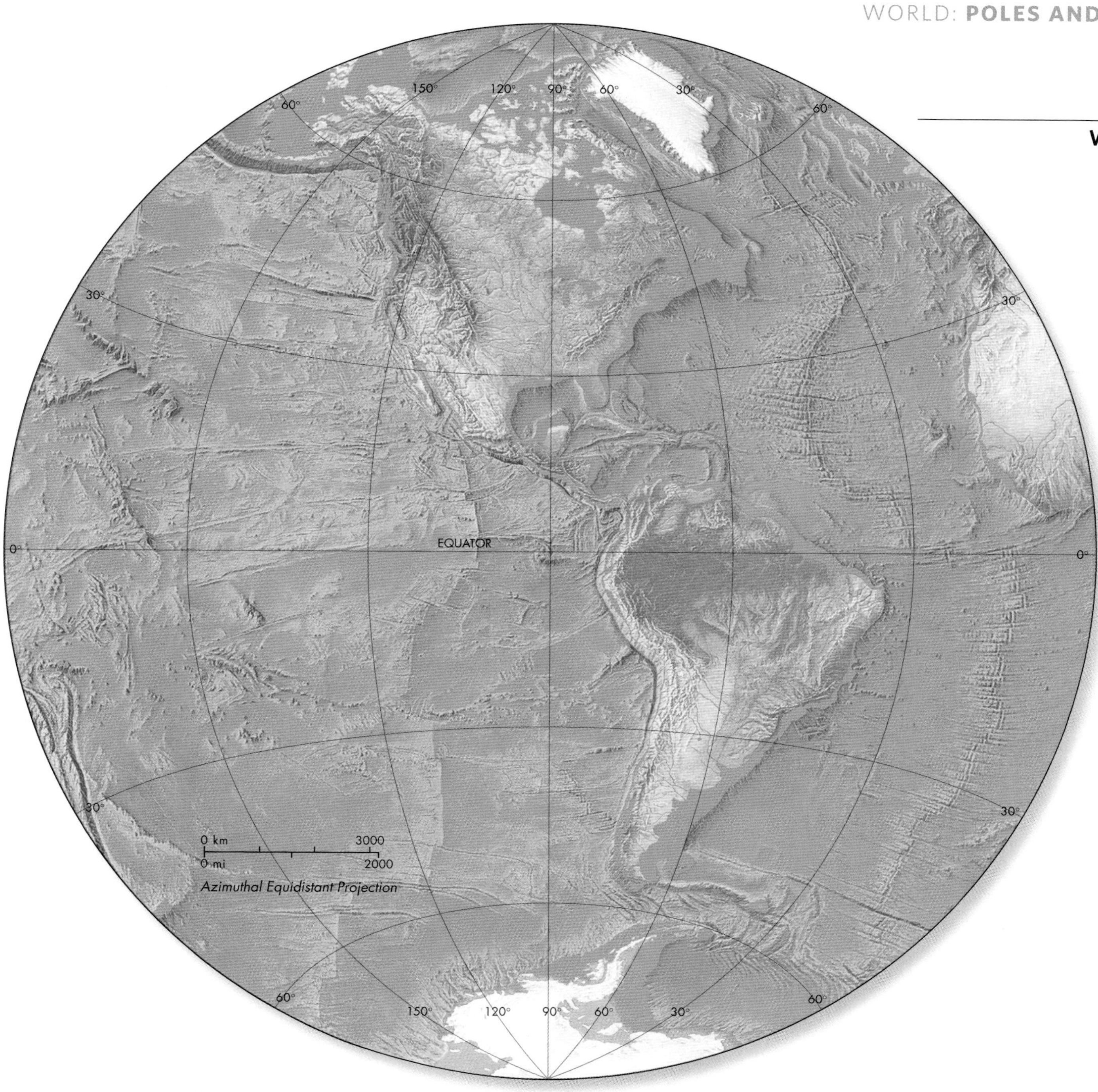

EQUATOR

0 km 3000
0 mi 2000
Azimuthal Equidistant Projection

Eastern Hemisphere

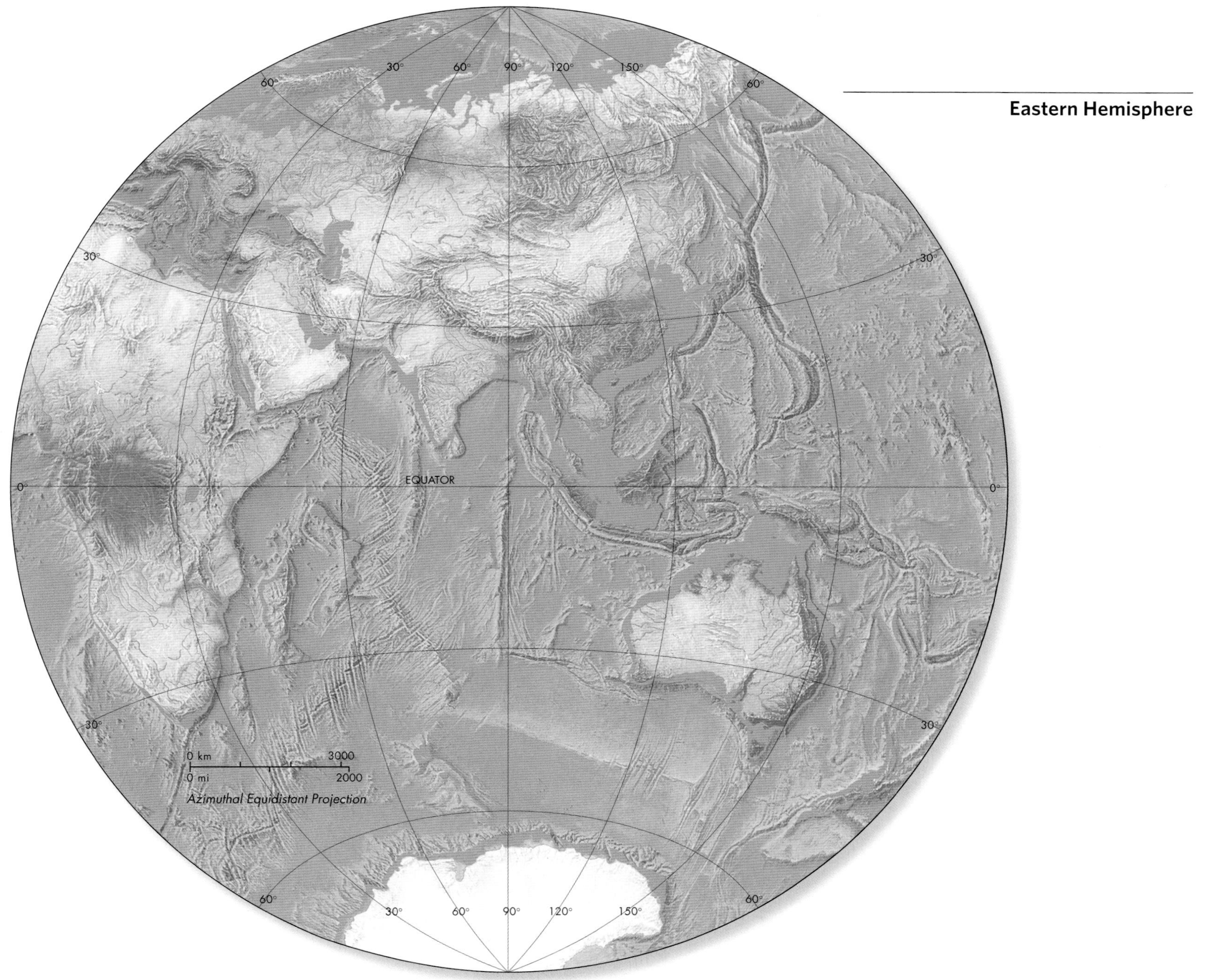
EQUATOR
0 km 3000
0 mi 2000
Azimuthal Equidistant Projection

Paleogeography

EARTH'S OUTERMOST LAYER (or lithosphere—see figure below) is broken into more than a dozen enormous slabs of rock, called plates (or tectonic plates), averaging thousands of miles wide and tens of miles thick. The lithosphere consists of Earth's crust and the solid upper part of a much thicker underlying denser, semisolid layer called the mantle. These rigid tectonic plates are in slow but constant motion, "floating" atop, and rafted by, the hotter, but still mobile mantle beneath (called the asthenosphere). As they move and grind against each other, they push up mountains, spawn volcanoes, and generate earthquakes. Although such cataclysmic events capture our attention, steady plate movements that cause them are imperceptible—a slow waltz of rafted rock that continues over eons. How slow? The Mid-Atlantic Ridge (see Plate Tectonics, pages 32-33) grows as molten rock (magma) oozes into the space created as the North and South American plates pull away from the Eurasian and African plates, at about the speed of a growing human fingernail.

The boundaries between plates generally mark zones of high volcanic and/or earthquake activity as plates gnash against each or one sinks beneath another. Within the notorious circum-Pacific Ring of Fire, disastrous earthquakes often strike in places like Kobe, Japan, and Los Angeles and San Francisco, California. Explosive eruptions are also common, as seen in Pinatubo, Philippines, and Mount St. Helens, Washington.

Paleogeography is a specialized field of geology and deals with how Earth's geography—its distribution of oceans and continents—has changed over geologic time. Plate tectonic movements and associated rise and fall of sea level, together with changes in climate (paleoclimate), are the dominant forces that control paleogeography.

STRUCTURE OF THE EARTH The composition of Earth's interior (cutaway diagram, below) is known from observing changes in the speed of seismic waves of large earthquakes as they pass through the earth.

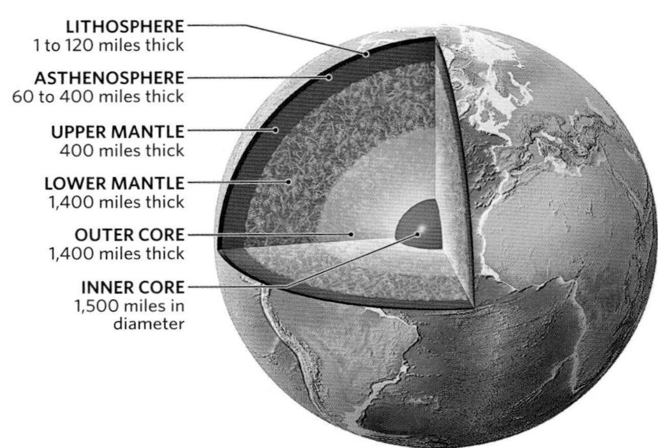
LITHOSPHERE
1 to 120 miles thick
ASTHENOSPHERE
60 to 400 miles thick
UPPER MANTLE
400 miles thick
LOWER MANTLE
1,400 miles thick
OUTER CORE
1,400 miles thick
INNER CORE
1,500 miles in diameter

Continents Adrift in Time

With unceasing movement of Earth's tectonic plates, continents "drift" over geologic time—repeatedly breaking apart, reassembling, and fragmenting. Three times during the past billion years, Earth's drifting landmasses have merged to form so-called supercontinents. Rodinia, a supercontinent in the late Precambrian, began breaking apart about 750 million years ago. In time, its pieces reassembled to form another supercontinent, which in turn later split into smaller landmasses during the Paleozoic. The largest of these were called Euramerica (ancestral Europe and North America) and Gondwana (ancestral Africa, Antarctica, Arabia, India, and Australia). More than 250 million years ago, these two landmasses recombined, forming Pangaea. In the Mesozoic era, Pangaea began to split and the Atlantic and Indian Oceans formed. Though the Atlantic is still widening today, scientists predict it will close as the seafloor recycles back into Earth's mantle. A new supercontinent, called Pangaea Ultima by some, will eventually form.

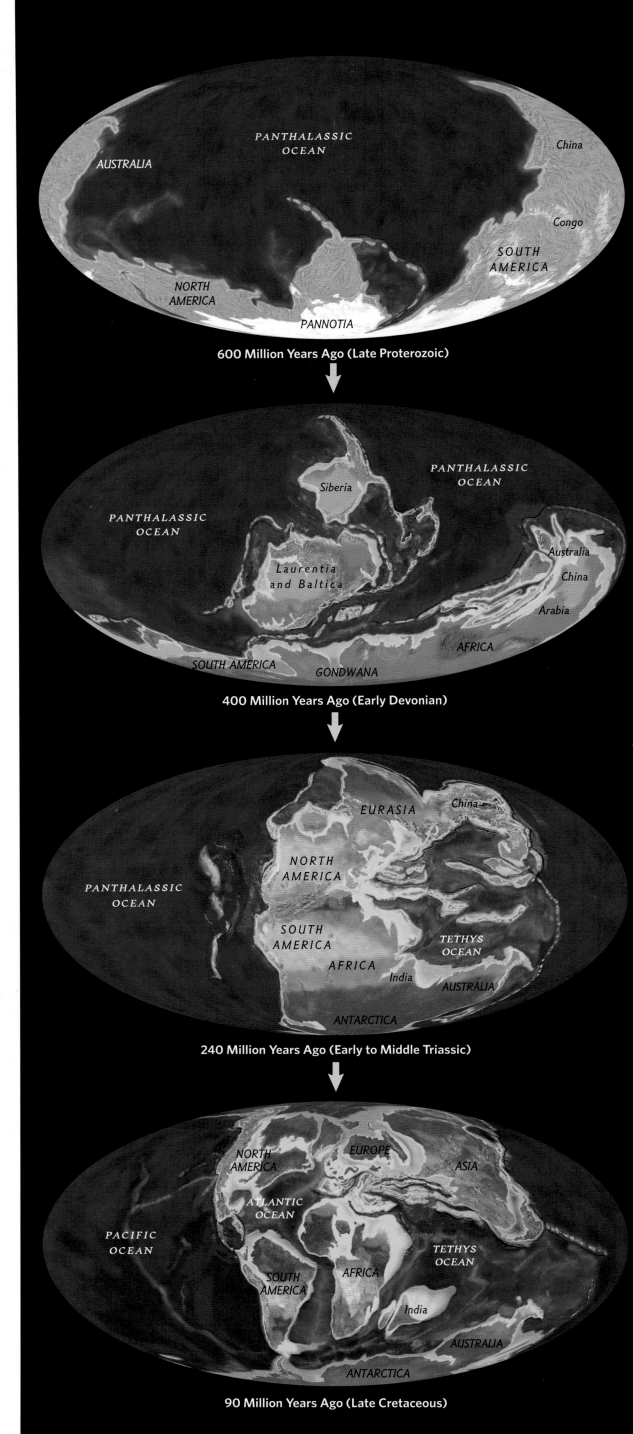

600 Million Years Ago (Late Proterozoic)

400 Million Years Ago (Early Devonian)

240 Million Years Ago (Early to Middle Triassic)

90 Million Years Ago (Late Cretaceous)

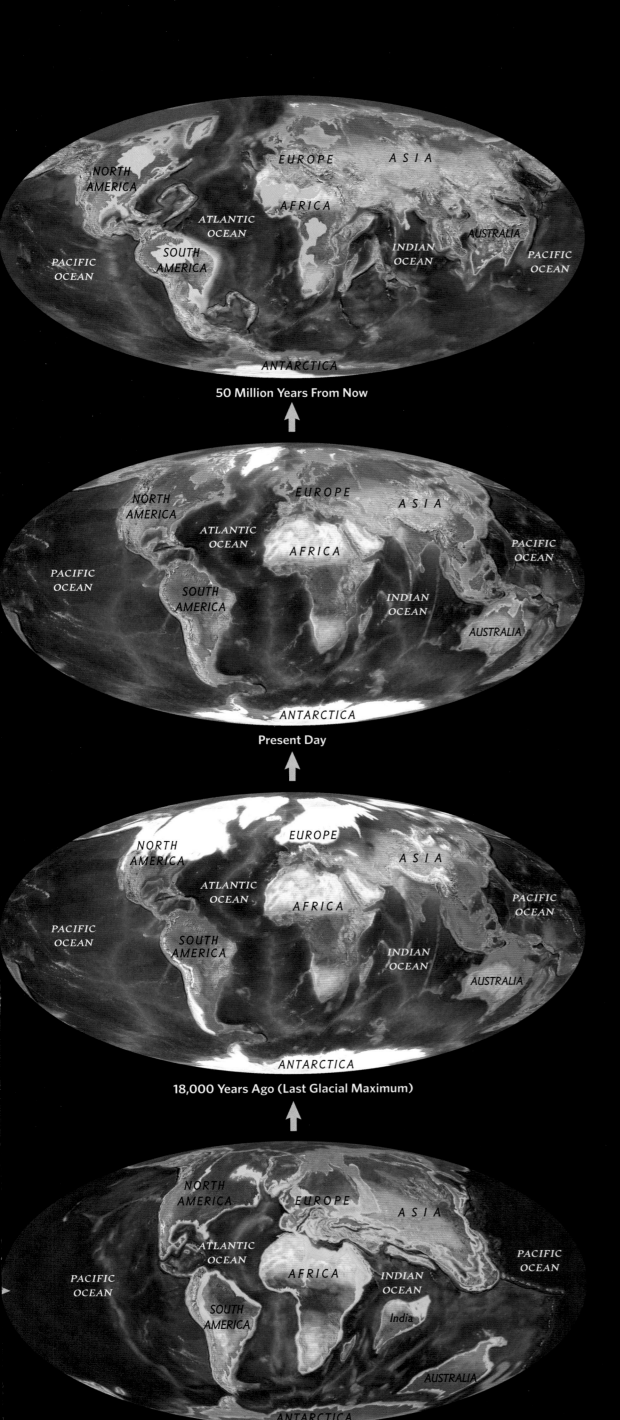

50 Million Years From Now

Present Day

18,000 Years Ago (Last Glacial Maximum)

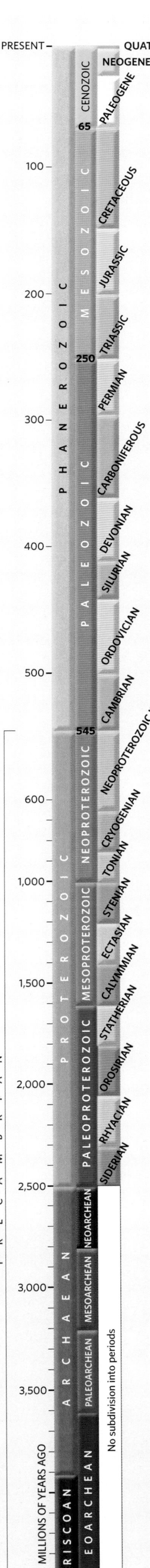
PRESENT
QUATERNARY
NEOGENE
PALEOGENE
CENOZOIC
65
100
CRETACEOUS
MESOZOIC
JURASSIC
200
TRIASSIC
250
PERMIAN
300
CARBONIFEROUS
PHANEROZOIC
DEVONIAN
400
SILURIAN
PALEOZOIC
ORDOVICIAN
500
CAMBRIAN
545
NEOPROTEROZOIC III
NEOPROTEROZOIC
600
CRYOGENIAN
TONIAN
1,000
STENIAN
MESOPROTEROZOIC
ECTASIAN
CALYMMIAN
1,500
STATHERIAN
PROTEROZOIC
OROSIRIAN
2,000
PALEOPROTEROZOIC
RHYACIAN
SIDERIAN
2,500
PRECAMBRIAN
NEOARCHEAN
3,000
MESOARCHEAN
ARCHAEAN
PALEOARCHEAN
3,500
No subdivision into periods
EOARCHEAN
PRISCOAN
MILLIONS OF YEARS AGO
4,500

Geologic Time

Before the emergence of modern geology in the 18th century, earlier peoples—reflecting religious teaching and tradition—generally believed that our planet is very young, having formed less than 6,000 to 10,000 years ago. In fact, in the 17th century, Irish bishop James Ussher very precisely calculated the date of Earth's creation to be October 23, 4004 B.C., based on a meticulous, scholarly study of the Bible.

Today, we of course know that Earth is much, much older than thought during previous centuries. The time of Earth's early formation—about 4.6 billion years ago—is solidly based on geological and paleontological studies (for example, erosion and sedimentation rates, time needed to build and wear down mountains, studies of fossil fauna and flora, and rates of tectonic plate motions), as well as on "age determinations" of rocks and meteorites using various isotropic dating techniques. Thus far, the oldest dated rock on Earth has an age in excess of 4 billion years.

In reconstructing the long history of our planet, scientists have devised various geologic timescales to provide temporal context for major changes affecting Earth. Time divisions, or "ages," which are given in millions or thousands of years before present (see timescale at left), are determined by fossil and radiometric dating studies. Because Earth has been continually reshaped by plate tectonics and associated geologic forces, the record of its earliest history has been mostly obliterated or obscured by later processes and phenomena. Thus, the history for the Precambrian eons (earlier than 545 million years ago) necessarily is very poorly understood compared with that for the Phanerozoic eon that followed. As new fossil and age-determination data become available, the age estimates of the boundaries between the timescale divisions can be refined, and new divisions and subdivisions can be proposed.

Key to Paleo-Geographic Maps

- Seafloor spreading ridge
- Subduction zone
- Landmass
- Continental shelf
- Glacier/ice cap

Plate Tectonics

EARTH (*TERRA FIRMA*, IN LATIN) actually is not terribly firm. Every place on our planet—be it on an ocean, island, or continent—is moving relative to one another, at average speeds ranging from a few tenths of an inch to nearly six inches per year. These movements are driven by plate tectonic forces (see below), which in turn have influenced, directly or indirectly, nearly all geologic processes, past or present. The notion that continents have not always been fixed in their position has existed since the late 16th century, perhaps even earlier. It was not until the early 20th century, however, that the German scientist Alfred Wegener developed a full-fledged scientific theory, called continental drift. Initially, earth scientists largely rejected his theory, mostly because it lacked a physically plausible mechanism to move continents. However, Wegener vigorously defended his theory until his death in 1930 at age 50, and decades later he was vindicated.

Beginning in the 1950s, a wealth of new evidence—especially from mapping the ocean floor—rekindled scientific interest and debate about continental drift, resulting in its transformation during the 1960s and 1970s to the theory of plate tectonics. According to this theory, Earth's outermost rigid layer (the lithosphere) is a mosaic of large and small slabs or "plates" (see map) that are moving relative to one another. These plates are piggybacked by a slowly flowing underlying layer of hotter, softer mantle (the asthenosphere). Plate movement represents the surface expression of a large-scale circulation system (convection), driven by Earth's escaping heat that extends deep into the mantle.

Some consider plate tectonics to be as important to the earth sciences as the discovery of atomic structure was to physics and as chemistry and theory of evolution were to the life sciences. Even though the plate tectonics theory is now widely accepted by the scientific community, aspects of it are still being hotly debated.

Kodiak-Bowie
Cobb
JUAN DE FUCA PLATE
ROCKY MOUNTAINS
Yellowstone
Raton
NORTH AMERICAN PLATE
Mid-Atlantic Ridge
Azores
New England
Cape Verde
Hawaiian Islands
Hawaiian-Emperor
Guadalupe-Baja
CARIBBEAN PLATE
COCOS PLATE
PACIFIC PLATE
Galápagos
ANDES
SOUTH AMERICAN PLATE
NASCA PLATE
Samoa
Tahiti-Society
Gambier
Easter
Trindade
Austral-Cooks
Juan Fernández
Louisville
SCOTIA PLATE
ANTARCTIC

Geologic Forces Change the Face of the Planet

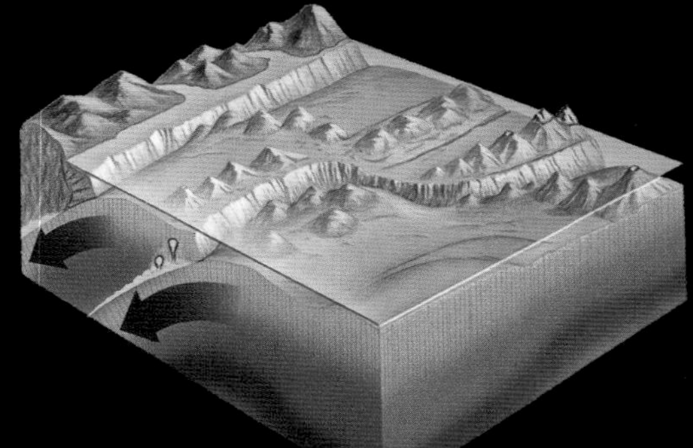

ACCRETION When oceanic parts of plates encroach—by subduction and faulting processes—the edges of continents or island arcs, pieces can break off. These pieces can slide under other plates, or are skimmed off to pile up in submarine trenches. Over geologic time, continents or island arcs can

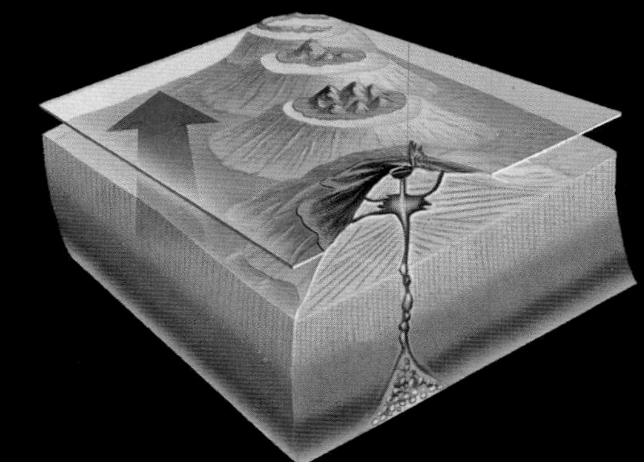

HOT SPOTS In Earth's convecting hot interior, some narrow zones are much hotter than others. These anomalous hot zones can cause local melting to produce magma to form and feed volcanoes. The passage of the Pacific plate over such a "hot spot" built a 3,700-mile-long chain of seamounts and

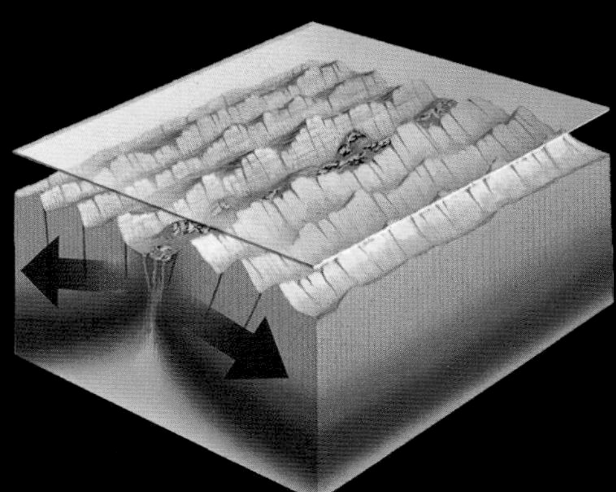

SPREADING Along divergent plate boundaries, magma oozes into the space created when plates pull apart, at rates from less than one inch to more than six inches per year. Over geologic time, such processes have built the global mid-ocean ridge—an immense submarine mountain chain (including the

Iceland

EURASIAN PLATE

ALPS

HIMALAYA

Plateau of Tibet

PACIFIC PLATE

ARABIAN PLATE

INDIAN PLATE

PHILIPPINE PLATE

Tibesti Uplift

Afar

AFRICAN PLATE

Great Rift Valley

East Africa

Caroline

Mid-Atlantic Ridge

Comoros

St. Helena

Réunion

Location Uncertain

AUSTRALIAN PLATE

Walvis Ridge

East Australia

Tasmantid

Crozet

Kerguelen

Bouvet

LATE

Winkel Tripel Projection

0 1000 2000 3000 KILOMETERS

0 1000 2000 3000 STATUTE MILES

Selected hot spots

Notable earthquake since 1900

Quake since 1900 greater than 6.5 magnitude

Volcanic eruption since 1900

Known volcanic eruption during the past 10,000 years

Diffuse plate boundary (may be more than 100 miles across)

Convergent boundary

Spreading boundary

Other fault zone

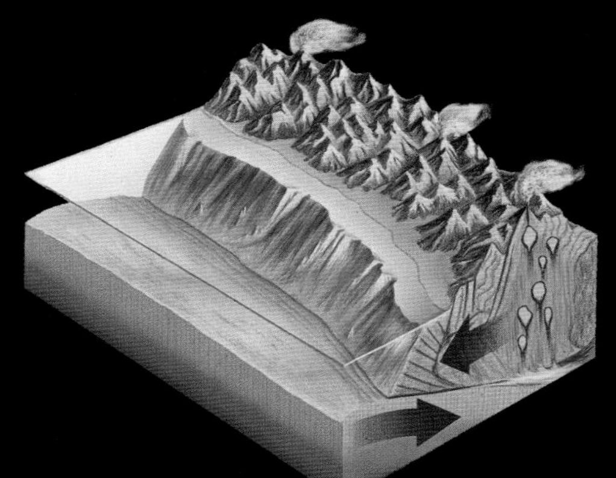

SUBDUCTION When the oceanic part of a plate encounters the continental or oceanic part of another plate, the colder, heavier oceanic part sinks beneath the lighter plate. The sinking (subducting) plate descends back into the Earth's hot interior and ultimately loses its physical identity and is recycled into the slowly flowing deep mantle.

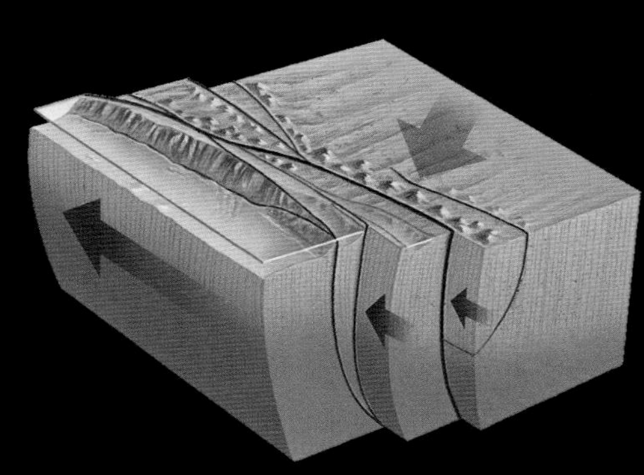

FAULTING Moving tectonic plates do not slide smoothly by or under one another. Stress and strain built up along plate boundaries may release gradually by a series of small movements and associated earthquakes. Prolonged buildup of stress can also be released suddenly, producing a major earthquake and significant ground rupture.

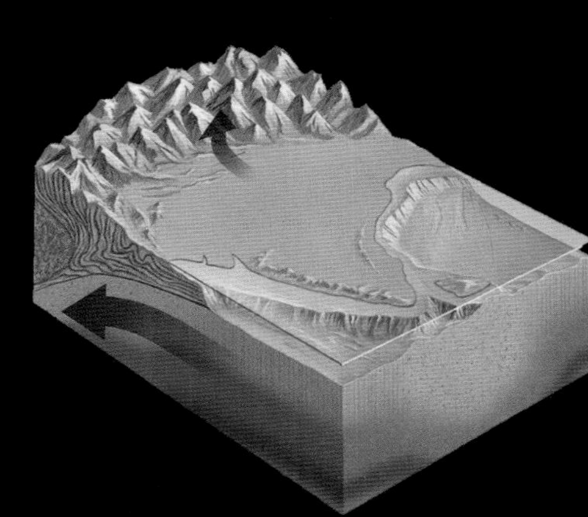

COLLISION When the continental parts of plates converge, the resulting "collision" can cause the most dramatic mountain-building processes on Earth. The Himalaya range — including Mount Everest, the world's highest peak — and the adjacent Tibetan plateau rose rapidly when the Indian subcontinent collided with Eurasia.

Landforms

SEVEN MAJOR LANDFORM TYPES are found on Earth's surface; except for ice caps, all result from tectonic movements and denudational forces.

The loftiest landforms, mountains, often define the edges of tectonic plates. In places where continental plates converge, Earth's crust crumples into high ranges such as the Himalaya. Where oceanic plates dive beneath continental ones, volcanic mountains can rise. Volcanoes are common along the west coast of South America, which is part of the so-called Pacific Ring of Fire, the world's most active mountain-building zone.

Widely spaced mountains are another type, and examples of this landform are seen in the Basin and Range province of the western United States. These features are actually the tops of heavily eroded, faulted mountains. The eroded material filled adjacent valleys, giving these old summits the look of widely spaced mountains.

Extensive, relatively flat lands that are higher than surrounding areas are called plateaus. Formed by uplift, they include the Guiana Highlands of South America. Hills and low plateaus are rounded natural elevations of land with some local relief. The Canadian Shield and Ozarks of North America provide good examples. Depressions are large basins delimited by higher lands, an example of which is the Tarim Basin in western China. Plains are extensive areas of level or rolling treeless country. Examples include the steppes of Eurasia, the Ganges River plains, and the outback of Australia.

Caused by the same tectonic forces, many of the landforms that occur on land also occur on the ocean floor (see pages 38–39), including the world's tallest mountain measured from its base (Mauna Kea in Hawai'i), and a 30,000-mile-long (48,280 kilometers) mountain chain, the Mid-Ocean Ridge System.

The forces of nature are usually gradual, often taking millions of years to shape landforms, but heavy rains and high winds can transform a landscape in a matter of hours. Human land use practices can also rapidly accelerate erosion, speeding the creation of floodplains and sand dunes.

Brooks Ra.
Alaska Ra.
Rocky Mountains
Canadian Shield
NORTH AMERICA
Cascade Ra.
Great Plains
Great Basin
2
Ozark Plateau
Appalachian Mts.
Coastal Plain
Sa. Madre Occidental
Sa. Madre Oriental
Gulf of Mexico
TROPIC OF CANCER
PACIFIC OCEAN
EQUATOR
Guiana Highlands
Amazon Basin
Andes
SOUTH AMERICA
Brazilian Highlands
TROPIC OF CAPRICORN
Pampas
4

Endogenic Landforms (landforms that result from "internal" processes)

Forces deep within Earth give rise to mountains and other endogenic landforms. Some mountains, such as the Himalaya, were born when continental plates collided. Others rose in the form of volcanoes as a result of tectonic plate subduction, like the Cascade Range, or as plates moved over hot spots in Earth's mantle, as in Hawai'i. Still others were thrust up by tectonic uplift. Rifting and faulting, which generally occur along plate boundaries, also generate vertical tectonic landforms.

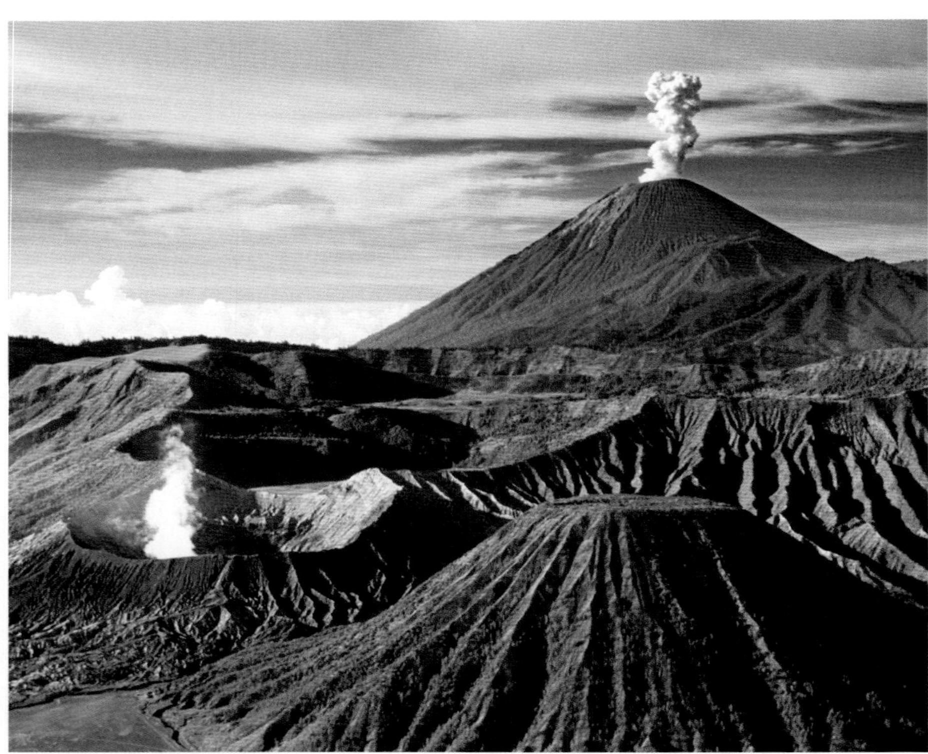

Mount Bromo, Indonesia ❶

Exogenic Landforms (landforms that result from "external" processes)

External agents create exogenic landforms. Weathering by wind, rain, groundwater, and other natural elements slowly breaks down rocks, such as the limestone in southeastern China's karst landscapes or the granite in an exfoliation dome, such as Yosemite's Half Dome. Erosion removes weathered material and transports it from place to place. In the American Southwest, erosion continues to shape the spires of Bryce Canyon (below) and the walls of narrow slot canyons.

Bryce Canyon Amphitheater, United States ❷

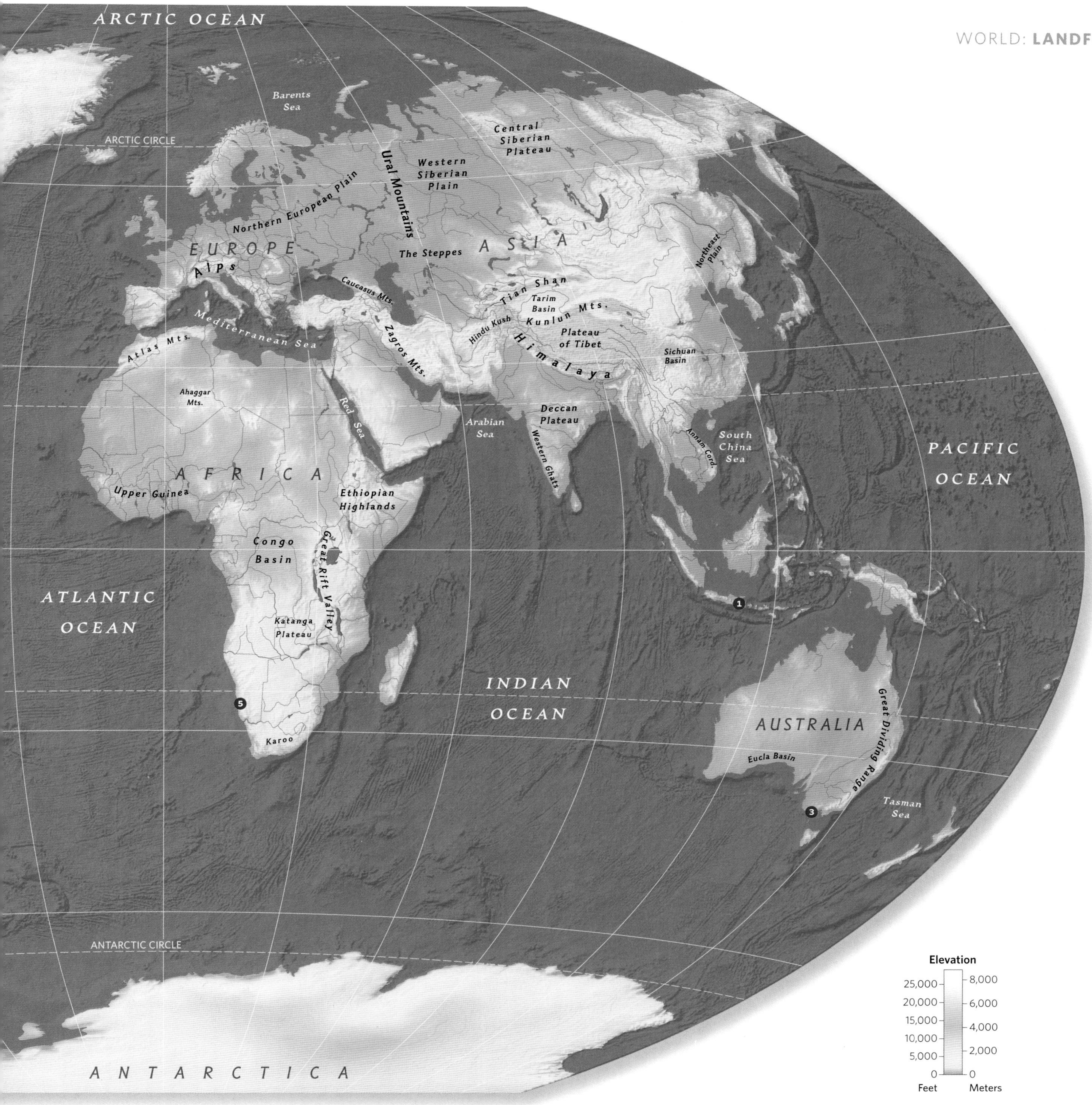

ARCTIC OCEAN
Barents Sea
ARCTIC CIRCLE
Central Siberian Plateau
Western Siberian Plain
Ural Mountains
Northern European Plain
EUROPE
Alps
The Steppes
ASIA
Northeast Plain
Caucasus Mts.
Tian Shan
Tarim Basin
Kunlun Mts.
Hindu Kush
Plateau of Tibet
Himalaya
Sichuan Basin
Mediterranean Sea
Atlas Mts.
Zagros Mts.
Ahaggar Mts.
Red Sea
Arabian Sea
Deccan Plateau
Western Ghats
Annam Cord.
South China Sea
PACIFIC OCEAN
AFRICA
Upper Guinea
Ethiopian Highlands
Congo Basin
Great Rift Valley
ATLANTIC OCEAN
Katanga Plateau
INDIAN OCEAN
AUSTRALIA
Great Dividing Range
Eucla Basin
Karoo
Tasman Sea
ANTARCTIC CIRCLE
ANTARCTICA

Elevation

Feet	Meters
25,000	8,000
20,000	6,000
15,000	4,000
10,000	2,000
5,000	0
0	

LANDFORMS CREATED BY WATER

Consistently powered by Earth's gravity (rivers and groundwater) and ceaseless ocean winds (breaking coastal waves), moving water produces dramatic changes in the land. Canyons and valleys are river-created landforms; river deltas form when water slows at a river's mouth, desspositing suspended sediments. But perhaps water's most easily observable creations are along Earth's coastlines.

The Twelve Apostles, Australia 3

LANDFORMS CREATED BY ICE

Among the legacies of Earth's most recent ice age are landforms shaped by glaciers. These large, slow-moving masses of ice can crush or topple anything in their paths. Glaciers are also powerful agents of erosion, grinding against the ground and picking up and carrying huge amounts of rock and soil, which they deposit at their margins as they melt; these deposits are called lateral and terminal moraines.

Perito Moreno Glacier, Argentina 4

LANDFORMS CREATED BY WIND

The term "eolian" (from Aeolus, the Greek god of the winds) describes landforms shaped by the wind. The erosive action of wind is characterized by deflation, or the removal of dust and sand from dry soil; sandblasting, the erosion of rock by windborne sand; and deposition, the laying down of sediments. Among desert landforms, sand dunes may be the most spectacular.

Namib Desert, Namibia 5

Land Cover

RELIABLE INFORMATION ON GLOBAL LAND COVER and land use is an important requirement for many Earth-system studies. The Earth's ecosystems are currently undergoing substantial and rapid change related to such processes as agricultural expansion, deforestation, urbanization, and climate change. The best source for information related to these processes is satellite data.

Such data allow for the creation of internally consistent, reproducible, and accurate land cover maps like the one at right, which is based on a year of global satellite imagery from NASA's Moderate Resolution Imaging Spectroradiometer (MODIS) at a spatial resolution of 500 meters. The change of vegetation through time, or its phenology, is captured in the satellite record and used to differentiate classes of land cover and land use. By recording the data at different wavelengths of the electromagnetic spectrum, scientists can derive land cover types through spectral variation. Maps made from this information help to both characterize the state of the planet and to identify places undergoing changes. Descriptions of the various land cover types are provided below.

NORTH AMERICA
ATLANTIC OCEAN
TROPIC OF CANCER
PACIFIC OCEAN
EQUATOR
SOUTH AMERICA
TROPIC OF CAPRICORN
Land Cover
Evergreen Needleleaf Forest
Evergreen Broadleaf Forest
Deciduous Needleleaf Forest
Deciduous Broadleaf Forest
Mixed Forest
Woody Savanna
Savanna
Closed Shrubland
Open Shrubland
Grassland
Cropland
Barren or Sparsely Vegetated
Urban and Built-up
Snow and Ice
Cropland/Natural Vegetation Mosaic
Permanent Wetland
Water

EVERGREEN NEEDLELEAF FOREST

More than 60 percent of the land is covered by a forest canopy; tree height exceeds 5 meters. These forests are typical of the boreal (northern subarctic) region; in many of them, trees are grown on plantations and logged for the making of paper and building products.

EVERGREEN BROADLEAF FOREST

More than 60 percent of the land is covered by a forest canopy; tree height exceeds 5 meters. These, which include rain forests, dominate in the tropics and have the greatest concentrations of biodiversity. In many areas, farms, ranches, and tree plantations are replacing this land cover.

DECIDUOUS NEEDLELEAF FOREST

More than 60 percent of the land is covered by forest canopy; tree height exceeds 5 meters. Trees respond to cold seasons by shedding their leaves simultaneously. This land cover class is dominant only in Siberia, taking the form of larch forests with a short June to August growing season.

DECIDUOUS BROADLEAF FOREST

More than 60 percent of the land is covered by a forest canopy; tree height exceeds 5 meters. In dry or cold seasons, trees shed their leaves simultaneously. Much of this forest has been converted to cropland in temperate regions, with large remnants found only on steep and remote slopes.

MIXED FOREST

More than 60 percent of the land is covered by a forest canopy; tree height exceeds 5 meters. Both needleleaf and deciduous types appear, with neither having coverage of less than 25 percent or more than 75 percent. This type is largely found between temperate deciduous and boreal evergreen forests.

WOODY SAVANNA

Land has herbaceous or woody understories and tree canopy cover of 40 to 60 percent; trees exceed 5 meters and may be evergreen or deciduous. This type is common in the tropics and is most highly degraded in areas with long histories of human habitation, such as West Africa.

SAVANNA

Land has herbaceous or woody understories and tree canopy cover of 10 to 40 percent; trees exceed 5 meters and may be evergreen or deciduous. This type includes classic African savanna, as well as open boreal woodlands that demarcate tree lines and the beginning of tundra ecosystems.

CLOSED SHRUBLAND

Bushes or shrubs dominate, with a canopy coverage of more than 40 percent. Bushes do not exceed 5 meters in height; shrubs or bushes can be evergreen or deciduous. Tree canopy is less than 10 percent. This land cover can be found where prolonged cold or dry seasons limit plant growth.

OPEN SHRUBLAND

Shrubs are dominant, with a canopy cover between 10 and 40 percent; they do not exceed 2 meters in height and can be evergreen or deciduous. The remaining land is either barren or characterized by annual herbaceous cover. This land cover type occurs in semiarid or severely cold regions.

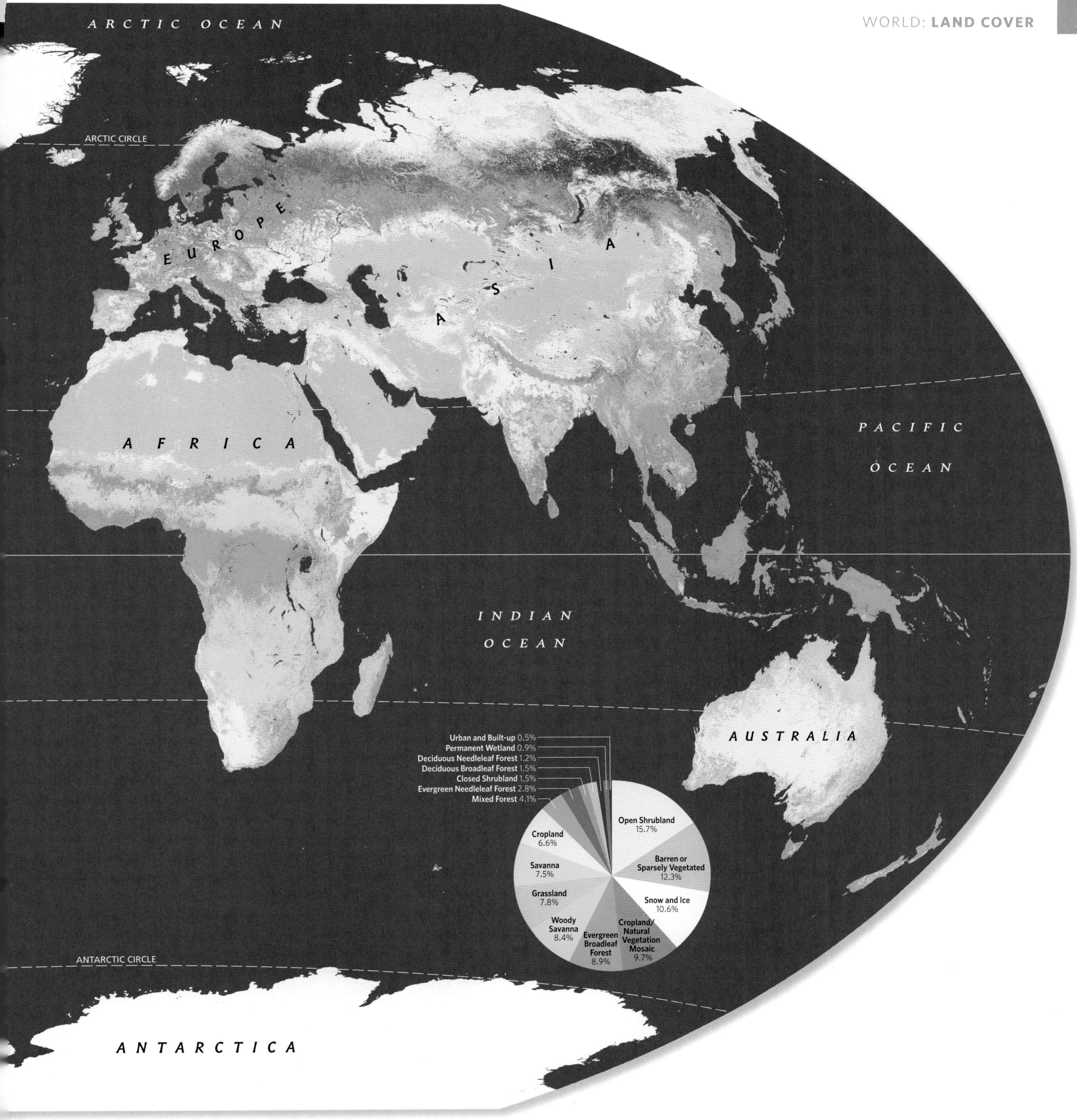

ARCTIC OCEAN

ARCTIC CIRCLE

EUROPE

ASIA

AFRICA

PACIFIC OCEAN

INDIAN OCEAN

AUSTRALIA

ANTARCTIC CIRCLE

ANTARCTICA

Urban and Built-up 0.5%
Permanent Wetland 0.9%
Deciduous Needleleaf Forest 1.2%
Deciduous Broadleaf Forest 1.5%
Closed Shrubland 1.5%
Evergreen Needleleaf Forest 2.8%
Mixed Forest 4.1%
Open Shrubland 15.7%
Barren or Sparsely Vegetated 12.3%
Snow and Ice 10.6%
Cropland/Natural Vegetation Mosaic 9.7%
Evergreen Broadleaf Forest 8.9%
Woody Savanna 8.4%
Grassland 7.8%
Savanna 7.5%
Cropland 6.6%

GRASSLAND
Land has continuous herbaceous cover and less than 10 percent tree or shrub canopy cover. This type occurs in a wide range of habitats. Perennial grasslands in the central United States and Russia, for example, are the most extensive and mark a line of decreased precipitation that limits agriculture.

CROPLAND
Crop-producing fields make up more than 80 percent of the landscape. Areas of high-intensity agriculture, including mechanized farming, stretch across temperate regions. Much agriculture in the developing world is fragmented, however, and occurs frequently on small plots of land.

BARREN OR SPARSELY VEGETATED
Exposed soil, sand, or rocks are typical; the land never has more than 10 percent vegetated cover during any time of year. Includes true deserts, such as the Sahara in Africa and Gobi in Asia. Desertification, the expansion of deserts due to land degradation or climate change, is a problem in some areas.

URBAN AND BUILT-UP
Land cover includes buildings, roads, and other man-made structures. This class was mapped using the populated places layer that is part of the "Digital Chart of the World" (Danko, 1992). Urban and built-up cover represents the most densely developed areas of human habitation.

SNOW AND ICE
Land has permanent snow and ice; it never has more than 10 percent vegetated cover at any time of year. The greatest expanses of this class can be seen in Greenland, on other Arctic islands, and in Antarctica. Glaciers at high elevations form significant examples in Alaska, the Himalaya, and Iceland.

CROPLAND/NATURAL VEGETATION MOSAIC
Lands with a mosaic of croplands, forests, shrublands, and grasslands in which no one component makes up more than 60 percent of the landscape. This land cover class can be seen in much of the U.S.; examples include southwestern Wisconsin and the Susquehanna River valley (pictured).

PERMANENT WETLAND
A permanent mixture of water and herbaceous or woody vegetation. The vegetation can be present in either salt, brackish, or fresh water. The Everglades (pictured) are one of the world's largest permanent wetlands. Other wetlands include Lake Chad and the Sundarbans of India and Bangladesh.

Oceans

THE ONLY PLANET IN OUR SOLAR SYSTEM with liquid water at the surface, Earth is known as the blue planet. The majority of Earth's surface (71 percent) is submerged beneath more than 300 million cubic miles of saline water, with the remaining 29 percent covered by less dense continental crust that rises above sea level. Of the total amount of water on Earth's surface, 97.2 percent is saline; approximately 3.5 percent of the total mass of the oceans is salt.

The global ocean is subdivided into five major basins, with the massive Pacific occupying roughly half. It is followed by—in descending order of size—the Atlantic, Indian, "Southern" (the ocean around Antarctica), and Arctic Ocean. The salt water that fills these ocean basins is slowly mixed by a giant density-driven current known as the global conveyor belt, which starts in the northern Atlantic and flows southward into the southern ocean basin and then onward to the Indian and Pacific, on a timescale of approximately a thousand years. This immense storage of ocean water plays a critical role in regulating Earth's surface temperature and climate (figure below right) and supports a diverse ecological system that is increasingly being impacted through human activities (figure below left).

Lying below an average ocean depth of more than 12,400 feet (3,800 meters) are towering mountains and the deepest valleys on Earth. The lithospheric plates that make up Earth's surface crust are continuously being created along the vast chain of undersea mountains known as mid-ocean ridges and pulled into the mantle at subduction zones in deep-sea trenches through the process of continental drift. Thus, new oceanic crust is formed along the Mid-Atlantic Ridge at a rate of approximately an inch (10 to 30 millimeters) per year, resulting in a progressive expansion of the Atlantic Ocean. In contrast, oceanic crust is destroyed at subduction zones located around the perimeter of the Pacific Ocean, which is characterized by numerous island and continental arc volcanoes known as the Ring of Fire.

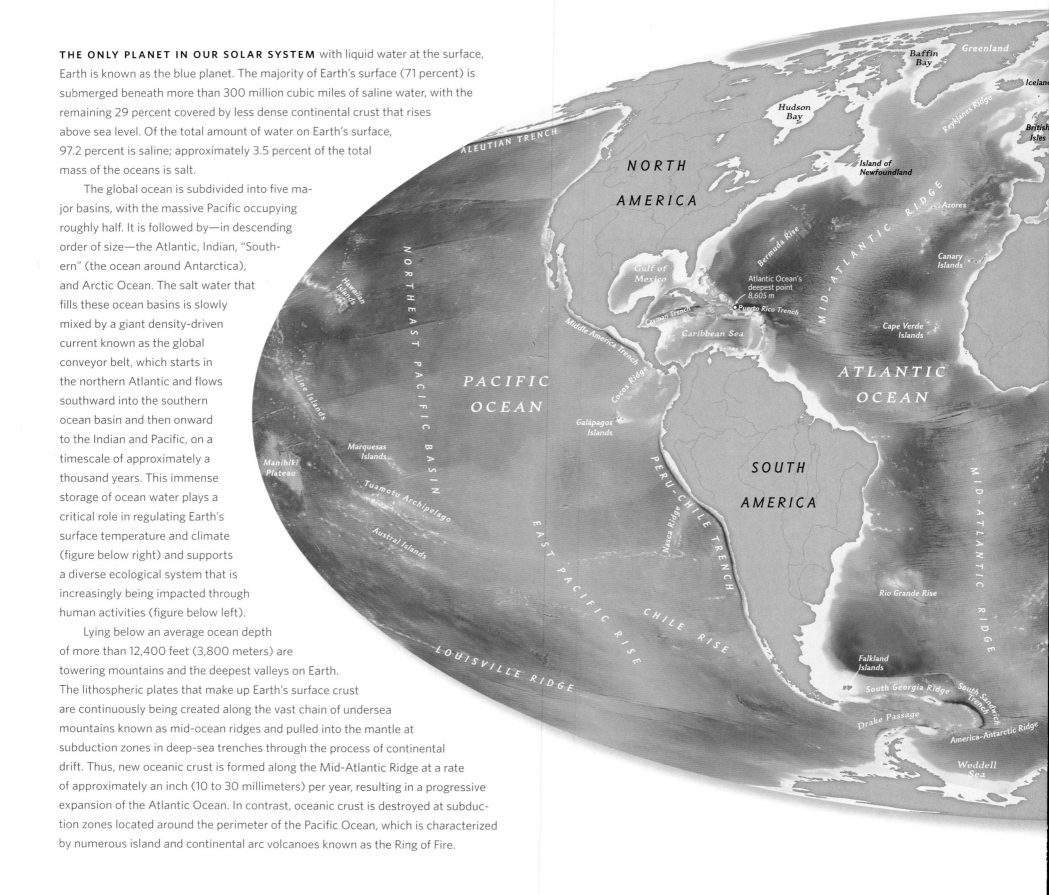

Human Impact on the Oceans

Human activities can affect the world's oceans in many different ways. This map shows the condition of the oceans as a result of the cumulative impact on marine ecosystems of 17 different human drivers of change, ranging from commercial fishing to climate change to land-based pollution.

To develop this map, the location of all marine ecosystems and intensity of the 17 drivers of change were plotted, and the unique vulnerability of each ecosystem to each driver was used to translate the overlap of these layers into the degree of impact, or degradation, of the ecosystems at any location. All the ecosystems were then combined to create a cumulative impact rating, which was used to define levels of ocean degradation. Colors range from relatively low impact levels (blue) to very high impact levels (red). More than 40 percent of the oceans' surface area is heavily impacted by human activities, while only a tiny percentage, mostly in polar regions, is relatively pristine.

The most severe areas of human impact are in the North Sea and in the South and East China Seas. These are, not coincidentally, adjacent to densely populated areas, and support heavy ship traffic and commercial fishing. Even some well-traveled transoceanic shipping routes are visible, appearing as thin, straight lines more highly impacted than their surroundings.

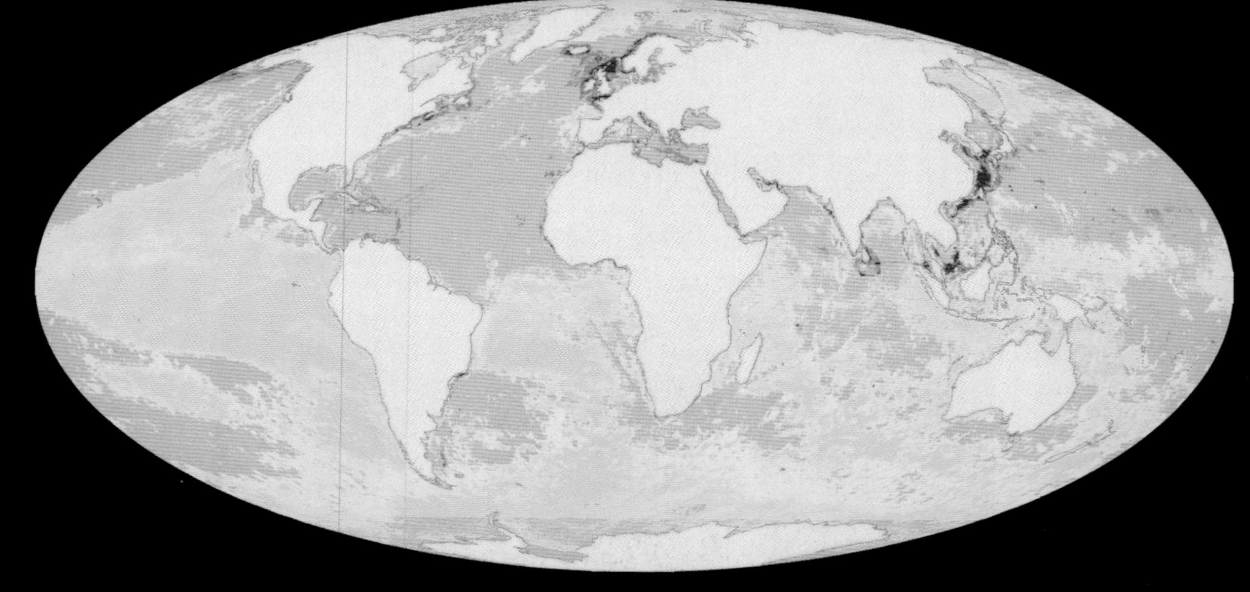

Human Impact

Very high
High
Medium high
Medium
Low
Very low

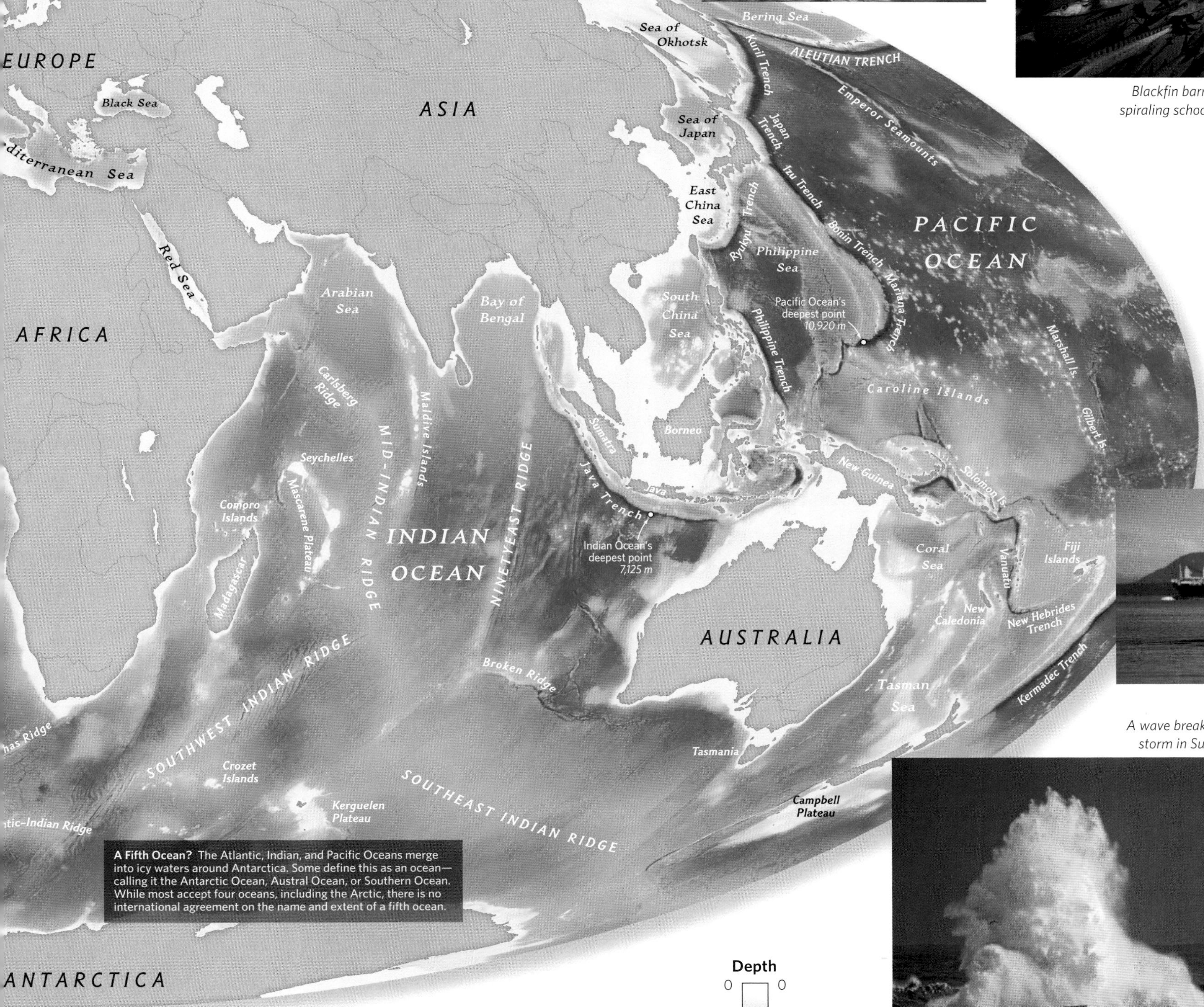

A dolphin surfs a large wave. Dolphins are found in nearly all of the world's oceans and seas.

Blackfin barracudas (Sphyraena qenie) form a spiraling school at 70 feet deep, Solomon Islands.

Orca (killer) whales (Orcinus orca) swim near an oil tanker, San Juan Islands, Washington State.

A wave breaks near a lighthouse during a winter storm in Sunderland, Tyne and Wear, England.

A Fifth Ocean? The Atlantic, Indian, and Pacific Oceans merge into icy waters around Antarctica. Some define this as an ocean—calling it the Antarctic Ocean, Austral Ocean, or Southern Ocean. While most accept four oceans, including the Arctic, there is no international agreement on the name and extent of a fifth ocean.

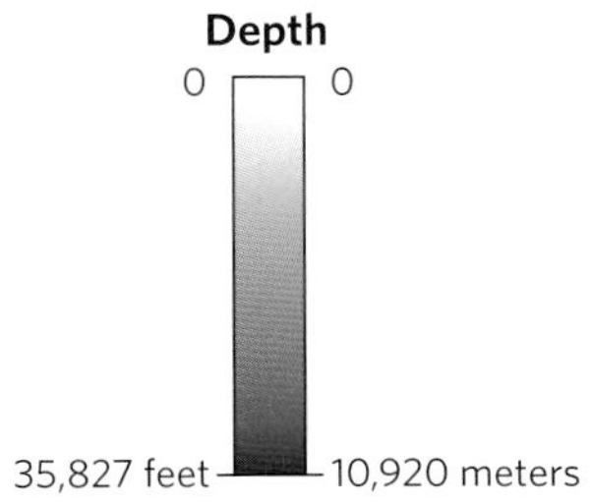

Depth

0 0

35,827 feet 10,920 meters

For more information, see the World Oceans section, pages 254–269.

Sea-surface Temperatures

A satellite image of sea-surface temperatures (from 2002 through early 2008) reveals warmer waters depicted in red and yellow near the tropical and subtropical regions surrounding the Equator, with the highest temperatures found in the Pacific between Asia and Australia. Green and pale blue colors represent intermediate temperatures located in temperate zones at mid-latitudes. The coldest water temperatures, indicated in dark purple, are observed in the high latitude areas of the Arctic and Antarctic.

Prevailing winds and giant ocean currents distort temperature patterns through clockwise fluid motion in the Northern Hemisphere and counterclockwise motion in the Southern Hemisphere, resulting in massive quantities of heat being transported from the Equator to the Poles. Thus, the western equatorial Pacific is warmer than the eastern side, and warm tropical currents move poleward in the form of major ocean currents such as the Kuroshio in the northwest Pacific and the Gulf Steam in the northwest Atlantic. The high heat capacity of water combined with constant fluid motion results in ocean temperatures falling within a far narrower range compared to temperature extremes recorded on land, and open ocean surface temperature variations rarely exceed 1°C on a daily basis. The oceans therefore act as a giant heat pump that modulates global temperatures and climate and make Earth a habitable planet.

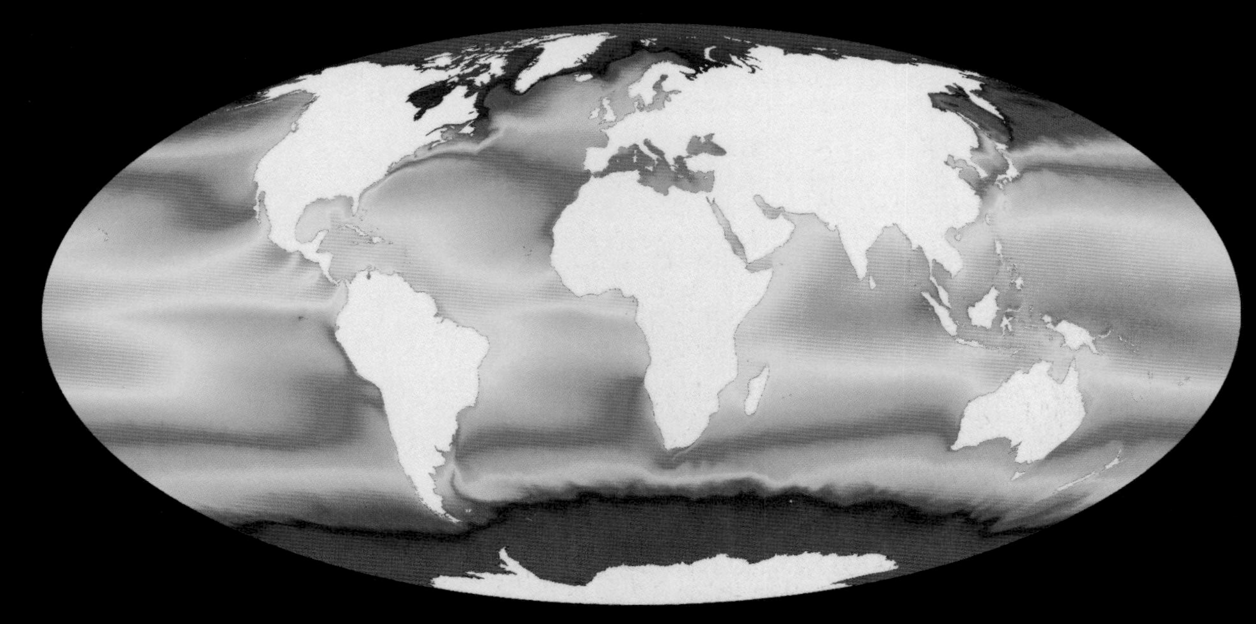

Fresh Water

THE WORLD'S FRESHWATER RESOURCES are essential to all life outside the oceans. Lakes, rivers, ponds, streams, and wetlands provide habitat for a wide variety of imperiled species, nourish the lands around them, and sustain human populations. People use fresh water for drinking resources, agricultural irrigation, transportation, electricity generation, industry and manufacturing, spiritual nourishment, and domestic purposes. As the world's population grows, the planet's strained freshwater resources are further taxed, resulting in the daunting problem of providing more with less.

Aside from sustaining natural and human communities, freshwater systems perform vital ecological functions. Rivers deliver essential nutrients downstream, and their floodplains filter their waters. Wetlands also act as filters, absorbing and processing pollutants and excess nutrients. However, as humans have used the world's fresh waters, they have altered them to better suit their purposes, often inadvertently jeopardizing the whole system. Dams interrupt fish migrations and often turn wetlands and running rivers into lakes. Levee systems disconnect rivers from their floodplains, disrupting the natural flow patterns. Pollutants foul waters, and overfishing decimates historically abundant fisheries.

These changes have had dramatic and disturbing results. Half of Earth's wetlands are estimated to have disappeared in the 20th century. Fisheries in major rivers around the world have shown dramatic declines. More than 20 percent of the world's known freshwater fish species have become extinct or imperiled in the last 50 years—a rate disproportionately higher than terrestrial species.

The challenge is to find a sustainable balance between human needs and the health of freshwater ecosystems, which, due to their often cross-boundary nature, can require international cooperation. Nonprofit agencies, governmental institutions, and local stakeholders can work together on systemwide plans for restoration and conservation. Examples include leveraging usage policies, teaching sustainable fishing techniques, restoring wetlands, and acquiring buffer lands for direct protection.

Greenland
NORTH AMERICA
ATLANTIC OCEAN
PACIFIC OCEAN
SOUTH AMERICA

Water Availability (in millimeters per person per year)
- More than 750
- 251–750
- 26–250
- Less than 26
- Primary watershed boundary
- Selected potential water disputes

For a map of the world's largest drainage basins, see pages 308–309.

Water Use

The pie charts at right illustrate just how precious little of Earth's water is suitable for most human use. Of the 2.5 percent of the planet's water that doesn't reside in the salty oceans, most is locked up in the massive ice caps of Antarctica and Greenland, leaving less than one percent that is exploitable for human use.

As with the distribution of fresh water on Earth's surface, water use varies around the world. Globally, the agricultural sector is the largest user of water, primarily for irrigating crops. Industrial uses are a distant second in the amount of water use, using fresh water mostly as a cooling agent for generators and machinery. The smallest percentage of fresh water is used by the domestic sector for purposes such as in-home use and drinking water; however, more than a billion people around the world lack access to safe drinking water. This population lives primarily in the developing world where funding is not readily available for water treatment and proper sanitation. In many countries around the world, fresh water is increasingly being left in rivers for in-stream uses such as aquatic species habitat and recreation.

In Africa, Asia, and South America, agriculture dominates water use, comprising more than 80 percent of freshwater usage. This large percentage is partly due to the lack of widespread industry. Europe and North America, however, show a different trend. Being significantly more industrialized, they use 30 to 40 percent of their water in the industrial sector, and are also much more liberal with their domestic usage, which tops 20 percent.

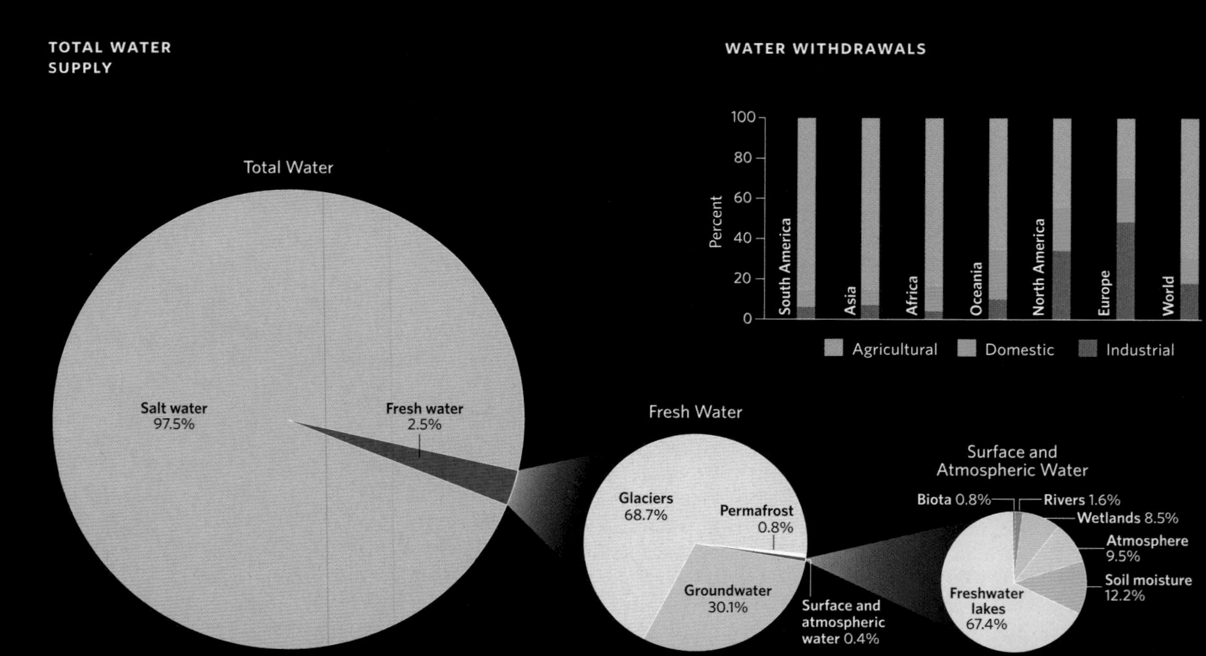

TOTAL WATER SUPPLY
Total Water
Salt water 97.5%
Fresh water 2.5%
Fresh Water
Glaciers 68.7%
Permafrost 0.8%
Groundwater 30.1%
Surface and atmospheric water 0.4%
Surface and Atmospheric Water
Biota 0.8%
Rivers 1.6%
Wetlands 8.5%
Atmosphere 9.5%
Soil moisture 12.2%
Freshwater lakes 67.4%
WATER WITHDRAWALS
100
80
60
40
20
0
Percent
South America
Asia
Africa
Oceania
North America
Europe
World
Agricultural
Domestic
Industrial

Lake Baikal, in Russia, is the largest freshwater lake in the world, based on volume. It contains about 20 percent of the world's total surface fresh water—as much as the Great Lakes of North America combined.

ARCTIC OCEAN

EUROPE

ASIA

PACIFIC OCEAN

AFRICA

INDIAN OCEAN

AUSTRALIA

ANTARCTICA

The Los Angeles Aqueduct system, in operation since 1913, delivers fresh water from the Eastern Sierra Nevada. Over the past ten years it has supplied roughly half of the city's water needs.

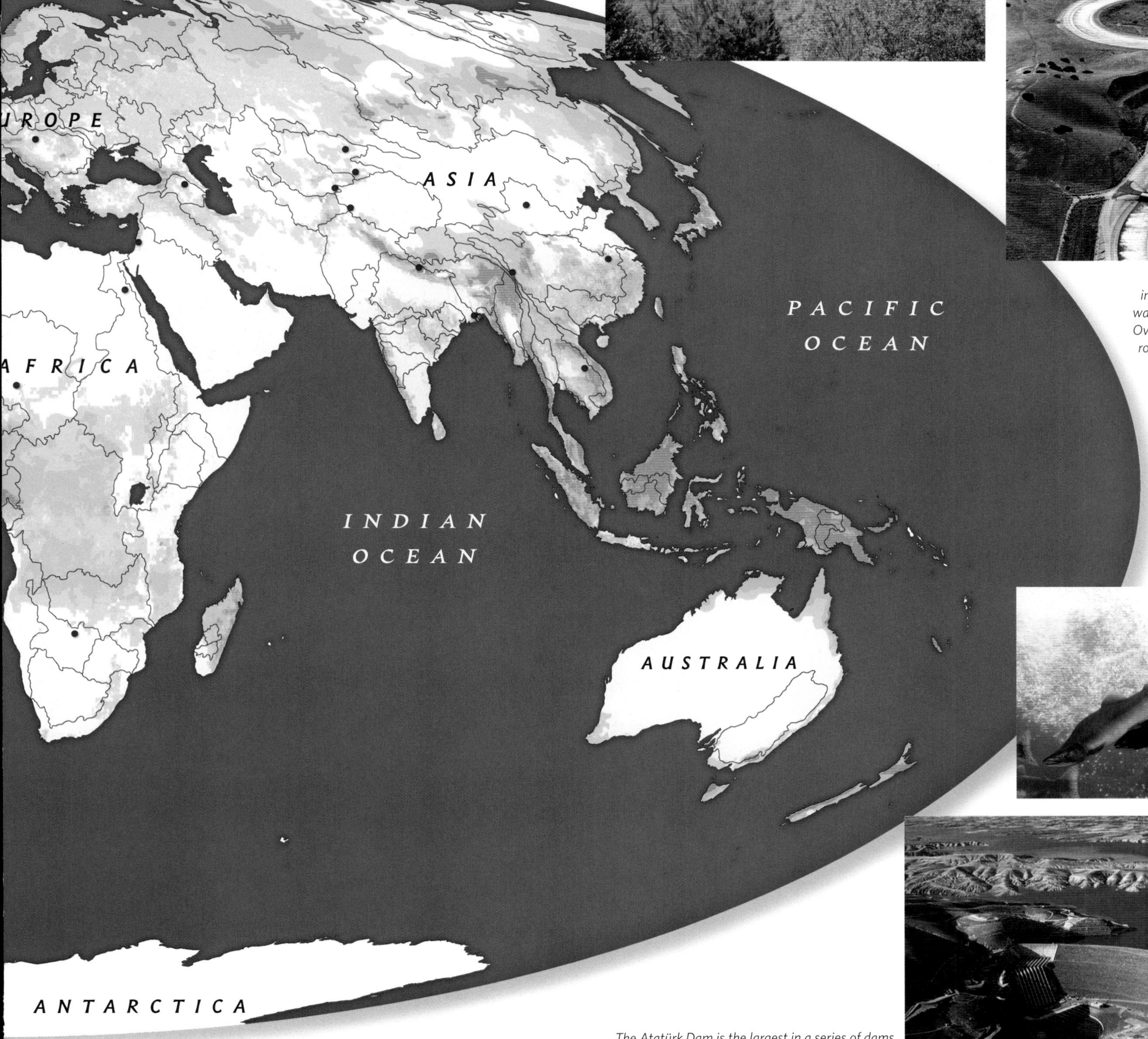

Salmon—which live in the ocean but return to fresh water to reproduce—are one of many species dependent on freshwater habitats.

The Atatürk Dam is the largest in a series of dams along the Tigris and Euphrates Rivers. Built mainly in the 1980s and 1990s, the dams provide irrigation water and electricity for arid southeastern Turkey.

Aquifers of the World

As water infiltrates the Earth's surface, it collects in large subsurface formations called aquifers, which are accessed through wells and used for agricultural, commercial, domestic, and industrial purposes. This groundwater accounts for more than 30 percent of the world's freshwater resources.

Annually, the world uses between 180 and 192 cubic miles (750–800 cubic kilometers) of groundwater, primarily for irrigation, but also to supply the majority of the world's municipalities. In the United States, half the population relies on groundwater for domestic uses. Around the world, groundwater resources are becoming increasingly scarce as human populations multiply, and as advances in technology allow more to be extracted. Annually, there is a 48-cubic-mile (200 cubic kilometers) overdraft, worldwide: This means that humans are pumping more water out of the ground than the hydrologic cycle puts back in to it.

The increase in withdrawals corresponds to the more than doubling of irrigated acreage around the world since the 1950s. In regions where groundwater is utilized for irrigation, groundwater managers are faced with problems of overdrafting and contamination—both challenges for

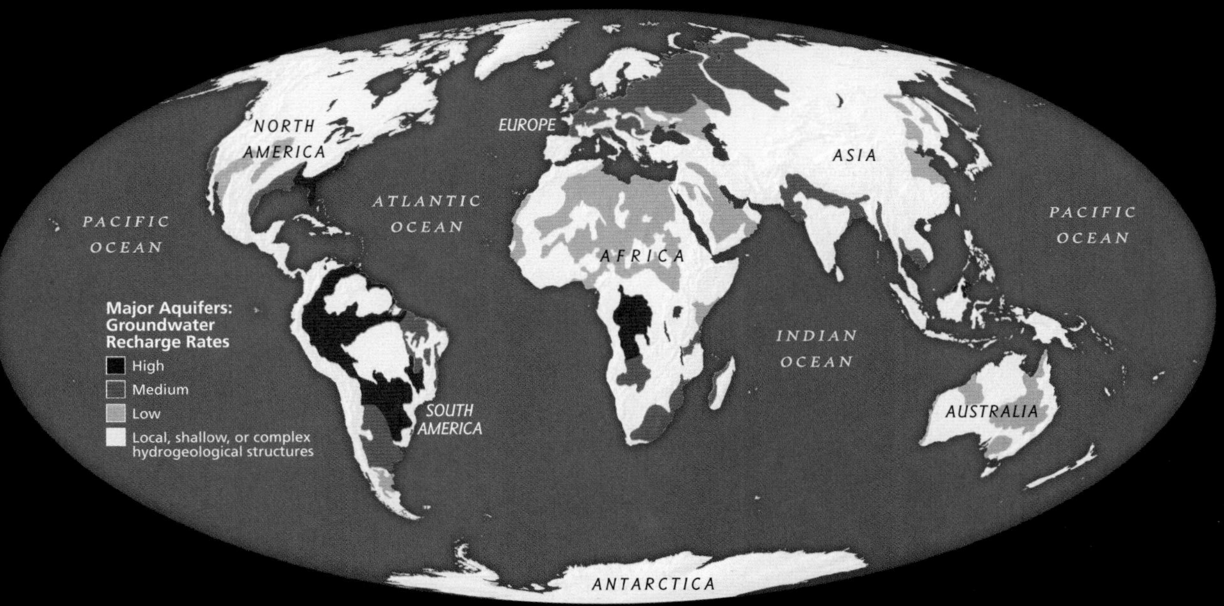

NORTH AMERICA
EUROPE
ASIA
PACIFIC OCEAN
ATLANTIC OCEAN
AFRICA
PACIFIC OCEAN
Major Aquifers: Groundwater Recharge Rates
High
Medium
Low
Local, shallow, or complex hydrogeological structures
SOUTH AMERICA
INDIAN OCEAN
AUSTRALIA
ANTARCTICA

Climate

THE TERM "CLIMATE" describes the average weather conditions, as measured over many years, that prevail at any given point around the world at a given time of the year. Daily weather may differ dramatically from that expected on the basis of climatic statistics.

Energy from the sun drives the global climate system. Much of this incoming energy is absorbed in the tropics. Outgoing heat radiation, much of which exits at high latitudes, balances the absorbed incoming solar energy. To achieve a balance across the globe, huge amounts of heat are moved from the tropics to polar regions by both the atmosphere and the oceans.

The tilt of Earth's axis leads to shifting patterns of incoming solar energy throughout the year. There is a bigger difference between the tropics and high latitudes in winter because higher latitudes have lower midday solar angles and shorter days in the winter. In the summer the lower midday sun angles in the high latitudes are partly offset by longer days.

More energy is transported to higher latitudes in winter than in summer, and hence the contrast in temperatures between the tropics and polar regions is greatest at this time of year—especially in the Northern Hemisphere.

Scientists present this data in many ways, using climographs (see pages 44–45), which show information about specific places. Alternatively, they produce maps, which show regional and worldwide data.

The effects of the climatic contrasts are seen in the distribution of Earth's life-forms. Temperature, precipitation, and the amount of sunlight all determine what plants can grow in a region and the animals that live there. People are more adaptable, but climate exerts powerful constraints on where we live.

Climatic conditions define planning decisions, such as how much heating oil we need for the winter, and the necessary rainfall for agriculture in the summer. Fluctuations from year to year (e.g., cold winters or summer droughts) make planning more difficult.

In the longer term, continued global warming may change climatic conditions around the world, which could dramatically alter temperature and precipitation patterns and lead to more frequent heat waves, floods, and droughts.

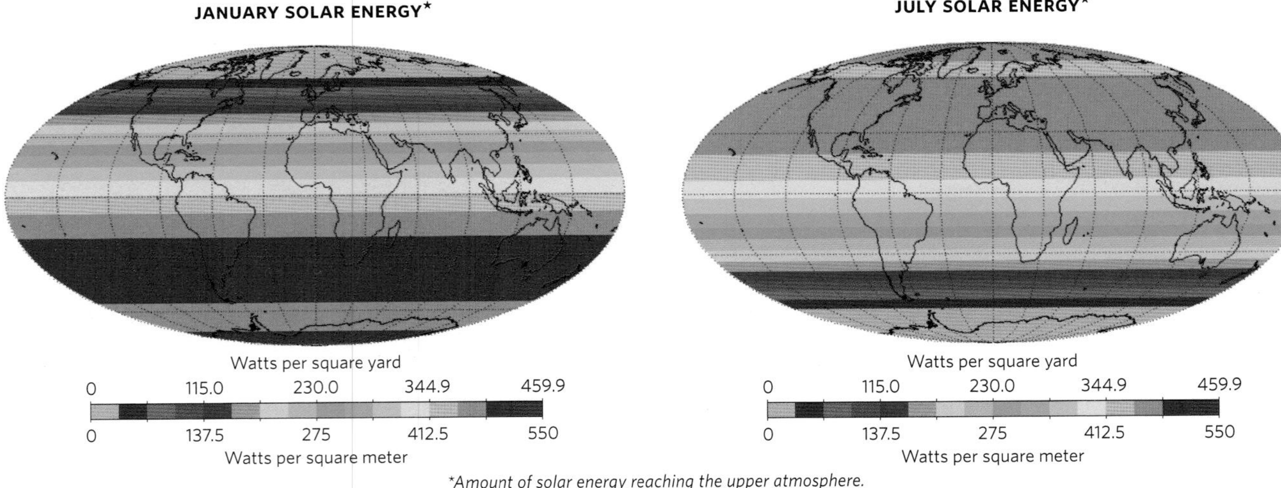
JANUARY SOLAR ENERGY*
JULY SOLAR ENERGY*
Watts per square yard
0 115.0 230.0 344.9 459.9
0 137.5 275 412.5 550
Watts per square meter

*Amount of solar energy reaching the upper atmosphere. Cloud patterns greatly modify the amount of solar radiation available at the Earth's surface.

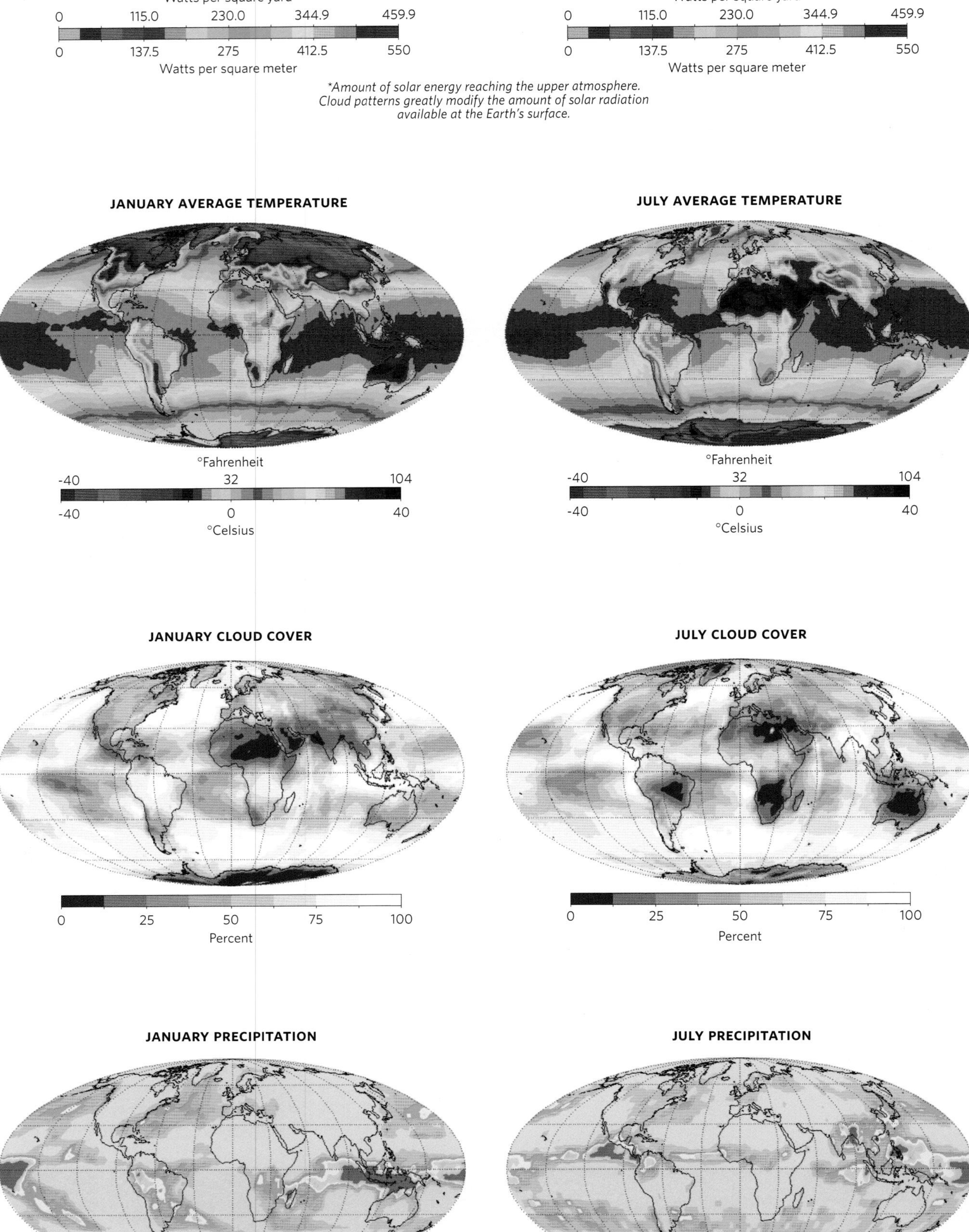
JANUARY AVERAGE TEMPERATURE
JULY AVERAGE TEMPERATURE
°Fahrenheit
-40 32 104
-40 0 40
°Celsius
JANUARY CLOUD COVER
JULY CLOUD COVER
0 25 50 75 100
Percent
JANUARY PRECIPITATION
JULY PRECIPITATION
Inches
0 4.9 9.8 14.8 19.7
0 125 250 375 500
Millimeters

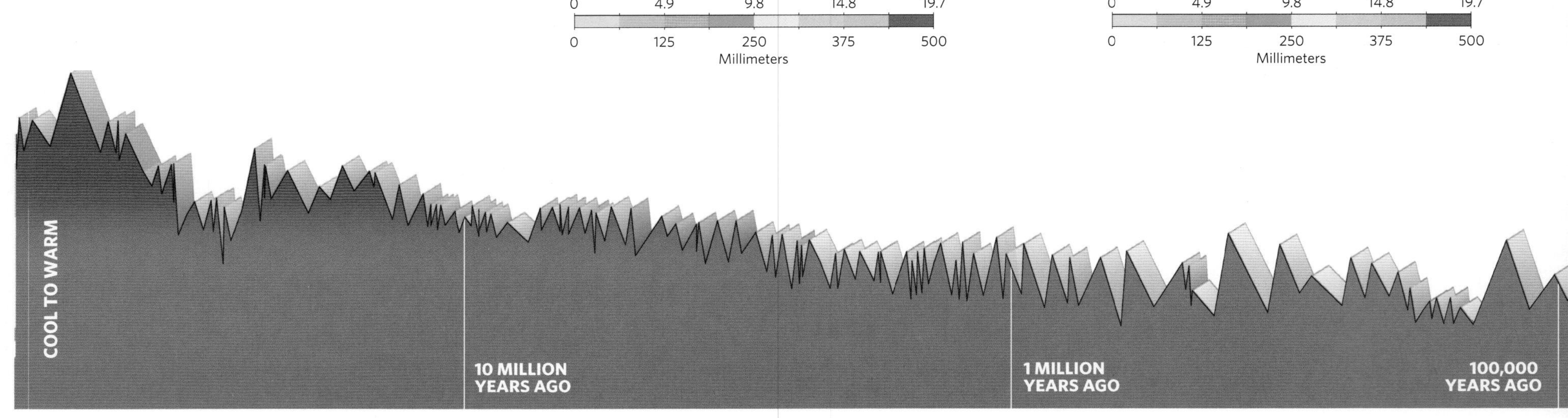
COOL TO WARM
10 MILLION YEARS AGO
1 MILLION YEARS AGO
100,000 YEARS AGO

Major Factors That Influence Climate

LATITUDE AND ANGLE OF THE SUN'S RAYS As Earth circles the sun, the tilt of its axis causes changes in the angle of the sun's rays and in the periods of daylight at different latitudes. Polar regions experience the greatest variation, with long periods of limited or no sunlight in winter and up to 24 hours of daylight in the summer.

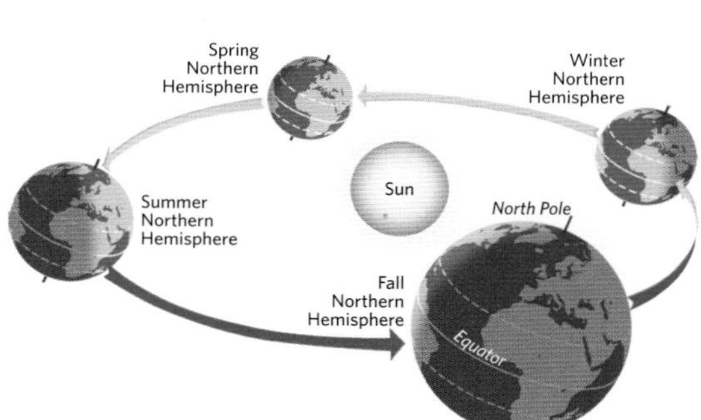

Spring Northern Hemisphere
Winter Northern Hemisphere
Summer Northern Hemisphere
Sun
North Pole
Fall Northern Hemisphere
Equator
South Pole

ELEVATION (ALTITUDE) In general, climatic conditions become colder as elevation increases, just as they do when latitude increases. "Life zones" on a high mountain reflect the changes: Plants at the base are the same as those in surrounding countryside. Farther up, treed vegetation distinctly ends at the tree line, and at the highest elevations, snow covers the mountain.

Fuji, Honshu, Japan

TOPOGRAPHY Mountain ranges are natural barriers to air movement. In California (see diagram at right), winds off the Pacific carry moisture-laden air toward the coast. The Coast Ranges allow for some condensation and light precipitation. Inland, the taller Sierra Nevada wrings more significant precipitation from the air. On the leeward slopes of the Sierra Nevada, sinking air warms from compression, clouds evaporate, and dry conditions prevail.

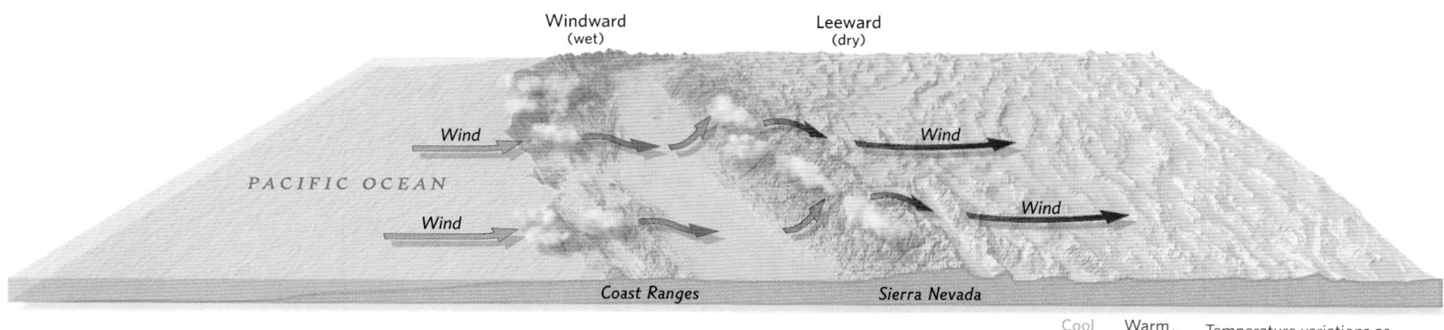

Windward (wet)
Leeward (dry)
Wind
Wind
Wind
Wind
PACIFIC OCEAN
Coast Ranges
Sierra Nevada
Cool Warm
Temperature variations as air moves over mountains

EFFECTS OF GEOGRAPHY The location of a place and its distance from mountains and bodies of water help determine its prevailing wind patterns and what types of air masses affect it. Coastal areas may enjoy refreshing breezes in summer, when cooler ocean air moves ashore. Places south and east of the Great Lakes can expect "lake effect" snow in winter, when cold air travels over relatively warmer waters. In spring and summer, people living in "Tornado Alley" in the central United States watch for thunderstorms. Here, three types of air masses often converge: cold and dry from the north, warm and dry from the southwest, and warm and moist from the Gulf of Mexico. The colliding air masses often spawn powerful tornadic storms.

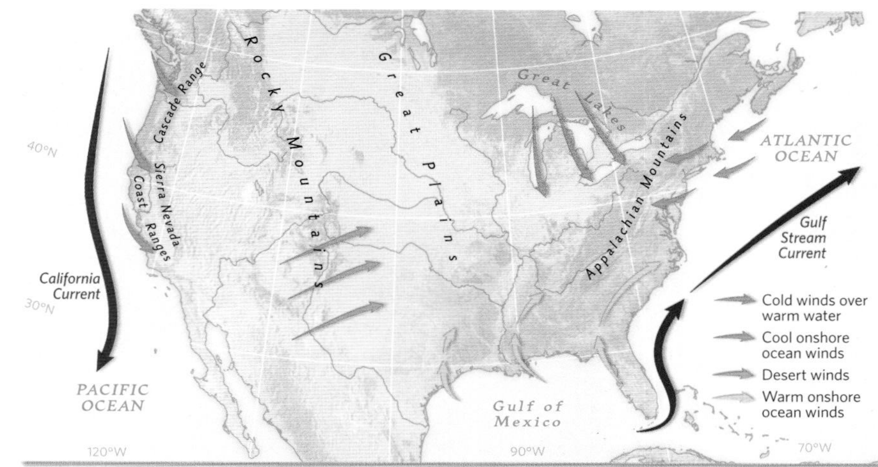

Cascade Range
Rocky Mountains
Great Plains
Great Lakes
Sierra Nevada
Coast Ranges
Appalachian Mountains
ATLANTIC OCEAN
Gulf Stream Current
California Current
PACIFIC OCEAN
Gulf of Mexico
40°N
30°N
120°W
90°W
70°W
Cold winds over warm water
Cool onshore ocean winds
Desert winds
Warm onshore ocean winds

PREVAILING GLOBAL WIND PATTERNS As shown at right, three large-scale wind patterns are found in the Northern Hemisphere and three are found in the Southern Hemisphere. These are average conditions and do not necessarily reflect those occurring on a particular day. As seasons change, the wind patterns shift north or south. So does the intertropical convergence zone, which moves back and forth across the Equator. Sailors called this zone the doldrums because its winds are typically weak.

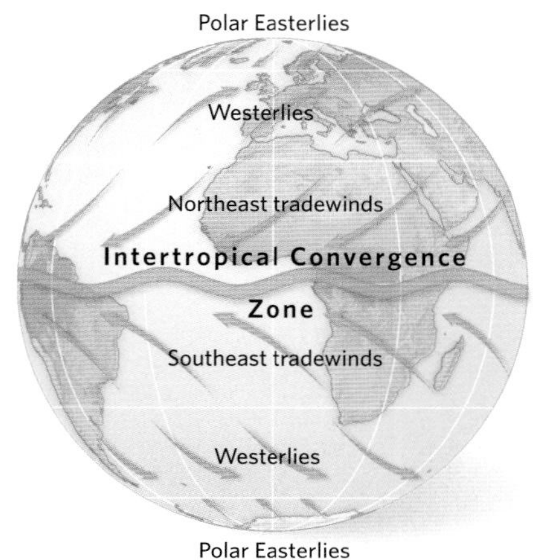

Polar Easterlies
Westerlies
Northeast tradewinds
Intertropical Convergence Zone
Southeast tradewinds
Westerlies
Polar Easterlies

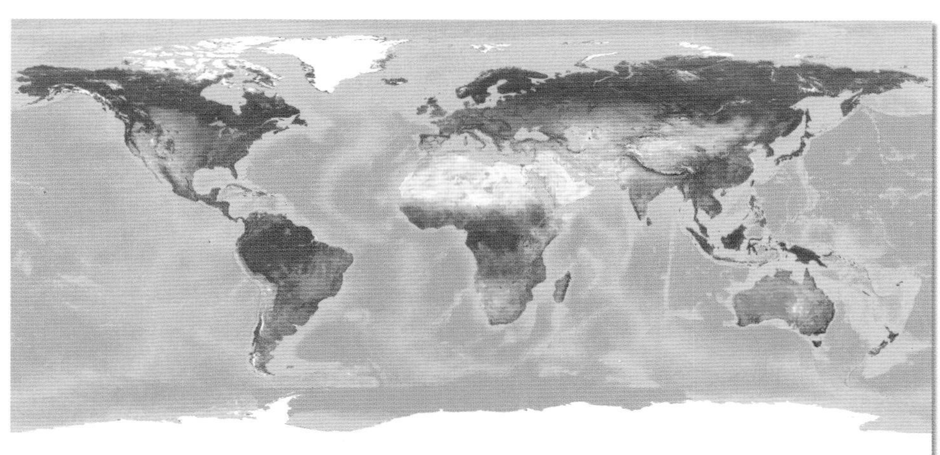

SURFACE OF THE EARTH Just look at any globe or a world map showing land cover, and you will see another important influence on climate: Earth's surface. The amount of sunlight that is absorbed or reflected by the surface determines how much atmospheric heating occurs. Darker areas, such as heavily vegetated regions, tend to be good absorbers; lighter areas, such as snow- and ice-covered regions, tend to be good reflectors. Oceans absorb a high proportion of the solar energy falling upon them, but release it more slowly. Both the oceans and the atmosphere distribute heat around the globe.

Temperature Change Over Time

Cold and warm periods punctuate Earth's long history. Some were fairly short (perhaps hundreds of years); others spanned hundreds of thousands of years. In some cold periods, glaciers grew and spread over large regions. In subsequent warm periods, the ice retreated. Each period profoundly affected plant and animal life. The most recent cool period, often called the little ice age, ended in western Europe around the year 1850.

Since the turn of the 20th century, temperatures have been rising rapidly throughout the world. Human activity, such as the burning of fossil fuels and the clearing of forests, is the main reason for the sudden warming of the globe. For more information on climate change, see pages 46–47.

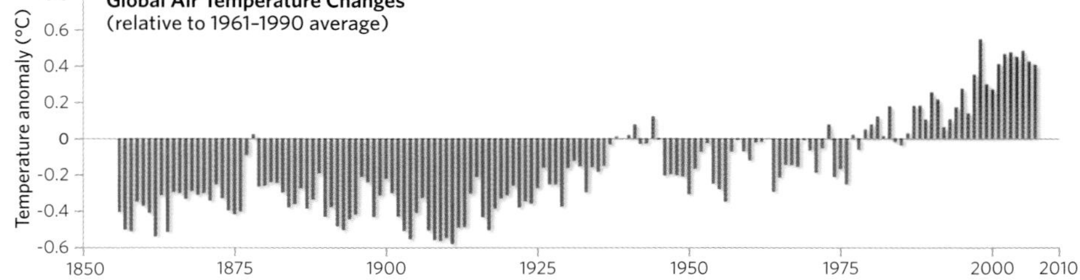

Global Air Temperature Changes
(relative to 1961–1990 average)
Temperature anomaly (°C)
0.8
0.6
0.4
0.2
0
-0.2
-0.4
-0.6
1850
1875
1900
1925
1950
1975
2000
2010

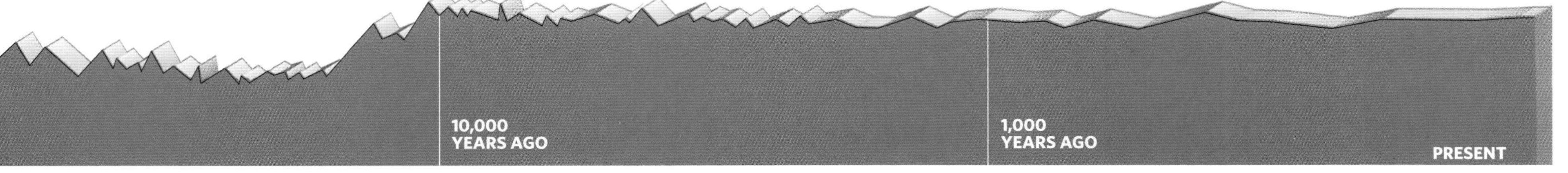

10,000 YEARS AGO
1,000 YEARS AGO
PRESENT

Climate (continued)

CLIMATE ZONES ARE PRIMARILY CONTROLLED BY LATITUDE— which governs the prevailing winds, the angle of the sun's rays, and the length of day throughout the year — and by geographical location with respect to mountains and oceans. Elevation, surface attributes, and other variables modify the primary controlling factors. Latitudinal banding of climate zones is most pronounced over Africa and Asia, where fewer north-south mountain ranges mean less disruption of the prevailing winds. In the Western Hemisphere, the high, almost continuous mountain range that extends from western Canada to southern South America helps create dry regions on its leeward slopes. Over the United States, where westerly winds prevail, areas to the east of the range lie in a "rain shadow" and are therefore drier. In northern parts of South America, where easterly trade winds prevail, the rain shadow lies west of the mountains. Ocean effects dominate much of western Europe and southern Australia.

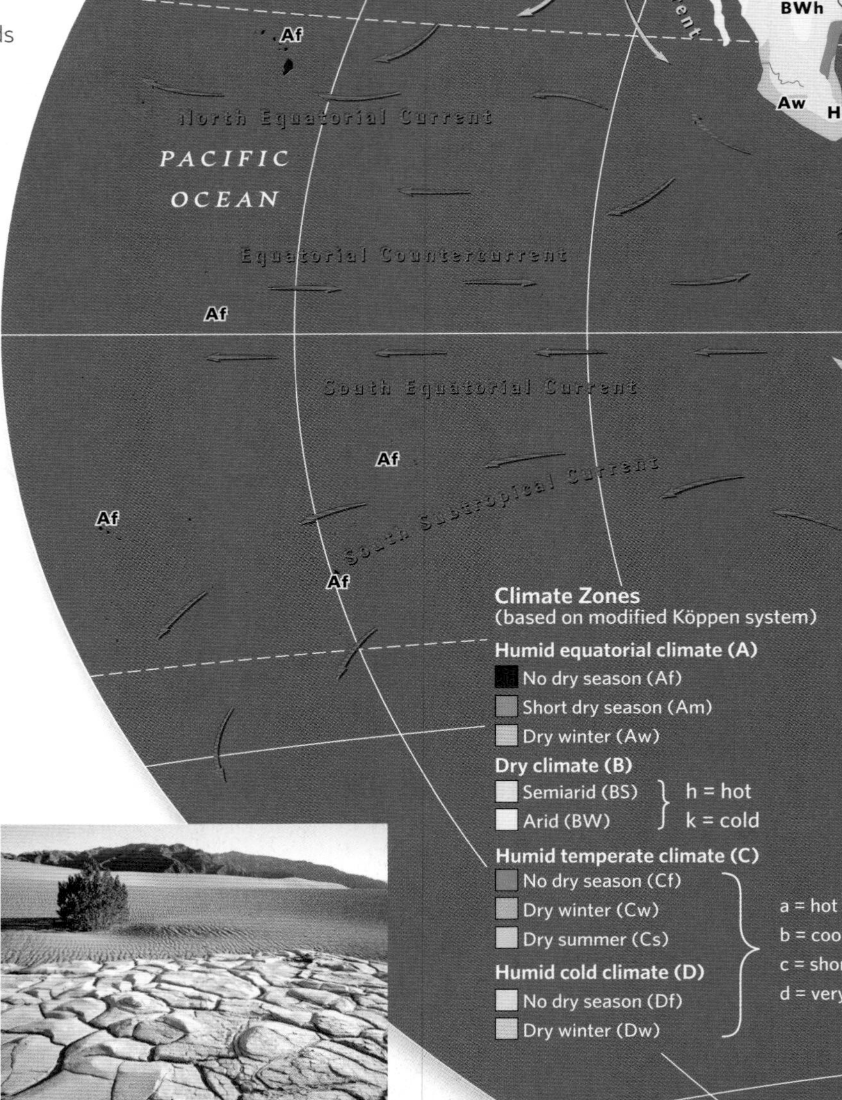

Beaufort Gyre
Alaska Current
Subarctic Current
North Pacific Drift
California Current
North Equatorial Current
PACIFIC OCEAN
Equatorial Countercurrent
South Equatorial Current
South Subtropical Current
Peru Current
Labrador Current
Gulf Stream
North Atlantic Drift
ATLANTIC OCEAN
Falkland Current
Denver
La Paz
Buenos Aires
Climate Zones
(based on modified Köppen system)
Humid equatorial climate (A)
No dry season (Af)
Short dry season (Am)
Dry winter (Aw)
Dry climate (B)
Semiarid (BS)
Arid (BW)
h = hot
k = cold
Humid temperate climate (C)
No dry season (Cf)
Dry winter (Cw)
Dry summer (Cs)
Humid cold climate (D)
No dry season (Df)
Dry winter (Dw)
a = hot summer
b = cool summer
c = short, cool summer
d = very cold winter
Cold polar climate (E)
Tundra and ice
Highland climate (H)
Unclassified highlands
Ocean current
Cold
Warm

Winter temperatures in Moscow often dip below 0°F (-18°C). One cold snap in 1940 produced the city's record low, -44°F (-42°C).

Death Valley is a desert of North American extremes, where temperatures reach 130°F (54°C), and parts of the valley receive less than 2 inches (50 mm) of rain annually.

Climographs

The map at right shows the global distribution of climate zones, while the following 12 climographs (graphs of monthly temperature and precipitation) provide snapshots of the climate at specific places. Each place has a different climate type, which is described in general terms. Rainfall is shown in a bar graph (in inches on the right side of the graph); temperature is expressed with a line graph (in degrees Fahrenheit on the left side).

SINGAPORE Located just 85 miles north of the Equator, Singapore experiences a tropical rain forest climate characterized by hot, humid weather year-round. There are no distinct seasons and there is little variation in conditions. Daytime temperatures range between 79°F (26°C) and 86°F (30°C), and humidity is usually above 75 percent. Winter is wettest, but rainfall is abundant all year.

Singapore

DA NANG, VIETNAM The coastal city of Da Nang, Vietnam, is located in a tropical monsoon climate with consistently high temperatures year-round. The city experiences two seasons as a result of the monsoon winds — a wet season from August to January, and a drier season from February to July. The average temperature is 79°F (26°C), while the average humidity is over 83 percent.

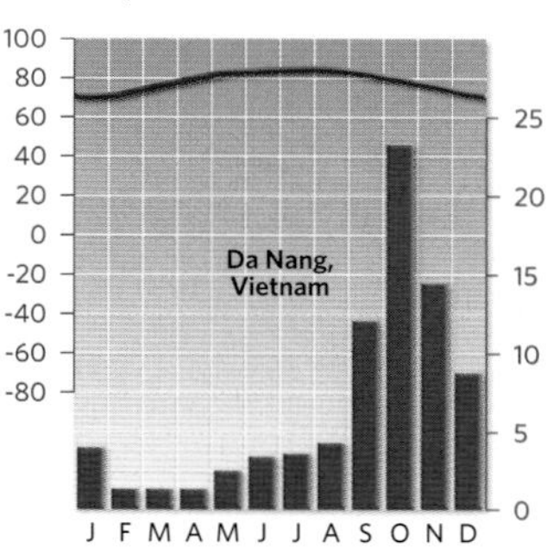

Da Nang, Vietnam
J F M A M J J A S O N D

MUMBAI, INDIA Located on the Arabian Sea in the outer tropics, Mumbai has very pronounced wet and dry seasons. Humidity is high between March and October, with highs over 86°F (30°C). Monsoon rains fall between June and September, bringing the majority of the annual precipitation. The dry season lasts from November through February and brings slightly cooler temperatures and lower humidity.

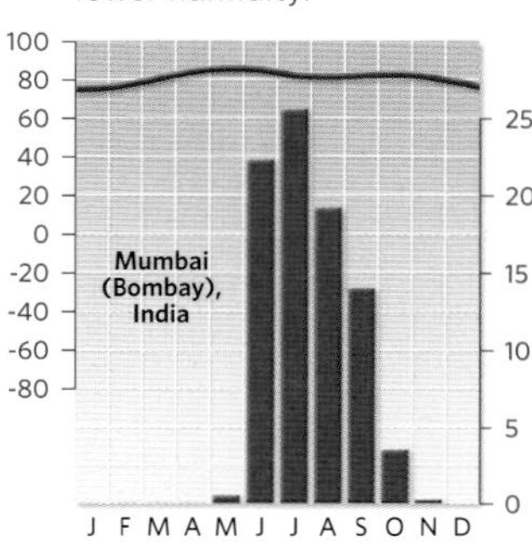

Mumbai (Bombay), India
J F M A M J J A S O N D

DENVER, UNITED STATES Located at the foot of the Rocky Mountains, Denver has a semiarid climate with about 300 days of sunshine each year. The mountains help shield the city from heavy precipitation, and warm winds moving down the mountain slopes keep temperatures mild. The average temperature in Denver is 50°F (10°C), and the average annual precipitation is 15.81 inches (402 mm).

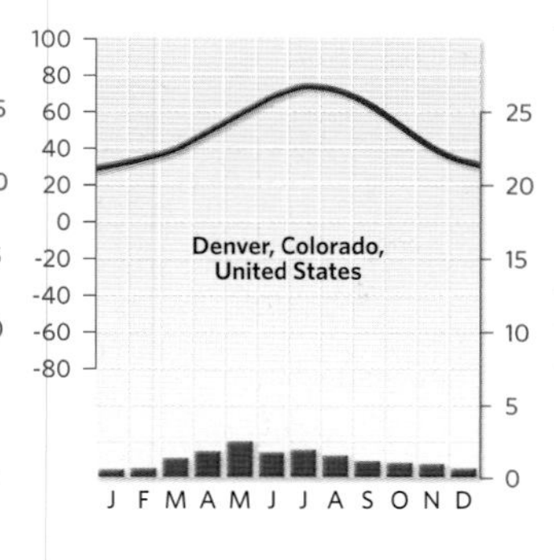

Denver, Colorado, United States
J F M A M J J A S O N D

CAIRO, EGYPT The desert city of Cairo receives less than 0.5 inch (13 mm) of rain each year. Temperatures are warm throughout the year and often surpass 104°F (40°C) in the summer. Gusty, hot winds arrive in the spring, bringing Saharan dust into the city. In the summer, humidity levels can reach 77 percent but are low the rest of the year.

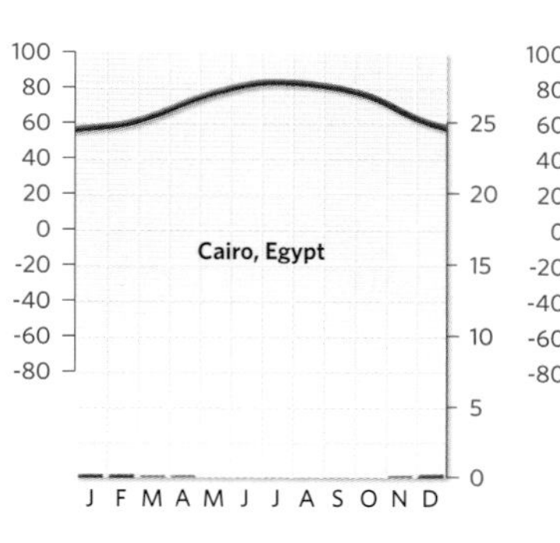

Cairo, Egypt
J F M A M J J A S O N D

LONDON, UNITED KINGDOM Like much of the British Isles, London has a temperate climate, with warm summers and moderate winters. Summers are humid, with high temperatures in July reaching 73°F (23°C). Low temperatures in January fall to 35°F (2°C). The city experiences regular precipitation throughout the year, often in the form of light rain. A few light snowfalls are generally seen each year.

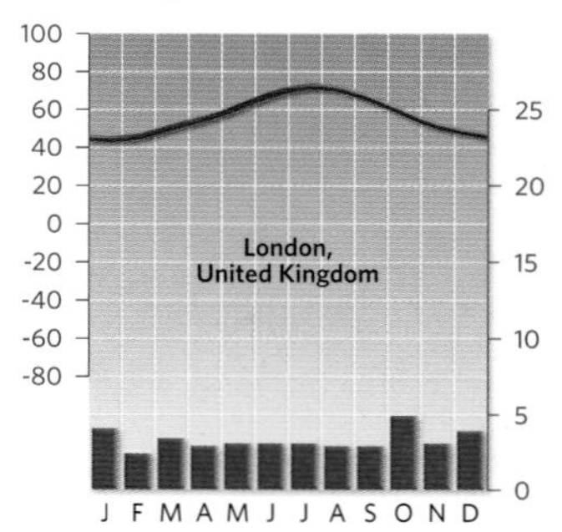

London, United Kingdom
J F M A M J J A S O N D

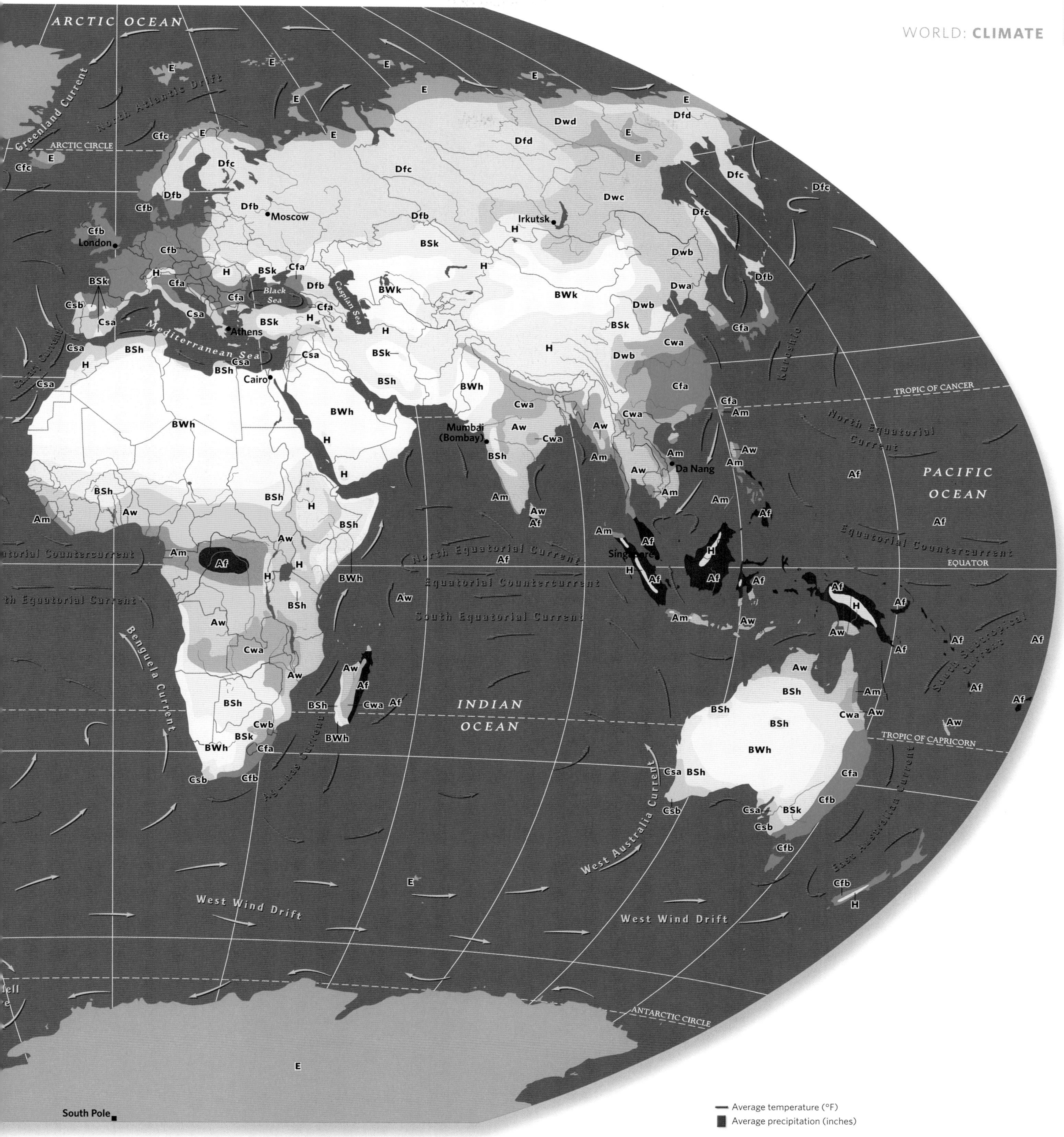

Average temperature (°F)
Average precipitation (inches)

BUENOS AIRES, ARGENTINA Buenos Aires experiences a humid temperate climate with a warm, wet summer from December to February due to its location in the Southern Hemisphere. High temperatures range from 86°F (30°C) in January to 59°F (15°C) in July. The heaviest rains fall during the southern summer, between October and March, and the winter months of June through September are drier.

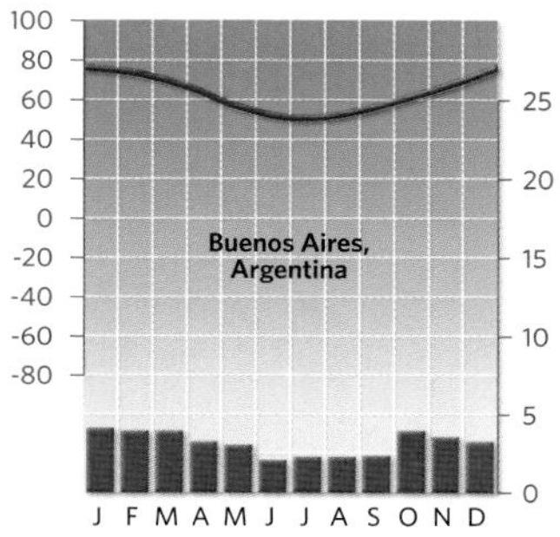

ATHENS, GREECE In the Mediterranean climate of Athens, most of the rainfall occurs in the winter months between October and April. Summers are sunny and dry with an occasional shower or thunderstorm, and heat waves are common. Temperatures can reach 104°F (40°C) during July and August and the city is prone to smog. Winters are generally mild and snowfall is rare.

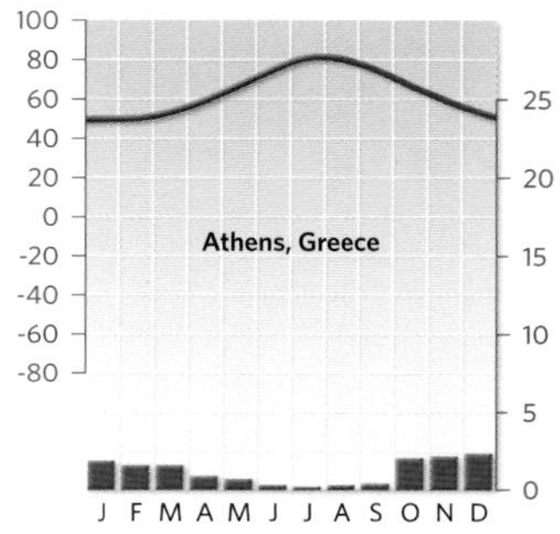

MOSCOW, RUSSIA Located well inland, Moscow's continental climate is characterized by very cold, long winters and warm summers. July and August are humid, with highs around 72°F (22°C). In winter, average lows dip to 11°F (-12°C). There is no significant variation in precipitation totals, although much of the precipitation falls as snow during the long winter. Overcast skies are common, especially in December.

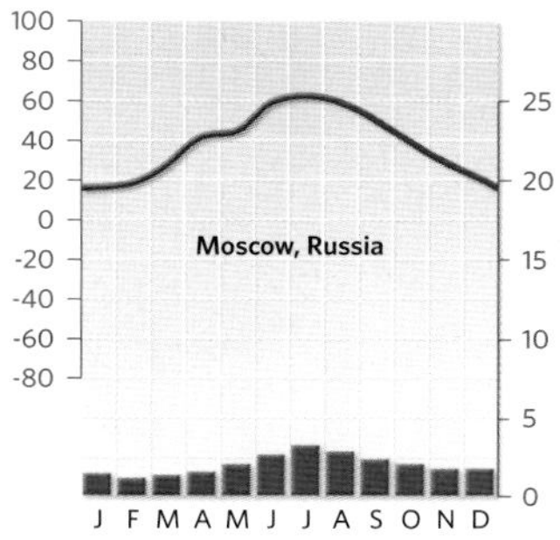

IRKUTSK, RUSSIA Located near Lake Baikal in southern Siberia, Irkutsk experiences a continental climate with extreme variation in temperature and precipitation. Average temperatures range from 64°F (18°C) in summer to -2°F (-19°C) in winter. Winters are dry, characterized by fluffy snow with a low moisture content. July, the wettest month, has an average of 4.7 inches (119 mm) of rain.

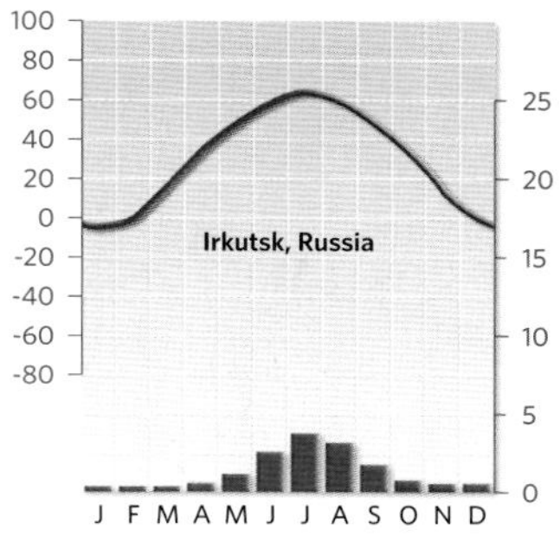

SOUTH POLE Lack of sunlight during the southern winter, along with a high altitude, creates one of the coldest climates on Earth at the South Pole. In winter, the temperatures can reach -85°F (-65°C), and in summer the average high is -14°F (-25°C). There is almost no precipitation, and humidity is near zero. However, windblown snow from other areas can create blinding conditions.

LA PAZ, BOLIVIA Located high in the Altiplano region at nearly 12,000 feet (3658 m) above sea level, La Paz experiences consistently cool temperatures year-round. During the southern winter, the average high is 59°F (15°C), and in the summer it is 72°F (22°C). Rain falls on most afternoons in the summer. There is typically a large diurnal temperature variation due to clear skies.

Buenos Aires, Argentina

Athens, Greece

Moscow, Russia

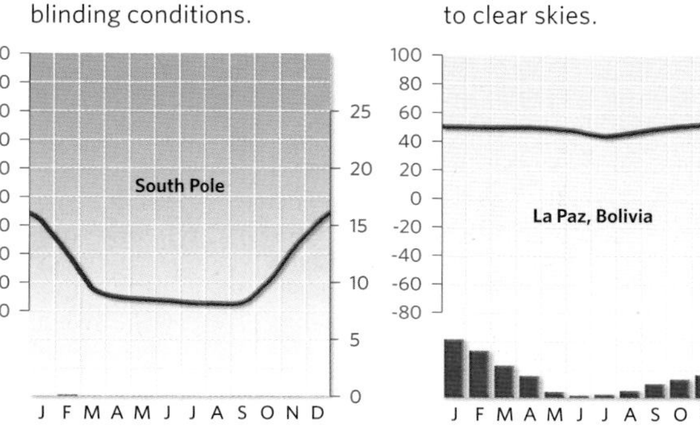
Irkutsk, Russia
South Pole
La Paz, Bolivia
J F M A M J J A S O N D

Climate Change

THE SCIENTIFIC EVIDENCE IS CLEAR: Surface temperatures on Earth are warming at a pace that signals a decisive shift in the global climate, one expected to last for centuries. Previous epochal changes of climate, such as the ice age that ended 11,500 years ago, were set in motion by natural causes—variations in Earth's orbit that affect the amount of sunlight warming the planet. In those cases, the cycles of cooling and warming unfolded slowly, over the course of millennia. This episode is different.

Climate is changing more rapidly than ever before. Human activity is the main cause. Burning of fossil fuels—oil, gas, coal—has flooded the atmosphere with heat-trapping carbon dioxide (CO_2), triggering a 1°F (0.6°C) spike in average global temperature in the past century, largely in the past 30 years. Already, impacts include altered precipitation patterns, melting glaciers, intensifying storms, and a rise in sea level. Unless CO_2 emissions are slashed, the planet will likely heat up even faster, fundamentally changing the world we live in.

Even a future with dramatic cuts in carbon emissions will see an additional temperature rise of 3.6°F (2°C) over the next century. Though a few regions, such as Russia and northern Europe, may benefit from warmer years, most of the world will suffer. Particularly hard hit will be those people in the tropics and in poorer countries without the funds to adapt. Changes that will most directly affect humans include increased water scarcity (see Environmental Stresses, pages 82-83), losses to vegetation and crops, increased flooding and disease, and population displacement due to rising sea levels.

Greenhouse Earth

Earth is hospitable to life because its atmosphere works like a greenhouse, retaining enough of the sun's heat to allow plants and animals to exist. This natural climate-control system depends on the trace presence of certain atmospheric gases—most important, carbon dioxide—to trap the sun's radiation.

But while these processes are essential to life on Earth, the "enhanced greenhouse effect," or continual rise in atmospheric greenhouse gas concentrations, is threatening to disrupt the global climate, civilizations, ecosystems, and natural resources. The system's stability has been jolted.

The primary source of carbon dioxide emissions is the burning of fossil fuels in power stations, industrial processes, and transportation; and these activities have hiked atmospheric CO_2 to levels unprecedented during human history. Greenhouse Earth is growing warmer. How much warmer it gets depends on the human response.

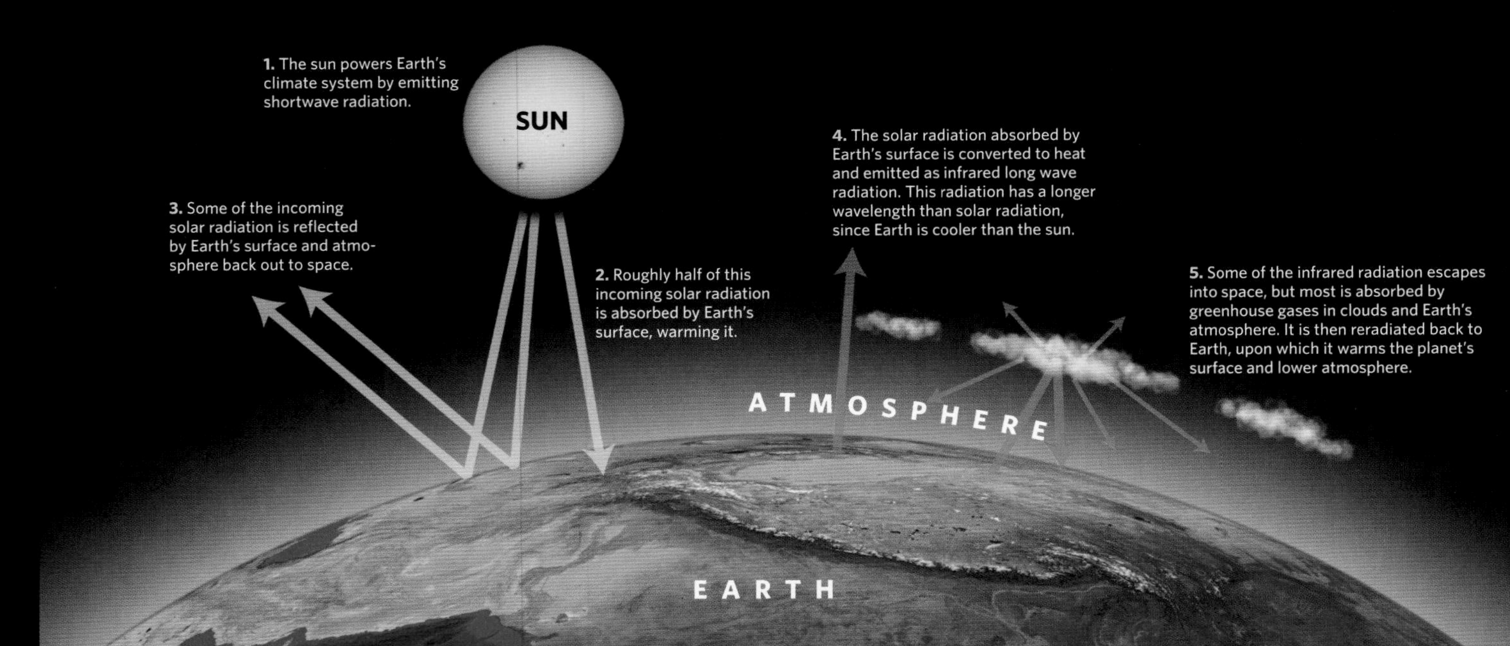
1. The sun powers Earth's climate system by emitting shortwave radiation.
SUN
2. Roughly half of this incoming solar radiation is absorbed by Earth's surface, warming it.
3. Some of the incoming solar radiation is reflected by Earth's surface and atmosphere back out to space.
4. The solar radiation absorbed by Earth's surface is converted to heat and emitted as infrared long wave radiation. This radiation has a longer wavelength than solar radiation, since Earth is cooler than the sun.
5. Some of the infrared radiation escapes into space, but most is absorbed by greenhouse gases in clouds and Earth's atmosphere. It is then reradiated back to Earth, upon which it warms the planet's surface and lower atmosphere.
ATMOSPHERE
EARTH

Ages of Ice and Heat

Carbon dioxide levels, as measured in Antarctic ice cores, have risen and fallen in step with global temperatures and sea levels over the past 400,000 years. The record shows that long ice ages have gripped the planet, interrupted by shorter warming periods. Historically, temperatures rose first, then CO_2 increased, accelerating temperature rise. What makes the present situation unpredictable is that never before has CO_2 climbed so fast and so high, far ahead of temperature.

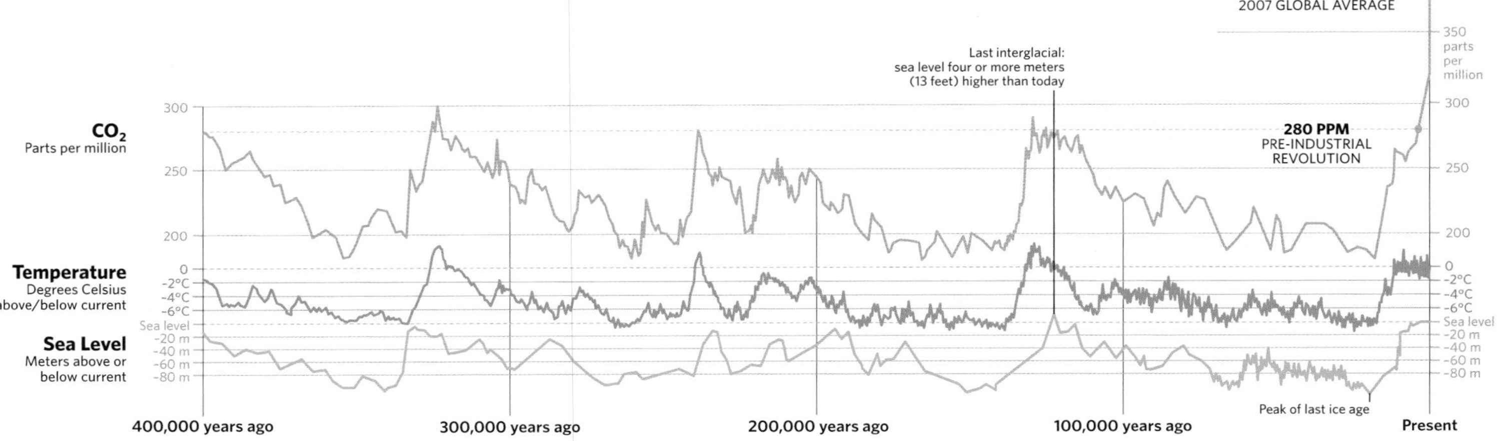
384 PPM
2007 GLOBAL AVERAGE
Last interglacial: sea level four or more meters (13 feet) higher than today
280 PPM
PRE-INDUSTRIAL REVOLUTION
CO2
Parts per million
300
250
200
350 parts per million
Temperature
Degrees Celsius above/below current
0
-2°C
-4°C
-6°C
Sea Level
Meters above or below current
Sea level
-20 m
-40 m
-60 m
-80 m
Peak of last ice age
400,000 years ago
300,000 years ago
200,000 years ago
100,000 years ago
Present

The Warming Earth

According to basic laws of physics, our copious CO_2 emissions should amplify the greenhouse effect and raise temperatures worldwide—and that's just what climate data show. Earth is, on average, 1.3°F (0.7°C) warmer today than in 1906, with increased surface temperatures recorded on every continent and ocean. The most dramatic changes have been in the Arctic, where temperatures have risen 4° to 5°F (2.2° to 2.7°C) in the past 50 years. Landmasses have warmed more quickly than oceans, which are natural heat sinks, and day-to-night temperature swings have narrowed as less heat escapes into space when the sun goes down.

The Arctic is experiencing the fastest rate of warming as its reflective covering of ice and snow shrinks. In the mid-latitudes there are now fewer cold nights; heat waves are more common. The Indian Ocean and the western Pacific Ocean are warmer than at any point in the past 11,500 years. Against the trend are certain pockets of the oceans that are cooled by deepwater upwellings. Ozone loss over the South Pole may have cooled parts of Antarctica.

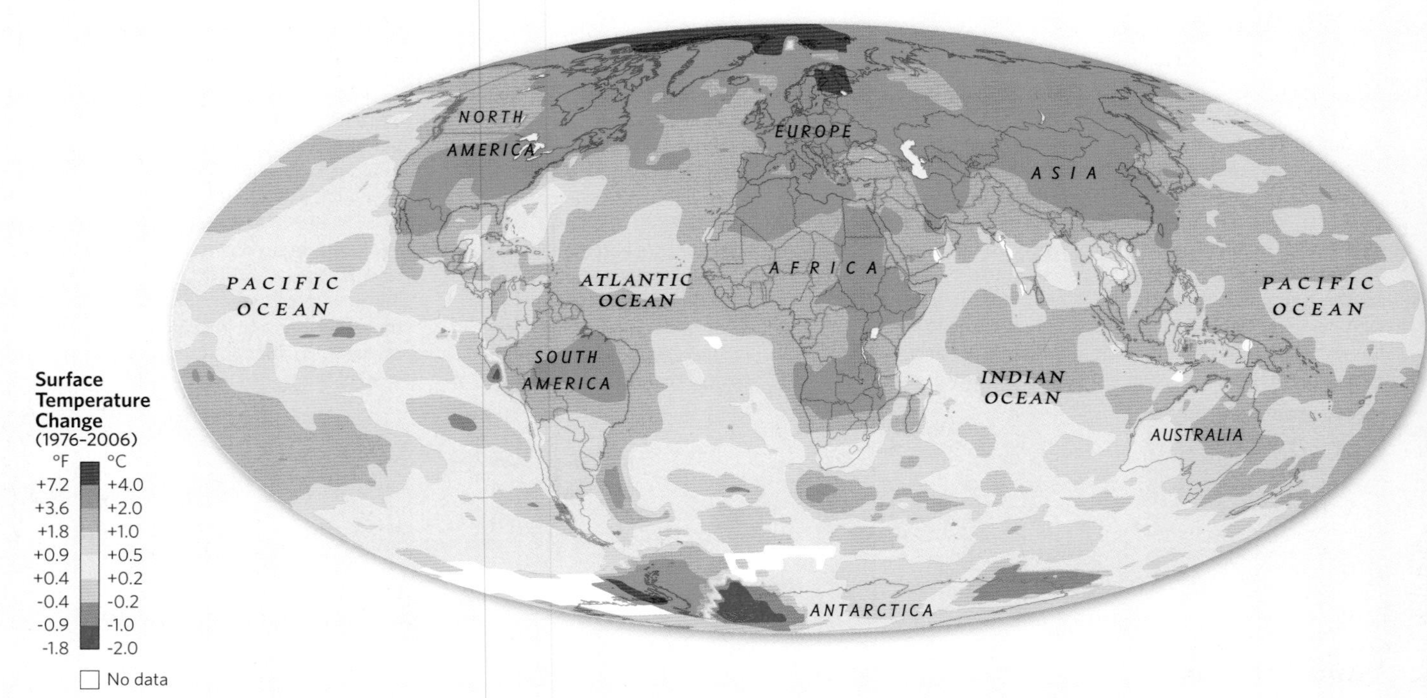
NORTH AMERICA
EUROPE
ASIA
AFRICA
PACIFIC OCEAN
ATLANTIC OCEAN
PACIFIC OCEAN
SOUTH AMERICA
INDIAN OCEAN
AUSTRALIA
ANTARCTICA
Surface Temperature Change (1976-2006)
°F °C
+7.2 +4.0
+3.6 +2.0
+1.8 +1.0
+0.9 +0.5
+0.4 +0.2
-0.4 -0.2
-0.9 -1.0
-1.8 -2.0
No data

1979
Sea ice extent, end of summer, 1979

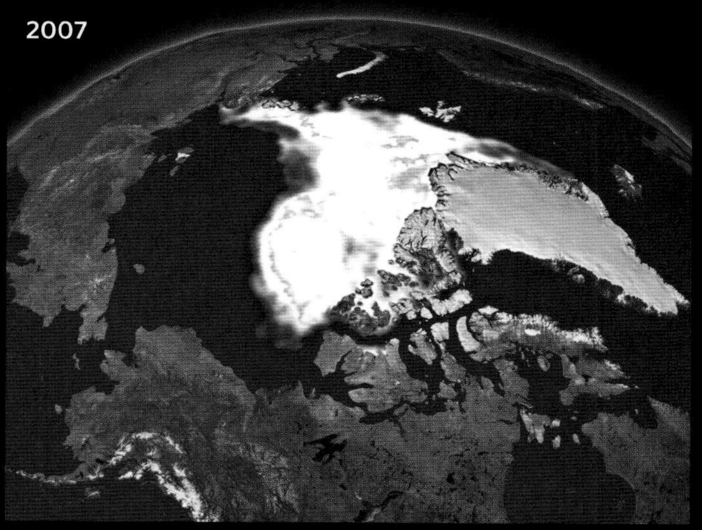
2007
Sea ice extent, end of summer, 2007

Shrinking Ice

Nowhere has global warming proceeded with more speed than in the Arctic Ocean, where the ice pack has been shrinking and thinning noticeably since the early 1990s. The changes caught the world's attention in late summer 2007, when normally icebound sea channels, like the Northwest Passage, opened to ships as the ice retreated drastically. That summer, Arctic ice coverage was nearly half a million square miles smaller than its previous minimum in 2005.

Although 2007 was unusually warm even by the standards of the recent Arctic regional warming trend, coming years promise to eclipse it. Researchers predict the Arctic Ocean will likely be ice-free in summer by 2030, opening legendary trade routes and sending countries scrambling to claim newly open waters.

Environmental Impacts

No region of the world is immune to the effects of climate change. The impacts are seen everywhere, from glacial mountaintops to inland lakes to low-lying islands in the middle of the ocean.

Plants and animals—whose existence depends on natural cues, such as the timing of spring, the presence of ice, or the number of days below freezing—have been the first to feel the heat. Polar species have been hit hardest; shrinking sea ice in particular spells trouble for polar bears, which depend on it to hunt, rest, and travel. As their numbers fall, the reality hits home.

For many people, climate change may still seem abstract, its impact felt mainly in the world's remote wild places. In actuality, it is already hitting us where we live, in the form of extreme weather events such as heat waves, droughts, floods, and more intense hurricanes—all signs of a new reality.

Climate change paradox: drought and desertification in some areas; melting and flooding in others

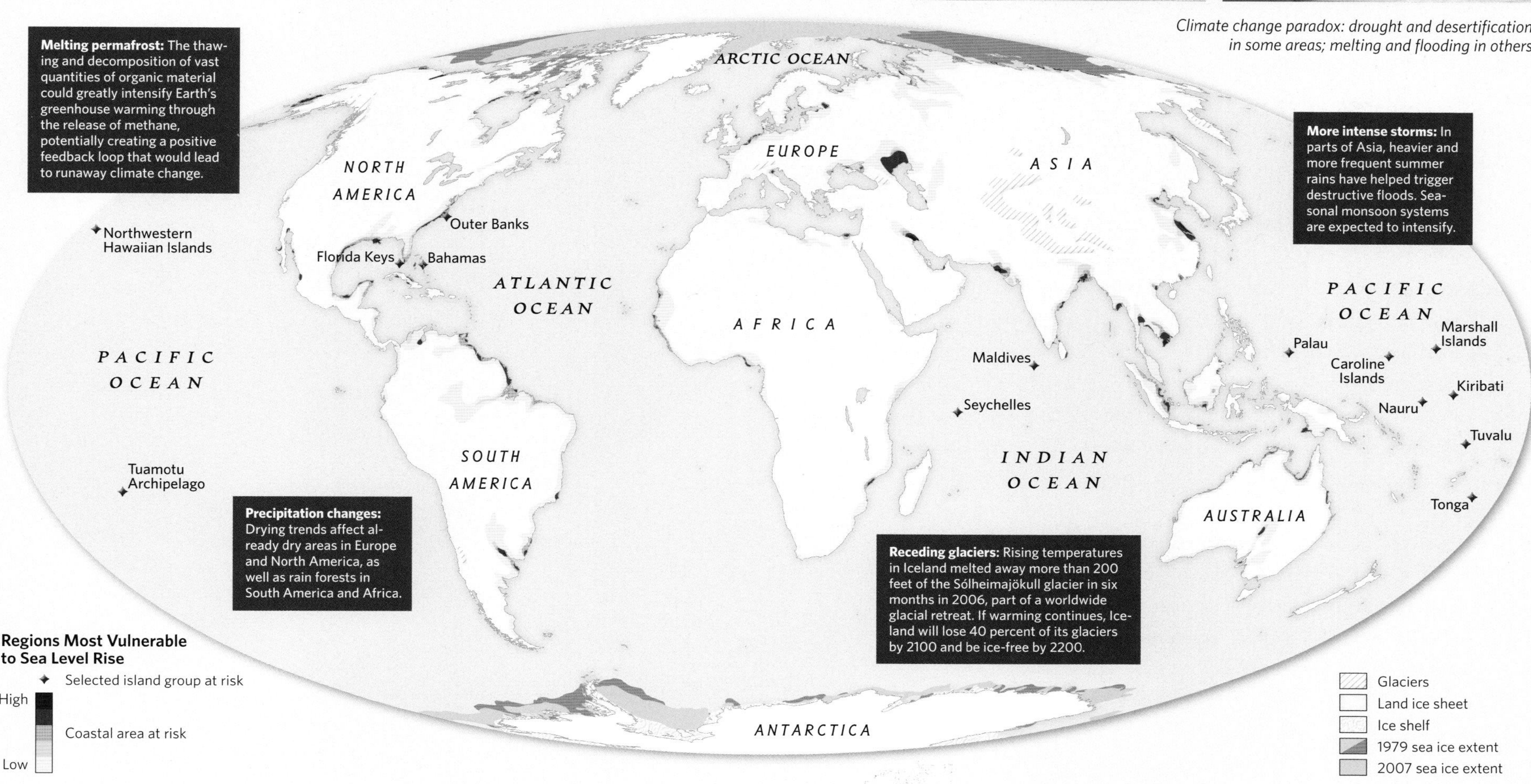
ARCTIC OCEAN
NORTH AMERICA
EUROPE
ASIA
Outer Banks
Florida Keys
Bahamas
Northwestern Hawaiian Islands
ATLANTIC OCEAN
AFRICA
PACIFIC OCEAN
PACIFIC OCEAN
Marshall Islands
Palau
Caroline Islands
Kiribati
Nauru
Tuvalu
Tonga
Maldives
Seychelles
INDIAN OCEAN
AUSTRALIA
SOUTH AMERICA
Tuamotu Archipelago
ANTARCTICA
Melting permafrost: The thawing and decomposition of vast quantities of organic material could greatly intensify Earth's greenhouse warming through the release of methane, potentially creating a positive feedback loop that would lead to runaway climate change.
More intense storms: In parts of Asia, heavier and more frequent summer rains have helped trigger destructive floods. Seasonal monsoon systems are expected to intensify.
Precipitation changes: Drying trends affect already dry areas in Europe and North America, as well as rain forests in South America and Africa.
Receding glaciers: Rising temperatures in Iceland melted away more than 200 feet of the Sólheimajökull glacier in six months in 2006, part of a worldwide glacial retreat. If warming continues, Iceland will lose 40 percent of its glaciers by 2100 and be ice-free by 2200.
Regions Most Vulnerable to Sea Level Rise
Selected island group at risk
High
Coastal area at risk
Low
Glaciers
Land ice sheet
Ice shelf
1979 sea ice extent
2007 sea ice extent

Ethical Considerations

Since 1950, there has been a distinct increase in the frequency of global extreme weather events, with about 15 events per decade during the 1950s and 1960s rising to about 58 events per decade during the 1980s and 1990s. Likewise, the global costs of extreme weather events increased dramatically since the 1970s. These results reflect rising populations, development in high-risk regions, and the tendency of global warming to amplify weather variability and extremes. During the past 50 to 100 years, the observational record suggests that very heavy precipitation events have become more frequent across much of the mid-latitudes.

Climate change should be viewed as an ethical issue. While the rich countries (e.g., the United States, China, and Germany) produce the greatest carbon emissions, the poorest countries (e.g., much of Africa) will likely endure the most health-related mortality triggered by climate change, including malaria, malnutrition, diarrhea, and flooding fatalities. According to the *UN Human Development Report 2007/2008*, "Climate change is the defining human development challenge of the 21st Century," and "the poorest countries and most vulnerable citizens will suffer the earliest and most damaging setbacks, though they have contributed the least to the problem."

COUNTRIES WITH THE HIGHEST LEVELS OF GREENHOUSE GAS EMISSIONS

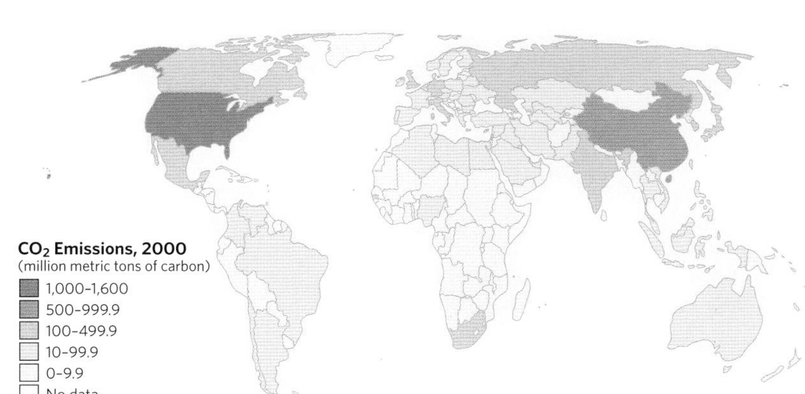
CO_2 Emissions, 2000
(million metric tons of carbon)
1,000–1,600
500–999.9
100–499.9
10–99.9
0–9.9
No data

COUNTRIES THAT WILL SUFFER THE MOST DUE TO CLIMATE CHANGE

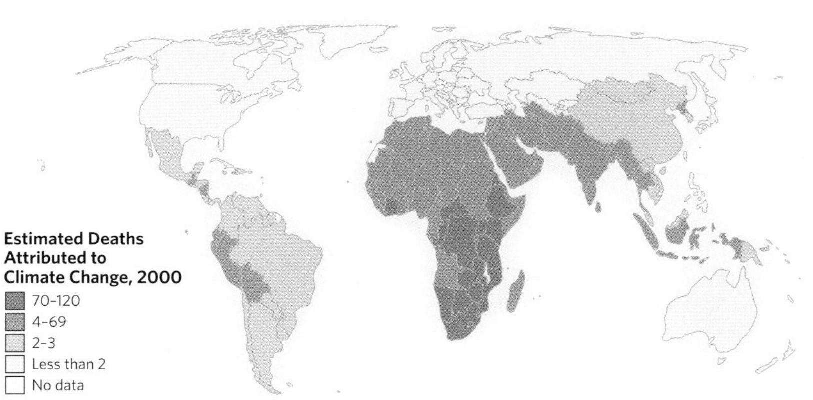
Estimated Deaths Attributed to Climate Change, 2000
70–120
4–69
2–3
Less than 2
No data

For more information on the related topics of climate and weather events, see pages 42–49.

Weather Events

AT ANY LOCATION ON EARTH AT ANY MOMENT, a set of atmospheric variables is at work creating short-term conditions that define what we refer to as "the weather." These variables include temperature, pressure, humidity, cloud cover, precipitation, and wind direction and speed. Although the terms "weather" and "climate" are sometimes used interchangeably, climate refers to the prevailing weather conditions in a given region based on a long period of record. For example, in the winter many people travel to places like Florida and Hawai'i because these areas are known for their warm and sunny climates, but a short-term change in the weather may bring several days of cold temperatures, much to the dismay of travelers.

Many weather conditions only cause minor inconveniences, such as an unplanned day of rain, snow, or wind. However, weather can also manifest itself in the form of extreme events that leave severe consequences in their wake. Tropical cyclones (called hurricanes in the Atlantic and typhoons in the Pacific) are giant seasonal storm systems that develop over warm tropical waters and bring torrential rains and wind speeds of up to 200 miles (322 kilometers) an hour. A cyclone "season" can be relatively calm or very active. For example, the 2004-05 South Pacific cyclone season was an intense one, with eight cyclones impacting various Pacific islands between January and April.

Tornadoes develop when a mass of cool air meets warm, humid air to create a spinning funnel that descends from a cloud to the ground. These funnels can move at speeds up to 300 miles (483 kilometers) per hour and are capable of uprooting trees and hurling large objects through the air. An average of one thousand tornadoes per year occur in the United States, and the central U.S. is known as the world's most tornado-prone area. Other extreme weather events include snowstorms, monsoons, dust storms, and wind and hail storms. In addition to their immediate impacts, many weather events trigger secondary effects, such as coastal erosion, storm surges, landslides, and avalanches.

Nearly every human on Earth is affected by severe weather. Impacts from these events include disruptions to communications, transportation, and other infrastructure; damage to agriculture, crops, and water resources; and economic effects, such as a reduction in tourism. Increases in economic damages are largely due to growing population, infrastructure, and wealth in regions prone to severe weather, such as coastal areas.

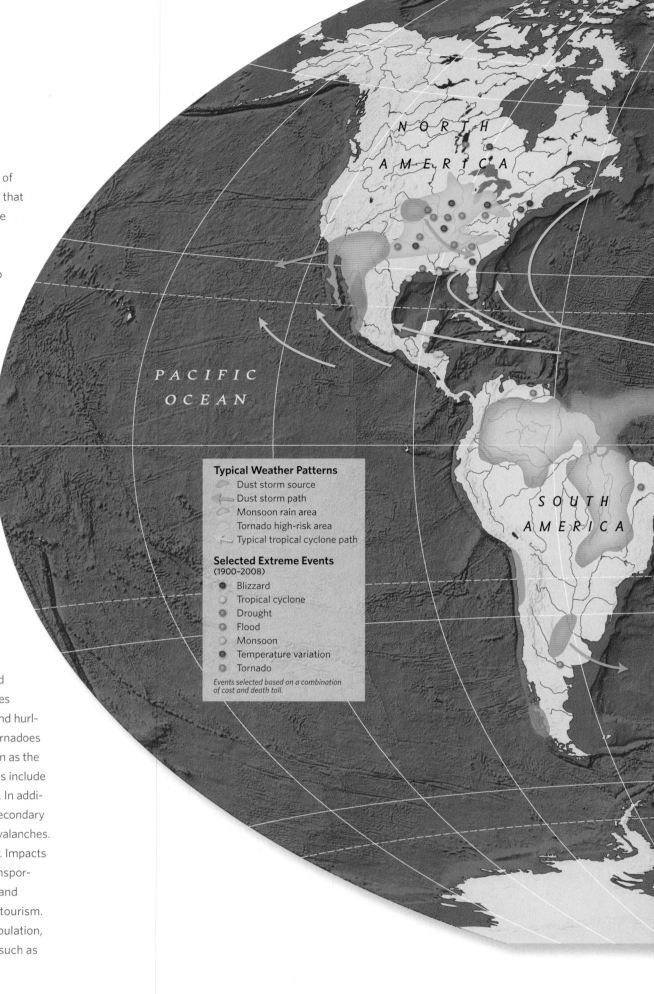

NORTH AMERICA
PACIFIC OCEAN
SOUTH AMERICA

Typical Weather Patterns
- Dust storm source
- Dust storm path
- Monsoon rain area
- Tornado high-risk area
- Typical tropical cyclone path

Selected Extreme Events (1900-2008)
- Blizzard
- Tropical cyclone
- Drought
- Flood
- Monsoon
- Temperature variation
- Tornado

Events selected based on a combination of cost and death toll.

El Niño

In the winter of 1997-98, the San Francisco Bay area experienced significant storm and flood damage. Waves up to six feet (1.8 meters) high washed over the city's Embarcadero waterfront area, and water from the Pacific Ocean rushed over the coastal highway at Ocean Beach. The extreme weather conditions resulted from wind-driven waves and unusually high sea levels.

Later analysis by scientists at the U.S. Geological Survey, based on a hundred years of sea-level data, revealed that the extreme storm conditions were the result of the El Niño-Southern Oscillation phenomenon.

During most years, trade winds typically blow from east to west and create warm surface waters and upwellings of cold, nutrient-rich bottom water in the tropical Pacific Ocean near the coast of Peru. Every few years, however, an El Niño cycle disrupts this pattern and the trade winds relax, or even reverse, which warms the surface waters off South America. This rise in sea-surface temperature has significant consequences for global weather, including heavy rainfall and flooding, severe storms, and drought. Asian monsoons have been linked to the Pacific rainfall patterns that accompany El Niño. Strong El Niño cycles can also disrupt plankton, fish, and seabird populations, due to nutrient-poor surface water conditions.

An El Niño cycle typically occurs about every three to four years, but intervals can be as long as seven to ten years. Some El Niño events are minor and last only a few months, while others last 12 to 15 months. The strongest El Niños in recent times occurred in 1982-83 and 1997-98. Because of their cyclic and variable nature, El Niños are difficult to predict, but new tools — such as the Tropical Ocean Atmosphere array of buoy instruments in the Pacific Ocean — are enabling researchers to better understand the physical processes related to this weather phenomenon.

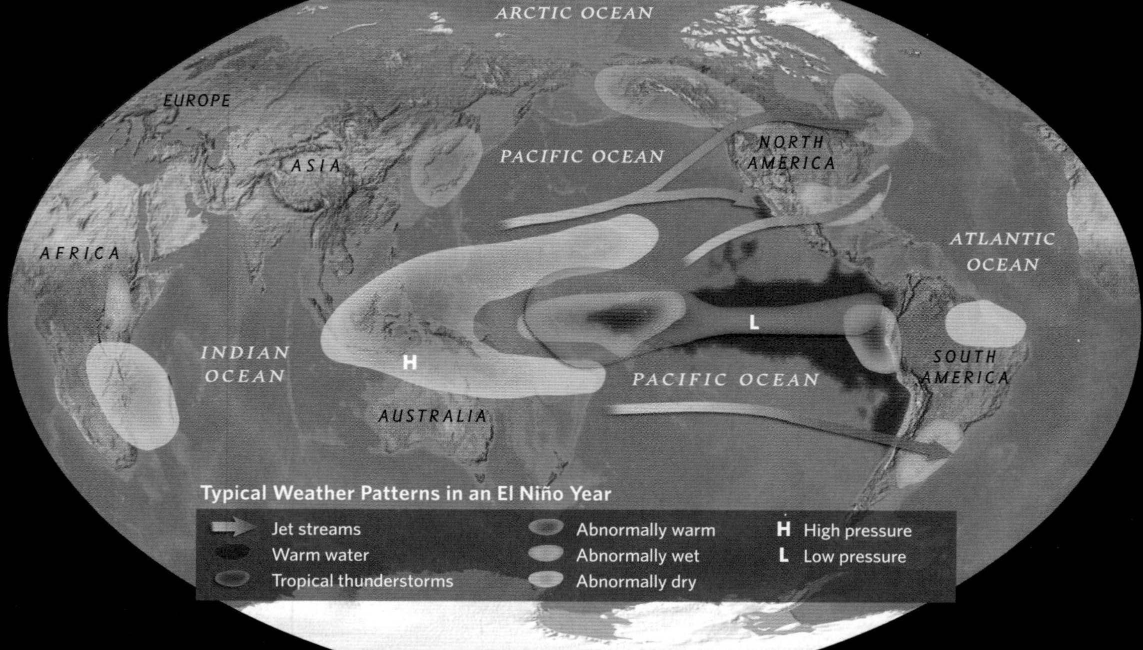
ARCTIC OCEAN
EUROPE
ASIA
PACIFIC OCEAN
NORTH AMERICA
ATLANTIC OCEAN
AFRICA
INDIAN OCEAN
H
L
PACIFIC OCEAN
SOUTH AMERICA
AUSTRALIA
Typical Weather Patterns in an El Niño Year
Jet streams
Warm water
Tropical thunderstorms
Abnormally warm
Abnormally wet
Abnormally dry
H High pressure
L Low pressure

ARCTIC OCEAN

EUROPE

ASIA

AFRICA

PACIFIC OCEAN

TLANTIC OCEAN

INDIAN OCEAN

AUSTRALIA

ANTARCTICA

NORTH AMERICA

EUROPE

ASIA

AFRICA

SOUTH AMERICA

AUSTRALIA

Average Number of Lightning Flashes (per sq km/year)

More than 50	6–9	0.4–0.7
30–50	2–5	0.1–0.3
10–29	0.8–1.9	Less than 0.1

The map at right is based on 11 years of lightning data collected by NASA's Optical Transient Detector and the Lightning Image Sensor.

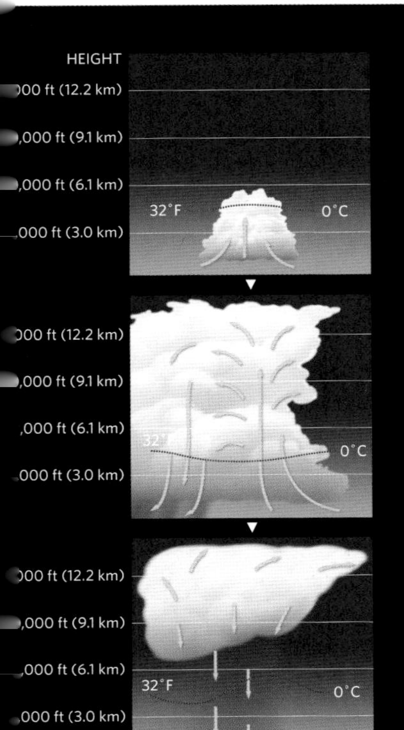
HEIGHT
00 ft (12.2 km)
,000 ft (9.1 km)
,000 ft (6.1 km)
,000 ft (3.0 km)
32°F
0°C

Thunderstorms

A thunderstorm is an intense local storm associated with a dense cumulonimbus cloud that has strong updrafts of air. As air rises and cools rapidly, unstable air masses bring intense localized rainfall, damaging winds, hail, and lightning. A thunderstorm is classified as "severe" when it has hailstones that are at least three-quarters of an inch (1.9 centimeters) in size, or wind gusts greater than 57.5 miles (92.5 kilometers) an hour. Because they develop so rapidly, thunderstorms are one of the most difficult weather events to predict. Generally short-lived, they affect only a small area (less than about 40 square miles/103.6 square kilometers), but they pack a powerful punch.

Many weather-related hazards are associated with thunderstorms. Lightning can cause fires and human deaths, hail can damage property and cause injury, and heavy rainfall in a short time period can generate flash floods — local floods of short duration but immense volume. In April 2008, six outdoor education students and their teacher were killed in New Zealand when a thunderstorm triggered a flash flood that roared through the Mangetepopo River Canyon. The storm caused the river to rise to 36 times its normal level in just 30 minutes.

According to the National Oceanic and Atmospheric Administration (NOAA), an estimated 100,000 thunderstorms develop around the world each year. In the United States, thunderstorms occur most frequently in Florida and the southeast plains of Colorado. Forecasters rely on computer models to decide whether conditions are right for a thunderstorm, and satellite data can help them track the growth of cumulus clouds into cumulonimbus clouds. A thunderstorm watch informs the public about when and where a severe thunderstorm is likely to occur, while a thunderstorm warning is issued when severe weather has been reported or indicated by radar

Lightning ripples through a cumulonimbus thunderstorm cloud. Cumulonimbus clouds are tall, dense clouds that generate thunderstorms and other severe weather. They typically form near oceans or over mountains, which force the air upward. If conditions are right, cumulonimbus clouds can further develop into supercells.

An isolated supercell thunderstorm threatened south-central Kansas on June 5, 2004, producing baseball-size hail. Supercells are convective storms with a rotating updraft that allows them to continue for up to several hours. They are capable of producing high winds, large hail, and strong tornadoes

Population

WHILE COUNTRY POPULATIONS IN many parts of the world are expanding, those of Europe—along with some other rich industrial areas, such as Japan—show little to no growth, or are shrinking due to very low birthrates. Many such countries must bring in immigrant workers to keep their economies thriving. A clear correlation exists between wealth and low birthrates: Higher incomes and educational levels result in lower rates of reproduction.

Many governments keep vital statistics, record births and deaths, and count their populations regularly to try to plan ahead. The United States has taken a census every ten years since 1790, recording the ages, the occupations, and other important facts about its people. The United Nations helps less developed countries carry out censuses and improve their demographic information.

Governments of some poor countries may find that half their populations are under the age of 20. They are faced with the overwhelming tasks of providing adequate education and jobs while encouraging better family planning programs. Governments of countries with low birthrates find themselves with growing numbers of elderly people but fewer workers able to provide tax support for health care and pensions.

In a mere 150 years, world population has grown fivefold, at an ever increasing pace. The industrial revolution helped bring about improvements in food supplies and advances in both medicine and public health, which allowed people to live longer and to have healthier babies. Today, 15,000 people are born into the world every hour, and nearly all of them in poor African, Asian, and Latin American countries. The world's least developed countries will need to make dramatic changes in order to adapt to their new population structures. This situation concerns planners, who look to demographers (professionals who study all aspects of population) for important data.

NORTH AMERICA
Chicago
Toronto
New York
Philadelphia
Los Angeles
Miami
Mexico City
Bogotá
SOUTH AMERICA
Lima
Belo Horizonte
São Paulo
Rio de Janeiro
Santiago
Buenos Aires

Population Density

A country's population density is estimated by calculating how many people, if they were all spread out evenly, would occupy each square mile. In reality, people live together most closely in cities, on seacoasts, and in river valleys. Singapore, a tiny country largely composed of a single city, has a high population density—more than 18,000 people per square mile. Greenland, by comparison, has less than one person per square mile because it is mostly covered by ice. Its people mainly fish for a living and dwell in small groups near the shore.

Regional Population Growth Disparities

Two centuries ago, the population of the world began a phenomenal expansion. Despite the opening of new lands in North America and Oceania, the far greater part of that growth took place in less developed countries. Two less developed countries, China and India, each now exceed one billion in population. Africa, which has the second greatest growth, does not yet approach Asia in numbers.

According to some experts, the world's population, now totaling more than 6.5 billion, might not start to level off until as late as the year 2200, when it could reach 11 billion. Nearly all the new growth will take place in Asia, Africa, and Latin America; however, Africa's share will be almost double that of its present level and China's share will decline.

Current regional population disparities are illustrated by the population pyramids below, which show the number of males (blue) and females (red) in each age group within a population. A pyramid for Nigeria reveals that more than half—about 55 percent—of the population is under the age of 20, while only 19 percent of Italy's population is younger than 20.

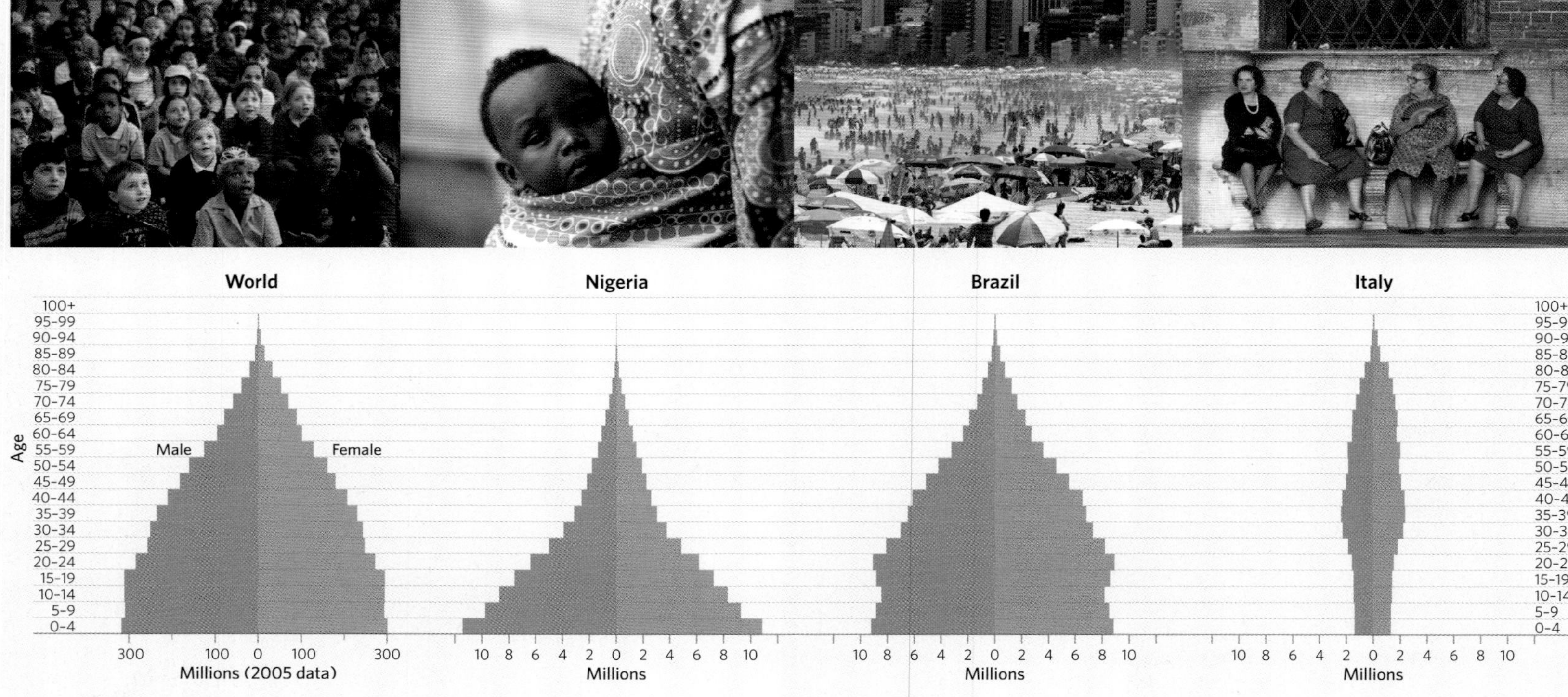
World
Nigeria
Brazil
Italy
100+
95-99
90-94
85-89
80-84
75-79
70-74
65-69
60-64
55-59
50-54
45-49
40-44
35-39
30-34
25-29
20-24
15-19
10-14
5-9
0-4
Age
Male
Female
300 100 0 100 300
Millions (2005 data)
10 8 6 4 2 0 2 4 6 8 10
Millions

50 100 150 200 250 300 350 400 450 500 550 600 650 700 750 800 850 900 950
Year

People Per Square Mile		People Per Square Kilometer
More than 500	■	More than 195
150-500	■	60-195
25-149	■	10-59
1-24	□	1-9
Less than 1	□	Less than 1
No data	□	No data

Urban Area Population, 2007

- ■ More than 20 million
- ▲ 15-20 million
- • 10-14.9 million
- ○ 5-9.9 million

PROJECTED POPULATION CHANGE, 2005-2050

By 2050, the world population is projected to pass nine billion, with virtually all of that growth in the developing countries of Africa, Asia, Latin America, and Oceania. But that projection makes the assumption that birthrates will continue to decline in those countries where they are currently doing so and begin to decline where they have not. Regardless of the ultimate total, there will be a continuing dramatic shift of the global population balance from today's wealthier countries to today's poorer countries.

Percent Population Change (2005-2050)

- 100 and above
- 26-99
- 0-25
- Population decline
- No data

The highest and lowest values for each continent are labeled individually.

REGIONAL POPULATION GROWTH OVER TIME

- Asia
- Africa
- Latin America
- Europe
- North America
- Australia/Oceania

Billions of people

Year

Population (continued)

Fertility

A country's birthrate is often given as the total fertility rate. It can also be expressed as the number of births per 1,000 population. In low-income countries, with limited educational opportunities for girls and women, fertility is often highest.

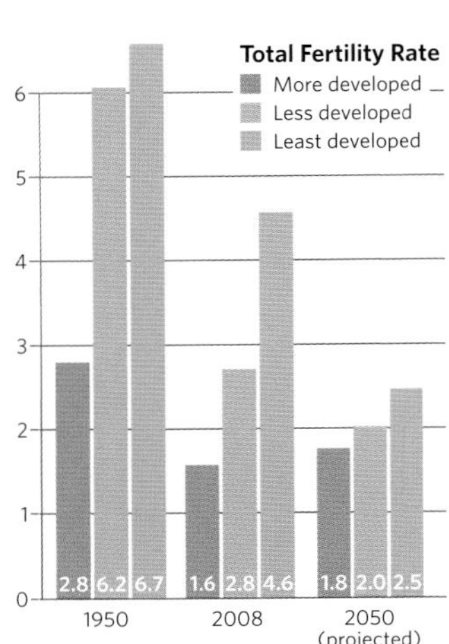

Total Fertility Rate
More developed
Less developed
Least developed
2.8 6.2 6.7
1.6 2.8 4.6
1.8 2.0 2.5
1950
2008
2050 (projected)

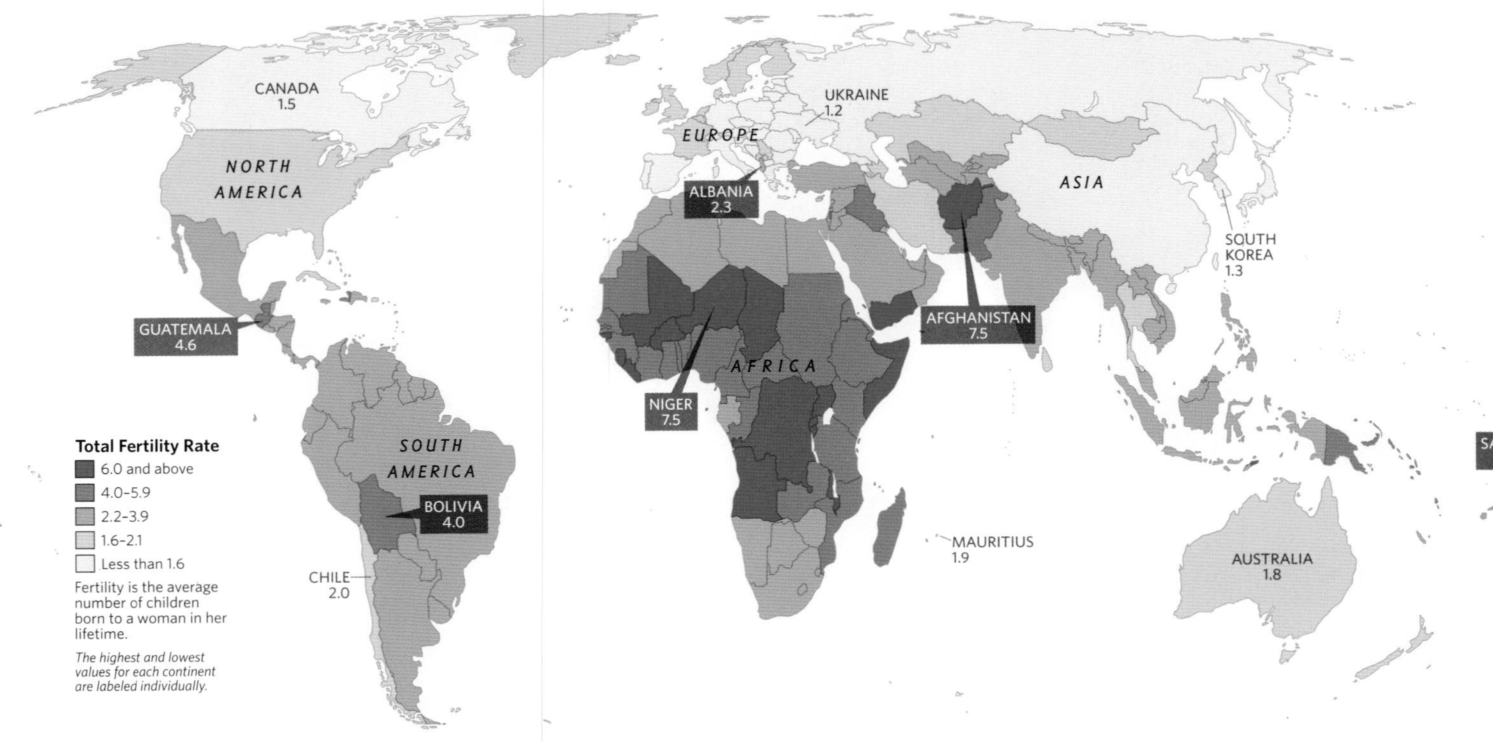

CANADA 1.5
NORTH AMERICA
GUATEMALA 4.6
SOUTH AMERICA
BOLIVIA 4.0
CHILE 2.0
EUROPE
UKRAINE 1.2
ALBANIA 2.3
ASIA
SOUTH KOREA 1.3
AFGHANISTAN 7.5
AFRICA
NIGER 7.5
MAURITIUS 1.9
AUSTRALIA 1.8
SAMOA 4.4
Total Fertility Rate
6.0 and above
4.0–5.9
2.2–3.9
1.6–2.1
Less than 1.6
Fertility is the average number of children born to a woman in her lifetime.
The highest and lowest values for each continent are labeled individually.

Urban Population Densities

People around the world are leaving farms and moving to cities, where jobs and opportunities are better. In 2008, half the world's people lived in towns or cities. The shift of population from the countryside to urban centers will probably continue in less developed countries for many years to come.

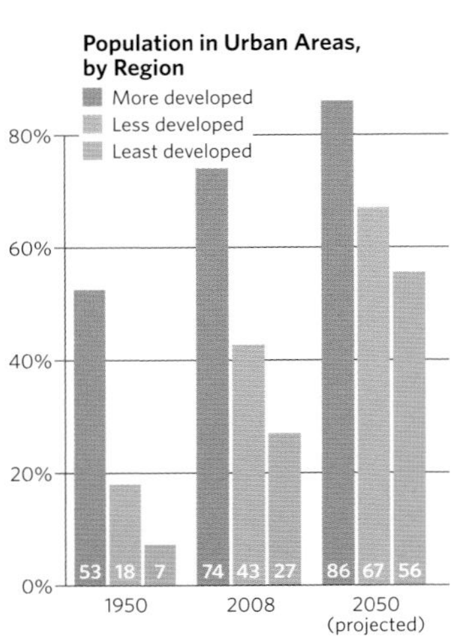

Population in Urban Areas, by Region
More developed
Less developed
Least developed
80%
60%
40%
20%
0%
53 18 7
74 43 27
86 67 56
1950
2008
2050 (projected)

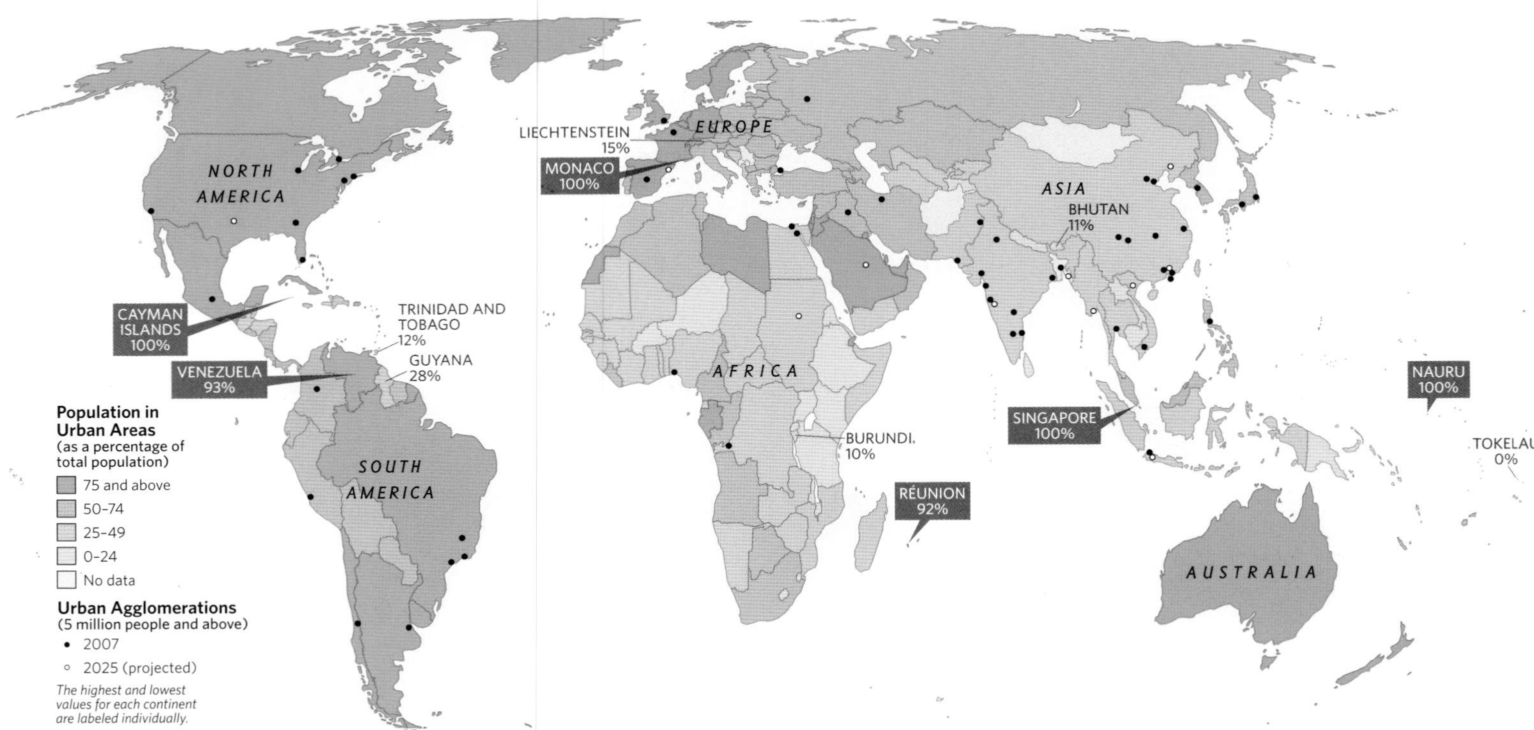

NORTH AMERICA
CAYMAN ISLANDS 100%
TRINIDAD AND TOBAGO 12%
GUYANA 28%
VENEZUELA 93%
SOUTH AMERICA
LIECHTENSTEIN 15%
MONACO 100%
EUROPE
ASIA
BHUTAN 11%
AFRICA
BURUNDI 10%
RÉUNION 92%
SINGAPORE 100%
NAURU 100%
TOKELAU 0%
AUSTRALIA
Population in Urban Areas (as a percentage of total population)
75 and above
50–74
25–49
0–24
No data
Urban Agglomerations (5 million people and above)
2007
2025 (projected)
The highest and lowest values for each continent are labeled individually.

Population Growth Cartogram

Viewed in terms of their population size, instead of geographic size, countries look very different. In the cartogram at right, each square represents one million people. With some geographical facsimile, countries are associated with neighboring countries and landmasses, but the size of an individual country is directly related to its population.

The population of the world is not distributed evenly. In this cartogram Canada is reduced to a small strip, while India looks enormous because its population is more than 34 times greater than Canada's. In geographic area, Canada is three times larger than India. The shape of almost every country looks distorted when populations are compared in this way.

Population sizes are constantly changing, however. In countries that are experiencing many more births than deaths, population totals are ballooning. In others, too few babies are born to replace the number of people who die, and populations are shrinking. A cartogram depicting population growth rates would show Africa as the largest area while Eastern Europe, with its declining population, would be largely absent.

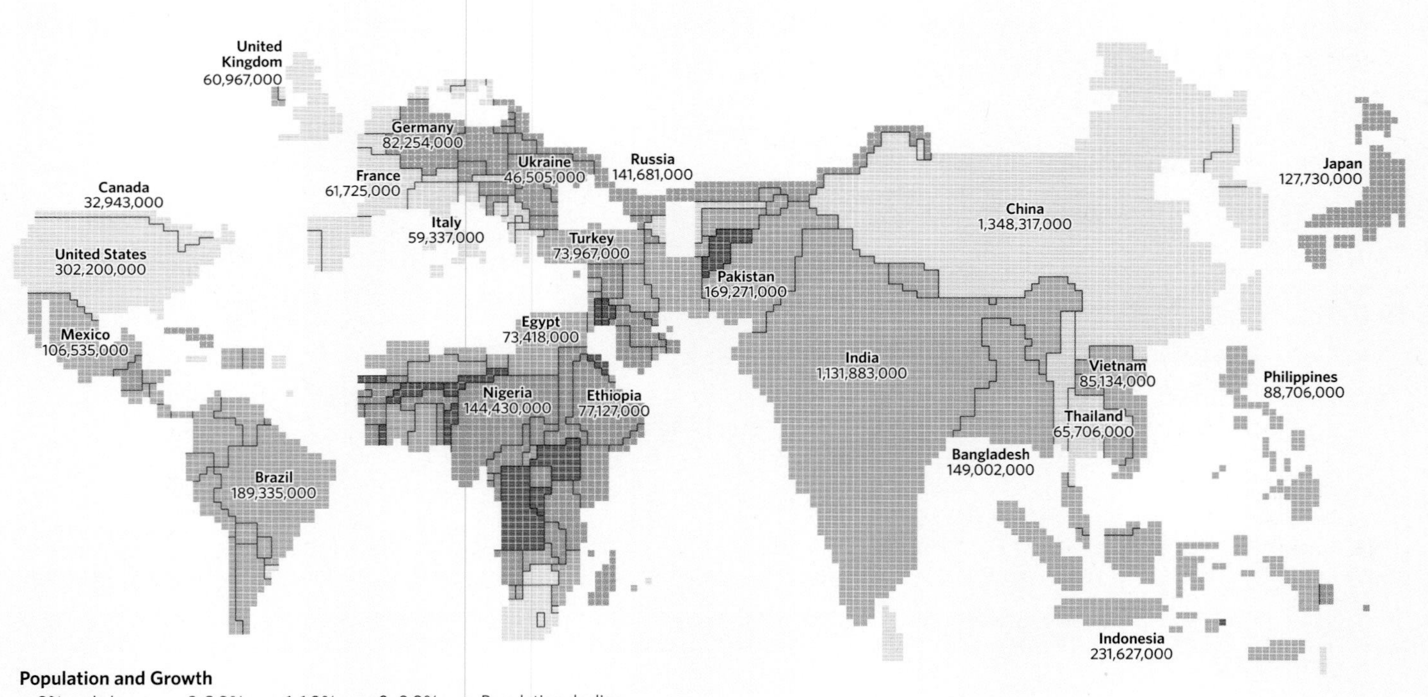

United Kingdom 60,967,000
Germany 82,254,000
France 61,725,000
Ukraine 46,505,000
Russia 141,681,000
Canada 32,943,000
Italy 59,337,000
Turkey 73,967,000
United States 302,200,000
China 1,348,317,000
Japan 127,730,000
Pakistan 169,271,000
Mexico 106,535,000
Egypt 73,418,000
India 1,131,883,000
Nigeria 144,430,000
Ethiopia 77,127,000
Vietnam 85,134,000
Philippines 88,706,000
Thailand 65,706,000
Bangladesh 149,002,000
Brazil 189,335,000
Indonesia 231,627,000
Population and Growth
3% and above
2–2.9%
1–1.9%
0–0.9%
Population decline
Each square represents one million people. Colors represent growth rates, excluding migration. (2007 data)

Life Expectancy

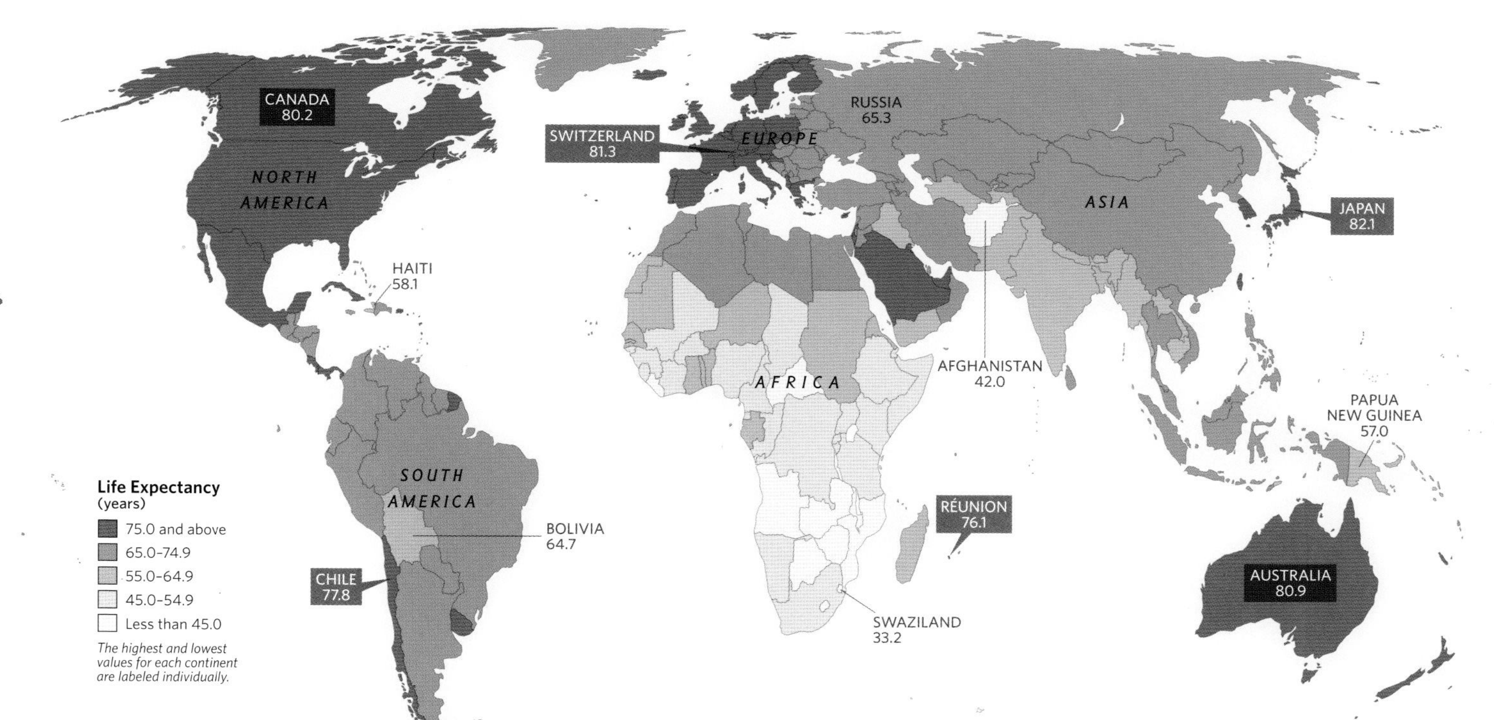
CANADA
80.2
NORTH AMERICA
HAITI
58.1
SWITZERLAND
81.3
EUROPE
RUSSIA
65.3
ASIA
JAPAN
82.1
AFRICA
AFGHANISTAN
42.0
PAPUA
NEW GUINEA
57.0
SOUTH AMERICA
BOLIVIA
64.7
CHILE
77.8
RÉUNION
76.1
SWAZILAND
33.2
AUSTRALIA
80.9
Life Expectancy
(years)
75.0 and above
65.0–74.9
55.0–64.9
45.0–54.9
Less than 45.0
The highest and lowest values for each continent are labeled individually.

Life expectancy at birth is the number of years, on average, a newborn baby can expect to live. However, during its lifetime, health conditions and infant mortality are likely to improve so that death rates decrease and the actual number of years lived is greater than it had been at birth.

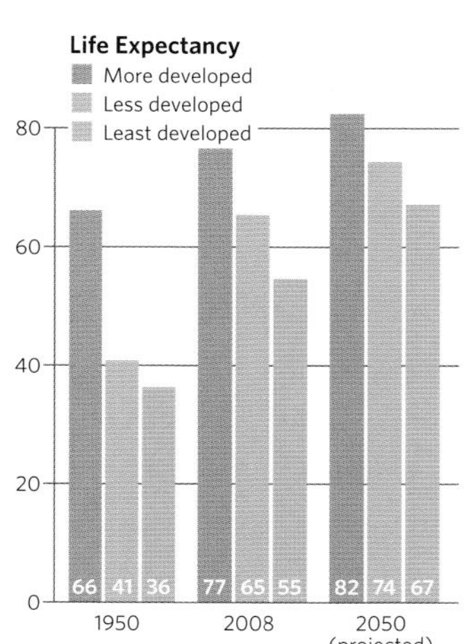
Life Expectancy
More developed
Less developed
Least developed
80
60
40
20
0
66 41 36
77 65 55
82 74 67
1950
2008
2050
(projected)

Migration

International migration has reached its highest level, with foreign workers now providing the labor in several Middle Eastern nations and immigrant workers proving essential to rich countries with low birthrates. Refugees continue to escape grim political and environmental conditions. Skilled and unskilled workers migrate to developed countries to fill shrinking labor forces.

NORTH AMERICA
ROMANIA
0.6%
ANDORRA
77.9%
EUROPE
ASIA
CHINA
0%
ANGUILLA
41.8%
EGYPT
0.2%
QATAR
78.3%
GUAM
66.9%
EL SALVADOR
0.3%
GUYANA
0.1%
AFRICA
PAPUA
NEW GUINEA
0.5%
SOUTH AMERICA
RÉUNION
18.1%
AUSTRALIA
FALKLAND ISLANDS
70.2%

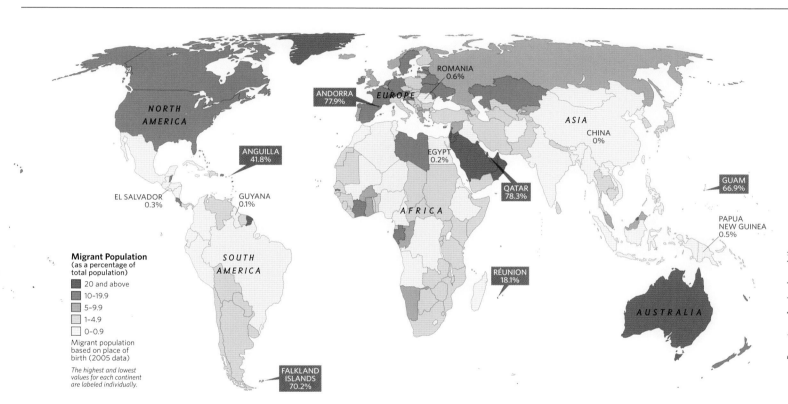

Migrant Population
(as a percentage of total population)
- 20 and above
- 10–19.9
- 5–9.9
- 1–4.9
- 0–0.9

Migrant population based on place of birth (2005 data)

The highest and lowest values for each continent are labeled individually.

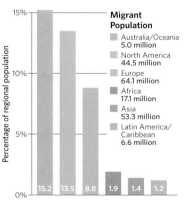

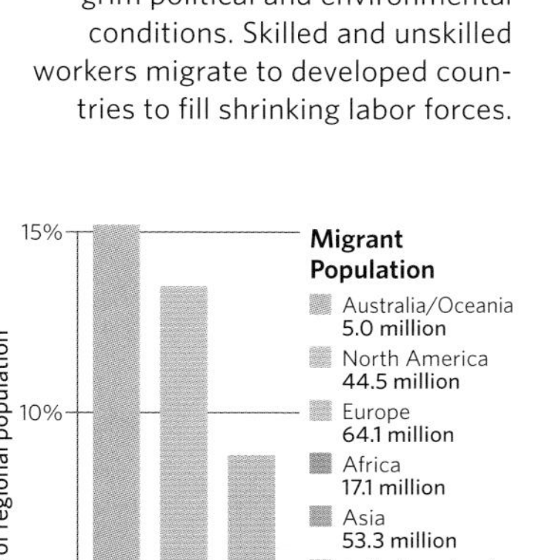
Migrant Population
Australia/Oceania
5.0 million
North America
44.5 million
Europe
64.1 million
Africa
17.1 million
Asia
53.3 million
Latin America/
Caribbean
6.6 million
Percentage of regional population
15%
10%
5%
0%
15.2
13.5
8.8
1.9
1.4
1.2

MOST POPULOUS COUNTRIES

2007 POPULATION FIGURES

1.	China	1,348,317,000
2.	India	1,131,883,000
3.	United States	302,200,000
4.	Indonesia	231,627,000
5.	Brazil	189,335,000
6.	Pakistan	169,271,000
7.	Bangladesh	149,002,000
8.	Nigeria	144,430,000
9.	Russia	141,681,000
10.	Japan	127,730,000
11.	Mexico	106,535,000
12.	Philippines	88,706,000
13.	Vietnam	85,134,000
14.	Germany	82,254,000
15.	Ethiopia	77,127,000
16.	Turkey	73,967,000
17.	Egypt	73,418,000
18.	Iran	71,208,000
19.	Thailand	65,706,000
20.	Dem. Rep. of the Congo	62,636,000
21.	France	61,725,000
22.	United Kingdom	60,967,000
23.	Italy	59,337,000
24.	Myanmar	49,805,000
25.	South Korea	48,456,000

MOST CROWDED PLACES

POPULATION DENSITY PER SQ KM

1.	Monaco	16,920
2.	Singapore	7,021
3.	Gibraltar (U.K.)	4,462
4.	Vatican City	1,995
5.	Malta	1,288
6.	Bermuda (U.K.)	1,208
7.	Bahrain	1,063
8.	Maldives	1,020
9.	Bangladesh	1,010
10.	Nauru	667
11.	Barbados	647
12.	Taiwan (China)	636
13.	Mauritius	618
14.	Mayotte (France)	524
15.	Aruba (Neth.)	513
16.	San Marino	508
17.	South Korea	488
18.	Puerto Rico (U.S.)	434
19.	Netherlands	394
20.	Comoros	382
21.	Tuvalu	379
22.	Lebanon	375
23.	Marshall Islands	370
24.	Martinique (France)	368
25.	Rwanda	355

LIFE EXPECTANCY

LOWEST (FEMALE):

33	Botswana
34	Swaziland
36	Lesotho

LOWEST (MALE):

33	Swaziland
35	Botswana, Lesotho
38	Zambia, Zimbabwe

HIGHEST (FEMALE):

86	Japan
84	France, Italy, San Marino, Switzerland
83	Aruba (Neth.), Australia, Austria, Canada, Finland, Gibraltar (U.K.), Iceland, Norway, Puerto Rico (U.S.), Spain, Sweden, Virgin Islands (U.S.)

HIGHEST (MALE):

79	Australia, Gibraltar (U.K.), Iceland, Japan, Liechtenstein, Sweden, Switzerland
78	Canada, Israel, Italy, Malta, Netherlands, New Zealand, Norway, San Marino, Singapore Switzerland
77	Austria, Costa Rica, France, Greece, Kuwait, Spain, U.A.E., United Kingdom

AGE STRUCTURE

HIGHEST % POPULATION UNDER AGE 15

49%	Uganda
48%	Mali, Niger
47%	Afghanistan, Dem. Rep. of the Congo, Guinea-Bissau, Liberia, Malawi
46%	Angola, Burkina Faso, Chad, Occupied Palestinian Terr., Yemen, Zambia

HIGHEST % POPULATION OVER AGE 65

20%	Italy, Japan
19%	Germany
18%	Greece
17%	Belgium, Bulgaria, Croatia, Estonia, Latvia, Portugal, Spain, Sweden,

LOWEST % POPULATION UNDER AGE 15

14%	Bulgaria, Germany, Greece, Italy, Japan, Latvia, Slovenia, Spain
15%	Czech Republic, Estonia, Russia, Ukraine

LOWEST % POPULATION OVER AGE 65

1%	Qatar, United Arab Emirates
2%	Afghanistan, Angola, Eritrea, Kuwait, Liberia, Papua New Guinea, Western Sahara, Yemen

Megacities

IN 1950, NEW YORK AND TOKYO were the only cities that had more than ten million inhabitants. In 2025, there will be 27 such megacities around the world, and 48 more will have populations between five and ten million. Urban areas of the less developed regions, including developing countries in Africa, Latin America, and Asia, are absorbing almost all population growth worldwide with a continuation of this trend expected in the future. Hence, population growth will be concentrated in cities of the world. Historically, rapid urbanization started in today's more developed regions, which were already 53 percent urban in 1950 compared with only 18 percent in less developed regions. Now, in developing countries, the race is on to urbanize. Cities in rapidly urbanizing countries such as China are swelling with new residents, most of whom are seeking jobs and a better life for themselves or their children. In 2008, for the first time ever, city dwellers worldwide outnumbered Earth's rural population, with the majority of urbanites living in cities of less than one million.

While cities in the developing world continue to grow at a feverish pace, the growth of megacities in the developed world has lost momentum. Natural population increases and rural to urban migration rates have fallen in the developed world, putting the brakes on the expansion of places like Tokyo, which has nearly stabilized with a population of over 35 million. Some cities are also experiencing a phenomenon called counter urbanization, whereby cities see residents escaping to smaller cities or rural areas in search of lower population density, pollution, and crime.

Cities—as centers of power, wealth, production, ideas, and culture—act as magnets for underemployed populations living elsewhere. New urbanites, often unskilled, may settle into worse poverty than they knew before. Where urban growth is at its fastest, vast, overcrowded slums sometimes encircle entire cities while others spring up within, alongside modern luxury buildings, highlighting the great gulf between the rich and poor. So far, many cities are unable to keep pace with growth, forcing slum dwellers to live without such basic municipal services as clean water, sewage disposal, or electricity. A few have succeeded in keeping down corruption and crime, establishing a sound tax base, and providing necessary services such as public transportation and health facilities.

Nevertheless, as the world becomes more urbanized, the environment suffers from a further depletion of resources and increased levels of pollution. The development of societies everywhere will depend on the understanding and management of city growth.

NORTH AMERICA

New York
19,040,000

Los Angeles
12,500,000

Mexico City
19,028,000

SOUTH AMERICA

São Paulo
18,845,000

Rio de Janeiro
11,748,000

Buenos Aires
12,795,000

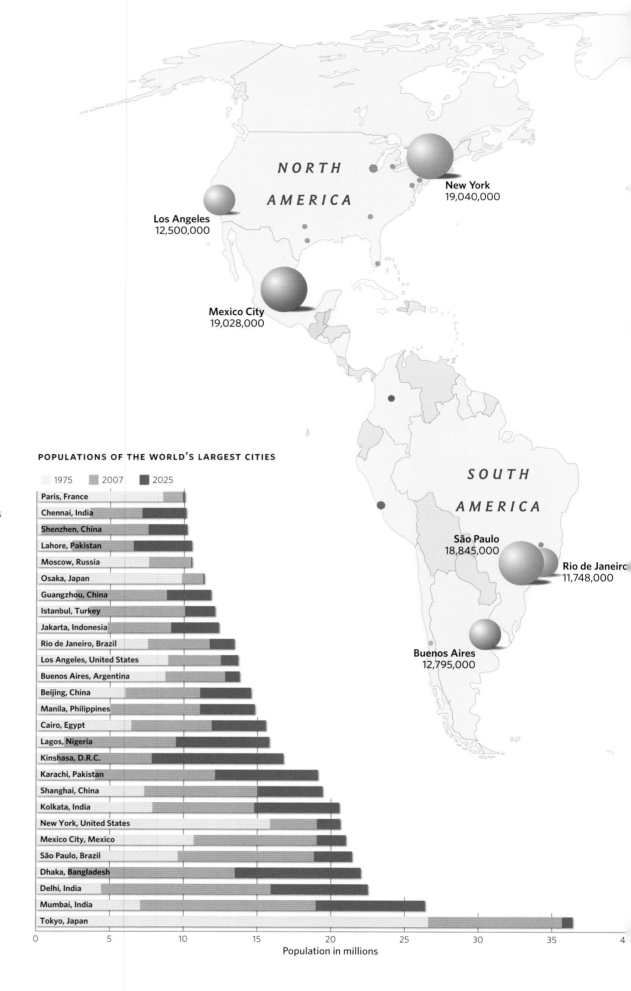

POPULATIONS OF THE WORLD'S LARGEST CITIES

1975 | 2007 | 2025

Paris, France
Chennai, India
Shenzhen, China
Lahore, Pakistan
Moscow, Russia
Osaka, Japan
Guangzhou, China
Istanbul, Turkey
Jakarta, Indonesia
Rio de Janeiro, Brazil
Los Angeles, United States
Buenos Aires, Argentina
Beijing, China
Manila, Philippines
Cairo, Egypt
Lagos, Nigeria
Kinshasa, D.R.C.
Karachi, Pakistan
Shanghai, China
Kolkata, India
New York, United States
Mexico City, Mexico
São Paulo, Brazil
Dhaka, Bangladesh
Delhi, India
Mumbai, India
Tokyo, Japan

0 5 10 15 20 25 30 35 40

Population in millions

MANILA, PHILIPPINES Manila was colonized by Spain in 1571 and quickly became the center of Spain's worldwide trade. The city remains a major seaport in a strategically important setting, but is also choking on its own pollution. Thousands of families scrape out a living in the city's massive dumps, scavenging daily for food, empty bottles, and other scraps. Heavy rains occasionally create dangerous garbage slides; hundreds were killed in a trash avalanche in 2000.

SÃO PAULO, BRAZIL Though founded by Jesuit missionaries in 1554, São Paulo languished for more than 300 years, until a coffee boom hit in the 1880s. Immigrants from Europe—and, notably, Japan—and their descendants made the city the largest in South America and the Southern Hemisphere. A modern cultural center, São Paulo is also Brazil's economic workhorse, attracting a multitude of commuters to its crowded streets and train stations.

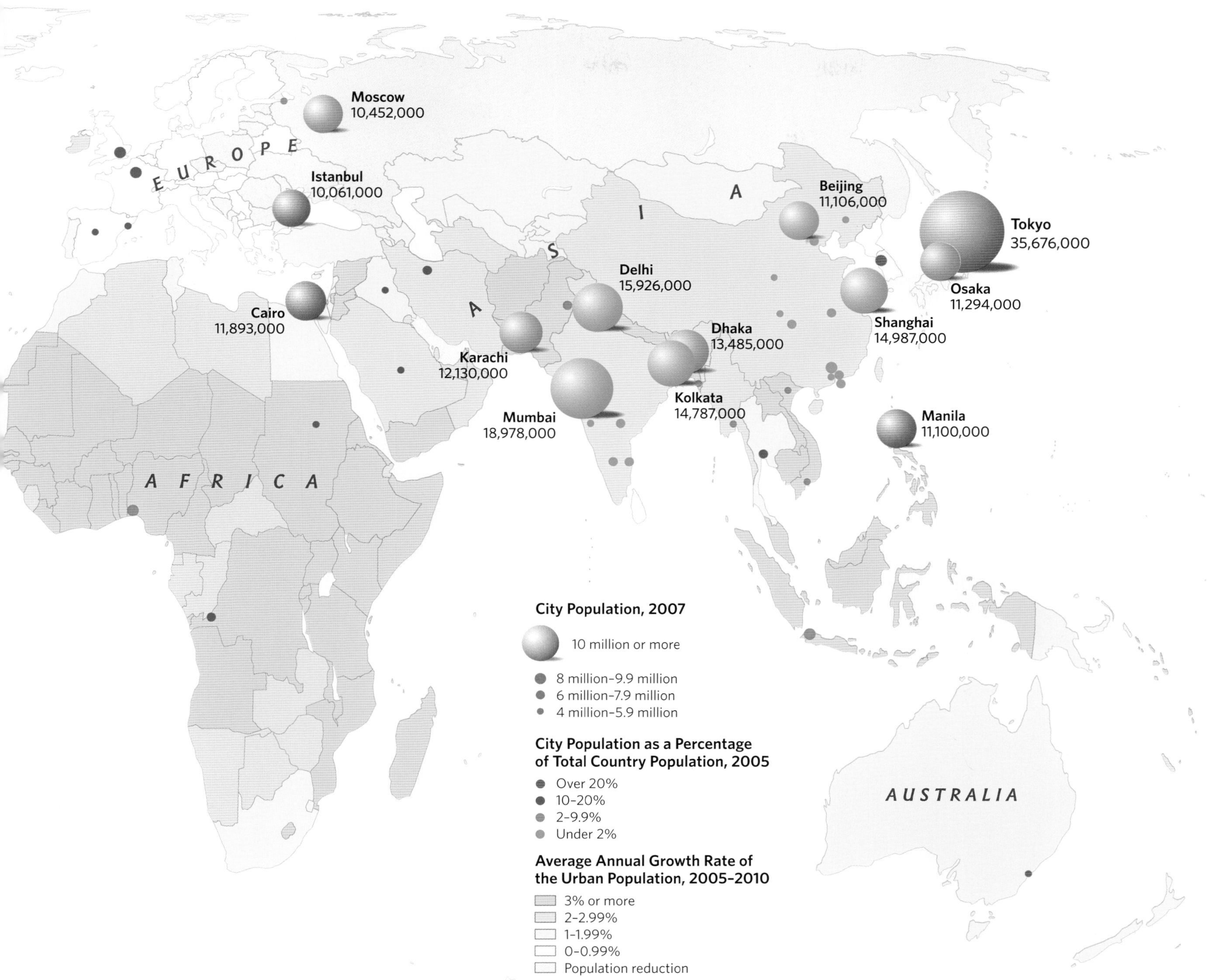

EUROPE
ASIA
AFRICA
AUSTRALIA

Moscow 10,452,000
Istanbul 10,061,000
Cairo 11,893,000
Karachi 12,130,000
Delhi 15,926,000
Mumbai 18,978,000
Dhaka 13,485,000
Kolkata 14,787,000
Beijing 11,106,000
Shanghai 14,987,000
Tokyo 35,676,000
Osaka 11,294,000
Manila 11,100,000

City Population, 2007

- 10 million or more
- 8 million–9.9 million
- 6 million–7.9 million
- 4 million–5.9 million

City Population as a Percentage of Total Country Population, 2005

- Over 20%
- 10–20%
- 2–9.9%
- Under 2%

Average Annual Growth Rate of the Urban Population, 2005–2010

- 3% or more
- 2–2.99%
- 1–1.99%
- 0–0.99%
- Population reduction

MEGACITIES OVER TIME

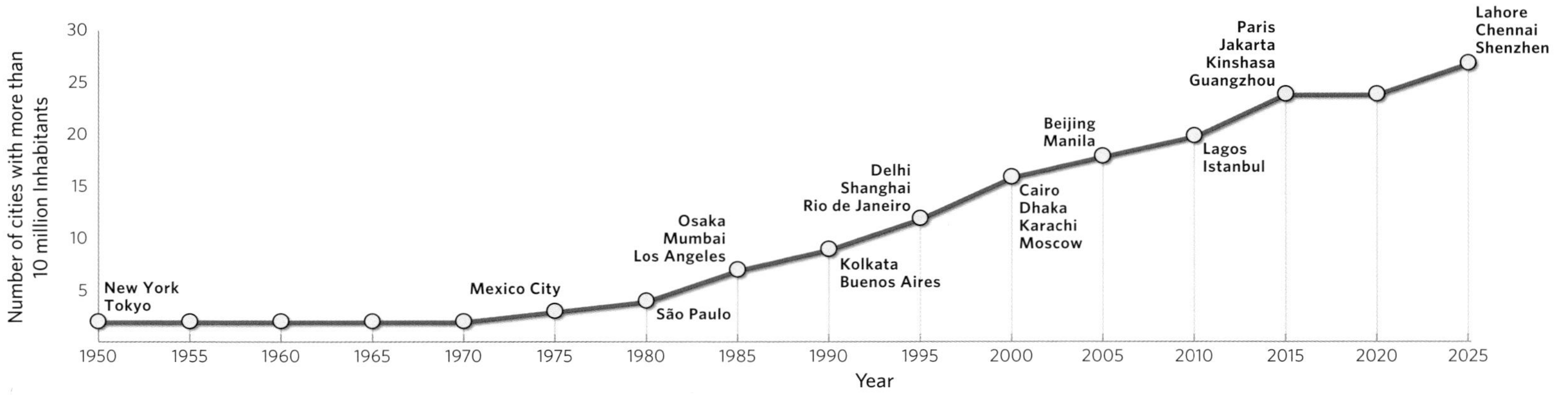

Number of cities with more than 10 million Inhabitants (0–30) by Year (1950–2025)

- 1950: New York, Tokyo
- 1970: Mexico City
- 1980: São Paulo
- 1985: Osaka, Mumbai, Los Angeles
- 1990: Kolkata, Buenos Aires
- 1995: Delhi, Shanghai, Rio de Janeiro
- 2000: Cairo, Dhaka, Karachi, Moscow
- 2005: Beijing, Manila
- 2010: Lagos, Istanbul
- 2015: Paris, Jakarta, Kinshasa, Guangzhou
- 2025: Lahore, Chennai, Shenzhen

BEIJING, CHINA Beijing, literally "northern capital," has been China's capital for most of the past 700 years, since Kublai Khan first established his court there. Beijing is the second largest city in China, trailing only Shanghai in economic and industrial production, and is unrivaled in its number of colleges and universities. Modern construction of all kinds is booming, spurred in part when Beijing was chosen to host the 2008 Olympic Summer Games.

NEW YORK, UNITED STATES The most populous U.S. city by 1810, New York grew even faster with the 1825 opening of the Erie Canal, which connected New York's harbor to the Midwest. The main port of entry for generations of immigrants to America, New York is one of the world's most cosmopolitan cities, and is the epitome of all the glitz, glamour, and bright lights of a big city. Always alive with activity, New York is truly the city that never sleeps.

Languages

A PERSON'S NATIONALITY AND LANGUAGE are often closely associated—most Germans speak German, for example. But there are only about 200 countries, while there are nearly 7,000 living languages. In a quarter of all countries, no single language is spoken by a majority of the inhabitants. Different countries manage this diversity in different ways. Canada is legally bilingual; India has 22 official languages; and French, Spanish, English, Portuguese, and German are each the official language of at least two countries.

Most languages are spoken by only a few hundred or a few thousand people. Only around 300 languages are spoken by more than a million people. Just over 80 languages have more than ten million speakers and of those, nine have more than a hundred million speakers. Not everyone agrees on how to define "a language." This makes it difficult to determine the exact number of languages. A dialect may be a specific variety of language used by a specific geographic or social group, with its own rules of grammar or pronunciation. If a dialect is distinct enough it may become recognized as a different language. Recognition of a language is closely related to the social status and identity of its speakers. Pidgins and creoles, languages that have come into existence as the result of contact between different groups, may not be recognized as full languages because they aren't used by a large number of speakers for a full range of functions.

Speaker population numbers are estimates of those who speak a language as their first language. There may be many more people who speak a language as their second or third language. Each language that a person speaks is used most for certain activities and functions and less for others. Thus a speaker may have very good proficiency in a language when talking about certain topics but lower proficiency in that language for other uses.

Languages diverge over time and geographic space, forming language families. Languages which have diverged little from each other are considered to be more closely related and are shown as being nearer each other on a family tree. Even languages that are quite distinct from each other may show some remnants of their earlier close relationship and provide evidence for the existence of an earlier "proto" language.

Voices of the World

ARCTIC OCEAN

ESKIMO-ALEUT

Of this family's dozen languages in Asia and North America, only Greenlandic Inuktitut, one of Greenland's official languages, may outlive this century.

AMERICAN INDIAN (NORTH)

More than 300 native languages were once spoken in the United States and Canada. Two-thirds survive, but the few speakers left are aging. Even as native languages fade, their sounds echo in place-names such as Chicago and Massachusetts.

1 Algonquian-Ritwan
2 Caddoan
3 Hokan
4 Iroquoian
5 Kiowa-Tanoan
6 Muskogean
7 Nadene
8 Penutian
9 Salishan
10 Siouan
11 Uto-Aztecan
12 Wakashan
13 Undetermined

AFRO-ASIATIC

The languages of ancient Babylon, Assyria, Egypt, and Palestine belonged to this family. Still thriving, the largest living Afro-Asiatic language Arabic, a complex of more than 35 closely-related spoken varieties, spreads in its classical form in tandem with Islam.

1 Berber
2 Chadic
3 Cushitic
4 Omotic
5 Semitic

AMERICAN INDIAN (MESO-)

K'iche' and Yucatec, Mayan languages, are the region's strongest indigenous tongues. Most languages faded after European contact, but a few were documented by missionaries. Alonso de Molina recorded Nahuatl, the Aztec language, in the mid-1500s.

1 Macro-Chibchan
2 Mayan
3 Mixe-Zoquean
4 Oto-Manguean
5 Totonacan
6 Uto-Aztecan

ATLANTIC OCEAN

PACIFIC OCEAN

ISOLATES

Dozens of unusual languages—such as Basque in Spain and France, Burushaski in Pakistan—persist as linguistic islands. Despite decades of research, links to other languages remain unclear and difficult to verify. Chukchi, spoken in Siberia, is an example of a member of an isolated small language family consisting of only 5 members.

Isolates and isolated small families

AMERICAN INDIAN (SOUTH)

Perhaps a thousand Indian languages that once had a voice here have disappeared. Two modest success stories: Quechua, the language of the Inca, though divided among many distinct varieties, has ten million speakers; Guaraní is the major language of Paraguay and is used by nearly everyone in the country as a symbol of national identity.

1 Arawakan
2 Kariban
3 Macro-Chibchan
4 Macro-Ge
5 Pano-Takanan
6 Quechumaran
7 Tukánoan
8 Tupían
9 Other
10 Undetermined

Evolution of Languages

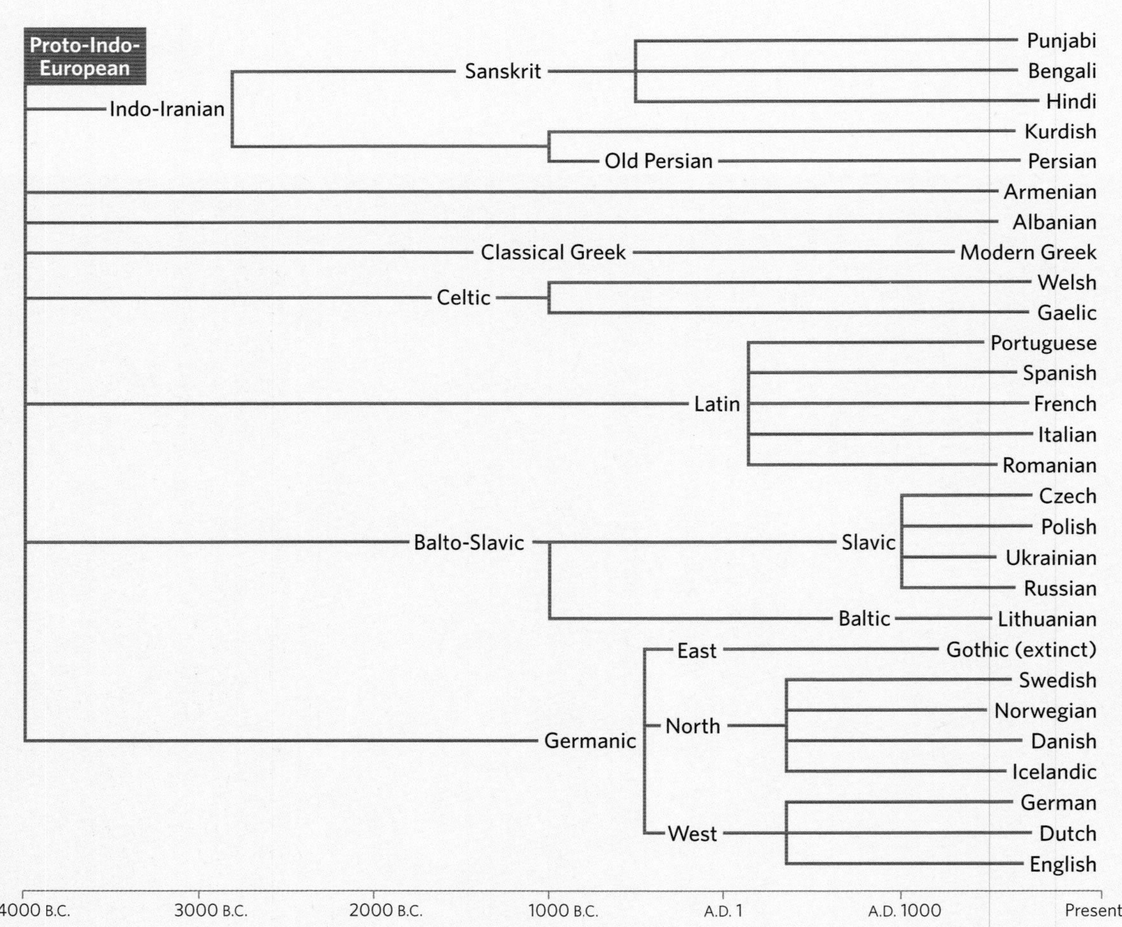

Proto-Indo-European
Indo-Iranian
Sanskrit
Old Persian
Punjabi
Bengali
Hindi
Kurdish
Persian
Armenian
Albanian
Classical Greek
Modern Greek
Celtic
Welsh
Gaelic
Latin
Portuguese
Spanish
French
Italian
Romanian
Balto-Slavic
Slavic
Czech
Polish
Ukrainian
Russian
Baltic
Lithuanian
Germanic
East
Gothic (extinct)
North
Swedish
Norwegian
Danish
Icelandic
West
German
Dutch
English
4000 B.C.
3000 B.C.
2000 B.C.
1000 B.C.
A.D. 1
A.D. 1000
Present

Vanishing Languages

Some 10,000 languages—or more—are thought to have once existed. The actual number is uncertain; unlike extinct animals, dead languages rarely left traces, as most lacked a written form. Nearly 7,000 still exist, but linguists fear that the rate of loss is quickening. Languages cease to exist as their speakers, shifting to other more prestigious or more advantageous languages, don't pass them on to their children. Fortunately, many indigenous communities are working to restore their abandoned heritage languages.

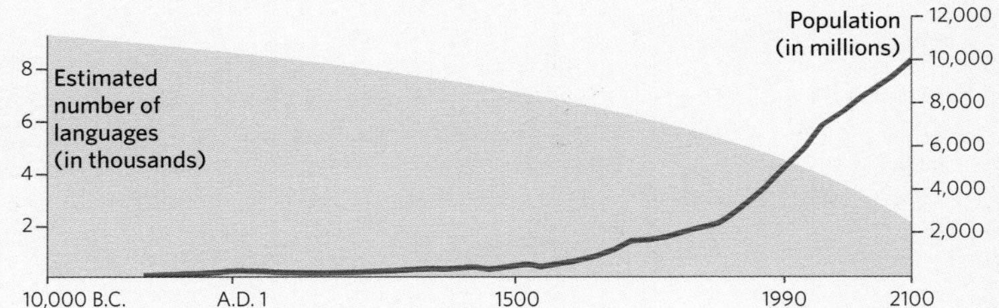

Estimated number of languages (in thousands)
8
6
4
2
Population (in millions)
12,000
10,000
8,000
6,000
4,000
2,000
10,000 B.C.
A.D. 1
1500
1990
2100

Above, Australian Aborigine elders. Many indigenous languages have no remaining speakers or are only remembered by older people. In some communities, elders teach younger apprentice language learners in an effort to keep the language alive. Other language revitalization and documentation approaches are also being tried.

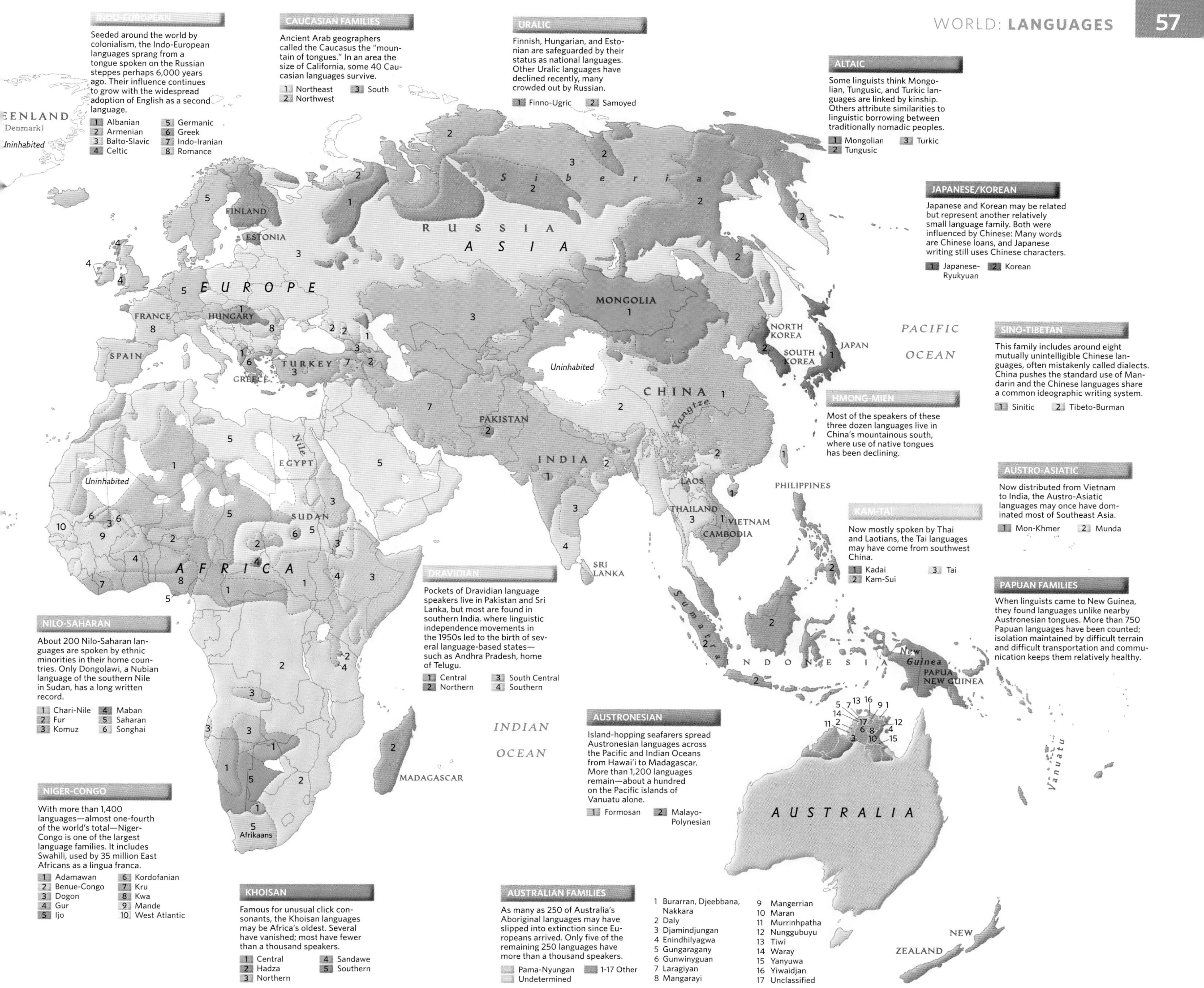

INDO-EUROPEAN

Seeded around the world by colonialism, the Indo-European languages sprang from a tongue spoken on the Russian steppes perhaps 6,000 years ago. Their influence continues to grow with the widespread adoption of English as a second language.

1 Albanian · 2 Armenian · 3 Balto-Slavic · 4 Celtic · 5 Germanic · 6 Greek · 7 Indo-Iranian · 8 Romance

CAUCASIAN FAMILIES

Ancient Arab geographers called the Caucasus the "mountain of tongues." In an area the size of California, some 40 Caucasian languages survive.

1 Northeast · 2 Northwest · 3 South

URALIC

Finnish, Hungarian, and Estonian are safeguarded by their status as national languages. Other Uralic languages have declined recently, many crowded out by Russian.

1 Finno-Ugric · 2 Samoyed

ALTAIC

Some linguists think Mongolian, Tungusic, and Turkic languages are linked by kinship. Others attribute similarities to linguistic borrowing between traditionally nomadic peoples.

1 Mongolian · 2 Tungusic · 3 Turkic

JAPANESE/KOREAN

Japanese and Korean may be related but represent another relatively small language family. Both were influenced by Chinese: Many words are Chinese loans, and Japanese writing still uses Chinese characters.

1 Japanese-Ryukyuan · 2 Korean

SINO-TIBETAN

This family includes around eight mutually unintelligible Chinese languages, often mistakenly called dialects. China pushes the standard use of Mandarin and the Chinese languages share a common ideographic writing system.

1 Sinitic · 2 Tibeto-Burman

HMONG-MIEN

Most of the speakers of these three dozen languages live in China's mountainous south, where use of native tongues has been declining.

AUSTRO-ASIATIC

Now distributed from Vietnam to India, the Austro-Asiatic languages may once have dominated most of Southeast Asia.

1 Mon-Khmer · 2 Munda

KAM-TAI

Now mostly spoken by Thai and Laotians, the Tai languages may have come from southwest China.

1 Kadai · 2 Kam-Sui · 3 Tai

PAPUAN FAMILIES

When linguists came to New Guinea, they found languages unlike nearby Austronesian tongues. More than 750 Papuan languages have been counted; isolation maintained by difficult terrain and difficult transportation and communication keeps them relatively healthy.

DRAVIDIAN

Pockets of Dravidian language speakers live in Pakistan and Sri Lanka, but most are found in southern India, where linguistic independence movements in the 1950s led to the birth of several language-based states—such as Andhra Pradesh, home of Telugu.

1 Central · 2 Northern · 3 South Central · 4 Southern

NILO-SAHARAN

About 200 Nilo-Saharan languages are spoken by ethnic minorities in their home countries. Only Dongolawi, a Nubian language of the southern Nile in Sudan, has a long written record.

1 Chari-Nile · 2 Fur · 3 Komuz · 4 Maban · 5 Saharan · 6 Songhai

NIGER-CONGO

With more than 1,400 languages—almost one-fourth of the world's total—Niger-Congo is one of the largest language families. It includes Swahili, used by 35 million East Africans as a lingua franca.

1 Adamawan · 2 Benue-Congo · 3 Dogon · 4 Gur · 5 Ijo · 6 Kordofanian · 7 Kru · 8 Kwa · 9 Mande · 10 West Atlantic

AUSTRONESIAN

Island-hopping seafarers spread Austronesian languages across the Pacific and Indian Oceans from Hawai'i to Madagascar. More than 1,200 languages remain—about a hundred on the Pacific islands of Vanuatu alone.

1 Formosan · 2 Malayo-Polynesian

KHOISAN

Famous for unusual click consonants, the Khoisan languages may be Africa's oldest. Several have vanished; most have fewer than a thousand speakers.

1 Central · 2 Hadza · 3 Northern · 4 Sandawe · 5 Southern

AUSTRALIAN FAMILIES

As many as 250 of Australia's Aboriginal languages may have slipped into extinction since Europeans arrived. Only five of the remaining 250 languages have more than a thousand speakers.

Pama-Nyungan · Undetermined · 1-17 Other

1 Burarran, Djeebbana, Nakkara
2 Daly
3 Djamindjungan
4 Enindhilyagwa
5 Gungaragany
6 Gunwinyguan
7 Laragiyan
8 Mangarayi
9 Mangerrian
10 Maran
11 Murrinhpatha
12 Nunggubuyu
13 Tiwi
14 Waray
15 Yanyuwa
16 Yiwaidjan
17 Unclassified

Living Languages

A living language is defined as one that has at least one speaker for whom it is their first language—but a language with only one speaker remaining is considered moribund and will not survive if it is not passed on and maintained from generation to generation. For a language to be maintained it must be used by a community of speakers for a broad range of social and communicative functions. The more functions a language is used for, the stronger it is.

Though writing in a language may contribute to its prestige and usefulness, unwritten languages can also have a broad range of oral uses and be maintained over many generations. Changes in usage patterns generally follow social and cultural changes in the community of speakers. Increased contact of formerly isolated groups of people with more powerful outsiders often lead to social changes that affect the prospects for maintenance of many of the world's smaller languages. These changes not only cause the loss of languages but may also foster the development of new ones. Spanish, French, Italian, and the other Romance languages came into being as the Roman Empire disintegrated and Latin was spoken by fewer people for fewer functions.

NORTH AMERICA
EUROPE
ASIA
AFRICA
SOUTH AMERICA
AUSTRALIA

Each dot represents a primary location of a living language listed in Ethnologue.com.

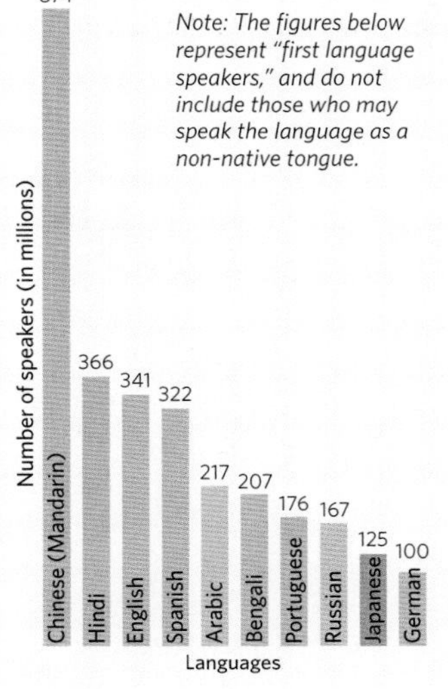
Note: The figures below represent "first language speakers," and do not include those who may speak the language as a non-native tongue.
Number of speakers (in millions)
874 Chinese (Mandarin)
366 Hindi
341 English
322 Spanish
217 Arabic
207 Bengali
176 Portuguese
167 Russian
125 Japanese
100 German
Languages

HOW MANY SPEAK WHAT?

Languages can paint vivid historical pictures of migration and colonization. English, Spanish, and Portuguese, for example, originated in parts of Europe with only a tenth of China's population and area; yet they rival Mandarin Chinese in total number of speakers. They spread because England, Spain, and Portugal built large overseas empires. India, which has been a part of several empires, currently has 22 official languages (in addition to English) and a population of 1.1 billion; only a fifth of its people speak Hindi.

Religions

THE GREAT POWER OF RELIGION comes from its ability to speak to the heart of individuals and societies. Since earliest human times, honoring nature spirits or the belief in a supreme being has brought comfort and security in the face of fundamental questions of life and death.

Billions of people are now adherents of Hinduism, Buddhism, Judaism, Christianity, and Islam, all of which began in Asia or the Middle East. Universal elements of these faiths include worship, sacred sites, saints and martyrs, ritual clothing, dietary laws and fasting, festivals and holy days, and special ceremonies for life's major moments. Each of these religions gives its followers ways to relate to the spiritual realm, as well as moral guidelines that attempt to make life better on Earth as well. Their tenets and goals are taught not only at the church, synagogue, mosque, or temple, but also through schools, storytelling, and artistic creations. In addition to the five great worldwide religions, people have been shaped by Chinese traditional religions (especially Daoism and Confucianism), Shinto and the New Religions of Japan, and Native American traditions.

The world's major religions blossomed from the teachings and revelations of individuals who transmitted the voice of God or discovered a way to salvation that could be understood by others. Abraham and Moses for Jews, the Buddha for Buddhists, Jesus Christ for Christians, and Muhammad for Muslims fulfilled the roles of religious teachers who experienced essential truths of existence. Throughout history, priests, rabbis, ministers, and imams have proclaimed the words of sacred texts to the faithful. The great religions have responded to a deep longing within the human mind for a sense of purpose in the universe, glimpses into the meaning of life. They have also provided communities for persons who share spiritual insights and ethical principles. Today the world's religions, with their guidance here on Earth and hopes and promises for the afterlife, continue to exert an extraordinary force on billions of people.

Major Religions: Geographic Distribution

NORTH AMERICA

EUROPE

ASIA

AFRICA

SOUTH AMERICA

There are almost a million more Jews living in the United States than there are in Israel.

The United States also has almost as many Muslims as Jews, approximately 5 million each.

The Caucasus are deeply divided, with Azerbaijan 88% Muslim and Georgia and Armenia 83% Christian.

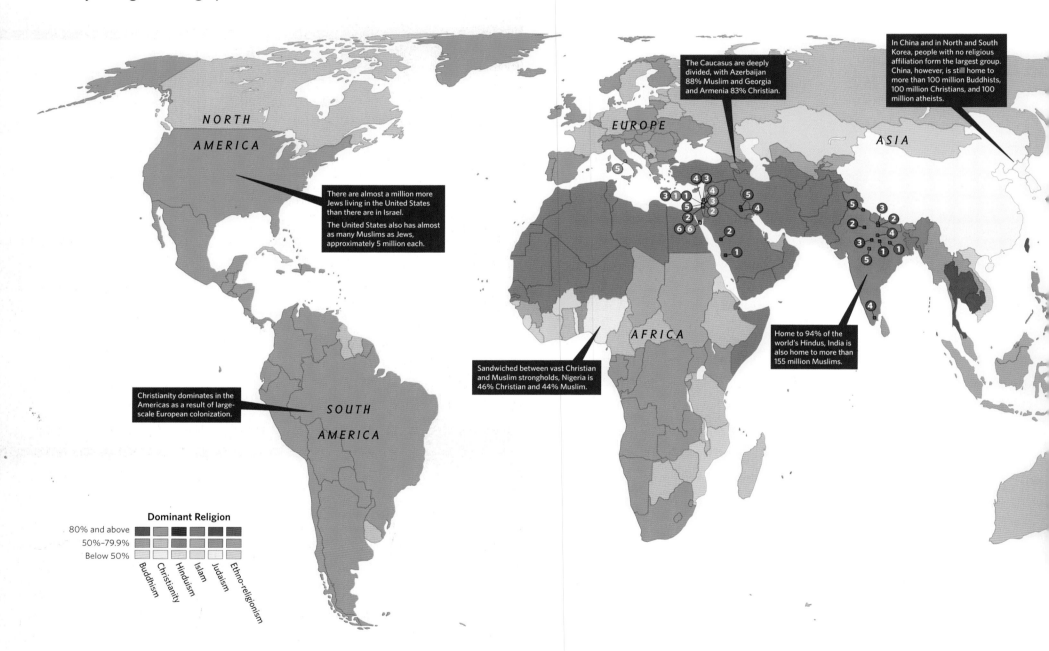

In China and in North and South Korea, people with no religious affiliation form the largest group. China, however, is still home to more than 100 million Buddhists, 100 million Christians, and 100 million atheists.

Sandwiched between vast Christian and Muslim strongholds, Nigeria is 46% Christian and 44% Muslim.

Home to 94% of the world's Hindus, India is also home to more than 155 million Muslims.

Christianity dominates in the Americas as a result of large-scale European colonization.

Dominant Religion

80% and above

50%–79.9%

Below 50%

Buddhism

Christianity

Hinduism

Islam

Judaism

Ethno-religionism

Adherents by Region

In terms of the total number of religious adherents, Asia ranks first. This is not only because half the world's people live on that continent, but also because three of the five major faiths are practiced there: Hinduism in South Asia; Buddhism in East and Southeast Asia; and Islam from Indonesia to the Central Asian republics to Turkey. Oceania, Europe, North America, and South America are overwhelmingly Christian. Africa, with many millions of Muslims and Christians, also retains large numbers of animists.

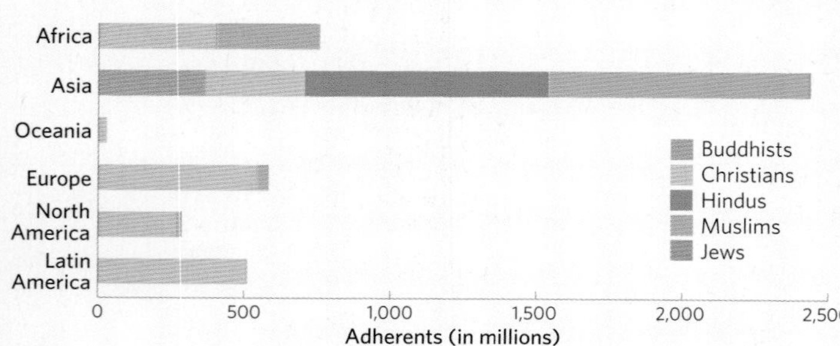

Africa
Asia
Oceania
Europe
North America
Latin America
Buddhists
Christians
Hindus
Muslims
Jews
0
500
1,000
1,500
2,000
2,500
Adherents (in millions)

COUNTRIES WITH THE MOST BUDDHISTS

COUNTRY	BUDDHISTS
1. China	110,710,000
2. Japan	71,771,000
3. Thailand	52,373,000
4. Vietnam	40,992,000
5. Myanmar	35,529,000
6. Sri Lanka	13,184,000
7. Cambodia	11,901,000
8. India	7,789,000
9. South Korea	7,234,000
10. Taiwan*	6,065,000
11. Laos	3,014,000
12. United States	2,811,000
13. Nepal	2,583,000
14. Indonesia	1,962,000
15. Malaysia	1,313,000

COUNTRIES WITH THE MOST CHRISTIANS

COUNTRY	CHRISTIANS
1. United States	245,931,000
2. Brazil	170,598,000
3. Russia	113,863,000
4. China	109,576,000
5. Mexico	99,946,000
6. Philippines	75,521,000
7. India	65,963,000
8. Nigeria	64,440,000
9. Germany	59,356,000
10. Dem. Rep. of the Congo	56,020,000
11. United Kingdom	48,738,000
12. Italy	47,580,000
13. Ethiopia	43,815,000
14. Colombia	43,033,000
15. France	42,265,000

COUNTRIES WITH THE MOST HINDUS

COUNTRY	HINDUS
1. India	826,499,000
2. Nepal	19,302,000
3. Bangladesh	14,765,000
4. Indonesia	7,217,000
5. Sri Lanka	2,160,000
6. Pakistan	2,057,000
7. Malaysia	1,608,000
8. United States	1,338,000
9. South Africa	1,141,000
10. Myanmar	818,000
11. Russia	742,000
12. United Kingdom	604,000
13. Mauritius	544,000
14. Tanzania	332,000
15. Canada	328,000

*Non-sovereign nation

All figures are estimates based on data for the year 2005.
Countries with the highest reported nonreligious populations include China, Russia, United States, Germany, India, Japan, North Korea, Vietnam, France, and Italy.

Religiosity and Wealth

A 2007 study by the Pew Global Attitudes Project revealed a strong link between the religiosity (which measures how religious a person or a group is) and the wealth of countries. When the per capita GDPs of 44 countries from around the world are plotted against their religiosity scores, a clear correlation is seen—the more religious a country is, the poorer it tends to be. But there are exceptions to every rule. Oil revenues have filled the pockets of the deeply religious Kingdom of Kuwait, while the United States is also much more religious than its high per capita GDP would predict.

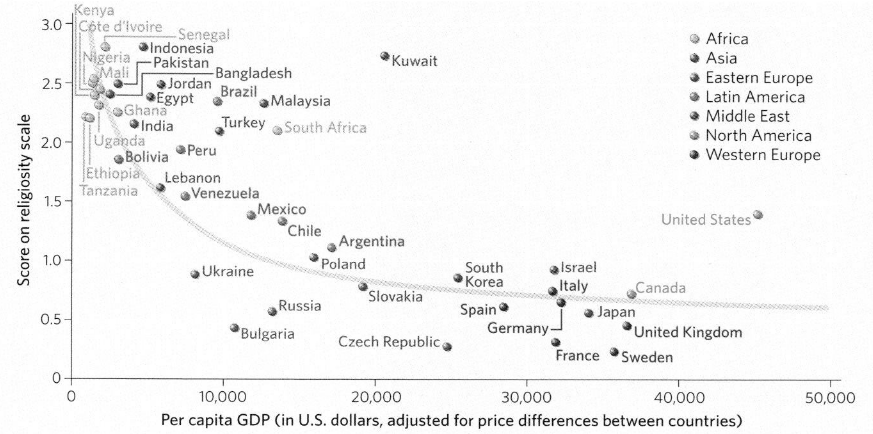
Kenya
Côte d'Ivoire
Senegal
Indonesia
Nigeria
Pakistan
Mali
Bangladesh
Jordan
Brazil
Egypt
Malaysia
Ghana
India
Turkey
South Africa
Uganda
Bolivia
Peru
Ethiopia
Lebanon
Tanzania
Venezuela
Mexico
Chile
Argentina
Poland
Ukraine
Slovakia
Russia
Bulgaria
Czech Republic
Kuwait
South Korea
Israel
Italy
Canada
Spain
Germany
Japan
United Kingdom
France
Sweden
United States
Africa
Asia
Eastern Europe
Latin America
Middle East
North America
Western Europe
Score on religiosity scale
0
0.5
1.0
1.5
2.0
2.5
3.0
0
10,000
20,000
30,000
40,000
50,000
Per capita GDP (in U.S. dollars, adjusted for price differences between countries)

Buddhism

Founded about 2,500 years ago by Shakyamuni Buddha (or Gautama Buddha), Buddhism teaches liberation from suffering through the threefold cultivation of morality, meditation, and wisdom. Buddhists revere the Three Jewels: Buddha (the Awakened One), Dharma (the Truth), and Sangha (the community of monks and nuns).

Christianity

Christian belief in eternal life is based on the example of Jesus Christ, a Jew born some 2,000 years ago. The New Testament tells of his teaching, persecution, crucifixion, and resurrection. Today Christianity is found around the world in three main forms: Roman Catholicism, Eastern Orthodoxy, and Protestantism.

Sacred Places

BUDDHISM

1. **Bodhgaya:** Where Buddha attained awakening
2. **Kusinagara:** Where Buddha entered nirvana
3. **Lumbini:** Place of Buddha's last human birth
4. **Sarnath:** Place where Buddha delivered his first sermon
5. **Sanchi:** Location of famous stupa containing relics of Buddha

CHRISTIANITY

1. **Jerusalem:** Church of the Holy Sepulchre, Jesus's crucifixion
2. **Bethlehem:** Jesus's birthplace
3. **Nazareth:** Hometown of Jesus Christ
4. **Shore of the Sea of Galilee:** Where Jesus gave the Sermon on the Mount
5. **Rome and the Vatican:** Tombs of St. Peter and St. Paul
6. **Mount Sinai:** Site of God's manifestation to Moses and the revelation of the Ten Commandments given to him by God

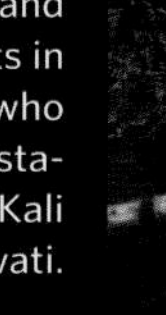

HINDUISM

1. **Varanasi (Benares):** Most holy Hindu site, home of Shiva
2. **Vrindavan:** Krishna's birthplace
3. **Allahabad:** At confluence of Ganges and Yamuna Rivers, purest place to bathe
4. **Madurai:** Temple of Minakshi, great goddess of the south
5. **Badrinath:** Vishnu's shrine

ISLAM

1. **Mecca:** The Prophet Muhammad's birthplace; destination of the pilgrimage, or hajj; houses the Kaaba (shrine that Muslims face when praying)
2. **Medina:** Burial place of the Prophet Muhammad; contains the tombs of the 2nd, 4th, 5th, and 6th Shiite imams
3. **Jerusalem:** The first Qibla (direction of the prayers) before replaced by Mecca; site of nightlong ascension of the Prophet Muhammad to the heavens
4. **Najaf (Shi'ite):** Tomb of the first imam, Ali; ancient center of Shiite learning; known as the "Vatican City" of Shiism
5. **Karbala (Shi'ite):** Tomb of the 3rd imam and martyr, Hussein

JUDAISM

1. **Jerusalem:** Location of the Western Wall and First and Second Temples; City of David; the ancient and modern capital of Israel
2. **Hebron:** Burial spot of patriarchs and matriarchs
3. **Safed:** Where Kabbalah (Jewish mysticism) flourished
4. **Tiberias:** Where Talmud (source of Jewish law) first composed
5. **Bethlehem:** Site of Rachel's tomb
6. **Mount Sinai**: Site of God's revelation, where God appeared to Moses and gave him the Ten Commandments

STRALIA

Hinduism

Hinduism began in India more than 4,000 years ago and is still flourishing. Sacred texts known as the Vedas form the basis of Hindu faith and ritual. Today most Hindus are devoted to one of the two Great Gods: Vishnu, who has been incarnated as Rama and Krishna at crucial points in human history, or Shiva, who also has feminine manifestations of power, such as Kali and Parvati.

Islam

Muslims believe that the Koran, Islam's sacred book, accurately records the spoken word of God (Allah) as revealed to the Prophet Muhammad, born in Mecca about A.D. 570. Strict adherents pray five times a day, fast during the holy month of Ramadan, and make at least one pilgrimage to Mecca, Islam's holiest city.

Judaism

The 4,000-year-old religion of the Jews stands as the oldest of the major faiths that believe in a single God. The foundations of Judaism's traditions, laws, and beliefs are in the Torah, the first five books of the Bible, with its stories of patriarchs/matriarchs such as Abraham and Sarah and the leadership of Moses in the Hebrews' exodus from Egypt.

COUNTRIES WITH THE MOST MUSLIMS

	COUNTRY	MUSLIMS
1.	Indonesia	203,832,000
2.	India	155,197,000
3.	Pakistan	151,568,000
4.	Bangladesh	135,764,000
5.	Turkey	71,068,000
6.	Iran	68,247,000
7.	Nigeria	62,391,000
8.	Egypt	61,816,000
9.	Algeria	32,221,000
10.	Morocco	29,994,000
11.	Iraq	27,171,000
12.	Ethiopia	26,732,000
13.	Sudan	26,309,000
14.	Afghanistan	25,006,000
15.	Saudi Arabia	21,927,000

COUNTRIES WITH THE MOST JEWS

	COUNTRY	JEWS
1.	United States	5,761,000
2.	Israel	4,844,000
3.	France	610,000
4.	Argentina	513,000
5.	Occ. Pal. Terr.*	445,000
6.	Canada	418,000
7.	United Kingdom	282,000
8.	Germany	225,000
9.	Russia	188,000
10.	Ukraine	182,000
11.	Brazil	141,000
12.	Mexico	129,000
13.	Australia	100,000
14.	Hungary	98,000
15.	South Africa	78,000

Adherents Worldwide

The growth of Islam and the decline of Chinese traditional religion stand out as significant changes over the past hundred years. Christianity, the largest of the world's main faiths, has remained fairly stable in its number of adherents. Today more than one in six people claim to be atheistic or nonreligious.

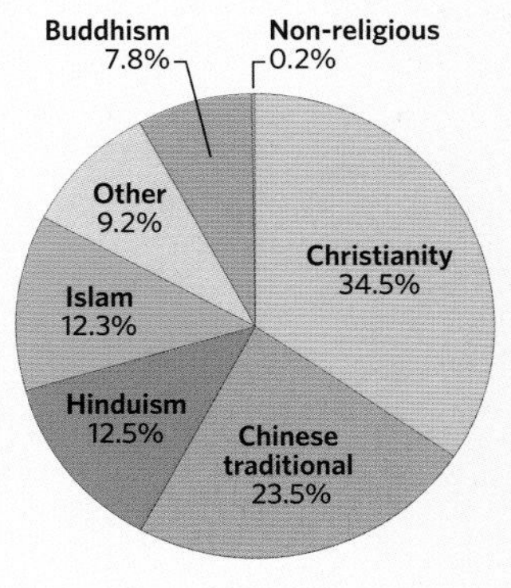
Buddhism 7.8%
Non-religious 0.2%
Other 9.2%
Christianity 34.5%
Islam 12.3%
Hinduism 12.5%
Chinese traditional 23.5%
1900

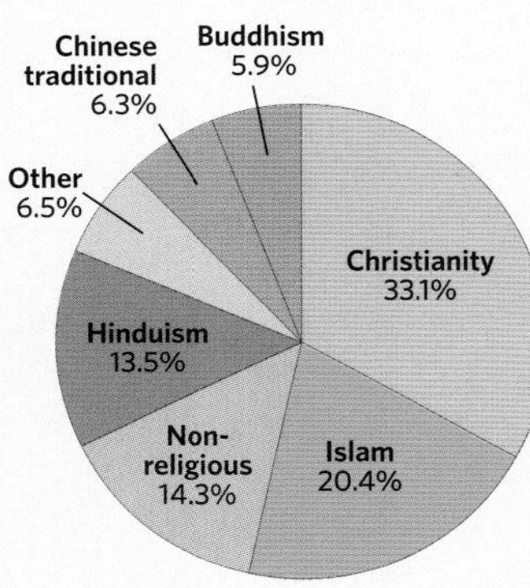
Chinese traditional 6.3%
Buddhism 5.9%
Other 6.5%
Christianity 33.1%
Hinduism 13.5%
Non-religious 14.3%
Islam 20.4%
2005

Health and Education

IN THE PAST 50 YEARS, health conditions have improved dramatically. With better economic and living conditions and access to immunization and other basic health services, global life expectancy has risen from 40 to 65 years; the death rate for children under five years old has fallen by half; and many infectious and parasitic diseases that once killed and disabled millions have been eradicated, eliminated, or greatly reduced in impact. Today, fully three-quarters of the world's children benefit from protection against six infectious diseases that were responsible in the past for many millions of infant and child deaths.

Despite major strides, however, infant and child mortality from infectious diseases remains relatively high in many of the poorest countries. Each year, nearly ten million children under five years old die—about four out of every ten of those deaths occur in sub-Saharan Africa and three in South Asia. Undernutrition is a major contributor to fully one-third of child deaths, and poor families are the hardest hit. In Indonesia, for example, a child born in a poor household is four times as likely to die by her fifth birthday as a child born to a well-off family.

The age-old link between social inequality and ill health is also manifested in the emergence of new health threats. The HIV/AIDS pandemic has erased decades of steady improvements in sub-Saharan Africa. The death toll in southern African countries, where adult prevalence exceeds 15 percent, is contributing to reversals in life expectancy—just 47 years instead of the estimated 62 years without AIDS. Because of both biological and social factors, adolescent girls are the most vulnerable: Three out of every four HIV-positive individuals ages 10 to 24 in southern Africa are female. And the impacts are felt across generations: An estimated 15 million children have lost one or both of their parents to the disease.

Increasingly, lifestyle diseases are also afflicting low-income countries, coming with demographic changes, urbanization, changes in eating habits and physical activity, and environmental degradation. Traffic accidents account for more than a million deaths and upward of 50 million injuries annually; with the rapid increase of automobile use, observers expect that by 2020 the number of traffic deaths will have increased by more than 80 percent in developing countries.

While many international leaders focus on high-profile infectious diseases, the looming challenges of chronic diseases may be even greater. In many high- and middle-income countries, chronic, lifestyle-related diseases such as cardiovascular disease, diabetes, and others are becoming the predominant cause of disability and death. In developed countries, smoking is the cause of more than one-third of male deaths in middle age, and about one in eight female deaths. Because the focus of policymakers has been on treatment rather than prevention, the costs of dealing with these ailments contributes to high (and rapidly increasing) health-care spending.

Health-Care Availability

Regional differences in health-care resources are striking. While countries in Europe and the Americas have relatively large numbers of physicians and nurses, nations with far higher burdens of disease (particularly African countries) are experiencing severe deficits in both health workers and health facilities.

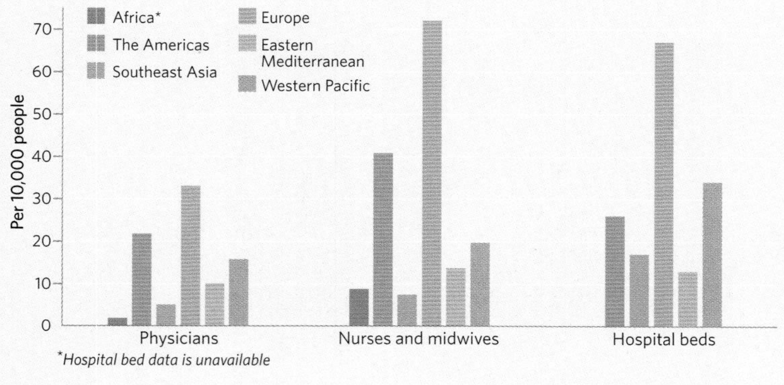
Africa*
The Americas
Southeast Asia
Europe
Eastern Mediterranean
Western Pacific
Per 10,000 people
0
10
20
30
40
50
60
70
Physicians
Nurses and midwives
Hospital beds

*Hospital bed data is unavailable

Income Levels: Indicators of Health and Literacy

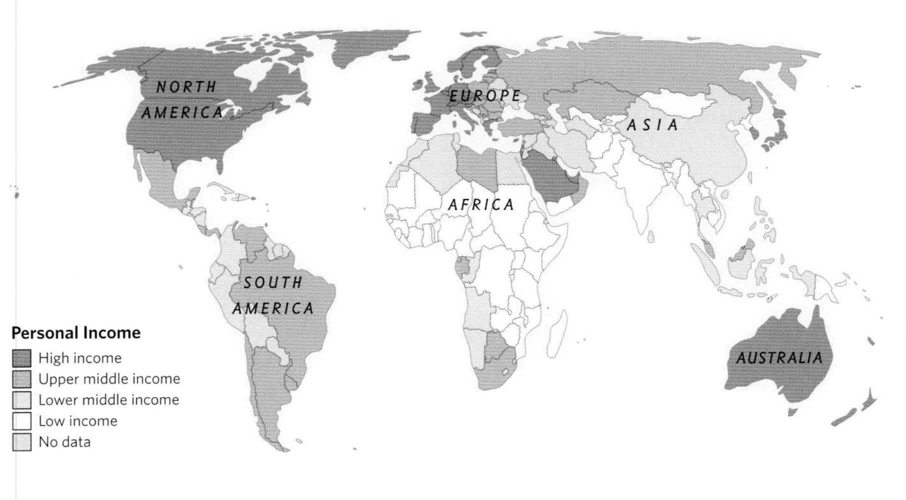
NORTH AMERICA
EUROPE
ASIA
AFRICA
SOUTH AMERICA
AUSTRALIA
Personal Income
High income
Upper middle income
Lower middle income
Low income
No data

Access to Improved Sanitation

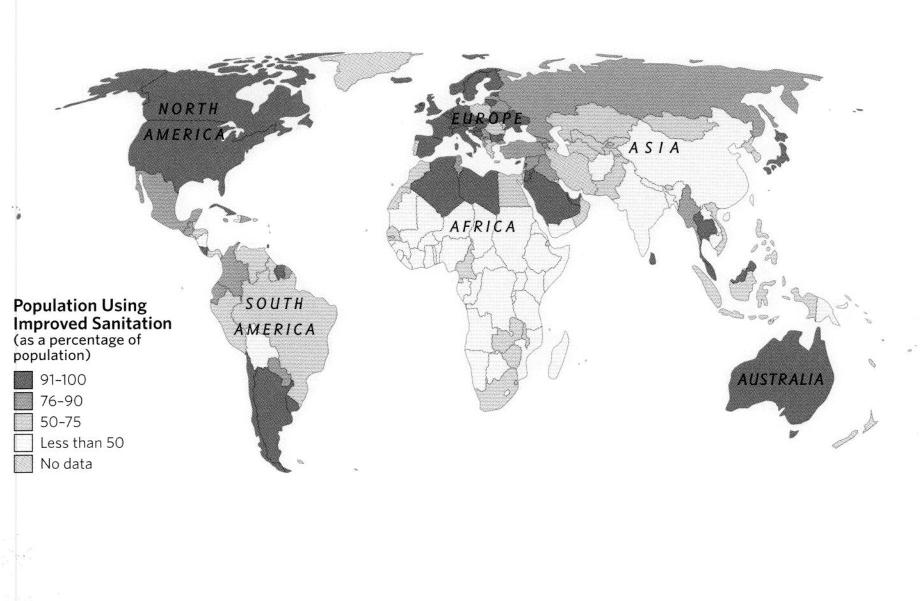
NORTH AMERICA
EUROPE
ASIA
AFRICA
SOUTH AMERICA
AUSTRALIA
Population Using Improved Sanitation
(as a percentage of population)
91-100
76-90
50-75
Less than 50
No data

Nutrition

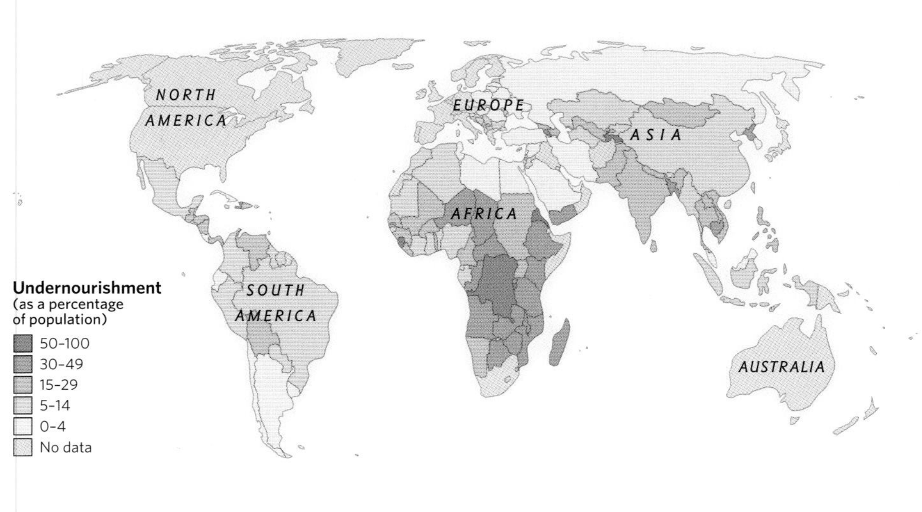
NORTH AMERICA
EUROPE
ASIA
AFRICA
SOUTH AMERICA
AUSTRALIA
Undernourishment
(as a percentage of population)
50-100
30-49
15-29
5-14
0-4
No data

HIV

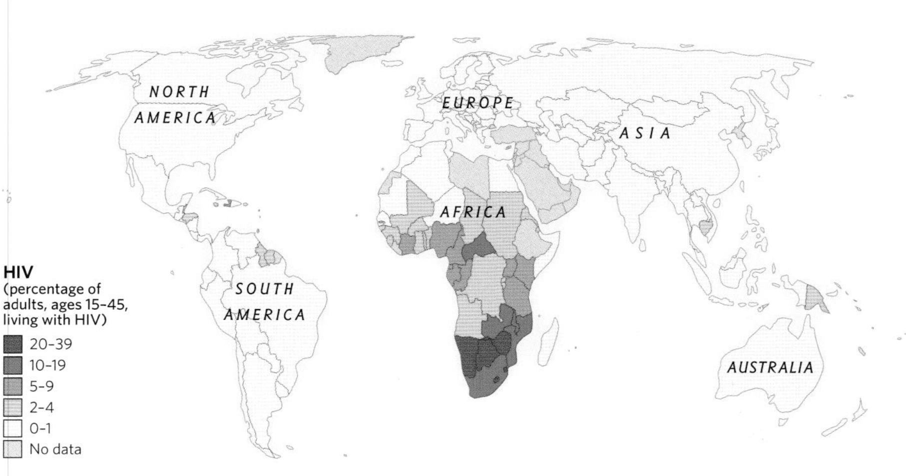
NORTH AMERICA
EUROPE
ASIA
AFRICA
SOUTH AMERICA
AUSTRALIA
HIV
(percentage of adults, ages 15-45, living with HIV)
20-39
10-19
5-9
2-4
0-1
No data

Global Disease Burden

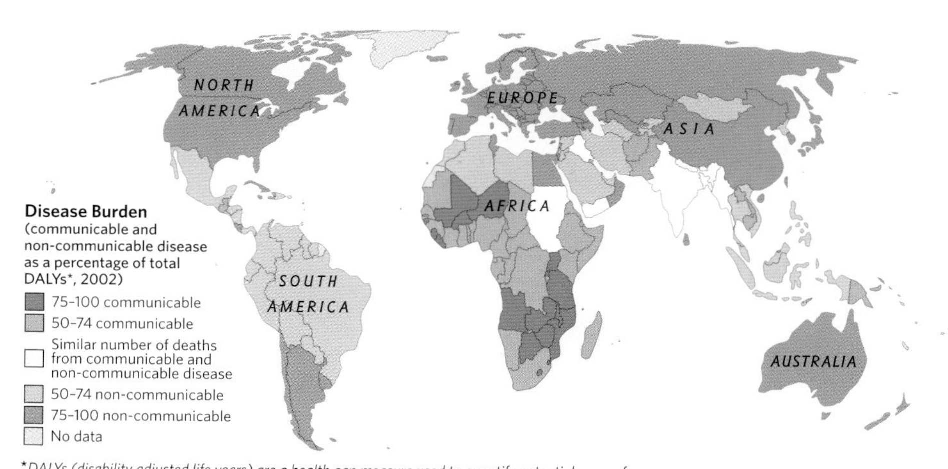
NORTH AMERICA
EUROPE
ASIA
AFRICA
SOUTH AMERICA
AUSTRALIA
Disease Burden
(communicable and non-communicable disease as a percentage of total DALYs*, 2002)
75–100 communicable
50–74 communicable
Similar number of deaths from communicable and non-communicable disease
50–74 non-communicable
75–100 non-communicable
No data

*DALYs (disability adjusted life years) are a health gap measure used to quantify potential years of life lost to illness or premature death. One DALY can be thought of as one lost year of "healthy" life.

While infectious and parasitic diseases account for nearly one-quarter of total deaths in developing countries, they result in relatively few deaths in wealthier countries. In contrast, cardiovascular diseases and cancer are more significant causes of death in industrialized countries. Over time, however, as fertility rates fall, social and living conditions improve, the population ages, and further advances are made against infectious diseases in poorer countries, the differences in causes of death between developed and developing countries will narrow and may eventually converge.

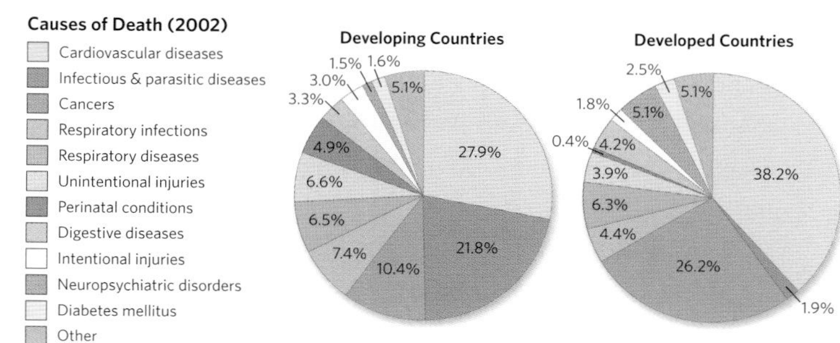
Causes of Death (2002)
Cardiovascular diseases
Infectious & parasitic diseases
Cancers
Respiratory infections
Respiratory diseases
Unintentional injuries
Perinatal conditions
Digestive diseases
Intentional injuries
Neuropsychiatric disorders
Diabetes mellitus
Other
Developing Countries
1.5% 1.6%
3.0%
3.3%
5.1%
4.9%
6.6%
6.5%
7.4%
10.4%
21.8%
27.9%
Developed Countries
2.5%
1.8%
5.1%
5.1%
0.4%
4.2%
3.9%
6.3%
4.4%
26.2%
38.2%
1.9%

Under-Five Mortality

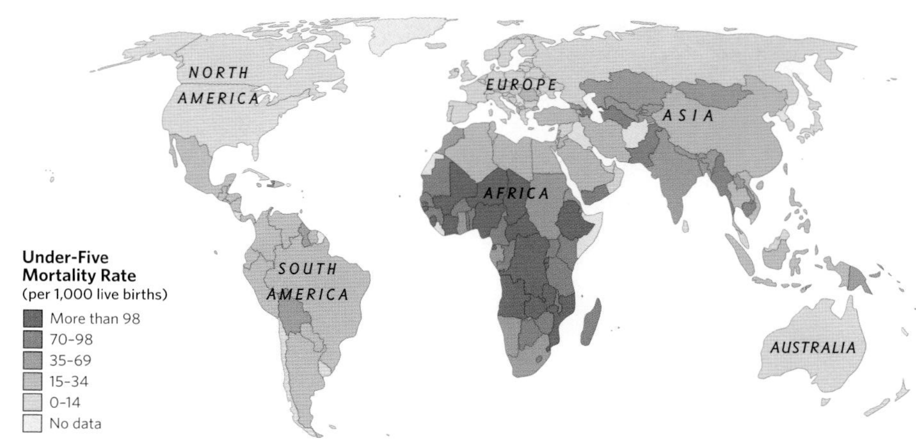
NORTH AMERICA
EUROPE
ASIA
AFRICA
SOUTH AMERICA
AUSTRALIA
Under-Five Mortality Rate
(per 1,000 live births)
More than 98
70–98
35–69
15–34
0–14
No data

Maternal Mortality

Under-five maternal mortality ratio per 100,000 live births*

COUNTRIES WITH THE HIGHEST MATERNAL MORTALITY RATES:		COUNTRIES WITH THE LOWEST MATERNAL MORTALITY RATES:	
1. Sierra Leone	2,100	1. Ireland	1
2. Niger	1,800	2. Sweden	3
3. Chad	1,500	3. Denmark	3
4. Angola	1,400	4. Italy	3
5. Rwanda	1,300	5. Greece	3
6. Guinea-Bissau	1,100	6. Bosnia and Herzegovina	3
7. Dem. Rep. of the Congo	1,100	7. Iceland	4
8. Burundi	1,100	8. Australia	4
9. Malawi	1,100	9. Spain	4
10. Nigeria	1,100	10. Austria	4

*Adjusted for underreporting and misclassification.
Countries with the same rates are listed in order of their UN Human Development Index rankings.

Education and Literacy

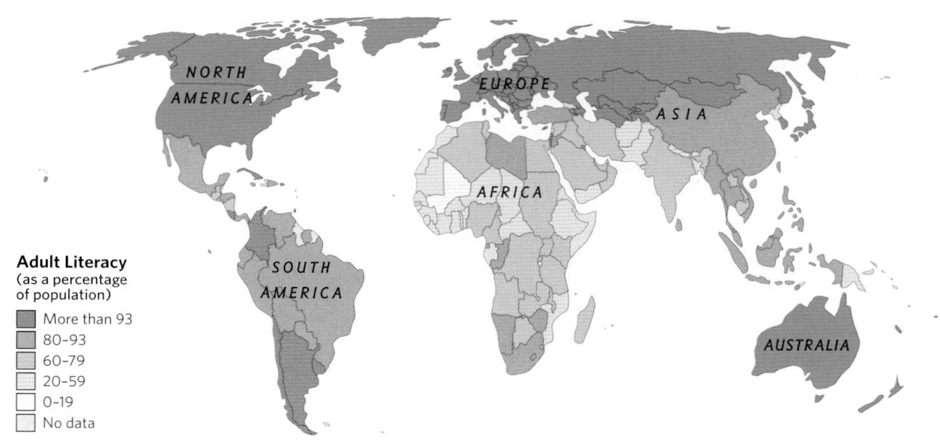
NORTH AMERICA
EUROPE
ASIA
AFRICA
SOUTH AMERICA
AUSTRALIA
Adult Literacy
(as a percentage of population)
More than 93
80–93
60–79
20–59
0–19
No data

Basic education is an investment for the long-term prosperity of a country, generating individual, household, and social benefits. Some countries, such as many in Europe, have long traditions of high educational attainment among both genders, and now have well-educated populations of all ages. In contrast, many low-income countries have only recently expanded access to primary education; girls still lag behind boys in enrollment and completion of primary school, and then in making the transition to secondary school. Socially excluded populations, including ethnic minorities, have the lowest rates of school entry and completion. Countries with low levels of education will have to wait many years before most individuals in the productive ages have even minimal levels of reading, writing, and basic arithmetic skills. The expansion of secondary schooling tends to lag even further behind, so countries with low educational attainment will likely be at a disadvantage for at least another generation.

The United Nations recognizes the urgent need for universal primary education. To help define the role of the UN in the 21st century, world leaders at the UN Millennium Summit in 2000 created the eight Millennium Development Goals, which are to be achieved by 2015. The UN is monitoring the progress of its goals, which aim to combat poverty, hunger, disease, illiteracy, environmental degradation, and discrimination against women.

While no one doubts that the key to long-term economic growth and poverty reduction lies in greater education opportunities for all, many poor countries face the tremendous challenge of paying for schools and teachers today, while having to wait 20 years for the economic returns from those investments.

School Enrollment for Girls

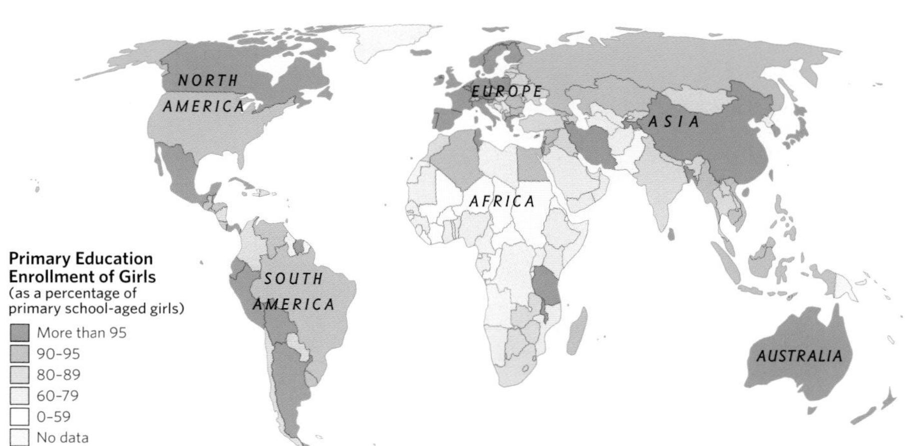
NORTH AMERICA
EUROPE
ASIA
AFRICA
SOUTH AMERICA
AUSTRALIA
Primary Education Enrollment of Girls
(as a percentage of primary school-aged girls)
More than 95
90–95
80–89
60–79
0–59
No data

DEVELOPING HUMAN CAPITAL In the pyramids below, more red and blue in the bars indicates a higher level of educational attainment, or "human capital," which contributes greatly to a country's ability for future economic growth. These two countries are similar in population size, but their human capital measures are significantly different.

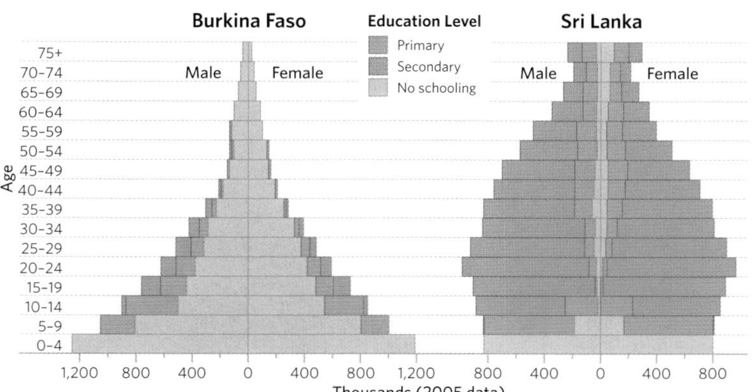
Burkina Faso
Education Level
Primary
Secondary
No schooling
Sri Lanka
Male
Female
Male
Female
Age
75+
70–74
65–69
60–64
55–59
50–54
45–49
40–44
35–39
30–34
25–29
20–24
15–19
10–14
5–9
0–4
1,200 800 400 0 400 800 1,200
800 400 0 400 800
Thousands (2005 data)

Economy

A GLOBAL ECONOMIC ACTIVITY MAP (right) reveals striking differences in the composition of output in advanced economies (such as the United States, Japan, and Western Europe) compared with less developed countries (such as Nigeria and China). Advanced economies tend to have high proportions of their GDP (gross domestic product) in services, while developing economies have relatively high proportions in agriculture and industry.

There are different ways of looking at the distribution of manufacturing industry activity. When examined by country, the United States leads in production in many industries, but Western European countries are also a major manufacturing force. Western Europe outpaces the U.S. in the production of cars, chemicals, and food.

The world's sixth largest economy is found in China, and it has been growing rapidly. Chinese workers take home only a fraction of the cash pocketed each week by their economic rivals in the West, but are quickly catching up to the global economy with their purchase of cell phones and motor vehicles—two basic consumer products of the modern age.

The Middle East—a number of whose countries enjoy relatively high per capita GDP values—produces more fuel than any other region, but it has virtually no other economic output besides that single commodity.

As patterns of trade and sourcing become increasingly complex, global economic interdependence is deepening. India and Eastern Europe have become major suppliers of global services, such as information technology. The Chinese economy has grown through manufacturing exports, but is now diversifying, in part due to domestic demand.

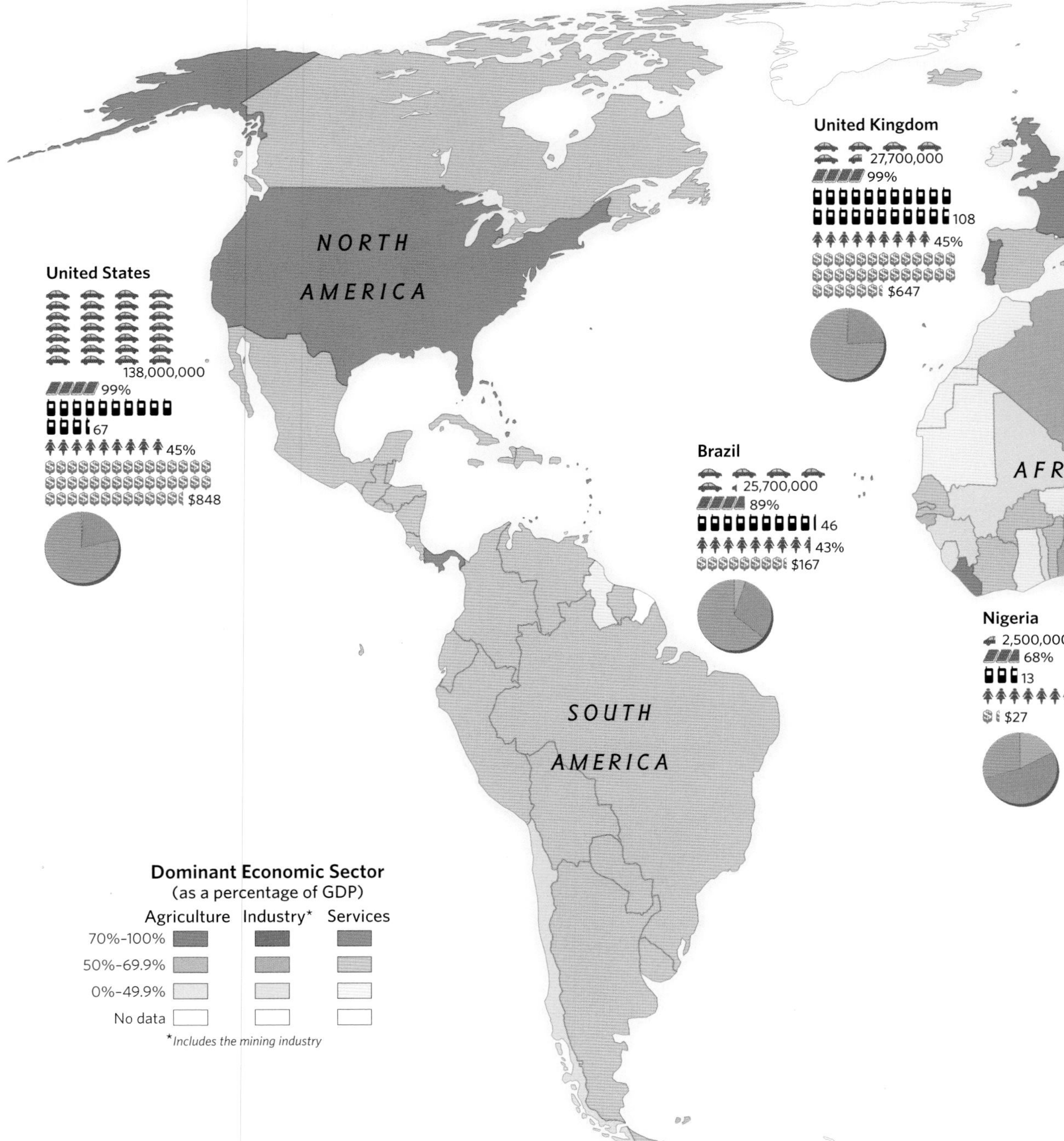

NORTH AMERICA
SOUTH AMERICA
AFRIC
United States
138,000,000
99%
67
45%
$848
United Kingdom
27,700,000
99%
108
45%
$647
Brazil
25,700,000
89%
46
43%
$167
Nigeria
2,500,000
68%
13
$27
Dominant Economic Sector
(as a percentage of GDP)
Agriculture Industry* Services
70%–100%
50%–69.9%
0%–49.9%
No data
*Includes the mining industry

Labor Migration

People in search of jobs gravitate toward the higher-income economies, unless immigration policies prevent them from doing so. Japan, for instance, has one of the world's most restrictive immigration policies and a population that is more than 99 percent Japanese. Some countries are "labor importers," while others are "labor exporters." In the mid-1990s, Malaysia was the largest Asian importer (close to a million workers) and the Philippines was the largest Asian exporter (4.2 million). The largest share of foreign workers in domestic employment is found in the Persian Gulf region and in Singapore.

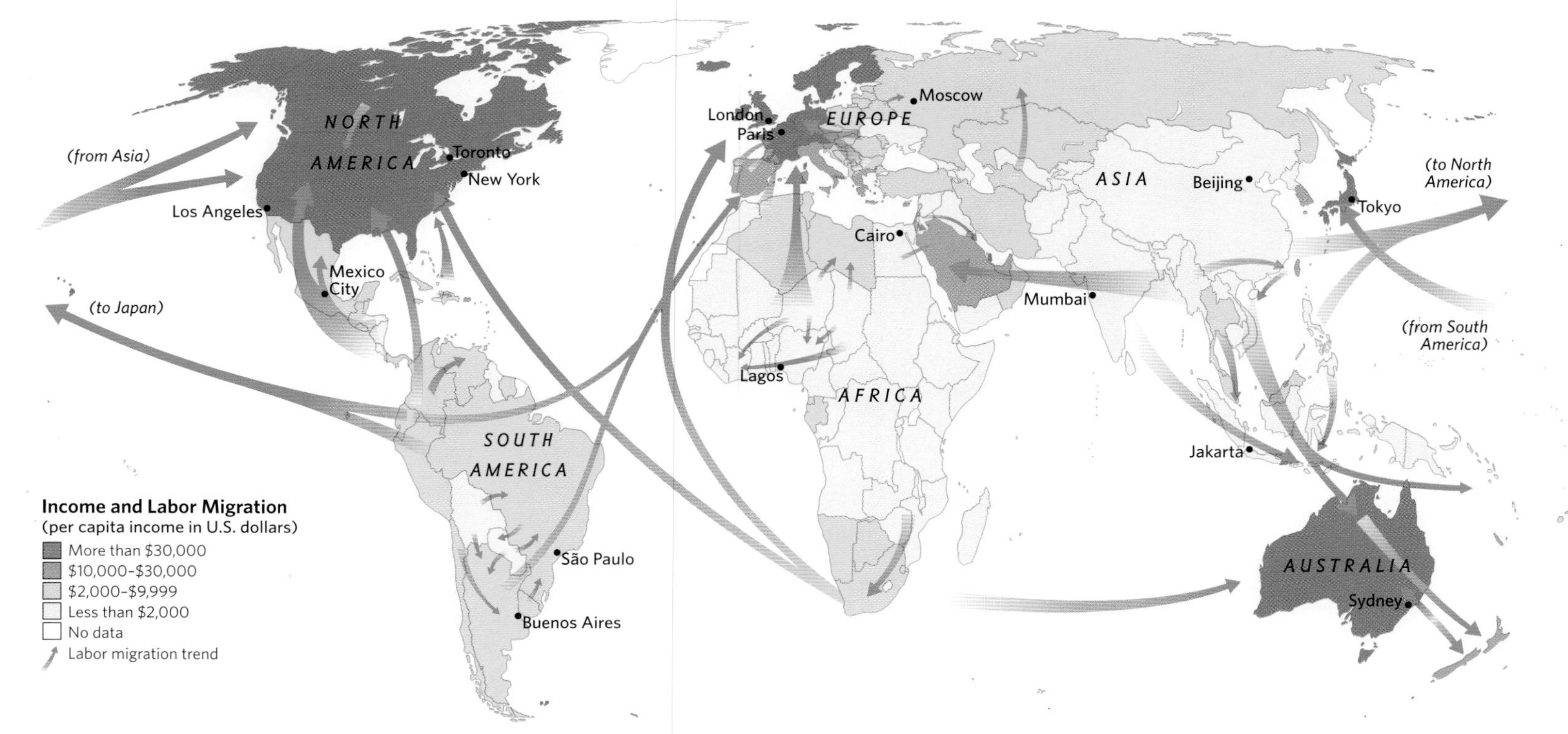

NORTH AMERICA
(from Asia)
Los Angeles
Toronto
New York
Mexico City
(to Japan)
SOUTH AMERICA
São Paulo
Buenos Aires
London
Paris
EUROPE
Moscow
Cairo
Lagos
AFRICA
ASIA
Beijing
Tokyo
Mumbai
Jakarta
(to North America)
(from South America)
AUSTRALIA
Sydney
Income and Labor Migration
(per capita income in U.S. dollars)
More than $30,000
$10,000–$30,000
$2,000–$9,999
Less than $2,000
No data
Labor migration trend

Top GDP Growth Rates

(based on PPP, or purchasing power parity)

COUNTRY	(2000–2007 AVERAGE)
1. Equatorial Guinea	19.4%
2. Azerbaijan	17.5%
3. Armenia	14.7%
4. Turkmenistan	14.5%
5. Angola	13.2%
6. Kazakhstan	12.0%
7. Latvia	11.9%
8. Afghanistan	11.8%
9. China	11.7%
10. Sierra Leone	11.5%

Source: International Monetary Fund (IMF)

The World's Richest Countries

COUNTRY	GDP PER CAPITA (PPP) (2007)
1. Luxembourg	$84,500
2. Ireland	$46,800
3. Norway	$45,500
4. United States	$45,200
5. Iceland	$41,200
6. Switzerland	$38,800
7. Denmark	$38,100
8. Austria	$37,500
9. Canada	$36,800
10. United Kingdom	$36,600

Source: International Monetary Fund (IMF)

The World's Poorest Countries

COUNTRY	GDP PER CAPITA (PPP) (2007)
1. Burundi	$725
2. Malawi	$746
3. Yemen	$764
4. Guinea-Bissau	$807
5. Tanzania	$861
6. Democratic Republic of the Congo	$900
7. Sierra Leone	$941
8. Niger	$980
9. Madagascar	$1,037
10. Eritrea	$1,038

Source: International Monetary Fund (IMF)

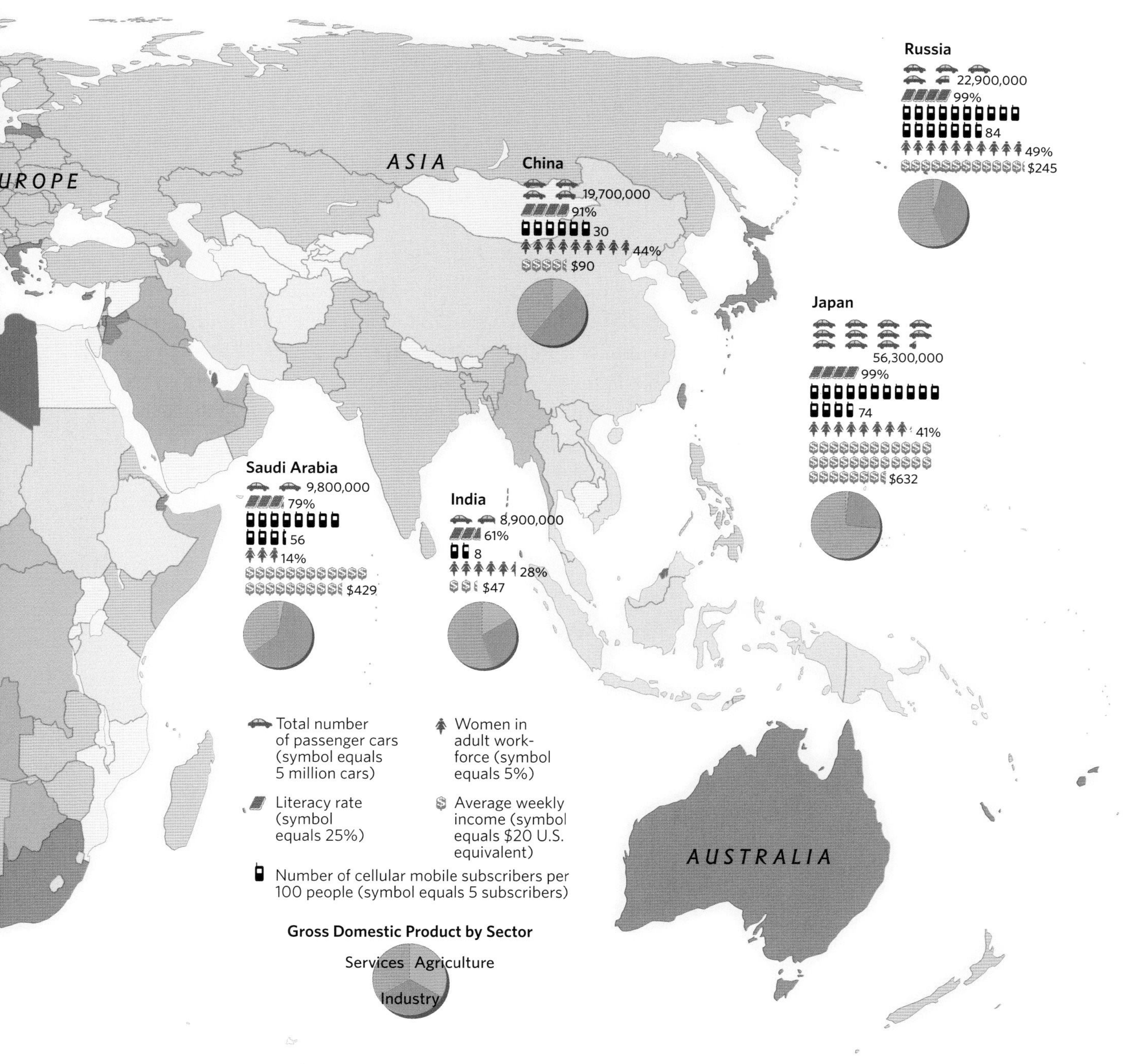

Russia
22,900,000
99%
84
49%
$245
ASIA
UROPE
China
19,700,000
91%
30
44%
$90
Japan
56,300,000
99%
74
41%
$632
Saudi Arabia
9,800,000
79%
56
14%
$429
India
8,900,000
61%
8
28%
$47
Total number of passenger cars (symbol equals 5 million cars)
Women in adult work-force (symbol equals 5%)
Literacy rate (symbol equals 25%)
Average weekly income (symbol equals $20 U.S. equivalent)
Number of cellular mobile subscribers per 100 people (symbol equals 5 subscribers)
Gross Domestic Product by Sector
Services
Agriculture
Industry
AUSTRALIA

Gross Domestic Product

The gross domestic product (GDP) is the total market value of goods and services produced by a country's economy in a given year using global currency exchange rates. It is a convenient way of calculating the level of a country's international purchasing power and economic strength, but it does not show average wealth of individuals or measure standards of living. For example, a country could have a high level of exports, but still have a low standard of living.

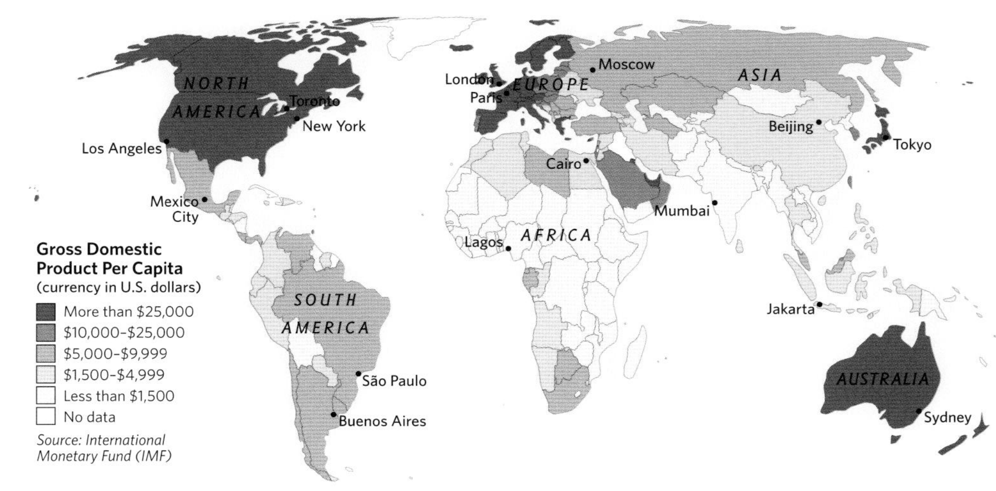

NORTH AMERICA
Toronto
New York
Los Angeles
Mexico City
London
Paris
EUROPE
Moscow
ASIA
Beijing
Tokyo
Cairo
Mumbai
Lagos
AFRICA
SOUTH AMERICA
São Paulo
Buenos Aires
Jakarta
AUSTRALIA
Sydney
Gross Domestic Product Per Capita
(currency in U.S. dollars)
More than $25,000
$10,000–$25,000
$5,000–$9,999
$1,500–$4,999
Less than $1,500
No data
Source: International Monetary Fund (IMF)

Gross Domestic Product: Purchasing Power Parity (PPP)

The PPP method calculates the relative value of currencies based on what each currency will buy in its country of origin, providing a good comparison between national economies. Per capita GDP at PPP is a very good but not perfect indicator of living standards. For instance, although workers in China earn only a fraction of the wage of American workers, (measured at current dollar rates) they also spend it in a lower-cost environment.

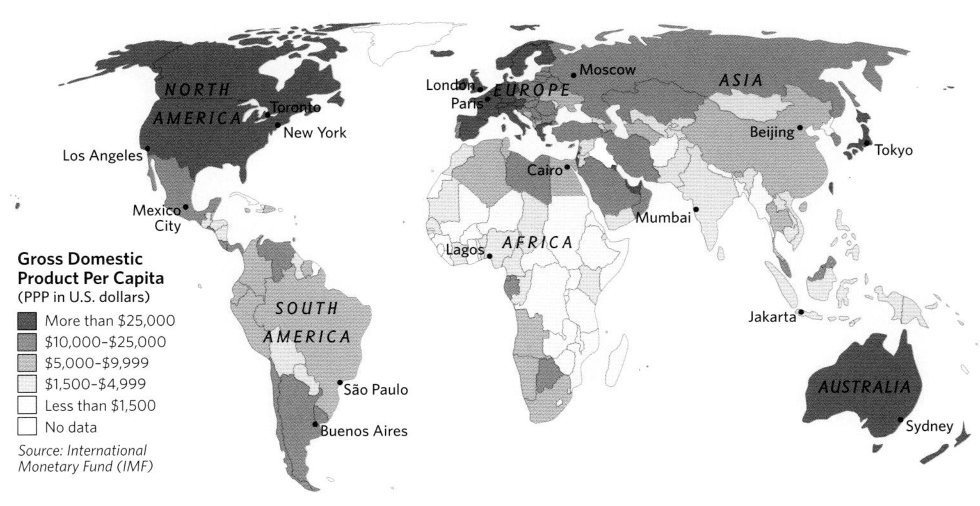

NORTH AMERICA
Toronto
New York
Los Angeles
Mexico City
London
Paris
EUROPE
Moscow
ASIA
Beijing
Tokyo
Cairo
Mumbai
Lagos
AFRICA
SOUTH AMERICA
São Paulo
Buenos Aires
Jakarta
AUSTRALIA
Sydney
Gross Domestic Product Per Capita
(PPP in U.S. dollars)
More than $25,000
$10,000–$25,000
$5,000–$9,999
$1,500–$4,999
Less than $1,500
No data
Source: International Monetary Fund (IMF)

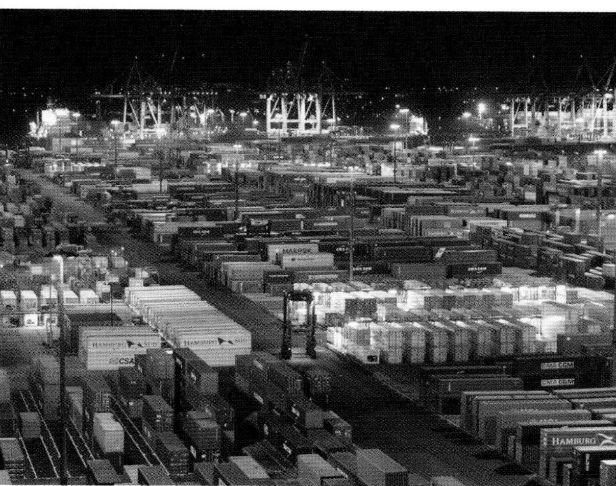

With its four large terminals on the Elbe River, the port of Hamburg, Germany, is the ninth largest container terminal in the world, handling about ten million shipping containers a year. From Hamburg, exports head for other markets while imported goods are efficiently distributed throughout much of Europe. For more on world trade, see pages 64–65.

Major Exporters

Manufacturing export activity remains heavily concentrated in North America, Western Europe, and Japan. But China is rapidly emerging as a global industrial power.

(Value of total exports in billions of U.S. dollars, 2006)

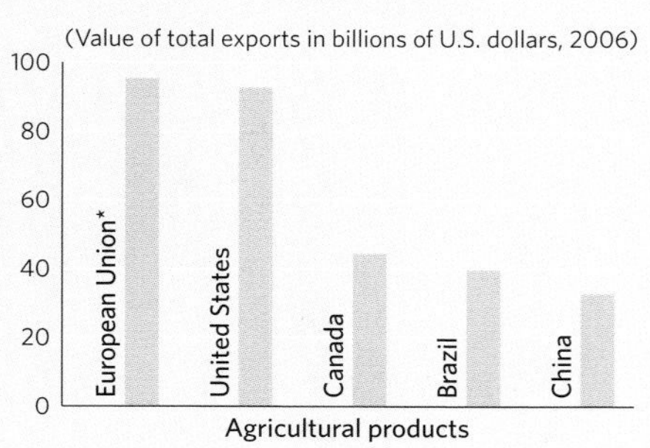

100
80
60
40
20
0
European Union*
United States
Canada
Brazil
China
Agricultural products

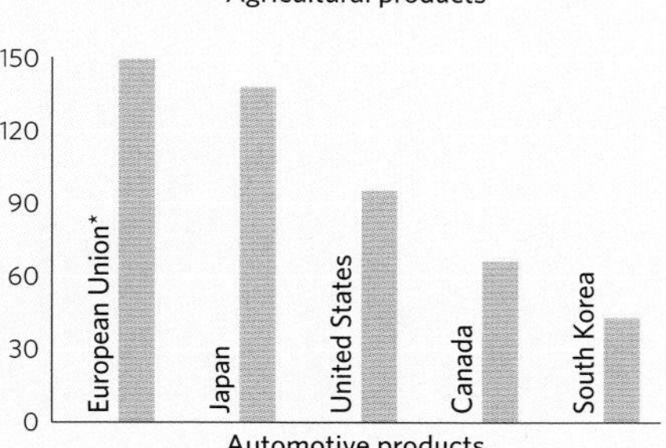

150
120
90
60
30
0
European Union*
Japan
United States
Canada
South Korea
Automotive products

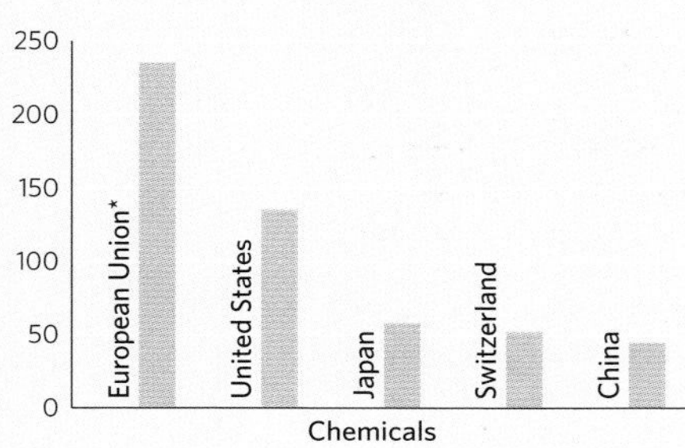

250
200
150
100
50
0
European Union*
United States
Japan
Switzerland
China
Chemicals

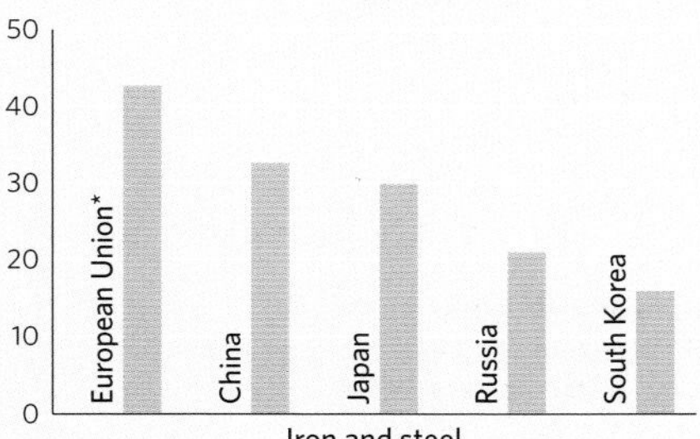

50
40
30
20
10
0
European Union*
China
Japan
Russia
South Korea
Iron and steel

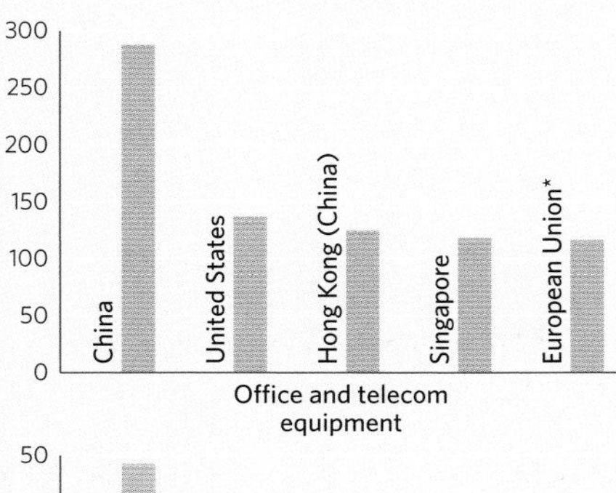

300
250
200
150
100
50
0
China
United States
Hong Kong (China)
Singapore
European Union*
Office and telecom equipment

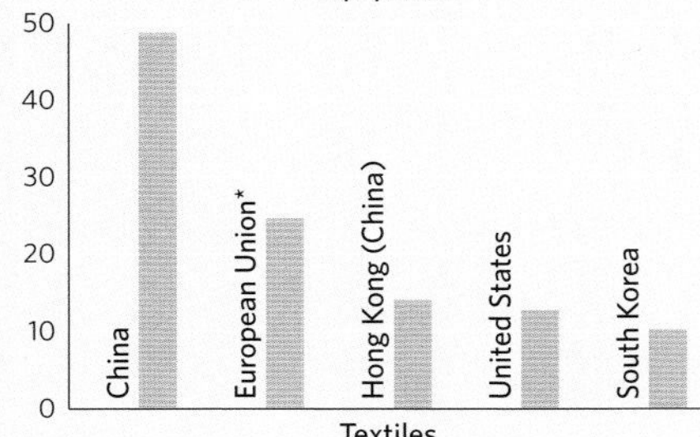

50
40
30
20
10
0
China
European Union*
Hong Kong (China)
United States
South Korea
Textiles

*European Union exports to non-European Union members.

Trade

WORLD TRADE HAS EXPANDED at a dizzying pace in the decades following World War II. The dollar value of world merchandise exports rose from $61 billion in 1950 to $10.1 trillion in 2005. Adjusted for price changes, world trade grew 30-fold over the past 55 years, much faster than world output. Trade in manufactures expanded much faster than that of mining products (including fuels) and agricultural products. In the last decades many developing countries have become important exporters of manufactures (e.g., China, South Korea, Mexico). However, there are still many less-developed countries—primarily in Africa and the Middle East—that are dependent on a few primary commodities for their export earnings. Commercial services exports have expanded rapidly over the past two decades, and amounted to $2.4 trillion in 2005.

While developed countries account for more than two-thirds of world services trade, some developing countries now gain most of their export earnings from services exports. Earnings from tourism in the Caribbean and those from software exports in India are prominent examples of developing countries' dynamic services exports.

Capital flows and worker remittances have gained in importance worldwide and are another important aspect of globalization. The stock of worldwide foreign direct investment was estimated to be close to $9 trillion at the end of 2004, $2.2 trillion of which was invested in developing countries. Capital markets in many developing countries remain small, fragile, and underdeveloped, which hampers household savings and the funding of local enterprises.

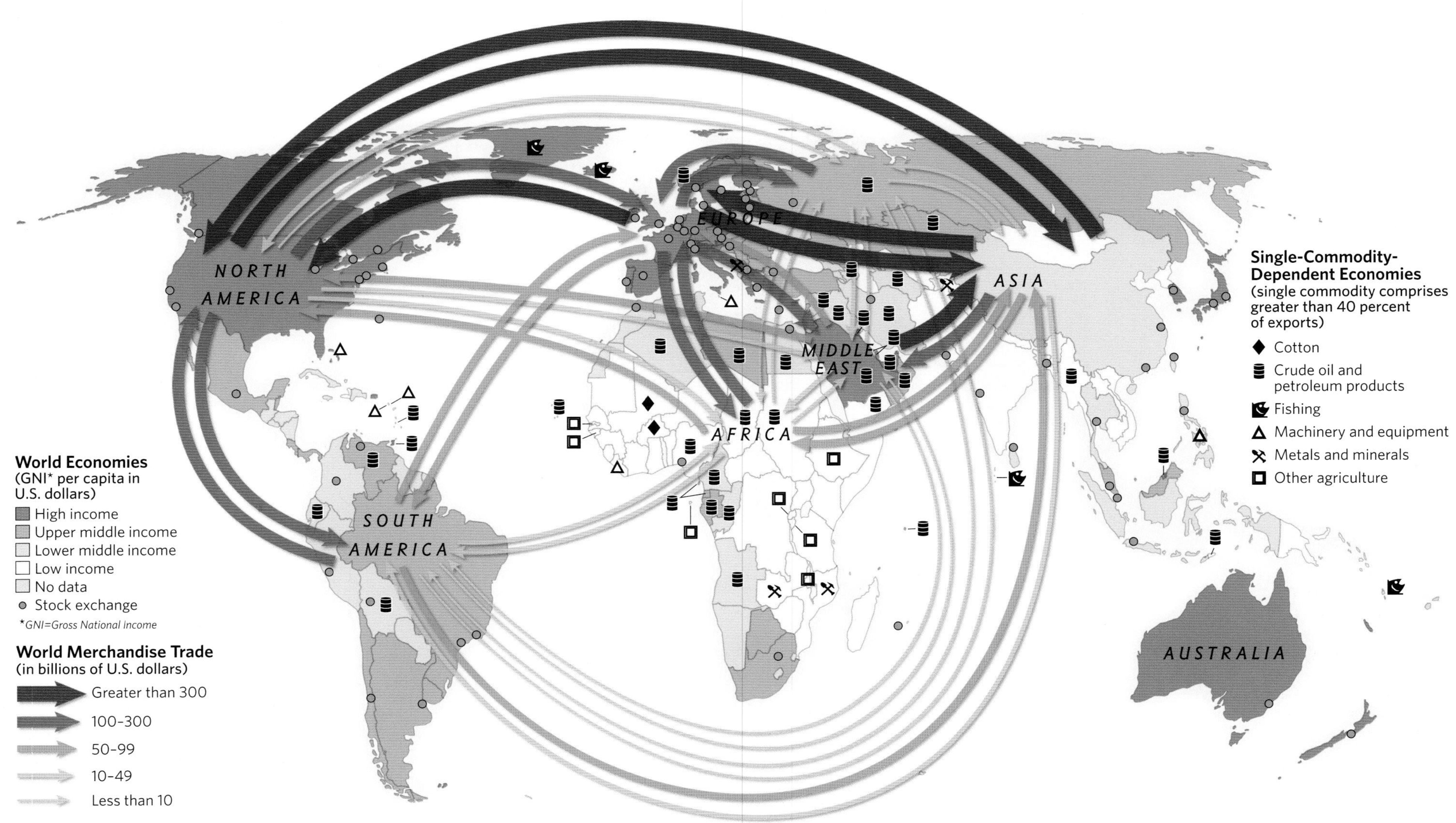
NORTH AMERICA
SOUTH AMERICA
EUROPE
AFRICA
MIDDLE EAST
ASIA
AUSTRALIA
World Economies
(GNI* per capita in U.S. dollars)
High income
Upper middle income
Lower middle income
Low income
No data
Stock exchange
*GNI=Gross National income
World Merchandise Trade
(in billions of U.S. dollars)
Greater than 300
100-300
50-99
10-49
Less than 10
Single-Commodity-Dependent Economies
(single commodity comprises greater than 40 percent of exports)
Cotton
Crude oil and petroleum products
Fishing
Machinery and equipment
Metals and minerals
Other agriculture

GROWTH OF WORLD TRADE Since 1950, trade in manufactured goods has grown at 7.5 percent, about twice the rate of agricultural and fuels and mining products. World trade should continue to grow as "vertical specialization" (where different countries produce only certain components of a final product) continues to remake the global manufacturing scene.

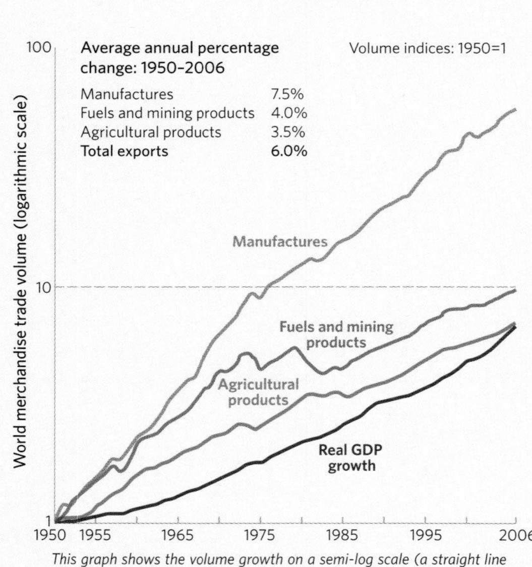
Average annual percentage change: 1950-2006
Manufactures 7.5%
Fuels and mining products 4.0%
Agricultural products 3.5%
Total exports 6.0%
Volume indices: 1950=1
World merchandise trade volume (logarithmic scale)
100
10
1
Manufactures
Fuels and mining products
Agricultural products
Real GDP growth
1950 1955 1965 1975 1985 1995 2006

This graph shows the volume growth on a semi-log scale (a straight line represents constant growth) rather than a standard scale (a straight line indicates a constant increase in the absolute values in each year).

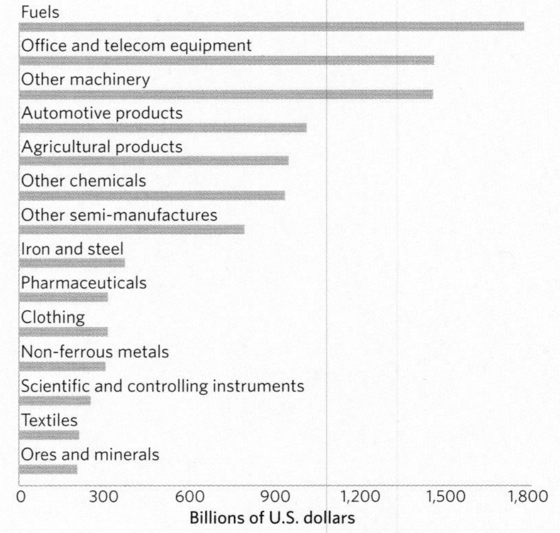
Fuels
Office and telecom equipment
Other machinery
Automotive products
Agricultural products
Other chemicals
Other semi-manufactures
Iron and steel
Pharmaceuticals
Clothing
Non-ferrous metals
Scientific and controlling instruments
Textiles
Ores and minerals
0 300 600 900 1,200 1,500 1,800
Billions of U.S. dollars

MERCHANDISE EXPORTS Manufactured goods account for three-quarters of world merchandise exports. Export values of two subtypes—machinery and office/telecom equipment—exceed the total export value of mining products; world exports in chemicals and automotive products exceed the export value of all agricultural products.

MAIN TRADING NATIONS The U.S., Germany, and Japan account for nearly 30 percent of total world merchandise trade. Ongoing negotiations among the 152 member countries of the World Trade Organization are tackling market-access barriers in agriculture, textiles, and clothing—areas where many developing countries hope to compete.

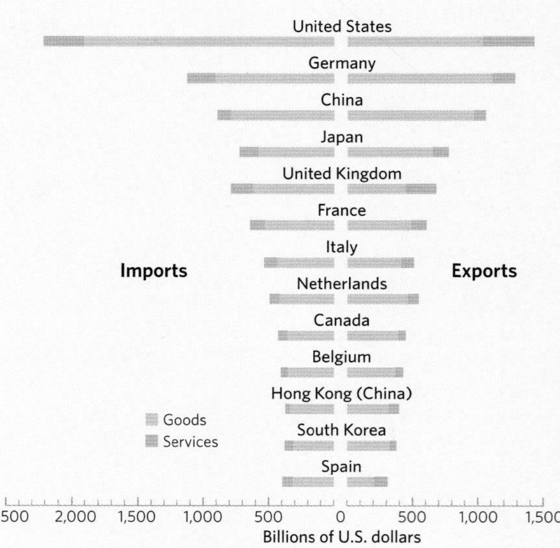
United States
Germany
China
Japan
United Kingdom
France
Italy
Netherlands
Canada
Belgium
Hong Kong (China)
South Korea
Spain
Imports
Exports
Goods
Services
2,500 2,000 1,500 1,000 500 0 500 1,000 1,500
Billions of U.S. dollars

Debt of Developing Countries

Measuring a country's outstanding foreign debt in relation to its GDP indicates the size of future income needed to pay back the debt; it also shows how much a country has relied in the past on foreign savings to finance investment and consumption expenditures. A high external debt ratio can pose a financial risk if debt service payments are not assured. A country's ability to finance its foreign debt depends directly on its economic growth, investment climate, and its ability to earn foreign exchange through exports.

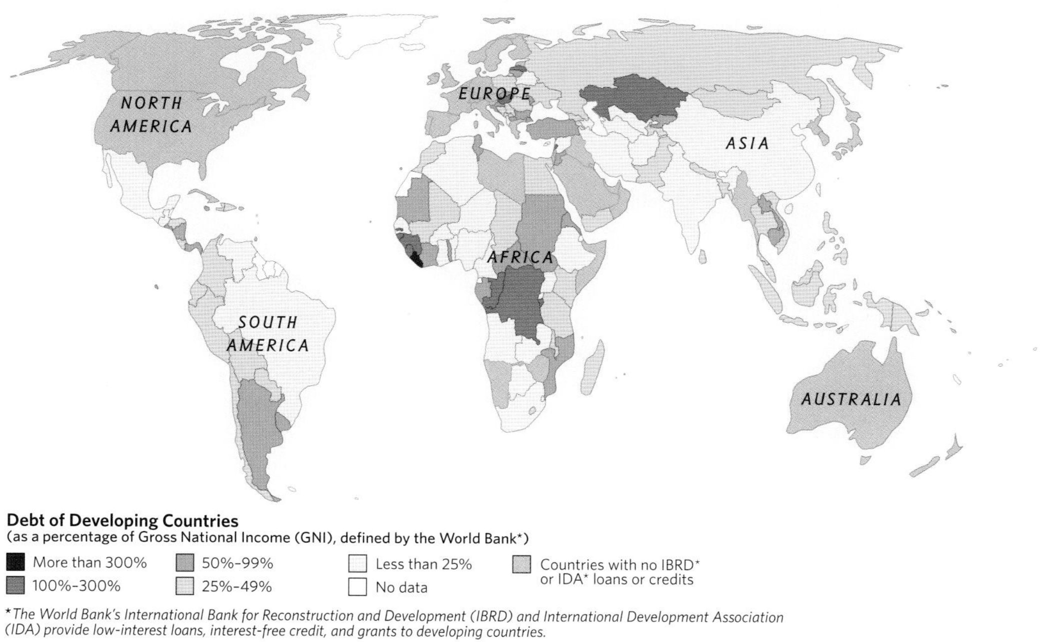
NORTH AMERICA
EUROPE
ASIA
AFRICA
SOUTH AMERICA
AUSTRALIA
Debt of Developing Countries
(as a percentage of Gross National Income (GNI), defined by the World Bank*)
More than 300%
100%–300%
50%–99%
25%–49%
Less than 25%
No data
Countries with no IBRD* or IDA* loans or credits

*The World Bank's International Bank for Reconstruction and Development (IBRD) and International Development Association (IDA) provide low-interest loans, interest-free credit, and grants to developing countries.

Trade Blocs

Regional trade is on the rise. Agreements between neighboring countries to offer each other trade benefits can create larger markets and improve the economy of the region as a whole. But they can also lead to discrimination, especially when more efficient suppliers outside the regional agreements are prevented from supplying their goods and services. With multilateral talks within the World Trade Organization at a standstill, bilateral and regional agreements will increasingly become the focus of trade liberalization efforts. So far the trend has not impeded the growth of global trade.

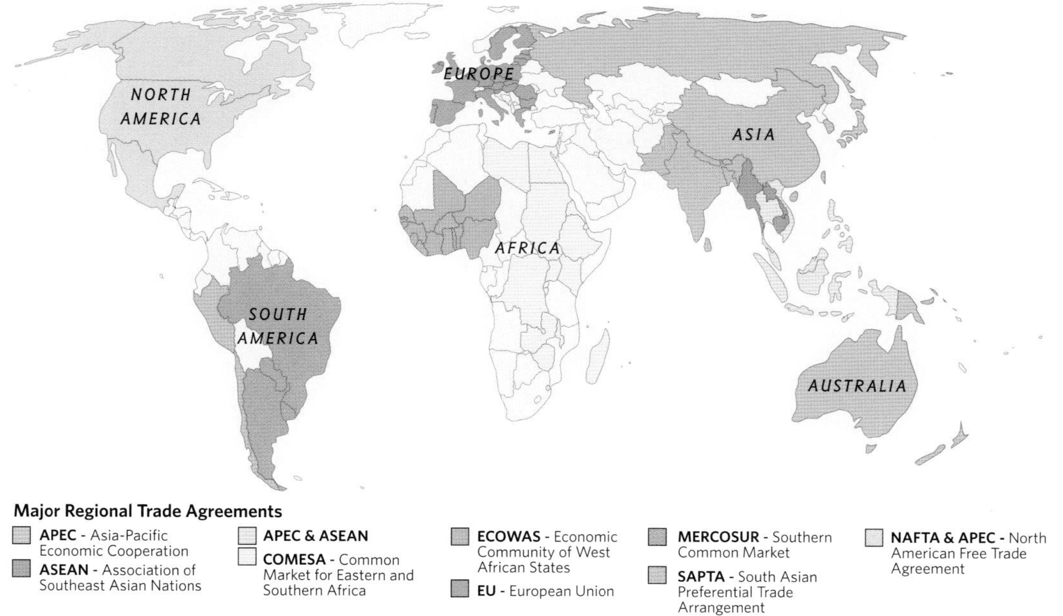
NORTH AMERICA
EUROPE
ASIA
AFRICA
SOUTH AMERICA
AUSTRALIA
Major Regional Trade Agreements
APEC - Asia-Pacific Economic Cooperation
ASEAN - Association of Southeast Asian Nations
APEC & ASEAN
COMESA - Common Market for Eastern and Southern Africa
ECOWAS - Economic Community of West African States
EU - European Union
MERCOSUR - Southern Common Market
SAPTA - South Asian Preferential Trade Arrangement
NAFTA & APEC - North American Free Trade Agreement

Trade Flow: Fuels

The leading exporters of fuel products are countries in the Middle East, Africa, Russia, and central and western Asia; all export more fuel than they consume. But intra-regional energy trade is growing, with some of the key producers—Canada, Mexico, Norway, and the United Kingdom, for example—located in regions that are net energy importers. Driving the growth in energy trade has been the rapid expansion of car ownership and electrical generation in China, India, and other fast-developing countries.

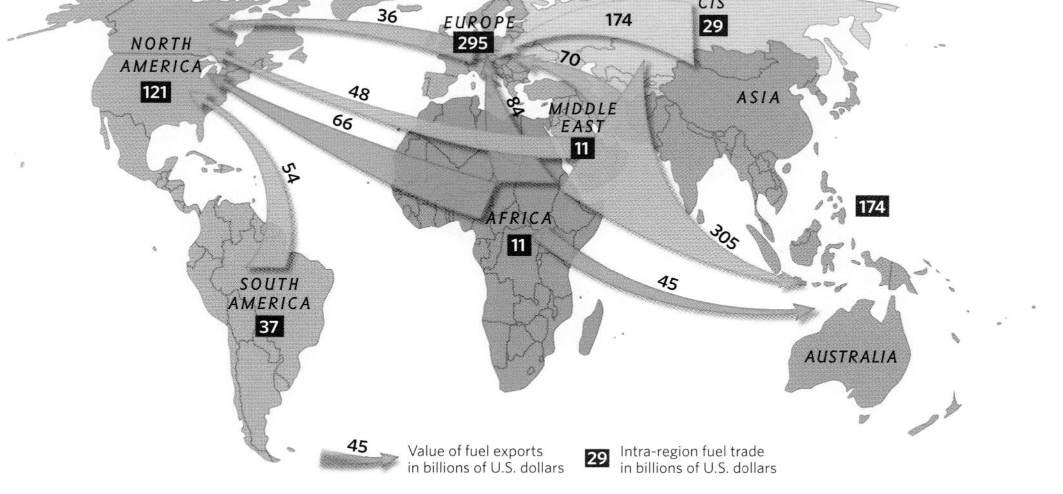
NORTH AMERICA
121
EUROPE
295
CIS
29
ASIA
174
MIDDLE EAST
11
AFRICA
11
SOUTH AMERICA
37
AUSTRALIA
36
174
70
48
66
84
54
305
45
45 Value of fuel exports in billions of U.S. dollars
29 Intra-region fuel trade in billions of U.S. dollars

Trade Flow: Agricultural Products

The world trade in agricultural products is less concentrated than trade in fuels, with processed goods making up the majority. Agricultural products encounter high export barriers, which limit the opportunities for some exporters to expand into foreign markets. Reducing such barriers is a major challenge for governments that are engaged in agricultural trade negotiations. Global trade barriers remain high against such commodities as dairy products, cotton, rice, and sugar—hurting millions of farmers in poor countries while leaving global markets more vulnerable to price shocks.

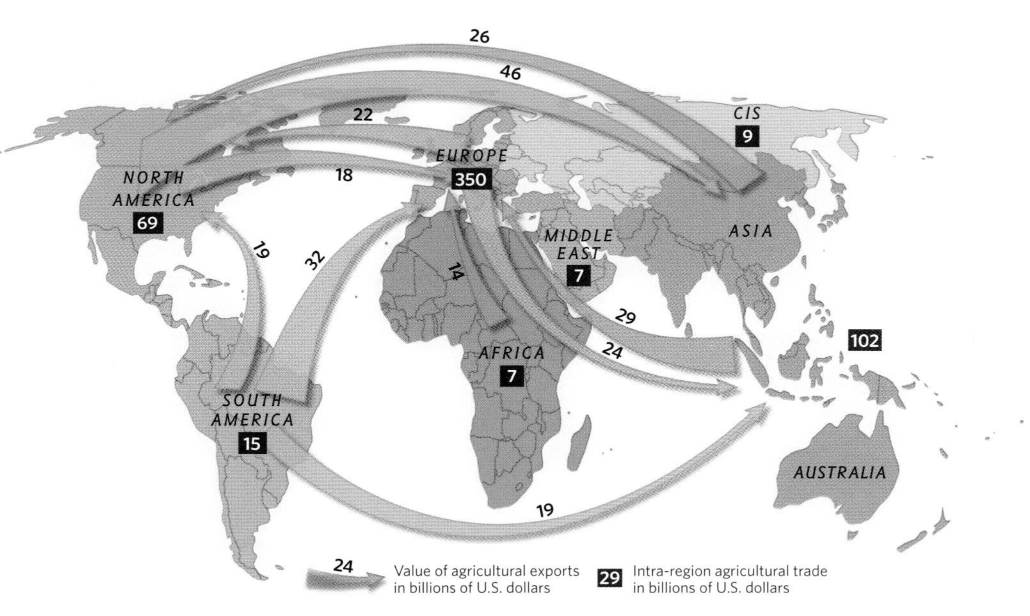
NORTH AMERICA
69
EUROPE
350
CIS
9
ASIA
102
MIDDLE EAST
7
AFRICA
7
SOUTH AMERICA
15
AUSTRALIA
26
46
22
18
19
32
14
29
24
19
24 Value of agricultural exports in billions of U.S. dollars
29 Intra-region agricultural trade in billions of U.S. dollars

Top Merchandise Exporters and Importers

TOP EXPORTERS

COUNTRY	PERCENTAGE OF WORLD TOTAL	VALUE (BILLIONS)
Germany	9.2	$1,112
United States	8.6	$1,038
China	8.0	$969
Japan	5.4	$650
France	4.1	$490
Netherlands	3.8	$462
United Kingdom	3.7	$448
Italy	3.4	$411
Canada	3.2	$390
Belgium	3.1	$369
South Korea	2.7	$326
Hong Kong (China)	2.7	$323
Russia	2.5	$305
Singapore	2.2	$272
Mexico	2.1	$250

TOP IMPORTERS

COUNTRY	PERCENTAGE OF WORLD TOTAL	VALUE (BILLIONS)
United States	15.5	$1,919
Germany	7.3	$909
China	6.4	$792
United Kingdom	5.0	$619
Japan	4.7	$580
France	4.3	$535
Italy	3.5	$437
Netherlands	3.4	$416
Canada	2.9	$358
Belgium	2.9	$354
Hong Kong (China)	2.7	$336
Spain	2.5	$316
South Korea	2.5	$309
Mexico	2.2	$268
Singapore	1.9	$239

Top Commercial Services Exporters and Importers

(includes transportation, travel, and other services)

TOP EXPORTERS

COUNTRY	PERCENTAGE OF WORLD TOTAL	VALUE (BILLIONS)
United States	14.1	$389
United Kingdom	8.3	$228
Germany	6.1	$169
Japan	4.4	$123
France	4.2	$115
Spain	3.8	$106
Italy	3.5	$98
China	3.3	$91
Netherlands	3.0	$83
India	2.7	$74
Hong Kong (China)	2.6	$73
Ireland	2.5	$68
Austria	2.1	$59
Canada	2.1	$59
Belgium	2.1	$59

TOP IMPORTERS

COUNTRY	PERCENTAGE OF WORLD TOTAL	VALUE (BILLIONS)
United States	11.6	$308
Germany	8.3	$219
United Kingdom	6.5	$172
Japan	5.4	$144
France	4.1	$109
China	3.8	$100
Italy	3.7	$98
Ireland	3.0	$79
Netherlands	2.9	$78
Spain	2.9	$78
Canada	2.7	$72
South Korea	2.6	$70
India	2.4	$64
Singapore	2.3	$61
Belgium	2.0	$54

Globalization

THERE IS A GROWING CONSENSUS that globalization is defined by increasing levels of interdependence over vast distances, not just in the economic dimension, but along the lines of person-to-person contact, technological connectivity, and political ties. In many important ways, global integration is continuing to deepen over the years—and ties between countries have continued to strengthen, despite deterrents such as acts of terror, stalling of trade talks, and divisions over international peace and security issues.

The annual A.T. Kearney/Foreign Policy magazine Globalization Index "reverse engineers" the globalization phenomenon and quantifies its most important component indicators—spanning trade, finance, political engagement, information technology, and personal contact—to determine the rankings of 72 places. Together, they account for 97 percent of the world's gross domestic product (GDP) and 88 percent of the world's population. Major regions of the world, including developed and developing countries, are covered to provide a comprehensive and comparative view of globalization. The index measures 12 variables, which are divided into four "baskets": economic integration, technological connectivity, personal contact, and political engagement.

In years past, Western European countries have claimed many of the top spots as engaged participants in the international system. Small trading countries like Singapore have tended to take top places in the index due in part to their particular reliance on other countries for trade, investment, and tourism.

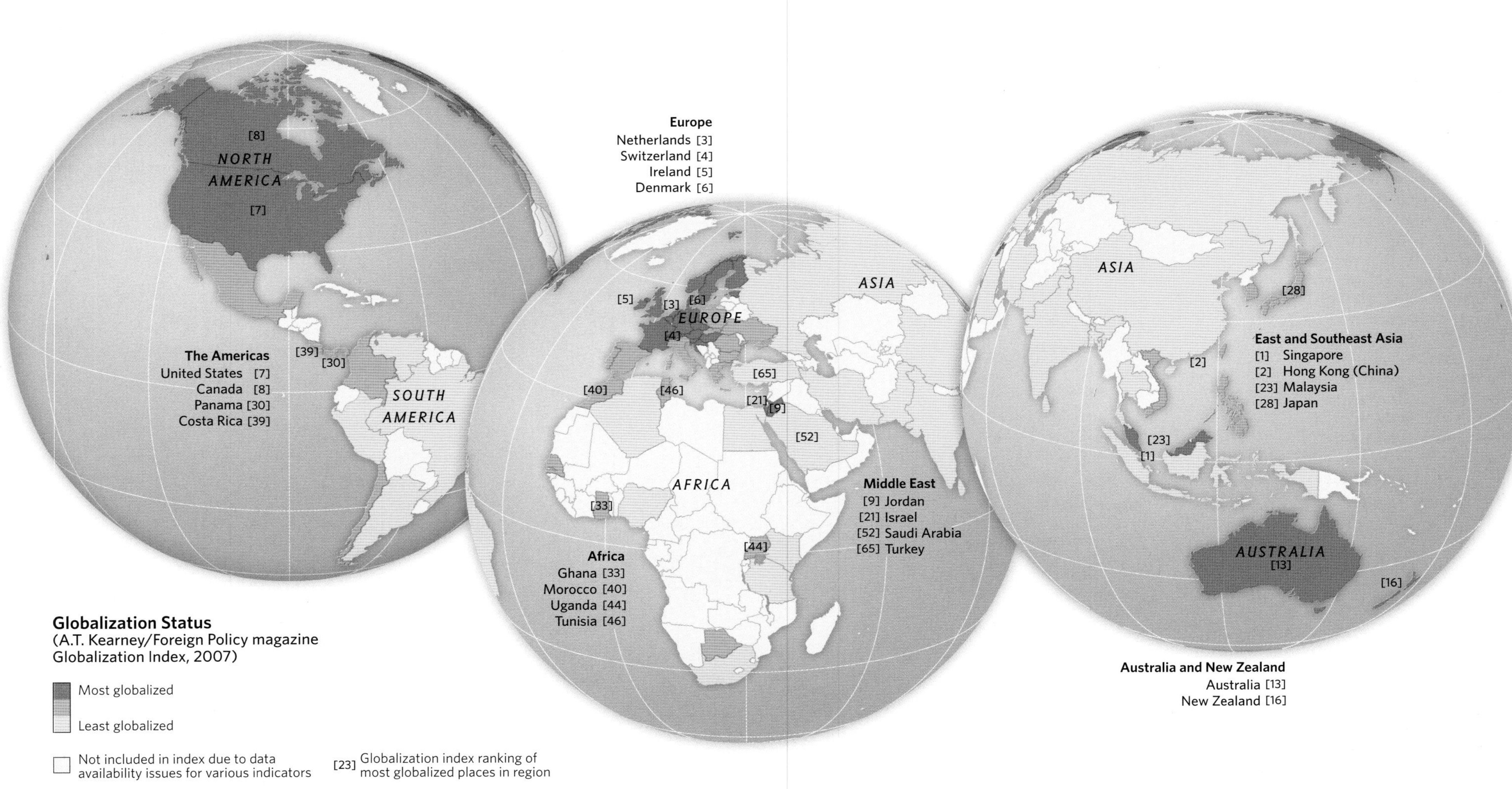
NORTH AMERICA
[8]
[7]
The Americas
United States [7]
Canada [8]
Panama [30]
Costa Rica [39]
[39]
[30]
SOUTH AMERICA
Europe
Netherlands [3]
Switzerland [4]
Ireland [5]
Denmark [6]
[5] [3] [6]
EUROPE
[4]
ASIA
[40] [46] [65]
[21] [9]
[52]
AFRICA
[33]
[44]
Africa
Ghana [33]
Morocco [40]
Uganda [44]
Tunisia [46]
Middle East
[9] Jordan
[21] Israel
[52] Saudi Arabia
[65] Turkey
ASIA
[28]
[2]
East and Southeast Asia
[1] Singapore
[2] Hong Kong (China)
[23] Malaysia
[28] Japan
[23]
[1]
AUSTRALIA
[13]
[16]
Australia and New Zealand
Australia [13]
New Zealand [16]

Globalization Status
(A.T. Kearney/Foreign Policy magazine Globalization Index, 2007)

Most globalized

Least globalized

Not included in index due to data availability issues for various indicators

[23] Globalization index ranking of most globalized places in region

Transnational Corporations

Transnational corporations (TNCs), as their name suggests, operate across national boundaries and are major players in the era of increased global integration. The sales, value added, and exports of some 78,000 TNCs and their 780,000 foreign affiliates accounted for 10 percent of world GDP and one-third of world exports in 2006. In fact, a number of TNCs have assets equivalent to or larger than the nominal GDP of some countries, as illustrated in the graph below. The United Nations Conference on Trade and Development (UNCTAD) ranks the largest nonfinancial TNCs by their foreign assets and financial firms according to a Spread Index that takes into account the number of foreign affiliates and the number of host countries.

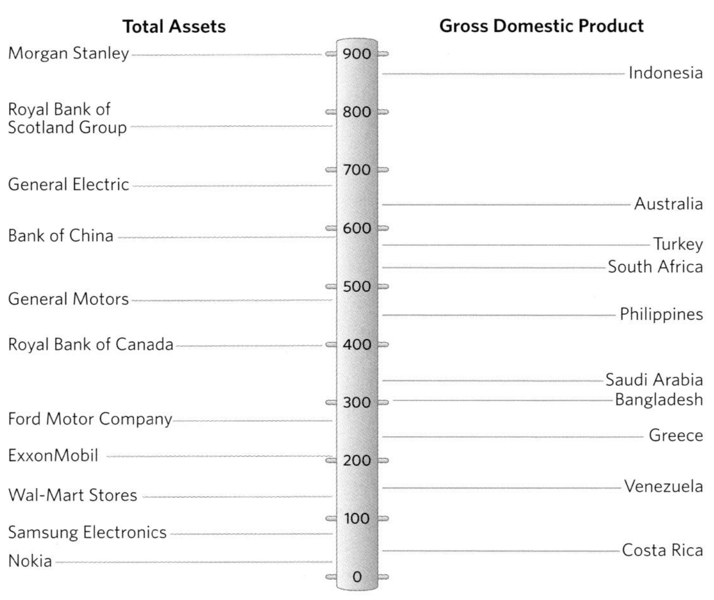
Total Assets
Gross Domestic Product
Morgan Stanley
Royal Bank of Scotland Group
General Electric
Bank of China
General Motors
Royal Bank of Canada
Ford Motor Company
ExxonMobil
Wal-Mart Stores
Samsung Electronics
Nokia
900
800
700
600
500
400
300
200
100
0
Indonesia
Australia
Turkey
South Africa
Philippines
Saudi Arabia
Bangladesh
Greece
Venezuela
Costa Rica
Billions of U.S. dollars (2005)

Extremes of Globalization

For the fourth time in seven years, Singapore tops the Globalization Index as the most globalized country in the world. Hong Kong debuted in the 2007 index in second place and distinguished itself with the highest scores in both the economic and the personal contact dimensions. Smaller countries tend to be more globalized. Eight of the index's top ten countries have land areas smaller than the U.S. state of Indiana; and seven have fewer than eight million citizens. Canada and the United States are the only large countries that consistently rank in the top ten. Countries such as Singapore and the Netherlands lack natural resources while countries like Denmark and Ireland can't rely on their limited domestic markets the way the United States can. To be globally competitive, these countries have no choice but to open up and attract trade and foreign investment. Yet a glance at this year's index suggests that those who seek to expand globalization's benefits have their work cut out for them. The bottom ten are home to more than three billion people. As many indicators are measured on a per capita basis, gains from globalization may be slow to reach the massive populations of these countries.

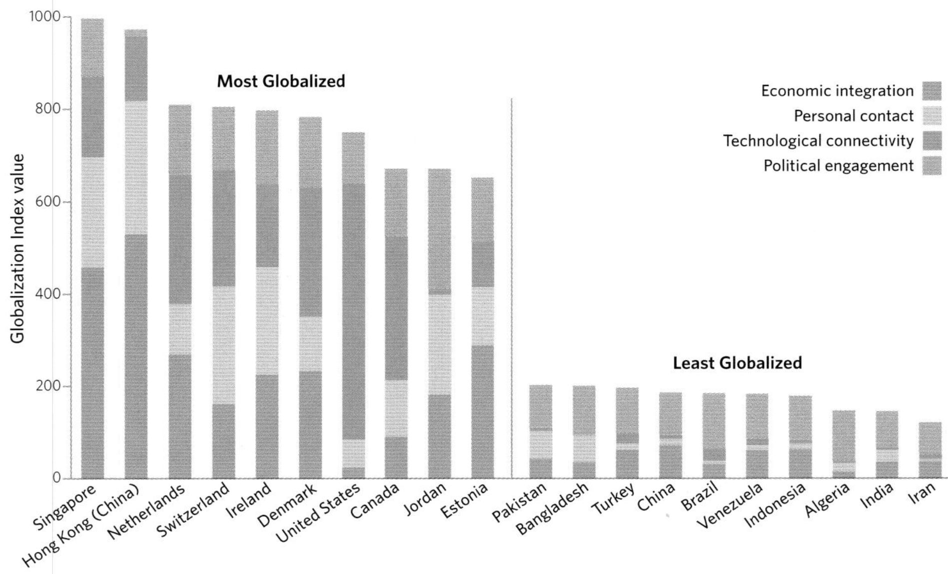
Globalization Index value
1000
800
600
400
200
0
Most Globalized
Least Globalized
Economic integration
Personal contact
Technological connectivity
Political engagement
Singapore
Hong Kong (China)
Netherlands
Switzerland
Ireland
Denmark
United States
Canada
Jordan
Estonia
Pakistan
Bangladesh
Turkey
China
Brazil
Venezuela
Indonesia
Algeria
India
Iran

Economic Integration

Economic integration combines data on trade and foreign direct investment (FDI). Measured as a percentage of GDP, foreign direct investment flows include investments in physical assets, such as plants and equipment, both into and out of a country. The Netherlands' high rank in the overall index is due in part to the merger of the Royal Dutch Petroleum Company and Britain's Shell Transport and Trading Company. Worth about $100 billion, the deal helped to increase foreign direct investment outflows for the Netherlands by more than 590 percent in 2005. Additionally, in tiny Estonia FDI accounted for about a quarter of the country's GDP, placing its FDI dependence just behind Hong Kong and the Netherlands.

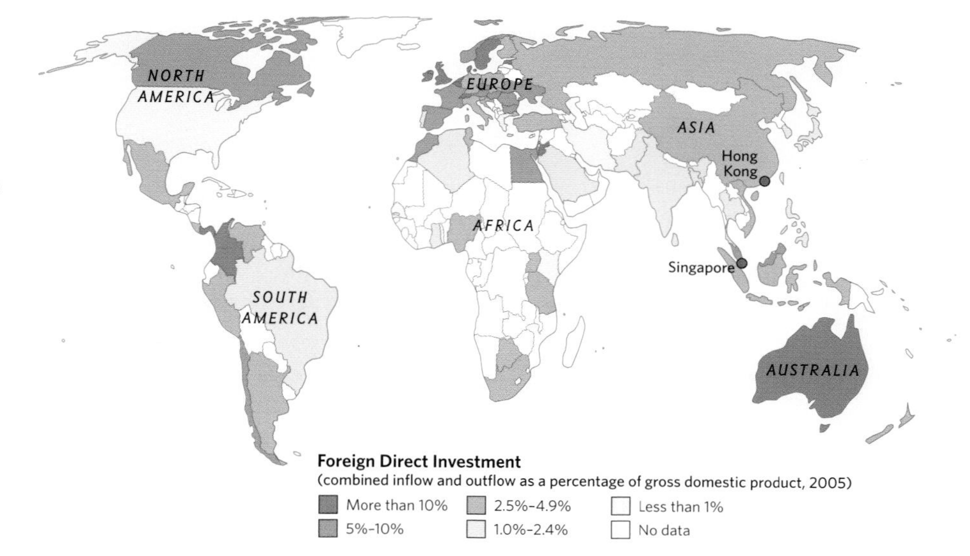
NORTH AMERICA
EUROPE
ASIA
Hong Kong
AFRICA
Singapore
SOUTH AMERICA
AUSTRALIA
Foreign Direct Investment
(combined inflow and outflow as a percentage of gross domestic product, 2005)
More than 10%
5%-10%
2.5%-4.9%
1.0%-2.4%
Less than 1%
No data

Personal Contact

Personal contact tracks international travel and tourism, international telephone traffic, and cross-border remittances and personal transfers (including worker remittances, compensation to employees, and other person-to-person and nongovernmental transfers). International telephone calls sum up the total number of minutes of telephone traffic into and out of a country on a per capita basis. Six of this year's tiny globalizers also ranked in the top ten on the personal dimension of globalization. High levels of personal contact via telephone and travel gave Hong Kong the top ranking in personal contact. Not surprisingly, its ties with mainland China helped propel it to the top.

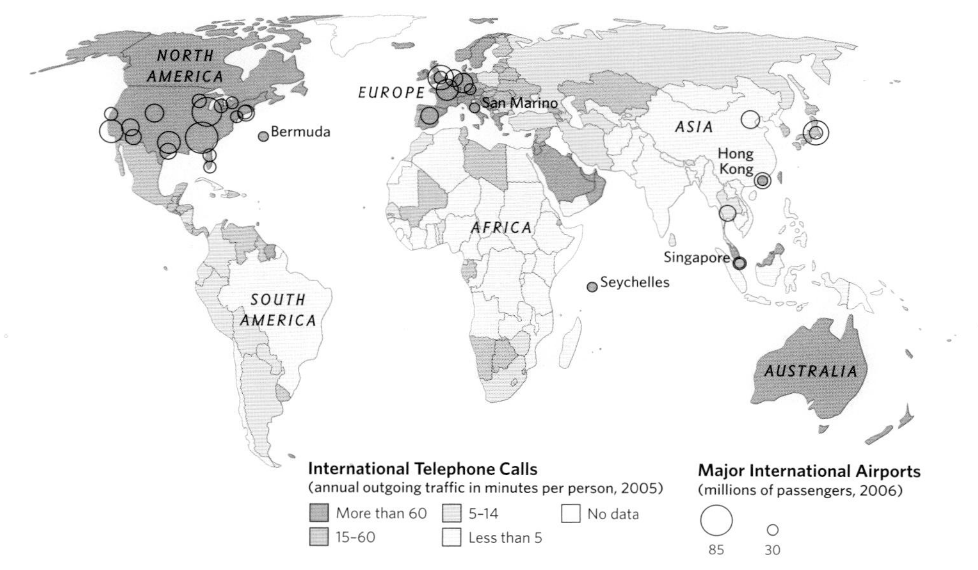
NORTH AMERICA
EUROPE
San Marino
Bermuda
ASIA
Hong Kong
AFRICA
Singapore
Seychelles
SOUTH AMERICA
AUSTRALIA
International Telephone Calls
(annual outgoing traffic in minutes per person, 2005)
More than 60
15-60
5-14
Less than 5
No data
Major International Airports
(millions of passengers, 2006)
85
30

Technological Connectivity

Technological connectivity counts the number of Internet users, Internet hosts, and secure servers through which encrypted transactions are carried out. The indicators used measure penetration—that is, how many Internet users there are out of every 100 people in the country—as well as how widespread the Internet infrastructure is. The United States routinely tops the technological connectivity ranking, thanks to high levels of Internet penetration. Sweden, the Netherlands, Australia, and South Korea have the highest number of Internet users per 100 people. Other countries, such as Japan, have aggressively promoted information and communication technologies development, resulting in a 30 percent increase in the number of Internet users in recent years.

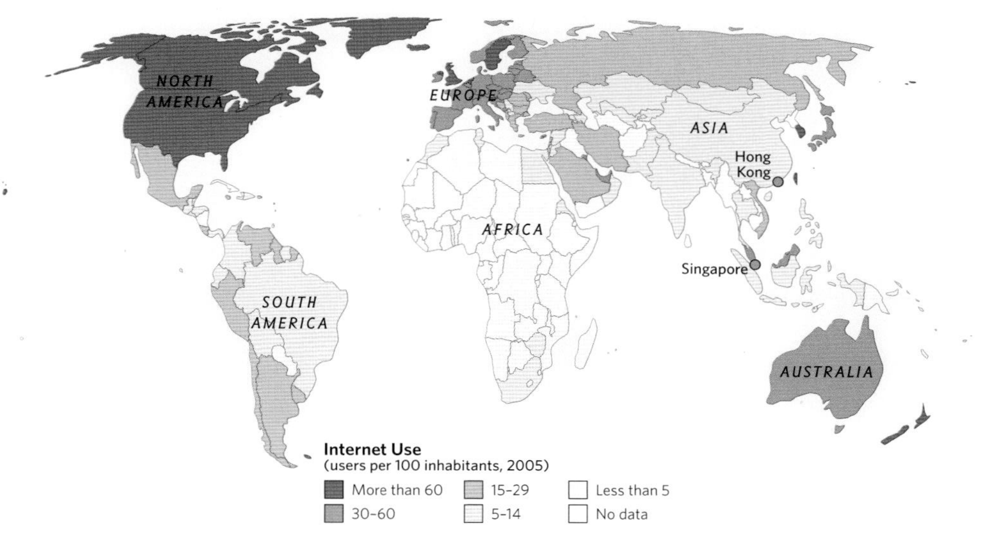
NORTH AMERICA
EUROPE
ASIA
Hong Kong
AFRICA
Singapore
SOUTH AMERICA
AUSTRALIA
Internet Use
(users per 100 inhabitants, 2005)
More than 60
30-60
15-29
5-14
Less than 5
No data

Political Engagement

Political engagement includes each country's memberships in a variety of representative international organizations, personnel and financial contributions to UN peacekeeping missions, ratification of selected multilateral treaties, and amounts of governmental transfer payments and receipts. The measures provide an indication of how various countries rank as participants of international arrangements relative to their economic and population sizes. Jordan performs well in the political rankings, as it has one of the highest levels of peacekeeping troop contributions of all UN member states, but is also one of the smallest countries, with a population of less than six million.

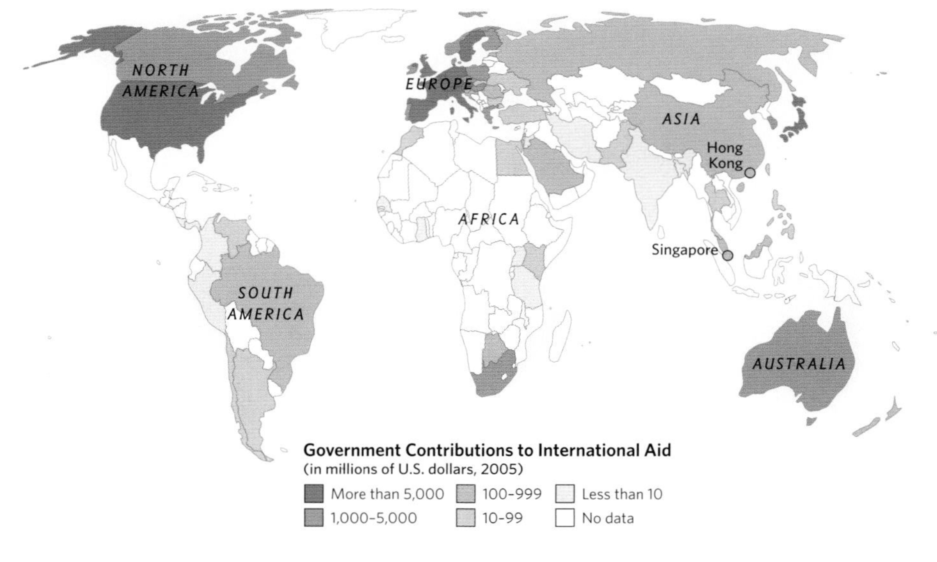
NORTH AMERICA
EUROPE
ASIA
Hong Kong
AFRICA
Singapore
SOUTH AMERICA
AUSTRALIA
Government Contributions to International Aid
(in millions of U.S. dollars, 2005)
More than 5,000
1,000-5,000
100-999
10-99
Less than 10
No data

International Outsourcing

Improvements in communication technologies, such as the Internet and digital telephone lines, are making it increasingly possible for firms to source their service inputs from suppliers abroad. Recent examples include call centers and computer software development services provided by India to the rest of the world. Until recently, global production networks mostly involved the offshoring of manufactured intermediate inputs, whereas now many services as well can be produced in one country and utilized in another.

TRENDS IN OUTSOURCING

International outsourcing of services has been steadily increasing but it is still at relatively low levels. Although U.S. business service imports have roughly doubled in each of the past several decades, they remained at less than one percent of total GDP in 2007. India, reported to be the recipient of significant outsourcing, itself outsources a large amount of services.

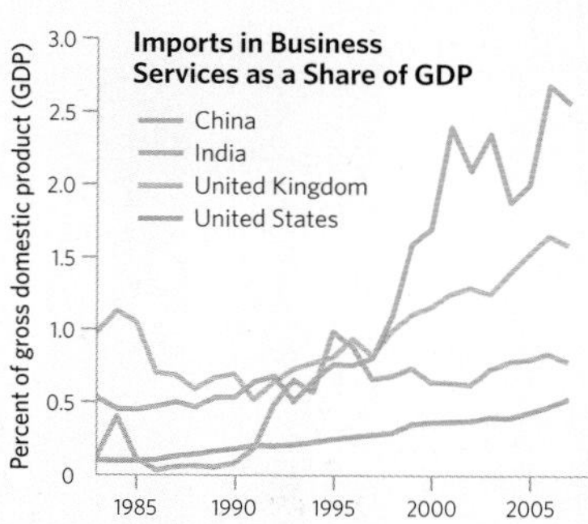
Imports in Business Services as a Share of GDP
China
India
United Kingdom
United States
Percent of gross domestic product (GDP)
3.0
2.5
2.0
1.5
1.0
0.5
0
1985
1990
1995
2000
2005

As shown in the graph below, the U.K. and the U.S. have significant net surpluses in business services. But this is not true for all industrialized countries. The data reveal no clear pattern of developing or industrial countries either being net exporters or net importers. For example, in addition to the U.K. and the U.S. having a net surplus in business services, India also does. Yet, Indonesia has a large net deficit in business services, as do Germany and Ireland.

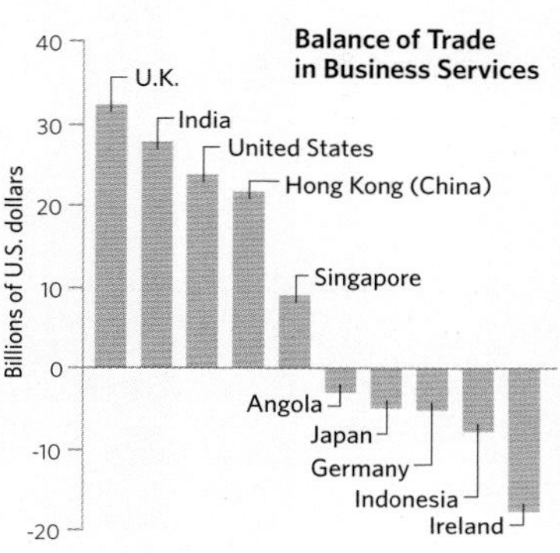
Balance of Trade in Business Services
Billions of U.S. dollars
40
30
20
10
0
-10
-20
U.K.
India
United States
Hong Kong (China)
Singapore
Angola
Japan
Germany
Indonesia
Ireland

TOP OUTSOURCERS OF BUSINESS SERVICES

VALUE (IN BILLIONS OF U.S. DOLLARS)

United States	52
Germany	46
France	34
Italy	32
Netherlands	31
United Kingdom	31
Japan	26
Ireland	26

In dollar value terms, the U.S. ranks highest in outsourcing of business services, but as a share of the country's overall GDP, its value is comparatively low (0.53 percent in 2007). In smaller countries, trade generally accounts for a larger percentage of GDP. Among the top relative outsourcers of business services are several small developing countries, such as Angola (16 percent of GDP), Lebanon (12 percent), Congo (10 percent), Azerbaijan (9 percent), and the Seychelles (8 percent).

Food

THE POPULATION OF THE PLANET, which already tops six and a half billion, continues to increase by 211,000 new mouths a day. What will they eat? Where will the additional food come from? Worldwide, agricultural production also continues to grow, but the food-producing regions are unevenly distributed around the globe. And though efforts to raise the levels of production even more (while relying less on chemical applications that damage the environment) are vitally important, they can go only so far in solving a great dilemma: How can we get more food to the millions of people who do not have enough to eat? Invariably, it is the economic situation of countries—which ones have food surpluses to sell; which ones need food and have or don't have enough money to buy it—that determines who goes hungry. For people in the world's poorest regions, the situation is grim. With prices for staple grains soaring in 2007 and 2008 due to higher demand, a new world hunger crisis could be just around the corner.

The UN Food and Agriculture Organization (FAO) reports that every night 815 million people in the developing world go to bed hungry and that malnourishment contributes to at least one-third of all child deaths. The FAO also says that 13 million people in southern Africa face famine. Most cases of malnutrition are found in the developing countries of the tropics, where rapid population growth and other factors are depleting agricultural and financial resources.

Croplands of the World

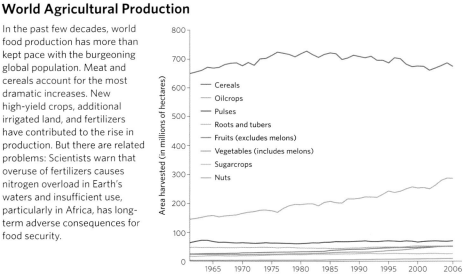

ARCTIC OCEAN
NORTH AMERICA
EUROPE
ASIA
ATLANTIC OCEAN
PACIFIC OCEAN
AFRICA
PACIFIC OCEAN
SOUTH AMERICA
INDIAN OCEAN
AUSTRALIA

Agricultural Extent

Nonagricultural land

100% Cropland

100% Grazing land

Caloric Supply

As shown at right, cereals (grains) dominate the caloric supply of people in Africa and Asia. Sugars, oils, and proteins comprise a much higher portion in other parts of the world, and the increasing consumption rates of these foods leads to obesity problems in many countries.

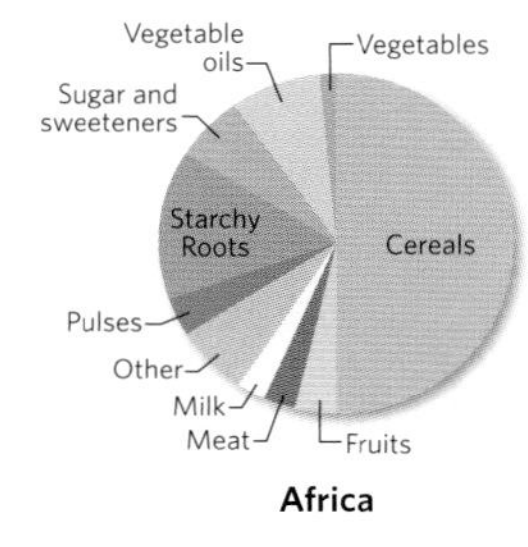
Vegetable oils
Vegetables
Sugar and sweeteners
Starchy Roots
Cereals
Pulses
Other
Milk
Meat
Fruits
Africa

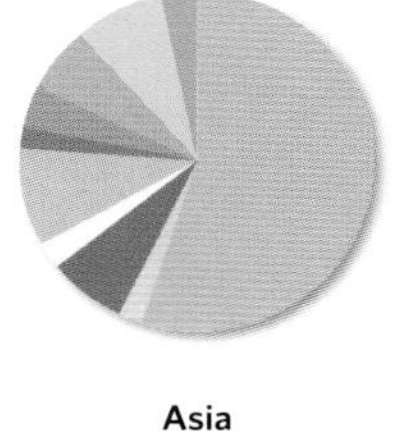
Asia

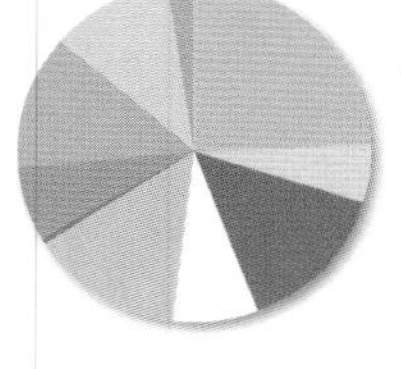
Australia/ Oceania

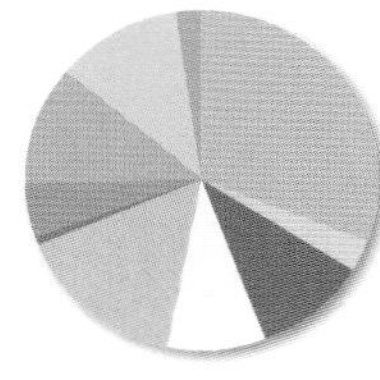
Europe

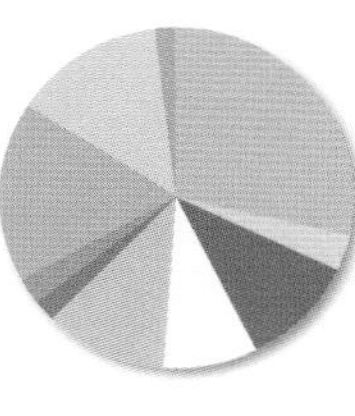
North/Central America

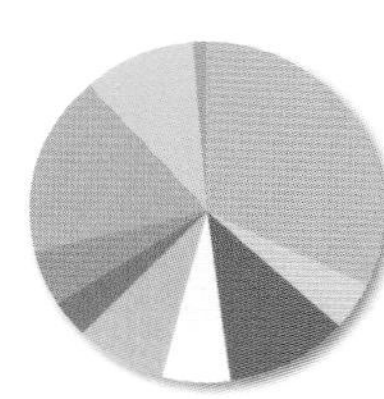
South America

Indicates breakdown of per capita calorie supply

World Agricultural Production

In the past few decades, world food production has more than kept pace with the burgeoning global population. Meat and cereals account for the most dramatic increases. New high-yield crops, additional irrigated land, and fertilizers have contributed to the rise in production. But there are related problems: Scientists warn that overuse of fertilizers causes nitrogen overload in Earth's waters and insufficient use, particularly in Africa, has long-term adverse consequences for food security.

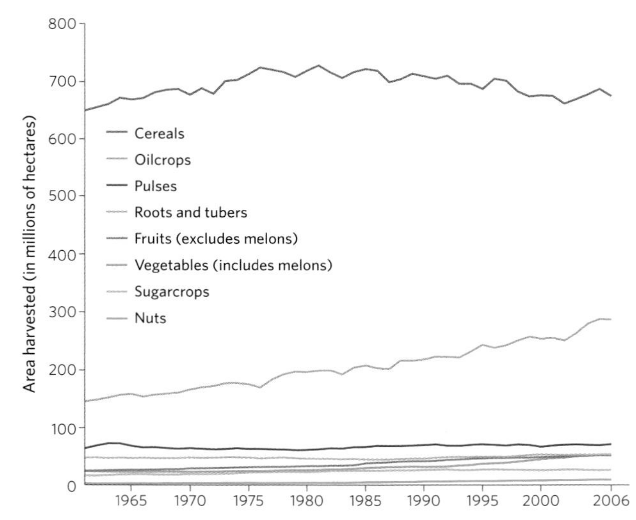
Area harvested (in millions of hectares)
800
700
600
500
400
300
200
100
0
Cereals
Oilcrops
Pulses
Roots and tubers
Fruits (excludes melons)
Vegetables (includes melons)
Sugarcrops
Nuts
1965
1970
1975
1980
1985
1990
1995
2000
2006

Undernourishment in the Developing World

More food than ever is produced, but its distribution is uneven. Africa, in particular, is a continent of contrasts: Almost half the people in central, eastern, and southern Africa are undernourished, while a much lower percentage of people in the north and west are undernourished. The United Nations estimates that more than 750 million people suffer from persistent malnourishment. Without access to adequate food, these populations cannot lead healthy, productive lives.

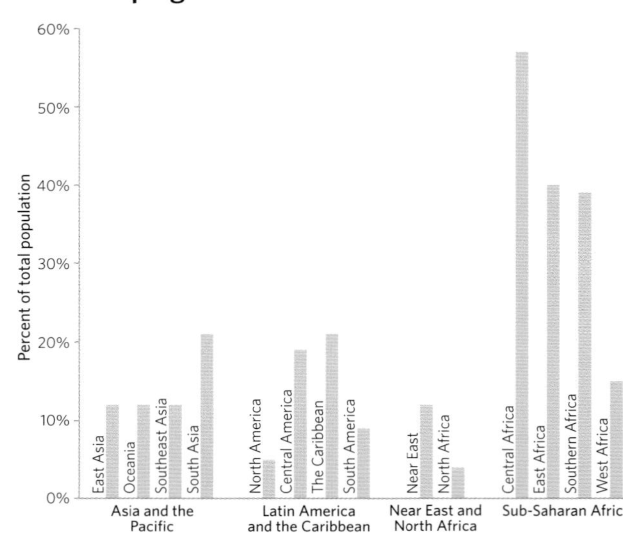
Percent of total population
60%
50%
40%
30%
20%
10%
0%
East Asia
Oceania
Southeast Asia
South Asia
North America
Central America
The Caribbean
South America
Near East
North Africa
Central Africa
East Africa
Southern Africa
West Africa
Asia and the Pacific
Latin America and the Caribbean
Near East and North Africa
Sub-Saharan Africa

Note: Regions are as defined by the FAO Statistics Division.

Land Use and Commercial Agriculture

Humans rely on plant sources for carbohydrates, with grains (the edible parts of cereal plants) providing 80 percent of the food energy (calorie) supply. This means that the major grains—maize, wheat, and rice—are the foods that fuel humanity. Most cereal grains are grown in the Northern Hemisphere, with the United States and France producing enough to be the largest exporters. Many parts of the world cannot grow cereal grains because they do not have productive farmland or the needed technology. Again and again throughout history, the actions of countries have been shaped by disparities in the supply and demand of grains, and by the knowledge that grains equal survival. Waverley Root, a food historian, once wrote: "[P]ossession of wheat or lack of it sways the destinies of nations; nor is it rare to find wheat being used as a political weapon.... [I]t is difficult to foresee any future in which it will not still exert a powerful influence on human history."

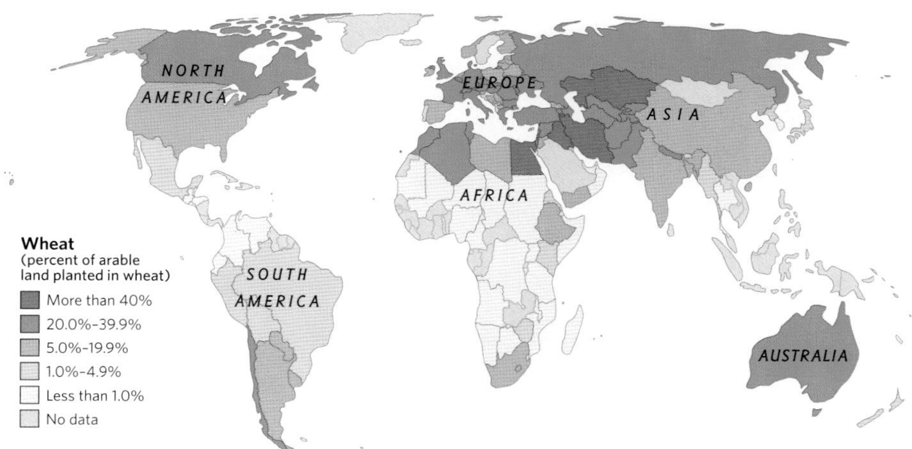
NORTH AMERICA
EUROPE
ASIA
AFRICA
SOUTH AMERICA
AUSTRALIA
Wheat
(percent of arable land planted in wheat)
More than 40%
20.0%–39.9%
5.0%–19.9%
1.0%–4.9%
Less than 1.0%
No data

NORTH AMERICA
EUROPE
ASIA
AFRICA
SOUTH AMERICA
AUSTRALIA
Rice
(percent of arable land planted in rice)
More than 40%
20.0%–39.9%
5.0%–19.9%
1.0%–4.9%
Less than 1.0%
No data

WHEAT Among the two oldest grains (barley is the other), wheat was important in ancient Mediterranean civilizations. Today, it is the most widely grown cereal—cultivated across the globe in many different varieties. Wheat grows best, however, in the temperate latitudes of the Northern Hemisphere. China, India, and the United States are the leading producers of the world's roughly 600 million metric tons of wheat produced annually; the U.S. and Canada lead the world in wheat exports. Largely used in baked goods such as bread, pasta, and noodles, wheat is a major source of calories for more than half the world's population.

RICE Originating in Asia many millennia ago, rice is the staple grain for about half the world's people. Rice continues to play a dominant role in the agriculture and diet of Asians. It is a labor-intensive plant that grows primarily in paddies (flooded fields) and thrives in the hot, humid tropics. Nearly 90 percent of the world's rice is produced and consumed in Asia, mostly on small family farms. While Thailand is the world's leading exporter of rice, of the 650 million metric tons produced annually, China and India produce about half. Large scale commercial cultivation of rice takes place in the southern United States, southern Australia, and the Amazon Basin.

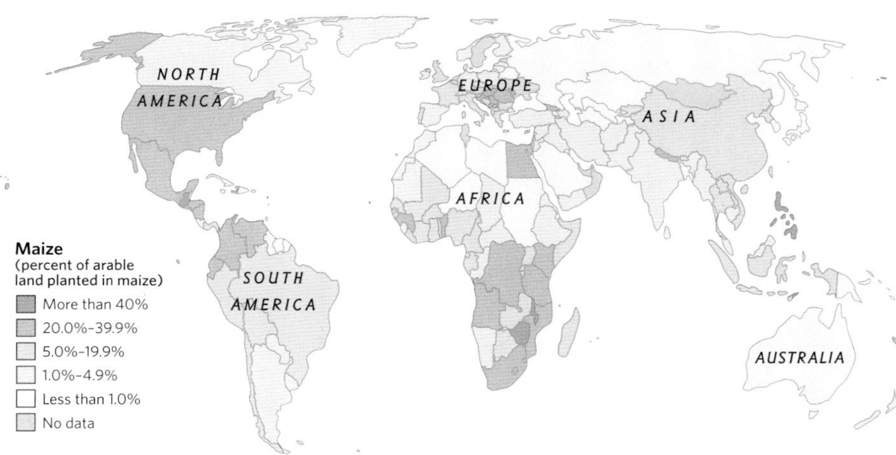
NORTH AMERICA
EUROPE
ASIA
AFRICA
SOUTH AMERICA
AUSTRALIA
Maize
(percent of arable land planted in maize)
More than 40%
20.0%–39.9%
5.0%–19.9%
1.0%–4.9%
Less than 1.0%
No data

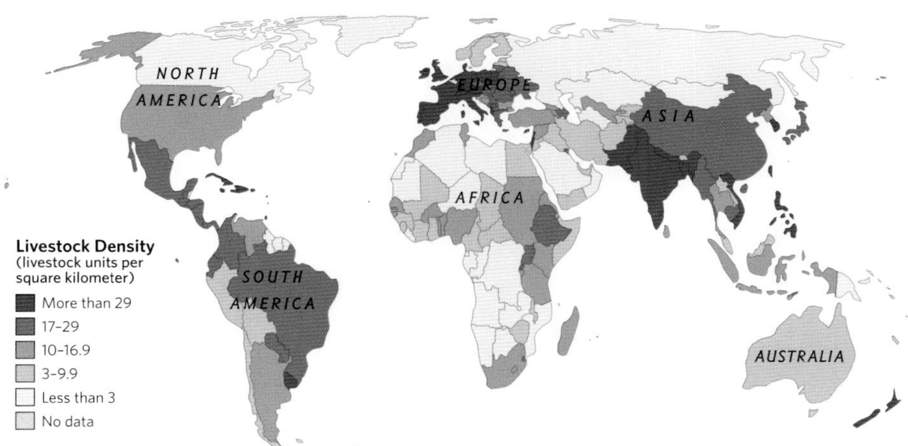
NORTH AMERICA
EUROPE
ASIA
AFRICA
SOUTH AMERICA
AUSTRALIA
Livestock Density
(livestock units per square kilometer)
More than 29
17–29
10–16.9
3–9.9
Less than 3
No data

MAIZE, OR CORN Maize was domesticated 6,000 years ago in Mexico. It is now intensively grown in the United States, China, along Africa's Rift Valley, and throughout eastern Europe. The United States is unrivaled in maize production and export, growing over 40 percent of the world's 700 million metric tons, and making up more than half the world's total exports. Although it remains a staple food, the majority of the world's harvest is for animal feed, with a growing amount being diverted to produce biofuels such as ethanol.

LIVESTOCK The global livestock sector has expanded rapidly due to increases in population, income, and urbanization such that it will soon provide 50 percent of global agricultural GDP. About 70 percent of the world's rural poor, whose livelihoods depend on livestock, have largely been bypassed by this development. The vigorous livestock sector growth and its concomitant structural changes have resulted in significant challenges related to the role of the sector in economic development, in disease (re)emergence, and affecting climate and natural resources.

Fishing and Aquaculture

Marine fisheries are vital for food security in developing countries, and are a heavily subsidized industry in developed countries. Today, no parts of the world's oceans are unaffected. Most fish are caught in coastal waters, with the most intense fishing in northern Europe, and off China and Southeast Asia. The world's reported catch has more than quadrupled since 1950, but peaked in the late 1980s and has been declining since. Fish-farming, called aquaculture, is one of the fastest growing areas of food production. The bulk of marine aquaculture occurs in developing countries, with China accounting for around two-thirds of total output.

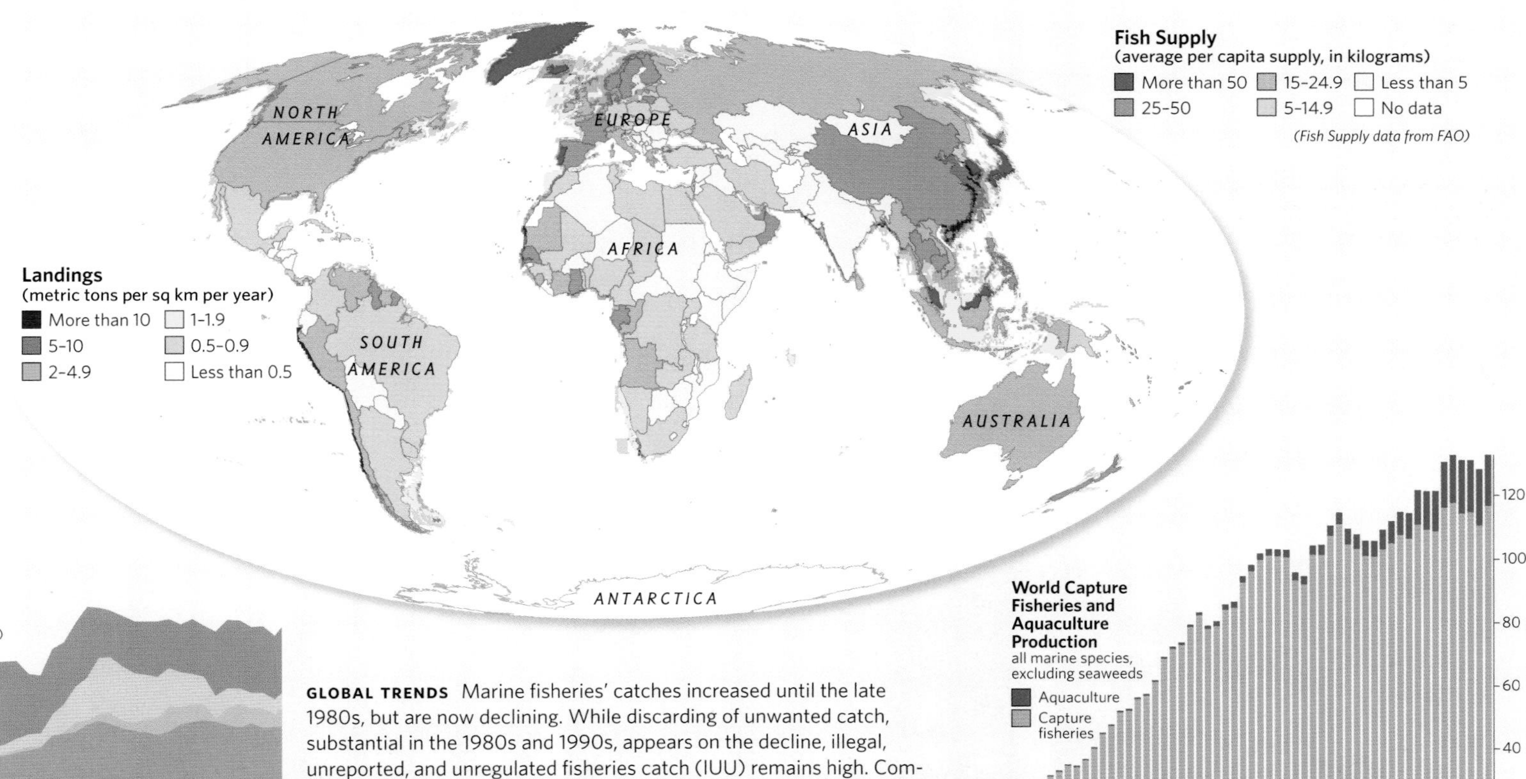
NORTH AMERICA
EUROPE
ASIA
AFRICA
SOUTH AMERICA
AUSTRALIA
ANTARCTICA
Landings
(metric tons per sq km per year)
More than 10
5–10
2–4.9
1–1.9
0.5–0.9
Less than 0.5
Fish Supply
(average per capita supply, in kilograms)
More than 50
25–50
15–24.9
5–14.9
Less than 5
No data
(Fish Supply data from FAO)

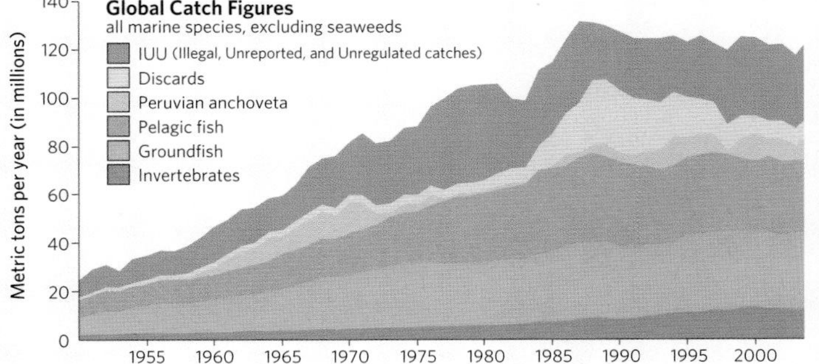
Global Catch Figures
all marine species, excluding seaweeds
IUU (Illegal, Unreported, and Unregulated catches)
Discards
Peruvian anchoveta
Pelagic fish
Groundfish
Invertebrates
Metric tons per year (in millions)
140
120
100
80
60
40
20
0
1955
1960
1965
1970
1975
1980
1985
1990
1995
2000

GLOBAL TRENDS Marine fisheries' catches increased until the late 1980s, but are now declining. While discarding of unwanted catch, substantial in the 1980s and 1990s, appears on the decline, illegal, unreported, and unregulated fisheries catch (IUU) remains high. Combined, discarding and IUU account for one-third of total ocean catches. Marine aquaculture (excluding seaweeds) accounts for 15 percent of the total fish available for human consumption, and is increasingly impacting marine ecosystems, due to its high demand for fish meal.

World Capture Fisheries and Aquaculture Production
all marine species, excluding seaweeds
Aquaculture
Capture fisheries
Metric tons (in millions)
120
100
80
60
40
20
0
1950
1960
1970
1980
1990
2000

Data for Fishing and Aquaculture section: Sea Around Us Project, www.seaaroundus.org

Energy

PRIMARY ENERGY comes in many different forms. Some fuels, such as animal dung and fuelwood, have a low energy content, while coal, natural gas, and oil contain much more. By adopting a common measurement that takes these differences into account, we can compare energy usage around the world. Today, the international standard is the "metric ton of oil equivalent" (toe), which translates all forms of energy (solid, liquid, or gas) to a common baseline. On this basis, global energy consumption is currently about 11.4 billion metric tons of oil equivalent a year.

The world's chief sources of energy are oil, coal, and natural gas. Resources and reserves of fossil fuels are unevenly distributed around the globe and do not always coincide with areas of high consumption. As a result, more and more energy is traded between producer and consumer countries. For several decades this has been true for oil and coal; it is now becoming the case for natural gas. Large historical importers like the United States, Western Europe, and Japan have now been joined by large fast-growing importers such as China and India. One of the consequences is the higher dependency or interdependency between producers and consumers. Security of supply and security of demand are now at the center of the economics and geopolitics of the energy market.

Consumption patterns show major differences worldwide. North America, with less than one-tenth of the world's population, uses about one-quarter of its energy while Africa, with twice the population of North America, consumes five times less energy. Fast-growing economies, like China and India, are using more than ever, and will continue to drive up worldwide demand for oil, coal, and natural gas.

As demand for energy grows, prices rise. Combined with high prices and a growing public awareness of the negative environmental impact of burning fossil fuels, energy efficiency programs and other energy sources (such as hydro and nuclear) become more attractive. In addition, technological advancements in the harnessing of renewable energies such as biofuels, geothermal, wind, and solar power will continue to increase their effectiveness—and their viability as primary energy sources of the future.

LNG to Japan
Oil to United States from Canada
NORTH AMERICA
Oil to United States from Middle East and Africa
Oil to Europe from Africa
ATLANTIC OCEAN
Oil to United States from Mexico
PACIFIC OCEAN
Oil to United States from Venezuela
LNG to United States and Spain
SOUTH AMERICA
Annual Energy Consumption Per Capita
(in metric tons of oil equivalent)
More than 5
3-5
1-2.9
Less than 1
No data
Major Coal, Natural Gas, and Oil Deposits
Coal
Natural gas
Oil
Liquefied natural gas (LNG) liquefication plant
Oil transit chokepoint

Energy Production

WORLD ENERGY PRODUCTION BY TYPE

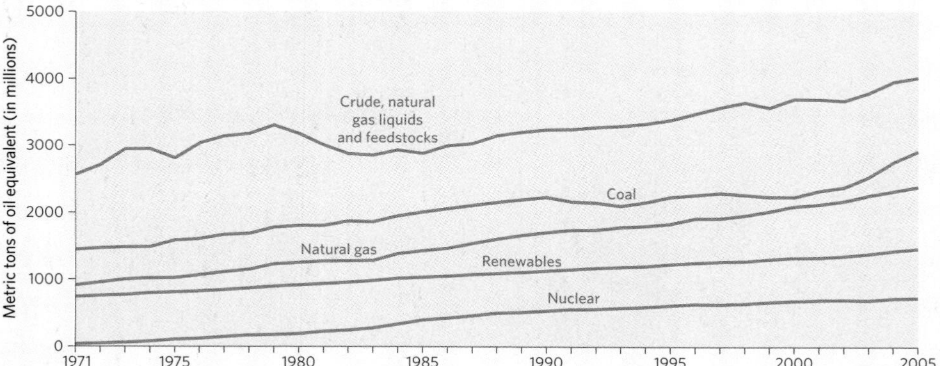
Metric tons of oil equivalent (in millions)
5000
4000
3000
2000
1000
0
Crude, natural gas liquids and feedstocks
Coal
Natural gas
Renewables
Nuclear
1971
1975
1980
1985
1990
1995
2000
2005

Since the industrial revolution, fossil fuels have overtaken biomass (mainly used in cooking and heating) and have become the world's energy production workhorse, with oil the leading source of energy worldwide. But with demand for oil—especially for transportation—climbing quickly, the world has been increasing its usage of coal, of which there are at least 900 billion tons in reserve. The challenge for energy producers of the future will be how to continue to meet humanity's growing thirst for energy while faced with declining reserves of fossil fuels and increasing levels of pollution created from the burning of those fuels.

WORLD ENERGY PRODUCTION BY REGION

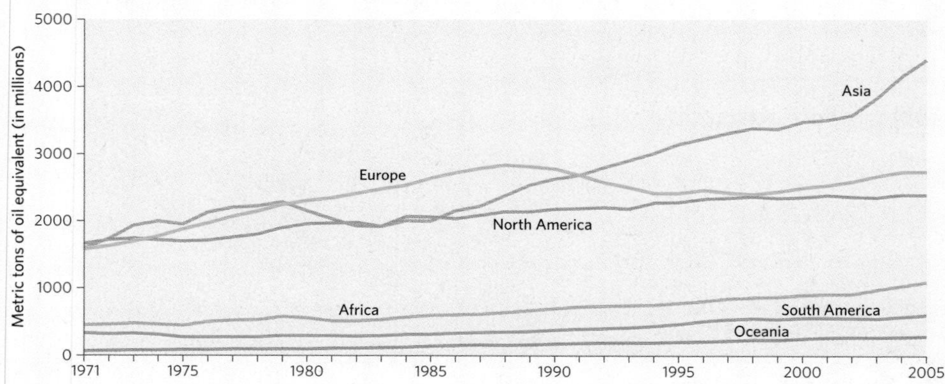
Metric tons of oil equivalent (in millions)
5000
4000
3000
2000
1000
0
Asia
Europe
North America
Africa
South America
Oceania
1971
1975
1980
1985
1990
1995
2000
2005

Reacting to the energy crises of 1973 and 1979, global demand for oil fell in the 1980s, creating excess supply and dramatically driving down prices. OPEC's subsequent reduction in oil output is responsible for the decrease in overall energy production in Asia (especially in the Middle East) and Africa in the early 1980s. The economic collapse of the Soviet Union (included in Europe on graph) led to a lengthy downturn in production for nearly every former Soviet republic. China's recent surge in coal production currently drives the spike in Asian energy production.

Pumpjacks, California

CRUDE OIL

Coal miners, Yongxing, China

COAL

Natural gas plant, Surgut, Russia

NATURAL GAS

Sherpa women carrying firewood, Nepal

FUELWOOD

Source for energy production graphs: International Energy Agency Statistics

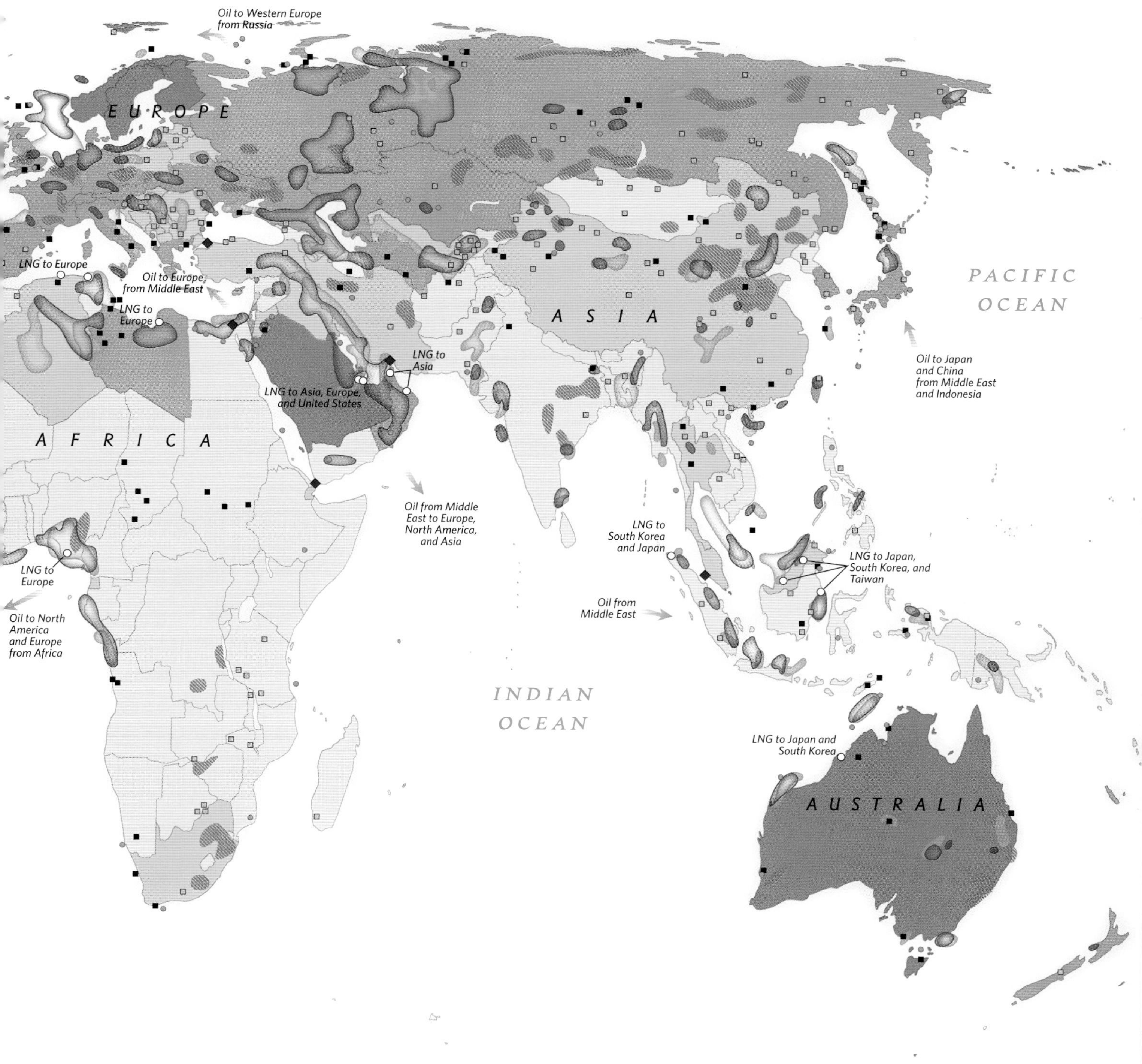

Oil to Western Europe from Russia

EUROPE

ASIA

AFRICA

AUSTRALIA

PACIFIC OCEAN

INDIAN OCEAN

LNG to Europe

Oil to Europe, from Middle East

LNG to Europe

LNG to Asia

LNG to Asia, Europe, and United States

Oil to Japan and China from Middle East and Indonesia

Oil from Middle East to Europe, North America, and Asia

LNG to South Korea and Japan

LNG to Japan, South Korea, and Taiwan

Oil from Middle East

LNG to Europe

Oil to North America and Europe from Africa

LNG to Japan and South Korea

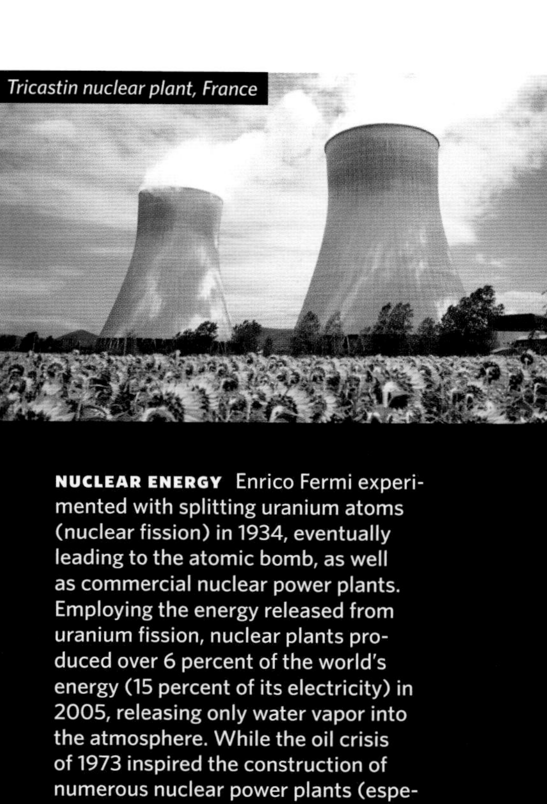
Tricastin nuclear plant, France

NUCLEAR ENERGY Enrico Fermi experimented with splitting uranium atoms (nuclear fission) in 1934, eventually leading to the atomic bomb, as well as commercial nuclear power plants. Employing the energy released from uranium fission, nuclear plants produced over 6 percent of the world's energy (15 percent of its electricity) in 2005, releasing only water vapor into the atmosphere. While the oil crisis of 1973 inspired the construction of numerous nuclear power plants (especially in France), subsequent problems have slowed construction of new nuclear plants to a crawl. Higher construction prices due to safety concerns (stemming from a fear of accidents) and the difficulties of safely storing nuclear waste have limited the number of nuclear plants (just over 400) since the late 1980s. However, as the costs of fossil fuels and concerns about climate change continue to rise, nuclear power plants appear poised for a renaissance.

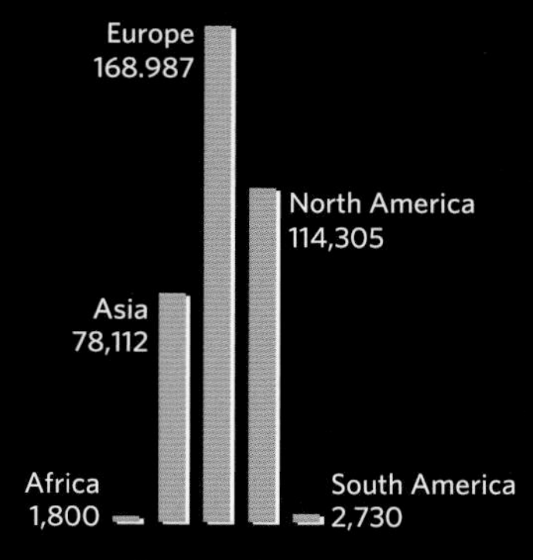

Europe 168.987

North America 114,305

Asia 78,112

Africa 1,800

South America 2,730

Nuclear Power Installed Capacity, 2008
(in megawatts)

Renewable Resources

Besides biomass already largely used, wind, solar, tidal, wave, and other technologies are promising sources of natural, renewable energy. In addition to being largely nonpolluting, renewable energy sources have the advantage of being mostly untapped at present. As the technology and economics of wind power improve, certain regions of the world could become "Saudi Arabias of wind." The amount of solar radiation received on Earth each year corresponds to several thousand times global energy consumption. Weaknesses of renewable energy sources include their intermittent nature and the lack of energy storage technologies, but as the world's demand for energy grows, and as people become more eco-conscious, renewable energy will gain in popularity.

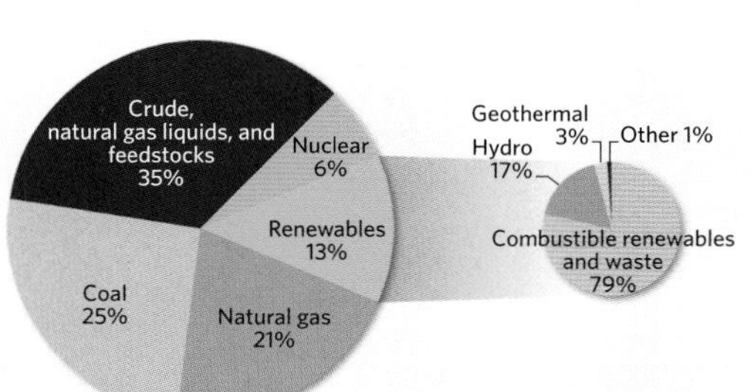

Crude, natural gas liquids, and feedstocks 35%
Nuclear 6%
Renewables 13%
Coal 25%
Natural gas 21%
Geothermal 3%
Other 1%
Hydro 17%
Combustible renewables and waste 79%

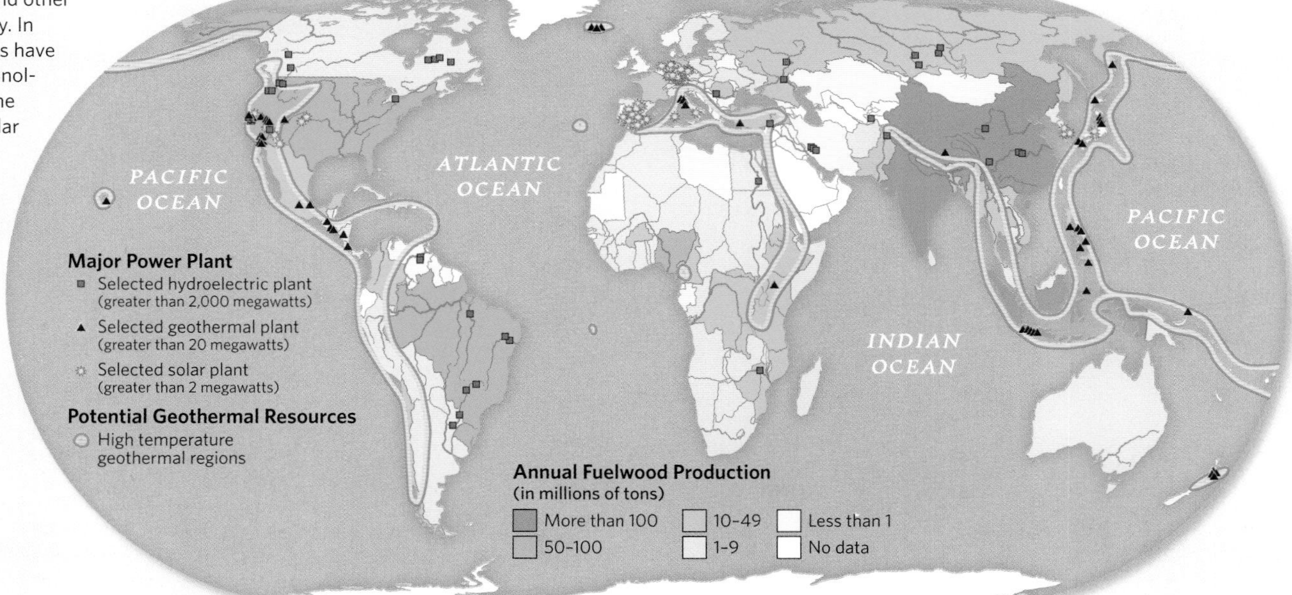

PACIFIC OCEAN
ATLANTIC OCEAN
PACIFIC OCEAN
INDIAN OCEAN
Major Power Plant
Selected hydroelectric plant (greater than 2,000 megawatts)
Selected geothermal plant (greater than 20 megawatts)
Selected solar plant (greater than 2 megawatts)
Potential Geothermal Resources
High temperature geothermal regions
Annual Fuelwood Production (in millions of tons)
More than 100
50-100
10-49
1-9
Less than 1
No data

The Geysers plant, Middletown, California

GEOTHERMAL

Field of solar troughs, California

SOLAR

Huitengxile Wind Farm, near Jining, China

WIND

John Day Dam, Oregon-Washington

HYDROELECTRIC

Mineral Resources

THE SPATIAL PATTERN of world mineral production is the result of several factors: geology, climate, economic systems, and social preferences. This pattern can be seen on the maps at right, which show the distribution of worldwide production and locate major production sites for major metallic mineral commodities and some important gemstones. The examples shown here certainly comprise more than 90 percent of the total tonnage of metallic minerals mined. However, many other metals are also required to manufacture the products of our modern world.

Metals such as those shown here are commodities with high unit values—whose prices are quoted in dollars to hundreds of dollars per ounce or pound. Of equal importance are much greater tonnages of less glamorous commodities such as cement, sand and gravel, sulfur, potash, and phosphates—materials with generally low unit values, measured in dollars to hundreds of dollars per ton.

The world's ability to feed its ever expanding population relies on fertilizer. The essential nutrients of phosphorous and potassium come from mines, are processed with sulfuric acid, and are combined with nitrogen from the air that has been transformed to ammonia by processing with methane gas. After fresh water, the availability of fertilizer (and the soil to which it is applied) is arguably more important than any of the metals discussed here.

Plate movements, volcanism, and sedimentation are geologic processes that form valuable concentrations of minerals. The same geologic forces that formed the Andes, for example, are responsible for the porphyry copper deposits along South America's Pacific coast. Other processes concentrate copper in sedimentary basins and in volcanic arcs. Climatic factors, such as the tropical conditions that contribute to bauxite formation, are also important.

Mineral consumption by industries is positively correlated with income and differs greatly among countries. Developed countries use larger volumes of materials and a wider variety of mineral commodities than less developed countries. In developed countries, annual copper use is typically five to ten kilograms per person; for less developed ones, usage is only a few kilograms per person. Recent economic growth has led to greater demand for many mineral resources. Meeting that need without causing harm to the environment will be one of the major challenges for societies in the 21st century.

Supply and Demand

PRICE PER POUND FOR IMPORTANT METALS, 2008

WORLD PRODUCTION OF MAJOR METALS BY VOLUME, 2007 (IN METRIC TONS)

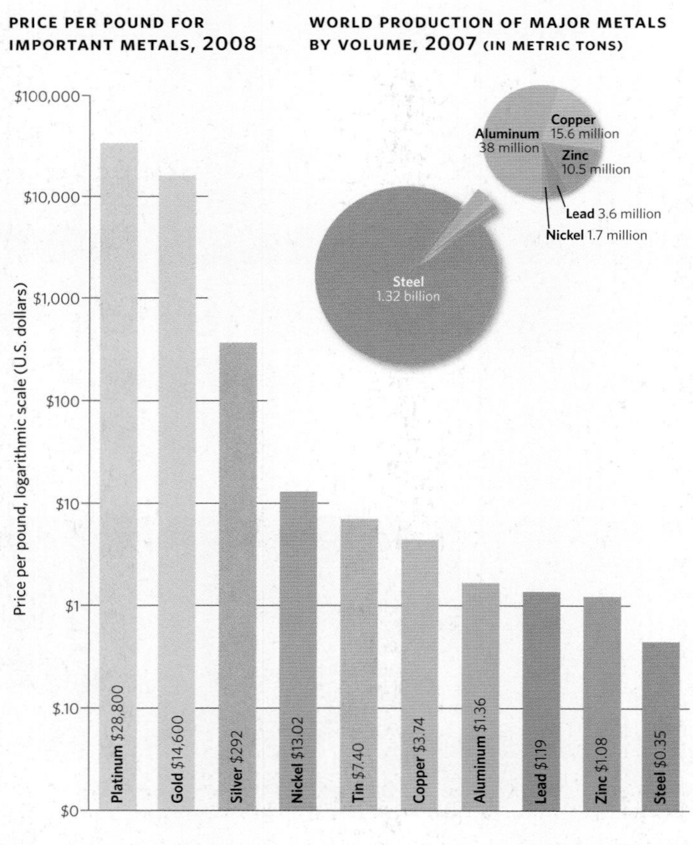

$100,000
$10,000
$1,000
$100
$10
$1
$.10
$0
Price per pound, logarithmic scale (U.S. dollars)
Platinum $28,800
Gold $14,600
Silver $292
Nickel $13.02
Tin $7.40
Copper $3.74
Aluminum $1.36
Lead $1.19
Zinc $1.08
Steel $0.35
Copper 15.6 million
Aluminum 38 million
Zinc 10.5 million
Lead 3.6 million
Nickel 1.7 million
Steel 1.32 billion

Iron Ore

Primary iron oxide ores range from 35 to 70 percent iron content—the richer ores (from Australia, Brazil, and South Africa) can be shipped directly to smelters while the rest require on-site grinding, separation, and concentration. The pie diagram for world steel production would be very different from the one at right—36 percent for China, 9 percent for Japan, 7 percent for the U.S., 5 percent for Russia, and the remaining 43 percent scattered across more than 50 other countries. The annual 1.4 billion tons of steel production requires large quantities of many other metals to make the specialty steels of our modern world.

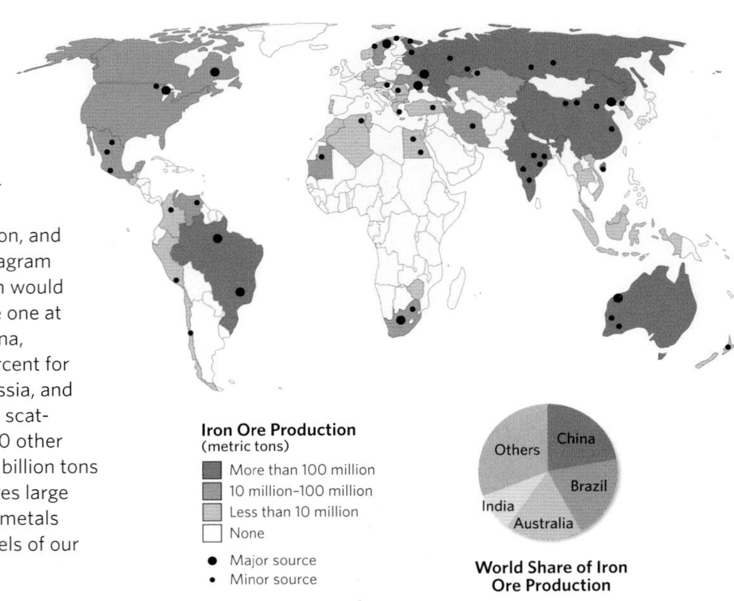

Iron Ore Production
(metric tons)
More than 100 million
10 million–100 million
Less than 10 million
None
Major source
Minor source
Others
China
Brazil
India
Australia
World Share of Iron Ore Production

Bauxite (aluminum ore)

Bauxite production comes from aluminous rocks that have spent millions of years near the surface of the Earth in tropical or subtropical climates. Deep, prolonged weathering leaches most elements from the parent rock, leaving aluminum and iron oxides. Despite this natural pretreatment, large amounts of energy are still required to convert the ore to aluminum metal. The ore is shipped to smelters where electricity is cheap; China, Russia, Canada, and the U.S. produce 58 percent of the world's aluminum metal. A significant percentage of the world's aluminum production comes from recycled products.

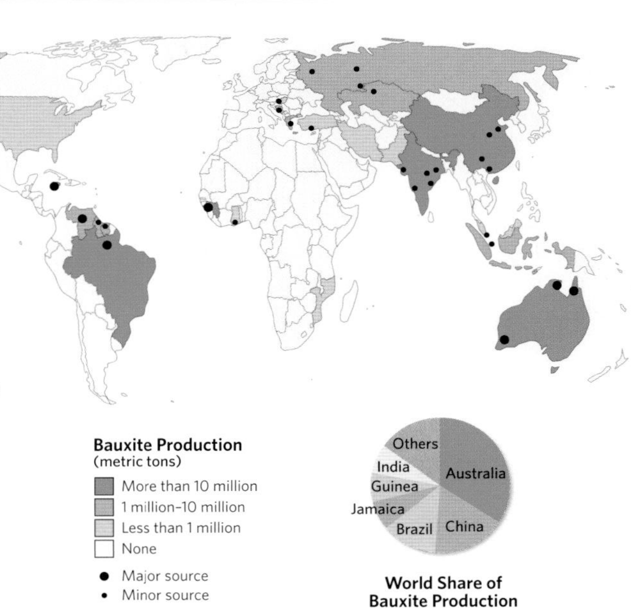

Bauxite Production
(metric tons)
More than 10 million
1 million–10 million
Less than 1 million
None
Major source
Minor source
Others
India
Guinea
Australia
Jamaica
Brazil
China
World Share of Bauxite Production

Zinc

Today, more than 50 percent of zinc is used in the production of galvanized steel while nearly 40 percent is consumed as zinc-based alloys and brass, the copper-zinc alloy. In ores, zinc sulfide is commonly found with copper sulfide minerals and thus the original brass was certainly an accidental product. Nearly all the primary cadmium (for nickel-cadmium batteries) and germanium (for fiber-optic cables) production comes as by-products from zinc mining. Thus the demand for galvanized steel influences the markets for batteries and fiber-optic glass.

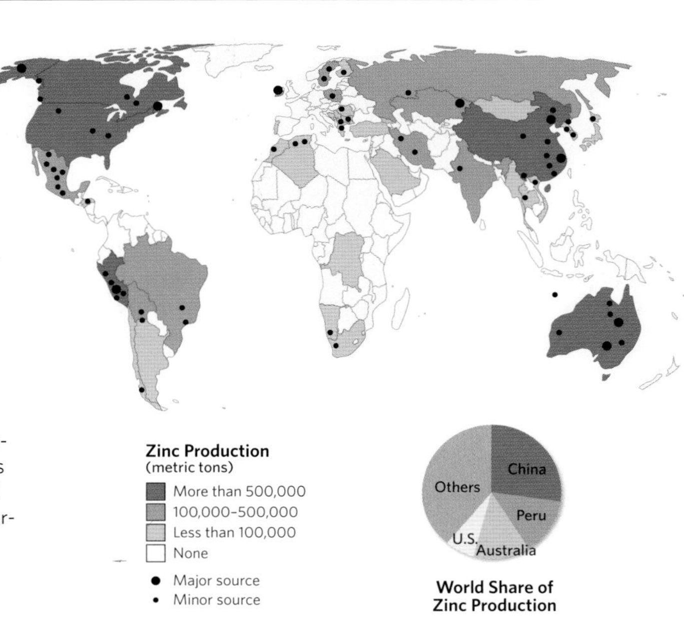

Zinc Production
(metric tons)
More than 500,000
100,000–500,000
Less than 100,000
None
Major source
Minor source
China
Others
Peru
U.S.
Australia
World Share of Zinc Production

Precious Metals (gold, silver, platinum)

Gold prices have nearly tripled in the last five years and have resulted in the breadth of production indicated on the map. Twenty years ago South Africa produced nearly 33 percent (21 percent ten years ago) of the global annual production from the world's deepest mines, which are now nearing technological exhaustion. Eighty percent of silver production comes from eight countries (Mexico leads with 15 percent) while South Africa accounts for 80 percent of the platinum ($2,000 per troy ounce*) mining. Other platinum group metals have prices that range from $300 to $10,000 per troy ounce.

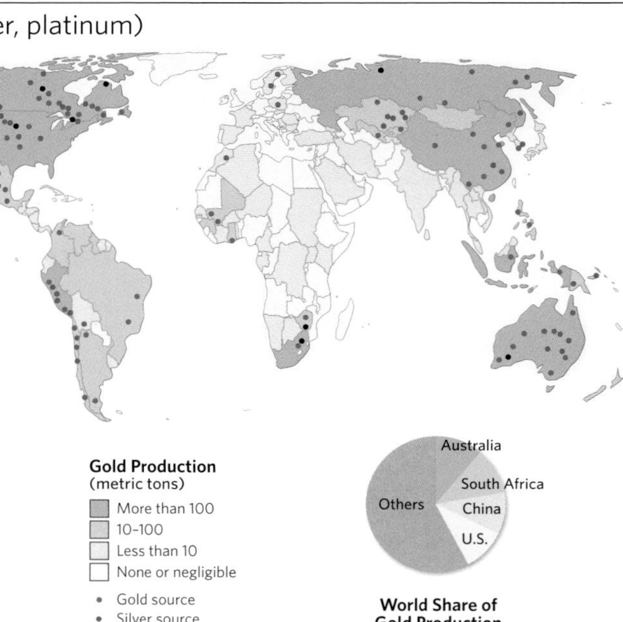

Gold Production
(metric tons)
More than 100
10–100
Less than 10
None or negligible
Gold source
Silver source
Platinum source
Australia
South Africa
Others
China
U.S.
World Share of Gold Production

**A troy ounce is equivalent to 0.0686 lbs. (0.0311 kg); it is the measure traditionally used for precious metals.*

Copper

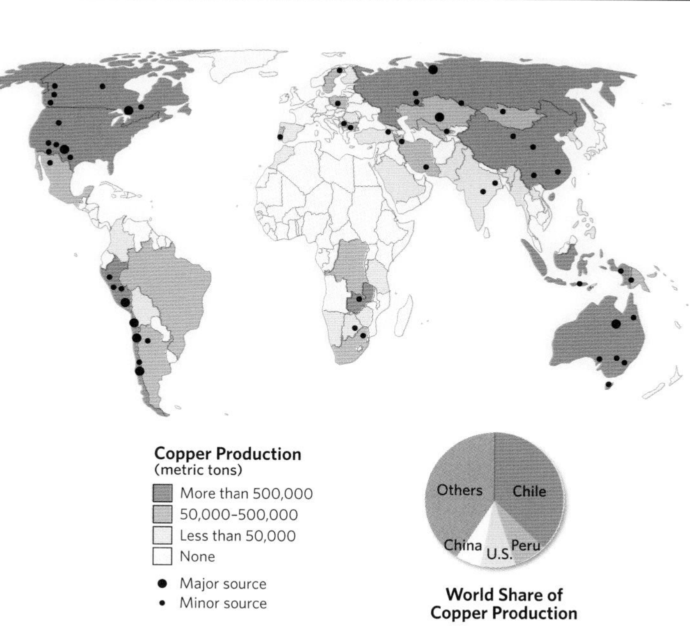
Copper Production
(metric tons)
More than 500,000
50,000-500,000
Less than 50,000
None
Major source
Minor source
Others
Chile
China
U.S.
Peru
World Share of Copper Production

Humans have used copper for at least 10,000 years and it ranks third after iron and aluminum in annual consumption. A soft metal, harder alloys with zinc (brass) and tin (bronze) allowed real tools and weapons to be formed, marking the end of the Stone Age. Most copper is recovered from sulfide minerals; historical open-hearth smelting led to severe acid rain problems. Building construction (51 percent) and electric and electronic products (19 percent) are the major consumers of copper and its alloys. Old scrap and recycled copper comprise 7 percent of U.S. consumption.

Nickel

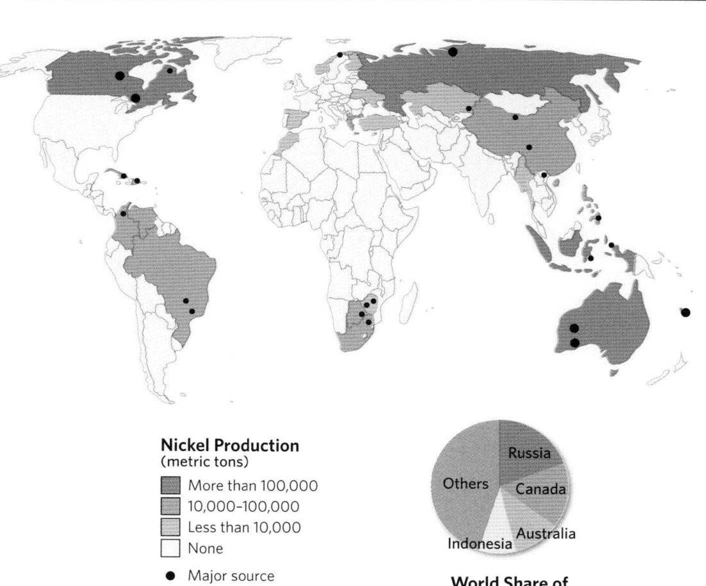
Nickel Production
(metric tons)
More than 100,000
10,000-100,000
Less than 10,000
None
Major source
Minor source
Russia
Others
Canada
Australia
Indonesia
World Share of Nickel Production

Globally, stainless steel (66 percent) and non-iron based alloys and superalloys account for nearly 90 percent of nickel consumption. China's dramatic expansion of its stainless steel industry is certainly the major cause of the nearly threefold price increase in nickel since 2005. A majority of land-based nickel reserves are contained in deeply weathered tropical settings—laterites —similar in their formation to the major ores of iron and aluminum. Traditional nickel sulfide ores contain the other 40 percent of identified resources.

Lead

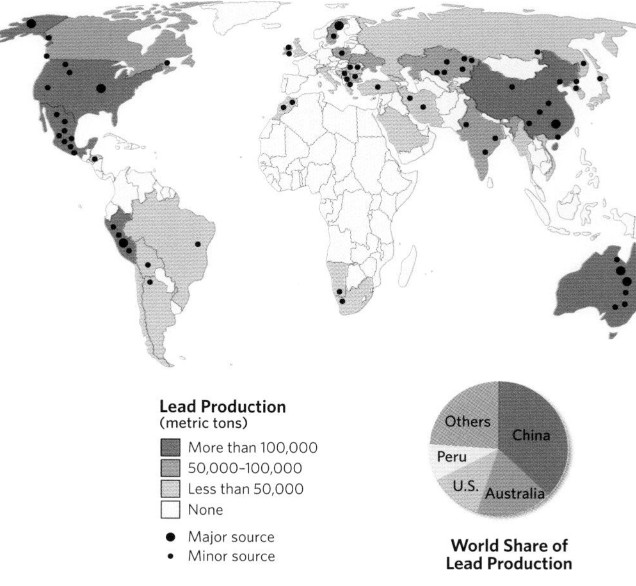
Lead Production
(metric tons)
More than 100,000
50,000-100,000
Less than 50,000
None
Major source
Minor source
Others
China
Peru
U.S.
Australia
World Share of Lead Production

Lead-acid batteries for cars and trucks continue to be the major end-product for lead sales, comprising 89 percent of U.S. consumption in 2007. Lead is also the recycling king—76 percent of U.S. consumption is recycled lead. Dramatic expansion of the transportation sector in China, however, has driven down global supplies and pushed prices to an all-time high. Lead sulfide is the primary product at many mines but it also occurs as a secondary product with copper, zinc, and, importantly, silver ores.

Gemstones

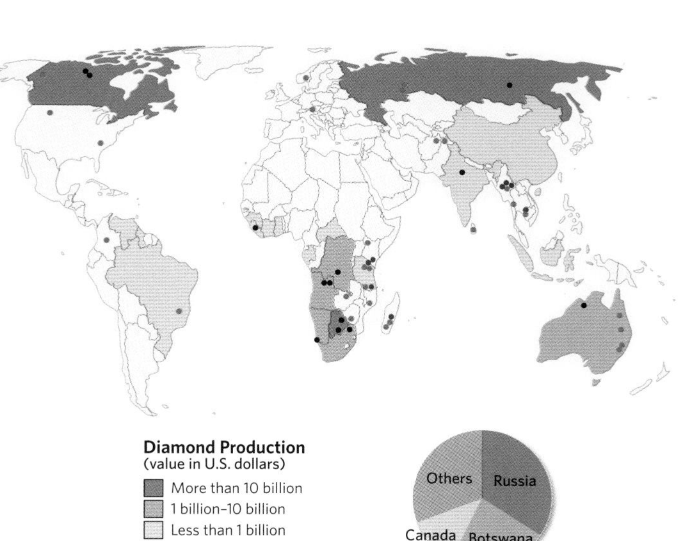
Diamond Production
(value in U.S. dollars)
More than 10 billion
1 billion-10 billion
Less than 1 billion
None
Diamond source
Ruby source
Sapphire source
Emerald source
Others
Russia
Canada
Botswana
World Share of Diamond Production

Diamonds dominate the world gemstone trade with roughly 100 million carats accounting for about $50 billion in sales in 2007. Canadian diamonds from the Northern Territories have been mined since 1999 and new deposits continue to be found, spurring further exploration across North America. Most diamonds are several billion years old and have been relatively recently brought to the surface as accidental inclusions in unusual volcanic rocks. Other gemstones such as rubies, sapphires, and emeralds occur in different geological settings and thus in different countries.

WORLD MINERALS BY ECONOMIC VALUE
(in billions of U.S. dollars)

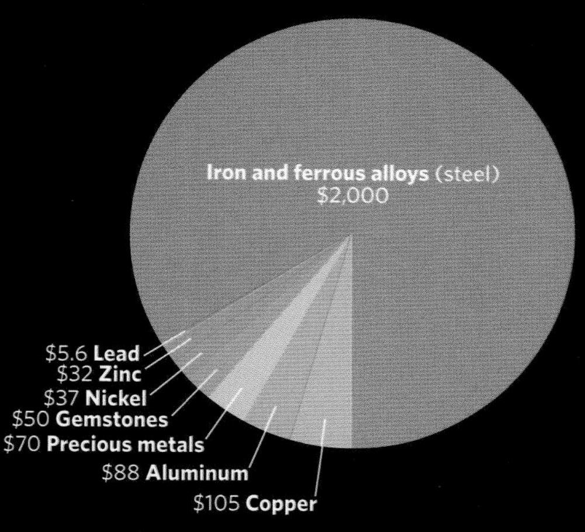
Iron and ferrous alloys (steel) $2,000
$5.6 Lead
$32 Zinc
$37 Nickel
$50 Gemstones
$70 Precious metals
$88 Aluminum
$105 Copper

Steel Production: Mining

Nearly all iron mining is done in open pits using huge electric or diesel shovels and trucks capable of hauling 200 to 300 tons at a time. Most ore needs to be drilled and blasted prior to processing. The iron-bearing minerals are generally extremely fine-grained and thus the rock must be ground to flour-size particles before separation, concentration, and shipping—usually as pellets.

Peña Colorada mine, Minatitlán, Mexico

Steel Production: Smelting

Concentrated iron oxides, limestone, and coke (a coal-derived fuel that doesn't smoke when burned) are combined in a furnace to reduce the iron oxides to iron metal. Impurities form slag, and large amounts of dust and gasses (largely water vapor and carbon dioxide) are given off. The molten iron is then combined with desired alloy metals to produce specific kinds of steel.

MAN B&W Diesel foundry, Augsburg, Germany

Steel Production: Finished Product

Molten steel may be cast as ingots for shipping, but it generally is formed into bars, beams, sheets, or wires at the foundry. Conversion of these steel raw materials into finished products, such as these rows and stacks of coiled steel wires in Hangzhou, China, involves either hot or cold rolling, drawing, or forming using large, powerful equipment.

Hangzhou Iron and Steel Company, Hangzhou, China

Military Strength

MILITARY STRENGTH among the world's sovereign states is difficult to measure since national power is typically perceived as a combination of economic, political, and military determinants. Nonetheless, traditional measures of military strength—such as sizes of standing armies, along with air and sea power—remain useful indicators of raw military power. These indicators have not changed much since the end of the Cold War; however, there have been two important evolutions in relative military strength since 1990: the ability to project military power beyond one's borders—either regionally or globally—and the availability of ungoverned space as a base of operations for violent transnational actions. Logistically, recent trends have included the increased use of precision-guided munitions and ISR (intelligence, surveillance, and reconnaissance) technologies. These, ironically, have often been countered with relatively low-tech weapons, such as roadside bombs and rockets (e.g., during the 2006 Israel-Lebanon conflict and the ongoing U.S. war in Iraq).

Since the beginning of contemporary global counterterror operations, the assessment of national power has become increasingly problematic. As the September 11 attacks against the United States so clearly demonstrated, a nontraditional, transnational military force can plan, resource, and conduct a military attack against a powerful sovereign state using ungoverned territory as a base of operations. While the security threats of the 20th century arose from powerful countries that embarked on aggressive courses, the key dimensions of the 21st century—globalization and the potential proliferation of weapons of mass destruction—mean great dangers can arise in and emanate from relatively weak states and ungoverned areas. Thus, the new security menace is transnational in nature and characterized by enemies without territory, borders, or traditional military forces. This situation cultivates other growing threats to global and regional security, including the export and franchising of terrorism, narcotrafficking, uncontrolled refugee flow, illegal immigration, slave trade, and piracy on the seas. Ungoverned spaces (areas outside of effective or viable government control) are also at particular risk of severe effects from humanitarian disasters and ethnic conflicts.

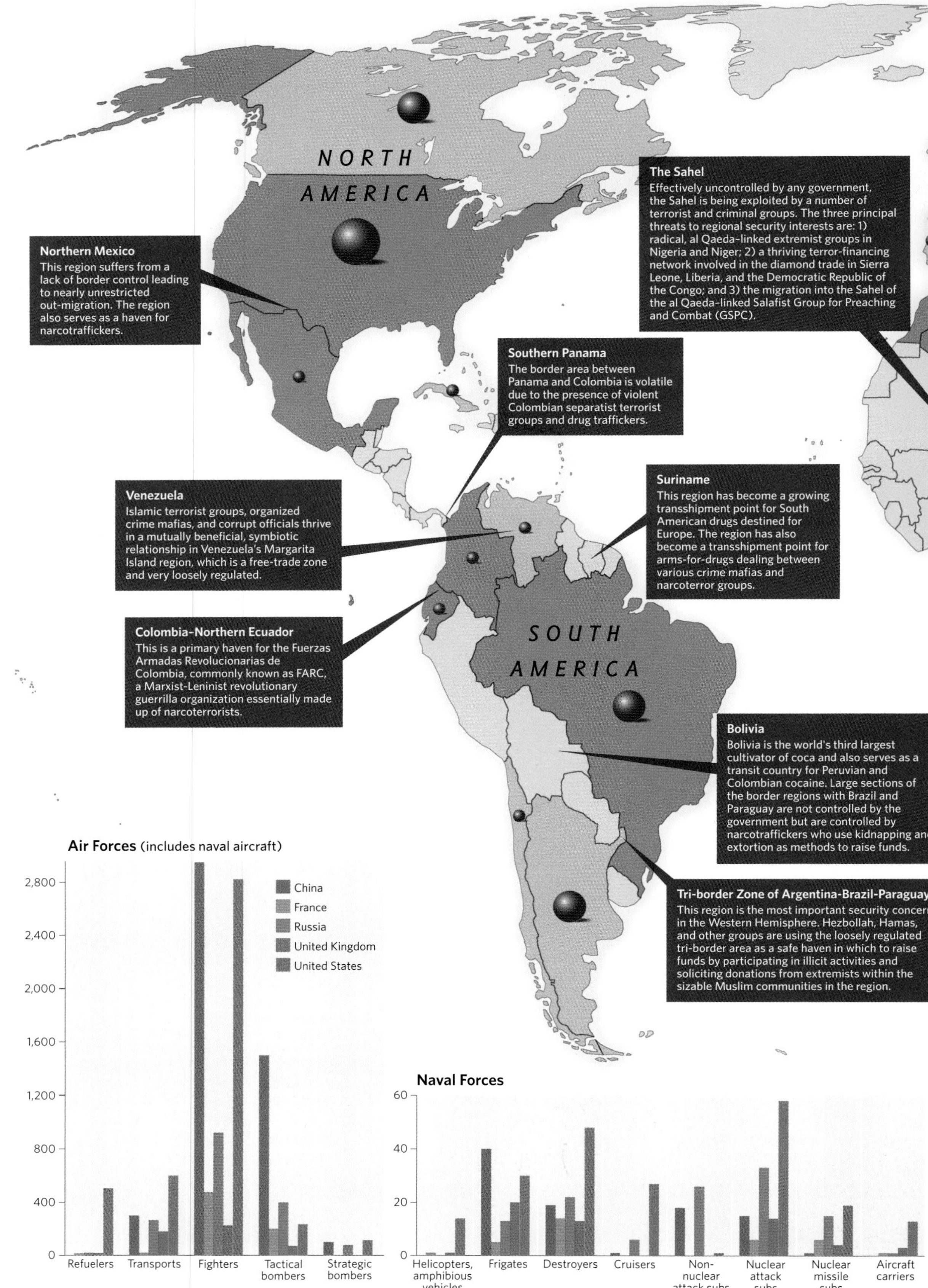
NORTH AMERICA
SOUTH AMERICA
Northern Mexico
This region suffers from a lack of border control leading to nearly unrestricted out-migration. The region also serves as a haven for narcotraffickers.
The Sahel
Effectively uncontrolled by any government, the Sahel is being exploited by a number of terrorist and criminal groups. The three principal threats to regional security interests are: 1) radical, al Qaeda-linked extremist groups in Nigeria and Niger; 2) a thriving terror-financing network involved in the diamond trade in Sierra Leone, Liberia, and the Democratic Republic of the Congo; and 3) the migration into the Sahel of the al Qaeda-linked Salafist Group for Preaching and Combat (GSPC).
Southern Panama
The border area between Panama and Colombia is volatile due to the presence of violent Colombian separatist terrorist groups and drug traffickers.
Venezuela
Islamic terrorist groups, organized crime mafias, and corrupt officials thrive in a mutually beneficial, symbiotic relationship in Venezuela's Margarita Island region, which is a free-trade zone and very loosely regulated.
Suriname
This region has become a growing transshipment point for South American drugs destined for Europe. The region has also become a transshipment point for arms-for-drugs dealing between various crime mafias and narcoterror groups.
Colombia-Northern Ecuador
This is a primary haven for the Fuerzas Armadas Revolucionarias de Colombia, commonly known as FARC, a Marxist-Leninist revolutionary guerrilla organization essentially made up of narcoterrorists.
Bolivia
Bolivia is the world's third largest cultivator of coca and also serves as a transit country for Peruvian and Colombian cocaine. Large sections of the border regions with Brazil and Paraguay are not controlled by the government but are controlled by narcotraffickers who use kidnapping and extortion as methods to raise funds.
Tri-border Zone of Argentina-Brazil-Paraguay
This region is the most important security concern in the Western Hemisphere. Hezbollah, Hamas, and other groups are using the loosely regulated tri-border area as a safe haven in which to raise funds by participating in illicit activities and soliciting donations from extremists within the sizable Muslim communities in the region.
Air Forces (includes naval aircraft)
China
France
Russia
United Kingdom
United States
2,800
2,400
2,000
1,600
1,200
800
400
0
Refuelers
Transports
Fighters
Tactical bombers
Strategic bombers
Naval Forces
60
40
20
0
Helicopters, amphibious vehicles
Frigates
Destroyers
Cruisers
Non-nuclear attack subs
Nuclear attack subs
Nuclear missile subs
Aircraft carriers
Note: France, United Kingdom: no data for non-nuclear attack subs, cruisers, or strategic bombers; Russia: no data for helicopters, amphibious vehicles; China: no data for refuelers

Nuclear Weapons in the World

The possession of a nuclear weapon is perceived by many states as the most important variable in today's strategic military calculus, magnifying a country's military strength. Thus, a number of countries have attempted to develop nuclear weapons during the past 25 years to join the so-called nuclear club. At present eight states have successfully incorporated nuclear weapons into their arsenals.

The 1970 Nuclear Non-Proliferation Treaty (NPT) conferred an internationally recognized "legal" nuclear status on five states: China, France, Russia, the United Kingdom, and the United States. However, three states that were not parties to the original treaty—India, Pakistan, and North Korea—have now conducted nuclear tests, with India and Pakistan having built sizable nuclear arsenals. It is also universally accepted that Israel possesses nuclear weapons.

In recent years Iran has been cited by the International Atomic Energy Agency Board of Governors for noncompliance with its NPT-required safeguards agreement. Iran has continued its dual-use nuclear activities, which has led to UN-imposed sanctions and heightened tensions in the Middle East. The Israeli Air Force has attacked and disabled nuclear reactors in Iraq and Syria, and in 2003 Libya abandoned its pursuit of nuclear weapons and later turned over all its materials for destruction. South Africa is the only country to have fully dismantled its nuclear weapons arsenal.

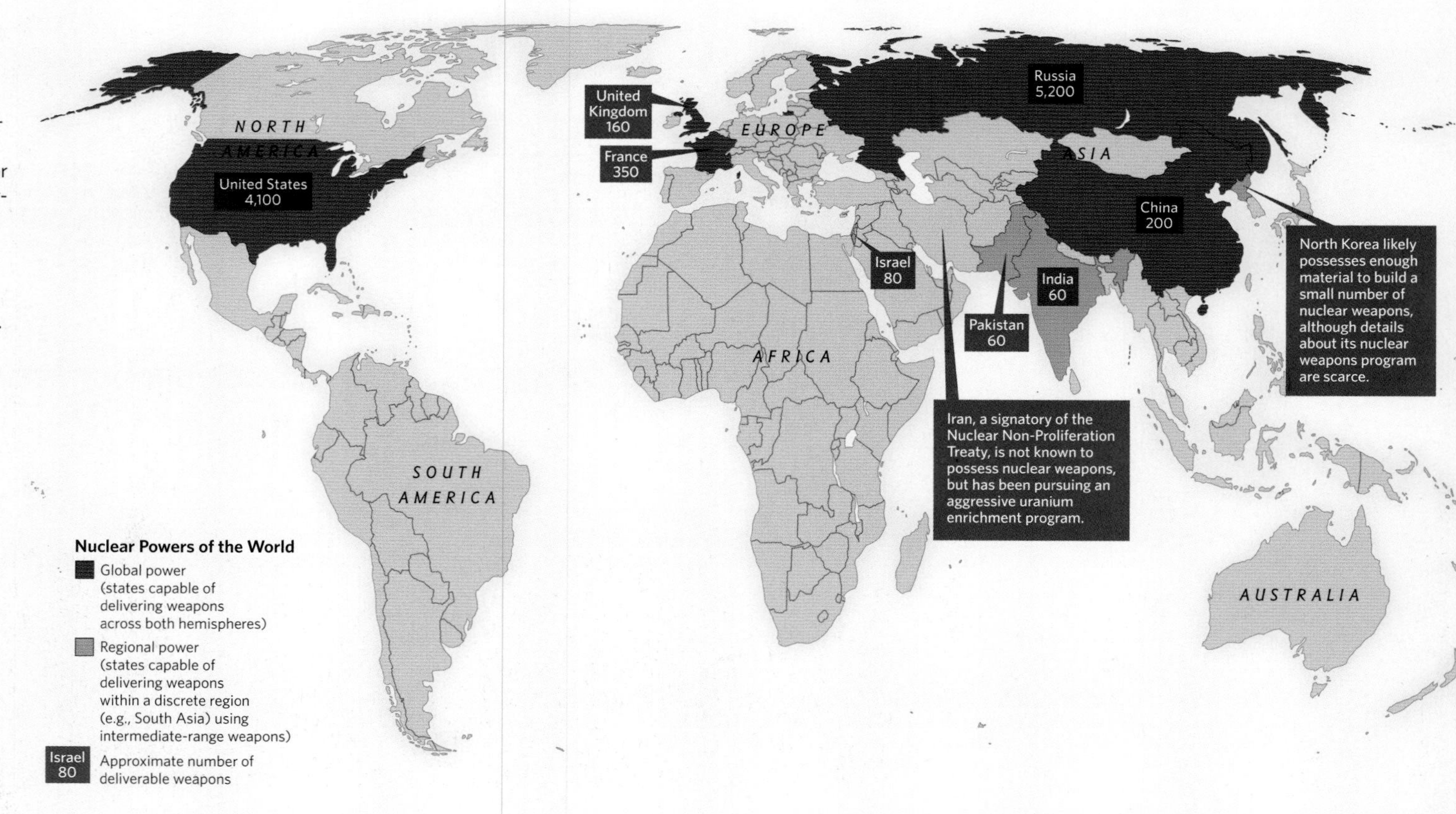
NORTH AMERICA
United States 4,100
United Kingdom 160
France 350
EUROPE
Russia 5,200
ASIA
China 200
Israel 80
India 60
Pakistan 60
AFRICA
SOUTH AMERICA
AUSTRALIA
North Korea likely possesses enough material to build a small number of nuclear weapons, although details about its nuclear weapons program are scarce.
Iran, a signatory of the Nuclear Non-Proliferation Treaty, is not known to possess nuclear weapons, but has been pursuing an aggressive uranium enrichment program.
Nuclear Powers of the World
Global power (states capable of delivering weapons across both hemispheres)
Regional power (states capable of delivering weapons within a discrete region (e.g., South Asia) using intermediate-range weapons)
Israel 80
Approximate number of deliverable weapons

EUROPE

ASIA

AFRICA

AUSTRALIA

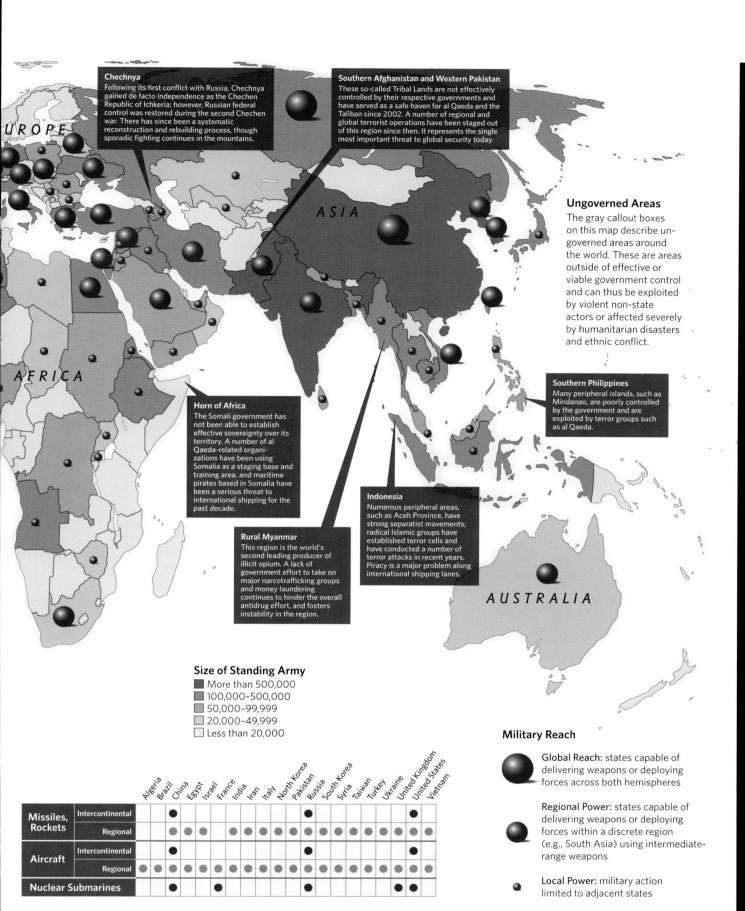

Chechnya
Following its first conflict with Russia, Chechnya gained de facto independence as the Chechen Republic of Ichkeria; however, Russian federal control was restored during the second Chechen war. There has since been a systematic reconstruction and rebuilding process, though sporadic fighting continues in the mountains.

Southern Afghanistan and Western Pakistan
These so-called Tribal Lands are not effectively controlled by their respective governments and have served as a safe haven for al Qaeda and the Taliban since 2002. A number of regional and global terrorist operations have been staged out of this region since then. It represents the single most important threat to global security today.

Ungoverned Areas

The gray callout boxes on this map describe ungoverned areas around the world. These are areas outside of effective or viable government control and can thus be exploited by violent non-state actors or affected severely by humanitarian disasters and ethnic conflict.

Southern Philippines
Many peripheral islands, such as Mindanao, are poorly controlled by the government and are exploited by terror groups such as al Qaeda.

Horn of Africa
The Somali government has not been able to establish effective sovereignty over its territory. A number of al Qaeda-related organizations have been using Somalia as a staging base and training area, and maritime pirates based in Somalia have been a serious threat to international shipping for the past decade.

Rural Myanmar
This region is the world's second leading producer of illicit opium. A lack of government effort to take on major narcotrafficking groups and money laundering continues to hinder the overall antidrug effort, and fosters instability in the region.

Indonesia
Numerous peripheral areas, such as Aceh Province, have strong separatist movements; radical Islamic groups have established terror cells and have conducted a number of terror attacks in recent years. Piracy is a major problem along international shipping lanes.

Size of Standing Army

- More than 500,000
- 100,000–500,000
- 50,000–99,999
- 20,000–49,999
- Less than 20,000

		Algeria	Brazil	China	Egypt	Israel	France	India	Iran	Italy	North Korea	Pakistan	Russia	South Korea	Syria	Taiwan	Turkey	Ukraine	United Kingdom	United States	Vietnam
Missiles, Rockets	Intercontinental			●									●							●	
	Regional			●	●	●		●	●	●	●	●	●	●	●	●	●	●	●	●	●
Aircraft	Intercontinental			●									●							●	
	Regional	●	●	●	●	●	●	●	●	●	●	●	●	●	●	●	●	●	●	●	●
Nuclear Submarines				●			●						●						●	●	

Military Reach

- **Global Reach:** states capable of delivering weapons or deploying forces across both hemispheres
- **Regional Power:** states capable of delivering weapons or deploying forces within a discrete region (e.g., South Asia) using intermediate-range weapons
- **Local Power:** military action limited to adjacent states

Military Technologies

Drones
The Global Hawk is an unmanned aircraft designed to provide global intelligence coverage. If a Global Hawk were flown from a U.S. West Coast base, it would be able to remain airborne over the East Coast for 24 hours, and use high-technology sensors to collect information on hundreds of square miles—all without having to place a pilot in harm's way.

Stealth
The F-22 Raptor is the newest stealth aircraft and represents one of the most advanced in the world. Stealth technology has revolutionized military capabilities because of the aircraft's virtual invisibility to radar. The F-22 is revolutionary because it is the first multirole aircraft, serving as both a fighter and a ground attack bomber.

Littoral Combat Ships
The Littoral Combat Ship is a next-generation Navy surface warship. It is designed to operate in heavily contested near-shore waters, thus enhancing the Navy's role in counterterror and antipiracy operations. These new vessels are designed to be small, fast and maneuverable, and employ modular "plug-and-fight" systems. Their versatility and modularity allows them to be reconfigured as needed for changing missions and technologies.

NORTH AMERICA

EUROPE

ASIA

AFRICA

SOUTH AMERICA

NATO Membership by Year

- 1949
- 1952
- 1955
- 1982
- 1990
- 1999
- 2004
- Expected in 2009

Since 1966, France has not been part of NATO's integrated military structure but has participated fully in all of NATO's political bodies. A decision to return to NATO's military structure will come in 2009.

NATO's Post-Cold War Activity

April 1993
Operation Deny Flight: Enforces a no-fly zone over Bosnia and Herzegovina.

June 1993 to October 1996
Operation Sharp Guard: Conducts peacekeeping operations in the former Yugoslavia.

August 1995
Operation Deliberate Force: Leads bombing campaign against the Serbian Army after the massacre in Srebrenica.

December 1996 to December 2004
Operation Joint Endeavor: Enforces peace in Bosnia and Herzegovina following the Dayton Accords.

March 1999
Operation Allied Force: Conducts an 11-week bombing campaign against the Federal Republic of Yugoslavia to stop ethnic cleansing by Serbian forces in Kosovo; deploys its ACE Mobile Land Force in Kosovo.

October 2001
Operation Active Endeavor: Conducts naval operations in the Mediterranean to prevent the movement of terrorists and weapons of mass destruction.

August 2003
Begins its first mission outside Europe when it assumes control of the International Security Assistance Force (ISAF) in Afghanistan.

NATO and Its Role in the World

Since the end of the Cold War, the North Atlantic Treaty Organization (NATO) has shown amazing resilience and ability to adapt, confounding those who expected its demise. As a military alliance, it was thought that NATO would become obsolete and disappear from the world stage with the dissolution of the Warsaw Pact. As this map indicates, however, NATO membership has grown over the past decade. NATO expanded incrementally from its original 12 member states in 1949 to 26 member states and into what is perhaps the strongest military alliance in history. Membership will expand to 28 with the addition of Croatia and Albania in 2009, while Ukraine, Georgia, and Macedonia are also likely to join NATO in the coming years.

There are many geopolitical factors contributing to NATO's growth, but from an assessment of military strength, NATO represents the largest block of military force in the world. As the map indicates, the alliance has increasingly flexed its might since the end of the Cold War. NATO was conceived as a defensive alliance, designed to defend Western Europe with the onset of the Cold War. Since that time, however, NATO's mission profile has changed and member states have provided military units in peace-keeping operations and offensive aerial campaigns. Most recently NATO began its first ever mission outside Europe when it assumed command and control of the International Security Assistance Force (ISAF) in Afghanistan.

Conflict

POLITICAL VIOLENCE, WAR, AND TERROR continue to plague many areas of the world in the early 21st century, despite dramatic decreases in major armed conflict since 1991. The 20th century is often described as the century of "total war," as modern weapons technologies made every facet of society a potential target in warfare. The globe was rocked by two world wars, self-determination wars in developing countries, and the encompassing threat of nuclear annihilation. Whereas the first half of the century was torn by interstate wars among the most powerful states, the latter half was consumed by protracted civil wars in the weakest states. The end of the Cold War emboldened international engagement, and concerted efforts toward peace had reduced armed conflicts more than half by early 2008.

While wars still smolder across the globe in the early 21st century, our apprehension is riveted on super-powerful states, super-empowered individuals, and the proliferation of "weapons of mass disruption." Globalization is bringing people closer together and making us ever more vulnerable. Though violence is generally subsiding and democracy spreading, greater competition over resources and markets increases global tensions, especially across the divide between the world's oil-producing and oil-consuming countries. Complicating the world's energy future are problems of global warming and the conversion of food grains to energy. Rising food and energy prices hit the poorer populations the hardest, increasing pressures on fragile states. A little-understood "war on terror" punctuates the hard-won peace and prods us toward an uncertain future. Prospects for an ever more peaceful world are good, yet much work remains to be done to meet the needs of the next generations.

The United States is the only country in the world currently directly engaged in foreign war. Its military operations in Iraq and Afghanistan were authorized by Congress, but in neither case was there a formal declaration of war.
That the U.S. rates low on the fragility map is a testament to its capacity to engage in a war halfway around the world (see the Military Reach map on pages 74–75). Other developed, low-fragility states have sent troops to assist the U.S. war efforts, but their support has been limited.
NORTH AMERICA
United States Iraq
United States "War on Terror"
ATLANTIC OCEAN
Algeria
Haiti
Guinea
Sierra Leone
Côte d'Ivoire
Liberia
Nigeria Niger Delta
PACIFIC OCEAN
Colombia
SOUTH AMERICA
Political Violence
Political violence in a localized region
Political violence affecting population generally
Recently ended or low-level political violence
Location of terrorist attack(s) resulting in 50 or more deaths, 2000 to early 2008

Based on data collection and analysis by the Center for Systemic Peace. Countries or areas color-coded on this map are—or recently have been—directly involved in sustained warfare resulting in at least 500 combat deaths.

Refugees and IDPs (Internally Displaced Persons)

Refugees are persons who have fled their country of origin due to fear of persecution for reasons of, for example, race, religion, or political opinion. IDPs are often displaced for the same reasons as refugees, but they still reside in their country of origin. By the end of 2006, the global number of refugees was nearly 10 million, with Asia hosting the largest number (46%), followed by Africa (26%), Europe (16%), North America (10%), Oceania (1%), and Latin America-Caribbean (0.4%). Afghanistan and Iraq were the top two countries of origin, with an estimated 2.5 million and 1.5 million refugees, respectively.

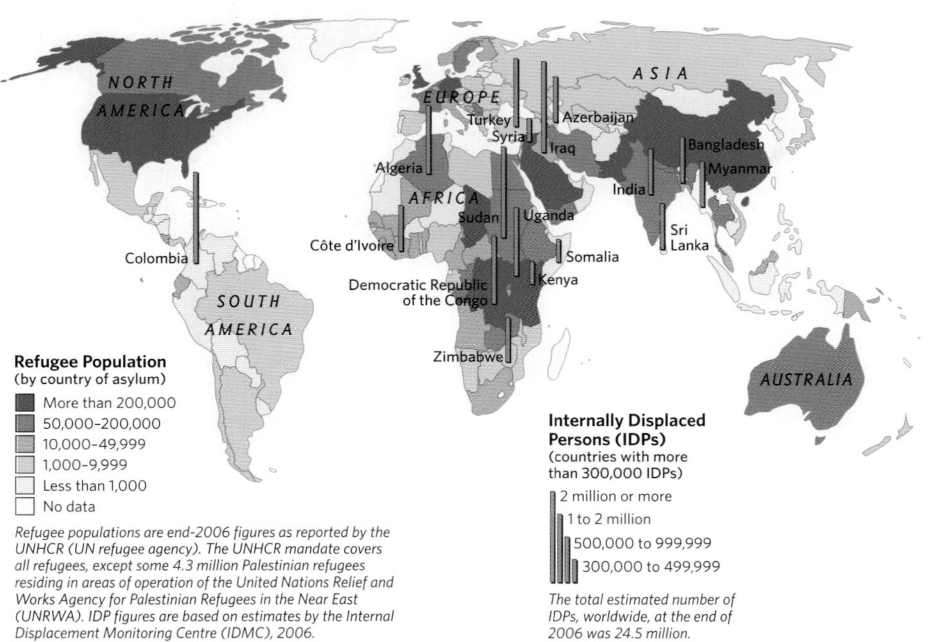

NORTH AMERICA
EUROPE
ASIA
Turkey
Syria
Azerbaijan
Iraq
Bangladesh
Myanmar
Algeria
AFRICA
India
Sudan
Uganda
Sri Lanka
Côte d'Ivoire
Somalia
Colombia
Kenya
Democratic Republic of the Congo
SOUTH AMERICA
Zimbabwe
AUSTRALIA
Refugee Population (by country of asylum)
More than 200,000
50,000–200,000
10,000–49,999
1,000–9,999
Less than 1,000
No data
Internally Displaced Persons (IDPs) (countries with more than 300,000 IDPs)
2 million or more
1 to 2 million
500,000 to 999,999
300,000 to 499,999

Refugee populations are end-2006 figures as reported by the UNHCR (UN refugee agency). The UNHCR mandate covers all refugees, except some 4.3 million Palestinian refugees residing in areas of operation of the United Nations Relief and Works Agency for Palestinian Refugees in the Near East (UNRWA). IDP figures are based on estimates by the Internal Displacement Monitoring Centre (IDMC), 2006.

The total estimated number of IDPs, worldwide, at the end of 2006 was 24.5 million.

Genocides and Politicides Since 1955

Our worst fears are realized when governments are directly involved in killing their own, unarmed citizens. Lethal repression is most often associated with autocratic regimes; its most extreme forms are termed genocide and politicide. These policies involve the intentional destruction, in whole or in part, of a communal or ethnic group (genocide) or opposition group (politicide). Death squads and ethnic cleansing have brutalized populations in 29 countries at various times since 1955. Humanitarian crises increase human suffering in the world's most fragile states.

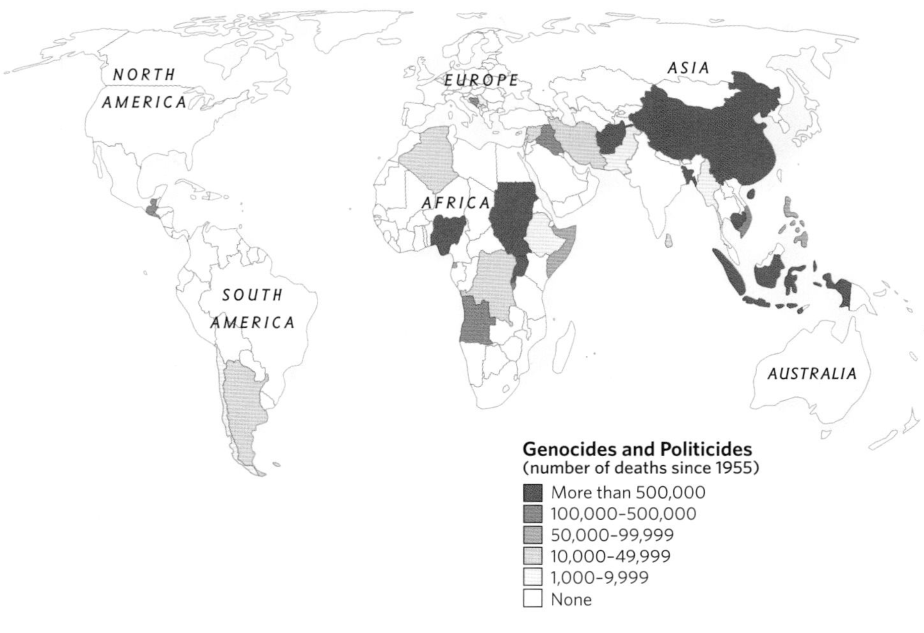

NORTH AMERICA
EUROPE
ASIA
AFRICA
SOUTH AMERICA
AUSTRALIA
Genocides and Politicides (number of deaths since 1955)
More than 500,000
100,000–500,000
50,000–99,999
10,000–49,999
1,000–9,999
None

Change in Magnitude of Ongoing Conflicts

Individual wars are scored on a ten-point magnitude scale and summed annually to chart warfare trends over time. The UN system was designed to control interstate wars and has been fairly successful. Societal wars, mainly in new and fragile states, increased during the Cold War but have fallen sharply since 1992

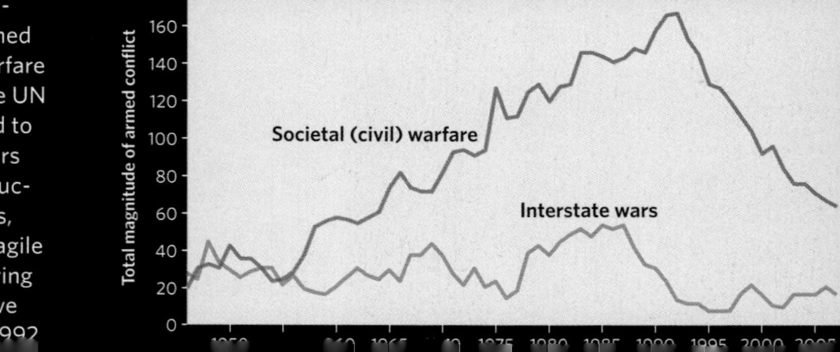

Total magnitude of armed conflict
180
160
140
120
100
80
60
40
20
0
Societal (civil) warfare
Interstate wars

Global Regimes by Type

Autocracy and democracy are two distinct and fairly stable forms of governance. Weakly autocratic or democratic regimes, and those with mixed forms of rule, are less able to provide basic needs and manage political conflict. The end of the Cold War is marked by dramatic changes in the nature of governance

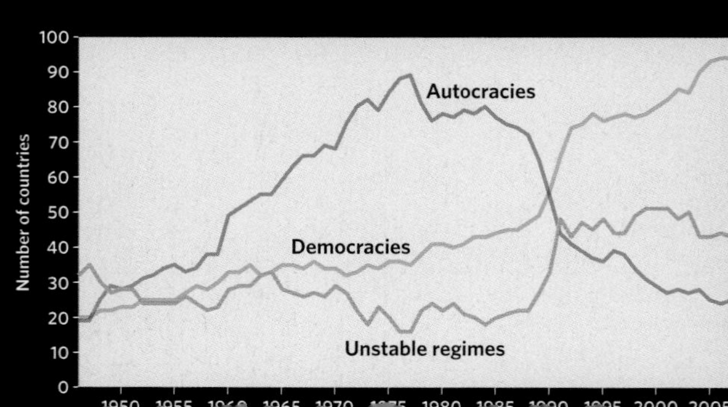

Number of countries
100
90
80
70
60
50
40
30
20
10
0
Autocracies
Democracies
Unstable regimes

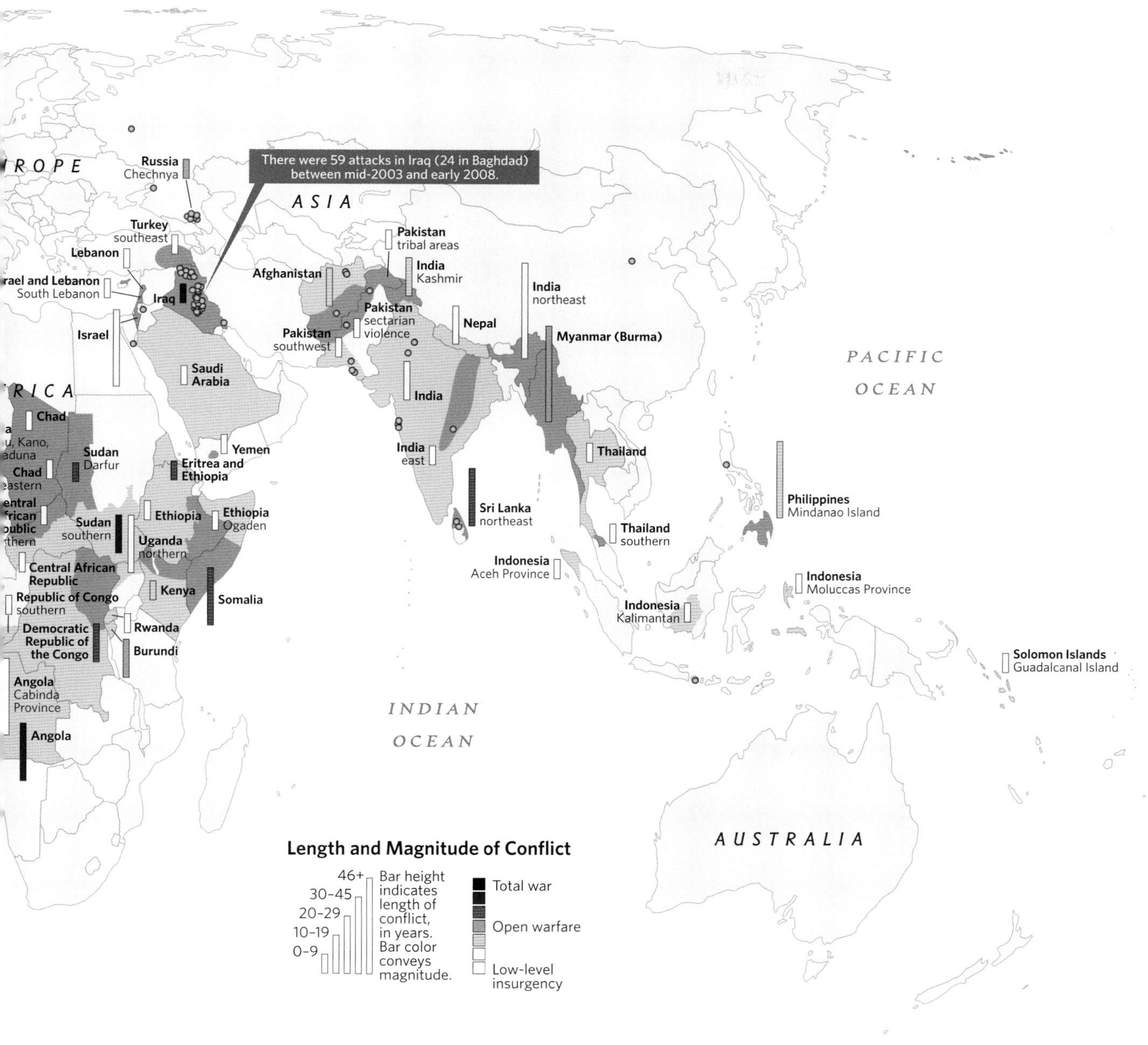
There were 59 attacks in Iraq (24 in Baghdad) between mid-2003 and early 2008.
EUROPE
ASIA
AFRICA
Russia Chechnya
Turkey southeast
Lebanon
Israel and Lebanon South Lebanon
Israel
Iraq
Afghanistan
Pakistan tribal areas
India Kashmir
Pakistan sectarian violence
Pakistan southwest
India northeast
Nepal
Myanmar (Burma)
Saudi Arabia
India
India east
Yemen
Sudan Darfur
Chad
Eritrea and Ethiopia
Ethiopia
Ethiopia Ogaden
Sudan southern
Uganda northern
Central African Republic
Kenya
Somalia
Republic of Congo southern
Rwanda
Democratic Republic of the Congo
Burundi
Angola Cabinda Province
Angola
Sri Lanka northeast
Thailand
Thailand southern
Philippines Mindanao Island
Indonesia Aceh Province
Indonesia Moluccas Province
Indonesia Kalimantan
Solomon Islands Guadalcanal Island
PACIFIC OCEAN
INDIAN OCEAN
AUSTRALIA
Length and Magnitude of Conflict
46+
30-45
20-29
10-19
0-9
Bar height indicates length of conflict, in years. Bar color conveys magnitude.
Total war
Open warfare
Low-level insurgency

Terrorist Attacks

Terrorism has a special connotation with violent attacks on civilians. The vast majority of such attacks are domestic; both state and non-state actors can engage in terror tactics. International terrorism is a special subset of attacks linked to globalization in which militants go abroad to strike their targets, select domestic targets linked to a foreign state, or attack international transports such as planes or ships. The intentional bombing of civilian targets has become a common tactic in the wars of the early 21st century.

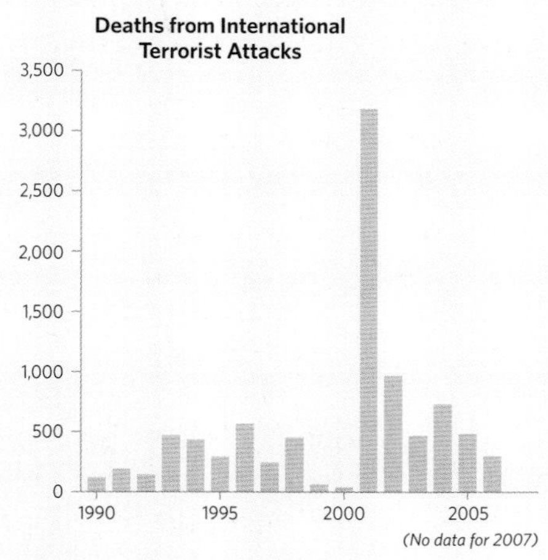
Deaths from International Terrorist Attacks
3,500
3,000
2,500
2,000
1,500
1,000
500
0
1990
1995
2000
2005
(No data for 2007)

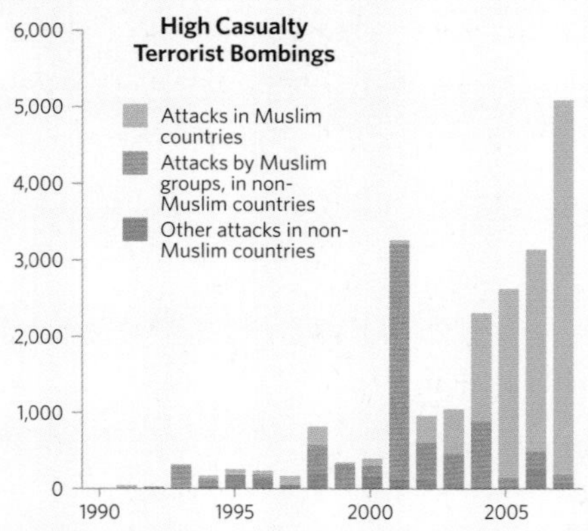
High Casualty Terrorist Bombings
6,000
5,000
4,000
3,000
2,000
1,000
0
Attacks in Muslim countries
Attacks by Muslim groups, in non-Muslim countries
Other attacks in non-Muslim countries
1990
1995
2000
2005

State Fragility

The quality of a government's response to rising tensions is the most crucial factor in the management of political conflict. State fragility gauges a country's vulnerability to civil disorder and political violence by evaluating government effectiveness and legitimacy in its four functions: security, political, economic, and social. Fragility is most serious when a government cannot provide reasonable levels of security; engages in brutal repression; lacks political accountability and responsiveness; excludes or marginalizes social groups; suffers poverty and inadequate development; fails to manage growth or reinvest; and neglects the well-being and key aspirations of its citizens. State fragility is an especially serious challenge in many African and Muslim countries.

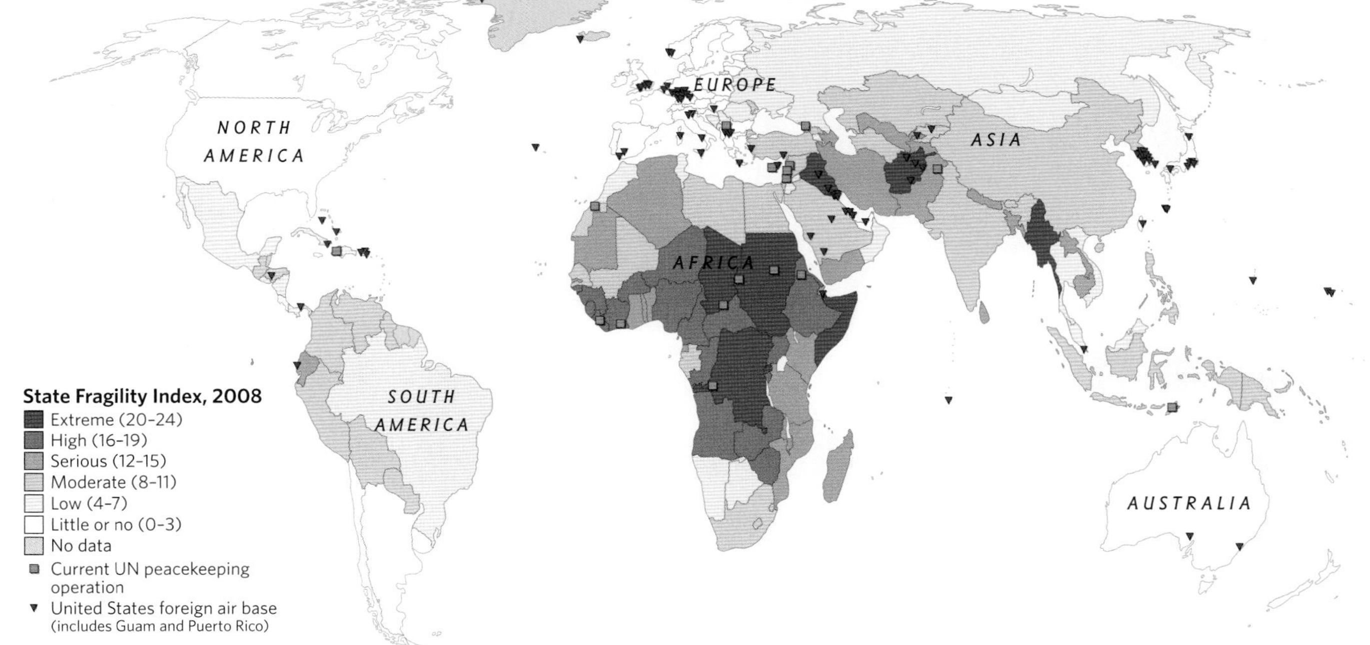
NORTH AMERICA
EUROPE
ASIA
AFRICA
SOUTH AMERICA
AUSTRALIA
State Fragility Index, 2008
Extreme (20-24)
High (16-19)
Serious (12-15)
Moderate (8-11)
Low (4-7)
Little or no (0-3)
No data
Current UN peacekeeping operation
United States foreign air base (includes Guam and Puerto Rico)

Weapons Possessions

The proliferation of weapons of mass destruction (WMDs) is a principal concern in the 21st century. State fragility and official corruption increase the possibilities that these modern technologies might fall into the wrong hands and be a source of terror, extortion, or war. Of equal concern is the proliferation of "weapons of mass disruption." Globalization has increased the spread of small arms, explosives, and missiles and the scope and strength of militant networks and organized crime. New communication and information technologies have contributed to the "super-empowered individual." At the same time, the proliferation of indiscriminant weapons such as antipersonnel land mines and cluster bombs has increased the danger to civilians in war zones, both during the fighting and long afterward, as unexploded ordnance litters the land, disabling a return to productive life.

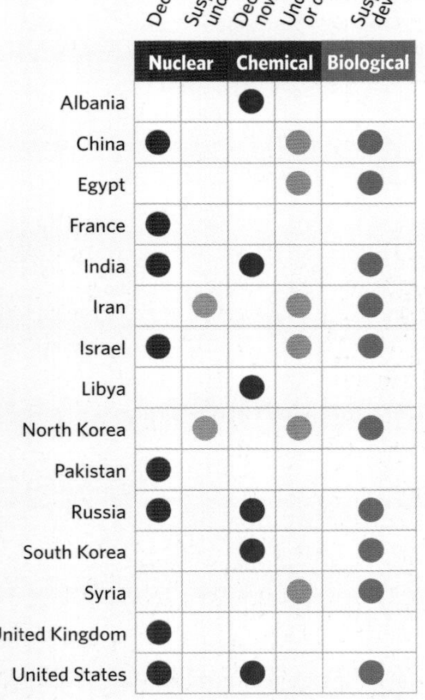

	Nuclear		Chemical		Biological
	Declared stockpile	Suspected or undeclared program	Declared stockpile now being destroyed	Undeclared stockpile or development program	Suspected offensive development program
Albania			●		
China	●			●	●
Egypt				●	●
France	●				
India	●		●		●
Iran		●		●	●
Israel	●			●	●
Libya			●		
North Korea		●		●	●
Pakistan	●				
Russia	●		●		●
South Korea			●		●
Syria				●	●
United Kingdom	●				
United States	●		●		●

Military Deployments and Bases

The reduction of armed conflicts since 1991 has led to an increase in peacekeeping and peacemaking operations. In early 2008, there were 17 UN peacekeeping operations across the world's most volatile and fragile regions. As the sole superpower, the U.S. has taken a leading role; its military is engaged in training, peacemaking, or combat operations in nearly 130 countries around the globe.

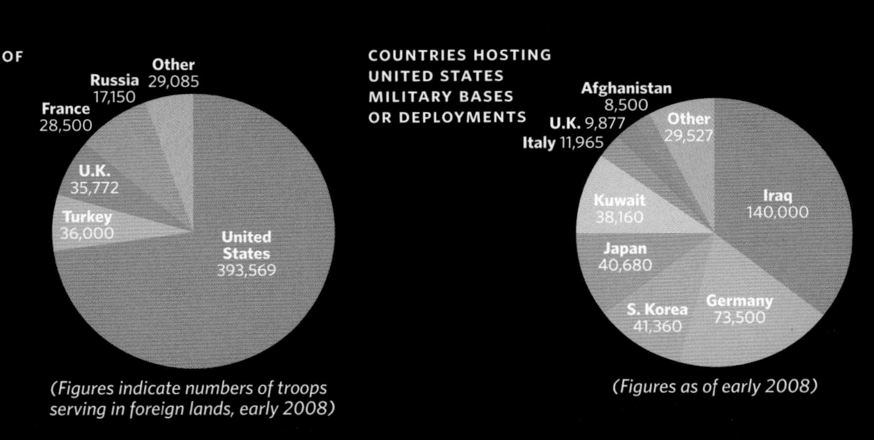
NUMBER OF TROOPS SERVING ABROAD
Other 29,085
Russia 17,150
France 28,500
U.K. 35,772
Turkey 36,000
United States 393,569
COUNTRIES HOSTING UNITED STATES MILITARY BASES OR DEPLOYMENTS
Afghanistan 8,500
U.K. 9,877
Italy 11,965
Other 29,527
Kuwait 38,160
Iraq 140,000
Japan 40,680
S. Korea 41,360
Germany 73,500

(Figures indicate numbers of troops serving in foreign lands, early 2008)

(Figures as of early 2008)

Technology and Communication

THE TECHNOLOGICAL REVOLUTION that began in the 1950s has given rise to a new Information Age in which global communications networks underpin every facet of modern life. Each day, trillions of dollars of goods and services are traded worldwide in the form of bits and bytes, speeding through space, beneath the waves, under our feet, and in the air around us. Information has never been so plentiful, nor so cheap. The world's first mass-produced book, the Gutenberg Bible, took up to two years to print and was beyond the means of all but a wealthy few. Today's Net-savvy generation routinely downloads books, music, radio and TV shows, and film clips over the Internet in minutes, for just a few cents.

The Internet itself has quickly evolved into a ubiquitous "network of networks" carrying everything from financial data to phone calls, TV, real-time gaming, online shopping, and social networking. Information flows are becoming near-impossible to restrict as the Internet goes wireless, and free content-sharing sites begin to break down old models of control and distribution. Inanimate objects are themselves becoming part of an intelligent "Internet of things," actively exchanging information without the need for human intervention. Tiny RFID tags are already being used to track items like retail goods and aircraft baggage; soon, they could be providing information about an individual's identity, buying and traveling habits, and more. At the same time, advanced new satellite mapping systems are providing an instant bird's-eye view of our planet — and our neighbors — on a global scale never before possible.

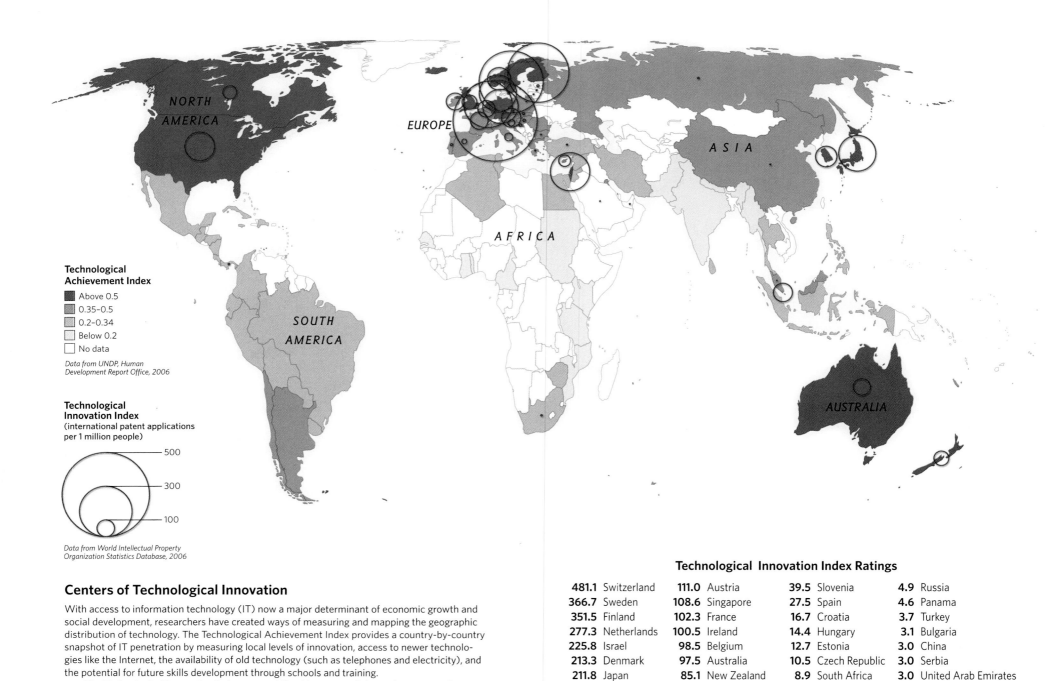

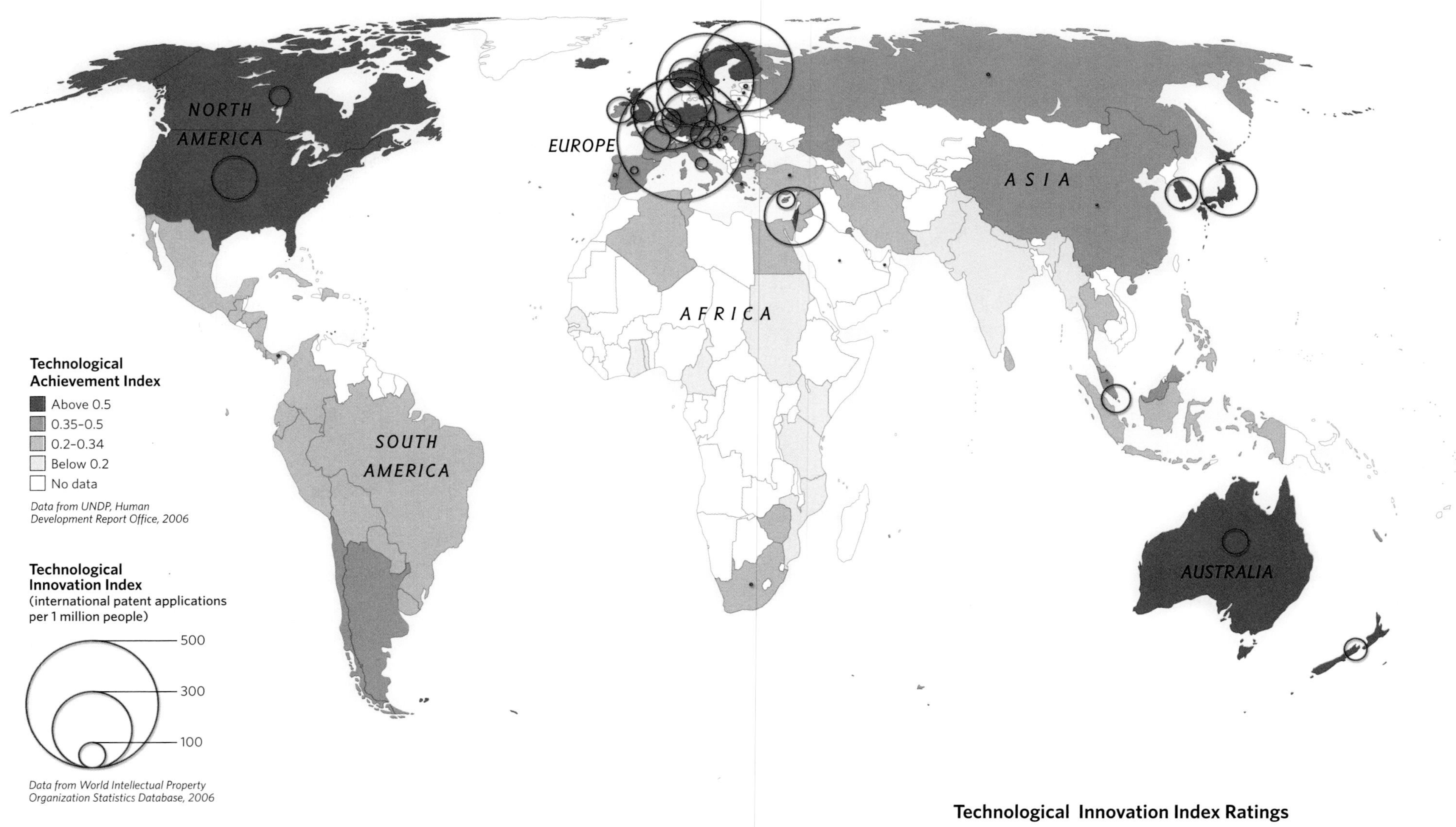

NORTH AMERICA
EUROPE
ASIA
AFRICA
SOUTH AMERICA
AUSTRALIA
Technological Achievement Index
Above 0.5
0.35–0.5
0.2–0.34
Below 0.2
No data
Data from UNDP, Human Development Report Office, 2006
Technological Innovation Index
(international patent applications per 1 million people)
500
300
100
Data from World Intellectual Property Organization Statistics Database, 2006

Centers of Technological Innovation

With access to information technology (IT) now a major determinant of economic growth and social development, researchers have created ways of measuring and mapping the geographic distribution of technology. The Technological Achievement Index provides a country-by-country snapshot of IT penetration by measuring local levels of innovation, access to newer technologies like the Internet, the availability of old technology (such as telephones and electricity), and the potential for future skills development through schools and training.

The Technological Innovation Index, meanwhile, shines a spotlight on the centers of innovation that are driving today's technological revolution. Each country is assigned an innovation score based on the number of patents generated by its residents, which is then weighted against national population figures to provide a global perspective. The results can be surprising, with some of the world's more dynamic smaller nations easily outstripping industrial giants.

Technological Innovation Index Ratings

481.1	Switzerland	**111.0**	Austria	**39.5**	Slovenia	**4.9**	Russia
366.7	Sweden	**108.6**	Singapore	**27.5**	Spain	**4.6**	Panama
351.5	Finland	**102.3**	France	**16.7**	Croatia	**3.7**	Turkey
277.3	Netherlands	**100.5**	Ireland	**14.4**	Hungary	**3.1**	Bulgaria
225.8	Israel	**98.5**	Belgium	**12.7**	Estonia	**3.0**	China
213.3	Denmark	**97.5**	Australia	**10.5**	Czech Republic	**3.0**	Serbia
211.8	Japan	**85.1**	New Zealand	**8.9**	South Africa	**3.0**	United Arab Emirates
203.1	Germany	**84.4**	United Kingdom	**7.6**	Greece	**2.9**	Lithuania
170.7	United States	**78.9**	Canada	**7.4**	Latvia	**2.7**	Poland
131.4	Norway	**67.9**	Cyprus	**6.4**	Portugal	**2.3**	Malaysia
122.7	South Korea	**46.3**	Italy	**5.8**	Slovakia	**2.3**	Saudi Arabia

Milestones in Technology

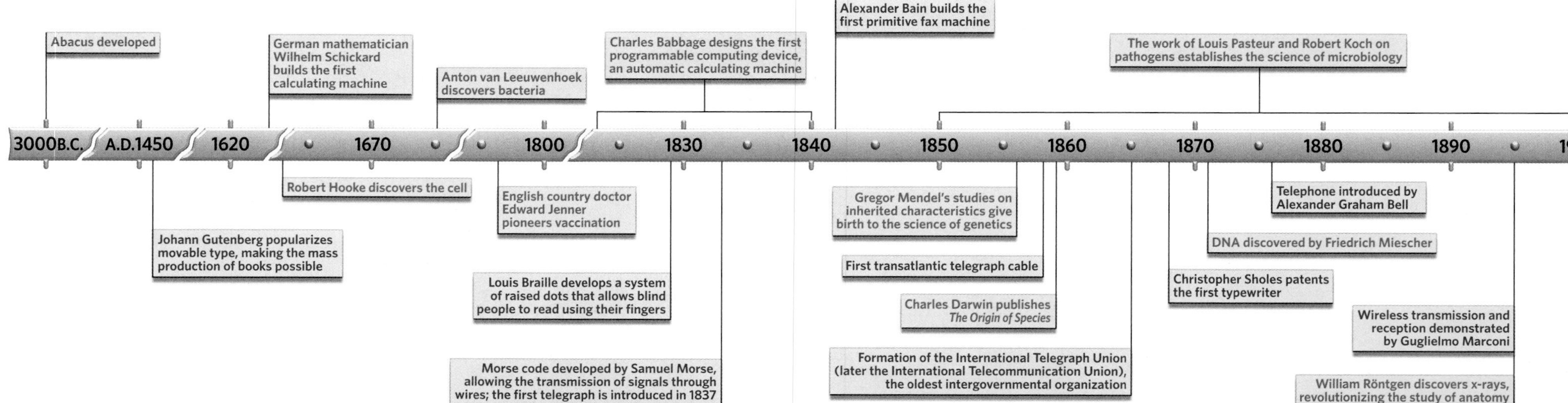

Abacus developed
German mathematician Wilhelm Schickard builds the first calculating machine
Anton van Leeuwenhoek discovers bacteria
Charles Babbage designs the first programmable computing device, an automatic calculating machine
Alexander Bain builds the first primitive fax machine
The work of Louis Pasteur and Robert Koch on pathogens establishes the science of microbiology
3000B.C.
A.D.1450
1620
1670
1800
1830
1840
1850
1860
1870
1880
1890
190
Robert Hooke discovers the cell
Johann Gutenberg popularizes movable type, making the mass production of books possible
English country doctor Edward Jenner pioneers vaccination
Louis Braille develops a system of raised dots that allows blind people to read using their fingers
Morse code developed by Samuel Morse, allowing the transmission of signals through wires; the first telegraph is introduced in 1837
Gregor Mendel's studies on inherited characteristics give birth to the science of genetics
First transatlantic telegraph cable
Charles Darwin publishes The Origin of Species
Formation of the International Telegraph Union (later the International Telecommunication Union), the oldest intergovernmental organization
Telephone introduced by Alexander Graham Bell
DNA discovered by Friedrich Miescher
Christopher Sholes patents the first typewriter
Wireless transmission and reception demonstrated by Guglielmo Marconi
William Röntgen discovers x-rays, revolutionizing the study of anatomy

The Digital Divide

If access to digital information is taken for granted in industrialized nations, information and communication technologies (ICTs) remain out of reach for many millions in the developing world. The result of widespread poverty and geographical challenges like mountainous terrain or widely dispersed communities, concerted efforts to bridge this "digital divide" are seeing the deployment of new technologies that leverage the power of low-cost long-range wireless, and new shared infrastructure models that cut the cost of network builds.

The International Telecommunication Union's Digital Opportunity Index is a composite model based on 11 different indicators of opportunity, infrastructure, and utilization. Among the information-rich, South Korea, Japan, and Denmark score highest, while countries beset by chronic poverty and civil strife fare worst, with Niger, Chad, Myanmar, Guinea-Bissau, and Eritrea all falling at the bottom end of the scale. Asia remains the world's fastest-growing region for ICT uptake, with China alone now boasting over 550 million mobile subscribers — more than twice that of the world's second-ranked mobile market, India.

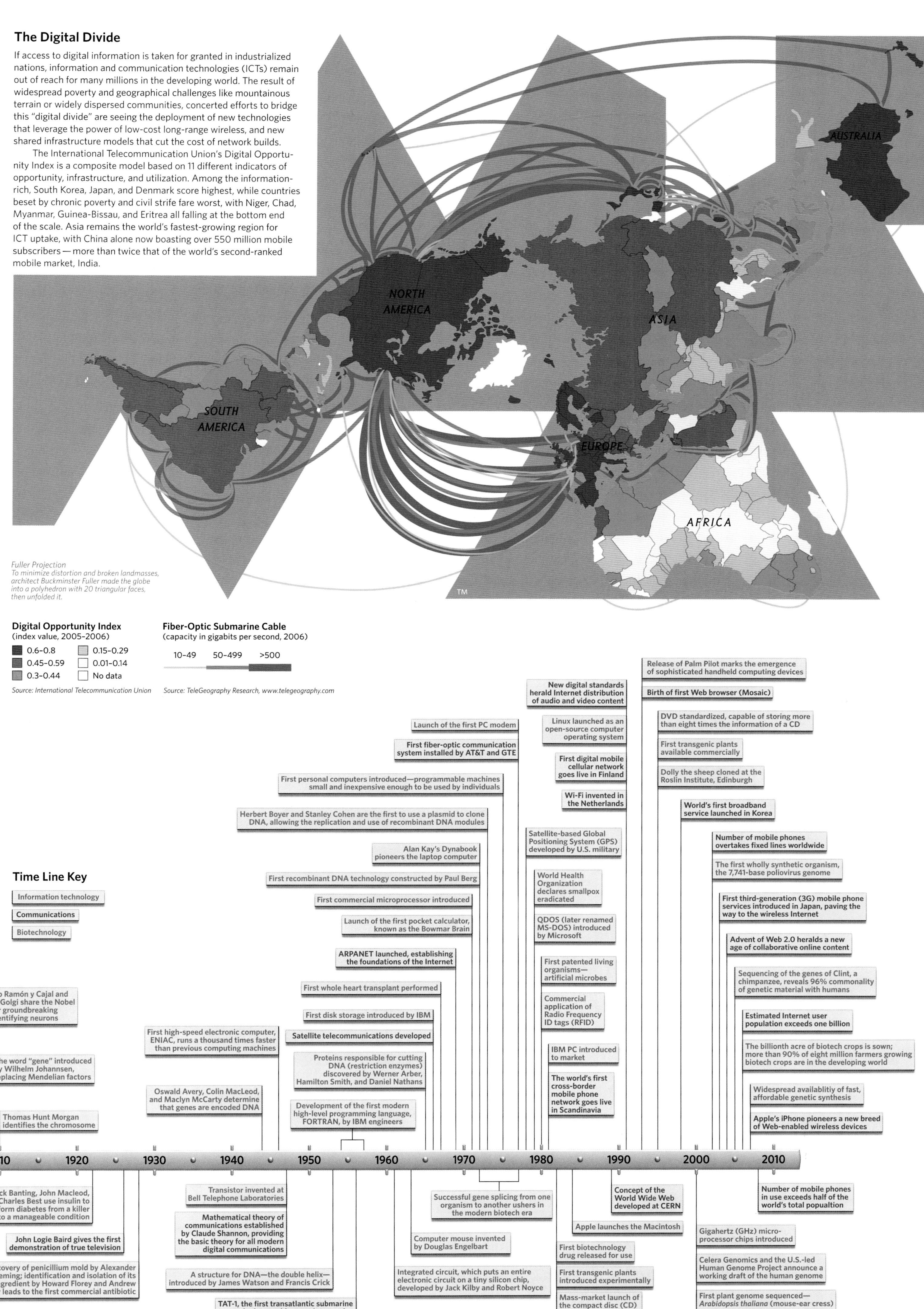
AUSTRALIA
NORTH AMERICA
ASIA
SOUTH AMERICA
EUROPE
AFRICA
TM
Digital Opportunity Index
(index value, 2005–2006)
0.6–0.8
0.45–0.59
0.3–0.44
0.15–0.29
0.01–0.14
No data
Fiber-Optic Submarine Cable
(capacity in gigabits per second, 2006)
10–49
50–499
>500
Time Line Key
Information technology
Communications
Biotechnology
antiago Ramón y Cajal and
amillo Golgi share the Nobel
rize for groundbreaking
work identifying neurons
The word "gene" introduced by Wilhelm Johannsen, replacing Mendelian factors
Thomas Hunt Morgan identifies the chromosome
First high-speed electronic computer, ENIAC, runs a thousand times faster than previous computing machines
Oswald Avery, Colin MacLeod, and Maclyn McCarty determine that genes are encoded DNA
Herbert Boyer and Stanley Cohen are the first to use a plasmid to clone DNA, allowing the replication and use of recombinant DNA modules
First personal computers introduced—programmable machines small and inexpensive enough to be used by individuals
Launch of the first PC modem
First fiber-optic communication system installed by AT&T and GTE
Alan Kay's Dynabook pioneers the laptop computer
First recombinant DNA technology constructed by Paul Berg
First commercial microprocessor introduced
Launch of the first pocket calculator, known as the Bowmar Brain
ARPANET launched, establishing the foundations of the Internet
First whole heart transplant performed
First disk storage introduced by IBM
Satellite telecommunications developed
Proteins responsible for cutting DNA (restriction enzymes) discovered by Werner Arber, Hamilton Smith, and Daniel Nathans
Development of the first modern high-level programming language, FORTRAN, by IBM engineers
New digital standards herald Internet distribution of audio and video content
Linux launched as an open-source computer operating system
First digital mobile cellular network goes live in Finland
Wi-Fi invented in the Netherlands
Satellite-based Global Positioning System (GPS) developed by U.S. military
World Health Organization declares smallpox eradicated
QDOS (later renamed MS-DOS) introduced by Microsoft
First patented living organisms—artificial microbes
Commercial application of Radio Frequency ID tags (RFID)
IBM PC introduced to market
The world's first cross-border mobile phone network goes live in Scandinavia
Release of Palm Pilot marks the emergence of sophisticated handheld computing devices
Birth of first Web browser (Mosaic)
DVD standardized, capable of storing more than eight times the information of a CD
First transgenic plants available commercially
Dolly the sheep cloned at the Roslin Institute, Edinburgh
World's first broadband service launched in Korea
Number of mobile phones overtakes fixed lines worldwide
The first wholly synthetic organism, the 7,741-base poliovirus genome
First third-generation (3G) mobile phone services introduced in Japan, paving the way to the wireless Internet
Advent of Web 2.0 heralds a new age of collaborative online content
Sequencing of the genes of Clint, a chimpanzee, reveals 96% commonality of genetic material with humans
Estimated Internet user population exceeds one billion
The billionth acre of biotech crops is sown; more than 90% of eight million farmers growing biotech crops are in the developing world
Widespread availablitiy of fast, affordable genetic synthesis
Apple's iPhone pioneers a new breed of Web-enabled wireless devices
1910
1920
1930
1940
1950
1960
1970
1980
1990
2000
2010
Frederick Banting, John Macleod, and Charles Best use insulin to transform diabetes from a killer
sease to a manageable condition
John Logie Baird gives the first demonstration of true television
Discovery of penicillium mold by Alexander Fleming; identification and isolation of its
active ingredient by Howard Florey and Andrew Moyer leads to the first commercial antibiotic
Transistor invented at Bell Telephone Laboratories
Mathematical theory of communications established by Claude Shannon, providing the basic theory for all modern digital communications
A structure for DNA—the double helix—introduced by James Watson and Francis Crick
TAT-1, the first transatlantic submarine telephone cable, goes into service
Computer mouse invented by Douglas Engelbart
Integrated circuit, which puts an entire electronic circuit on a tiny silicon chip, developed by Jack Kilby and Robert Noyce
Successful gene splicing from one organism to another ushers in the modern biotech era
Apple launches the Macintosh
First biotechnology drug released for use
First transgenic plants introduced experimentally
Mass-market launch of the compact disc (CD)
Concept of the World Wide Web developed at CERN
Gigahertz (GHz) micro-processor chips introduced
Celera Genomics and the U.S.-led Human Genome Project announce a working draft of the human genome
First plant genome sequenced—*Arabidopsis thaliana* (mouse-ear cress)
Number of mobile phones in use exceeds half of the world's total popualtion

Fuller Projection
To minimize distortion and broken landmasses, architect Buckminster Fuller made the globe into a polyhedron with 20 triangular faces, then unfolded it.

Source: International Telecommunication Union

Source: TeleGeography Research, www.telegeography.com

Internet

THE "COOPERATIVE ANARCHY" of the global Internet, a vast collection of interconnected computer networks communicating through specific protocols (information exchange rules), defies easy characterization or measurement of its behavior. Still, a lack of understanding has not stalled development of technologies that enable and support Internet growth.

Old behavior models for telephone networks no longer apply to packet delivery (data sent over a network) and to application support over multiple links, routers, and Internet Service Providers (ISPs). The sheer volume of traffic and the high capacity of electronic pathways have made Internet monitoring and analysis a more challenging endeavor. Users and providers both benefit from measurements that detect and isolate problems, but watching every link is not practical or particularly effective.

Each ISP monitors its own infrastructure and quality of service; however, business and policy concerns often keep ISPs from sharing such information. Common sense supports creation of a measurement infrastructure that would yield maximal Internet coverage for a reasonable price. But dynamically changing network configurations, as well as complex business and geopolitical concerns, make it difficult to acquire a worldwide view of the Internet.

A Brief Overview

1960s: ARPANET, a system designed to promote the sharing of supercomputers by researchers in the United States, is commissioned by the Department of Defense.

1970s: People begin to use ARPANET to collaborate on research projects and discuss common interests. In 1974, a commercial version goes online for the first time.

1980s: Corporations begin to use the Internet for e-mail. As the Internet grows in importance, viruses start to create concerns about online privacy and security. New terms such as "hacker" come into use.

1990s: After the introduction of browsers for navigating the World Wide Web, Internet use expands rapidly (see graph below). By the late 1990s, 200 million people are connected, with online consumer spending totaling in the tens of billions of dollars. During this time, Internet-related companies attract enormous amounts of money from investors.

EARLY 2000s: Internet stock values take a deep plunge following the "dotcom" crash of April 2000. But rapid Internet growth continues, with more than 100 million new users each year. Satellite communications technology allows people to easily access the Internet with handheld devices.

MID- TO LATE 2000s: The trend in rapid Internet growth continues and the number of worldwide users surpasses one billion. Significant growth is seen in the Middle East, Africa, Latin America, and the Caribbean. New uses of the Internet such as peer-to-peer file sharing, Internet telephony, Video-on-Demand, and social networking come into use.

Mapping the Spread of a Computer Virus

The graphics below detail the spread of the Nyxem e-mail virus during early 2006. This virus operates in much the same way other viruses do, running as an e-mail attachment that attempts to disable antivirus software and harvest e-mail addresses to automatically spread itself. However, the Nyxem virus stands out because it exhibits the rare behavior of reporting its progress to a single Web site, thus allowing researchers to undertake a detailed analysis of its activity. These images, generated with a geographic visualization tool called Cuttlefish, highlight the correlation between human activity at certain times of the day (for example, booting computers and reading e-mail), the spread of the virus, and the corresponding geographical locations of the infected computers.

The image at upper left includes a key that maps colors to the number of infected hosts. Circles of varying diameter and color depict the number of infected hosts in each region. At top right is a histogram showing the number of infected hosts over the roughly two-week period of analysis.

Newly Infected Nyxem Hosts
(per location, in thousands)

329–1,399 · 77–328 · 18–76 · 5–17 · 2–4 · 1

Circle diameter represents a logarithmic scale of the number of hosts affected per location at a given time.

**Coordinated Universal Time (UTC) is the international time standard. It is the current term for what was commonly referred to as Greenwich Meridian Time (GMT). Zero (0) hours UTC is midnight in Greenwich, England, which lies on the zero longitudinal meridian. Universal Time is based on a 24-hour clock; therefore, afternoon hours such as 5 pm UTC are expressed as 17:00 UTC (seventeen hours, zero minutes).*

Newly Infected Nyxem Hosts (Global)
(daily)

24-hour period represented in series of maps below

Number of hosts (thousands): 0, 2, 4, 6, 8, 9
Day: 0 1 2 3 4 5 6 7 8 9 10

00:00 UTC

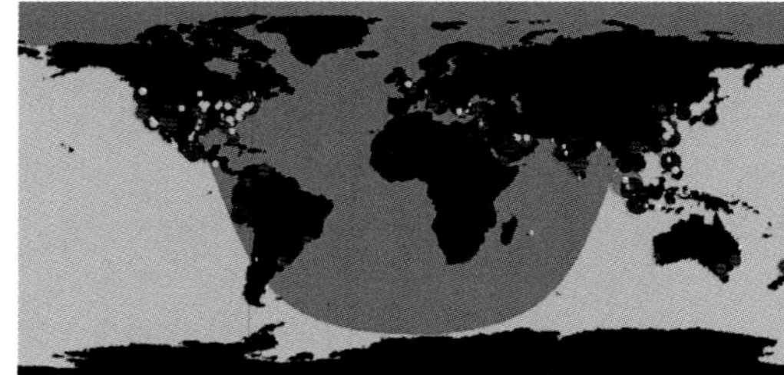

12:00 UTC

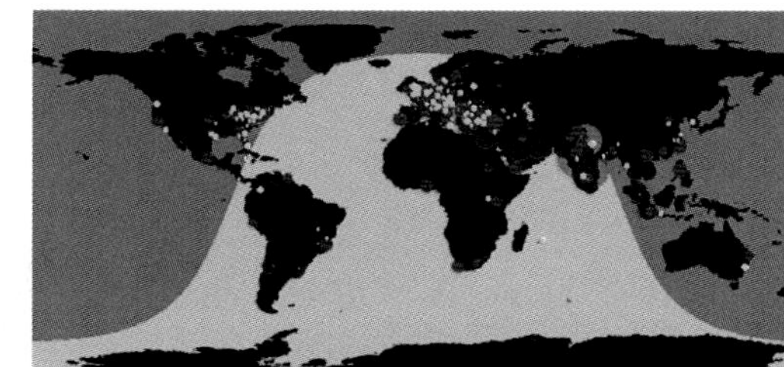

03:00 UTC

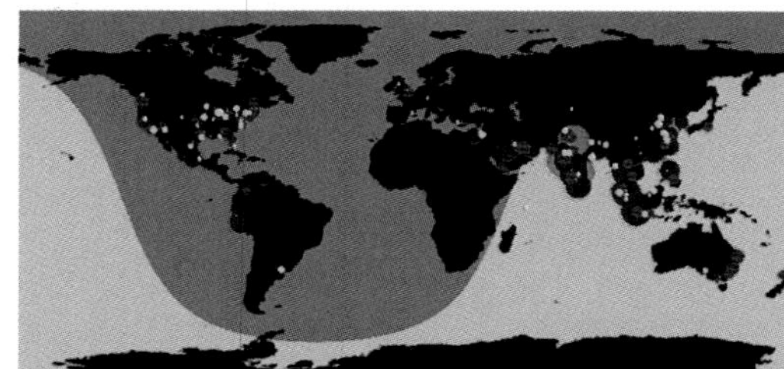

15:00 UTC

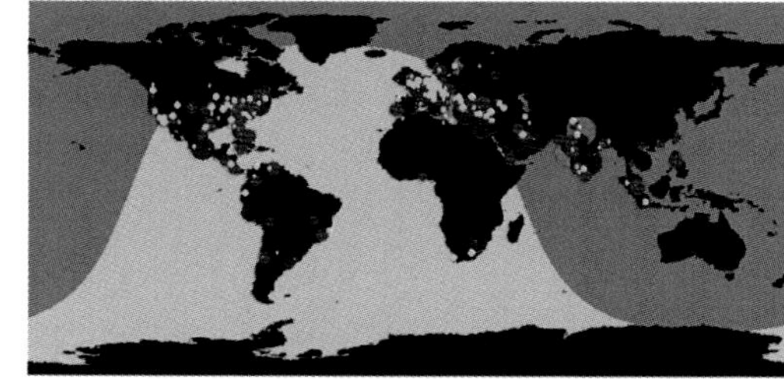

06:00 UTC

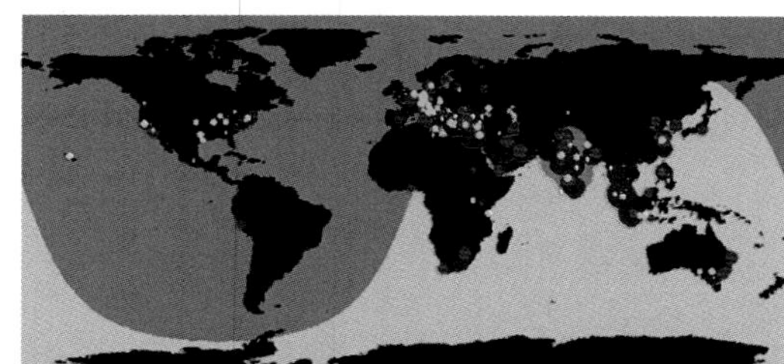

18:00 UTC

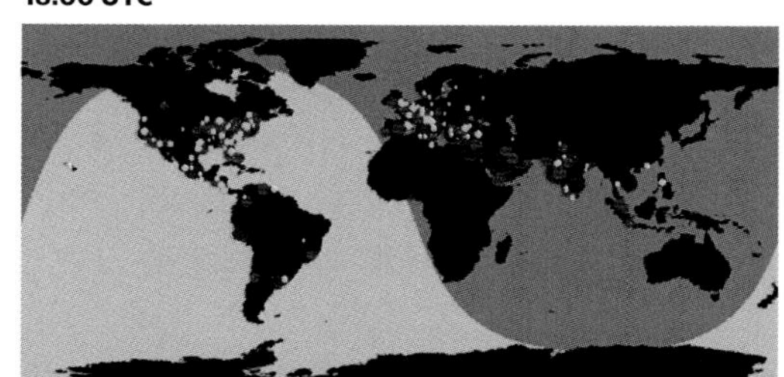

09:00 UTC

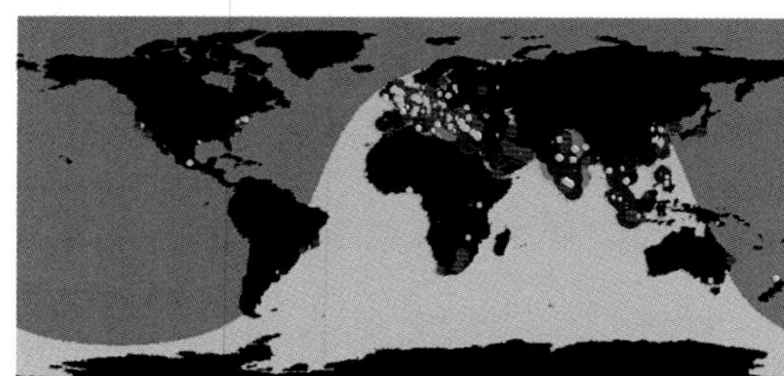

21:00 UTC

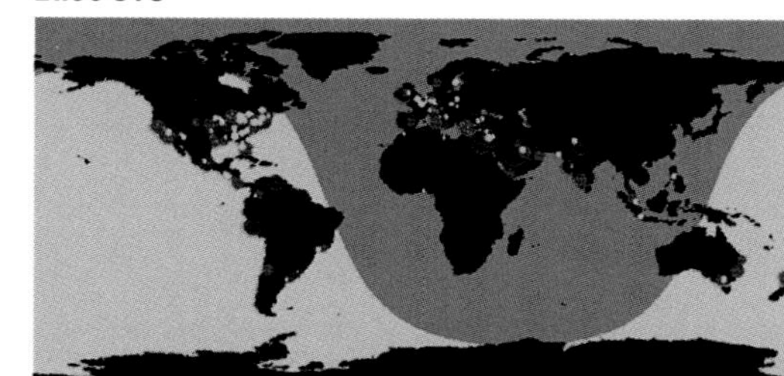

Estimated Internet Users Worldwide, 1996–2006

1996: **74 million**
1997: **117 million**
1998: **183 million**
1999: **277 million**
2000: **399 million**
2001: **502 million**

7473(Singapore Tel.)
3904(Hutchison)
4637(Reach)
4766(Korea Tel)
703(UUNET)
3786(DACOM)
20485(JSC)
2516(KDDI)
10026(Asia Netcom)
15412(Flag)
7714(TelstraClear)
3320(Deutsche Telekom)
8928(Interoute)
1299(TeliaNet)
702(MCI)
1273(CW)
786(JANET)
5459(London IX)
3356(Level 3)
701(UUNET)
174(Cogent)
3257(Tiscali)
1239(Sprint)
7018(AT&T)
3549(Global Crossing)
5511(France Tel)
209(Qwest)
6453(Teleglobe)
2914(NTT)
6461(Abovenet)
7132(SBC)
3491(Beyond)
4323(Time Warner)
2828(XO)
3561(Savvis)

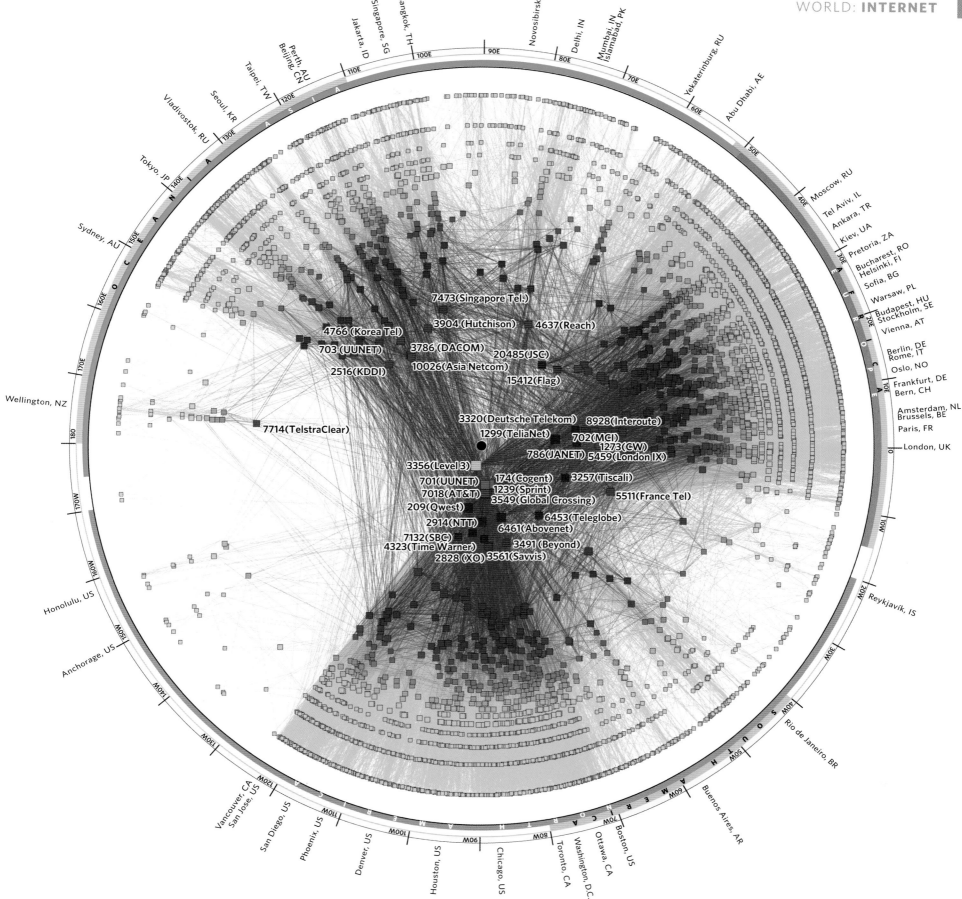

Global Internet Connectivity

The above graph is a macroscopic snapshot of the Internet core, based on data collected from January 1st to January 17th, 2008. Internet Service Providers (ISPs) are represented by squares, with better-connected ISPs found toward the center. The colors indicate "outdegree" (the number of "next-hop" systems that were observed accepting traffic from a link), from lowest (blue) to highest (yellow).

Both technical (cabling and router placement and management) and policy factors (business and cost models, geopolitical considerations) contribute to the ISP associations represented in this graph. In recent years, researchers have noticed a trend toward globalization of the core, which was more United States-centric a few years ago. Compared with similar visualizations from previous years, the number of connections between and within Asia and Europe have increased. Service provider Level 3 has also become increasingly prominent relative to its closest rival, UUnet.

Key to Internet Country Codes

Code	Country	Code	Country	Code	Country
AE	United Arab Emirates	ES	Spain	NZ	New Zealand
AQ	Antarctica	FI	Finland	PK	Pakistan
AR	Argentina	FR	France	PL	Poland
AT	Austria	HU	Hungary	RO	Romania
AU	Australia	ID	Indonesia	RU	Russia
BD	Bangladesh	IL	Israel	SA	Saudi Arabia
BE	Belgium	IN	India	SE	Sweden
BG	Bulgaria	IS	Iceland	SG	Singapore
BR	Brazil	IT	Italy	TH	Thailand
CA	Canada	JP	Japan	TR	Turkey
CH	Switzerland	KR	South Korea	TW	Taiwan, China
CN	China	MX	Mexico	UA	Ukraine
DE	Germany	NG	Nigeria	UK	United Kingdom
DK	Denmark	NL	Netherlands	US	United States
EG	Egypt	NO	Norway	ZA	South Africa

Worldwide Distribution of Internet Resources

The worldwide distribution of Internet resources—ISPs, Autonomous System (AS) routers, address space—is highly non-uniform and is unrelated to a region's size or population. For this graph, Internet addresses of routable paths announced on March 21, 2006, were mapped to physical locations and compared with public demographic data.

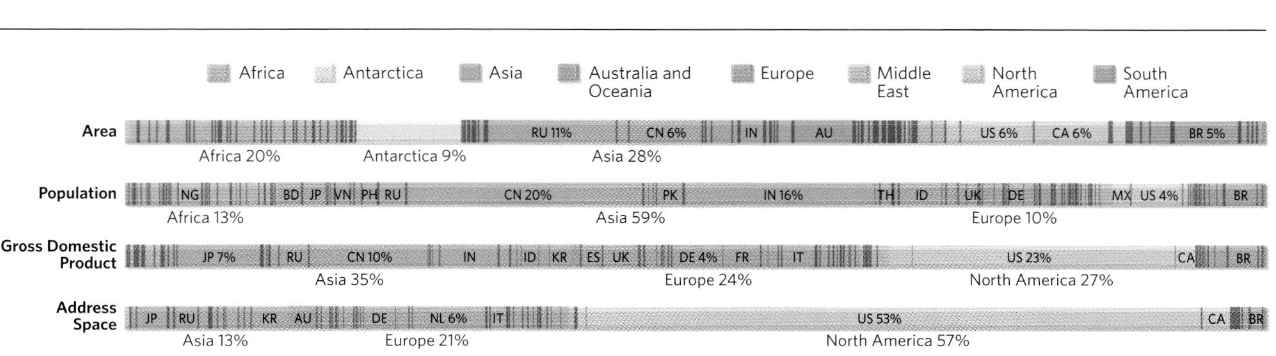
Africa
Antarctica
Asia
Australia and Oceania
Europe
Middle East
North America
South America
Area
Africa 20%
Antarctica 9%
Asia 28%
RU 11%
CN 6%
US 6%
CA 6%
BR 5%
Population
Africa 13%
Asia 59%
Europe 10%
CN 20%
IN 16%
US 4%
Gross Domestic Product
Asia 35%
Europe 24%
North America 27%
JP 7%
CN 10%
DE 4%
US 23%
Address Space
Asia 13%
Europe 21%
North America 57%
NL 6%
US 53%

2002: **619 million**
2003: **724 million**
2004: **870 million**
2005: **1 billion**
2006: **1.1 billion**

Environmental Stresses

MOST ENVIRONMENTAL DAMAGE is due to human activity. Some harmful actions are inadvertent—the release, for example, of chlorofluorocarbons (CFCs), once thought to be inert gases, into the atmosphere. Others are deliberate and include such acts as the disposal of sewage into rivers.

Among the root causes of human-induced damage are excessive consumption (mainly in industrialized countries) and rapid population growth (primarily in the developing countries). So, even though scientists may develop products and technologies that have no adverse effects on the environment, their efforts will be muted if both population and consumption continue to increase worldwide.

Socioeconomic and environmental indicators can reveal much about long-term trends; unfortunately, such data are not collected routinely in many countries. In addition, many are difficult to portray visually. With respect to stresses from urban areas, suitable indicators would include electricity consumption, numbers of automobiles, and rates of land conversion from rural to urban. The rapid conversion of countryside to built-up areas during the last 25 to 50 years is a strong indicator that change is occurring at an ever quickening pace. Many types of environmental stress are interrelated and may have far-reaching consequences. Global warming, for one, will likely increase water scarcity, desertification, deforestation, and coastal flooding (due to rising sea level)—all of which can have a significant impact on human populations.

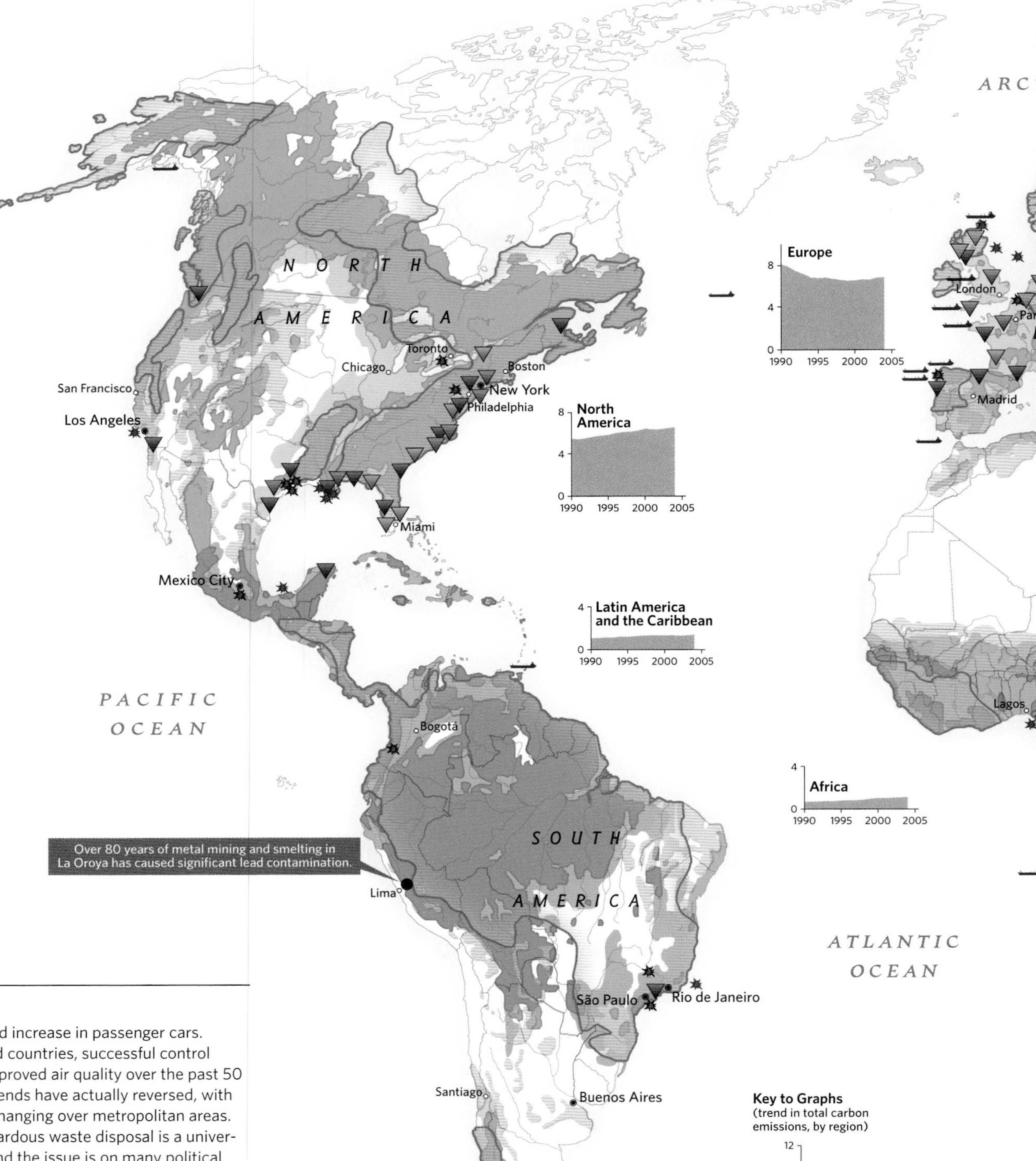
ARCTI
NORTH AMERICA
SOUTH AMERICA
PACIFIC OCEAN
ATLANTIC OCEAN
San Francisco
Los Angeles
Chicago
Toronto
Boston
New York
Philadelphia
Miami
Mexico City
Bogotá
Lima
São Paulo
Rio de Janeiro
Santiago
Buenos Aires
London
Paris
Madrid
Lagos
Over 80 years of metal mining and smelting in La Oroya has caused significant lead contamination.
Europe
North America
Latin America and the Caribbean
Africa
1990 1995 2000 2005
Key to Graphs
(trend in total carbon emissions, by region)
Metric tons of CO2 (in trillions)
Year
Regions as defined by the UNFCCC (UN Framework Convention on Climate Change)

Pollution

Examples of water and soil pollution include the contamination of groundwater, salinization of irrigated lands in semiarid regions, and the so-called chemical time bomb issue, where accumulated toxins are suddenly mobilized following a change in external conditions. Oceans and estuaries are also increasingly polluted. A growing problem is the creation of "dead zones" (areas of oxygen depletion), mostly due to agricultural runoff and municipal effluents. Addressing the problem requires prevention or reduction at the source; safely disposing of and cleaning up pollution should be strategies of last resort. The modernization of industrial plants, additional staff training, a better understanding of the problems, effective policies, and greater public support are needed.

Urban air quality remains a serious problem, particularly in developing countries. One of the main reasons is the rapid increase in passenger cars. In some developed countries, successful control measures have improved air quality over the past 50 years; in others, trends have actually reversed, with brown haze often hanging over metropolitan areas.

Solid and hazardous waste disposal is a universal urban strain, and the issue is on many political agendas. In the world's poorest countries, "garbage pickers" (usually women and children) are symbols of abject poverty. In North America, toxic wastes are frequently transported long distances; this introduces the risk of ocean, highway, and rail accidents, causing serious local contamination.

Pollution also often occurs as a result of armed conflict. Lebanon, for example, suffered extensive environmental damage after its oil depots were hit by Israeli bombers in 2006.

Depletion of the Ozone Layer

The ozone layer in the stratosphere has long shielded the biosphere from harmful solar ultraviolet radiation. Since the 1970s, however, the layer has been thinning over Antarctica—and more recently elsewhere. If the process continues, there will be significant effects on human health, including more cases of skin cancer and eye cataracts, and on biological systems. Fortunately, scientific understanding of the phenomenon came rather quickly.

Beginning in the 1950s, increasing amounts of CFCs (and other ozone-depleting substances) were released into the atmosphere. CFCs are chemically inert in the lower atmosphere but decompose in the stratosphere, subsequently destroying ozone. This understanding provided the basis for successful United Nations actions (Vienna Convention, 1985; Montréal Protocol, 1987) to phase out these gases.

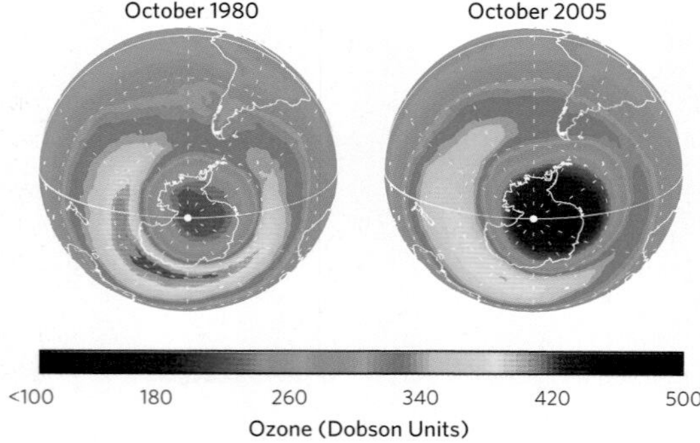
October 1980
October 2005
<100
180
260
340
420
500>
Ozone (Dobson Units)

Deforestation

Widespread deforestation in the wet tropics is largely the result of short-term and unsustainable uses. In Mexico, Brazil, and Peru, only 30, 42, and 45 percent (respectively) of the total land area still has a closed forest cover. International agencies such as FAO, UNEP, UNESCO, WWF/IUCN, and others are working to improve the situation through education, restoration, and land protection. Venezuela enjoys a very high level of forest protection (63 percent); by comparison, Russia protects just 2 percent.

Forest loss has contributed to the atmospheric buildup of carbon dioxide (a greenhouse gas; see sidebar opposite), changes in rainfall patterns (in Brazil at least), soil erosion, and soil nutrient losses. Deforestation in the wet tropics, where more than half of the world's species and millions of forest people live, is the main cause of biodiversity loss. In contrast, forest cover in temperate zones has increased slightly in the last 50 years because of the adoption of conservation practices and because forests have replaced some abandoned farmlands.

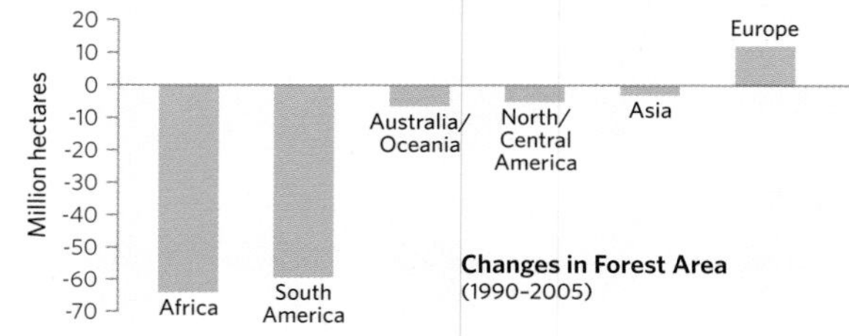
20
10
0
-10
-20
-30
-40
-50
-60
-70
Million hectares
Africa
South America
Australia/ Oceania
North/ Central America
Asia
Europe
Changes in Forest Area (1990-2005)

Land Degradation and Desertification

Deserts exist where rainfall is too little and too erratic to support life except in a few favored localities. Even in these "oases," occasional sandstorms may inhibit agricultural activity. In semiarid zones, lands can easily become degraded or desert-like if they are overused or subject to long or frequent drought.

Often, an extended drought over a wide area can trigger desertification if the land has already been degraded by human actions. Causes of degradation include overgrazing, deforestation, overcultivation, overconsumption of groundwater, and the salinization/waterlogging of irrigated lands. An emerging issue is the effect of climate warming on desertification: Warming will probably lead to increasing drought in more parts of the world.

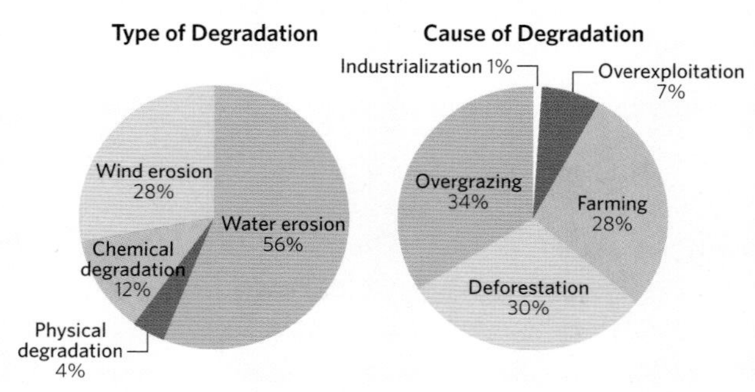
Type of Degradation
Wind erosion 28%
Water erosion 56%
Chemical degradation 12%
Physical degradation 4%
Cause of Degradation
Industrialization 1%
Overexploitation 7%
Overgrazing 34%
Farming 28%
Deforestation 30%

Mining and smelting operations have devastated the Norilsk area with particulates and heavy metal pollution.

The legacy of the Chernobyl nuclear disaster lingers, and has resulted in thousands of cancer deaths.

Dzerzhinsk: A major site for Cold War era manufacturing, industrial chemicals have polluted local water supplies; area death rates are above average.

Dated technologies, a lack of pollution controls, and improper disposal of industrial waste have left Sumgayit contaminated.

Expanding and unregulated industry based on local coal and other resources has given Linfen the worst air quality in China.

Tianying: average lead content in the air and soil are up to 10 times higher than national standards.

Waste rock and untreated water from Sukinda mines impacts local water supplies. The air and soils are also heavily affected.

More than 50 industrial estates discharge heavy metals, pesticides, and chemical waste in Vapi. Mercury in the groundwater is 96 times higher than WHO standards.

Unregulated lead mining and smelting operations in Kabwe, Zambia, have resulted in lead dust covering large areas; children's blood levels are up to ten times the recommended maximum.

ASIA
PACIFIC OCEAN
INDIAN OCEAN
AUSTRALIA
Moscow
Istanbul
Baghdad
Tehran
Cairo
Riyadh
Tashkent
Lahore
Delhi
Karachi
Ahmadabad
Mumbai (Bombay)
Hyderabad
Bangalore
Chennai (Madras)
Kolkata (Calcutta)
Dhaka
Beijing
Tianjin
Seoul
Tokyo
Osaka
Shanghai
Wuhan
Guangzhou
Hong Kong
Manila
Bangkok
Ho Chi Minh City
Jakarta

Asia and the Pacific (1990, 1995, 2000, 2005; 0, 4, 8, 12)

West Asia (1990, 1995, 2000, 2005; 0, 4)

Jet traffic in Newark, New Jersey

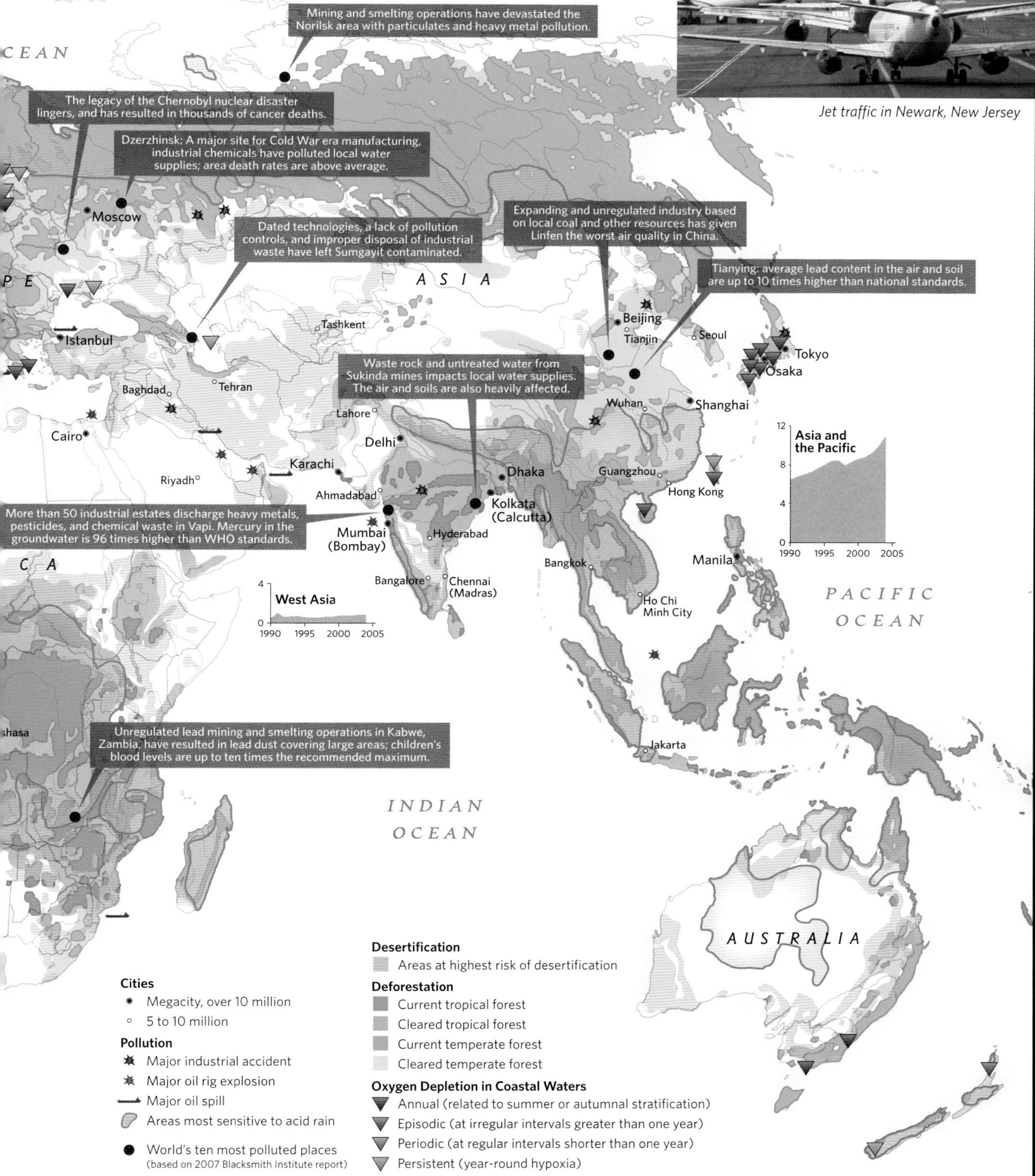

Cities
- Megacity, over 10 million
- 5 to 10 million

Pollution
- Major industrial accident
- Major oil rig explosion
- Major oil spill
- Areas most sensitive to acid rain
- World's ten most polluted places (based on 2007 Blacksmith Institute report)

Desertification
- Areas at highest risk of desertification

Deforestation
- Current tropical forest
- Cleared tropical forest
- Current temperate forest
- Cleared temperate forest

Oxygen Depletion in Coastal Waters
- Annual (related to summer or autumnal stratification)
- Episodic (at irregular intervals greater than one year)
- Periodic (at regular intervals shorter than one year)
- Persistent (year-round hypoxia)

Overfishing is another significant stress on the planet's resources. For more information on global fisheries, see page 69.

Global Climate Change

(see also pages 46–47)

The world's climate is constantly changing—over decades, centuries, and millennia. Currently, several lines of reasoning support the idea that we are likely to live in a much warmer world before the end of this century. Atmospheric concentrations of carbon dioxide and other greenhouse gases are now well above historical levels, and emissions from human activities are the main drivers of change. Simulation models predict that these gases will result in a warming of the lower atmosphere (particularly in polar regions) but a cooling of the stratosphere. Experimental evidence supports these predictions.

Indeed, throughout the last decade the globally averaged annual surface temperature was higher than the hundred-year average. Model simulations of the impacts of this warming—and studies indicating significant reductions already occurring in polar permafrost and sea ice cover—are so alarming that most scientists and many policy people believe that immediate action must be taken to curb emissions and adapt to change.

PER CAPITA CO_2 (CARBON DIOXIDE) EMISSIONS, BY REGION

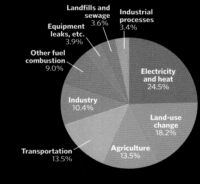

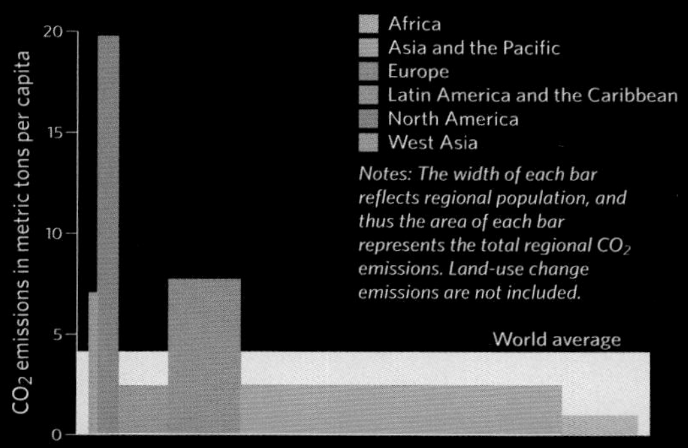

- Africa
- Asia and the Pacific
- Europe
- Latin America and the Caribbean
- North America
- West Asia

Notes: The width of each bar reflects regional population, and thus the area of each bar represents the total regional CO_2 emissions. Land-use change emissions are not included.

World average

CO_2 emissions in metric tons per capita (0, 5, 10, 15, 20)

CO_2 EMISSIONS, BY SOURCE The energy that propels modern industrial societies is the main human activity contributing to the climate change crisis. Burning fossil fuels—oil, coal, and natural gas—accounts for 80 percent of the extra CO_2 that now holds more heat in the atmosphere. Most of the rest comes from land-use changes, primarily in tropical forests. Tropical deforestation releases huge amounts of carbon into the atmosphere each year; when left standing, forests act as "carbon sinks," helping to absorb it. Large tracts of forest in Indonesia and the Amazon are particularly significant carbon sinks. The demand for permanent agriculture accounts for the bulk of forest loss.

Electricity and heat 24.5%
Land-use change 18.2%
Agriculture 13.5%
Transportation 13.5%
Industry 10.4%
Other fuel combustion 9.0%
Equipment leaks, etc. 3.9%
Landfills and sewage 3.6%
Industrial processes 3.4%

Water Scarcity

Shortages of drinking water are increasing in many parts of the world, and the United Nations' Global Environment Outlook (GEO-4) predicts that by 2025, if present trends continue, 1.8 billion people will be living in countries or regions with absolute water scarcity and that two-thirds of the world population could be subject to water stress.

Water is a pillar of human development and economic growth. It is essential for health, hygiene, agriculture, power generation, industry, and transportation, as well as for maintaining healthy freshwater habitats. With increasing pressures from population growth, industrialization, higher standards of living, and climate change, the situation can only worsen. Water scarcity will continue to be a major obstacle to economic development in many of the world's poorest regions, from Asia through Central and South America and across most of Africa (see map below).

Some countries are pumping groundwater more rapidly than it can be replaced, an activity that will lead to even greater water shortages down the road. In river basins where water is shared among several jurisdictions, political tensions are likely to increase. This is particularly so in the Middle East, North Africa, and East Africa, where the availability of fresh water is less than 1,300 cubic yards (1,000 cubic meters) per person per year; water-rich countries such as Iceland, New Zealand, and Canada enjoy more than a hundred times as much.

Irrigation can be a particularly wasteful use of water, with up to 70 percent of the water being lost through leaky pipes before arriving at its destination. In many of the world's cities, aging water distribution systems are not faring much better, with losses from leakages exceeding 40 percent in cities across North America and Europe.

Many individuals and organizations believe that water scarcity is the major environmental issue of the 21st century. The solutions, they say, lie in better management of the resource.

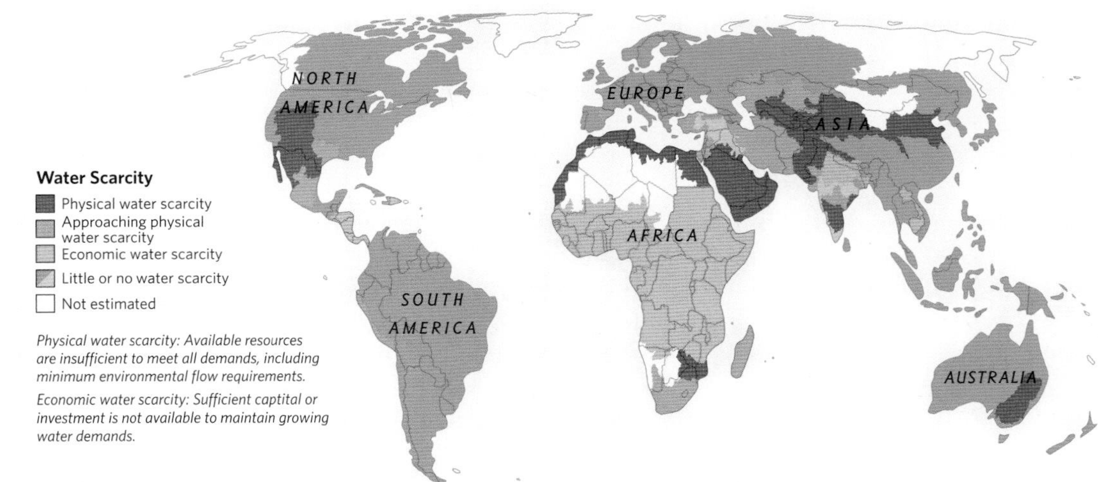
NORTH AMERICA
EUROPE
ASIA
AFRICA
SOUTH AMERICA
AUSTRALIA
Water Scarcity
Physical water scarcity
Approaching physical water scarcity
Economic water scarcity
Little or no water scarcity
Not estimated
Physical water scarcity: Available resources are insufficient to meet all demands, including minimum environmental flow requirements.
Economic water scarcity: Sufficient captital or investment is not available to maintain growing water demands.

Irrigation in a barren desert, Wadi Rum, Jordan

Wildlands

WILDLANDS ARE THOSE AREAS on Earth that bear the least evidence of human influence: the relatively unaltered tracts like North America's boreal forests, central Asia's steppes, and Africa's deserts. As human populations expand, so do their needs, and thus their demands upon the environment, further reducing the last of the wildlands.

Landscapes of arable soil have disappeared rapidly, having been converted to agricultural purposes to feed burgeoning populations. Between 1950 and 1990, close to 70 percent of global temperate grasslands, savannas, and shrublands were paved or plowed. Other ecosystems disappeared at similar rates. Around 60 percent of Mediterranean forests, woodlands, and scrublands; approximately 50 percent of tropical and subtropical dry broadleaf forests; and more than 40 percent of flooded grasslands and savannas and tropical and subtropical grasslands, savannas, and shrublands were lost. Landscapes that were inaccessible or economically unfeasible to exploit—such as tundras, deserts, and far northern boreal forests—fared better because of the high cost and low incentive of development.

Aside from direct conversion, the wildlands of the planet face a number of other threats, including invasive species, incompatible land management practices, pollution, alterations to natural hydrology, suppression of natural fire cycles, and other human interferences. The disappearance and degradation of these ecosystems directly impacts the species that rely upon them. Between 1970 and 2003, a nonrandom sample of 1,300 vertebrates showed an overall decline of 30 percent. Tropical species suffered the most severe declines, averaging 55 percent.

While conservation organizations seek to preserve the world's remaining wildlands for their own sake and for the sake of their natural inhabitants, the lands are also essential to balancing human needs with the biosphere's ability to sustainably produce resources.

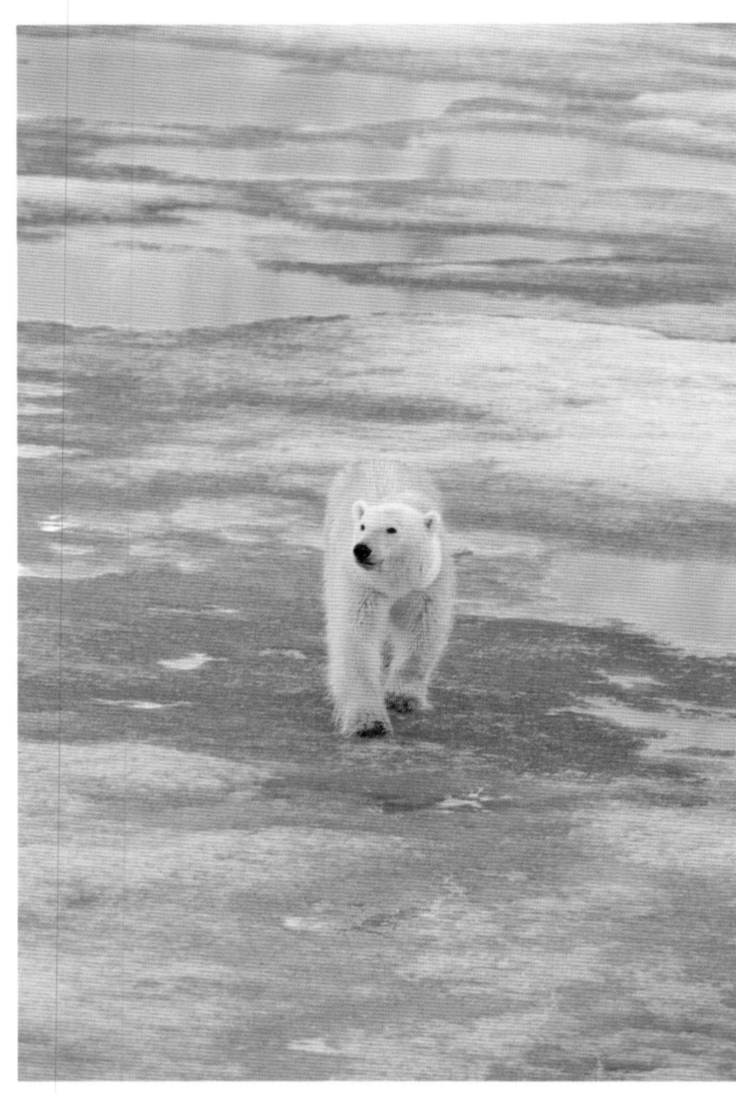

Polar Bear on Pack Ice, Svalbard, Norway

A polar bear crosses pack ice on the Svalbard archipelago in the Arctic Ocean. In 2002, Norway passed the Svalbard Environmental Protection Act to safeguard the archipelago's pristine wilderness areas, landscape elements, flora, and fauna. Access to cultural heritage areas received protection as well. This was the first time that an area's total environmental legislation was bundled in a single act, breaking ground for simpler and more effective implementation and monitoring. Svalbard is one of Europe's last remaining wilderness areas.

Bull Moose Looking at Beaver Ponds, Denali National Park, Alaska, U.S.

Denali National Park and Preserve, with its six million acres of wilderness, is larger than the state of Massachusetts. Made up of boreal forest and subarctic tundra, the park and preserve contains just a single, 91-mile-long road—along which visitors are required to travel by bus. The area is home to 39 mammal species, including the "big five" many visitors aim to see: moose, caribou, Dall sheep, wolf, and grizzly bear.

Impala, Mana Pools National Park, Zimbabwe

Above, an impala stands of the edge of Lake Chivero, which is covered in water hyacinth. The 848 square miles (2,196 square kilometers) of Mana Pools make up one of the least developed national parks in southern Africa. Situated on the shores of the Zambezi River, it is home to a striking array of wildlife, including elephants, lions, impalas, zebras, varied aquatic species, and nearly 400 different species of birds.

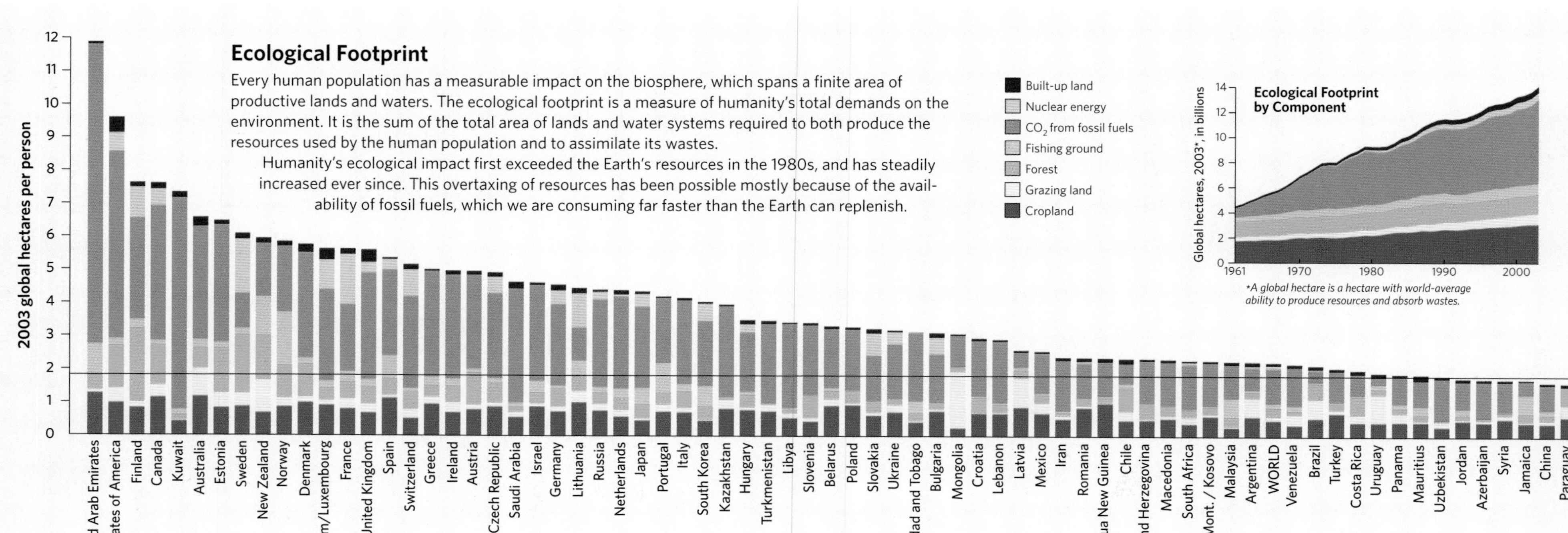

2003 global hectares per person
0
1
2
3
4
5
6
7
8
9
10
11
12
Built-up land
Nuclear energy
CO_2 from fossil fuels
Fishing ground
Forest
Grazing land
Cropland
Ecological Footprint by Component
Global hectares, 2003*, in billions
0
2
4
6
8
10
12
14
1961
1970
1980
1990
2000
*A global hectare is a hectare with world-average ability to produce resources and absorb wastes.
United Arab Emirates
United States of America
Finland
Canada
Kuwait
Australia
Estonia
Sweden
New Zealand
Norway
Denmark
Belgium/Luxembourg
France
United Kingdom
Spain
Switzerland
Greece
Ireland
Austria
Czech Republic
Saudi Arabia
Israel
Germany
Lithuania
Russia
Netherlands
Japan
Portugal
Italy
South Korea
Kazakhstan
Hungary
Turkmenistan
Libya
Slovenia
Belarus
Poland
Slovakia
Ukraine
Trinidad and Tobago
Bulgaria
Mongolia
Croatia
Lebanon
Latvia
Mexico
Iran
Romania
Papua New Guinea
Chile
Bosnia and Herzegovina
Macedonia
South Africa
Serbia / Mont. / Kosovo
Malaysia
Argentina
WORLD
Venezuela
Brazil
Turkey
Costa Rica
Uruguay
Panama
Mauritius
Uzbekistan
Jordan
Azerbaijan
Syria
Jamaica
China
Paraguay
Dominican Republic

Ecological Footprint

Every human population has a measurable impact on the biosphere, which spans a finite area of productive lands and waters. The ecological footprint is a measure of humanity's total demands on the environment. It is the sum of the total area of lands and water systems required to both produce the resources used by the human population and to assimilate its wastes.

Humanity's ecological impact first exceeded the Earth's resources in the 1980s, and has steadily increased ever since. This overtaxing of resources has been possible mostly because of the availability of fossil fuels, which we are consuming far faster than the Earth can replenish.

Human Footprint

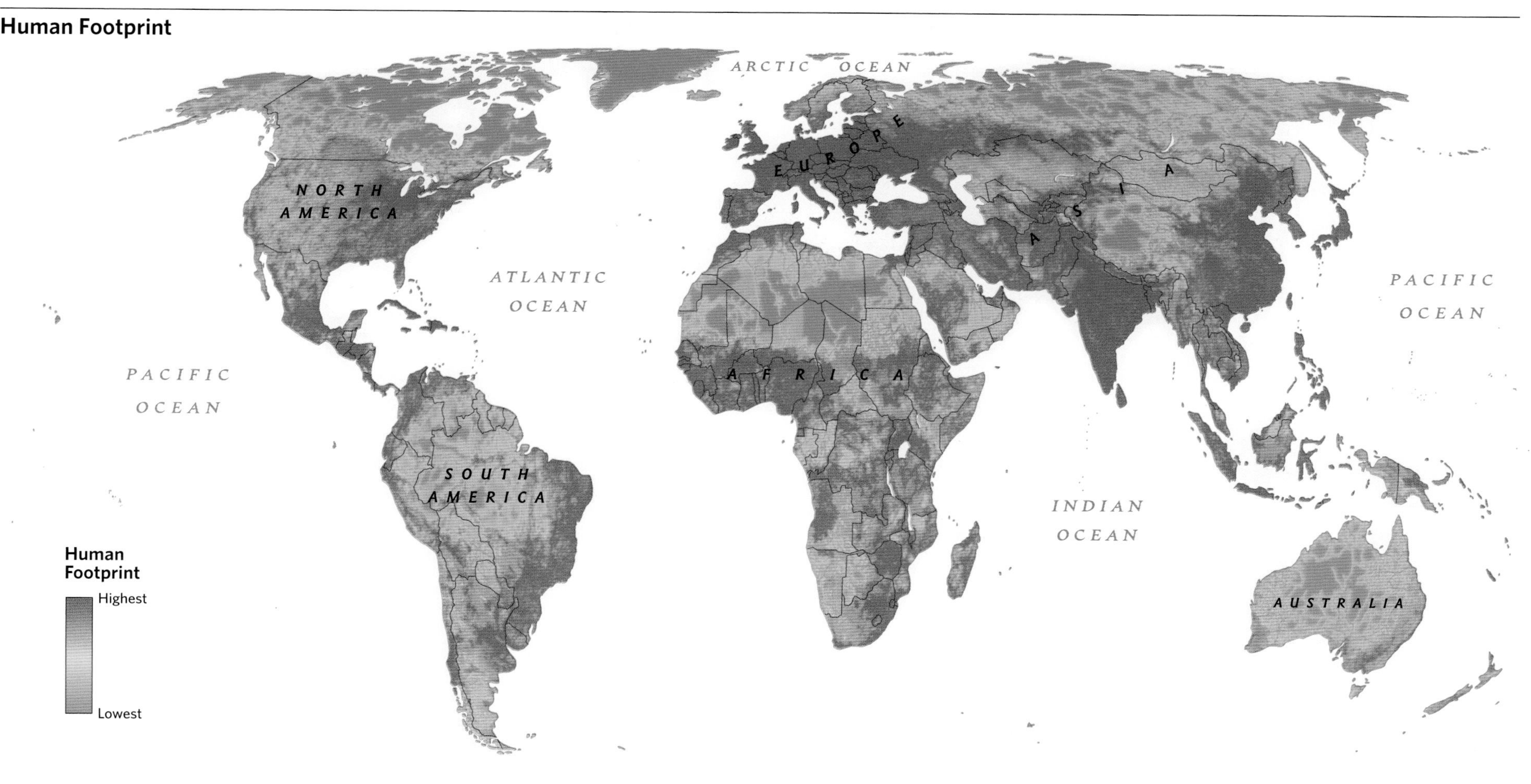
ARCTIC OCEAN
NORTH AMERICA
EUROPE
ASIA
ATLANTIC OCEAN
PACIFIC OCEAN
PACIFIC OCEAN
AFRICA
SOUTH AMERICA
INDIAN OCEAN
AUSTRALIA
Human Footprint
Highest
Lowest

Last of the Wild

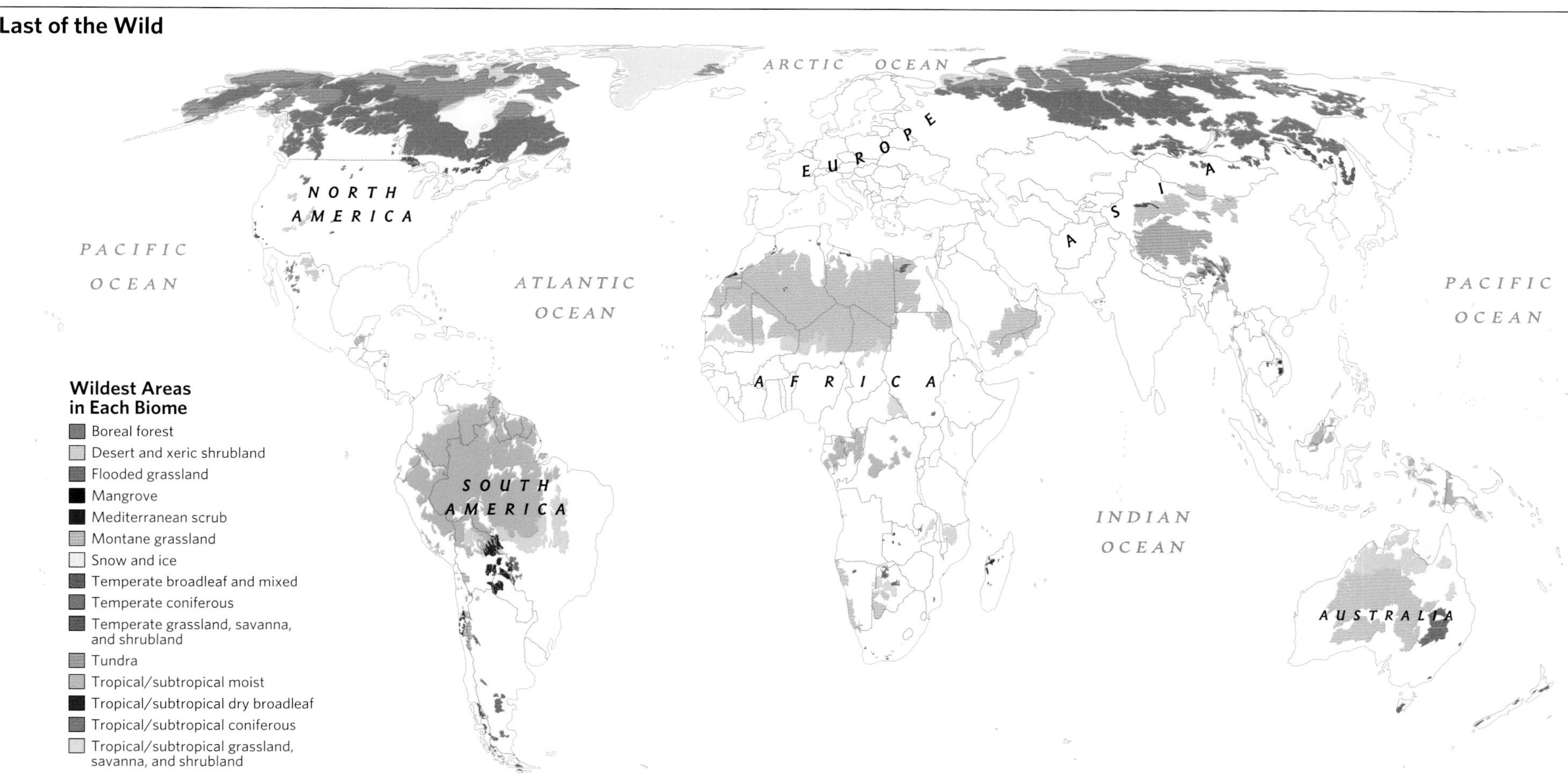
ARCTIC OCEAN
NORTH AMERICA
EUROPE
ASIA
PACIFIC OCEAN
ATLANTIC OCEAN
PACIFIC OCEAN
AFRICA
SOUTH AMERICA
INDIAN OCEAN
AUSTRALIA
Wildest Areas in Each Biome
Boreal forest
Desert and xeric shrubland
Flooded grassland
Mangrove
Mediterranean scrub
Montane grassland
Snow and ice
Temperate broadleaf and mixed
Temperate coniferous
Temperate grassland, savanna, and shrubland
Tundra
Tropical/subtropical moist
Tropical/subtropical dry broadleaf
Tropical/subtropical coniferous
Tropical/subtropical grassland, savanna, and shrubland

▲
Human Footprint and the Last of the Wild

Created as a collaboration between the Wildlife Conservation Society and the Center for International Earth Science Information Network at Columbia University, these maps chart the maximum and minimum areas of human influence on the planet. The top map shows an estimate of the total human influence on the lands of the world. (Antarctica, the wildest and least human-influenced area on Earth, was not evaluated.)

Still, more than 80 percent of Earth's land area is directly affected by human population density. The map also includes areas that regularly produce enough light at night to be seen from space. Arable lands capable of sustaining rice, wheat, or maize (corn) production are similarly influenced at a rate of 98 percent.

The lower map shows the largest tracts of land in all of the planet's biomes that are the least influenced by humans by the same criteria used in determining an area's "human footprint." Biomes are large-scale regional ecosystems. There are 568 of these "Last of the Wild" areas, though they vary widely in size, biodiversity, and ecological productivity. The areas were selected as the ten largest, 10 percent wildest lands in each biome. These are places where the full range of native inhabitants, ecosystems, and natural processes exist with minimum human interference.

These two maps were created as a starting point for global conservation efforts. While they provide information at a scale too broad for local environmental efforts, they do provide a rough portrait of the level of human influence on the natural world and an estimate of the remaining wild lands.

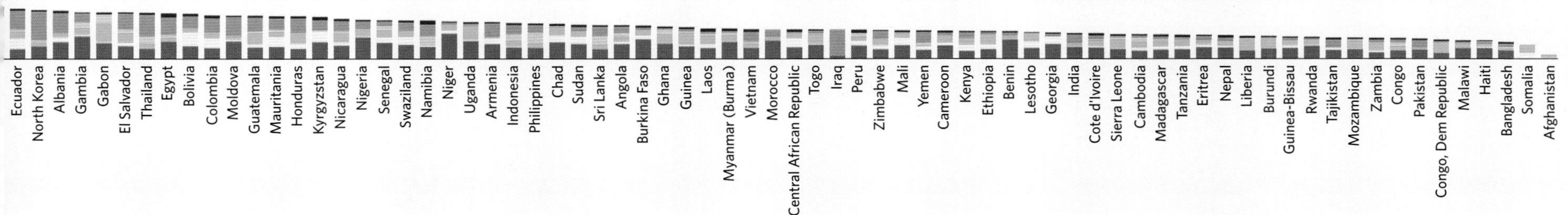
2003 world biocapacity per person: 1.8 global hectares, ignoring the needs of wild species
Ecuador
North Korea
Albania
Gambia
Gabon
El Salvador
Thailand
Egypt
Bolivia
Colombia
Moldova
Guatemala
Mauritania
Honduras
Kyrgyzstan
Nicaragua
Nigeria
Senegal
Swaziland
Namibia
Niger
Uganda
Armenia
Indonesia
Philippines
Chad
Sudan
Sri Lanka
Angola
Burkina Faso
Ghana
Guinea
Laos
Myanmar (Burma)
Vietnam
Morocco
Central African Republic
Togo
Iraq
Peru
Zimbabwe
Mali
Yemen
Cameroon
Kenya
Ethiopia
Benin
Lesotho
Georgia
India
Cote d'Ivoire
Sierra Leone
Cambodia
Madagascar
Tanzania
Eritrea
Nepal
Liberia
Burundi
Guinea-Bissau
Rwanda
Tajikistan
Mozambique
Zambia
Congo
Pakistan
Congo, Dem Republic
Malawi
Haiti
Bangladesh
Somalia
Afghanistan

Biodiversity

BIODIVERSITY REFERS TO THREE MEASURES of Earth's intricate web of life: the number of different species, the genetic diversity within a species, and the variety of ecosystems in which species live. Greatest in the wet tropics, biodiversity is important for many reasons, including helping to provide food and medicine, breathable air, drinkable water, livable climates, protection from pests and diseases, and ecosystem stability.

Humankind is only one species in a vast array of life-forms. It is, however, an especially influential and increasingly disruptive actor in the huge cast of characters on the stage of planet Earth. Estimates of the total number of plant and animal species range from ten million to a hundred million; of these, fewer than two million have been described. Yet a substantial number of those species may be gone before we even have a chance to understand their value.

For most of human history, people have often looked at plants and animals simply as resources for meeting their own basic needs. Scientists today count more than a quarter million plant species, of which just nine provide three-quarters of all our food; in that respect, biodiversity has been an unimaginable luxury. It is ironic that as humankind's power to destroy other species grows, so does our ingenuity in finding new and beneficial uses for them.

Sometimes the benefits of preserving a species may have nothing to do with food or medicine. Before a worldwide ban on exports of elephant ivory, the estimated value of such exports was 40 million dollars a year for all of Africa. Now, in Kenya alone, the viewing value of elephants by tourists is thought to be 25 million dollars a year.

Species Diversity

Among fauna and flora, insects make up the largest classification in terms of sheer number of species, with fungi ranked a distant second. At the other extreme, the categories with the lowest numbers—mammals, birds, and mollusks—also happen to be the classes with the greatest percentage of threatened species. This is not just a matter of proportion: These groups include the most at-risk species in terms of absolute numbers as well.

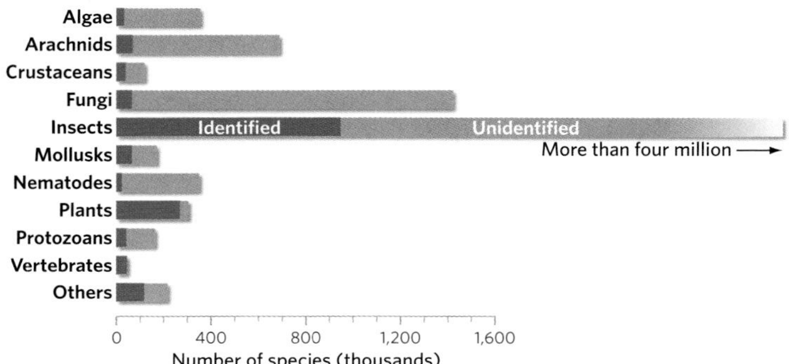
Algae
Arachnids
Crustaceans
Fungi
Insects
Identified
Unidentified
More than four million
Mollusks
Nematodes
Plants
Protozoans
Vertebrates
Others
0
400
800
1,200
1,600
Number of species (thousands)

Threatened Ecoregions

British ecologist Norman Myers defined the "biodiversity hotspot" concept in 1988 to help address the dilemma of identifying conservation priorities. To qualify as a hotspot, a region must meet two strict criteria: It must contain at least 1,500 species of vascular plants (more than 0.5 percent of the world's total) as endemics, and it has to have lost at least 70 percent of its original habitat.

Today there are 34 biodiversity hotspots, covering 15.7 percent of the Earth's land surface. In all, 86 percent of the habitat in these areas has already been destroyed, such that the intact remnants now cover only 2.3 percent of the Earth's land surface. Between them, the hotspots hold at least 150,000 plant species as endemics, 50 percent of the world's total. The total number of terrestrial vertebrates endemic to them is 11,980, representing 42 percent of all terrestrial vertebrate species.

While the world's 34 hotspots clearly hold astounding levels of species endemism, this is not sufficient to describe the extent to which they represent the history of life. A measurement of hotspot endemism at the higher taxonomic levels of genera and families also finds an extremely high concentration of biodiversity at these levels, even compared with what we would expect based on their levels of species endemism.

More than half of the planet's species are endemic to only 15.7 percent of its land area. If we consider only the extent of remaining habitat (2.3 percent), these numbers are even more remarkable. Biodiversity hotspots represent a conservation challenge. Unless we succeed in conserving this small fraction of the planet's land area, we will lose more than half of our natural heritage.

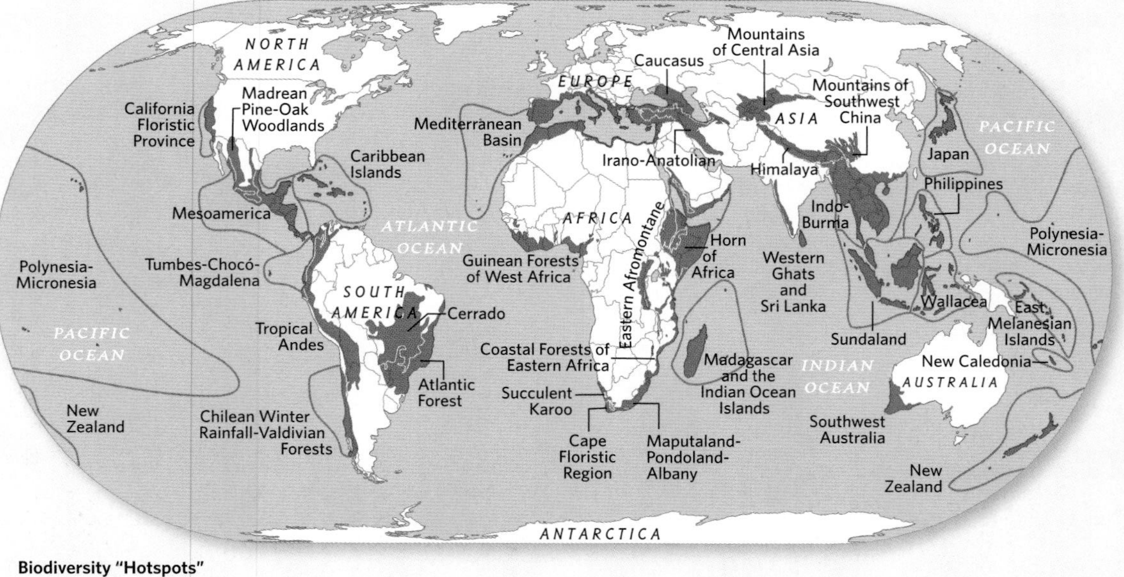
NORTH AMERICA
California Floristic Province
Madrean Pine-Oak Woodlands
Caribbean Islands
Mesoamerica
Polynesia-Micronesia
Tumbes-Chocó-Magdalena
PACIFIC OCEAN
ATLANTIC OCEAN
SOUTH AMERICA
Cerrado
Tropical Andes
Atlantic Forest
Chilean Winter Rainfall-Valdivian Forests
New Zealand
EUROPE
Mediterranean Basin
Caucasus
Mountains of Central Asia
Mountains of Southwest China
ASIA
Irano-Anatolian
Himalaya
AFRICA
Eastern Afromontane
Guinean Forests of West Africa
Horn of Africa
Coastal Forests of Eastern Africa
Succulent Karoo
Cape Floristic Region
Maputaland-Pondoland-Albany
Madagascar and the Indian Ocean Islands
INDIAN OCEAN
Western Ghats and Sri Lanka
Indo-Burma
Japan
Philippines
PACIFIC OCEAN
Sundaland
Wallacea
East Melanesian Islands
Polynesia-Micronesia
New Caledonia
AUSTRALIA
Southwest Australia
New Zealand
ANTARCTICA

Biodiversity "Hotspots"

Hotspot regions

ARCTIC OCEAN

TERRESTRIAL AND MARINE ECOREGIONS OF THE WORLD The many hundreds of terrestrial and coastal marine areas shown on this map represent ecoregions defined by the World Wildlife Fund (WWF) and the Nature Conservancy. Each ecoregion has unique species and communities, found nowhere else on Earth. For detailed information on each region, see the online maps at: worldwildlife.org/wildworld and worldwildlife.org/MEOW.

EUROPE

ASIA

PACIFIC OCEAN

AFRICA

INDIAN OCEAN

AUSTRALIA

ANTARCTICA

Note: For the Global 200 Ecoregions map (showing the 200 areas with exceptional levels of biodiversity), see pages 88–89.

Threatened Species, by Continent

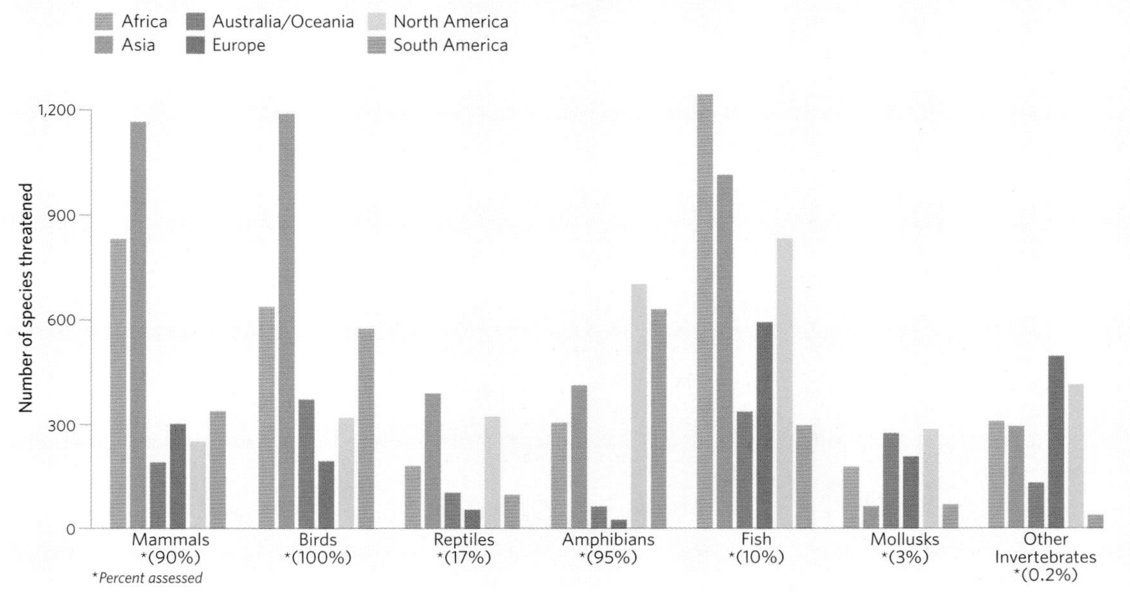
Africa
Asia
Australia/Oceania
Europe
North America
South America
Number of species threatened
1,200
900
600
300
0
Mammals *(90%)
Birds *(100%)
Reptiles *(17%)
Amphibians *(95%)
Fish *(10%)
Mollusks *(3%)
Other Invertebrates *(0.2%)
*Percent assessed

The red-knobbed hornbill (above) is endemic to the island of Sulawesi, in the Wallacea biodiversity hotspot region. Asia has the greatest number of threatened species, with birds accounting for the majority. Nearly 1,200 known bird species are threatened in Asia alone.

Global 200 Ecoregions

Limited funding compels the conservation community to be strategic and earmark the greatest amount of resources for the most outstanding and representative areas of biodiversity. World Wildlife Fund's Global 200 is a first attempt to identify a set of ecoregions whose conservation would achieve the goal of saving a broad diversity of the Earth's ecosystems. These ecoregions include those with exceptional levels of biodiversity, such as high species richness or endemism, or those with unusual ecological or evolutionary phenomena.

Tropical rain forests deservedly garner much conservation attention, as they may contain half of the world's species. However, a comprehensive strategy for conserving global biodiversity must strive to include the other 50 percent of species and habitats, such that all species and the distinctive ecosystems that support them are conserved. Habitats like tropical dry forests, tundra, polar seas, desert springs, and mangroves all harbor unique species, communities, adaptations, and phenomena.

To lose examples of these assemblages would represent an enormous loss of global biodiversity. For this reason, the Global 200 aims to represent all of the world's biodiversity by identifying outstanding ecoregions in all of the world's biomes and biogeographic realms. These represent the places where WWF is initially focusing its conservation efforts to develop biodiversity visions; ecoregion conservation is currently underway in many of these areas.

TERRESTRIAL

Tropical and Subtropical Moist Broadleaf Forests

AFROTROPICAL

1 Guinean Moist Forests—*Benin, Côte d'Ivoire, Ghana, Guinea, Liberia, Sierra Leone, Togo*

2 Congolian Coastal Forests—*Angola, Cameroon, Congo, Dem. Rep. of the Congo, Equatorial Guinea, Gabon, Nigeria, Sao Tome and Principe*

3 Cameroon Highlands Forests—*Cameroon, Equatorial Guinea, Nigeria*

4 Northeastern Congo Basin Moist Forests—*Central African Republic, Dem. Rep. of the Congo*

5 Central Congo Basin Moist Forests—*Dem. Rep. of the Congo*

6 Western Congo Basin Moist Forests Forests—*Cameroon, Central African Republic, Congo, Dem. Rep. of the Congo*

7 Albertine Rift Montane Forests—*Burundi, Dem. Rep. of the Congo, Rwanda, Tanzania, Uganda*

8 East African Coastal Forests—*Kenya, Somalia, Tanzania*

9 Eastern Arc Montane Forests—*Kenya, Tanzania*

10 Madagascar Forests and Shrublands—*Madagascar*

11 Seychelles and Mascarenes Moist Forests—*Mauritius, Réunion (France), Seychelles*

AUSTRALASIA

12 Sulawesi Moist Forests—*Indonesia*

13 Moluccas Moist Forests—*Indonesia*

14 Southern New Guinea Lowland Forests—*Indonesia, Papua New Guinea*

15 New Guinea Montane Forests—*Indonesia, Papua New Guinea*

16 Solomons-Vanuatu-Bismarck Moist Forests—*Papua New Guinea, Solomon Islands, Vanuatu*

17 Queensland Tropical Forests—*Australia*

18 New Caledonia Moist Forests—*New Caledonia (France)*

19 Lord Howe-Norfolk Islands Forests—*Australia*

INDO-MALAYAN

20 Southwestern Ghats Moist Forests—*India*

21 Sri Lankan Moist Forests—*Sri Lanka*

22 Northern Indochina Subtropical Moist Forests—*China, Laos, Myanmar, Thailand, Vietnam*

23 Southeast China-Hainan Moist Forests—*China, Vietnam*

24 Taiwan Montane Forests—*China*

25 Annamite Range Moist Forests—*Cambodia, Laos, Vietnam*

26 Sumatran Islands Lowland and Montane Forests—*Indonesia*

27 Philippines Moist Forests—*Philippines*

28 Palawan Moist Forests—*Philippines*

29 Kayah-Karen/Tenasserim Moist Forests—*Malaysia, Myanmar, Thailand*

30 Peninsular Malaysian Lowland and Mountain Forests—*Indonesia, Malaysia, Singapore, Thailand*

31 Borneo Lowland and Montane Forests—*Brunei, Indonesia, Malaysia*

32 Nansei Shoto Archipelago Forests—*Japan*

33 Eastern Deccan Plateau Moist Forests—*India*

34 Naga-Manipuri-Chin Hills Moist Forests—*Bangladesh, India, Myanmar*

35 Cardamom Mountains Moist Forests—*Cambodia, Thailand*

36 Western Java Mountain Forests—*Indonesia*

NEOTROPICAL

37 Greater Antillean Moist Forests—*Cuba, Dominican Republic, Haiti, Jamaica, Puerto Rico (United States)*

38 Talamancan and Isthmian Pacific Forests—*Costa Rica, Panama*

39 Chocó-Darién Moist Forests—*Colombia, Ecuador, Panama*

40 Northern Andean Montane Forests—*Colombia, Ecuador, Peru, Venezuela*

41 Coastal Venezuela Montane Forests—*Venezuela*

42 Guianan Moist Forests—*Brazil, French Guiana (France), Guyana, Suriname, Venezuela*

43 Napo Moist Forests—*Colombia, Ecuador, Peru*

44 Río Negro-Juruá Moist Forests—*Brazil, Colombia, Peru, Venezuela*

45 Guayanan Highlands Forests—*Brazil, Colombia, Guyana, Suriname, Venezuela*

46 Central Andean Yungas—*Argentina, Bolivia, Peru*

47 Southwestern Amazonian Moist Forests—*Bolivia, Brazil, Peru*

48 Atlantic Forests—*Argentina, Brazil, Paraguay*

OCEANIA

49 South Pacific Islands Forests—*American Samoa (United States), Cook Islands (New Zealand), Fiji Islands, French Polynesia (France), Niue (New Zealand), Samoa, Tonga, Wallis and Futuna Islands (France)*

50 Hawai'i Moist Forests—*Hawai'i (United States)*

Tropical and Subtropical Dry Broadleaf Forests

AFROTROPICAL

51 Madagascar Dry Forests—*Madagascar*

AUSTRALASIA

52 Nusu Tenggara Dry Forests—*Indonesia, Timor-Leste*

53 New Caledonia Dry Forests—*New Caledonia (France)*

INDO-MALAYAN

54 Indochina Dry Forests—*Cambodia, Laos, Thailand, Vietnam*

55 Chhota-Nagpur Dry Forests—*India*

NEOTROPICAL

56 Mexican Dry Forests—*Guatemala, Mexico*

57 Tumbesian-Andean Valleys Dry Forests—*Colombia, Ecuador, Peru*

58 Chiquitano Dry Forests—*Bolivia, Brazil*

59 Atlantic Dry Forests—*Brazil*

OCEANIA

60 Hawai'i's Dry Forests—*Hawai'i (United States)*

Tropical and Suptropical Coniferous Forests

NEARCTIC

61 Sierra Madre Oriental and Occidental Pine-Oak Forests—*Mexico, United States*

NEOTROPICAL

62 Greater Antillean Pine Forests—*Cuba, Dominican Republic, Haiti*

63 Mesoamerican Pine-Oak Forests—*El Salvador, Guatemala, Honduras, Mexico, Nicaragua*

Temperate Broadleaf and Mixed Forests

AUSTRALASIA

64 Eastern Australia Temperate Forests—*Australia*

65 Tasmanian Temperate Rain Forests—*Australia*

66 New Zealand Temperate Forests—*New Zealand*

INDO-MALAYAN

67 Eastern Himalayan Broadleaf and Conifer Forests—*Bhutan, China, India, Myanmar, Nepal*

68 Western Himalayan Temperate Forests—*Afghanistan, India, Nepal, Pakistan*

NEARCTIC

69 Appalachian and Mixed Mesophytic Forests—*United States*

PALEARCTIC

70 Southwest China Temperate Forests—*China*

71 Russian Far East Temperate Forests—*Russia*

Temperate Coniferous Forests

NEARCTIC

72 Pacific Temperate Rain Forests—*Canada, United States*

73 Klamath-Siskiyou Coniferous Forests—*United States*

74 Sierra Nevada Coniferous Forests—*United States*

75 Southeastern Coniferous and Broadleaf Forests—*United States*

NEOTROPICAL

76 Valdivian Temperate Rain Forests/Juan Fernandez Islands—*Argentina, Chile*

PALEARCTIC

77 European-Mediterranean Montane Mixed Forests—*Albania, Algeria, Andorra, Austria, Bosnia and Herzegovina, Bulgaria, Croatia, Czech Republic, France, Germany, Greece, Italy, Liechtenstein, Macedonia, Montenegro, Morocco, Poland, Romania, Russia, Slovakia, Slovenia*

78 Caucasus-Anatolian-Hyrcanian Temperate Forests—*Armenia, Azerbaijan, Bulgaria, Georgia, Iran, Russia, Turkey, Turkmenistan*

79 Altai-Sayan Montane Forests—*China, Kazakhstan, Mongolia, Russia*

80 Hengduan Shan Coniferous Forests—*China*

Boreal Forests/Taiga

NEARCTIC

81 Muskwa/Slave Lake Boreal Forests—*Canada*

82 Canadian Boreal Forests—*Canada*

PALEARCTIC

83 Ural Mountains Taiga—*Russia*

84 Eastern Siberian Taiga—*Russia*

85 Kamchatka Taiga and Grasslands—*Russia*

Tropical and Subtropical Grasslands, Savannas, and Shrublands

AFROTROPICAL

86 Horn of Africa Acacia Savannas—*Eritrea, Ethiopia, Kenya, Somalia, Sudan*

87 East African Acacia Savannas—*Ethiopia, Kenya, Sudan, Tanzania, Uganda*

88 Central and Eastern Miombo Woodlands—*Angola, Botswana, Burundi, Dem. Rep. of the Congo, Malawi, Mozambique, Namibia, Tanzania, Zambia, Zimbabwe*

89 Sudanian Savannas—*Cameroon, Central African Republic, Chad, Nigeria, Dem. Rep. of the Congo, Eritrea, Ethiopia, Kenya, Sudan, Uganda*

AUSTRALASIA

90 Northern Australia and Trans-Fly Savannas—*Australia, Indonesia, Papua New Guinea*

INDO-MALAYAN

91 Terai-Duar Savannas and Grasslands—*Bangladesh, Bhutan, India, Nepal*

NEOTROPICAL

92 Llanos Savannas—*Colombia, Venezuela*

93 Cerrado Woodlands and Savannas—*Bolivia, Brazil, Paraguay*

Temperate Grasslands, Savannas, and Shrublands

NEARCTIC

94 Northern Prairie—*Canada, United States*

NEOTROPICAL

95 Patagonian Steppe—*Argentina, Chile*

PALEARCTIC

96 Daurian Steppe—*China, Mongolia, Russia*

Flooded Grasslands and Savannas

AFROTROPICAL

97 Sudd-Sahelian Flooded Grasslands and Savannas—*Cameroon, Chad, Ethiopia, Mali, Niger, Nigeria, Sudan, Uganda*

98 Zambezian Flooded Savannas—*Angola, Botswana, Dem. Rep. of the Congo, Malawi, Mozambique, Namibia, Tanzania, Zambia*

INDO-MALAYAN

99 Rann of Kutch Flooded Grasslands—*India, Pakistan*

NEOTROPICAL

100 Everglades Flooded Grasslands—*United States*

101 Pantanal Flooded Savannas—*Bolivia, Brazil, Paraguay*

Montane Grasslands and Shrublands

AFROTROPICAL

102 Ethiopian Highlands—*Eritrea, Ethiopia, Sudan*

103 Southern Rift Montane Woodlands—*Malawi, Mozambique, Tanzania, Zambia*

104 East African Moorlands—*Dem. Rep. of the Congo, Kenya, Rwanda, Tanzania, Uganda*

105 Drakensberg Montane Shrublands and Woodlands—*Lesotho, South Africa, Swaziland*

AUSTRALASIA

106 Central Range Subalpine Grasslands—*Indonesia, Papua New Guinea*

INDO-MALAYAN

107 Kinabalu Montane Scrub—*Malaysia*

NEOTROPICAL

108 Northern Andean Paramo—*Colombia, Ecuador, Peru, Venezuela*

109 Central Andean Dry Puna—*Argentina, Bolivia, Chile, Peru*

PALEARCTIC

110 Tibetan Plateau Steppe—*Afghanistan, China, India, Pakistan, Tajikistan*

111 Middle Asian Montane Steppe and Woodlands—*Afghanistan, China, Kazakhstan, Kyrgyzstan, Tajikistan, Turkmenistan, Uzbekistan*

112 Eastern Himalayan Alpine Meadows—*Bhutan, China, India, Myanmar, Nepal*

Tundra

NEARCTIC

113 Alaskan North Slope Coastal Tundra—*Canada, United States*

114 Canadian Low Arctic Tundra—*Canada*

PALEARCTIC

115 Fenno-Scandia Alpine Tundra and Taiga—*Finland, Norway, Russia, Sweden*

116 Taimyr and Siberian Coastal Tundra—*Russia*

117 Chukote Coastal Tundra—*Russia*

Mediterranean Forests, Woodlands and Scrub

AFROTROPICAL

118 Fynbos—*South Africa*

AUSTRALASIA

119 Southwestern Australia Forests and Scrub—*Australia*

120 Southern Australia Mallee and Woodlands—*Australia*

NEARCTIC

121 California Chaparral and Woodlands—*Mexico, United States*

NEOTROPICAL

122 Chilean Matorral—*Chile*

PALEARCTIC

123 Mediterranean Forests, Woodlands, and Scrub—*Albania, Algeria, Bosnia and Herzegovina, Bulgaria, Canary Islands (Spain), Croatia, Cyprus, Egypt, France, Gibraltar (United Kingdom), Greece, Iraq, Israel, Italy, Jordan, Lebanon, Libya, Macedonia, Madeira Islands (Portugal), Malta, Monaco, Montenegro, Morocco, Portugal, San Marino, Serbia, Slovenia, Spain, Syria, Tunisia, Turkey, Western Sahara (Morocco)*

Deserts and Xeric Shrublands

AFROTROPICAL

124 Namib-Karoo-Kaokeveld Deserts—*Angola, Namibia, South Africa*

125 Madagascar Spiny Thicket—*Madagascar*

126 Socotra Island Desert—*Yemen*

127 Arabian Highland Woodlands and Shrublands—*Oman, Saudi Arabia, United Arab Emirates, Yemen*

AUSTRALASIA

128 Carnavon Xeric Scrub—*Australia*

129 Great Sandy-Tanami Deserts—*Australia*

NEARCTIC

130 Sonoran-Baja Deserts—*Mexico, United States*

131 Chihuahuan-Tehuacán Deserts—*Mexico, United States*

NEOTROPICAL

132 Galápagos Islands Scrub—*Ecuador*

ARCTIC OCEAN
EUROPE
ASIA
AFRICA
PACIFIC OCEAN
INDIAN OCEAN
AUSTRALIA
ANTARCTICA

For the Terrestrial and Marine Ecoregions map (a detailed breakdown of the more than 800 ecoregions all around the world), see pages 86–87.

133 Atacama-Sechura Deserts—*Chile, Peru*

PALEARCTIC
134 Central Asian Deserts—*Kazakhstan, Kyrgyzstan, Turkmenistan, Uzbekistan*

Mangroves

AFROTROPICAL
135 Gulf of Guinea Mangroves—*Angola, Cameroon, Dem. Rep. of the Congo, Equatorial Guinea, Gabon, Ghana, Nigeria*
136 East African Mangroves—*Kenya, Mozambique, Somalia, Tanzania*
137 Madagascar Mangroves—*Madagascar*

AUSTRALASIA
138 New Guinea Mangroves—*Indonesia, Papua New Guinea*

INDO-MALAYAN
139 Sundarbans Mangroves—*Bangladesh, India*
140 Greater Sundas Mangroves—*Brunei, Indonesia, Malaysia*

NEOTROPICAL
141 Guianan-Amazon Mangroves—*Brazil, French Guiana (France), Suriname, Trinidad and Tobago, Venezuela*
142 Panama Bight Mangroves—*Colombia, Ecuador, Panama, Peru*

FRESHWATER

Large Rivers

AFROTROPICAL
143 Congo River and Flooded Forests—*Angola, Congo, Dem. Rep. of the Congo*

INDO-MALAYAN
144 Mekong River—*Cambodia, China, Laos, Myanmar, Thailand, Vietnam*

NEARCTIC
145 Colorado River—*Mexico, United States*
146 Lower Mississippi River—*United States*

NEOTROPICAL
147 Amazon River and Flooded Forests—*Brazil, Colombia, Peru*
148 Orinoco River and Flooded Forests—*Brazil, Colombia, Venezuela*

PALEARCTIC
149 Yangtze River and Lakes—*China*

Large River Headwaters

AFROTROPICAL
150 Congo Basin Piedmont Rivers and Streams—*Angola, Cameroon, Central African Republic, Congo, Dem. Rep. of the Congo, Gabon, Sudan*

NEARCTIC
151 Mississippi Piedmont Rivers and Streams—*United States*

NEOTROPICAL
152 Upper Amazon Rivers and Streams—*Bolivia, Brazil, Colombia, Ecuador, French Guiana (France), Guyana, Peru, Suriname, Venezuela*
153 Upper Paraná Rivers and Streams—*Argentina, Brazil, Paraguay*
154 Brazilian Shield Amazonian Rivers and Streams—*Bolivia, Brazil, Paraguay*

Large River Deltas

AFROTROPICAL
155 Niger River Delta—*Nigeria*

INDO-MALAYAN
156 Indus River Delta—*India, Pakistan*

PALEARCTIC
157 Volga River Delta—*Kazakhstan, Russia*
158 Mesopotamian Delta and Marshes—*Iran, Iraq, Kuwait*
159 Danube River Delta—*Bulgaria, Macedonia, Moldova, Romania, Serbia, Ukraine*
160 Lena River Delta—*Russia*

Small Rivers

AFROTROPICAL
161 Upper Guinea Rivers and Streams—*Côte d'Ivoire, Guinea, Liberia, Sierra Leone*
162 Madagascar Freshwater—*Madagascar*
163 Gulf of Guinea Rivers and Streams—*Angola, Cameroon, Congo, Dem. Rep. of the Congo, Equatorial Guinea, Gabon, Nigeria*
164 Cape Rivers and Streams—*South Africa*

AUSTRALASIA
165 New Guinea Rivers and Streams—*Indonesia, Papua New Guinea*
166 New Caledonia Rivers and Streams—*New Caledonia (France)*
167 Kimberley Rivers and Streams—*Australia*
168 Southwest Australia Rivers and Streams—*Australia*
169 Eastern Australia Rivers and Streams—*Australia*

INDO-MALAYAN
170 Xi Jiang Rivers and Streams—*China, Vietnam*
171 Western Ghats Rivers and Streams—*India*
172 Southwestern Sri Lanka Rivers and Streams—*Sri Lanka*
173 Salween River—*China, Myanmar, Thailand*
174 Sundaland Rivers and Swamps—*Brunei, Indonesia, Malaysia, Singapore*

NEARCTIC
175 Southeastern Rivers and Streams—*United States*
176 Pacific Northwest Coastal Rivers and Streams—*United States*
177 Gulf of Alaska Coastal Rivers and Streams—*Canada, United States*

NEOTROPICAL
178 Guianan Freshwater—*Brazil, French Guiana (France), Guyana, Suriname, Venezuela*
179 Greater Antillean Freshwater—*Cuba, Dominican Republic, Haiti, Puerto Rico (United States)*

PALEARCTIC
180 Balkan Rivers and Streams—*Albania, Bosnia and Herzegovina, Bulgaria, Croatia, Greece, Macedonia, Serbia, Turkey*
181 Russian Far East Rivers and Wetlands—*China, Mongolia, Russia*

Large Lakes

AFROTROPICAL
182 Rift Valley Lakes—*Burundi, Dem. Rep. of the Congo, Ethiopia, Kenya, Malawi, Mozambique, Rwanda, Tanzania, Uganda, Zambia*

NEOTROPICAL
183 High Andean Lakes—*Argentina, Bolivia, Chile, Peru*

PALEARCTIC
184 Lake Baikal—*Russia*
185 Lake Biwa—*Japan*

Small Lakes

AFROTROPICAL
186 Cameroon Crater Lakes—*Cameroon*

AUSTRALASIA
187 Lakes Kutubu and Sentani—*Indonesia, Papua New Guinea*
188 Central Sulawesi Lakes—*Indonesia*

INDO-MALAYAN
189 Philippines Freshwater—*Philippines*
190 Lake Inle—*Myanmar*
191 Yunnan Lakes and Streams—*China*

NEOTROPICAL
192 Mexican Highland Lakes—*Mexico*

Xeric Basins

AUSTRALASIA
193 Central Australian Freshwater—*Australia*

NEARCTIC
194 Chihuahuan Freshwater—*Mexico, United States*

PALEARCTIC
195 Anatolian Freshwater—*Syria, Turkey*

MARINE

Polar Seas

ANTARCTIC
196 Antarctic Peninsula and Weddell Sea—*Antarctic Peninsula and Weddell Sea*

ARCTIC
197 Bering Sea—*Canada, Russia, United States*
198 Barents-Kara Sea—*Norway, Russia*

Temperate Shelves and Seas

MEDITERRANEAN
199 Mediterranean Sea—*Albania, Algeria, Bosnia and Herzegovina, Croatia, Cyprus, Egypt, France, Gibraltar (United Kingdom), Greece, Israel, Italy, Lebanon, Libya, Malta, Monaco, Montenegro, Morocco, Slovenia, Spain, Syria, Tunisia, Turkey*

NORTH TEMPERATE ATLANTIC
200 Northeast Atlantic Shelf Marine—*Belgium, Denmark, Estonia, Finland, France, Germany, Ireland, Latvia, Lithuania, Netherlands, Norway, Poland, Russia, Sweden, United Kingdom*
201 Grand Banks—*Canada, St. Pierre and Miquelon (France), United States*
202 Chesapeake Bay—*United States*

NORTH TEMPERATE INDO-PACIFIC
203 Yellow Sea—*China, North Korea, South Korea*
204 Okhotsk Sea—*Japan, Russia*

SOUTHERN OCEAN
205 Patagonian Southwest Atlantic—*Argentina, Brazil, Chile, Uruguay*
206 Southern Australian Marine—*Australia*
207 New Zealand Marine—*New Zealand*

Temperate Upwelling

NORTH TEMPERATE INDO-PACIFIC
208 Californian Current—*Canada, Mexico, United States*

SOUTH TEMPERATE ATLANTIC
209 Benguela Current—*Namibia, South Africa*

SOUTH TEMPERATE INDO-PACIFIC
210 Humboldt Current—*Chile, Ecuador, Peru*
211 Agulhas Current—*Mozambique, South Africa*

Tropical Upwelling

212 Western Australian Marine—*Australia*

EASTERN INDO-PACIFIC
213 Panama Bight—*Colombia, Ecuador, Panama*
214 Gulf of California—*Mexico*
215 Galápagos Marine—*Ecuador*

EASTERN TROPICAL ATLANTIC
216 Canary Current—*Canary Islands (Spain), Gambia, Guinea-Bissau, Mauritania, Morocco, Senegal, Western Sahara (Morocco)*

Tropical Coral

CENTRAL INDO-PACIFIC
217 Nansei Shoto—*Japan*
218 Sulu-Sulawesi Seas—*Indonesia, Malaysia, Philippines*
219 Bismarck-Solomon Seas—*Indonesia, Papua New Guinea, Solomon Islands*
220 Banda-Flores Sea—*Indonesia, Timor-Leste*
221 New Caledonia Barrier Reef—*New Caledonia (France)*
222 Great Barrier Reef—*Australia*
223 Lord Howe-Norfolk Islands Marine—*Australia*
224 Palau Marine—*Palau*
225 Andaman Sea—*Andaman and Nicobar Islands (India), Indonesia, Malaysia, Myanmar, Thailand*

EASTERN INDO-PACIFIC
226 Tahitian Marine—*Cook Islands (New Zealand), French Polynesia (France)*
227 Hawaiian Marine—*Hawai'i (United States)*
228 Rapa Nui—*Chile*
229 Fiji Barrier Reef—*Fiji Islands*

WESTERN INDO-PACIFIC
230 Maldives, Chagos, Lakshadweep Atolls—*Chagos Archipelago (United Kingdom), India, Maldives, Sri Lanka*
231 Red Sea—*Djibouti, Egypt, Eritrea, Israel, Jordan, Saudi Arabia, Sudan, Yemen*
232 Arabian Sea—*Djibouti, Iran, Oman, Pakistan, Qatar, Saudi Arabia, United Arab Emirates, Yemen*
233 East African Marine—*Kenya, Mozambique, Somalia, Tanzania*
234 West Madagascar Marine—*Comoros, Madagascar, Mayotte and Îles Glorieuses (France), Seychelles*

WESTERN TROPICAL ATLANTIC
235 Mesoamerican Reef—*Belize, Guatemala, Honduras, Mexico*
236 Greater Antillean Marine—*Bahamas, Cayman Islands (United Kingdom), Cuba, Dominican Republic, Haiti, Jamaica, Puerto Rico (United States), Turks and Caicos Islands (United Kingdom), United States*
237 Southern Caribbean Sea—*Aruba (Netherlands), Colombia, Netherlands Antilles (Netherlands), Panama, Trinidad and Tobago, Venezuela*
238 Northeast Brazil Shelf Marine—*Brazil*

Protected Areas

THERE ARE MORE THAN 100,000 protected areas around the globe—on every continent and in every ocean. When thinking of protected areas, one often imagines exotic landscapes harboring rare and imperiled plants and animals. While many protected areas are indeed of this nature, there are many reasons why lands and waters are granted protection. Some habitats are protected to preserve specific species, while others are protected to ensure the survival of whole ecosystems. Aside from ecological value and the promotion of biodiversity, areas are also protected to preserve their ability to supply natural resources or because they offer valuable spiritual, scientific, educational, or recreational opportunities. Landscapes are also protected not for their own sake, but for the sake of neighboring areas. So-called buffer zones ensure that neighboring ecosystems remain undisturbed and often act as migration corridors for wildlife.

The International Union for Conservation of Nature (IUCN) categorizes protected areas in seven categories. In descending order of strictness, they are: strict nature reserve, wilderness area, national park, national monument, habitat/species management area, protected landscape/seascape, and managed resource protection area. The categories are based on the level of protection granted, the area's designated purpose, and access available to humans. The largest protected area on Earth is Denmark's 375,300-square-mile (972,000 square kilometers) Northeast Greenland National Park.

The World Database on Protected Areas (WDPA) is a joint venture of the United Nations Environment Programme (UNEP) and the IUCN. Compiling data from a wide variety of sources, it is the world's most comprehensive resource on protected areas, storing information about each area's official designation, total area, date of establishment, legal status, boundaries, geographical locations, and relationships to programs and organizations. Aside from offering comprehensive information about the world's protected areas, the WDPA offers an important tool for evaluating the success of environmental conservation efforts and for making strategic policy and planning decisions.

A wide range of environmental agencies and local, national, and international governments collaborate to provide protection to these areas. Agencies like WWF (World Wildlife Fund), the Nature Conservancy, and Conservation International work with one another, local shareholders and officials, national agencies, and international organizations like the United Nations to ensure that environmental and cultural goals can be met while also striving to preserve the livelihoods and traditions of local peoples.

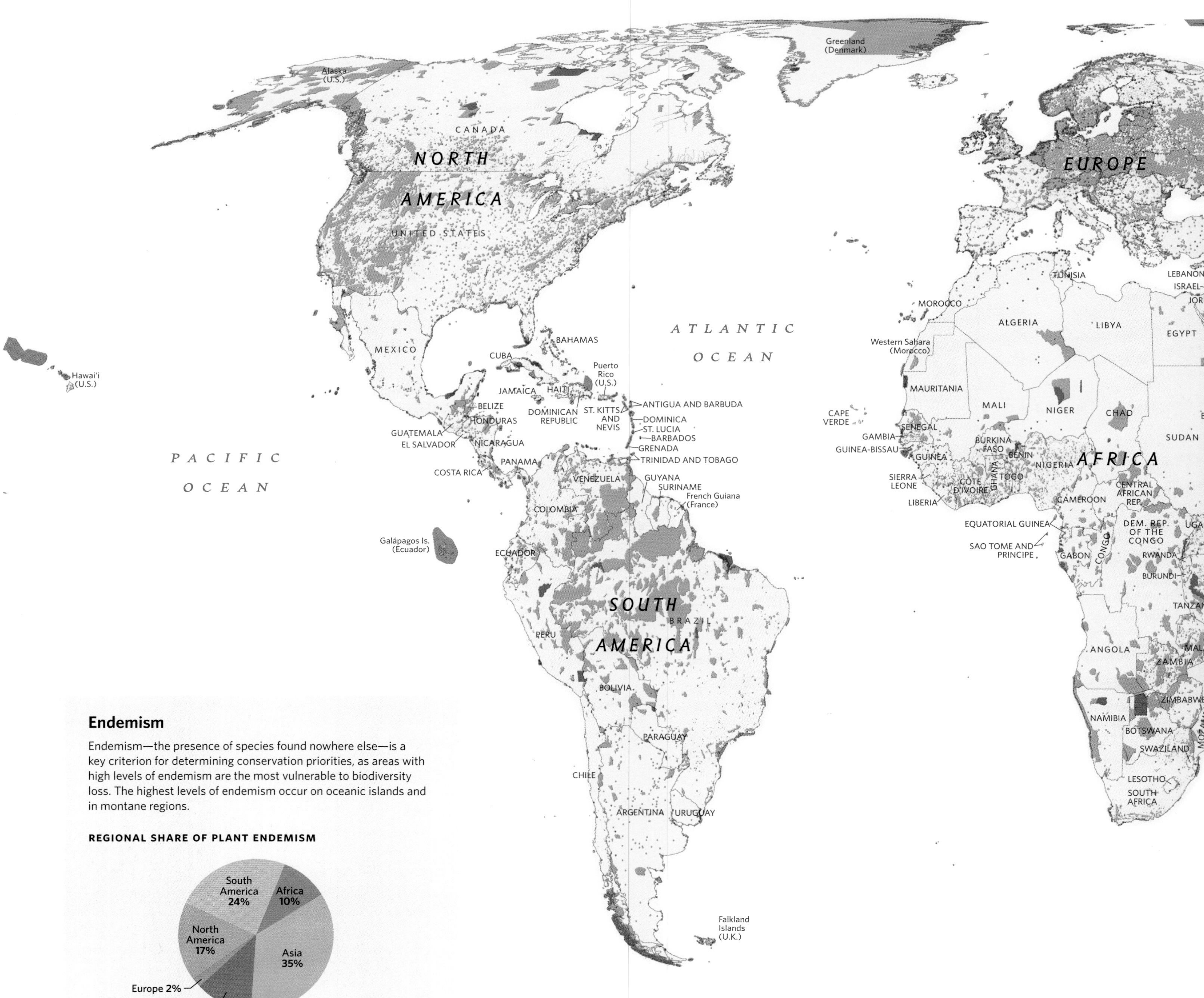

Greenland (Denmark)
Alaska (U.S.)
CANADA
NORTH AMERICA
UNITED STATES
EUROPE
Hawai'i (U.S.)
MEXICO
BAHAMAS
CUBA
JAMAICA
HAITI
Puerto Rico (U.S.)
BELIZE
HONDURAS
GUATEMALA
EL SALVADOR
NICARAGUA
DOMINICAN REPUBLIC
ST. KITTS AND NEVIS
ANTIGUA AND BARBUDA
DOMINICA
ST. LUCIA
BARBADOS
GRENADA
TRINIDAD AND TOBAGO
PANAMA
COSTA RICA
VENEZUELA
GUYANA
SURINAME
French Guiana (France)
COLOMBIA
ECUADOR
Galápagos Is. (Ecuador)
PACIFIC OCEAN
ATLANTIC OCEAN
SOUTH AMERICA
BRAZIL
PERU
BOLIVIA
PARAGUAY
CHILE
ARGENTINA
URUGUAY
Falkland Islands (U.K.)
MOROCCO
Western Sahara (Morocco)
ALGERIA
TUNISIA
LIBYA
EGYPT
LEBANON
ISRAEL
MAURITANIA
MALI
NIGER
CHAD
SUDAN
CAPE VERDE
SENEGAL
GAMBIA
GUINEA-BISSAU
GUINEA
BURKINA FASO
BENIN
NIGERIA
AFRICA
SIERRA LEONE
LIBERIA
CÔTE D'IVOIRE
GHANA
TOGO
CENTRAL AFRICAN REP.
CAMEROON
EQUATORIAL GUINEA
SAO TOME AND PRINCIPE
GABON
CONGO
DEM. REP. OF THE CONGO
RWANDA
BURUNDI
ANGOLA
ZAMBIA
ZIMBABWE
NAMIBIA
BOTSWANA
SWAZILAND
LESOTHO
SOUTH AFRICA

Endemism

Endemism—the presence of species found nowhere else—is a key criterion for determining conservation priorities, as areas with high levels of endemism are the most vulnerable to biodiversity loss. The highest levels of endemism occur on oceanic islands and in montane regions.

REGIONAL SHARE OF PLANT ENDEMISM

South America 24%
Africa 10%
North America 17%
Asia 35%
Europe 2%
Australia/Oceania 12%

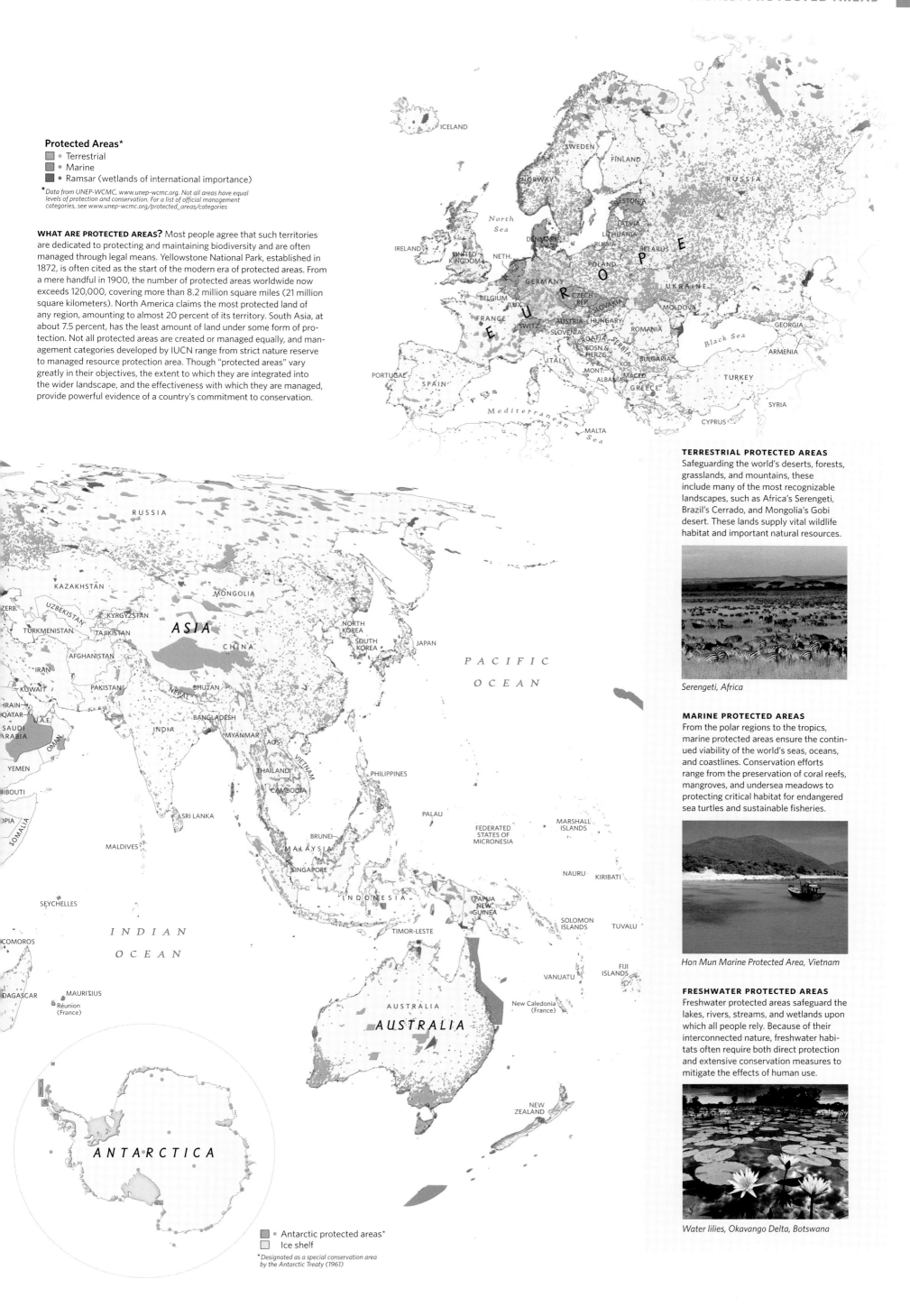

Protected Areas*

- Terrestrial
- Marine
- Ramsar (wetlands of international importance)

*Data from UNEP-WCMC, www.unep-wcmc.org. Not all areas have equal levels of protection and conservation. For a list of official management categories, see www.unep-wcmc.org/protected_areas/categories

WHAT ARE PROTECTED AREAS? Most people agree that such territories are dedicated to protecting and maintaining biodiversity and are often managed through legal means. Yellowstone National Park, established in 1872, is often cited as the start of the modern era of protected areas. From a mere handful in 1900, the number of protected areas worldwide now exceeds 120,000, covering more than 8.2 million square miles (21 million square kilometers). North America claims the most protected land of any region, amounting to almost 20 percent of its territory. South Asia, at about 7.5 percent, has the least amount of land under some form of protection. Not all protected areas are created or managed equally, and management categories developed by IUCN range from strict nature reserve to managed resource protection area. Though "protected areas" vary greatly in their objectives, the extent to which they are integrated into the wider landscape, and the effectiveness with which they are managed, provide powerful evidence of a country's commitment to conservation.

TERRESTRIAL PROTECTED AREAS

Safeguarding the world's deserts, forests, grasslands, and mountains, these include many of the most recognizable landscapes, such as Africa's Serengeti, Brazil's Cerrado, and Mongolia's Gobi desert. These lands supply vital wildlife habitat and important natural resources.

Serengeti, Africa

MARINE PROTECTED AREAS

From the polar regions to the tropics, marine protected areas ensure the continued viability of the world's seas, oceans, and coastlines. Conservation efforts range from the preservation of coral reefs, mangroves, and undersea meadows to protecting critical habitat for endangered sea turtles and sustainable fisheries.

Hon Mun Marine Protected Area, Vietnam

FRESHWATER PROTECTED AREAS

Freshwater protected areas safeguard the lakes, rivers, streams, and wetlands upon which all people rely. Because of their interconnected nature, freshwater habitats often require both direct protection and extensive conservation measures to mitigate the effects of human use.

Water lilies, Okavango Delta, Botswana

- Antarctic protected areas*
- Ice shelf

*Designated as a special conservation area by the Antarctic Treaty (1961)

World Heritage Sites

MORE THAN 800 PROPERTIES AROUND the world are inscribed on the World Heritage List of the United Nations Educational, Scientific and Cultural Organization (UNESCO). These unique landscapes, ecosystems, buildings, monuments, and cities are selected to represent the natural and cultural heritage of the world. From Floridian Everglades to French cathedrals, the listed sites are identified, protected, monitored, and preserved for the benefit of all of humanity. The catalyst to create the List was the decision to build the Aswan High Dam in Egypt and thus flood the valley where the Abu Simbel temples were located. In 1959, UNESCO launched an international campaign to safeguard the site, accelerating on-site archaeological research and eventually dismantling and relocating the temples. The campaign's successes demonstrated the vast potential of international cooperation and resulted in other campaigns and, ultimately, the Convention Concerning the Protection of the World Cultural and Natural Heritage, which was adopted by the General Conference of UNESCO on November 16, 1972.

The Convention's stated mission is to encourage countries to join as States Parties and identify, maintain, preserve, and manage cultural and natural sites important to the heritage of humanity as a whole. Coordinated from the World Heritage Centre in Paris and overseen by the World Heritage Committee, the World Heritage programs assist countries in the preservation of their sites by supplying technical and professional training, emergency assistance to immediately threatened sites, and support for public awareness campaigns. Work is done at every level, from promoting awareness in local populations to facilitating international cooperation. Aside from determining which sites will be inscribed on the List, the World Heritage Committee also allocates financial assistance to States Parties and examines reports on the state of conservation of listed sites to determine whether the property is being managed properly and interceding if necessary. Funding for management, preservation, and other activities is provided by the World Heritage Fund, which is mostly supported by compulsory contributions from States Parties and other voluntary contributions. Profits from World Heritage publications and funds-in-trust supplement the program's income.

Sites are selected for listing based primarily on their importance to the natural and cultural heritage of humanity. Protected areas are sometimes granted World Heritage status in order to raise awareness, increase protection, enhance funding, improve management practices, and harness tourism.

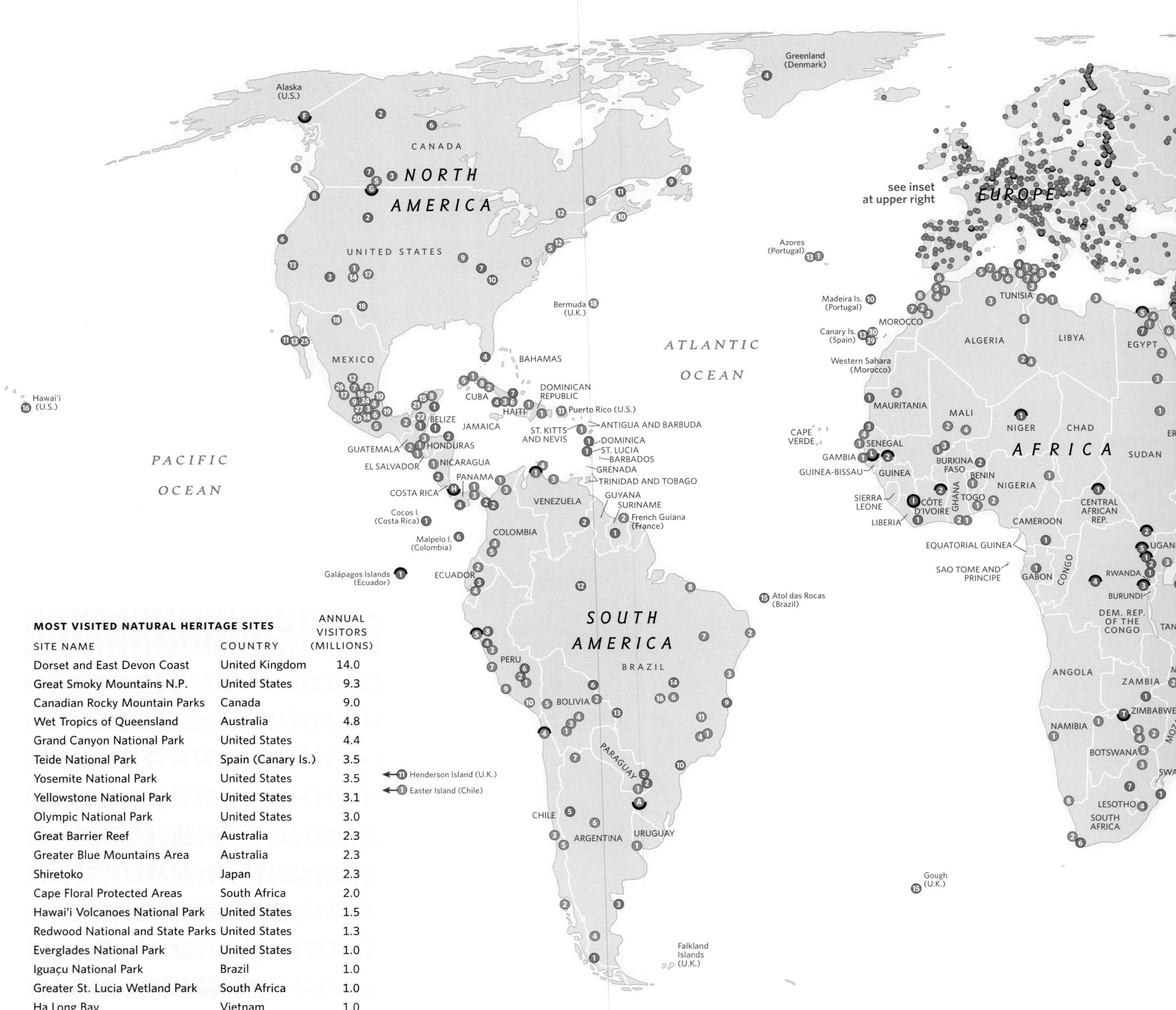

NORTH AMERICA
CANADA
UNITED STATES
Alaska (U.S.)
Greenland (Denmark)
MEXICO
Hawai'i (U.S.)
PACIFIC OCEAN
ATLANTIC OCEAN
see inset at upper right
EUROPE
Azores (Portugal)
Bermuda (U.K.)
BAHAMAS
CUBA
HAITI
DOMINICAN REPUBLIC
Puerto Rico (U.S.)
JAMAICA
BELIZE
GUATEMALA
HONDURAS
EL SALVADOR
NICARAGUA
COSTA RICA
PANAMA
ST. KITTS AND NEVIS
ANTIGUA AND BARBUDA
DOMINICA
ST. LUCIA
BARBADOS
GRENADA
TRINIDAD AND TOBAGO
Cocos I. (Costa Rica)
Malpelo I. (Colombia)
Galápagos Islands (Ecuador)
VENEZUELA
GUYANA
SURINAME
French Guiana (France)
COLOMBIA
ECUADOR
PERU
BOLIVIA
BRAZIL
SOUTH AMERICA
PARAGUAY
CHILE
ARGENTINA
URUGUAY
Atol das Rocas (Brazil)
Falkland Islands (U.K.)
Henderson Island (U.K.)
Easter Island (Chile)
Gough (U.K.)
Madeira Is. (Portugal)
Canary Is. (Spain)
Western Sahara (Morocco)
MOROCCO
ALGERIA
TUNISIA
LIBYA
EGYPT
CAPE VERDE
MAURITANIA
MALI
NIGER
CHAD
SUDAN
SENEGAL
GAMBIA
GUINEA-BISSAU
GUINEA
SIERRA LEONE
LIBERIA
CÔTE D'IVOIRE
GHANA
TOGO
BENIN
BURKINA FASO
NIGERIA
CAMEROON
CENTRAL AFRICAN REP.
EQUATORIAL GUINEA
SAO TOME AND PRINCIPE
GABON
CONGO
AFRICA
UGANDA
RWANDA
BURUNDI
DEM. REP. OF THE CONGO
ANGOLA
ZAMBIA
ZIMBABWE
NAMIBIA
BOTSWANA
LESOTHO
SOUTH AFRICA

MOST VISITED NATURAL HERITAGE SITES

SITE NAME	COUNTRY	ANNUAL VISITORS (MILLIONS)
Dorset and East Devon Coast	United Kingdom	14.0
Great Smoky Mountains N.P.	United States	9.3
Canadian Rocky Mountain Parks	Canada	9.0
Wet Tropics of Queensland	Australia	4.8
Grand Canyon National Park	United States	4.4
Teide National Park	Spain (Canary Is.)	3.5
Yosemite National Park	United States	3.5
Yellowstone National Park	United States	3.1
Olympic National Park	United States	3.0
Great Barrier Reef	Australia	2.3
Greater Blue Mountains Area	Australia	2.3
Shiretoko	Japan	2.3
Cape Floral Protected Areas	South Africa	2.0
Hawai'i Volcanoes National Park	United States	1.5
Redwood National and State Parks	United States	1.3
Everglades National Park	United States	1.0
Iguaçu National Park	Brazil	1.0
Greater St. Lucia Wetland Park	South Africa	1.0
Ha Long Bay	Vietnam	1.0
West Norwegian Fjords	Norway	1.0

World Heritage Sites

- Cultural property
- Natural property
- Mixed property (cultural and natural)
- Transnational property
- Property currently inscribed on the List of World Heritage in Danger

Number indicates site order by year of inscription within each country.

http://whc.unesco.org

WORLD HERITAGE LIST The World Heritage List was established under the terms of the 1972 UNESCO Convention Concerning the Protection of the World Cultural and Natural Heritage. The first 12 sites were named in 1978; among them were L'Anse aux Meadows in Canada, the site of the first Viking settlement in North America; the Galápagos Islands; the cathedral of Aachen, Germany; the historic city center of Kraków, Poland; the island of Gorée, off Senegal; and Mesa Verde and Yellowstone National Parks in the United States. New sites are added annually. At the time of publication, the list comprised 851 sites, with 660 cultural, 166 natural, and 25 mixed sites, located in 141 countries.

NATURAL HERITAGE SITE
On the border between Alaska and Canada, the U.S.'s Wrangell-St. Elias and Glacier Bay National Parks and Canada's Kluane and Tatshenshini-Alsek protected areas compose the first bi-national entry on the list. In addition to a vast chain of glaciers, the site has forests and tundras which provide valuable species habitats.

Wrangell-St. Elias National Park

CULTURAL HERITAGE SITE
Prague's historic areas and structures, many of which date from the Middle Ages, illustrate the city's impressive architectural and cultural legacy. Europe claims about half of the world's cultural heritage sites, with more than 300.

Historic Center of Prague

MIXED HERITAGE SITE
Originally called Ayers Rock-Mount Olga National Park, Uluru-Kata Tjuta was added to the List in 1987. Its designation as a Mixed site stems from its unique geological formations in combination with its Aboriginal cultural heritage.

Uluru-Kata Tjuta National Park, Australia

World Heritage Sites (continued)

Key

- Cultural property
- Natural property
- Mixed property (cultural and natural)
- Transnational property
- Property currently inscribed on the List of World Heritage in Danger **(labeled in bold)**

1979 Year in which each of the 184 States Parties adhered to the World Heritage Convention

A variety of dangers due to natural causes or human intervention are constantly threatening World Heritage. As a result, 30 properties (in bold on the list) are currently inscribed on the List of World Heritage in Danger and are thus entitled to particular attention and emergency conservation action.

AFGHANISTAN 1979
1. **Minaret and Archaeological Remains of Jam**
2. **Cultural Landscape and Archaeological Remains of the Bamian Valley**

ALBANIA 1989
1. Butrint
2. Museum-City of Gjirokastra

ALGERIA 1974
1. Al Qal'a of Beni Hammad
2. Tassili n'Ajjer
3. M'Zab Valley
4. Djémila
5. Tipasa
6. Timgad
7. Kasbah of Algiers

ANDORRA 1997
1. Madriu-Perafita-Claror Valley

ANGOLA 1991

ANTIGUA AND BARBUDA 1983

ARGENTINA 1978
1. Los Glaciares
2. Iguazu National Park
3. Península Valdés
4. Cueva de las Manos, Río Pinturas
5. Ischigualasto/Talampaya Natural Parks
6. Jesuit Block and Estancias of Córdoba
7. Quebrada de Humahuaca

ARMENIA 1993
1. Monasteries of Haghpat and Sanahin
2. Cathedral and Churches of Echmiatsin and the Archaeological Site of Zvartnots
3. Monastery of Geghard and the Upper Azat Valley

AUSTRALIA 1974
1. Kakadu National Park
2. Great Barrier Reef
3. Willandra Lakes Region
4. Tasmanian Wilderness
5. Lord Howe Island Group
6. Gondwana Rainforests of Australia
7. Uluru-Kata Tjuta National Park
8. Wet Tropics of Queensland
9. Shark Bay, Western Australia
10. Fraser Island
11. Australian Fossil Mammal Sites (Riversleigh/Naracoorte)
12. Heard and McDonald Islands
13. Macquarie Island
14. Greater Blue Mountains Area
15. Purnululu National Park
16. Royal Exhibition Building and Carlton Gardens
17. Sydney Opera House

AUSTRIA 1992
1. Historic Centre of Salzburg
2. Palace and Gardens of Schönbrunn
3. Hallstatt-Dachstein Salzkammergut Cultural Landscape
4. Semmering Railway
5. City of Graz—Historic Centre
6. Wachau Cultural Landscape
7. Historic Centre of Vienna

AZERBAIJAN 1993
1. **Walled City of Baku with the Shirvanshah's Palace and Maiden Tower**
2. Gobustan Rock Art Cultural Landscape

BAHRAIN 1991
1. Qal'at al-Bahrain—Ancient Harbour and Capital of Dilmun

BANGLADESH 1983
1. Historic Mosque City of Bagerhat
2. Ruins of the Buddhist Vihara at Paharpur
3. The Sundarbans

BARBADOS 2002

BELARUS 1988
1. Mir Castle Complex
2. Architectural, Residential and Cultural Complex of the Radziwill Family at Nesvizh

BELGIUM 1996
1. La Grand-Place, Brussels
2. Flemish Béguinages
3. The Four Lifts on the Canal du Centre and their Environs, La Louvière and Le Roeulx (Hainault)
4. Historic Centre of Brugge
5. Major Town Houses of the Architect Victor Horta (Brussels)
6. Neolithic Flint Mines at Spiennes (Mons)
7. Notre-Dame Cathedral in Tournai
8. Plantin-Moretus House-Workshops-Museum Complex

BELIZE 1990
1. Belize Barrier Reef Reserve System

BENIN 1982
1. Royal Palaces of Abomey

BHUTAN 2001

BOLIVIA 1976
1. City of Potosí
2. Jesuit Missions of the Chiquitos
3. Historic City of Sucre
4. Fuerte de Samaipata
5. Tiwanaku: Spiritual and Political Centre of the Tiwanaku Culture
6. Noel Kempff Mercado National Park

BOSNIA AND HERZEGOVINA 1993
1. Old Bridge Area of the Old City of Mostar
2. Mehmed Paša Sokolović Bridge in Višegrad

BOTSWANA 1998
1. Tsodilo

BRAZIL 1977
1. Historic Town of Ouro Preto
2. Historic Centre of the Town of Olinda
3. Historic Centre of Salvador de Bahia
4. Sanctuary of Bom Jesus do Congonhas
5. Iguaçu National Park
6. Brasília
7. Serra da Capivara National Park
8. Historic Centre of São Luís
9. Discovery Coast Atlantic Forest Reserves
10. Atlantic Forest South-East Reserves
11. Historic Centre of the Town of Diamantina
12. Central Amazon Conservation Complex
13. Pantanal Conservation Area
14. Cerrado Protected Areas: Chapada dos Veadeiros and Emas National Parks
15. Brazilian Atlantic Islands: Fernando de Noronha and Atol das Rocas Reserves
16. Historic Centre of the Town of Goiás

BULGARIA 1974
1. Boyana Church
2. Madara Rider
3. Thracian Tomb of Kazanlak
4. Rock-Hewn Churches of Ivanovo
5. Ancient City of Nessebar
6. Rila Monastery
7. Srebarna Nature Reserve
8. Pirin National Park
9. Thracian Tomb of Sveshtari

BURKINA FASO 1987

BURUNDI 1982

CAMBODIA 1991
1. Angkor

CAMEROON 1982
1. Dja Faunal Reserve

CANADA 1976
1. L'Anse aux Meadows National Historic Site
2. Nahanni National Park
3. Dinosaur Provincial Park
4. SGang Gwaay
5. Head-Smashed-In Buffalo Jump
6. Wood Buffalo National Park
7. Canadian Rocky Mountain Parks
8. Historic District of Old Québec
9. Gros Morne National Park
10. Old Town Lunenburg
11. Miguasha National Park
12. Rideau Canal

CAPE VERDE 1988

CENTRAL AFRICAN REPUBLIC 1980
1. **Manovo-Gounda St Floris National Park**

CHAD 1999

CHILE 1980
1. Rapa Nui National Park
2. Churches of Chiloé
3. Historic Quarter of the Seaport City of Valparaíso
4. **Humberstone and Santa Laura Saltpeter Works**
5. Sewell Mining Town

CHINA 1985
1. Mount Taishan
2. The Great Wall
3. Imperial Palaces of the Ming and Qing Dynasties in Beijing and Shenyang
4. Mogao Caves
5. Mausoleum of the First Qin Emperor
6. Peking Man Site at Zhoukoudian
7. Mount Huangshan
8. Jiuzhaigou Valley Scenic and Historic Interest Area
9. Huanglong Scenic and Historic Interest Area
10. Wulingyuan Scenic and Historic Interest Area
11. Mountain Resort and its Outlying Temples, Chengde
12. Temple and Cemetery of Confucius and the Kong Family Mansion in Qufu
13. Ancient Building Complex in the Wudang Mountains
14. Historic Ensemble of the Potala Palace, Lhasa
15. Lushan National Park
16. Mount Emei Scenic Area, including Leshan Giant Buddha Scenic Area
17. Ancient City of Ping Yao
18. Classical Gardens of Suzhou
19. Old Town of Lijiang
20. Temple of Heaven: an Imperial Sacrificial Altar in Beijing
21. Summer Palace, an Imperial Garden in Beijing
22. Mount Wuyi
23. Dazu Rock Carvings
24. Mount Qingcheng and the Dujiangyan Irrigation System
25. Ancient Villages in Southern Anhui—Xidi and Hongcun
26. Longmen Grottoes
27. Imperial Tombs of the Ming and Qing Dynasties
28. Yungang Grottoes
29. Three Parallel Rivers of Yunnan Protected Areas
30. Capital Cities and Tombs of the Ancient Koguryo Kingdom
31. Historic Centre of Macao
32. Sichuan Giant Panda Sanctuary—Wolong, Mt. Siguniang, and Jiajin Mountains
33. Yin Xu
34. Kaiping Diaolou and Villages
35. South China Karst

COLOMBIA 1983
1. Port, Fortresses and Group of Monuments, Cartagena
2. Los Katios National Park
3. Historic Centre of Santa Cruz de Mompox
4. National Archaeological Park of Tierradentro
5. San Agustín Archaeological Park
6. Malpelo Fauna and Flora Sanctuary

COMOROS 2000

CONGO 1987

CONGO, DEM. REP. OF THE 1974
1. **Virunga National Park**
2. **Garamba National Park**
3. **Kahuzi-Biega National Park**
4. **Salonga National Park**
5. **Okapi Wildlife Reserve**

COSTA RICA 1977
1. Cocos Island National Park
2. Area de Conservación Guanacaste

CÔTE D'IVOIRE 1981
1. Taï National Park
2. **Comoé National Park**

CROATIA 1992
1. Old City of Dubrovnik
2. Historical Complex of Split with the Palace of Diocletian
3. Plitvice Lakes National Park
4. Episcopal Complex of the Euphrasian Basilica in the Historic Centre of Poreč
5. Historic City of Trogir
6. Cathedral of St James in Šibenik

CUBA 1981
1. Old Havana and its Fortifications
2. Trinidad and the Valle de los Ingenios
3. San Pedro de la Roca Castle, Santiago de Cuba
4. Desembarco del Granma National Park
5. Viñales Valley
6. Archaeological Landscape of the First Coffee Plantations in the South-East of Cuba
7. Alejandro de Humboldt National Park
8. Urban Historic Centre of Cienfuegos

CYPRUS 1975
1. Paphos
2. Painted Churches in the Troodos Region
3. Choirokoitia

CZECH REPUBLIC 1993
1. Historic Centre of Prague
2. Historic Centre of Český Krumlov
3. Historic Centre of Telč
4. Pilgrimage Church of St John of Nepomuk at Zelená Hora
5. Kutná Hora: Historical Town Centre with the Church of St Barbara and the Cathedral of Our Lady of Sedlec
6. Lednice-Valtice Cultural Landscape
7. Holašovice Historical Village Reservation
8. Gardens and Castle at Kroměříž
9. Litomyšl Castle
10. Holy Trinity Column in Olomouc
11. Tugendhat Villa in Brno
12. Jewish Quarter and St Procopius' Basilica in Třebíč

DENMARK 1979
1. Jelling Mounds, Runic Stones and Church
2. Roskilde Cathedral
3. Kronborg Castle
4. Ilulissat Icefjord

DOMINICA 1995
1. Morne Trois Pitons National Park

DOMINICAN REPUBLIC 1985
1. Colonial City of Santo Domingo

ECUADOR 1975
1. **Galápagos Islands**
2. City of Quito
3. Sangay National Park
4. Historic Centre of Santa Ana de los Ríos de Cuenca

EGYPT 1974
1. Memphis and its Necropolis—the Pyramid Fields from Giza to Dahshur
2. Ancient Thebes with its Necropolis
3. Nubian Monuments from Abu Simbel to Philae
4. Historic Cairo
5. **Abu Mena**
6. Saint Catherine Area
7. Wadi Al-Hitan (Whale Valley)

EL SALVADOR 1991
1. Joya de Cerén Archaeological Site

ERITREA 2001

ESTONIA 1995
1. Historic Centre (Old Town) of Tallinn

ETHIOPIA 1977
1. **Simien National Park**
2. Rock-Hewn Churches, Lalibela
3. Fasil Ghebbi, Gondar Region
4. Lower Valley of the Awash
5. Tiya
6. Aksum
7. Lower Valley of the Omo
8. Harar Jugol, the Fortified Historical Town

FIJI ISLANDS 1990

FINLAND 1987
1. Old Rauma
2. Fortress of Suomenlinna
3. Petäjävesi Old Church
4. Verla Groundwood and Board Mill
5. Bronze Age Burial Site of Sammallahdenmäki

FRANCE 1975
1. Mont-Saint-Michel and its Bay
2. Chartres Cathedral
3. Palace and Park of Versailles
4. Vézelay, Church and Hill
5. Prehistoric Sites and Decorated Caves of the Vézère Valley
6. Palace and Park of Fontainebleau
7. Amiens Cathedral
8. Roman Theatre and its Surroundings and the "Triumphal Arch" of Orange

PROTECTED LAND AREAS BY REGION

REGION	%PROTECTED	SQ. KM.
Africa	12.4	3,778,894
Antarctica	0.03	1,749
Asia	12.8	4,071,088
Australia/Oceania	16.3	1,386,543
Europe	10.7	2,460,036
North America	17.7	3,995,314
South America	25.7	4,557,333
World	13.6	20,250,957

COUNTRIES WITH HIGHEST % PROTECTED AREA

COUNTRY	%PROTECTED	SQ. KM.
Seychelles	99.5	452
Kiribati	99.2	804
Palau	87.1	399
Malta	83.0	262
Venezuela	71.4	651,191
Estonia	65.5	29,642
Benin	59.3	66,834
Colombia	56.3	641,274
Monaco	56.0	1.1
Dominican Republic	50.9	24,819

COUNTRIES WITH LOWEST % PROTECTED AREA

COUNTRY	%PROTECTED	SQ. KM.
Cape Verde	0	0
Maldives	0	0
San Marino	0	0
United Arab Emirates	0	0
Sao Tome and Principe	0.02	0.2
Syria	0.05	100
Djibouti	0.13	30
Qatar	0.15	17
Libya	0.18	3,121
Lesotho	0.24	72

9 Arles, Roman and Romanesque Monuments
10 Cistercian Abbey of Fontenay
11 Royal Saltworks of Arc-et-Senans
12 Place Stanislas, Place de la Carrière and Place d'Alliance in Nancy
13 Abbey Church of Saint-Savin sur Gartempe
14 Gulf of Porto: Calanche of Piana, Gulf of Girolata, Scandola Reserve
15 Pont du Gard (Roman Aqueduct)
16 Strasbourg — Grande Île
17 Paris, Banks of the Seine
18 Cathedral of Notre-Dame, Former Abbey of Saint-Remi and Palace of Tau, Reims
19 Bourges Cathedral
20 Historic Centre of Avignon: Papal Palace, Episcopal Ensemble and Avignon Bridge
21 Canal du Midi
22 Historic Fortified City of Carcassonne
23 Historic Site of Lyons
24 Routes of Santiago de Compostela in France
25 Jurisdiction of Saint-Emilion
26 Loire Valley between Sully-sur-Loire and Chalonnes
27 Provins, Town of Medieval Fairs
28 Le Havre, the City Rebuilt by Auguste Perret
29 Bordeaux, Port of the Moon

GABON 1986
1 Ecosystem and Relict Cultural Landscape of Lopé-Okanda

GAMBIA 1987
1 James Island and Related Sites

GEORGIA 1992
1 Historical Monuments of Mtskheta
2 Bagrati Cathedral and Gelati Monastery
3 Upper Svaneti

GERMANY 1976
1 Aachen Cathedral
2 Speyer Cathedral
3 Würzburg Residence with the Court Gardens and Residence Square
4 Pilgrimage Church of Wies
5 Castles of Augustusburg and Falkenlust at Brühl
6 St Mary's Cathedral and St Michael's Church at Hildesheim
7 Roman Monuments, Cathedral of St Peter and Church of Our Lady in Trier
8 Hanseatic City of Lübeck
9 Palaces and Parks of Potsdam and Berlin
10 Abbey and Altenmünster of Lorsch
11 Mines of Rammelsberg and Historic Town of Goslar
12 Town of Bamberg
13 Maulbronn Monastery Complex
14 Collegiate Church, Castle and Old Town of Quedlinburg
15 Völklingen Ironworks
16 Messel Pit Fossil Site
17 Cologne Cathedral
18 Bauhaus and its Sites in Weimar and Dessau
19 Luther Memorials in Eisleben and Wittenberg
20 Classical Weimar
21 Wartburg Castle
22 Museumsinsel (Museum Island), Berlin
23 Monastic Island of Reichenau
24 Garden Kingdom of Dessau-Wörlitz
25 Zollverein Coal Mine Industrial Complex in Essen
26 Historic Centres of Stralsund and Wismar
27 Upper Middle Rhine Valley
28 **Dresden Elbe Valley**
29 Town Hall and Roland on the Marketplace of Bremen
30 Old Town of Regensburg with Stadtamhof

GHANA 1975
1 Forts and Castles, Volta Greater Accra, Central and Western Regions
2 Asante Traditional Buildings

GREECE 1981
1 Temple of Apollo Epicurius at Bassae
2 Archaeological Site of Delphi
3 Acropolis, Athens
4 Mount Athos
5 Meteora
6 Paleochristian and Byzantine Monuments of Thessaloníka
7 Sanctuary of Asklepios at Epidaurus
8 Medieval City of Rhodes
9 Archaeological Site of Mystras
10 Archaeological Site of Olympia
11 Delos
12 Monasteries of Daphni, Hosios Loukas and Nea Moni of Chios
13 Pythagoreion and Heraion of Samos
14 Archaeological Site of Aigai (modern name Vergina)
15 Archaeological Sites of Mycenae and Tiryns
16 Historic Centre (Chorá) with the Monastery of Saint John "the Theologian" and the Cave of the Apocalypse on the Island of Pátmos
17 Old Town of Corfu

GRENADA 1998

GUATEMALA 1979
1 Tikal National Park
2 Antigua Guatemala
3 Archaeological Park and Ruins of Quirigua

GUINEA 1979

GUINEA-BISSAU 2006

GUYANA 1977

HAITI 1980
1 National History Park — Citadel, Sans Souci, Ramiers

HONDURAS 1979
1 Maya Site of Copan
2 Río Plátano Biosphere Reserve

HUNGARY 1985
1 Budapest, including the Banks of the Danube, the Buda Castle Quarter and Andrássy Avenue
2 Old Village of Hollókő and its Surroundings
3 Millenary Benedictine Abbey of Pannonhalma and its Natural Environment
4 Hortobágy National Park — the *Puszta*
5 Early Christian Necropolis of Pécs (Sopianae)
6 Tokaj Wine Region Historic Cultural Landscape

ICELAND 1995
1 Thingvellir National Park

INDIA 1977
1 Ajanta Caves
2 Ellora Caves
3 Agra Fort
4 Taj Mahal
5 Sun Temple, Konârak
6 Group of Monuments at Mahabalipuram
7 Kaziranga National Park
8 **Manas Wildlife Sanctuary**
9 Keoladeo National Park
10 Churches and Convents of Goa
11 Khajuraho Group of Monuments
12 Group of Monuments at Hampi
13 Fatehpur Sikri
14 Group of Monuments at Pattadakal
15 Elephanta Caves
16 Great Living Chola Temples
17 Sundarbans National Park
18 Nanda Devi and Valley of Flowers National Parks
19 Buddhist Monuments at Sanchi
20 Humayun's Tomb, Delhi
21 Qutb Minar and its Monuments, Delhi
22 Mountain Railways of India
23 Mahabodhi Temple Complex at Bodh Gaya
24 Rock Shelters of Bhimbetka
25 Champaner-Pavagadh Archaeological Park

Old Bridge Area of the Old City of Mostar, Bosnia and Herzegovina

26 Chhatrapati Shivaji Terminus (formerly Victoria Terminus) Station
27 Red Fort Complex

INDONESIA 1989
1 Borobudur Temple Compounds
2 Ujung Kulon National Park
3 Komodo National Park
4 Prambanan Temple Compounds
5 Sangiran Early Man Site
6 Lorentz National Park
7 Tropical Rainforest Heritage of Sumatra

IRAN 1975
1 Tchogha Zanbil
2 Persepolis
3 Meidan Emam, Isfahan
4 Takht-e Soleyman
5 Pasargadae
6 **Bam and its Cultural Landscape**
7 Soltaniyeh
8 Bisotun

IRAQ 1974
1 Hatra
2 **Ashur (Qal'at Sherqat)**
3 **Samarra Archaeological City**

IRELAND 1991
1 Archaeological Ensemble of the Bend of the Boyne
2 Skellig Michael

ISRAEL 1999
1 Masada
2 Old City of Acre
3 White City of Tel-Aviv — the Modern Movement
4 Biblical Tels — Megiddo, Hazor, Beer Sheba
5 Incense Route — Desert Cities in the Negev

ITALY 1978
1 Rock Drawings in Valcamonica
2 Church and Dominican Convent of Santa Maria delle Grazie with "The Last Supper" by Leonardo da Vinci
3 Historic Centre of Florence
4 Venice and its Lagoon
5 Piazza del Duomo, Pisa
6 Historic Centre of San Gimignano
7 The Sassi and the Park of the Rupestrian Churches of Matera
8 City of Vicenza and the Palladian Villas of the Veneto
9 Historic Centre of Siena
10 Historic Centre of Naples
11 Crespi d'Adda
12 Ferrara, City of the Renaissance and its Po Delta
13 Castel del Monte
14 The *trulli* of Alberobello
15 Early Christian Monuments of Ravenna
16 Historic Centre of the City of Pienza
17 18th-Century Royal Palace at Caserta with the Park, the Aqueduct of Vanvitelli and San Leucio Complex
18 Residences of the Royal House of Savoy
19 Botanical Garden (Orto Botanico), Padua
20 Cathedral, Torre Civica and Piazza Grande, Modena
21 Archaeological Areas of Pompei, Herculanum and Torre Annunziata
22 Villa Romana del Casale
23 Su Nuraxi di Barumini
24 Portovenere, Cinque Terre and the Islands (Palmaria, Tino and Tinetto)
25 Costiera Amalfitana
26 Archaeological Area of Agrigento
27 Archaeological Area and the Patriarchal Basilica of Aquileia
28 Cilento and Vallo di Diano National Park with the Archaeological Sites of Paestum and Velia and the Certosa de Padula
29 Historic Centre of Urbino
30 Villa Adriana (Tivoli)
31 City of Verona
32 Isole Eolie (Aeolian Islands)
33 Assisi, the Basilica of San Francesco and other Franciscan Sites
34 Villa d'Este, Tivoli
35 Late Baroque Towns of the Val di Noto (South-Eastern Sicily)
36 Sacri Monti of Piedmont and Lombardy
37 Etruscan Necropolises of Cerveteri and Tarquinia
38 Val d'Orcia
39 Syracuse and the Rocky Necropolis of Pantalica
40 Genoa: The *Strade Nuove* and the system of the *Palazzi dei Rolli*

JAMAICA 1983

JAPAN 1992
1 Buddhist Monuments in the Horyu-ji Area
2 Himeji-jo
3 Yakushima
4 Shirakami-Sanchi
5 Historic Monuments of Ancient Kyoto (Kyoto, Uji and Otsu Cities)
6 Historic Villages of Shirakawa-go and Gokayama
7 Hiroshima Peace Memorial (Genbaku Dome)
8 Itsukushima Shinto Shrine
9 Historic Monuments of Ancient Nara
10 Shrines and Temples of Nikko

Pitons Management Area, Saint Lucia

11 Gusuku Sites and Related Properties of the Kingdom of Ryukyu
12 Sacred Sites and Pilgrimage Routes in the Kii Mountain Range
13 Shiretoko
14 Iwami Ginzan Silver Mine and its Cultural Landscape

JERUSALEM
(Site proposed by Jordan)
1 **Old City of Jerusalem and its Walls**

JORDAN 1975
1 Petra
2 Quseir Amra
3 Um er-Rasas (Kastrom Mefa'a)

KAZAKHSTAN 1994
1 Mausoleum of Khoja Ahmed Yasawi
2 Petroglyphs within the Archaeological Landscape of Tamgaly

KENYA 1991
1 Mount Kenya National Park/ Natural Forest
2 Lake Turkana National Parks
3 Lamu Old Town

KIRIBATI 2000

KUWAIT 2002

KYRGYZSTAN 1995

LAOS 1987
1 Town of Luang Prabang
2 Vat Phou and Associated Ancient Settlements within the Champasak Cultural Landscape

LATVIA 1995
1 Historic Centre of Riga

LEBANON 1983
1 Anjar
2 Baalbek
3 Byblos
4 Tyre
5 Ouadi Qadisha (the Holy Valley) and the Forest of the Cedars of God (Horsh Arz el-Rab)

LESOTHO 2003

LIBERIA 2002

LIBYA 1978
1 Archaeological Site of Leptis Magna
2 Archaeological Site of Sabratha
3 Archaeological Site of Cyrene
4 Rock-Art Sites of Tadrart Acacus
5 Old Town of Ghadamès

LITHUANIA 1992
1 Vilnius Historic Centre
2 Kernavė Archaeological Site (Cultural Reserve of Kernavė)

LUXEMBOURG 1983
1 City of Luxembourg: its Old Quarters and Fortifications

MACEDONIA 1997
1 Natural and Cultural Heritage of the Ohrid Region

MADAGASCAR 1983
1 Tsingy de Bemaraha Strict Nature Reserve
2 Royal Hill of Ambohimanga
3 Rainforests of the Atsinanana

MALAWI 1982
1 Lake Malawi National Park
2 Chongoni Rock Art Area

MALAYSIA 1988
1 Kinabalu Park
2 Gunung Mulu National Park

MALDIVES 1986

MALI 1977
1 Old Towns of Djénné
2 Timbuktu
3 Cliff of Bandiagara (Land of the Dogons)
4 Tomb of Askia

World Heritage Sites (continued)

MALTA 1978
1. Hal Saflieni Hypogeum
2. City of Valletta
3. Megalithic Temples of Malta

MARSHALL ISLANDS 2002

MAURITANIA 1981
1. Banc d'Arguin National Park
2. Ancient *Ksour* of Ouadane, Chinguetti, Tichitt and Oualata

MAURITIUS 1995
1. Aapravasi Ghat

MEXICO 1984
1. Sian Ka'an
2. Pre-Hispanic City and National Park of Palenque
3. Historic Centre of Mexico City and Xochimilco
4. Pre-Hispanic City of Teotihuacán
5. Historic Centre of Oaxaca and Archaeological Site of Monte Albán
6. Historic Centre of Puebla
7. Historic Town of Guanajuato and Adjacent Mines
8. Pre-Hispanic City of Chichén-Itzá
9. Historic Centre of Morelia
10. El Tajín, Pre-Hispanic City
11. Whale Sanctuary of El Vizcaíno
12. Historic Centre of Zacatecas
13. Rock Paintings of the Sierra de San Francisco
14. Earliest 16th-Century Monasteries on the Slopes of Popocatepetl
15. Pre-Hispanic Town of Uxmal
16. Historic Monuments Zone of Querétaro
17. Hospicio Cabañas, Guadalajara
18. Archaeological Zone of Paquimé, Casas Grandes
19. Historic Monuments Zone of Tlacotalpán
20. Archaeological Monuments Zone of Xochicalco
21. Historic Fortified Town of Campeche
22. Ancient Maya City of Calakmul, Campeche
23. Franciscan Missions in the Sierra Gorda of Querétaro
24. Luis Barragán House and Studio
25. Islands and Protected Areas of the Gulf of California
26. Agave Landscape and Ancient Industrial Facilities of Tequila
27. Central University City Campus of the *Universidad Nacional Autónoma de México (UNAM)*

MICRONESIA, FED. STATES OF 2002

MOLDOVA 2002

MONACO 1978

MONGOLIA 1990
1. Orkhon Valley Cultural Landscape

MONTENEGRO 2006
1. Natural and Culturo-Historical Region of Kotor
2. Durmitor National Park

MOROCCO 1975
1. Medina of Fez
2. Medina of Marrakesh
3. Ksar of Ait-Ben-Haddou
4. Historic City of Meknes
5. Archaeological Site of Volubilis
6. Medina of Tétouan (formerly known as Titawin)
7. Medina of Essaouira (Ancient Mogador)
8. Portuguese City of Mazagan (El Jadida)

MOZAMBIQUE 1982
1. Island of Mozambique

MYANMAR 1994

NAMIBIA 2000
1. Twyfelfontein or /Ui-//aes

NEPAL 1978
1. Sagarmatha National Park
2. Kathmandu Valley
3. Royal Chitwan National Park
4. Lumbini, the Birthplace of the Lord Buddha

NETHERLANDS 1992
1. Schokland and Surroundings
2. Defence Line of Amsterdam
3. Mill Network at Kinderdijk-Elshout
4. Historical Area of Willemstad, Inner City and Harbour, Netherlands Antilles
5. Ir.D.F. Woudagemaal (D.F. Wouda Steam Pumping Station)
6. Droogmakerij de Beemster (Beemster Polder)
7. Rietveld Schröderhuis (Rietveld Schröder House)

NEW ZEALAND 1984
1. Te Wahipounamu — South-West New Zealand
2. Tongariro National Park
3. New Zealand Sub-Antarctic Islands

NICARAGUA 1979
1. Ruins of León Viejo

NIGER 1974
1. **Aïr and Ténéré Natural Reserves**
2. W National Park of Niger

NIGERIA 1974
1. Sukur Cultural Landscape
2. Osun-Osogbo Sacred Grove

NIUE (New Zealand) 2001

NORTH KOREA 1998
1. Complex of Koguryo Tombs

NORWAY 1977
1. Urnes Stave Church
2. Bryggen
3. Røros Mining Town
4. Rock Art of Alta
5. Vegaøyan — The Vega Archipelago
6. West Norwegian Fjords — Geirangerfjord and Nærøyfjord

OMAN 1981
1. Bahla Fort
2. Archaeological Sites of Bat, Al-Khutm and Al-Ayn
3. Land of Frankincense
4. *Aflaj* Irrigation Systems of Oman

PAKISTAN 1976
1. Archaeological Ruins at Moenjodaro
2. Taxila
3. Buddhist Ruins of Takht-i-Bahi and Neighbouring City Remains at Sahr-i-Bahlol
4. Historical Monuments of Thatta
5. **Fort and Shalamar Gardens in Lahore**
6. Rohtas Fort

PALAU 2002

PANAMA 1978
1. Fortifications on the Caribbean Side of Panama: Portobelo-San Lorenzo
2. Darien National Park
3. Archaeological Site of Panamá Viejo and Historic District of Panamá
4. Coiba National Park and its Special Zone of Marine Protection

PAPUA NEW GUINEA 1997

PARAGUAY 1988
1. Jesuit Missions of La Santísima Trinidad de Paraná and Jesús de Tavarangue

PERU 1982
1. City of Cuzco
2. Historic Sanctuary of Machu Picchu
3. Chavin (Archaeological Site)
4. Huascarán National Park
5. **Chan Chan Archaeological Zone**
6. Manú National Park
7. Historic Centre of Lima
8. Río Abiseo National Park
9. Lines and Geoglyphs of Nasca and Pampas de Jumana
10. Historical Centre of the City of Arequipa

PHILIPPINES 1985
1. Tubbataha Reef Marine Park
2. Baroque Churches of the Philippines
3. **Rice Terraces of the Philippine Cordilleras**
4. Puerto-Princesa Subterranean River National Park
5. Historic Town of Vigan

POLAND 1976
1. Kraków's Historic Centre
2. Wieliczka Salt Mine
3. Auschwitz Birkenau German Nazi Concentration and Extermination Camp (1940-1945)
4. Historic Centre of Warsaw
5. Old City of ZamoĐć
6. Medieval Town of Toruń
7. Castle of the Teutonic Order in Malbork
8. Kalwaria Zebrzydowska: the Mannerist Architecture and Park Landscape Complex and Pilgrimage Park
9. Churches of Peace in Jawor and Swidnica
10. Wooden Churches of Southern Little Poland
11. Centennial Hall in Wrocław

PORTUGAL 1980
1. Central Zone of the Town of Angra do Heroismo in the Azores
2. Monastery of the Hieronymites and Tower of Belém in Lisbon
3. Monastery of Batalha
4. Convent of Christ in Tomar
5. Historic Centre of Évora
6. Monastery of Alcobaça
7. Cultural Landscape of Sintra
8. Historic Centre of Oporto
9. Prehistoric Rock-Art Sites in the Côa Valley
10. Laurisilva of Madeira
11. Alto Douro Wine Region
12. Historic Centre of Guimarães
13. Landscape of the Pico Island Vineyard Culture

QATAR 1984

ROMANIA 1990
1. Danube Delta
2. Villages with Fortified Churches in Transylvania
3. Monastery of Horezu
4. Churches of Moldavia
5. Dacian Fortresses of the Orastie Mountains
6. Historic Centre of SighiĐoara
7. Wooden Churches of MaramureĐ

RUSSIA 1988
1. Historic Centre of Saint Petersburg and Related Groups of Monuments
2. Kizhi Pogost
3. Kremlin and Red Square, Moscow
4. Historic Monuments of Novgorod and Surroundings
5. Cultural and Historic Ensemble of the Solovetsky Islands
6. White Monuments of Vladimir and Suzdal
7. Architectural Ensemble of the Trinity Sergius Lavra in Sergiev Posad
8. Church of the Ascension, Kolomenskoye
9. Virgin Komi Forests
10. Lake Baikal
11. Volcanoes of Kamchatka
12. Golden Mountains of Altai
13. Western Caucasus
14. Historic and Architectural Complex of the Kazan Kremlin
15. Ensemble of Ferapontov Monastery
16. Central Sikhote-Alin
17. Citadel, Ancient City and Fortress Buildings of Derbent
18. Ensemble of the Novodevichy Convent
19. Natural System of Wrangel Island Reserve
20. Historical Centre of the City of Yaroslavl

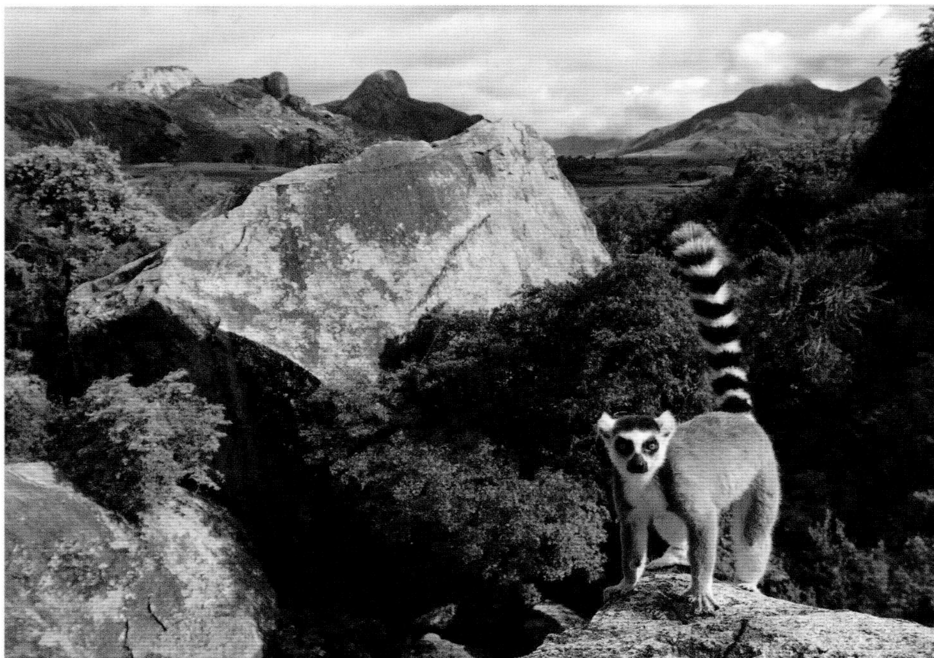

Rainforests of the Atsinanana, Madagascar

RWANDA 2000

SAINT KITTS AND NEVIS 1986
1. Brimstone Hill Fortress National Park

SAINT LUCIA 1991
1. Pitons Management Area

SAINT VINCENT AND THE GRENADINES 2003

SAMOA 2001

SAN MARINO 1991

SAO TOME AND PRINCIPE 2006

SAUDI ARABIA 1978

SENEGAL 1976
1. Island of Gorée
2. **Niokolo-Koba National Park**
3. Djoudj National Bird Sanctuary
4. Island of Saint-Louis

SERBIA 2001 (includes Kosovo)
1. Stari Ras and Sopoćani
2. Studenica Monastery
3. **Medieval Monuments in Kosovo**
4. Gamzigrad-Romuliana, Palace of Galerius

SEYCHELLES 1980
1. Aldabra Atoll
2. Vallée de Mai Nature Reserve

SIERRA LEONE 2005

SLOVAKIA 1993
1. Vlkolínec
2. Historic Town of Banská Štiavnica and the Technical Monuments in its Vicinity
3. Spišský Hrad and its Associated Cultural Monuments
4. Bardejov Town Conservation Reserve

SLOVENIA 1992
1. Škocjan Caves

SOLOMON ISLANDS 1992
1. East Rennell

SOUTH AFRICA 1997
1. Greater St Lucia Wetland Park
2. Robben Island
3. Fossil Hominid Sites of Sterkfontein, Swartkrans, Kromdraai and Environs
4. uKhahlamba/Drakensberg Park
5. Mapungubwe Cultural Landscape
6. Cape Floral Region Protected Areas
7. Vredefort Dome
8. Richtersveld Cultural and Botanical Landscape

SOUTH KOREA 1988
1. Seokguram Grotto and Bulguksa Temple
2. Haeinsa Temple Janggyeong Panjeon, the Depositories for the *Tripitaka Koreana* Woodblocks
3. Jongmyo Shrine
4. Changdeokgung Palace Complex
5. Hwaseong Fortress
6. Gyeongju Historic Areas
7. Gochang, Hwasun and Ganghwa Dolmen Sites
8. Jeju Volcanic Island and Lava Tubes

SPAIN 1982
1. Historic Centre of Córdoba
2. Alhambra, Generalife and Albayzín, Granada
3. Burgos Cathedral
4. Monastery and Site of the Escurial, Madrid
5. Works of Antoni Gaudí
6. Altamira Cave
7. Old Town of Segovia and its Aqueduct
8. Monuments of Oviedo and the Kingdom of the Asturias
9. Santiago de Compostela (Old Town)
10. Old Town of Ávila with its Extra-Muros Churches
11. Mudejar Architecture of Aragon
12. Historic City of Toledo
13. Garajonay National Park
14. Old Town of Cáceres

Site of Palmyra, Syria

15 Cathedral, Alcázar and Archivo de Indias in Seville
16 Old City of Salamanca
17 Poblet Monastery
18 Archaeological Ensemble of Mérida
19 Royal Monastery of Santa María de Guadalupe
20 Route of Santiago de Compostela
21 Doñana National Park
22 Historic Walled Town of Cuenca
23 La Lonja de la Seda de Valencia
24 Las Médulas
25 Palau de la Música Catalana and Hospital de Sant Pau, Barcelona
26 San Millán Yuso and Suso Monasteries
27 Rock Art of the Mediterranean Basin on the Iberian Peninsula
28 University and Historic Precinct of Alcalá de Henares
29 Ibiza, Biodiversity and Culture
30 San Cristóbal de La Laguna
31 Archaeological Ensemble of Tárraco
32 Palmeral of Elche
33 Roman Walls of Lugo
34 Catalan Romanesque Churches of the Vall de Boí
35 Archaeological Site of Atapuerca
36 Aranjuez Cultural Landscape
37 Renaissance Monumental Ensembles of Úbeda and Baeza
38 Vizcaya Bridge
39 Teide National Park

SRI LANKA 1980
1 Sacred City of Anuradhapura
2 Ancient City of Polonnaruwa
3 Ancient City of Sigiriya
4 Sinharaja Forest Reserve
5 Sacred City of Kandy
6 Old Town of Galle and its Fortifications
7 Golden Temple of Dambulla

SUDAN 1974
1 Gebel Barkal and the Sites of the Napatan Region

SURINAME 1997
1 Central Suriname Nature Reserve
2 Historic Inner City of Paramaribo

SWAZILAND 2005

SWEDEN 1985
1 Royal Domain of Drottningholm
2 Birka and Hovgården
3 Engelsberg Ironworks
4 Rock Carvings in Tanum
5 Skogskyrkogården
6 Hanseatic Town of Visby
7 Laponian Area
8 Church Village of Gammelstad, Luleå
9 Naval Port of Karlskrona
10 Agricultural Landscape of Southern Öland
11 Mining Area of the Great Copper Mountain in Falun
12 Varberg Radio Station

SWITZERLAND 1975
1 Convent of St Gall
2 Benedictine Convent of St John at Müstair
3 Old City of Bern
4 Three Castles, Defensive Wall and Ramparts of the Market-Town of Bellinzone
5 Jungfrau-Aletsch-Bietschhorn
6 Monte San Giorgio
7 Lavaux, Vineyard Terraces

SYRIA 1975
1 Ancient City of Damascus
2 Ancient City of Bosra
3 Site of Palmyra
4 Ancient City of Aleppo
5 Crac des Chevaliers and Qal'at Salah El-Din

TAJIKISTAN 1992

TANZANIA 1977
1 Ngorongoro Conservation Area
2 **Ruins of Kilwa Kisiwani and Ruins of Songo Mnara**
3 Serengeti National Park
4 Selous Game Reserve
5 Kilimanjaro National Park
6 Stone Town of Zanzibar
7 Kondoa Rock Art Sites

THAILAND 1987
1 Historic Town of Sukhothai
2 Historic City of Ayutthaya
3 Thungyai-Huai Kha Khaeng Wildlife Sanctuaries
4 Ban Chiang Archaeological Site
5 Dong Phayayen-Khao Yai Forest Complex

TOGO 1998
1 Koutammakou, the Land of the Batammariba

TONGA 2004

TRINIDAD AND TOBAGO 2005

TUNISIA 1975
1 Medina of Tunis
2 Site of Carthage
3 Amphitheatre of El Jem
4 Ichkeul National Park
5 Punic Town of Kerkuane and its Necropolis
6 Medina of Sousse
7 Kairouan
8 Dougga/Thugga

TURKEY 1983
1 Historic Areas of Istanbul
2 Göreme National Park and the Rock Sites of Cappadocia
3 Great Mosque and Hospital of Divriği
4 Hattusha: the Hittite Capital
5 Nemrut Dağ
6 Xanthos-Letoon
7 Hierapolis-Pamukkale
8 City of Safranbolu
9 Archaeological Site of Troy

TURKMENISTAN 1994
1 State Historical and Cultural Park "Ancient Merv"
2 Kunya-Urgench
3 Parthian Fortresses of Nisa

UGANDA 1987
1 Bwindi Impenetrable National Park
2 Rwenzori Mountains National Park
3 Tombs of Buganda Kings at Kasubi

UKRAINE 1988
1 Kiev: Saint-Sophia Cathedral and Related Monastic Buildings, Kiev-Pechersk Lavra
2 L'viv—the Ensemble of the Historic Centre

UNITED ARAB EMIRATES 2001

UNITED KINGDOM 1984
1 Giant's Causeway and Causeway Coast
2 Durham Castle and Cathedral
3 Ironbridge Gorge
4 Studley Royal Park including the Ruins of Fountains Abbey
5 Stonehenge, Avebury and Associated Sites
6 Castles and Town Walls of King Edward in Gwynedd
7 St Kilda
8 Blenheim Palace
9 City of Bath
10 Westminster Palace, Westminster Abbey and Saint Margaret's Church
11 Henderson Island
12 Tower of London
13 Canterbury Cathedral, St Augustine's Abbey and St Martin's Church
14 Old and New Towns of Edinburgh
15 Gough and Inaccessible Islands
16 Maritime Greenwich
17 Heart of Neolithic Orkney
18 Historic Town of St George and Related Fortifications, Bermuda
19 Blaenavon Industrial Landscape
20 Dorset and East Devon Coast
21 Derwent Valley Mills
22 New Lanark
23 Saltaire
24 Royal Botanic Gardens, Kew
25 Liverpool—Maritime Mercantile City
26 Cornwall and West Devon Mining Landscape

UNITED STATES 1973
1 Mesa Verde National Park
2 Yellowstone National Park
3 Grand Canyon National Park
4 Everglades National Park
5 Independence Hall
6 Redwood National Park
7 Mammoth Cave National Park
8 Olympic National Park
9 Cahokia Mounds State Historic Site
10 Great Smoky Mountains National Park
11 La Fortaleza and San Juan National Historic Site in Puerto Rico
12 Statue of Liberty
13 Yosemite National Park
14 Chaco Culture
15 Monticello and the University of Virginia in Charlottesville
16 Hawai'i Volcanoes National Park
17 Pueblo de Taos
18 Carlsbad Caverns National Park

URUGUAY 1989
1 Historic Quarter of the City of Colonia del Sacramento

UZBEKISTAN 1993
1 Itchan Kala
2 Historic Centre of Bukhara
3 Historic Centre of Shakhrisyabz
4 Samarqand—Crossroads of Cultures

VANUATU 2002

VATICAN CITY 1982
1 Vatican City

VENEZUELA 1990
1 **Coro and its Port**
2 Canaima National Park
3 Ciudad Universitaria de Caracas

VIETNAM 1987
1 Complex of Hué Monuments
2 Ha Long Bay
3 Hoi An Ancient Town
4 My Son Sanctuary
5 Phong Nha-Ke Bang National Park

YEMEN 1980
1 Old Walled City of Shibam
2 Old City of Sana'a
3 **Historic Town of Zabid**

ZAMBIA 1984

ZIMBABWE 1982
1 Mana Pools National Park, Sapi and Chewore Safari Areas
2 Great Zimbabwe National Monument
3 Khami Ruins National Monument
4 Matobo Hills

Transnational Sites

Twenty properties are nominated and managed by more than one State Party.

ARGENTINA and **BRAZIL**
A Jesuit Missions of the Guaranis

AUSTRIA and **HUNGARY**
B Fertö/Neusiedlersee Cultural Landscape

BELARUS and **POLAND**
C Belovezhskaya Pushcha/ Białowieża Forest

BELARUS/ESTONIA/ FINLAND/LATVIA/ LITHUANIA/MOLDOVA/ NORWAY/RUSSIA/ SWEDEN/UKRAINE
D Struve Geodetic Arc

BELGIUM and **FRANCE**
E Belfries of Belgium and France

CANADA and **UNITED STATES**
F Kluane/Wrangell-St Elias/Glacier Bay/Tatshenshini-Alsek
G Waterton Glacier International Peace Park

COSTA RICA and **PANAMA**
H Talamanca Range-La Amistad Reserves/La Amistad National Park

CÔTE D'IVOIRE and **GUINEA**
I Mount Nimba Strict Nature Reserve

FINLAND and **SWEDEN**
J Kvarken Archipelago/ High Coast

FRANCE and **SPAIN**
K Pyrénées—Mount Perdu

GAMBIA and **SENEGAL**
L Stone Circles of Senegambia

GERMANY and **POLAND**
M Muskauer Park/Park Muzakowski

GERMANY and **UNITED KINGDOM**
N Frontiers of the Roman Empire

HUNGARY and **SLOVAKIA**
O Caves of Aggtelek Karst and Slovak Karst

ITALY and **VATICAN CITY**
P Historic Centre of Rome

LITHUANIA and **RUSSIA**
Q Curonian Spit

MONGOLIA and **RUSSIA**
R Uvs Nuur Basin

SLOVAKIA and **UKRAINE**
S Primeval Beech Forests of the Carpathians

ZAMBIA and **ZIMBABWE**
T Mosi-oa-Tunya/Victoria Falls

UNESCO World Heritage Information

DONATIONS TO THE WORLD HERITAGE FUND The granting of international assistance from the World Heritage Fund to finance World Heritage conservation projects is an important tool establishing by the Convention. If you would like to participate in conserving World Heritage, please send a contribution. Please indicate that the contribution is a donation to the World Heritage Fund.

Donations in USD should be made to:
UNESCO account: 949-1-191558
CHASE JP MORGAN BANK
International Money Transfer Division
4 Metrotech Center, Brooklyn
New York, NY 11245, U.S.A.
Swift code: CHASUS 33-ABA: 0210-0002-1

Donations in EUR should be made to:
UNESCO account: 30003-03301-00037291909-97
SOCIETE GENERALE
Paris Seine Amont
10 rue Thénard
75005 Paris, France
Swift code: SOGEFRPPAFS

UNESCO WORLD HERITAGE CENTRE The map of World Heritage properties is produced each year by the UNESCO World Heritage Centre. If you would like to receive more information about the World Heritage Convention and World Heritage conservation, please contact:

UNESCO World Heritage Centre
7, place de Fontenoy, 75352 Paris 07 SP, France
Telephone: + 33 (0)1 45 68 18 76
Fax: + 33 (0)1 45 68 55 70
E-mail: wh-info@unesco.org

Explore World Heritage sites on the Internet at http://whc.unesco.org
World Heritage donations online: http://whc.unesco.org/en/donation/

COAST TO COAST, A VAST CONTINENT WAS TRANSFORMED within a few centuries of the arrival of Europeans. The New World they found was far from empty; some of the great pre-Columbian urban centers of present-day Mexico and Central America rivaled European cities in size. But superior European weaponry and foreign diseases combined to vanquish the indigenous populations. The United States and Mexico fought to sever colonial ties, while the transformation was generally a peaceful one for Central American countries and Canada. Meanwhile the relentless westward expansion of the United States brought the country into conflict with American Indian tribes and Mexico.

Beyond Native American ruins and old Spanish town centers, North America's array of World Heritage sites is weighted toward natural wonders. They range from the world-famous — the awesome depths of the Grand Canyon, the geysers and hot springs of Yellowstone, the fiery volcanoes of Hawai'i — to the equally impressive but less well known, like the Belize Barrier Reef — the largest reef found outside of Australian waters — and the isolated forests and mountain ranges of western Canada and Alaska.

KEY Cultural World Heritage Site Natural World Heritage Site Mixed World Heritage Site

North America

Lower Yellowstone Falls (above) thunders down a canyon in the western United States' Yellowstone National Park, one of Earth's most active geothermal hot spots. Other World Heritage sites around North America include (left, top to bottom): the massive cliff dwellings of Mesa Verde National Park, abandoned by the Ancient Pueblo people in the face of persistent drought; Kilauea, a Hawaiian volcano that is one of the most active in the world; Monte Albán, one of the earliest cities in North America, founded around 500 B.C. in present-day Oaxaca, Mexico; and Wrangell-St. Elias National Park and Preserve in Alaska, where kaleidoscopic colors explode across the fall landscape.

ARCTIC OCEAN
North Magnetic Pole 2008
GREENLAND SEA
NORWEGIAN SEA
BEAUFORT SEA
BAFFIN BAY
LABRADOR SEA
HUDSON BAY
GULF OF ALASKA
BERING SEA
PACIFIC
ATLANTIC OCEAN
SIBERIA
ASIA
GREENLAND
ICELAND
Faroe Islands
Jan Mayen
QUEEN ELIZABETH ISLANDS
PARRY ISLANDS
Ellesmere Island
Axel Heiberg Island
Devon I.
Baffin Island
Victoria Island
Banks Island
Melville I.
Bathurst I.
Cornwallis I.
Somerset Island
Prince of Wales I.
Prince Patrick Island
Southampton Island
Coats I.
Mansel I.
Belcher Islands
Akimiski I.
Prince Charles I.
Bylot Island
ISLAND OF NEWFOUNDLAND
NOVA SCOTIA
Prince Edward I.
Cape Breton Island
Anticosti I.
Sable I.
Vancouver I.
Queen Charlotte Is.
Alexander Archipelago
Kodiak Island
St. Lawrence Island
Nunivak I.
KNUD RASMUSSEN LAND
Peary Land
Crown Prince Christian Land
King Frederik VIII Land
King Wilhelm Land
King Christian X Land
King Christian IX Land
King Frederik VI Coast
Cape Morris Jesup
Cape Farewell
Cape York
Hayes Pen.
Denmark Strait
Davis Strait
Hudson Strait
Lincoln Sea
Bering Strait
The north and south geomagnetic poles, distinct from the more familiar geographic and magnetic poles, mark the axis of the Earth's magnetic field.
North Geomagnetic Pole 2008
CANADIAN SHIELD
Labrador
Ungava Peninsula
Laurentide Scarp
Laurentian Scarp
ROCKY MOUNTAINS
COAST MOUNTAINS
YUKON PLATEAU
Brooks Range
North Slope
Alaska Range
Kuskokwim Mts.
White Mts.
Mt. McKinley (Denali) 6194 20320 ft
Highest point in North America
Mackenzie Mts.
Richardson Mts.
Franklin Mts.
Selwyn Mts.
Ogilvie Mountains
Davidson Mts.
Chugach Mts.
Cassiar Mts.
Caribou Mts.
Birch Mts.
Columbia Mts.
Selkirk Mts.
Bitterroot Ra.
Torngat Mts.
Long Range Mts.
Seward Peninsula
Kenai Peninsula
Melville Pen.
Melville Hills
Boothia Peninsula
Borden Pen.
Brodeur Pen.
Collinson Peninsula
Wollaston Peninsula
Cumberland Peninsula
Meta Incognita Peninsula
Foxe Pen.
Gaspé Pen.
Avalon Peninsula
Great Bear Lake
Great Slave Lake
Lake Athabasca
Wollaston Lake
Reindeer Lake
Lake Winnipeg
Lake Winnipegosis
Lake Manitoba
Lake of the Woods
Lake Nipigon
Lake Abitibi
Lake St. Joseph
Trout Lake
Lac la Ronge
Dubawnt Lake
Williston Lake
Réservoir Caniapiscau
Smallwood Reservoir
Rés. Manicouagan
Rés. Gouin
L. Superior
Mackenzie
Yukon
Porcupine
Peace
Athabasca
Saskatchewan
N. Saskatchewan
S. Saskatchewan
Churchill
Nelson
Severn
Attawapiskat
Thelon
Back
Fraser
Source of the Yukon
Source of the Mackenzie-Peace
Source of the Missouri-Red Rock
Source of the Mississippi (Lake Itasca)
Hudson Bay
James Bay
Foxe Basin
Queen Maud Gulf
Amundsen Gulf
Franklin Bay
Mackenzie Bay
Gulf of St. Lawrence
Bay of Fundy
Cabot Str.
Cape Churchill
Cape Tatnam
Cape Dobbs
Point Barrow
Cape Prince Alfred
Cape Flattery
Mt. Rainier 4392
Mt. St. Helens 2550
Mt. Logan 5959
Mt. Katahdin 1606
Mt. Washington 1917
Mont Tremblant 968
Monts Otish 1135
Gunnbjørn 3700
Mont Forel 3360
J.A.D. Jensen Nunatakker 1680
Cook Inlet
Prince William Sd.
Norton Sound
Hecate Str.
Str. of Georgia
Virginia Falls
Baird Mts.
Missouri
Yellowstone
Badlands
Upper Pen.
Ottawa
Georgian Bay
L. Champlain
Adirondack Mts.
Cape Sable
Cape Harrison
Killiniq Island
Cape Blanco
Great Sandy Desert
Columbia

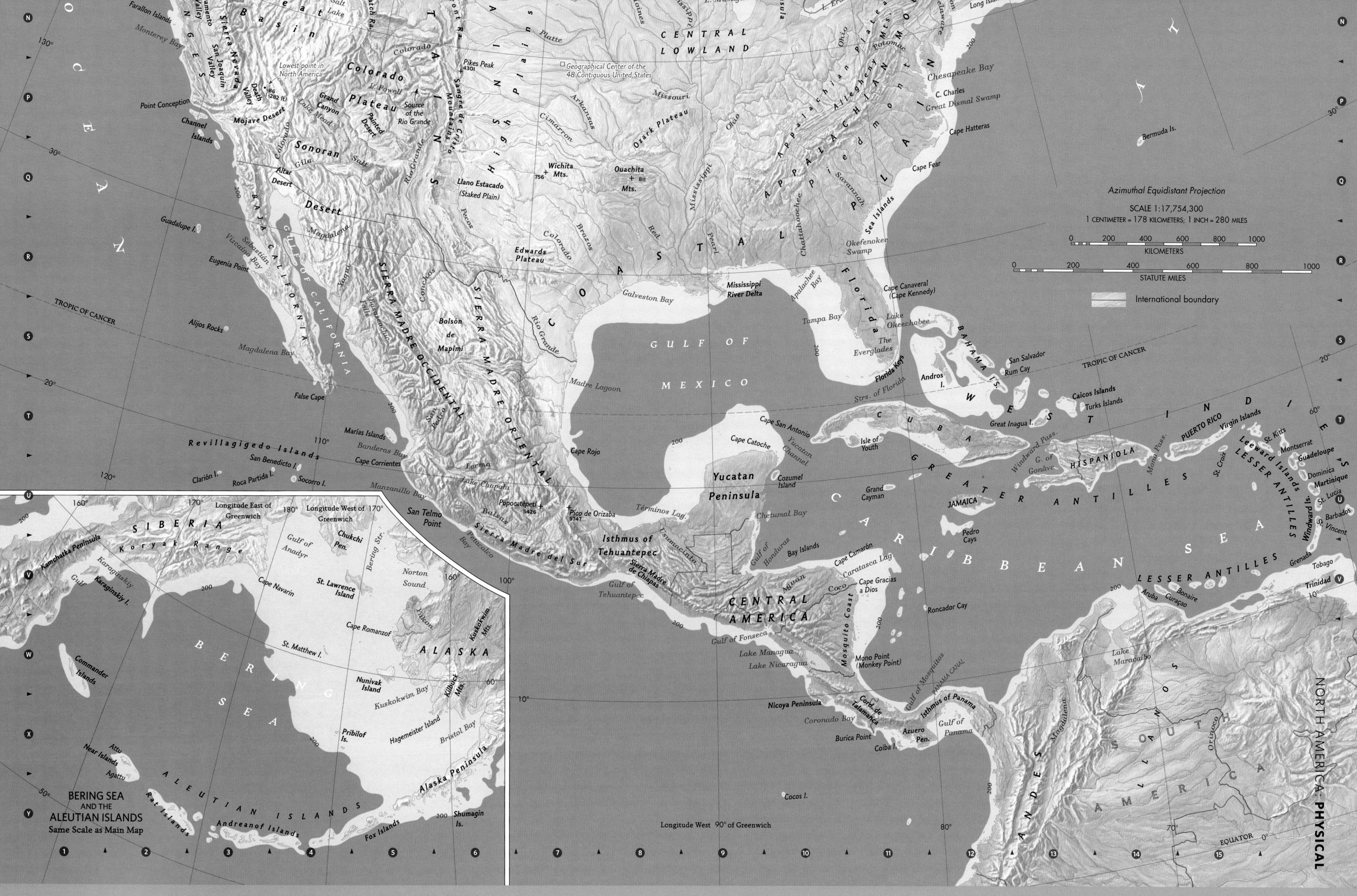
Azimuthal Equidistant Projection
SCALE 1:17,754,300
1 CENTIMETER = 178 KILOMETERS; 1 INCH = 280 MILES
KILOMETERS
STATUTE MILES
International boundary
GULF OF MEXICO
CARIBBEAN SEA
WEST INDIES
GREATER ANTILLES
LESSER ANTILLES
BAHAMA IS.
CUBA
HISPANIOLA
JAMAICA
PUERTO RICO
Yucatan Peninsula
CENTRAL AMERICA
Isthmus of Tehuantepec
Isthmus of Panama
SIERRA MADRE ORIENTAL
SIERRA MADRE OCCIDENTAL
Sierra Madre del Sur
BAJA CALIFORNIA
GULF OF CALIFORNIA
Colorado Plateau
Sonoran Desert
Mojave Desert
Death Valley
Sierra Nevada
San Joaquin Valley
Pikes Peak 4301
Sangre de Cristo Mountains
Llano Estacado (Staked Plain)
Edwards Plateau
Ozark Plateau
Ouachita Mts.
Wichita Mts.
CENTRAL LOWLAND
Mississippi River Delta
Florida
Florida Keys
Cape Canaveral (Cape Kennedy)
Cape Hatteras
Cape Fear
Chesapeake Bay
TROPIC OF CANCER
ANDES
SOUTH AMERICA
EQUATOR
BERING SEA
ALEUTIAN ISLANDS
ALASKA
SIBERIA
BERING SEA AND THE ALEUTIAN ISLANDS
Same Scale as Main Map
Longitude West 90° of Greenwich

ASIA
RUSSIA
ARCTIC OCEAN
ATLANTIC OCEAN
PACIFIC
CHUKCHI SEA
BERING SEA
BEAUFORT SEA
GULF OF ALASKA
NORWEGIAN SEA
GREENLAND SEA
LABRADOR SEA
Denmark Strait
Davis Strait
BAFFIN BAY
Hudson Strait
HUDSON BAY
Foxe Basin
James Bay
Ungava Bay
Lincoln Sea
ARCTIC CIRCLE
North Magnetic Pole 2008
North Geomagnetic Pole 2008
The north and south geomagnetic poles, distinct from the more familiar geographic and magnetic poles, mark the axis of the Earth's magnetic field.
GREENLAND (KALAALLIT NUNAAT)
Denmark
KNUD RASMUSSEN LAND
ICELAND
Reykjavík
QUEEN ELIZABETH ISLANDS
PARRY ISLANDS
Ellesmere Island
Devon Island
Banks Island
Victoria Island
Baffin Island
Viscount Melville Sound
M'Clintock Chan.
G. of Boothia
Boothia Peninsula
Prince of Wales Island
Somerset Island
Southampton Island
CANADA
NUNAVUT
NORTHWEST TERRITORIES
YUKON
BRITISH COLUMBIA
ALBERTA
SASKATCHEWAN
MANITOBA
ONTARIO
QUEBEC
NEWFOUNDLAND AND LABRADOR
NOVA SCOTIA
ROCKY MOUNTAINS
ALASKA
Brooks Range
North Slope
Seward Peninsula
Norton Sound
Bering Str.
U.S.
CANADA
WASH.
OREGON
IDAHO
MONTANA
NORTH DAKOTA
MINN.
WIS.
ME.
N.H.
VT.
N.B.
P.E.I.
Alert
Eureka
Resolute
Iqaluit
Whitehorse
Yellowknife
Anchorage
Fairbanks
Juneau
Vancouver
Victoria
Seattle
Portland
Edmonton
Calgary
Regina
Winnipeg
Thunder Bay
Ottawa
MONTRÉAL
Québec
Halifax
St. John's
Nuuk (Godthåb)
Nunap Isua (Cape Farewell)

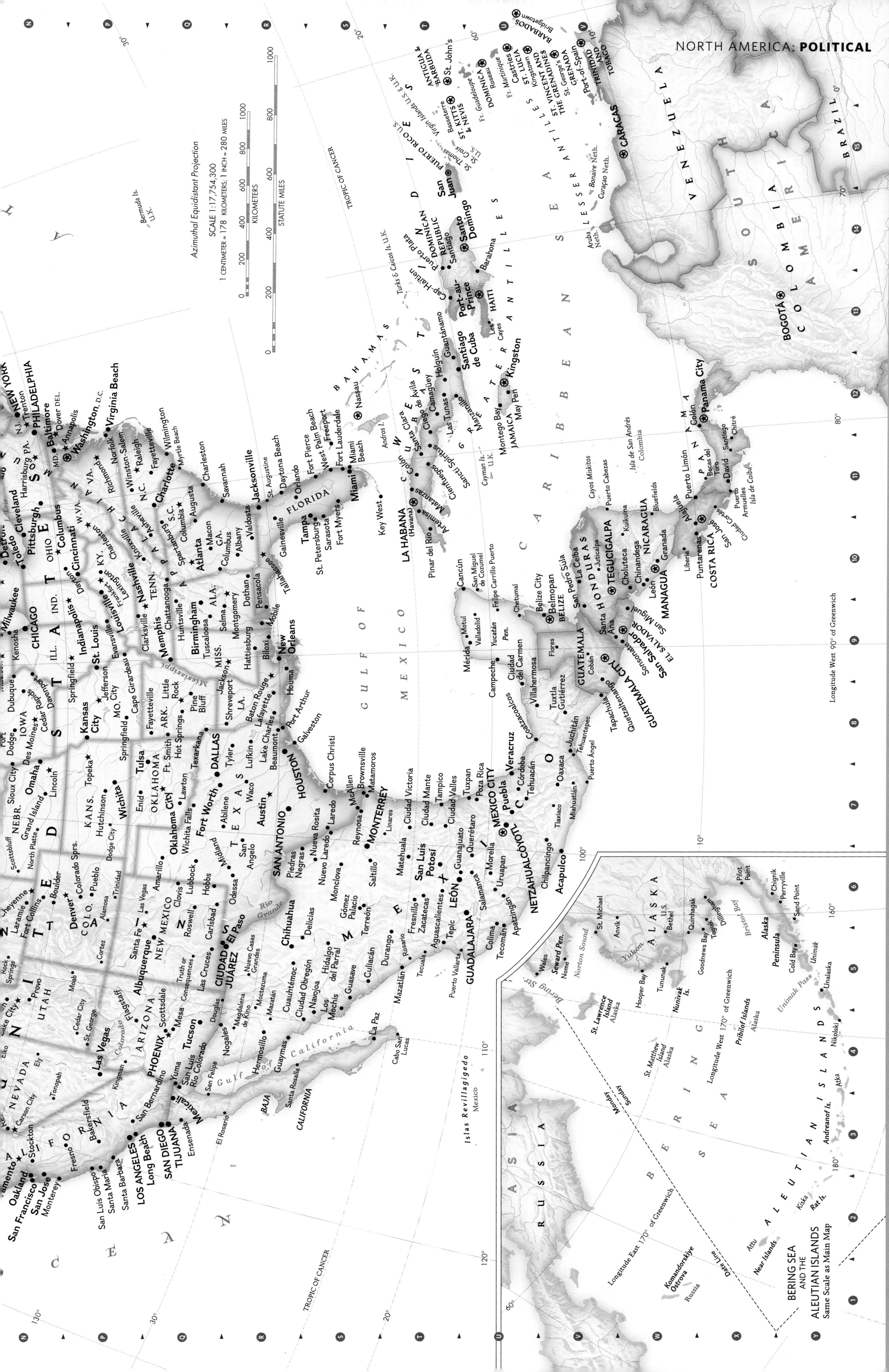

Azimuthal Equidistant Projection

SCALE 1:17,754,300

1 CENTIMETER = 178 KILOMETERS; 1 INCH = 280 MILES

KILOMETERS 0 200 400 600 800 1000

STATUTE MILES 0 200 400 600 800 1000

BERING SEA AND THE ALEUTIAN ISLANDS

Same Scale as Main Map

North America: Themes

Continental Facts

TOTAL NUMBER OF COUNTRIES: 23

TOTAL AREA: 24,474,000 sq km (9,449,000 sq mi)

FIRST INDEPENDENT COUNTRY: United States, July 4, 1776

"YOUNGEST" COUNTRY: St. Kitts and Nevis, Sept. 19, 1983

MOST POPULOUS COUNTRY: United States 302,200,000

LEAST POPULOUS COUNTRY: St. Kitts and Nevis 47,000

LARGEST COUNTRY BY AREA: Canada 9,984,670 sq km (3,855,101 sq mi)

SMALLEST COUNTRY BY AREA: St. Kitts and Nevis 269 sq km (104 sq mi)

HIGHEST ELEVATION: Mount McKinley (Denali), Alaska, United States 6,194 m (20,320 ft)

LOWEST ELEVATION: Death Valley, California, United States -86 m (-282 ft)

Water Availability

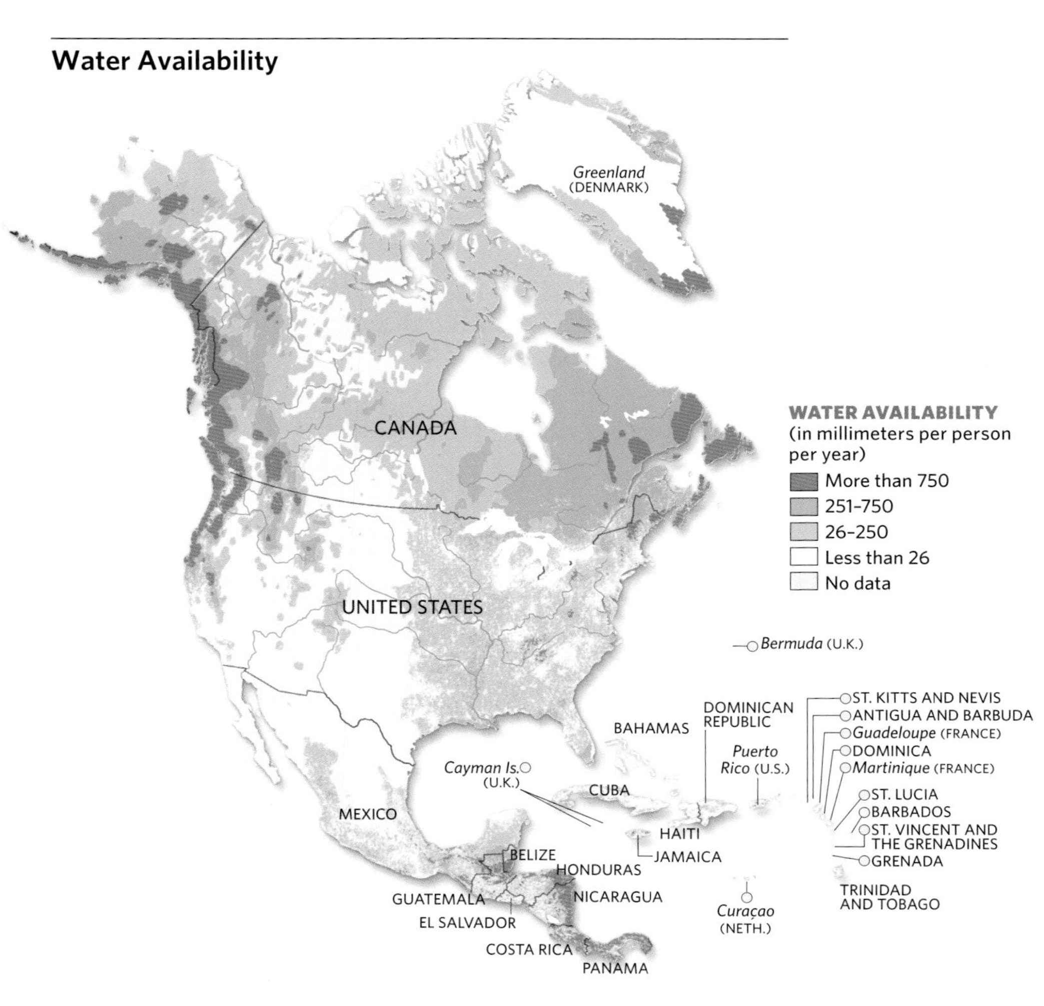

Greenland (DENMARK)
CANADA
UNITED STATES
MEXICO
Bermuda (U.K.)
BAHAMAS
DOMINICAN REPUBLIC
Puerto Rico (U.S.)
ST. KITTS AND NEVIS
ANTIGUA AND BARBUDA
Guadeloupe (FRANCE)
DOMINICA
Martinique (FRANCE)
ST. LUCIA
BARBADOS
ST. VINCENT AND THE GRENADINES
GRENADA
TRINIDAD AND TOBAGO
Curaçao (NETH.)
Cayman Is. (U.K.)
CUBA
HAITI
JAMAICA
BELIZE
HONDURAS
NICARAGUA
GUATEMALA
EL SALVADOR
COSTA RICA
PANAMA
WATER AVAILABILITY
(in millimeters per person per year)
More than 750
251–750
26–250
Less than 26
No data

Climate Zones

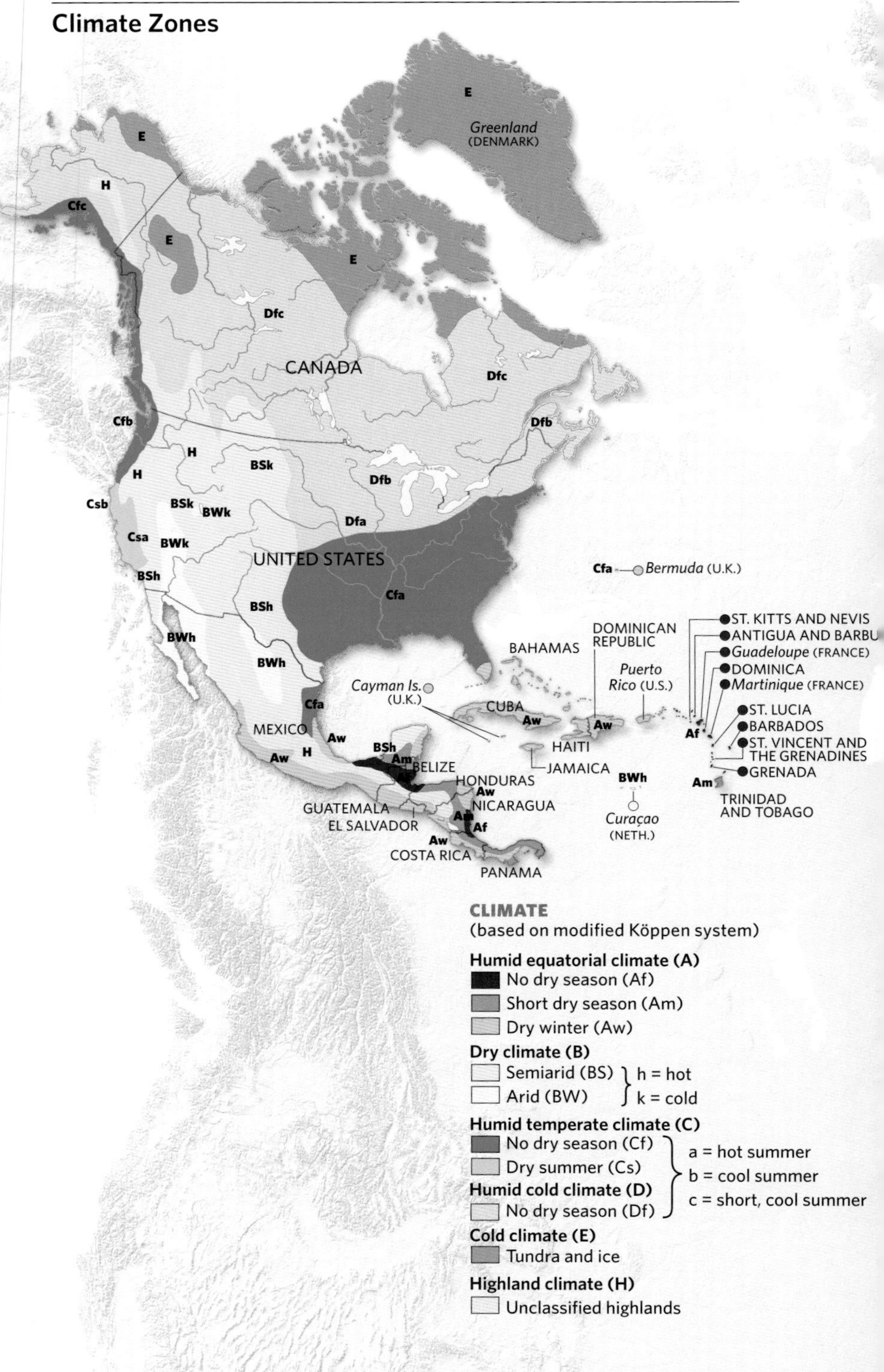

Greenland (DENMARK)
CANADA
UNITED STATES
MEXICO
E
H
Dfc
Cfc
Cfb
Dfb
Dfa
BSk
BWk
Csb
Csa
BSh
BWh
Cfa
Aw
Am
Af
Bermuda (U.K.)
BAHAMAS
DOMINICAN REPUBLIC
Puerto Rico (U.S.)
Cayman Is. (U.K.)
CUBA
HAITI
JAMAICA
BELIZE
HONDURAS
NICARAGUA
GUATEMALA
EL SALVADOR
COSTA RICA
PANAMA
Curaçao (NETH.)
ST. KITTS AND NEVIS
ANTIGUA AND BARBUDA
Guadeloupe (FRANCE)
DOMINICA
Martinique (FRANCE)
ST. LUCIA
BARBADOS
ST. VINCENT AND THE GRENADINES
GRENADA
TRINIDAD AND TOBAGO
CLIMATE
(based on modified Köppen system)
Humid equatorial climate (A)
No dry season (Af)
Short dry season (Am)
Dry winter (Aw)
Dry climate (B)
Semiarid (BS)
Arid (BW)
h = hot
k = cold
Humid temperate climate (C)
No dry season (Cf)
Dry summer (Cs)
Humid cold climate (D)
No dry season (Df)
a = hot summer
b = cool summer
c = short, cool summer
Cold climate (E)
Tundra and ice
Highland climate (H)
Unclassified highlands

Natural Events

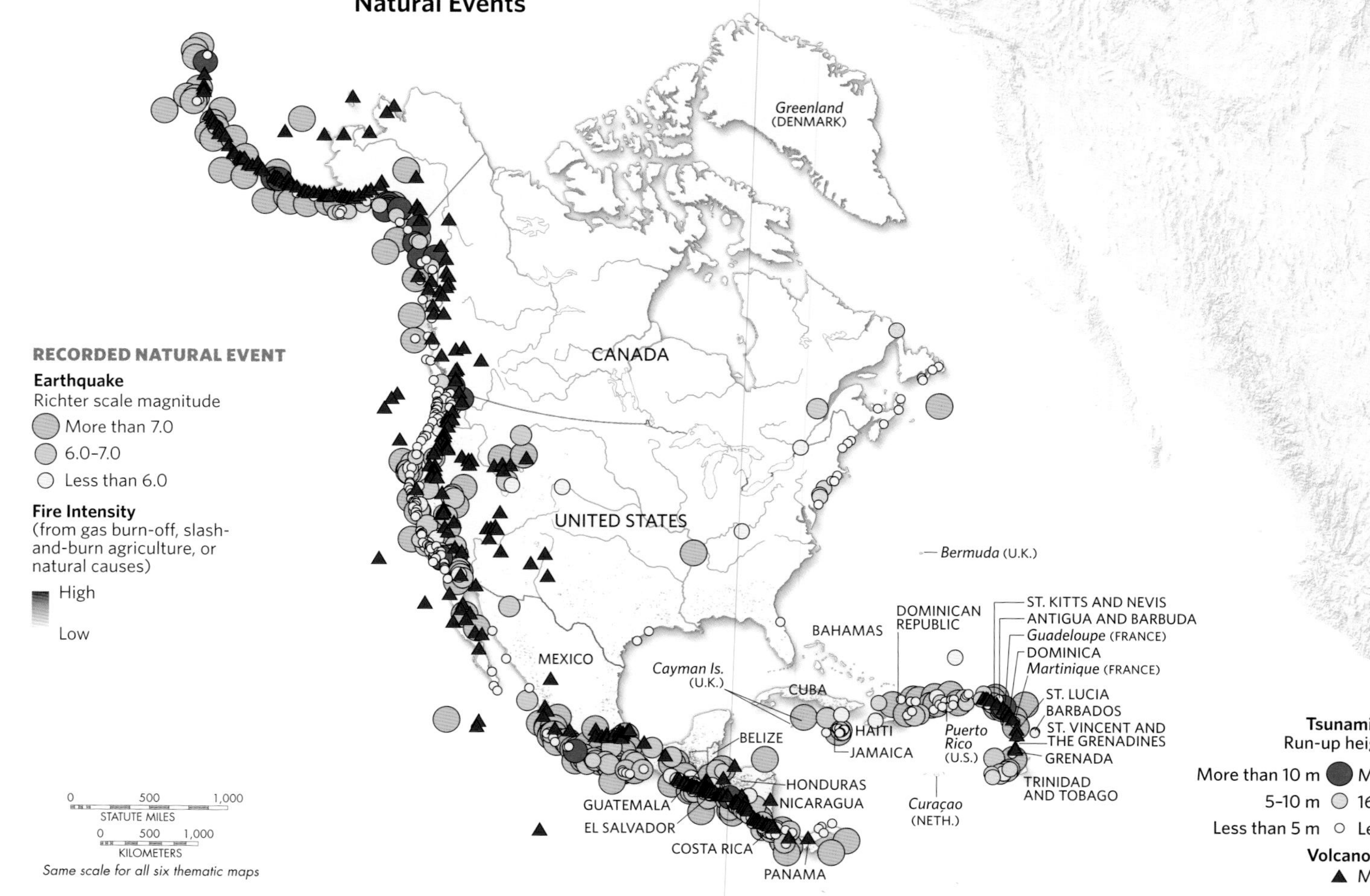

Greenland (DENMARK)
CANADA
UNITED STATES
MEXICO
Bermuda (U.K.)
BAHAMAS
DOMINICAN REPUBLIC
Puerto Rico (U.S.)
Cayman Is. (U.K.)
CUBA
HAITI
JAMAICA
BELIZE
HONDURAS
NICARAGUA
GUATEMALA
EL SALVADOR
COSTA RICA
PANAMA
Curaçao (NETH.)
ST. KITTS AND NEVIS
ANTIGUA AND BARBUDA
Guadeloupe (FRANCE)
DOMINICA
Martinique (FRANCE)
ST. LUCIA
BARBADOS
ST. VINCENT AND THE GRENADINES
GRENADA
TRINIDAD AND TOBAGO
RECORDED NATURAL EVENT
Earthquake
Richter scale magnitude
More than 7.0
6.0–7.0
Less than 6.0
Fire Intensity
(from gas burn-off, slash-and-burn agriculture, or natural causes)
High
Low
Tsunami
Run-up height
More than 10 m
More than 32 ft
5-10 m
16-32 ft
Less than 5 m
Less than 16 ft
Volcano
Major eruption
0 500 1,000
STATUTE MILES
0 500 1,000
KILOMETERS
Same scale for all six thematic maps

Population Density

Energy Consumption

Dominant Economy

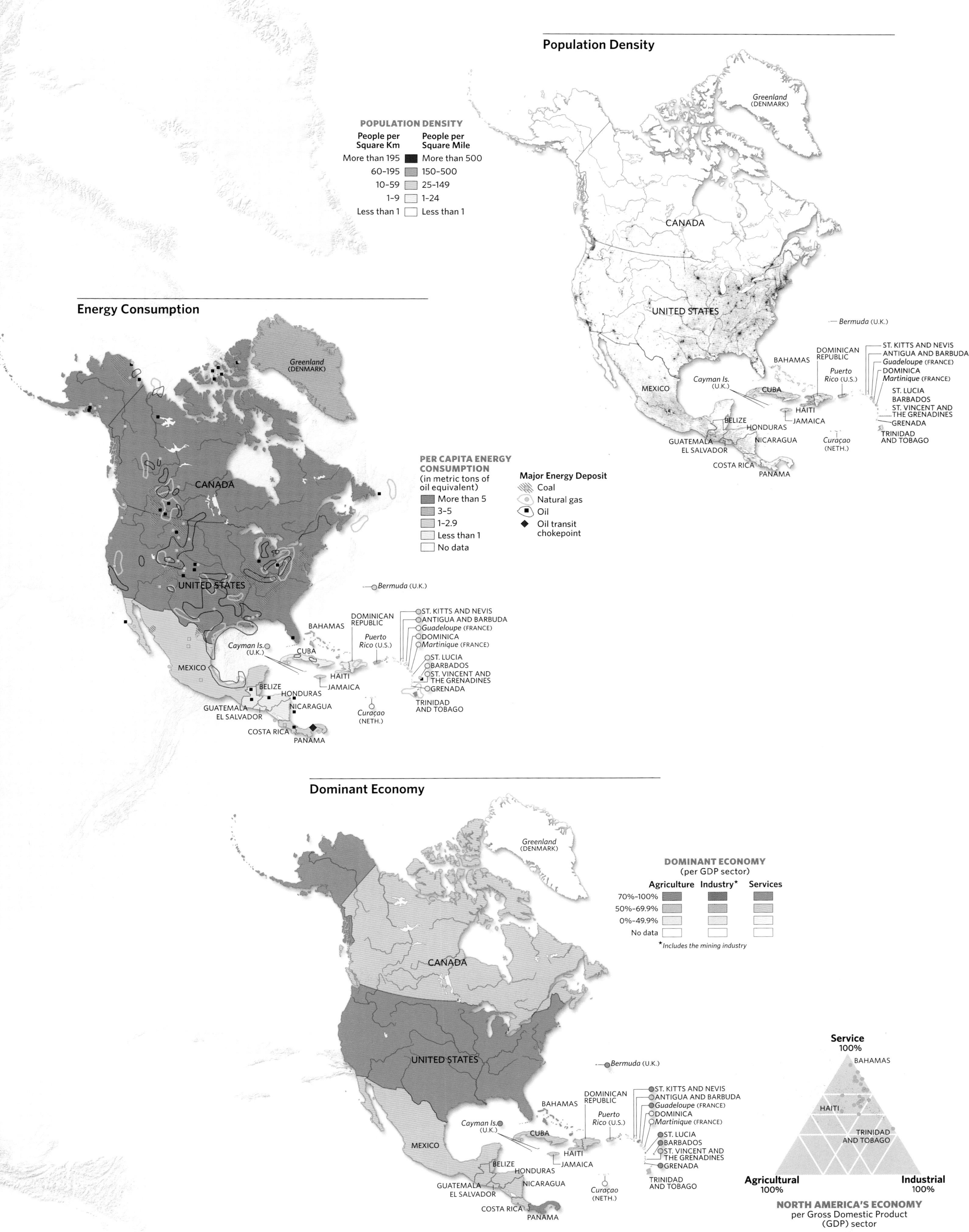
POPULATION DENSITY
People per Square Km
People per Square Mile
More than 195 | More than 500
60-195 | 150-500
10-59 | 25-149
1-9 | 1-24
Less than 1 | Less than 1
Greenland (DENMARK)
CANADA
UNITED STATES
MEXICO
Bermuda (U.K.)
BAHAMAS
DOMINICAN REPUBLIC
Puerto Rico (U.S.)
Cayman Is. (U.K.)
CUBA
HAITI
JAMAICA
BELIZE
HONDURAS
GUATEMALA
EL SALVADOR
NICARAGUA
COSTA RICA
PANAMA
Curaçao (NETH.)
ST. KITTS AND NEVIS
ANTIGUA AND BARBUDA
Guadeloupe (FRANCE)
DOMINICA
Martinique (FRANCE)
ST. LUCIA
BARBADOS
ST. VINCENT AND THE GRENADINES
GRENADA
TRINIDAD AND TOBAGO
PER CAPITA ENERGY CONSUMPTION
(in metric tons of oil equivalent)
More than 5
3-5
1-2.9
Less than 1
No data
Major Energy Deposit
Coal
Natural gas
Oil
Oil transit chokepoint
DOMINANT ECONOMY
(per GDP sector)
Agriculture
Industry*
Services
70%-100%
50%-69.9%
0%-49.9%
No data
*Includes the mining industry
Service 100%
Agricultural 100%
Industrial 100%
NORTH AMERICA'S ECONOMY
per Gross Domestic Product (GDP) sector

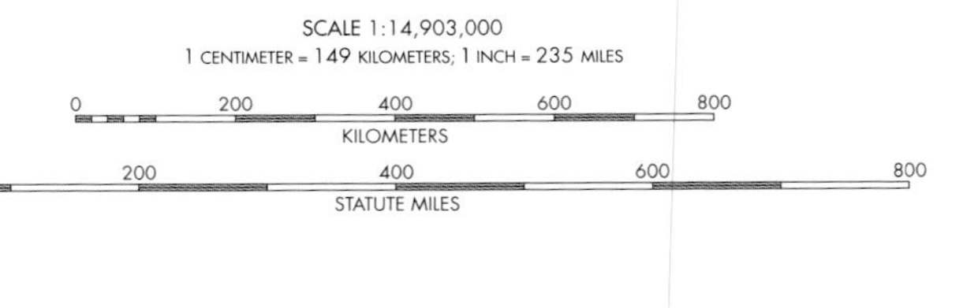
Azimuthal Equidistant Projection
SCALE 1:14,903,000
1 CENTIMETER = 149 KILOMETERS; 1 INCH = 235 MILES
0 200 400 600 800
KILOMETERS
0 200 400 600 800
STATUTE MILES

Kluane/Wrangell-St. Elias/Glacier Bay/Tatshenshini-Alsek ❶

Covering more than 24 million acres and comprising the world's third largest terrestrial protected area, this joint Canadian-U.S. region extends from the Gulf of Alaska, over the coastal Chugach and St. Elias Mountains, and deep into the southwest Yukon Territory. The relatively inaccessible wilderness includes Mount Logan, Canada's highest mountain at 19,520 feet; the largest nonpolar icefield in the world with 350 valley glaciers; rivers that provide the only vegetated, ice-free linkage for animal migration; one of the last stronghold's of North America's grizzly bear and sanctuary for endangered humpback whales; and a diversity of vegetation that attracts the blue-gray "Glacier" bear, a rare color of the black bear found nowhere else in Canada.

Canadian Rocky Mountain Parks, British Columbia and Alberta ❷

Comprised of four contiguous national parks and three provincial parks spanning more than 7,800 square miles, this protected site includes the Burgess Shale, one of the world's most significant fossil remains of soft-bodied marine animals. Snow on mountain peaks compresses to form glaciers and as the temperature rises, ice melts and races down mountainsides, boring holes in thousand-foot-thick glaciers and finally emerging as giant waterfalls filling the lakes with blue-green water.

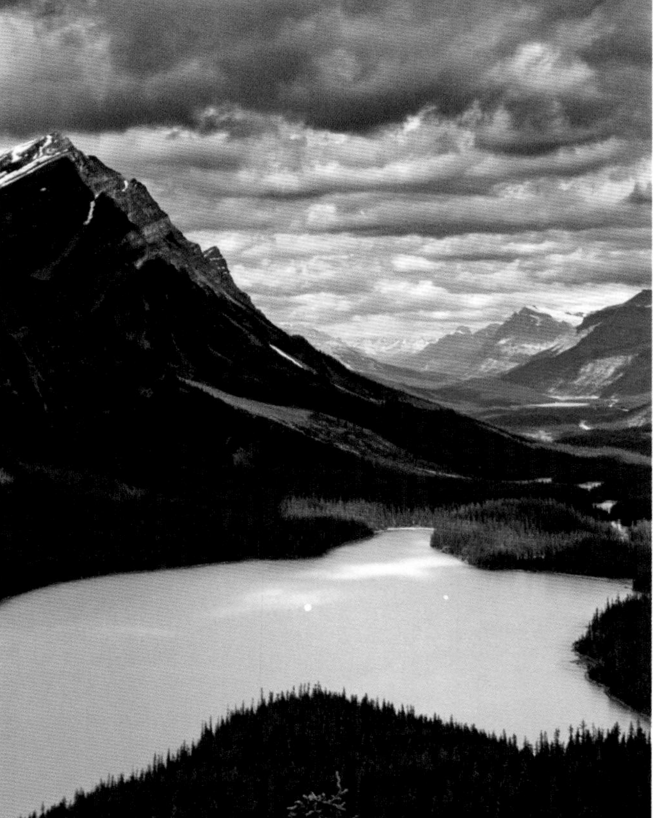

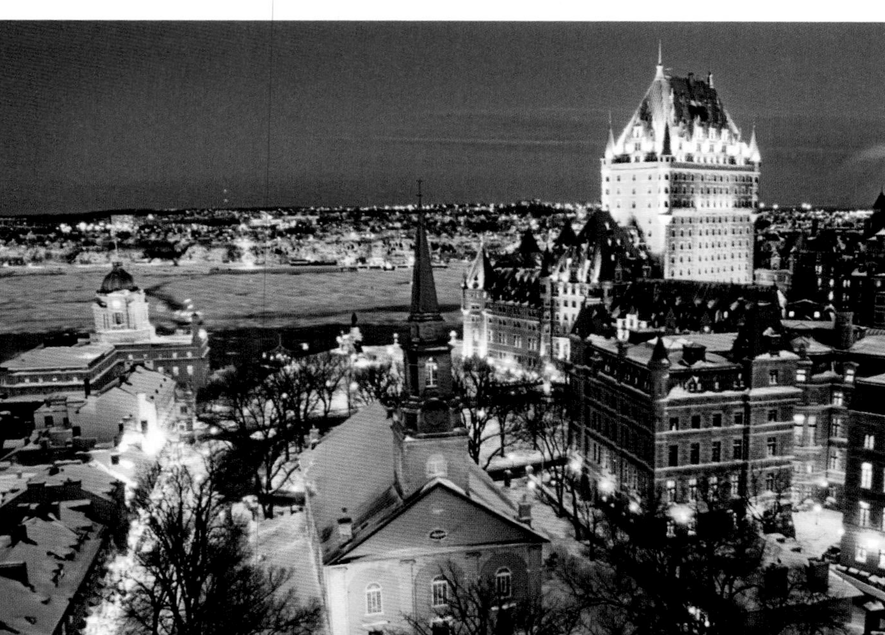

Historic District of Old Québec, Québec ❸

Founded on a steep plateau in 1608 by the French explorer Samuel de Champlain, the former capital of New France is surrounded by its ramparts, bastions, and gates, and is the only North American city to have preserved its original defensive fortifications. The Upper Town, which remains the administrative and religious center, lies on the cliff where monuments such as Château Frontenac and the Citadel still stand. The Lower Town encompasses the Notre-Dame-des-Victoires Church, 17th- and 18th-century houses, and the harbor where ships delivered manufactured goods from Europe and loaded precious pelts from the North.

Canada

Canada
North
America

Gros Morne National Park,
4 Newfoundland and Labrador

Nearly 4,500 years ago, maritime Indians inhabited this area on Newfoundland's west coast. The park is a rare example of the process of continental drift, where deep ocean crust and rocks of Earth's mantle lie exposed. Site of the world's most well-known fossil collection of extinct animals trapped in rock layers, more recent glacial action has resulted in coastal lowlands, alpine plateaus, glacial valleys, fjords, waterfalls, and pristine lakes.

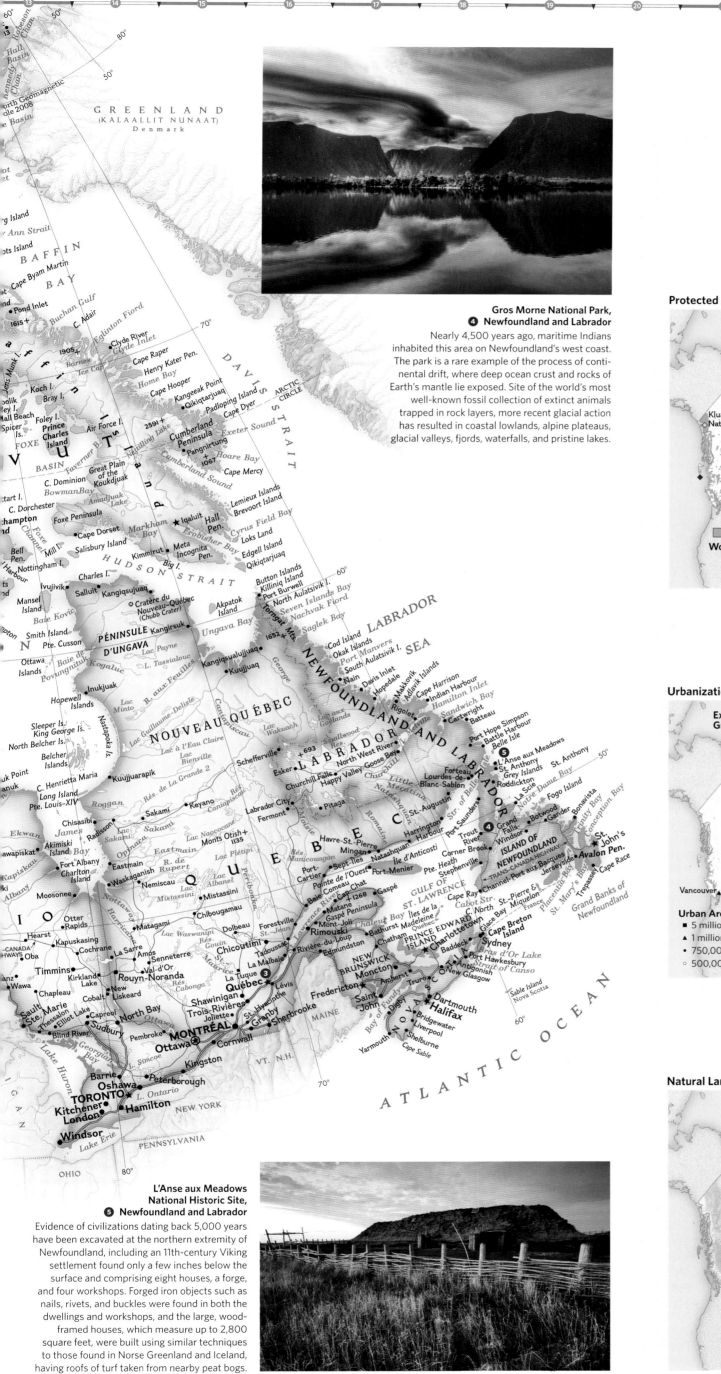

Protected Areas and World Heritage Sites

Kluane
National Park
CANADA
Canadian Rocky
Mountain Parks
L'Anse aux
Meadows
Gros Morne
National Park
Québec
Protected areas
World Heritage Sites
Cultural
Natural
8.9%
Canada
Percent of Land Area Protected

Urbanization and Largest Cities

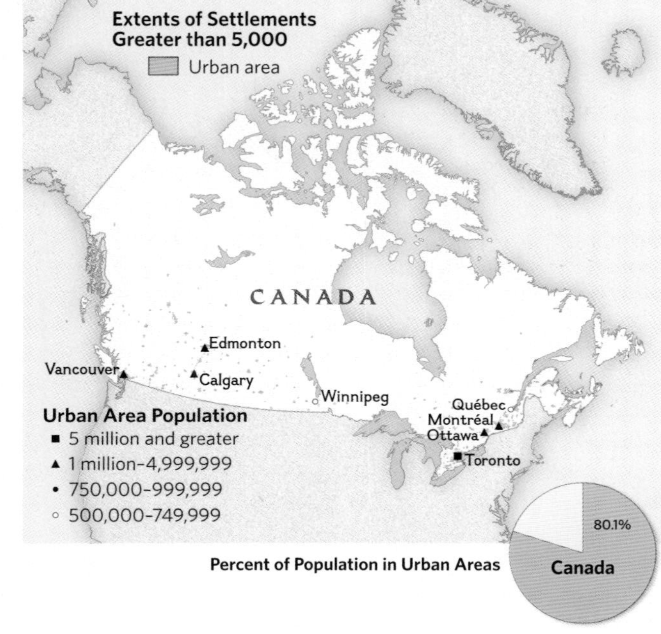
Extents of Settlements
Greater than 5,000
Urban area
CANADA
Edmonton
Vancouver
Calgary
Winnipeg
Québec
Montréal
Ottawa
Toronto
Urban Area Population
5 million and greater
1 million–4,999,999
750,000–999,999
500,000–749,999
80.1%
Canada
Percent of Population in Urban Areas

Natural Land Cover

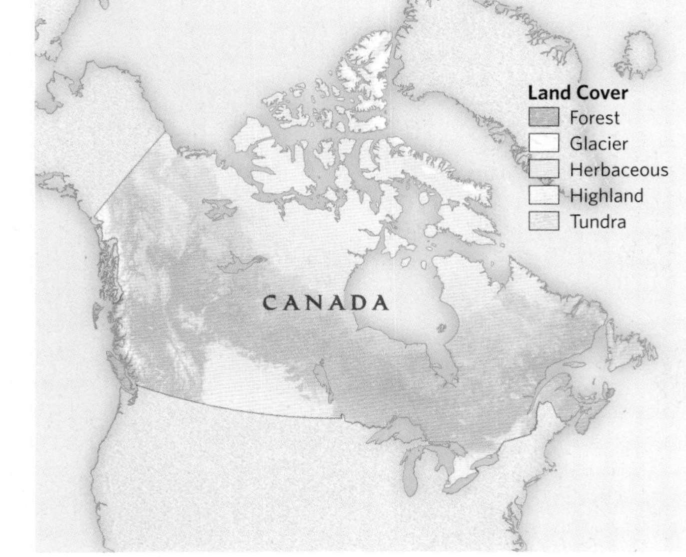
Land Cover
Forest
Glacier
Herbaceous
Highland
Tundra
CANADA

L'Anse aux Meadows
National Historic Site,
5 Newfoundland and Labrador

Evidence of civilizations dating back 5,000 years have been excavated at the northern extremity of Newfoundland, including an 11th-century Viking settlement found only a few inches below the surface and comprising eight houses, a forge, and four workshops. Forged iron objects such as nails, rivets, and buckles were found in both the dwellings and workshops, and the large, wood-framed houses, which measure up to 2,800 square feet, were built using similar techniques to those found in Norse Greenland and Iceland, having roofs of turf taken from nearby peat bogs.

PACIFIC OCEAN
CAN
ROCKY MOUNTAINS
GREAT PLAINS
COAST RANGES
CASCADE RANGE
SIERRA NEVADA
GREAT BASIN
Columbia Plateau
COLORADO PLATEAU
MEXICO
Mt. Baker 10778
Mt. Olympus 7980
Mt. Rainier 14411
Mt. St. Helens 8365
Mt. Adams 12307
Mt. Hood 11239
Mt. Shasta 14162
Lassen Peak 10457
Mt. Whitney 14494 (4418 m)
Death Valley -282' (-86 m)
Great Salt Lake
Grand Canyon
Mojave Desert
Sonoran Desert
Llano Estacado
Edwards Plateau
Great Divide Basin
Continental Divide
Pikes Peak 14110
Mt. Elbert 14433
Longs Peak 14255
Grand Teton 13770
Geographical Center of the 50 United States
Geographical Center of the 48 Contiguous United States
ALASKA
BROOKS RANGE
ALASKA RANGE
Mt. McKinley (Denali) 20320 (6194 m)
BEAUFORT SEA
GULF OF ALASKA
ALASKA PENINSULA
ALEUTIAN RANGE
SEWARD PENINSULA
KENAI PENINSULA
ALEXANDER ARCHIPELAGO
COAST MOUNTAINS
ARCTIC CIRCLE
0 100 200 300 km
0 50 100 150 statute mi

ATLANTIC OCEAN
GULF OF MEXICO
GULF OF MAINE
CENTRAL LOWLAND
APPALACHIAN MOUNTAINS
Appalachian Plateau
Allegheny Mountains
Blue Ridge
Piedmont
Cumberland Plateau
Ozark Plateau
Lake Superior
Lake Michigan
Lake Huron
Lake Erie
Lake Ontario
Upper Peninsula
Lower Peninsula
Mt. Katahdin 5268
Mt. Washington 6288
Mt. Mansfield 4393
Mt. Marcy 5344
Adirondack Mts.
Catskill Mts.
Slide Mt. 4180
Mt. Greylock 3491
Mt. Frissell 2380
Jerimoth Hill 812
High Pt. 1803
Mt. Davis 3213
Backbone Mt. 3360
Spruce Knob 4863
Mt. Rogers 5729
Black Mt. 4145
Mt. Mitchell 6684
Clingmans Dome 6643
Great Smoky Mts.
Sassafras Mt. 3560
Brasstown Bald 4784
Cheaha Mt. 2407
Woodall Mt. 806
Campbell Hill 1550
Charles Mound 1235
Timms Hill 1951
Mt. Arvon 1979
Eagle Mt. 2301
Taum Sauk Mt. 1772
Boston Mts.
Ouachita Mts.
Magazine Mt. 2753
Driskill Mt. 535
Black Belt
Sea Islands
Florida Keys
Straits of Florida
The Everglades
Lake Okeechobee
Cape Canaveral
Cape Hatteras
Cape Lookout
Cape Fear
Cape Charles
Cape Cod
Cape Ann
Chesapeake Bay
Delaware Bay
Long Island Sd.
Pine Barrens
Mississippi River Delta
BAHAMAS
CUBA
HAITI
TROPIC OF CANCER
Albers Conic Equal-Area Projection
SCALE 1:9,864,700
1 CENTIMETER = 99 KILOMETERS; 1 INCH = 156 MILES
KILOMETERS
STATUTE MILES
elevations in feet
10,000
9,000
8,000
7,000
6,000
5,000
4,000
3,000
2,000
1,000
250
0 (sea level)
Longitude West 90° of Greenwich
PRINCIPAL HAWAIIAN ISLANDS
PACIFIC OCEAN
KAUA'I
O'AHU
MOLOKA'I
LĀNA'I
MAUI
HAWAI'I
NI'IHAU
Kawaikini 5243
Mauna Kea 13796
Mauna Loa 13679
Kilauea 4077
Kalae (South Cape)
100 km
100 statute mi
Longitude West 159° of Greenwich

Albers Conic Equal-Area Projection
SCALE 1:9,864,700
1 CENTIMETER = 99 KILOMETERS; 1 INCH = 156 MILES
KILOMETERS
STATUTE MILES
Elevations in feet
BRITISH COLUMBIA
ALBERTA
CANADA
SASKATCHEWAN
MANITOBA
ROCKY
PACIFIC OCEAN
WASHINGTON
OREGON
IDAHO
MONTANA
WYOMING
NORTH DAKOTA
SOUTH DAKOTA
NEBRASKA
KANSAS
OKLAHOMA
CALIFORNIA
NEVADA
UTAH
COLORADO
ARIZONA
NEW MEXICO
TEXAS
MEXICO
GREAT BASIN
SIERRA NEVADA
COLORADO PLATEAU
Str. of Georgia
Str. of Juan de Fuca
Seattle
Bellingham
Everett
Tacoma
Olympia
Spokane
Yakima
Portland
Salem
Eugene
Boise
Helena
Missoula
Billings
Great Falls
Butte
Cheyenne
Casper
Salt Lake City
Ogden
Provo
Reno
Carson City
Las Vegas
Sacramento
San Francisco
Oakland
San Jose
Fresno
Bakersfield
LOS ANGELES
Long Beach
SAN DIEGO
Denver
Colorado Springs
Pueblo
Santa Fe
Albuquerque
PHOENIX
Tucson
El Paso
SAN ANTONIO
Austin
Fort Worth
Oklahoma City
Wichita
Bismarck
Pierre
Lubbock
Amarillo
Laredo
Brownsville
ARCTIC OCEAN
BEAUFORT SEA
CHUKCHI SEA
BERING SEA
GULF OF ALASKA
PACIFIC OCEAN
RUSSIA
ALASKA
BROOKS RANGE
ALASKA RANGE
North Slope
YUKON
CANADA U.S.
Barrow
Prudhoe Bay
Nome
Fairbanks
Anchorage
Juneau
Kodiak Island
Mt. McKinley (Denali) 20320
ALASKA
0 100 200 300 km
0 50 100 150 statute mi

Yellowstone National Park, Wyoming 1

Established as the world's first national park in 1872 and covering nearly 3,500 square miles, Yellowstone is home to grizzly bears, bison, and bald eagles, and has more than 300 geysers, two-thirds of all those on Earth. Located where molten rock rises in a column from deep in Earth's mantle, it contains half of the world's known geothermal features, including the 370-foot-diameter Grand Prismatic Spring, tinted by algae and bacteria that thrive in its hot water.

United States

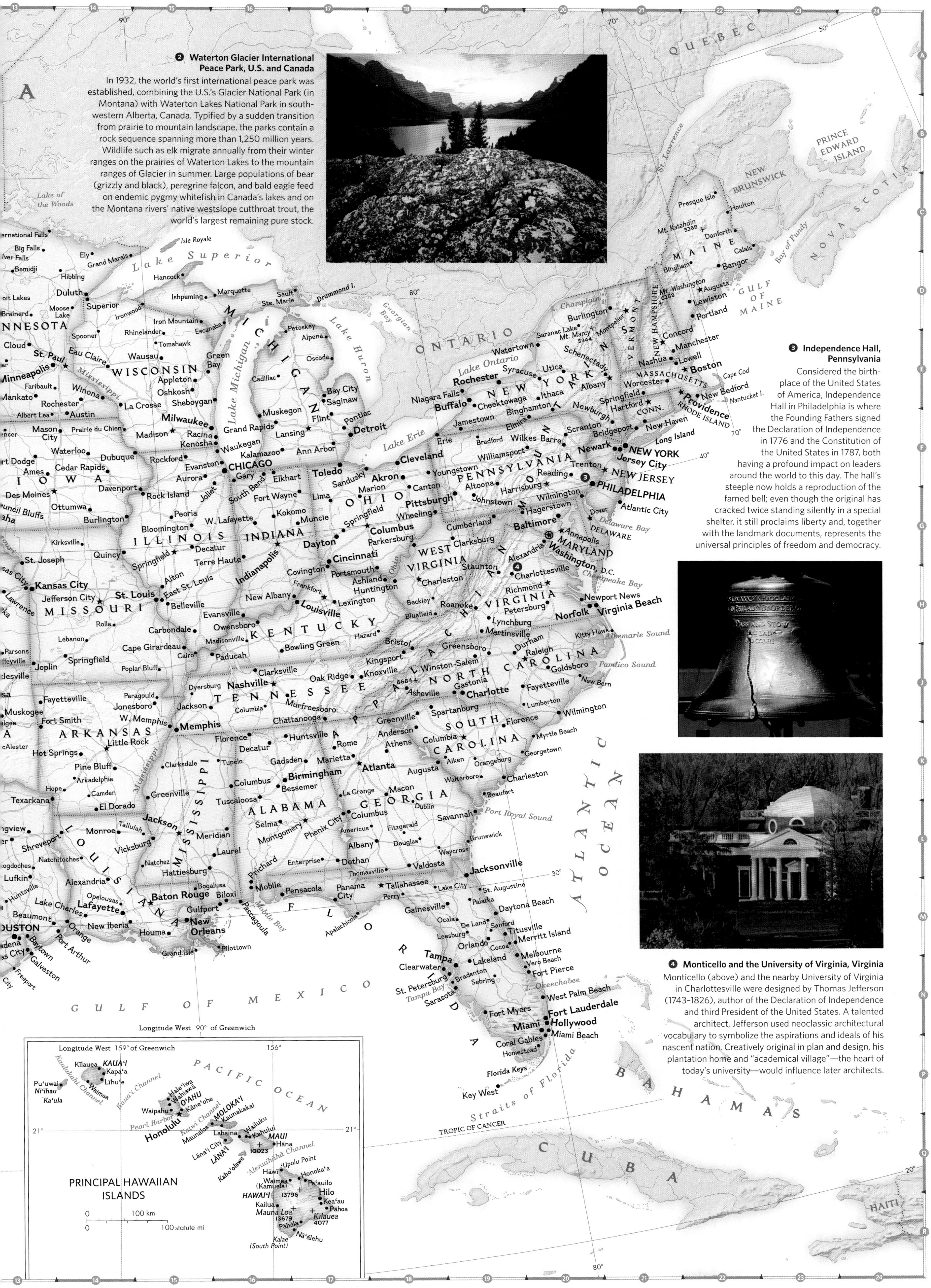

❷ Waterton Glacier International Peace Park, U.S. and Canada

In 1932, the world's first international peace park was established, combining the U.S.'s Glacier National Park (in Montana) with Waterton Lakes National Park in southwestern Alberta, Canada. Typified by a sudden transition from prairie to mountain landscape, the parks contain a rock sequence spanning more than 1,250 million years. Wildlife such as elk migrate annually from their winter ranges on the prairies of Waterton Lakes to the mountain ranges of Glacier in summer. Large populations of bear (grizzly and black), peregrine falcon, and bald eagle feed on endemic pygmy whitefish in Canada's lakes and on the Montana rivers' native westslope cutthroat trout, the world's largest remaining pure stock.

❸ Independence Hall, Pennsylvania

Considered the birthplace of the United States of America, Independence Hall in Philadelphia is where the Founding Fathers signed the Declaration of Independence in 1776 and the Constitution of the United States in 1787, both having a profound impact on leaders around the world to this day. The hall's steeple now holds a reproduction of the famed bell; even though the original has cracked twice standing silently in a special shelter, it still proclaims liberty and, together with the landmark documents, represents the universal principles of freedom and democracy.

❹ Monticello and the University of Virginia, Virginia

Monticello (above) and the nearby University of Virginia in Charlottesville were designed by Thomas Jefferson (1743–1826), author of the Declaration of Independence and third President of the United States. A talented architect, Jefferson used neoclassic architectural vocabulary to symbolize the aspirations and ideals of his nascent nation. Creatively original in plan and design, his plantation home and "academical village"—the heart of today's university—would influence later architects.

PRINCIPAL HAWAIIAN ISLANDS

Protected Areas: National Parks and Reserves

Natural Risks: Risk to Property from Natural Disasters

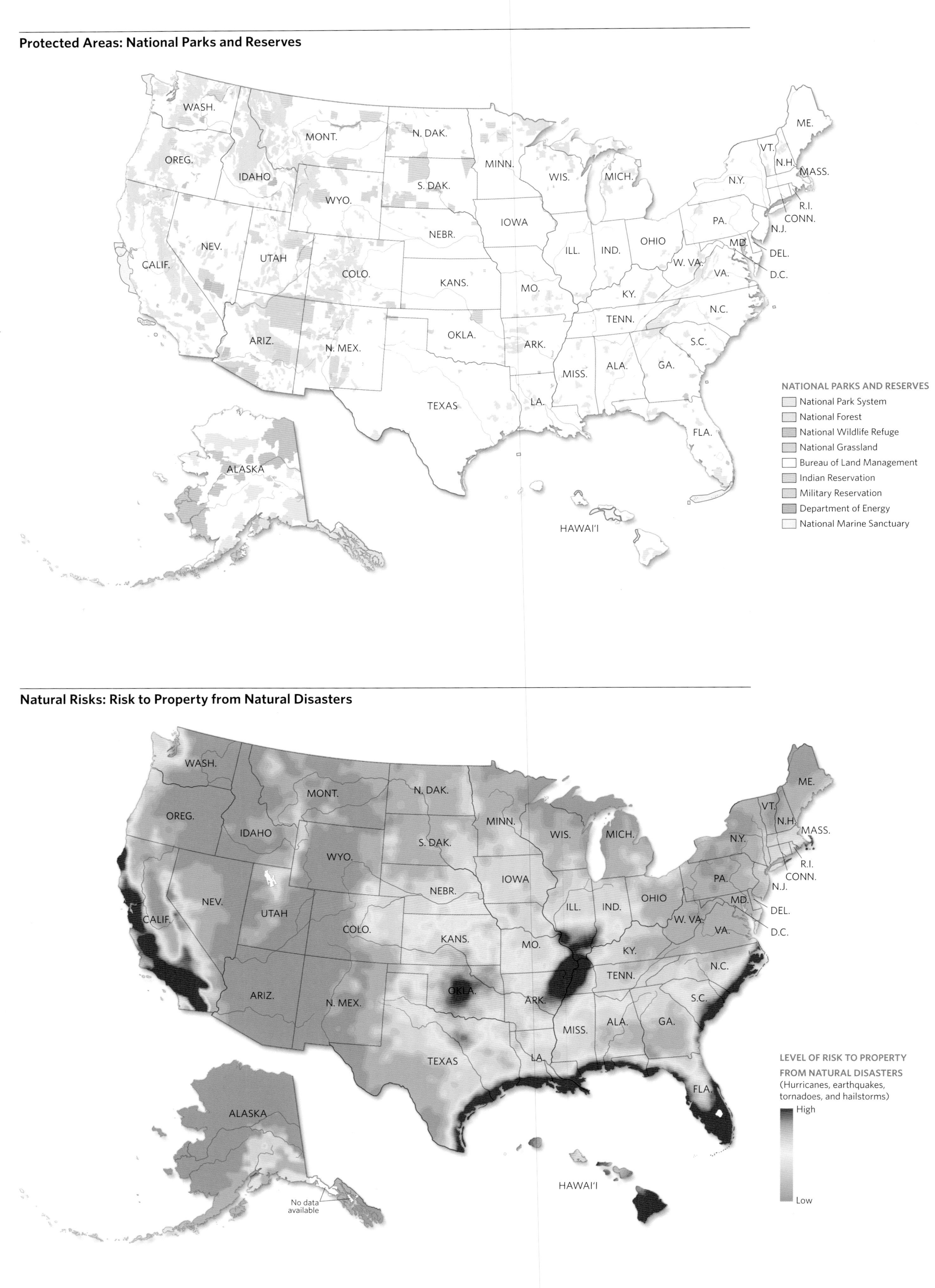
WASH.
OREG.
CALIF.
NEV.
IDAHO
MONT.
WYO.
UTAH
ARIZ.
COLO.
N. MEX.
N. DAK.
S. DAK.
NEBR.
KANS.
OKLA.
TEXAS
MINN.
IOWA
MO.
ARK.
LA.
WIS.
ILL.
MICH.
IND.
OHIO
KY.
TENN.
MISS.
ALA.
GA.
FLA.
S.C.
N.C.
VA.
W. VA.
PA.
N.Y.
MD.
DEL.
D.C.
N.J.
CONN.
R.I.
MASS.
VT.
N.H.
ME.
ALASKA
HAWAI'I
NATIONAL PARKS AND RESERVES
National Park System
National Forest
National Wildlife Refuge
National Grassland
Bureau of Land Management
Indian Reservation
Military Reservation
Department of Energy
National Marine Sanctuary
No data available
LEVEL OF RISK TO PROPERTY FROM NATURAL DISASTERS
(Hurricanes, earthquakes, tornadoes, and hailstorms)
High
Low

United States: Themes

TOTAL AREA: 9,826,630 sq km (3,794,083 sq mi)

FIRST STATE TO RATIFY THE CONSTITUTION: Delaware, Dec. 7, 1787

MOST POPULOUS STATE: California, 36,553,215

LEAST POPULOUS STATE: Wyoming, 522,830

MOST POPULOUS CITY: New York, 8,214,426

LARGEST STATE BY AREA: Alaska, 1,717,862 sq km (663,267 sq mi)

SMALLEST STATE BY AREA: Rhode Island, 4,002 sq km (1,545 sq mi)

LARGEST LAKE: Lake Superior, 82,100 sq km (31,700 sq mi)

LONGEST RIVER: Mississippi-Missouri, 5,971 km (3,710 mi)

LOWEST TEMPERATURE RECORDED: Minus 62.2°C (-80°F) at Prospect Creek, Alaska, January 23, 1971

HIGHEST TEMPERATURE RECORDED: 56.6°C (134°F) at Death Valley, California, July 10, 1913

RAINIEST SPOT: Wai'ale'ale (mountain), Hawai'i average annual rainfall 1,168 cm (460 in)

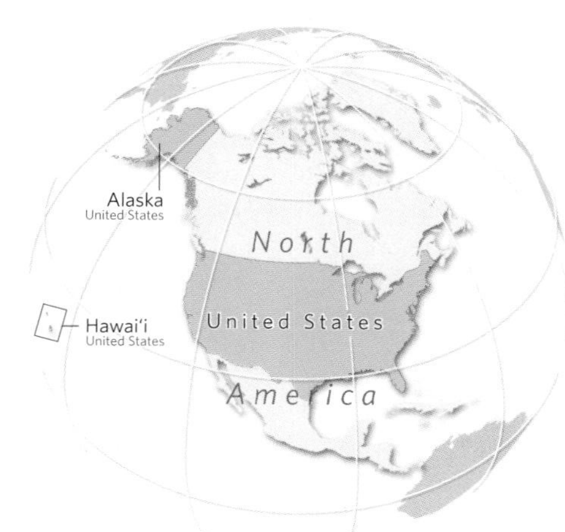

Alaska
United States
Hawai'i
United States
North
United States
America

Protected Areas and World Heritage Sites

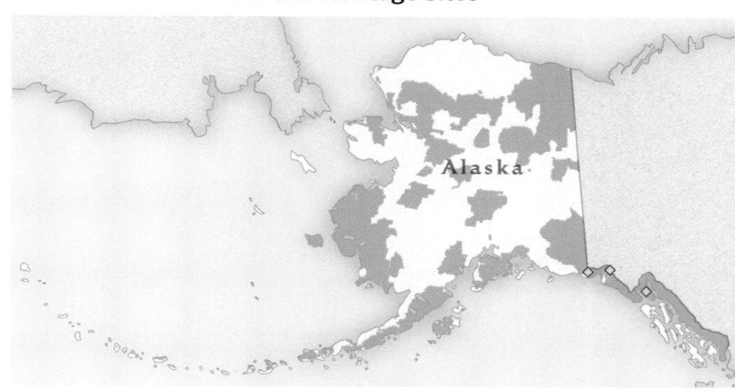

Alaska

Protected areas

World Heritage Sites
- ◆ Cultural
- ◇ Natural

Hawai'i

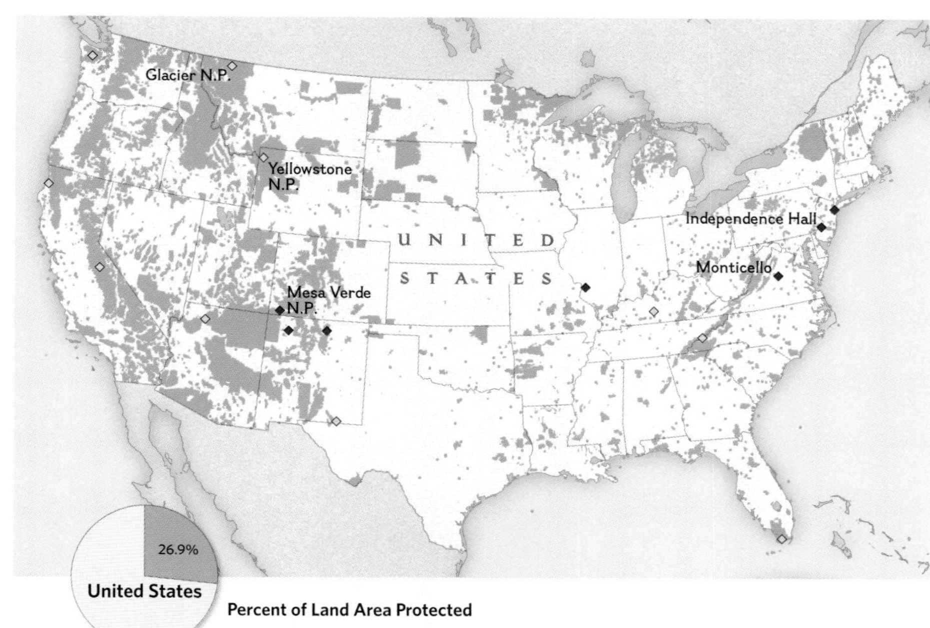

Glacier N.P.
Yellowstone N.P.
UNITED STATES
Mesa Verde N.P.
Independence Hall
Monticello
26.9%
United States

Percent of Land Area Protected

Urbanization and Largest Cities

Alaska

Extents of Settlements Greater than 5,000

Urban area

Urban Area Population
- ■ 10 million and greater
- ▲ 5 million–9,999,999
- • 2 million–4,999,999
- ◦ 1,500,000–1,999,999

Hawai'i

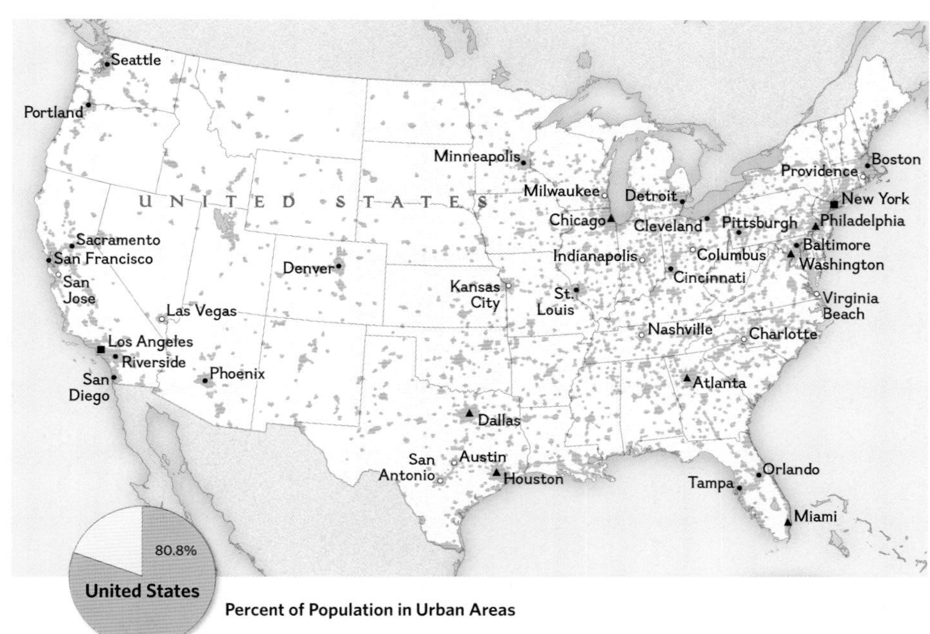

Seattle
Portland
UNITED STATES
Minneapolis
Boston
Providence
Milwaukee
Detroit
New York
Chicago
Cleveland
Pittsburgh
Philadelphia
Sacramento
San Francisco
Indianapolis
Columbus
Baltimore
Washington
Denver
Cincinnati
San Jose
Kansas City
St. Louis
Virginia Beach
Las Vegas
Nashville
Charlotte
Los Angeles
Riverside
Phoenix
San Diego
Atlanta
Dallas
San Antonio
Austin
Houston
Orlando
Tampa
Miami
80.8%
United States

Percent of Population in Urban Areas

Natural Land Cover

Alaska

Land Cover

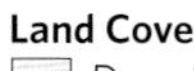

- Desert
- Forest
- Glacier
- Herbaceous
- Highland
- Tundra

Hawai'i

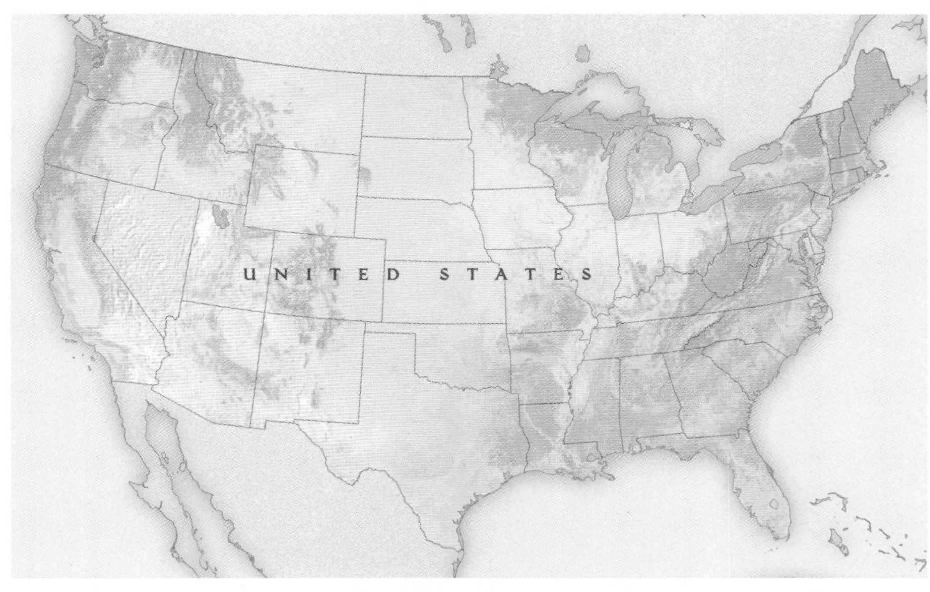

UNITED STATES

UNITED S
NEW MEXICO
ARIZONA
CALIFORNIA
TEX
SONORA
CHIHUAHUA
COAHUILA
DURANGO
SINALOA
ZACATECAS
NAYARIT
BAJA CALIFORNIA
BAJA CALIFORNIA SUR
SIERRA MADRE OCCIDENTAL
SIERRA MADRE ORIENTAL
GOLFO DE CALIFORNIA
MAR DE CORTÉS
PACIFIC OC
Longitude West 105° of Greenwich
Albers Conic Equal-Area Projection
SCALE 1:7,000,000
1 CENTIMETER = 70 KILOMETERS; 1 INCH = 110 MILES
KILOMETERS
STATUTE MILES
Islas Revillagigedo
TIJUANA
Mexicali
Ensenada
CIUDAD JUÁREZ
Chihuahua
Hermosillo
Guaymas
Ciudad Obregón
Culiacán
Mazatlán
La Paz
Cabo San Lucas
Durango
Torreón
Saltillo
MONTERREY
Nuevo Laredo
Zacatecas
Aguascalientes
GUADALAJARA
LEÓN
Morelia
Acapulco

Pre-Hispanic City of Chichén Itzá ❶
The remains of Chichén Itzá, a Mayan city that prospered between the ninth and thirteenth centuries, lie hidden in the dense forests of the Yucatán Peninsula. Toltec warriors migrated from the north in the tenth century, imposing the ritual of human sacrifice on the Mayan. Gradually, the cultures began to merge by borrowing traits from one another, creating, for example, the combined Mayan and Toltec vision of the universe revealed in the site's stone monuments and artistic works: The sun rises in the east and sleeps in the west; at night, it fights against the underworld gods in the south; and, passing through the top of the world in the north where the gods in the sky reside, the sun is reborn.

Mexico

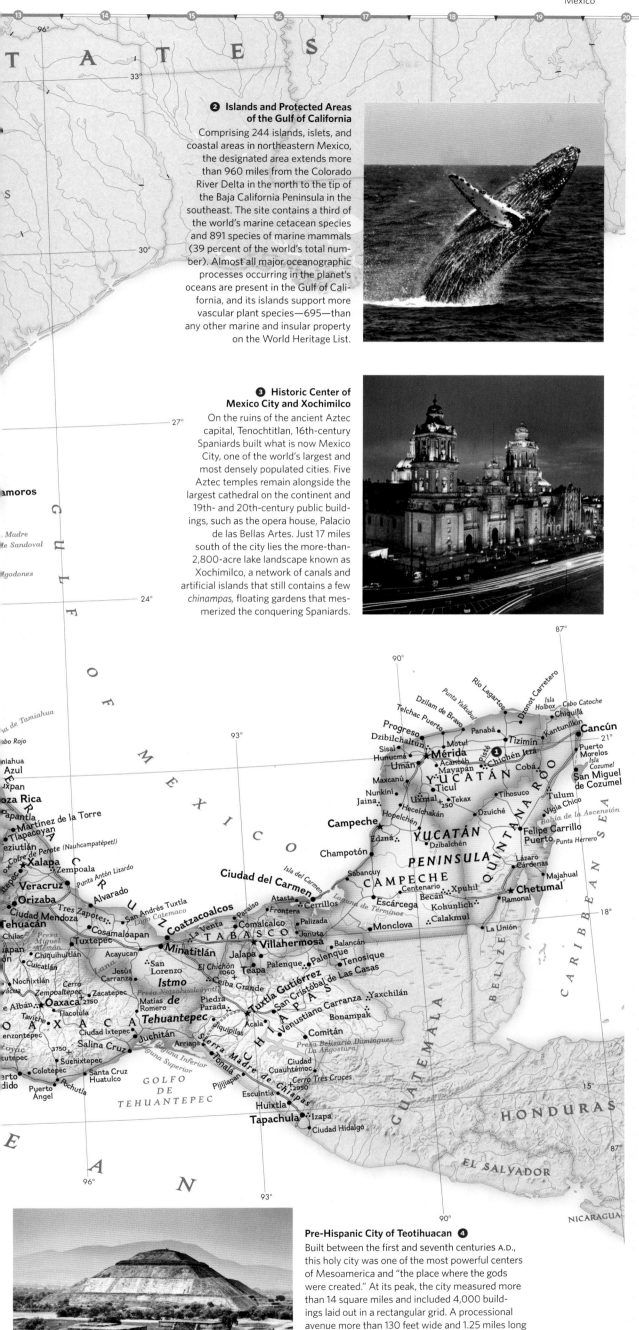

❷ Islands and Protected Areas of the Gulf of California

Comprising 244 islands, islets, and coastal areas in northeastern Mexico, the designated area extends more than 960 miles from the Colorado River Delta in the north to the tip of the Baja California Peninsula in the southeast. The site contains a third of the world's marine cetacean species and 891 species of marine mammals (39 percent of the world's total number). Almost all major oceanographic processes occurring in the planet's oceans are present in the Gulf of California, and its islands support more vascular plant species—695—than any other marine and insular property on the World Heritage List.

❸ Historic Center of Mexico City and Xochimilco

On the ruins of the ancient Aztec capital, Tenochtitlan, 16th-century Spaniards built what is now Mexico City, one of the world's largest and most densely populated cities. Five Aztec temples remain alongside the largest cathedral on the continent and 19th- and 20th-century public buildings, such as the opera house, Palacio de las Bellas Artes. Just 17 miles south of the city lies the more-than-2,800-acre lake landscape known as Xochimilco, a network of canals and artificial islands that still contains a few *chinampas*, floating gardens that mesmerized the conquering Spaniards.

Pre-Hispanic City of Teotihuacan ❹

Built between the first and seventh centuries A.D., this holy city was one of the most powerful centers of Mesoamerica and "the place where the gods were created." At its peak, the city measured more than 14 square miles and included 4,000 buildings laid out in a rectangular grid. A processional avenue more than 130 feet wide and 1.25 miles long bisected the city, linking markets, plazas, and the huge monuments on the avenue's border, including the Pyramid of the Sun, located in direct relation to the position of the sun at its zenith.

North
America
Mexico

Protected Areas and World Heritage Sites

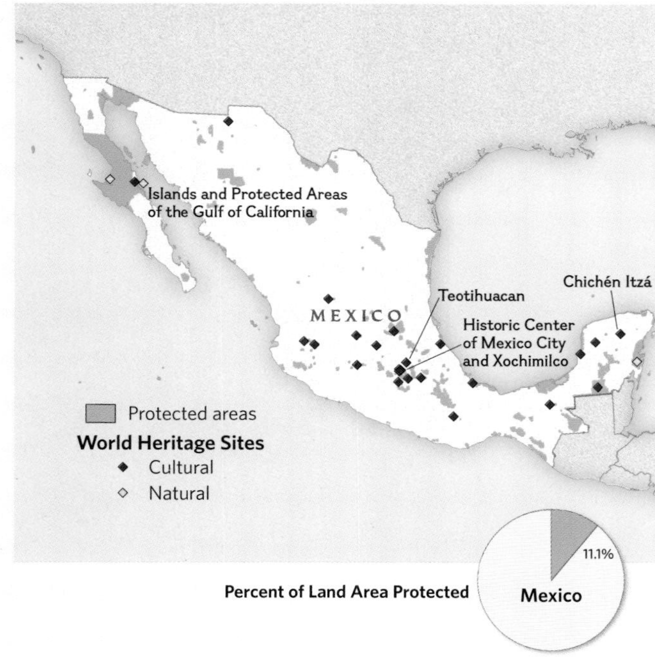
Islands and Protected Areas of the Gulf of California
MEXICO
Teotihuacan
Chichén Itzá
Historic Center of Mexico City and Xochimilco
Protected areas
World Heritage Sites
Cultural
Natural
11.1%
Mexico
Percent of Land Area Protected

Urbanization and Largest Cities

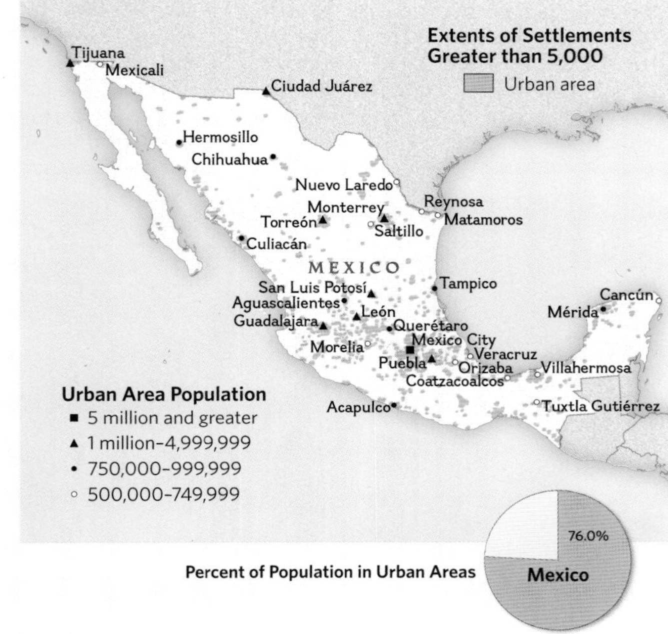
Extents of Settlements Greater than 5,000
Urban area
Tijuana
Mexicali
Ciudad Juárez
Hermosillo
Chihuahua
Nuevo Laredo
Monterrey
Reynosa
Matamoros
Torreón
Saltillo
Culiacán
MEXICO
San Luis Potosí
Tampico
Aguascalientes
León
Guadalajara
Querétaro
Mexico City
Morelia
Puebla
Veracruz
Orizaba
Coatzacoalcos
Villahermosa
Mérida
Cancún
Acapulco
Tuxtla Gutiérrez
Urban Area Population
5 million and greater
1 million–4,999,999
750,000–999,999
500,000–749,999
76.0%
Mexico
Percent of Population in Urban Areas

Natural Land Cover

MEXICO
Land Cover
Desert
Forest
Herbaceous
Highland
Savanna

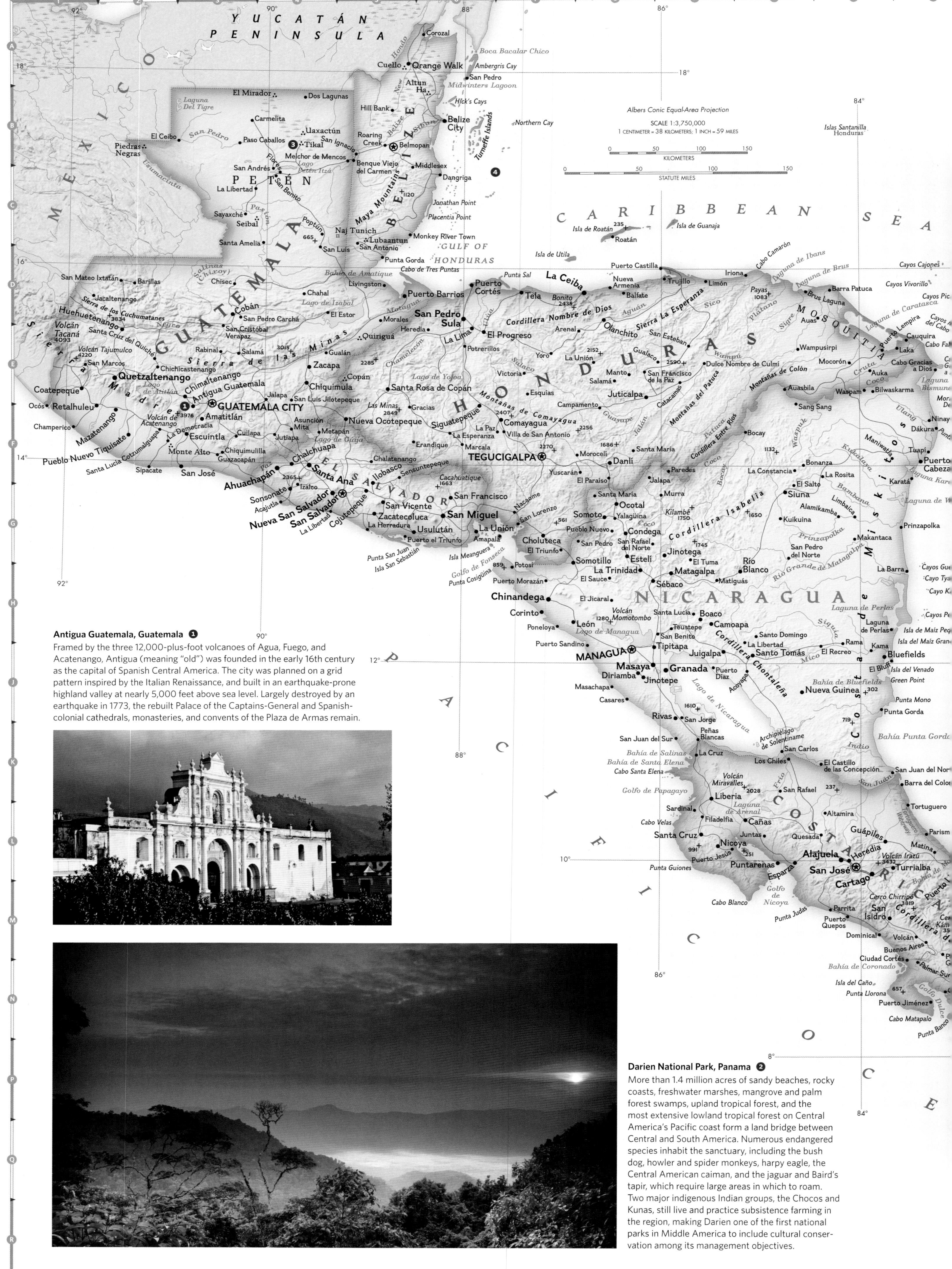
YUCATÁN PENINSULA
MEXICO
GUATEMALA
PETÉN
BELIZE
HONDURAS
EL SALVADOR
NICARAGUA
COSTA RICA
CARIBBEAN SEA
PACIFIC OCEAN
GULF OF HONDURAS
Albers Conic Equal-Area Projection
SCALE 1:3,750,000
1 CENTIMETER = 38 KILOMETERS; 1 INCH = 59 MILES
KILOMETERS
STATUTE MILES
GUATEMALA CITY
Antigua Guatemala
Quetzaltenango
Belize City
Belmopan
Orange Walk
Corozal
Tikal
Flores
San Pedro Sula
La Ceiba
Puerto Cortés
Puerto Barrios
TEGUCIGALPA
Comayagua
Choluteca
San Salvador
Santa Ana
San Miguel
MANAGUA
León
Chinandega
Granada
Masaya
Matagalpa
Bluefields
Lago de Nicaragua
Lago de Managua
San José
Alajuela
Cartago
Liberia
Puntarenas
Golfo de Fonseca
Golfo de Nicoya
Golfo de Papagayo
Isla de Roatán
Isla de Guanaja
Sierra Madre
Cordillera Isabelia
Montañas de Comayagua
Maya Mountains

Antigua Guatemala, Guatemala 1

Framed by the three 12,000-plus-foot volcanoes of Agua, Fuego, and Acatenango, Antigua (meaning "old") was founded in the early 16th century as the capital of Spanish Central America. The city was planned on a grid pattern inspired by the Italian Renaissance, and built in an earthquake-prone highland valley at nearly 5,000 feet above sea level. Largely destroyed by an earthquake in 1773, the rebuilt Palace of the Captains-General and Spanish-colonial cathedrals, monasteries, and convents of the Plaza de Armas remain.

Darien National Park, Panama 2

More than 1.4 million acres of sandy beaches, rocky coasts, freshwater marshes, mangrove and palm forest swamps, upland tropical forest, and the most extensive lowland tropical forest on Central America's Pacific coast form a land bridge between Central and South America. Numerous endangered species inhabit the sanctuary, including the bush dog, howler and spider monkeys, harpy eagle, the Central American caiman, and the jaguar and Baird's tapir, which require large areas in which to roam. Two major indigenous Indian groups, the Chocos and Kunas, still live and practice subsistence farming in the region, making Darien one of the first national parks in Middle America to include cultural conservation among its management objectives.

Population Density
POPULATION DENSITY
People per Square Km
People per Square Mile
More than 195 | More than 500
60-195 | 150-500
10-59 | 25-149
1-9 | 1-24
Less than 1 | Less than 1
VENEZUELA
GUYANA
SURINAME
French Guiana (FRANCE)
COLOMBIA
ECUADOR
Galápagos Islands (ECUADOR)
St. Peter and St. Paul Rocks (BRAZIL)
Arquipélago Fernando de Noronha
Atol das Rocas (BRAZIL)
PERU
BRAZIL
BOLIVIA
PARAGUAY
CHILE
Is. Martin Vaz
I. de Trindade (BRAZIL)
I. San Félix
Isla San Ambrosio (CHILE)
URUGUAY
Archipiélago Juan Fernández (CHILE)
ARGENTINA
Falkland Islands (U.K.)
Is. Diego Ramírez (CHILE)
Energy Consumption
VENEZUELA
GUYANA
SURINAME
French Guiana (FRANCE)
COLOMBIA
ECUADOR
Galápagos Islands (ECUADOR)
PERU
BRAZIL
BOLIVIA
PARAGUAY
CHILE
ARGENTINA
URUGUAY
Falkland Islands (U.K.)
PER CAPITA ENERGY CONSUMPTION
(in metric tons of oil equivalent)
More than 5
3-5
1-2.9
Less than 1
No data
Major Energy Deposit
Coal
Natural gas
Oil
Oil pipeline
Dominant Economy
VENEZUELA
GUYANA
SURINAME
French Guiana (FRANCE)
COLOMBIA
ECUADOR
Galápagos Islands (ECUADOR)
PERU
BRAZIL
BOLIVIA
PARAGUAY
CHILE
URUGUAY
ARGENTINA
Falkland Islands (U.K.)
DOMINANT ECONOMY
(per GDP sector)
Agriculture | Industry* | Services
70%-100%
50%-69.9%
0%-49.9%
No data
*Includes the mining industry
Service 100%
PERU
GUYANA
CHILE
Agricultural 100%
Industrial 100%
SOUTH AMERICA'S ECONOMY
per Gross Domestic Product (GDP) sector

San Agustín Archaeological Park, Colombia ❶
San Agustín is the largest group of religious monuments and megalithic sculptures in South America, numbering more than 300, and was occupied by a flourishing pre-Colombian civilization from the 6th century B.C. to the 12th century A.D. Three locales form the park, where, in styles ranging from abstract to realist, the Agustinian Culture skillfully represented gods with threatening faces, warriors armed with clubs, and animals such as the jaguar, with razor-sharp teeth and stealthy eyes. The stonework, a combination of sculpture, painting, graffiti, and funerary stelae, survives, but the people vanished, wiped out by the Spanish conquest.

CARIBBEAN SEA
PACIFIC OCEAN
COLOMBIA
VENEZUELA
PANAMA
ECUADOR
PERU
Península de la Guajira
Pen. de Paraguaná
Aruba Neth.
Curaçao
Bonaire
Netherlands
Islas Los Roques
Isla Orchila
Golfo de Venezuela
Lago de Maracaibo
Golfo de Urabá
Golfo de Cupica
Golfo de Tibugá
G. de Morrosquillo
Ensenada Docampadó
Bahía de Ancón de Sardinas
Riohacha
Santa Marta
BARRANQUILLA
CARTAGENA
MARACAIBO
Ciénaga
Soledad
Valledupar
Montería
Sincelejo
Cúcuta
San Cristóbal
Bucaramanga
Barrancabermeja
MEDELLÍN
Quibdó
Manizales
Pereira
Armenia
Ibagué
BOGOTÁ
Tunja
Sogamoso
Villavicencio
Neiva
CALI
Palmira
Buga
Tuluá
Buenaventura
Popayán
Pasto
Ipiales
Tumaco
Florencia
Mocoa
San Agustín
Mitú
Leticia
La Pedrera
Tarapacá
Puerto Leguízamo
Puerto Carreño
Puerto Ayacucho
San Fernando de Apure
Barinas
Mérida
Barquisimeto
VALENCIA
Maracay
CARACAS
Puerto Cabello
Coro
Punto Fijo
Los Teques
Calabozo
Guanare
Acarigua
EQUATOR
Amazonas
Caquetá
Putumayo
Guaviare
Meta
Orinoco
Apure
Vaupés
Magdalena
Cauca
Cordillera de Mérida
Raudal Yupurari (Devils Cataract)
Pico da Neblina 3014

Ciudad Universitaria de Caracas, Venezuela ❷
Having outgrown its original location in the Santa Rosa Seminary in the city's main square, the university relocated to the city's outskirts in the 1940s. Designed by the Venezuelan architect Carlos Raúl Villanueva, the new campus integrated urban planning with artistic and architectural movements of the day. In 1947, the symmetrical construction of the first buildings (School of Medicine, 1945) was abandoned for avant-garde ideas, such as the use of bare concrete structures conceived as sculptures. Another key element, introduced in the School of Architecture, is contrasting volumes: Low buildings set against the tall, prismatic towers of the Central Library.

Port, Fortresses, and Group of Monuments, Cartagena, Colombia ❸
Founded in 1533 by Spaniards on a tiny archipelago in the Caribbean, Cartagena with its natural defenses of narrow channels and a succession of bays was the perfect treasure cache for Spanish bureaucrats rich on trade between the New World and Old. Six massive fortresses with high walls and cannon protected stolen emeralds, gold, pearls, and silver, and officials built up the city with gardens, fountains, and balconied white houses that reminded them of their Andalusian roots. They divided Cartagena into three districts corresponding to the major social categories: San Pedro, where the nobles resided in palaces, San Diego for middle-class merchants and craftsmen, and Gethsemani, the "popular quarter."

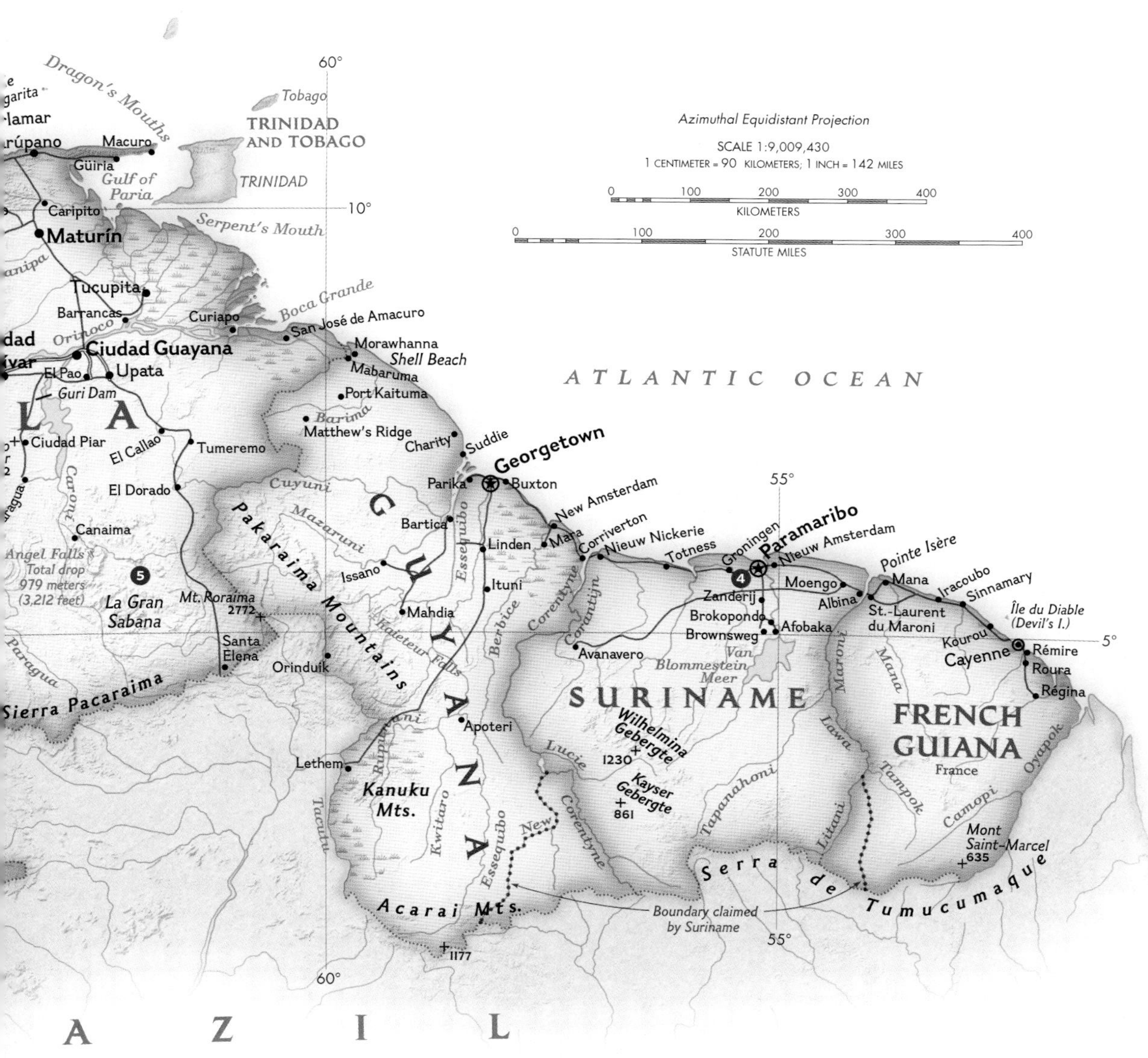
Azimuthal Equidistant Projection
SCALE 1:9,009,430
1 CENTIMETER = 90 KILOMETERS; 1 INCH = 142 MILES
KILOMETERS
STATUTE MILES
ATLANTIC OCEAN
TRINIDAD AND TOBAGO
Tobago
TRINIDAD
Dragon's Mouths
Gulf of Paria
Serpent's Mouth
Boca Grande
Macuro
Güiria
Caripito
Maturín
Tucupita
Barrancas
Curiapo
San José de Amacuro
Ciudad Guayana
Upata
El Pao
Guri Dam
Ciudad Piar
El Callao
Tumeremo
El Dorado
Canaima
Angel Falls Total drop 979 meters (3,212 feet)
La Gran Sabana
Mt. Roraima 2772
Santa Elena
Sierra Pacaraima
Morawhanna
Shell Beach
Mabaruma
Port Kaituma
Matthew's Ridge
Charity
Suddie
Georgetown
Parika
Buxton
Bartica
Linden
Ituni
Issano
Mahdia
Orinduik
Pakaraima Mountains
GUYANA
Apoteri
Lethem
Kanuku Mts.
Acarai Mts.
1177
New Amsterdam
Mara
Corriverton
Nieuw Nickerie
Totness
Groningen
Paramaribo
Nieuw Amsterdam
Zanderij
Brokopondo
Brownsweg
Afobaka
Moengo
Albina
Avanavero
Blommestein Meer
SURINAME
Wilhelmina Gebergte
1230
Kayser Gebergte
861
Boundary claimed by Suriname
Serra de Tumucumaque
Pointe Isère
Mana
St.-Laurent du Maroni
Iracoubo
Sinnamary
Île du Diable (Devil's I.)
Kourou
Cayenne
Rémire
Roura
Régina
FRENCH GUIANA
France
Mont Saint-Marcel
635
BRAZIL

Venezuela
Colombia
Guyana
Suriname
French Guiana
France
South America

Protected Areas and World Heritage Sites

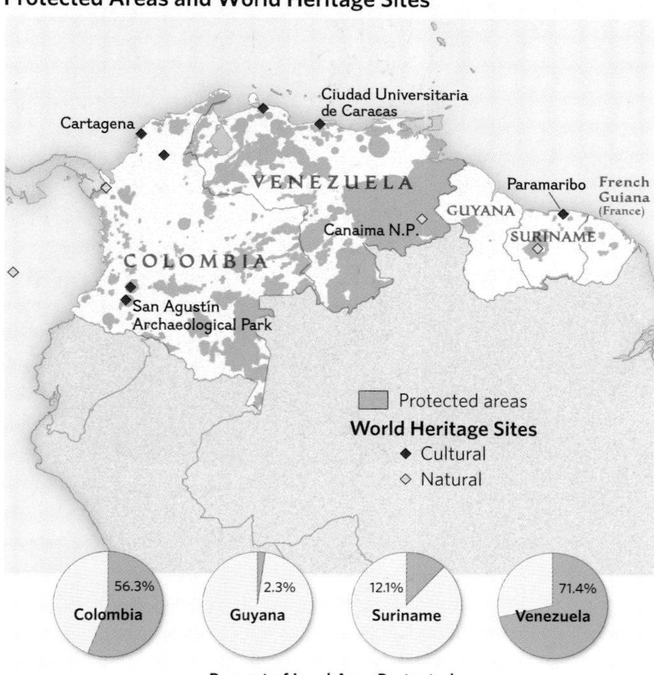
Cartagena
Ciudad Universitaria de Caracas
VENEZUELA
Canaima N.P.
Paramaribo
GUYANA
SURINAME
French Guiana (France)
COLOMBIA
San Agustín Archaeological Park
Protected areas
World Heritage Sites
Cultural
Natural
56.3% Colombia
2.3% Guyana
12.1% Suriname
71.4% Venezuela
Percent of Land Area Protected

Historic Inner City of ❹ Paramaribo, Suriname

The Dutch colonized the northern coast of tropical South America from the 17th century and directed settlers toward sugarcane and tobacco cultivation to meet demand from Europe for tropical products. By the end of the 18th century, more than 600 plantations were in operation. As owners migrated to Paramaribo, the plantations declined, especially after slavery was abolished in 1863. To work the remaining fields, the government brought in thousands of laborers from China, the West Indies, India, and Java. Paramaribo quickly grew, and with two nearby fortresses, the town didn't need fortifying. Fusing Dutch architecture with local techniques and materials, craftsmen from the diverse population built symmetrical, rectangular houses with steep roofs on spacious lots along wide streets.

Urbanization and Largest Cities

Barranquilla
Cartagena
Maracaibo
Valencia
Caracas
Barcelona
Maracay
Barquisimeto
Maturín
Ciudad Guayana
Cúcuta
Bucaramanga
Medellín
Pereira
Bogotá
Cali
VENEZUELA
COLOMBIA
GUYANA
SURINAME
French Guiana (France)
Extents of Settlements Greater than 5,000
Urban area
Urban Area Population
5 million and greater
1 million–4,999,999
750,000–999,999
500,000–749,999
72.7% Colombia
28.2% Guyana
73.9% Suriname
93.4% Venezuela
Percent of Population in Urban Areas

Canaima National Park, Venezuela ❺

Dubbed "The Lost World" by author Sir Arthur Conan Doyle, more than a hundred flat-topped, sheer-walled mountains in southeastern Venezuela stretch across nearly 7.5 million acres of green savanna and forests of the Guyana Highlands. The world's highest waterfall at 3,287 feet, Angel Falls cascades down 8,398-foot-tall Table Mountain, eventually turning to spray that provides moisture for the tropical forest. The highlands are the remnants of a lakebed formed some 200 million years ago, when South America was connected to Africa, forming part of the supercontinent Gondwanaland. When the mantle rose, the lake floor elevated. Wind and rain then eroded the softer rocks, resulting in *tepuis*, or table mountains, on top of which prevails high humidity perfect for moss fields. In turn, these beds foster hundreds of endemic plant species that have evolved to adapt to the weathered, rocky surfaces.

Natural Land Cover

VENEZUELA
COLOMBIA
GUYANA
SURINAME
French Guiana (France)
Land Cover
Forest
Glacier
Herbaceous
Highland
Savanna

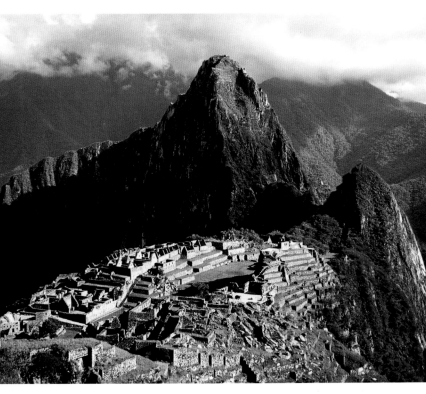

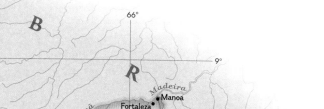

Galápagos Islands, Ecuador ❶
Isolated more than 600 miles off the Pacific coast of Ecuador lie more than 60 islands and islets, a "living showcase of evolution." At the confluence of three sea currents bringing mixed conditions, the Galápagos archipelago was formed by volcanic activity relatively recently in geologic terms, between three to five million years ago, and is a melting pot of species: Penguins share an ecosystem with flamingos; endangered giant tortoises calmly breed on beaches among colorful crabs; and fur seals dive alongside marine iguanas, the only seagoing lizard species.

Historic Sanctuary of ❷ Machu Picchu, Peru
The endangered Andean cat and vulnerable spectacled bear roam more than 80,000 acres of tropical forest on the eastern slopes of the Andes, where, at nearly 8,000 feet above sea level, the Inca Empire established its last stronghold. Dating to the 15th century and manually carved into continuous rock escarpments, the ruins of giant walls, ramps, and stairs are separated into two sectors, the first with distinct industrial, religious, and royal sections, and the surrounding agricultural area with huge terraces cultivated and transformed into hanging gardens.

Historic Center of Arequipa, Peru ❸
Rising more than 7,500 feet in the desert mountains of the Andes, Arequipa was founded by a handful of Spanish conquistadores in 1540, but the Incas were the first to realize the importance of the region, connecting centrally located Cusco with the ocean. Numerous earthquakes forced several rebuildings, as natives integrated European and local techniques and constructed robust walls, extensive archways, courtyards, and intricate baroque facades using *sillar*, pink- and pearl-colored volcanic rock that is tremor-resistant.

Jesuit Missions of the Chiquitos, Bolivia ❹
To ensure the conquest of the indigenous communities of South America, the Spanish crown sent Jesuit fathers to spread Christianity. They built ten missions between 1696 and 1760—six remain today—using a model inspired by the ideal cities of humanist philosophers such as Thomas Moore. They selected sites that couldn't be flooded and constructed wooden houses for the Indians, spacing them regularly along three sides of a rectangular square, the fourth occupied by workshops, schools, and the church.

COLOMBIA
ECUADOR
EQUATOR
QUITO
GUAYAQUIL
Esmeraldas
Ibarra
Santo Domingo de los Colorados
Manta
Portoviejo
Quevedo
Ambato
Riobamba
Milagro
Cuenca
Machala
Loja
Tumbes
Talara
Sullana
Piura
Chiclayo
Lambayeque
Chachapoyas
Cajamarca
Trujillo
Chimbote
Huaraz
Huánuco
Cerro de Pasco
Pucallpa
Iquitos
Cordillera Occidental
Cordillera Oriental
Cordillera Negra
Golfo de Guayaquil
Bahía de Sechura
Amazonas
Marañón
Ucayali
Napo
Putumayo
Fortaleza
Manoa
Guayaramerín
Riberalta
Cobija
Esperanza
Puerto Portillo
Atalaya
Sepahua
La Merced
Satipo
Junín
Huacho
Tingo María
Moyobamba
Tarapoto
Yurimaguas
Requena
Nauta
Pebas
Caballococha
Amelia
Puerto Alegre
Tournavista
Nevado Huascarán
6768
Chimborazo
6310
Cotopaxi
5897
Cayambe
5790
Sangay
5230
0°
3°
6°
9°
63°
66°
69°
72°
75°
78°
81°

Bolivia Ecuador Peru

BOLIVIA
PERU
CHILE
ARGENTINA
PARAGUAY
PACIFIC OCEAN
La Paz
Administrative capital
Sucre
Constitutional capital
Santa Cruz
Cochabamba
Oruro
Potosí
Tarija
Trinidad
Arequipa
Cusco
Tacna
Puno
Juliaca
Altiplano
Cordillera Oriental
Cord. Occidental
Cordillera de los Frailes
Cordillera de Chichas
Cordillera de Lípez
Salar de Uyuni
Salar de Coipasa
Lago Titicaca
Lago Poopó
Machu Picchu
Transverse Mercator Projection
SCALE 1:8,000,000
1 CENTIMETER = 80 KILOMETERS; 1 INCH = 126 MILES
Longitude West 63° of Greenwich
GALÁPAGOS ISLANDS
(ARCHIPIÉLAGO DE COLÓN)
Ecuador
Isla Isabela (Albemarle)
Isla Santa Cruz (Chaves, Indefatigable)
Isla San Cristóbal (Chatham)
Isla San Salvador (Santiago, James)
Isla Fernandina (Narborough)
Isla Santa María (Floreana, Charles)
Isla Española (Hood)
Isla Marchena (Bindloe)
Isla Pinta (Abingdon)
Isla Genovesa (Tower)
Isla Darwin (Culpepper)
Isla Wolf (Wenman)
EQUATOR
Protected Areas and World Heritage Sites
Protected areas
World Heritage Sites
Cultural
Natural
Mixed
Jesuit Missions of the Chiquitos
Bolivia 23.5%
Ecuador 27.1%
Peru 19.5%
Percent of Land Area Protected
Urbanization and Largest Cities
Extents of Settlements Greater than 5,000
Urban area
Urban Area Population
5 million and greater
1 million–4,999,999
750,000–999,999
500,000–749,999
Quito
Guayaquil
Chiclayo
Trujillo
Lima
Bolivia 64.2%
Ecuador 62.8%
Peru 72.6%
Percent of Population in Urban Areas
Natural Land Cover
ECUADOR
Land Cover
Desert
Forest
Glacier
Herbaceous
Highland
South America
Galápagos Islands

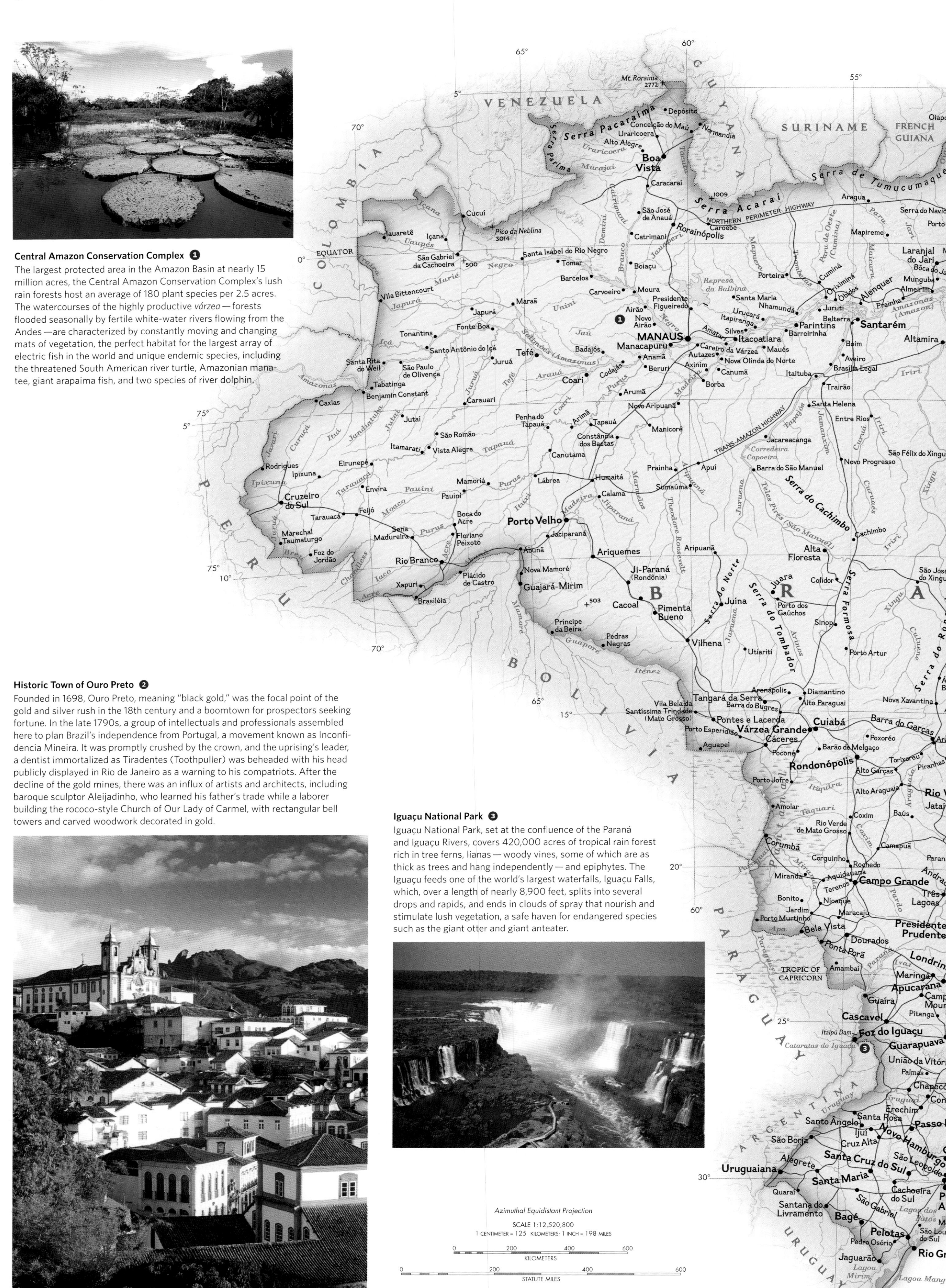
VENEZUELA
GUYANA
SURINAME
FRENCH GUIANA
COLOMBIA
PERU
BOLIVIA
PARAGUAY
ARGENTINA
URUGUAY
B R A
EQUATOR
TROPIC OF CAPRICORN
Mt. Roraima 2772
Pico da Neblina 3014
Serra Pacaraima
Serra Parima
Serra Acaraí
Serra de Tumucumaque
Serra do Cachimbo
Serra Formosa
Serra do Tombador
Serra do Norte
Serra do Roncador
NORTHERN PERIMETER HIGHWAY
TRANS-AMAZON HIGHWAY
Boa Vista
Caracaraí
Rorainópolis
MANAUS
Manacapuru
Santarém
Altamira
Itaituba
Parintins
Itacoatiara
Tefé
Coari
Porto Velho
Rio Branco
Cruzeiro do Sul
Guajará-Mirim
Ariquemes
Ji-Paraná (Rondônia)
Cacoal
Pimenta Bueno
Vilhena
Humaitá
Lábrea
Tabatinga
Benjamin Constant
São Gabriel da Cachoeira
Cuiabá
Várzea Grande
Cáceres
Rondonópolis
Corumbá
Campo Grande
Dourados
Ponta Porã
Presidente Prudente
Londrina
Maringá
Cascavel
Foz do Iguaçu
Guarapuava
Cataratas do Iguaçu
Itaipú Dam
Passo Fundo
Santa Maria
Uruguaiana
Bagé
Pelotas
Rio Grande
Santa Vitória do Palmar
Chuí
Azimuthal Equidistant Projection
SCALE 1:12,520,800
1 CENTIMETER = 125 KILOMETERS; 1 INCH = 198 MILES
KILOMETERS
STATUTE MILES

Central Amazon Conservation Complex ❶

The largest protected area in the Amazon Basin at nearly 15 million acres, the Central Amazon Conservation Complex's lush rain forests host an average of 180 plant species per 2.5 acres. The watercourses of the highly productive *várzea*—forests flooded seasonally by fertile white-water rivers flowing from the Andes—are characterized by constantly moving and changing mats of vegetation, the perfect habitat for the largest array of electric fish in the world and unique endemic species, including the threatened South American river turtle, Amazonian manatee, giant arapaima fish, and two species of river dolphin.

Historic Town of Ouro Preto ❷

Founded in 1698, Ouro Preto, meaning "black gold," was the focal point of the gold and silver rush in the 18th century and a boomtown for prospectors seeking fortune. In the late 1790s, a group of intellectuals and professionals assembled here to plan Brazil's independence from Portugal, a movement known as Inconfidencia Mineira. It was promptly crushed by the crown, and the uprising's leader, a dentist immortalized as Tiradentes (Toothpuller) was beheaded with his head publicly displayed in Rio de Janeiro as a warning to his compatriots. After the decline of the gold mines, there was an influx of artists and architects, including baroque sculptor Aleijadinho, who learned his father's trade while a laborer building the rococo-style Church of Our Lady of Carmel, with rectangular bell towers and carved woodwork decorated in gold.

Iguaçu National Park ❸

Iguaçu National Park, set at the confluence of the Paraná and Iguaçu Rivers, covers 420,000 acres of tropical rain forest rich in tree ferns, lianas—woody vines, some of which are as thick as trees and hang independently—and epiphytes. The Iguaçu feeds one of the world's largest waterfalls, Iguaçu Falls, which, over a length of nearly 8,900 feet, splits into several drops and rapids, and ends in clouds of spray that nourish and stimulate lush vegetation, a safe haven for endangered species such as the giant otter and giant anteater.

Brazil

4 Historic Center of Salvador de Bahia

Discovered by Amerigo Vespucci in 1502, Salvador de Bahia was the first capital of Brazil, holding the honor from 1549 to 1763. The upper city is built on a ridgeline parallel to the Atlantic coast and easily defendable. It overlooks the commercial activities of the lower city's port, which became the first slave market of the New World in 1558, when slaves first arrived to work on the sugar plantations. The colonial streets are lined with brightly colored houses expertly decorated in stucco.

Protected Areas and World Heritage Sites

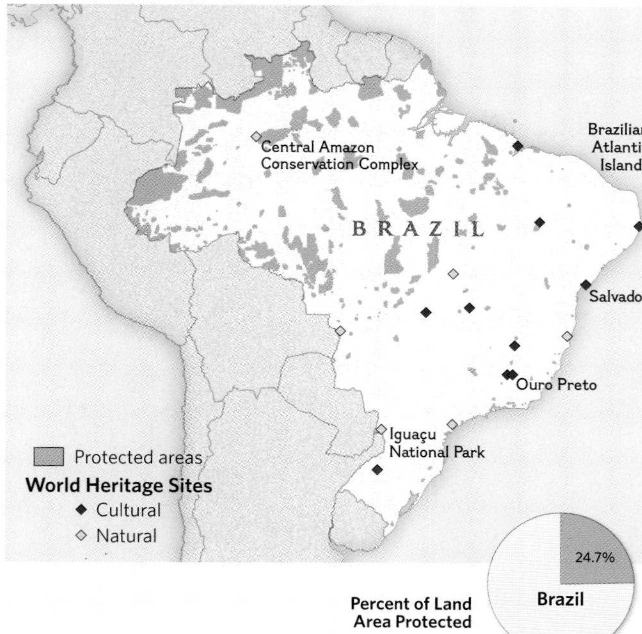

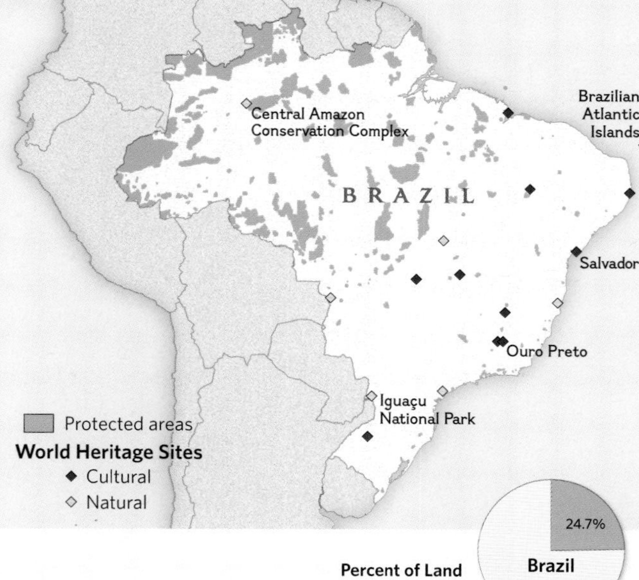

Central Amazon Conservation Complex
Brazilian Atlantic Islands
BRAZIL
Salvador
Ouro Preto
Iguaçu National Park
Protected areas
World Heritage Sites
Cultural
Natural
24.7%
Brazil
Percent of Land Area Protected

Urbanization and Largest Cities

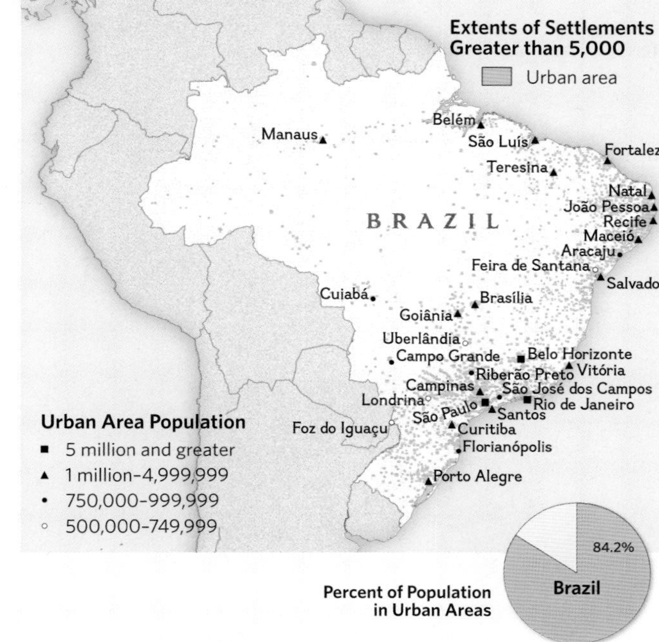

Extents of Settlements Greater than 5,000
Urban area
Manaus
Belém
São Luís
Fortaleza
Teresina
Natal
João Pessoa
Recife
Maceió
Aracaju
Feira de Santana
Salvador
BRAZIL
Cuiabá
Brasília
Goiânia
Uberlândia
Campo Grande
Belo Horizonte
Ribeirão Preto
Vitória
Campinas
São José dos Campos
Rio de Janeiro
Londrina
São Paulo
Santos
Foz do Iguaçu
Curitiba
Florianópolis
Porto Alegre
Urban Area Population
5 million and greater
1 million–4,999,999
750,000–999,999
500,000–749,999
84.2%
Brazil
Percent of Population in Urban Areas

5 Brazilian Atlantic Islands: Fernando de Noronha and Atol das Rocas Reserves

Off northeast Brazil, peaks of a South Atlantic marine ridge rise more than 13,000 feet from the seafloor to form the Fernando de Noronha Archipelago. Reefs growing on the submerged mountains make up the Rocas Atoll, the only atoll in the South Atlantic Ocean and one of the world's smallest. Representing more than 50 percent of the South Atlantic's island surface, the atoll has the largest concentration of tropical seabirds in the western Atlantic, and its waters are vital feeding and spawning grounds for tuna, shark, dolphin, and the hawksbill turtle, the world's second most threatened species. At high tide, only two sandy islands stand above water, but at low tide, the Rocas Atoll reveals lagoons and tidal pools teeming with fish.

Natural Land Cover

BRAZIL
Land Cover
Forest
Herbaceous
Savanna

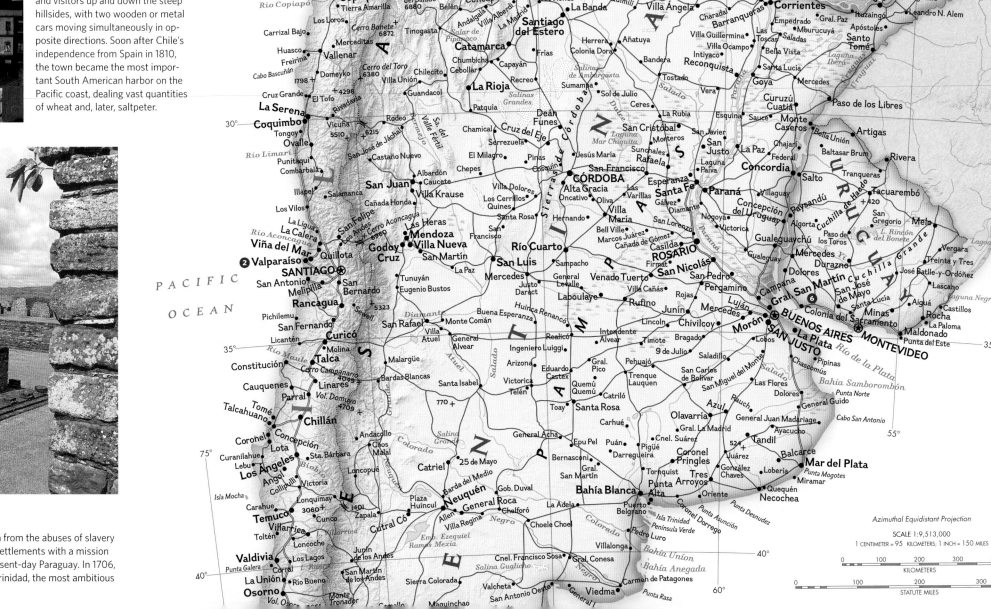

Rapa Nui National Park,
❶ Easter Island, Chile

Around 300 A.D., a Stone Age society of Polynesians settled between Tahiti and Chile on Rapa Nui, the island's indigenous name. Between the 10th and 16th centuries, isolated and free from external influences, they used simple picks made from hard basalt to carve *moai*, the famous monumental stone statues. Nearly a thousand still exist, ranging in size from 6 to 65 feet tall, and are believed to represent ancestors watching over the villages. Archaeologists have found a clear stylistic evolution from the earlier small, round-headed, round-eyed figures to the more well-known large statues with carefully carved fingers, nostrils, and long ears.

Historic Quarter of the Seaport City of Valparaíso, Chile ❷

Located on an amphitheater-like bay that opens north to the Pacific, the colonial city of Valparaíso conforms to a series of terraces formed by the regressions and abrasions of the sea tides. Thirty cable car elevators, of which 15 remain, took citizens and visitors up and down the steep hillsides, with two wooden or metal cars moving simultaneously in opposite directions. Soon after Chile's independence from Spain in 1810, the town became the most important South American harbor on the Pacific coast, dealing vast quantities of wheat and, later, saltpeter.

Jesuit Missions of La Santísima Trinidad de Paraná and Jesús de Tavarangue, Paraguay ❸

To protect the South American natives in a region known as Guayrá from the abuses of slavery under the Spanish colonials, Jesuit priests created 30 *reducciones,* settlements with a mission as its focal point, in the Río de la Plata Basin, 8 of which were in present-day Paraguay. In 1706, Jesuit architect Juan Bautista Primoli built the stone La Santísima Trinidad, the most ambitious of these missions and the eventual capital of Guayrá.

Refer to pages 244–245 for Isla de Pascua ❶ *(Easter Island)*

PACIFIC OCEAN

Azimuthal Equidistant Projection
SCALE 1:9,513,000
1 CENTIMETER = 95 KILOMETERS; 1 INCH = 150 MILES
0 100 200 300 400 KILOMETERS
0 100 200 300 400 STATUTE MILES

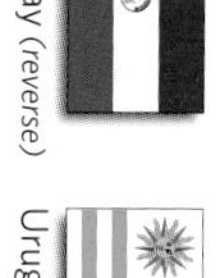
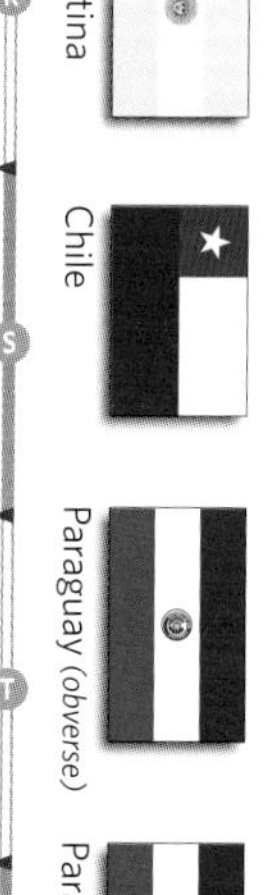

Argentina Chile Paraguay *(obverse)* Paraguay *(reverse)* Uruguay

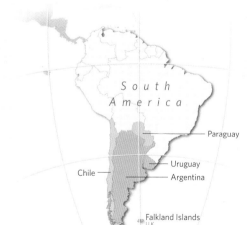

Cueva de los Manos, Río Pinturas, Argentina ❹
From 9,500 to 13,000 years ago, the first hunter-gatherers of South America stenciled outlines of their hands in this cave; they also painted hunting scenes on the rock shelters and walls. Hunters are shown surrounding animals, trapping them in ambushes, and throwing *bolas* (round stones) at them. Depictions also include the feet of an American ostrich and the guanaco, a deerlike mammal related to the camel but lacking a dorsal hump, that was the main prey of the hunters.

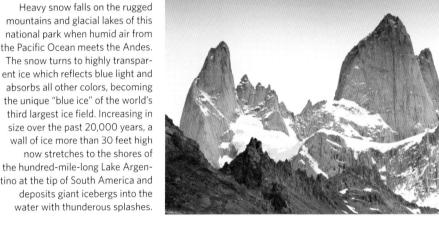

❺ **Los Glaciares, Argentina**
Heavy snow falls on the rugged mountains and glacial lakes of this national park when humid air from the Pacific Ocean meets the Andes. The snow turns to highly transparent ice which reflects blue light and absorbs all other colors, becoming the unique "blue ice" of the world's third largest ice field. Increasing in size over the past 20,000 years, a wall of ice more than 30 feet high now stretches to the shores of the hundred-mile-long Lake Argentino at the tip of South America and deposits giant icebergs into the water with thunderous splashes.

Historic Quarter of Colonia
❺ **del Sacramento, Uruguay**
By order of their prince regent, the Portuguese founded this city in 1680 on the Río de la Plata, or "river of silver," one of the most strategic regions of South America. Located at the mouth of estuaries that led to the mines of Peru and adjacent to Brazil's farmlands, Sacramento was constantly besieged by the Spanish. The colonial town lacks the typical checkerboard layout common to Spanish and Portuguese settlements, and, instead, conforms to the topography with church tower and lighthouse rising above the former town houses of patricians and humbler dwellings of artisans and shopkeepers.

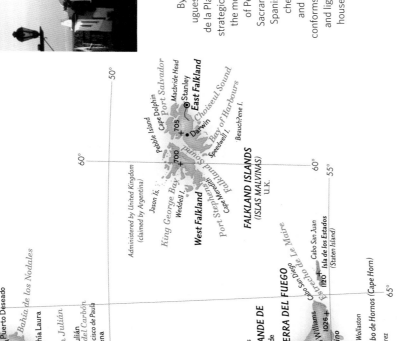

ATLANTIC OCEAN

FALKLAND ISLANDS (ISLAS MALVINAS) U.K.

Administered by United Kingdom (claimed by Argentina)

Protected Areas and World Heritage Sites

Protected areas
World Heritage Sites
◆ Cultural
◇ Natural
PARAGUAY
Jesuit Missions of La Santísima Trinidad de Paraná and Jesús de Tavarangue
CHILE
Valparaíso
URUGUAY
Colonia del Sacramento
ARGENTINA
Cueva de los Manos, Río Pinturas
Los Glaciares
9.4% Argentina
24.0% Chile
24.8% Paraguay
3.7% Uruguay
Percent of Land Area Protected

Urbanization and Largest Cities

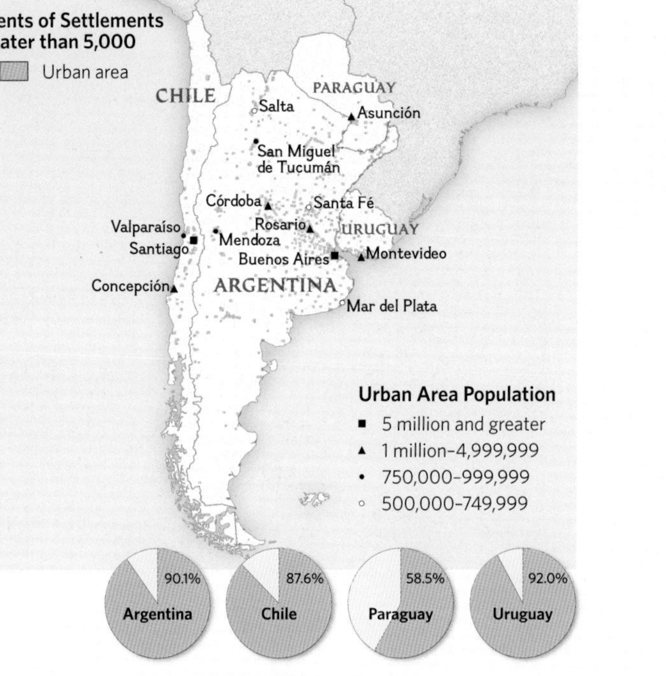
Extents of Settlements Greater than 5,000
Urban area
CHILE
PARAGUAY
Salta
Asunción
San Miguel de Tucumán
Córdoba
Santa Fé
Rosario
URUGUAY
Valparaíso
Santiago
Mendoza
Buenos Aires
Montevideo
Concepción
ARGENTINA
Mar del Plata
Urban Area Population
■ 5 million and greater
▲ 1 million–4,999,999
• 750,000–999,999
◦ 500,000–749,999
90.1% Argentina
87.6% Chile
58.5% Paraguay
92.0% Uruguay
Percent of Population in Urban Areas

Natural Land Cover

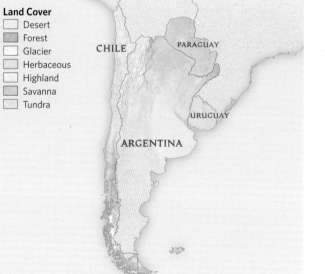

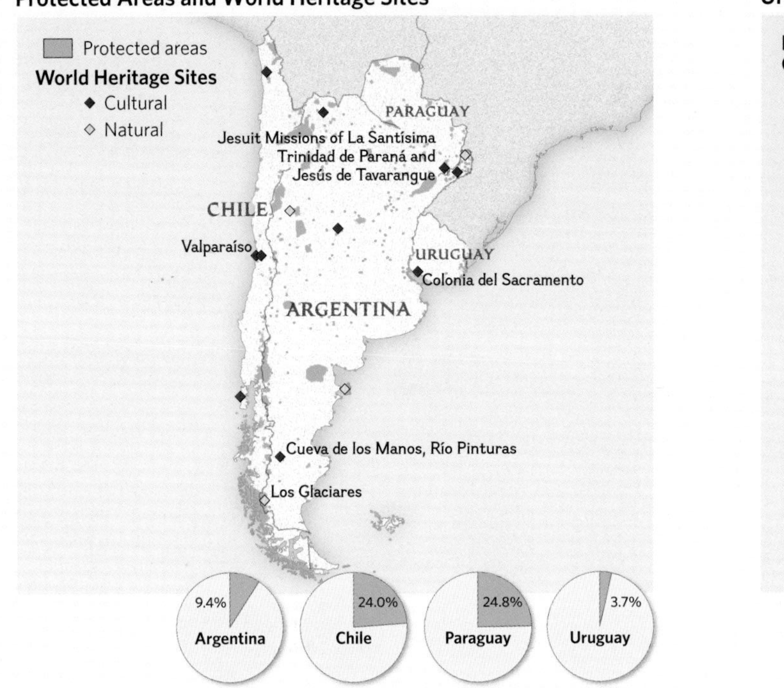
Land Cover
Desert
Forest
Glacier
Herbaceous
Highland
Savanna
Tundra
CHILE
PARAGUAY
URUGUAY
ARGENTINA

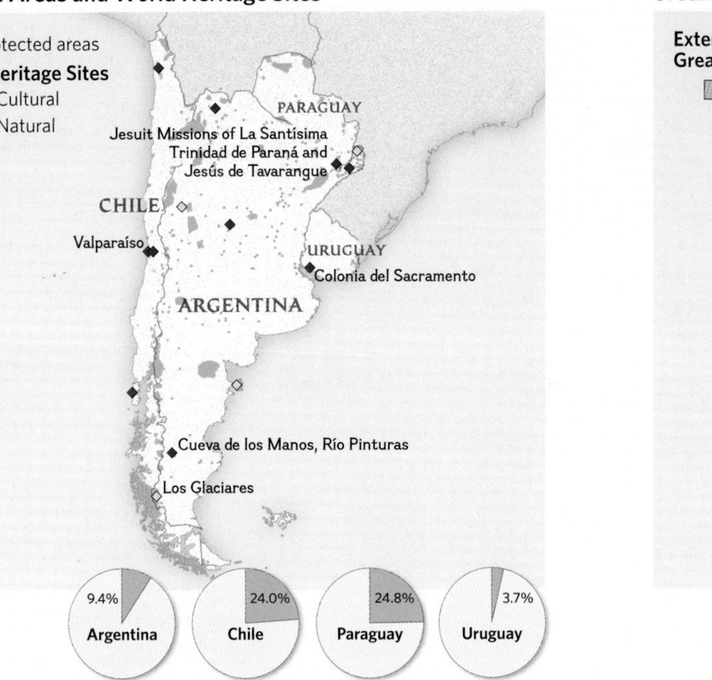

South America
Paraguay
Uruguay
Argentina
Chile
Falkland Islands U.K.

KEY
Cultural World Heritage Site
Natural World Heritage Site
Mixed World Heritage Site

THROUGH THE POWER OF IDEAS AS WELL AS FORCE of arms, Europe rose to dominate world affairs as the modern age dawned. The continent is heir to the legacy of classical Greece, where democracy took root some 25 centuries ago. The subsequent rise of Rome would for the first time unite much of the continent under a single government that established cities, built roads and public works, and established legal traditions, all of which endure to this day. Europe became the bastion of Christianity after the Roman Empire's conversion in the fourth century A.D. The faith would later develop in eastern and western forms when the empire split, a cultural fault line that remains.

Beginning in the 16th century, the Reformation and later the Enlightenment were intellectual earthquakes. The contrasting ideas and ideologies that followed—individual freedom, liberal democracy, free markets, nationalism, socialism—continue to inspire passionate responses. European culture was carried by force to every corner of the world through the establishment of colonies across Asia, Africa, and the Americas. Today, as the continent again moves toward solidarity under the European Union, it remains a place of sharply etched national and cultural identities.

Europe

Manarola (above), one of the five seaside villages of Italy's historic and picturesque Cinque Terre coast, perches above the Gulf of Genoa. Other World Heritage sites around Europe include (left, top to bottom): Athens's sacred hill, the Acropolis, where a finely carved Ionic column and capital help support a temple roof; France's walled city of Carcassonne, a key example of a medieval fortified town; the mysterious standing rocks of the Stonehenge circle, which Neolithic peoples began building more than 5,000 years ago in southern England; and the historic center of the Czech Republic's charming capital, Prague, where graceful bridges span the Vltava River.

Azimuthal Equidistant Projection
SCALE 1:11,154,300
1 CENTIMETER = 112 KILOMETERS; 1 INCH = 176 MILES
0 100 200 300 400 500
KILOMETERS
0 100 200 300 400 500
STATUTE MILES
International boundary
ICELAND
Breiðafjörður
Húnaflói
Faxaflói
Reykjanes
Hekla 1491
Surtsey
Vestmannaeyjar (Westman Is.)
Hvannadalshnúkur 2119
Rifstangi
Langanes
Vopnafjörður
NORWEGIAN SEA
ARCTIC CIRCLE
ATLANTIC OCEAN
Faroe Islands
Shetland Islands
Orkney Islands
Outer Hebrides
Inner Hebrides
Moray Firth
Rattray Head
Ben Nevis 1343
Highlands
Grampian Mts.
BRITISH ISLES
GREAT BRITAIN
Firth of Forth
Southern Uplands
Donegal B.
L. Neagh
IRELAND
Shannon
Carrantuohill 1041
IRISH SEA
Isle of Man
The Pennines
Snowdon 1085
Cambrian Mts.
Spurn Head
The Wash
Thames
CELTIC SEA
Land's End
English Channel
Str. of Dover
Channel Islands
Point St.-Mathieu
Armorican Massif
PARIS BASIN
Seine
Loire
BAY OF BISCAY
AQUITAINE BASIN
Garonne
Puy de Sancy 1886
MASSIF CENTRAL
Cévennes
Rhône
Saône
Jura Mts.
Vosges
Black Forest
Source of the Danube
Lake Constance
Sources of the Rhine
Lake of Geneva
Mont Blanc 4810
Matterhorn 4478
ALPS
Piedmont
L. Como
L. Garda
Po
Grossglockner 3798
Cape Finisterre
Cantabrian Mountains
Douro
Ebro
IBERIAN PENINSULA
Iberian Mountains
MESETA
Tagus
Guadiana
Sierra Morena
Guadalquivir
Baetic Mountains
Mulhacén 3481
Cape St. Vincent
Strait of Gibraltar
ALBORAN SEA
Er Rif
PYRENEES
Pico de Aneto 3404
Gulf of Lions
BALEARIC SEA
BALEARIC ISLANDS
Minorca
Majorca
Iviza
LIGURIAN SEA
Riviera
CORSICA
SARDINIA
Cape Carbonara
TYRRHENIAN SEA
MEDITERRANEAN SEA
APENNINES
Corno Grande 2912
Tiber
Vesuvius 1281
Calabria
SICILY
Etna 3315
Cape Passero
Malta
MALTESE ISLANDS
Pelagian Is.
IONIAN SEA
Strait of Otranto
IONIAN ISLANDS
Gulf of Venice
ADRIATIC SEA
DINARIC ALPS
Dalmatia
Durmitor 2522
Sava
Drava
Tisza
Danube
Bakony
Balaton
Great Hungarian Plain
Neusiedler Lake
CARPATHIAN MTS.
Gerlach 2655
L. Ohrid
Pindus Mts.
Olympus 2917
Thessaly
Parnassus 2457
PELOPONNESUS
ATLAS MOUNTAINS
AFRICA
SAHARA
Gulf of Sidra
Longitude West 5° of Greenwich
Longitude East 5° of Greenwich
NORTH SEA
Skagerrak
Kattegat
The Skaw
JUTLAND
Blavands Point
FYN
ZEALAND
Schleswig
Frisian Islands
IJsselmeer
Rhine
Meuse
Ardennes
Moselle
Main
Weser
Elbe
MITTELLAND CANAL
Harz 1141
NORTHERN EUROPEAN PLAIN
Ore Mts.
Sudeten 1602
Bohemian Forest
Danube
Oder
Rügen
Pomerania
Notéc
Vistula
Bug
Gulf of Gdańsk
Neman
SCANDINAVIA
Sognefjorden
Hardangerfjorden
Telemark
Galdhøpiggen 2469
Glåma
Mjøsa
Klarälven
Siljan
Svealand
Vänern
Vättern
Götland
Skåne
Gotland
Öland
Trondheimsfjorden
Ångermanälven
Umeälven
Indalsälven
Lofoten
Vesterålen
Vestfjorden
Kebnekaise 2111
Torneälven
Luleälven
Storavan
Finnmark Plateau
North Cape
Inari
Saari Ridge
Kemi
Hailuoto
Oulujärvi
Suomen
Päijänne
GULF OF BOTHNIA
Åland Is.
GULF OF FINLAND
Hiiumaa
Saaremaa
Gulf of Riga
Venta
BALTIC SEA

EUROPE–ASIA BOUNDARY

A commonly accepted division between Asia and Europe–marked here with a green line–is formed by the Ural Mountains, Ural River, Caspian Sea, Caucasus Mountains, and the Black Sea with its outlets, the Bosporus and Dardanelles. From north to south, the Europe–Asia boundary divides the nations of Russia, Kazakhstan, Azerbaijan, Georgia, and Turkey, placing territory of each country in both continents.

Lowest point in Europe

Caspian Sea: Surface elevation -28 (-92 ft)

Highest point in Europe

El'brus 5642 (18510 ft)

World's lowest point

Dead Sea -421 (-1380 ft)

URAL MOUNTAINS

WEST SIBERIAN PLAIN

EUROPEAN PLAIN

CENTRAL RUSSIAN UPLAND

OKA-DON PLAIN

THE STEPPES

CAUCASUS MOUNTAINS

BLACK SEA

CASPIAN SEA

ANATOLIA (ASIA MINOR)

MESOPOTAMIA

SYRIAN DESERT

ARABIAN PENINSULA

ASIA

Azimuthal Equidistant Projection
SCALE 1:11,154,300
1 CENTIMETER = 112 KILOMETERS; 1 INCH = 176 MILES
0 100 200 300 400 500
KILOMETERS
0 100 200 300 400 500
STATUTE MILES
□ Small country
ICELAND
Reykjavík
Akureyri
Keflavík
Ísafjörður
Neskaupstaður
Höfn
Surtsey
Vestmannaeyjar
ARCTIC CIRCLE
N O R W E G I A N
S E A
Meridian of Greenwich (London)
FAROE ISLANDS (FØROYAR) Denmark
Tórshavn
SHETLAND ISLANDS
Mainland
Lerwick
ORKNEY ISLANDS
Kirkwall
Rockall U.K.
A T L A N T I C
O C E A N
Isle of Lewis
Outer Hebrides
Stornoway
Thurso
Island of Skye
Inverness
Aberdeen
SCOTLAND
Perth
Dundee
Greenock
Edinburgh
Glasgow
Londonderry
NORTHERN IRELAND
Belfast
Sligo
Dundalk
Baile Átha Cliath (Dublin)
Galway
IRELAND
Limerick
Tralee
Cork
Waterford
IRISH SEA
Newcastle
Sunderland
UNITED
KINGDOM
Leeds
Liverpool
Manchester
Sheffield
WALES
ENGLAND
BIRMINGHAM
Swansea
Cardiff
Bristol
LONDON
Southampton
Plymouth
CELTIC SEA
Isles of Scilly
ENGLISH CHANNEL
Channel Islands U.K.
N O R T H
S E A
Tromsø
Vesterålen
Lofoten
Svolvær
Harstad
Narvik
Bodø
Mo i Rana
Mosjøen
Namsos
Steinkjer
Trondheim
Kristiansund
Molde
Ålesund
Florø
Sognefjorden
Bergen
Odda
Haugesund
Stavanger
Egersund
Kristiansand
Mandal
Arendal
Lillehammer
Gjøvik
Hamar
Hønefoss
Drammen
Oslo
Skien
Fredrikstad
Røros
Glåma
N O R W A Y
Kiruna
Gällivare
Arvidsjaur
Storuman
Gäddede
Östersund
Örnsköldsvik
Kramfors
Sundsvall
Bollnäs
Falun
Borlänge
Gävle
Karlstad
Västerås
Uppsala
Stockholm
Örebro
Vänern
Norrköping
Linköping
Trollhättan
Göteborg
Jönköping
Borås
Växjö
Halmstad
Kalmar
ÖLAND
Karlskrona
Helsingborg
Malmö
GOTLAND
Visby
S W E D E N
L A P L A N D
Piteå
Luleå
Skellefteå
Umeå
GULF OF BOTHNIA
ÅLAND
Sørøya
Hammerfest
Alta
Lakselv
Kautokeino
Inari
Ivalo
Kittilä
Kemijärvi
Rovaniemi
Kemi
Boden
Oulu
Raahe
Kokkola
Jakobstad
Vaasa
Seinäjoki
Jyväskylä
Pori
Tampere
Rauma
Hämeenlinna
Turku
Helsinki
GULF OF FINLAND
Tallinn
Pärnu
Gulf of Riga
Ventspils
Riga
Liepāja
Šiauliai
Jelgava
Panevėžys
Klaipėda
Kaliningrad
Russia
EAST PRUSSIA
Vilnius
BALTIC SEA
BORNHOLM
DENMARK
JUTLAND
Frederikshavn
Ålborg
Randers
Århus
Esbjerg
Odense
København (Copenhagen)
Kiel
Lübeck
Rostock
HAMBURG
Bremerhaven
Oldenburg
Bremen
Groningen
NETHERLANDS
Amsterdam
Den Haag
Rotterdam
Hannover
Braunschweig
BERLIN
Bielefeld
Magdeburg
Essen
Dortmund
Köln
Bonn
G E R M A N Y
Leipzig
Erfurt
Dresden
Chemnitz
Zwickau
Wiesbaden
Frankfurt
Darmstadt
Würzburg
Mannheim
Karlsruhe
Nürnberg
Stuttgart
Augsburg
MÜNCHEN (Munich)
Freiburg
Elbe
Oder
Rhine
Donau
Antwerpen
(Brussels) Bruxelles
Lille
BELGIUM
Charleroi
LUXEMBOURG
Luxembourg
Szczecin
Słupsk
Koszalin
Gdańsk
Olsztyn
Bydgoszcz
Toruń
Białystok
Poznań
WARSZAWA (Warsaw)
Łódź
P O L A N D
Wrocław
Wałbrzych
Radom
Częstochowa
Kielce
Lublin
Katowice
Kraków
Rzeszów
Przemyśl
Wisła
PRAHA (Prague)
Plzeň
CZECH REP.
České Budějovice
Brno
Olomouc
Ostrava
WIEN (Vienna)
Linz
Salzburg
Innsbruck
A U S T R I A
Graz
Bratislava
SLOVAKIA
Košice
C A R P A T H I A N
Miskolc
Nyíregyháza
Debrecen
Győr
BUDAPEST
H U N G A R Y
Szeged
Oradea
Cluj-Napoca
Arad
Timișoara
Cherbourg-Octeville
Le Havre
Caen
Brest
Amiens
Rouen
Seine
PARIS
Reims
Rennes
Lorient
Alençon
Le Mans
Troyes
Nancy
Strasbourg
Angers
Nantes
Orléans
Tours
Loire
Dijon
Mulhouse
Besançon
F R A N C E
La Rochelle
Poitiers
Limoges
Clermont-Ferrand
MASSIF CENTRAL
Saint-Étienne
Lyon
Grenoble
Valence
Bordeaux
Garonne
Agen
Montauban
Toulouse
Pau
Rhône
Nîmes
Montpellier
Aix-en-Provence
Marseille
Toulon
Nice
MONACO
Perpignan
ANDORRA
Andorra
BAY OF BISCAY
Basel
Bern
Zürich
LIECHTENSTEIN
Lausanne
Genève
SWITZERLAND
Bolzano
Trento
Bergamo
MILANO (Milan)
Brescia
Verona
Padova
Venezia (Venice)
Torino
Genova (Genoa)
Modena
Po
Ferrara
Bologna
Riviera
La Spezia
Pisa
Firenze
Rimini
SAN MARINO
Ancona
Perugia
Terni
Teramo
Pescara
Civitavecchia
VATICAN CITY
(Rome) ROMA
I T A L Y
Foggia
Benevento
(Naples) NAPOLI
Salerno
Potenza
Bari
Brindisi
Taranto
Lecce
Castrovillari
Cosenza
Catanzaro
Reggio di Calabria
Messina
Palermo
Marsala
SICILY
Catania
Ragusa
Siracusa
A L P S
A P E N N I N E S
ADRIATIC SEA
TYRRHENIAN SEA
IONIAN SEA
Bastia
Elba
CORSE (CORSICA) France
Ajaccio
Sassari
Olbia
Nuoro
SARDEGNA (SARDINIA) Italy
Oristano
Iglesias
Carbonia
Cagliari
SLOVENIA
Ljubljana
Maribor
Trieste
Zagreb
CROATIA
Osijek
Banja Luka
Tuzla
BOSNIA & HERZEGOVINA
Sarajevo
Split
Zadar
Mostar
Dubrovnik
MONTENEGRO
Podgorica
Shkodër
Tiranë (Tirana)
Elbasan
ALBANIA
Vlorë
Korçë
Durrës
Novi Sad
BEOGRAD (Belgrade)
S E R B I A
Kragujevac
Niš
Novi Pazar
Priština
KOSOVO
SOFIYA (Sofia)
Vratsa
Skopje
MACEDONIA
Bitola
Thessaloníki
Ioánina
Kérkira (Corfu)
Lefkáda
Kefalonia
Zákinthos
Pátra
PELOPONNISOS
Kalamáta
G R E E C E
Santiago de Compostela
A Coruña
Gijón
Oviedo
Lugo
Vigo
Ourense
León
Santander
Bilbao
Donostia-San Sebastián
Vitória-Gasteiz
Burgos
Bayonne
Pamplona
Ebro
Porto
Braga
Vila Real
Duero
Valladolid
Salamanca
Zaragoza
Lleida
Tarragona
BARCELONA
Coimbra
Segovia
MADRID
Castelo Branco
Santarém
(Lisbon) Lisboa
Setúbal
P O R T U G A L
S P A I N
Tajo
Cáceres
Toledo
Mérida
Badajoz
Guadiana
Ciudad Real
Castelló de la Plana
Valencia
Albacete
Córdoba
Linares
Jaén
Lucena
Sevilla
Huelva
Faro
Cádiz
Jerez
Granada
Murcia
Alicante
Cartagena
Almería
Málaga
Algeciras
GIBRALTAR U.K.
Strait of Gibraltar
Ceuta Sp.
Melilla Sp.
Alborán Spain
ALBORAN SEA
BALEARIC SEA
Menorca
Palma de Mallorca
Mallorca
BALEARIC ISLANDS Spain
Ibiza
M E D I T E R R A N E A N
S E A
ALGER (Algiers)
Oran
Constantine
TUNIS
Sfax
T U N I S I A
Pantelleria Italy
Isole Pelagie Italy
MALTA
Valletta
RABAT
CASABLANCA
M O R O C C O
A L G E R I A
TARĀBULUS (Tripoli)
Banghāzī (Benghazi)
L I B Y A
A F R I C A
Longitude West 5° of Greenwich
Longitude East 5° of Greenwich

EUROPE–ASIA BOUNDARY

A commonly accepted division between Asia and Europe–marked here with a green line–is formed by the Ural Mountains, Ural River, Caspian Sea, Caucasus Mountains, and the Black Sea with its outlets, the Bosporus and Dardanelles. From north to south, the Europe–Asia boundary divides the nations of Russia, Kazakhstan, Azerbaijan, Georgia, and Turkey, placing territory of each country in both continents.

Cyprus marks the southeastern extent of Europe. Its cultural and historic ties to the continent include joining the European Union in 2004.

Europe: Themes

Continental Facts

TOTAL NUMBER OF COUNTRIES: 46

TOTAL AREA: 9,947,000 sq km (3,841,000 sq mi)

FIRST INDEPENDENT COUNTRY: San Marino, Sept. 3, 301

"YOUNGEST" COUNTRY: Kosovo, Feb. 17, 2008

MOST POPULOUS COUNTRY: *Russia 141,681,000

LEAST POPULOUS COUNTRY: Vatican City 798

LARGEST COUNTRY BY AREA: *Russia 17,075,400 sq km (6,592,850 sq mi)

SMALLEST COUNTRY BY AREA: Vatican City 0.4 sq km (0.2 sq mi)

HIGHEST ELEVATION: El'brus, Russia 5,642 m (18,510 ft)

LOWEST ELEVATION: Caspian Sea -28 m (-92 ft)

The world's largest country, Russia, straddles both Asia and Europe. Area and population figures reflect the total of both its Asian and European regions.

Climate Zones

Svalbard (NORWAY)
ICELAND
Faroe Islands (DENMARK)
NORWAY
SWEDEN
FINLAND
RUSSIA
UNITED KINGDOM
IRELAND
DEN.
EST.
LAT.
LITH.
BELARUS
NETH.
BELG.
GERMANY
POLAND
Channel Is. (U.K.)
LUX.
CZECH REP.
LIECH.
SLOVAKIA
UKRAINE
KAZ.
FRANCE
SWITZ.
AUST.
HUNG.
MOLD.
SLOV.
CROATIA
ROMANIA
BOSN. & HERZG.
SERBIA
MONACO
SAN MARINO
PORTUGAL
SPAIN
ANDORRA
ITALY
MONT.
KOSOVO
ALBAN.
BULGARIA
TURKEY
GEORGIA
AZERB.
GREECE
VATICAN CITY
MACED.
CYPRUS
MALTA
Gibraltar (U.K.)
CLIMATE
(based on modified Köppen system)
Dry climate (B)
Semiarid (BS)
Arid (BW)
k = cold
Humid temperate climate (C)
No dry season (Cf)
Dry summer (Cs)
a = hot summer
b = cool summer
c = short, cool summer
Humid cold climate (D)
No dry season (Df)
Cold climate (E)
Tundra and ice
Highland climate (H)
Unclassified highlands

Water Availability

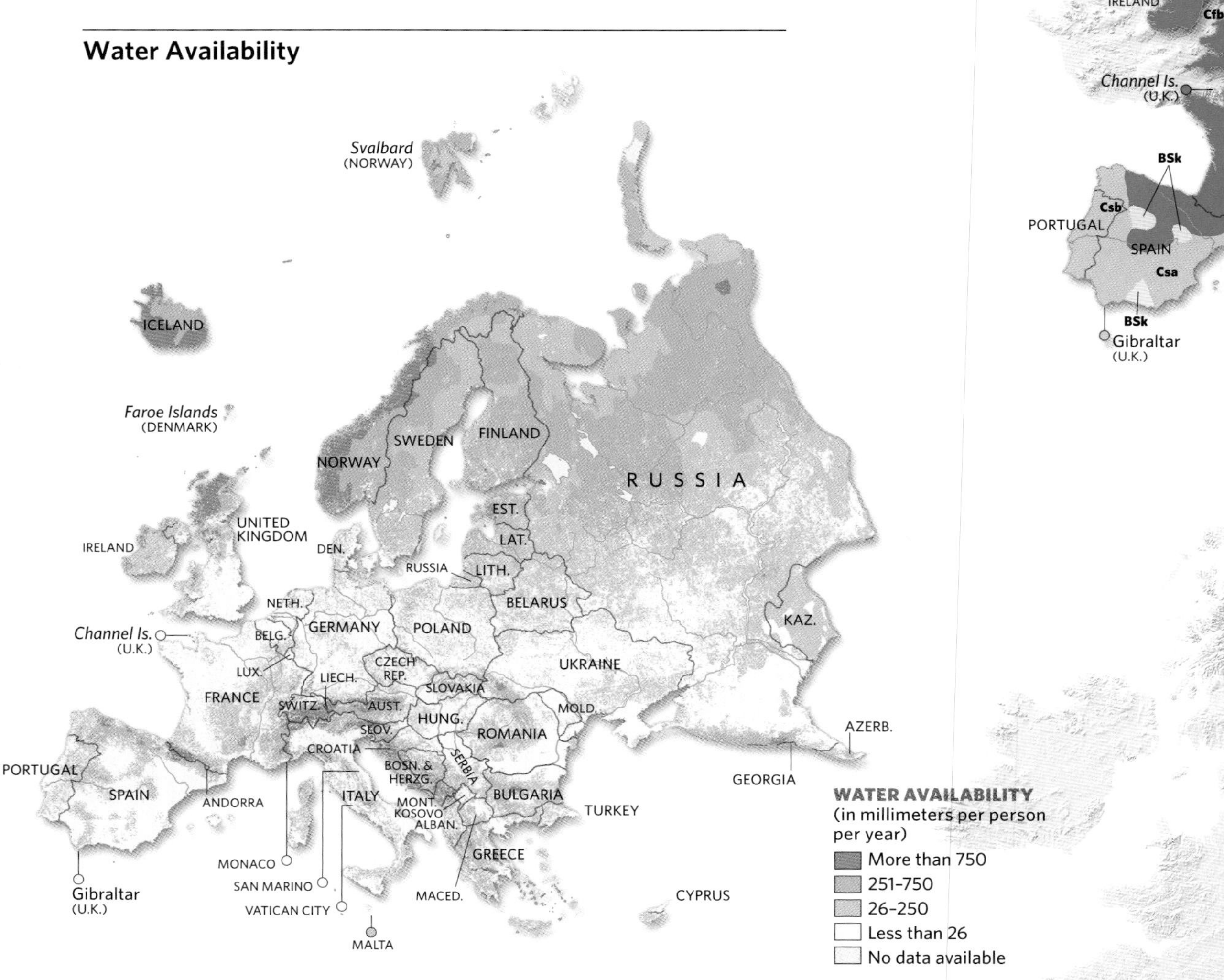

Svalbard (NORWAY)
ICELAND
Faroe Islands (DENMARK)
NORWAY
SWEDEN
FINLAND
RUSSIA
UNITED KINGDOM
IRELAND
DEN.
EST.
LAT.
LITH.
BELARUS
NETH.
GERMANY
POLAND
Channel Is. (U.K.)
BELG.
LUX.
CZECH REP.
LIECH.
SLOVAKIA
UKRAINE
KAZ.
FRANCE
SWITZ.
AUST.
HUNG.
MOLD.
SLOV.
ROMANIA
CROATIA
BOSN. & HERZG.
SERBIA
PORTUGAL
SPAIN
ANDORRA
ITALY
MONT.
KOSOVO
ALBAN.
BULGARIA
TURKEY
GEORGIA
AZERB.
GREECE
MONACO
SAN MARINO
VATICAN CITY
MACED.
CYPRUS
MALTA
Gibraltar (U.K.)
WATER AVAILABILITY
(in millimeters per person per year)
More than 750
251-750
26-250
Less than 26
No data available

Natural Events

Svalbard (NORWAY)
ICELAND
Faroe Islands (DENMARK)
NORWAY
SWEDEN
FINLAND
RUSSIA
UNITED KINGDOM
IRELAND
DEN.
EST.
LAT.
LITH.
BELARUS
NETH.
GERMANY
POLAND
Channel Is. (U.K.)
BELG.
LUX.
LIECH.
CZECH REP.
SLOVAKIA
UKRAINE
KAZ.
FRANCE
SWITZ.
AUST.
HUNG.
ROMANIA
MOLD.
AZERB.
GEORGIA
PORTUGAL
ANDORRA
SLOV.
SPAIN
CROATIA
ITALY
BOSN. & HERZG.
SERBIA
BULGARIA
KOSOVO
MACED.
TURKEY
ALBANIA
GREECE
CYPRUS
MALTA
MONTENEGRO
Gibraltar (U.K.)
RECORDED NATURAL EVENT
Earthquake
Richter scale magnitude
More than 7.0
6.0-7.0
Less than 6.0
Fire Intensity
(from gas burn-off, slash-and-burn agriculture, or natural causes)
High
Low
Tsunami
Run-up height
More than 10 m
More than 32 ft
5-10 m
16-32 ft
Less than 5 m
Less than 16 ft
Volcano
Major eruption
0 500 1,000
STATUTE MILES
0 500 1,000
KILOMETERS
Same scale for all six thematic maps

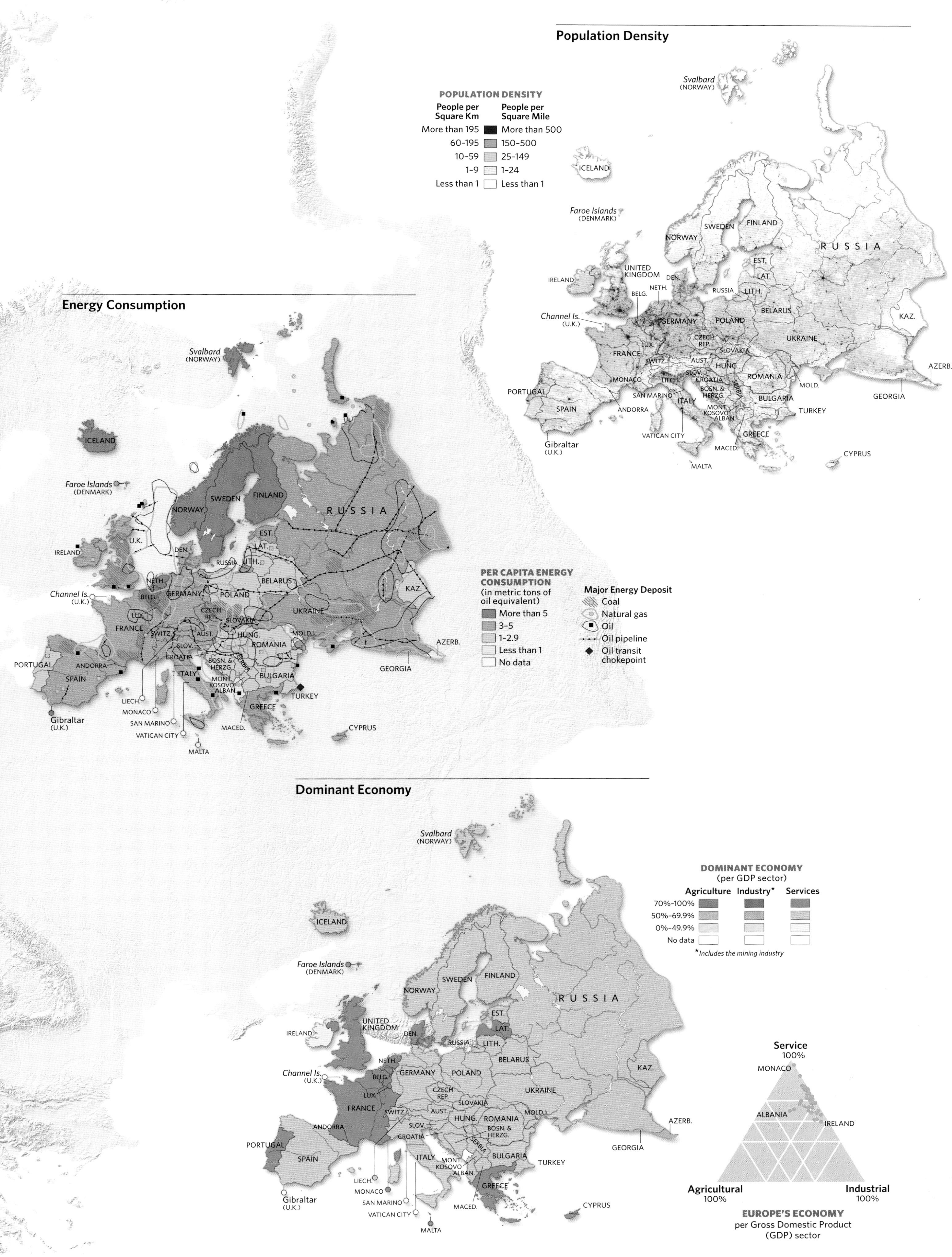

Population Density
POPULATION DENSITY
People per Square Km
People per Square Mile
More than 195 More than 500
60-195 150-500
10-59 25-149
1-9 1-24
Less than 1 Less than 1
Svalbard (NORWAY)
ICELAND
Faroe Islands (DENMARK)
NORWAY
SWEDEN
FINLAND
RUSSIA
EST.
LAT.
LITH.
UNITED KINGDOM
IRELAND
DEN.
NETH.
BELG.
BELARUS
KAZ.
Channel Is. (U.K.)
GERMANY
POLAND
LUX.
CZECH REP.
SLOVAKIA
UKRAINE
FRANCE
SWITZ.
AUST.
HUNG.
SLOV.
CROATIA
ROMANIA
MOLD.
AZERB.
MONACO
LIECH.
BOSN. & HERZG.
SERBIA
PORTUGAL
SAN MARINO
ITALY
MONT.
KOSOVO
ALBAN.
BULGARIA
GEORGIA
SPAIN
ANDORRA
TURKEY
VATICAN CITY
GREECE
Gibraltar (U.K.)
MACED.
CYPRUS
MALTA
Energy Consumption
PER CAPITA ENERGY CONSUMPTION
(in metric tons of oil equivalent)
More than 5
3-5
1-2.9
Less than 1
No data
Major Energy Deposit
Coal
Natural gas
Oil
Oil pipeline
Oil transit chokepoint
Dominant Economy
DOMINANT ECONOMY
(per GDP sector)
Agriculture
Industry*
Services
70%-100%
50%-69.9%
0%-49.9%
No data
*Includes the mining industry
Service 100%
MONACO
ALBANIA
IRELAND
Agricultural 100%
Industrial 100%
EUROPE'S ECONOMY
per Gross Domestic Product (GDP) sector

Bryggen, Norway 1
One of the oldest trading posts in northern Europe, Bryggen, Bergen's historic harbor district, has retained its original medieval appearance, with wooden houses running parallel to the docks, a common courtyard, and warehouses made of stone built behind the homes to protect them from fire. The old wharf of Bergen belonged to the aristocracy, who had a monopoly on fish trading from the 11th to 14th century, before becoming part of the Hanseatic League's trading empire into the 1700s.

2 Hanseatic Town of Visby, Sweden
In the island region of Gotland, Visby dates back to the early Viking age and was central to Baltic trade of Russia's fur, wax, tar, and timber. With a 13th-century town wall fortified with gates, towers, and turrets, ruins of more than a dozen churches and some 200 warehouses and merchants' homes from the Romanesque period still remain on a medieval street plan, which suddenly broadens and narrows.

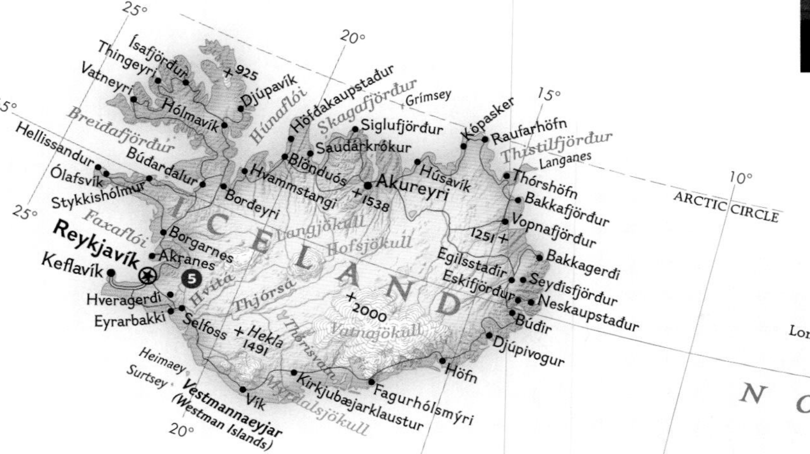
ICELAND
Reykjavík
Keflavík
Ísafjörður
Akureyri
Húsavík
Siglufjörður
Sauðárkrókur
Blönduós
Borgarnes
Akranes
Hveragerði
Eyrarbakki
Selfoss
Hekla 1491
Vík
Vestmannaeyjar (Westman Islands)
Heimaey
Surtsey
Kirkjubæjarklaustur
Fagurhólsmýri
Höfn
Djúpivogur
Búðir
Neskaupstaður
Seyðisfjörður
Eskifjörður
Egilsstaðir
Bakkagerði
Vopnafjörður
Bakkafjörður
Þórshöfn
Raufarhöfn
Kópasker
Grímsey
Vatnajökull
Hofsjökull
Langjökull
Mýrdalsjökull
Faxaflói
Breiðafjörður
Húnaflói
Skagafjörður
ARCTIC CIRCLE

Longitude West 5° of Greenwich

Longitude East 5° of Greenwich

NORWEGIAN SEA

ATLANTIC OCEAN

FAROE ISLANDS (FØROYAR) Denmark

Tórshavn

SHETLAND ISLANDS United Kingdom

ORKNEY ISLANDS United Kingdom

Meridian of Greenwich (London)

NORTH SEA

DENMARK

Kristiansund

Molde

Ålesund 4

Bergen 1

Haugesund

Stavanger

Egersund

Azimuthal Equidistant Projection

SCALE 1:8,024,000

1 CENTIMETER = 80 KILOMETERS; 1 INCH = 127 MILES

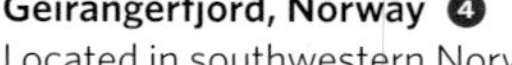
0 100 200 300
KILOMETERS

0 100 200 300
STATUTE MILES

Petäjävesi Old Church, Finland 3
A peasant and master builder constructed this Lutheran country church from logs in 1763-64 and situated it on a peninsula where two lakes meet, thereby accommodating the congregation who reached it by boat. It has a steeply pitched roof reminiscent of Gothic architecture, while also drawing from the Renaissance with a circular design at the top of an octagonal dome.

Geirangerfjord, Norway 4
Located in southwestern Norway, Geirangerfjord is among the world's longest and deepest fjords, stretching more than 90 miles and extending more than 1,600 feet below sea level. Rivers, which have escaped hydroelectric power development, drain glacial lakes as they flow through rugged mountains, clad in deciduous and coniferous forests, to cascade in numerous waterfalls from the steep crystalline walls that rise nearly a mile above the Norwegian Sea.

5 Thingvellir N.P., Iceland
In 930, Viking inhabitants agreed on a convenient meeting area for their farming community and created Althing, an open-air national assembly where no central authority existed. A loose association of the principal chieftains set and maintained laws as a covenant between free men, and disputes were resolved based on mutual agreement until 1798. Today, turf and stone fragments of booths still exist, and the natural site is considered the centerpiece for Icelandic national pride.

Denmark

Finland

Iceland

Norway

Sweden

Svalbard
Norway
Iceland
Sweden
Faroe Islands
Denmark
Norway
Denmark
Finland
Europe

Protected Areas and World Heritage Sites

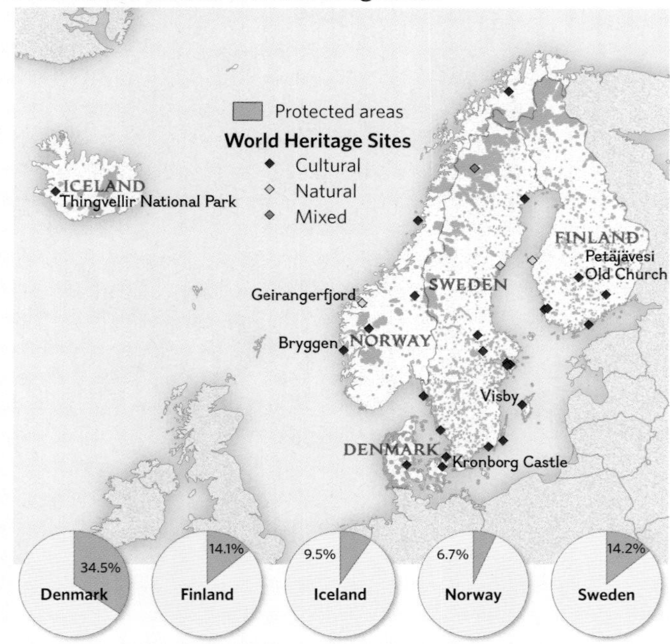
Protected areas
World Heritage Sites
Cultural
Natural
Mixed
ICELAND
Thingvellir National Park
FINLAND
Petäjävesi Old Church
SWEDEN
Geirangerfjord
Bryggen
NORWAY
Visby
DENMARK
Kronborg Castle
34.5%
Denmark
14.1%
Finland
9.5%
Iceland
6.7%
Norway
14.2%
Sweden

Percent of Land Area Protected

Urbanization and Largest Cities

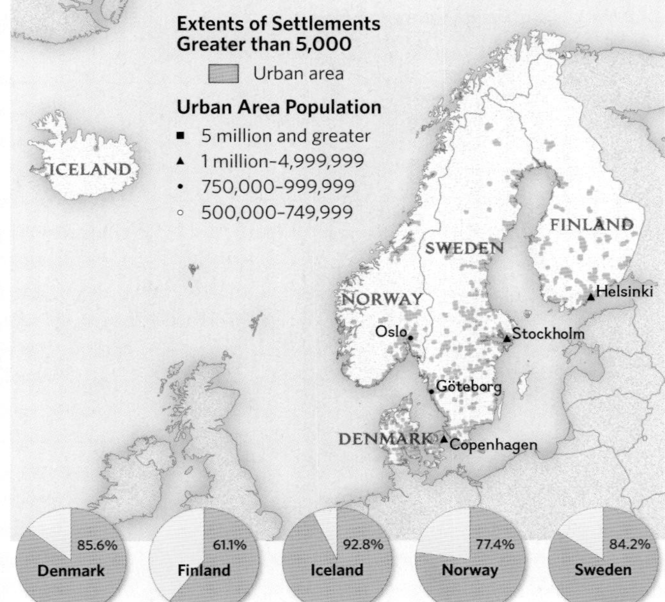
Extents of Settlements Greater than 5,000
Urban area
Urban Area Population
5 million and greater
1 million–4,999,999
750,000–999,999
500,000–749,999
ICELAND
FINLAND
SWEDEN
Helsinki
NORWAY
Oslo
Stockholm
Göteborg
DENMARK
Copenhagen
85.6%
Denmark
61.1%
Finland
92.8%
Iceland
77.4%
Norway
84.2%
Sweden

Percent of Population in Urban Areas

6 Kronborg Castle, Denmark Known as Elsinore in Shakespeare's *Hamlet*, the Kronborg Castle juts into Øresund Sound, the waterway separating Denmark and Sweden; it was constructed in the north European Renaissance style between 1574 and 1585. Because the castle commands a view over a two-mile-wide stretch of the sound, Danish kings once used it as a site to levy taxes on ships passing between the North and Baltic seas.

Natural Land Cover

ICELAND
FINLAND
SWEDEN
NORWAY
DENMARK
Land Cover
Forest
Glacier
Herbaceous
Highland
Tundra

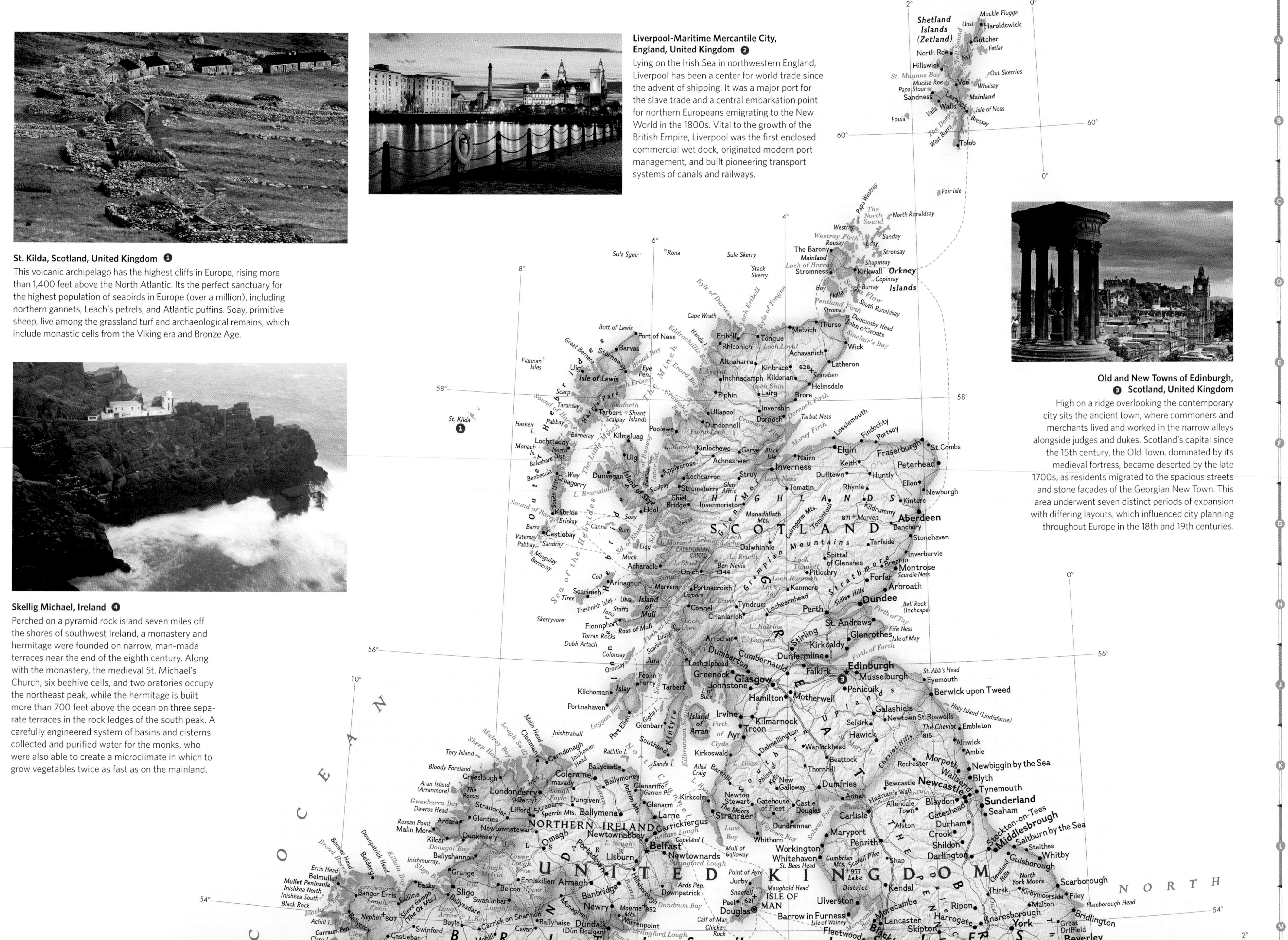
Shetland Islands (Zetland)
Orkney Islands
SCOTLAND
HIGHLANDS
Grampian Mountains
NORTHERN IRELAND
UNITED KINGDOM
ISLE OF MAN
OCEAN
NORTH
Edinburgh
Glasgow
Aberdeen
Dundee
Inverness
Perth
Stirling
Belfast
Londonderry
Newcastle
Sunderland
Carlisle
Berwick upon Tweed
Middlesbrough
Scarborough
York
Douglas
St. Kilda
Fair Isle
Outer Hebrides
Isle of Lewis
Island of Skye
Island of Mull

St. Kilda, Scotland, United Kingdom ❶

This volcanic archipelago has the highest cliffs in Europe, rising more than 1,400 feet above the North Atlantic. Its the perfect sanctuary for the highest population of seabirds in Europe (over a million), including northern gannets, Leach's petrels, and Atlantic puffins. Soay, primitive sheep, live among the grassland turf and archaeological remains, which include monastic cells from the Viking era and Bronze Age.

Skellig Michael, Ireland ❹

Perched on a pyramid rock island seven miles off the shores of southwest Ireland, a monastery and hermitage were founded on narrow, man-made terraces near the end of the eighth century. Along with the monastery, the medieval St. Michael's Church, six beehive cells, and two oratories occupy the northeast peak, while the hermitage is built more than 700 feet above the ocean on three separate terraces in the rock ledges of the south peak. A carefully engineered system of basins and cisterns collected and purified water for the monks, who were also able to create a microclimate in which to grow vegetables twice as fast as on the mainland.

Liverpool-Maritime Mercantile City, England, United Kingdom ❷

Lying on the Irish Sea in northwestern England, Liverpool has been a center for world trade since the advent of shipping. It was a major port for the slave trade and a central embarkation point for northern Europeans emigrating to the New World in the 1800s. Vital to the growth of the British Empire, Liverpool was the first enclosed commercial wet dock, originated modern port management, and built pioneering transport systems of canals and railways.

Old and New Towns of Edinburgh, ❸ Scotland, United Kingdom

High on a ridge overlooking the contemporary city sits the ancient town, where commoners and merchants lived and worked in the narrow alleys alongside judges and dukes. Scotland's capital since the 15th century, the Old Town, dominated by its medieval fortress, became deserted by the late 1700s, as residents migrated to the spacious streets and stone facades of the Georgian New Town. This area underwent seven distinct periods of expansion with differing layouts, which influenced city planning throughout Europe in the 18th and 19th centuries.

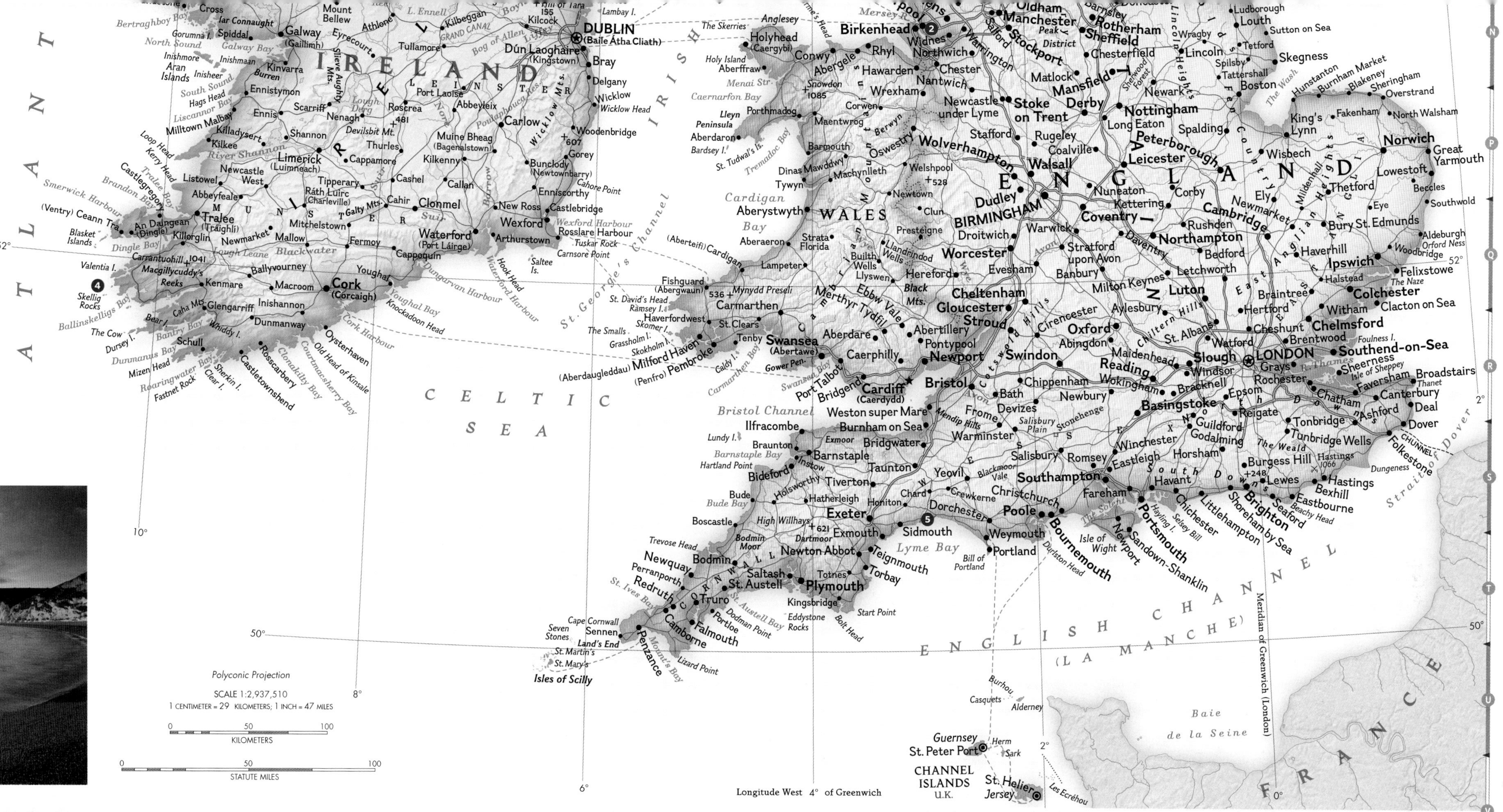

Ireland
United Kingdom

Dorset and East Devon Coast, England, United Kingdom 5

A pristine fossil forest of the late Jurassic period, whose trees are preserved in their original soils from more than 140 million years ago, lies on this undeveloped south coast of Britain. The area contains one of the only examples of rock strata and animal life from the Mesozoic era's 185 million years. The bays, sea stacks, and grasslands atop landslide cliffs support more than 20,000 migratory wildfowl, while Chesil Beach and Fleet Lagoon are renowned grounds for the study of beach formation and the evolution of a retreating coastline.

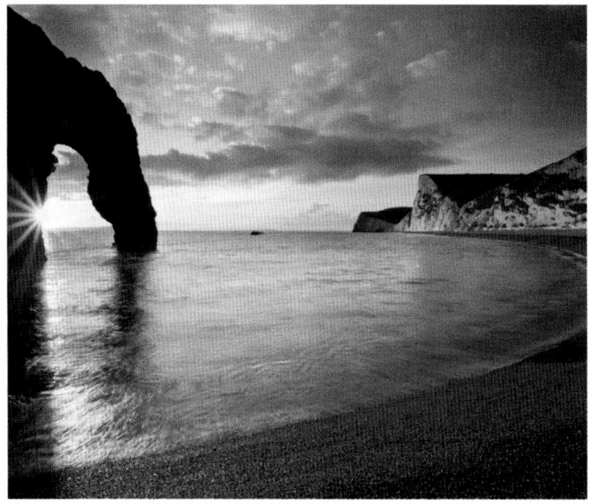

Polyconic Projection

SCALE 1:2,937,510

1 CENTIMETER = 29 KILOMETERS; 1 INCH = 47 MILES

0 50 100 KILOMETERS

0 50 100 STATUTE MILES

Longitude West 4° of Greenwich

Protected Areas and World Heritage Sites

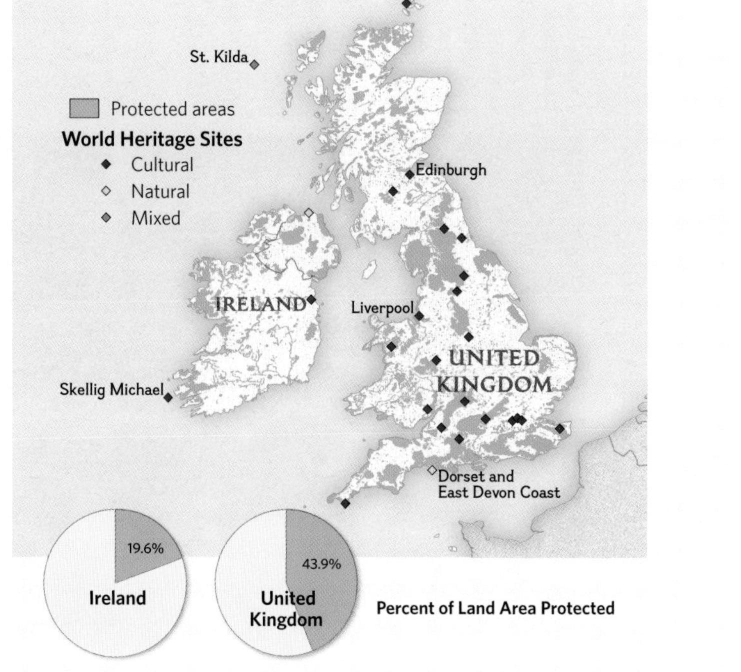
Protected areas
World Heritage Sites
Cultural
Natural
Mixed
St. Kilda
Edinburgh
Liverpool
IRELAND
UNITED KINGDOM
Skellig Michael
Dorset and East Devon Coast
19.6%
Ireland
43.9%
United Kingdom
Percent of Land Area Protected

Urbanization and Largest Cities

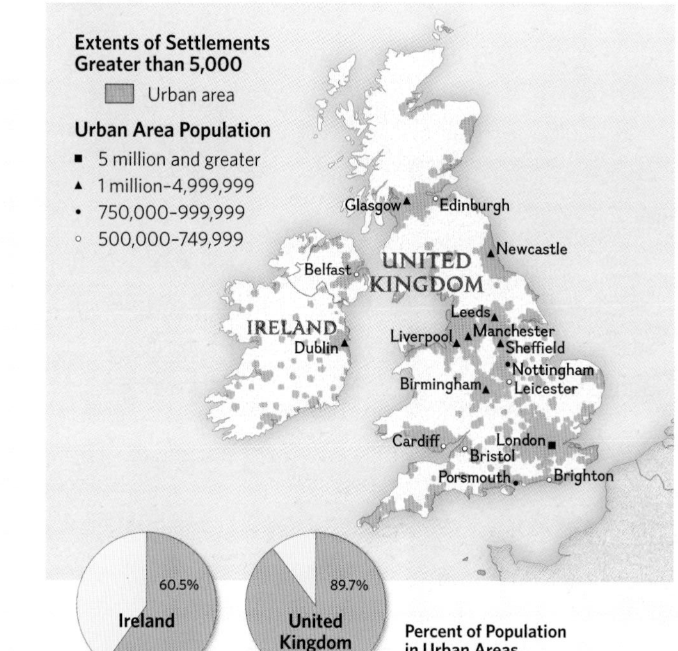
Extents of Settlements Greater than 5,000
Urban area
Urban Area Population
5 million and greater
1 million–4,999,999
750,000–999,999
500,000–749,999
Glasgow
Edinburgh
Newcastle
Belfast
UNITED KINGDOM
IRELAND
Dublin
Leeds
Liverpool
Manchester
Sheffield
Nottingham
Birmingham
Leicester
Cardiff
Bristol
London
Porsmouth
Brighton
60.5%
Ireland
89.7%
United Kingdom
Percent of Population in Urban Areas

Natural Land Cover

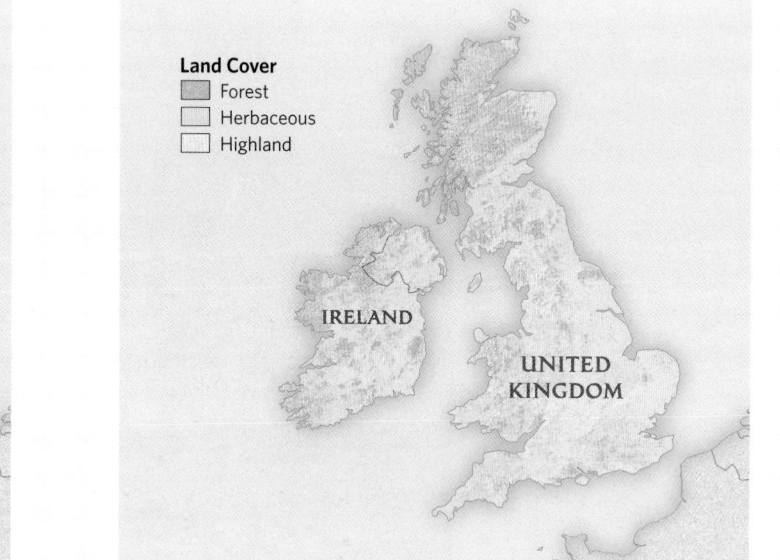
Land Cover
Forest
Herbaceous
Highland
IRELAND
UNITED KINGDOM
Ireland
United Kingdom
Europe

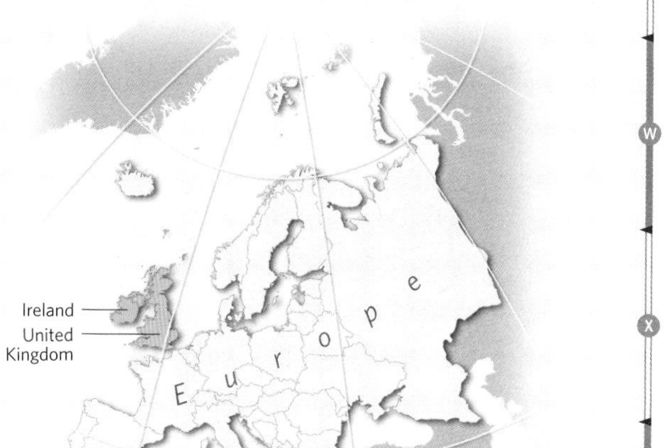

Alto Douro Wine Region, Portugal ❶

For nearly 2,000 years, communities have cultivated the rocky soil of these narrow, boxed-in valleys and capitalized on the region's hot, dry microclimate. Generations of farmers adapted the steep slopes for the vine by building terraces supported by hundreds of miles of stone walls. The result is world-famous port wine, the region's major export since the 1700s.

Sintra, Portugal ❷

In the 19th century, cool summers and mild winters lured Ferdinand II to Sintra, where he built a royal palace out of monastic ruins. A vast park of local and exotic trees and fountains surrounds the castle; it and the mix of parks and gardens in the nearby *quintas* (country houses) influenced landscape architecture throughout Europe.

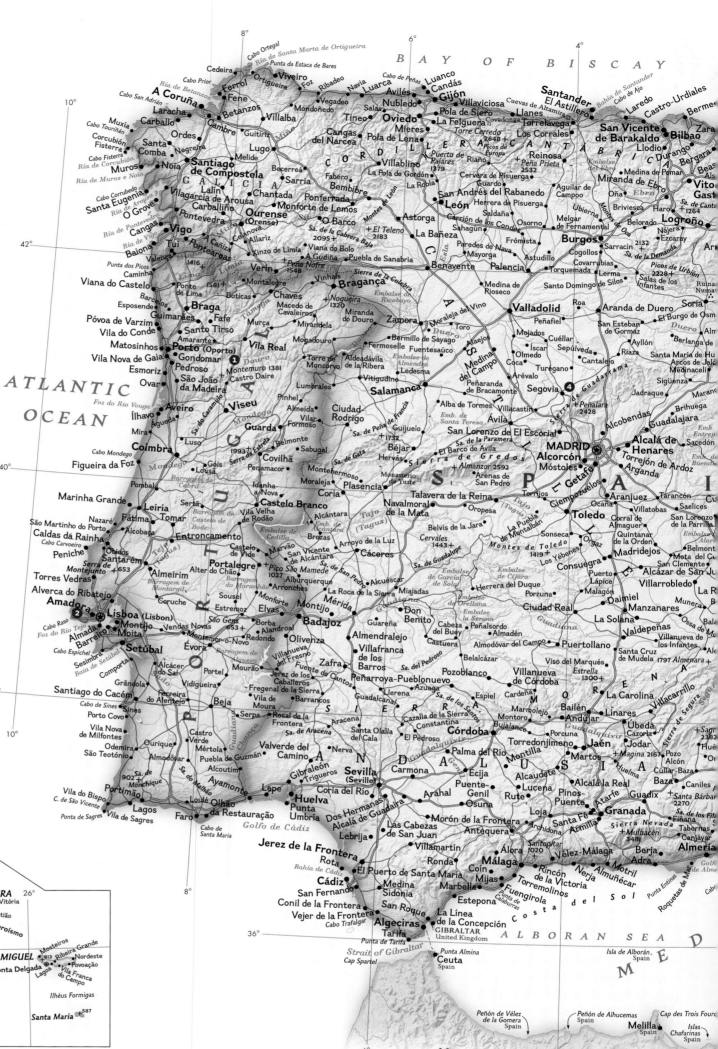

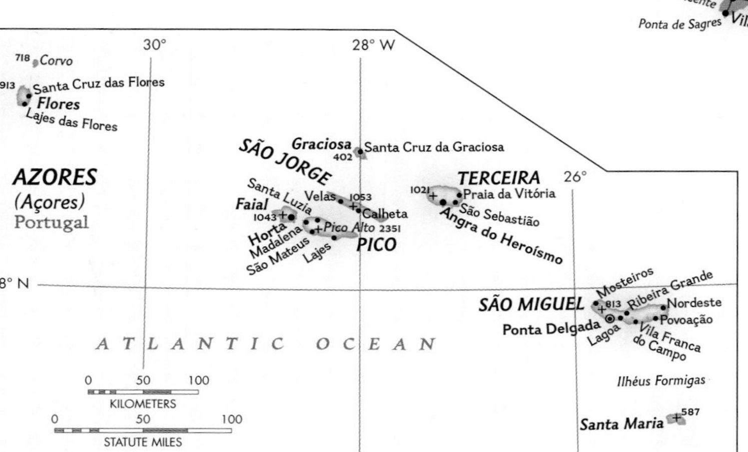
AZORES
(Açores)
Portugal
Corvo
Santa Cruz das Flores
Flores
Lajes das Flores
Graciosa
Santa Cruz da Graciosa
SÃO JORGE
TERCEIRA
Praia da Vitória
São Sebastião
Angra do Heroísmo
Faial
Horta
Velas
Calheta
Pico Alto 2351
PICO
Lajes
SÃO MIGUEL
Ponta Delgada
Nordeste
Povoação
Vila Franca do Campo
Ribeira Grande
Ilhéus Formigas
Santa Maria
ATLANTIC OCEAN
30°
28° W
26°
38° N
KILOMETERS
STATUTE MILES

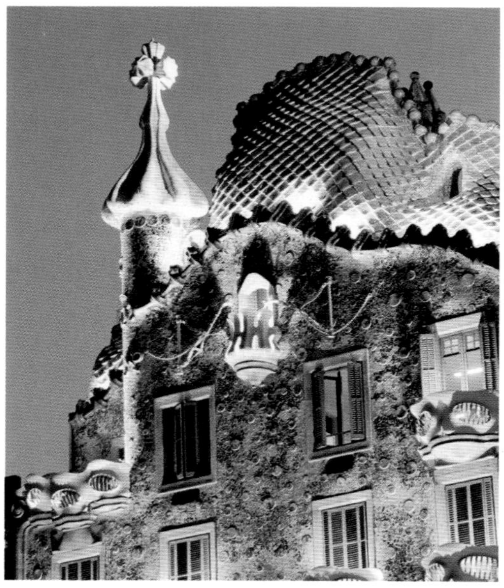

The Works of Antoni Gaudí (Barcelona), Spain ❸

In the late 19th and early 20th centuries, Gaudí demonstrated his belief that a building should be a total work of art, employing his full range of talents as architect, builder, artist, engineer, and craftsman. Seven sites in or near the city (including the residence Casa Batlló, left) exemplify this approach, which drew from nature and other influences including the arts and crafts movement, symbolism, expressionism, and rationalism.

Old Town of Segovia ❹ and its Aqueduct, Spain

Built by the Romans in the first century A.D., this aqueduct has 128 arched pillars and carried water from a river 11 miles away. A medieval wall encircles the historic district that includes the most Romanesque churches in Europe and Alcázar castle, where Queen Isabel promised Columbus the financial backing he needed to discover America.

Portugal
Spain

Albers Conic Equal-Area Projection
SCALE 1:3,290,000
1 CENTIMETER = 118 KILOMETERS; 1 INCH = 187 MILES
For more detail on Andorra, see pages 170–171
BALEARIC ISLANDS
MALLORCA (MAJORCA)
MENORCA (MINORCA)
IBIZA (IVISA)
BARCELONA
MEDITERRANEAN SEA
ALGERIA

❻ Ibiza, Balearic Islands, Spain
Ibiza is one of only 25 heritage sites considered both culturally and naturally significant. The Upper Town of Ibiza is an acropolis built during the Renaissance, while nearby Phoenician ruins include archaic urban configurations of scattered buildings linked by irregular streets and triangular public areas. Dense, threatened prairies of oceanic sea grass found only in the Mediterranean Basin thrive and support the highest concentration of marine species in the Mediterranean Sea.

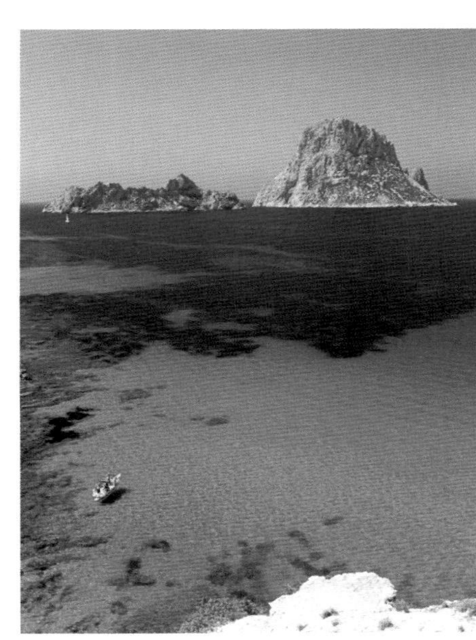

❺ Walled City of Cuenca, Spain
Built by the Moors, this archetypal fortress-town epitomizes landscape architecture by conforming to the surroundings. The *casas colgadas* (hanging houses) of the upper town teeter on cliffs over the Huécar River, while the suburban area twists on streets that mold to the steep topography.

Europe
Azores
Portugal
Spain

Protected Areas and World Heritage Sites

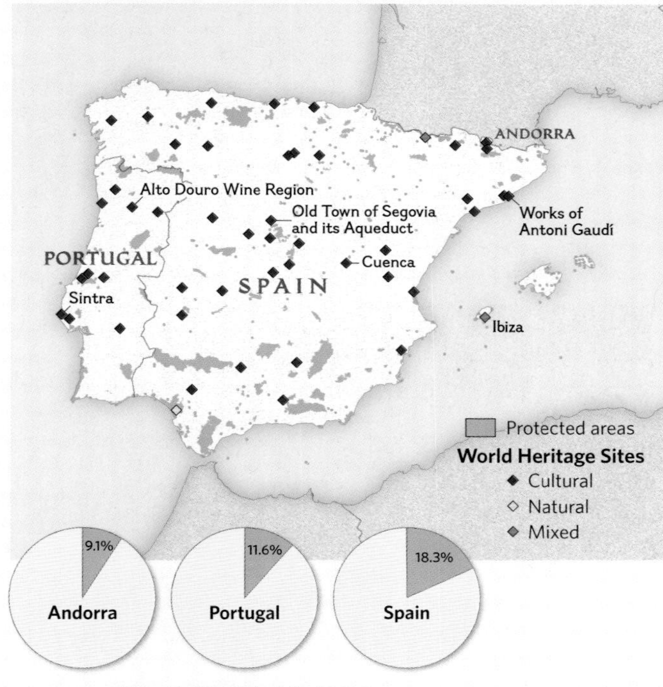
ANDORRA
Alto Douro Wine Region
Old Town of Segovia and its Aqueduct
Works of Antoni Gaudí
PORTUGAL
Sintra
SPAIN
Cuenca
Ibiza
Protected areas
World Heritage Sites
Cultural
Natural
Mixed
9.1%
Andorra
11.6%
Portugal
18.3%
Spain

Percent of Land Area Protected

Urbanization and Largest Cities

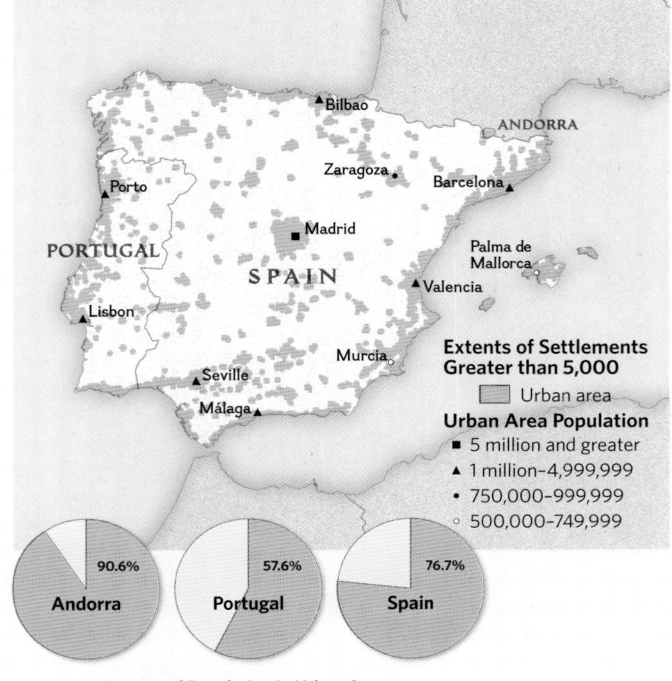
Bilbao
ANDORRA
Zaragoza
Barcelona
Porto
Madrid
PORTUGAL
SPAIN
Palma de Mallorca
Valencia
Lisbon
Murcia
Seville
Málaga
Extents of Settlements Greater than 5,000
Urban area
Urban Area Population
5 million and greater
1 million–4,999,999
750,000–999,999
500,000–749,999
90.6%
Andorra
57.6%
Portugal
76.7%
Spain

Percent of Population in Urban Areas

Natural Land Cover

ANDORRA
PORTUGAL
SPAIN
Land Cover
Desert
Forest
Herbaceous
Highland

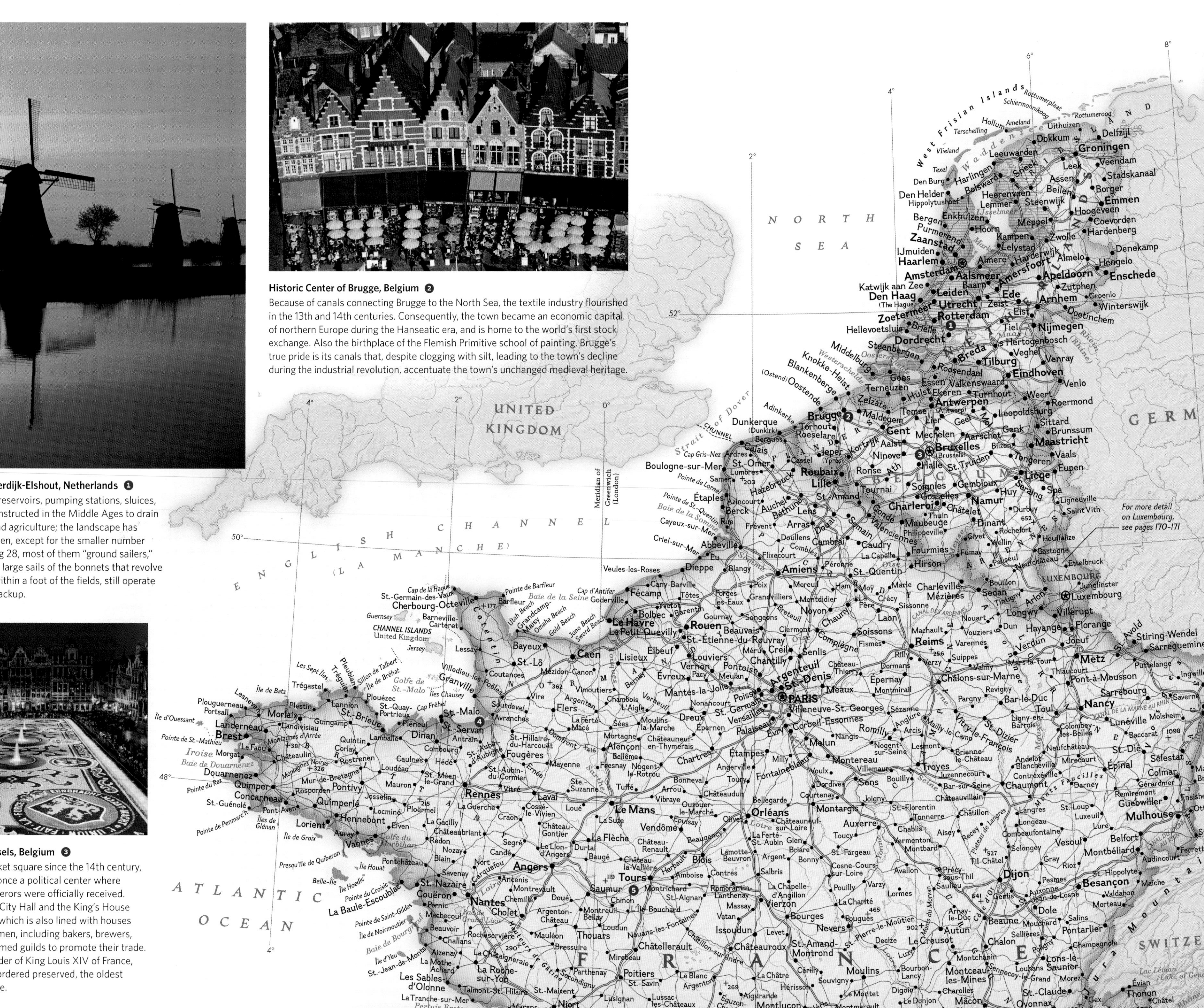
NORTH SEA
UNITED KINGDOM
ENGLISH CHANNEL (LA MANCHE)
ATLANTIC OCEAN
GERMANY
SWITZERLAND
FRANCE
LUXEMBOURG
West Frisian Islands
Strait of Dover
CHANNEL ISLANDS
United Kingdom
Meridian of Greenwich (London)
For more detail on Luxembourg, see pages 170-171
PARIS
Bruxelles
Luxembourg
Den Haag (The Hague)
Amsterdam

Historic Center of Brugge, Belgium 2

Because of canals connecting Brugge to the North Sea, the textile industry flourished in the 13th and 14th centuries. Consequently, the town became an economic capital of northern Europe during the Hanseatic era, and is home to the world's first stock exchange. Also the birthplace of the Flemish Primitive school of painting, Brugge's true pride is its canals that, despite clogging with silt, leading to the town's decline during the industrial revolution, accentuate the town's unchanged medieval heritage.

Mill Network at Kinderdijk-Elshout, Netherlands 1

This system of dikes, reservoirs, pumping stations, sluices, and windmills was constructed in the Middle Ages to drain land for settlement and agriculture; the landscape has changed little since then, except for the smaller number of mills. The remaining 28, most of them "ground sailers," so-called because the large sails of the bonnets that revolve with the wind come within a foot of the fields, still operate as emergency flood backup.

La Grand-Place, Brussels, Belgium 3

The city's central market square since the 14th century, the Grand-Place was once a political center where dukes, kings, and emperors were officially received. The massive tower of City Hall and the King's House dominate the square, which is also lined with houses once owned by craftsmen, including bakers, brewers, and butchers, who formed guilds to promote their trade. Bombed in 1695 by order of King Louis XIV of France, the Grand-Place was ordered preserved, the oldest record of such a decree.

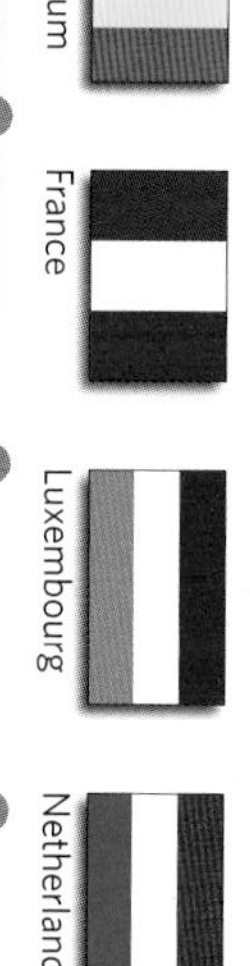
Belgium
France
Luxembourg
Netherlands

Mont-St.-Michel and Its Bay, France 4

Built in the Middle Ages, this Benedictine abbey and surrounding village seem lost between land and sea, perched on a rocky island a half mile in circumference and more than a mile from solid ground. The mount has survived the rough tides of the bay between Normandy and Brittany, and the medieval fortifications withstood sieges from English and French troops before becoming a prison after the French Revolution.

The Loire Valley, France 5

With the end of the Hundred Years' War in the mid-15th century, the Renaissance took root in the Loire Valley. Once home to Leonardo da Vinci, Balzac, and Alexandre Dumas, this 170-mile stretch of valley is dotted with isolated farms, villages, and historic provincial towns. French ornamental gardens, replete with fountains, originated here, and the area's limestone and black slate were used to build world-famous monuments, including the Château de Chambord.

BAY OF BISCAY
MEDITERRANEAN SEA
Golfe du Lion
SPAIN
ANDORRA
ITALY
MONACO
Bordeaux
Toulouse
Montpellier
Marseille
Toulon
Nice
Lyon
Grenoble
St.-Étienne
Clermont-Ferrand
Limoges
Perpignan
Nîmes
Avignon
Aix-en-Provence
Bayonne
Biarritz
Pau
Tarbes
Carcassonne
Béziers
Longitude West 2° of Greenwich
Longitude East 2° of Greenwich
For more detail on Andorra, see pages 170-171
For more detail on Monaco, see pages 170-171
Refer to pages 158-159 for Corsica
To Corse (Corsica)
Albers Conic Equal-Area Projection
SCALE 1:3,556,000
1 CENTIMETER = 36 KILOMETERS; 1 INCH = 56 MILES
KILOMETERS
STATUTE MILES

Protected Areas and World Heritage Sites

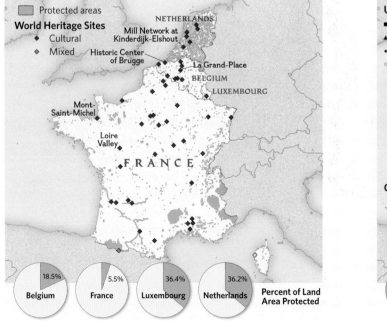

Protected areas

World Heritage Sites
- Cultural
- Mixed

Mill Network at Kinderdijk-Elshout; Historic Center of Brugge; La Grand-Place; Mont-Saint-Michel; Loire Valley; NETHERLANDS; BELGIUM; LUXEMBOURG; FRANCE

Percent of Land Area Protected: Belgium 18.5%; France 5.5%; Luxembourg 36.4%; Netherlands 36.2%

Urbanization and Largest Cities

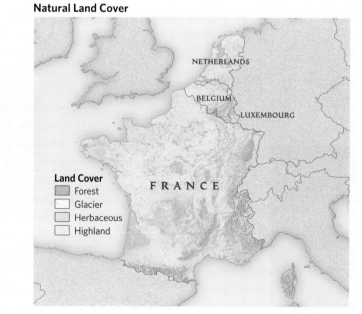

Urban Area Population
- 5 million and greater
- 1 million–4,999,999
- 750,000–999,999
- 500,000–749,999

Extents of Settlements Greater than 5,000
- Urban area

Amsterdam; Antwerp; Brussels; Liège; Lille; Rouen; Paris; Strasbourg; Rennes; Nantes; Lyon; Grenoble; Bordeaux; Montpellier; Nice; Toulouse; Marseille; Toulon

Percent of Population in Urban Areas: Belgium 97.2%; France 76.7%; Luxembourg 82.8%; Netherlands 80.2%

Natural Land Cover

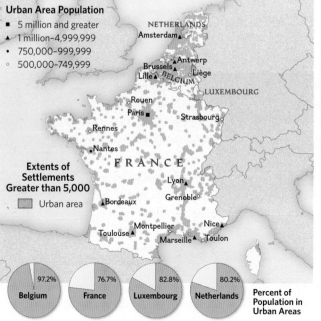

Land Cover
- Forest
- Glacier
- Herbaceous
- Highland

NETHERLANDS; BELGIUM; LUXEMBOURG; FRANCE

Europe: Netherlands; Belgium; Luxembourg; France

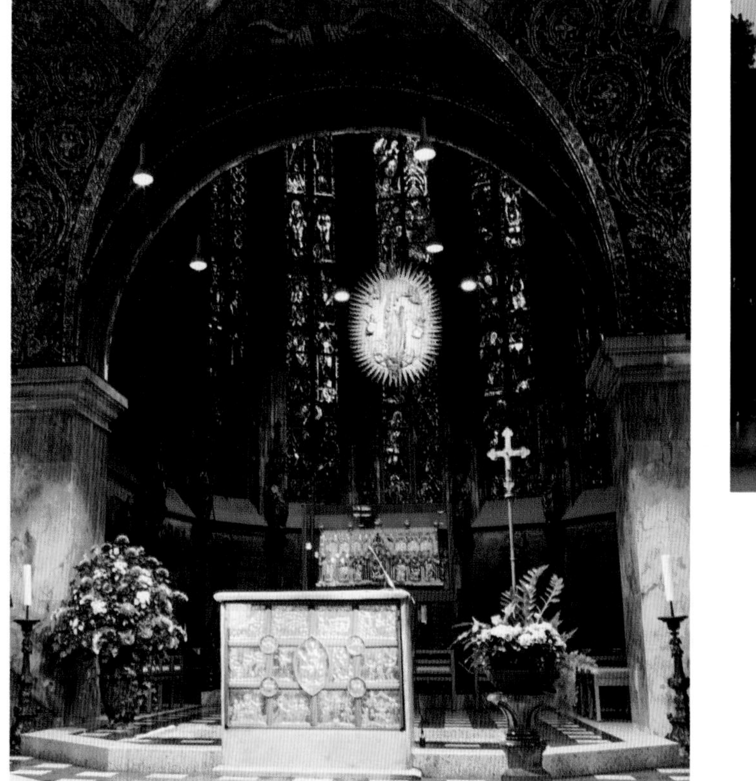

Aachen Cathedral, Germany ❶

With an octagonal dome, columns of Greek and Italian marble, and a bronze gate and door, this palatine chapel was the first vaulted structure north of the Alps prior to the Middle Ages. Built by Roman Emperor Charlemagne in the late eighth century, its collection of relics is the most significant in central Europe, including what is said to be remnants of Jesus' loincloth worn on the Cross.

Lavaux Vineyard Terraces, Switzerland ❺

Stretching more than 18 miles along Lake Geneva, these steep, narrow stone terraces interlacing villages and hamlets have produced Chasselas grapes since Benedictine and Cistercian monks managed the land in the 11th century. Winegrowers constantly innovated traditional viticulture to optimize production, resulting in more than 270 miles of retaining walls supporting more than 10,000 terraces.

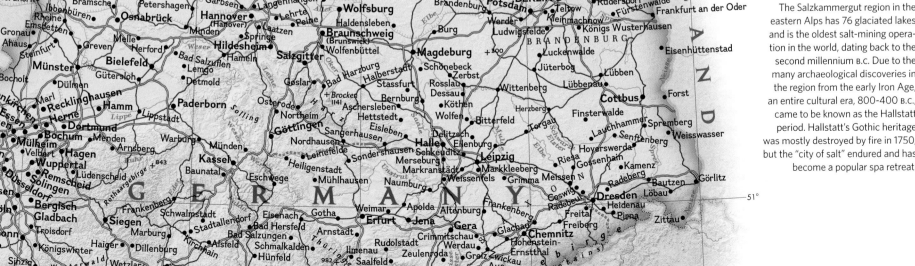

Museumsinsel (Museum Island), Berlin, Germany ❷

Built between 1824 and 1930, this group of five buildings in Berlin exhibits the evolution of the modern public art museum in the 20th century from one enjoyed only by royalty, to one accessible to the masses, with different wings for various gallery holdings. Its world-renowned art collection includes ancient Egyptian, Near East, and Islamic art, sculptures from the Middle Ages, and coinage dating back to the seventh century B.C.

❸ **Wachau Cultural Landscape, Austria**

The vast forests and grasslands along this stretch of the Danube River Valley have been inhabited since the Paleolithic period. As landowners alternated between viticulture and apricot-growing with changing market demands, they avoided technological and industrial encroachment, leaving the natural surroundings virtually untouched. Nearly 5,000 monuments dating back to the Middle Ages dot the landscape, including baroque monasteries, well-preserved castle ruins, and medieval market towns.

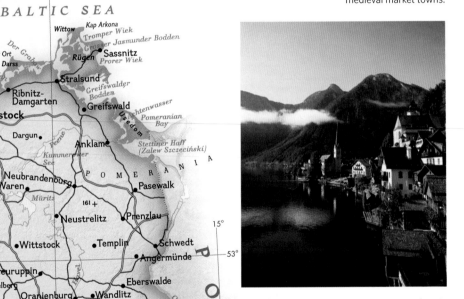

Hallstatt-Dachstein Salzkammergut Cultural ❹ **Landscape, Austria**

The Salzkammergut region in the eastern Alps has 76 glaciated lakes and is the oldest salt-mining operation in the world, dating back to the second millennium B.C. Due to the many archaeological discoveries in the region from the early Iron Age, an entire cultural era, 800-400 B.C., came to be known as the Hallstatt period. Hallstatt's Gothic heritage was mostly destroyed by fire in 1750, but the "city of salt" endured and has become a popular spa retreat.

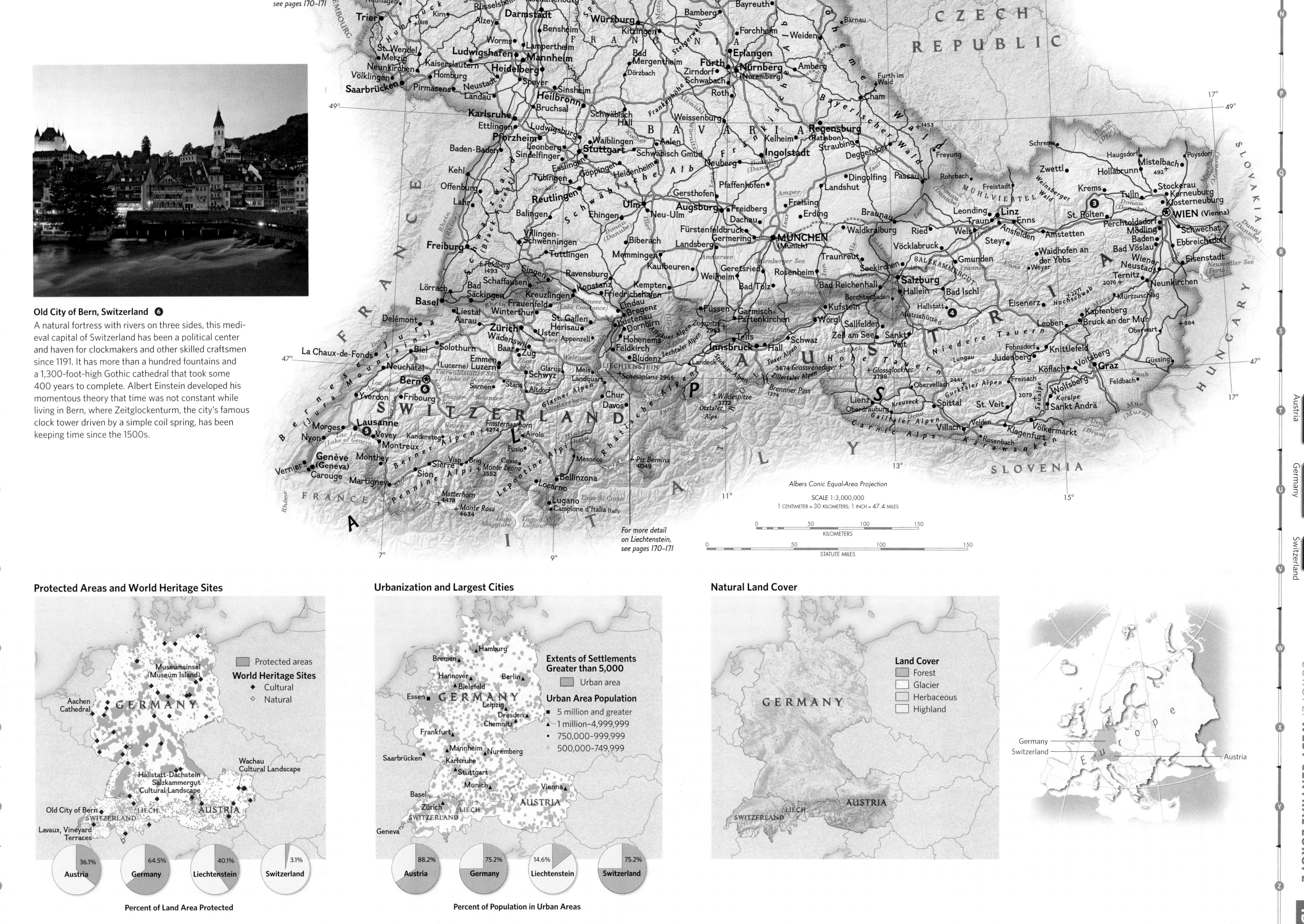
Austria
Germany
Switzerland
CZECH REPUBLIC
SLOVAKIA
HUNGARY
SLOVENIA
ITALY
FRANCE
SWITZERLAND
AUSTRIA
BAVARIA
FRANCONIA
WIEN (Vienna)
MÜNCHEN (Munich)
Stuttgart
Nürnberg (Nuremberg)
Zürich
Bern
Salzburg
Innsbruck
Graz
Linz
Genève (Geneva)
Lausanne
Basel
Albers Conic Equal-Area Projection
SCALE 1:3,000,000
1 CENTIMETER = 30 KILOMETERS; 1 INCH = 47.4 MILES
KILOMETERS
STATUTE MILES
For more detail on Liechtenstein, see pages 170-171
For more detail on Luxembourg, see pages 170-171
Protected Areas and World Heritage Sites
Protected areas
World Heritage Sites
Cultural
Natural
Museumsinsel (Museum Island)
Aachen Cathedral
Hallstatt-Dachstein Salzkammergut Cultural Landscape
Wachau Cultural Landscape
Old City of Bern
Lavaux, Vineyard Terraces
36.1% Austria
64.5% Germany
40.1% Liechtenstein
3.1% Switzerland
Percent of Land Area Protected
Urbanization and Largest Cities
Extents of Settlements Greater than 5,000
Urban area
Urban Area Population
5 million and greater
1 million–4,999,999
750,000–999,999
500,000–749,999
88.2% Austria
75.2% Germany
14.6% Liechtenstein
75.2% Switzerland
Percent of Population in Urban Areas
Natural Land Cover
Land Cover
Forest
Glacier
Herbaceous
Highland
Europe
Germany
Switzerland
Austria

Old City of Bern, Switzerland 6

A natural fortress with rivers on three sides, this medieval capital of Switzerland has been a political center and haven for clockmakers and other skilled craftsmen since 1191. It has more than a hundred fountains and a 1,300-foot-high Gothic cathedral that took some 400 years to complete. Albert Einstein developed his momentous theory that time was not constant while living in Bern, where Zeitglockenturm, the city's famous clock tower driven by a simple coil spring, has been keeping time since the 1500s.

Historic Center of Český Krumlov, Czech Republic ❶
Founded on the banks of the Vltava River in the 1300s as the government seat of Bohemia, this town became the center for trade in central Europe. Influential families ruled from Hrádek Castle, built on a rock promontory sculpted by the river and comprising 40 buildings around five courtyards. Across the river, the settlement Làtran, the surrounding medieval town, and the 15th-century Church of St. Vitus remain undisturbed.

Spišský Hrad, Slovakia ❷
Spis Castle sits high above the western plains on an area occupied since the fifth century B.C. Built on a fault line and ravaged by war, it was rebuilt four times in medieval times. Although left to ruin after a fire in 1780, it is one of the largest and finest medieval castles in eastern Europe. It is surrounded by some of the oldest Slovak settlements.

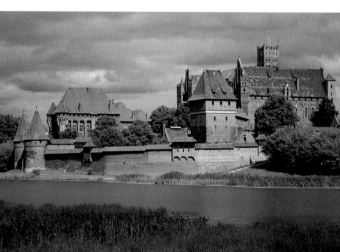

❸ Białowieża Forest, Poland
Białowieża Forest is the site of the successful reintroduction of European bison in 1929 and, at more than 140,000 acres, forms part of the largest and last old-growth virgin forest in central Europe (another 165,000 acres crosses the border into Belarus). Situated on the watershed of the Baltic and Black Seas, the range, with its evergreen and broad-leafed trees, peat bogs, and two major rivers, is a buffer to human encroachment, and the perfect habitat for the rare lynx, gray wolf, northern birch moose, otter, and Poland's only population of masked shrew.

Castle of the Teutonic Order in Malbork, Poland ❹
Malbork Castle was built in the late 13th century by crusading knights hired by the Polish state to bring Christianity to the Pruzzi, or Prussians, a tribe of Baltic pagans who had lived here since prehistoric times. Constructed in red brick surrounded by bastions, ramparts, and moats, the High Castle was composed of a square convent and central courtyard with living spaces for the knights, refectories, kitchens, and a church. The Middle Castle, restyled from an exercise area, housed an infirmary, commander's quarters, chapel, and guest wing for visiting dignitaries. The Fore Castle holds servants' quarters, workshops, cannon foundries, stables, and the wagon house.

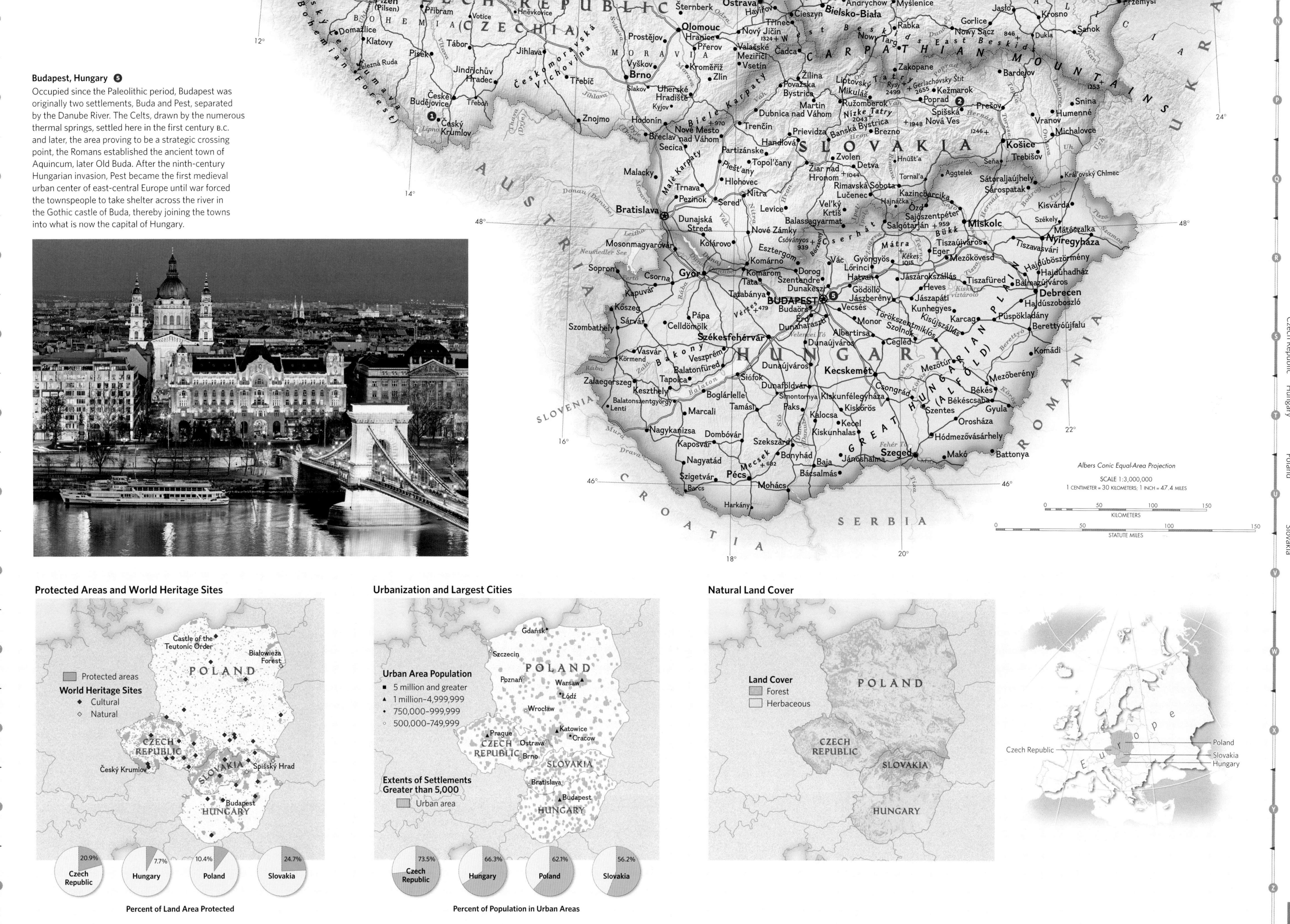
Czech Republic
Hungary
Poland
Slovakia
CZECH REPUBLIC (CZECHIA)
SLOVAKIA
HUNGARY
AUSTRIA
SLOVENIA
CROATIA
SERBIA
ROMANIA
UKRAINE
CARPATHIAN MOUNTAINS
GREAT HUNGARIAN PLAIN (ALFÖLD)
BUDAPEST
Bratislava
Albers Conic Equal-Area Projection
SCALE 1:3,000,000
1 CENTIMETER = 30 KILOMETERS; 1 INCH = 47.4 MILES
KILOMETERS
STATUTE MILES
Protected Areas and World Heritage Sites
Protected areas
World Heritage Sites
Cultural
Natural
Castle of the Teutonic Order
Białowieża Forest
Český Krumlov
Spišský Hrad
20.9% Czech Republic
7.7% Hungary
10.4% Poland
24.7% Slovakia
Percent of Land Area Protected
Urbanization and Largest Cities
Urban Area Population
5 million and greater
1 million–4,999,999
750,000–999,999
500,000–749,999
Extents of Settlements Greater than 5,000
Urban area
73.5% Czech Republic
66.3% Hungary
62.1% Poland
56.2% Slovakia
Percent of Population in Urban Areas
Natural Land Cover
Land Cover
Forest
Herbaceous
Europe

Budapest, Hungary 5

Occupied since the Paleolithic period, Budapest was originally two settlements, Buda and Pest, separated by the Danube River. The Celts, drawn by the numerous thermal springs, settled here in the first century B.C. and later, the area proving to be a strategic crossing point, the Romans established the ancient town of Aquincum, later Old Buda. After the ninth-century Hungarian invasion, Pest became the first medieval urban center of east-central Europe until war forced the townspeople to take shelter across the river in the Gothic castle of Buda, thereby joining the towns into what is now the capital of Hungary.

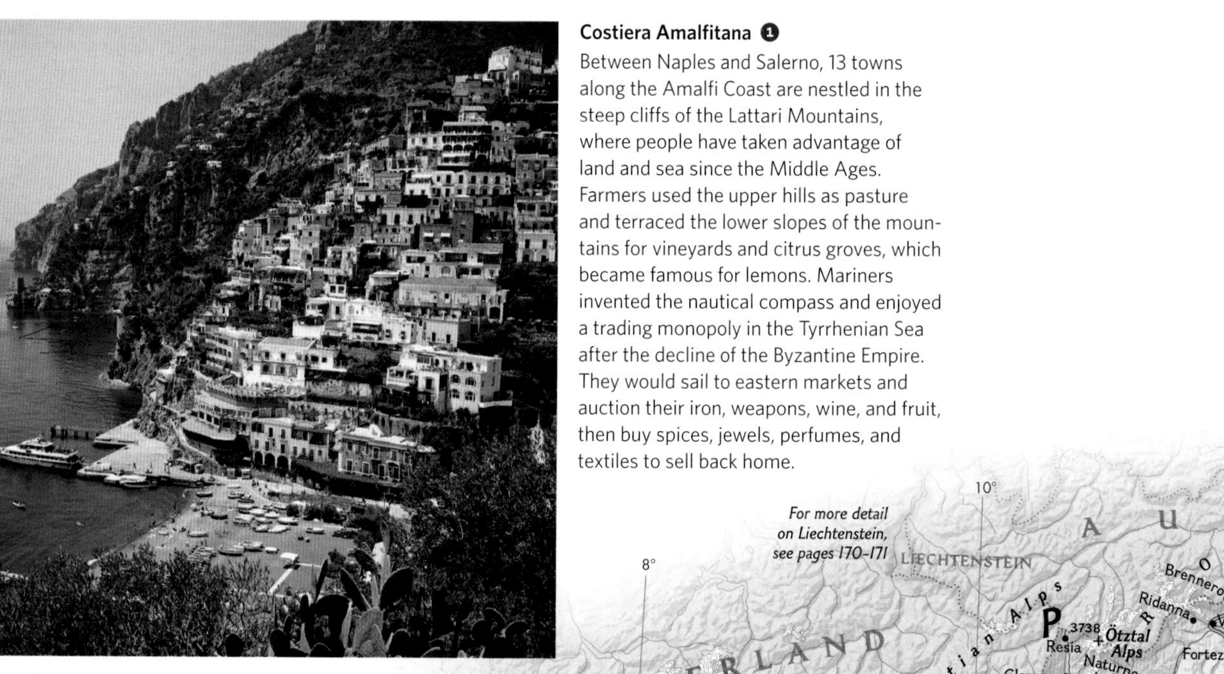

Costiera Amalfitana ❶

Between Naples and Salerno, 13 towns along the Amalfi Coast are nestled in the steep cliffs of the Lattari Mountains, where people have taken advantage of land and sea since the Middle Ages. Farmers used the upper hills as pasture and terraced the lower slopes of the mountains for vineyards and citrus groves, which became famous for lemons. Mariners invented the nautical compass and enjoyed a trading monopoly in the Tyrrhenian Sea after the decline of the Byzantine Empire. They would sail to eastern markets and auction their iron, weapons, wine, and fruit, then buy spices, jewels, perfumes, and textiles to sell back home.

❷ Val d'Orcia

In the 14th and 15th centuries, residents of the Siena city-state planned and designed this agricultural area 15 miles to the southwest. Fortified settlements were grouped on the summits of conical hills decorated by cypress trees, inspiring painters of the Renaissance. Families lived on and cultivated the merchant-owned estates, paying rent in grain, olives, fruits, and vegetables, which the merchants then sold, reinvesting the profits into the land and villages.

❸ Venice and its Lagoon

In the fifth century, Venetian mainlanders fleeing Barbarian raids hid on the 118 sandy islands of the shallow lagoon, which covers nearly 8,000 square miles. Venice grew out of these settlements of peasants and fishermen and became a major maritime power in the tenth century, commanding an area stretching from the shores of the eastern Mediterranean Sea to Crete and the islands of the Ionian Sea. The city seems to float on the waters of the lagoon and boasts one of the highest concentrations of art and architectural masterpieces in the world.

Historic Center of Urbino ❹

A fortified Roman settlement once sat on the hill now occupied by the Ducal Palace. Rooms are adorned with inlaid doors, bas-reliefs, and walls painted by masters such as Paolo Uccello, Piero della Francesca, and Raphael. Because Urbino filled with scholars and artists during the Renaissance, it was a favorite stopover for royal courts traveling between Rome and Europe, and thereby strongly influenced European culture.

For more detail on Liechtenstein, see pages 170–171

For more detail on Monaco, see pages 170–171

For more detail on San Marino, see pages 170–171

For more detail on Vatican City, see pages 170–171

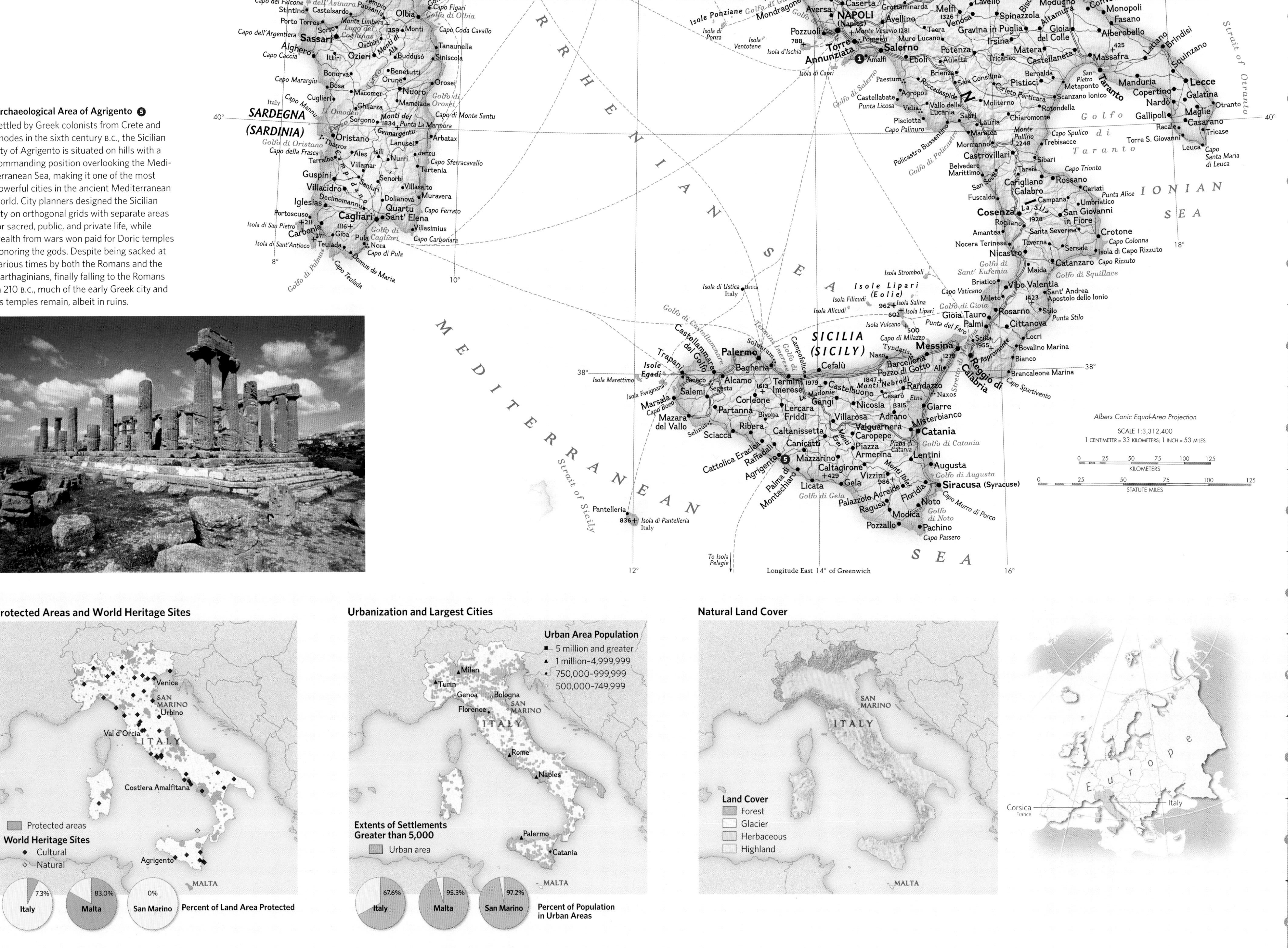
Italy
SARDEGNA
(SARDINIA)
SICILIA
(SICILY)
NAPOLI
(Naples)
Palermo
Messina
Catania
Siracusa (Syracuse)
Agrigento
Cagliari
Sassari
Salerno
Taranto
Lecce
Brindisi
Reggio di Calabria
Cosenza
Catanzaro
Crotone
Trapani
Marsala
Pantelleria
Isole Lipari (Eolie)
Isole Egadi
Isole Ponziane
Isola di Capri
IONIAN SEA
MEDITERRANEAN
Strait of Sicily
Strait of Otranto
Golfo di Taranto
Golfo di Squillace
Golfo di Catania
Golfo di Gela
Golfo di Castellammare
Golfo di Salerno
Golfo di Policastro
Longitude East 14° of Greenwich
To Isola Pelagie
Albers Conic Equal-Area Projection
SCALE 1:3,312,400
1 CENTIMETER = 33 KILOMETERS; 1 INCH = 53 MILES
KILOMETERS
STATUTE MILES

Archaeological Area of Agrigento 5

Settled by Greek colonists from Crete and Rhodes in the sixth century B.C., the Sicilian city of Agrigento is situated on hills with a commanding position overlooking the Mediterranean Sea, making it one of the most powerful cities in the ancient Mediterranean world. City planners designed the Sicilian city on orthogonal grids with separate areas for sacred, public, and private life, while wealth from wars won paid for Doric temples honoring the gods. Despite being sacked at various times by both the Romans and the Carthaginians, finally falling to the Romans in 210 B.C., much of the early Greek city and its temples remain, albeit in ruins.

Protected Areas and World Heritage Sites

Venice
SAN MARINO
Urbino
Val d'Orcia
ITALY
Costiera Amalfitana
Agrigento
MALTA
Protected areas
World Heritage Sites
Cultural
Natural
Italy 7.3%
Malta 83.0%
San Marino 0%
Percent of Land Area Protected

Urbanization and Largest Cities

Urban Area Population
5 million and greater
1 million–4,999,999
750,000–999,999
500,000–749,999
Milan
Turin
Genoa
Bologna
SAN MARINO
Florence
ITALY
Rome
Naples
Palermo
Catania
MALTA
Extents of Settlements Greater than 5,000
Urban area
Italy 67.6%
Malta 95.3%
San Marino 97.2%
Percent of Population in Urban Areas

Natural Land Cover

SAN MARINO
ITALY
MALTA
Land Cover
Forest
Glacier
Herbaceous
Highland
Europe
Corsica
France
Italy

Albania

Bosnia and Herzegovina

Bulgaria

Dubrovnik, Croatia ❷
Protected by a stone-and-lime wall measuring 20 feet at its thickest and 50 feet at its tallest, this medieval port city fended off assaults from Arabs, Turks, and Napoleon, but many of the buildings were destroyed in Croatia's war for independence from Yugoslavia in 1991. Scholars discovered original materials and designs in ancient manuscripts, while experts replicated archaic tools and supervised volunteer citizens and local craftsmen who undertook the restoration.

Mostar, Bosnia and Herzegovina ❶
In 1566, Süleyman the Magnificent ordered the Old Bridge reconstructed in stone to accommodate the trade route across the Neretva River to the Adriatic Sea. Mostar became a frontier town of the Ottoman Empire, as Turks built mosques, a religious school, and a public bath. A prolonged siege during the Bosnian war of the early 1990s destroyed most of the historic town, but the Old Bridge, ancient Turkish homes, and several Turkish mosques and shrines have been restored.

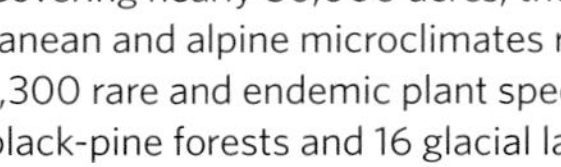

Durmitor N.P., Montenegro ❸
Covering nearly 80,000 acres, the park's Mediterranean and alpine microclimates result in more than 1,300 rare and endemic plant species. The dense black-pine forests and 16 glacial lakes shelter gray wolves, chamois, salmon, and eagles, while the Tara River canyon has the deepest gorges in Europe, measuring more than 4,000 feet deep.

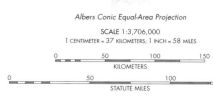

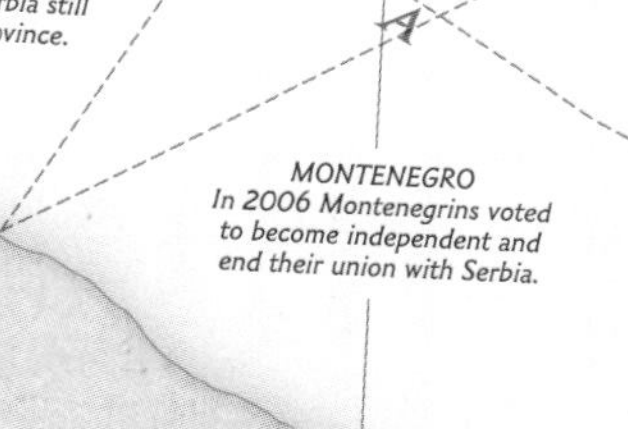
KOSOVO
On February 17, 2008, Kosovo declared its independence. Serbia still claims it as a province.
MONTENEGRO
In 2006 Montenegrins voted to become independent and end their union with Serbia.

Ohrid, Macedonia ❹
Lake Ohrid covers 140 square miles of this former Yugoslav republic and is geographically isolated by Albania to the west. Its seclusion and relatively pollution-free environment make it the perfect habitat for snail, worm, crab, and sponge species that have inhabited Earth for 50 million years. Humans have lived on Ohrid's shores since the Stone Age. In the sixth century B.C., Illyrian tribes founded the old town of Ohrid, which prospered under Roman rule because it lay on the main trade route between the Aegean and Adriatic Seas. The arrival of Saints Clement and Naum in the ninth century A.D. inspired intellectual growth and the construction of schools, libraries, and churches, some of which still perch on rocky promontories above the lake.

Albers Conic Equal-Area Projection
SCALE 1:3,706,000
1 CENTIMETER = 37 KILOMETERS; 1 INCH = 58 MILES
0 50 100 150 KILOMETERS
0 50 100 STATUTE MILES

Croatia

Kosovo

Macedonia

Montenegro

Romania

Serbia

Slovenia

Villages with Fortified Churches ❺ in Transylvania, Romania

At the invitation of Hungarian kings, German-speaking artisans, farmers, and merchants colonized Transylvania in the 13th century. These Transylvania Saxons settled seven villages in the foothills of the Carpathian Mountains, but lacked the resources to fortify the towns. Instead they built fortresses around their churches to fend off sieges and grouped their houses nearby.

UKRAINE
MOLDOVA
ROMANIA
BULGARIA
TURKEY
BLACK SEA
CARPATHIAN MOUNTAINS
TRANSYLVANIA
BUCOVINA
MOLDAVIA
DOBRUDJA
Baia Mare
Satu Mare
Sighetul Marmaţiei
Suceava
Botoşani
Iaşi
Piatra Neamţ
Roman
Bacău
Vaslui
Huşi
Bârlad
Cluj-Napoca
Târgu Mureş
Sighişoara
Alba Iulia
Sibiu
Braşov
Focşani
Galaţi
Brăila
Tulcea
Buzău
Ploieşti
Piteşti
Râmnicu Vâlcea
Târgovişte
BUCUREŞTI (Bucharest)
Constanţa
Mangalia
Craiova
Ruse
Giurgiu
Silistra
Dobrich
Varna
Shumen
Pleven
Veliko Tŭrnovo
Gabrovo
SOFIYA (Sofia)
Plovdiv (Philippopolis)
Stara Zagora
Sliven
Yambol
Burgas
Haskovo
Kŭrdzhali
Blagoevgrad
Danube
Delta
Ludogorsko Plato
THE BALKANS
The Balkan Peninsula consists of Albania, Bosnia and Herzegovina, Bulgaria, Croatia, Greece, Kosovo, Macedonia, Montenegro, Romania, Slovenia, Serbia, and the European part of Turkey.

Montenegro
Croatia
Slovenia
Bosnia and Herzegovina
Albania
Macedonia
Kosovo
Serbia
Romania
Bulgaria
Europe

Protected Areas and World Heritage Sites

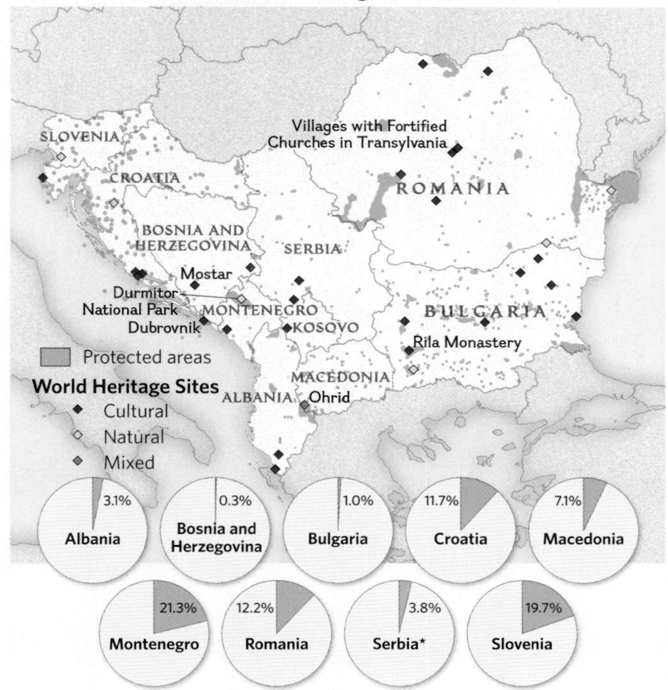

SLOVENIA
CROATIA
BOSNIA AND HERZEGOVINA
SERBIA
ROMANIA
MONTENEGRO
KOSOVO
BULGARIA
MACEDONIA
ALBANIA
Villages with Fortified Churches in Transylvania
Mostar
Durmitor National Park
Dubrovnik
Rila Monastery
Ohrid
Protected areas
World Heritage Sites
Cultural
Natural
Mixed

Country	Percent of Land Area Protected
Albania	3.1%
Bosnia and Herzegovina	0.3%
Bulgaria	1.0%
Croatia	11.7%
Macedonia	7.1%
Montenegro	21.3%
Romania	12.2%
Serbia*	3.8%
Slovenia	19.7%

Percent of Land Area Protected

* includes Kosovo

Urbanization and Largest Cities

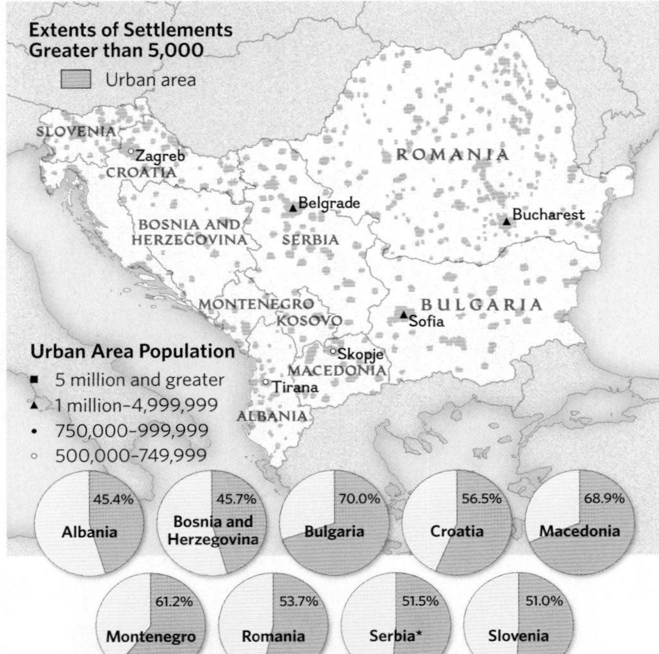

Extents of Settlements Greater than 5,000
Urban area
SLOVENIA
Zagreb
CROATIA
BOSNIA AND HERZEGOVINA
Belgrade
SERBIA
ROMANIA
Bucharest
MONTENEGRO
KOSOVO
BULGARIA
Sofia
Skopje
MACEDONIA
Tirana
ALBANIA
Urban Area Population
5 million and greater
1 million–4,999,999
750,000–999,999
500,000–749,999

Country	Percent of Population in Urban Areas
Albania	45.4%
Bosnia and Herzegovina	45.7%
Bulgaria	70.0%
Croatia	56.5%
Macedonia	68.9%
Montenegro	61.2%
Romania	53.7%
Serbia*	51.5%
Slovenia	51.0%

Percent of Population in Urban Areas

* includes Kosovo

Natural Land Cover

SLOVENIA
CROATIA
BOSNIA AND HERZEGOVINA
SERBIA
ROMANIA
MONTENEGRO
KOSOVO
BULGARIA
MACEDONIA
ALBANIA
Land Cover
Forest
Herbaceous
Highland

❻ Rila Monastery, Bulgaria

Founded in the tenth century by a critic of the clergy and Bulgarian court, St. John of Rila, this five-domed monastery became a center for religion and culture in the mountain wilderness of western Bulgaria. Its rugged exterior resembles a fortress and repelled bandits and Muslim invaders, while the courtyard's red-and-white-striped arcades visually link it to the church; baroque frescoes and carved wooden ceilings decorate the 250 or so guest rooms.

Meteora ❶

From the 11th century onward, monks prayed and meditated in the 24 monasteries perched on a cluster of almost inaccessible sandstone peaks in western Thessaly. Meaning "suspended in the air," Meteora is the largest and most important group of monasteries in Greece after those of Mount Athos. The leading icon painter of the early 16th century, Theophanes the Cretan, executed frescoes that became the reference of the fundamental features of post-Byzantine painting. Built under impossible conditions with no possibility of roads for transportation of materials, these "columns of the sky" required the monks to be hoisted up alongside the sheer cliffs. Though only four of the original monasteries continue to house religious communities, they are a testimony to the restoration of the hermitic ideals in the early Christian church.

❷ Acropolis, Athens

Formerly a walled citadel used by the Mycenaeans in the 13th century B.C., the layout of the limestone outcropping known as the Acropolis was redesigned under the Greek statesman Pericles, who, in the 5th century B.C., ordered a religious sanctuary erected to honor the city's patron, Athena the Virgin, goddess of wisdom and war. It took more than 50 years to complete construction of the shrines, and by the latter half of the century, several holy buildings rose high on the rocky hill, including the Parthenon, a marble Doric temple dedicated to Athena. Inside stood a 40-foot gold and ivory statue of Athena in full armor carrying Nike, the goddess of victory, to the Athenians. Although only ruins remain today, the Parthenon's pediments depicted compositions from the goddess's life, including her birth, as she sprang from the head of Zeus before the assembled gods.

❸ Mount Athos

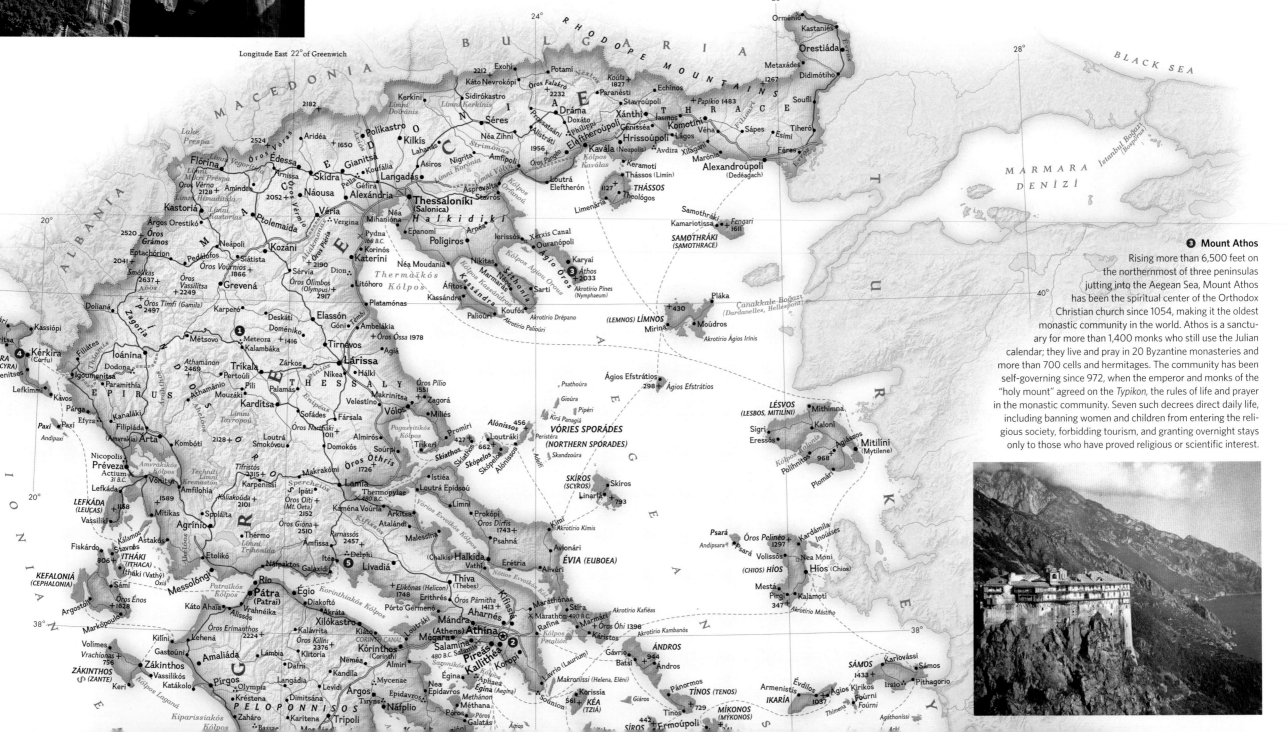

Rising more than 6,500 feet on the northernmost of three peninsulas jutting into the Aegean Sea, Mount Athos has been the spiritual center of the Orthodox Christian church since 1054, making it the oldest monastic community in the world. Athos is a sanctuary for more than 1,400 monks who still use the Julian calendar; they live and pray in 20 Byzantine monasteries and more than 700 cells and hermitages. The community has been self-governing since 972, when the emperor and monks of the "holy mount" agreed on the *Typikon*, the rules of life and prayer in the monastic community. Seven such decrees direct daily life, including banning women and children from entering the religious society, forbidding tourism, and granting overnight stays only to those who have proved religious or scientific interest.

Greece

Conic Projection, Standard Parallels 40° 30' and 36° 00'
SCALE 1:2,601,000
1 CENTIMETER = 26 KILOMETERS; 1 INCH = 41 MILES
KILOMETERS
STATUTE MILES
Messíni
Spárti (Sparta)
Kosmás
Pílos
Methóni
Koróni
Sapiéntza
Kardamíli
Skála
Gíthio
Moláoi
Areópoli
Itilo
Máni
Monemvassía
Neápoli
Lakonikós Kólpos
Messiniakós Kólpos
Geroliménas
Akrotírio Ténaro (Taenarum)
Akrotírio Maléas
Agía Pelagía
KÍTHIRA (CERIGO, CYTHERA)
Kíthira
Velopoúla
Falkonéra
Karávia
Potamós
Andikíthira
SEA OF CRETE
MEDITERRANEAN SEA
Kólpos Kissámou
Kólpos Chaníon
Haniá (Canea, Cydonia)
Réthimno
Iráklio (Heráklion, Candia)
Cnossus (Knossos)
Óros Ídi (Psiloreitis) 2456
Kándanos
Samaria Gorge
Agía Rouméli
Sfakiá
Palaiochóra
Gávdos
Phaestus
Gortyn
Mália
Ágios Nikólaos
Óros Díkti
Ierápetra
Sitía
Palékastro
Zákros
Kamárai
Apolonia
SÍFNOS
MÍLOS (MELOS)
Páros
NÁXOS
AMORGÓS
ÍOS
THÍRA (SANTORINI)
ANÁFI
ASTIPÁLEA
KÁLIMNOS
Kos
KOS (COS)
DODECANESE (DODEKÁNISOS)
Ródos (Rhodes)
RÓDOS (RHODES)
Líndos
KÁRPATHOS (CARPATHOS)
Kássos
AEGEAN SEA

Old Corfu 4

Eritreans from the southwestern coast of the Red Sea annexed the island of Corfu to the Greeks in the early seventh century B.C., and Mediterranean powers from the Romans and Goths to the Normans and Byzantians fought over the Ionian island until the Republic of Venice took control in 1386. Strategically located at the entrance to the Adriatic Sea, the island was perfect for Venetians seeking a safe harbor to resupply their trade ships en route to the Black Sea. Building three fortresses protecting the harbors and constantly refortifying the port town to complement its forces, they also used Corfu for the next 400 years as one of four bases to defend their maritime interests against the Ottoman Empire.

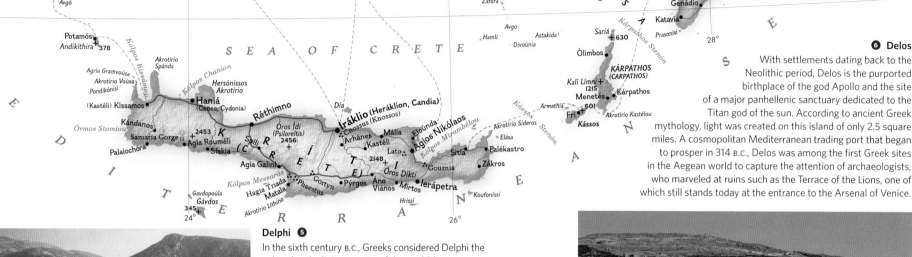

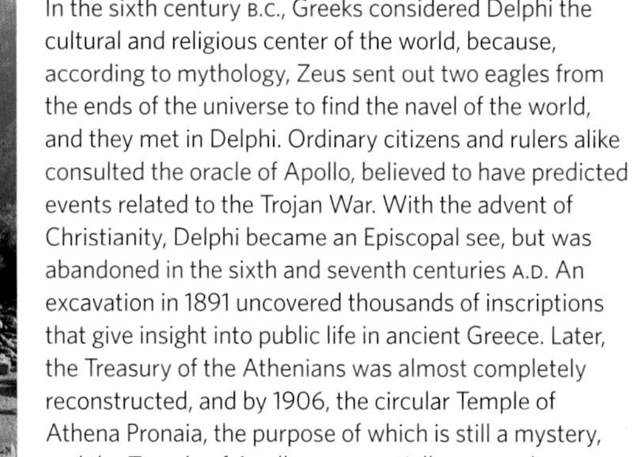

Delphi 5

In the sixth century B.C., Greeks considered Delphi the cultural and religious center of the world, because, according to mythology, Zeus sent out two eagles from the ends of the universe to find the navel of the world, and they met in Delphi. Ordinary citizens and rulers alike consulted the oracle of Apollo, believed to have predicted events related to the Trojan War. With the advent of Christianity, Delphi became an Episcopal see, but was abandoned in the sixth and seventh centuries A.D. An excavation in 1891 uncovered thousands of inscriptions that give insight into public life in ancient Greece. Later, the Treasury of the Athenians was almost completely reconstructed, and by 1906, the circular Temple of Athena Pronaia, the purpose of which is still a mystery, and the Temple of Apollo were partially restored.

6 Delos

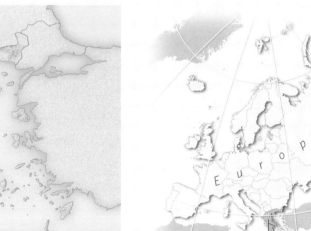

With settlements dating back to the Neolithic period, Delos is the purported birthplace of the god Apollo and the site of a major panhellenic sanctuary dedicated to the Titan god of the sun. According to ancient Greek mythology, light was created on this island of only 2.5 square miles. A cosmopolitan Mediterranean trading port that began to prosper in 314 B.C., Delos was among the first Greek sites in the Aegean world to capture the attention of archaeologists, who marveled at ruins such as the Terrace of the Lions, one of which still stands today at the entrance to the Arsenal of Venice.

Protected Areas and World Heritage Sites

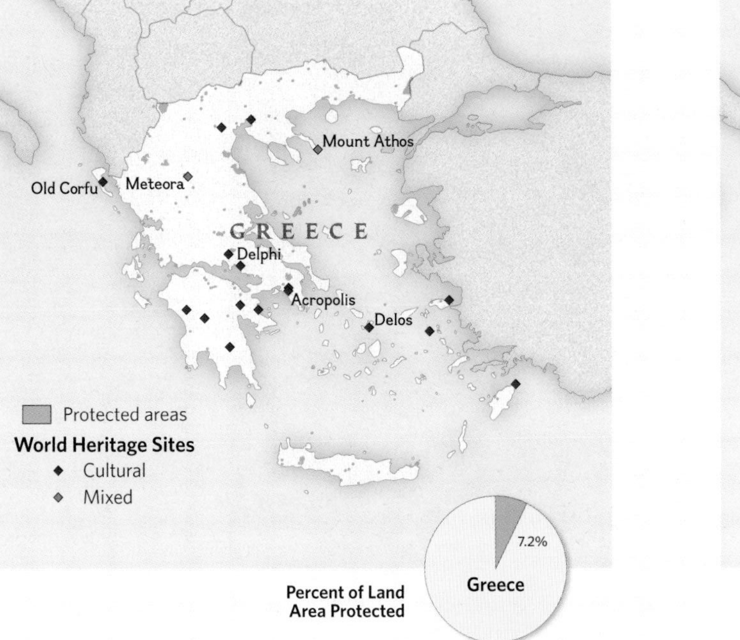
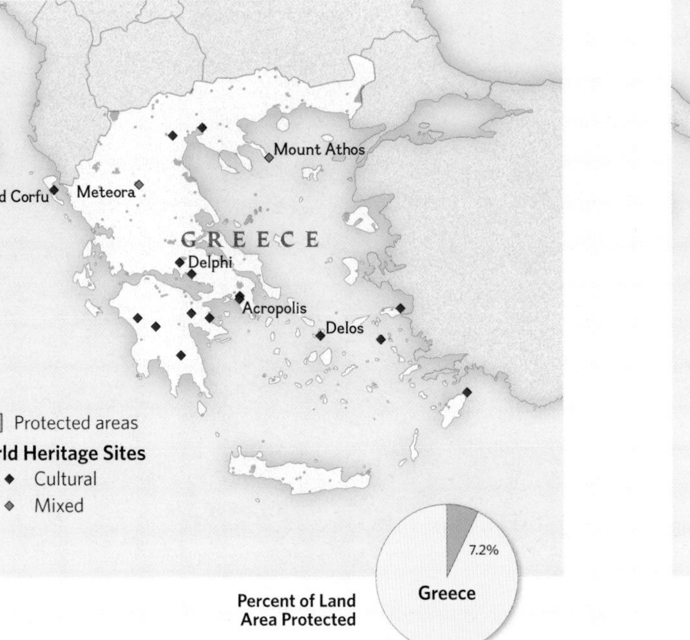
Old Corfu
Meteora
Mount Athos
GREECE
Delphi
Acropolis
Delos
Protected areas
World Heritage Sites
Cultural
Mixed
7.2%
Greece
Percent of Land Area Protected

Urbanization and Largest Cities

Extents of Settlements Greater than 5,000
Urban area
Thessaloníki
GREECE
Athens
Urban Area Population
5 million and greater
1 million–4,999,999
750,000–999,999
500,000–749,999
59.0%
Greece
Percent of Population in Urban Areas

Natural Land Cover

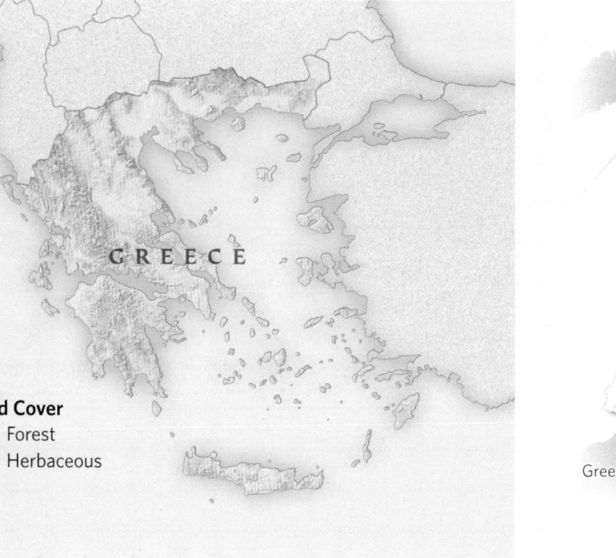

GREECE
Land Cover
Forest
Herbaceous
Europe
Greece

Historic Center (Old Town) of Tallinn, Estonia ❶

Tallinn, settled off the Gulf of Finland more than 3,500 years ago, was used as a port and trading post by Vikings sailing to Constantinople. The Danes built a stone castle on the limestone plateau of Toompea; the knights of the Teutonic Order later reinforced it with 30-foot walls and a 155-foot tower. Under Hanseatic rule from the 14th to 16th century, the strategic town became one of the most remote and powerful outposts in northeastern Europe because it lay on the trade route between western Europe and Russia. Tallinn fell to Tsar Peter I in 1710; after almost 300 more years of occupation, Estonians finally gained their independence with ceremonies held at Toompea Castle.

Historic Center of Riga, Latvia ❷

Established by Bishop Albert in 1201, German settlers built castles for the bishop and the crusading knights who accompanied him on sacred missions. Riga became part of the Hanseatic League—which controlled commerce on the Baltic and North Seas—prospering from the 13th through 15th centuries as a trade center with central and eastern Europe. It was ruled by Poland, Sweden, then Russia, and in the mid-1800s, the bourgeoisie poured their wealth into totally rebuilding the medieval city with sweeping boulevards and buildings using the Finnish Jugendstil, or art nouveau style. By 1897, Riga had become the fifth largest city in the Russian Empire.

BENETTON

Vilnius Historic Center, Lithuania ❸

A wooden castle was built at the confluence of the Vilnia and Neris Rivers at the start of the 11th century, but Vilnius only developed as a town in the 13th century, during the Baltic struggles against German invaders. By 1323, it had become the political center of the Grand Duchy of Lithuania, an honor it retained until the end of the 18th century. During that time, it was a major trade link between eastern and western Europe, spreading western culture into Ukraine and present-day Belarus. Today, Vilnius is once again a political and cultural center, this time of the Republic of Lithuania.

TRANSDNIESTRIA
Since the break-up of the Soviet Union, Ukrainian and Russian minorities have been struggling for independence from Moldova.

Transverse Mercator Projection
SCALE 1:6,865,285
1 CENTIMETER = 69 KILOMETERS; 1 INCH = 108 MILES

Longitude East 36° of Greenwich

Belarus | Estonia | Latvia | Lithuania | Moldova | Russia | Ukraine

Historic Center of St. Petersburg and Related Groups of Monuments, Russia ❹

Known as Leningrad in the former U.S.S.R., St. Petersburg was the capital city of Peter the Great, who, in 1703, demanded the forced labor of Russian soldiers, Swedish and Ottoman prisoners of war, and Finnish and Estonian workers. In less than 20 years, the colossal detachment transformed an inhospitable coastal area into a city where palaces, churches, convents, and two-story stone houses fit into the designs of Frenchman Alexandre Leblond. Later, rulers such as Catherine the Great and Alexander I continued Peter's tradition, turning St. Petersburg into the "Venice of the north": A network of canals running beneath more than 400 bridges was gradually built, followed by a rivalry among an array of foreign architects, who directed the construction of disparate styles ranging from baroque to neoclassical, yet preserving an overall logic shown by the Admiralty, the Winter Palace, and the Hermitage.

Kremlin and Red Square, Moscow, Russia ❺

A 70-acre, triangular fortification built between the 14th and 17th centuries, the Kremlin is the prototypical citadel at the center of Russian towns of the day. Reinforced by 29 towers with five gates, it was the residence of the grand prince, and its palaces, churches, and cathedrals have been the center for political and spiritual power since 1263, when Moscow was established as a principality. Beneath the Kremlin's east wall lies the 18-acre Red Square with the Mausoleum of Lenin, the epitome of Soviet symbolic monuments, and St. Basil's Basilica, a foremost edifice of Russian Orthodox art and architecture.

Kiev: St.-Sophia Cathedral and Related Monastic Buildings, Kiev-Pechersk Lavra, Ukraine ❻

St.-Sophia Cathedral was designed to rival the then-Byzantine church of Hagia Sophia in Constantinople, and establish Kiev as "the new Constantinople." Its 13 cupolas symbolize Christ and the Twelve Apostles, and mosaic masterpieces include the "Virgin Mary at Prayer" and the "Communion of the Apostles." The cathedral is complimented by Kiev-Pechersk Lavra, a 60-acre monastic complex that comprises the Clock Tower, the Refectory Church, and a printshop that issued devotional literature from the 17th to 19th century, contributing to the spread of Orthodox thought and faith in Russia.

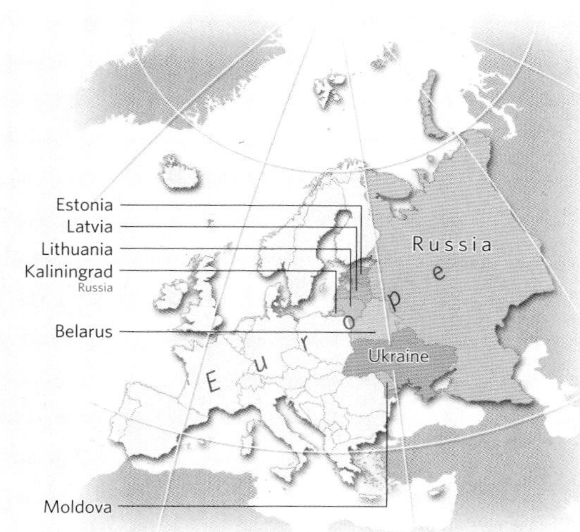
Estonia
Latvia
Lithuania
Kaliningrad
Russia
Belarus
Moldova
Russia
Ukraine
Europe

Protected Areas and World Heritage Sites

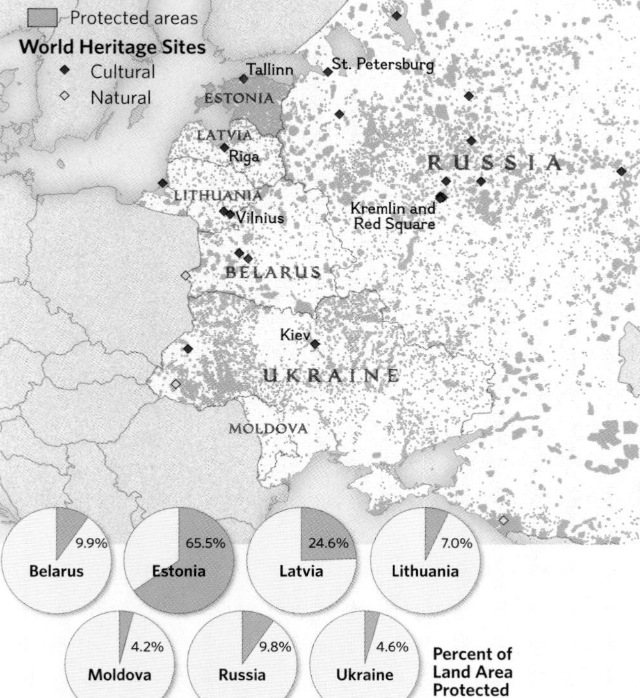
Protected areas
World Heritage Sites
Cultural
Natural
Tallinn
St. Petersburg
ESTONIA
LATVIA
Riga
RUSSIA
LITHUANIA
Vilnius
Kremlin and Red Square
BELARUS
Kiev
UKRAINE
MOLDOVA
9.9% Belarus
65.5% Estonia
24.6% Latvia
7.0% Lithuania
4.2% Moldova
9.8% Russia
4.6% Ukraine
Percent of Land Area Protected

Urbanization and Largest Cities

see pages 168–169 for continuation of Russia

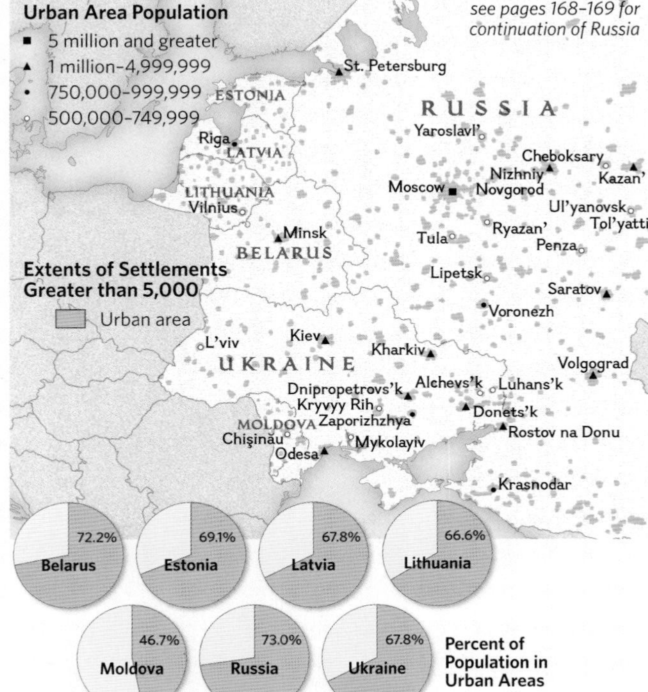
Urban Area Population
5 million and greater
1 million–4,999,999
750,000–999,999
500,000–749,999
Extents of Settlements Greater than 5,000
Urban area
St. Petersburg
ESTONIA
RUSSIA
Yaroslavl'
Riga
LATVIA
Cheboksary
Nizhniy Novgorod
Kazan'
Moscow
LITHUANIA
Vilnius
Ul'yanovsk
Tol'yatti
Minsk
Tula
Ryazan'
Penza
BELARUS
Lipetsk
Saratov
Voronezh
L'viv
Kiev
Kharkiv
Volgograd
UKRAINE
Dnipropetrovs'k
Alchevs'k
Luhans'k
Kryvyy Rih
Donets'k
MOLDOVA
Zaporizhzhya
Chişinău
Mykolayiv
Rostov na Donu
Odesa
Krasnodar
72.2% Belarus
69.1% Estonia
67.8% Latvia
66.6% Lithuania
46.7% Moldova
73.0% Russia
67.8% Ukraine
Percent of Population in Urban Areas

Natural Land Cover

ESTONIA
LATVIA
LITHUANIA
RUSSIA
BELARUS
UKRAINE
MOLDOVA
Land Cover
Forest
Herbaceous
Highland

Architectural Ensemble of the Trinity Sergius Lavra in Sergiyev Posad ❶

In the mid-1300s, Sergius, spiritual adviser to the Great Prince of Moscow and eventual patron saint, precisely planned monastic cells around a rectangular courtyard, with a church and refectory at its center. Strategically located on the road to Moscow, the complex grew to include a 300-foot belfry, the tsar's palace, and the Cathedral of the Assumption, all surrounded by a mile-long, three-level stone wall defending the heart of the Orthodox church.

❷ Kizhi Pogost

A landmark to sailors navigating the White Sea, two 18th-century wooden churches and an octagonal bell tower sit on the island of Kizhi in Lake Onega. The *pogost,* or enclosure, was centrally located to villages scattered over northernmost Russia. Used in summer, the Church of the Transfiguration has rooftops shaped like tulip buds topped with 22 bulbous cupolas, while the Winter Church's octagonal second level has eight cupolas around a central dome rising nearly 90 feet.

Two-Point Equidistant Projection

SCALE 1:19,775,000
1 CENTIMETER = 198 KILOMETERS; 1 INCH = 312 MILES

A commonly accepted division between Asia and Europe–here marked by a green line–is formed by the Ural Mountains, Ural River, Caspian Sea, Caucasus Mountains, and the Black Sea with its outlets, the Bosporus and Dardanelles.

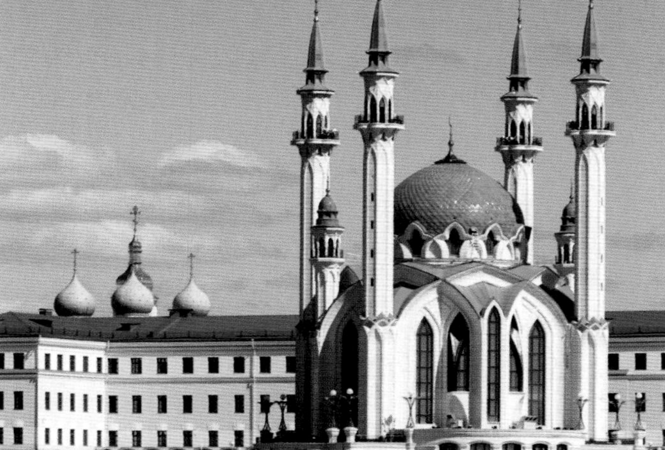

Kazan Kremlin ❸

Built on a site dating to the seventh millennium B.C., the Kazan Kremlin represents the northwestern limit of the spread of Islam and was the stronghold of the Kazan Khanate Golden Horde of the Muslim period. Later conquered by Ivan the Terrible in 1552, it became the Christian capital of the Volga Land. With fortifications and buildings partly constructed from the remains of structures dating from the 10th through 16th centuries, it is the only surviving Tatar citadel in Russia and the world's only place of pilgrimage for the Tatar republic.

❹ Golden Mountains of Altay

Domain of the endangered snow leopard, these mountains in southern Siberia are the region's source for the Ob River, the world's seventh longest at more than 3,300 miles. The Altay Mountains, with curving moraines, drumlins, outwash plains, and tectonic lakes, offer the most complete sequence of altitudinal vegetation zones in central Siberia, and, due to the high number of undisturbed glaciers, the area has universal importance in assessing the effects of global warming in mountain ecosystems.

Russia

❺ Volcanoes of Kamchatka

In the Russian Far East lies the Kamchatka Peninsula, an integral part of the Pacific Ring of Fire, with the most concentrated number of active volcanoes. A moist, mild climate bears lush vegetation of more than 700 plant species in moist, coniferous taiga forests, coastal wetlands, and subalpine shrub and mountain tundra. Abundant snow rams, wolverines, and brown bears roam the glaciers, rivers, and hot springs; Steller's sea eagles and gyrfalcons prey on the largest known variety of salmon, which come to spawn; and more than half of the world's population of Aleutian tern nest by the Bering Sea.

KURIL ISLANDS
The southern Kuril Islands of Iturup (Etorofu), Kunashir (Kunashiri), Shikotan, and the Habomai group were lost by Japan to the Soviet Union in 1945. Japan continues to claim these Russian-administered islands.

Protected Areas and World Heritage Sites

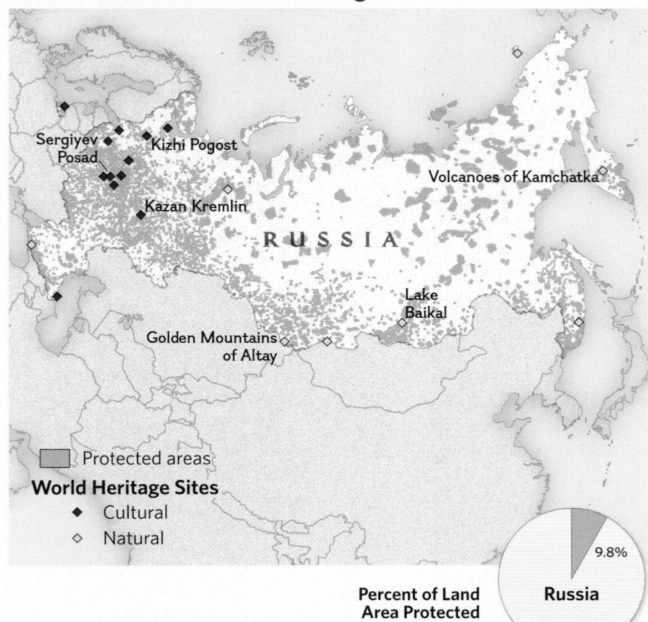

Sergiyev Posad
Kizhi Pogost
Volcanoes of Kamchatka
Kazan Kremlin
RUSSIA
Lake Baikal
Golden Mountains of Altay
Protected areas
World Heritage Sites
Cultural
Natural
9.8%
Russia
Percent of Land Area Protected

Urbanization and Largest Cities

Saint Petersburg
Moscow
Nizhniy Novgorod
Kazan'
Izhevsk
Perm
Samara
Saratov
Ufa
Yekaterinburg
Tyumen'
Volgograd
Rostov na Donu
Krasnodar
Orenburg
Chelyabinsk
Omsk
Makhachkala
RUSSIA
Novosibirsk
Barnaul
Krasnoyarsk
Novokuznetsk
Irkutsk
Khabarovsk
Vladivostok
Extents of Settlements Greater than 5,000
Urban area
Urban Area Population
5 million and greater
1 million–4,999,999
750,000–999,999
500,000–749,999
see map on pages 166–167 for more urban areas
73.0%
Russia
Percent of Population in Urban Areas

Natural Land Cover

RUSSIA
Land Cover
Forest
Glacier
Herbaceous
Highland
Tundra

Lake Baikal ❻

Isolated in southeast Siberia, the "Galápagos of Russia" is a living laboratory of evolution and the oldest (25 million years) and deepest (5,370 feet) lake in the world. Sandy shores adjoin taiga and deciduous forests, which rise to mountain steppes and grasslands surmounted by jagged, snow-clad peaks. Lake Baikal, covering 7.78 million acres and holding 20 percent of the world's fresh water, has limited chemical and mineral contact, making the water pure and transparent to a depth of 130 feet. The Baikal seal, normally a marine mammal, is endemic only to this lake and can swim nearly a thousand feet down, where one-third of the world's shrimp thrive.

NORTH SEA
BALTIC SEA
ATLANTIC OCEAN
LUXEMBOURG
LIECHTENSTEIN
MONACO
ANDORRA
SAN MARINO
VATICAN CITY
BLACK SEA
MEDITERRANEAN SEA
MALTA
CYPRUS
kilometers 900
statute miles 600

Smallest Countries of Europe

The eight smallest countries in Europe have a combined area less than the state of Connecticut. But these countries are big in other ways. Monaco and Malta are among Europe's most densely populated and most visited countries. Luxembourg boasts the world's highest per capita income. Andorra, nestled in the towering Pyrenees, is Europe's highest country, San Marino its oldest republic. And Vatican City, heart of the Roman Catholic Church, oversees St. Peter's Basilica, the world's largest church.

City of Luxembourg: Its Old Quarters and Fortifications, Luxembourg 1

At a major Roman crossroad in the 10th century, the city has been coveted as a strategic military location by Spaniards, French, Austrians, and Prussians. Sandwiched between present-day Germany, France, and Belgium, the city and nation's architectural and cultural heritage has been shaped and appended by foreign powers, all of whom reconstructed and enlarged the fortress and increased the number of fortifications. Not until the Treaty of London in 1867 confirmed the city's perpetual neutrality was the fortress evacuated and the fortifications ordered demolished. Among the remains are the Grand Ducal Palace and its Renaissance and baroque facades; the 17th-century Cathedral of Notre-Dame de Luxembourg, its pointed towers prominent in the skyline; and the lower town with a 16th-century sluice built by the Austrians as a defensive fortification that could inundate the surrounding valleys. More than three times smaller than Rhode Island, the country's central location, political stability, and tax incentives make the city a major financial center.

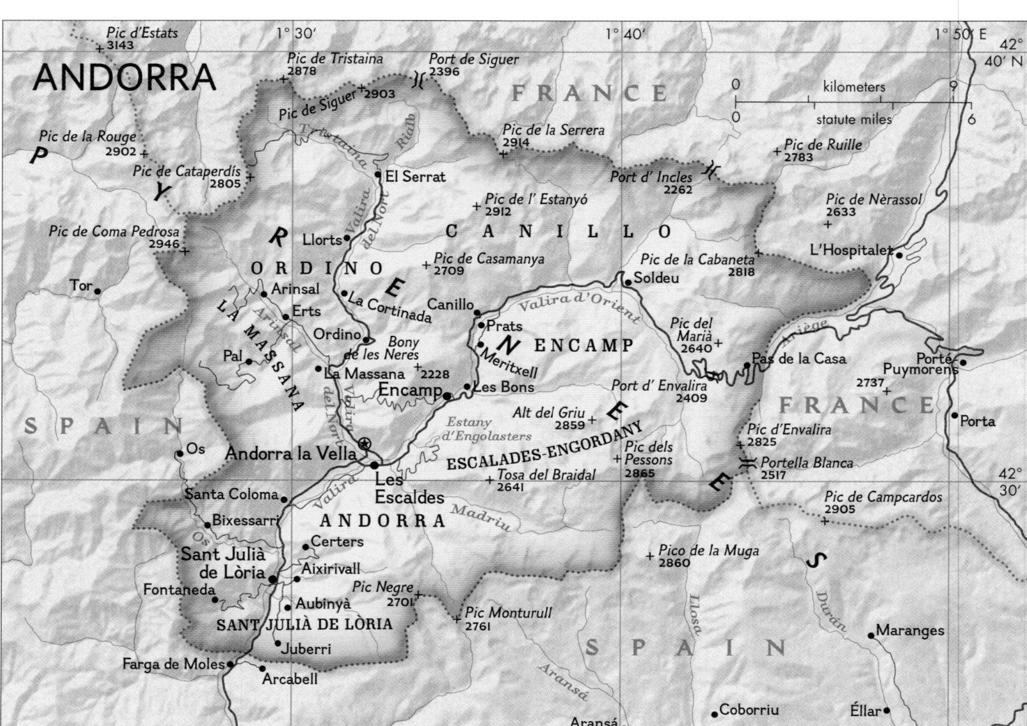
ANDORRA
FRANCE
SPAIN
CANILLO
ORDINO
LA MASSANA
ENCAMP
ESCALADES-ENGORDANY
ANDORRA
SANT JULIÀ DE LÒRIA
Andorra la Vella
Les Escaldes
El Serrat
Llorts
Arinsal
Erts
La Cortinada
Ordino
Canillo
Soldeu
Prats
Meritxell
Les Bons
Encamp
La Massana
Pal
Os
Santa Coloma
Bixessarri
Certers
Sant Julià de Lòria
Aixirivall
Fontaneda
Aubinyà
Juberri
Farga de Moles
Arcabell
Pas de la Casa
L'Hospitalet
Porté-Puymorens
Porta
Maranges
Aransá
Coborriu
Éllar
Pic d'Estats 3143
Pic de Tristaina 2878
Port de Siguer 2396
Pic de la Serrera 2914
Pic de Ruille 2783
Port d' Incles 2262
Pic de Nérassol 2633
Pic de l' Estanyó 2912
Pic de Casamanya 2709
Pic de la Cabaneta 2818
Pic del Maià 2640
Port d' Envalira 2409
Alt del Griu 2859
Pic d'Envalira 2825
Pic dels Pessons 2865
Portella Blanca 2517
Tosa del Braidal 2641
Pic de Campcardos 2905
Pico de la Muga 2860
Pic Negre 2701
Pic Monturull 2761
Pic de Coma Pedrosa 2946
Pic de la Rouge 2902
Pic de Cataperdis 2805
kilometers 9
statute miles 6

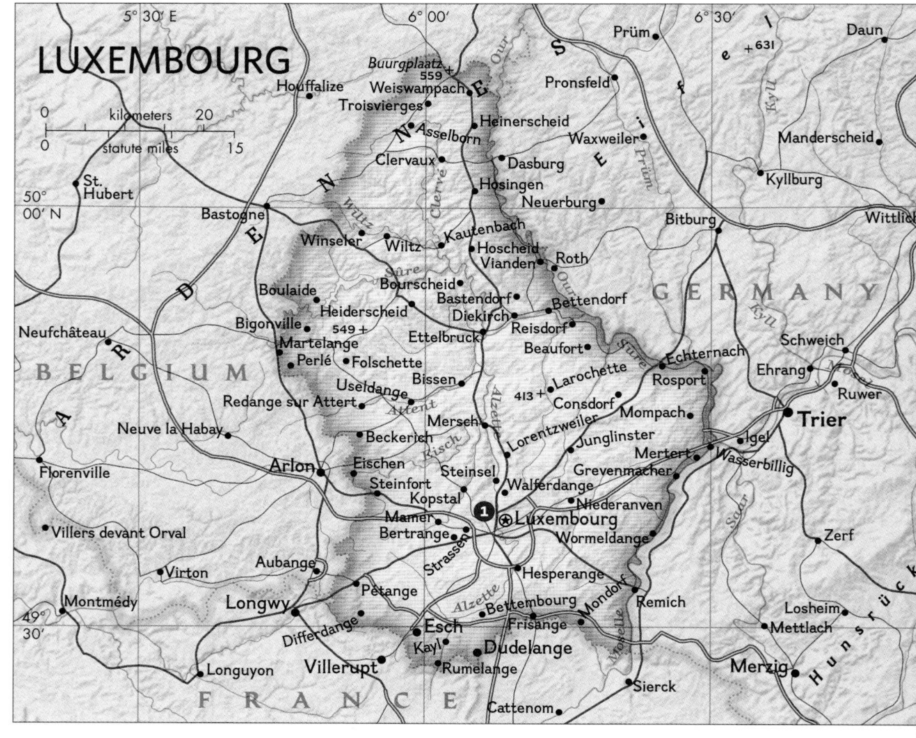
LUXEMBOURG
BELGIUM
GERMANY
FRANCE
ARDENNES
Luxembourg
Trier
Arlon
Esch
Dudelange
Longwy
Villerupt
Bastogne
Houffalize
Troisvierges
Clervaux
Wiltz
Vianden
Diekirch
Ettelbruck
Echternach
Remich
Grevenmacher
Mersch
Bettembourg
Differdange
Pétange
Bitburg
Prüm
Daun
Merzig
Sierck
Cattenom
Longuyon
Virton
Florenville
Neufchâteau
St. Hubert
Wittlich
Schweich
kilometers 20
statute miles 15
Buurgplaatz 559

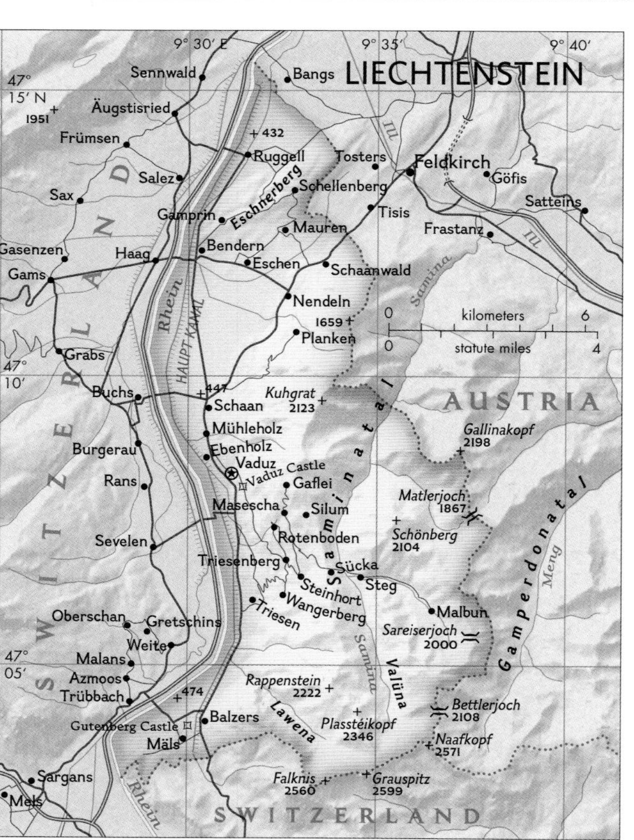
LIECHTENSTEIN
AUSTRIA
SWITZERLAND
Vaduz
Schaan
Balzers
Triesen
Triesenberg
Eschen
Mauren
Ruggell
Schellenberg
Gamprin
Bendern
Nendeln
Planken
Malbun
Steg
Feldkirch
Buchs
Sargans
Sevelen
Rhein
kilometers 6
statute miles 4
Grauspitz 2599

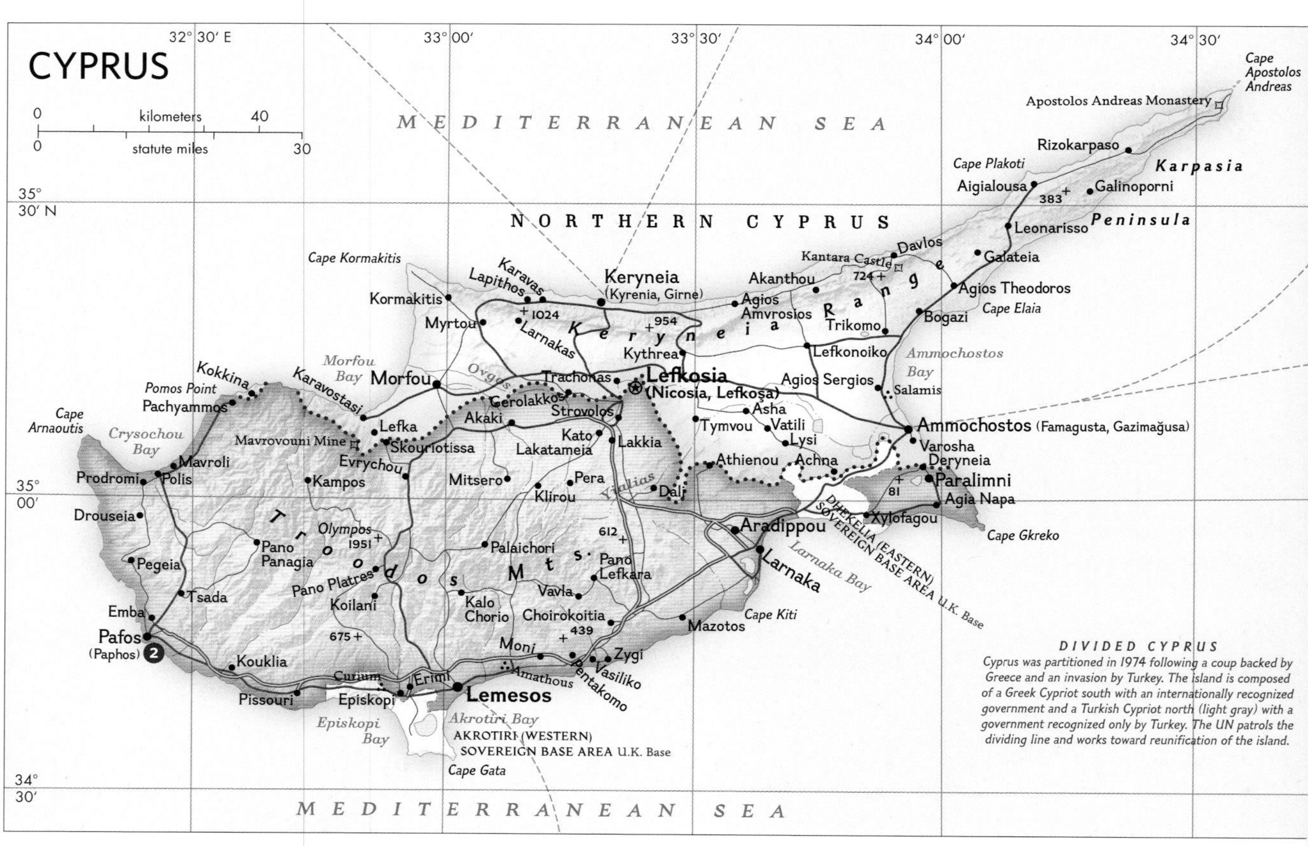
CYPRUS
MEDITERRANEAN SEA
NORTHERN CYPRUS
Lefkosia (Nicosia, Lefkoşa)
Keryneia (Kyrenia, Girne)
Ammochostos (Famagusta, Gazimağusa)
Lemesos
Larnaka
Pafos (Paphos)
Morfou
Paralimni
Agia Napa
Karpasia Peninsula
Troodos Mts
Kyrenia Range
Olympos 1951
Akrotiri (Western) Sovereign Base Area U.K. Base
Dhekelia (Eastern) Sovereign Base Area U.K. Base
Cape Apostolos Andreas
Cape Kormakitis
Cape Arnaoutis
Cape Gkreko
Cape Gata
Cape Kiti
Morfou Bay
Larnaka Bay
Episkopi Bay
Chrysochou Bay
Ammochostos Bay
kilometers 40
statute miles 30
DIVIDED CYPRUS
Cyprus was partitioned in 1974 following a coup backed by Greece and an invasion by Turkey. The island is composed of a Greek Cypriot south with an internationally recognized government and a Turkish Cypriot north (light gray) with a government recognized only by Turkey. The UN patrols the dividing line and works toward reunification of the island.

Andorra

Cyprus

Liechtenstein

Luxembourg

Malta

Monaco

San Marino

Vatican City

Paphos, Cyprus ❷

Birthplace of the mythical Aphrodite, ideal of beauty and love in Homer's poetry, Paphos has been inhabited since the Stone Age and is one of the earliest Mycenaean settlements. A three-chambered temple devoted to the fertility goddess dates back to the 12th century B.C., and thrived as a sanctuary through Phoenician, Egyptian, and Roman rule. Eight hundred years later, King Nicocles built New Paphos, a harbor and eventual center for Christianity. Ruins of baths, theaters, and tombs surrounded by rock columns remain, along with villas and palaces decorated with rare mosaics from the Hellenistic and Byzantine eras.

Valletta, Malta ❸

Outnumbered five to one, the knights of St. John of Jerusalem, a charitable and military Christian order, defeated 30,000 Turks under Süleyman the Magnificent and halted the Ottoman Empire's conquest of the West. The knights then fortified the city in 1566 and named it after their Grand Master, Jean de la Valette. One of the most concentrated historic areas in the world with 320 monuments in an area of 135 acres, Valletta's houses and palaces rise in tiers and are built on a baroque-style grid which follows the contours of the peninsula's terrain. Prized for its strategic location on the Mediterranean Sea, the capital of Malta is the southernmost extension of Europe and survived ten successive powers, from the Phoenicians and Romans to the Arabs and British, before gaining its independence in 1964.

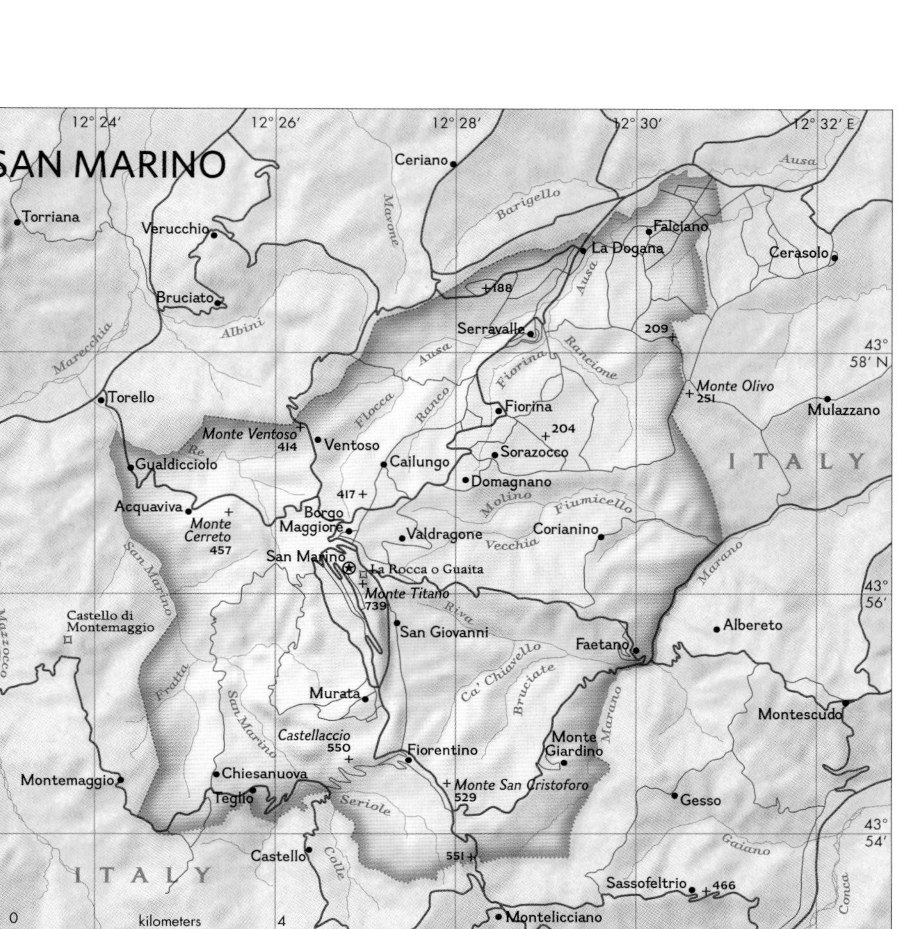
SAN MARINO
12° 24′
12° 26′
12° 28′
12° 30′
12° 32′ E
43° 58′ N
43° 56′
43° 54′
Torriana
Verucchio
Ceriano
Bruciato
Falciano
La Dogana
Cerasolo
Serravalle
Torello
Monte Olivo 251
Mulazzano
Monte Ventoso 414
Ventoso
Gualdicciolo
Fiorina
Cailungo
Sorazocco
Domagnano
Acquaviva
Monte Cerreto 457
Borgo Maggiore
Valdragone
Corianino
San Marino
La Rocca o Guaita
Monte Titano 739
San Giovanni
Castello di Montemaggio
Faetano
Alberteto
Murata
Montescudo
Castellaccio 550
Fiorentino
Monte Giardino
Montemaggio
Chiesanuova
Teglio
Monte San Cristoforo 529
Gesso
Castello
Sassofeltrio
Montelicciano
ITALY
kilometers
statute miles

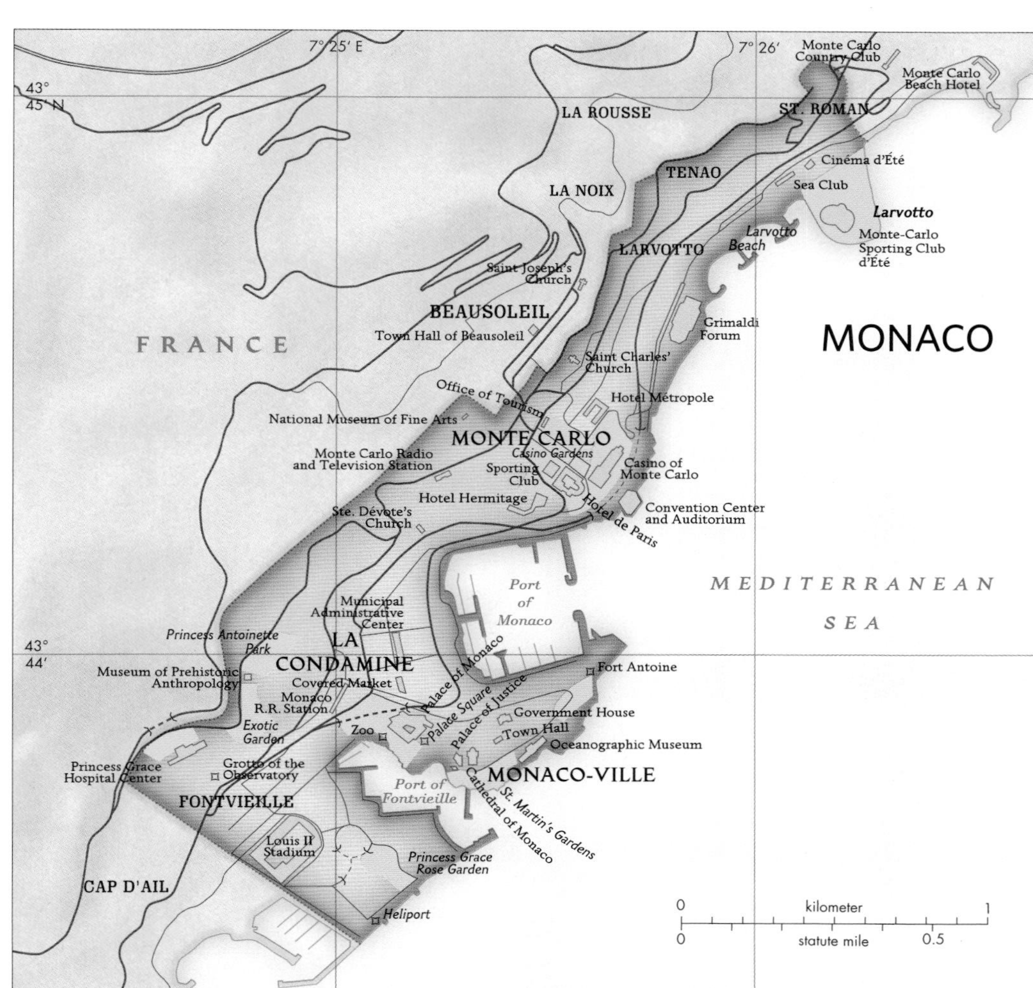
7° 25′ E
7° 26′
43° 45′ N
43° 44′
Monte Carlo Country Club
Monte Carlo Beach Hotel
LA ROUSSE
ST. ROMAN
LA NOIX
TENAO
Cinéma d'Été
Sea Club
Larvotto
Monte-Carlo Sporting Club d'Été
LARVOTTO
Larvotto Beach
Saint Joseph's Church
BEAUSOLEIL
Town Hall of Beausoleil
FRANCE
Grimaldi Forum
MONACO
Saint Charles' Church
Office of Tourism
Hotel Métropole
National Museum of Fine Arts
MONTE CARLO
Casino Gardens
Monte Carlo Radio and Television Station
Sporting Club
Casino of Monte Carlo
Hotel Hermitage
Hotel de Paris
Convention Center and Auditorium
Ste. Devote's Church
MEDITERRANEAN SEA
Port of Monaco
Municipal Administrative Center
Princess Antoinette Park
LA CONDAMINE
Museum of Prehistoric Anthropology
Covered Market
Monaco R.R. Station
Fort Antoine
Palace of Monaco
Palace Square
Palace of Justice
Exotic Garden
Zoo
Government House
Town Hall
Oceanographic Museum
Princess Grace Hospital Center
Grotto of the Observatory
MONACO-VILLE
FONTVIEILLE
Port of Fontvieille
Cathedral of Monaco
St. Martin's Gardens
Louis II Stadium
Princess Grace Rose Garden
CAP D'AIL
Heliport
kilometer
statute mile

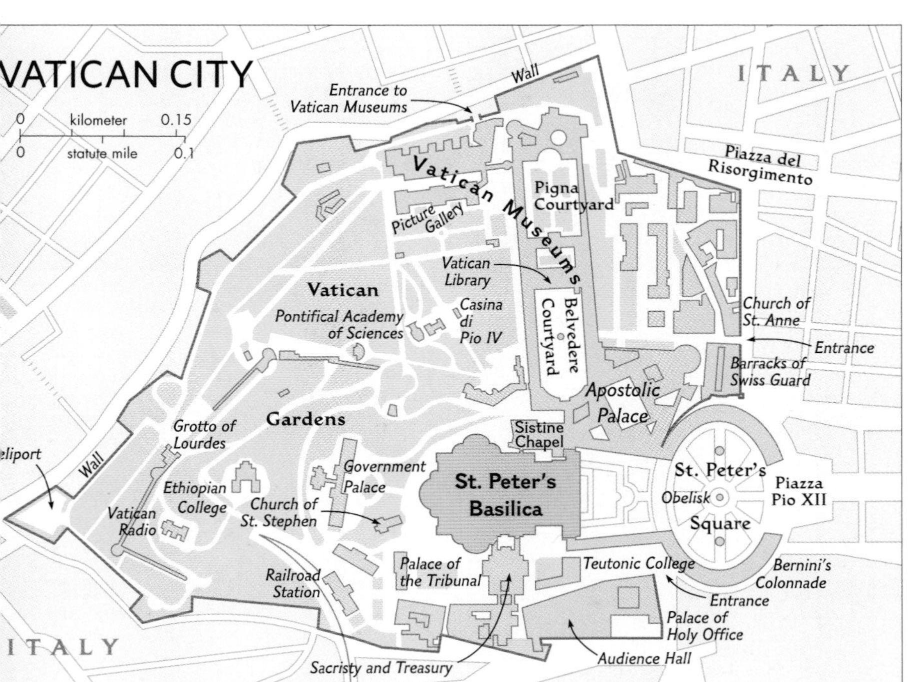
VATICAN CITY
kilometer
statute mile
Entrance to Vatican Museums
Wall
ITALY
Piazza del Risorgimento
Vatican Museums
Pigna Courtyard
Picture Gallery
Vatican Library
Vatican
Pontifical Academy of Sciences
Casina di Pio IV
Belvedere Courtyard
Church of St. Anne
Entrance
Barracks of Swiss Guard
Apostolic Palace
Gardens
Grotto of Lourdes
Sistine Chapel
Heliport
Government Palace
St. Peter's Basilica
St. Peter's Square
Obelisk
Piazza Pio XII
Ethiopian College
Church of St. Stephen
Vatican Radio
Railroad Station
Palace of the Tribunal
Teutonic College
Bernini's Colonnade
Entrance
Palace of Holy Office
Audience Hall
Sacristy and Treasury

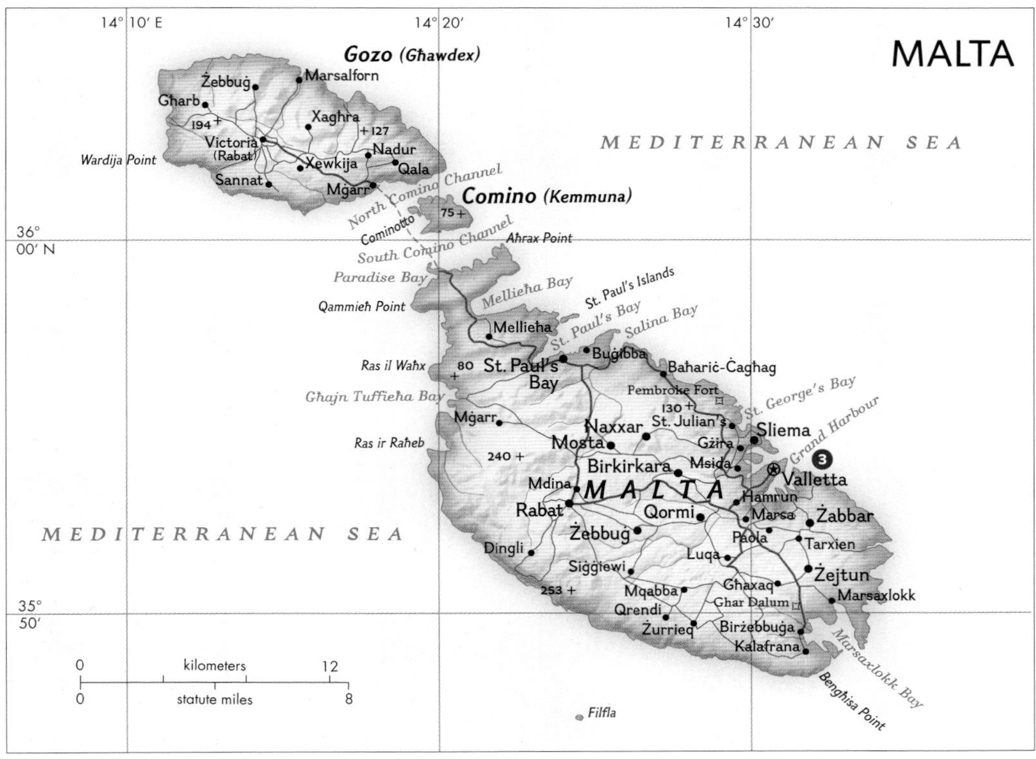
14° 10′ E
14° 20′
14° 30′
MALTA
Gozo (Ghawdex)
Żebbuġ
Marsalforn
Gharb
Xaghra
Victoria (Rabat)
Nadur
Wardija Point
Xewkija
Qala
Sannat
Mgarr
MEDITERRANEAN SEA
North Comino Channel
Comino (Kemmuna)
Cominotto
South Comino Channel
Ahrax Point
36° 00′ N
Paradise Bay
Mellieha Bay
St. Paul's Islands
Qammieh Point
Mellieha
St. Paul's Bay
Salina Bay
Ras il Wahx
Buġibba
Bahariċ-Ċaghaq
Ghajn Tuffieha Bay
Pembroke Fort
St. George's Bay
Mgarr
Naxxar
St. Julian's
Sliema
Grand Harbour
Ras ir Raheb
Mosta
Gżira
Birkirkara
Msida
Valletta
Mdina
MALTA
Hamrun
Rabat
Marsa
Żabbar
Qormi
Żebbuġ
Paola
Dingli
Tarxien
Siġġiewi
Luqa
Żejtun
Mqabba
Ghaxaq
Marsaxlokk
Qrendi
Ghar Dalam
Żurrieq
Birżebbuġa
Kalafrana
Marsaxlokk Bay
Benghisa Point
Filfla
35° 50′
kilometers
statute miles

IT'S NEARLY IMPOSSIBLE TO SUM UP ASIA NEATLY, given its vast size and diversity, except to note that its cultural heritage and natural riches are unsurpassed. It is a continent of superlatives — largest in area, highest in population, home to the world's tallest mountains. Asia is a place of beginnings: People first mastered agriculture in Mesopotamia (in present-day Iraq) more than 10,000 years ago, and later created what many scholars regard as the first civilization, Sumeria. As well, the world's major religions, eastern and western ones alike, all took root in Asia before believers carried them elsewhere.

From ancient times, the great dynasties of Persia, India, and China rose and fell, assembling large empires and leaving impressive ruins. Cultural interplay was a constant factor — whether through the unification of China under the Qin dynasty, the rapid expansion of Islam, or the world-shaking invasions of Genghis Khan's Mongols. Trade was an integrating factor as well. Caravans passed each other on the Silk Road, a system of trading routes that spanned Asia and helped blur the boundaries between East and West.

KEY • Cultural World Heritage Site • Natural World Heritage Site • Mixed World Heritage Site

Asia

A watchtower (above) crowns a hill in Badaling, where the Ming dynasty built the final sections of China's Great Wall during its reign from the 14th to the 17th centuries. Other World Heritage sites across Asia, either on the list or tentatively proposed, include (left, top to bottom): Kumano Nachi Shrine in Japan's Kii Mountains, which reflects a unique fusion of Buddhism and Shinto; Göreme National Park in Turkey's Cappadocia region, where early Christians carved churches and cities in hills of volcanic ash; ancient spires of Buddhist temples in Bagan, Myanmar, the capital of the first Burmese empire; and the Jiuzhaigou Valley in China, famed for the brilliant blue waters of its lakes.

ATLANTIC OCEAN
ARCTIC
North Pole
Ireland
BRITISH ISLES
Great Britain
NORTH SEA
NORWEGIAN SEA
Meridian of Greenwich (London)
ARCTIC CIRCLE
SVALBARD
FRANZ JOSEF LAND
Komsomolets
October Revolution
BARENTS SEA
IBERIAN PENINSULA
SCANDINAVIA
NORTHERN EUROPEAN PLAIN
EUROPE
Gulf of Bothnia
BALTIC SEA
Kola Peninsula
White Sea
NOVAYA ZEMLYA
KARA SEA
Yenisey Gulf
Gyda Pen.
Gulf of Ob
Yamal Peninsula
Yenisey
Taz
Ob
ATLAS MOUNTAINS
ALPS
MEDITERRANEAN SEA
Lake Ladoga
Lake Onega
Narodnaya 1895
URAL MOUNTAINS
Volga
Kama
WEST SIBERIAN PLAIN
Irtysh
Vasyugan'ye
Tobol
Ishim Steppe
BALKAN PENINSULA
AEGEAN SEA
Dardanelles
Bosporus
Crimea
BLACK SEA
Don
EUROPE
ASIA
Ural
ANATOLIA (ASIA MINOR)
Taurus Mts.
3916
Cyprus
Caucasus Mountains
El'brus 5642
Caspian Depression
CASPIAN SEA
THE STEPPES
Lake Tengiz
Kazakh Uplands
Belukha 4506
ALTAI
Black Irtysh
Mt. Ararat 5137
L. Van
Lake Urmia
Kura
Aral Sea
Ustyurt Plateau
Syr Darya
Balkhash
Lake
Betpaqdala Desert
Ili
Dzungarian Basin
AFRICA
TROPIC OF CANCER
Levant Coast
3088
Euphrates
Tigris
Mesopotamia
Syrian Desert
SUEZ CANAL
SINAI
Dead Sea
-421 (-1380 ft) World's lowest point
Gulf of Aqaba
2285
Nile
-28
Garabogaz Bay
Turan Lowland
Amu Darya
Qizilqum
Elburz Mts. 5671
Kopet Mts.
Garagum
Victory Peak 7439
TIAN SHAN
Turpan Depression
Tarim
Lop Nur
SAHARA
Hejaz
An Nafūd
1137
ARABIAN PENINSULA
Zagros Mountains
4548
Dasht-e Kavīr
Dasht-e Lūt
3494
7495
TARIM BASIN
Taklimakan Desert
Altun Shan
7690
Hindu Kush
Karakoram Ra.
K2 (Godwin Austen) 8611
Muztag 6638
KUNLUN MOUNTAINS
RED SEA
Ad Dahnā'
Hasa Plain
PERSIAN GULF
Helmand
Indus
PLATEAU OF TIBET
Source of the Yangtze
Nganglong Range
Gangdise Ra.
7059
HIMALAYA
2386
Tuwayq Mountains
Tihamah
2093
1454
Sutlej
Great Indian Desert
World's highest point
Mt. Everest 8850
ETHIOPIAN HIGHLANDS
3760
Rub al Khali
2980
GULF OF OMAN
Ra's al Hadd
Ganges Plain
Ganges
Gulf of Kutch
Gulf of Masira
Hadhramaut
1730
Vindhya Range
Narmada
1350
Chota Nagpur Plateau
643
GULF OF ADEN
Gulf of Khambhat
1293
DECCAN PLATEAU
Krishna
Eastern Ghats
1589
Western Ghats
Socotra
ARABIAN SEA
Somali Peninsula
Coromandel Coast
BAY OF BENGAL
Lakshadweep
LACCADIVE SEA
Malabar Coast
2695
EQUATOR
Cape Comorin
2524
Sri Lanka
Maldive Islands
INDIAN OCEAN
Seychelles
Comoro Is.
Chagos Archipelago
Longitude East 80° of Greenwich

Two-Point Equidistant Projection

SCALE 1:24,575,500

1 CENTIMETER = 246 KILOMETERS; 1 INCH = 388 MILES

0 200 400 600 800 1000 KILOMETERS

0 200 400 600 800 1000 STATUTE MILES

International boundary

Disputed or undefined boundary

EUROPE–ASIA BOUNDARY

A commonly accepted division between Asia and Europe—marked here with a green line—is formed by the Ural Mountains, Ural River, Caspian Sea, Caucasus Mountains, and the Black Sea with its outlets, the Bosporus and Dardanelles. From north to south, the Europe-Asia boundary divides the nations of Russia, Kazakhstan, Azerbaijan, Georgia, and Turkey, placing territory of each country in both continents.

North Pole
ATLANTIC OCEAN
NORWEGIAN SEA
ARCTIC CIRCLE
ARCTIC
Meridian of Greenwich (London)
Spitsbergen
Edgeøya
Nordaustlandet
SVALBARD
Norway
FRANZ JOSEF LAND
(Zemlya Frantsa Iosifa)
Russia
BARENTS SEA
Ostrov Komsomolets
O. Oktyabr'skoy Revolyutsii
Novaya Zemlya
KARA SEA
Dikson
Yeniseyskiy Zaliv
Gulf of Ob'
Lisboa
(Lisbon)
PORTUGAL
SPAIN
MADRID
MOROCCO
ALGER
(Algiers)
ALGERIA
TUNIS
TUNISIA
MALTA
LIBYA
TARĀBULUS
(Tripoli)
IRELAND
Baile Átha Cliath
(Dublin)
UNITED KINGDOM
LONDON
NORTH SEA
Amsterdam
NETHERLANDS
Bruxelles
(Brussels)
BELGIUM
LUXEMBOURG
PARIS
FRANCE
Bern
SWITZERLAND
DENMARK
København
(Copenhagen)
BERLIN
GERMANY
PRAHA
(Prague)
CZECH REP.
AUSTRIA
WIEN
(Vienna)
Bratislava
SLOVAKIA
SLOVENIA
Ljubljana
CROATIA
Zagreb
BOSNIA & HERZEGOVINA
Sarajevo
HUNGARY
BUDAPEST
ITALY
ROMA
(Rome)
MEDITERRANEAN SEA
MONTENEGRO
Podgorica
SERBIA
BEOGRAD
(Belgrade)
KOSOVO
Tiranë
ALBANIA
Skopje
MACEDONIA
GREECE
Athína
(Athens)
SOFIYA
(Sofia)
BULGARIA
ROMANIA
BUCUREȘTI
(Bucharest)
MOLDOVA
Chișinău
UKRAINE
KYIV
(Kiev)
Crimea
BLACK SEA
Bosporus
İSTANBUL
AEGEAN SEA
OSLO
NORWAY
SWEDEN
Stockholm
LAPLAND
FINLAND
Gulf of Bothnia
Helsinki
Tallinn
ESTONIA
BALTIC SEA
Riga
LATVIA
LITHUANIA
Vilnius
Kaliningrad
Russia
POLAND
WARSZAWA
(Warsaw)
MINSK
BELARUS
Murmansk
Kandalaksha
BELOYE MORE
(WHITE SEA)
Severodvinsk
Arkhangel'sk
Segezha
Petrozavodsk
Ladozhskoye Ozero
SANKT-PETERBURG
(St. Petersburg)
Mezen'
Pechora
Nar'yan Mar
Vorkuta
Severnaya Dvina
Vologda
Tver'
MOSKVA
(Moscow)
Yaroslavl'
Smolensk
Tula
Bryansk
Orel
Kursk
Ryazan'
Tambov
Voronezh
Penza
NIZHNIY NOVGOROD
Volga
KAZAN'
Kama
Kirov
Perm'
Izhevsk
Ul'yanovsk
SAMARA
Saratov
Ufa
Syktyvkar
Ukhta
RUSSIA
URAL MOUNTAINS
Salekhard
Ob'
Nadym
Novyy Urengoy
Igarka
Dudinka
Khanty-Mansiysk
Surgut
Nizhnevartovsk
Serov
Nizhniy Tagil
Tavda
YEKATERINBURG
Tyumen'
Tobol'sk
Irtysh
CHELYABINSK
Kolpashevo
Volgograd
ROSTOV NA DONU
Krasnodar
Stavropol'
Sochi
ABKHAZIA
Vladikavkaz
Groznyy
Astrakhan'
EUROPE
ASIA
Oral
Ural
Orenburg
Orsk
Magnitogorsk
Aqtöbe
Qostanay
Petropavlovsk
Kökshetaū
Ekibastuz
OMSK
NOVOSIBIRSK
Tomsk
Achinsk
Kemerovo
Barnaul
Prokop'yevsk
Novokuznetsk
Biysk
Pavlodar
Astana
Qaraghandy
Semey
Rubtsovsk
Öskemen
Zaysan Köli
Altay
KAZAKHSTAN
Atyraū
Oktyabr'sk
Fort Shevchenko
Aqtaū
Aral Sea
Aral
Qazaly
Syr Darya
Qyzylorda
Balqash Köli
Balqash
Ayaköz
Tacheng
Saryözek
Taldyqorghan
ALMATY
Yining
Shihezi
Ürümqi
Turpan
Korla
Kuqa
Aksu
TIAN SHAN
SINKIANG
Tarim
Taklimakan Shamo
Qiemo
ALTUN SHAN
KUNLUN SHAN
Kashi
Shache
Hotan
Plateau of Tibet
CHINA
Boundary claimed by India
KASHMIR
Gilgit
Bishkek
KYRGYZSTAN
Namangan
Farg'ona
Taraz
Shymkent
TOSHKENT
(Tashkent)
Samarqand
UZBEKISTAN
Nukus
Daşoguz
Amu Darya
Türkmenbaşy
TURKMENISTAN
Aşgabat
Türkmenabat
Buxoro
(Bukhara)
Mary
Termiz
TAJIKISTAN
Dushanbe
Kondoz
Mazar-e Sharif
AFGHANISTAN
Herat
KABOL
(Kabul)
Farah
Kandahar
Zābol
Islamabad
SRINAGAR
PESHAWAR
RAWALPINDI
LAHORE
FAISALABAD
AMRITSAR
Jalandhar
Quetta
Nushki
MULTAN
Bahawalpur
LUDHIANA
PAKISTAN
Khanpur
Indus
Sukkur
Turbat
KARACHI
HYDERABAD
DELHI
New Delhi
Meerut
JAIPUR
AGRA
LUCKNOW
Jodhpur
KANPUR
Gwalior
Ganga
(Ganges)
NEPAL
Kathmandu
Thimphu
Xigazê
Gyangzê
HIMALAYA
PATNA
VARANASI
Allahabad
Kota
Udaipur
INDIA
AHMADABAD
Rajkot
VADODARA
BHOPAL
INDORE
Jabalpur
Ranchi
Khulna
DHAKA
Jamshedpur
KOLKATA
(Calcutta)
BANGLADESH
SURAT
Amravati
NAGPUR
Nasik
MUMBAI
(Bombay)
KALYAN
PUNE
Sholapur
HYDERABAD
Kolhapur
Vishakhapatnam
Guntur
Vijayawada
Hubli
Nellore
BANGALORE
Mysore
Salem
CHENNAI (Madras)
Puducherry (Pondicherry)
Kozhikode
COIMBATORE
Tiruchchirappalli
Kochi
(Cochin)
Madurai
Jaffna
Thiruvananthapuram
(Trivandrum)
SRI LANKA
Colombo
Galle
BAY OF BENGAL
Lakshadweep
India
ARABIAN SEA
Maldive Islands
Maale
(Male)
MALDIVES
British Indian Ocean Territory
Chagos Archipelago
(Oil Islands)
Diego Garcia
INDIAN OCEAN
Longitude East 80° of Greenwich
SEYCHELLES
Victoria
Mahé I.
Moroni
COMOROS
TURKEY
BURSA
Eskişehir
ANKARA
İZMİR
Konya
Samsun
Kayseri
ADANA
Iskenderun
Trabzon
GEORGIA
T'BILISI
ARMENIA
YEREVAN
AZERBAIJAN
BAKI
(Baku)
CASPIAN SEA
Diyarbakır
CYPRUS
(Nicosia) Lefkosia
(Beirut) BEYROUTH
LEBANON
HALAB
(Aleppo)
SYRIA
DIMASHQ
(Damascus)
ISRAEL
Jerusalem
GAZA STRIP
WEST BANK
'AMMĀN
JORDAN
EL QĀHIRA
(Cairo)
EGYPT
Nile
SUEZ CANAL
Sinai
TROPIC OF CANCER
AL MAWṢIL
IRAQ
KARKŪK
Euphrates
Tigris
MESOPOTAMIA
BAGHDĀD
Karbalā'
An Najaf
An Nāṣirīyah
AL BAṢRAH
KUWAIT
Al Kuwayt
TABRĪZ
Ardabīl
Rasht
Qazvīn
Hamadān
Sanandaj
TEHRĀN
QOM
Kermānshāh
Arāk
IRAN
EṢFAHĀN
Ahvāz
Ābādān
Yazd
SHĪRĀZ
Būshehr
Jahrom
Kermān
Bam
Zāhedān
Mashhad
Sabzevār
Bojnūrd
KHORĀSĀN
Bīrjand
Bābol
Bandar-e 'Abbās
BALUCHISTAN
PERSIAN GULF
Gulf of Oman
Tabūk
Dawmat al Jandal
Ḥā'il
Buraydah
AL HIJĀZ
Yanbu' al Baḥr
AL MADĪNAH
(Medina)
SAUDI ARABIA
AR RIYĀḌ
(Riyadh)
Ad Dammām
Al Hufūf
Al Manāmah
(Manama)
BAHRAIN
Ad Dawḥah
(Doha)
QATAR
UNITED ARAB EMIRATES
DUBAI
Abu Dhabi
'Ibrī
Masqaṭ (Muscat)
Ṣūr
OMAN
Jazīrat Maṣīrah
Ṣalālah
JEDDAH
MAKKAH
(Mecca)
Aṭ Ṭā'if
Khamīs Mushayṭ
'ASĪR
Qal'at Bīshah
Ar Rub' al Khālī
(Empty Quarter)
Jīzān
Ṣa'dah
RED SEA
Al Ḥudaydah
ṢAN'Ā'
Ta'izz
YEMEN
Saywūn
Ash Shiḥr
Al Mukallā
'Adan (Aden)
GULF OF ADEN
Suquṭrā (Socotra)
Yemen
MIDDLE EAST
Turkey, Cyprus, Syria, Lebanon, Israel, Jordan, Egypt, Iraq, Iran, and the countries of the Arabian Peninsula form the heart of the Middle East region.
SUDAN
KHARTOUM
El Bahr el Abyad
(White Nile)
ERITREA
Asmara
DJIBOUTI
Djibouti
ĀDĪS ĀBEBA
(Addis Ababa)
ETHIOPIA
SOMALILAND
Hargeysa
SOMALIA
MUQDISHO
(Mogadishu)
UGANDA
Lake Victoria
KENYA
NAIROBI
EQUATOR
Dodoma
TANZANIA
DAR ES SALAAM
MOZAMBIQUE

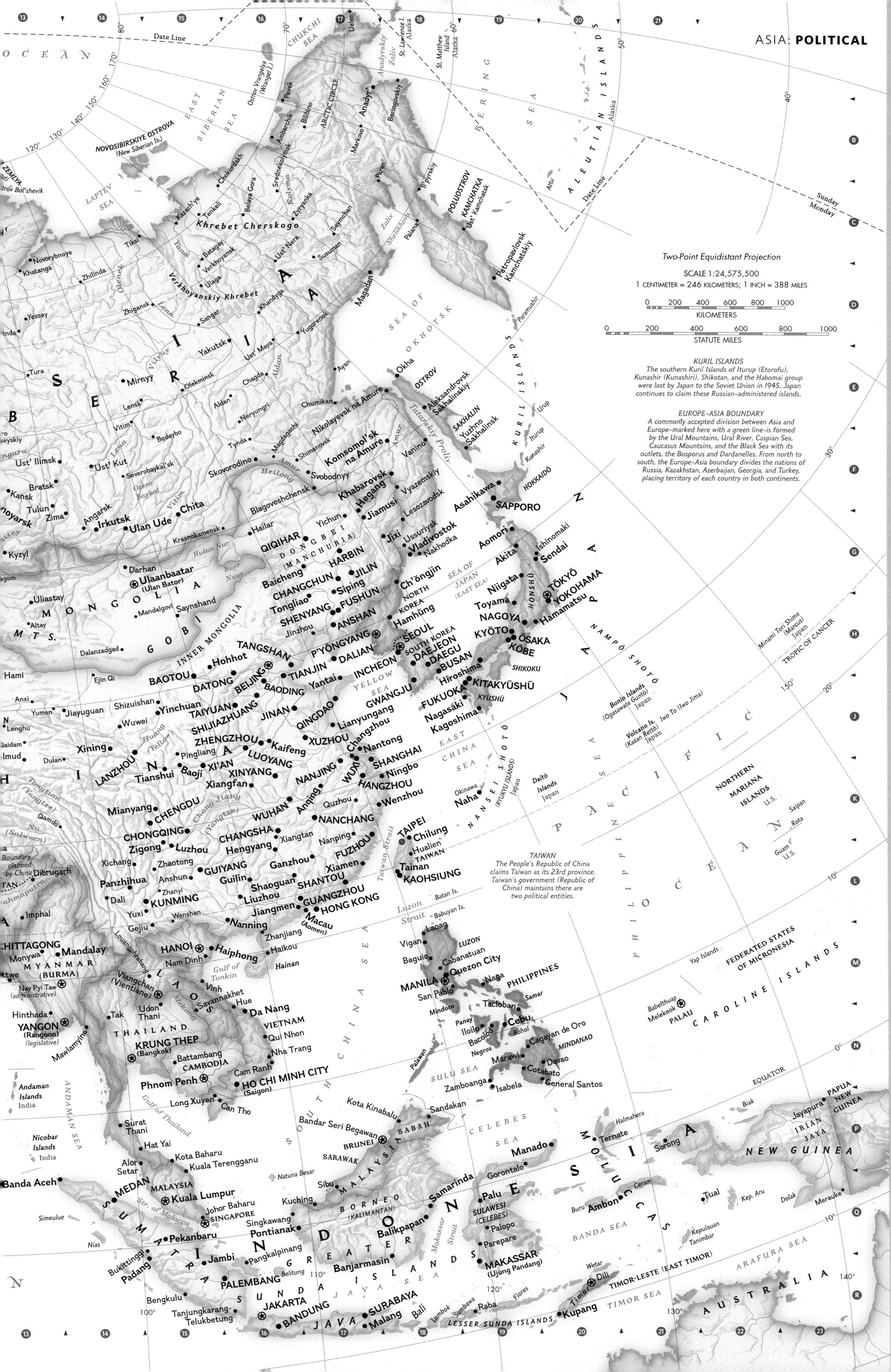

Two-Point Equidistant Projection

SCALE 1:24,575,500

1 CENTIMETER = 246 KILOMETERS; 1 INCH = 388 MILES

0 200 400 600 800 1000 KILOMETERS

0 200 400 600 800 1000 STATUTE MILES

KURIL ISLANDS

The southern Kuril Islands of Iturup (Etorofu), Kunashir (Kunashiri), Shikotan, and the Habomai group were lost by Japan to the Soviet Union in 1945. Japan continues to claim these Russian-administered islands.

EUROPE-ASIA BOUNDARY

A commonly accepted division between Asia and Europe–marked here with a green line–is formed by the Ural Mountains, Ural River, Caspian Sea, Caucasus Mountains, and the Black Sea with its outlets, the Bosporus and Dardanelles. From north to south, the Europe-Asia boundary divides the nations of Russia, Kazakhstan, Azerbaijan, Georgia, and Turkey, placing territory of each country in both continents.

TAIWAN

The People's Republic of China claims Taiwan as its 23rd province. Taiwan's government (Republic of China) maintains there are two political entities.

Asia: Themes

Continental Facts

TOTAL NUMBER OF COUNTRIES: 46

TOTAL AREA: 44,570,000 sq km (17,208,000 sq mi)

FIRST INDEPENDENT COUNTRY: Japan, 660 B.C.

"YOUNGEST" COUNTRY: Timor-Leste, May 20, 2002

MOST POPULOUS COUNTRY: China 1,348,317,000

LEAST POPULOUS COUNTRY: Maldives 304,000

LARGEST COUNTRY BY AREA: *China 9,596,960 sq km (3,705,405 sq mi)

SMALLEST COUNTRY BY AREA: Maldives 298 sq km (115 sq mi)

HIGHEST ELEVATION: Mount Everest, China-Nepal 8,850 m (29,035 ft)

LOWEST ELEVATION: Dead Sea, Israel-Jordan -421 m (-1,380 ft)

**The world's largest country, Russia, straddles both Asia and Europe. China, which is entirely within Asia, is considered the continent's largest country.*

Climate Zones

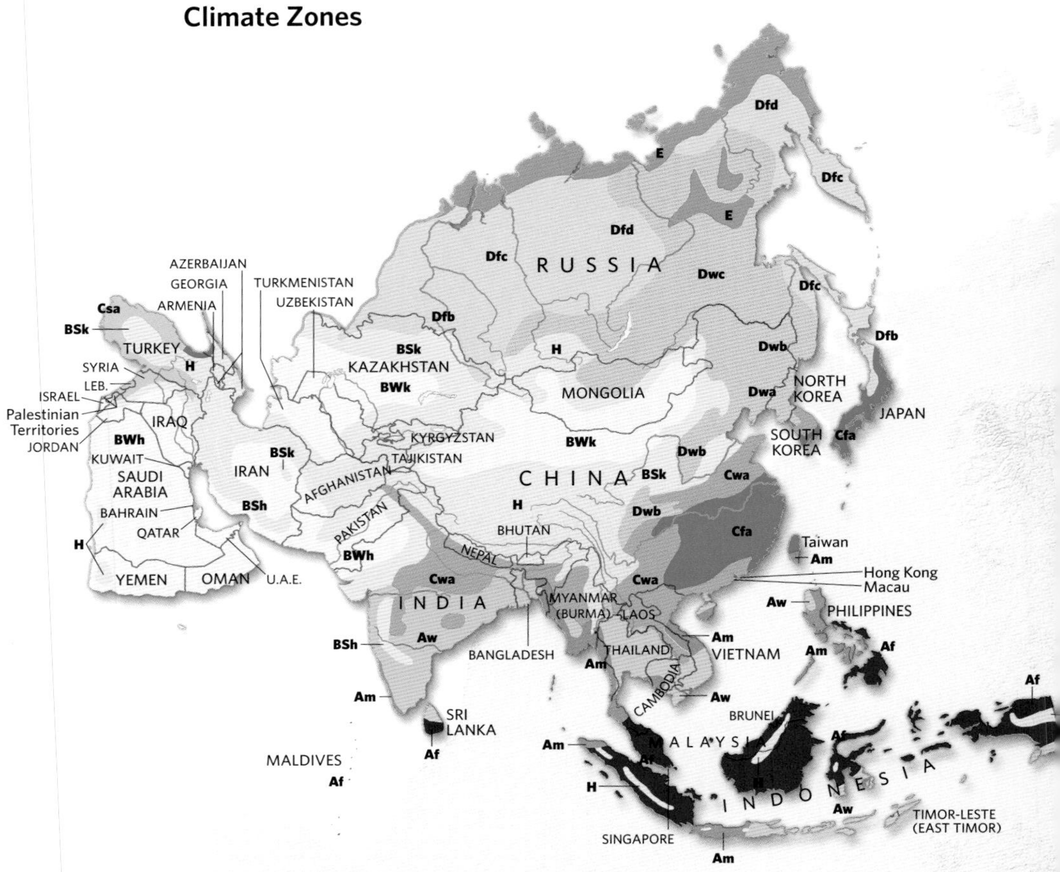

AZERBAIJAN
GEORGIA
ARMENIA
TURKMENISTAN
UZBEKISTAN
TURKEY
SYRIA
LEB.
ISRAEL
Palestinian Territories
JORDAN
IRAQ
KUWAIT
SAUDI ARABIA
BAHRAIN
QATAR
YEMEN
OMAN
U.A.E.
IRAN
KAZAKHSTAN
KYRGYZSTAN
TAJIKISTAN
AFGHANISTAN
PAKISTAN
RUSSIA
MONGOLIA
CHINA
NORTH KOREA
SOUTH KOREA
JAPAN
NEPAL
BHUTAN
INDIA
BANGLADESH
SRI LANKA
MALDIVES
MYANMAR (BURMA)
LAOS
THAILAND
CAMBODIA
VIETNAM
Taiwan
Hong Kong
Macau
PHILIPPINES
BRUNEI
MALAYSIA
SINGAPORE
INDONESIA
TIMOR-LESTE (EAST TIMOR)

CLIMATE
(based on modified Köppen system)

Humid equatorial climate (A)
- No dry season (Af)
- Short dry season (Am)
- Dry winter (Aw)

Dry climate (B)
- Semiarid (BS)
- Arid (BW)

h = hot
k = cold

Humid temperate climate (C)
- No dry season (Cf)
- Dry winter (Cw)
- Dry summer (Cs)

Humid cold climate (D)
- No dry season (Df)
- Dry winter (Dw)

a = hot summer
b = cool summer
c = short, cool summer
d = very cold winter

Cold climate (E)
- Tundra and ice

Highland climate (H)
- Unclassified highlands

Water Availability

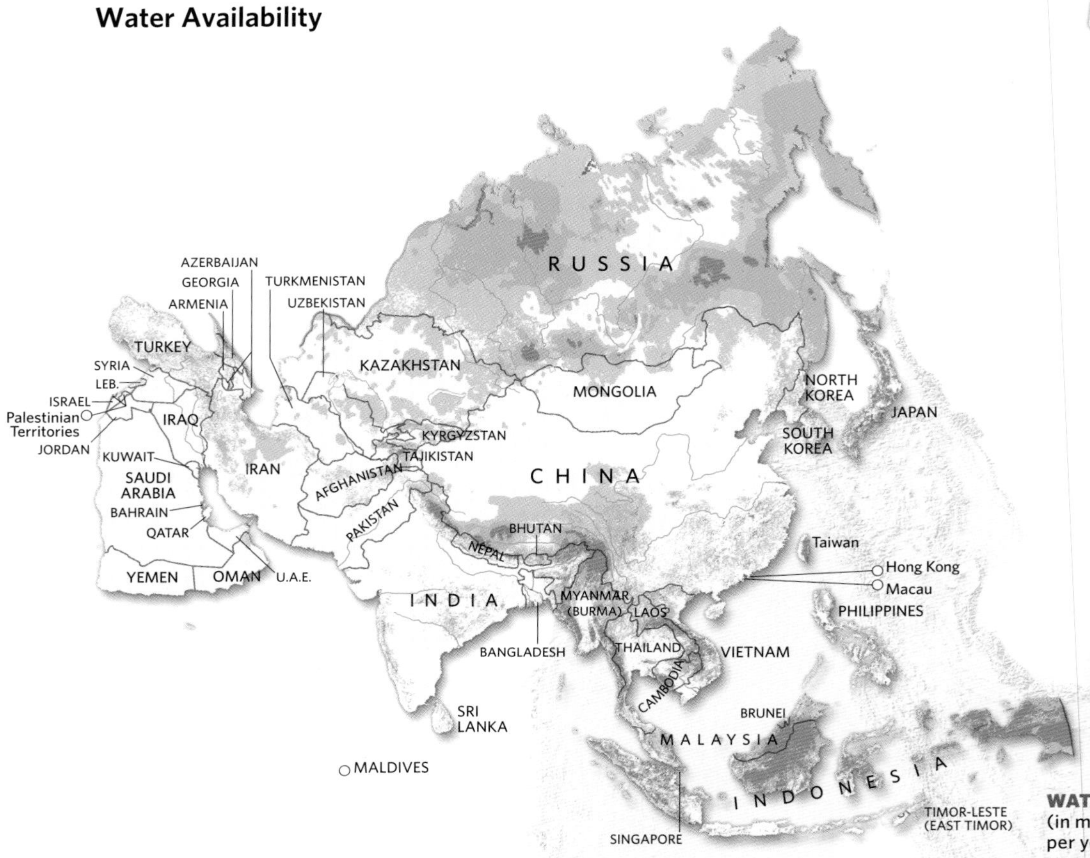

AZERBAIJAN
GEORGIA
ARMENIA
TURKMENISTAN
UZBEKISTAN
TURKEY
SYRIA
LEB.
ISRAEL
Palestinian Territories
JORDAN
IRAQ
KUWAIT
SAUDI ARABIA
BAHRAIN
QATAR
YEMEN
OMAN
U.A.E.
IRAN
KAZAKHSTAN
KYRGYZSTAN
TAJIKISTAN
AFGHANISTAN
PAKISTAN
RUSSIA
MONGOLIA
CHINA
NORTH KOREA
SOUTH KOREA
JAPAN
NEPAL
BHUTAN
INDIA
BANGLADESH
SRI LANKA
MALDIVES
MYANMAR (BURMA)
LAOS
THAILAND
CAMBODIA
VIETNAM
Taiwan
Hong Kong
Macau
PHILIPPINES
BRUNEI
MALAYSIA
SINGAPORE
INDONESIA
TIMOR-LESTE (EAST TIMOR)

WATER AVAILABILITY
(in millimeters per person per year)
- More than 750
- 251–750
- 26–250
- Less than 26

Natural Events

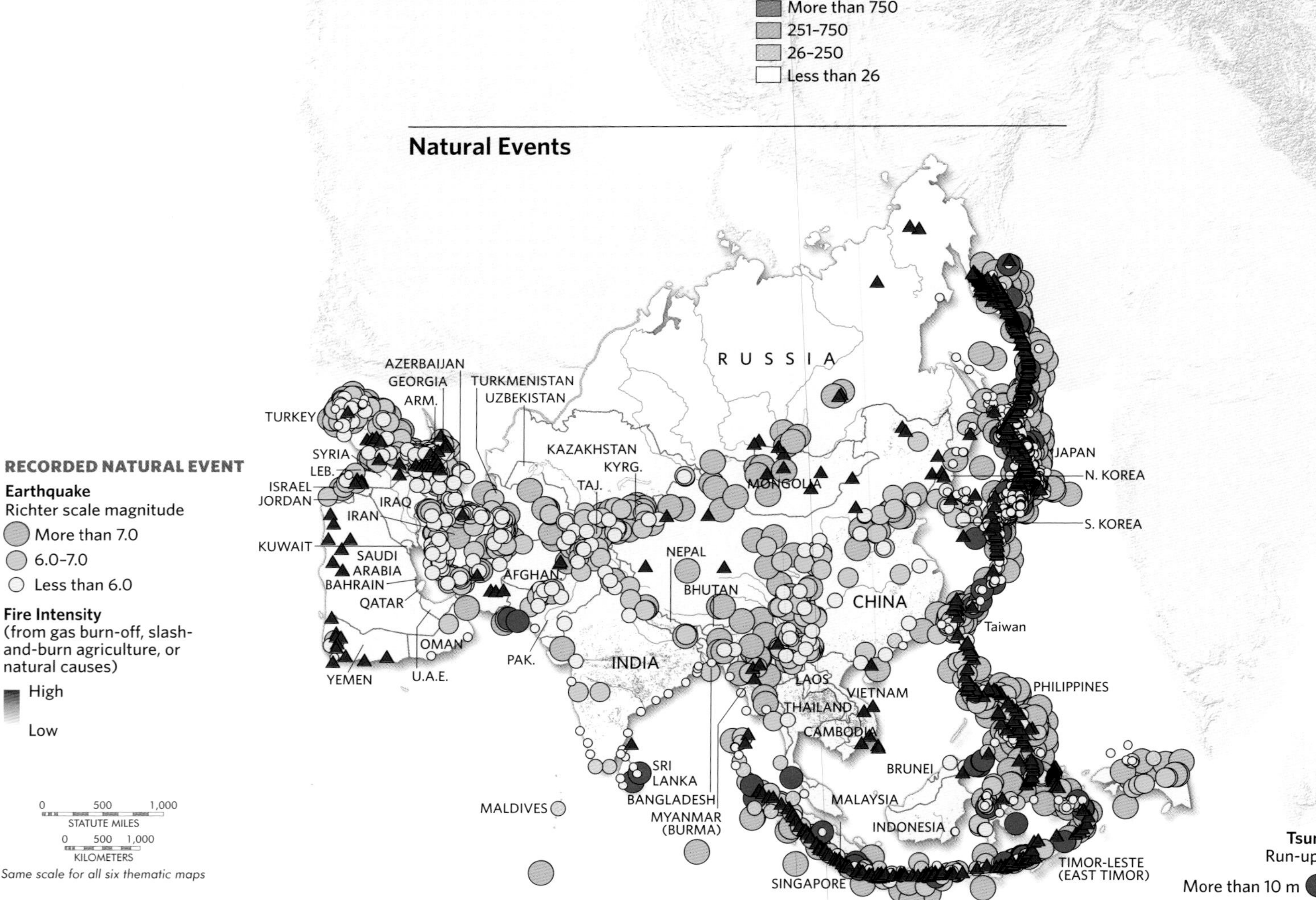
RUSSIA
AZERBAIJAN
GEORGIA
ARM.
TURKMENISTAN
UZBEKISTAN
TURKEY
SYRIA
LEB.
ISRAEL
JORDAN
IRAQ
IRAN
KUWAIT
SAUDI ARABIA
BAHRAIN
QATAR
OMAN
U.A.E.
YEMEN
KAZAKHSTAN
KYRG.
TAJ.
AFGHAN.
PAK.
MONGOLIA
NEPAL
BHUTAN
INDIA
CHINA
JAPAN
N. KOREA
S. KOREA
Taiwan
PHILIPPINES
LAOS
VIETNAM
THAILAND
CAMBODIA
SRI LANKA
BANGLADESH
MYANMAR (BURMA)
MALDIVES
BRUNEI
MALAYSIA
INDONESIA
SINGAPORE
TIMOR-LESTE (EAST TIMOR)
RECORDED NATURAL EVENT
Earthquake
Richter scale magnitude
More than 7.0
6.0–7.0
Less than 6.0
Fire Intensity
(from gas burn-off, slash-and-burn agriculture, or natural causes)
High
Low
0 500 1,000
STATUTE MILES
0 500 1,000
KILOMETERS
Same scale for all six thematic maps
Tsunami
Run-up height
More than 10 m More than 32 ft
5–10 m 16–32 ft
Less than 5 m Less than 16 ft
Volcano
Major eruption

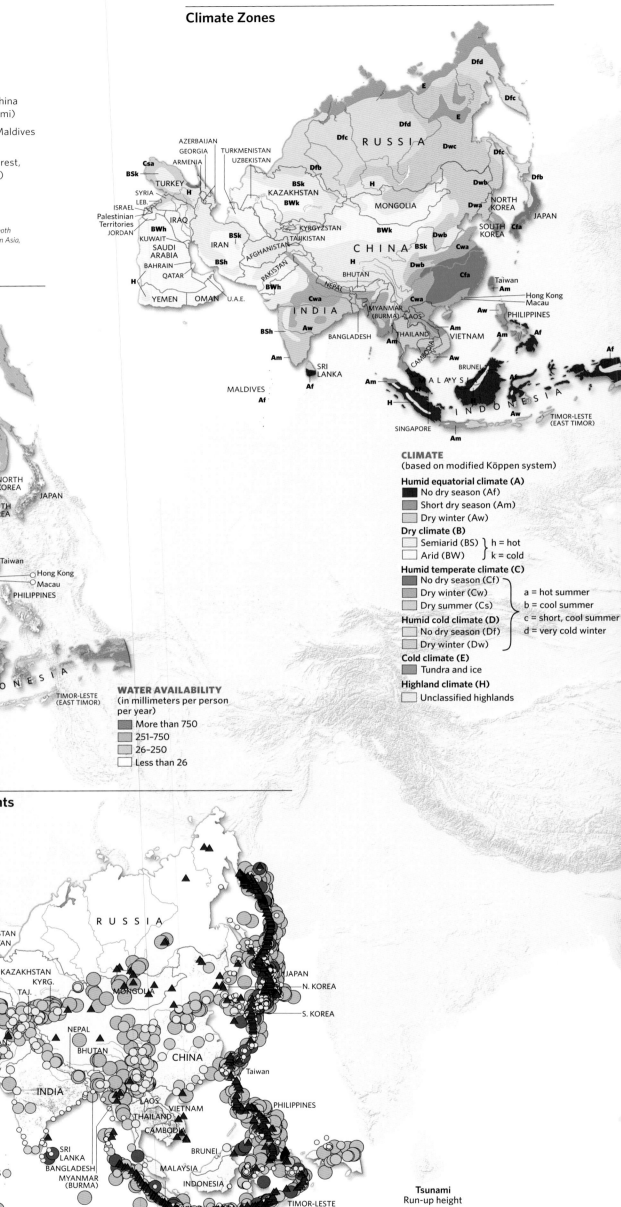

Population Density

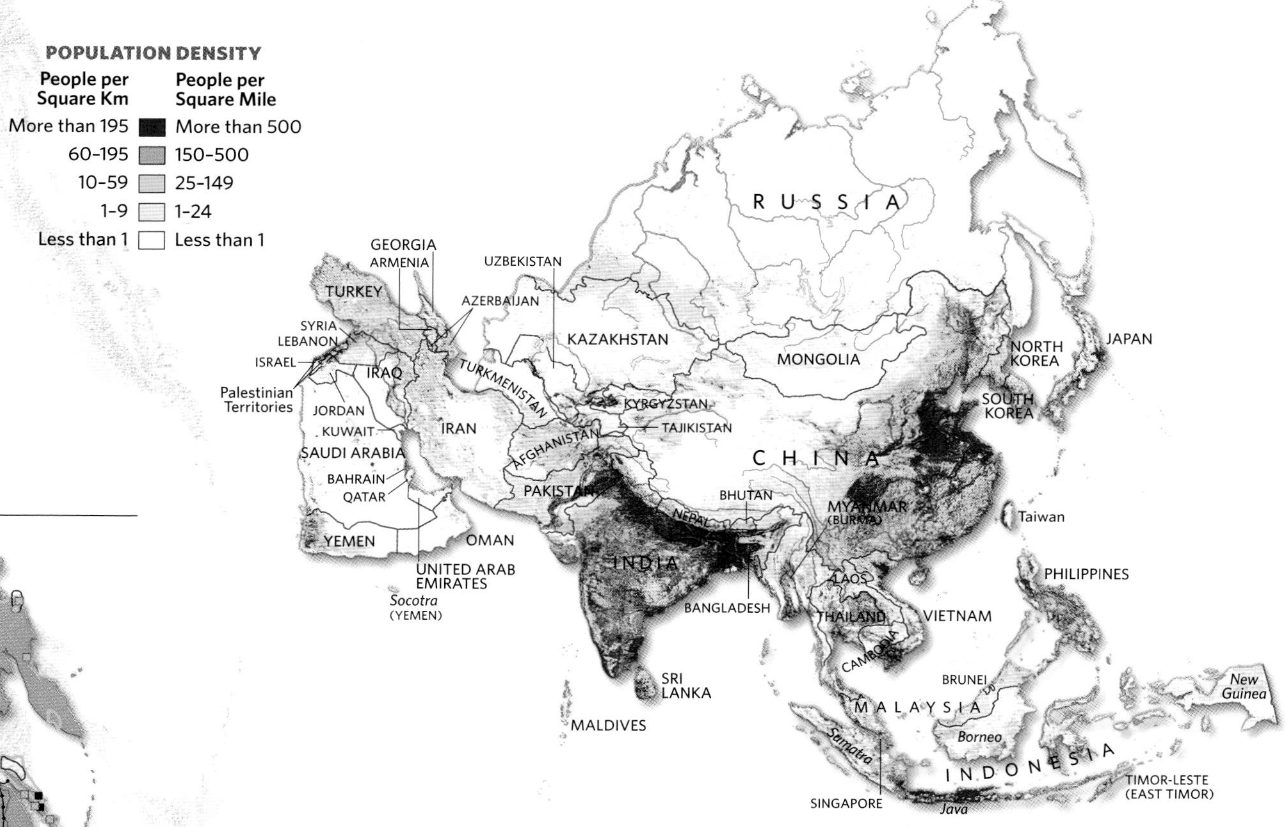

POPULATION DENSITY

People per Square Km	People per Square Mile
More than 195	More than 500
60–195	150–500
10–59	25–149
1–9	1–24
Less than 1	Less than 1

Energy Consumption

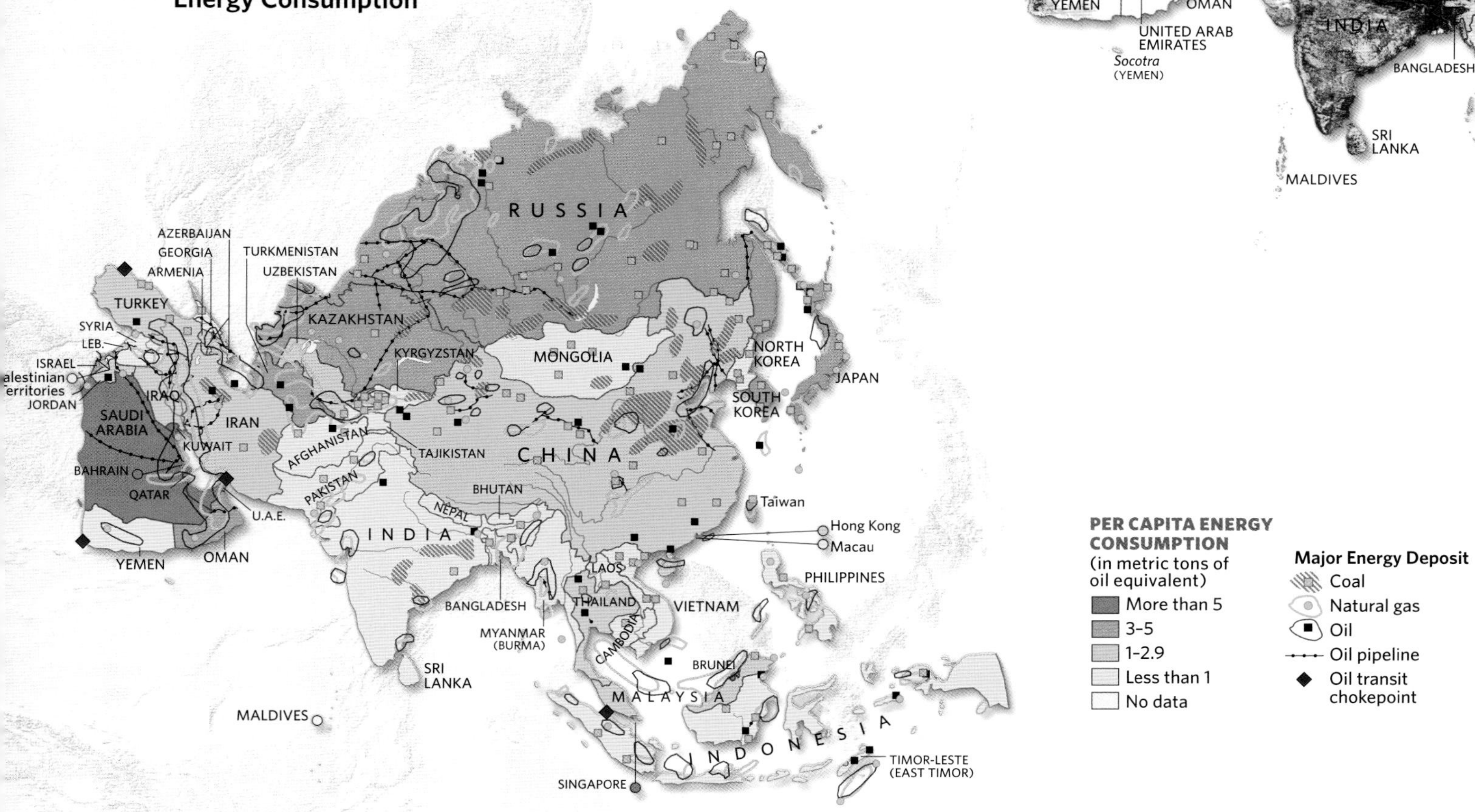

PER CAPITA ENERGY CONSUMPTION
(in metric tons of oil equivalent)

- More than 5
- 3–5
- 1–2.9
- Less than 1
- No data

Major Energy Deposit

- Coal
- Natural gas
- Oil
- Oil pipeline
- Oil transit chokepoint

Dominant Economy

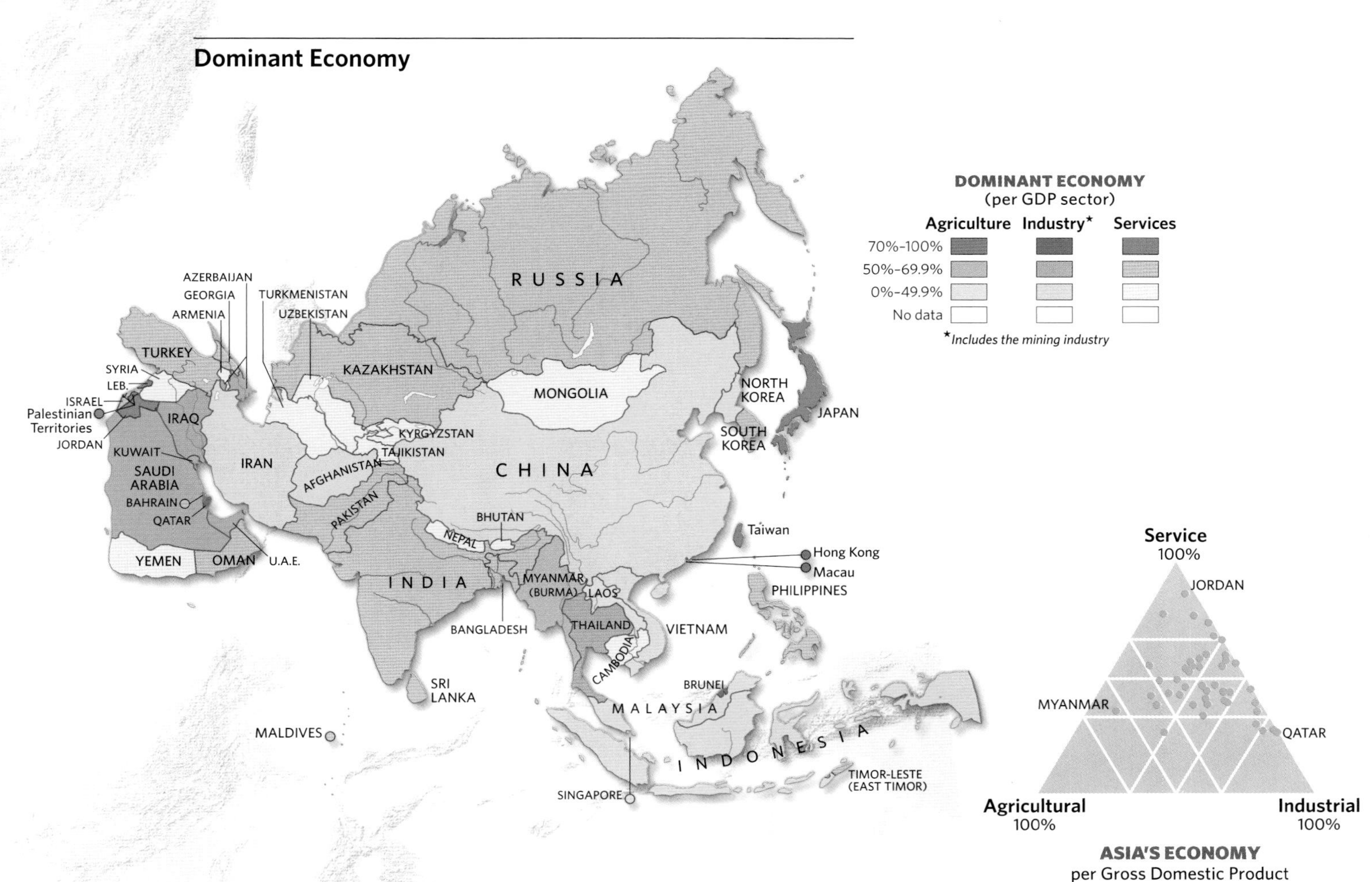
RUSSIA
KAZAKHSTAN
MONGOLIA
CHINA
INDIA
IRAN
AZERBAIJAN
GEORGIA
ARMENIA
TURKMENISTAN
UZBEKISTAN
TURKEY
SYRIA
LEB.
ISRAEL
Palestinian Territories
JORDAN
IRAQ
KUWAIT
SAUDI ARABIA
BAHRAIN
QATAR
YEMEN
OMAN
U.A.E.
KYRGYZSTAN
TAJIKISTAN
AFGHANISTAN
PAKISTAN
NEPAL
BHUTAN
BANGLADESH
MYANMAR (BURMA)
LAOS
THAILAND
CAMBODIA
VIETNAM
NORTH KOREA
SOUTH KOREA
JAPAN
Taiwan
Hong Kong
Macau
PHILIPPINES
SRI LANKA
MALDIVES
BRUNEI
MALAYSIA
INDONESIA
SINGAPORE
TIMOR-LESTE (EAST TIMOR)

DOMINANT ECONOMY
(per GDP sector)

	Agriculture	Industry*	Services
70%–100%			
50%–69.9%			
0%–49.9%			
No data			

*Includes the mining industry

Service 100%
JORDAN
MYANMAR
QATAR
Agricultural 100%
Industrial 100%

ASIA'S ECONOMY
per Gross Domestic Product (GDP) sector

Historic Areas of Istanbul, Turkey ❶

The soaring dome and spires of the Sultan Ahmed Mosque (left) — also called the Blue Mosque — tower over one of the key cities in world history. Istanbul straddles the Bosporus strait, a dividing line between Asia and Europe long seen as the crossroads of East and West. Once called Byzantium, then New Rome, it served briefly as the Roman capital. Renamed Constantinople, it was the seat of the Byzantine Empire. When it fell to the Ottomans, the city assumed its current name. As the tides of history swept over it, Istanbul accumulated a huge legacy of art and architecture, including the fourth-century Hippodrome of Constantine and the sixth-century Hagia Sophia — Christendom's largest cathedral for a millennium, then a mosque for five centuries, now a museum. Today pollution and Istanbul's expanding population of well over ten million threaten the sites.

Conic Projection

SCALE 1:4,771,100
1 CENTIMETER = 47.7 KILOMETERS; 1 INCH = 75.3 MILES

ISTANBUL
The only city to span two continents, Europe and Asia, its foundation dates to the 7th century B.C. — past names include Byzantium and Constantinople. Today it is one of the largest cities in Europe and the cultural and financial center of Turkey.

ABKHAZIA
Separatists defeated Georgian troops to gain control of this region in 1993 — negotiations continue resolving the conflict.

BLACK SEA

MEDITERRANEAN SEA

CYPRUS

For more detail on Cyprus, see pages 170-171

Longitude East 30° of Greenwich

Göreme National Park and the Rock Sites of Cappadocia, Turkey ❷

This dreamlike desert region of western Turkey was named a World Heritage site both for its fantastical rock formations and for human-made features: subterranean churches, houses, even entire cities carved into the soft local rock. Ancient eruptions covered the region with a layer of tuff — solidified volcanic ash that erodes easily into spires and pinnacles, some here standing up to 131 feet high. In the fourth century, monks moved into small cells carved into rock faces, and thereafter, underground building spread. In search of refuge from invasions, local people began excavating underground towns like Kaymakli and Derinkuyu. The latter, reaching 279 feet deep, may have housed tens of thousands of people, and featured a winery, schools, and a church. In addition, monastic communities carved beautiful sanctuaries into the cliffs and spires of Cappadocia and adorned them with frescoes that number among the finest examples of Byzantine art.

Upper Svaneti, Georgia ❸

Quaint medieval villages perch on mountain slopes in this remote area of northwestern Georgia. The region's architecture is renowned — particularly tower houses like these in the village of Chazhashi (below). An ancient design, they were everyday residences as well as family fortresses in times of war.

❹ Monasteries of Haghpat and Sanahin, Armenia

Located two miles apart in craggy northern Armenia, these monastic complexes are the best examples of church architecture in the first nation to accept Christianity as its state religion. The building of Haghpat (right) and Sanahin began in the tenth century, soon after Armenia reemerged from under Arab rule. They blend local and Byzantine building styles, with monumental main churches dominating the surrounding smaller worship buildings. Repeatedly sacked by invaders in medieval times, they endured as centers of learning and guardians of national identity.

RUSSIA
SOUTH OSSETIA
Ethnic Ossetians, a majority in South Ossetia, seceded from Georgia in 1990. In 1992 and 2006, South Ossetia voted for full independence but has not achieved international recognition.
NAGORNO-KARABAKH
Since a cease-fire in 1994 ethnic Armenians in Azerbaijan's Nagorno-Karabakh region have exercised autonomous control over the region. International mediation to resolve the conflict continues.
KURDISTAN
Kurds, the largest ethnic minority in Turkey at some 14 million, live in the southeastern highlands—Turkey's poorest region. Clashes between militants of the Kurdistan Workers' Party (PKK) and Turkish armed forces have left villages in ruins and thousands dead.
GEORGIA
ARMENIA
AZERBAIJAN
CASPIAN SEA
IRAN
IRAQ
T'BILISI (Tbilisi)
YEREVAN
BAKI (Baku)
Sukhumi
Zugdidi
K'ut'aisi
Gori
Rust'avi
Batumi
Gyumri
Vanadzor
Gäncä
Sumqayit
Stepanakert
Naxçıvan
Länkäran
Erzurum
Kars
Van
Batman
Siirt
Ağrı
Mingäçevir
Kura Lowland
Van Gölü
42°
45°
48°
39°

Turkey
Armenia
Georgia
Azerbaijan

Protected Areas and World Heritage Sites

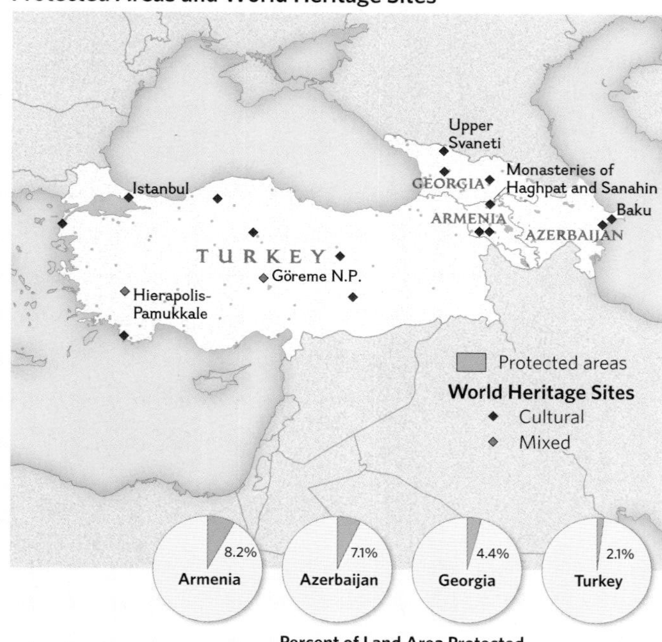
Upper Svaneti
Monasteries of Haghpat and Sanahin
Baku
Istanbul
GEORGIA
ARMENIA
AZERBAIJAN
TURKEY
Göreme N.P.
Hierapolis-Pamukkale
Protected areas
World Heritage Sites
Cultural
Mixed
Armenia 8.2%
Azerbaijan 7.1%
Georgia 4.4%
Turkey 2.1%
Percent of Land Area Protected

Urbanization and Largest Cities

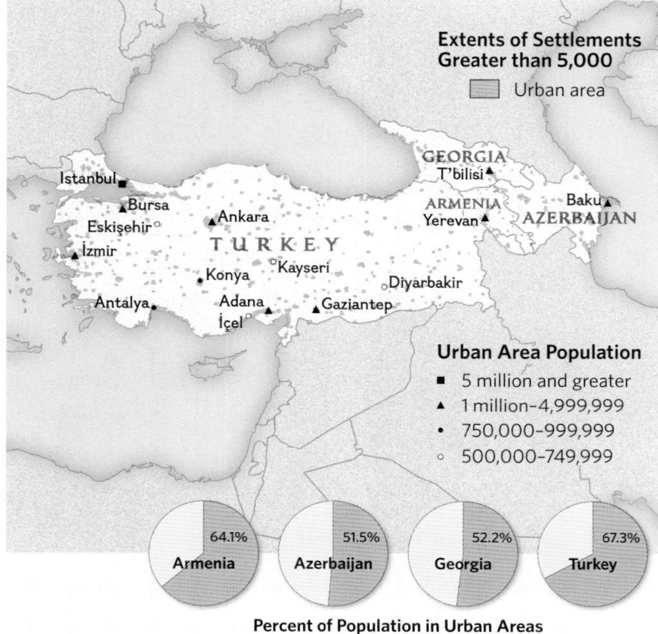
Extents of Settlements Greater than 5,000
Urban area
GEORGIA
T'bilisi
Baku
ARMENIA
Yerevan
AZERBAIJAN
Istanbul
Bursa
Eskişehir
İzmir
Ankara
TURKEY
Kayseri
Konya
Diyarbakir
Antalya
Adana
İçel
Gaziantep
Urban Area Population
5 million and greater
1 million–4,999,999
750,000–999,999
500,000–749,999
Armenia 64.1%
Azerbaijan 51.5%
Georgia 52.2%
Turkey 67.3%
Percent of Population in Urban Areas

Hierapolis-Pamukkale, Turkey ❺

Terraced pools (below) formed by mineral-laden waters from hot springs spill down a calcified slope in southwestern Turkey. The Greeks used the area as a retreat in the second century B.C., followed by Rome, which took control in 129 B.C. and built the spa city of Hierapolis. Romans attributed healing powers to the 95°F water, and they built basins for swimming and soaking. When the Ottomans conquered the region, they aptly named this area Pamukkale, or "cotton castle," because of the dazzling whiteness of its soaring travertine cliffs, cascades, and terraces. After more than 2,000 years as a tourist attraction, Pamukkale continues to draw crowds.

Walled City of Baku, Azerbaijan ❻

An ornate portal leads into the Shirvanshah's Palace (above) erected in the 15th century for Azerbaijan's ruling dynasty. The country was absorbed the following century by the Safavids, then captured by the Ottomans 50 years later, and finally taken by Russia in the 18th century. Baku's labyrinthine medieval core preserves the threads of this tumultuous history, but it was rocked by a 2000 earthquake, and today is endangered by uncontrolled reconstruction and encroaching development.

Natural Land Cover

GEORGIA
AZERBAIJAN
ARMENIA
TURKEY
Land Cover
Desert
Forest
Herbaceous
Highland

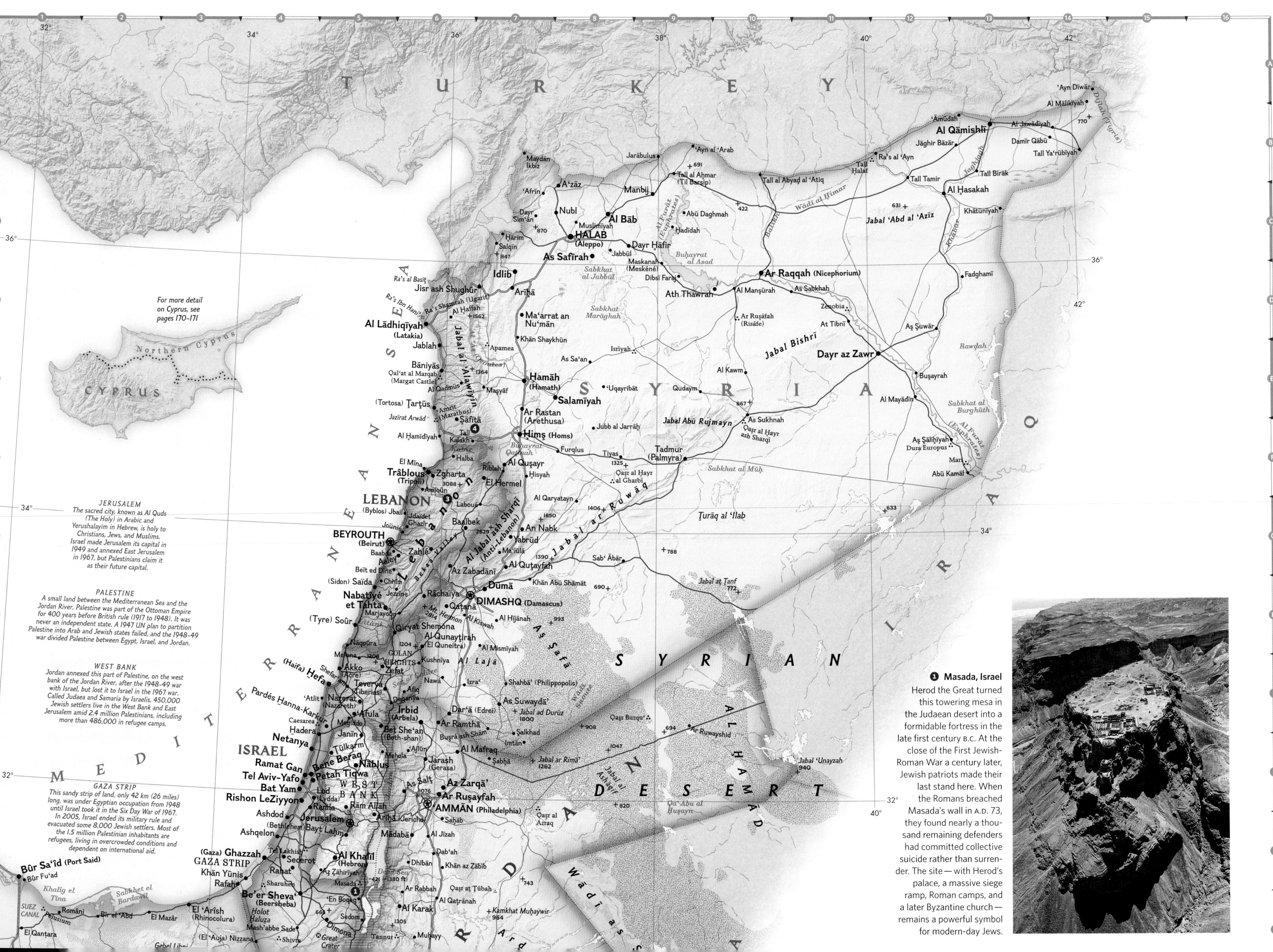
T U R K E Y
S Y R I A
I R A Q
LEBANON
ISRAEL
GAZA STRIP
WEST BANK
GOLAN HEIGHTS
CYPRUS
Northern Cyprus
M E D I T E R R A N E A N S E A
S Y R I A N D E S E R T
J O R D A N
AL ḤAMĀD
HALAB (Aleppo)
Al Lādhiqīyah (Latakia)
Ḥamāh (Hamath)
Ḥimṣ (Homs)
DIMASHQ (Damascus)
BEYROUTH (Beirut)
Trâblous (Tripoli)
Ar Raqqah (Nicephorium)
Dayr az Zawr
Al Qāmishlī
Al Ḥasakah
Tadmur (Palmyra)
AMMĀN (Philadelphia)
Jerusalem
Tel Aviv-Yafo
(Haifa) Ḥefa
(Gaza) Ghazzah
Būr Sa'īd (Port Said)
Jabal al 'Alawīyīn
Jabal Bishrī
Jabal 'Abd al 'Azīz
Jabal Abū Rujmayn
Al Jabal ash Sharqī (Anti-Lebanon)
Jabal ar Ruwāq
Lebanon
Ṭurāq al 'Ilab
Dijlah (Tigris)
Al Furāt (Euphrates)
Buḥayrat al Asad
Dead Sea
Wādī as Sirḥān
For more detail on Cyprus, see pages 170–171

JERUSALEM
The sacred city, known as Al Quds (The Holy) in Arabic and Yerushalayim in Hebrew, is holy to Christians, Jews, and Muslims. Israel made Jerusalem its capital in 1949 and annexed East Jerusalem in 1967, but Palestinians claim it as their future capital.

PALESTINE
A small land between the Mediterranean Sea and the Jordan River, Palestine was part of the Ottoman Empire for 400 years before British rule (1917 to 1948). It was never an independent state. A 1947 UN plan to partition Palestine into Arab and Jewish states failed, and the 1948-49 war divided Palestine between Egypt, Israel, and Jordan.

WEST BANK
Jordan annexed this part of Palestine, on the west bank of the Jordan River, after the 1948-49 war with Israel, but lost it to Israel in the 1967 war. Called Judaea and Samaria by Israelis, 450,000 Jewish settlers live in the West Bank and East Jerusalem amid 2.4 million Palestinians, including more than 486,000 in refugee camps.

GAZA STRIP
This sandy strip of land, only 42 km (26 miles) long, was under Egyptian occupation from 1948 until Israel took it in the Six Day War of 1967. In 2005, Israel ended its military rule and evacuated some 8,000 Jewish settlers. Most of the 1.5 million Palestinian inhabitants are refugees, living in overcrowded conditions and dependent on international aid.

1 Masada, Israel
Herod the Great turned this towering mesa in the Judaean desert into a formidable fortress in the late first century B.C. At the close of the First Jewish-Roman War a century later, Jewish patriots made their last stand here. When the Romans breached Masada's wall in A.D. 73, they found nearly a thousand remaining defenders had committed collective suicide rather than surrender. The site — with Herod's palace, a massive siege ramp, Roman camps, and a later Byzantine church — remains a powerful symbol for modern-day Jews.

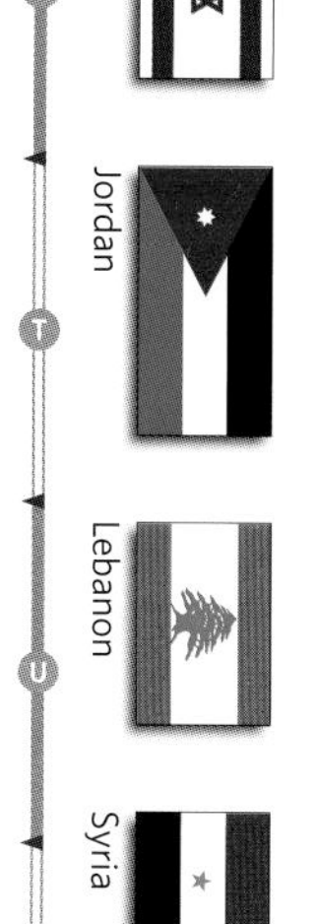
Israel
Jordan
Lebanon
Syria

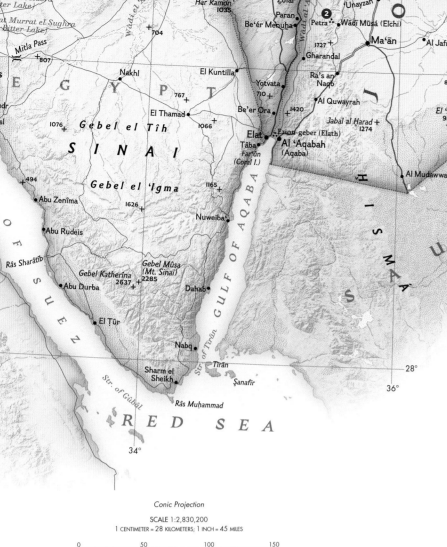

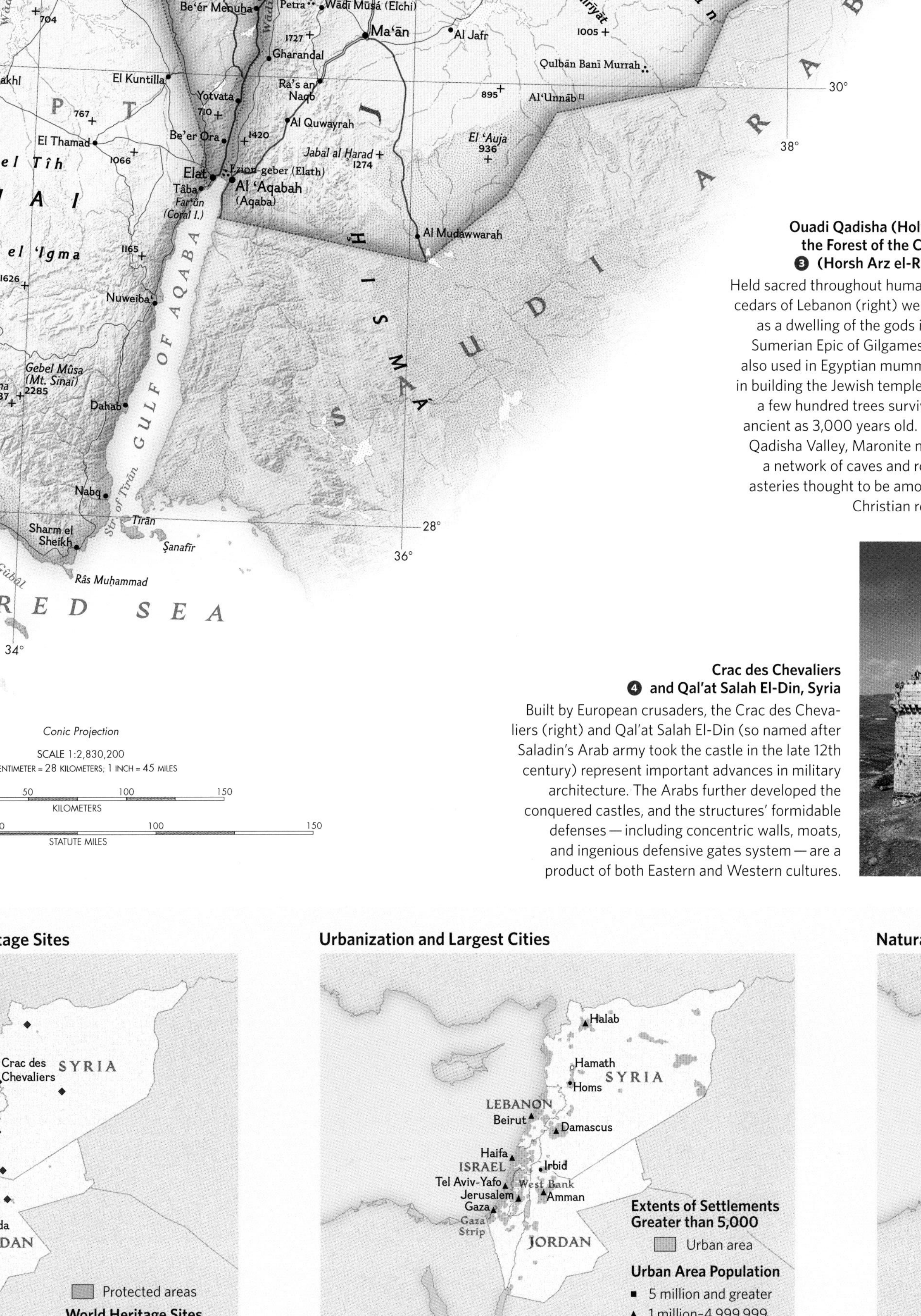
EGYPT
SINAI
Gebel el Tîh
Gebel el 'Igma
El Suweis (Suez)
El Kûbri
Buheirat Murrat el Sughra (Little Bitter Lake)
SUEZ CANAL
Mitla Pass
Nakhl
El Thamad
El Kuntilla
Sudr
Asl
Abu Zenîma
Abu Rudeis
Râs Sharâtîb
Gebel Katherina 2637
Gebel Mûsa (Mt. Sinai) 2285
Abu Durba
El Tûr
Dahab
Nuweiba
Nabq
Sharm el Sheikh
Râs Muhammad
Tîrân
Şanâfir
Str. of Tîrân
Str. of Gûbâl
GULF OF SUEZ
GULF OF AQABA
RED SEA
Elat
Tâba
Far'ûn (Coral I.)
Be'er Ora
Yotvata
Be'ér Menuha
Paran
Zofar
Har Ramon 1035
Petra
Wādī Mūsá (Elchi)
'Unayzah
Ma'ān
Gharandal
Ra's an Naqb
Al Quwayrah
Jabal al Harad 1274
Ezion-geber (Elath)
Al 'Aqabah (Aqaba)
Al Jafr
Qā' al Jafr
Jibāl al 'Adhiriyāt
Qulbān Banī Murrah
Al 'Unnāb
El 'Auja 936
Al Mudawwarah
HISMÁ
SAUDI ARABIA
30°
28°
34°
36°
38°
Conic Projection
SCALE 1:2,830,200
1 CENTIMETER = 28 KILOMETERS; 1 INCH = 45 MILES
KILOMETERS
STATUTE MILES
0
50
100
150

Petra, Jordan ❷
This capital city of ancient Nabataea is renowned for monumental buildings—including the so-called Treasury (below)—cut into sandstone cliff faces. Little is known about this trade-based Arabic culture today. Though their capital is situated on a main caravan route connecting Egypt and Arabia, it is hidden deep in narrow gorges, and remained unknown to the Western world until it was discovered by a 19th-century French explorer. Located in present-day Jordan, Petra has become an iconic location and a setting for numerous films, including *Indiana Jones and the Last Crusade*.

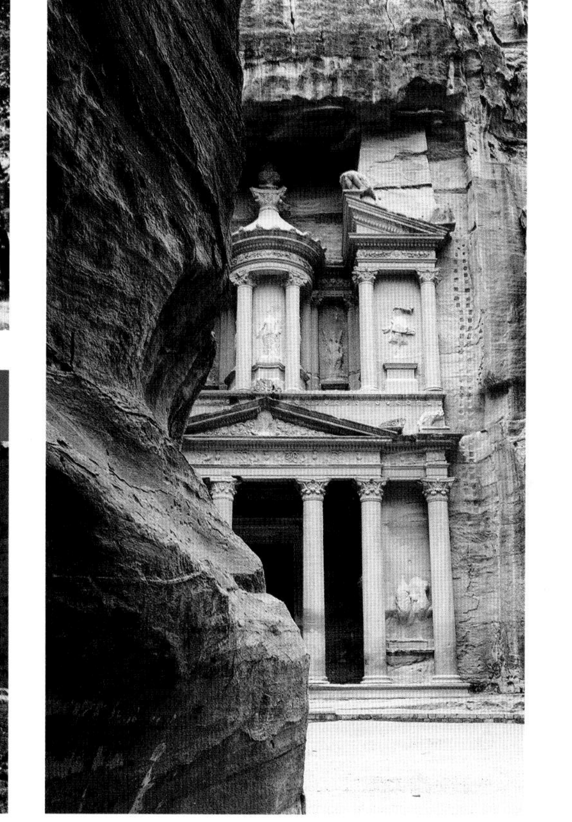

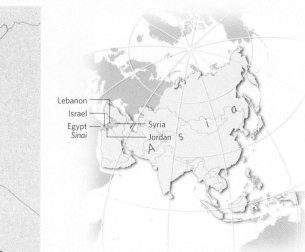

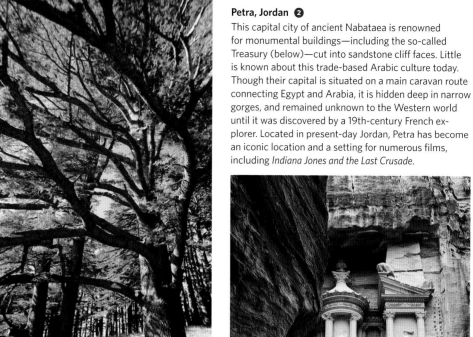

Ouadi Qadisha (Holy Valley) and the Forest of the Cedars of God ❸ (Horsh Arz el-Rab), Lebanon
Held sacred throughout human history, the cedars of Lebanon (right) were mentioned as a dwelling of the gods in the ancient Sumerian Epic of Gilgamesh. They were also used in Egyptian mummification and in building the Jewish temples. Today only a few hundred trees survive — some as ancient as 3,000 years old. In the nearby Qadisha Valley, Maronite monks inhabit a network of caves and rock-cut monasteries thought to be among the oldest Christian religious sites.

Crac des Chevaliers ❹ and Qal'at Salah El-Din, Syria
Built by European crusaders, the Crac des Chevaliers (right) and Qal'at Salah El-Din (so named after Saladin's Arab army took the castle in the late 12th century) represent important advances in military architecture. The Arabs further developed the conquered castles, and the structures' formidable defenses — including concentric walls, moats, and ingenious defensive gates system — are a product of both Eastern and Western cultures.

Protected Areas and World Heritage Sites

SYRIA
Crac des Chevaliers
Ouadi Qadisha
LEBANON
West Bank
Gaza Strip
ISRAEL
Masada
JORDAN
Petra
Protected areas
World Heritage Sites
Cultural
Percent of Land Area Protected
19.7% Israel
10.4% Jordan
5.6% Lebanon
0.1% Syria

Urbanization and Largest Cities

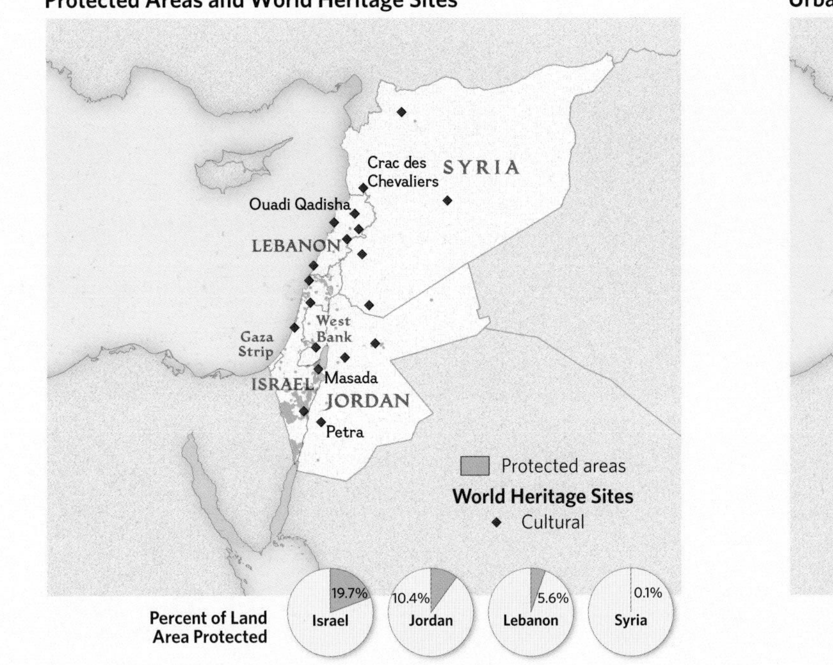
Halab
Hamath
Homs
SYRIA
LEBANON
Beirut
Damascus
Haifa
ISRAEL
Irbid
Tel Aviv-Yafo
West Bank
Jerusalem
Amman
Gaza
Gaza Strip
JORDAN
Extents of Settlements Greater than 5,000
Urban area
Urban Area Population
5 million and greater
1 million–4,999,999
750,000–999,999
500,000–749,999
Percent of Population in Urban Areas
91.6% Israel
82.3% Jordan
86.6% Lebanon
50.6% Syria

Natural Land Cover

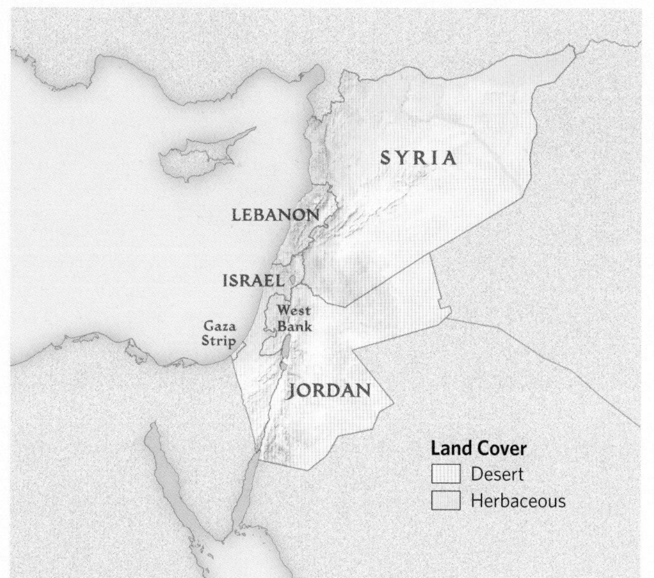
SYRIA
LEBANON
ISRAEL
West Bank
Gaza Strip
JORDAN
Land Cover
Desert
Herbaceous

Lebanon
Israel
Egypt
Sinai
Syria
Jordan

Lambert Conformal Conic Projection
SCALE 1:7,975,400
1 CENTIMETER = 80 KILOMETERS; 1 INCH = 126 MILES
KILOMETERS
STATUTE MILES
S Y R I A N D E S E R T
I R A Q
JORDAN
ISRAEL
EGYPT
SUDAN
ETHIOPIA
ERITREA
DJIBOUTI
S A U D I A R A B I A
Y E
RED SEA
TROPIC OF CANCER
Longitude East 44° of Greenwich
Al Qurayyāt
Ṭurayf
'Ar'ar
Sakākah
Dawmat al Jandal (Al Jawf)
Al 'Uwayqīlah
Rafḥā'
Ḥafar al Bāṭin
An Nafūd
Tabūk
Taymā'
Ḥā'il
Buraydah
'Unayzah
Al Wajh
Umm Lajj
AL MADĪNAH (Medina)
Yanbu' al Baḥr
Rābigh
JEDDAH
MAKKAH (Mecca)
Aṭ Ṭā'if
Al Qunfudhah
Abhā
Khamīs Mushayt
Najrān
Jīzān
Ṣa'dah
ṢAN'Ā' (Sanaa)
Al Ḥudaydah
Dhamār
Ibb
Ta'izz
Al Mukhā
'Adan (Aden)
Bab el Mandeb
Ma'rib
As Sulayyil
Ḍubā
Al Bad'
Ḥaql
Maqnah
Al 'Ulā
Ḥarrat Khaybar
Ḥarrat al 'Uwayriḍ
Jabal Rāf 979
Jabal Raḍwā 1814
Jabal Sawdā' 3133
Al Bāḥah
Qal'at Bīshah
Turabah
'Afīf
Ad Dawādimī
Jazā'ir Farasān

Qal'at al-Bahrain — Ancient Harbor and Capital of Dilmun, Bahrain ❶
A 16th-century Portuguese fort dominates the site, sitting atop a tell — a small hill formed by the accumulated rubble of thousands of years of habitation. Long buried within the tell, and now partially excavated (left) are the palaces and other buildings of the capital of ancient Dilmun, a realm that arose on the island of Bahrain in the Persian Gulf in the late third millennium B.C. and went on to become an important trading center.

Land of Frankincense, Oman ❷
Omani frankincense sellers set the aromatic tree resin alight for a customer. Said to produce the world's finest frankincense, Oman has numerous archaeological sites that were key to a trade that helped tie the ancient world together: The Wadi Dawkah Frankincense Park preserves frankincense trees, while the caravan oasis of Shisr/Ubar was a key distribution point.

Archaeological Sites of Bat, Al-Khutm and Al-Ayn, Oman ❸
These well-preserved third-millennium B.C. settlements and necropolises provide a window into the life of Bronze Age civilizations in the Arabian Peninsula. Copper exported from the area may have passed through the port of Dilmun on its way to Sumeria. Hundreds of stone tombs (below) survive, along with ruins of residences and towers up to 65.5 feet high.

Bahla Fort, Oman ❹
Until restoration efforts in recent years bore fruit, each rainy season washed away more of the massive adobe fortress that dominates the Bahla oasis. It was built in stages over hundreds of years, assuming its current form while the oasis was ruled by the Banu Nebhan tribe, rulers of the region from the 12th to the 15th centuries. Now physically stabilized, UNESCO has removed it from the List of World Heritage in Danger.

Bahrain | Oman | Qatar | Saudi Arabia | United Arab Emirates | Yemen

5 Old Walled City of Shibam, Yemen
Hundreds of densely packed tower houses crowd together like skyscrapers in this small Yemeni city, leading to its nickname the "Manhattan of the desert." Urbanists consider Shibam, with houses up to eight stories tall, a prime early example of the vertical development. The residents probably began building skyward in the 16th century to escape the predations of nomadic raiding parties, using the towers as forts in times of trouble. A number of even older buildings remain, including a 10th-century mosque and a 13th-century castle.

Saudi Arabia
Qatar
Yemen
Oman
Bahrain
United Arab Emirates
Asia

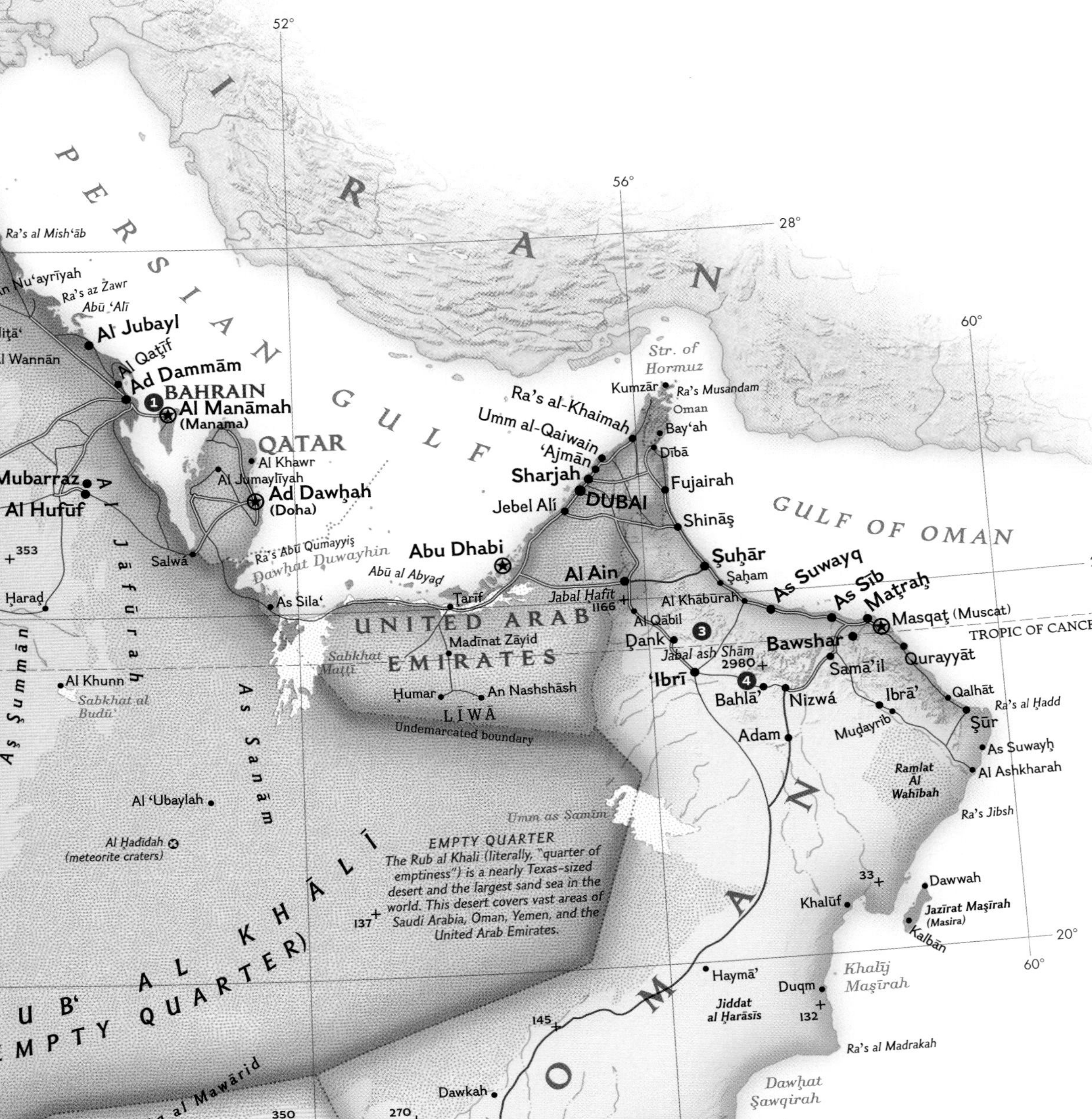

IRAN
PERSIAN GULF
GULF OF OMAN
Str. of Hormuz
Ra's al Mish'āb
Al Jubayl
Ad Dammām
BAHRAIN
Al Manāmah (Manama)
QATAR
Ad Dawḩah (Doha)
Al Mubarraz
Al Hufūf
Abu Dhabi
Ra's al-Khaimah
Umm al-Qaiwain
'Ajmān
Sharjah
DUBAI
Jebel Alī
Fujairah
Shināş
Şuḩār
As Suwayq
As Sīb
Maţraḩ
Masqaţ (Muscat)
TROPIC OF CANCER
Al Ain
UNITED ARAB EMIRATES
LIWA
Undemarcated boundary
'Ibrī
Bahlā'
Nizwá
Bawshar
Sama'il
Qurayyāt
Şūr
Al Ashkharah
Ramlat Al Wahibah
Jazīrat Maşīrah (Masira)
EMPTY QUARTER
The Rub al Khali (literally, "quarter of emptiness") is a nearly Texas-sized desert and the largest sand sea in the world. This desert covers vast areas of Saudi Arabia, Oman, Yemen, and the United Arab Emirates.
RUB' AL KHĀLĪ (EMPTY QUARTER)
OMAN
Haymā'
Duqm
Khalīj Maşīrah
Ra's al Madrakah
ZUFĀR
Şalālah
Mirbāţ
Thamarīt
ARABIAN SEA
HADRAMAWT
Sayḩūt
Al Ghaydah
Nishtūn
Mukallā
Ash Shiḩr
GULF OF ADEN
Suquţrá (Socotra) Yemen
Al Ikhwān (The Brothers)
'Abd al Kūrī

6 Old City of Sanaa, Yemen
One of the world's most picturesque cities, the Yemeni capital has many intricately decorated buildings built atop rock outcroppings. Sanaa, with more than a hundred mosques exceeding a thousand years old, was a major force in the spread of Islam. The Grand Mosque—Islam's third oldest—was the first built outside of the city of Medina.

Protected Areas and World Heritage Sites

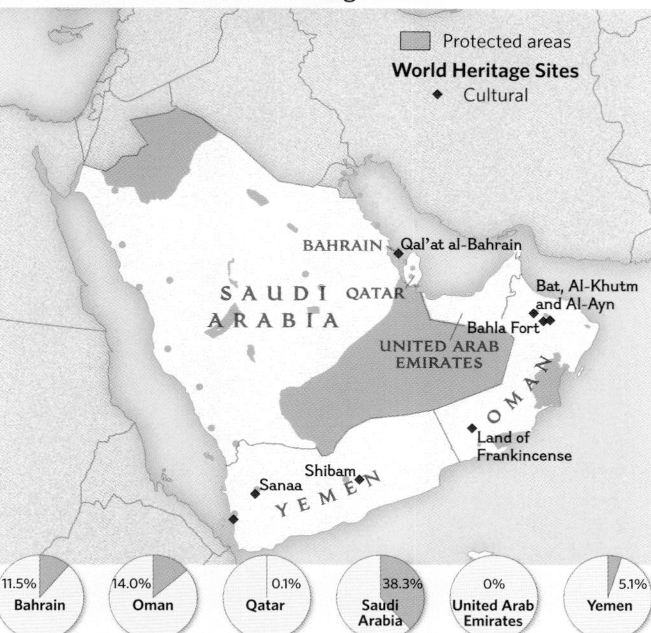

Protected areas
World Heritage Sites
Cultural
Qal'at al-Bahrain
Bat, Al-Khutm and Al-Ayn
Bahla Fort
Land of Frankincense
Shibam
Sanaa

Bahrain	Oman	Qatar	Saudi Arabia	United Arab Emirates	Yemen
11.5%	14.0%	0.1%	38.3%	0%	5.1%

Percent of Land Area Protected

Urbanization and Largest Cities

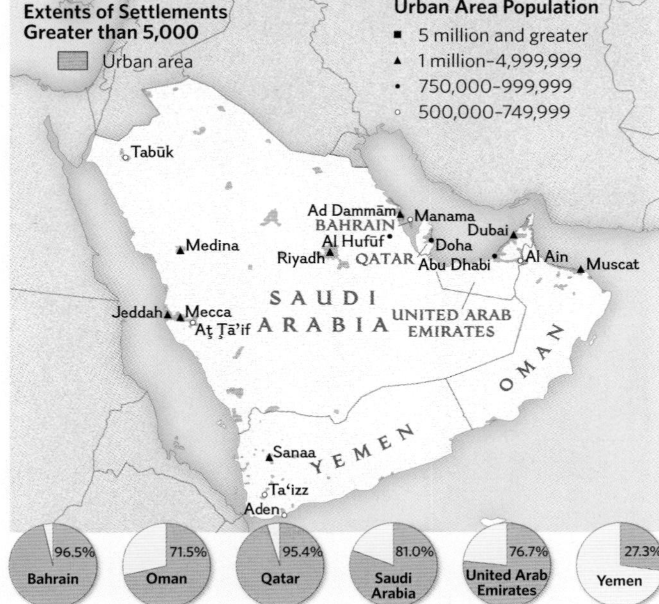

Extents of Settlements Greater than 5,000
Urban area
Urban Area Population
5 million and greater
1 million–4,999,999
750,000–999,999
500,000–749,999
Tabūk
Medina
Riyadh
Jeddah
Mecca
Aţ Ţā'if
Ad Dammām
Manama
Al Hufūf
Doha
Dubai
Abu Dhabi
Al Ain
Muscat
Sanaa
Ta'izz
Aden

Bahrain	Oman	Qatar	Saudi Arabia	United Arab Emirates	Yemen
96.5%	71.5%	95.4%	81.0%	76.7%	27.3%

Percent of Population in Urban Areas

Natural Land Cover

Land Cover
Desert
Herbaceous
BAHRAIN
QATAR
SAUDI ARABIA
UNITED ARAB EMIRATES
OMAN
YEMEN

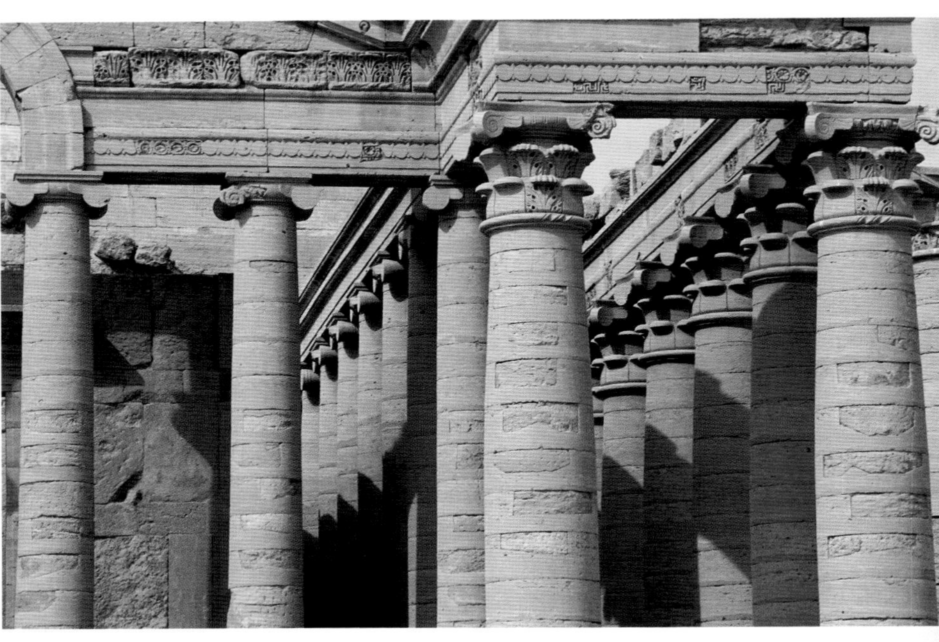

Hatra, Iraq ❶

The Greek-inspired ruins of a sun temple grace the destroyed city of Hatra, once an important trade and religious center of the Parthian empire. The Parthians, members of an Iranian dynasty that styled itself the successor of the Achaemenid Persian Empire, clashed often with Rome to the west. The frontier city of Hatra — built in a circular defensive plan — was an important bastion in the struggle, repulsing assaults by Trajan and Septimius Severus in the second century A.D. It fell the following century to the Sassanid, a resurgant Persian dynasty.

Marshlands of Mesopotamia, Iraq (Tentative List) ❷

The destruction of southern Iraq's extensive wetlands — nominated as a World Heritage site — is both a human and an environmental catastrophe. Decades of dam-building combined with Saddam Hussein's marsh-drainage projects in the 1990s to render most of the area a salt-encrusted desert, threatening the culture of the Ma'dan people, who have lived there for millennia, along with waterfowl that nest there.

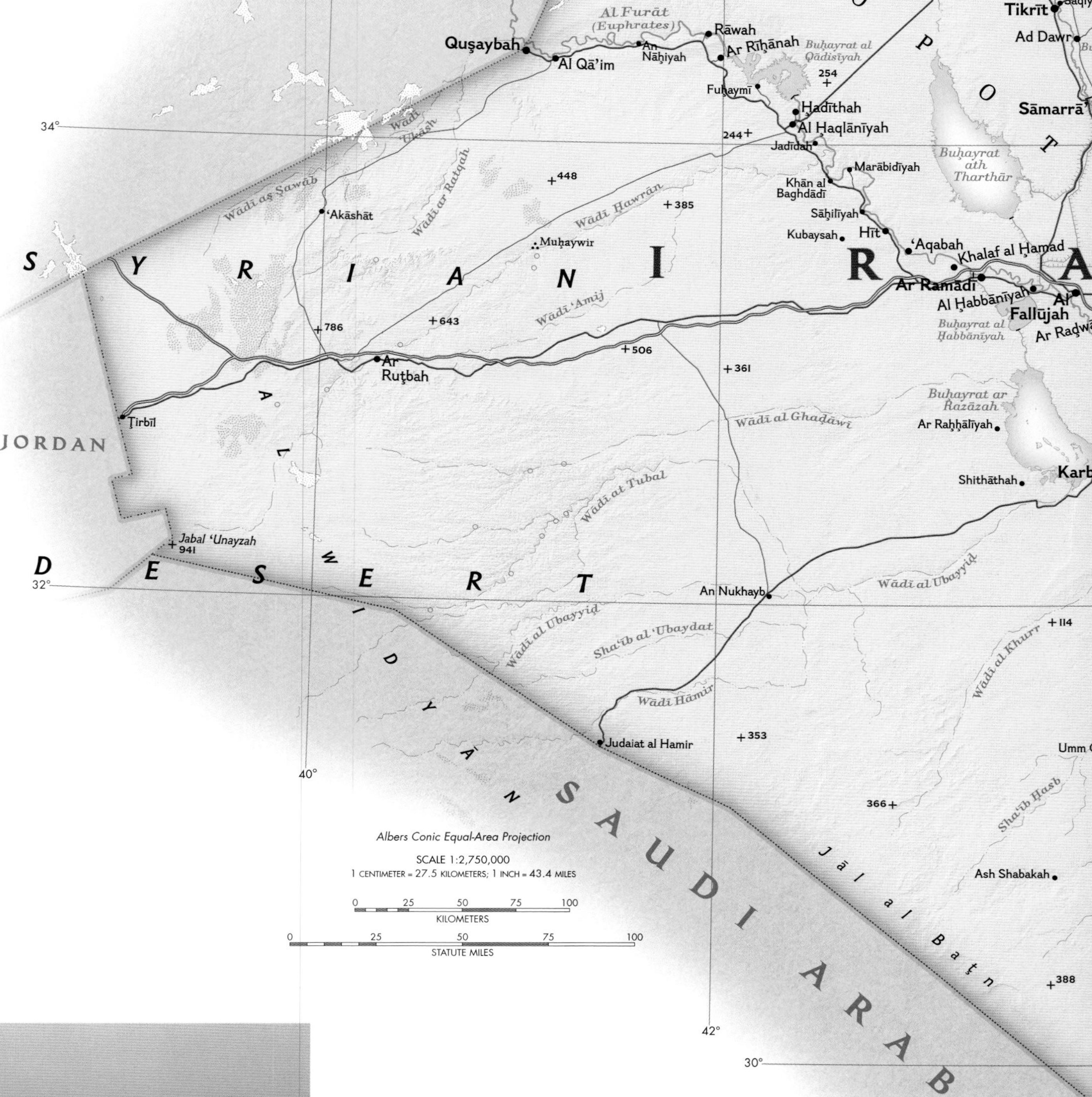
Longitude East 42° of Greenwich
TURKEY
SYRIA
JORDAN
SAUDI ARABIA
SYRIAN DESERT
MESOPOTAMIA
IRA
MESOPOTAMIA
Modern Iraq occupies ancient Mesopotamia, site of the world's earliest civilizations, and exhibits the ruins of fabled cities: Ashhur, Hatra, Nimrūd, Nineveh, and Sāmarrā' in northern Iraq; in the south, Babylon and Ūr—with its famed ziggurat (stepped pyramid).
Zakho
Faysh Khābūr
Al 'Amādīyah
Sawārah Tūkā
Sarsing
Zāwīta
Summēl
Dihōk
Rabī'ah
Tall 'Uwaynāt
'Ayn Sifnī
Bā'idrah
Bāqasrah
Kalakchī
Tall Kayf
Bardarash
Al Ḥuqnah
Askī Mawṣil
Jabal Sinjār
Sinjār
Tall 'Afar
Tu'aym
AL MAŞIL (Mosul)
Nineveh
Bartalah
'Ayn al Ghazāl
Tall Banāt
Qabr Ḥajar
Bulayj
Ḥammām al 'Alīl
Nimrūd
Demir Dāgh
Al Bi'āj
Ash Shūrah
Al Kuwayr
Al Bādī
Al Qayyārah
Ḥajj 'Alī
Khunayfis
Hatra
Al Ḥaḍr
Ḥadrānīyah
Ashhur
Safīnah
Ash Sharqāt
Ash Sharīy'ah
Shūmayt
Zarārīyah
Zuwiyya
Shaykh
Sunaysilah
Milḥat Ashqar
Bayjī
Tikrīt
Ad Dawr
Sāmarrā'
Al Furāt (Euphrates)
Quşaybah
Al Qā'im
An Nāḥiyah
Rāwah
Ar Riḥānah
Buḥayrat al Qādisīyah
Fuḥaymī
Ḥadīthah
Al Ḥaqlānīyah
Jadīdah
Buḥayrat ath Tharthār
Marābidīyah
Khān al Baghdādī
Ṣāḥilīyah
Kubaysah
Hīt
'Aqabah
Khalaf al Ḥamad
Ar Ramādī
Al Ḥabbānīyah
Fallūjah
Ar Raḍwān
Buḥayrat al Ḥabbānīyah
Buḥayrat ar Razāzah
Ar Raḥḥālīyah
Shithāthah
Karbal
'Akāshāt
Muḥaywir
Wādī Ḥawrān
Wādī 'Amij
Wādī al Ghadāwī
Wādī aṭ Ṭubal
Wādī al Ubayyiḍ
Sha'īb al 'Ubaydat
Wādī Ḥāmir
Wādī al Khurr
Sha'īb Ḥasb
Ar Ruṭbah
Ṭirbīl
Jabal 'Unayzah 941
An Nukhayb
Judaiat al Hamir
Umm Gh
Ash Shabakah
Jāl al Baṭn
Albers Conic Equal-Area Projection
SCALE 1:2,750,000
1 CENTIMETER = 27.5 KILOMETERS; 1 INCH = 43.4 MILES
KILOMETERS
STATUTE MILES

Sacred Complex of Babylon, Iraq (Tentative List) ❸

The heart of the Mesopotamian city of Babylon was a huge religious complex dedicated to the city's patron deity, Marduk. The Esagila temple was completed in the sixth century B.C. by Nebuchadnezzer of biblical fame, as was the Etemenanki, a giant ziggurat popularly regarded as the Tower of Babel mentioned in the Book of Genesis. Only ruins remain today. Elsewhere around the ancient city, a reconstruction program begun by Saddam Hussein — including a private palace built on the ruins — has marred the site, as did the construction of a U.S. military base and helicopter landing pads within the site in 2003.

Iraq  Kuwait

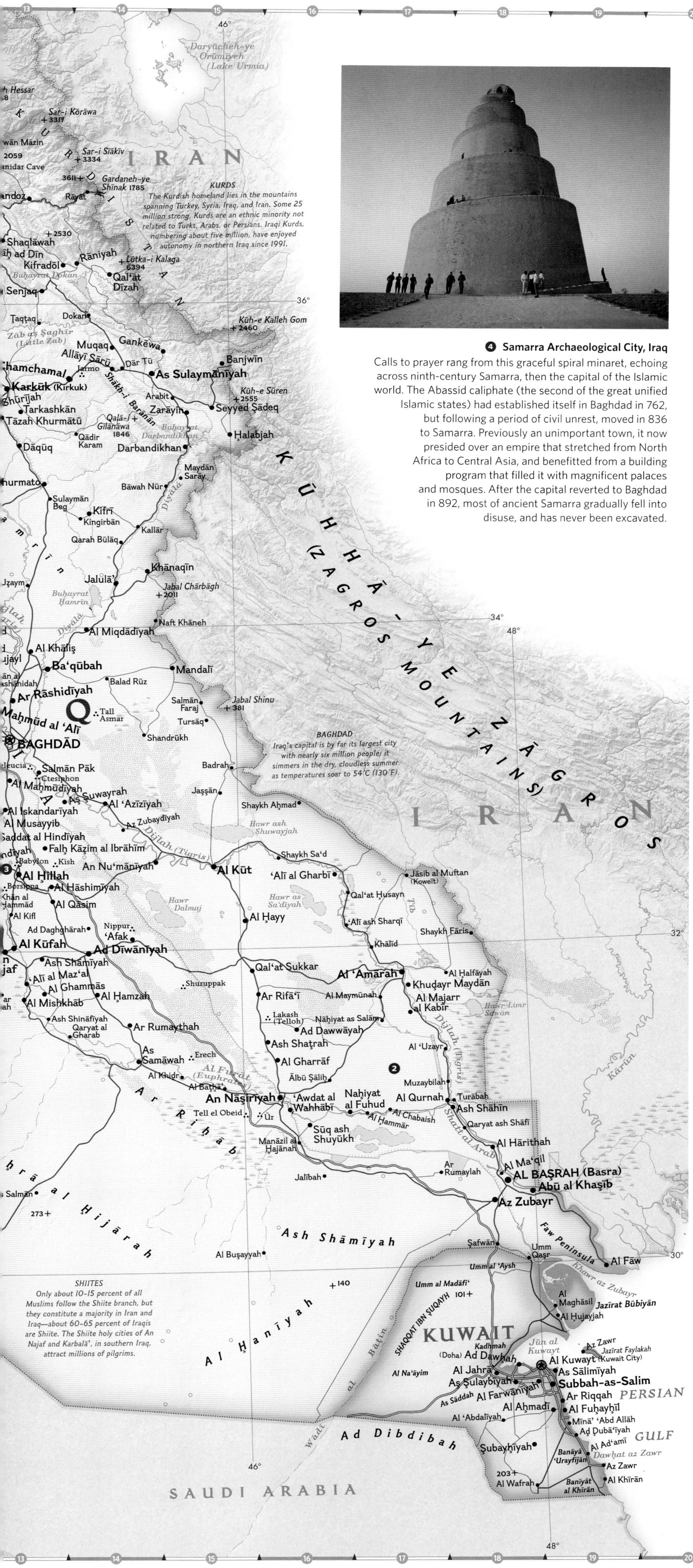

KURDS
The Kurdish homeland lies in the mountains spanning Turkey, Syria, Iraq, and Iran. Some 25 million strong, Kurds are an ethnic minority not related to Turks, Arabs, or Persians. Iraqi Kurds, numbering about five million, have enjoyed autonomy in northern Iraq since 1991.

BAGHDAD
Iraq's capital is by far its largest city with nearly six million people; it simmers in the dry, cloudless summer as temperatures soar to 54°C (130°F).

SHIITES
Only about 10–15 percent of all Muslims follow the Shiite branch, but they constitute a majority in Iran and Iraq—about 60–65 percent of Iraqis are Shiite. The Shiite holy cities of An Najaf and Karbalā', in southern Iraq, attract millions of pilgrims.

4 Samarra Archaeological City, Iraq
Calls to prayer rang from this graceful spiral minaret, echoing across ninth-century Samarra, then the capital of the Islamic world. The Abassid caliphate (the second of the great unified Islamic states) had established itself in Baghdad in 762, but following a period of civil unrest, moved in 836 to Samarra. Previously an unimportant town, it now presided over an empire that stretched from North Africa to Central Asia, and benefitted from a building program that filled it with magnificent palaces and mosques. After the capital reverted to Baghdad in 892, most of ancient Samarra gradually fell into disuse, and has never been excavated.

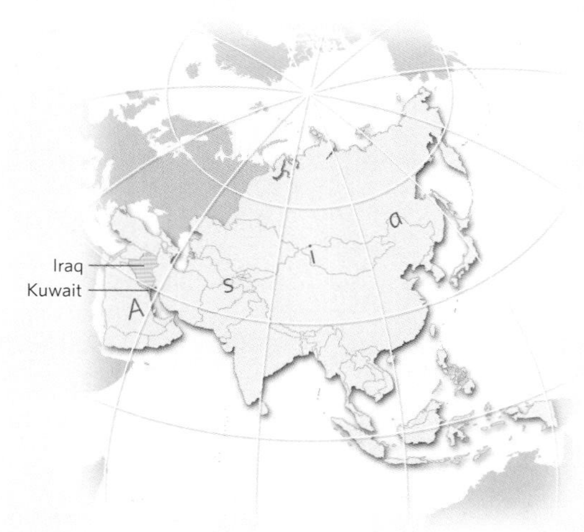
Iraq
Kuwait

Protected Areas and World Heritage Sites

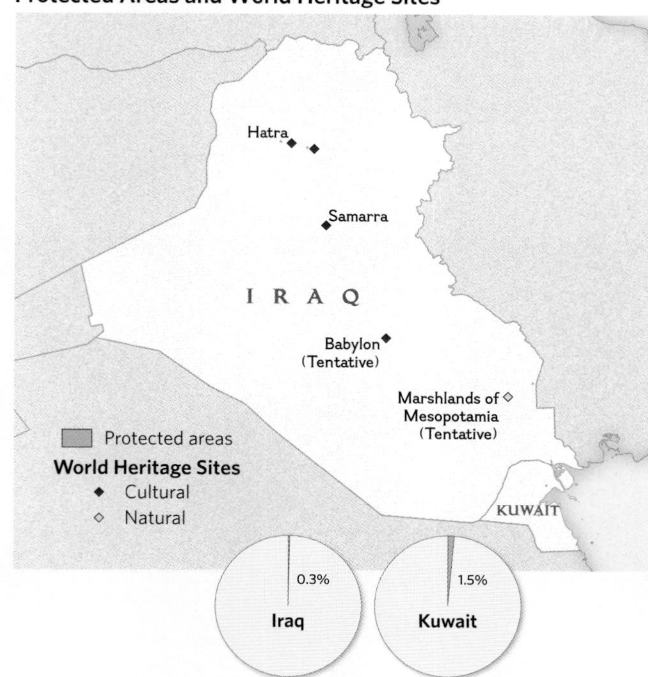
Hatra
Samarra
IRAQ
Babylon (Tentative)
Marshlands of Mesopotamia (Tentative)
KUWAIT
Protected areas
World Heritage Sites
Cultural
Natural
0.3%
Iraq
1.5%
Kuwait
Percent of Land Area Protected

Urbanization and Largest Cities

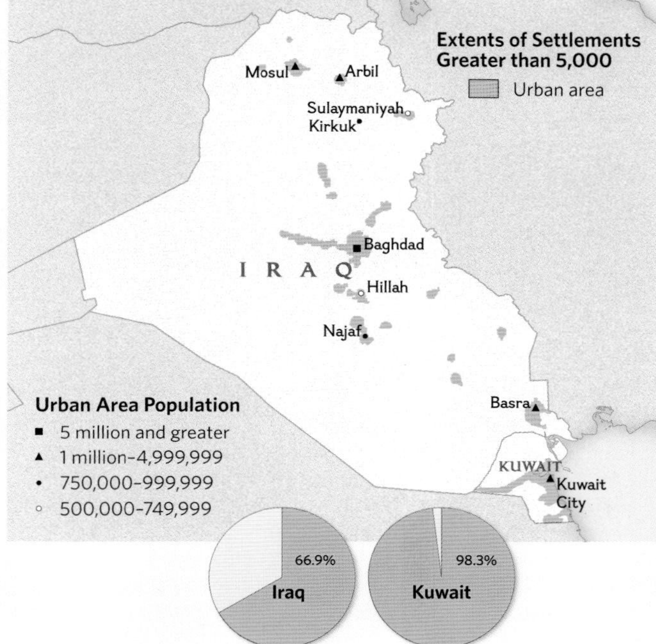
Extents of Settlements Greater than 5,000
Urban area
Mosul
Arbil
Sulaymaniyah
Kirkuk
Baghdad
IRAQ
Hillah
Najaf
Basra
KUWAIT
Kuwait City
Urban Area Population
5 million and greater
1 million–4,999,999
750,000–999,999
500,000–749,999
66.9%
Iraq
98.3%
Kuwait

Percent of Population in Urban Areas

Natural Land Cover

IRAQ
KUWAIT
Land Cover
Desert
Forest
Herbaceous
Highland

Soltaniyeh 1

The early 14th-century Mausoleum of Oljaytu is an important Persian architectural milestone—Iran's earliest example of a double-shelled dome construction similar to that later used to build India's better-known Taj Mahal. The mausoleum is the main extant feature of Soltaniyeh, capital city of the Ilkhanid, a Mongol dynasty descended from Ghengis Khan that ruled Iran in the 13th and 14th centuries. Towering 177 feet high, the dome's exterior is undergoing extensive repairs, but the interior, covered in fine mosaics and murals, is in far better shape.

Meidan Emam, Esfahan 2

The ornate Portico of Qaysariyyeh (above) leads from the Meidan Emam, also called the Royal Square of Esfahan, into the city's bustling Grand Bazaar. The square, surrounded by monumental buildings and the Royal Mosque, was the heart of the 17th-century capital of the Safavid empire. Truly a multipurpose space, it hosted polo matches some days and public executions on others.

Persepolis 3

Built on a giant stone terrace above a plain, Persepolis was both a city and a monument to the power of the Persian (or Achaemenid) Empire. Darius I and his successors met foreign delegations presenting gifts (as depicted on this carved staircase) surrounded by jaw-dropping splendor—until Alexander's army burned it down in 331 B.C. Now partly restored, Persepolis is a proud reminder of past glory for modern Iranians.

AZERBAIJAN REGION

The ancient Azerbaijan region, divided between the countries of Azerbaijan and Iran, holds a mostly Shiite and Turkic-speaking people. The Azeri community in Iran surpasses 17 million—Iran's largest minority.

Longitude East 50° of Greenwich

Albers Conic Equal-Area Projection

SCALE 1:5,500,000

1 CENTIMETER = 55 KILOMETERS; 1 INCH = 87 MILES

0 50 100 150 200 KILOMETERS

0 50 100 150 200 STATUTE MILES

❹ Pasargadae

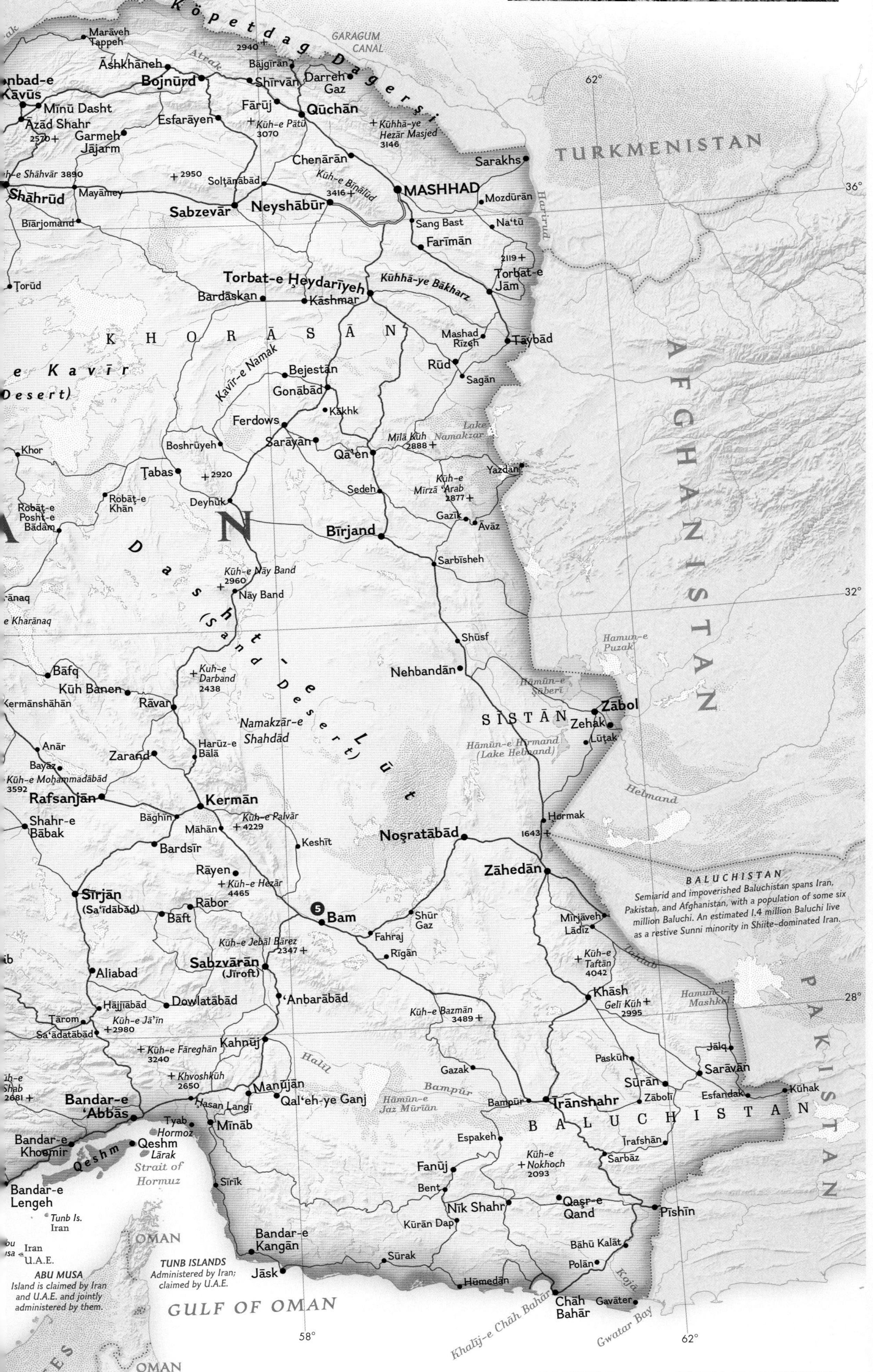

The austere tomb of Cyrus the Great, founder of the Persian Empire around 550 B.C., stands amid the ruins of his capital, Pasargadae. Cyrus freed the Jews from the Babylonian captivity and has often been called a model ruler. His city offers impressive examples of royal Achaemenid art and architecture, as well as of Persian civilization.

BALUCHISTAN
Semiarid and impoverished Baluchistan spans Iran, Pakistan, and Afghanistan, with a population of some six million Baluchi. An estimated 1.4 million Baluchi live as a restive Sunni minority in Shiite-dominated Iran.

TUNB ISLANDS
Administered by Iran; claimed by U.A.E.

ABU MUSA
Island is claimed by Iran and U.A.E. and jointly administered by them.

❺ Bam and Its Cultural Landscape

Built of mud but beautiful nevertheless, the Citadel of Bam (in background) and nearby historic districts crumbled in a 2003 earthquake. Founded in pre-Islamic days, Bam reached its height in the centuries after conversion to Islam. Ingenious buried irrigation canals — qanāts — made the city an oasis; it was famed for textiles and palm groves. Iran is now investing heavily to restore Bam, which has been placed on the List of World Heritage in Danger.

Iran

Protected Areas and World Heritage Sites

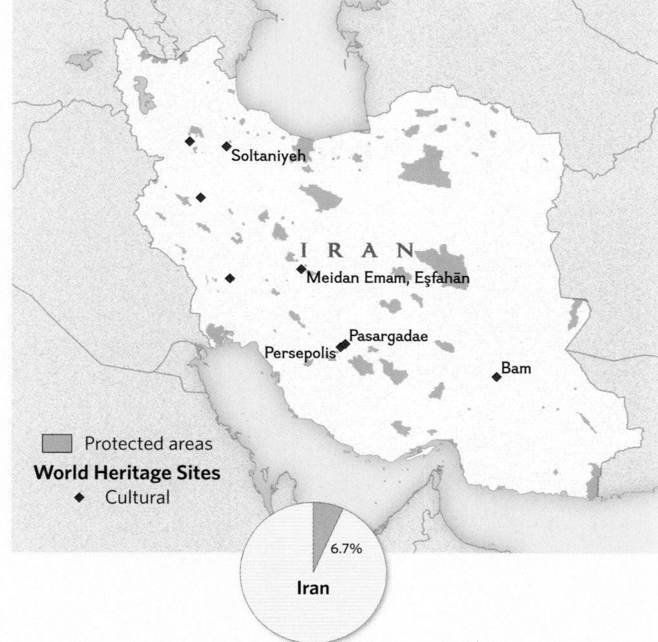
Soltaniyeh
IRAN
Meidan Emam, Eşfahān
Pasargadae
Persepolis
Bam
Protected areas
World Heritage Sites
Cultural
6.7%
Iran

Percent of Land Area Protected

Urbanization and Largest Cities

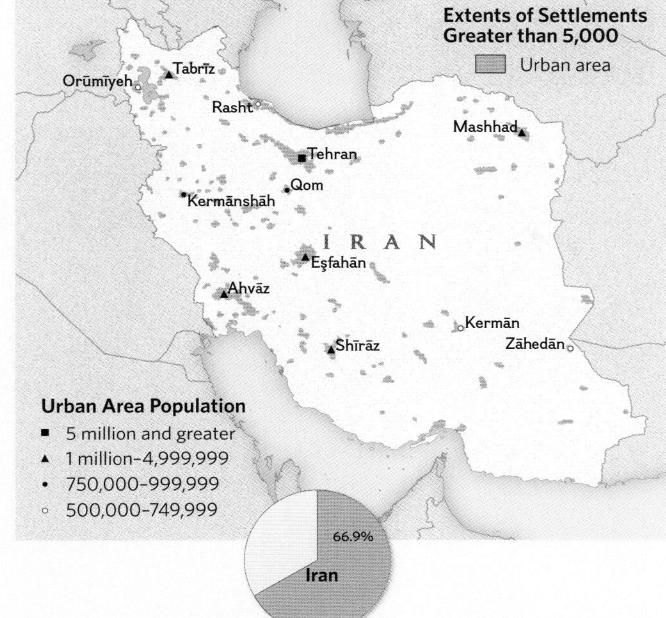
Extents of Settlements Greater than 5,000
Urban area
Orūmīyeh
Tabrīz
Rasht
Mashhad
Tehran
Qom
Kermānshāh
IRAN
Eşfahān
Ahvāz
Kermān
Zāhedān
Shīrāz
Urban Area Population
5 million and greater
1 million–4,999,999
750,000–999,999
500,000–749,999
66.9%
Iran

Percent of Population in Urban Areas

Natural Land Cover

IRAN
Land Cover
Desert
Forest
Glacier
Herbaceous
Highland

Cultural Landscape and Archaeological Remains of the Bamiyan Valley, Afghanistan ❶

Once a major Buddhist monastic center as well as a stop on the Silk Road trade route, Bamiyan Valley witnessed one of the worst cultural crimes of recent decades. In 2001, the Taliban regime, adherents of an extreme version of Islam, destroyed two giant Buddha statues carved into cliff faces some 1,600 years ago. Only hollow sockets now remain overlooking the valley (below). Though the Taliban claimed the fifth-century statues were idols forbidden by Islam, strict Islamic governments around the world joined in a chorus of condemnation. The site has been placed on the List of World Heritage in Danger, and plans are under way to piece together the rubble of the larger Buddha, which stood 174 feet tall. The caves that riddle the valley walls, used in ancient times by the Bamiyan monks, were reinhabited in the 20th century by refugees displaced by decades of war.

Minaret and Archaeological Remains of Jam, Afghanistan ❷

Hidden away in a rocky gorge, a 213-foot-tall minaret was built in the late 12th century in the summer capital of the Ghurid dynasty, which was extinguished a few decades later by the Mongol invasion. The brick minaret, decorated with geometric patterns and turquoise glazing, survives, along with ruins of castles and towers and a medieval Jewish graveyard.

Taxila, Pakistan ❸

Intricately carved plaster Buddhas and Bodhisattvas adorn the sides of a stupa (above), a type of Buddhist shrine, in the Jaulian Monastery, one of several monasteries affiliated with Taxila. The monastery is the best preserved remnant of ancient Taxila, one of the oldest current cities in the Indian subcontinent, with origins in the fourth millennium B.C. Over the course of several hundred years, ending with the destruction of the monasteries by invaders in the fifth century A.D., Taxila was the capital of several ruling dynasties, a major cultural center, and a focal point of higher learning.

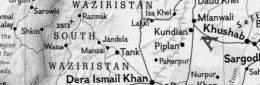

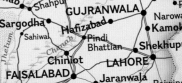

Longitude East 69° of Greenwich
TAJIKISTAN
UZBEKISTAN
TURKMENISTAN
AFGHANISTAN
CHINA
IRAN
KASHMIR
HIMALAYA
LADAKH
HAZARAJAT
KASHMIR
A 1947–49 war partitioned Kashmir between India and Pakistan. This land of snowcapped mountains, alpine forests, and 12 million people remains divided by a militarized border—the Line of Control—that is monitored by UN forces.
KHYBER PASS
A gateway for invasions and trade, this vital land link between Central Asia and the Indian subcontinent twists for 45 kilometers (28 miles) through the arid mountains separating Afghanistan and Pakistan.
WAZIRISTAN
Populated by Pashtun tribes, like the Wazir, the mountainous Pakistani region of Waziristan has become a refuge for Pashtun fighters from Afghanistan—aligned with the Taliban and al Qaeda.
KABOL (Kabul)
PESHAWAR
Islamabad
RAWALPINDI
LAHORE
FAISALABAD
GUJRANWALA
Kandahar
Herat (Hirat)
Mazar-e Sharif
Bamian (Bamiyan)
Jalalabad
Ghazni
Kondoz (Kunduz)
Baghlan
Feyzabad
Mardan
Mingaora
Sialkot
Sargodha
Dera Ismail Khan
Khost (Khowst)
Gardiz
Chitral
Gilgit
Abbottabad
Wah Cantonment
Kohat
Jhelum
Naomid Plain
Khash Desert
Torkestan Mountains
Safed Kuh Mountains
Paropamisus Range
Hindu Kush
Karakoram Range
Salt Range
Line of Control

Afghanistan

Pakistan

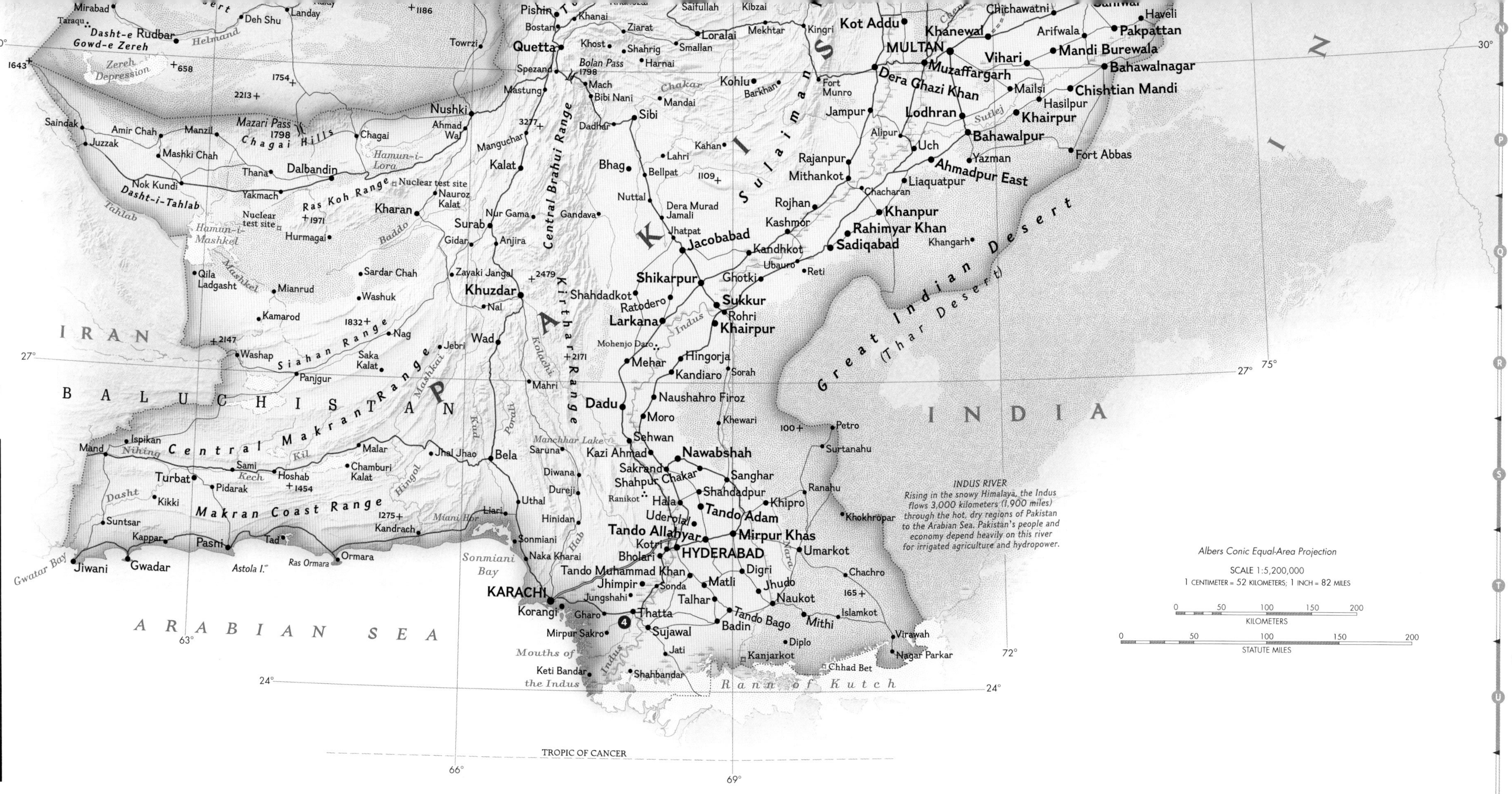

Historical Monuments of Thatta, Pakistan ❹

Redbrick vaults (below) stretch into the distance in the Mosque of Shah Jahan, built in 1647 by the same Mughal ruler who commissioned the Taj Mahal. The mosque's tilework is said to be the most elaborate on the Indian subcontinent. The city of Thatta—the capital of successive dynasties that ruled the Sindh region of Pakistan—is the site of a number of important mausoleums as well as half a million other burial sites, making it the world's largest Muslim necropolis.

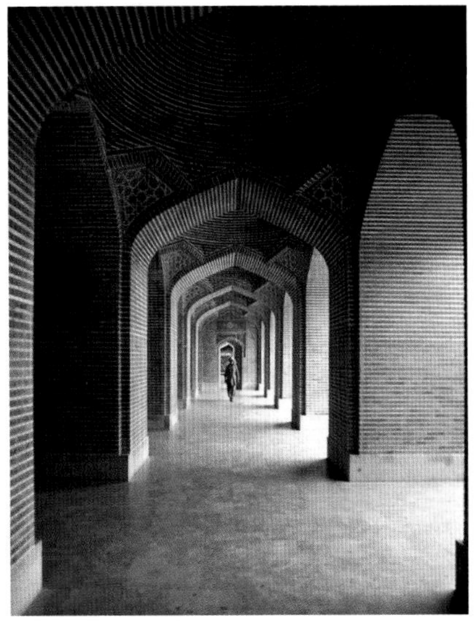

INDUS RIVER
Rising in the snowy Himalaya, the Indus flows 3,000 kilometers (1,900 miles) through the hot, dry regions of Pakistan to the Arabian Sea. Pakistan's people and economy depend heavily on this river for irrigated agriculture and hydropower.

Albers Conic Equal-Area Projection
SCALE 1:5,200,000
1 CENTIMETER = 52 KILOMETERS; 1 INCH = 82 MILES
0 50 100 150 200 KILOMETERS
0 50 100 150 200 STATUTE MILES

Protected Areas and World Heritage Sites

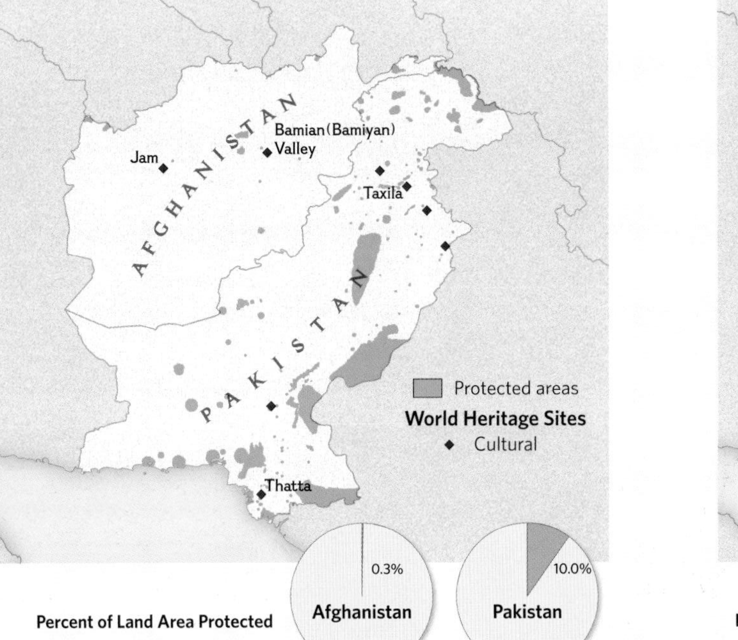
AFGHANISTAN
PAKISTAN
Jam
Bamian (Bamiyan) Valley
Taxila
Thatta
Protected areas
World Heritage Sites
Cultural
Percent of Land Area Protected
Afghanistan 0.3%
Pakistan 10.0%

Urbanization and Largest Cities

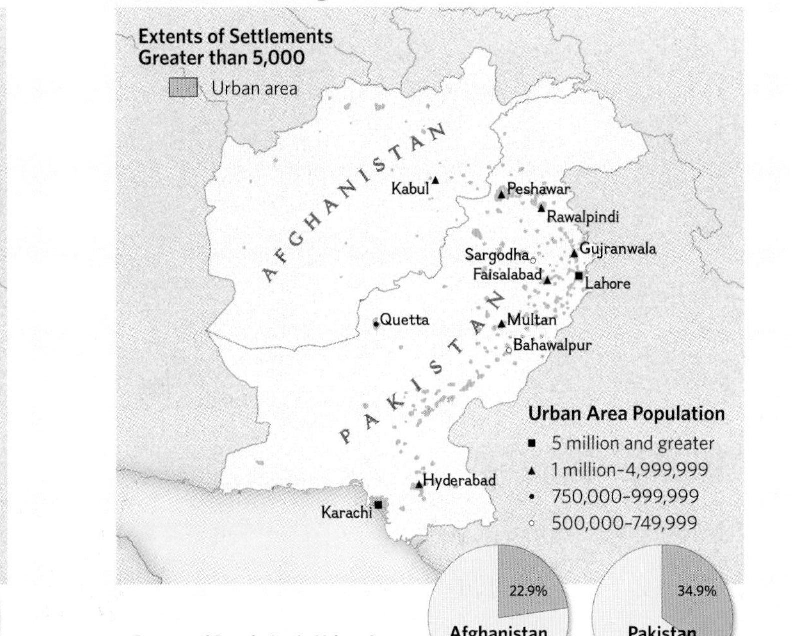
Extents of Settlements Greater than 5,000
Urban area
AFGHANISTAN
PAKISTAN
Kabul
Peshawar
Rawalpindi
Gujranwala
Sargodha
Faisalabad
Lahore
Quetta
Multan
Bahawalpur
Hyderabad
Karachi
Urban Area Population
5 million and greater
1 million–4,999,999
750,000–999,999
500,000–749,999
Percent of Population in Urban Areas
Afghanistan 22.9%
Pakistan 34.9%

Natural Land Cover

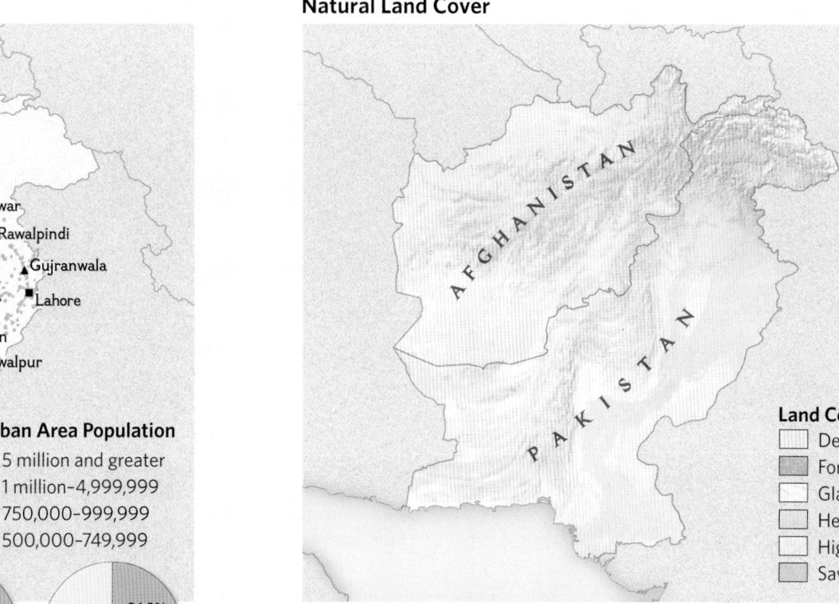
AFGHANISTAN
PAKISTAN
Land Cover
Desert
Forest
Glacier
Herbaceous
Highland
Savanna

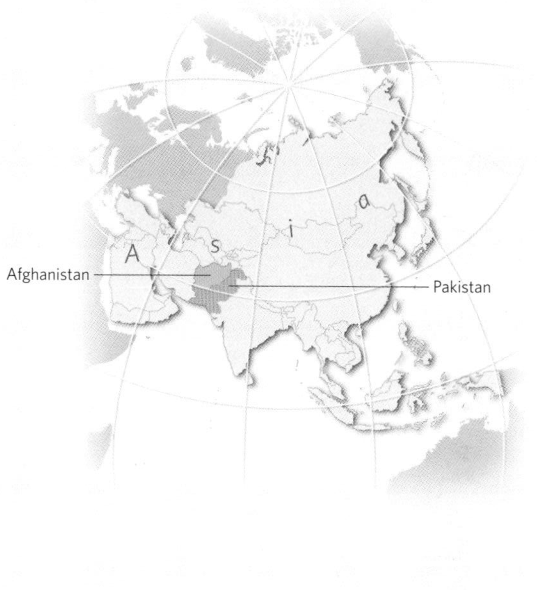

Afghanistan
Pakistan

Mausoleum of Khoja Ahmed Yasawi, Kazakhstan ❶
The emperor Timur, known in the West as the fearsome Tamerlane, commissioned this gorgeously ornamented mausoleum to honor a teacher of Sufism who was key in spreading the mystical strain of Islam in Central Asia. Although left unfinished after Timur's death in 1405, the mausoleum, with its two turquoise blue domes, had served its purpose as a sort of sketchpad for testing new building materials and techniques. What was learned in the building of this structure would be put to use in the construction of the Timurid empire's new capital in Samarkand, in present-day Uzbekistan.

ARAL SEA
Once the world's fourth largest lake, the Aral Sea today is less than half its 1960 extent. Soviet-era irrigation canals divert river water—causing the sea to shrink and changing the former lake bed into desert. A UN study predicts the Aral Sea could disappear by 2016.

BAYKONUR COSMODROME
Russian-administered

Samarkand—Crossroads of Cultures, Uzbekistan ❷
A modern monument (below) recalls Samarkand's key spot on the ancient caravan route linking East Asia with India, Persia, and the Mediterranean world. The city, nicknamed the "heart of the Silk Road," has been a cultural, religious, and economic bastion of Central Asia for more than 2,000 years. Over the course of history, the city fell under the domain of scores of rulers, but it reached its height starting in the 14th century, when Timur—known for his conquests and the resulting massacres—based the Timurid empire here. The treasures of Samarkand include the Bibi Khanum Mosque, built in honor of Timur's wife; the Shakhi-Zinda ensemble, a collection of mosques, tombs, and madrassas constructed between the 11th and 19th centuries; and the Registan, the civic and religious center of the ancient city.

Itchan Kala, Uzbekistan ❸
Powerful crenellated walls surround Itchan Kala, the inner town of the oasis of Khiwa. The old town preserves scores of historic monuments—mosques, mausoleums, and madrassas—in an exotic setting that's said to be reminiscent of *One Thousand and One Nights.* Many structures in the current walled town were built in the 17th and 18th centuries (though the foundations are more than a thousand years old), and Itchan Kala seems to have been practically frozen in time since then, giving visitors a glimpse of Central Asia at the beginning of the 19th century.

Kazakhstan Kyrgyzstan Tajikistan Turkmenistan Uzbekistan

Lambert Conformal Conic Projection

SCALE 1:8,875,000
1 CENTIMETER = 89 KILOMETERS; 1 INCH = 140 MILES

0 100 200 300 KILOMETERS

0 100 200 300 STATUTE MILES

Turkmenistan
Uzbekistan
Kazakhstan
Kyrgyzstan
Tajikistan

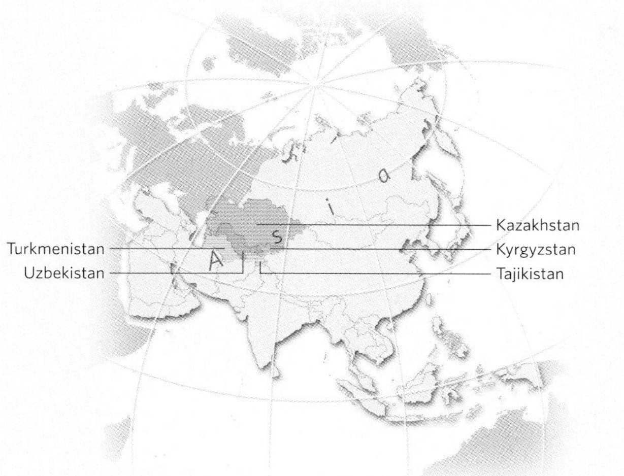

Protected Areas and World Heritage Sites

Protected areas
World Heritage Sites
Cultural
KAZAKHSTAN
Mausoleum of Khoja Ahmed Yasawi
UZBEKISTAN
KYRGYZSTAN
Itchan Kala
Buxoro (Bukhara)
Samarqand (Samarkand)
TURKMENISTAN
TAJIKISTAN
Parthian fortresses of Nisa
2.8% Kazakhstan
24.3% Kyrgyzstan
14.3% Tajikistan
2.5% Turkmenistan
2.1% Uzbekistan
Percent of Land Area Protected

Urbanization and Largest Cities

Urban Area Population
5 million and greater
1 million–4,999,999
750,000–999,999
500,000–749,999
Extents of Settlements Greater than 5,000
Urban area
KAZAKHSTAN
Almaty
Bishkek
Namangan
KYRGYZSTAN
Tashkent
Andijon
Farg'ona
UZBEKISTAN
TURKMENISTAN
Samarqand
TAJIKISTAN
Ashgabat
Dushanbe
57.3% Kazakhstan
35.8% Kyrgyzstan
24.7% Tajikistan
46.2% Turkmenistan
36.7% Uzbekistan
Percent of Population in Urban Areas

Historic Center of Bukhara, Uzbekistan 5

Bukhara first appears in history in 500 B.C. as part of Darius the Great's Achaemenid Empire, but likely it had been an inhabited oasis thousands of years earlier. Today, after passing through the hands of various Persian and Arab dynasties, this important cultural and religious center is considered the most complete example of a medieval Central Asian city. The city's architectural jewel is the tenth-century mausoleum of Ismail Samani, as well as madrassas (below) and mosques unchanged over several centuries.

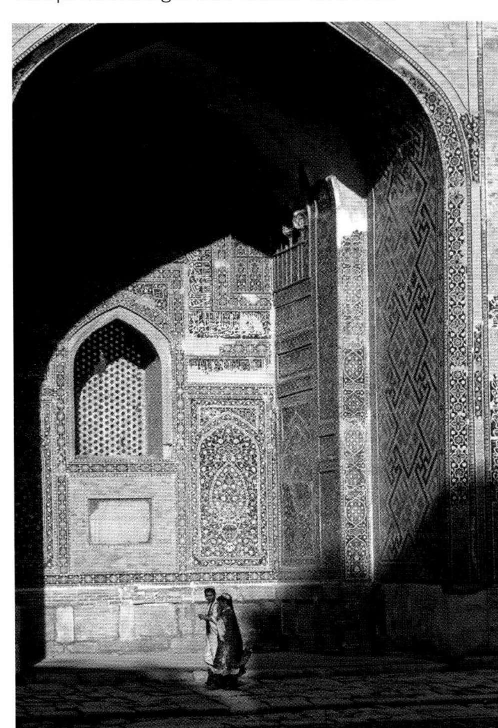

4 Parthian Fortresses of Nisa, Turkmenistan

Two partially excavated mounds are all that remain of a city that may have been the first capital of the Parthian empire, which controlled much of central Asia from the third century B.C. to the third century A.D. Despite Parthia's size and power, little is known about this Iranian civilization compared to those before and after it. The long-buried halls and palaces of Nisa may provide some clues.

Natural Land Cover

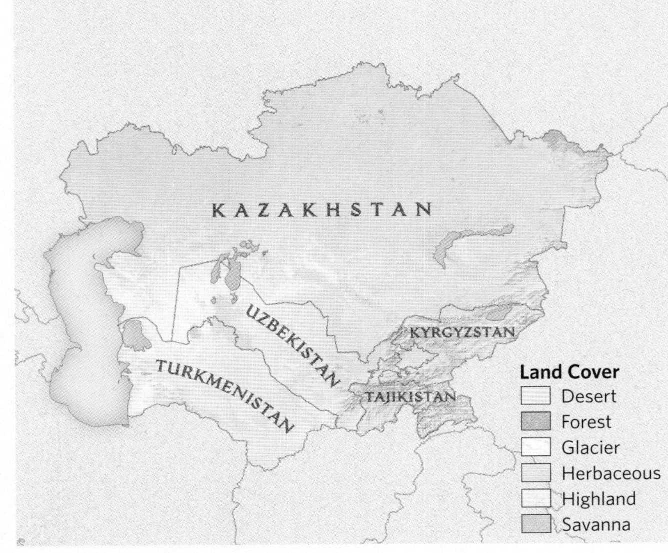
KAZAKHSTAN
UZBEKISTAN
KYRGYZSTAN
TURKMENISTAN
TAJIKISTAN
Land Cover
Desert
Forest
Glacier
Herbaceous
Highland
Savanna

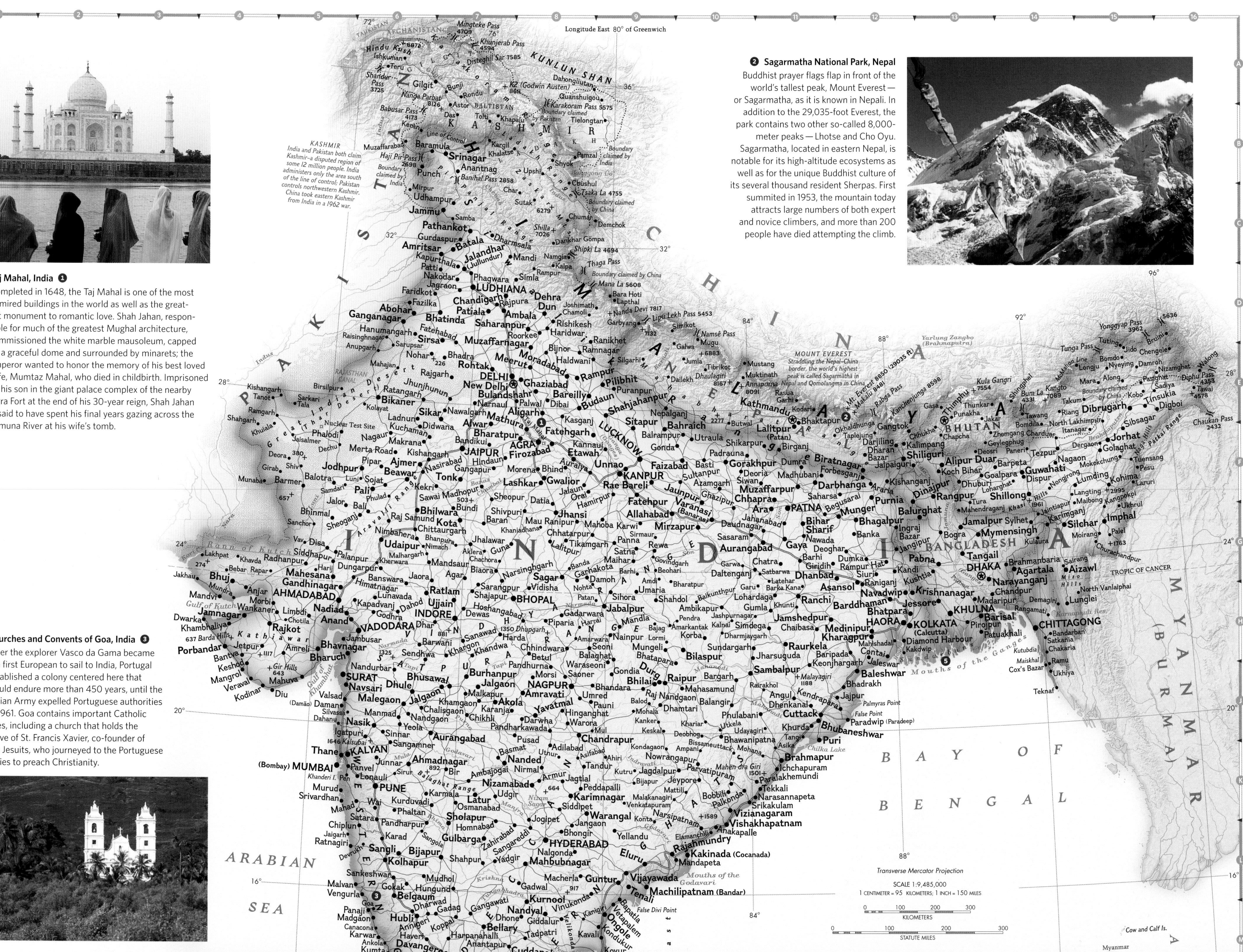
Longitude East 80° of Greenwich
KUNLUN SHAN
KASHMIR
KASHMIR India and Pakistan both claim Kashmir–a disputed region of some 12 million people. India administers only the area south of the line of control; Pakistan controls northwestern Kashmir. China took eastern Kashmir from India in a 1962 war.
PAKISTAN
CHINA
NEPAL
BHUTAN
INDIA
BANGLADESH
MYANMAR (BURMA)
MOUNT EVEREST Straddling the Nepal-China border, the world's highest peak is called Sagarmatha in Nepal and Qomolangma in China.
Mt. Everest 8850 (29035 ft)
ARABIAN SEA
BAY OF BENGAL
TROPIC OF CANCER
Thar Desert
Mouths of the Ganges
Mouths of the Godavari
Gulf of Kutch
Gulf of Khambhat
Rann of Kutch
DELHI
New Delhi
KOLKATA (Calcutta)
(Bombay) MUMBAI
HYDERABAD
DHAKA
Transverse Mercator Projection
SCALE 1:9,485,000
1 CENTIMETER = 95 KILOMETERS; 1 INCH = 150 MILES
KILOMETERS
STATUTE MILES

Taj Mahal, India ❶

Completed in 1648, the Taj Mahal is one of the most admired buildings in the world as well as the greatest monument to romantic love. Shah Jahan, responsible for much of the greatest Mughal architecture, commissioned the white marble mausoleum, capped by a graceful dome and surrounded by minarets; the emperor wanted to honor the memory of his best loved wife, Mumtaz Mahal, who died in childbirth. Imprisoned by his son in the giant palace complex of the nearby Agra Fort at the end of his 30-year reign, Shah Jahan is said to have spent his final years gazing across the Yamuna River at his wife's tomb.

Churches and Convents of Goa, India ❸

After the explorer Vasco da Gama became the first European to sail to India, Portugal established a colony centered here that would endure more than 450 years, until the Indian Army expelled Portuguese authorities in 1961. Goa contains important Catholic sites, including a church that holds the grave of St. Francis Xavier, co-founder of the Jesuits, who journeyed to the Portuguese Indies to preach Christianity.

❷ **Sagarmatha National Park, Nepal**

Buddhist prayer flags flap in front of the world's tallest peak, Mount Everest—or Sagarmatha, as it is known in Nepali. In addition to the 29,035-foot Everest, the park contains two other so-called 8,000-meter peaks—Lhotse and Cho Oyu. Sagarmatha, located in eastern Nepal, is notable for its high-altitude ecosystems as well as for the unique Buddhist culture of its several thousand resident Sherpas. First summited in 1953, the mountain today attracts large numbers of both expert and novice climbers, and more than 200 people have died attempting the climb.

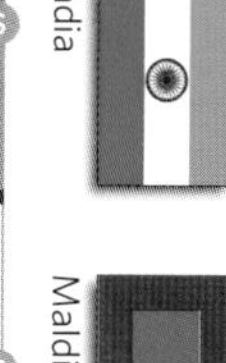

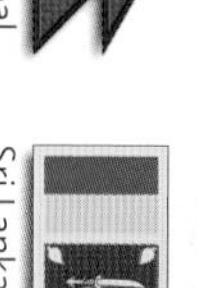

Bangladesh Bhutan India Maldives Nepal Sri Lanka

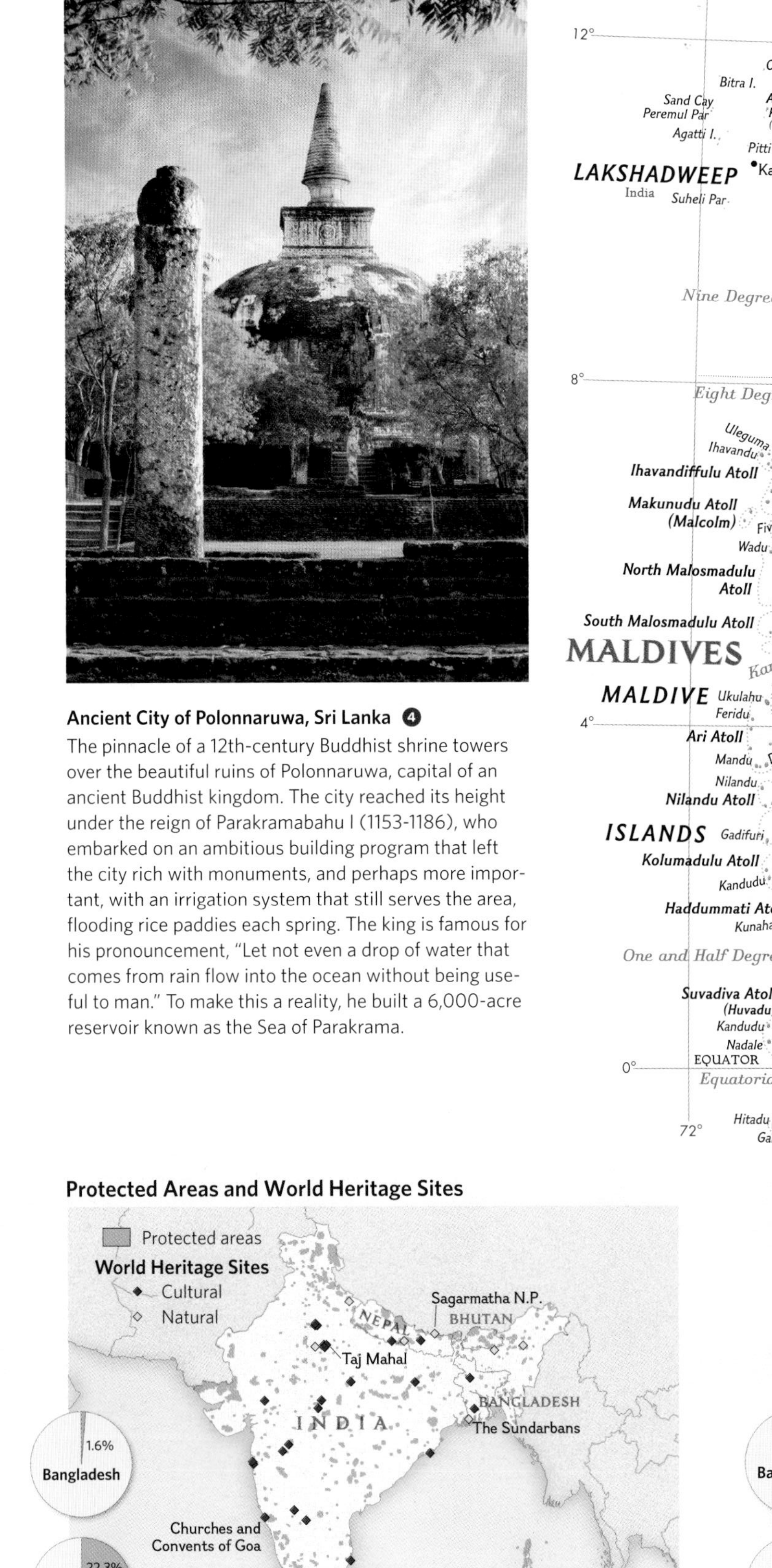

Ancient City of Polonnaruwa, Sri Lanka 4

The pinnacle of a 12th-century Buddhist shrine towers over the beautiful ruins of Polonnaruwa, capital of an ancient Buddhist kingdom. The city reached its height under the reign of Parakramabahu I (1153-1186), who embarked on an ambitious building program that left the city rich with monuments, and perhaps more important, with an irrigation system that still serves the area, flooding rice paddies each spring. The king is famous for his pronouncement, "Let not even a drop of water that comes from rain flow into the ocean without being useful to man." To make this a reality, he built a 6,000-acre reservoir known as the Sea of Parakrama.

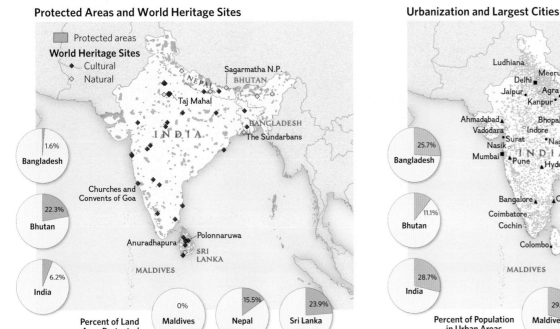

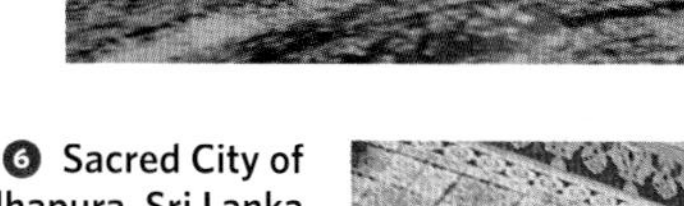

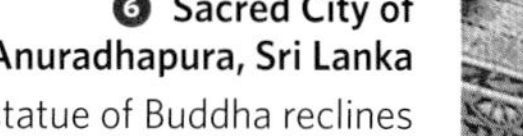

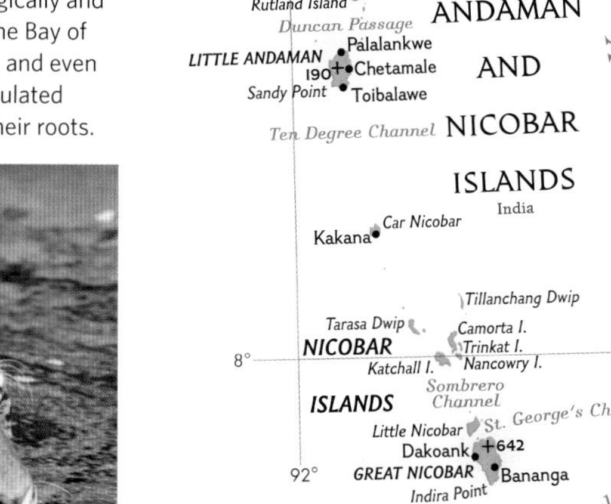
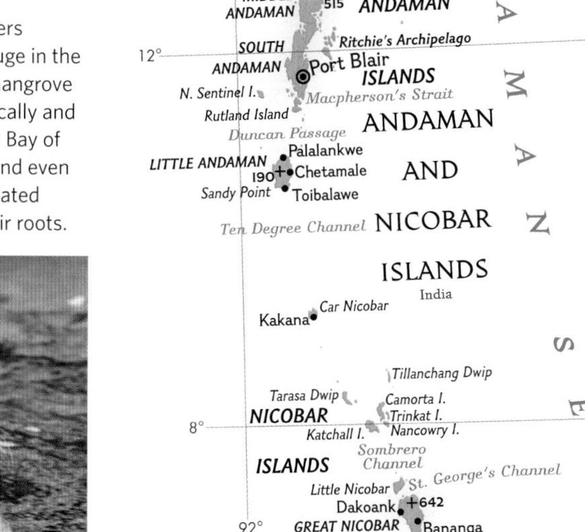
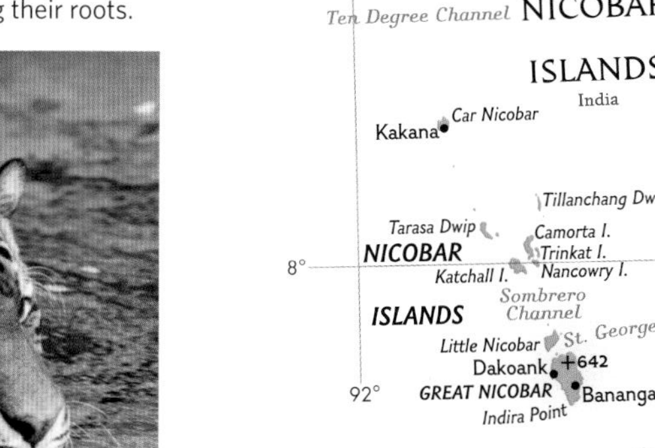

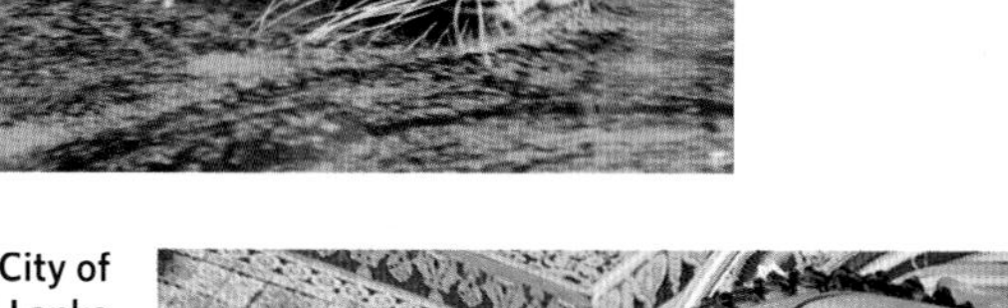

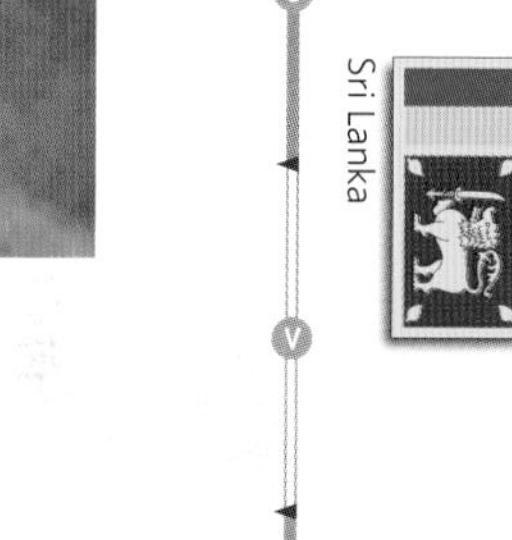

BANGALORE
CHENNAI (Madras)
Mangalore
Mysore
Kozhikode (Calicut)
Coimbatore
Tiruppur
Kumbakonam
Thanjavur (Tanjore)
Tiruchchirappalli
Ernakulam
(Cochin) Kochi
(Alleppey) Alappuzha
(Quilon) Kollam
Madurai
Tuticorin
Tirunelveli
Thiruvananthapuram (Trivandrum)
Nagercoil
Cape Comorin
Puducherry (Pondicherry)
Cuddalore
Jaffna
Point Pedro
Palk Strait
Palk Bay
Gulf of Mannar
Trincomalee
Anuradhapura
Kandy
Colombo
Adam's Peak 2243
Galle
Matara
SRI LANKA (CEYLON)
LAKSHADWEEP
India
Kavaratti
Nine Degree Channel
Minicoy Island
India
Eight Degree Channel
MALDIVES
MALDIVE ISLANDS
Maale (Male)
One and Half Degree Channel
Equatorial Channel
EQUATOR
Addu Atoll
LACCADIVE SEA
INDIAN OCEAN
ANDAMAN SEA
ANDAMAN AND NICOBAR ISLANDS
India
Port Blair
Ten Degree Channel
Car Nicobar
GREAT NICOBAR
Indira Point
Great Channel
INDONESIA

The Sundarbans, Bangladesh 5

A Bengal tiger, one of less than 2,500 tigers surviving in the wild worldwide, finds refuge in the lush Sundarbans, a 4,000-square-mile mangrove forest wetland that's crucial both ecologically and economically to Bangladesh. Fronting the Bay of Bengal, the mangroves prevent erosion, and even help build new land for the densely populated country by catching sediment among their roots.

6 Sacred City of Anuradhapura, Sri Lanka

A statue of Buddha reclines in Anuradhapura, an ancient capital of Sri Lanka. Founded in the fourth century B.C., the city later developed around a tree reputedly grown from a cutting taken from the tree under which the Buddha attained enlightenment. Abandoned in favor of Polonnaruwa after an invasion in the late tenth century A.D., many of the city's religious monuments were lost for centuries to the jungle.

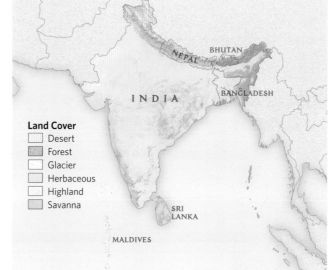

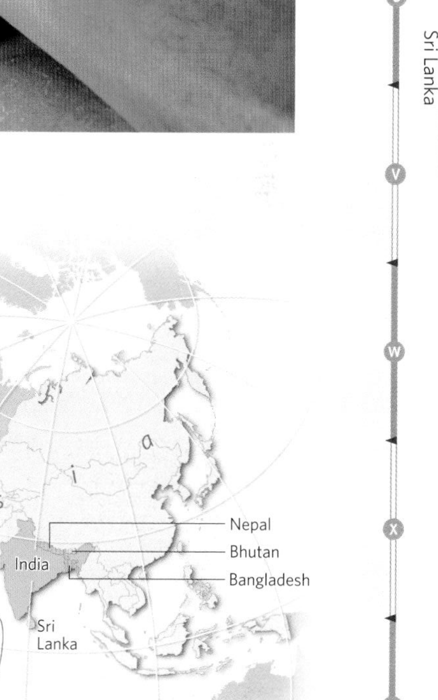
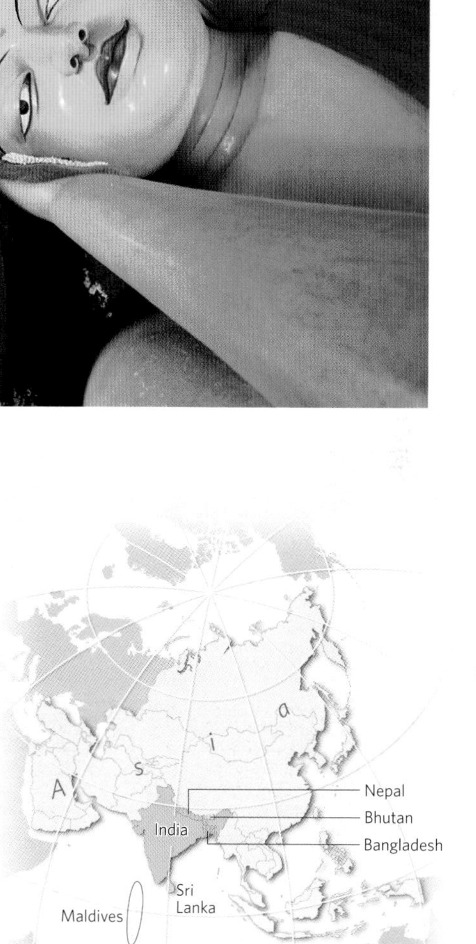

Protected Areas and World Heritage Sites

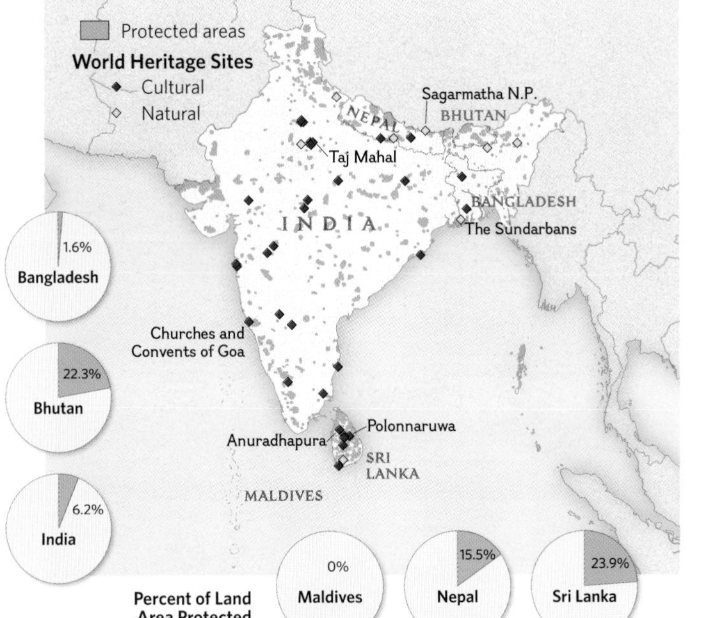

Protected areas
World Heritage Sites
Cultural
Natural
Sagarmatha N.P.
NEPAL
BHUTAN
Taj Mahal
INDIA
BANGLADESH
The Sundarbans
Churches and Convents of Goa
Anuradhapura
Polonnaruwa
SRI LANKA
MALDIVES
1.6% Bangladesh
22.3% Bhutan
6.2% India
0% Maldives
15.5% Nepal
23.9% Sri Lanka
Percent of Land Area Protected

Urbanization and Largest Cities

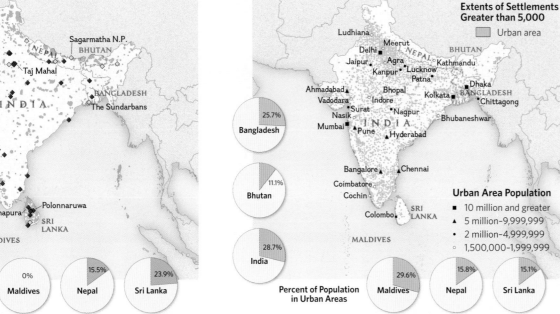

Extents of Settlements Greater than 5,000
Urban area
Ludhiana
Meerut
Delhi
Agra
Jaipur
Kanpur
Lucknow
Kathmandu
Patna
NEPAL
BHUTAN
Dhaka
BANGLADESH
Chittagong
Ahmadabad
Vadodara
Bhopal
Indore
Kolkata
Surat
Nagpur
Nasik
Mumbai
Pune
Hyderabad
Bhubaneshwar
INDIA
Bangalore
Chennai
Coimbatore
Cochin
Colombo
SRI LANKA
MALDIVES
Urban Area Population
10 million and greater
5 million–9,999,999
2 million–4,999,999
1,500,000–1,999,999
25.7% Bangladesh
11.1% Bhutan
28.7% India
29.6% Maldives
15.8% Nepal
15.1% Sri Lanka
Percent of Population in Urban Areas

Natural Land Cover

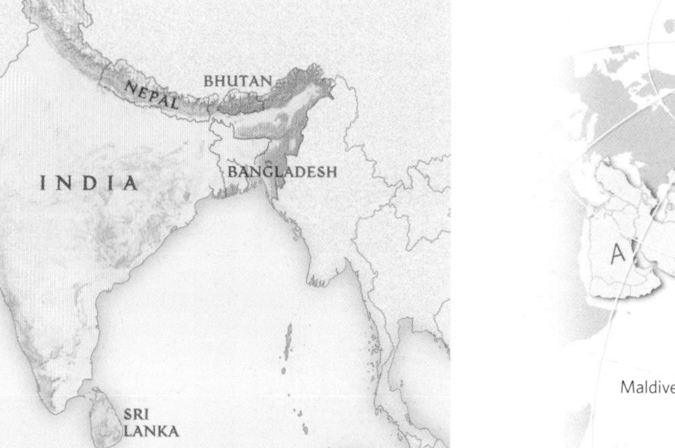

NEPAL
BHUTAN
BANGLADESH
INDIA
SRI LANKA
MALDIVES
Land Cover
Desert
Forest
Glacier
Herbaceous
Highland
Savanna
ASIA
India
Nepal
Bhutan
Bangladesh
Sri Lanka
Maldives

Mausoleum of the First Qin Emperor, China ❶
One of the world's most amazing archaeological sites, the necropolis built for the first ruler to unify China, Qin Shi Huang, contains the so-called Terra-cotta Army. Thousands of individually crafted terra-cotta warriors—and their associated horses, chariots, and weapons—were buried prior to the emperor's death in 210 B.C. to provide Qin with a powerful military in the afterlife.

Orkhon Valley Cultural Landscape, Mongolia ❷
Horses graze near the camp of Mongolian nomads in the Orkhon Valley, a pastureland in central Mongolia that was the heartland of the medieval Mongol Empire. The site covers several hundred square miles and includes the ruins of Kharkhorum, Ghengis Khan's capital, as well as the remnants of the older Uighur capital of Khar Balgas, and several 16th- and 17th-century Buddhist monasteries.

KAZAKHSTAN
KYRGYZSTAN
TAJIKISTAN
PAKISTAN
NEPAL
BHUTAN
BANGLADESH
INDIA
MYANMAR (BURMA)
LAOS
ALTAY MOUNTAINS
TIAN SHAN
TARIM PENDI
Taklimakan Shamo
KUNLUN SHAN
ALTUN SHAN
QING ZANG GAOYUAN (PLATEAU OF TIBET)
Tanggula Shan
Gangdisê Shan
HIMALAYA
SINKIANG
TIBET
Junggar Pendi (Dzungarian Basin)
Qaidam Pendi
Qilian Shan
ÜRÜMQI
Kashi (Kashgar)
Hotan
Aksu
Korla
Turpan
Hami (Kumul)
Golmud
Lhasa
Xigazê
Mount Everest (Qomolangma, Sagarmatha) +8850 (29,035 ft)
LANZHOU
Xining
CHENGDU
KUNMING
Dali
Lijiang
Leshan
Ulaangom
Hovd
Uliastay
Altay
Jiayuguan
Dunhuang
TROPIC OF CANCER

Albers Conic Equal-Area Projection
SCALE 1:14,000,000
1 CENTIMETER = 140 KILOMETERS; 1 INCH = 225 MILES
0 200 400 600 KILOMETERS
0 200 400 600 STATUTE MILES

Historic Ensemble of the Potala Palace, Lhasa, China ❸
A visual icon of Tibetan Buddhism, the Potala Palace was the primary residence of the Dalai Lama from the 17th century until 1959, when the Tibetan government went into exile following a failed uprising against China. Today, the hilltop complex, including the Red Palace, the White Palace, and the Namgyel Dratshang—the private monastery of the Dalai Lama—is a museum of Tibetan history and culture overseen by China. Housed within is a huge collection of Buddhist art and religious relics.

Mount Emei Scenic Area, Including Leshan Giant Buddha ❹ Scenic Area, China
The face of the tallest—233 feet—Buddha in the world (right) overlooks the confluence of three rivers near Mount Emei, long one of the holiest Buddhist sites. The first Buddhist temple in China was built in this part of western Sichuan Province in the first century A.D. It was followed by a succession of other important monuments, culminating in the construction of the huge Leshan Giant Buddha, carved out of a cliff in the eighth century.

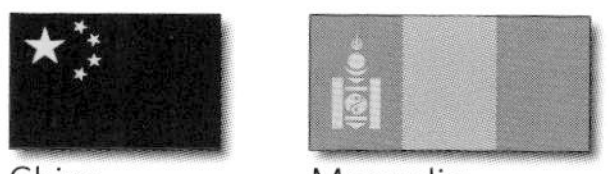

TAIWAN
The People's Republic of China claims Taiwan as its 23rd province. Taiwan's government (Republic of China) maintains that there are two political entities.

Mongolia
China
Asia

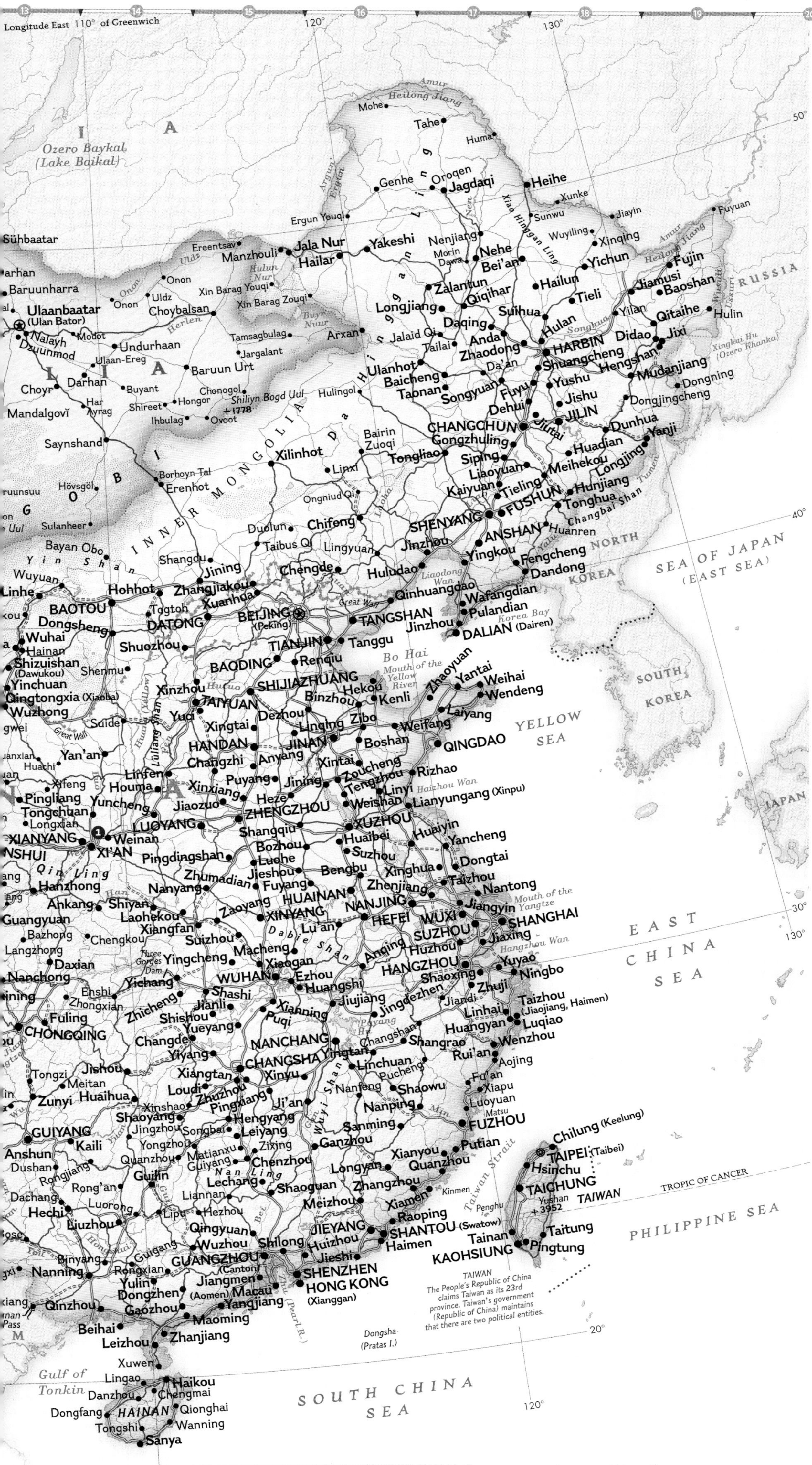

Protected Areas and World Heritage Sites

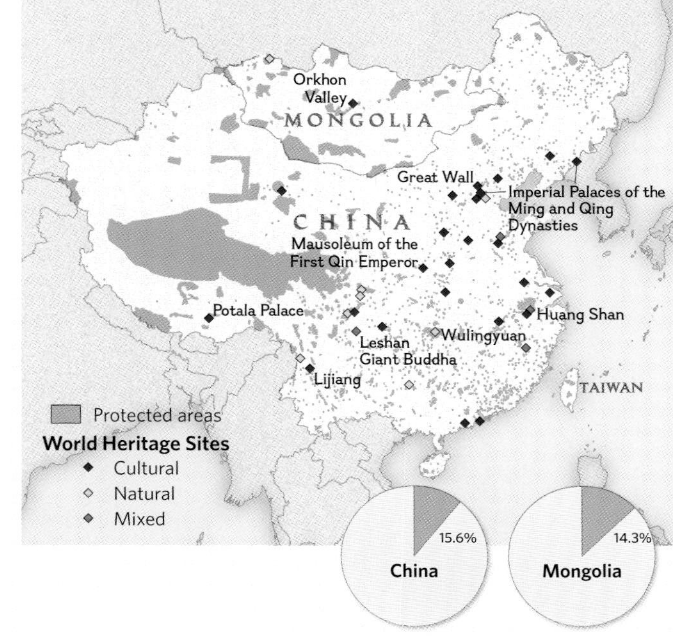
Orkhon Valley
MONGOLIA
Great Wall
Imperial Palaces of the Ming and Qing Dynasties
CHINA
Mausoleum of the First Qin Emperor
Potala Palace
Huang Shan
Leshan Giant Buddha
Wulingyuan
Lijiang
TAIWAN
Protected areas
World Heritage Sites
Cultural
Natural
Mixed
15.6%
China
14.3%
Mongolia

Percent of Land Area Protected

Urbanization and Largest Cities

Extents of Settlements Greater than 5,000
Urban area
MONGOLIA
Ürümqi
Harbin
Changchun
Jilin
Shenyang
Anshan
Dalian
Tangshan
Beijing
Tianjin
Shijiazhuang
Taiyuan
Jinan
Zibo
Qingdao
Lanzhou
Luoyang
Zhengzhou
Xi'an
Nanjing
CHINA
Xinyang
Wuxi
Shanghai
Chengdu
Wuhan
Hangzhou
Chongqing
Changsha
Nanchang
Guiyang
Fuzhou
Taipei
Kunming
Taichung
Shantou
TAIWAN
Guangzhou
Kaohsiung
Nanning
Hong Kong
Zhanjiang
Urban Area Population
10 million and greater
5 million–9,999,999
2 million–4,999,999
1,500,000–1,999,999
40.4%
China
56.7%
Mongolia

Percent of Population in Urban Areas

Natural Land Cover

MONGOLIA
CHINA
TAIWAN
Land Cover
Desert
Forest
Glacier
Herbaceous
Highland

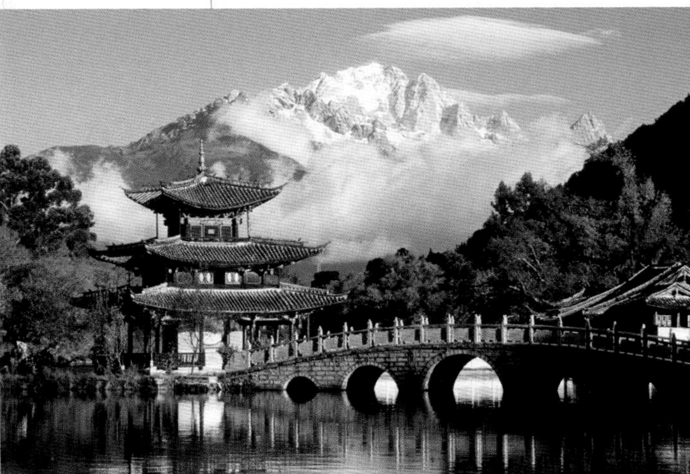

Old Town of Lijiang, China 5

One of the foremost destinations for domestic Chinese tourism, beautiful Lijiang is the main city of the minority Naxi people, a matrilineal culture that speaks a Sino-Tibetan language. The old town, a cultural and economic center in China's southern Yunnan Province for hundreds of years, may also be the best preserved medieval urban core in the country. The complex system of canals that cuts through the city has effectively delivered water to residents for centuries, and lends a picturesque atmosphere to the city, enhanced by the hundreds of bridges of various styles that cross the canals.

SEA OF JAPAN
(EAST SEA)
NORTH KOREA
SOUTH KOREA
KOREA BAY
BO HAI
YELLOW SEA
EAST CHINA SEA
KOREA STRAIT
TSUSHIMA STRAIT
Albers Equal-Area Projection
SCALE 1:6,000,000
1 CENTIMETER = 60 KILOMETERS; 1 INCH = 94 MILES
KILOMETERS
STATUTE MILES
MONGOLIA
NEI MONGOL GAOYUAN
NEI MONGOL
HEBEI
SHANXI
SHAANXI
HENAN
SHANDONG
JIANGSU
ANHUI
HUBEI
ZHEJIANG
SICHUAN
CHONGQING
NINGXIA HUIZU
BEIJING
TIANJIN
SHANGHAI
SHENYANG
NANJING
WUHAN
ZHENGZHOU
XI'AN
HEFEI
HANGZHOU
NANCHANG
TAIYUAN
SHIJIAZHUANG
JINAN
HOHHOT
YINCHUAN
THREE GORGES DAM
China is due to complete the largest hydroelectric dam on Earth by 2009

China

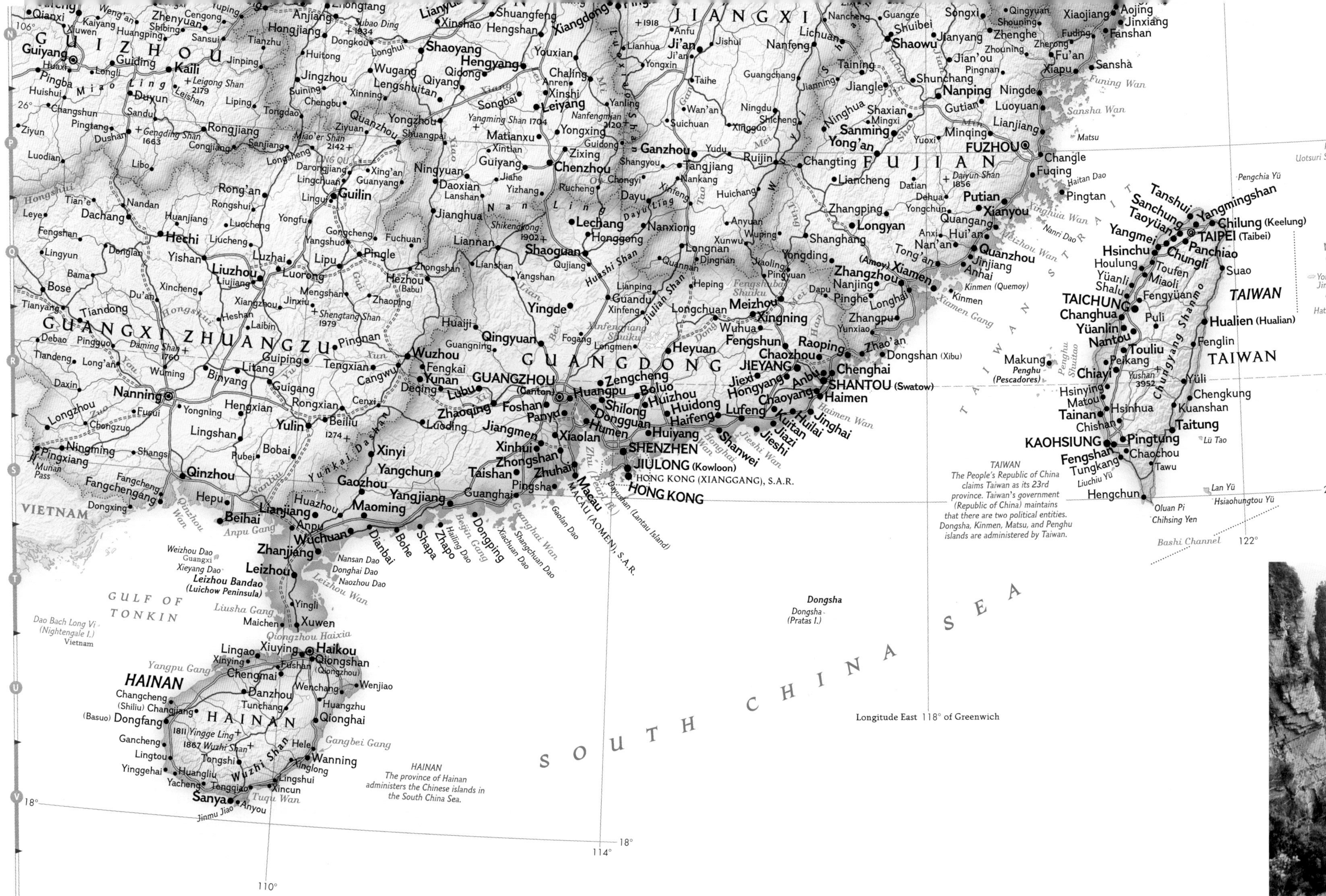

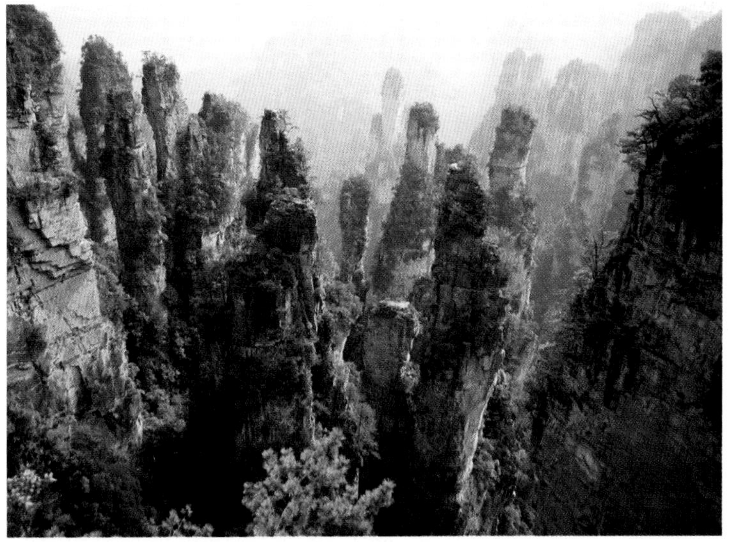

TAIWAN
The People's Republic of China claims Taiwan as its 23rd province. Taiwan's government (Republic of China) maintains that there are two political entities. Dongsha, Kinmen, Matsu, and Penghu islands are administered by Taiwan.

HAINAN
The province of Hainan administers the Chinese islands in the South China Sea.

Senkaku Shotō (Diaoyu Qundao) Administered by Japan Claimed by China

Longitude East 118° of Greenwich

Wulingyuan Scenic and Historic Interest Area ❸
More than 3,000 towering sandstone pillars create a fantastic landscape—one that is cut by gorges and punctuated by waterfalls and two huge natural bridges. Located in the Hunan Province of central China, the 64,000-acre Wulingyuan National Park is important for more than dramatic topography—it harbors rare plants and animals, including leopards, giant salamanders, and pangolins, or scaly anteaters.

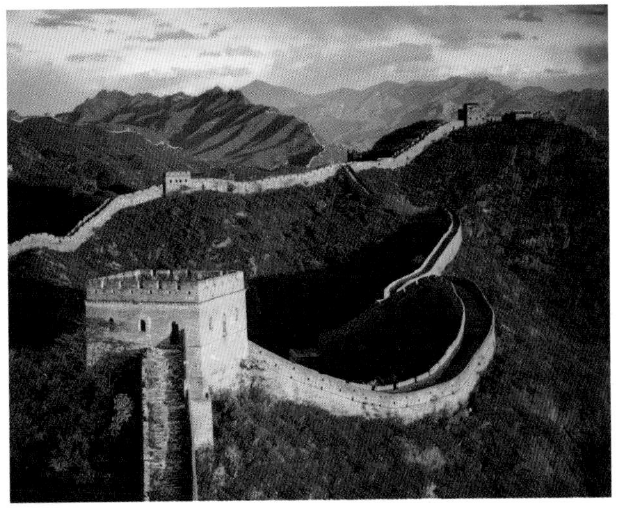

The Great Wall ❶
The Great Wall is the world's single largest building project—but the legend that it can be seen from the moon by the naked eye is false. Emperor Qin Shi Huang, who united China in the third century B.C., began piecing the wall together from fragments of earlier defensive structures in order to guard against invaders from the north. Some 16 centuries later, the Ming dynasty still worked on the wall, which eventually stretched some 4,200 miles from east to west. While some of the wall remains in good shape, much of it has been lost or lies in disrepair.

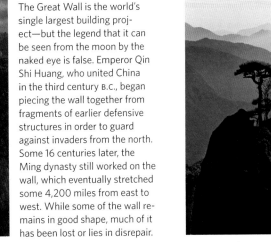

Huang Shan ❷
One of China's greatest natural monuments, Huang Shan is a magnificent landscape of granite peaks piercing a sea of clouds, while misty valleys lie below. The beautiful scenery has inspired Chinese writers and visual artists to heights of creativity since ancient times. The area was named Huang Shan, or "yellow mountain," by royal decree after the eighth-century poet Li Bai called it that in his work. Around Huang Shan, poetry from various ages of Chinese literature is carved into the gorges and precipices.

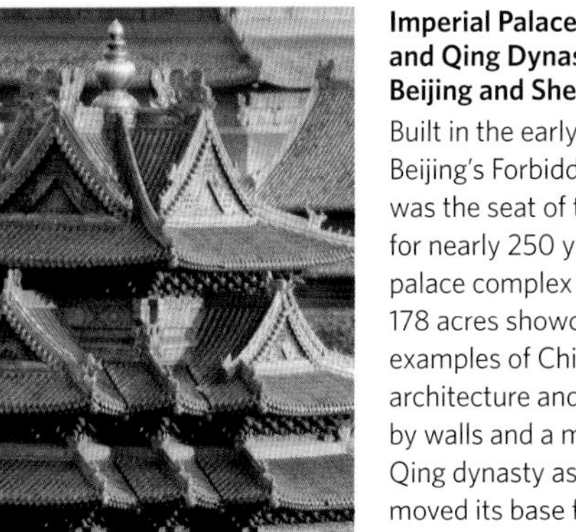

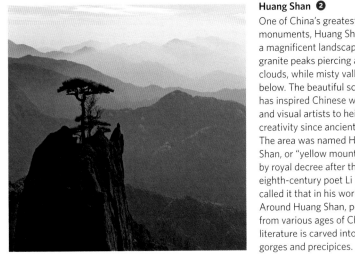

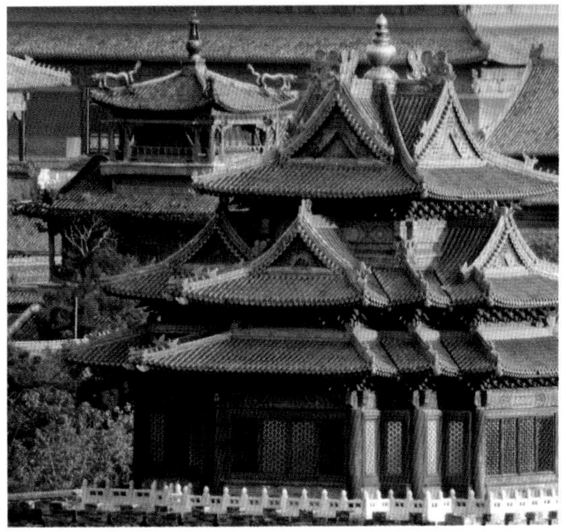

Imperial Palaces of the Ming and Qing Dynasties in Beijing and Shenyang ❹
Built in the early 15th century, Beijing's Forbidden City (left) was the seat of the Ming dynasty for nearly 250 years. The largest palace complex in the world, its 178 acres showcase important examples of Chinese imperial architecture and are surrounded by walls and a moat. When the Qing dynasty assumed power, it moved its base from Shenyang to Beijing and turned Shenyang Imperial Palace, built in 1625, into a secondary palace; today, it displays the unique heritage of the Qing's Manchu ethnicity.

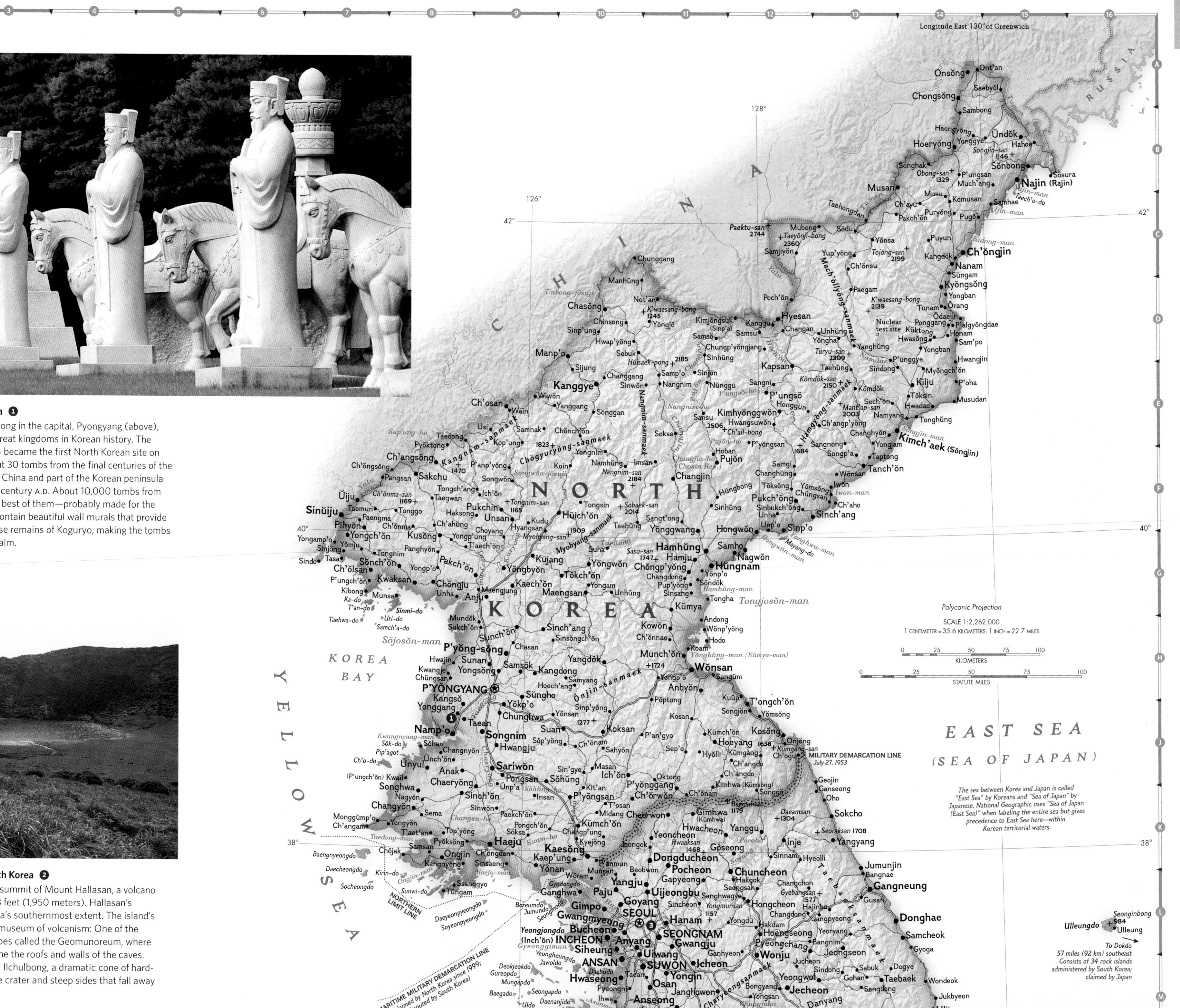
NORTH KOREA
CHINA
RUSSIA
EAST SEA
(SEA OF JAPAN)
YELLOW SEA
KOREA BAY
Longitude East 130° of Greenwich
P'YONGYANG
SEOUL
Polyconic Projection
SCALE 1:2,262,000
1 CENTIMETER = 35.6 KILOMETERS; 1 INCH = 22.7 MILES
KILOMETERS
STATUTE MILES
MILITARY DEMARCATION LINE
July 27, 1953
NORTHERN LIMIT LINE
MARITIME MILITARY DEMARCATION LINE
(claimed by North Korea since 1999; disputed by South Korea)
The sea between Korea and Japan is called "East Sea" by Koreans and "Sea of Japan" by Japanese. National Geographic uses "Sea of Japan (East Sea)" when labeling the entire sea but gives precedence to East Sea here—within Korean territorial waters.
To Dokdo
57 miles (92 km) southeast
Consists of 34 rock islands administered by South Korea; claimed by Japan
Ulleungdo
Paektu-san 2744
Wŏnsan
Hamhŭng
Ch'ŏngjin
Najin (Rajin)
Kaesŏng
Sinŭiju
Nampo
Haeju
INCHEON
SUWON
Chuncheon
Gangneung
Donghae

Complex of Koguryo Tombs, North Korea ❶

At the Mausoleum of the King of Tongmyong in the capital, Pyongyang (above), modern statues hark back to one of the great kingdoms in Korean history. The Koguryo Tombs complex—which in 2004 became the first North Korean site on the World Heritage List—comprises about 30 tombs from the final centuries of the Koguryo Kingdom, which ruled northeast China and part of the Korean peninsula from the third century B.C. to the seventh century A.D. About 10,000 tombs from the period have been discovered, and the best of them—probably made for the royal family and important aristocrats—contain beautiful wall murals that provide a glimpse at life in ancient Korea. Little else remains of Koguryo, making the tombs the primary testament to the vanished realm.

Jeju Volcanic Island and Lava Tubes, South Korea ❷

A jewel-like lake lies in a crater below the summit of Mount Hallasan, a volcano that is the highest peak in Korea, at 6,398 feet (1,950 meters). Hallasan's eruptions created Jeju Island—South Korea's southernmost extent. The island's protected natural features are a veritable museum of volcanism: One of the most famous is a large complex of lava tubes called the Geomunoreum, where unique multicolored carbonate deposits line the roofs and walls of the caves. On the island's coast stands the Seongsan Ilchulbong, a dramatic cone of hardened volcanic ash; it has a broad, bowl-like crater and steep sides that fall away into the sea.

North Korea

South Korea

Jongmyo Shrine, South Korea ❸

A South Korean man (left) venerates royal ancestors during the Jongmyo Jerye, an important ceremony held yearly at the Jongmyo Shrine in Seoul. The oldest and best-preserved Confucian royal shrine, it was originally built in the late 14th century to house memorial rites for the ancestors of the Joseon Dynasty, rulers of Korea until the early 20th century. The shrine was burned down in 1592 during a Japanese invasion, but rebuilt soon thereafter in its current form. Continuously expanded since then, the shrine is the highest expression of traditional Korean building styles and remains an important site of research for modern-day architects.

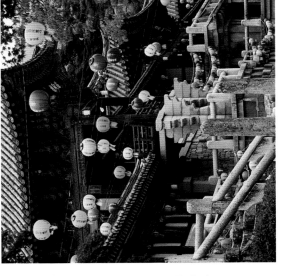

Seokguram Grotto and Bulguksa ❹ Temple, South Korea

Constructed more than 13 centuries ago, the Bulguksa Temple (right)—famed for its spectacular pair of ornamental stone pagodas—is one of Korea's most precious examples of Buddhist architecture. On a nearby mountain slope overlooking the Sea of Japan (East Sea), Seokguram Grotto—constructed of stone slabs at the same time as the Bulguksa Temple—holds a beautiful Buddha statue surrounded by relief carvings of Buddhist deities, Bodhisattvas, and other religious figures. Although modest in size, the grotto is a major treasure of Asian religious art.

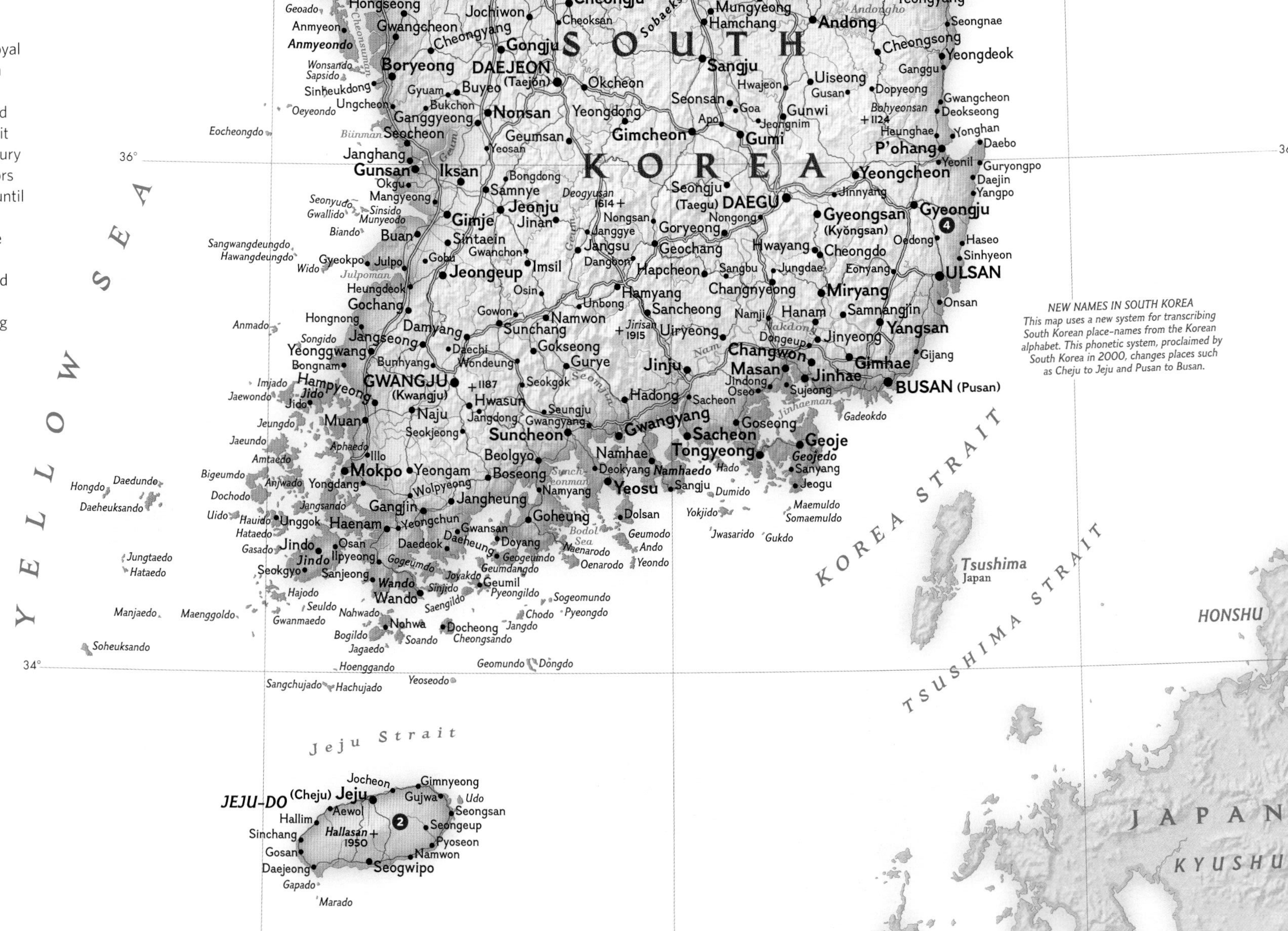
SOUTH KOREA
YELLOW SEA
KOREA STRAIT
TSUSHIMA STRAIT
Jeju Strait
JAPAN
HONSHU
KYUSHU
Tsushima
Japan
JEJU-DO (Cheju) Jeju
Hallasan + 1950
Seogwipo
DAEJEON (Taejŏn)
GWANGJU (Kwangju)
DAEGU (Taegu)
BUSAN (Pusan)
ULSAN
Gyeongju
P'ohang
Andong
Jeonju
Mokpo
Yeosu
Suncheon
Changwon
Masan
Jinju
Gimhae
Yangsan
Gunsan
Iksan
Gongju
Boryeong
Gimcheon
Gumi
Sangju
Mungyeong
Miryang
Geoje
Tongyeong
Sacheon
Gyeongsan (Kyŏngsan)
Yeongcheon
Jeongeup
Gimje
Namwon
Naju
Haenam
Jindo
Wando
Goheung
Gwangyang
NEW NAMES IN SOUTH KOREA
This map uses a new system for transcribing South Korean place-names from the Korean alphabet. This phonetic system, proclaimed by South Korea in 2000, changes places such as Cheju to Jeju and Pusan to Busan.
36°
34°
126°
130°
Longitude East 128° of Greenwich

Protected Areas and World Heritage Sites

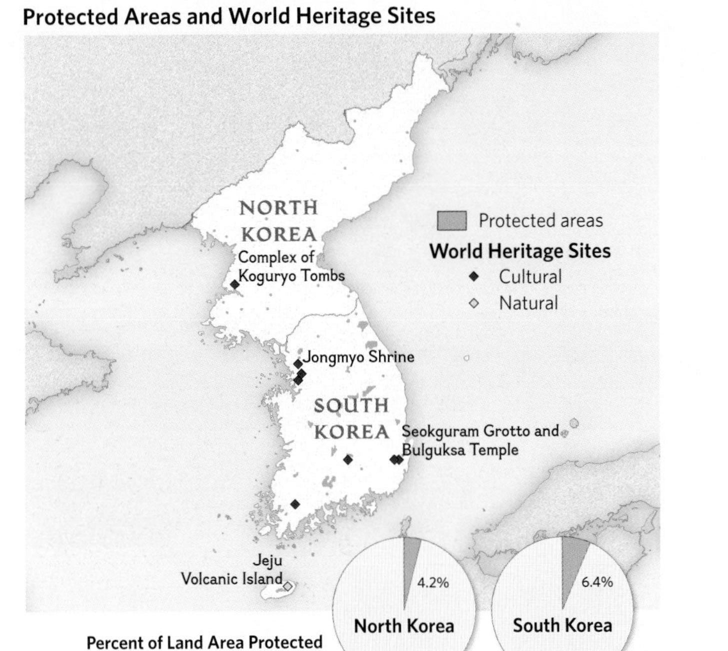
NORTH KOREA
SOUTH KOREA
Complex of Koguryo Tombs
Jongmyo Shrine
Seokguram Grotto and Bulguksa Temple
Jeju Volcanic Island
Protected areas
World Heritage Sites
◆ Cultural
◇ Natural
4.2%
North Korea
6.4%
South Korea
Percent of Land Area Protected

Urbanization and Largest Cities

Extents of Settlements Greater than 5,000
Urban area

Urban Area Population
- ■ 5 million and greater
- ▲ 1 million–4,999,999
- • 750,000–999,999
- ○ 500,000–749,999

NORTH KOREA: Sinŭiju, Hamhŭng, P'yŏngyang
SOUTH KOREA: Seoul, Incheon, Cheongju, Daejeon, Jeonju, Daegu, Ulsan, Changwon, Gwangju, Busan

Percent of Population in Urban Areas: North Korea 61.6%; South Korea 80.8%

Natural Land Cover

NORTH KOREA
SOUTH KOREA

Land Cover
- Forest
- Herbaceous

North Korea
South Korea
ASIA

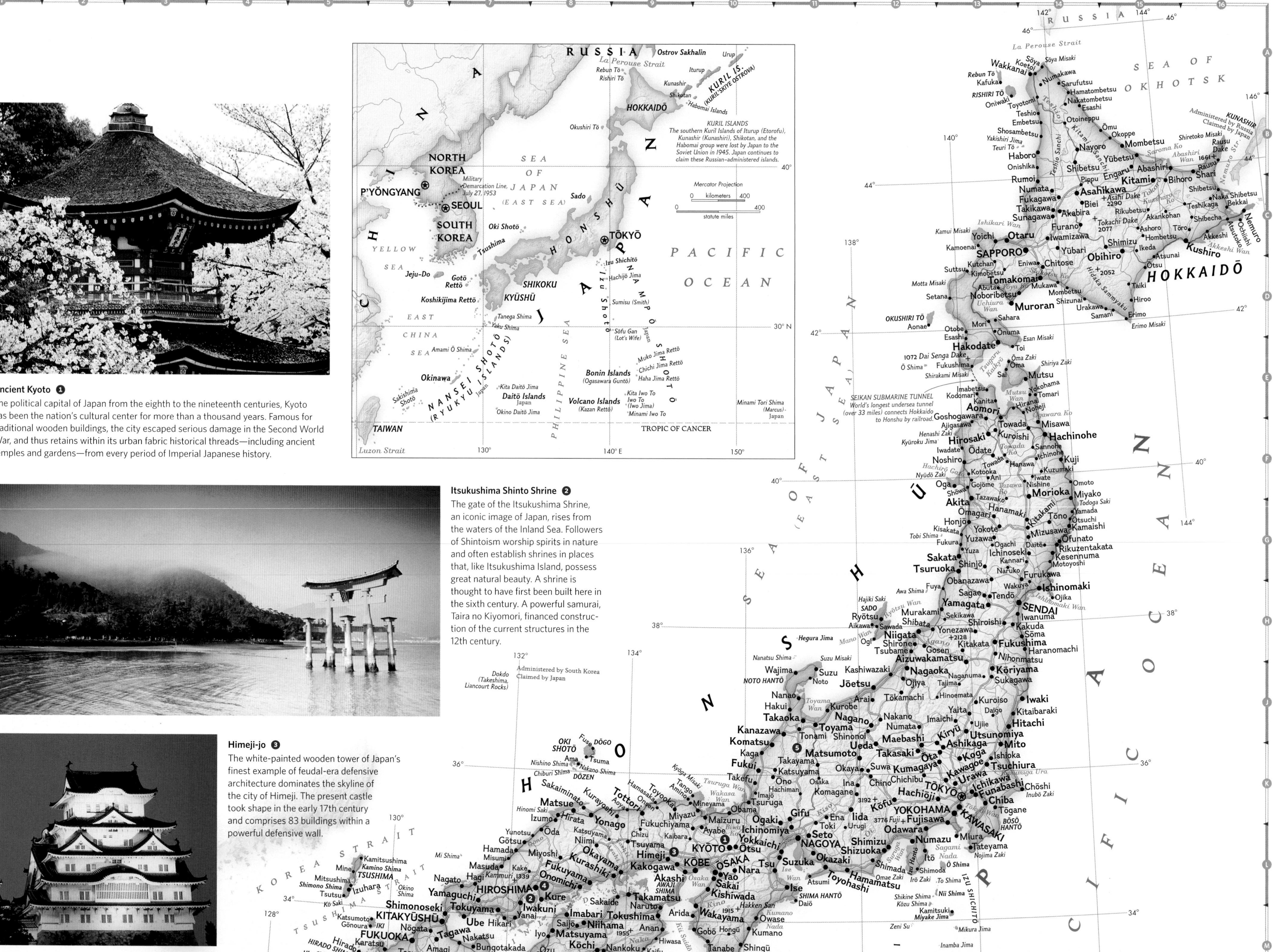
RUSSIA
SEA OF OKHOTSK
La Perouse Strait
HOKKAIDŌ
KUNASHIR Administered by Russia Claimed by Japan
SEA OF JAPAN (EAST SEA)
HONSHŪ
PACIFIC OCEAN
SEIKAN SUBMARINE TUNNEL World's longest undersea tunnel (over 33 miles) connects Hokkaido to Honshu by railroad.
SAPPORO
SENDAI
TŌKYŌ
YOKOHAMA
KAWASAKI
NAGOYA
KYŌTO
ŌSAKA
KŌBE
HIROSHIMA
KITAKYŪSHŪ
FUKUOKA
KOREA STRAIT
TSUSHIMA
OKI SHOTŌ
Dokdo (Takeshima, Liancourt Rocks) Administered by South Korea Claimed by Japan
IZU SHICHITŌ
RUSSIA
Ostrov Sakhalin
KURIL IS. (KURIL'SKIYE OSTROVA)
KURIL ISLANDS The southern Kuril Islands of Iturup (Etorofu), Kunashir (Kunashiri), Shikotan, and the Habomai group were lost by Japan to the Soviet Union in 1945. Japan continues to claim these Russian-administered islands.
Mercator Projection
kilometers
statute miles
CHINA
NORTH KOREA
P'YŎNGYANG
Military Demarcation Line, July 27, 1953
SEOUL
SOUTH KOREA
YELLOW SEA
EAST CHINA SEA
JAPAN
SHIKOKU
KYŪSHŪ
Izu Shotō
NAMPŌ SHOTŌ
Bonin Islands (Ogasawara Guntō)
Volcano Islands (Kazan Rettō)
Daitō Islands Japan
NANSEI SHOTŌ (RYUKYU ISLANDS)
Okinawa
PHILIPPINE SEA
TAIWAN
Luzon Strait
TROPIC OF CANCER
Minami Tori Shima (Marcus) Japan

Ancient Kyoto 1

The political capital of Japan from the eighth to the nineteenth centuries, Kyoto has been the nation's cultural center for more than a thousand years. Famous for traditional wooden buildings, the city escaped serious damage in the Second World War, and thus retains within its urban fabric historical threads—including ancient temples and gardens—from every period of Imperial Japanese history.

Itsukushima Shinto Shrine 2

The gate of the Itsukushima Shrine, an iconic image of Japan, rises from the waters of the Inland Sea. Followers of Shintoism worship spirits in nature and often establish shrines in places that, like Itsukushima Island, possess great natural beauty. A shrine is thought to have first been built here in the sixth century. A powerful samurai, Taira no Kiyomori, financed construction of the current structures in the 12th century.

Himeji-jo 3

The white-painted wooden tower of Japan's finest example of feudal-era defensive architecture dominates the skyline of the city of Himeji. The present castle took shape in the early 17th century and comprises 83 buildings within a powerful defensive wall.

Japan

Polyconic Projection
SCALE 1:5,323,000
1 CENTIMETER = 53.3 KILOMETERS; 1 INCH = 84 MILES

Longitude East 130° of Greenwich

Hiroshima Peace Memorial (Genbaku Dome) 4

A visitor to the Hiroshima Peace Memorial bows his head in honor of the more than 100,000 people, mostly civilians, killed in Hiroshima in 1945 when the United States dropped an atomic bomb on the city. At the center of the memorial is the skeleton of the Hiroshima Prefectural Industrial Promotion Hall, which survived less than 500 feet from ground zero. The ruin, which came to be known as the Genbaku ("atomic bomb") Dome, has been allowed to stand as a silent plea for the eradication of nuclear weapons from Earth.

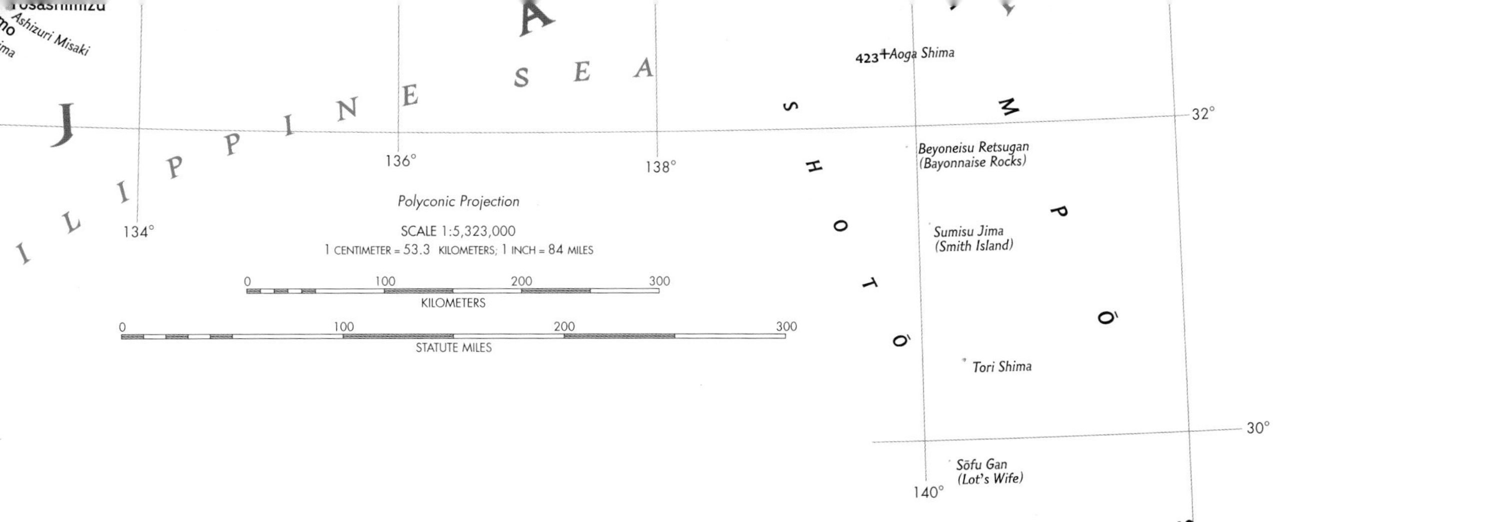

Historic Villages of Shirakawa-go and Gokayama 5

Surrounded by steep mountains, the farming villages in these areas were mostly cut off from the rest of Japan until the 1950s; thus they developed unique cultural and architectural traditions. Most obvious among these is the distinctive *gassho*-style house found in the villages of Ogimachi, Ainokura, and Suginuma. It is much larger than the typical Japanese farmhouse, and its steep, gabled roofs—an aid in shedding the heavy snowfalls of the region—allow for multiple levels that provide room for large extended families, or can be used for agricultural purposes, such as raising silkworms and storing crops.

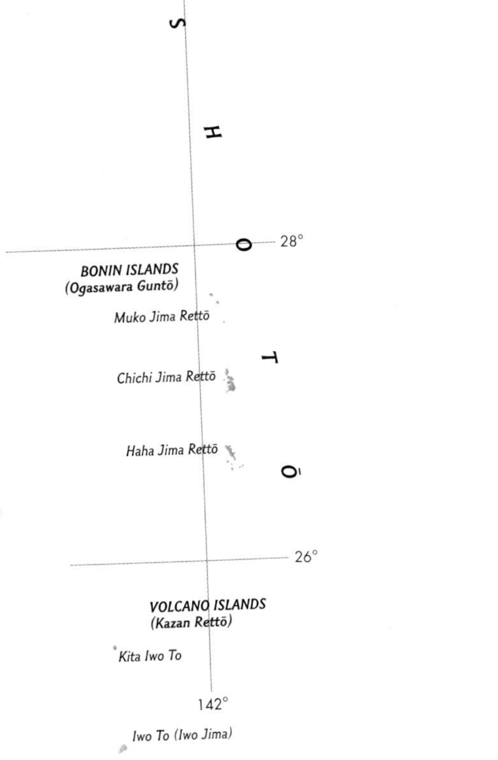

Protected Areas and World Heritage Sites

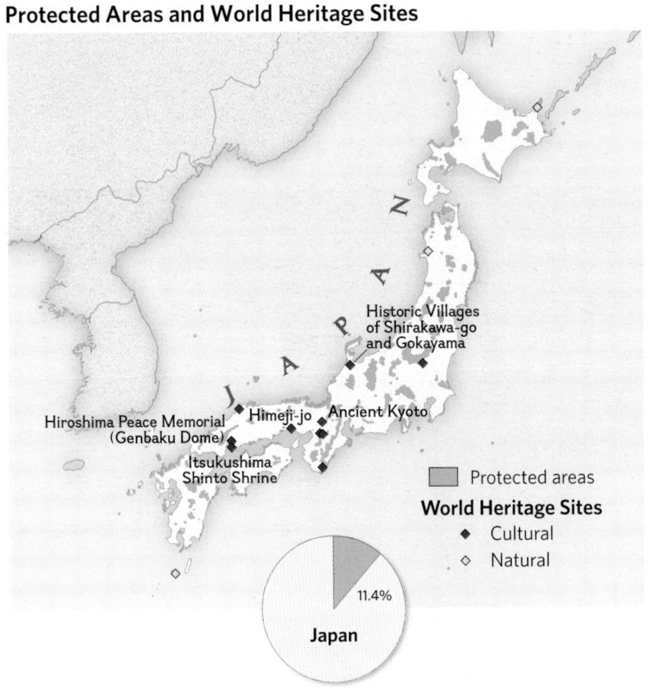

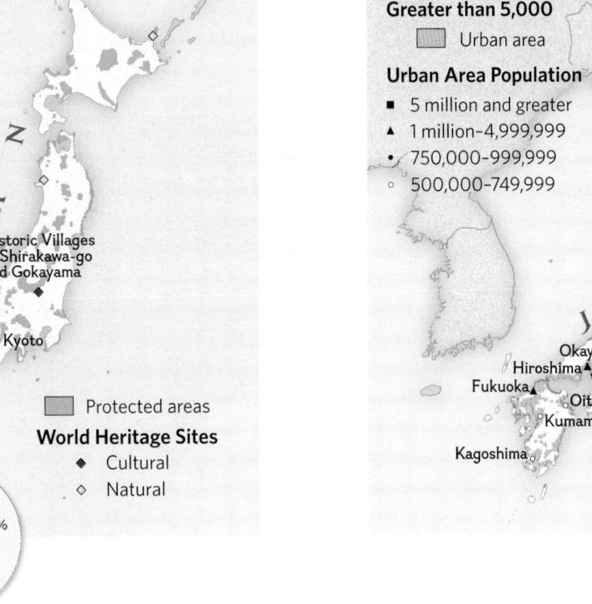
JAPAN
Historic Villages of Shirakawa-go and Gokayama
Ancient Kyoto
Himeji-jo
Hiroshima Peace Memorial (Genbaku Dome)
Itsukushima Shinto Shrine
Protected areas
World Heritage Sites
Cultural
Natural

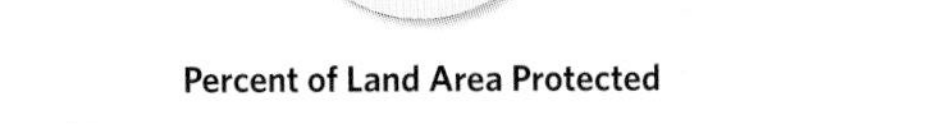
11.4%
Japan

Percent of Land Area Protected

Urbanization and Largest Cities

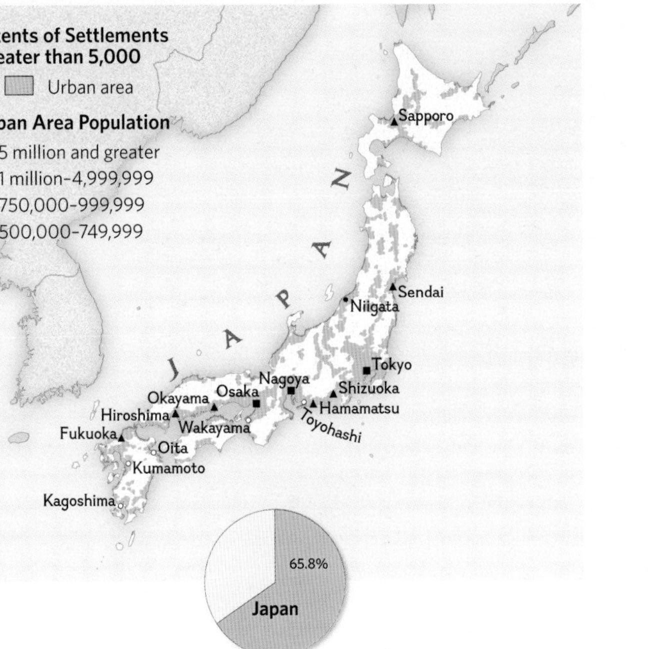
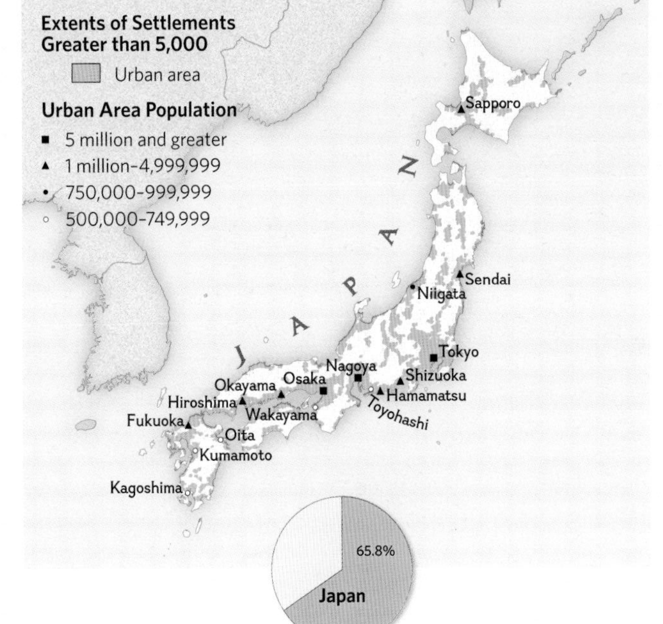
Extents of Settlements Greater than 5,000
Urban area
Urban Area Population
5 million and greater
1 million–4,999,999
750,000–999,999
500,000–749,999
JAPAN
Sapporo
Sendai
Niigata
Tokyo
Shizuoka
Hamamatsu
Toyohashi
Nagoya
Osaka
Wakayama
Okayama
Hiroshima
Fukuoka
Oita
Kumamoto
Kagoshima
65.8%
Japan

Percent of Population in Urban Areas

Natural Land Cover

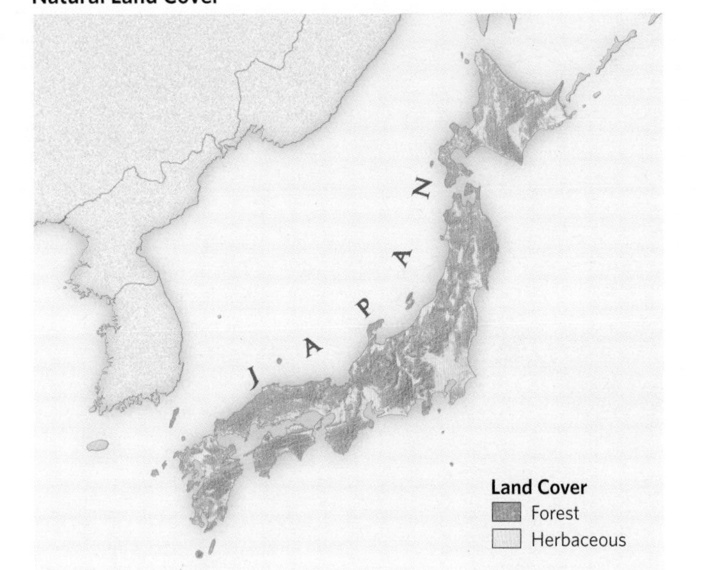
JAPAN
Land Cover
Forest
Herbaceous

Complex of Hue Monuments, Vietnam ❶

The sun sinks behind the monumental gate of the Temple of Letters—a sanctuary dedicated to prominent scholars of Confucianism—in the 19th-century capital of unified Vietnam. The Nguyen dynasty built Hue after consolidating rule of the country in 1802. The Perfume River winds through the royal complex, past palaces, temples, mausoleums, and defensive structures of a city widely admired for the beauty and harmony of its architecture.

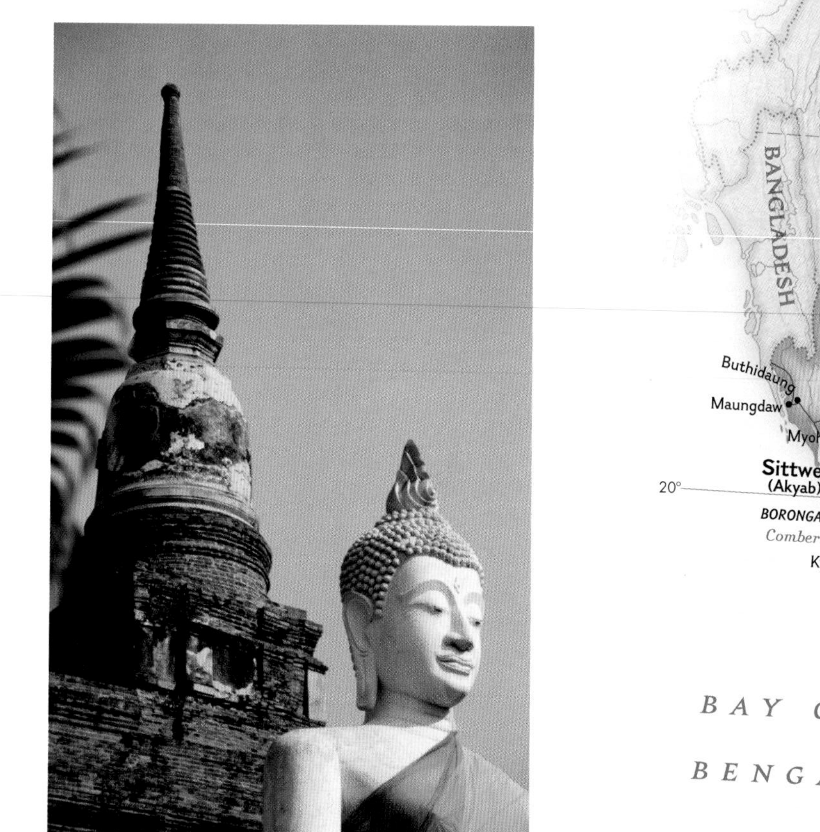

Historic City of Ayutthaya, Thailand ❸

The spire of Wat Ya Chai Mongkon Buddhist temple towers above the ruins of Ayutthaya, established in 1350 as the capital of Siam, soon to become the dominant kingdom in Thailand. Ayutthaya is one of Thailand's gems of historical religious architecture—filled with the impressive remnants of the hundreds of monasteries and temples that thrived here until 1767, the year that the Burmese destroyed the city after a protracted siege.

❷ Ha Long Bay, Vietnam

Hotel junks ferry tourists through the spectacular seascape of Ha Long Bay. Nearly 2,000 islands and islets jut steeply out of the this large bay on the Gulf of Tonkin, some of which are little more than dramatic pillars of limestone topped with vegetation. Within some of the islands are spectacular grottoes that have become major tourist draws. The sea life of the bay supports several fishing villages where residents live in houses that float on the water. Ha Long Bay has long been inhabited; archaeological finds indicate it was a significant port on Asian trade routes in prehistoric times.

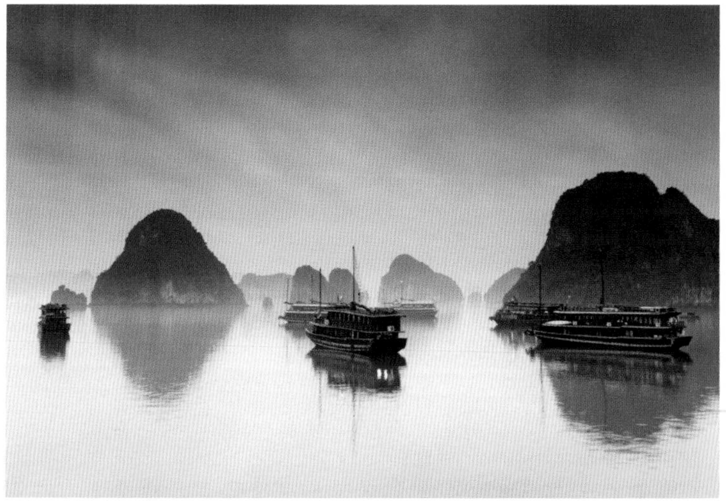

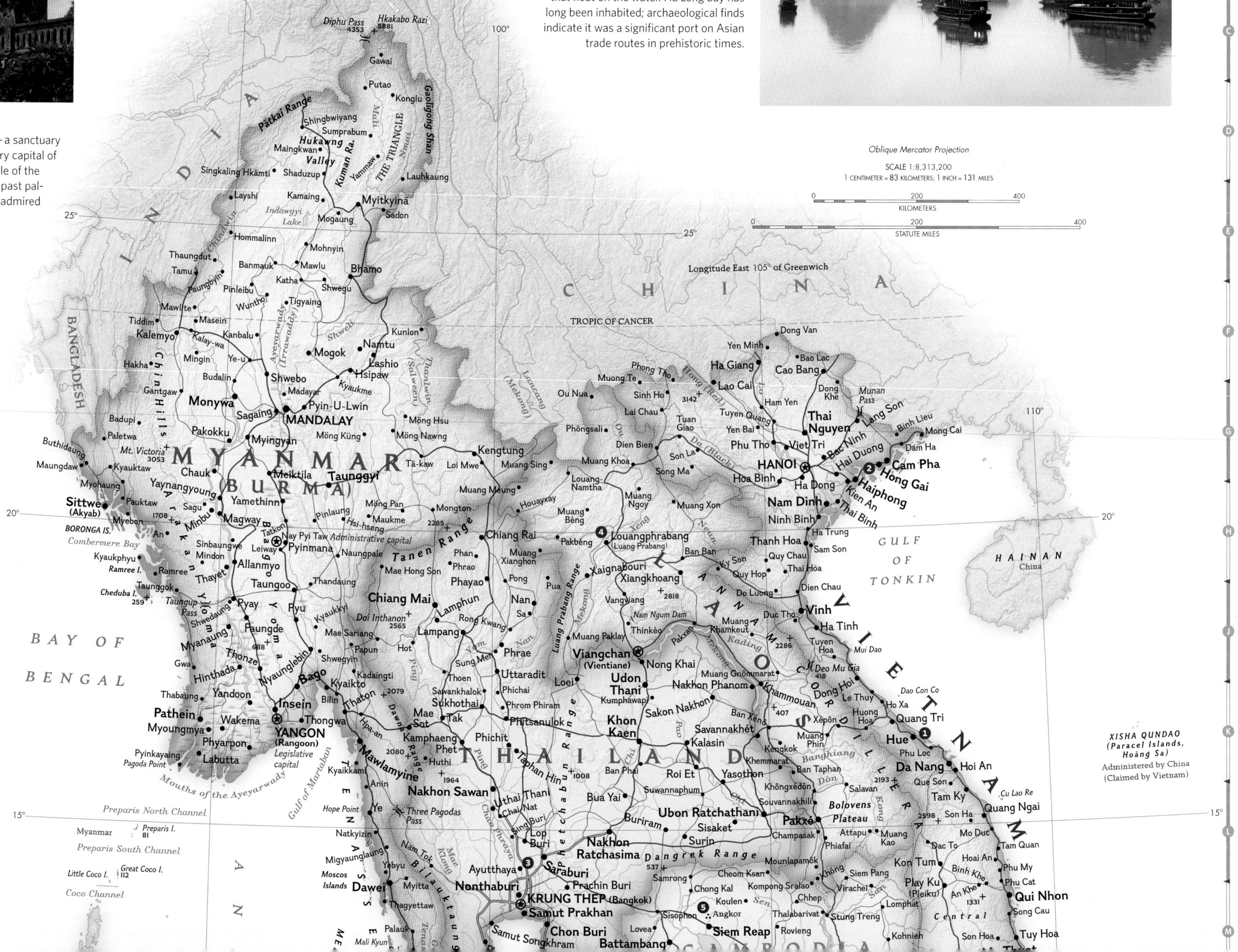

Oblique Mercator Projection

SCALE 1:8,313,200

1 CENTIMETER = 83 KILOMETERS; 1 INCH = 131 MILES

0 200 400 KILOMETERS

0 200 400 STATUTE MILES

Longitude East 105° of Greenwich

TROPIC OF CANCER

XISHA QUNDAO (Paracel Islands, Hoàng Sa) Administered by China (Claimed by Vietnam)

INDIA · CHINA · MYANMAR (BURMA) · LAOS · THAILAND · VIETNAM · CAMBODIA · BANGLADESH · HAINAN China

BAY OF BENGAL · GULF OF TONKIN · Gulf of Martaban · ANDAMAN SEA

MANDALAY · YANGON (Rangoon) · Nay Pyi Taw Administrative capital · HANOI · Viangchan (Vientiane) · KRUNG THEP (Bangkok) · Louangphrabang · Hue · Da Nang · Haiphong · Chiang Mai · Sittwe (Akyab) · Siem Reap · Angkor

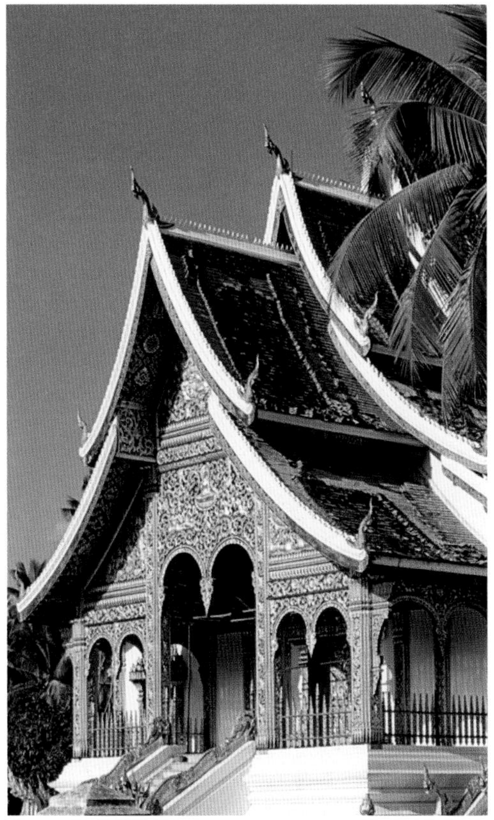

Cambodia | Laos | Myanmar | Thailand | Vietnam

Refer to pages 206-207 for Borneo

Town of Luang Prabang, Laos 4

An ornate Buddhist temple graces the Haw Kham, or Royal Palace (above), in the former royal capital of Laos. The early 20th-century palace was built when the country was part of French Indochina, and like much of Luang Prabang's architecture, exhibits a harmonious blend of local and French building styles. In addition to the unique urban feel of the old colonial capital, dozens of temples and shrines contribute to a spiritual atmosphere in this picturesque city on the bank of the Mekong River.

Angkor, Cambodia 5

Over several centuries this capital of the Khmer Empire grew into what is thought to have been the largest pre-industrial settlement the world has seen, covering well over a thousand square miles. The ruins of the Angkor Wat temple complex (below) are the best known of the many religious monuments throughout the area.

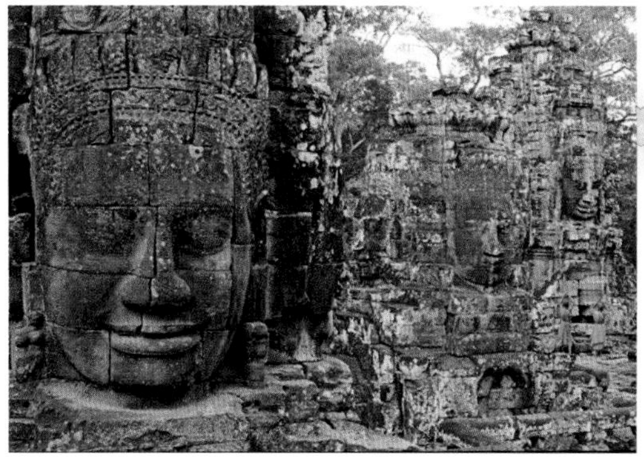

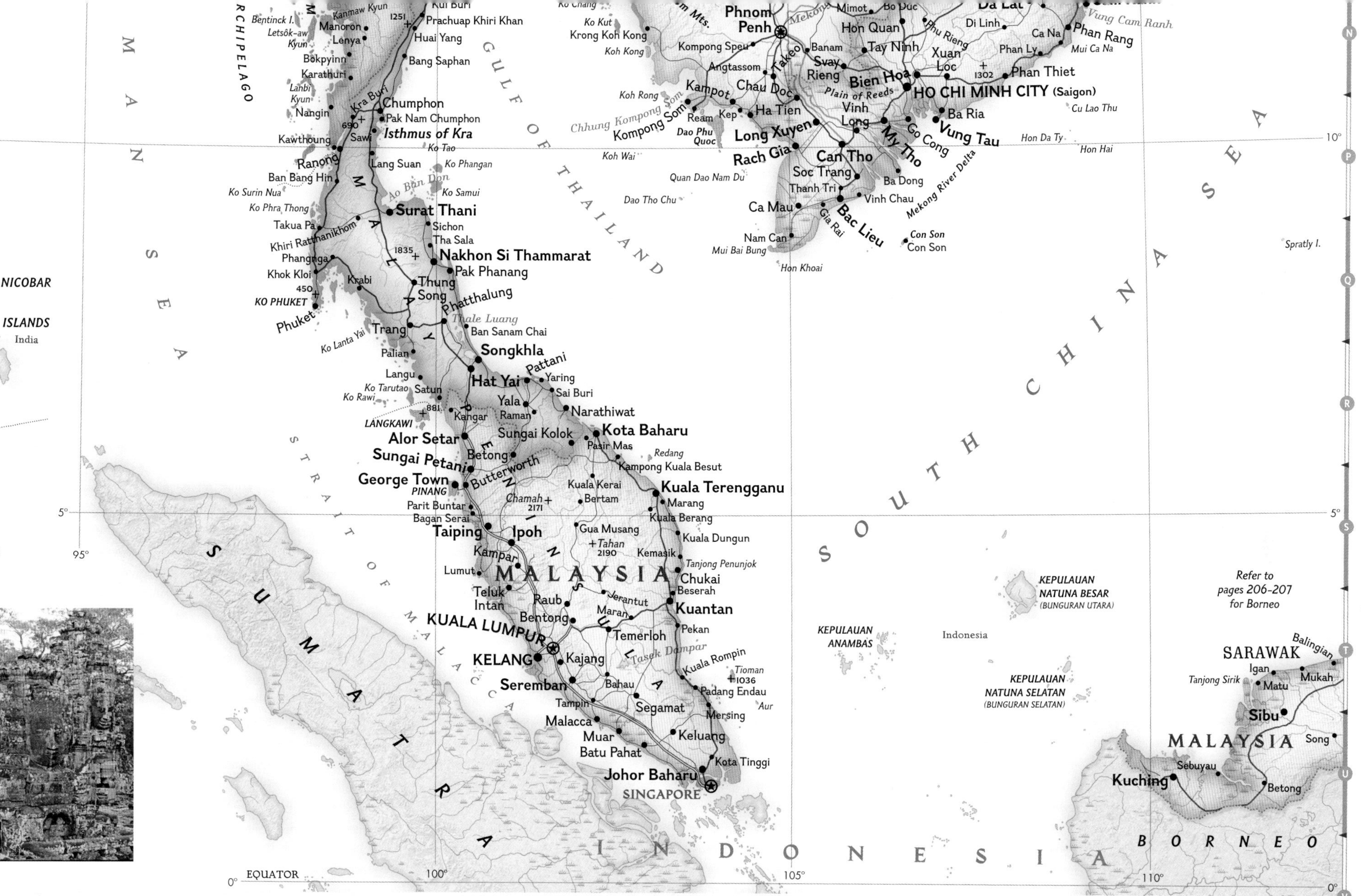

Protected Areas and World Heritage Sites

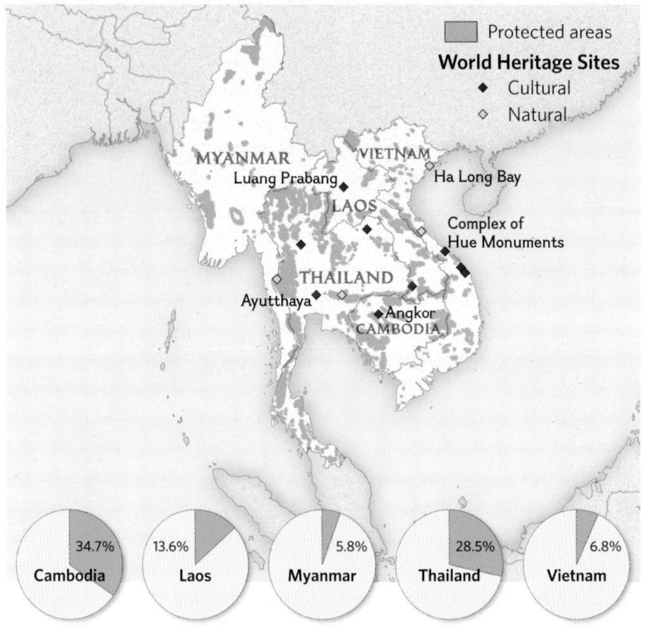

Protected areas

World Heritage Sites
- Cultural
- Natural

Luang Prabang, Ha Long Bay, Complex of Hue Monuments, Ayutthaya, Angkor

Percent of Land Area Protected

Cambodia	Laos	Myanmar	Thailand	Vietnam
34.7%	13.6%	5.8%	28.5%	6.8%

Urbanization and Largest Cities

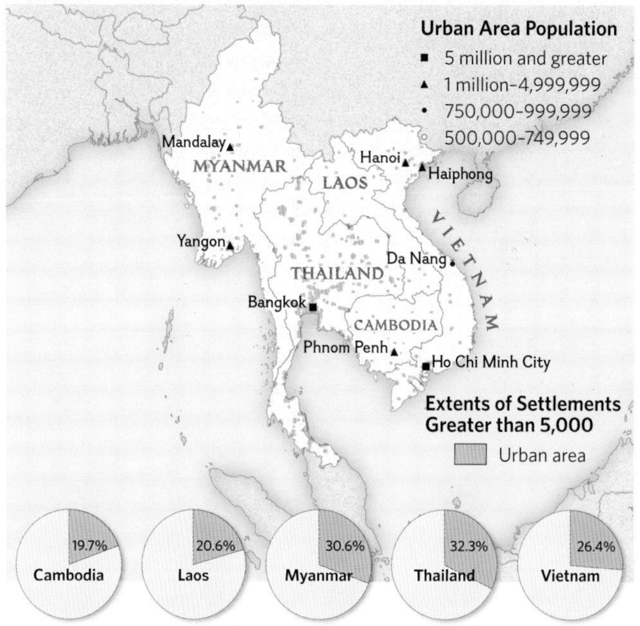

Urban Area Population
- 5 million and greater
- 1 million–4,999,999
- 750,000–999,999
- 500,000–749,999

Mandalay, Yangon, Hanoi, Haiphong, Da Nang, Bangkok, Phnom Penh, Ho Chi Minh City

Extents of Settlements Greater than 5,000

Urban area

Percent of Population in Urban Areas

Cambodia	Laos	Myanmar	Thailand	Vietnam
19.7%	20.6%	30.6%	32.3%	26.4%

Natural Land Cover

Land Cover
- Forest
- Herbaceous
- Savanna

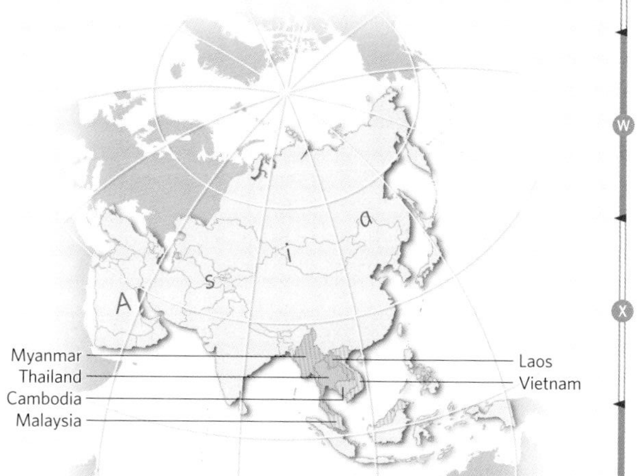

Myanmar, Thailand, Cambodia, Malaysia, Laos, Vietnam

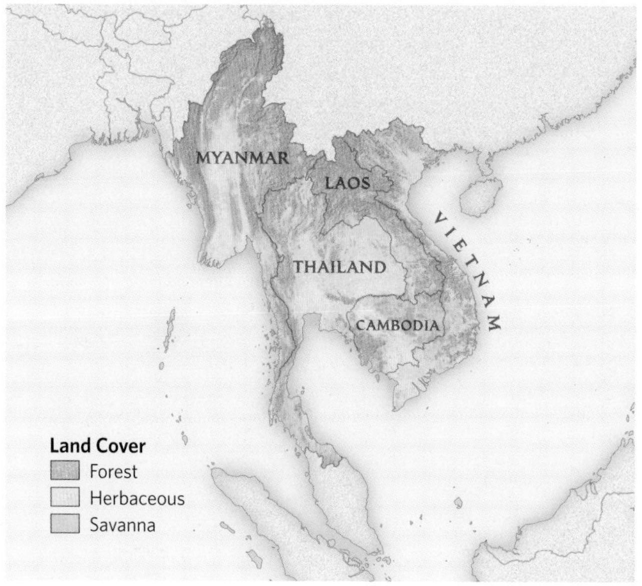

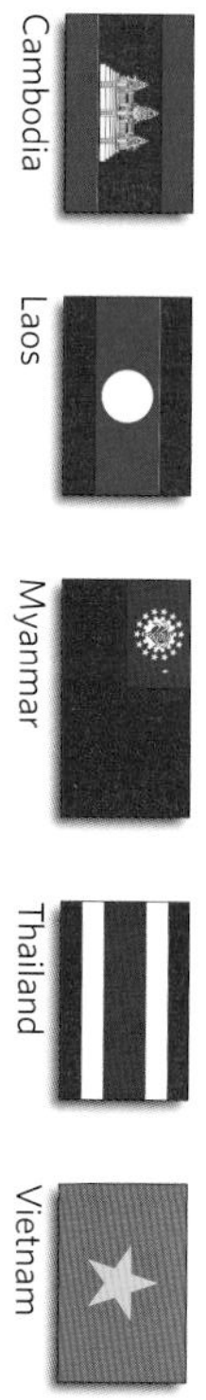

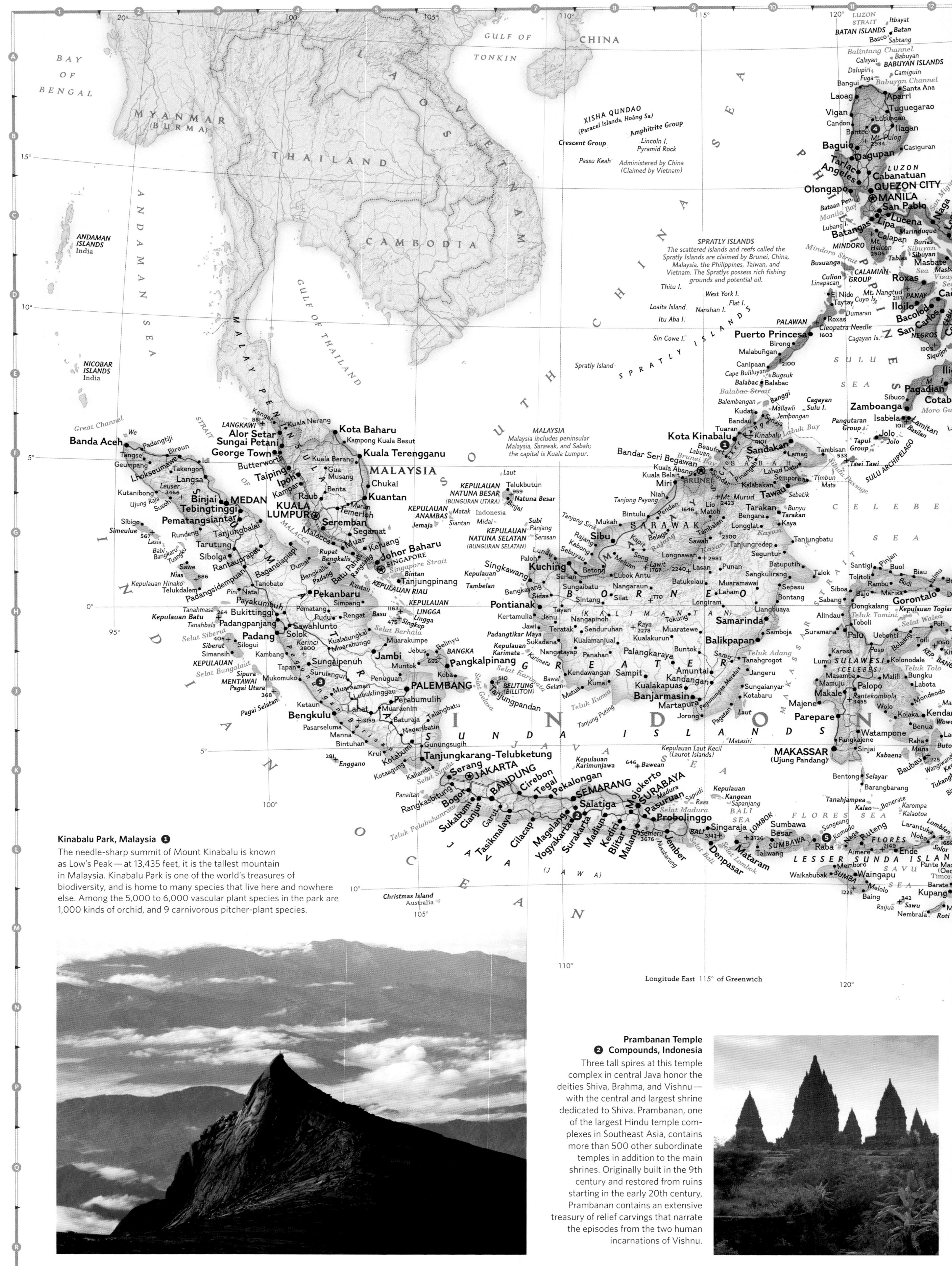

BAY OF BENGAL
GULF OF TONKIN
CHINA
MYANMAR (BURMA)
LAOS
THAILAND
VIETNAM
CAMBODIA
ANDAMAN SEA
GULF OF THAILAND
ANDAMAN ISLANDS India
NICOBAR ISLANDS India
SOUTH CHINA SEA
XISHA QUNDAO (Paracel Islands, Hoàng Sa)
Amphitrite Group
Crescent Group
Lincoln I.
Pyramid Rock
Passu Keah
Administered by China (Claimed by Vietnam)
SPRATLY ISLANDS
The scattered islands and reefs called the Spratly Islands are claimed by Brunei, China, Malaysia, the Philippines, Taiwan, and Vietnam. The Spratlys possess rich fishing grounds and potential oil.
MALAYSIA
Malaysia includes peninsular Malaysia, Sarawak, and Sabah; the capital is Kuala Lumpur.
MALAY PENINSULA
STRAIT OF MALACCA
KUALA LUMPUR
Kota Baharu
Kuala Terengganu
Kuantan
George Town
Ipoh
Johor Baharu
SINGAPORE
Banda Aceh
MEDAN
Padang
Pekanbaru
Jambi
PALEMBANG
Bengkulu
Pangkalpinang
Tanjungkarang-Telukbetung
JAKARTA
BANDUNG
SEMARANG
SURABAYA
Yogyakarta
Denpasar
Mataram
Pontianak
Kuching
Sibu
Miri
Bandar Seri Begawan
BRUNEI
Kota Kinabalu
Sandakan
Samarinda
Balikpapan
Banjarmasin
BORNEO (KALIMANTAN)
SARAWAK
SABAH
SUNDA ISLANDS
JAVA (JAWA)
LESSER SUNDA ISLANDS
MAKASSAR (Ujung Pandang)
SULAWESI (CELEBES)
CELEBES SEA
SULU SEA
PHILIPPINES
LUZON
MANILA
QUEZON CITY
Puerto Princesa
PALAWAN
Zamboanga
INDIAN OCEAN
Christmas Island Australia
Longitude East 115° of Greenwich

Kinabalu Park, Malaysia ❶

The needle-sharp summit of Mount Kinabalu is known as Low's Peak—at 13,435 feet, it is the tallest mountain in Malaysia. Kinabalu Park is one of the world's treasures of biodiversity, and is home to many species that live here and nowhere else. Among the 5,000 to 6,000 vascular plant species in the park are 1,000 kinds of orchid, and 9 carnivorous pitcher-plant species.

❷ Prambanan Temple Compounds, Indonesia

Three tall spires at this temple complex in central Java honor the deities Shiva, Brahma, and Vishnu—with the central and largest shrine dedicated to Shiva. Prambanan, one of the largest Hindu temple complexes in Southeast Asia, contains more than 500 other subordinate temples in addition to the main shrines. Originally built in the 9th century and restored from ruins starting in the early 20th century, Prambanan contains an extensive treasury of relief carvings that narrate the episodes from the two human incarnations of Vishnu.

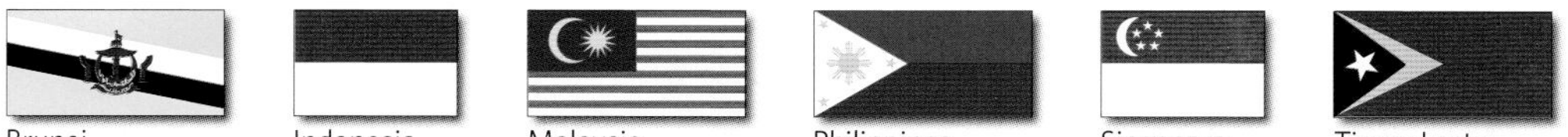

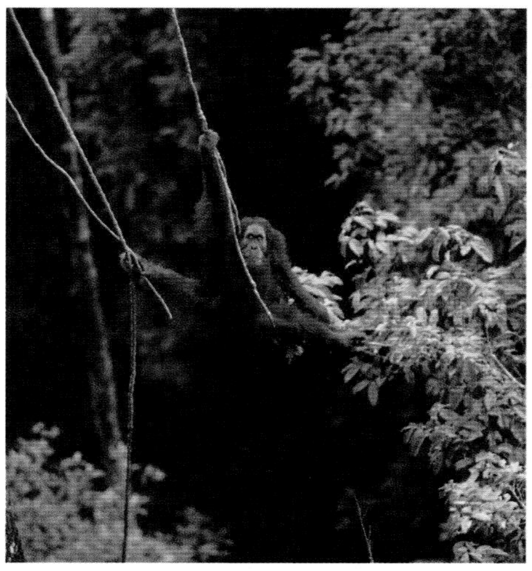

Brunei | Indonesia | Malaysia | Philippines | Singapore | Timor-Leste

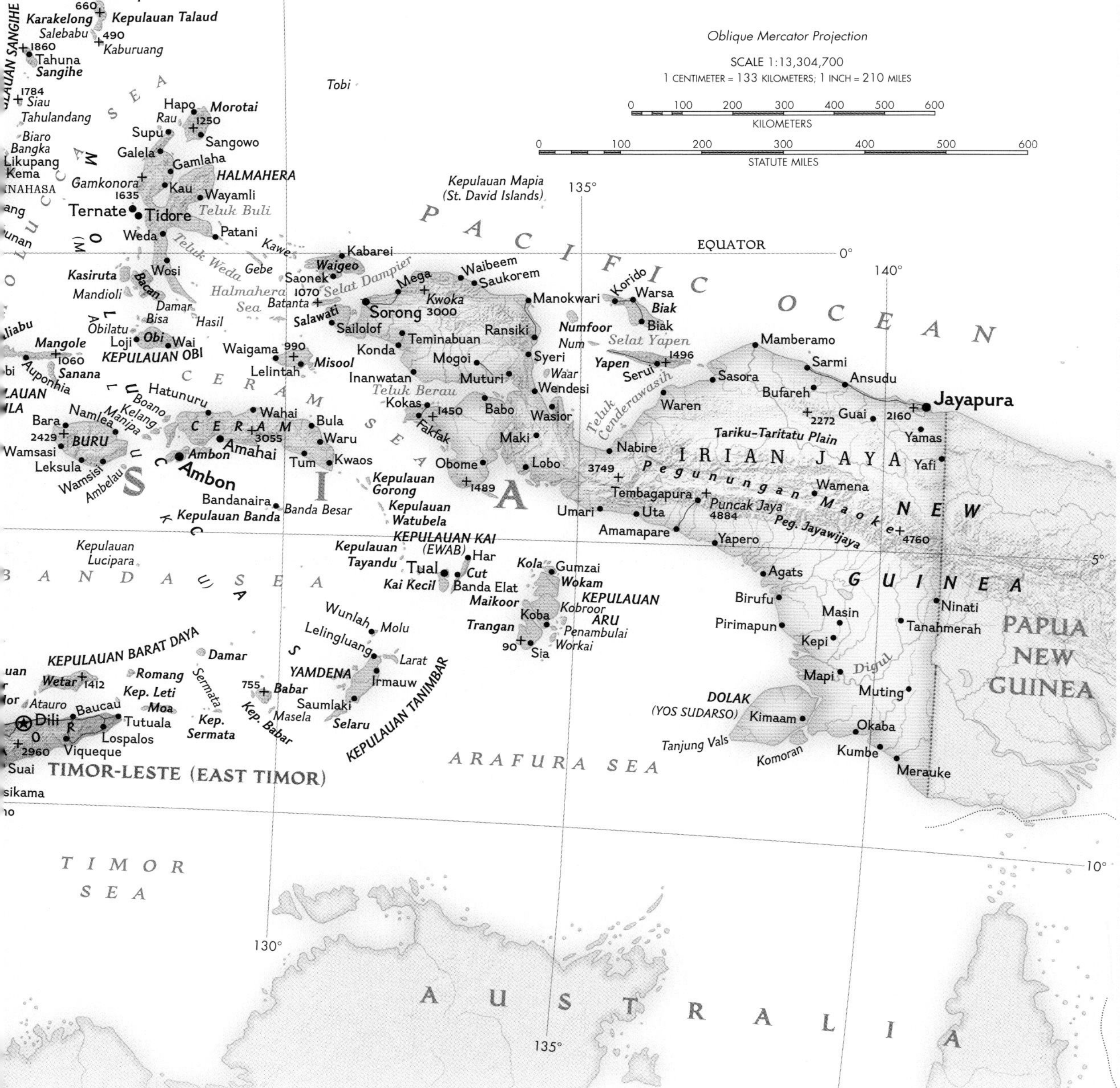

Tropical Rainforest Heritage of Sumatra, Indonesia ❸

An orangutan swings on vines through the forest on the Indonesian island of Sumatra, one of the most biodiverse places on the planet. Covering more than 6.1 million acres, this World Heritage site pulls together three ecologically precious national parks that retain tracts of the ancient Sumatran forest. The parks today shelter numerous endangered and threatened species.

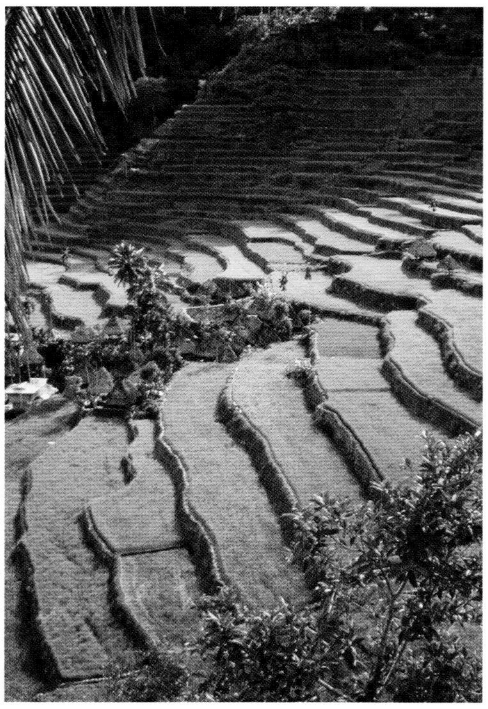

Rice Terraces of the Philippine Cordilleras, Philippines ❹

For 2,000 years or more, farmers in this mountainous part of Luzon have laboriously built terraces for rice paddies on slopes of up to 70 degrees. The terraces cover thousands of square miles but are deteriorating as young people quit farming, causing their inscription on the List of World Heritage in Danger.

Oblique Mercator Projection

SCALE 1:13,304,700

1 CENTIMETER = 133 KILOMETERS; 1 INCH = 210 MILES

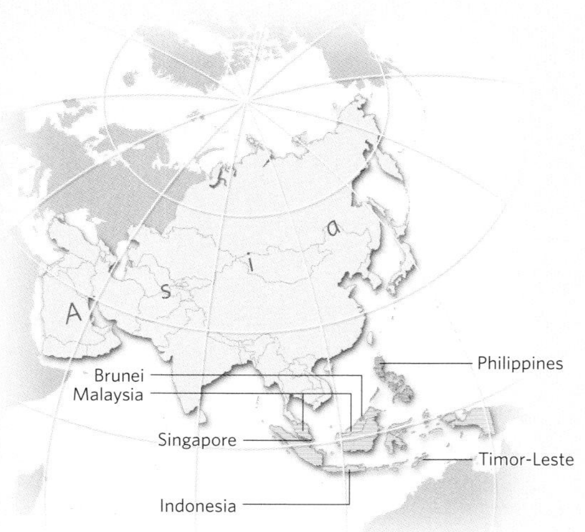

Brunei
Malaysia
Singapore
Indonesia
Philippines
Timor-Leste

Protected Areas and World Heritage Sites

Rice Terraces of the Philippine Cordilleras
PHILIPPINES
BRUNEI
MALAYSIA
Kinabalu Park
INDONESIA
Rainforest of Sumatra
Prambanan Temple Compounds
Komodo N.P.
TIMOR-LESTE
Protected areas
World Heritage Sites
Cultural
Natural
24.5% Brunei
17.9% Indonesia
9.3% Malaysia

26.5% Philippines | 4.6% Singapore | 2.0% Timor-Leste

Percent of Land Area Protected

Urbanization and Largest Cities

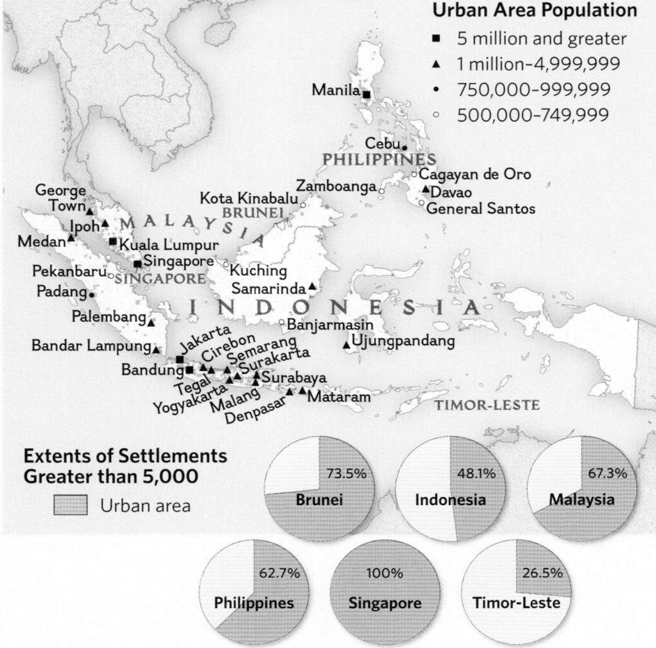

Urban Area Population
5 million and greater
1 million–4,999,999
750,000–999,999
500,000–749,999
Manila
Cebu
PHILIPPINES
Cagayan de Oro
Zamboanga
Davao
General Santos
George Town
Kota Kinabalu
BRUNEI
Ipoh
Medan
Kuala Lumpur
Singapore
SINGAPORE
Pekanbaru
Padang
Kuching
Samarinda
Palembang
INDONESIA
Banjarmasin
Bandar Lampung
Jakarta
Ujungpandang
Bandung
Cirebon
Semarang
Tegal
Surakarta
Yogyakarta
Surabaya
Malang
Denpasar
Mataram
TIMOR-LESTE
Extents of Settlements Greater than 5,000
Urban area
73.5% Brunei
48.1% Indonesia
67.3% Malaysia

62.7% Philippines | 100% Singapore | 26.5% Timor-Leste

Percent of Population in Urban Areas

Natural Land Cover

Land Cover
Forest
Herbaceous
Highland
Savanna
PHILIPPINES
BRUNEI
MALAYSIA
SINGAPORE
INDONESIA
TIMOR-LESTE

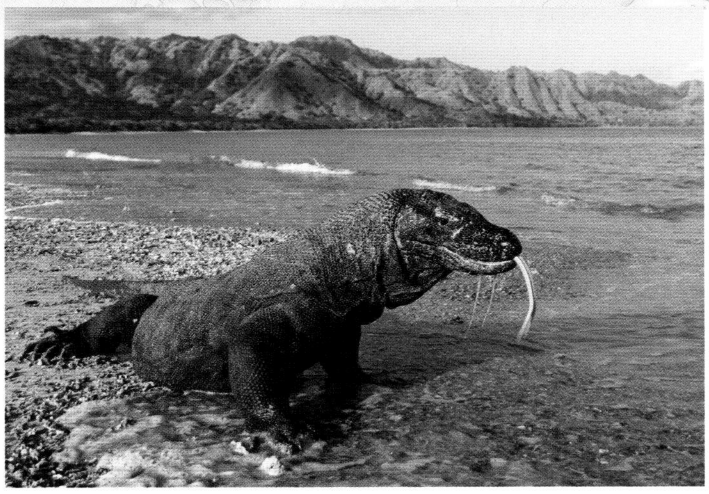

Komodo National Park, Indonesia ❺

Perhaps looking for a bite of fish, a Komodo dragon ventures into the surf in the Indonesian national park created to safeguard this largest of all lizard species. The forked tongue—used for smelling as well as tasting—may be extended because the animal senses an intruder. About 5,700 of the scaly giants live in the park, which comprises Komodo Island and all or parts of several other islands. Since it is practically the only place in the world the lizards live, the park is key to their survival. Lacking any natural competition as predators, Komodo dragons can grow to weigh more than 150 pounds on a diet of any kind of meat they can find, no matter whether it's fresh or scavenged.

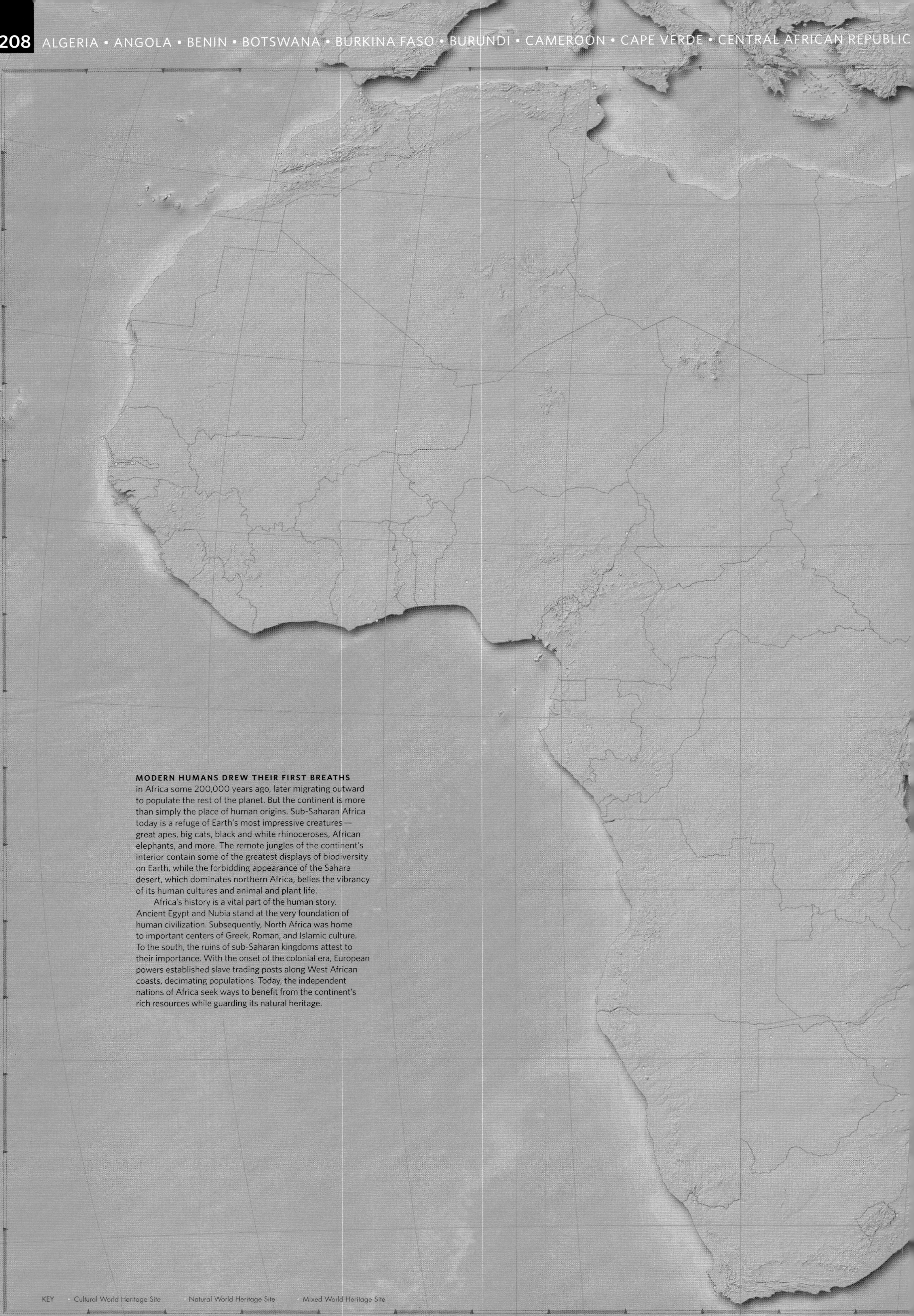

MODERN HUMANS DREW THEIR FIRST BREATHS in Africa some 200,000 years ago, later migrating outward to populate the rest of the planet. But the continent is more than simply the place of human origins. Sub-Saharan Africa today is a refuge of Earth's most impressive creatures—great apes, big cats, black and white rhinoceroses, African elephants, and more. The remote jungles of the continent's interior contain some of the greatest displays of biodiversity on Earth, while the forbidding appearance of the Sahara desert, which dominates northern Africa, belies the vibrancy of its human cultures and animal and plant life.

Africa's history is a vital part of the human story. Ancient Egypt and Nubia stand at the very foundation of human civilization. Subsequently, North Africa was home to important centers of Greek, Roman, and Islamic culture. To the south, the ruins of sub-Saharan kingdoms attest to their importance. With the onset of the colonial era, European powers established slave trading posts along West African coasts, decimating populations. Today, the independent nations of Africa seek ways to benefit from the continent's rich resources while guarding its natural heritage.

KEY • Cultural World Heritage Site • Natural World Heritage Site • Mixed World Heritage Site

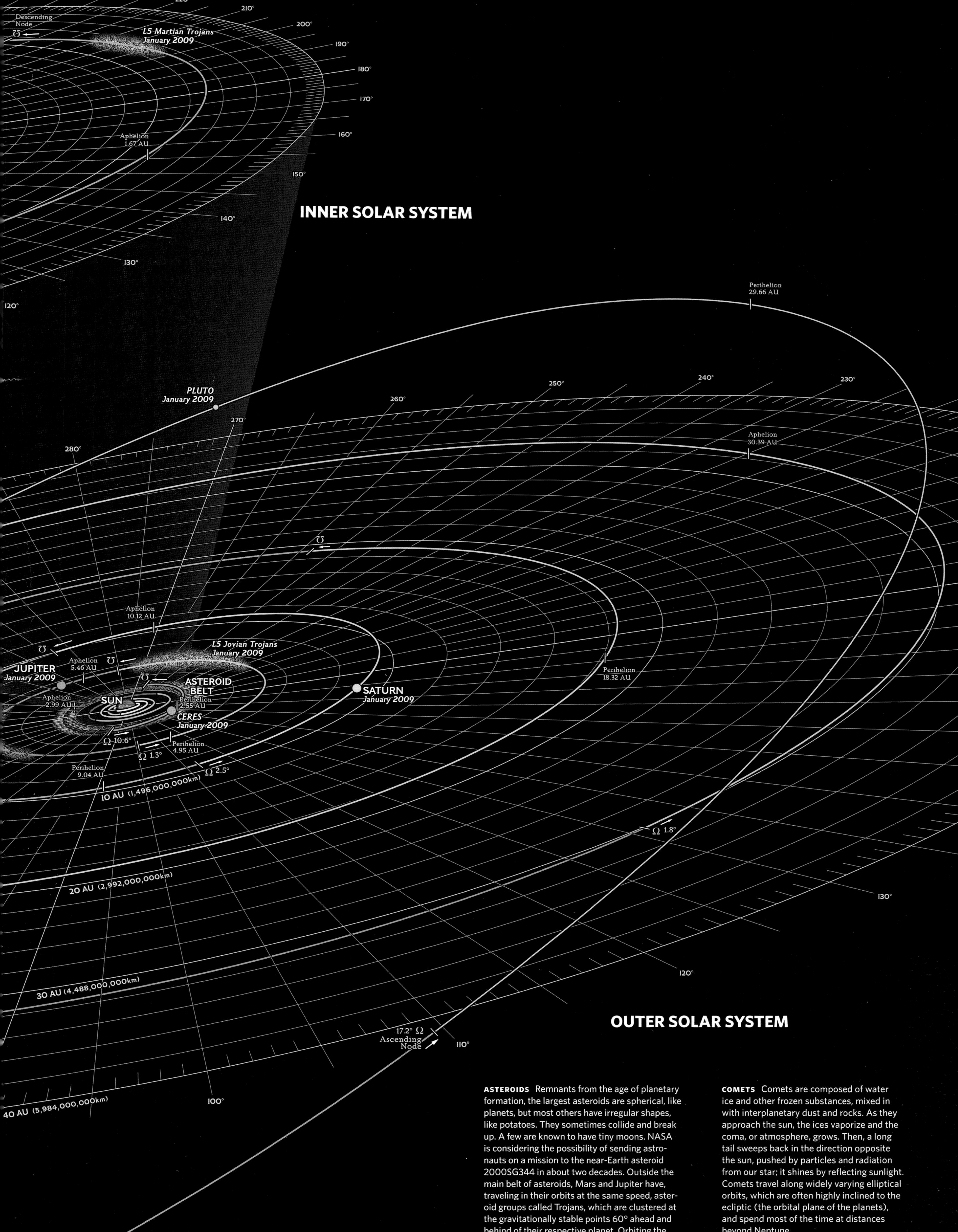
INNER SOLAR SYSTEM
Descending Node
L5 Martian Trojans
January 2009
Aphelion
1.67 AU
OUTER SOLAR SYSTEM
Perihelion
29.66 AU
PLUTO
January 2009
Aphelion
30.39 AU
Aphelion
10.12 AU
L5 Jovian Trojans
January 2009
JUPITER
January 2009
Aphelion
5.46 AU
ASTEROID BELT
SUN
Aphelion
2.99 AU
Perihelion
2.55 AU
CERES
January 2009
Perihelion
4.95 AU
Perihelion
9.04 AU
SATURN
January 2009
Perihelion
18.32 AU
10 AU (1,496,000,000km)
20 AU (2,992,000,000km)
30 AU (4,488,000,000km)
40 AU (5,984,000,000km)
17.2° Ω
Ascending Node

ASTEROIDS Remnants from the age of planetary formation, the largest asteroids are spherical, like planets, but most others have irregular shapes, like potatoes. They sometimes collide and break up. A few are known to have tiny moons. NASA is considering the possibility of sending astronauts on a mission to the near-Earth asteroid 2000SG344 in about two decades. Outside the main belt of asteroids, Mars and Jupiter have, traveling in their orbits at the same speed, asteroid groups called Trojans, which are clustered at the gravitationally stable points 60° ahead and behind of their respective planet. Orbiting the sun 60° ahead of Neptune is another group of Trojans, shown at lower left.

COMETS Comets are composed of water ice and other frozen substances, mixed in with interplanetary dust and rocks. As they approach the sun, the ices vaporize and the coma, or atmosphere, grows. Then, a long tail sweeps back in the direction opposite the sun, pushed by particles and radiation from our star; it shines by reflecting sunlight. Comets travel along widely varying elliptical orbits, which are often highly inclined to the ecliptic (the orbital plane of the planets), and spend most of the time at distances beyond Neptune.

The Planets

What Is a Planet?

Our solar system has two classes of planets whose origins can be partially explained or understood. The terrestrial, or inner planets (Mercury, Venus, Earth, and Mars), are small and have solid surfaces and mean densities that suggest an iron core surrounded by a rocky, partially molten mantle. The jovian, or outer planets (Jupiter, Saturn, Uranus, and Neptune), are very large bodies consisting primarily of hydrogen and helium in gas and liquid forms; thus, they have much lower average densities than the terrestrial planets. Planets within our solar system vary widely in other ways as well: For example, in whether they have moons, rings,or internal heat sources, and whether they rotate rapidly or slowly.

In the past two decades, a large number of rocky, icy bodies have been discovered beyond the orbit of Neptune, in the general vicinity of Pluto, in a region known as the Kuiper belt. A few of these Kuiper belt objects are not much smaller than Pluto. One of them, Eris, is slightly larger than Pluto and has a moon, Dysnomia. The Kuiper belt can thus be considered an icy, distant analog of the asteroid belt between Mars and Jupiter, which contains many small, rocky bodies, the largest of which is Ceres. Astronomers hope to learn more about Pluto and the Kuiper belt when the New Horizons spacecraft (launched in 2006) reaches Pluto in 2015. This should provide new clues to the origin of the solar system.

In 2006, the International Astronomical Union (IAU), an organization of professional astronomers, decided to reclassify Pluto as a "dwarf planet" rather than a genuine planet. Eris and Ceres are also now considered to be dwarf planets; they orbit the sun, and they are large enough to be roughly spherical, but they are not large enough to clear most other, smaller bodies out of their orbital regions. All of the other, smaller objects are now known as "small solar-system bodies," although some of them will probably become reclassified as dwarf planets if they are sufficiently large to be roughly spherical. In 2008 those dwarf planets outside Neptune's orbit were subclassified as plutoids, which currently are known to include Pluto and Eris.

However, not all astronomers agree with the IAU demotion of Pluto from planetary status. The exact definition of a planet is still being debated. So, although our solar system is now said to have only eight planets, the consensus could change in the future.

Also, improvements in telescopic observation have led astronomers to detect evidence of large bodies orbiting other stars than our sun. Of the more than 300 such "exoplanets" or "extrasolar planets" discovered in the past two decades, many have strange, unexpected properties, such as giant planets orbiting very close to stars ("hot Jupiters"), planets with highly eccentric (elliptical) orbits, bloated planets, and planets with ferocious winds. There are even three small "planets" known to orbit a neutron star—a tiny, ultra-dense stellar remnant that formed when the massive star exploded at the end of its life.

JUPITER

SATURN

RELATIVE SCALE
The planets are shown here in proportionate size to one another and the sun, whose edge is shown across the top. The dwarf planets are less than 3,000 kilometers in diameter—much smaller than Mercury. See the Planetary Orbits diagram in the upper right of this plate for their proper relationship to the sun.

URANUS

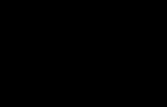

NEPTUNE

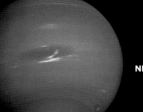

EARTH

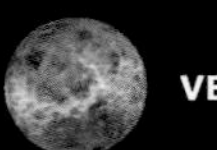

VENUS

MARS

Inner Planets ▶

MERCURY	
Average distance from the sun:	57,900,000 km
Perihelion:	46,000,000 km
Aphelion:	69,820,000 km
Revolution period:	88 days
Average orbital speed:	47.9 km/s
Average temperature:	167°C
Rotation period:	58.9 days
Equatorial diameter:	4,879 km
Mass (Earth=1):	0.055
Density:	5.43 g/cm^3
Surface gravity (Earth=1):	0.38
Known satellites:	none

Image by: Mariner 10

Outer Planets ▶

JUPITER	
Average distance from the sun:	778,600,000 km
Perihelion:	740,520,000 km
Aphelion:	816,620,000 km
Revolution period:	11.87 years
Average orbital speed:	13.1 km/s
Average temperature:	-110°C
Rotation period:	9.9 hours
Equatorial diameter:	142,984 km
Mass (Earth=1):	317.8
Density:	1.33 g/cm^3
Surface gravity (Earth=1):	2.36
Known satellites:	49
Largest satellites:	Ganymede, Callisto, Io, Europa

Image by: Cassini Orbiter

Perihelion and aphelion define the orbit's closest and farthest points from the sun. Mass and surface gravity data for each planet are expressed in proportional relation to Earth. Approximate values for Earth are given in both categories, allowing comparison between planets.

SUN

Average surface temperature:	5,505°C
Average core temperature:	16,000,000°C
Rotation period:	25 days
Equatorial diameter:	1,392,000 km
Mass (Earth=1):	332,950
Density:	1.41 g/cm^3
Surface gravity (Earth=1):	28.0

Planetary Orbits *(See also pages 276-277)*

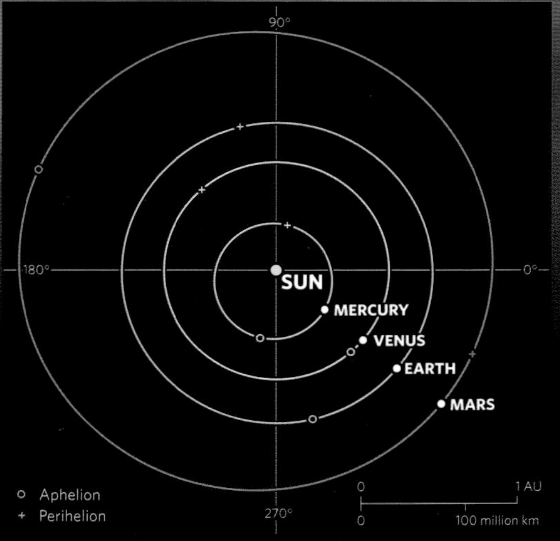
90°
180°
0°
270°
SUN
MERCURY
VENUS
EARTH
MARS
Aphelion
Perihelion
0
1 AU
0
100 million km

Inner Planets

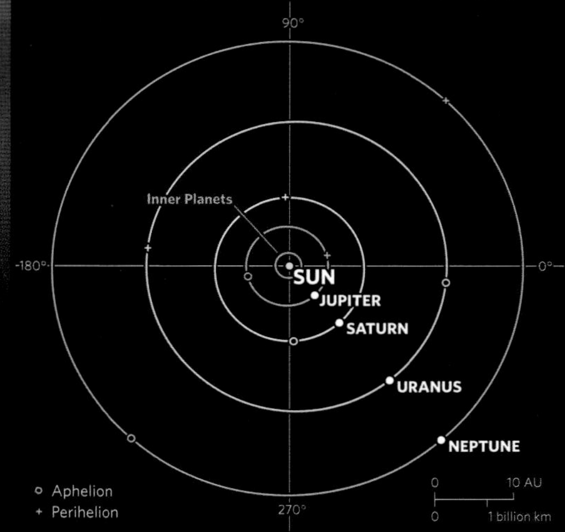
90°
180°
0°
270°
Inner Planets
SUN
JUPITER
SATURN
URANUS
NEPTUNE
Aphelion
Perihelion
0
10 AU
0
1 billion km

Outer Planets

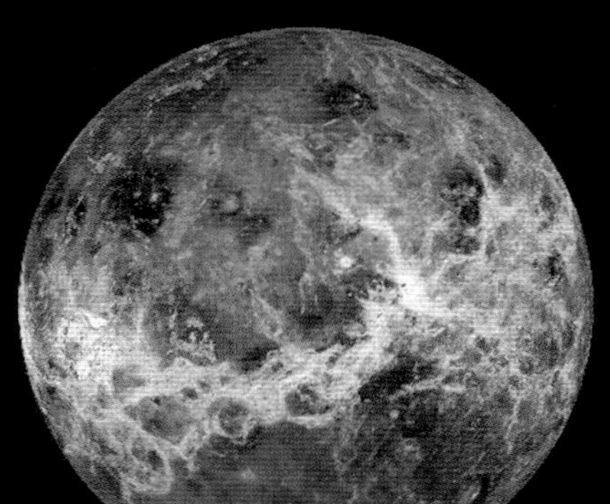

VENUS

Average distance from the sun:	108,200,000 km
Perihelion:	107,480,000 km
Aphelion:	108,940,000 km
Revolution period:	224.7 days
Average orbital speed:	35 km/s
Average temperature:	464°C
Rotation period:	244 days
Equatorial diameter:	12,104 km
Mass (Earth=1):	0.816
Density:	5.24 g/cm^3
Surface gravity (Earth=1):	0.91
Known satellites:	none

Image by: Magellan

EARTH

Average distance from the sun:	149,600,000 km
Perihelion:	147,090,000 km
Aphelion:	152,100,000 km
Revolution period:	365.2 days
Average orbital speed:	29.8 km/s
Average temperature:	15°C
Rotation period:	23.9 hours
Equatorial diameter:	12,756 km
Mass:	5,973,600,000,000,000,000,000 metric tons
Density:	5.52 g/cm^3
Surface gravity:	9.81 m/s^2
Known satellites:	1
Largest satellite:	Earth's moon

Image by: Galileo Orbiter

MARS

Average distance from the sun:	227,900,000 km
Perihelion:	206,620,000 km
Aphelion:	249,230,000 km
Revolution period:	687 days
Average orbital speed:	24.1 km/s
Average temperature:	-65°C
Rotation period:	24.6 hours
Equatorial diameter:	6,794 km
Mass (Earth=1):	0.107
Density:	3.93 g/cm^3
Surface gravity (Earth=1):	0.38
Known satellites:	2
Largest satellites:	Phobos, Deimos

Image by: Mars Global Surveyor

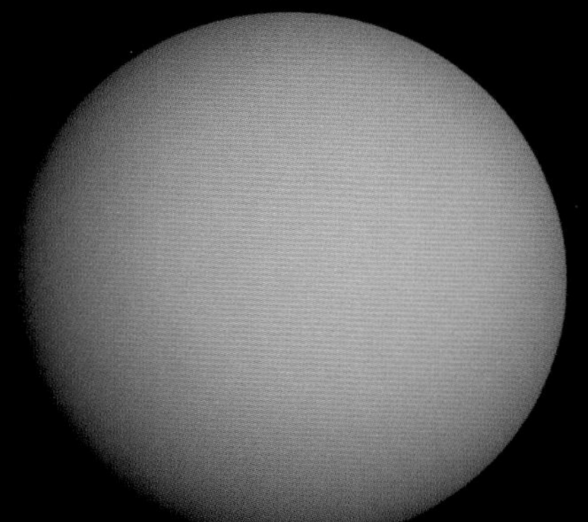

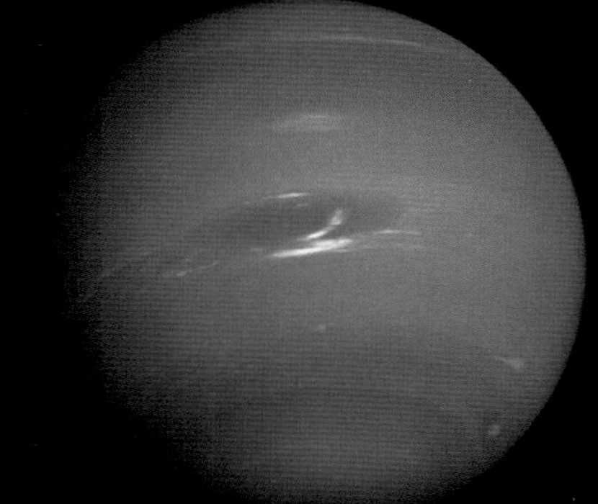

SATURN

Average distance from the sun:	1,433,500,000 km
Perihelion:	1,352,550,000 km
Aphelion:	1,514,500,000 km
Revolution period:	29.44 years
Average orbital speed:	9.7 km/s
Average temperature:	-140°C
Rotation period:	10.7 hours
Equatorial diameter:	120,536 km
Mass (Earth=1):	95.2
Density:	0.69 g/cm^3
Surface gravity (Earth=1):	0.92
Known satellites:	52
Largest satellites:	Titan, Rhea, Iapetus, Dione, Tethys

Image by: Cassini Orbiter

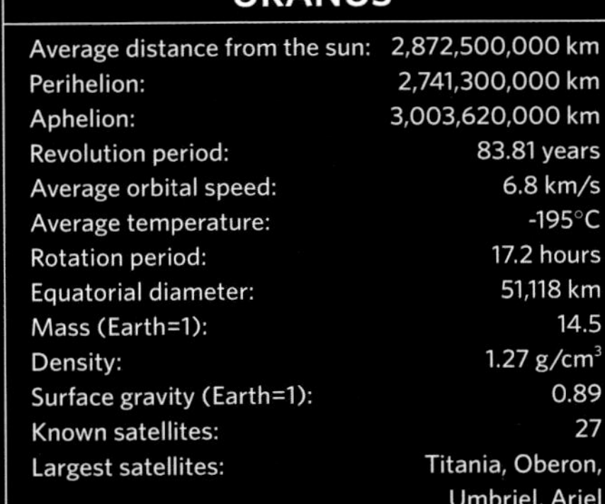

URANUS

Average distance from the sun:	2,872,500,000 km
Perihelion:	2,741,300,000 km
Aphelion:	3,003,620,000 km
Revolution period:	83.81 years
Average orbital speed:	6.8 km/s
Average temperature:	-195°C
Rotation period:	17.2 hours
Equatorial diameter:	51,118 km
Mass (Earth=1):	14.5
Density:	1.27 g/cm^3
Surface gravity (Earth=1):	0.89
Known satellites:	27
Largest satellites:	Titania, Oberon, Umbriel, Ariel

Image by: Hubble Space Telescope

NEPTUNE

Average distance from the sun:	4,495,100,000 km
Perihelion:	4,444,450,000 km
Aphelion:	4,545,670,000 km
Revolution period:	163.84 years
Average orbital speed:	5.4 km/s
Average temperature:	-200°C
Rotation period:	16.1 hours
Equatorial diameter:	49,528 km
Mass (Earth=1):	17.1
Density:	1.64 g/cm^3
Surface gravity (Earth=1):	1.12
Known satellites:	13
Largest satellite:	Triton

Image by: Voyager II

Mars

THE MARTIAN LANDSCAPE is both familiar and alien. All of its features, from rugged riverbeds to shifting sand dunes, are also found on Earth. Yet Mars, with its lower gravity and much thinner atmosphere, imprints its own character on these features: The volcanoes are taller, the canyons wider, and the ice caps more ephemeral than on Earth.

Compiled from NASA spacecraft data, the map at right depicts the remarkable terrain of the orange-red planet. Mars's polar caps have frozen water, like our Arctic and Antarctic, but during the winters frozen carbon dioxide also coats the poles. The huge crater at far left is a caldera atop Olympus Mons, a Missouri-size volcano more than two times the height of Mount Everest. Three more large calderas, to the right of Olympus Mons, mark the peaks of three other volcanoes along the Tharsis rise. To the right of Tharsis, the dark canyons of the Valles Marineris (Mariner Valleys) extend more than 2,500 miles (4,000 kilometers), nearly the entire width of the United States. To the right of center, the dark patch running north-south is Syrtis Major, often the easiest feature to spot with a small telescope.

Studies of Mars are continuing in earnest. For example, the Mars Reconnaissance orbiter is making detailed maps of Mars and its two moons, showing objects as small as a card table. Scientists are combining the pictures with elevation readings to produce spectacular three-dimensional views. In June 2008, the Phoenix Mars lander conducted several analyses of soil in the Martian arctic, finding some water-soluble elements and compounds that are necessary for life.

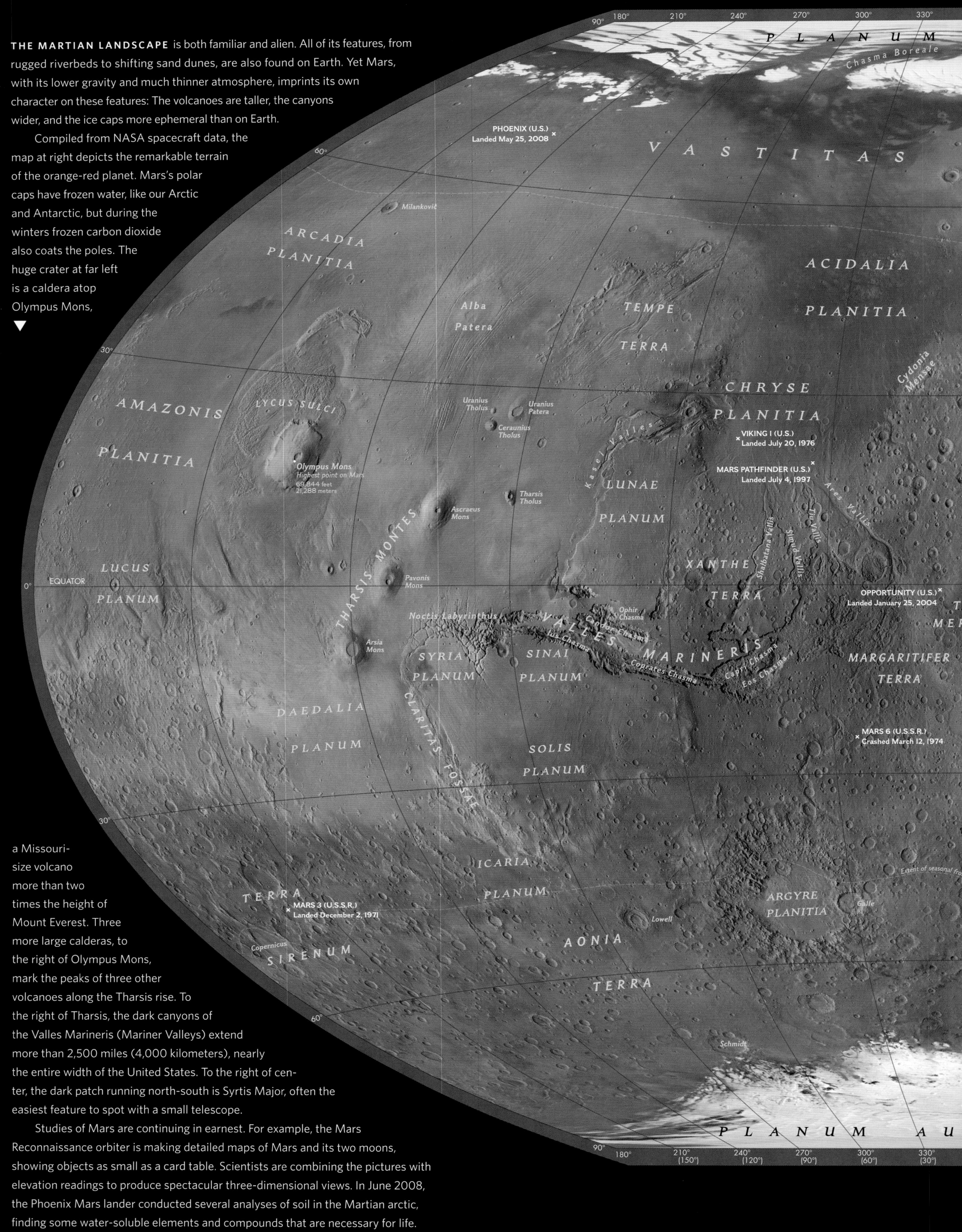

PLANUM
Chasma Boreale
PHOENIX (U.S.)
Landed May 25, 2008
VASTITAS
Milanković
ARCADIA PLANITIA
ACIDALIA PLANITIA
Alba Patera
TEMPE TERRA
AMAZONIS PLANITIA
LYCUS SULCI
Uranius Tholus
Uranius Patera
Ceraunius Tholus
CHRYSE PLANITIA
Cydonia Mensae
VIKING I (U.S.)
Landed July 20, 1976
MARS PATHFINDER (U.S.)
Landed July 4, 1997
Kasei Valles
Olympus Mons
Highest point on Mars
69,844 feet
21,288 meters
Tharsis Tholus
LUNAE PLANUM
Ascraeus Mons
Ares Vallis
THARSIS MONTES
XANTHE TERRA
Shalbatana Vallis
Simud Vallis
Tiu Vallis
LUCUS PLANUM
EQUATOR
Pavonis Mons
OPPORTUNITY (U.S.)
Landed January 25, 2004
Ophir Chasma
Candor Chasma
Noctis Labyrinthus
VALLES MARINERIS
Ius Chasma
Coprates Chasma
Capri Chasma
Eos Chasma
Arsia Mons
SYRIA PLANUM
SINAI PLANUM
MARGARITIFER TERRA
DAEDALIA PLANUM
CLARITAS FOSSAE
MARS 6 (U.S.S.R.)
Crashed March 12, 1974
SOLIS PLANUM
ICARIA PLANUM
Extent of seasonal frost
TERRA SIRENUM
MARS 3 (U.S.S.R.)
Landed December 2, 1971
ARGYRE PLANITIA
Galle
Lowell
Copernicus
AONIA TERRA
Schmidt
PLANUM AU
90°
180°
210°
240°
270°
300°
330°
60°
30°
0°
(150°)
(120°)
(90°)
(60°)
(30°)

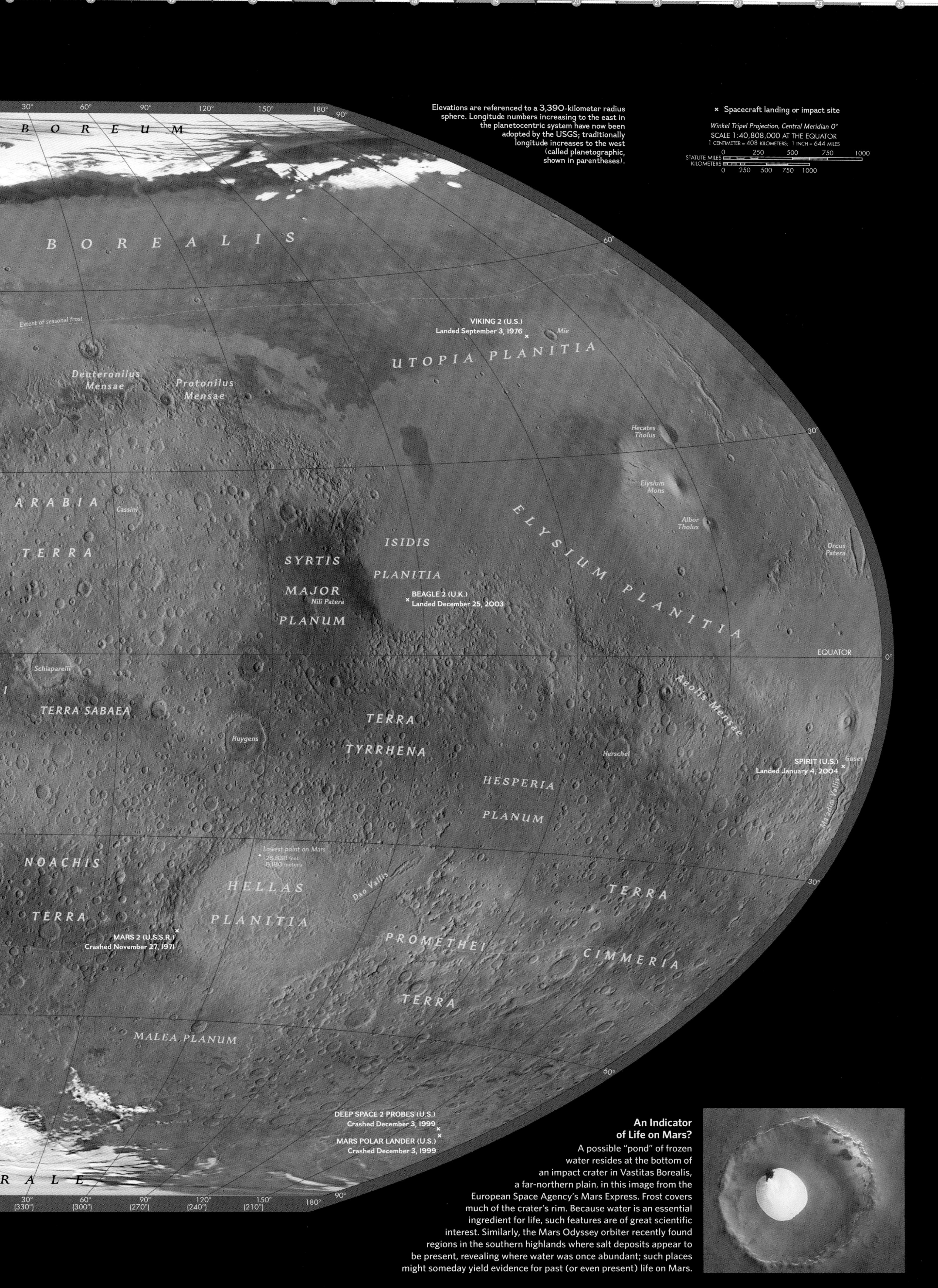
Elevations are referenced to a 3,390-kilometer radius sphere. Longitude numbers increasing to the east in the planetocentric system have now been adopted by the USGS; traditionally longitude increases to the west (called planetographic, shown in parentheses).
× Spacecraft landing or impact site
Winkel Tripel Projection, Central Meridian 0°
SCALE 1:40,808,000 AT THE EQUATOR
1 CENTIMETER = 408 KILOMETERS; 1 INCH = 644 MILES
STATUTE MILES 0 250 500 750 1000
KILOMETERS 0 250 500 750 1000
BOREUM
BOREALIS
Extent of seasonal frost
VIKING 2 (U.S.)
Landed September 3, 1976
Mie
UTOPIA PLANITIA
Deuteronilus Mensae
Protonilus Mensae
Hecates Tholus
Elysium Mons
Albor Tholus
ARABIA
TERRA
Cassini
ELYSIUM PLANITIA
ISIDIS
PLANITIA
SYRTIS
MAJOR
Nili Patera
PLANUM
BEAGLE 2 (U.K.)
Landed December 25, 2003
Orcus Patera
EQUATOR
Schiaparelli
TERRA SABAEA
Huygens
TERRA
TYRRHENA
Aeolis Mensae
Herschel
SPIRIT (U.S.)
Landed January 4, 2004
Gusev
Ma'adim Vallis
HESPERIA
PLANUM
NOACHIS
TERRA
Lowest point on Mars
26,838 feet
-8,180 meters
HELLAS
PLANITIA
Dao Vallis
MARS 2 (U.S.S.R.)
Crashed November 27, 1971
PROMETHEI
TERRA
CIMMERIA
TERRA
MALEA PLANUM
DEEP SPACE 2 PROBES (U.S.)
Crashed December 3, 1999
MARS POLAR LANDER (U.S.)
Crashed December 3, 1999
RALE
30° 60° 90° 120° 150° 180°
30° (330°) 60° (300°) 90° (270°) 120° (240°) 150° (210°) 180°
60° 30° 0° 30° 60° 90°

An Indicator of Life on Mars?

A possible "pond" of frozen water resides at the bottom of an impact crater in Vastitas Borealis, a far-northern plain, in this image from the European Space Agency's Mars Express. Frost covers much of the crater's rim. Because water is an essential ingredient for life, such features are of great scientific interest. Similarly, the Mars Odyssey orbiter recently found regions in the southern highlands where salt deposits appear to be present, revealing where water was once abundant; such places might someday yield evidence for past (or even present) life on Mars.

Universe

Looking Back in Time for Origins

Supercomputer calculations simulate the structure of the early universe. The formation of great chains of protogalaxies was probably triggered by seed concentrations of as yet unidentified dark matter. The first stars in the 13.7 billion-year-old universe may have formed as early as 200 to 300 million years after the dawn of time, and a total of only 500 to 800 million years elapsed until the first galaxies formed. Hydrogen and helium from the big bang were transformed by nuclear reactions in stars and supernova explosions into all the other chemical elements found on Earth.

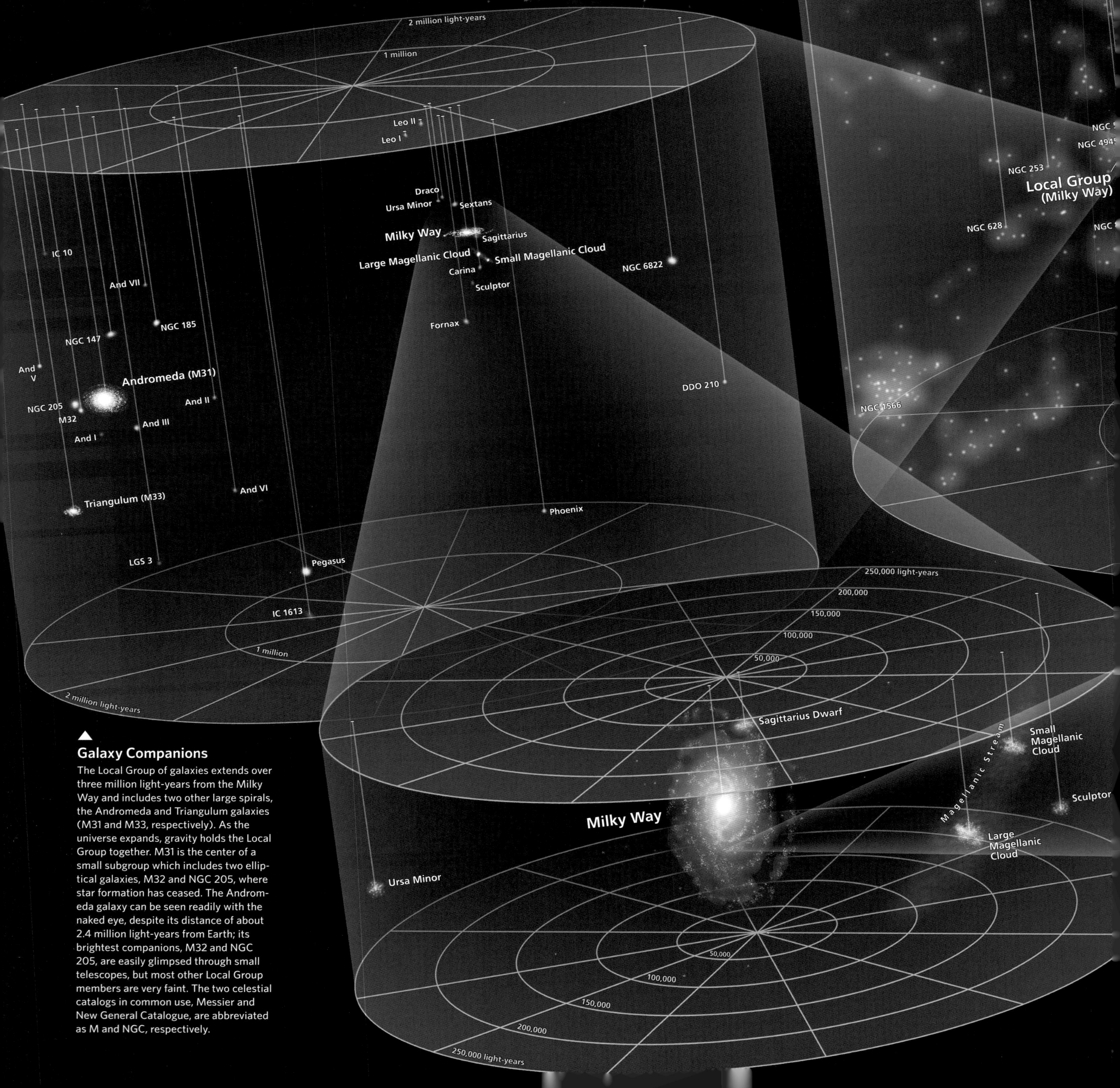

▲

Galaxy Companions

The Local Group of galaxies extends over three million light-years from the Milky Way and includes two other large spirals, the Andromeda and Triangulum galaxies (M31 and M33, respectively). As the universe expands, gravity holds the Local Group together. M31 is the center of a small subgroup which includes two elliptical galaxies, M32 and NGC 205, where star formation has ceased. The Andromeda galaxy can be seen readily with the naked eye, despite its distance of about 2.4 million light-years from Earth; its brightest companions, M32 and NGC 205, are easily glimpsed through small telescopes, but most other Local Group members are very faint. The two celestial catalogs in common use, Messier and New General Catalogue, are abbreviated as M and NGC, respectively.

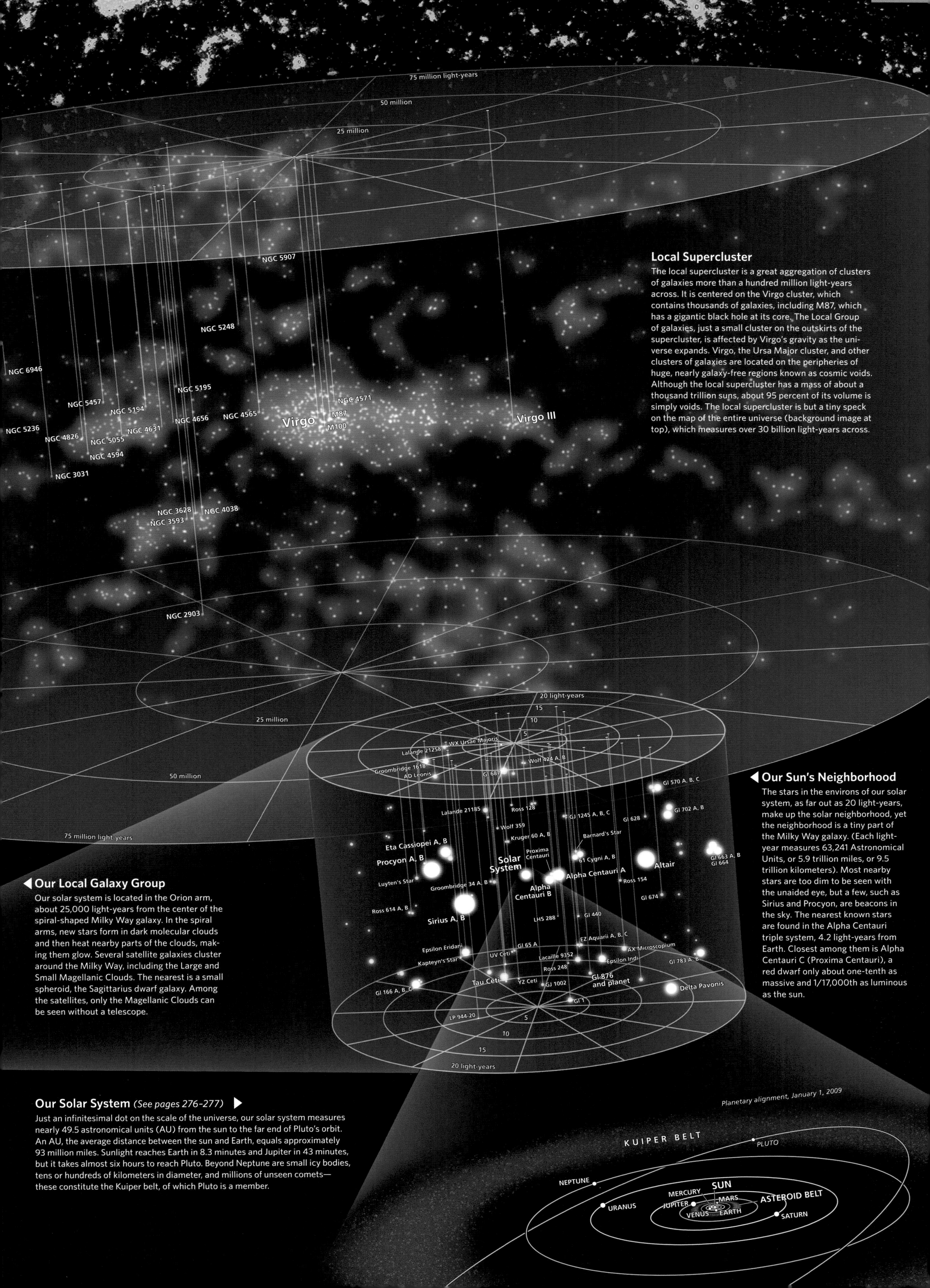

Local Supercluster

The local supercluster is a great aggregation of clusters of galaxies more than a hundred million light-years across. It is centered on the Virgo cluster, which contains thousands of galaxies, including M87, which has a gigantic black hole at its core. The Local Group of galaxies, just a small cluster on the outskirts of the supercluster, is affected by Virgo's gravity as the universe expands. Virgo, the Ursa Major cluster, and other clusters of galaxies are located on the peripheries of huge, nearly galaxy-free regions known as cosmic voids. Although the local supercluster has a mass of about a thousand trillion suns, about 95 percent of its volume is simply voids. The local supercluster is but a tiny speck on the map of the entire universe (background image at top), which measures over 30 billion light-years across.

◀ Our Sun's Neighborhood

The stars in the environs of our solar system, as far out as 20 light-years, make up the solar neighborhood, yet the neighborhood is a tiny part of the Milky Way galaxy. (Each light-year measures 63,241 Astronomical Units, or 5.9 trillion miles, or 9.5 trillion kilometers). Most nearby stars are too dim to be seen with the unaided eye, but a few, such as Sirius and Procyon, are beacons in the sky. The nearest known stars are found in the Alpha Centauri triple system, 4.2 light-years from Earth. Closest among them is Alpha Centauri C (Proxima Centauri), a red dwarf only about one-tenth as massive and 1/17,000th as luminous as the sun.

◀ Our Local Galaxy Group

Our solar system is located in the Orion arm, about 25,000 light-years from the center of the spiral-shaped Milky Way galaxy. In the spiral arms, new stars form in dark molecular clouds and then heat nearby parts of the clouds, making them glow. Several satellite galaxies cluster around the Milky Way, including the Large and Small Magellanic Clouds. The nearest is a small spheroid, the Sagittarius dwarf galaxy. Among the satellites, only the Magellanic Clouds can be seen without a telescope.

Our Solar System *(See pages 276-277)* ▶

Just an infinitesimal dot on the scale of the universe, our solar system measures nearly 49.5 astronomical units (AU) from the sun to the far end of Pluto's orbit. An AU, the average distance between the sun and Earth, equals approximately 93 million miles. Sunlight reaches Earth in 8.3 minutes and Jupiter in 43 minutes, but it takes almost six hours to reach Pluto. Beyond Neptune are small icy bodies, tens or hundreds of kilometers in diameter, and millions of unseen comets—these constitute the Kuiper belt, of which Pluto is a member.

Planetary alignment, January 1, 2009

Flags & Facts

NATIONAL
GEOGRAPHIC
SOCIETY

Flags and Facts

THE FOLLOWING PAGES present a general overview for all 194 independent countries recognized by the National Geographic Society in the spring of 2008, including the youngest nation, Kosovo, gaining independence in 2008. Abbreviated entries for other areas including dependencies and areas of special status have also been included. Dependencies, such as territories, are nonindependent political entities having an association with an independent nation. These sovereign nations are listed in parentheses. Locator maps in the upper right corner of each spread show the location of the political entities found on those two pages. Colors used match those used on political maps throughout this atlas.

Flags of each independent country, having been created using design specifications from expert vexillologists, symbolize diverse cultures and histories. The statistical data provide highlights of geography, demography, and economy. These details offer a brief overview of each entity; they present general characteristics and are not intended to be comprehensive studies. For example, not every language spoken in a specific region can be listed. Thus, languages shown are provided as the most representative of that area.

A Flags and Facts key explaining the categories presented below and their sources can be found at the end of the list on page 301.

A Special Flags section including international, regional, and religious flags is on pages 302-303.

Afghanistan
ISLAMIC REPUBLIC OF AFGHANISTAN

CONTINENT Asia
AREA 652,090 sq km (251,773 sq mi)
POPULATION 31,890,000
DEMONYM Afghan(s)
CAPITAL Kabul 3,324,000
RELIGION Sunni Muslim, Shiite Muslim
LANGUAGE Afghan Persian (Dari), Pashto, Turkic languages (primarily Uzbek and Turkmen), Baluchi, 30 minor languages (including Pashai)
LITERACY 28%
LIFE EXPECTANCY 42 years
GDP PER CAPITA $800
CURRENCY afghani (AFN)
ECONOMY **IND:** small-scale production of textiles, soap, furniture, shoes; handwoven carpets; natural gas **AGR:** opium, wheat, fruits, nuts; wool, mutton **EXP:** opium, fruits and nuts, handwoven carpets, wool, cotton, precious and semiprecious gems
MAP pages 190-191

Albania
REPUBLIC OF ALBANIA

CONTINENT Europe
AREA 28,748 sq km (11,100 sq mi)
POPULATION 3,174,000
DEMONYM Albanian(s)
CAPITAL Tirana 406,000
RELIGION Muslim, Albanian Orthodox, Roman Catholic
LANGUAGE Albanian, Greek, Vlach, Romani, Slavic dialects
LITERACY 99%
LIFE EXPECTANCY 75 years
GDP PER CAPITA $5,500
CURRENCY lek (ALL); note: the plural of lek is leke
ECONOMY **IND:** food processing, textiles and clothing, lumber, oil, cement, chemicals **AGR:** wheat, corn, potatoes, fruits and vegetables; meat **EXP:** textiles, footwear, asphalt, metals and metallic ores, crude oil, fruits and vegetables, tobacco
MAP pages 162-163

Algeria
PEOPLE'S DEMOCRATIC REPUBLIC OF ALGERIA

CONTINENT Africa
AREA 2,381,741 sq km (919,595 sq mi)
POPULATION 34,104,000
DEMONYM Algerian(s)
CAPITAL Algiers 3,355,000
RELIGION Sunni Muslim
LANGUAGE Arabic, French, Berber dialects
LITERACY 70%
LIFE EXPECTANCY 72 years
GDP PER CAPITA $8,100
CURRENCY Algerian dinar (DZD)
ECONOMY **IND:** petroleum, natural gas, light industries, mining **AGR:** wheat, barley, oats, grapes, olives; sheep **EXP:** petroleum, natural gas, petroleum products
MAP pages 216-217

American Samoa (U.S.)
TERRITORY OF AMERICAN SAMOA

CONTINENT Australia/Oceania
AREA 199 sq km (77 sq mi)
POPULATION 67,000
DEMONYM American Samoan(s) (U.S. nationals)
CAPITAL Pago Pago 58,000
RELIGION Christian Congregationalist, Roman Catholic, Protestant
LANGUAGE Samoan
MAP pages 244-245

Andorra
PRINCIPALITY OF ANDORRA

CONTINENT Europe
AREA 468 sq km (181 sq mi)
POPULATION 81,000
DEMONYM Andorran(s)
CAPITAL Andorra la Vella 24,000
RELIGION Roman Catholic
LANGUAGE Catalan, French, Castilian, Portuguese
LITERACY 100%
LIFE EXPECTANCY NA
GDP PER CAPITA $38,800
CURRENCY euro (EUR)
ECONOMY **IND:** tourism (particularly skiing), cattle raising, timber, banking **AGR:** rye, wheat, barley, oats, vegetables; sheep **EXP:** tobacco products, furniture
MAP pages 170-171

Angola
REPUBLIC OF ANGOLA

CONTINENT Africa
AREA 1,246,700 sq km (481,354 sq mi)
POPULATION 16,293,000
DEMONYM Angolan(s)
CAPITAL Luanda 4,007,000
RELIGION indigenous beliefs, Roman Catholic, Protestant
LANGUAGE Portuguese, Bantu and other African languages
LITERACY 67%
LIFE EXPECTANCY 41 years
GDP PER CAPITA $6,500
CURRENCY kwanza (AOA)
ECONOMY **IND:** petroleum, diamonds, iron ore, phosphates **AGR:** bananas, sugarcane, coffee, sisal; livestock; forest products; fish **EXP:** crude oil, diamonds, petroleum products, gas
MAP pages 224-225

Anguilla (U.K.)
ANGUILLA

CONTINENT North America
AREA 96 sq km (37 sq mi)
POPULATION 14,000
DEMONYM Anguillan(s)
CAPITAL The Valley 1,000
RELIGION Anglican, Methodist, other Protestant, Roman Catholic
LANGUAGE English
MAP pages 120-121

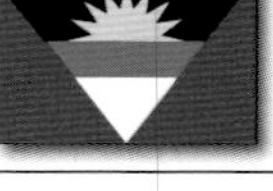

Antigua and Barbuda
ANTIGUA AND BARBUDA

CONTINENT North America
AREA 442 sq km (171 sq mi)
POPULATION 86,000
DEMONYM Antiguan(s), Barbudan(s)
CAPITAL St. John's 26,000
RELIGION Anglican, Seventh-day Adventist, Pentecostal, Moravian, Roman Catholic, Methodist, Baptist, Church of God, other Christian
LANGUAGE English, local dialects
LITERACY 86%
LIFE EXPECTANCY 72 years
GDP PER CAPITA $10,900
CURRENCY East Caribbean dollar (XCD)
ECONOMY **IND:** tourism, construction, light manufacturing (clothing, alcohol, household appliances) **AGR:** cotton, fruits, vegetables, bananas; livestock **EXP:** petroleum products, manufactures, machinery and transport equipment, food and live animals
MAP pages 120-121

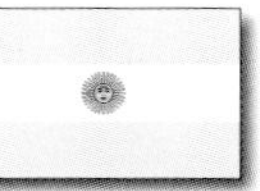

Argentina
ARGENTINE REPUBLIC

CONTINENT South America
AREA 2,780,400 sq km (1,073,518 sq mi)
POPULATION 39,356,000
DEMONYM Argentine(s)
CAPITAL Buenos Aires 12,795,000
RELIGION Roman Catholic
LANGUAGE Spanish, English, Italian, German, French
LITERACY 97%
LIFE EXPECTANCY 75 years
GDP PER CAPITA $13,000
CURRENCY Argentine peso (ARS)
ECONOMY **IND:** food processing, motor vehicles, consumer durables, textiles **AGR:** sunflower seeds, lemons, soybeans, grapes; livestock **EXP:** soybeans and derivatives, petroleum and gas, vehicles, corn, wheat
MAP pages 138-139

Armenia
REPUBLIC OF ARMENIA

CONTINENT Asia
AREA 29,743 sq km (11,484 sq mi)
POPULATION 3,014,000
DEMONYM Armenian(s)
CAPITAL Yerevan 1,102,000
RELIGION Armenian Apostolic, other Christian
LANGUAGE Armenian
LITERACY 99%
LIFE EXPECTANCY 71 years
GDP PER CAPITA $5,700
CURRENCY dram (AMD)
ECONOMY **IND:** diamond-processing, metal-cutting machine tools, forging-pressing machines, electric motors **AGR:** fruits (especially grapes), vegetables; livestock **EXP:** diamonds, mineral products, foodstuffs, energy
MAP pages 180-181

Aruba (Netherlands)
ARUBA

CONTINENT North America
AREA 193 sq km (75 sq mi)
POPULATION 99,000
DEMONYM Aruban(s)
CAPITAL Oranjestad 32,000
RELIGION Roman Catholic, Protestant, other (includes Hindu, Muslim, Confucian, Jewish)
LANGUAGE Papiamento, Spanish, English, Dutch
MAP pages 120-121

Flags in Front of The United Nations

Flags of its Member States stand in front of the 39-floor United Nations Secretariat Building in New York City. The flags are displayed in alphabetical order, running along First Avenue at UN Headquarters, an international zone belonging to its 192 members.

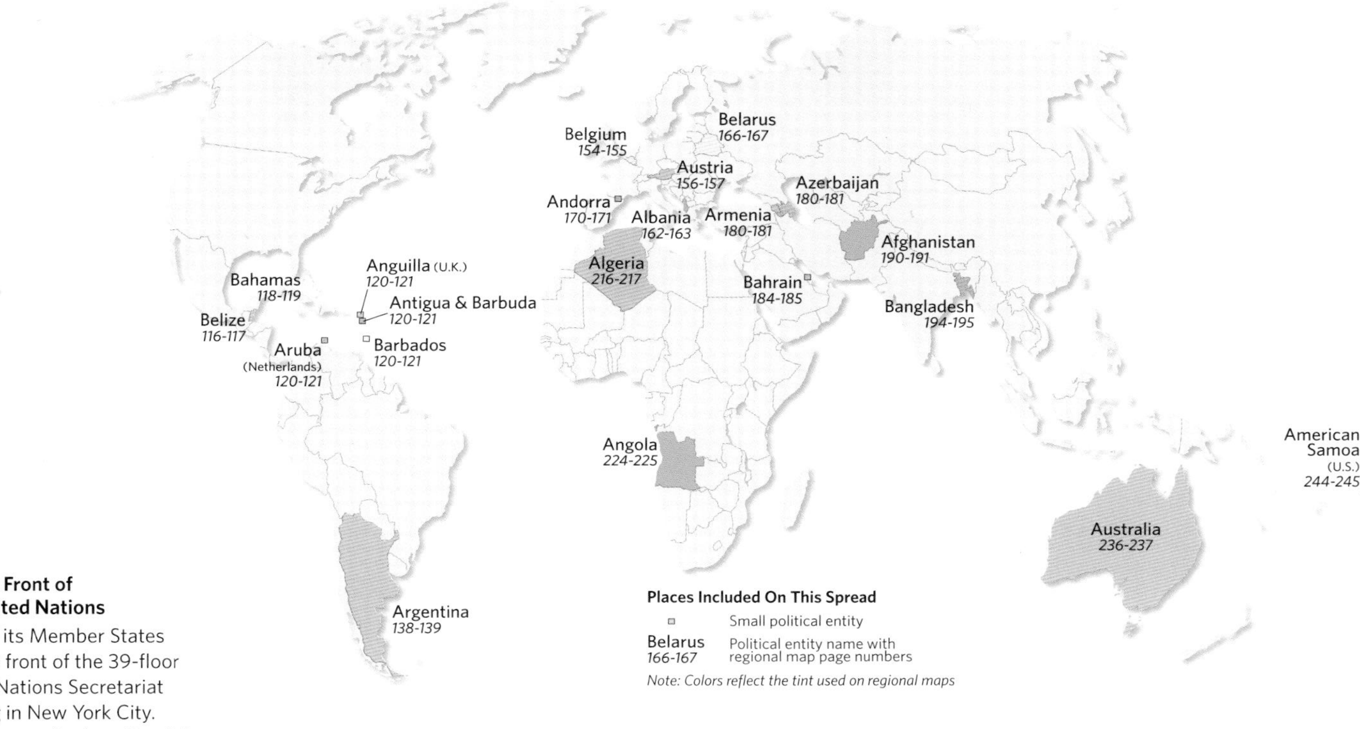
Belgium
154-155
Belarus
166-167
Austria
156-157
Azerbaijan
180-181
Andorra
170-171
Albania
162-163
Armenia
180-181
Afghanistan
190-191
Algeria
216-217
Bahrain
184-185
Bangladesh
194-195
Bahamas
118-119
Anguilla (U.K.)
120-121
Antigua & Barbuda
120-121
Belize
116-117
Aruba
(Netherlands)
120-121
Barbados
120-121
Angola
224-225
American Samoa
(U.S.)
244-245
Australia
236-237
Argentina
138-139
Places Included On This Spread
Small political entity
Belarus
166-167
Political entity name with regional map page numbers
Note: Colors reflect the tint used on regional maps

Australia
COMMONWEALTH OF AUSTRALIA

CONTINENT Australia/Oceania
AREA 7,692,024 sq km (2,969,906 sq mi)
POPULATION 21,000,000
DEMONYM Australian(s)
CAPITAL Canberra 378,000
RELIGION Roman Catholic, Anglican
LANGUAGE English
LITERACY 99%
LIFE EXPECTANCY 81 years
GDP PER CAPITA $37,500
CURRENCY Australian dollar (AUD)
ECONOMY **IND:** mining, industrial and transportation equipment, food processing, chemicals **AGR:** wheat, barley, sugarcane, fruits; cattle **EXP:** coal, iron ore, gold, meat, wool, alumina
MAP pages 236-237

Austria
REPUBLIC OF AUSTRIA

CONTINENT Europe
AREA 83,858 sq km (32,378 sq mi)
POPULATION 8,315,000
DEMONYM Austrian(s)
CAPITAL Vienna 2,315,000
RELIGION Roman Catholic, Protestant, Muslim
LANGUAGE German
LITERACY 98%
LIFE EXPECTANCY 80 years
GDP PER CAPITA $39,000
CURRENCY euro (EUR)
ECONOMY **IND:** construction, machinery, vehicles, food **AGR:** grains, potatoes, sugar beets, wine; dairy products; lumber **EXP:** machinery and equipment, motor vehicles, paper, metal goods
MAP pages 156-157

Azerbaijan
REPUBLIC OF AZERBAIJAN

CONTINENT Europe/Asia
AREA 86,600 sq km (33,436 sq mi)
POPULATION 8,581,000
DEMONYM Azerbaijani(s)
CAPITAL Baku 1,892,000
RELIGION Muslim
LANGUAGE Azerbaijani (Azeri)
LITERACY 99%
LIFE EXPECTANCY 72 years
GDP PER CAPITA $9,000
CURRENCY Azerbaijani manat (AZM)
ECONOMY **IND:** petroleum and natural gas products, oilfield equipment, steel, iron ore, cement **AGR:** cotton, grain, rice, grapes; cattle, pigs **EXP:** oil and gas, machinery, cotton, foodstuffs
MAP pages 180-181

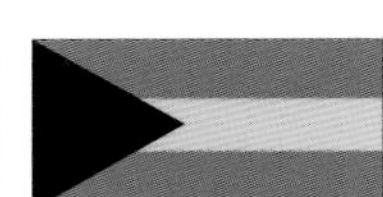

Bahamas
COMMONWEALTH OF THE BAHAMAS

CONTINENT North America
AREA 13,939 sq km (5,382 sq mi)
POPULATION 334,000
DEMONYM Bahamian(s)
CAPITAL Nassau 240,000
RELIGION Baptist, Anglican, Roman Catholic, Pentecostal, Church of God
LANGUAGE English, Creole
LITERACY 96%
LIFE EXPECTANCY 71 years
GDP PER CAPITA $22,700
CURRENCY Bahamian dollar (BSD)
ECONOMY **IND:** tourism, banking, cement, oil transshipment **AGR:** citrus, vegetables; poultry **EXP:** mineral products and salt, animal products, rum, chemicals
MAP pages 118-119

Bahrain
KINGDOM OF BAHRAIN

CONTINENT Asia
AREA 717 sq km (277 sq mi)
POPULATION 762,000
DEMONYM Bahraini(s)
CAPITAL Manama 157,000
RELIGION Muslim (Shiite and Sunni), Christian
LANGUAGE Arabic, English, Farsi, Urdu
LITERACY 87%
LIFE EXPECTANCY 74 years
GDP PER CAPITA $34,700
CURRENCY Bahraini dinar (BHD)
ECONOMY **IND:** petroleum processing and refining, aluminum smelting, iron pelletization, fertilizers **AGR:** fruits, vegetables; poultry; shrimp, fish **EXP:** petroleum and petroleum products, aluminum, textiles
MAP pages 184-185

Bangladesh
PEOPLE'S REPUBLIC OF BANGLADESH

CONTINENT Asia
AREA 147,570 sq km (56,977 sq mi)
POPULATION 149,002,000
DEMONYM Bangladeshi(s)
CAPITAL Dhaka 13,485,000
RELIGION Muslim, Hindu
LANGUAGE Bangla (Bengali), English
LITERACY 43%
LIFE EXPECTANCY 62 years
GDP PER CAPITA $1,400
CURRENCY taka (BDT)
ECONOMY **IND:** cotton textiles, jute, garments, tea processing **AGR:** rice, jute, tea, wheat, sugarcane; beef **EXP:** garments, jute and jute goods, leather, frozen fish
MAP pages 194-195

Barbados
BARBADOS

CONTINENT North America
AREA 430 sq km (166 sq mi)
POPULATION 278,000
DEMONYM Barbadian(s) or Bajan (colloquial)
CAPITAL Bridgetown 116,000
RELIGION Anglican, Pentecostal, Methodist, other Protestant, Roman Catholic
LANGUAGE English
LITERACY 100%
LIFE EXPECTANCY 76 years
GDP PER CAPITA $19,700
CURRENCY Barbadian dollar (BBD)
ECONOMY **IND:** tourism, sugar, light manufacturing, component assembly for export **AGR:** sugarcane, vegetables, cotton **EXP:** manufactures, sugar and molasses, rum, other foods and beverages
MAP pages 120-121

Belarus
REPUBLIC OF BELARUS

CONTINENT Europe
AREA 207,595 sq km (80,153 sq mi)
POPULATION 9,696,000
DEMONYM Belarusian(s)
CAPITAL Minsk 1,806,000
RELIGION Eastern Orthodox, other (includes Roman Catholic, Protestant, Jewish, Muslim)
LANGUAGE Belarusian, Russian
LITERACY 100%
LIFE EXPECTANCY 70 years
GDP PER CAPITA $10,200
CURRENCY Belarusian ruble (BYR)
ECONOMY **IND:** metal-cutting machine tools, tractors, trucks, earthmovers **AGR:** grain, potatoes, vegetables, sugar beets; beef **EXP:** machinery and equipment, mineral products, chemicals, metals
MAP pages 166-167

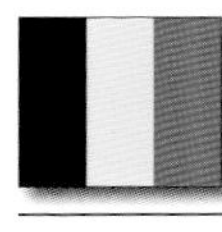

Belgium
KINGDOM OF BELGIUM

CONTINENT Europe
AREA 30,528 sq km (11,787 sq mi)
POPULATION 10,611,000
DEMONYM Belgian(s)
CAPITAL Brussels 1,743,000
RELIGION Roman Catholic, other (includes Protestant)
LANGUAGE Dutch, French
LITERACY 99%
LIFE EXPECTANCY 79 years
GDP PER CAPITA $36,500
CURRENCY euro (EUR)
ECONOMY **IND:** engineering and metal products, motor vehicle assembly, transportation equipment, scientific instruments **AGR:** sugar beets, fresh vegetables, fruits, grain; beef **EXP:** machinery and equipment, chemicals, diamonds, metals and metal products
MAP pages 154-155

Belize
BELIZE

CONTINENT North America
AREA 22,965 sq km (8,867 sq mi)
POPULATION 311,000
DEMONYM Belizean(s)
CAPITAL Belmopan 16,000
RELIGION Roman Catholic, Protestant (includes Pentecostal, Anglican, Seventh-day Adventist, Mennonite, Methodist)
LANGUAGE Spanish, Creole, Mayan dialects, English, Garifuna (Carib), German
LITERACY 77%
LIFE EXPECTANCY 70 years
GDP PER CAPITA $7,800
CURRENCY Belizean dollar (BZD)
ECONOMY **IND:** garment production, food processing, tourism, construction **AGR:** bananas, cacao, citrus, sugar; lumber; fish **EXP:** sugar, bananas, citrus, clothing, fish products
MAP pages 116-117

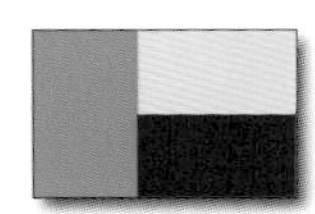

Benin
REPUBLIC OF BENIN

CONTINENT Africa
AREA 112,622 sq km (43,484 sq mi)
POPULATION 9,033,000
DEMONYM Beninese (singular and plural)
CAPITAL Porto-Novo (constitutional) 257,000; Cotonou (seat of government) 762,000
RELIGION Christian (includes Roman Catholic, Celestial, Methodist), Muslim, Vodoun
LANGUAGE French, Fon, Yoruba, tribal languages
LITERACY 35%
LIFE EXPECTANCY 56 years
GDP PER CAPITA $1,500
CURRENCY Communauté Financière Africaine franc (XOF)
ECONOMY **IND:** textiles, food processing, construction materials, cement **AGR:** cotton, corn, cassava (tapioca), yams; livestock **EXP:** cotton, cashews, shea butter, textiles, palm products
MAP pages 220-221

Bermuda (U.K.)
BERMUDA

CONTINENT North America
AREA 53 sq km (21 sq mi)
POPULATION 64,000
DEMONYM Bermudian(s)
CAPITAL Hamilton 11,000
RELIGION Anglican, Roman Catholic, African Methodist Episcopal, other Protestant
LANGUAGE English, Portuguese
MAP pages 118-119

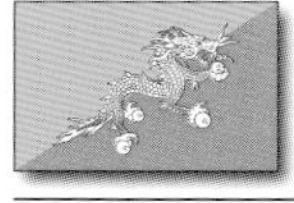

Bhutan
KINGDOM OF BHUTAN

CONTINENT Asia
AREA 46,500 sq km (17,954 sq mi)
POPULATION 896,000
DEMONYM Bhutanese (singular and plural)
CAPITAL Thimphu 83,000
RELIGION Lamaistic Buddhist, Indian- and Nepalese-influenced Hindu
LANGUAGE Dzongkha, Tibetan dialects, Nepalese dialects
LITERACY 47%
LIFE EXPECTANCY 64 years
GDP PER CAPITA $1,400
CURRENCY ngultrum (BTN); Indian rupee (INR)
ECONOMY **IND:** cement, wood products, processed fruits, alcoholic beverages **AGR:** rice, corn, root crops, citrus; dairy products **EXP:** electricity (to India), cardamom, gypsum, timber
MAP pages 194-195

Bolivia
REPUBLIC OF BOLIVIA

CONTINENT South America
AREA 1,098,581 sq km (424,164 sq mi)
POPULATION 9,815,000
DEMONYM Bolivian(s)
CAPITAL La Paz (administrative) 1,590,000; Sucre (legal) 243,000
RELIGION Roman Catholic, Protestant (includes Evangelical Methodist)
LANGUAGE Spanish, Quechua, Aymara
LITERACY 87%
LIFE EXPECTANCY 65 years
GDP PER CAPITA $4,400
CURRENCY boliviano (BOB)
ECONOMY **IND:** mining, smelting, petroleum, food and beverages **AGR:** soybeans, coffee, coca, cotton; timber **EXP:** natural gas, soybeans and soy products, crude petroleum, zinc ore
MAP pages 134-135

Bosnia and Herzegovina
BOSNIA AND HERZEGOVINA

CONTINENT Europe
AREA 51,129 sq km (19,741 sq mi)
POPULATION 3,845,000
DEMONYM Bosnian(s), Herzegovinian(s)
CAPITAL Sarajevo 377,000
RELIGION Muslim, Orthodox, Roman Catholic
LANGUAGE Bosnian, Croatian, Serbian
LITERACY 97%
LIFE EXPECTANCY 74 years
GDP PER CAPITA $6,600
CURRENCY konvertibilna marka (convertible mark) (BAM)
ECONOMY **IND:** steel, coal, iron ore, lead, zinc, vehicle assembly **AGR:** wheat, corn, fruits, vegetables; livestock **EXP:** metals, clothing, wood products
MAP pages 162-163

Botswana
REPUBLIC OF BOTSWANA

CONTINENT Africa
AREA 581,730 sq km (224,607 sq mi)
POPULATION 1,753,000
DEMONYM Motswana (singular), Batswana (plural)
CAPITAL Gaborone 224,000
RELIGION Christian, Badimo
LANGUAGE Setswana, Kalanga
LITERACY 81%
LIFE EXPECTANCY 34 years
GDP PER CAPITA $14,700
CURRENCY pula (BWP)
ECONOMY **IND:** diamonds, copper, nickel, salt, livestock processing **AGR:** livestock, sorghum, maize, millet, beans **EXP:** diamonds, copper, nickel, soda ash, meat
MAP pages 228-229

Brazil
FEDERATIVE REPUBLIC OF BRAZIL

CONTINENT South America
AREA 8,547,403 sq km (3,300,169 sq mi)
POPULATION 189,335,000
DEMONYM Brazilian(s)
CAPITAL Brasília 3,594,000
RELIGION Roman Catholic, Protestant
LANGUAGE Portuguese
LITERACY 89%
LIFE EXPECTANCY 72 years
GDP PER CAPITA $9,700
CURRENCY real (BRL)
ECONOMY **IND:** textiles, shoes, chemicals, cement, lumber **AGR:** coffee, soybeans, wheat, rice, corn; beef **EXP:** transport equipment, iron ore, soybeans, shoes
MAP pages 136-137

British Virgin Islands (U.K.)
BRITISH VIRGIN ISLANDS

CONTINENT North America
AREA 153 sq km (59 sq mi)
POPULATION 23,000
DEMONYM British Virgin Islander(s)
CAPITAL Road Town 9,000
RELIGION Protestant (includes Methodist, Anglican, Church of God, Seventh-day Adventist), Roman Catholic
LANGUAGE English
MAP pages 120-121

Brunei
NEGARA BRUNEI DARUSSALAM

CONTINENT Asia
AREA 5,765 sq km (2,226 sq mi)
POPULATION 372,000
DEMONYM Bruneian(s)
CAPITAL Bandar Seri Begawan 22,000
RELIGION Muslim, Buddhist, Christian, other (includes indigenous beliefs)
LANGUAGE Malay, English, Chinese
LITERACY 93%
LIFE EXPECTANCY 75 years
GDP PER CAPITA $25,600
CURRENCY Bruneian dollar (BND)
ECONOMY **IND:** petroleum, petroleum refining, liquefied natural gas, construction **AGR:** rice, vegetables, fruits; chickens, water buffalo **EXP:** crude oil, natural gas, refined products, clothing
MAP pages 206-207

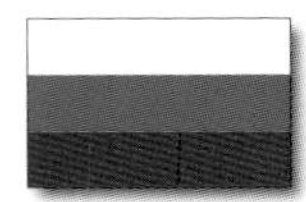

Bulgaria
REPUBLIC OF BULGARIA

CONTINENT Europe
AREA 110,994 sq km (42,855 sq mi)
POPULATION 7,660,000
DEMONYM Bulgarian(s)
CAPITAL Sofia 1,186,000
RELIGION Bulgarian Orthodox, Muslim
LANGUAGE Bulgarian, Turkish, Roma
LITERACY 98%
LIFE EXPECTANCY 73 years
GDP PER CAPITA $11,800
CURRENCY lev (BGL)
ECONOMY **IND:** electricity, gas, food and beverages, machinery and equipment **AGR:** vegetables, fruits, tobacco, wine; livestock **EXP:** clothing, footwear, iron and steel, machinery and equipment
MAP pages 162-163

Burkina Faso
BURKINA FASO

CONTINENT Africa
AREA 274,200 sq km (105,869 sq mi)
POPULATION 14,784,000
DEMONYM Burkinabe (singular and plural)
CAPITAL Ouagadougou 1,148,000
RELIGION Muslim, indigenous beliefs, Christian (mainly Roman Catholic)
LANGUAGE French, native African languages
LITERACY 22%
LIFE EXPECTANCY 51 years
GDP PER CAPITA $1,200
CURRENCY Communauté Financière Africaine franc (XOF)
ECONOMY **IND:** cotton lint, beverages, agricultural processing, soap **AGR:** cotton, peanuts, shea nuts, sesame; livestock **EXP:** cotton, livestock, gold
MAP pages 220-221

Burundi
REPUBLIC OF BURUNDI

CONTINENT Africa
AREA 27,834 sq km (10,747 sq mi)
POPULATION 8,508,000
DEMONYM Burundian(s)
CAPITAL Bujumbura 430,000
RELIGION Roman Catholic, indigenous beliefs, Muslim, Protestant
LANGUAGE Kirundi, French, Swahili
LITERACY 59%
LIFE EXPECTANCY 49 years
GDP PER CAPITA $800
CURRENCY Burundi franc (BIF)
ECONOMY **IND:** light consumer goods, assembly of imported components, public works construction, food processing **AGR:** coffee, cotton, tea, corn, sorghum; beef **EXP:** coffee, tea, sugar, cotton
MAP pages 226-227

Cambodia
KINGDOM OF CAMBODIA

CONTINENT Asia
AREA 181,035 sq km (69,898 sq mi)
POPULATION 14,364,000
DEMONYM Cambodian(s)
CAPITAL Phnom Penh 1,465,000
RELIGION Theravada Buddhist
LANGUAGE Khmer
LITERACY 74%
LIFE EXPECTANCY 63 years
GDP PER CAPITA $1,800
CURRENCY riel (KHR)
ECONOMY **IND:** tourism, garments, rice milling, fishing **AGR:** rice, rubber, corn, vegetables, cashews **EXP:** clothing, timber, rubber, rice, fish,
MAP pages 204-205

Cameroon
REPUBLIC OF CAMEROON

CONTINENT Africa
AREA 475,442 sq km (183,569 sq mi)
POPULATION 18,060,000
DEMONYM Cameroonian(s)
CAPITAL Yaoundé 1,610,000
RELIGION indigenous beliefs, Christian, Muslim
LANGUAGE 24 major African language groups, English, French
LITERACY 68%
LIFE EXPECTANCY 50 years
GDP PER CAPITA $2,300
CURRENCY Communauté Financière Africaine franc (XAF)
ECONOMY **IND:** petroleum production and refining, aluminum production, food processing, light consumer goods **AGR:** coffee, cocoa, cotton, rubber; livestock; timber **EXP:** crude oil and petroleum products, lumber, cocoa beans, aluminum
MAP pages 222-223

Canada
CANADA

CONTINENT North America
AREA 9,984,670 sq km (3,855,101 sq mi)
POPULATION 32,943,000
DEMONYM Canadian(s)
CAPITAL Ottawa 1,143,000
RELIGION Roman Catholic, Protestant (includes United Church, Anglican), other Christian
LANGUAGE English, French
LITERACY 99%
LIFE EXPECTANCY 80 years
GDP PER CAPITA $38,200
CURRENCY Canadian dollar (CAD)
ECONOMY **IND:** transportation equipment, chemicals, minerals, food products **AGR:** wheat, barley, oilseed, tobacco; dairy products; forest products; fish **EXP:** vehicles, industrial machinery, aircraft, telecommunications equipment
MAP pages 106-107

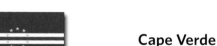

Cape Verde
REPUBLIC OF CAPE VERDE

CONTINENT Africa
AREA 4,036 sq km (1,558 sq mi)
POPULATION 494,000
DEMONYM Cape Verdean(s)
CAPITAL Praia 125,000
RELIGION Roman Catholic (infused with indigenous beliefs), Protestant (mostly Church of the Nazarene)
LANGUAGE Portuguese, Crioulo
LITERACY 77%
LIFE EXPECTANCY 71 years
GDP PER CAPITA $7,000
CURRENCY Cape Verdean escudo (CVE)
ECONOMY **IND:** food and beverages, fish processing, shoes and garments, salt mining **AGR:** bananas, corn, beans, sweet potatoes; fish **EXP:** fuel, shoes, garments, fish, hides
MAP pages 230-231

Cayman Islands (U.K.)
CAYMAN ISLANDS

CONTINENT North America
AREA 262 sq km (101 sq mi)
POPULATION 46,000
DEMONYM Caymanian(s)
CAPITAL George Town 28,000
RELIGION United Church (Presbyterian and Congregational), Anglican, Baptist, Church of God, other Protestant, Roman Catholic
LANGUAGE English
MAP pages 118-119

Central African Republic
CENTRAL AFRICAN REPUBLIC

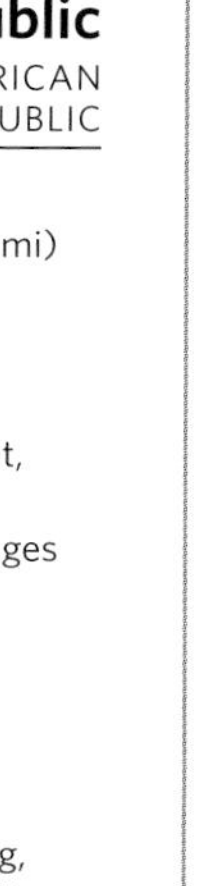

CONTINENT Africa
AREA 622,984 sq km (240,535 sq mi)
POPULATION 4,343,000
DEMONYM Central African(s)
CAPITAL Bangui 672,000
RELIGION indigenous beliefs, Protestant, Roman Catholic, Muslim
LANGUAGE French, Sangho, tribal languages
LITERACY 51%
LIFE EXPECTANCY 43 years
GDP PER CAPITA $700
CURRENCY Communauté Financière Africaine franc (XAF)
ECONOMY **IND:** gold and diamond mining, logging, brewing, textiles **AGR:** cotton, coffee, tobacco, manioc (tapioca); timber **EXP:** diamonds, timber, cotton, coffee, tobacco
MAP pages 222-223

Chad
REPUBLIC OF CHAD

CONTINENT Africa
AREA 1,284,000 sq km (495,755 sq mi)
POPULATION 10,781,000
DEMONYM Chadian(s)
CAPITAL N'Djamena 987,000
RELIGION Muslim, Catholic, Protestant, animist
LANGUAGE French, Arabic, Sara, over 120 languages and dialects
LITERACY 48%
LIFE EXPECTANCY 51 years
GDP PER CAPITA $1,600
CURRENCY Communauté Financière Africaine franc (XAF)
ECONOMY **IND:** oil, cotton textiles, meatpacking, beer brewing **AGR:** cotton, sorghum, millet, peanuts; cattle **EXP:** oil, cotton, cattle, gum arabic
MAP pages 222-223

Chile
REPUBLIC OF CHILE

CONTINENT South America
AREA 756,096 sq km (291,930 sq mi)
POPULATION 16,598,000
DEMONYM Chilean(s)
CAPITAL Santiago 5,719,000
RELIGION Roman Catholic, Evangelical
LANGUAGE Spanish
LITERACY 96%
LIFE EXPECTANCY 78 years
GDP PER CAPITA $14,400
CURRENCY Chilean peso (CLP)
ECONOMY **IND:** copper, other minerals, foodstuffs, fish processing **AGR:** grapes, apples, pears, onions; beef; timber; fish **EXP:** copper, fruits, fish products, paper, pulp
MAP pages 138-139

China
PEOPLE'S REPUBLIC OF CHINA

CONTINENT Asia
AREA 9,596,960 sq km (3,705,405 sq mi)
POPULATION 1,348,317,000
DEMONYM Chinese (singular and plural)
CAPITAL Beijing 11,106,000
RELIGION Taoist, Buddhist, Christian
LANGUAGE Standard Chinese or Mandarin, Yue, Wu, Minbei, Minnan, Xiang, Gan, Hakka dialects, minority languages
LITERACY 91%
LIFE EXPECTANCY 72 years
GDP PER CAPITA $5,300
CURRENCY renminbi (RMB); also referred to by the unit yuan (CNY)
ECONOMY **IND:** mining and ore processing (iron, steel, aluminum), coal, machine building, armaments **AGR:** rice, wheat, potatoes, corn; pork; fish **EXP:** machinery, electrical products, data processing equipment, apparel
MAP pages 196-197

Canada 106-107
Croatia 162-163
Bulgaria 162-163
Bosnia & Herzegovina 162-163
Bermuda (U.K.) 118-119
China 196-197
Cyprus 170-171
Cuba 118-119
British Virgin Islands (U.K.) 120-121
Burkina Faso 220-221
Chad 222-223
Bhutan 194-195
Cayman Islands (U.K.) 118-119
Cape Verde 230-231
Colombia 132-133
Central African Republic 222-223
Costa Rica 116-117
Cambodia 204-205
Brunei 206-207
Côte d'Ivoire 220-221
Burundi 226-227
Benin 220-221
Congo 224-225
Comoros 230-231
Cameroon 222-223
Brazil 136-137
Bolivia 134-135
Cook Islands (N.Z.) 244-245
Botswana 228-229
Chile 138-139
Places Included On This Spread
Small political entity
Brazil 136-137 Political entity name with regional map page numbers
Note: Colors reflect the tint used on regional maps

Colombia
REPUBLIC OF COLOMBIA

CONTINENT South America
AREA 1,141,748 sq km (440,831 sq mi)
POPULATION 46,156,000
DEMONYM Colombian(s)
CAPITAL Bogotá 7,764,000
RELIGION Roman Catholic
LANGUAGE Spanish
LITERACY 93%
LIFE EXPECTANCY 72 years
GDP PER CAPITA $7,200
CURRENCY Colombian peso (COP)
ECONOMY **IND:** textiles, food processing, oil, clothing and footwear **AGR:** coffee, cut flowers, bananas, rice; forest products; shrimp **EXP:** petroleum, coffee, coal, emeralds
MAP pages 132-133

Comoros
UNION OF THE COMOROS

CONTINENT Africa
AREA 1,862 sq km (719 sq mi)
POPULATION 711,000
DEMONYM Comoran(s)
CAPITAL Moroni 46,000
RELIGION Sunni Muslim
LANGUAGE Arabic, French, Shikomoro
LITERACY 57%
LIFE EXPECTANCY 64 years
GDP PER CAPITA $600
CURRENCY Comoran franc (KMF)
ECONOMY **IND:** fishing, tourism, perfume distillation **AGR:** vanilla, cloves, ylang-ylang, perfume essences, copra, bananas **EXP:** vanilla, perfume essences, cloves, copra
MAP pages 230-231

Congo
REPUBLIC OF THE CONGO

CONTINENT Africa
AREA 342,000 sq km (132,047 sq mi)
POPULATION 3,801,000
DEMONYM Congolese (singular and plural)
CAPITAL Brazzaville 1,332,000
RELIGION Christian, animist
LANGUAGE French, Lingala, Monokutuba, local languages
LITERACY 84%
LIFE EXPECTANCY 52 years
GDP PER CAPITA $3,700
CURRENCY Communauté Financière Africaine franc (XAF)
ECONOMY **IND:** petroleum extraction, cement, lumber, brewing **AGR:** cassava (tapioca), sugar, rice, corn; forest products **EXP:** petroleum, lumber, plywood, sugar, cocoa
MAP pages 224-225

Cook Islands (N.Z.)
COOK ISLANDS

CONTINENT Australia/Oceania
AREA 240 sq km (93 sq mi)
POPULATION 11,000
DEMONYM Cook Islander(s)
CAPITAL Avarua 10,000
RELIGION Cook Islands Christian Church, Roman Catholic, Seventh-day Adventist, Church of Latter-day Saints, other Protestant
LANGUAGE English, Maori
MAP pages 244-245

Costa Rica
REPUBLIC OF COSTA RICA

CONTINENT North America
AREA 51,100 sq km (19,730 sq mi)
POPULATION 4,477,000
DEMONYM Costa Rican(s)
CAPITAL San José 1,284,000
RELIGION Roman Catholic, Evangelical
LANGUAGE Spanish, English
LITERACY 96%
LIFE EXPECTANCY 79 years
GDP PER CAPITA $13,500
CURRENCY Costa Rican colon (CRC)
ECONOMY **IND:** microprocessors, food processing, textiles and clothing, construction materials **AGR:** bananas, pineapples, coffee, melons; beef; timber **EXP:** bananas, pineapples, coffee, melons, ornamental plants
MAP pages 116-117

Côte d'Ivoire (Ivory Coast)
REPUBLIC OF CÔTE D'IVOIRE

CONTINENT Africa
AREA 322,462 sq km (124,503 sq mi)
POPULATION 20,237,000
DEMONYM Ivoirian(s)
CAPITAL Abidjan (administrative) 3,801,000; Yamoussoukro (legislative) 669,000
RELIGION Muslim, indigenous beliefs, Christian
LANGUAGE French, Dioula, other native dialects
LITERACY 51%
LIFE EXPECTANCY 51 years
GDP PER CAPITA $1,800
CURRENCY Communauté Financière Africaine franc (XOF)
ECONOMY **IND:** foodstuffs, beverages, wood products, oil refining, automobile assembly **AGR:** coffee, cocoa beans, bananas, palm kernels; timber **EXP:** cocoa, coffee, timber, petroleum, cotton
MAP pages 220-221

Croatia
REPUBLIC OF CROATIA

CONTINENT Europe
AREA 56,542 sq km (21,831 sq mi)
POPULATION 4,448,000
DEMONYM Croat(s), Croatian(s)
CAPITAL Zagreb 689,000
RELIGION Roman Catholic, Orthodox
LANGUAGE Croatian
LITERACY 98%
LIFE EXPECTANCY 75 years
GDP PER CAPITA $15,500
CURRENCY kuna (HRK)
ECONOMY **IND:** chemicals and plastics, machine tools, fabricated metal, electronics **AGR:** wheat, corn, sugar beets, sunflower seed; livestock **EXP:** transport equipment, textiles, chemicals, foodstuffs
MAP pages 162-163

Cuba
REPUBLIC OF CUBA

CONTINENT North America
AREA 110,860 sq km (42,803 sq mi)
POPULATION 11,248,000
DEMONYM Cuban(s)
CAPITAL Havana 2,178,000
RELIGION Roman Catholic, Protestant, Jehovah's Witness, Jewish, Santeria
LANGUAGE Spanish
LITERACY 100%
LIFE EXPECTANCY 77 years
GDP PER CAPITA $4,500
CURRENCY Cuban peso (CUP)
ECONOMY **IND:** sugar, petroleum, tobacco, construction **AGR:** sugar, tobacco, citrus, coffee; livestock **EXP:** sugar, nickel, tobacco, fish, medical products
MAP pages 118-119

Cyprus
REPUBLIC OF CYPRUS

CONTINENT Europe
AREA 9,251 sq km (3,572 sq mi)
POPULATION 1,023,000
DEMONYM Cypriot(s)
CAPITAL Nicosia 233,000
RELIGION Greek Orthodox, Muslim, Maronite, Armenian Apostolic
LANGUAGE Greek, Turkish, English
LITERACY 98%
LIFE EXPECTANCY 78 years
GDP PER CAPITA $27,100; Northern Cyprus: $7,135
CURRENCY euro (EUR); new Turkish lira (TRY) in Northern Cyprus
ECONOMY **IND:** tourism, food and beverage processing, cement and gypsum production, ship repair **AGR:** citrus, vegetables, barley, grapes; poultry **EXP:** citrus, potatoes, dairy, pharmaceuticals, cement
MAP pages 170-171

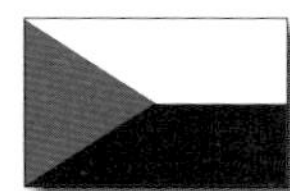

Czech Republic (Czechia)

CZECH REPUBLIC

CONTINENT Europe
AREA 78,866 sq km (30,450 sq mi)
POPULATION 10,305,000
DEMONYM Czech(s)
CAPITAL Prague 1,162,000
RELIGION Roman Catholic
LANGUAGE Czech
LITERACY 99%
LIFE EXPECTANCY 76 years
GDP PER CAPITA $24,400
CURRENCY Czech koruna (CZK)
ECONOMY **IND:** metallurgy, machinery and equipment, motor vehicles, glass, armaments **AGR:** wheat, potatoes, sugar beets, hops; pigs **EXP:** machinery and transport equipment, chemicals, raw materials, fuel
MAP pages 158-159

Democratic Republic of the Congo

DEMOCRATIC REPUBLIC OF THE CONGO

CONTINENT Africa
AREA 2,344,885 sq km (905,365 sq mi)
POPULATION 62,636,000
DEMONYM Congolese (singular and plural)
CAPITAL Kinshasa 7,851,000
RELIGION Roman Catholic, Protestant, Kimbanguist, Muslim, syncretic sects, indigenous beliefs
LANGUAGE French, Lingala, Kingwana, Kikongo, Tshiluba
LITERACY 66%
LIFE EXPECTANCY 45 years
GDP PER CAPITA $300
CURRENCY Congolese franc (CDF)
ECONOMY **IND:** mining (diamonds, copper, zinc), mineral processing, consumer products, cement **AGR:** coffee, sugar, palm oil, rubber; wood products **EXP:** diamonds, copper, crude oil, coffee
MAP pages 224-225

Denmark

KINGDOM OF DENMARK

CONTINENT Europe
AREA 43,098 sq km (16,640 sq mi)
POPULATION 5,454,000
DEMONYM Dane(s)
CAPITAL Copenhagen 1,086,000
RELIGION Evangelical Lutheran, other Protestant, Roman Catholic
LANGUAGE Danish, Faroese, Greenlandic, German, English as second language
LITERACY 99%
LIFE EXPECTANCY 78 years
GDP PER CAPITA $37,400
CURRENCY Danish krone (DKK)
ECONOMY **IND:** iron, steel, nonferrous metals, chemicals **AGR:** barley, wheat, potatoes, sugar beets; pork; fish **EXP:** machinery and instruments, meat, meat products, dairy products, fish
MAP pages 148-149

Djibouti

REPUBLIC OF DJIBOUTI

CONTINENT Africa
AREA 23,200 sq km (8,958 sq mi)
POPULATION 833,000
DEMONYM Djiboutian(s)
CAPITAL Djibouti 583,000
RELIGION Muslim, Christian
LANGUAGE French, Arabic, Somali, Afar
LITERACY 68%
LIFE EXPECTANCY 54 years
GDP PER CAPITA $1,000
CURRENCY Djiboutian franc (DJF)
ECONOMY **IND:** construction, agricultural processing **AGR:** fruits, vegetables; goats, sheep, camels **EXP:** reexports, hides and skins, coffee (in transit)
MAP pages 226-227

Dominica

COMMONWEALTH OF DOMINICA

CONTINENT North America
AREA 751 sq km (290 sq mi)
POPULATION 70,000
DEMONYM Dominican(s)
CAPITAL Roseau 14,000
RELIGION Roman Catholic, Seventh-day Adventist, Pentecostal, Baptist, Methodist, other Christian
LANGUAGE English, French patois
LITERACY 94%
LIFE EXPECTANCY 74 years
GDP PER CAPITA $3,800
CURRENCY East Caribbean dollar (XCD)
ECONOMY **IND:** soap, coconut oil, tourism, copra, furniture **AGR:** bananas, citrus, mangoes, root crops; forest and fishery potential not exploited **EXP:** bananas, soap, bay oil, vegetables, grapefruit
MAP pages 120-121

Dominican Republic

DOMINICAN REPUBLIC

CONTINENT North America
AREA 48,442 sq km (18,704 sq mi)
POPULATION 9,366,000
DEMONYM Dominican(s)
CAPITAL Santo Domingo 2,154,000
RELIGION Roman Catholic
LANGUAGE Spanish
LITERACY 87%
LIFE EXPECTANCY 72 years
GDP PER CAPITA $9,200
CURRENCY Dominican peso (DOP)
ECONOMY **IND:** tourism, sugar processing, ferronickel and gold mining, textiles **AGR:** sugarcane, coffee, cotton, cocoa; cattle **EXP:** ferro-nickel, sugar, gold, silver, coffee
MAP pages 118-119

Ecuador

REPUBLIC OF ECUADOR

CONTINENT South America
AREA 283,560 sq km (109,483 sq mi)
POPULATION 13,473,000
DEMONYM Ecuadorian(s)
CAPITAL Quito 1,697,000
RELIGION Roman Catholic
LANGUAGE Spanish, Quechua, other Amerindian languages
LITERACY 91%
LIFE EXPECTANCY 75 years
GDP PER CAPITA $7,100
CURRENCY US dollar (USD)
ECONOMY **IND:** petroleum, food processing, textiles, wood products **AGR:** bananas, coffee, cocoa, rice; cattle; balsa wood; fish **EXP:** petroleum, bananas, cut flowers, shrimp
MAP pages 134-135

Egypt

ARAB REPUBLIC OF EGYPT

CONTINENT Africa
AREA 1,002,000 sq km (386,874 sq mi)
POPULATION 73,418,000
DEMONYM Egyptian(s)
CAPITAL Cairo 11,893,000
RELIGION Muslim (mostly Sunni), Coptic Christian
LANGUAGE Arabic, English, French
LITERACY 71%
LIFE EXPECTANCY 71 years
GDP PER CAPITA $5,400
CURRENCY Egyptian pound (EGP)
ECONOMY **IND:** textiles, food processing, tourism, chemicals **AGR:** cotton, rice, corn, wheat, beans; cattle **EXP:** crude oil and petroleum products, cotton, textiles, metal products
MAP pages 218-219

El Salvador

REPUBLIC OF EL SALVADOR

CONTINENT North America
AREA 21,041 sq km (8,124 sq mi)
POPULATION 6,877,000
DEMONYM Salvadoran(s)
CAPITAL San Salvador 1,433,000
RELIGION Roman Catholic, Protestant
LANGUAGE Spanish, Nahua
LITERACY 80%
LIFE EXPECTANCY 71 years
GDP PER CAPITA $5,200
CURRENCY US dollar (USD)
ECONOMY **IND:** food processing, beverages, petroleum, chemicals **AGR:** coffee, sugar, corn, rice; beef; shrimp **EXP:** offshore assembly exports, coffee, sugar, shrimp
MAP pages 116-117

Equatorial Guinea

REPUBLIC OF EQUATORIAL GUINEA

CONTINENT Africa
AREA 28,051 sq km (10,831 sq mi)
POPULATION 507,000
DEMONYM Equatorial Guinean(s) or Equatoguinean(s)
CAPITAL Malabo 96,000
RELIGION Christian (predominantly Roman Catholic), pagan practices
LANGUAGE Spanish, French, Fang, Bubi
LITERACY 86%
LIFE EXPECTANCY 49 years
GDP PER CAPITA $44,100
CURRENCY Communauté Financière Africaine franc (XAF)
ECONOMY **IND:** petroleum, fishing, sawmilling, natural gas **AGR:** coffee, cocoa, rice, yams; livestock; timber **EXP:** petroleum, methanol, timber, cocoa
MAP pages 222-223

Eritrea

STATE OF ERITREA

CONTINENT Africa
AREA 121,144 sq km (46,774 sq mi)
POPULATION 4,851,000
DEMONYM Eritrean(s)
CAPITAL Asmara 600,000
RELIGION Muslim, Coptic Christian, Roman Catholic, Protestant
LANGUAGE Afar, Arabic, Tigre, Kunama, Tigrinya, other Cushitic languages
LITERACY 59%
LIFE EXPECTANCY 57 years
GDP PER CAPITA $1,000
CURRENCY nakfa (ERN)
ECONOMY **IND:** food processing, beverages, clothing and textiles, light manufacturing **AGR:** sorghum, lentils, vegetables, corn; livestock; fish **EXP:** livestock, sorghum, textiles, food, small manufactures
MAP pages 226-227

Estonia

REPUBLIC OF ESTONIA

CONTINENT Europe
AREA 45,227 sq km (17,462 sq mi)
POPULATION 1,341,000
DEMONYM Estonian(s)
CAPITAL Tallinn 397,000
RELIGION Evangelical Lutheran, Orthodox
LANGUAGE Estonian, Russian
LITERACY 100%
LIFE EXPECTANCY 73 years
GDP PER CAPITA $21,800
CURRENCY Estonian kroon (EEK)
ECONOMY **IND:** engineering, electronics, wood and wood products, textiles **AGR:** potatoes, vegetables; livestock and dairy products; fish **EXP:** machinery and equipment, wood and paper, textiles, food products
MAP pages 166-167

Ethiopia

FEDERAL DEMOCRATIC REPUBLIC OF ETHIOPIA

CONTINENT Africa
AREA 1,133,380 sq km (437,600 sq mi)
POPULATION 77,127,000
DEMONYM Ethiopian(s)
CAPITAL Addis Ababa 3,102,000
RELIGION Christian (Orthodox, Protestant), Muslim, traditional
LANGUAGE Amharic, Oromigna, Tigrinya, Guaragigna, Somali
LITERACY 43%
LIFE EXPECTANCY 49 years
GDP PER CAPITA $700
CURRENCY birr (ETB)
ECONOMY **IND:** food processing, beverages, textiles, leather **AGR:** cereals, pulses, coffee, oilseed; hides; fish **EXP:** coffee, qat, gold, leather products, live animals
MAP pages 226-227

Falkland Islands (U.K.)

FALKLAND ISLANDS

CONTINENT South America
AREA 12,173 sq km (4,700 sq mi)
POPULATION 2,900
DEMONYM Falkland Islander(s)
CAPITAL Stanley 2,000
RELIGION Anglican, Roman Catholic, United Free Church, Evangelist Church, Jehovah's Witness, Lutheran, Seventh-day Adventist
LANGUAGE English
MAP pages 138-139

Faroe Islands (Denmark)

FAROE ISLANDS

CONTINENT Europe
AREA 1,399 sq km (540 sq mi)
POPULATION 48,000
DEMONYM Faroese (singular and plural)
CAPITAL Tórshavn 20,000
RELIGION Evangelical Lutheran
LANGUAGE Faroese, Danish
MAP pages 148-149

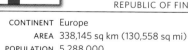

Fiji Islands

REPUBLIC OF THE FIJI ISLANDS

CONTINENT Australia/Oceania
AREA 18,376 sq km (7,095 sq mi)
POPULATION 862,000
DEMONYM Fijian(s)
CAPITAL Suva 224,000
RELIGION Christian (Methodist, Roman Catholic, Assembly of God), Hindu (Sanatan), Muslim (Sunni)
LANGUAGE English, Fijian, Hindustani
LITERACY 94%
LIFE EXPECTANCY 68 years
GDP PER CAPITA $4,100
CURRENCY Fijian dollar (FJD)
ECONOMY **IND:** tourism, sugar, clothing, copra, gold, silver **AGR:** sugarcane, coconuts, cassava (tapioca), rice; cattle; fish **EXP:** sugar, garments, gold, timber, fish
MAP pages 244-245

Finland

REPUBLIC OF FINLAND

CONTINENT Europe
AREA 338,145 sq km (130,558 sq mi)
POPULATION 5,288,000
DEMONYM Finn(s)
CAPITAL Helsinki 1,115,000
RELIGION Lutheran Church of Finland
LANGUAGE Finnish, Swedish
LITERACY 100%
LIFE EXPECTANCY 79 years
GDP PER CAPITA $35,500
CURRENCY euro (EUR)
ECONOMY **IND:** metals and metal products, electronics, machinery and scientific instruments, shipbuilding **AGR:** barley, wheat, sugar beets, potatoes; dairy cattle; fish **EXP:** machinery and equipment, chemicals, metals, timber
MAP pages 148-149

Places Included On This Spread
Small political entity
Greece 164-165 Political entity name with regional map page numbers
Note: Colors reflect the tint used on regional maps

France
FRENCH REPUBLIC

CONTINENT Europe
AREA 543,965 sq km (210,026 sq mi)
POPULATION 61,725,000
DEMONYM Frenchman(men), Frenchwoman(women)
CAPITAL Paris 9,902,000
RELIGION Roman Catholic, Muslim
LANGUAGE French
LITERACY 99%
LIFE EXPECTANCY 81 years
GDP PER CAPITA $33,800
CURRENCY euro (EUR)
ECONOMY **IND:** machinery, chemicals, automobiles, metallurgy **AGR:** wheat, cereals, sugar beets, potatoes; beef; fish **EXP:** machinery and transportation equipment, aircraft, plastics, chemicals
MAP pages 154-155

French Guiana (France)
OVERSEAS DEPARTMENT OF FRANCE

CONTINENT South America
AREA 86,504 sq km (33,400 sq mi)
POPULATION 207,000
DEMONYM Frenchman(men), Frenchwoman(women)
CAPITAL Cayenne 63,000
RELIGION Roman Catholic
LANGUAGE French
MAP pages 132-133

French Polynesia (France)
OVERSEAS LANDS OF FRENCH POLYNESIA

CONTINENT Australia/Oceania
AREA 4,167 sq km (1,608 sq mi)
POPULATION 261,000
DEMONYM French Polynesian(s)
CAPITAL Papeete 131,000
RELIGION Protestant, Roman Catholic
LANGUAGE French, Polynesian
MAP pages 244-245

Gabon
GABONESE REPUBLIC

CONTINENT Africa
AREA 267,667 sq km (103,347 sq mi)
POPULATION 1,331,000
DEMONYM Gabonese (singular and plural)
CAPITAL Libreville 576,000
RELIGION Christian, animist
LANGUAGE French, Fang, Myene, Nzebi, Bapounou/Eschira, Bandjabi
LITERACY 63%
LIFE EXPECTANCY 57 years
GDP PER CAPITA $13,800
CURRENCY Communauté Financière Africaine franc (XAF)
ECONOMY **IND:** petroleum extraction and refining, manganese and gold mining, chemicals, ship repair **AGR:** cocoa, coffee, sugar, palm oil; okoume (a tropical softwood); fish **EXP:** crude oil, timber, manganese, uranium
MAP pages 224-225

Gambia
REPUBLIC OF THE GAMBIA

CONTINENT Africa
AREA 11,295 sq km (4,361 sq mi)
POPULATION 1,517,000
DEMONYM Gambian(s)
CAPITAL Banjul 407,000
RELIGION Muslim, Christian
LANGUAGE English, Mandinka, Wolof, Fula, other indigenous vernaculars
LITERACY 40%
LIFE EXPECTANCY 58 years
GDP PER CAPITA $800
CURRENCY dalasi (GMD)
ECONOMY **IND:** peanut, fish, and hide processing; tourism, beverages, agricultural machinery assembly **AGR:** rice, millet, sorghum, peanuts, corn; cattle **EXP:** peanut products, fish, cotton lint, palm kernels
MAP pages 220-221

Gaza Strip
OCCUPIED PALESTINIAN TERRITORY

CONTINENT Asia
AREA 365 sq km (141 sq mi)
POPULATION 1,444,000
DEMONYM NA
CAPITAL NA
RELIGION Muslim (mostly Sunni)
LANGUAGE Arabic, Hebrew, English widely understood
MAP pages 182-183

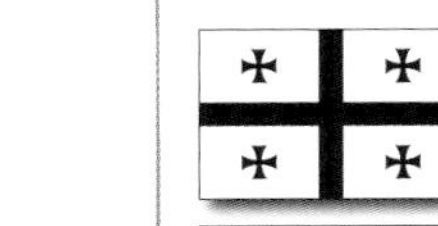

Georgia
GEORGIA

CONTINENT Europe/Asia
AREA 69,700 sq km (26,911 sq mi)
POPULATION 4,524,000
DEMONYM Georgian(s)
CAPITAL T'bilisi 1,099,000
RELIGION Orthodox Christian, Muslim, Armenian-Gregorian
LANGUAGE Georgian, Russian, Armenian, Azeri, Abkhaz
LITERACY 100%
LIFE EXPECTANCY 73 years
GDP PER CAPITA $4,200
CURRENCY lari (GEL)
ECONOMY **IND:** steel, aircraft, machine tools, electrical appliances **AGR:** citrus, grapes, tea, hazelnuts; livestock **EXP:** scrap metal, wine, mineral water, ores, vehicles
MAP pages 180-181

Germany
FEDERAL REPUBLIC OF GERMANY

CONTINENT Europe
AREA 357,022 sq km (137,847 sq mi)
POPULATION 82,254,000
DEMONYM German(s)
CAPITAL Berlin 3,405,000
RELIGION Protestant, Roman Catholic, Muslim
LANGUAGE German
LITERACY 99%
LIFE EXPECTANCY 79 years
GDP PER CAPITA $34,400
CURRENCY euro (EUR)
ECONOMY **IND:** iron, steel, coal, cement, chemicals, machinery **AGR:** potatoes, wheat, barley, sugar beets; cattle **EXP:** machinery, vehicles, chemicals, metals and manufactures
MAP pages 156-157

Ghana
REPUBLIC OF GHANA

CONTINENT Africa
AREA 238,537 sq km (92,100 sq mi)
POPULATION 22,995,000
DEMONYM Ghanaian(s)
CAPITAL Accra 2,120,000
RELIGION Christian (Pentecostal/Charismatic, Protestant, Roman Catholic, other), Muslim, traditional beliefs
LANGUAGE Asante, Ewe, Fante, Boron (Brong), Dagomba, Dangme, Dagarte (Dagaba), Akyem, Ga, English
LITERACY 58%
LIFE EXPECTANCY 59 years
GDP PER CAPITA $1,400
CURRENCY Ghana cedi (GHC)
ECONOMY **IND:** mining, lumbering, light manufacturing, aluminum smelting **AGR:** cocoa, rice, cassava (tapioca), peanuts; timber **EXP:** gold, cocoa, timber, tuna, bauxite, aluminum
MAP pages 220-221

Gibraltar (U.K.)
GIBRALTAR

CONTINENT Europe
AREA 6.5 sq km (2.5 sq mi)
POPULATION 29,000
DEMONYM Gibraltarian(s)
CAPITAL Gibraltar 29,000
RELIGION Roman Catholic, Church of England, Muslim, other Christian
LANGUAGE English, Spanish, Italian, Portuguese
MAP pages 152-153

Greece
HELLENIC REPUBLIC

CONTINENT Europe
AREA 131,957 sq km (50,949 sq mi)
POPULATION 11,189,000
DEMONYM Greek(s)
CAPITAL Athens 3,242,000
RELIGION Greek Orthodox
LANGUAGE Greek
LITERACY 96%
LIFE EXPECTANCY 79 years
GDP PER CAPITA $30,500
CURRENCY euro (EUR)
ECONOMY **IND:** tourism, food and tobacco processing, textiles, chemicals **AGR:** wheat, corn, barley, sugar beets; beef **EXP:** food and beverages, manufactured goods, petroleum products, chemicals
MAP pages 164-165

Greenland (Denmark)
GREENLAND

CONTINENT North America
AREA 2,166,086 sq km (836,086 sq mi)
POPULATION 57,000
DEMONYM Greenlander(s)
CAPITAL Nuuk (Godthåb) 15,000
RELIGION Evangelical Lutheran
LANGUAGE Greenlandic, Danish, English
MAP pages 102-103

Grenada
GRENADA

CONTINENT North America
AREA 344 sq km (133 sq mi)
POPULATION 99,000
DEMONYM Grenadian(s)
CAPITAL St. George's 32,000
RELIGION Roman Catholic, Anglican, other Protestant
LANGUAGE English, French patois
LITERACY 96%
LIFE EXPECTANCY 65 years
GDP PER CAPITA $3,900
CURRENCY East Caribbean dollar (XCD)
ECONOMY **IND:** food and beverages, textiles, light assembly operations, tourism **AGR:** bananas, cocoa, nutmeg, mace, citrus **EXP:** bananas, cocoa, nutmeg, fruits and vegetables, mace
MAP pages 120-121

Guadeloupe (France)
OVERSEAS DEPARTMENT OF FRANCE

CONTINENT North America
AREA 1,705 sq km (658 sq mi)
POPULATION 467,000
DEMONYM Frenchman(men), Frenchwoman(women)
CAPITAL Basse-Terre 12,000
RELIGION Roman Catholic
LANGUAGE French
MAP pages 120-121

Guam (U.S.)
TERRITORY OF GUAM

CONTINENT Australia/Oceania
AREA 561 sq km (217 sq mi)
POPULATION 173,000
DEMONYM Guamanian(s) (U.S. citizens)
CAPITAL Hagåtña (Agana) 149,000
RELIGION Roman Catholic
LANGUAGE English, Chamorro, Philippine languages, other Pacific island and Asian languages
MAP pages 244-245

Guatemala
REPUBLIC OF GUATEMALA

CONTINENT North America
AREA 108,889 sq km (42,042 sq mi)
POPULATION 13,354,000
DEMONYM Guatemalan(s)
CAPITAL Guatemala City 1,025,000
RELIGION Roman Catholic, Protestant, indigenous Mayan beliefs
LANGUAGE Spanish, 23 officially recognized Amerindian languages
LITERACY 69%
LIFE EXPECTANCY 69 years
GDP PER CAPITA $5,400
CURRENCY quetzal (GTQ)
ECONOMY **IND:** sugar, textiles and clothing, furniture, chemicals **AGR:** sugarcane, corn, bananas, coffee; cattle **EXP:** coffee, sugar, petroleum, apparel, bananas
MAP pages 116-117

Guinea
REPUBLIC OF GUINEA

CONTINENT Africa
AREA 245,857 sq km (94,926 sq mi)
POPULATION 10,112,000
DEMONYM Guinean(s)
CAPITAL Conakry 1,494,000
RELIGION Muslim, Christian, indigenous beliefs
LANGUAGE French, ethnic languages
LITERACY 30%
LIFE EXPECTANCY 54 years
GDP PER CAPITA $1,000
CURRENCY Guinean franc (GNF)
ECONOMY **IND:** bauxite, gold, diamonds, alumina refining **AGR:** rice, coffee, pineapples, palm kernels; cattle; timber **EXP:** bauxite, alumina, gold, diamonds, coffee
MAP pages 220-221

Guinea-Bissau
REPUBLIC OF GUINEA-BISSAU

CONTINENT Africa
AREA 36,125 sq km (13,948 sq mi)
POPULATION 1,695,000
DEMONYM Guinean(s)
CAPITAL Bissau 330,000
RELIGION indigenous beliefs, Muslim, Christian
LANGUAGE Portuguese, Crioulo, African languages
LITERACY 42%
LIFE EXPECTANCY 46 years
GDP PER CAPITA $600
CURRENCY Communauté Financière Africaine franc (XOF)
ECONOMY **IND:** agricultural products processing, beer, soft drinks **AGR:** rice, corn, beans, cassava (tapioca); timber; fish **EXP:** cashew nuts, shrimp, peanuts, palm kernels, sawn lumber
MAP pages 220-221

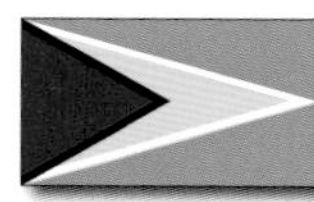

Guyana
CO-OPERATIVE REPUBLIC OF GUYANA

CONTINENT South America
AREA 214,969 sq km (83,000 sq mi)
POPULATION 763,000
DEMONYM Guyanese (singular and plural)
CAPITAL Georgetown 133,000
RELIGION Christian, Hindu, Muslim
LANGUAGE English, Amerindian dialects, Creole, Hindustani, Urdu
LITERACY 99%
LIFE EXPECTANCY 65 years
GDP PER CAPITA $5,300
CURRENCY Guyanese dollar (GYD)
ECONOMY **IND:** bauxite, sugar, rice milling, timber **AGR:** sugarcane, rice, vegetable oils; beef; shrimp **EXP:** sugar, gold, bauxite, alumina, rice,
MAP pages 132-133

Haiti
REPUBLIC OF HAITI

CONTINENT North America
AREA 27,750 sq km (10,714 sq mi)
POPULATION 8,967,000
DEMONYM Haitian(s)
CAPITAL Port-au-Prince 2,002,000
RELIGION Roman Catholic, Protestant (Baptist, Pentecostal, other)
LANGUAGE French, Creole
LITERACY 53%
LIFE EXPECTANCY 58 years
GDP PER CAPITA $1,900
CURRENCY gourde (HTG)
ECONOMY **IND:** sugar refining, flour milling, textiles, cement **AGR:** coffee, mangoes, sugarcane, rice; wood **EXP:** apparel, manufactures, oils, cocoa, mangoes
MAP pages 118-119

Honduras
REPUBLIC OF HONDURAS

CONTINENT North America
AREA 112,492 sq km (43,433 sq mi)
POPULATION 7,106,000
DEMONYM Honduran(s)
CAPITAL Tegucigalpa 947,000
RELIGION Roman Catholic, Protestant
LANGUAGE Spanish, Amerindian dialects
LITERACY 80%
LIFE EXPECTANCY 71 years
GDP PER CAPITA $3,300
CURRENCY lempira (HNL)
ECONOMY **IND:** sugar, coffee, textiles, clothing, wood products **AGR:** bananas, coffee, citrus; beef; timber; shrimp, tilapia **EXP:** coffee, bananas, gold, lobster
MAP pages 116-117

Hong Kong (China)
HONG KONG SPECIAL ADMINISTRATIVE REGION

CONTINENT Asia
AREA 1,104 sq km (426 sq mi)
POPULATION 6,936,000
DEMONYM Chinese/Hong Konger
CAPITAL NA
RELIGION eclectic mixture of local religions, Christian
LANGUAGE Chinese (Cantonese), other Chinese dialects, English
MAP pages 198-199

Hungary
REPUBLIC OF HUNGARY

CONTINENT Europe
AREA 93,030 sq km (35,919 sq mi)
POPULATION 10,058,000
DEMONYM Hungarian(s)
CAPITAL Budapest 1,675,000
RELIGION Roman Catholic, Calvinist, Lutheran
LANGUAGE Hungarian
LITERACY 99%
LIFE EXPECTANCY 73 years
GDP PER CAPITA $19,500
CURRENCY forint (HUF)
ECONOMY **IND:** mining, metallurgy, construction materials, processed foods **AGR:** wheat, corn, sunflower seed, potatoes; pigs **EXP:** machinery and equipment, other manufactures, food products, raw materials
MAP pages 158-159

Iceland
REPUBLIC OF ICELAND

CONTINENT Europe
AREA 103,000 sq km (39,769 sq mi)
POPULATION 313,000
DEMONYM Icelander(s)
CAPITAL Reykjavík 192,000
RELIGION Lutheran Church of Iceland
LANGUAGE Icelandic, English, Nordic languages, German
LITERACY 99%
LIFE EXPECTANCY 81 years
GDP PER CAPITA $39,400
CURRENCY Icelandic krona (ISK)
ECONOMY **IND:** fish processing, aluminum smelting, ferrosilicon production, geothermal power **AGR:** potatoes, green vegetables; mutton, dairy products; fish **EXP:** fish and fish products, aluminum, animal products, ferrosilicon, diatomite
MAP pages 148-149

India
REPUBLIC OF INDIA

CONTINENT Asia
AREA 3,287,270 sq km (1,269,221 sq mi)
POPULATION 1,131,883,000
DEMONYM Indian(s)
CAPITAL New Delhi 15,926,000 (part of Delhi metropolitan area)
RELIGION Hindu, Muslim
LANGUAGE Hindi, English, 21 other official languages, Hindustani (popular Hindi/Urdu variant in the north)
LITERACY 61%
LIFE EXPECTANCY 64 years
GDP PER CAPITA $2,700
CURRENCY Indian rupee (INR)
ECONOMY **IND:** textiles, chemicals, food processing, steel **AGR:** rice, wheat, oilseed, cotton; cattle; fish **EXP:** petroleum products, textile goods, gems and jewelry, engineering goods
MAP pages 194-195

Indonesia
REPUBLIC OF INDONESIA

CONTINENT Asia
AREA 1,922,570 sq km (742,308 sq mi)
POPULATION 231,627,000
DEMONYM Indonesian(s)
CAPITAL Jakarta 9,143,000
RELIGION Muslim, Protestant, Roman Catholic
LANGUAGE Bahasa Indonesia (modified form of Malay), English, Dutch, Javanese, local dialects
LITERACY 90%
LIFE EXPECTANCY 69 years
GDP PER CAPITA $3,400
CURRENCY Indonesian rupiah (IDR)
ECONOMY **IND:** petroleum and natural gas, textiles, apparel, footwear **AGR:** rice, cassava (tapioca), peanuts, rubber; poultry **EXP:** oil and gas, electrical appliances, plywood, textiles, rubber
MAP pages 206-207

Iran
ISLAMIC REPUBLIC OF IRAN

CONTINENT Asia
AREA 1,648,000 sq km (636,296 sq mi)
POPULATION 71,208,000
DEMONYM Iranian(s)
CAPITAL Tehran 7,875,000
RELIGION Shiite Muslim, Sunni Muslim
LANGUAGE Persian, Turkic, Kurdish, Luri, Baluchi, Arabic
LITERACY 77%
LIFE EXPECTANCY 70 years
GDP PER CAPITA $12,300
CURRENCY Iranian rial (IRR)
ECONOMY **IND:** petroleum, petrochemicals, fertilizers, caustic soda **AGR:** wheat, rice, other grains, sugar beets; dairy products; caviar **EXP:** petroleum, chemical and petrochemical products, fruits and nuts, carpets
MAP pages 188-189

Iraq
REPUBLIC OF IRAQ

CONTINENT Asia
AREA 437,072 sq km (168,754 sq mi)
POPULATION 28,993,000
DEMONYM Iraqi(s)
CAPITAL Baghdad 5,500,000
RELIGION Shiite Muslim, Sunni Muslim
LANGUAGE Arabic, Kurdish, Assyrian, Armenian
LITERACY 74%
LIFE EXPECTANCY 57 years
GDP PER CAPITA $3,600
CURRENCY Iraqi dinar (IQD)
ECONOMY **IND:** petroleum, chemicals, textiles, leather **AGR:** wheat, barley, rice, vegetables; cattle **EXP:** crude oil, crude materials excluding fuels, food and live animals
MAP pages 186-187

Ireland
IRELAND

CONTINENT Europe
AREA 70,273 sq km (27,133 sq mi)
POPULATION 4,369,000
DEMONYM Irishman(men), Irishwoman(women), Irish (collective plural)
CAPITAL Dublin 1,060,000
RELIGION Roman Catholic, Church of Ireland
LANGUAGE Irish (Gaelic), English
LITERACY 99%
LIFE EXPECTANCY 78 years
GDP PER CAPITA $45,600
CURRENCY euro (EUR)
ECONOMY **IND:** mining processing (steel, lead, zinc, aluminum), food products, brewing, textiles **AGR:** turnips, barley, potatoes, sugar beets; beef **EXP:** machinery and equipment, computers, chemicals, pharmaceuticals
MAP pages 150-151

Israel
STATE OF ISRAEL

CONTINENT Asia
AREA 22,145 sq km (8,550 sq mi)
POPULATION 7,347,000
DEMONYM Israeli(s)
CAPITAL Jerusalem 736,000
RELIGION Jewish, Muslim
LANGUAGE Hebrew, Arabic, English
LITERACY 97%
LIFE EXPECTANCY 80 years
GDP PER CAPITA $28,800
CURRENCY new Israeli sheqel (ILS)
ECONOMY **IND:** high-technology projects (aviation, communications), wood and paper products, potash and phosphates, food **AGR:** citrus, vegetables, cotton; beef, poultry **EXP:** machinery and equipment, software, diamonds, agricultural products
MAP pages 182-183

Italy
ITALIAN REPUBLIC

CONTINENT Europe
AREA 301,333 sq km (116,345 sq mi)
POPULATION 59,337,000
DEMONYM Italian(s)
CAPITAL Rome 3,340,000
RELIGION Roman Catholic, Protestant, Jewish, Muslim
LANGUAGE Italian, German, French, Slovene
LITERACY 98%
LIFE EXPECTANCY 81 years
GDP PER CAPITA $31,000
CURRENCY euro (EUR)
ECONOMY **IND:** tourism, machinery, iron, steel, chemicals **AGR:** fruits, vegetables, grapes, potatoes; beef; fish **EXP:** engineering products, textiles and clothing, production machinery, motor vehicles
MAP pages 160-161

Jamaica
JAMAICA

CONTINENT North America
AREA 10,991 sq km (4,244 sq mi)
POPULATION 2,680,000
DEMONYM Jamaican(s)
CAPITAL Kingston 581,000
RELIGION Protestant (Church of God, Seventh-day Adventist, Pentecostal, Baptist, Anglican, other)
LANGUAGE English, English patois
LITERACY 88%
LIFE EXPECTANCY 72 years
GDP PER CAPITA $4,800
CURRENCY Jamaican dollar (JMD)
ECONOMY **IND:** tourism, bauxite/alumina, agro-processing, light manufactures **AGR:** sugarcane, bananas, coffee, citrus; poultry; crustaceans **EXP:** alumina, bauxite, sugar, bananas, rum, yams
MAP pages 118-119

Japan
JAPAN

CONTINENT Asia
AREA 377,887 sq km (145,902 sq mi)
POPULATION 127,730,000
DEMONYM Japanese (singular and plural)
CAPITAL Tokyo 35,676,000
RELIGION Shinto, Buddhist
LANGUAGE Japanese
LITERACY 99%
LIFE EXPECTANCY 82 years
GDP PER CAPITA $33,800
CURRENCY yen (JPY)
ECONOMY **IND:** motor vehicles, electronic equipment, machine tools, steel and nonferrous metals **AGR:** rice, sugar beets, vegetables, fruit; pork; fish **EXP:** transport equipment, motor vehicles, semiconductors, electrical machinery
MAP pages 202-203

Jordan
HASHEMITE KINGDOM OF JORDAN

CONTINENT Asia
AREA 89,342 sq km (34,495 sq mi)
POPULATION 5,728,000
DEMONYM Jordanian(s)
CAPITAL Amman 1,064,000
RELIGION Sunni Muslim, Christian
LANGUAGE Arabic, English
LITERACY 90%
LIFE EXPECTANCY 72 years
GDP PER CAPITA $4,700
CURRENCY Jordanian dinar (JOD)
ECONOMY **IND:** clothing, phosphate mining, fertilizers, pharmaceuticals **AGR:** citrus, tomatoes, cucumbers, olives; sheep **EXP:** clothing, pharmaceuticals, potash, phosphates
MAP pages 182-183

Kazakhstan
REPUBLIC OF KAZAKHSTAN

CONTINENT Europe/Asia
AREA 2,717,300 sq km (1,049,155 sq mi)
POPULATION 15,486,000
DEMONYM Kazakhstani(s)
CAPITAL Astana 594,000
RELIGION Muslim, Russian Orthodox
LANGUAGE Kazakh (Qazaq), Russian
LITERACY 100%
LIFE EXPECTANCY 66 years
GDP PER CAPITA $11,100
CURRENCY tenge (KZT)
ECONOMY **IND:** oil, coal, iron ore, manganese, agricultural machinery **AGR:** grain (mostly spring wheat), cotton; livestock **EXP:** oil and oil products, ferrous metals, chemicals, machinery
MAP pages 192-193

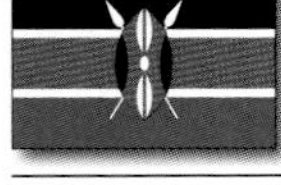

Kenya
REPUBLIC OF KENYA

CONTINENT Africa
AREA 580,367 sq km (224,081 sq mi)
POPULATION 36,914,000
DEMONYM Kenyan(s)
CAPITAL Nairobi 3,011,000
RELIGION Protestant, Roman Catholic, Muslim, indigenous beliefs
LANGUAGE English, Kiswahili, many indigenous languages
LITERACY 85%
LIFE EXPECTANCY 53 years
GDP PER CAPITA $1,600
CURRENCY Kenyan shilling (KES)
ECONOMY **IND:** small-scale consumer goods (plastic, furniture), agricultural products, horticulture, oil refining **AGR:** tea, coffee, corn, wheat; dairy products **EXP:** tea, horticultural products, coffee, petroleum products, fish
MAP pages 226-227

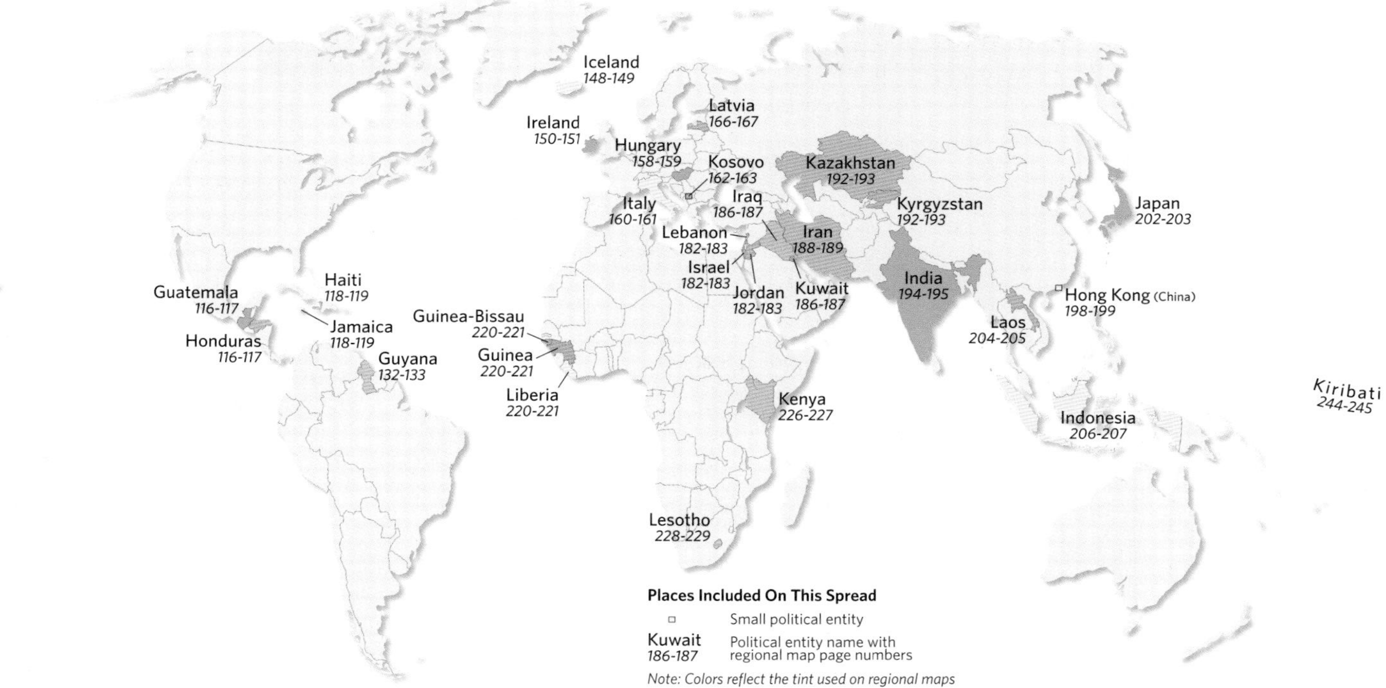
Iceland 148-149
Latvia 166-167
Ireland 150-151
Hungary 158-159
Kosovo 162-163
Kazakhstan 192-193
Iraq 186-187
Italy 160-161
Kyrgyzstan 192-193
Japan 202-203
Lebanon 182-183
Iran 188-189
Israel 182-183
Jordan 182-183
Kuwait 186-187
India 194-195
Haiti 118-119
Guatemala 116-117
Jamaica 118-119
Guinea-Bissau 220-221
Hong Kong (China) 198-199
Laos 204-205
Honduras 116-117
Guyana 132-133
Guinea 220-221
Liberia 220-221
Kenya 226-227
Kiribati 244-245
Indonesia 206-207
Lesotho 228-229
Places Included On This Spread
Small political entity
Kuwait 186-187 Political entity name with regional map page numbers
Note: Colors reflect the tint used on regional maps

Kiribati
REPUBLIC OF KIRIBATI

CONTINENT Australia/Oceania
AREA 811 sq km (313 sq mi)
POPULATION 96,000
DEMONYM I-Kiribati (singular and plural)
CAPITAL Tarawa 42,000
RELIGION Roman Catholic, Protestant (Congregational)
LANGUAGE I-Kiribati, English
LITERACY NA
LIFE EXPECTANCY 62 years
GDP PER CAPITA $1,800
CURRENCY Australian dollar (AUD)
ECONOMY **IND:** fishing, handicrafts **AGR:** copra, taro, breadfruit, sweet potatoes; fish **EXP:** copra, coconuts, seaweed, fish
MAP pages 244-245

Kosovo
REPUBLIC OF KOSOVO

CONTINENT Europe
AREA 10,887 sq km (4,203 sq mi)
POPULATION 1,900,000
DEMONYM Kosovar (Albanian) and Kosovac (Serbian); the neutral term Kosovan is sometimes also used
CAPITAL Pristina 600,000
RELIGION Muslim, Serbian Orthodox, Roman Catholic
LANGUAGE Albanian, Serbian, Bosniak, Turkish, Roma
LITERACY 94%
LIFE EXPECTANCY 75 years
GDP PER CAPITA $1,800
CURRENCY euro (EUR); Serbian dinar (RSD)
ECONOMY **IND:** mineral mining, construction materials, base metals, leather, machinery, appliances **AGR:** wheat, corn, fruits, vegetables, wine; beef **EXP:** mining and processed metal products, scrap metals, leather products, machinery, appliances
MAP pages 162-163

Kuwait
STATE OF KUWAIT

CONTINENT Asia
AREA 17,818 sq km (6,880 sq mi)
POPULATION 2,778,000
DEMONYM Kuwaiti(s)
CAPITAL Kuwait 2,061,000
RELIGION Sunni Muslim, Shiite Muslim, other (includes Christian, Hindu, Parsi)
LANGUAGE Arabic, English
LITERACY 93%
LIFE EXPECTANCY 78 years
GDP PER CAPITA $55,300
CURRENCY Kuwaiti dinar (KWD)
ECONOMY **IND:** petroleum, petrochemicals, cement, shipbuilding and repair **AGR:** practically no crops; fish **EXP:** oil and refined products, fertilizers
MAP pages 186-187

Kyrgyzstan
KYRGYZ REPUBLIC

CONTINENT Asia
AREA 199,900 sq km (77,182 sq mi)
POPULATION 5,216,000
DEMONYM Kyrgyzstani(s)
CAPITAL Bishkek 837,000
RELIGION Muslim, Russian Orthodox
LANGUAGE Kyrgyz, Uzbek, Russian
LITERACY 99%
LIFE EXPECTANCY 66 years
GDP PER CAPITA $2,000
CURRENCY som (KGS)
ECONOMY **IND:** small machinery, textiles, food processing, cement **AGR:** tobacco, cotton, potatoes, vegetables; sheep **EXP:** cotton, wool, meat, gold, mercury, uranium
MAP pages 192-193

Laos
LAO PEOPLE'S DEMOCRATIC REPUBLIC

CONTINENT Asia
AREA 236,800 sq km (91,429 sq mi)
POPULATION 5,862,000
DEMONYM Lao(s) or Laotian(s)
CAPITAL Vientiane 746,000
RELIGION Buddhist, animist
LANGUAGE Lao, French, English, various ethnic languages
LITERACY 69%
LIFE EXPECTANCY 55 years
GDP PER CAPITA $1,900
CURRENCY kip (LAK)
ECONOMY **IND:** copper, tin, and gypsum mining, timber, electric power, agricultural processing **AGR:** sweet potatoes, vegetables, corn, coffee; water buffalo **EXP:** garments, wood products, coffee, electricity, tin
MAP pages 204-205

Latvia
REPUBLIC OF LATVIA

CONTINENT Europe
AREA 64,589 sq km (24,938 sq mi)
POPULATION 2,275,000
DEMONYM Latvian(s)
CAPITAL Riga 722,000
RELIGION Lutheran, Roman Catholic, Russian Orthodox
LANGUAGE Latvian, Russian, Lithuanian
LITERACY 100%
LIFE EXPECTANCY 72 years
GDP PER CAPITA $17,700
CURRENCY Latvian lat (LVL)
ECONOMY **IND:** buses, vans, street and railroad cars, synthetic fibers **AGR:** grain, sugar beets, potatoes, vegetables; beef; fish **EXP:** wood and wood products, machinery and equipment, metals, textiles
MAP pages 166-167

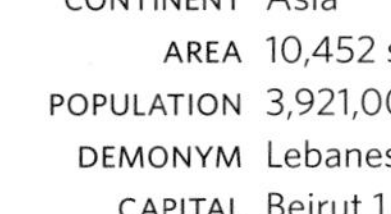

Lebanon
LEBANESE REPUBLIC

CONTINENT Asia
AREA 10,452 sq km (4,036 sq mi)
POPULATION 3,921,000
DEMONYM Lebanese (singular and plural)
CAPITAL Beirut 1,857,000
RELIGION Muslim, Christian
LANGUAGE Arabic, French, English, Armenian
LITERACY 87%
LIFE EXPECTANCY 71 years
GDP PER CAPITA $10,400
CURRENCY Lebanese pound (LBP)
ECONOMY **IND:** banking, tourism, food processing, jewelry **AGR:** citrus, grapes, tomatoes, apples; sheep **EXP:** authentic jewelry, inorganic chemicals, miscellaneous consumer goods, fruits
MAP pages 182-183

Lesotho
KINGDOM OF LESOTHO

CONTINENT Africa
AREA 30,355 sq km (11,720 sq mi)
POPULATION 1,798,000
DEMONYM Mosotho (singular), Basotho (plural)
CAPITAL Maseru 212,000
RELIGION Christian, indigenous beliefs
LANGUAGE Sesotho, English, Zulu, Xhosa
LITERACY 85%
LIFE EXPECTANCY 36 years
GDP PER CAPITA $1,500
CURRENCY loti (LSL); South African rand (ZAR)
ECONOMY **IND:** food, beverages, textiles, apparel assembly **AGR:** corn, wheat, pulses, sorghum; livestock **EXP:** clothing, footwear, road vehicles, wool, mohair, animals
MAP pages 228-229

Liberia
REPUBLIC OF LIBERIA

CONTINENT Africa
AREA 111,370 sq km (43,000 sq mi)
POPULATION 3,750,000
DEMONYM Liberian(s)
CAPITAL Monrovia 1,165,000
RELIGION Christian, indigenous beliefs, Muslim
LANGUAGE English, 20 ethnic languages
LITERACY 58%
LIFE EXPECTANCY 45 years
GDP PER CAPITA $500
CURRENCY Liberian dollar (LRD)
ECONOMY **IND:** rubber processing, palm oil processing, timber, diamonds **AGR:** rubber, coffee, cocoa, rice; sheep; timber **EXP:** rubber, timber, iron, diamonds, cocoa, coffee
MAP pages 220-221

Libya

GREAT SOCIALIST PEOPLE'S LIBYAN ARAB JAMAHIRIYA

CONTINENT Africa
AREA 1,759,540 sq km (679,362 sq mi)
POPULATION 6,160,000
DEMONYM Libyan(s)
CAPITAL Tripoli 2,188,000
RELIGION Sunni Muslim
LANGUAGE Arabic, Italian, English
LITERACY 83%
LIFE EXPECTANCY 73 years
GDP PER CAPITA $13,100
CURRENCY Libyan dinar (LYD)
ECONOMY **IND:** petroleum, iron and steel, food processing, textiles **AGR:** wheat, barley, olives, dates, citrus; cattle **EXP:** crude oil, refined petroleum products, natural gas, chemicals
MAP pages 216-217

Liechtenstein

PRINCIPALITY OF LIECHTENSTEIN

CONTINENT Europe
AREA 160 sq km (62 sq mi)
POPULATION 35,000
DEMONYM Liechtensteiner(s)
CAPITAL Vaduz 5,000
RELIGION Roman Catholic, Protestant
LANGUAGE German, Alemannic dialect
LITERACY 100%
LIFE EXPECTANCY 80 years
GDP PER CAPITA $25,000
CURRENCY Swiss franc (CHF)
ECONOMY **IND:** electronics, metal manufacturing, dental products, ceramics **AGR:** wheat, barley, corn, potatoes; livestock **EXP:** small machinery, audio/video connectors, vehicle parts, dental products
MAP pages 170-171

Lithuania

REPUBLIC OF LITHUANIA

CONTINENT Europe
AREA 65,300 sq km (25,212 sq mi)
POPULATION 3,376,000
DEMONYM Lithuanian(s)
CAPITAL Vilnius 543,000
RELIGION Roman Catholic, Russian Orthodox
LANGUAGE Lithuanian, Russian, Polish
LITERACY 100%
LIFE EXPECTANCY 71 years
GDP PER CAPITA $16,700
CURRENCY litas (LTL)
ECONOMY **IND:** metal-cutting machine tools, electric motors, televisions, refrigerators, freezers **AGR:** grain, potatoes, sugar beets, flax; beef; fish **EXP:** mineral products, textiles and clothing, machinery and equipment, chemicals
MAP pages 166-167

Luxembourg

GRAND DUCHY OF LUXEMBOURG

CONTINENT Europe
AREA 2,586 sq km (998 sq mi)
POPULATION 466,000
DEMONYM Luxembourger(s)
CAPITAL Luxembourg 84,000
RELIGION Roman Catholic, Protestant, Jewish, Muslim
LANGUAGE Luxembourgish, German, French
LITERACY 100%
LIFE EXPECTANCY 78 years
GDP PER CAPITA $80,800
CURRENCY euro (EUR)
ECONOMY **IND:** banking, financial services, iron, steel, information technology, telecommunications **AGR:** wine, grapes, barley, oats; dairy products **EXP:** machinery and equipment, steel products, chemicals, rubber products
MAP pages 170-171

Macau (China)

MACAU SPECIAL ADMINISTRATIVE REGION

CONTINENT Asia
AREA 28 sq km (11 sq mi)
POPULATION 488,100
DEMONYM Chinese
CAPITAL NA
RELIGION Buddhist, Roman Catholic
LANGUAGE Chinese (Cantonese, other dialects)
MAP pages 198-199

Macedonia

REPUBLIC OF MACEDONIA

CONTINENT Europe
AREA 25,713 sq km (9,928 sq mi)
POPULATION 2,047,000
DEMONYM Macedonian(s)
CAPITAL Skopje 480,000
RELIGION Macedonian Orthodox, Muslim
LANGUAGE Macedonian, Albanian, Turkish
LITERACY 96%
LIFE EXPECTANCY 74 years
GDP PER CAPITA $8,400
CURRENCY Macedonian denar (MKD)
ECONOMY **IND:** food processing, beverages, textiles, chemicals **AGR:** grapes, wine, tobacco, vegetables; milk **EXP:** food, beverages, tobacco, textiles, iron and steel
MAP pages 162-163

Madagascar

REPUBLIC OF MADAGASCAR

CONTINENT Africa
AREA 587,041 sq km (226,658 sq mi)
POPULATION 18,252,000
DEMONYM Malagasy (singular and plural)
CAPITAL Antananarivo 1,697,000
RELIGION indigenous beliefs, Christian, Muslim
LANGUAGE English, French, Malagasy
LITERACY 69%
LIFE EXPECTANCY 57 years
GDP PER CAPITA $1,000
CURRENCY Madagascar ariary (MGA)
ECONOMY **IND:** meat processing, seafood, soap, breweries **AGR:** coffee, vanilla, sugarcane, cloves; livestock products **EXP:** coffee, vanilla, shellfish, sugar, chromite
MAP pages 228-229

Malawi

REPUBLIC OF MALAWI

CONTINENT Africa
AREA 118,484 sq km (45,747 sq mi)
POPULATION 13,070,000
DEMONYM Malawian(s)
CAPITAL Lilongwe 732,000
RELIGION Christian, Muslim
LANGUAGE Chichewa, Chinyanja, Chiyao, Chitumbuka
LITERACY 63%
LIFE EXPECTANCY 40 years
GDP PER CAPITA $800
CURRENCY Malawian kwacha (MWK)
ECONOMY **IND:** tobacco, tea, sugar, sawmill products **AGR:** tobacco, sugarcane, cotton, tea; cattle **EXP:** tobacco, tea, sugar, cotton, coffee
MAP pages 228-229

Malaysia

MALAYSIA

CONTINENT Asia
AREA 329,847 sq km (127,355 sq mi)
POPULATION 27,160,000
DEMONYM Malaysian(s)
CAPITAL Kuala Lumpur 1,448,000
RELIGION Muslim, Buddhist, Christian, Hindu
LANGUAGE Bahasa Malaysia, English, Chinese, Tamil, Telugu, Malayalam, Panjabi, Thai, indigenous languages
LITERACY 89%
LIFE EXPECTANCY 74 years
GDP PER CAPITA $14,400
CURRENCY ringgit (MYR)
ECONOMY **IND:** rubber and palm oil processing and manufacturing, light manufacturing, logging, petroleum production **AGR:** rubber, coconuts, rice, palm oil; timber **EXP:** electronic equipment, petroleum and liquefied natural gas, wood and wood products, palm oil
MAP pages 206-207

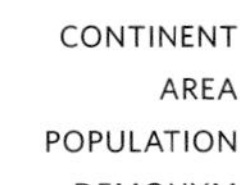

Maldives

REPUBLIC OF MALDIVES

CONTINENT Asia
AREA 298 sq km (115 sq mi)
POPULATION 304,000
DEMONYM Maldivian(s)
CAPITAL Male 111,000
RELIGION Sunni Muslim
LANGUAGE Maldivian Dhivehi, English
LITERACY 96%
LIFE EXPECTANCY 70 years
GDP PER CAPITA $3,900
CURRENCY rufiyaa (MVR)
ECONOMY **IND:** tourism, fish processing, shipping, boat building **AGR:** coconuts, corn, sweet potatoes; fish **EXP:** fish
MAP pages 194-195

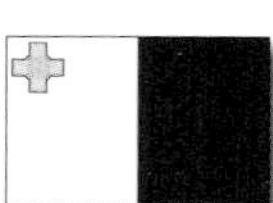

Mali

REPUBLIC OF MALI

CONTINENT Africa
AREA 1,240,192 sq km (478,841 sq mi)
POPULATION 12,337,000
DEMONYM Malian(s)
CAPITAL Bamako 1,494,000
RELIGION Muslim, indigenous beliefs
LANGUAGE Bambara, French, numerous African languages
LITERACY 46%
LIFE EXPECTANCY 53 years
GDP PER CAPITA $1,200
CURRENCY Communauté Financière Africaine franc (XOF)
ECONOMY **IND:** food processing, construction, phosphate and gold mining **AGR:** cotton, millet, rice, corn, vegetables; cattle **EXP:** cotton, gold, livestock
MAP pages 220-221

Malta

REPUBLIC OF MALTA

CONTINENT Europe
AREA 316 sq km (122 sq mi)
POPULATION 407,000
DEMONYM Maltese (singular and plural)
CAPITAL Valletta 199,000
RELIGION Roman Catholic
LANGUAGE Maltese, English
LITERACY 93%
LIFE EXPECTANCY 80 years
GDP PER CAPITA $23,200
CURRENCY euro (EUR)
ECONOMY **IND:** tourism, electronics, ship building and repair, construction **AGR:** potatoes, cauliflower, grapes, wheat; pork **EXP:** machinery and transport equipment, manufactures
MAP pages 170-171

Marshall Islands

REPUBLIC OF THE MARSHALL ISLANDS

CONTINENT Australia/Oceania
AREA 181 sq km (70 sq mi)
POPULATION 67,000
DEMONYM Marshallese (singular and plural)
CAPITAL Majuro 28,000
RELIGION Protestant, Assembly of God, Roman Catholic
LANGUAGE Marshallese
LITERACY 94%
LIFE EXPECTANCY 70 years
GDP PER CAPITA $2,900
CURRENCY US dollar (USD)
ECONOMY **IND:** copra, tuna processing, tourism; craft items from shell, wood, and pearls **AGR:** coconuts, tomatoes, melons, taro; pigs **EXP:** copra cake, coconut oil, handicrafts, fish
MAP pages 244-245

Martinique (France)

OVERSEAS DEPARTMENT OF FRANCE

CONTINENT North America
AREA 1,100 sq km (425 sq mi)
POPULATION 405,000
DEMONYM Frenchman(men), Frenchwoman(women)
CAPITAL Fort-de-France 92,000
RELIGION Roman Catholic, Protestant
LANGUAGE French, Creole patois
MAP pages 120-121

Mauritania

ISLAMIC REPUBLIC OF MAURITANIA

CONTINENT Africa
AREA 1,030,700 sq km (397,955 sq mi)
POPULATION 3,124,000
DEMONYM Mauritanian(s)
CAPITAL Nouakchott 673,000
RELIGION Muslim
LANGUAGE Arabic, Pulaar, Soninke, French, Hassaniya, Wolof
LITERACY 51%
LIFE EXPECTANCY 62 years
GDP PER CAPITA $1,800
CURRENCY ouguiya (MRO)
ECONOMY **IND:** fish processing, mining of iron ore and gypsum **AGR:** dates, millet, sorghum, rice, corn; cattle **EXP:** iron ore, fish and fish products, gold
MAP pages 220-221

Mauritius

REPUBLIC OF MAURITIUS

CONTINENT Africa
AREA 2,040 sq km (788 sq mi)
POPULATION 1,261,000
DEMONYM Mauritian(s)
CAPITAL Port Louis 150,000
RELIGION Hindu, Roman Catholic, Muslim, other Christian
LANGUAGE Creole, Bhojpuri, French
LITERACY 84%
LIFE EXPECTANCY 72 years
GDP PER CAPITA $11,900
CURRENCY Mauritian rupee (MUR)
ECONOMY **IND:** food processing (largely sugar milling), textiles, clothing, mining **AGR:** sugarcane, tea, corn, potatoes; cattle; fish **EXP:** clothing and textiles, sugar, cut flowers, molasses
MAP pages 230-231

Mayotte (France)

TERRITORIAL COLLECTIVITY OF MAYOTTE

CONTINENT Africa
AREA 374 sq km (144 sq mi)
POPULATION 196,000
DEMONYM Mahorais (singular and plural)
CAPITAL Mamoudzou NA
RELIGION Muslim, Roman Catholic
LANGUAGE Mahorian (a Swahili dialect), French
MAP pages 228-229

Mexico

UNITED MEXICAN STATES

CONTINENT North America
AREA 1,964,375 sq km (758,449 sq mi)
POPULATION 106,535,000
DEMONYM Mexican(s)
CAPITAL Mexico City 19,028,000
RELIGION Roman Catholic, Protestant
LANGUAGE Spanish, Mayan, Nahuatl, other indigenous languages
LITERACY 91%
LIFE EXPECTANCY 75 years
GDP PER CAPITA $12,500
CURRENCY Mexican peso (MXN)
ECONOMY **IND:** food and beverages, tobacco, chemicals, iron and steel **AGR:** corn, wheat, soybeans, rice; beef; wood products **EXP:** manufactured goods, oil and oil products, silver, fruits and vegetables
MAP pages 114-115

Micronesia

FEDERATED STATES OF MICRONESIA

CONTINENT Australia/Oceania
AREA 702 sq km (271 sq mi)
POPULATION 108,000
DEMONYM Micronesian(s)
CAPITAL Palikir 7,000
RELIGION Roman Catholic, Protestant
LANGUAGE English, Trukese, Pohnpeian, Yapese, other indigenous languages
LITERACY 89%
LIFE EXPECTANCY 67 years
GDP PER CAPITA $2,300
CURRENCY US dollar (USD)
ECONOMY **IND:** tourism, construction, fish processing, specialized aquaculture **AGR:** black pepper, tropical fruits and vegetables, coconuts, sakau (kava); pigs; fish **EXP:** fish, garments, bananas, black pepper, sakau (kava), betel nuts
MAP pages 244-245

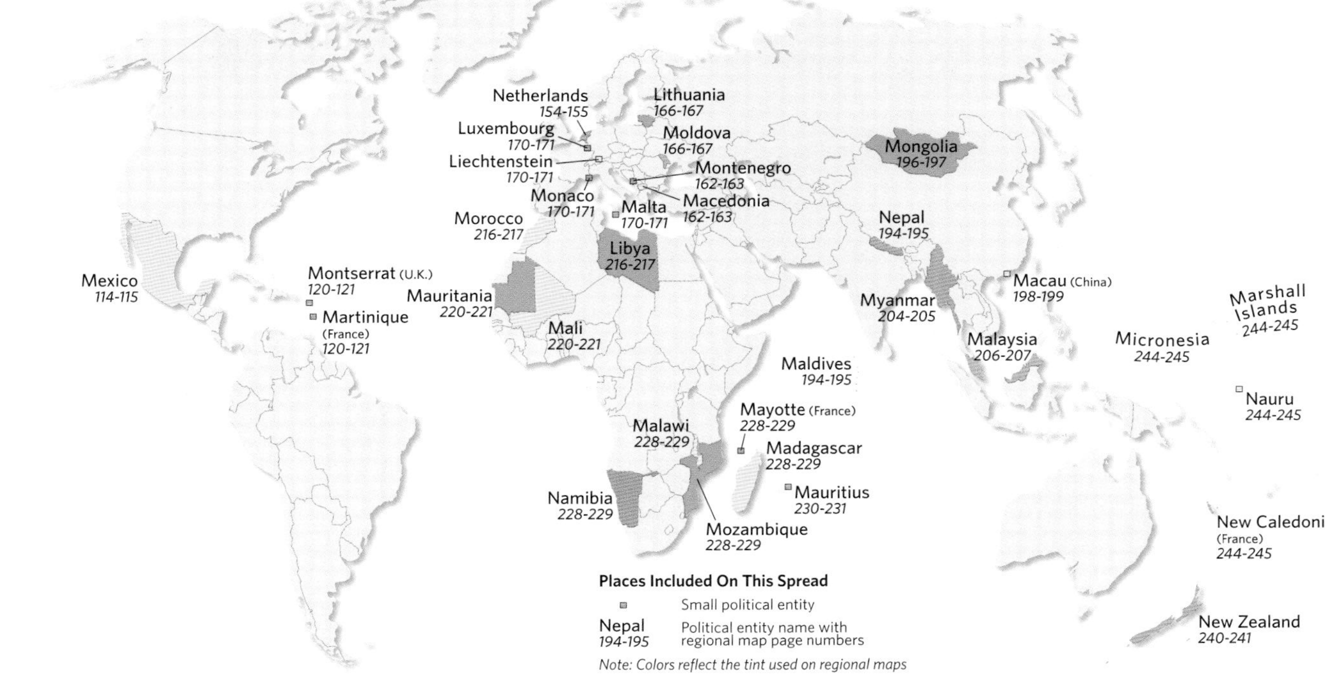

Netherlands 154-155
Lithuania 166-167
Luxembourg 170-171
Moldova 166-167
Liechtenstein 170-171
Montenegro 162-163
Monaco 170-171
Malta 170-171
Macedonia 162-163
Morocco 216-217
Libya 216-217
Mongolia 196-197
Nepal 194-195
Mexico 114-115
Montserrat (U.K.) 120-121
Martinique (France) 120-121
Mauritania 220-221
Mali 220-221
Myanmar 204-205
Macau (China) 198-199
Malaysia 206-207
Marshall Islands 244-245
Micronesia 244-245
Maldives 194-195
Mayotte (France) 228-229
Malawi 228-229
Madagascar 228-229
Mauritius 230-231
Namibia 228-229
Mozambique 228-229
Nauru 244-245
New Caledonia (France) 244-245
New Zealand 240-241
Places Included On This Spread
Small political entity
Nepal 194-195 Political entity name with regional map page numbers
Note: Colors reflect the tint used on regional maps

Moldova
REPUBLIC OF MOLDOVA

CONTINENT Europe
AREA 33,800 sq km (13,050 sq mi)
POPULATION 3,991,000
DEMONYM Moldovan(s)
CAPITAL Chisinau 592,000
RELIGION Eastern Orthodox
LANGUAGE Moldovan, Russian, Gagauz
LITERACY 99%
LIFE EXPECTANCY 69 years
GDP PER CAPITA $2,200
CURRENCY Moldovan leu (MDL)
ECONOMY **IND:** sugar, vegetable oil, food processing, agricultural machinery **AGR:** vegetables, fruits, wine, grain, sugar beets; beef **EXP:** foodstuffs, textiles, machinery
MAP pages 166-167

Monaco
PRINCIPALITY OF MONACO

CONTINENT Europe
AREA 2.0 sq km (0.8 sq mi)
POPULATION 33,000
DEMONYM Monegasque(s) or Monacan(s)
CAPITAL Monaco 33,000
RELIGION Roman Catholic
LANGUAGE French, English, Italian, Monegasque
LITERACY 99%
LIFE EXPECTANCY NA
GDP PER CAPITA $30,000
CURRENCY euro (EUR)
ECONOMY **IND:** tourism, construction, small-scale industrial and consumer products **AGR:** none **EXP:** none
MAP pages 170-171

Mongolia
MONGOLIA

CONTINENT Asia
AREA 1,564,116 sq km (603,909 sq mi)
POPULATION 2,610,000
DEMONYM Mongolian(s)
CAPITAL Ulaanbaatar 884,000
RELIGION Buddhist Lamaist, Shamanist, Christian, Muslim
LANGUAGE Khalkha Mongol, Turkic, Russian
LITERACY 98%
LIFE EXPECTANCY 66 years
GDP PER CAPITA $2,900
CURRENCY togrog/tugrik (MNT)
ECONOMY **IND:** construction and construction materials, mining (coal, copper, molybdenum, fluorspar, tin, tungsten, gold), oil, food and beverages **AGR:** wheat, barley, vegetables, forage crops; sheep **EXP:** copper, apparel, livestock, animal products, cashmere
MAP pages 196-197

Montenegro
REPUBLIC OF MONTENEGRO

CONTINENT Europe
AREA 14,026 sq km (5,415 sq mi)
POPULATION 626,000
DEMONYM Montenegrin(s)
CAPITAL Podgorica 142,000
RELIGION Orthodox, Muslim, Roman Catholic
LANGUAGE Serbian (Ijekavian dialect), Bosnian, Albanian, Croatian
LITERACY NA
LIFE EXPECTANCY 73 years
GDP PER CAPITA $3,800
CURRENCY euro (EUR)
ECONOMY **IND:** steelmaking, aluminum, agricultural processing, consumer goods, tourism **AGR:** grains, tobacco, potatoes, citrus fruits; sheepherding; negligible commercial fishing **EXP:** none
MAP pages 162-163

Montserrat (U.K.)
MONTSERRAT

CONTINENT North America
AREA 102 sq km (39 sq mi)
POPULATION 6,000
DEMONYM Montserratian(s)
CAPITAL Brades (administrative) 1,000; Plymouth (abandoned) 0
RELIGION Anglican, Methodist, Roman Catholic, Pentecostal, Seventh-day Adventist, other Christian
LANGUAGE English
MAP pages 120-121

Morocco
KINGDOM OF MOROCCO

CONTINENT Africa
AREA 710,850 sq km (274,461 sq mi)
POPULATION 31,711,000
DEMONYM Moroccan(s)
CAPITAL Rabat 1,705,000
RELIGION Muslim
LANGUAGE Arabic, Berber dialects, French
LITERACY 52%
LIFE EXPECTANCY 70 years
GDP PER CAPITA $3,800
CURRENCY Moroccan dirham (MAD)
ECONOMY **IND:** phosphate rock mining and processing, food processing, leather goods, textiles **AGR:** barley, wheat, citrus, wine, vegetables; livestock **EXP:** clothing and textiles, electric components, inorganic chemicals, transistors
MAP pages 216-217

Mozambique
REPUBLIC OF MOZAMBIQUE

CONTINENT Africa
AREA 799,380 sq km (308,642 sq mi)
POPULATION 20,359,000
DEMONYM Mozambican(s)
CAPITAL Maputo 1,445,000
RELIGION Roman Catholic, Muslim, Zionist Christian
LANGUAGE Emakhuwa, Xichangana, Portuguese, Elomwe, Cisena, Echuwabo, other local languages
LITERACY 48%
LIFE EXPECTANCY 43 years
GDP PER CAPITA $900
CURRENCY metical (MZM)
ECONOMY **IND:** food, beverages, chemicals, aluminum **AGR:** cotton, cashew nuts, sugarcane, tea; beef **EXP:** aluminum, prawns, cashews, cotton, sugar
MAP pages 228-229

Myanmar (Burma)
UNION OF MYANMAR

CONTINENT Asia
AREA 676,552 sq km (261,218 sq mi)
POPULATION 49,805,000
DEMONYM Burmese (singular and plural)
CAPITAL Nay Pyi Taw (administrative) 418,000; Yangon (Rangoon) (legislative) 4,088,000
RELIGION Buddhist, Christian, Muslim
LANGUAGE Burmese, minority ethnic languages
LITERACY 90%
LIFE EXPECTANCY 60 years
GDP PER CAPITA $1,900
CURRENCY kyat (MMK)
ECONOMY **IND:** agricultural processing, wood and wood products, copper, tin **AGR:** rice, pulses, beans, sesame; hardwood; fish and fish products **EXP:** gas, wood products, pulses, beans, fish, rice
MAP pages 204-205

Namibia
REPUBLIC OF NAMIBIA

CONTINENT Africa
AREA 824,292 sq km (318,261 sq mi)
POPULATION 2,074,000
DEMONYM Namibian(s)
CAPITAL Windhoek 313,000
RELIGION Lutheran, other Christian, indigenous beliefs
LANGUAGE Afrikaans, German, English
LITERACY 85%
LIFE EXPECTANCY 52 years
GDP PER CAPITA $5,200
CURRENCY Namibian dollar (NAD); South African rand (ZAR)
ECONOMY **IND:** meatpacking, fish processing, dairy products, mining (diamonds, lead, zinc) **AGR:** millet, sorghum, peanuts, grapes; livestock; fish **EXP:** diamonds, copper, gold, karakul skins
MAP pages 228-229

Nauru
REPUBLIC OF NAURU

CONTINENT Australia/Oceania
AREA 21 sq km (8 sq mi)
POPULATION 14,000
DEMONYM Nauruan(s)
CAPITAL Yaren 10,000
RELIGION Protestant, Roman Catholic
LANGUAGE Nauruan, English
LITERACY NA
LIFE EXPECTANCY 62 years
GDP PER CAPITA $5,000
CURRENCY Australian dollar (AUD)
ECONOMY **IND:** phosphate mining, offshore banking, coconut products **AGR:** coconuts **EXP:** phosphates
MAP pages 244-245

Nepal
NEPAL

CONTINENT Asia
AREA 147,181 sq km (56,827 sq mi)
POPULATION 27,828,000
DEMONYM Nepalese (singular and plural)
CAPITAL Kathmandu 895,000
RELIGION Hindu, Buddhist, Muslim, Kirant
LANGUAGE Nepali, Maithali, Bhojpuri, Tharu, Tamang, Newar, Magar
LITERACY 49%
LIFE EXPECTANCY 62 years
GDP PER CAPITA $1,100
CURRENCY Nepalese rupee (NPR)
ECONOMY **IND:** tourism, carpet, textiles; small rice, jute, sugar, mills **AGR:** rice, corn, wheat, sugarcane, jute; milk **EXP:** carpets, clothing, leather goods, jute goods
MAP pages 194-195

Netherlands
KINGDOM OF THE NETHERLANDS

CONTINENT Europe
AREA 41,528 sq km (16,034 sq mi)
POPULATION 16,368,000
DEMONYM Dutchman(men), Dutchwoman(women)
CAPITAL Amsterdam 1,031,000
RELIGION Roman Catholic, Dutch Reformed, Calvinist, Muslim
LANGUAGE Dutch, Frisian
LITERACY 99%
LIFE EXPECTANCY 80 years
GDP PER CAPITA $38,600
CURRENCY euro (EUR)
ECONOMY **IND:** agro-industries, metal and engineering products, electrical machinery and equipment, chemicals **AGR:** grains, potatoes, sugar beets, fruits; livestock **EXP:** machinery and equipment, chemicals, fuels, foodstuffs
MAP pages 154-155

New Caledonia (France)
TERRITORY OF NEW CALEDONIA AND DEPENDENCIES

CONTINENT Australia/Oceania
AREA 19,060 sq km (7,359 sq mi)
POPULATION 242,000
DEMONYM New Caledonian(s)
CAPITAL Nouméa 156,000
RELIGION Roman Catholic, Protestant
LANGUAGE French, 33 Melanesian-Polynesian dialects
MAP pages 244-245

New Zealand
NEW ZEALAND

CONTINENT Australia/Oceania
AREA 270,534 sq km (104,454 sq mi)
POPULATION 4,184,000
DEMONYM New Zealander(s)
CAPITAL Wellington 366,000
RELIGION Anglican, Roman Catholic, Presbyterian, other Christian
LANGUAGE English, Maori
LITERACY 99%
LIFE EXPECTANCY 80 years
GDP PER CAPITA $27,300
CURRENCY New Zealand dollar (NZD)
ECONOMY **IND:** food processing, wood and paper products, textiles, machinery **AGR:** wheat, barley, potatoes, pulses; dairy, wool; fish **EXP:** dairy products, meat, wood and wood products, fish
MAP pages 240-241

Nicaragua
REPUBLIC OF NICARAGUA

CONTINENT North America
AREA 130,000 sq km (50,193 sq mi)
POPULATION 5,620,000
DEMONYM Nicaraguan(s)
CAPITAL Managua 920,000
RELIGION Roman Catholic, Evangelical
LANGUAGE Spanish
LITERACY 68%
LIFE EXPECTANCY 71 years
GDP PER CAPITA $3,200
CURRENCY gold cordoba (NIO)
ECONOMY **IND:** food processing, chemicals, machinery and metal products, textiles **AGR:** coffee, bananas, sugarcane, cotton; beef, shrimp **EXP:** coffee, beef, shrimp and lobster, tobacco, sugar
MAP pages 116-117

Niger
REPUBLIC OF NIGER

CONTINENT Africa
AREA 1,267,000 sq km (489,191 sq mi)
POPULATION 14,226,000
DEMONYM Nigerien(s)
CAPITAL Niamey 915,000
RELIGION Muslim, other (includes indigenous beliefs and Christian)
LANGUAGE French, Hausa, Djerma
LITERACY 29%
LIFE EXPECTANCY 56 years
GDP PER CAPITA $700
CURRENCY Communauté Financière Africaine franc (XOF)
ECONOMY **IND:** uranium mining, cement, brick, soap, textiles **AGR:** cowpeas, cotton, peanuts, millet; cattle **EXP:** uranium ore, livestock, cowpeas, onions
MAP pages 222-223

Nigeria
FEDERAL REPUBLIC OF NIGERIA

CONTINENT Africa
AREA 923,768 sq km (356,669 sq mi)
POPULATION 144,430,000
DEMONYM Nigerian(s)
CAPITAL Abuja 1,579,000
RELIGION Muslim, Christian, indigenous beliefs
LANGUAGE English, Hausa, Yoruba, Igbo (Ibo), Fulani
LITERACY 68%
LIFE EXPECTANCY 47 years
GDP PER CAPITA $2,200
CURRENCY naira (NGN)
ECONOMY **IND:** crude oil, coal, tin, palm oil, hides **AGR:** cocoa, peanuts, palm oil, corn; cattle; timber; fish **EXP:** petroleum, petroleum products, cocoa, rubber
MAP pages 222-223

Niue (N.Z.)
NIUE

CONTINENT Australia/Oceania
AREA 263 sq km (102 sq mi)
POPULATION 1,000
DEMONYM Niuean(s)
CAPITAL Alofi 1,000
RELIGION Ekalesia Niue, Church of Latter-day Saints, Roman Catholic
LANGUAGE Niuean, English
MAP pages 244-245

Norfolk Island (Australia)
TERRITORY OF NORFOLK ISLAND

CONTINENT Australia/Oceania
AREA 35 sq km (14 sq mi)
POPULATION 2,000
DEMONYM Norfolk Islander(s)
CAPITAL Kingston NA
RELIGION Anglican, Roman Catholic, Uniting Church in Australia
LANGUAGE English, Norfolk
MAP pages 244-245

North Korea
DEMOCRATIC PEOPLE'S REPUBLIC OF KOREA

CONTINENT Asia
AREA 120,538 sq km (46,540 sq mi)
POPULATION 23,301,000
DEMONYM Korean(s)
CAPITAL Pyongyang 3,301,000
RELIGION Buddhist, Confucianist, some Christian and syncretic Chondogyo
LANGUAGE Korean
LITERACY 99%
LIFE EXPECTANCY 71 years
GDP PER CAPITA $1,900
CURRENCY North Korean won (KPW)
ECONOMY **IND:** military products, machine building, electric power, chemicals **AGR:** rice, corn, potatoes, soybeans; cattle **EXP:** minerals, metallurgical products, manufactures (including armaments), textiles
MAP pages 200-201

Northern Mariana Islands (U.S.)
COMMONWEALTH OF THE NORTHERN MARIANA ISLANDS

CONTINENT Australia/Oceania
AREA 477 sq km (184 sq mi)
POPULATION 82,000
DEMONYM NA (U.S. citizens)
CAPITAL Saipan 76,000
RELIGION Christian (mostly Roman Catholic), traditional beliefs
LANGUAGE Philippine languages, Chinese, Chamorro, English, other Pacific island languages
MAP pages 244-245

Norway
KINGDOM OF NORWAY

CONTINENT Europe
AREA 323,758 sq km (125,004 sq mi)
POPULATION 4,702,000
DEMONYM Norwegian(s)
CAPITAL Oslo 834,000
RELIGION Church of Norway (Lutheran)
LANGUAGE Bokmal Norwegian, Nynorsk Norwegian, Sami
LITERACY 100%
LIFE EXPECTANCY 80 years
GDP PER CAPITA $55,600
CURRENCY Norwegian krone (NOK)
ECONOMY **IND:** petroleum and gas, food processing, shipbuilding, pulp and paper products **AGR:** barley, wheat, potatoes; pork, beef, veal; fish **EXP:** petroleum and petroleum products, machinery and equipment, metals, chemicals
MAP pages 148-149

Oman
SULTANATE OF OMAN

CONTINENT Asia
AREA 309,500 sq km (119,500 sq mi)
POPULATION 2,706,000
DEMONYM Omani(s)
CAPITAL Muscat 621,000
RELIGION Ibadhi Muslim, Sunni Muslim, Shiite Muslim, Hindu
LANGUAGE Arabic, English, Baluchi, Urdu, Indian dialects
LITERACY 81%
LIFE EXPECTANCY 74 years
GDP PER CAPITA $19,100
CURRENCY Omani rial (OMR)
ECONOMY **IND:** crude oil production and refining, natural and liquefied natural gas (LNG) production, construction, cement **AGR:** dates, limes, bananas, alfalfa; camels; fish **EXP:** petroleum, reexports, fish, metals, textiles
MAP pages 184-185

Pakistan
ISLAMIC REPUBLIC OF PAKISTAN

CONTINENT Asia
AREA 796,095 sq km (307,374 sq mi)
POPULATION 169,271,000
DEMONYM Pakistani(s)
CAPITAL Islamabad 780,000
RELIGION Sunni Muslim, Shiite Muslim
LANGUAGE Punjabi, Sindhi, Siraiki, Pashto, Urdu, Baluchi, Hindko, English
LITERACY 50%
LIFE EXPECTANCY 62 years
GDP PER CAPITA $2,600
CURRENCY Pakistani rupee (PKR)
ECONOMY **IND:** textiles and apparel, food processing, pharmaceuticals, construction materials **AGR:** cotton, wheat, rice, sugarcane; milk, beef **EXP:** textiles (garments, bed linen, cotton cloth, yarn, carpet), rice, leather goods, sports goods
MAP pages 190-191

Palau
REPUBLIC OF PALAU

CONTINENT Australia/Oceania
AREA 489 sq km (189 sq mi)
POPULATION 20,000
DEMONYM Palauan(s)
CAPITAL Melekeok NA
RELIGION Roman Catholic, Protestant, Modekngei, Seventh-day Adventist
LANGUAGE Palauan, Filipino, English, Chinese
LITERACY 92%
LIFE EXPECTANCY 71 years
GDP PER CAPITA $7,600
CURRENCY US dollar (USD)
ECONOMY **IND:** tourism, craft items (from shell, wood, pearls), construction, garment making **AGR:** coconuts, copra, cassava (tapioca), sweet potatoes; fish **EXP:** shellfish, tuna, copra, garments
MAP pages 244-245

Panama
REPUBLIC OF PANAMA

CONTINENT North America
AREA 75,517 sq km (29,157 sq mi)
POPULATION 3,340,000
DEMONYM Panamanian(s)
CAPITAL Panama City 1,280,000
RELIGION Roman Catholic, Protestant
LANGUAGE Spanish, English
LITERACY 92%
LIFE EXPECTANCY 75 years
GDP PER CAPITA $9,000
CURRENCY balboa (PAB); US dollar (USD)
ECONOMY **IND:** construction, brewing, cement and other construction materials, sugar milling **AGR:** bananas, rice, corn, coffee; livestock; shrimp **EXP:** bananas, shrimp, sugar, coffee, clothing
MAP pages 116-117

Papua New Guinea
INDEPENDENT STATE OF PAPUA NEW GUINEA

CONTINENT Australia/Oceania
AREA 462,840 sq km (178,703 sq mi)
POPULATION 6,331,000
DEMONYM Papua New Guinean(s)
CAPITAL Port Moresby 299,000
RELIGION indigenous beliefs, Roman Catholic, Lutheran, other Protestant
LANGUAGE Melanesian Pidgin, 820 indigenous languages
LITERACY 57%
LIFE EXPECTANCY 57 years
GDP PER CAPITA $2,900
CURRENCY kina (PGK)
ECONOMY **IND:** copra crushing, palm oil processing, plywood production, wood chip production **AGR:** coffee, cocoa, copra, palm kernels; poultry; shellfish **EXP:** oil, gold, copper ore, logs, palm oil
MAP pages 240-241

Paraguay
REPUBLIC OF PARAGUAY

CONTINENT South America
AREA 406,752 sq km (157,048 sq mi)
POPULATION 6,126,000
DEMONYM Paraguayan(s)
CAPITAL Asunción 1,870,000
RELIGION Roman Catholic, Protestant
LANGUAGE Spanish, Guarani
LITERACY 94%
LIFE EXPECTANCY 71 years
GDP PER CAPITA $4,000
CURRENCY guarani (PYG)
ECONOMY **IND:** sugar, cement, textiles, beverages, wood products **AGR:** cotton, sugarcane, soybeans, corn; beef; timber **EXP:** soybeans, feed, cotton, meat, edible oils
MAP pages 136-137

Peru
REPUBLIC OF PERU

CONTINENT South America
AREA 1,285,216 sq km (496,224 sq mi)
POPULATION 27,903,000
DEMONYM Peruvian(s)
CAPITAL Lima 8,007,000
RELIGION Roman Catholic
LANGUAGE Spanish, Quechua, Aymara, minor Amazonian languages
LITERACY 88%
LIFE EXPECTANCY 70 years
GDP PER CAPITA $7,600
CURRENCY nuevo sol (PEN)
ECONOMY **IND:** mining and refining of minerals, steel, metal fabrication, petroleum extraction and refining **AGR:** asparagus, coffee, cotton, sugarcane; poultry, guinea pigs; fish **EXP:** copper, gold, zinc, petroleum, coffee, asparagus
MAP pages 134-135

Philippines
REPUBLIC OF THE PHILIPPINES

CONTINENT Asia
AREA 300,000 sq km (115,831 sq mi)
POPULATION 88,706,000
DEMONYM Filipino(s)
CAPITAL Manila 11,100,000
RELIGION Roman Catholic, Muslim, other Christian
LANGUAGE Filipino (based on Tagalog), English
LITERACY 93%
LIFE EXPECTANCY 69 years
GDP PER CAPITA $3,300
CURRENCY Philippine peso (PHP)
ECONOMY **IND:** electronics assembly, garments, footwear, pharmaceuticals **AGR:** sugarcane, coconuts, rice, corn; pork; fish **EXP:** semiconductors, electronics, transport equipment, garments, copper
MAP pages 206-207

Pitcairn Islands (U.K.)
PITCAIRN, HENDERSON, DUCIE, AND OENO ISLANDS

CONTINENT Australia/Oceania
AREA 47 sq km (18 sq mi)
POPULATION 45
DEMONYM Pitcairn Islander(s)
CAPITAL Adamstown 45
RELIGION Seventh-day Adventist
LANGUAGE English, Pitcairnese
MAP pages 244-245

Poland
REPUBLIC OF POLAND

CONTINENT Europe
AREA 312,685 sq km (120,728 sq mi)
POPULATION 38,109,000
DEMONYM Pole(s)
CAPITAL Warsaw 1,707,000
RELIGION Roman Catholic
LANGUAGE Polish
LITERACY 100%
LIFE EXPECTANCY 75 years
GDP PER CAPITA $16,200
CURRENCY zloty (PLN)
ECONOMY **IND:** machine building, iron, steel, coal mining, chemicals **AGR:** potatoes, fruits, vegetables, wheat; poultry **EXP:** machinery and transport equipment, other manufactured goods, food, animals
MAP pages 158-159

Portugal
PORTUGUESE REPUBLIC

CONTINENT Europe
AREA 92,345 sq km (35,655 sq mi)
POPULATION 10,667,000
DEMONYM Portuguese (singular and plural)
CAPITAL Lisbon 2,811,000
RELIGION Roman Catholic
LANGUAGE Portuguese, Mirandese
LITERACY 93%
LIFE EXPECTANCY 78 years
GDP PER CAPITA $21,800
CURRENCY euro (EUR)
ECONOMY **IND:** textiles and footwear; wood pulp, paper, and cork; metals and metalworking; oil refining **AGR:** grain, potatoes, tomatoes, olives; sheep; fish **EXP:** clothing and footwear, machinery, chemicals, cork and paper products
MAP pages 152-153

Puerto Rico (U.S.)
COMMONWEALTH OF PUERTO RICO

CONTINENT North America
AREA 9,086 sq km (3,508 sq mi)
POPULATION 3,947,000
DEMONYM Puerto Rican(s) (U.S. citizens)
CAPITAL San Juan 2,689,000
RELIGION Roman Catholic, Protestant
LANGUAGE Spanish, English
MAP pages 118-119

Qatar
STATE OF QATAR

CONTINENT Asia
AREA 11,521 sq km (4,448 sq mi)
POPULATION 882,000
DEMONYM Qatari(s)
CAPITAL Doha 386,000
RELIGION Muslim, Christian
LANGUAGE Arabic, English commonly a second language
LITERACY 89%
LIFE EXPECTANCY 73 years
GDP PER CAPITA $75,900
CURRENCY Qatari rial (QAR)
ECONOMY **IND:** crude oil production and refining, ammonia, fertilizers, petrochemicals **AGR:** fruits, vegetables; poultry, dairy products; fish **EXP:** liquefied natural gas (LNG), petroleum products, fertilizers, steel
MAP pages 184-185

Réunion (France)
OVERSEAS DEPARTMENT OF FRANCE

CONTINENT Africa
AREA 2,507 sq km (968 sq mi)
POPULATION 801,000
DEMONYM Frenchman(men), Frenchwoman(women)
CAPITAL St.-Denis 143,000
RELIGION Roman Catholic, Hindu, Muslim, Buddhist
LANGUAGE French, Creole
MAP pages 230-231

Romania
ROMANIA

CONTINENT Europe
AREA 238,391 sq km (92,043 sq mi)
POPULATION 21,550,000
DEMONYM Romanian(s)
CAPITAL Bucharest 1,940,000
RELIGION Eastern Orthodox, Protestant, Roman Catholic
LANGUAGE Romanian, Hungarian
LITERACY 97%
LIFE EXPECTANCY 71 years
GDP PER CAPITA $11,100
CURRENCY new leu (RON)
ECONOMY **IND:** textiles and footwear, light machinery and auto assembly, mining, timber **AGR:** wheat, corn, barley, sugar beets; eggs **EXP:** textiles and footwear, metals and metal products, machinery and equipment, minerals and fuels
MAP pages 162-163

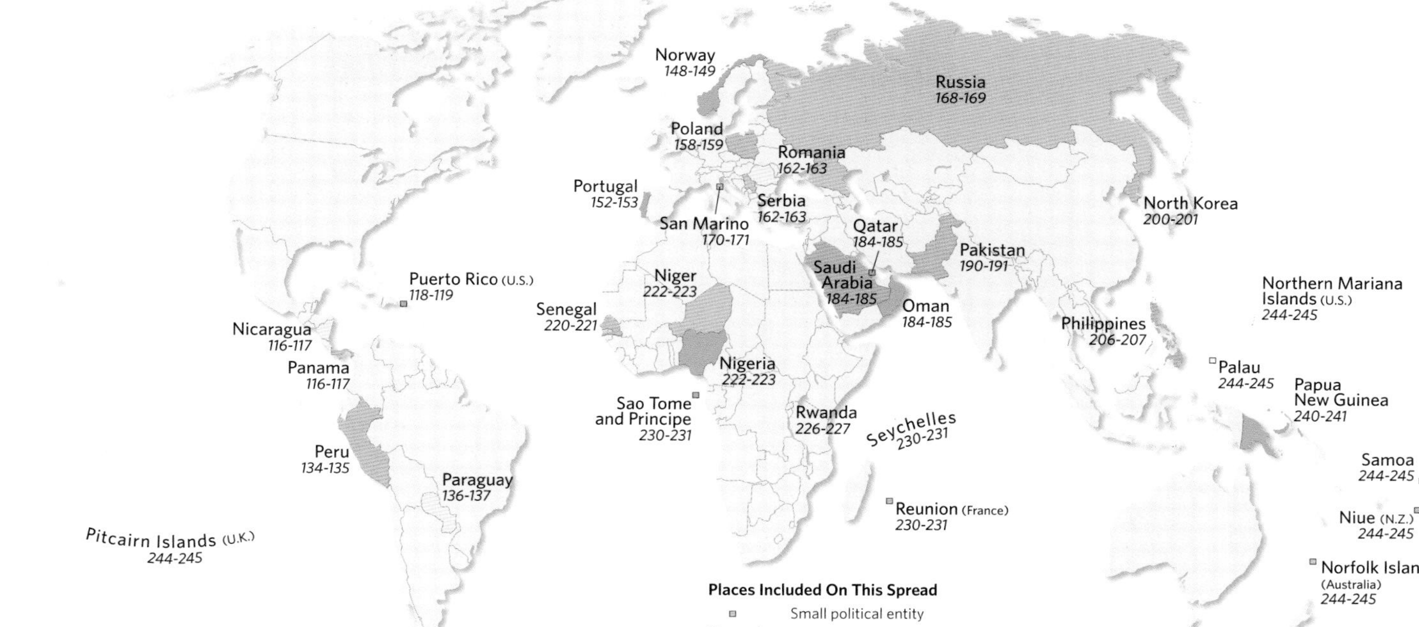

Norway 148-149
Russia 168-169
Poland 158-159
Romania 162-163
Portugal 152-153
Serbia 162-163
San Marino 170-171
Qatar 184-185
North Korea 200-201
Pakistan 190-191
Puerto Rico (U.S.) 118-119
Niger 222-223
Saudi Arabia 184-185
Oman 184-185
Northern Mariana Islands (U.S.) 244-245
Senegal 220-221
Nicaragua 116-117
Philippines 206-207
Panama 116-117
Nigeria 222-223
Palau 244-245
Papua New Guinea 240-241
Sao Tome and Principe 230-231
Rwanda 226-227
Seychelles 230-231
Peru 134-135
Samoa 244-245
Paraguay 136-137
Reunion (France) 230-231
Niue (N.Z.) 244-245
Pitcairn Islands (U.K.) 244-245
Norfolk Island (Australia) 244-245
Places Included On This Spread
Small political entity
Rwanda 226-227 Political entity name with regional map page numbers
Note: Colors reflect the tint used on regional maps

Russia
RUSSIAN FEDERATION

CONTINENT Europe/Asia
AREA 17,075,400 sq km (6,592,850 sq mi)
POPULATION 141,681,000
DEMONYM Russian(s)
CAPITAL Moscow 10,452,000
RELIGION Russian Orthodox, Muslim
LANGUAGE Russian, many minority languages
LITERACY 99%
LIFE EXPECTANCY 65 years
GDP PER CAPITA $14,600
CURRENCY Russian ruble (RUR)
ECONOMY **IND:** mining industries (coal, oil, gas), machine building, defense industries, transportation equipment **AGR:** grain, sugar beets, sunflower seed, vegetables; beef **EXP:** petroleum and petroleum products, natural gas, wood and wood products, metals
MAP pages 168-169

Rwanda
REPUBLIC OF RWANDA

CONTINENT Africa
AREA 26,338 sq km (10,169 sq mi)
POPULATION 9,347,000
DEMONYM Rwandan(s)
CAPITAL Kigali 852,000
RELIGION Roman Catholic, Protestant, Adventist, Muslim
LANGUAGE Kinyarwanda, French, English, Kiswahili
LITERACY 70%
LIFE EXPECTANCY 47 years
GDP PER CAPITA $1,000
CURRENCY Rwandan franc (RWF)
ECONOMY **IND:** cement, agricultural products, small-scale beverages, soap **AGR:** coffee, tea, pyrethrum (insecticide made from chrysanthemums), bananas; livestock **EXP:** coffee, tea, hides, tin ore
MAP pages 226-227

Samoa
INDEPENDENT STATE OF SAMOA

CONTINENT Australia/Oceania
AREA 2,831 sq km (1,093 sq mi)
POPULATION 187,000
DEMONYM Samoan(s)
CAPITAL Apia 43,000
RELIGION Congregationalist, Roman Catholic, Methodist, Church of Latter-day Saints, Assembly of God, Seventh-day Adventist
LANGUAGE Samoan (Polynesian), English
LITERACY 100%
LIFE EXPECTANCY 73 years
GDP PER CAPITA $2,100
CURRENCY tala (SAT)
ECONOMY **IND:** food processing, building materials, auto parts **AGR:** coconuts, bananas, taro, yams, coffee **EXP:** fish, coconut oil and cream, copra, taro, automotive parts
MAP pages 244-245

San Marino
REPUBLIC OF SAN MARINO

CONTINENT Europe
AREA 61 sq km (24 sq mi)
POPULATION 31,000
DEMONYM Sammarinese (singular and plural)
CAPITAL San Marino 4,000
RELIGION Roman Catholic
LANGUAGE Italian
LITERACY 96%
LIFE EXPECTANCY 81 years
GDP PER CAPITA $34,100
CURRENCY euro (EUR)
ECONOMY **IND:** tourism, banking, textiles, electronics **AGR:** wheat, grapes, corn, olives; cattle, pigs **EXP:** building stone, lime, wood, chestnuts, wheat
MAP pages 170-171

Sao Tome and Principe
DEMOCRATIC REPUBLIC OF SAO TOME AND PRINCIPE

CONTINENT Africa
AREA 1,001 sq km (386 sq mi)
POPULATION 155,000
DEMONYM Sao Tomean(s)
CAPITAL São Tomé 58,000
RELIGION Roman Catholic, Evangelical
LANGUAGE Portuguese
LITERACY 85%
LIFE EXPECTANCY 64 years
GDP PER CAPITA $1,200
CURRENCY dobra (STD)
ECONOMY **IND:** light construction, textiles, soap, beer **AGR:** cocoa, coconuts, palm kernels, copra; poultry; fish **EXP:** cocoa, copra, coffee, palm oil
MAP pages 230-231

Saudi Arabia
KINGDOM OF SAUDI ARABIA

CONTINENT Asia
AREA 1,960,582 sq km (756,985 sq mi)
POPULATION 27,601,000
DEMONYM Saudi(s)
CAPITAL Riyadh 4,462,000
RELIGION Muslim
LANGUAGE Arabic
LITERACY 79%
LIFE EXPECTANCY 75 years
GDP PER CAPITA $20,700
CURRENCY Saudi riyal (SAR)
ECONOMY **IND:** crude oil production, petroleum refining, basic petrochemicals, ammonia **AGR:** wheat, barley, tomatoes, melons; mutton **EXP:** petroleum and petroleum products
MAP pages 184-185

Senegal
REPUBLIC OF SENEGAL

CONTINENT Africa
AREA 196,722 sq km (75,955 sq mi)
POPULATION 12,379,000
DEMONYM Senegalese (singular and plural)
CAPITAL Dakar 2,603,000
RELIGION Muslim, Christian (mostly Roman Catholic)
LANGUAGE French, Wolof, Pulaar, Jola, Mandinka
LITERACY 39%
LIFE EXPECTANCY 62 years
GDP PER CAPITA $1,700
CURRENCY Communauté Financière Africaine franc (XOF)
ECONOMY **IND:** agricultural and fish processing, phosphate mining, fertilizer production, petroleum refining **AGR:** peanuts, millet, corn, sorghum; cattle; fish **EXP:** fish, groundnuts (peanuts), petroleum products, phosphates, cotton
MAP pages 220-221

Serbia
REPUBLIC OF SERBIA

CONTINENT Europe
AREA 88,361 sq km (34,116 sq mi)
POPULATION 7,625,000
DEMONYM Serb(s)
CAPITAL Belgrade 1,100,000
RELIGION Serbian Orthodox, Roman Catholic, Muslim
LANGUAGE Serbian, Hungarian, Albanian
LITERACY 96%
LIFE EXPECTANCY 72 years
GDP PER CAPITA $7,700
CURRENCY Serbian dinar (RSD)
ECONOMY **IND:** sugar, agricultural machinery, electrical and communication equipment, paper and pulp **AGR:** wheat, maize, sugar beets, sunflowers; beef **EXP:** manufactured goods, food and live animals, machinery and transport equipment
MAP pages 162-163

Seychelles
REPUBLIC OF SEYCHELLES

CONTINENT Africa
AREA 455 sq km (176 sq mi)
POPULATION 86,000
DEMONYM Seychellois (singular and plural)
CAPITAL Victoria 26,000
RELIGION Roman Catholic, Anglican, other Christian
LANGUAGE Creole, English
LITERACY 92%
LIFE EXPECTANCY 72 years
GDP PER CAPITA $18,400
CURRENCY Seychelles rupee (SCR)
ECONOMY **IND:** fishing, tourism, processing of coconuts and vanilla, coir (coconut fiber) rope **AGR:** coconuts, cinnamon, vanilla, sweet potatoes; poultry; tuna **EXP:** canned tuna, frozen fish, cinnamon bark, copra, petroleum product reexports
MAP pages 230-231

Sierra Leone
REPUBLIC OF SIERRA LEONE

CONTINENT Africa
AREA 71,740 sq km (27,699 sq mi)
POPULATION 5,335,000
DEMONYM Sierra Leonean(s)
CAPITAL Freetown 826,000
RELIGION Muslim, indigenous beliefs, Christian
LANGUAGE English, Mende, Temne, Krio
LITERACY 35%
LIFE EXPECTANCY 48 years
GDP PER CAPITA $800
CURRENCY leone (SLL)
ECONOMY **IND:** diamond mining, small-scale manufacturing, petroleum refining, small ship repair **AGR:** rice, coffee, cocoa, palm kernels; poultry; fish **EXP:** diamonds, rutile, cocoa, coffee, fish
MAP pages 220-221

Singapore
REPUBLIC OF SINGAPORE

CONTINENT Asia
AREA 660 sq km (255 sq mi)
POPULATION 4,634,000
DEMONYM Singaporean(s)
CAPITAL Singapore 4,634,000
RELIGION Buddhist, Muslim, Taoist, Roman Catholic, Hindu, other Christian
LANGUAGE Mandarin, English, Malay, Hokkien, Cantonese, Teochew, Tamil
LITERACY 93%
LIFE EXPECTANCY 80 years
GDP PER CAPITA $48,900
CURRENCY Singapore dollar (SGD)
ECONOMY **IND:** electronics, chemicals, financial services, oil drilling equipment **AGR:** rubber, copra, fruit, orchids; poultry; fish, ornamental fish **EXP:** machinery and equipment (including electronics), consumer goods, chemicals, mineral fuels
MAP pages 206-207

Slovakia
SLOVAK REPUBLIC

CONTINENT Europe
AREA 49,035 sq km (18,932 sq mi)
POPULATION 5,396,000
DEMONYM Slovak(s)
CAPITAL Bratislava 424,000
RELIGION Roman Catholic, Protestant, Greek Catholic
LANGUAGE Slovak, Hungarian
LITERACY 100%
LIFE EXPECTANCY 74 years
GDP PER CAPITA $19,800
CURRENCY Slovak koruna (SKK)
ECONOMY **IND:** metal and metal products, food and beverages, electricity, gas **AGR:** grains, potatoes, sugar beets, hops; pigs; forest products **EXP:** vehicles, machinery and electrical equipment, base metals, chemicals and minerals
MAP pages 158-159

Slovenia
REPUBLIC OF SLOVENIA

CONTINENT Europe
AREA 20,273 sq km (7,827 sq mi)
POPULATION 2,014,000
DEMONYM Slovene(s)
CAPITAL Ljubljana 244,000
RELIGION Roman Catholic
LANGUAGE Slovene, Serbo-Croatian
LITERACY 100%
LIFE EXPECTANCY 78 years
GDP PER CAPITA $27,300
CURRENCY euro (EUR)
ECONOMY **IND:** ferrous metallurgy and aluminum products, lead and zinc smelting, electronics, trucks **AGR:** potatoes, hops, wheat, sugar beets; cattle **EXP:** manufactured goods, machinery and transport equipment, chemicals, food
MAP pages 162-163

Solomon Islands
SOLOMON ISLANDS

CONTINENT Australia/Oceania
AREA 28,370 sq km (10,954 sq mi)
POPULATION 495,000
DEMONYM Solomon Islander(s)
CAPITAL Honiara 66,000
RELIGION Church of Melanesia, Roman Catholic, South Seas Evangelical, Seventh-day Adventist, United Church, other Christian
LANGUAGE Melanesian pidgin, 120 indigenous languages
LITERACY NA
LIFE EXPECTANCY 62 years
GDP PER CAPITA $600
CURRENCY Solomon Islands dollar (SBD)
ECONOMY **IND:** fish (tuna), mining, timber **AGR:** cocoa beans, coconuts, palm kernels, rice; cattle; timber; fish **EXP:** timber, fish, copra, palm oil, cocoa
MAP pages 244-245

Somalia
SOMALIA

CONTINENT Africa
AREA 637,657 sq km (246,201 sq mi)
POPULATION 9,119,000
DEMONYM Somali(s)
CAPITAL Mogadishu 1,450,000
RELIGION Sunni Muslim
LANGUAGE Somali, Arabic, Italian, English
LITERACY 38%
LIFE EXPECTANCY 48 years
GDP PER CAPITA $600
CURRENCY Somali shilling (SOS)
ECONOMY **IND:** sugar refining, textiles, wireless communication **AGR:** bananas, sorghum, corn, coconuts; cattle; fish **EXP:** livestock, bananas, hides, fish, charcoal
MAP pages 226-227

South Africa
REPUBLIC OF SOUTH AFRICA

CONTINENT Africa
AREA 1,219,090 sq km (470,693 sq mi)
POPULATION 47,867,000
DEMONYM South African(s)
CAPITAL Pretoria (administrative) 1,336,000; Bloemfontein (judicial) 417,000; Cape Town (legislative) 3,211,000
RELIGION Zion Christian, Pentecostal, Catholic, Methodist, Dutch Reformed, Anglican, other Christian
LANGUAGE IsiZulu, IsiXhosa, Afrikaans, Sepedi, English, Setswana, Sesotho, Xitsonga
LITERACY 86%
LIFE EXPECTANCY 51 years
GDP PER CAPITA $10,600
CURRENCY rand (ZAR)
ECONOMY **IND:** mining (platinum, gold, chromium), automobile assembly, metalworking, machinery **AGR:** corn, wheat, sugarcane, fruits, vegetables; beef **EXP:** gold, diamonds, platinum, other metals and minerals, machinery and equipment
MAP pages 228-229

South Korea
REPUBLIC OF KOREA

CONTINENT Asia
AREA 99,250 sq km (38,321 sq mi)
POPULATION 48,456,000
DEMONYM Korean(s)
CAPITAL Seoul 9,799,000
RELIGION Christian, Buddhist
LANGUAGE Korean, English
LITERACY 98%
LIFE EXPECTANCY 79 years
GDP PER CAPITA $24,600
CURRENCY South Korean won (KRW)
ECONOMY **IND:** electronics, telecommunications, automobile production, chemicals **AGR:** rice, root crops, barley, vegetables; cattle; fish **EXP:** semiconductors, wireless telecommunications equipment, motor vehicles, computers
MAP pages 200-201

Spain
KINGDOM OF SPAIN

CONTINENT Europe
AREA 505,988 sq km (195,363 sq mi)
POPULATION 45,332,000
DEMONYM Spaniard(s)
CAPITAL Madrid 5,567,000
RELIGION Roman Catholic
LANGUAGE Castilian Spanish, Catalan, Galician, Basque
LITERACY 98%
LIFE EXPECTANCY 80 years
GDP PER CAPITA $33,700
CURRENCY euro (EUR)
ECONOMY **IND:** textiles and apparel, food and beverages, metals and metal manufactures, chemicals **AGR:** grain, vegetables, olives, wine grapes; beef; fish **EXP:** machinery, motor vehicles, foodstuffs, pharmaceuticals
MAP pages 152-153

Sri Lanka
DEMOCRATIC SOCIALIST REPUBLIC OF SRI LANKA

CONTINENT Asia
AREA 65,525 sq km (25,299 sq mi)
POPULATION 20,087,000
DEMONYM Sri Lankan(s)
CAPITAL Colombo 656,000
RELIGION Buddhist, Muslim, Hindu, Christian
LANGUAGE Sinhala, Tamil
LITERACY 91%
LIFE EXPECTANCY 74 years
GDP PER CAPITA $4,100
CURRENCY Sri Lankan rupee (LKR)
ECONOMY **IND:** processing of rubber, tea, coconuts, tobacco, and other agricultural commodities; telecommunications, insurance, banking **AGR:** rice, sugarcane, grains, pulses; milk; fish **EXP:** textiles and apparel, tea, spices, diamonds, emeralds, rubies
MAP pages 194-195

St. Helena (U.K.)
SAINT HELENA

CONTINENT Africa
AREA 411 sq km (159 sq mi)
POPULATION 6,000
DEMONYM St. Helenian(s); referred to locally as Saints
CAPITAL Jamestown 1,000
RELIGION Anglican, Baptist, Seventh-day Adventist, Roman Catholic
LANGUAGE English
MAP pages 212-213

St. Kitts and Nevis
FEDERATION OF SAINT KITTS AND NEVIS

CONTINENT North America
AREA 269 sq km (104 sq mi)
POPULATION 47,000
DEMONYM Kittitian(s), Nevisian(s)
CAPITAL Basseterre 13,000
RELIGION Anglican, other Protestant, Roman Catholic
LANGUAGE English
LITERACY 98%
LIFE EXPECTANCY 70 years
GDP PER CAPITA $8,200
CURRENCY East Caribbean dollar (XCD)
ECONOMY **IND:** tourism, cotton, salt, copra, clothing **AGR:** sugarcane, rice, yams, vegetables; fish **EXP:** machinery, food, electronics, beverages, tobacco
MAP pages 120-121

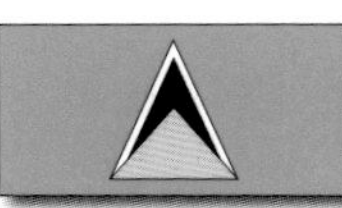

St. Lucia
SAINT LUCIA

CONTINENT North America
AREA 616 sq km (238 sq mi)
POPULATION 170,000
DEMONYM St. Lucian(s)
CAPITAL Castries 14,000
RELIGION Roman Catholic, Seventh-day Adventist, Pentecostal
LANGUAGE English, French patois
LITERACY 90%
LIFE EXPECTANCY 74 years
GDP PER CAPITA $4,800
CURRENCY East Caribbean dollar (XCD)
ECONOMY **IND:** clothing, assembly of electronic components, beverages, corrugated cardboard boxes **AGR:** bananas, coconuts, vegetables, citrus **EXP:** bananas, clothing, cocoa, vegetables, fruits
MAP pages 120-121

St. Vincent and the Grenadines
SAINT VINCENT AND THE GRENADINES

CONTINENT North America
AREA 389 sq km (150 sq mi)
POPULATION 111,000
DEMONYM St. Vincentian(s) or Vincentian(s)
CAPITAL Kingstown 26,000
RELIGION Anglican, Methodist, Roman Catholic
LANGUAGE English, French patois
LITERACY 96%
LIFE EXPECTANCY 71 years
GDP PER CAPITA $3,600
CURRENCY East Caribbean dollar (XCD)
ECONOMY **IND:** food processing, cement, furniture, clothing **AGR:** bananas, coconuts, sweet potatoes, spices; small numbers of cattle; fish **EXP:** bananas, eddoes and dasheen (taro), arrowroot starch, tennis racquets
MAP pages 120-121

St.-Pierre and Miquelon (France)
TERRITORIAL COLLECTIVITY OF SAINT PIERRE AND MIQUELON

CONTINENT North America
AREA 242 sq km (93 sq mi)
POPULATION 7,000
DEMONYM Frenchman(men), Frenchwoman(women)
CAPITAL St.-Pierre 6,000
RELIGION Roman Catholic
LANGUAGE French
MAP pages 106-107

Sudan
REPUBLIC OF THE SUDAN

CONTINENT Africa
AREA 2,505,813 sq km (967,500 sq mi)
POPULATION 38,560,000
DEMONYM Sudanese (singular and plural)
CAPITAL Khartoum 4,762,000
RELIGION Sunni Muslim, indigenous beliefs, Christian
LANGUAGE Arabic, Nubian, Ta Bedawie, many diverse dialects of Nilotic, Nilo-Hamitic, Sudanic languages, English
LITERACY 61%
LIFE EXPECTANCY 58 years
GDP PER CAPITA $2,500
CURRENCY Sudanese pound (SDG)
ECONOMY **IND:** oil, cotton ginning, textiles, cement, edible oils **AGR:** cotton, groundnuts (peanuts), sorghum, millet; sheep **EXP:** oil and petroleum products, cotton, sesame, livestock, groundnuts
MAP pages 218-219

Suriname

REPUBLIC OF SURINAME

- CONTINENT South America
- AREA 163,265 sq km (63,037 sq mi)
- POPULATION 503,000
- DEMONYM Surinamer(s)
- CAPITAL Paramaribo 252,000
- RELIGION Hindu, Protestant (predominantly Moravian), Roman Catholic, Muslim, indigenous beliefs
- LANGUAGE Dutch, English, Sranang Tongo, Hindustani, Javanese
- LITERACY 90%
- LIFE EXPECTANCY 69 years
- GDP PER CAPITA $7,800
- CURRENCY Surinam dollar (SRD)
- ECONOMY **IND:** bauxite and gold mining, alumina production, oil, lumbering **AGR:** paddy rice, bananas, palm kernels, coconuts; beef; forest products; shrimp **EXP:** alumina, gold, crude oil, lumber, shrimp and fish
- MAP pages 132-133

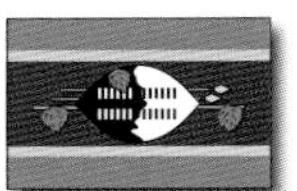

Swaziland

KINGDOM OF SWAZILAND

- CONTINENT Africa
- AREA 17,363 sq km (6,704 sq mi)
- POPULATION 1,133,000
- DEMONYM Swazi(s)
- CAPITAL Mbabane (administrative) 78,000; Lobamba (legislative and royal) NA
- RELIGION Zionist, Roman Catholic, Muslim
- LANGUAGE English, siSwati
- LITERACY 82%
- LIFE EXPECTANCY 33 years
- GDP PER CAPITA $4,800
- CURRENCY lilangeni (SZL)
- ECONOMY **IND:** coal, wood pulp, sugar, soft drink concentrates **AGR:** sugarcane, cotton, corn, tobacco; cattle **EXP:** soft drink concentrates, sugar, wood pulp, cotton yarn, refrigerators
- MAP pages 228-229

Sweden

KINGDOM OF SWEDEN

- CONTINENT Europe
- AREA 449,964 sq km (173,732 sq mi)
- POPULATION 9,146,000
- DEMONYM Swede(s)
- CAPITAL Stockholm 1,264,000
- RELIGION Lutheran
- LANGUAGE Swedish, small Sami- and Finnish-speaking minorities
- LITERACY 99%
- LIFE EXPECTANCY 81 years
- GDP PER CAPITA $36,900
- CURRENCY Swedish krona (SEK)
- ECONOMY **IND:** iron and steel, precision equipment (bearings, radio and telephone parts, armaments), wood pulp and paper products, processed foods **AGR:** barley, wheat, sugar beets; meat, milk **EXP:** machinery, motor vehicles, paper products, pulp and wood
- MAP pages 148-149

Switzerland

SWISS CONFEDERATION

- CONTINENT Europe
- AREA 41,284 sq km (15,940 sq mi)
- POPULATION 7,532,000
- DEMONYM Swiss (singular and plural)
- CAPITAL Bern 337,000
- RELIGION Roman Catholic, Protestant, Muslim
- LANGUAGE German, French, Italian, Romansh
- LITERACY 99%
- LIFE EXPECTANCY 81 years
- GDP PER CAPITA $39,800
- CURRENCY Swiss franc (CHF)
- ECONOMY **IND:** machinery, chemicals, watches, textiles **AGR:** grains, fruits, vegetables; meat, eggs **EXP:** machinery, chemicals, metals, watches, agricultural products
- MAP pages 156-157

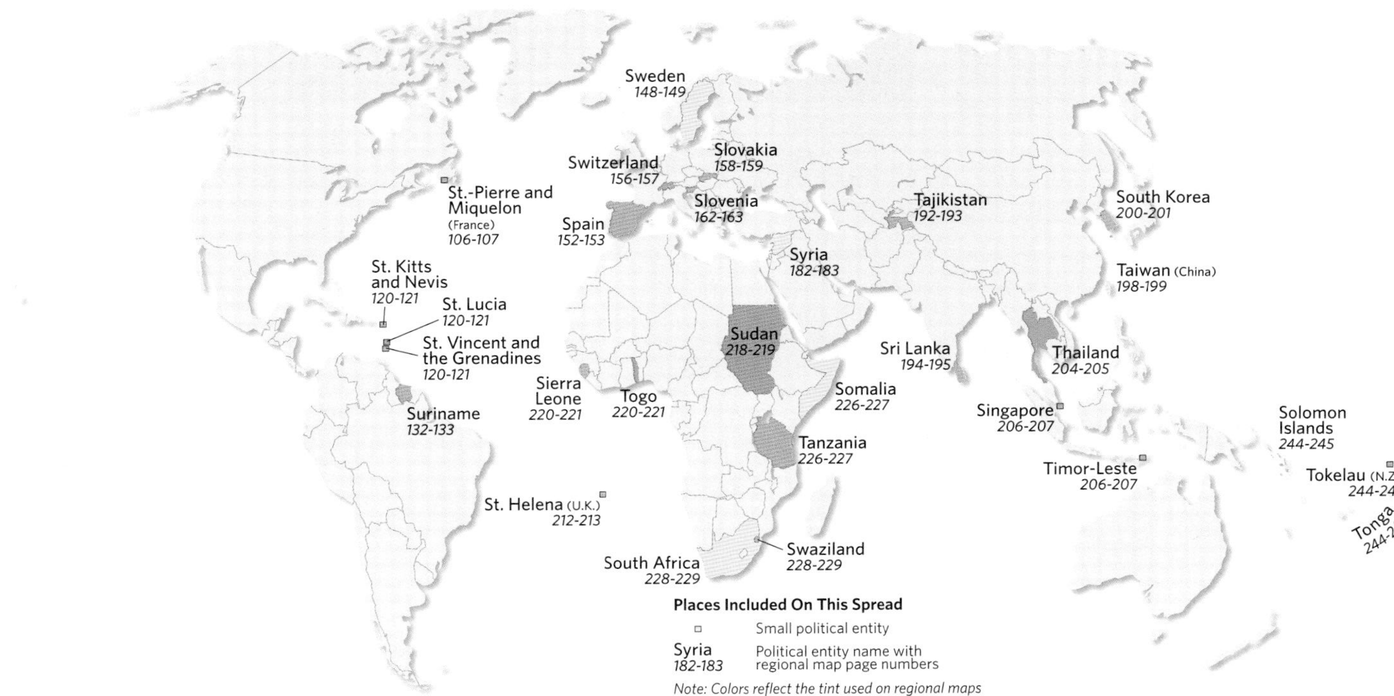

Sweden 148-149
Slovakia 158-159
Switzerland 156-157
St.-Pierre and Miquelon (France) 106-107
Slovenia 162-163
Tajikistan 192-193
South Korea 200-201
Spain 152-153
Syria 182-183
St. Kitts and Nevis 120-121
St. Lucia 120-121
Taiwan (China) 198-199
St. Vincent and the Grenadines 120-121
Sudan 218-219
Sri Lanka 194-195
Thailand 204-205
Sierra Leone 220-221
Togo 220-221
Somalia 226-227
Suriname 132-133
Singapore 206-207
Solomon Islands 244-245
Tanzania 226-227
Timor-Leste 206-207
Tokelau (N.Z.) 244-245
St. Helena (U.K.) 212-213
Tonga 244-245
Swaziland 228-229
South Africa 228-229
Places Included On This Spread
Small political entity
Syria 182-183
Political entity name with regional map page numbers
Note: Colors reflect the tint used on regional maps

Syria

SYRIAN ARAB REPUBLIC

- CONTINENT Asia
- AREA 185,180 sq km (71,498 sq mi)
- POPULATION 19,929,000
- DEMONYM Syrian(s)
- CAPITAL Damascus 2,467,000
- RELIGION Sunni, other Muslim (includes Alawite, Druze), Christian
- LANGUAGE Arabic, Kurdish, Armenian, Aramaic, Circassian; French and English somewhat understood
- LITERACY 80%
- LIFE EXPECTANCY 73 years
- GDP PER CAPITA $4,500
- CURRENCY Syrian pound (SYP)
- ECONOMY **IND:** petroleum, textiles, food processing, beverages **AGR:** wheat, barley, cotton, lentils, chickpeas; beef **EXP:** crude oil, petroleum products, fruits and vegetables, cotton fiber
- MAP pages 182-183

Taiwan (China)

TAIWAN

- CONTINENT Asia
- AREA 35,980 sq km (13,892 sq mi)
- POPULATION 22,901,000
- DEMONYM Taiwan (singular and plural)
- CAPITAL Taipei 2,603,000
- RELIGION Buddhist, Taoist, Christian
- LANGUAGE Mandarin Chinese, Taiwanese (Min), Hakka dialects
- MAP pages 198-199

Tajikistan

REPUBLIC OF TAJIKISTAN

- CONTINENT Asia
- AREA 143,100 sq km (55,251 sq mi)
- POPULATION 7,133,000
- DEMONYM Tajikistani(s)
- CAPITAL Dushanbe 553,000
- RELIGION Sunni Muslim, Shiite Muslim
- LANGUAGE Tajik, Russian
- LITERACY 100%
- LIFE EXPECTANCY 64 years
- GDP PER CAPITA $1,600
- CURRENCY somoni (TJS)
- ECONOMY **IND:** aluminum, zinc, lead; chemicals and fertilizers, cement, vegetable oil **AGR:** cotton, grain, grapes, other fruits, vegetables; cattle **EXP:** aluminum, electricity, cotton, fruits, vegetable oil
- MAP pages 192-193

Tanzania

UNITED REPUBLIC OF TANZANIA

- CONTINENT Africa
- AREA 945,087 sq km (364,900 sq mi)
- POPULATION 38,738,000
- DEMONYM Tanzanian(s)
- CAPITAL Dar es Salaam (administrative) 2,930,000; Dodoma (legislative) 183,000
- RELIGION Muslim, indigenous beliefs, Christian
- LANGUAGE Swahili, Kiunguja (Swahili in Zanzibar), English, Arabic, local languages
- LITERACY 69%
- LIFE EXPECTANCY 50 years
- GDP PER CAPITA $1,100
- CURRENCY Tanzanian shilling (TZS)
- ECONOMY **IND:** agricultural processing (sugar, beer, cigarettes, sisal twine); diamond, gold, and iron mining; salt **AGR:** coffee, sisal, tea, cotton, pyrethrum; cattle **EXP:** gold, coffee, cashew nuts, manufactures, cotton
- MAP pages 226-227

Thailand

KINGDOM OF THAILAND

- CONTINENT Asia
- AREA 513,115 sq km (198,115 sq mi)
- POPULATION 65,706,000
- DEMONYM Thai (singular and plural)
- CAPITAL Bangkok 6,706,000
- RELIGION Buddhist, Muslim
- LANGUAGE Thai, English, ethnic dialects
- LITERACY 93%
- LIFE EXPECTANCY 71 years
- GDP PER CAPITA $8,000
- CURRENCY baht (THB)
- ECONOMY **IND:** tourism, textiles and garments, agricultural processing, beverages **AGR:** rice, cassava (tapioca), rubber, corn, sugarcane **EXP:** textiles and footwear, fishery products, rice, rubber, jewelry
- MAP pages 204-205

Timor-Leste (East Timor)

DEMOCRATIC REPUBLIC OF TIMOR-LESTE

- CONTINENT Asia
- AREA 14,609 sq km (5,640 sq mi)
- POPULATION 1,048,000
- DEMONYM Timorese
- CAPITAL Dili 159,000
- RELIGION Roman Catholic
- LANGUAGE Tetum, Portuguese, Indonesian, English, indigenous languages
- LITERACY 59%
- LIFE EXPECTANCY 58 years
- GDP PER CAPITA $2,000
- CURRENCY US dollar (USD)
- ECONOMY **IND:** printing, soap manufacturing, handicrafts, woven cloth **AGR:** coffee, rice, corn, cassava, sweet potatoes **EXP:** coffee, sandalwood, marble; potential for oil and vanilla
- MAP pages 206-207

Togo

TOGOLESE REPUBLIC

- CONTINENT Africa
- AREA 56,785 sq km (21,925 sq mi)
- POPULATION 6,585,000
- DEMONYM Togolese (singular and plural)
- CAPITAL Lomé 1,451,000
- RELIGION indigenous beliefs, Christian, Muslim
- LANGUAGE French, Ewe, Mina, Kabye, Dagomba
- LITERACY 61%
- LIFE EXPECTANCY 58 years
- GDP PER CAPITA $900
- CURRENCY Communauté Financière Africaine franc (XOF)
- ECONOMY **IND:** phosphate mining, agricultural processing, cement, handicrafts **AGR:** coffee, cocoa, cotton, yams; livestock; fish **EXP:** reexports, cotton, phosphates, coffee, cocoa
- MAP pages 220-221

Tokelau (N.Z.)

TOKELAU

- CONTINENT Australia/Oceania
- AREA 12 sq km (5 sq mi)
- POPULATION 2,000
- DEMONYM Tokelauan(s)
- CAPITAL none
- RELIGION Congregational Christian Church, Roman Catholic
- LANGUAGE Tokelauan (a Polynesian language), English
- MAP pages 244-245

Tonga

KINGDOM OF TONGA

- CONTINENT Australia/Oceania
- AREA 748 sq km (289 sq mi)
- POPULATION 101,000
- DEMONYM Tongan(s)
- CAPITAL Nuku'alofa 25,000
- RELIGION Christian
- LANGUAGE Tongan, English
- LITERACY 99%
- LIFE EXPECTANCY 71 years
- GDP PER CAPITA $2,200
- CURRENCY pa'anga (TOP)
- ECONOMY **IND:** tourism, fishing **AGR:** squash, coconuts, copra, bananas; fish **EXP:** squash, fish, vanilla beans, root crops
- MAP pages 244-245

Trinidad and Tobago
REPUBLIC OF TRINIDAD AND TOBAGO

CONTINENT North America
AREA 5,128 sq km (1,980 sq mi)
POPULATION 1,387,000
DEMONYM Trinidadian(s), Tobagonian(s)
CAPITAL Port-of-Spain 54,000
RELIGION Roman Catholic, Hindu, Anglican, Baptist, Pentecostal, Muslim,
LANGUAGE English, Caribbean Hindustani, French, Spanish, Chinese
LITERACY 99%
LIFE EXPECTANCY 69 years
GDP PER CAPITA $21,700
CURRENCY Trinidad and Tobago dollar (TTD)
ECONOMY **IND:** petroleum, chemicals, tourism, food processing **AGR:** cocoa, rice, citrus, coffee; poultry **EXP:** petroleum, petroleum products, liquefied natural gas (LNG), methanol, ammonia
MAP pages 120-121

Tunisia
TUNISIAN REPUBLIC

CONTINENT Africa
AREA 163,610 sq km (63,170 sq mi)
POPULATION 10,225,000
DEMONYM Tunisian(s)
CAPITAL Tunis 746,000
RELIGION Muslim
LANGUAGE Arabic, French
LITERACY 74%
LIFE EXPECTANCY 74 years
GDP PER CAPITA $7,500
CURRENCY Tunisian dinar (TND)
ECONOMY **IND:** petroleum, mining (phosphate, iron ore), tourism, textiles **AGR:** olives and olive oil, grain, tomatoes, citrus fruits; beef **EXP:** clothing, semi-finished goods and textiles, agricultural products, mechanical goods
MAP pages 216-217

Turkey
REPUBLIC OF TURKEY

CONTINENT Europe/Asia
AREA 779,452 sq km (300,948 sq mi)
POPULATION 73,967,000
DEMONYM Turk(s)
CAPITAL Ankara 3,715,000
RELIGION Muslim (mostly Sunni)
LANGUAGE Turkish, Kurdish, Dimli (Zaza), Azeri, Kabardian, Gagauz
LITERACY 87%
LIFE EXPECTANCY 72 years
GDP PER CAPITA $9,400
CURRENCY new Turkish lira (TRY)
ECONOMY **IND:** textiles, food processing, automobiles, electronics **AGR:** tobacco, cotton, grain, olives; livestock **EXP:** apparel, foodstuffs, textiles, metal manufactures
MAP pages 180-181

Turkmenistan
TURKMENISTAN

CONTINENT Asia
AREA 488,100 sq km (188,456 sq mi)
POPULATION 5,409,000
DEMONYM Turkmen(s)
CAPITAL Ashgabat 744,000
RELIGION Muslim, Eastern Orthodox
LANGUAGE Turkmen, Russian, Uzbek
LITERACY 99%
LIFE EXPECTANCY 62 years
GDP PER CAPITA $9,200
CURRENCY Turkmen manat (TMM)
ECONOMY **IND:** natural gas, oil, petroleum products, textiles **AGR:** cotton, grain; livestock **EXP:** gas, crude oil, petrochemicals, cotton
MAP pages 192-193

Turks and Caicos Islands (U.K.)
TURKS AND CAICOS ISLANDS

CONTINENT North America
AREA 430 sq km (166 sq mi)
POPULATION 36,000
DEMONYM none
CAPITAL Grand Turk (Cockburn Town) 6,000
RELIGION Baptist, Anglican, Methodist
LANGUAGE English
MAP pages 118-119

Tuvalu
TUVALU

CONTINENT Australia/Oceania
AREA 26 sq km (10 sq mi)
POPULATION 10,000
DEMONYM Tuvaluan(s)
CAPITAL Funafuti 5,000
RELIGION Church of Tuvalu (Congregationalist)
LANGUAGE Tuvaluan, English, Samoan, Kiribati
LITERACY NA
LIFE EXPECTANCY 64 years
GDP PER CAPITA $1,600
CURRENCY Australian dollar (AUD); Tuvaluan dollar (TVD)
ECONOMY **IND:** fishing, tourism, copra **AGR:** coconuts; fish **EXP:** copra, fish
MAP pages 244-245

Uganda
REPUBLIC OF UGANDA

CONTINENT Africa
AREA 241,139 sq km (93,104 sq mi)
POPULATION 28,530,000
DEMONYM Ugandan(s)
CAPITAL Kampala 1,420,000
RELIGION Protestant, Roman Catholic, Muslim
LANGUAGE English, Ganda, other local languages, Swahili, Arabic
LITERACY 67%
LIFE EXPECTANCY 47 years
GDP PER CAPITA $1,100
CURRENCY Ugandan shilling (UGX)
ECONOMY **IND:** sugar, brewing, tobacco, cotton textiles **AGR:** coffee, tea, cotton, tobacco, cassava (tapioca); beef **EXP:** coffee, fish and fish products, tea, cotton, flowers
MAP pages 226-227

Ukraine
UKRAINE

CONTINENT Europe
AREA 603,700 sq km (233,090 sq mi)
POPULATION 46,505,000
DEMONYM Ukrainian(s)
CAPITAL Kiev 2,705,000
RELIGION Ukrainian Orthodox, Orthodox, Ukrainian Greek Catholic
LANGUAGE Ukrainian, Russian
LITERACY 99%
LIFE EXPECTANCY 68 years
GDP PER CAPITA $6,900
CURRENCY hryvnia (UAH)
ECONOMY **IND:** coal, electric power, ferrous and nonferrous metals, machinery and transport equipment **AGR:** grain, sugar beets, sunflower seeds, vegetables; beef **EXP:** ferrous and nonferrous metals, fuel and petroleum products, chemicals, machinery and transport equipment
MAP pages 166-167

United Arab Emirates
UNITED ARAB EMIRATES

CONTINENT Asia
AREA 77,700 sq km (30,000 sq mi)
POPULATION 4,424,000
DEMONYM Emirati(s)
CAPITAL Abu Dhabi 604,000
RELIGION Muslim
LANGUAGE Arabic, Persian, English, Hindi, Urdu
LITERACY 78%
LIFE EXPECTANCY 79 years
GDP PER CAPITA $55,200
CURRENCY Emirati dirham (AED)
ECONOMY **IND:** petroleum and petrochemicals, fishing, aluminum, cement **AGR:** dates, vegetables, watermelons; poultry; fish **EXP:** crude oil, natural gas, reexports, dried fish, dates
MAP pages 184-185

United Kingdom
UNITED KINGDOM OF GREAT BRITAIN AND NORTHERN IRELAND

CONTINENT Europe
AREA 242,910 sq km (93,788 sq mi)
POPULATION 60,967,000
DEMONYM Briton(s), British (collective plural)
CAPITAL London 8,566,000
RELIGION Anglican, Roman Catholic, Presbyterian, Methodist
LANGUAGE English, Welsh, Scottish form of Gaelic
LITERACY 99%
LIFE EXPECTANCY 79 years
GDP PER CAPITA $35,300
CURRENCY British pound (GBP)
ECONOMY **IND:** machine tools, electric power equipment, automation equipment, railroad equipment **AGR:** cereals, oilseed, potatoes, vegetables; cattle; fish **EXP:** manufactured goods, fuels, chemicals, food and beverages, tobacco
MAP pages 150-151

United States
UNITED STATES OF AMERICA

CONTINENT North America
AREA 9,826,630 sq km (3,794,083 sq mi)
POPULATION 302,200,000
DEMONYM American(s)
CAPITAL Washington, D.C. 4,338,000
RELIGION Protestant, Roman Catholic
LANGUAGE English, Spanish, other Indo-European languages, Asian and Pacific island languages
LITERACY 99%
LIFE EXPECTANCY 78 years
GDP PER CAPITA $46,000
CURRENCY US dollar (USD)
ECONOMY **IND:** petroleum, steel, motor vehicles, aerospace **AGR:** wheat, corn, other grains, fruits; beef; forest products; fish **EXP:** agricultural products (soybeans, fruit), industrial supplies (organic chemicals), capital goods (transistors, aircraft), consumer goods (automobiles, medicines)
MAP pages 110-111

Uruguay
ORIENTAL REPUBLIC OF URUGUAY

CONTINENT South America
AREA 176,215 sq km (68,037 sq mi)
POPULATION 3,324,000
DEMONYM Uruguayan(s)
CAPITAL Montevideo 1,514,000
RELIGION Roman Catholic
LANGUAGE Spanish
LITERACY 98%
LIFE EXPECTANCY 75 years
GDP PER CAPITA $10,700
CURRENCY Uruguayan peso (UYU)
ECONOMY **IND:** food processing, electrical machinery, transportation equipment, petroleum products **AGR:** rice, wheat, corn, barley; livestock; fish **EXP:** meat, rice, leather products, wool, fish
MAP pages 138-139

Uzbekistan
REPUBLIC OF UZBEKISTAN

CONTINENT Asia
AREA 447,400 sq km (172,742 sq mi)
POPULATION 26,499,000
DEMONYM Uzbekistani
CAPITAL Tashkent 2,184,000
RELIGION Muslim (mostly Sunni), Eastern Orthodox
LANGUAGE Uzbek, Russian, Tajik
LITERACY 99%
LIFE EXPECTANCY 67 years
GDP PER CAPITA $2,200
CURRENCY Uzbekistani soum (UZS)
ECONOMY **IND:** textiles, food processing, machine-building, metallurgy **AGR:** cotton, vegetables, fruits, grain; livestock **EXP:** cotton, gold, energy products, mineral fertilizers, metals
MAP pages 192-193

Vanuatu
REPUBLIC OF VANUATU

CONTINENT Australia/Oceania
AREA 12,190 sq km (4,707 sq mi)
POPULATION 235,000
DEMONYM Ni-Vanuatu (singular and plural)
CAPITAL Port-Vila 40,000
RELIGION Presbyterian, Anglican, Roman Catholic, Seventh-day Adventist, other Christian, indigenous beliefs
LANGUAGE over 100 local languages, pidgin (known as Bislama or Bichelama)
LITERACY 74%
LIFE EXPECTANCY 67 years
GDP PER CAPITA $2,900
CURRENCY vatu (VUV)
ECONOMY **IND:** food and fish freezing, wood processing, meat canning **AGR:** copra, coconuts, cocoa, coffee; beef; fish **EXP:** copra, beef, cocoa, timber, kava, coffee
MAP pages 244-245

Vatican City
THE HOLY SEE

CONTINENT Europe
AREA 0.4 sq km (0.2 sq mi)
POPULATION 798
DEMONYM NA
CAPITAL Vatican City 798
RELIGION Roman Catholic
LANGUAGE Italian, Latin, French
LITERACY 100%
LIFE EXPECTANCY NA
GDP PER CAPITA NA
CURRENCY euro (EUR)
ECONOMY **IND:** printing; production of coins, medals, and postage stamps; mosaics and staff uniforms; worldwide banking and financial activities **AGR:** none **EXP:** none
MAP pages 170-171

Venezuela
BOLIVARIAN REPUBLIC OF VENEZUELA

CONTINENT South America
AREA 912,050 sq km (352,144 sq mi)
POPULATION 27,483,000
DEMONYM Venezuelan(s)
CAPITAL Caracas 2,986,000
RELIGION Roman Catholic
LANGUAGE Spanish, numerous indigenous dialects
LITERACY 93%
LIFE EXPECTANCY 73 years
GDP PER CAPITA $12,800
CURRENCY bolivar (VEB)
ECONOMY **IND:** petroleum, construction materials, food processing, textiles **AGR:** corn, sorghum, sugarcane, rice; beef; fish **EXP:** petroleum, bauxite and aluminum, steel, chemicals
MAP pages 132-133

Vietnam
SOCIALIST REPUBLIC OF VIETNAM

CONTINENT Asia
AREA 331,114 sq km (127,844 sq mi)
POPULATION 85,134,000
DEMONYM Vietnamese (singular and plural)
CAPITAL Hanoi 4,377,000
RELIGION Buddhist, Catholic
LANGUAGE Vietnamese, English, French, Chinese, Khmer
LITERACY 90%
LIFE EXPECTANCY 72 years
GDP PER CAPITA $2,600
CURRENCY dong (VND)
ECONOMY **IND:** food processing, garments, shoes, machine-building **AGR:** paddy rice, coffee, rubber, cotton; poultry; fish **EXP:** crude oil, marine products, rice, coffee
MAP pages 204-205

Virgin Islands (U.S.)
UNITED STATES VIRGIN ISLANDS

CONTINENT North America
AREA 386 sq km (149 sq mi)
POPULATION 108,000
DEMONYM Virgin Islander(s) (US citizens)
CAPITAL Charlotte Amalie 53,000
RELIGION Baptist, Roman Catholic, Episcopalian
LANGUAGE English, Spanish or Spanish Creole, French or French Creole
MAP pages 120-121

Wallis and Futuna Islands (France)
TERRITORY OF THE WALLIS AND FUTUNA ISLANDS

CONTINENT Australia/Oceania
AREA 161 sq km (62 sq mi)
POPULATION 15,000
DEMONYM Wallisian(s), Futunan(s), or Wallis and Futuna Islanders
CAPITAL Matâ'utu 1,000
RELIGION Roman Catholic
LANGUAGE Wallisian, Futunian, French
MAP pages 244-245

West Bank
OCCUPIED PALESTINIAN TERRITORY

CONTINENT Asia
AREA 5,655 sq km (2,183 sq mi)
POPULATION 2,697,000
DEMONYM NA
CAPITAL NA
RELIGION Muslim (mostly Sunni), Jewish, Christian
LANGUAGE Arabic, Hebrew, English widely understood
MAP pages 182-183

Western Sahara (Morocco)
WESTERN SAHARA

CONTINENT Africa
AREA 252,120 sq km (97,344 sq mi)
POPULATION 480,000
DEMONYM Sahrawi(s), Sahraoui(s)
CAPITAL NA
RELIGION Muslim
LANGUAGE Hassaniya Arabic, Moroccan Arabic
MAP pages 216-217

United Kingdom 150-151
Ukraine 166-167
Uzbekistan 192-193
United States 110-111
Vatican City 170-171
Western Sahara (Morocco) 216-217
Turks and Caicos Islands (U.K.) 118-119
Tunisia 216-217
West Bank 182-183
Turkey 180-181
Turkmenistan 192-193
United Arab Emirates 184-185
Virgin Islands (U.S.) 120-121
Vietnam 204-205
Trinidad and Tobago 120-121
Yemen 184-185
Venezuela 132-133
Uganda 226-227
Zambia 224-225
Tuvalu 244-245
Vanuatu 244-245
Zimbabwe 228-229
Wallis and Futuna Islands (France) 244-245
Uruguay 138-139
Places Included On This Spread
Small political entity
Ukraine 166-167 Political entity name with regional map page numbers
Note: Colors reflect the tint used on regional maps

Yemen
REPUBLIC OF YEMEN

CONTINENT Asia
AREA 536,869 sq km (207,286 sq mi)
POPULATION 22,389,000
DEMONYM Yemeni(s)
CAPITAL Sanaa 2,008,000
RELIGION Muslim including Shaf'i (Sunni) and Zaydi (Shiite)
LANGUAGE Arabic
LITERACY 50%
LIFE EXPECTANCY 60 years
GDP PER CAPITA $2,400
CURRENCY Yemeni rial (YER)
ECONOMY **IND:** crude oil production, petroleum refining, cotton textiles, leather goods **AGR:** grain, fruits, vegetables, pulses; dairy products; fish **EXP:** crude oil, coffee, dried and salted fish
MAP pages 184-185

Zambia
REPUBLIC OF ZAMBIA

CONTINENT Africa
AREA 752,614 sq km (290,586 sq mi)
POPULATION 11,477,000
DEMONYM Zambian(s)
CAPITAL Lusaka 1,328,000
RELIGION Christian, Muslim, Hindu
LANGUAGE English, Bemba, Kaonda, Lozi, Lunda, Luvale, Nyanja, Tonga, about 70 other indigenous languages
LITERACY 81%
LIFE EXPECTANCY 38 years
GDP PER CAPITA $1,400
CURRENCY Zambian kwacha (ZMK)
ECONOMY **IND:** copper mining and processing, construction, foodstuffs, beverages **AGR:** corn, sorghum, rice, peanuts, sunflower seeds; cattle **EXP:** copper, cobalt, electricity, tobacco, flowers
MAP pages 224-225

Zimbabwe
REPUBLIC OF ZIMBABWE

CONTINENT Africa
AREA 390,757 sq km (150,872 sq mi)
POPULATION 13,349,000
DEMONYM Zimbabwean(s)
CAPITAL Harare 1,572,000
RELIGION Syncretic (part Christian, part indigenous beliefs), Christian, indigenous beliefs
LANGUAGE English, Shona, Sindebele, numerous minor tribal dialects
LITERACY 91%
LIFE EXPECTANCY 37 years
GDP PER CAPITA $500
CURRENCY Zimbabwean dollar (ZWD)
ECONOMY **IND:** mining (coal, gold, platinum), steel, wood products, cement **AGR:** corn, cotton, tobacco, wheat, coffee; sheep **EXP:** platinum, cotton, tobacco, gold, ferroalloys
MAP pages 228-229

Key to the Flags and Facts

The entry for each nation listed above includes its flag, as well as important statistical data. The entries for dependencies and areas of special status, which can be identified by the use of a smaller typeface and lack of a flag, provide an abbreviated list of statistical data. Dependencies are nonindependent political entities associated in some way with a particular independent nation. These administering independent nations are denoted in parenthesis.

The statistical data provide highlights of geography, demography, and economy. These details offer a brief overview of each political entity; they present general characteristics and are not intended to be comprehensive studies. The structured nature of the text results in some generic collective or umbrella terms. The industry category, for instance, includes services in addition to traditional manufacturing sectors. Space and source limitations dictate the amount of information included.

Entries are arranged alphabetically by the conventional short forms of the country or dependency names. The conventional long form names appear below the conventional short form; if there is no long form, the short form is repeated. Except where otherwise noted, all statistical data are derived from the *CIA World Factbook* (https://www.cia.gov/library/publications/the-world-factbook/index.html). When NA is listed for a category, it indicates that data are not applicable or not available.

To the left of the name of each independent nation is its **FLAG.** The term "national flag" is a simplification. Some countries have different flags for use at sea (ensign), by governments (state flag), private citizens (civil flag), the military (standard), and by private individuals. Thus German citizens use a simple tricolor, the government flag adds the German coat of arms, and the navy flag is swallowtailed. Although there is no international requirement that a country display its flag on land—or even that it have a national flag—it is significant that the last sovereign country without a flag was Bhutan in 1949. Flags play important roles internationally but even more so in the local politics of countries. Recording changes in flag designs, symbolism, and usage is undertaken by a number of institutions, including the source for the flags shown here, the Flag Research Center (Winchester, Massachusetts). The scientific discipline concerned with the history, usage, and significance of flags is known as vexillology, based on the Latin word for flag *(vexillum)*.

CONTINENT simply lists the continent where the political entity can be found, assisting the reader in locating the region on the locator map and throughout the atlas.

AREA accounts for the total area of a region, including all land and inland water delimited by international boundaries, intranational boundaries, or coastlines. It does not include any territorial waters.

POPULATION figures are mid-2007 figures from the 2007 World Population Data Sheet from the Population Reference Bureau (http://www.prb.org) in Washington, D.C. These figures are estimates rounded to the nearest thousand. Estimates are based on a recent census, official national data, or UN and U.S. Census Bureau projections. The effects of refugee movements, large numbers of foreign workers, and population shifts due to contemporary political events are taken into account to the extent possible.

DEMONYM, more commonly known as nationality, provides the identifying term for citizens of a country or dependency. For example, someone from Spain is referred to as a Spaniard. A demonym can be in either noun or adjective form. The term listed for this category is a noun, referring to a person or group of people, such as Spaniard(s), and not an adjective, which is often the same term but not always, as in Spanish.

Next to **CAPITAL** is the name of the seat of government, followed by the city's metropolitan area population. Capital city populations for both independent nations and dependencies are 2007 estimates from the *World Urbanization Prospects: The 2007 Revision* produced by the United Nations Department of Economic and Social Affairs, Population Division (http://www.unpopulation.org). These estimates represent the populations of urban agglomerations, which include city proper population plus all suburban areas lying outside of but being adjacent to the city boundaries. Several nations have more than one official capital. In these cases, each capital is listed with its function in parentheses followed by its population.

Under **RELIGION,** the most widely practiced faith appears first, followed by additional religions in rank order. "Traditional" or "indigenous" connotes beliefs of important local sects, such as the Maya in Middle America. Under **LANGUAGE,** the most widely spoken language is listed first, followed by other languages in rank order. These entries do not list every religion or language but generally list those that are practiced or spoken by roughly 3 percent or more of the population as determined by the CIA.

LITERACY generally indicates the percentage of the population (rounded to the nearest whole number) above the age of 15 who can read and write. There are no universal standards of literacy, so these estimates are based on the most common definition available for a nation. Information on literacy, while not a perfect measure of educational results, is easily available and valid for international comparisons.

LIFE EXPECTANCY presents the average number of years a 2007 newborn infant can expect to live under current mortality levels. Figures are from the 2007 World Population Data Sheet published by the Population Reference Bureau. This is an average of both sexes, though females generally live longer. Life expectancy at birth is a measure of overall quality of life in a country and summarizes the mortality at all ages.

GDP PER CAPITA is gross domestic product (GDP) divided by midyear population estimates. GDP is the value of all final goods and services produced within a region in a given year. These estimates use the purchasing power parity (PPP) conversion factor designed to equalize the purchasing powers of different currencies by converting to U.S. purchasing value. Individual income estimates such as GDP per capita are among the many indicators used to assess a nation's well-being. As statistical averages, they hide extremes of poverty and wealth. Furthermore, they take no account of factors that affect quality of life, such as environmental degradation, educational opportunities, and health care.

CURRENCY, or money, identifies the national medium of exchange and, in parenthesis, gives the International Organization for Standardization (ISO) three-character alphabetic currency code for each country or dependency.

ECONOMY information for the independent nations and dependencies is divided into three general categories: industry, agriculture, and exports. Because of structural limitations, only the primary industries (IND), agricultural commodities (AGR), and export commodities (EXP) are reported, starting with the most important. Agriculture serves as an umbrella term for not only crops but also livestock, products, and fish. In the interest of conciseness, agriculture for the independent nations presents, when applicable, four major crops, followed respectively by leading entries for livestock, products, and fish.

MAP provides the page numbers of the political map where the country or dependency is shown. For example, the entry for Mozambique lists pages 228-229 where the regional Southern Africa political map containing this country, can be found. These page numbers can also be found on the locator map in the upper right corner of each spread showing the locations of regions listed on those two pages.

Special Flags

IF WE COULD BRING A SNAPSHOT BACK FROM THE FUTURE, few images would tell us more about what lies ahead than a flag chart showing the banners of all countries. The independence of new nations, the breakup of empires, even changing political and religious currents—all would be reflected in the symbols and colors of the national flags. This is dramatically evident in the changing flag of the United States (lower right), but similar visual statements could be made for most countries.

Germany provides another example. In the Middle Ages, a gold banner with a black eagle proclaimed its Holy Roman Emperor a successor to the Caesars. A united 19th-century German Empire adopted a black-white-red tricolor for Bismarck's "blood and iron" policies. The liberal Weimar and Federal Republics (1919-1933 and since 1949) hailed a black-red-gold tricolor. The Nazi regime (1933-1945) flew the swastika flag. These and similar flags in other countries are more than visual aids to history: Their development and use are a fundamental part of the political and social life of a community.

Like maps, flags communicate information in condensed form. The study of flags is known as vexillology (from the Latin *vexillum,* for "small sail" or "flag"). Books, journals, Web sites, and other sources convey information on vexillology; there are also organizations and institutions around the world linked by the International Federation of Vexillological Associations. Students can gain understanding of countries, populations, political changes, religious movements, and historical events by learning about flags.

All flags embody myths and historical facts, whether they are carried by protesters, placed at a roadside shrine, or arrayed at a ceremony of national significance, such as a presidential inauguration. Flags are powerful symbols, attractive to groups of all kinds; hence their once prominent display by Nazis and Communists to manipulate the masses, their waving by the East Timorese after a successful struggle for independence, and their spontaneous use by people in the United States after September 11, 2001.

Flags of nations may be the most significant flags today, but they are far from the only ones. Sport teams, business enterprises, religious groups, ethnic groups, schools, and international organizations frequently rally, reward, and inspire people through the use of flags. An observant person will also notice advertising banners, nautical signals, warning flags, decorative pennants, the rank flags of important individuals, and many related symbols such as coats of arms and logos.

The messages inherent in flags often provoke emotional responses. Thus in 2008, Russian scientists literally marked their polar claims with a 90° N flagpole. Flag images—such as the iconic 1945 photo of Iwo Jima—deeply influence patriotism especially in warfare and times of political change. No flag has an inherent meaning—such as duty, honor, and comradeship—but those who understand how to use flags are capable of inspiring great deeds. Thus in the American Civil War, for example, when a battle standard fell because its bearer had fallen, it was a point of honor for other soldiers to seize that banner immediately, keeping it from the enemy. However, flags do not inspire solely in circumstances of war and political competition. When the Stars and Stripes was first displayed on the moon, millions worldwide felt it a victory for all humankind. Scientists have yet to understand fully the extraordinary power of that piece of cloth we call a flag.

Flags are listed in alphabetical order within each section.

International Flags

GAY PRIDE The Rainbow Flag, made in various configurations, has been flown since 1978 by the gay and lesbian community and their families. Other groups — including pacifists — also use rainbow flags.

OLYMPIC GAMES The colors refer to those most often found in the flags of participating nations. The Olympic flag was designed by Pierre de Coubertin and was first used in the 1920 Olympics.

OPEC Organized in 1960, the Organization of Petroleum Exporting Countries works to coordinate policies of countries where petroleum is a major export. Its flag, derived from the UN blue, uses stylized initials.

PEACE FLAG Gerald Holtom's 1958 Peace Symbol was based on the signal code for N and D (referring to nuclear disarmament). Now one of the best known symbols, it appears on many flags.

RED CRESCENT In Muslim nations, Geneva Convention organizations rejected the red cross in favor of a red crescent, officially recognized in 1906. Iran's red lion and sun symbol was used 1929-1979.

RED CROSS The Geneva Convention chose its symbol and flag in 1864 to identify people, vehicles, and buildings protected during wartime. A Swiss, Henri Dunant, created the Red Cross symbol.

RED CRYSTAL The official medical services symbol of Israel has been used in times of need since 1948, but not until 2006 did the Geneva Convention reach an agreement recognizing the Red Crystal.

TRUCE/PEACE For a thousand years the white flag has served as a symbol of truce, surrender, noncombatant status, neutrality, and peace. Ironically, the royal French battle flag was also plain white.

UNITED NATIONS Olive branches of peace and a world map form the symbol adopted by the United Nations in 1946. The flag dates from 1947. There is no official symbolism for the color blue.

Regional Flags

ARAB LEAGUE The color green and the crescent are often symbols in the member countries of the League of Arab States, founded in 1945. The wreath on the flag stands for the fertility of Arab lands.

ASEAN A stylized bundle of rice, the principal local crop, appears on the flag of the Association of South East Asian Nations (ASEAN). Blue is for peace and stability, red for courage and dynamism.

COMMONWEALTH Once the British Empire, the modern Commonwealth under this flag informally links countries with common goals. The C and "spears" suggest the organization's many activities.

COMMONWEALTH OF INDEPENDENT STATES Following the demise of the Soviet Union, Russia sought to maintain its influence by creating a regional "commonwealth" among the former Soviet republics.

EUROPEAN UNION The number of stars for this flag, adopted in 1955, is permanently set at 12. The ring is a symbol of unity. The flag is usually flown jointly with national flags of members.

LA RAZA Crosses for the ships of Columbus and a golden Inca sun recall the Spanish and Indian heritage of Latin Americans. Angel Camblor created this "flag of the race" in 1932.

NATO After World War II, Europeans and North Americans formed the North Atlantic Treaty Organization to defend against possible Soviet threats. Today, NATO meets new challenges worldwide.

OAS Flags of member nations appear on the flag of the Organization of American States; each new member prompts a flag change. Simón Bolívar's 1826 Pan-American unity conference inspired the OAS.

PACIFIC COMMISSION The palm tree, surf, and sailboat are found in all of the member nations; each star on the flag represents a country. The flag of the South Pacific Forum is similar.

Religious Flags

BUDDHISM Designed in 1885 by American Henry Olcott, the Buddhist flag features the auras associated with the Buddha. The flag, honoring his life, helped Buddhists unite.

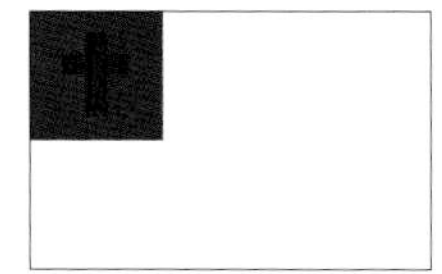

CHRISTIANITY The sacrifice of Christ on the Cross is heralded in this 1897 flag, which features a white field for purity. Many different sects have alternate Christian flags.

ISLAM "There Is No God But Allah; Muhammad Is the Prophet of Allah" is written on this widely used but unofficial flag. The *shahadah* states the fundamental principles of all Muslims.

MASONS The unofficial flag of Masonry displays their traditional logo with its symbolic square and compass. That design inspired the triangles in the official Cuban, Philippine, and Puerto Rican flags.

MOUNT ATHOS For more than a thousand years Greek Orthodox monks have made this peninsula their exclusive ecclesiastical home. Although part of Greece, its flag is an ancient Byzantine banner.

MOURNING The black flag signals death, piracy, protest, and danger. It is also a symbol of mourning for the dead. Given its symbolism, black is rarely the principal color in a national flag.

ORDER OF MALTA The Order long helped protect Christian pilgrims in the Near East. Its modern humanitarian work is carried out from headquarters in Rome under its ancient Maltese cross symbol.

ROMAN CATHOLIC CHURCH Popes for centuries ruled the Papal States, a major European country. Today the Vatican City, a tiny state in Rome, manages Catholic Church affairs.

SIKHISM Since 1469, Sikh garb — and their flag — have borne swords for bravery and spirituality. Many of this faith of six million, based in northwest India, seek independence for "Khalistan."

Community Flags

AFRICAN AMERICANS America welcomes immigrants, each with their own symbols. African Americans, forcibly removed from Africa, acquired their flag through the efforts of Marcus Garvey in 1920.

AMERICAN INDIANS While American Indians traditionally used few flags, many 20th-century tribes created flags featuring ancient symbols. Today, many tribes have flags, including the Mohawk, shown here.

BOY SCOUTS Created in 1961, this flag displays the traditional Boy Scout fleur-de-lis within a rope tied with a reef knot. The fleur-de-lis is the compass point, aiming Scouts in the right path.

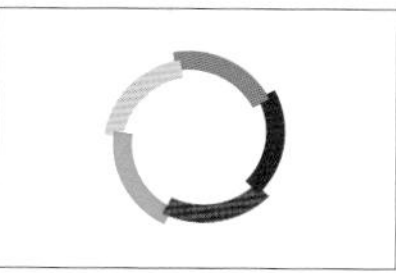

FRANCOPHONIE French-speaking countries share their common language and culture in activities held under this flag. Likewise, Dutch and Portuguese speakers participate in international communities.

GIRL SCOUTS A trefoil with a compass needle adorns the World Flag of Girl Guides and Girl Scouts, adopted May 1991. The 1930 flag was blue with a yellow trefoil resembling a flame for love of humankind.

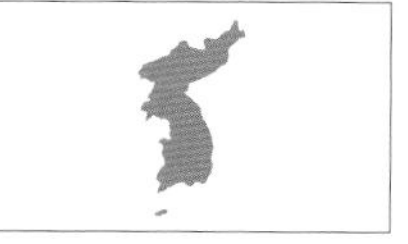

KOREAN OLYMPICS The Korean nation, separated by deep political differences, expresses the desire for unity between north and south by using a special Olympic flag bearing a map of the whole peninsula.

PALESTINIANS Since 1922 Palestinians have used this flag, with the four traditional Arab dynastic colors, as a symbol of the statehood they desire and their solidarity with other Arabs.

ROMA (GYPSIES) Against a background of blue sky and green grass, a wheel represents the vehicles (and homes) of the nomadic Roma people. The wheel was added to their 1933 flag in 1959.

TAIWAN The Red Army brought China under Communist rule in 1949, except for the island of Taiwan. In the Olympic Games Taiwan has a special flag and uses the name "Taipei Olympic Team."

Specialized Flags

ABKHAZIA After the Soviet Union ended, Russia helped South Ossetia, Abkhazia, and Ajaria maintain unrecognized independence under their own flags. They serve to pressure pro-Western Georgia.

ANARCHISTS Opposition to all forms of authority is hinted at in the "hand-drawn" rendition of an encircled *A* in the anarchist flag. Their philosophy of anarchism is used to justify violence.

ANTARCTICA Since Norwegians first reached the South Pole in 1911, many flags have flown there. An unofficial Antarctic flag features stylized hands for environmental protection and a dove of peace.

BLUE FLAG One campaign for the improvement of the environment presents this flag as an award for success. The program, focusing on improving beaches and marinas worldwide, began in 1987.

CIRCLE CROSS This ancient religious symbol, historically related to the swastika, is widely used as a neo-Nazi symbol in Europe and North America. Black symbolizes strength and death.

DIVER FLAG Warning nearby boats, this flag flies wherever divers are underwater nearby—and at divers' clubhouses. The official "diver down" flag is signal code BRAVO, a white and blue pennant.

ESPERANTO On the flag that promotes Esperanto as a world language, the star signifies unity. Green traditionally is a symbol of hope. Other artificial languages also have their own flags.

GREEN CROSS Organizations that display this flag promote public safety in natural disasters, transportation, and the workplace as well as programs concerned with preserving the environment.

N.A.V.A. Vexillologists study flag history and symbolism. Vexillology derives from the Latin *vexillum,* meaning "small sail" or "flag." Members of the North American Vexillological Association fly this flag.

NORTH POLE In 2008 a Russian flag on a "pole" was planted by Russian scientists in the North Polar floor. Canada, Denmark, and the United States also claim territory there.

POW·MIA

POW-MIA Aside from Old Glory, no U.S. flag is as popular as the one saluting war prisoners and those missing in action. The flag recalls those lost but not forgotten.

SOMALIA Somalia, although recognized by the UN as independent, has long had no central government. Unrecognized "nations"—Somaliland, Puntland, and Maakhir—control shifting portions of land.

Development of the Stars and Stripes

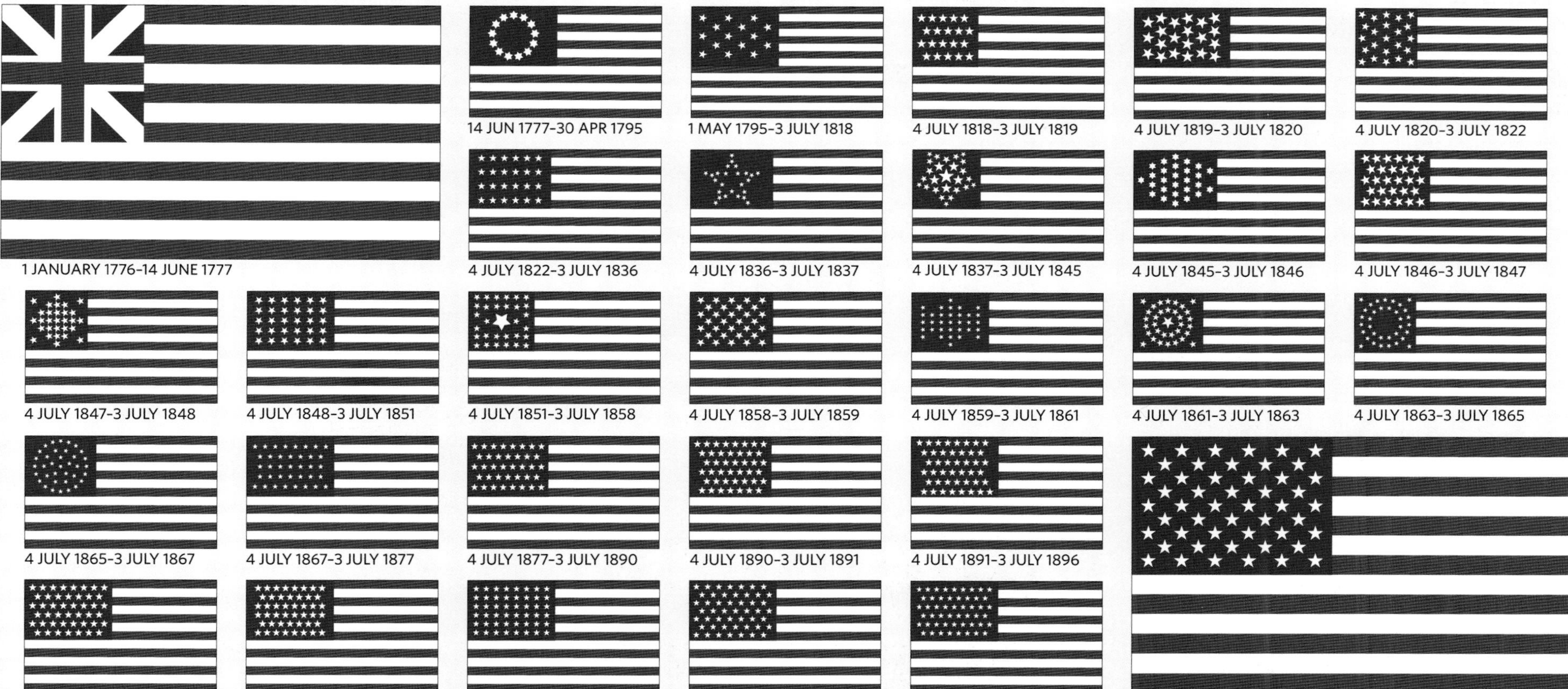

1 JANUARY 1776–14 JUNE 1777; 14 JUN 1777–30 APR 1795; 1 MAY 1795–3 JULY 1818; 4 JULY 1818–3 JULY 1819; 4 JULY 1819–3 JULY 1820; 4 JULY 1820–3 JULY 1822; 4 JULY 1822–3 JULY 1836; 4 JULY 1836–3 JULY 1837; 4 JULY 1837–3 JULY 1845; 4 JULY 1845–3 JULY 1846; 4 JULY 1846–3 JULY 1847; 4 JULY 1847–3 JULY 1848; 4 JULY 1848–3 JULY 1851; 4 JULY 1851–3 JULY 1858; 4 JULY 1858–3 JULY 1859; 4 JULY 1859–3 JULY 1861; 4 JULY 1861–3 JULY 1863; 4 JULY 1863–3 JULY 1865; 4 JULY 1865–3 JULY 1867; 4 JULY 1867–3 JULY 1877; 4 JULY 1877–3 JULY 1890; 4 JULY 1890–3 JULY 1891; 4 JULY 1891–3 JULY 1896; 4 JULY 1896–3 JULY 1908; 4 JULY 1908–3 JULY 1912; 4 JULY 1912–3 JULY 1959; 4 JULY 1959–3 JULY 1960; FUTURE (51-STAR)?; 4 JULY 1960–PRESENT

No country has changed its flag as frequently as the United States. The Continental Colors (top left) represented the Colonies during the early years of the American Revolution. Its British Union Jack, which signified loyalty to the crown, was replaced on June 14, 1777, by "13 stars . . . representing a new constellation." Congressman Francis Hopkinson was the designer.

The number of stars and stripes was increased to 15 in 1795. In 1817 Congressman Peter Wendover wrote the current flag law. The number of stripes was permanently limited to 13; the stars were to correspond to the number of states, with new stars added to the flag the following Fourth of July.

Star arrangement was not specified, however, and throughout the 19th century a variety of exuberant star designs—"great luminaries," rings, ovals, and diamonds—were actually used. With the increasing number of states, the modern alternating rows of stars became standard. Finally, in 1912, President Taft set forth exact regulations for all flag details.

If a new state joins the Union, a 51-star flag will be needed. There is a logical design for it: alternating rows of nine and eight stars, as shown above. The U.S. flag design, especially the use of stars, has been widely followed by other countries.

Appendix

Abbreviations

Adm.	*Administrative*
Af.	*Africa*
Afghan.	*Afghanistan*
Agr.	*Agriculture*
Ala.	*Alabama*
Alas.	*Alaska*
Alban.	*Albania*
Alg.	*Algeria*
Alta.	*Alberta*
Arch.	*Archipelago, Archipiélago*
Arg.	*Argentina*
Ariz.	*Arizona*
Ark.	*Arkansas*
Arm.	*Armenia*
Atl. Oc.	*Atlantic Ocean*
Aust.	*Austria*
Austral.	*Australia*
Azerb.	*Azerbaijan*
B.	*Baai, Baía, Baie, Bahía, Bay, Buḩayrat*
B.C.	*British Columbia*
Belg.	*Belgium*
Bol.	*Bolivia*
Bosn. & Herzg.	*Bosnia and Herzegovina*
Braz.	*Brazil*
Bulg.	*Bulgaria*
C.	*Cabo, Cap, Cape, Capo*
Calif.	*California*
Can.	*Canada*
Cen. Af. Rep.	*Central African Republic*
C.H.	*Court House*
Chan.	*Channel*
Chap.	*Chapada*
Cmte.	*Comandante*
Cnel.	*Coronel*
Co.-s.	*Cerro-s*
Col.	*Colombia*
Colo.	*Colorado*
Conn.	*Connecticut*
Cord.	*Cordillera*
C.R.	*Costa Rica*
Cr.	*Creek, Crique*
C.S.I. Terr.	*Coral Sea Islands Territory*
D.C.	*District of Columbia*
Del.	*Delaware*
Den.	*Denmark*
Dom. Rep.	*Dominican Republic*
D.R.C.	*Democratic Republic of the Congo*
E.	*East-ern*
Ecua.	*Ecuador*
El Salv.	*El Salvador*
Eng.	*England*
Ens.	*Ensenada*
Eq.	*Equatorial*
Est.	*Estonia*
Eth.	*Ethiopia*
Exp.	*Exports*
Falk. Is.	*Falkland Islands*
Fd.	*Fiord, Fiordo, Fjord*
Fin.	*Finland*
Fk.	*Fork*
Fla.	*Florida*
Fn.	*Fortín*
Fr.	*France, French*
F.S.M.	*Federated States of Micronesia*
ft	*feet*
Ft.	*Fort*
G.	*Golfe, Golfo, Gulf*
Ga.	*Georgia*
Ger.	*Germany*
Gl.	*Glacier*
Gr.	*Greece*
Gral.	*General*
Hbr.	*Harbor, Harbour*
Hist.	*Historic, -al*
Hond.	*Honduras*
Hts.	*Heights*
Hung.	*Hungary*
Hwy.	*Highway*
I.-s.	*Île-s, Ilha-s, Isla-s, Island-s, Isle, Isol-a, -e*
Ice.	*Iceland*
I.H.S.	*International Historic Site*
Ill.	*Illinois*
Ind.	*Indiana*
Ind.	*Industry*
Ind. Oc.	*Indian Ocean*
Intl.	*International*
Ire.	*Ireland*
It.	*Italy*
Jap.	*Japan*
Jct.	*Jonction, Junction*
Kans.	*Kansas*
Kaz.	*Kazakhstan*
Kep.	*Kepulauan*
Ky.	*Kentucky*
Kyrg.	*Kyrgyzstan*
L.	*Lac, Lago, Lake, Límni, Loch, Lough*
La.	*Louisiana*
Lab.	*Labrador*
Lag.	*Laguna*
Latv.	*Latvia*
Leb.	*Lebanon*
Lib.	*Libya*
Liech.	*Liechtenstein*
Lith.	*Lithuania*
Lux.	*Luxembourg*
m	*meters*
Maced.	*Macedonia*
Madag.	*Madagascar*
Maurit.	*Mauritius*
Mass.	*Massachusetts*
Md.	*Maryland*
Me.	*Maine*
Medit. Sea	*Mediterranean Sea*
Mex.	*Mexico*
Mgne.	*Montagne*
Mich.	*Michigan*
Minn.	*Minnesota*
Miss.	*Mississippi*
Mo.	*Missouri*
Mon.	*Monument*
Mont.	*Montana*
Mont.	*Montenegro*
Mor.	*Morocco*
Mt.-s.	*Mont-s, Mount-ain-s*
N.	*North-ern*
Nat.	*National*
Nat. Mem.	*National Memorial*
Nat. Mon.	*National Monument*
N.B.	*National Battlefield*
N.B.	*New Brunswick*
N.C.	*North Carolina*
N. Dak.	*North Dakota*
N.E.	*Northeast*
Nebr.	*Nebraska*
Neth.	*Netherlands*
Nev.	*Nevada*
Nfld.	*Newfoundland*
N.H.	*New Hampshire*
Nicar.	*Nicaragua*
Nig.	*Nigeria*
N. Ire.	*Northern Ireland*
N.J.	*New Jersey*
N. Mex.	*New Mexico*
N.M.P.	*National Military Park*
N.M.S.	*National Marine Sanctuary*
Nor.	*Norway*
N.P.	*National Park*
N.S.	*Nova Scotia*
N.S.W.	*New South Wales*
N.V.M.	*National Volcanic Monument*
N.W.T.	*Northwest Territories*
N.Y.	*New York*
N.Z.	*New Zealand*
O.	*Ostrov, Oued*
Oc.	*Ocean*
Okla.	*Oklahoma*
Ont.	*Ontario*
Oreg.	*Oregon*
Oz.	*Ozero*
Pa.	*Pennsylvania*
Pac. Oc.	*Pacific Ocean*
Pak.	*Pakistan*
Pan.	*Panama*
Para.	*Paraguay*
Pass.	*Passage*
Peg.	*Pegunungan*
P.E.I.	*Prince Edward Island*
Pen.	*Peninsula, Péninsule*
Pk.	*Peak*
P.N.G.	*Papua New Guinea*
Pol.	*Poland*
Pol.	*Poluostrov*
Port.	*Portugal, Portuguese*
P.R.	*Puerto Rico*
Prov.	*Province, Provincial*
Pt.-e.	*Point-e*
Pta.	*Ponta, Punta*
Qnsld.	*Queensland*
Que.	*Quebec*
R.	*Río, River, Rivière*
Ra.-s.	*Range-s*
Rec.	*Recreation*
Rep.	*Republic*
Res.	*Reservoir, Reserve, Reservatório*
R.I.	*Rhode Island*
Rom.	*Romania*
Russ.	*Russia*
S.	*South-ern*
Sa.-s.	*Serra, Sierra-s*
S. Af.	*South Africa*
Sask.	*Saskatchewan*
S.C.	*South Carolina*
Scot.	*Scotland*
Sd.	*Sound*
S. Dak.	*South Dakota*
Serb.	*Serbia*
Sev.	*Severn-yy, -aya, -oye*
Sk.	*Shankou*
Slov.	*Slovenia*
Sp.	*Spain, Spanish*
Spr.-s.	*Spring-s*
Sta.	*Santa*
St.-e.	*Saint-e, Sankt, Sint*
Str.-s.	*Straat, Strait-s*
Switz.	*Switzerland*
Syr.	*Syria*
Taj.	*Tajikistan*
Tas.	*Tasmania*
Tenn.	*Tennessee*
Terr.	*Territory*
Tex.	*Texas*
Tg.	*Tanjung*
Thai.	*Thailand*
Trin.	*Trinidad*
Tun.	*Tunisia*
Turk.	*Turkey*
Turkm.	*Turkmenistan*
U.A.E.	*United Arab Emirates*
U.K.	*United Kingdom*
Ukr.	*Ukraine*
U.N.	*United Nations*
Uru.	*Uruguay*
U.S.	*United States*
Uzb.	*Uzbekistan*
Va.	*Virginia*
Vdkhr.	*Vodokhranilishche*
Vdskh.	*Vodoskhovyshche*
Venez.	*Venezuela*
V.I.	*Virgin Islands*
Vic.	*Victoria*
Viet.	*Vietnam*
Vol.	*Volcán, Volcano*
Vt.	*Vermont*
W.	*Wadi, Wādī, Webi*
W.	*West-ern*
Wash.	*Washington*
Wis.	*Wisconsin*
W. Va.	*West Virginia*
Wyo.	*Wyoming*
Zakh.	*Zakhod-ni, -nyaya, -nye*
Zimb.	*Zimbabwe*

Metric Conversions

Quick Reference: **Metric to English Conversion**

1 METER	1 METER = 100 CENTIMETERS
1 FOOT	1 FOOT = 12 INCHES
1 KILOMETER	1 KILOMETER = 1,000 METERS
1 MILE	1 MILE = 5,280 FEET

METERS	1	10	20	50	100	200	500	1,000	2,000	5,000	10,000
FEET	3.281	32.81	65.62	164.04	328.1	656.2	1,640.4	3,280.8	6,561.7	16,404.2	32,808.4

KILOMETERS	1	10	20	50	100	200	500	1,000	2,000	5,000	10,000
MILES	0.621	6.21	12.43	31.07	62.1	124.3	310.7	621.4	1,242.7	3,106.9	6,213.7

Conversion Table: **From Metric Measures**

SYMBOL	WHEN YOU KNOW	MULTIPLY BY	TO FIND	SYMBOL
		LENGTH		
cm	centimeters	0.39	inches	in
m	meters	3.28	feet	ft
m	meters	1.09	yards	yd
km	kilometers	0.62	miles	mi
		AREA		
cm^2	square centimeters	0.16	square inches	in^2
m^2	square meters	10.76	square feet	ft^2
m^2	square meters	1.20	square yards	yd^2
km^2	square kilometers	0.39	square miles	mi^2
ha	hectares	2.47	acres	--
		MASS		
g	grams	0.04	ounces	oz
kg	kilograms	2.20	pounds	lb
t	metric tons	1.10	short tons	--
		VOLUME		
mL	milliliters	0.06	cubic inches	in^3
mL	milliliters	0.03	liquid ounces	liq oz
L	liters	2.11	pints	pt
L	liters	1.06	quarts	qt
L	liters	0.26	gallons	gal
m^3	cubic meters	35.31	cubic feet	ft^3
m^3	cubic meters	1.31	cubic yards	yd^3
		TEMPERATURE		
°C	degrees Celsius (centigrade)	9/5 then add 32	degrees Fahrenheit	°F

Conversion Table: **To Metric Measures**

SYMBOL	WHEN YOU KNOW	MULTIPLY BY	TO FIND	SYMBOL
		LENGTH		
in	inches	2.54	centimeters	cm
ft	feet	0.30	meters	m
yd	yards	0.91	meters	m
mi	miles	1.61	kilometers	km
		AREA		
in^2	square inches	6.45	square centimeters	cm^2
ft^2	square feet	0.09	square meters	m^2
yd^2	square yards	0.84	square meters	m^2
mi^2	square miles	2.59	square kilometers	km^2
--	acres	0.40	hectares	ha
		MASS		
oz	ounces	28.35	grams	g
lb	pounds	0.45	kilograms	kg
--	short tons	0.91	metric tons	t
		VOLUME		
in^3	cubic inches	16.39	milliliters	mL
liq oz	liquid ounces	29.57	milliliters	mL
pt	pints	0.47	liters	L
qt	quarts	0.95	liters	L
gal	gallons	3.79	liters	L
ft^3	cubic feet	0.03	cubic meters	m^3
yd^3	cubic yards	0.76	cubic meters	m^3
		TEMPERATURE		
°F	degrees Fahrenheit	5/9 after subtracting 32	degrees Celsius (centigrade)	°C

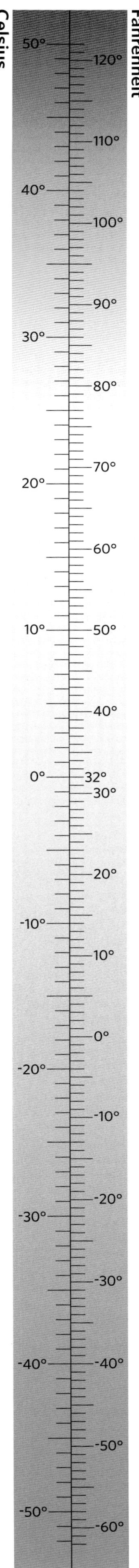
Celsius
Fahrenheit
50°
40°
30°
20°
10°
0°
-10°
-20°
-30°
-40°
-50°
120°
110°
100°
90°
80°
70°
60°
50°
40°
32°
30°
20°
10°
0°
-10°
-20°
-30°
-40°
-50°
-60°

Foreign Terms

Aaglet *well*
Aain *spring*
Aauinat *spring*
Āb *river, water*
Ache *stream*
Açude *reservoir*
Ada,-si *island*
Adrar *mountain-s, plateau*
Aguada *dry lake bed*
Aguelt *water hole, well*
ʻAin, Aïn *spring, well*
Aïoun-et *spring-s, well*
Aivi *mountain*
Ákra, Akrotírion *cape, promontory*
Alb *mountain, ridge*
Alföld *plain*
Alin' *mountain range*
Alpe-n *mountain-s*
Altiplanicie *high-plain, plateau*
Alto *hill-s, mountain-s, ridge*
Älv-en *river*
Āmba *hill, mountain*
Anou *well*
Anse *bay, inlet*
Ao *bay, cove, estuary*
Ap *cape, point*
Archipel, Archipiélago *archipelago*
Arcipelago, Arkhipelag *archipelago*
Arquipélago *archipelago*
Arrecife-s *reef-s*
Arroio, Arroyo *brook, gully, rivulet, stream*
Ås *ridge*
Ava *channel*
Aylagy *gulf*
ʻAyn *spring, well*

Ba *intermittent stream, river*
Baai *bay, cove, lagoon*
Bāb *gate, strait*
Badia *bay*
Bælt *strait*
Bagh *bay*
Bahar *drainage basin*
Bahía *bay*
Bahr, Baḩr *bay, lake, river, sea, wadi*
Baía, Baie *bay*
Bajo-s *shoal-s*
Ban *village*
Bañado-s *flooded area, swamp-s*
Banc, Banco-s *bank-s, sandbank-s, shoal-s*
Band *lake*
Bandao *peninsula*
Baño-s *hot spring-s, spa*
Baraj-ı *dam, reservoir*
Barra *bar, sandbank*
Barrage, Barragem *dam, lake, reservoir*
Barranca *gorge, ravine*
Bazar *marketplace*
Ben, Benin *mountain*
Belt *strait*
Bereg *bank, coast, shore*
Berg-e *mountain-s*
Bil *lake*
Biqʻat *plain, valley*
Bir, Bîr, Biʼr *spring, well*
Birket *lake, pool, swamp*
Bjerg-e *mountain-s, range*
Boca, Bocca *channel, river, mouth*
Bocht *bay*
Bodden *bay*
Boğaz, -i *strait*
Bögeni *reservoir*
Boka *gulf, mouth*
Bol'sh-oy, -aya, -oye *big*
Bolsón *inland basin*
Boubairet *lagoon, lake*
Bras *arm, branch of a stream*
Braţ, -ul *arm, branch of a stream*
Bre, -en *glacier, ice cap*
Bredning *bay, broad water*
Bruch *marsh*
Bucht *bay*
Bugt-en *bay*
Buḩayrat, Buheirat *lagoon, lake, marsh*
Bukhta, Bukta, Bukt-en *bay*
Bulak, Bulaq *spring*
Bum *hill, mountain*
Burnu, Burun *cape, point*
Busen *gulf*
Buuraha *hill-s, mountain-s*
Buyuk *big, large*

Cabeza-s *head-s, summit-s*
Cabo *cape*
Cachoeira *rapids, waterfall*
Cal *hill, peak*
Caleta *cove, inlet*
Campo-s *field-s, flat country*
Canal *canal, channel, strait*
Caño *channel, stream*
Cao Nguyen *mountain, plateau*
Cap, Capo *cape*
Capitán *captain*
Càrn *mountain*
Castillo *castle, fort*
Catarata-s *cataract-s, waterfall-s*
Causse *upland*
Çay *brook, stream*
Cay-s, Cayo-s *island-s, key-s, shoal-s*
Cerro-s *hill-s, peak-s*
Chaîne, Chaînons *mountain chain, range*
Chapada-s *plateau, upland-s*
Chedo *archipelago*
Chenal *river channel*
Chersónisos *peninsula*
Chhung *bay*
Chi *lake*
Chiang *bay*
Chiao *cape, point, rock*
Ch'ih *lake*
Chink *escarpment*
Chott *intermittent salt lake, salt marsh*
Chou *island*
Ch'ü *canal*
Ch'üntao *archipelago, islands*
Chute-s *cataract-s, waterfall-s*
Chyrvony *red*
Cima *mountain, peak, summit*
Ciudad *city*
Co *lake*
Col *pass*
Collina, Colline *hill, mountains*
Con *island*
Cordillera *mountain chain*
Corno *mountain, peak*
Coronel *colonel*
Corredeira *cascade, rapids*
Costa *coast*
Côte *coast, slope*
Coxilha, Cuchilla *range of low hills*
Crique *creek, stream*
Csatorna *canal, channel*
Cul de Sac *bay, inlet*

Da *great, greater*
Daban *pass*
Dağ, -ı, Dagh *mountain*
Dağlar, -ı *mountains*
Dahr *cliff, mesa*
Dake *mountain, peak*
Dal-en *valley*
Dala *steppe*
Dan *cape, point*
Danau *lake*
Dao *island*
Dar'ya *lake, river*
Daryācheh *lake, marshy lake*
Dasht *desert, plain*
Dawan *pass*
Dawḩat *bay, cove, inlet*
Deniz, -i *sea*
Dent-s *peak-s*
Deo *pass*
Desēt *hummock, island, land-tied island*
Desierto *desert*
Détroit *channel, strait*
Dhar *hills, ridge, tableland*
Ding *mountain*
Distrito *district*
Djebel *mountain, range*
Do *island-s, rock-s*
Doi *hill, mountain*
Dome *ice dome*
Dong *village*
Dooxo *floodplain*
Dzong *castle, fortress*

Eiland-en *island-s*
Eilean *island*
Ejland *island*
Elv *river*
Embalse *lake, reservoir*
Emi *mountain, rock*
Enseada, Ensenada *bay, cove*
Ér *rivulet, stream*
Erg *sand dune region*
Est *east*
Estación *railroad station*
Estany *lagoon, lake*
Estero *estuary, inlet, lagoon, marsh*
Estrecho *strait*
Étang *lake, pond*
Eylandt *island*
Ežeras *lake*
Ezers *lake*

Falaise *cliff, escarpment*
Farvand-et *channel, sound*
Fell *mountain*
Feng *mount, peak*
Fiord-o *inlet, sound*
Fiume *river*
Fjäll-et *mountain*
Fjällen *mountains*
Fjärd-en *fjord*
Fjarđar, Fjörđur *fjord*
Fjeld *mountain*
Fjell-ene *mountain-s*
Fjöll *mountain-s*
Fjord-en *inlet, fjord*
Fleuve *river*
Fljót *large river*
Flói *bay, marshland*
Foci *river mouths*
Főcsatorna *principal canal*
Förde *fjord, gulf, inlet*
Forsen *rapids, waterfall*
Fortaleza *fort, fortress*
Fortín *fortified post*
Foss-en *waterfall*
Foum *pass, passage*
Foz *mouth of a river*
Fuerte *fort, fortress*
Fwafwate *waterfalls*

Gacan-ka *hill, peak*
Gal *pond, spring, water hole, well*
Gang *harbor*
Gangri *peak, range*
Gaoyuan *plateau*
Garaet, Gara'et *lake, lake bed, salt lake*
Gardaneh *pass*
Garet *hill, mountain*
Gat *channel*
Gata *bay, inlet, lake*
Gattet *channel, strait*
Gaud *depression, saline tract*
Gave *mountain stream*
Gebel *mountain-s, range*
Gebergte *mountain range*
Gebirge *mountains, range*
Geçidi *mountain pass, passage*
Geçit *mountain pass, passage*
Gezâir *islands*
Gezîra-t, Gezîret *island, peninsula*
Ghats *mountain range*
Ghubb-at, -et *bay, gulf*
Giri *mountain*
Gletscher *glacier*
Gobernador *governor*
Gobi *desert*
Gol *river, stream*
Göl, -ü *lake*
Golets *mountain, peak*
Golf, -e, -o *gulf*
Gor-a, -y, Gór-a, -y *mountain,-s*
Got *point*
Gowd *depression*
Goz *sand ridge*
Gran, -de *great, large*
Gryada *mountains, ridge*
Guan *pass*
Guba *bay, gulf*
Guelta *well*
Guntō *archipelago*
Gunung *mountain*
Gura *mouth, passage*
Guyot *table mount*

Haḑabat *plateau*
Haehyŏp *strait*
Haff *lagoon*
Hai *lake, sea*
Haihsia *strait*
Haixia *channel, strait*
Hakau *reef, rock*
Hakuchi *anchorage*
Halvø, Halvøy-a *peninsula*
Hama *beach*
Hamada, Ḩammādah *rocky desert*
Hamn *harbor, port*
Hāmūn, Hamun *depression, lake*
Hana *cape, point*
Hantō *peninsula*
Har *hill, mound, mountain*
Ḩarrat *lava field*
Hasi, Hassi *spring, well*
Hauteur *elevation, height*
Hav-et *sea*
Havn, Havre *harbor, port*
Hawr *lake, marsh*
Häyk' *lake, reservoir*
He *canal, lake, river*
Hegy, -ség *mountain, -s, range*
Heiau *temple*
Hoek *hook, point*
Hög-en *high, hill*
Höhe, -n *height, high*
Høj *height, hill*
Holm, -e, Holmene *island-s, islet -s*
Ḩoloţ *dunes*
Hon *island-s*
Hor-a, -y *mountain, -s*
Horn *horn, peak*
Houma *point*
Hoved *headland, peninsula, point*
Hraun *lava field*
Hsü *island*
Hu *lake, reservoir*
Huk *cape, point*
Hüyük *hill, mound*

Idehan *sand dunes*
Île-s, Ilha-s, Illa-s, Îlot-s *island-s, islet-s*
Îlet, Ilhéu-s *islet, -s*
Irhil *mountain-s*
'Irq *sand dune-s*
Isblink *glacier, ice field*
Is-en *glacier*
Isla-s, Islote *island-s, islet*
Isol-a, -e *island, -s*
Istmo *isthmus*
Iwa *island, islet, rock*

Jabal, Jebel *mountain-s, range*
Järv, -i, Jaure, Javrre *lake*
Jazā'ir, Jazīrat, Jazīreh *island-s*
Jehīl *lake*
Jezero, Jezioro *lake*
Jiang *river, stream*
Jiao *cape*
Jibāl *hill, mountain, ridge*
Jima *island-s, rock-s*
Jøkel, Jökull *glacier, ice cap*
Joki, Jokka *river*
Jökulsá *river from a glacier*
Jūn *bay*

Kaap *cape*
Kafr *village*
Kaikyō *channel, strait*
Kaise *mountain*
Kaiwan *bay, gulf, sea*
Kanal *canal, channel*
Kangri *mountain, peak*
Kap, Kapp *cape*
Kavīr *salt desert*
Kefar *village*
Kënet' *lagoon, lake*
Kep *cape, point*
Kepulauan *archipelago, islands*
Khalîg, Khalīj *bay, gulf*
Khirb-at, -et *ancient site, ruins*
Khrebet *mountain range*
Kinh *canal*
Klint *bluff, cliff*
Kō *bay, cove, harbor*
Ko *island, lake*
Koh *island, mountain, range*
Köl-i *lake*
Kólpos *gulf*
Kong *mountain*
Körfez, -i *bay, gulf*
Kosa *spit of land*
Kou *estuary, river mouth*
Kowtal-e *pass*
Krasn-yy, -aya, -oye *red*
Kryazh *mountain range, ridge*
Kuala *estuary, river mouth*
Kuan *mountain pass*
Kūh, Kūhhā *mountain-s, range*
Kul', Kuli *lake*
Kum *sandy desert*
Kundo *archipelago*
Kuppe *hill-s, mountain-s*
Kust *coast, shore*
Kyst *coast*
Kyun *island*

La *pass*
Lac, Lac-ul, -us *lake*
Lae *cape, point*
Lago, -a *lagoon, lake*
Lagoen, Lagune *lagoon*
Laguna-s *lagoon-s, lake-s*
Laht *bay, gulf, harbor*
Laje *reef, rock ledge*
Laut *sea*
Lednik *glacier*
Leida *channel*
Lhari *mountain*
Li *village*
Liedao *archipelago, islands*
Liehtao *archipelago, islands*
Liman-ı *bay, estuary*
Límni *lake*
Ling *mountain-s, range*
Linn *pool, waterfall*
Lintasan *passage*
Liqen *lake*
Llano-s *plain-s*
Loch, Lough *lake, arm of the sea*
Loma-s *hill-s, knoll-s*

Mal ... *mountain, range*
Mal-yy, -aya, -oye ... *little, small*
Mamarr ... *pass, path*
Man ... *bay*
Mar, Mare ... *large lake, sea*
Marsa, Marsá ... *bay, inlet*
Masabb ... *mouth of river*
Massif ... *mountain-s*
Mauna ... *mountain*
Mēda ... *plain*
Meer ... *lake, sea*
Melkosopochnik ... *undulating plain*
Mesa, Meseta ... *plateau, tableland*
Mierzeja ... *sandspit*
Minami ... *south*
Mios ... *island*
Misaki ... *cape, peninsula, point*
Mochun ... *passage*
Mong ... *town, village*
Mont-e, -i, -s ... *mount, -ain, -s*
Montagne, -s ... *mount, -ain, -s*
Montaña, -s ... *mountain, -s*
More ... *sea*
Morne ... *hill, peak*
Morro ... *bluff, headland, hill*
Motu, -s ... *islands*
Mouïet ... *well*
Mouillage ... *anchorage*
Muang ... *town, village*
Mui ... *cape, point*
Mull ... *headland, promontory*
Munkhafad ... *depression*
Munte ... *mountain*
Munţi-i ... *mountains*
Muong ... *town, village*
Mynydd ... *mountain*
Mys ... *cape*

Nacional ... *national*
Nada ... *gulf, sea*
Næs, Näs ... *cape, point*
Nafūd ... *area of dunes, desert*
Nagor'ye ... *mountain range, plateau*
Nahar, Nahr ... *river, stream*
Nakhon ... *town*
Namakzār ... *salt waste*
Ne ... *island, reef, rock-s*
Neem ... *cape, point, promontory*
Nes, Ness ... *peninsula, point*
Nevado-s ... *snow-capped mountain-s*
Nez ... *cape, promontory*
Ni ... *village*
Nisi, Nísia, Nisís, Nísoi ... *island-s, islet-s*
Nisídhes ... *islets*
Nizhn-iy, -yaya, -eye ... *lower*
Nizmennost' ... *low country*
Noord ... *north*
Nord-re ... *north-ern*
Nørre ... *north-ern*
Nos ... *cape, nose, point*
Nosy ... *island, reef, rock*
Nov-yy, -aya, -oye ... *new*
Nudo ... *mountain*
Numa ... *lake*
Nunatak, -s, -ker ... *peak-s surrounded by ice cap*
Nur ... *lake, salt lake*
Nuruu ... *mountain range, ridge*
Nut-en ... *peak*
Nuur ... *lake*

Ö-n, Ø-er ... *island-s*
Oblast' ... *administrative division, province, region*
Oceanus ... *ocean*
Odde-n ... *cape, point*
Øer-ne ... *islands*
Oglat ... *group of wells*
Oguilet ... *well*
Ór-os, -i ... *mountain, -s*
Órmos ... *bay, port*
Ort ... *place, point*
Øst-er ... *east*
Ostrov, -a, Ostrv-o, -a ... *island, -s*
Otoci, Otok ... *islands, island*
Ouadi, Oued ... *river, watercourse*
Øy-a ... *island*
Øyane ... *islands*
Ozer-o, -a ... *lake, -s*

Pää ... *mountain, point*
Palus ... *marsh*
Pampa-s ... *grassy plain-s*
Pantà ... *lake, reservoir*
Pantanal ... *marsh, swamp*
Pao, P'ao ... *lake*
Parbat ... *mountain*
Parque ... *park*
Pas, -ul ... *pass*
Paso, Passo ... *pass*
Passe ... *channel, pass*
Pasul ... *pass*
Pedra ... *rock*
Pegunungan ... *mountain range*
Pellg ... *bay, bight*
Peña ... *cliff, rock*
Pendi ... *basin*
Penedo-s ... *rock-s*
Péninsule ... *peninsula*
Peñón ... *point, rock*
Pereval ... *mountain pass*
Pertuis ... *strait*
Peski ... *sands, sandy region*
Phnom ... *hill, mountain, range*
Phou ... *mountain range*
Phu ... *mountain*
Piana-o ... *plain*
Pic, Pik, Piz ... *peak*
Picacho ... *mountain, peak*
Pico-s ... *peak-s*
Pistyll ... *waterfall*
Piton-s ... *peak-s*
Pivdennyy ... *southern*
Plaja, Playa ... *beach, inlet, shore*
Planalto, Plato ... *plateau*
Planina ... *mountain, plateau*
Plassen ... *lake*
Ploskogor'ye ... *plateau, upland*
Pointe ... *point*
Polder ... *reclaimed land*
Poluostrov ... *peninsula*
Pongo ... *water gap*
Ponta, -l ... *cape, point*
Ponte ... *bridge*
Poolsaar ... *peninsula*
Portezuelo ... *pass*
Porto ... *port*
Poulo ... *island*
Praia ... *beach, seashore*
Presa ... *reservoir*
Presidente ... *president*
Presqu'île ... *peninsula*
Prokhod ... *pass*
Proliv ... *strait*
Promontorio ... *promontory*
Průsmyk ... *mountain pass*
Przylądek ... *cape*
Puerto ... *bay, pass, port*
Pulao ... *island-s*
Pulau, Pulo ... *island*
Puncak ... *peak, summit, top*
Punt, Punta, -n ... *point, -s*
Pun ... *peak*
Pu'u ... *hill, mountain*
Puy ... *peak*

Qā' ... *depression, marsh, mud flat*
Qal'at ... *fort*
Qal'eh ... *castle, fort*
Qanâ ... *canal*
Qārat ... *hill-s, mountain-s*
Qaşr ... *castle, fort, hill*
Qila ... *fort*
Qiryat ... *settlement, suburb*
Qolleh ... *peak*
Qooriga ... *anchorage, bay*
Qoz ... *dunes, sand ridge*
Qu ... *canal*
Quebrada ... *ravine, stream*
Qullai ... *peak, summit*
Qum ... *desert, sand*
Qundao ... *archipelago, islands*
Qurayyāt ... *hills*

Raas ... *cape, point*
Rabt ... *hill*
Rada ... *roadstead*
Rade ... *anchorage, roadstead*
Rags ... *point*
Ramat ... *hill, mountain*
Rand ... *ridge of hills*
Rann ... *swamp*
Raqaba ... *wadi, watercourse*
Ras, Râs, Ra's ... *cape*
Ravnina ... *plain*
Récif-s ... *reef-s*
Regreg ... *marsh*
Represa ... *reservoir*
Reservatório ... *reservoir*
Restinga ... *barrier, sand area*
Rettō ... *chain of islands*
Ri ... *mountain range, village*
Ría ... *estuary*
Ribeirão ... *stream*
Río, Rio ... *river*
Roca-s ... *cliff, rock-s*
Roche-r, -s ... *rock-s*
Rosh ... *mountain, point*
Rt ... *cape, point*
Rubha ... *headland*
Rupes ... *scarp*

Saar ... *island*
Saari, Sari ... *island*
Sabkha-t, Sabkhet ... *lagoon, marsh, salt lake*
Sagar ... *lake, sea*
Sahara, Şaḩrā' ... *desert*
Sahl ... *plain*
Saki ... *cape, point*
Salar ... *salt flat*
Salina ... *salt pan*
Salin-as, -es ... *salt flat-s, salt marsh-es*
Salto ... *waterfall*
Sammyaku ... *mountain range*
San ... *hill, mountain*
San, -ta, -to ... *saint*
Sandur ... *sandy area*
Sankt ... *saint*
Sanmaek ... *mountain range*
São ... *saint*
Sarīr ... *gravel desert*
Sasso ... *mountain, stone*
Savane ... *savanna*
Scoglio ... *reef, rock*
Se ... *reef, rock-s, shoal-s*
Sebjet ... *salt lake, salt marsh*
Sebkha ... *salt lake, salt marsh*
Sebkhet ... *lagoon, salt lake*
See ... *lake, sea*
Selat ... *strait*
Selkä ... *lake, ridge*
Semenanjung ... *peninsula*
Sen ... *mountain*
Seno ... *bay, gulf*
Serra, Serranía ... *range of hills or mountains*
Severn-yy, -aya, -oye ... *northern*
Sgùrr ... *peak*
Sha ... *island, shoal*
Sha'ib ... *ravine, watercourse*
Shamo ... *desert*
Shan ... *island-s, mountain-s, range*
Shankou ... *mountain pass*
Shanmo ... *mountain range*
Sharm ... *cove, creek, harbor*
Shaţţ ... *large river*
Shi ... *administrative division, municipality*
Shima ... *island-s, rock-s*
Shō ... *island, reef, rock*
Shotō ... *archipelago*
Shott ... *intermittent salt lake*
Shuiku ... *reservoir*
Shuitao ... *channel*
Shyghanaghy ... *bay, gulf*
Sierra ... *mountain range*
Silsilesi ... *mountain chain, ridge*
Sint ... *saint*
Sinus ... *bay, sea*
Sjö-n ... *lake*
Skarv-et ... *barren mountain*
Skerry ... *rock*
Slieve ... *mountain*
Sø ... *lake*
Sønder, Søndre ... *south-ern*
Sopka ... *conical mountain, volcano*
Sor ... *lake, salt lake*
Sør, Sör ... *south-ern*
Sory ... *salt lake, salt marsh*
Spitz-e ... *peak, point, top*
Sredn-iy, -yaya, -eye ... *central, middle*
Stagno ... *lake, pond*
Stantsiya ... *station*
Stausee ... *reservoir*
Stenón ... *channel, strait*
Step'-i ... *steppe-s*
Štít ... *summit, top*
Stor-e ... *big, great*
Straat ... *strait*
Straum-en ... *current-s*
Strelka ... *spit of land*
Stretet, Stretto ... *strait*
Su ... *reef, river, rock, stream*
Sud ... *south*
Sudo ... *channel, strait*
Suidō ... *channel, strait*
Şummān ... *rocky desert*
Sund ... *sound, strait*
Sunden ... *channel, inlet, sound*
Svyat-oy, -aya, -oye ... *holy, saint*
Sziget ... *island*

Tagh ... *mountain-s*
Tall ... *hill, mound*
T'an ... *lake*
Tanezrouft ... *desert*
Tang ... *plain, steppe*
Tangi ... *peninsula, point*
Tanjong, Tanjung ... *cape, point*
Tao ... *island-s*
Tarso ... *hill-s, mountain-s*
Tassili ... *plateau, upland*
Tau ... *mountain-s, range*
Taūy ... *hills, mountains*
Tchabal ... *mountain-s*
Te Ava ... *tidal flat*
Tel-l ... *hill, mound*
Telok, Teluk ... *bay*
Tepe, -si ... *hill, peak*
Tepui ... *mesa, mountain*
Terara ... *hill, mountain, peak*
Testa ... *bluff, head*
Thale ... *lake*
Thang ... *plain, steppe*
Tien ... *lake*
Tierra ... *land, region*
Ting ... *hill, mountain*
Tir'at ... *canal*
Tó ... *lake, pool*
To, Tō ... *island-s, rock-s*
Tonle ... *lake*
Tope ... *hill, mountain, peak*
Top-pen ... *peak-s*
Träsk ... *bog, lake*
Tso ... *lake*
Tsui ... *cape, point*
Tübegi ... *peninsula*
Tulu ... *hill, mountain*
Tunturi-t ... *hill-s, mountain-s*

Uad ... *wadi, watercourse*
Udde-m ... *point*
Ujong, Ujung ... *cape, point*
Umi ... *bay, lagoon, lake*
Ura ... *bay, inlet, lake*
'Urūq ... *dune area*
Uul, Uula ... *mountain, range*
'Uyûn ... *springs*

Vaara ... *mountain*
Vaart ... *canal*
Vær ... *fishing station*
Vaïn ... *channel, strait*
Valle, Vallée ... *valley, wadi*
Vallen ... *waterfall*
Valli ... *lagoon, lake*
Vallis ... *valley*
Vanua ... *land*
Varre ... *mountain*
Vatn, Vatten, Vatnet ... *lake, water*
Veld ... *grassland, plain*
Verkhn-iy, -yaya, -eye ... *higher, upper*
Vesi ... *lake, water*
Vest-er ... *west*
Via ... *road*
Vidda ... *plateau*
Vig, Vík, Vik, -en ... *bay, cove*
Vinh ... *bay, gulf*
Vodokhranilishche ... *reservoir*
Vodoskhovyshche ... *reservoir*
Volcan, Volcán ... *volcano*
Vostochn-yy, -aya, -oye ... *eastern*
Vötn ... *stream*
Vozvyshennost' ... *plateau, upland*
Vozyera ... *lake-s*
Vrchovina ... *mountains*
Vrch-y ... *mountain-s*
Vrh ... *hill, mountain*
Vrŭkh ... *mountain*
Vyaliki ... *big, large*
Vysočina ... *highland*

Wabē ... *stream*
Wadi, Wādī, Wādī ... *valley, watercourse*
Wāhāt, Wāḩat ... *oasis*
Wald ... *forest, wood*
Wan ... *bay, gulf*
Water ... *harbor*
Webi ... *stream*
Wiek ... *cove, inlet*

Xia ... *gorge, strait*
Xiao ... *lesser, little*

Yanchi ... *salt lake*
Yang ... *ocean*
Yarymadasy ... *peninsula*
Yazovir ... *reservoir*
Yōlto ... *island group*
Yoma ... *mountain range*
Yü ... *island*
Yumco ... *lake*
Yunhe ... *canal*
Yuzhn-yy, -aya, -oye ... *southern*

Zaki ... *cape, point*
Zaliv ... *bay, gulf*
Zan ... *mountain, ridge*
Zangbo ... *river, stream*
Zapadn-yy, -aya, -oye ... *western*
Zatoka ... *bay, gulf*
Zee ... *bay, sea*
Zemlya ... *land*
Zhotsy ... *mountains*

Geographic Comparisons

EARTH

PLANET FACTS

Age: Formed 4.54 billion years ago. Life appeared on its surface within a billion years.

Location: Third planet from the sun. Earth is the largest of the terrestrial planets in the solar system in diameter, mass, and density.

Interior: Remains active, with a thick layer of relatively solid mantle, a liquid outer core that generates a magnetic field, and a solid iron inner core.

Mass: 5,973,600,000,000,000,000,000 (5.9736 sextillion) metric tons

Total Area: 510,066,000 sq km (196,938,000 sq mi)

Surface: About 71% of the surface is covered with saltwater oceans, the remainder consisting of continents and islands.

Land Area: 148,647,000 sq km (57,393,000 sq mi), 29.1% of total

Water Area: 361,419,000 sq km (139,545,000 sq mi), 70.9% of total

Atmosphere Composition: Dry air is 78.08% Nitrogen (N_2), 20.95% Oxygen (O_2), 0.93% Argon (Ar), 0.038% Carbon dioxide (CO_2), and 0.002% other gases. Water vapor is variable and typically about 1%.

Orbit: Earth orbits the sun once for every 366.26 times it rotates about its axis. This length of time is a sidereal year, which is equal to 365.26 solar days.

Equatorial Circumference: 40,075 km (24,902 mi)

Polar Circumference: 40,008 km (24,860 mi)

Equatorial Radius: 6,378 km (3,963 mi)

Polar Radius: 6,357 km (3,950 mi)

EARTH'S EXTREMES

Hottest Place: Dalol, Danakil Desert, Ethiopia, annual average temperature 34°C (93°F)

Coldest Place: Plateau Station, Antarctica, annual average temperature -56.7°C (-70°F)

Hottest Recorded Temperature: Al Aziziyah, Libya 58°C (136.4°F), September 3, 1922

Coldest Recorded Temperature: Vostok Research Station, Antarctica -89.2°C (-128.6°F), July 21, 1983

Wettest Place: Mawsynram, Assam, India, annual average rainfall 1,187 cm (467 in)

Driest Place: Arica, Atacama Desert, Chile, rainfall barely measurable

Largest Hot Desert: Sahara, Africa 9,000,000 sq km (3,475,000 sq mi)

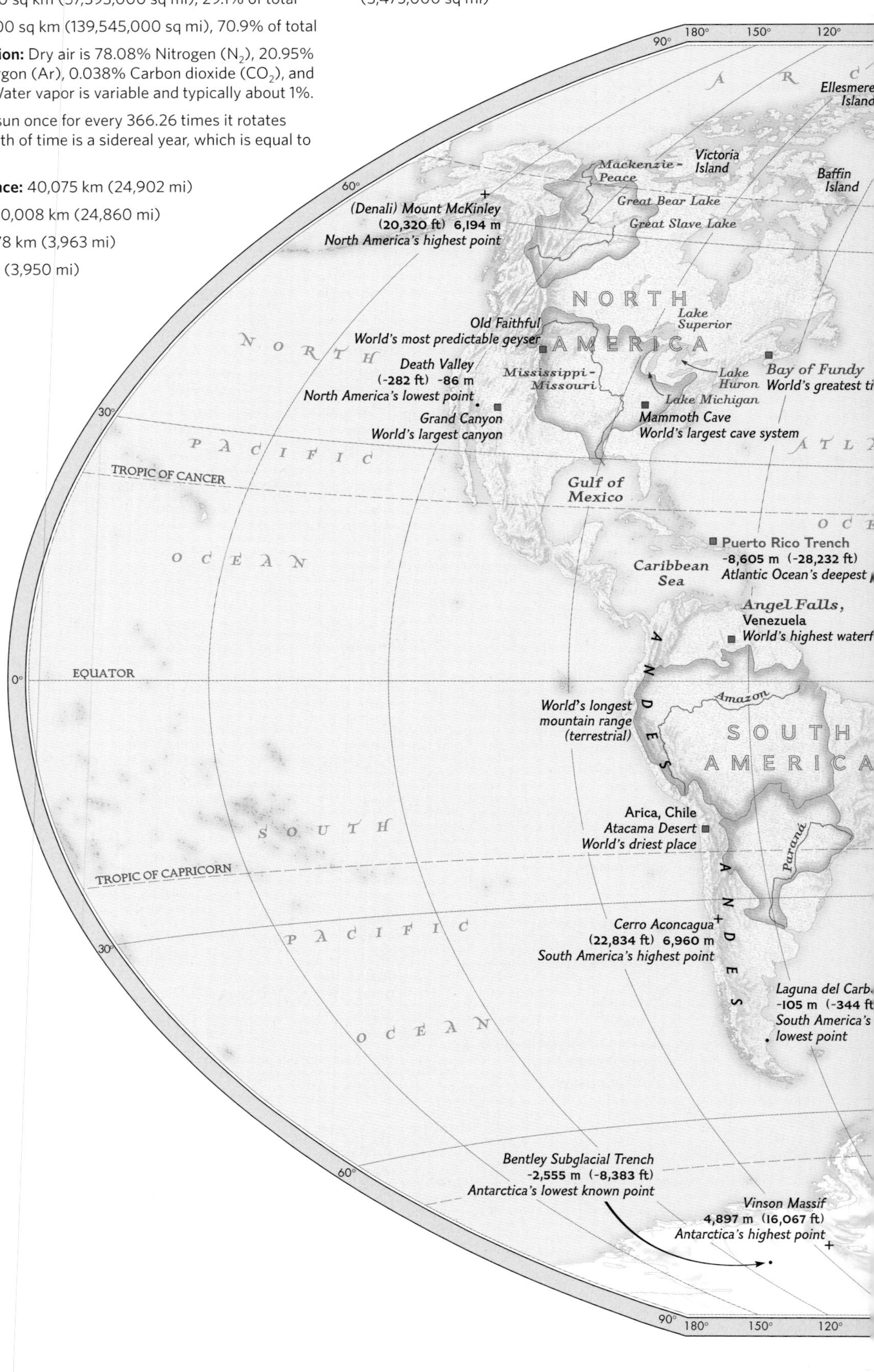

Ellesmere Island
Mackenzie-Peace
Victoria Island
Baffin Island
Great Bear Lake
Great Slave Lake
(Denali) Mount McKinley
(20,320 ft) 6,194 m
North America's highest point
NORTH AMERICA
Lake Superior
Old Faithful
World's most predictable geyser
Death Valley
(-282 ft) -86 m
North America's lowest point
Mississippi-Missouri
Lake Huron
Bay of Fundy
World's greatest ti
Lake Michigan
Grand Canyon
World's largest canyon
Mammoth Cave
World's largest cave system
PACIFIC OCEAN
TROPIC OF CANCER
Gulf of Mexico
Puerto Rico Trench
-8,605 m (-28,232 ft)
Atlantic Ocean's deepest
Caribbean Sea
Angel Falls, Venezuela
World's highest waterf
EQUATOR
World's longest mountain range (terrestrial)
ANDES
Amazon
SOUTH AMERICA
Arica, Chile
Atacama Desert
World's driest place
Paraná
TROPIC OF CAPRICORN
SOUTH PACIFIC OCEAN
Cerro Aconcagua
(22,834 ft) 6,960 m
South America's highest point
Laguna del Carb
-105 m (-344 ft
South America's lowest point
Bentley Subglacial Trench
-2,555 m (-8,383 ft)
Antarctica's lowest known point
Vinson Massif
4,897 m (16,067 ft)
Antarctica's highest point

Land

LAND EXTREMES

Largest Country: Russia 17,075,400 sq km (6,592,850 sq mi)

Smallest Country: Vatican City 0.4 sq km (0.2 sq mi)

Longest Mountain Range (Terrestrial): Andes, South America, approximately 7,200 km (4,500 mi)

Longest Mountain Range (Submarine): Mid-Atlantic Ridge, Atlantic Ocean, approximately 19,700 km (12,240 mi)

Largest Cave Chamber: Sarawak Cave, Gunung Mulu National Park, Malaysia, 16 hectares and 79 meters high (40.2 acres and 260 feet)

Largest Cave System: Mammoth Cave, Kentucky, over 530 km (330 mi) of passageways mapped

AREA OF EACH CONTINENT

	SQ KM	SQ MI	% OF EARTH'S LAND
Asia	44,570,000	17,208,000	30.0
Africa	30,065,000	11,608,000	20.2
North America	24,474,000	9,449,000	16.5
South America	17,819,000	6,880,000	12.0
Antarctica	13,209,000	5,100,000	8.9
Europe	9,947,000	3,841,000	6.7
Australia	7,692,000	2,970,000	5.2

LOWEST SURFACE POINT ON EACH CONTINENT

	METERS	FEET
Dead Sea, Asia	-421	-1,380
Lake Assal, Africa	-156	-512
Laguna del Carbón, South America	-105	-344
Death Valley, North America	-86	-282
Caspian Sea, Europe	-28	-92
Lake Eyre, Australia	-16	-52
Bentley Subglacial Trench, Antarctica	-2,555	-8,383

HIGHEST POINT ON EACH CONTINENT

	METERS	FEET
Mount Everest, Asia	8,850	29,035
Cerro Aconcagua, South America	6,960	22,834
Mount McKinley (Denali), N. America	6,194	20,320
Kilimanjaro, Africa	5,895	19,340
El'brus, Europe	5,642	18,510
Vinson Massif, Antarctica	4,897	16,067
Mount Kosciuszko, Australia	2,228	7,310

LARGEST ISLANDS

	AREA	SQ KM	SQ MI
1	Greenland	2,166,000	836,000
2	New Guinea	792,500	306,000
3	Borneo	725,500	280,100
4	Madagascar	587,000	226,600
5	Baffin Island	507,500	196,000
6	Sumatra	427,300	165,000
7	Honshu	227,400	87,800
8	Great Britain	218,100	84,200
9	Victoria Island	217,300	83,900
10	Ellesmere Island	196,200	75,800

Rivers and Lakes

LONGEST RIVERS

		KM	MI
1	Nile, Africa	6,825	4,241
2	Amazon, South America	6,437	4,000
3	Chang Jiang (Yangtze), Asia	6,380	3,964
4	Mississippi-Missouri, N. America	5,971	3,710
5	Yenisey-Angara, Asia	5,536	3,440
6	Huang (Yellow), Asia	5,464	3,395
7	Ob-Irtysh, Asia	5,410	3,362
8	Amur, Asia	4,416	2,744
9	Lena, Asia	4,400	2,734
10	Congo, Africa	4,370	2,715

LARGEST DRAINAGE BASINS

	AREA	SQ KM	SQ MI
1	Amazon, South America	7,050,000	2,721,000
2	Congo, Africa	3,700,000	1,428,000
3	Mississippi-Missouri, North America	3,250,000	1,255,000
4	Paraná, South America	3,100,000	1,197,000
5	Yenisey-Angara, Asia	2,700,000	1,042,000
6	Ob-Irtysh, Asia	2,430,000	938,000
7	Lena, Asia	2,420,000	934,000
8	Nile, Africa	1,900,000	733,400
9	Amur, Asia	1,840,000	710,000
10	Mackenzie-Peace, North America	1,765,000	681,000

EARTH'S EXTREMES *(continued)*

Largest Ice Desert: Antarctica, 13,209,000 sq km (5,100,000 sq mi)

Largest Canyon: Grand Canyon, Colorado River, Arizona, U.S., 446 km (277 mi) long along river, 180 m (600 ft) to 29 km (18 mi) wide, about 1.8 km (1.1 mi) deep

Most Predictable Geyser: Old Faithful, Wyoming, U.S., annual average interval 66 to 80 minutes

Longest Reef: Great Barrier Reef, Australia, 2,300 km (1,429 mi)

Greatest Tidal Range: Bay of Fundy, Canadian Atlantic Coast, 16 m (52 ft)

Highest Waterfall: Angel Falls, Venezuela 979 m (3,212 ft)

Human Geography

GEOPOLITICAL EXTREMES

Population: 6,624,528,000

Most Populous Country: China 1,348,317,000 people

Least Populous Country: Vatican City 798 people

Most Crowded Country: Monaco 16,920 per sq km (44,000 per sq mi)

Least Crowded Country: Mongolia 1.7 per sq km (4.3 per sq mi)

Largest Metropolitan Area: Tokyo 35,676,000 people

Country with the Greatest Number of Bordering Countries: China 14, Russia 14

ENGINEERING WONDERS

Tallest Office Building (in current use): Taipei 101, Taipei, Taiwan 509 m (1,670 ft)

Tallest Tower (Freestanding): CN Tower, Toronto, Canada 553 m (1,815 ft)

Tallest Manmade Structure: Burj Dubai, United Arab Emirates (under construction) to be completed in 2009 at over 800 m (2,600 ft)

Longest Wall: Great Wall of China, approximately 3,460 km (2,150 mi)

Longest Road: Pan-American highway (not including gap in Panama and Colombia), more than 24,140 km (15,000 mi)

Longest Railroad: Trans-Siberian Railroad, Russia 9,288 km (5,772 mi)

Highest Bridge (over water): Millau Viaduct, France 343 m (1,125 ft) above water

Longest Highway Bridge: Lake Pontchartrain Causeway, Louisiana 38.4 km (23.9 mi)

Longest Suspension Bridge: Akashi-Kaikyo Bridge, Japan, total length 3,911 m (12,831 ft), longest span 1,991 m (6,532 ft)

Largest Artificial Lake: Lake Volta, Volta River, Ghana 9,065 sq km (3,500 sq mi)

Tallest Dam: Rogun Dam, Vakhsh River, Tajikistan 335 m (1,099 ft)

Tallest Pyramid: Great Pyramid of Khufu, Egypt 137 m (450 ft)

Deepest Mine: TauTona Mine, South Africa 3,902 m (12,802 ft) deep

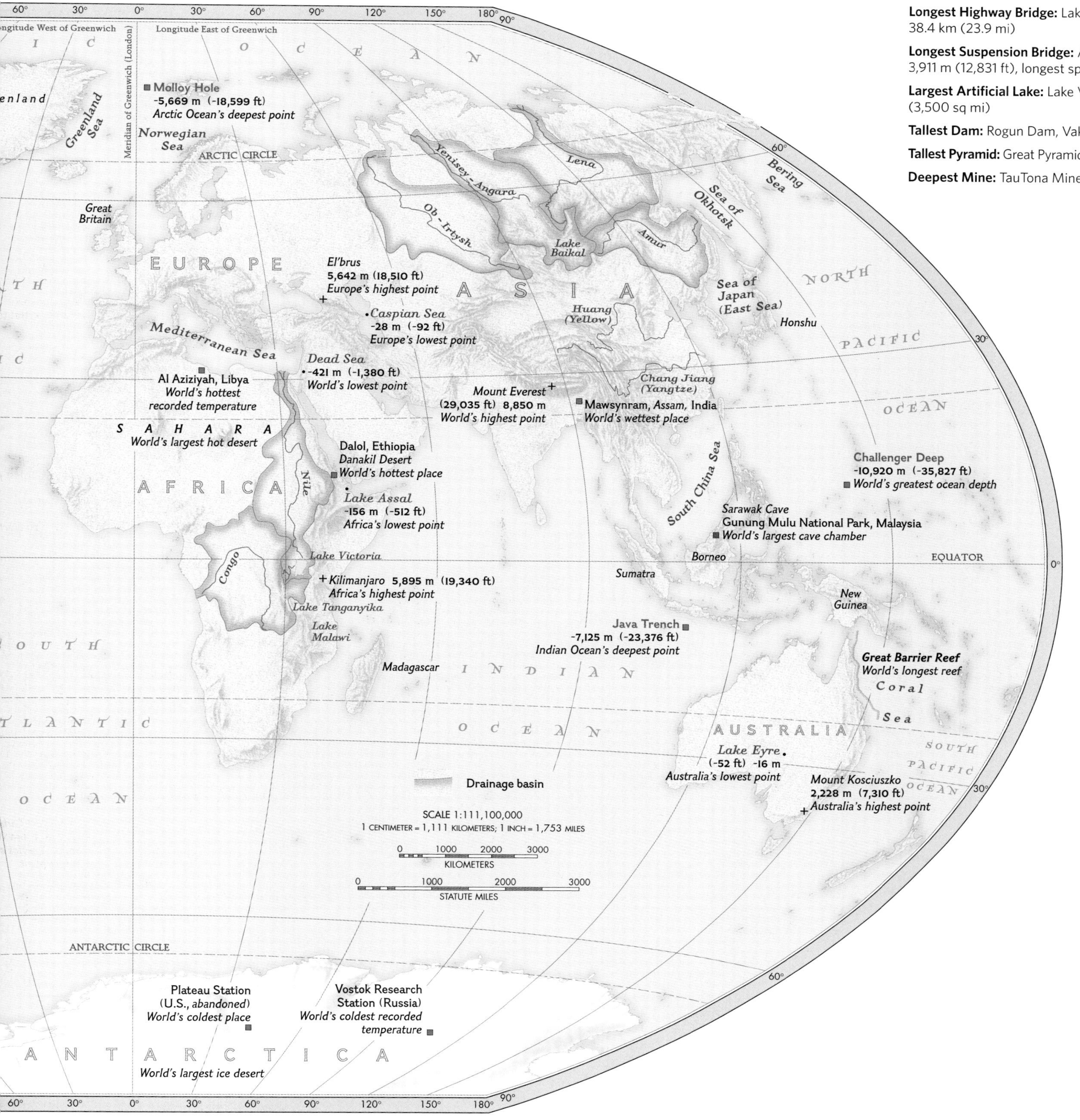
Longitude East of Greenwich
Meridian of Greenwich (London)
Molloy Hole
-5,669 m (-18,599 ft)
Arctic Ocean's deepest point
Greenland Sea
Norwegian Sea
ARCTIC CIRCLE
Great Britain
EUROPE
El'brus
5,642 m (18,510 ft)
Europe's highest point
Caspian Sea
-28 m (-92 ft)
Europe's lowest point
Mediterranean Sea
Dead Sea
-421 m (-1,380 ft)
World's lowest point
Al Aziziyah, Libya
World's hottest recorded temperature
SAHARA
World's largest hot desert
Dalol, Ethiopia
Danakil Desert
World's hottest place
Lake Assal
-156 m (-512 ft)
Africa's lowest point
AFRICA
Nile
Congo
Lake Victoria
Kilimanjaro 5,895 m (19,340 ft)
Africa's highest point
Lake Tanganyika
Lake Malawi
Madagascar
Yenisey-Angara
Ob-Irtysh
Lena
Amur
Lake Baikal
ASIA
Huang (Yellow)
Chang Jiang (Yangtze)
Mount Everest
(29,035 ft) 8,850 m
World's highest point
Mawsynram, Assam, India
World's wettest place
Sea of Okhotsk
Bering Sea
Sea of Japan (East Sea)
Honshu
NORTH PACIFIC OCEAN
Challenger Deep
-10,920 m (-35,827 ft)
World's greatest ocean depth
South China Sea
Sarawak Cave
Gunung Mulu National Park, Malaysia
World's largest cave chamber
Borneo
Sumatra
EQUATOR
New Guinea
Java Trench
-7,125 m (-23,376 ft)
Indian Ocean's deepest point
INDIAN OCEAN
Great Barrier Reef
World's longest reef
Coral Sea
AUSTRALIA
Lake Eyre
(-52 ft) -16 m
Australia's lowest point
Mount Kosciuszko
2,228 m (7,310 ft)
Australia's highest point
SOUTH PACIFIC OCEAN
Drainage basin
SCALE 1:111,100,000
1 CENTIMETER = 1,111 KILOMETERS; 1 INCH = 1,753 MILES
KILOMETERS
STATUTE MILES
ANTARCTIC CIRCLE
Plateau Station
(U.S., abandoned)
World's coldest place
Vostok Research Station (Russia)
World's coldest recorded temperature
ANTARCTICA
World's largest ice desert

LARGEST LAKES BY AREA

		AREA		MAX. DEPTH	
		SQ KM	SQ MI	METERS	FEET
1	Caspian Sea	371,000	143,200	1,025	3,363
2	Lake Superior	82,100	31,700	406	1,332
3	Lake Victoria	69,500	26,800	82	269
4	Lake Huron	59,600	23,000	229	751
5	Lake Michigan	57,800	22,300	281	922
6	Lake Tanganyika	32,600	12,600	1,470	4,823
7	Lake Baikal	31,500	12,200	1,637	5,371
8	Great Bear Lake	31,300	12,100	446	1,463
9	Lake Malawi	28,900	11,200	695	2,280
10	Great Slave Lake	28,600	11,000	614	2,014

Oceans and Seas

DEEPEST POINT IN EACH OCEAN

	METERS	FEET
Challenger Deep, Pacific Ocean	-10,920	-35,827
Puerto Rico Trench, Atlantic Ocean	-8,605	-28,232
Java Trench, Indian Ocean	-7,125	-23,376
Molloy Hole, Arctic Ocean	-5,669	-18,599

AREA OF EACH OCEAN

	SQ KM	SQ MI	% OF EARTH'S WATER AREA
Pacific	169,479,000	65,436,200	46.8
Atlantic	91,526,400	35,338,500	25.3
Indian	74,694,800	28,839,800	20.6
Arctic	13,960,100	5,390,000	3.9

LARGEST SEAS BY AREA

		AREA		AVG. DEPTH	
		SQ KM	SQ MI	METERS	FEET
1	Coral Sea	4,183,510	1,615,260	2,471	8,107
2	South China Sea	3,596,390	1,388,570	1,180	3,871
3	Caribbean Sea	2,834,290	1,094,330	2,596	8,517
4	Bering Sea	2,519,580	972,810	1,832	6,010
5	Mediterranean Sea	2,469,100	953,320	1,572	5,157
6	Sea of Okhotsk	1,625,190	627,490	814	2,671
7	Gulf of Mexico	1,531,810	591,430	1,544	5,066
8	Norwegian Sea	1,425,280	550,300	1,768	5,801
9	Greenland Sea	1,157,850	447,050	1,443	4,734
10	Sea of Japan	1,008,260	389,290	1,647	5,404

World Time Zones

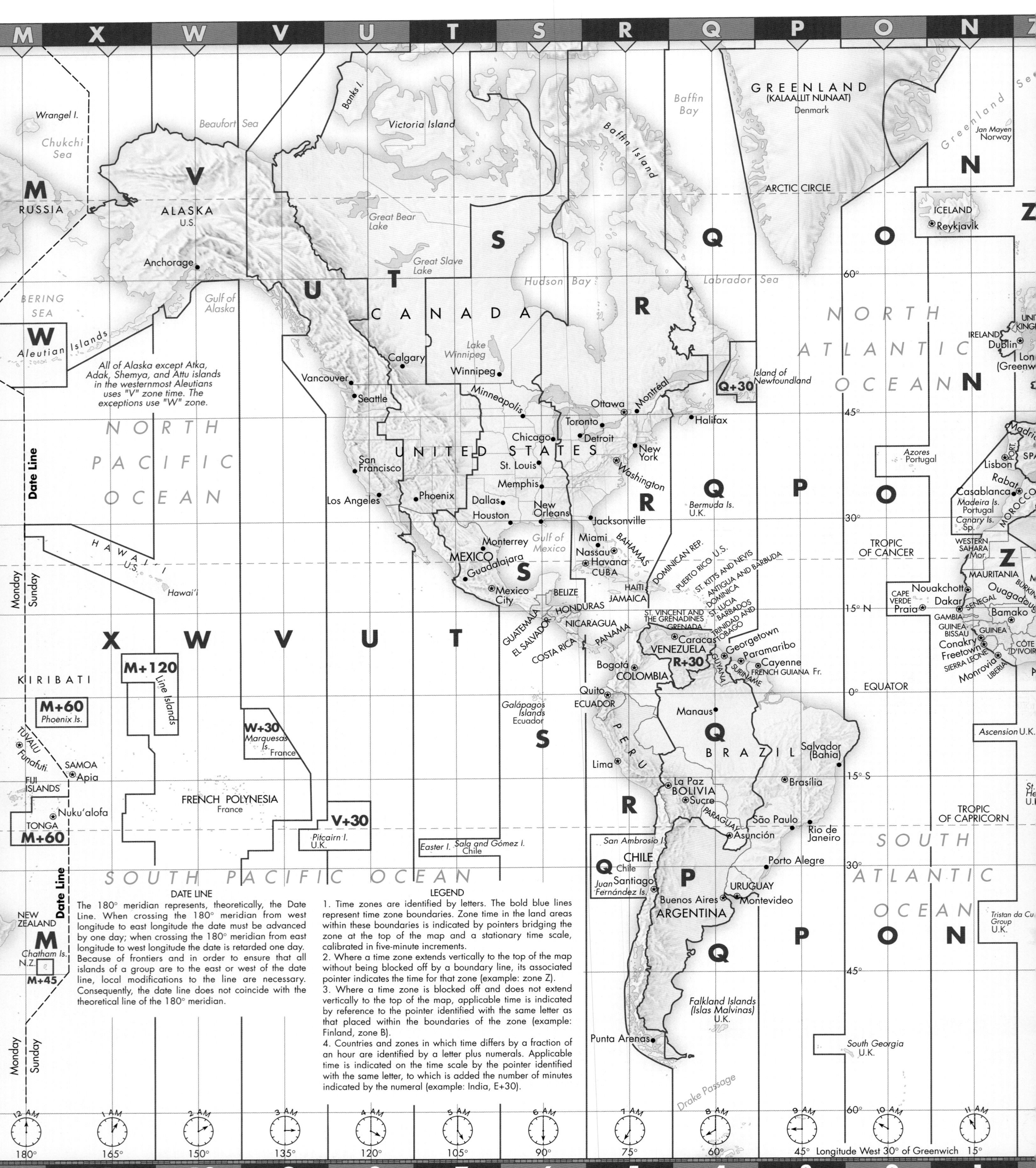
M X W V U T S R Q P O N
DATE LINE
The 180° meridian represents, theoretically, the Date Line. When crossing the 180° meridian from west longitude to east longitude the date must be advanced by one day; when crossing the 180° meridian from east longitude to west longitude the date is retarded one day. Because of frontiers and in order to ensure that all islands of a group are to the east or west of the date line, local modifications to the line are necessary. Consequently, the date line does not coincide with the theoretical line of the 180° meridian.
LEGEND
1. Time zones are identified by letters. The bold blue lines represent time zone boundaries. Zone time in the land areas within these boundaries is indicated by pointers bridging the zone at the top of the map and a stationary time scale, calibrated in five-minute increments.
2. Where a time zone extends vertically to the top of the map without being blocked off by a boundary line, its associated pointer indicates the time for that zone (example: zone Z).
3. Where a time zone is blocked off and does not extend vertically to the top of the map, applicable time is indicated by reference to the pointer identified with the same letter as that placed within the boundaries of the zone (example: Finland, zone B).
4. Countries and zones in which time differs by a fraction of an hour are identified by a letter plus numerals. Applicable time is indicated on the time scale by the pointer identified with the same letter, to which is added the number of minutes indicated by the numeral (example: India, E+30).
All of Alaska except Atka, Adak, Shemya, and Attu islands in the westernmost Aleutians uses "V" zone time. The exceptions use "W" zone.
Date Line
Monday Sunday
NORTH PACIFIC OCEAN
SOUTH PACIFIC OCEAN
NORTH ATLANTIC OCEAN
SOUTH ATLANTIC OCEAN
CANADA
UNITED STATES
GREENLAND (KALAALLIT NUNAAT) Denmark
ALASKA U.S.
RUSSIA
MEXICO
BRAZIL
ARGENTINA
CHILE
M+120
M+60 Phoenix Is.
M+45
W+30 Marquesas Is. France
V+30
Q+30
R+30
FRENCH POLYNESIA France
12 AM 1 AM 2 AM 3 AM 4 AM 5 AM 6 AM 7 AM 8 AM 9 AM 10 AM 11 AM
180° 165° 150° 135° 120° 105° 90° 75° 60° 45° Longitude West 30° of Greenwich 15°
+12- -11 -10 -9 -8 -7 -6 -5 -4 -3 -2 -1

The numeral in each tab directly above shows the number of hours to be added to, or subtracted from, Coordinated Universal Time (UTC), formerly Greenwich Mean Time (GMT).

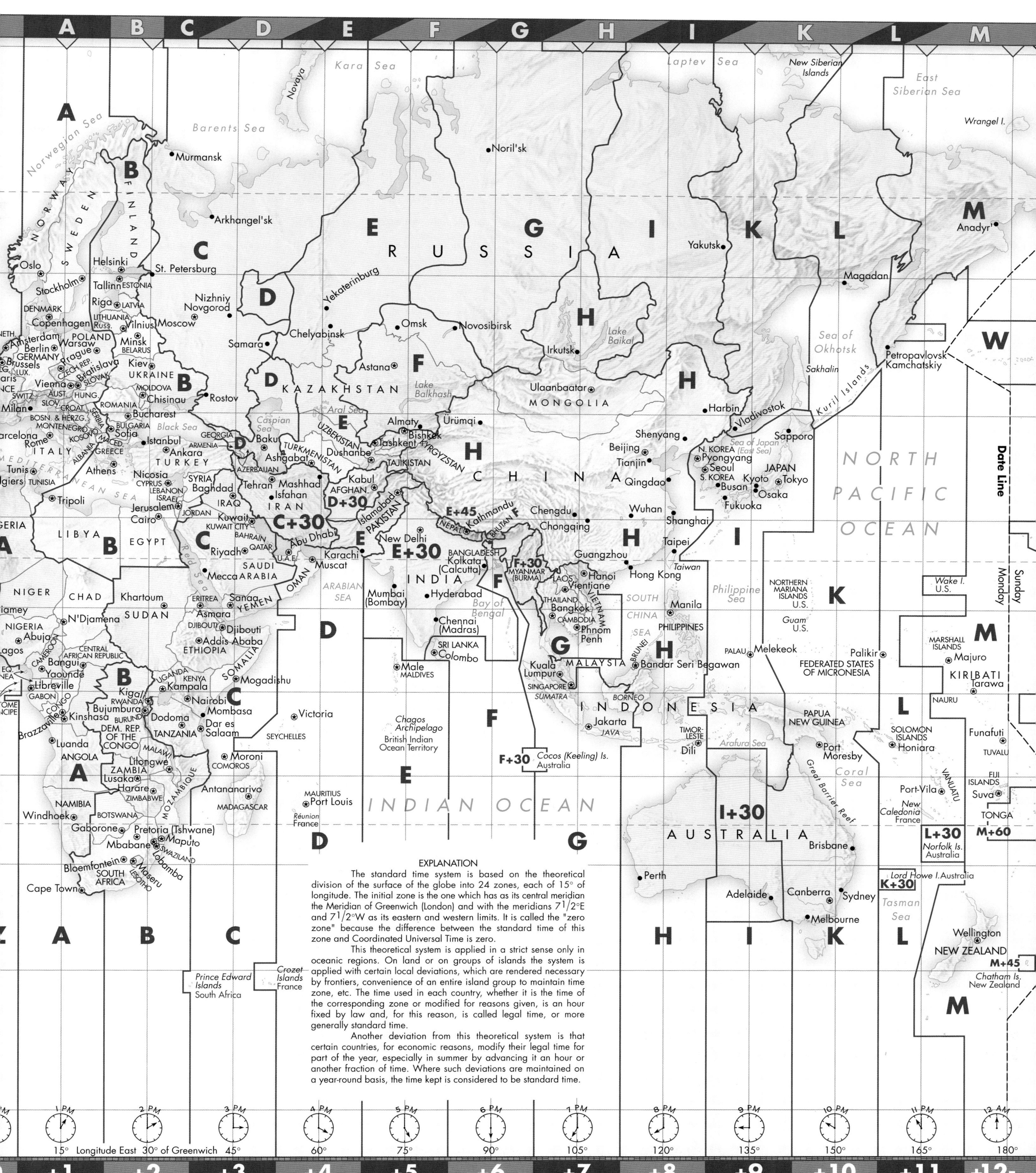

A B C D E F G H I K L M
Kara Sea
Laptev Sea
New Siberian Islands
East Siberian Sea
Wrangel I.
Barents Sea
Norwegian Sea
Novaya
Murmansk
Noril'sk
NORWAY
SWEDEN
FINLAND
Arkhangel'sk
R U S S I A
Yakutsk
Anadyr'
Oslo
Helsinki
St. Petersburg
Stockholm
Tallinn ESTONIA
Nizhniy Novgorod
Yekaterinburg
Magadan
DENMARK
Copenhagen
Riga LATVIA
LITHUANIA
RUSS.
Vilnius
Moscow
POLAND
Amsterdam
Berlin
GERMANY
Warsaw
Minsk BELARUS
Samara
Chelyabinsk
Omsk
Novosibirsk
Irkutsk
Lake Baikal
Sea of Okhotsk
Petropavlovsk Kamchatskiy
W
Brussels
LUX.
Prague
CZECH REP.
Bratislava
SLOVAK.
Kiev
UKRAINE
Astana
Sakhalin
Kuril Islands
Vienna
AUST.
HUNG.
MOLDOVA
Chisinau
Rostov
SWITZ.
SLOV.
CROAT.
ROMANIA
K A Z A K H S T A N
Lake Balkhash
Ulaanbaatar
M O N G O L I A
Milan
BOSN. & HERZG.
MONTENEGRO
SERBIA
Bucharest
BULGARIA
Sofia
Black Sea
Caspian Sea
Aral Sea
Almaty
Bishkek
Ürümqi
Harbin
Vladivostok
Barcelona
Rome
KOSOVO
MACED.
ITALY
ALBANIA
GREECE
Istanbul
Ankara
TURKEY
GEORGIA
ARMENIA
Baku
AZERBAIJAN
Ashgabat
TURKMENISTAN
UZBEKISTAN
Tashkent
Dushanbe
TAJIKISTAN
KYRGYZSTAN
Shenyang
Beijing
Tianjin
N. KOREA
Pyongyang
Seoul
S. KOREA
Busan
Sea of Japan (East Sea)
Sapporo
JAPAN
Tokyo
Kyoto
Osaka
Fukuoka
NORTH PACIFIC OCEAN
Date Line
Tunis
TUNISIA
Athens
Nicosia
CYPRUS
LEBANON
SYRIA
ISRAEL
Baghdad
IRAQ
Tehran
Mashhad
Isfahan
IRAN
Kabul
AFGHAN.
Islamabad
PAKISTAN
C H I N A
Qingdao
Tripoli
Jerusalem
JORDAN
Cairo
Kuwait
KUWAIT CITY
BAHRAIN
QATAR
Riyadh
Abu Dhabi
U.A.E.
Karachi
Muscat
OMAN
New Delhi
E+30
E+45
D+30
C+30
NEPAL
Kathmandu
BHUTAN
Chengdu
Chongqing
Wuhan
Shanghai
Taipei
Taiwan
LIBYA
EGYPT
Red Sea
SAUDI ARABIA
Mecca
BANGLADESH
Kolkata (Calcutta)
INDIA
F+30
MYANMAR (BURMA)
LAOS
Hanoi
Vientiane
Guangzhou
Hong Kong
NIGER
CHAD
Khartoum
SUDAN
ERITREA
Asmara
Sanaa
YEMEN
ARABIAN SEA
Mumbai (Bombay)
Hyderabad
Bay of Bengal
THAILAND
Bangkok
VIETNAM
CAMBODIA
Phnom Penh
SOUTH CHINA SEA
Manila
PHILIPPINES
Philippine Sea
NORTHERN MARIANA ISLANDS U.S.
Guam U.S.
Wake I. U.S.
Sunday
Monday
NIGERIA
Abuja
N'Djamena
DJIBOUTI
Djibouti
Addis Ababa
ETHIOPIA
SOMALIA
Chennai (Madras)
SRI LANKA
Colombo
Male
MALDIVES
Kuala Lumpur
MALAYSIA
SINGAPORE
BRUNEI
Bandar Seri Begawan
PALAU
Melekeok
FEDERATED STATES OF MICRONESIA
Palikir
MARSHALL ISLANDS
Majuro
KIRIBATI
Tarawa
CENTRAL AFRICAN REPUBLIC
CAMEROON
Bangui
Yaoundé
Libreville
GABON
CONGO
Brazzaville
Kinshasa
DEM. REP. OF THE CONGO
UGANDA
Kampala
KENYA
Kigali
RWANDA
Bujumbura
BURUNDI
Nairobi
Mombasa
Mogadishu
Victoria
SEYCHELLES
Dodoma
TANZANIA
Dar es Salaam
SUMATRA
BORNEO
I N D O N E S I A
Jakarta
JAVA
TIMOR-LESTE
Dili
Arafura Sea
PAPUA NEW GUINEA
Port Moresby
NAURU
SOLOMON ISLANDS
Honiara
Funafuti
TUVALU
Luanda
ANGOLA
ZAMBIA
Lusaka
MALAWI
Lilongwe
Harare
ZIMBABWE
MOZAMBIQUE
Moroni
COMOROS
Chagos Archipelago
British Indian Ocean Territory
F+30
Cocos (Keeling) Is. Australia
Coral Sea
Great Barrier Reef
VANUATU
Port-Vila
FIJI ISLANDS
Suva
NAMIBIA
Windhoek
BOTSWANA
Gaborone
Antananarivo
MADAGASCAR
MAURITIUS
Port Louis
Réunion France
INDIAN OCEAN
I+30
AUSTRALIA
New Caledonia France
TONGA
M+60
Pretoria (Tshwane)
Maputo
Mbabane
SWAZILAND
Bloemfontein
Maseru
Lobamba
SOUTH AFRICA
LESOTHO
Cape Town
Perth
Brisbane
L+30
Norfolk Is. Australia
Lord Howe I. Australia
K+30
Adelaide
Canberra
Sydney
Melbourne
Tasman Sea
Wellington
NEW ZEALAND
M+45
Chatham Is. New Zealand
Prince Edward Islands South Africa
Crozet Islands France
1 PM
2 PM
3 PM
4 PM
5 PM
6 PM
7 PM
8 PM
9 PM
10 PM
11 PM
12 AM
15° Longitude East 30° of Greenwich 45°
60°
75°
90°
105°
120°
135°
150°
165°
180°
+1 +2 +3 +4 +5 +6 +7 +8 +9 +10 +11 +12-
Mercator Projection

EXPLANATION

The standard time system is based on the theoretical division of the surface of the globe into 24 zones, each of 15° of longitude. The initial zone is the one which has as its central meridian the Meridian of Greenwich (London) and with the meridians 7 1/2°E and 7 1/2°W as its eastern and western limits. It is called the "zero zone" because the difference between the standard time of this zone and Coordinated Universal Time is zero.

This theoretical system is applied in a strict sense only in oceanic regions. On land or on groups of islands the system is applied with certain local deviations, which are rendered necessary by frontiers, convenience of an entire island group to maintain time zone, etc. The time used in each country, whether it is the time of the corresponding zone or modified for reasons given, is an hour fixed by law and, for this reason, is called legal time, or more generally standard time.

Another deviation from this theoretical system is that certain countries, for economic reasons, modify their legal time for part of the year, especially in summer by advancing it an hour or another fraction of time. Where such deviations are maintained on a year-round basis, the time kept is considered to be standard time.

Place-name Index

THE FOLLOWING SYSTEM is used to locate a place on a map in this atlas. The boldface type after an entry refers to the page on which the map is found; the letter-number combination refers to the grid square in which the particular place-name is located. The edge of each map is marked horizontally with numbers and vertically with letters. In between, at equally spaced intervals, are small triangles. If these small triangles were connected with lines, each page would be divided into a grid. Take the town of Tullah, for example. The index entry reads "**Tullah**, *Tas., Austral.* **237 Q22**." On page 237, Tullah is located within the grid square where row Q and column 22 intersect (see diagram, right).

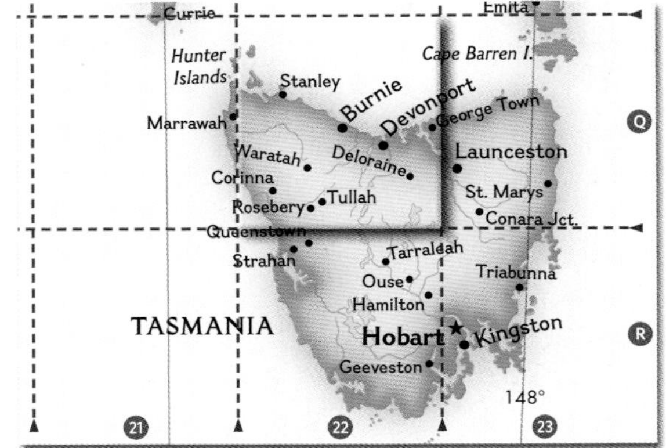

Currie
Emita
Hunter Islands
Stanley
Cape Barren I.
Burnie
Devonport
George Town
Marrawah
Waratah
Deloraine
Launceston
Corinna
Rosebery
Tullah
St. Marys
Conara Jct.
Queenstown
Strahan
Tarraleah
Ouse
Hamilton
Triabunna
TASMANIA
Hobart
Kingston
Geeveston
148°
Q
R
21
22
23

feature description — Montemuro, peak, Port. 152 E7 — page number, grid square, country
feature name — Tayan, Indonesia 206 H7 — page number, grid square

A place-name may appear on several maps, but the index lists only the best presentation. Usually, this means that a feature is indexed to the largest-scale map on which it appears in its entirety. (Note: Rivers are often labeled multiple times even on a single map. In such cases, the rivers are indexed to labels that are closest to their mouths.) The name of the country or continent in which a feature lies is shown in italic type and is sometimes abbreviated.

The index lists more than proper names. Some entries include a feature description (in colored type), as in "**Susak**, island, *Croatia* **162 G5**." In languages other than English, the description of a physical feature may be part of the name; e.g., the "Ozero" in "**Pskovskoye Ozero**, *Russ.* **166 D7**" means "lake." The Glossary of Foreign Terms on page 306 translates such terms into English. When a feature or place can be referred to by more than one name, both may appear in the index with cross-references. For example, the entry for Constantinople reads "**Constantinople** *see* **İstanbul**, *Turk.* **180 F3**." That entry is "**İstanbul (Constantinople)**, *Turk.* **180 F3**."

C

F

Í

O

P

Q

W

Z

Moon Index

LUNAR EQUIVALENTS

Lacus .... lake
Mare .... sea
Montes .... range
Oceanus .... ocean
Palus .... marsh
Rupes .... scarp
Sinus .... bay
Vallis .... valley

All other entries are craters.

SPACECRAFT LANDING OR IMPACT SITES

All landing dates are based on the UTC time zone.

Mars Index

MARTIAN EQUIVALENTS

Chasma .... canyon
Fossae .... trenches
Labyrinthus .... labyrinth
Mensae .... mesas
Mons .... mountain
Montes .... mountains
Patera .... crater
Planitia .... plain
Planum .... plateau
Sulci .... ridges
Terra .... region
Tholus .... hill
Vallis .... valley
Vastitas .... waste
All other entries are craters.

SPACECRAFT LANDING OR IMPACT SITES

All landing dates are based on the UTC time zone.

Acknowledgments

World Thematic Section

PALEOGEOGRAPHY pp. 30–31

CONSULTANTS

Robert Tilling
Volcano Hazards Team, U.S. Geological Survey (USGS)

Ron Blakey
Northern Arizona University

GRAPHICS

CONTINENTS ADRIFT IN TIME: Ron Blakey, Northern Arizona University

LAYERS OF THE EARTH: Tibor G. Tóth

PLATE TECTONICS pp. 32–33

CONSULTANT

Robert Tilling
Volcano Hazards Team, U.S. Geological Survey (USGS)

GRAPHICS

GEOLOGIC FORCES CHANGE THE FACE OF THE PLANET: Susan Sanford

LANDFORMS pp. 34–35

CONSULTANTS

Mike Slattery
Texas Christian University

PHOTOGRAPHS

PAGE 34, (LE) Diehm/Getty Images; (RT) Frank Krahmer/Getty Images
PAGE 35, (LE) John W. Banagan/Getty Images; (CT) Momatiuk-Eastcott/CORBIS; (RT) Jeremy Woodhouse/Getty Images

LAND COVER pp. 36–37

CONSULTANTS

Paul Davis
The Global Land Cover Facility, University of Maryland

Mark Friedl and Damien Sulla-Menashe
Global Land Cover Project, Boston University

SATELLITE IMAGES

GLOBAL LAND COVER: Boston University Department of Geography and Environment Global Land Cover Project. Source data provided by NASA's Moderate Resolution Imaging Spectroradiometer.

PHOTOGRAPHS

PAGE 36, (UP LE) Tom and Pat Leeson/Photo Researchers, Inc.; (UP RT) Michael Nichols/NationalGeographicStock.com; (LO-A), Stephen J. Krasemann/Photo Researchers, Inc.; (LO-A), Stephen J. Krasemann/Photo Researchers, Inc.; (LO-B), Rod Planck/Photo Researchers, Inc.; (LO-C), James Steinberg/Photo Researchers, Inc.; (LO-D), Matthew C. Hansen; (LO-E), Gregory G. Dimijian/Photo Researchers, Inc.; (LO-F), Dr. Sharon G. Johnson; (LO-G), Georg Gerster/Photo Researchers, Inc.
PAGE 37 (A): Rod Planck/Photo Researchers, Inc.; (B): Jim Richardson; (C): George Steinmetz; (D): Steve McCurry; (E): B. and C. Alexander/Photo Researchers, Inc.; (F): Robert Estall/CORBIS; (G): James Randklev/Getty Images

OCEANS pp. 38–39

CONSULTANTS

Benjamin S. Halpern
National Center for Ecological Analysis and Synthesis

S. Bradley Moran and Lewis Rothstein
University of Rhode Island

GRAPHICS

SEA-SURFACE TEMPERATURES: Gene Carl Feldman, NASA/Goddard Space Flight Center Aqua-MODIS

HUMAN IMPACT: Halpern, B.S., S. Walbridge, K.A. Selkoe, C.V. Kappel, F. Micheli, C. D'Agrosa, J. Bruno, K.S. Casey, C. Ebert, H.E. Fox, R. Fujita, D. Heinemann, H.S. Lenihan, E.M.P. Madin, M. Perry, E. Selig, M. Spalding, R. Steneck, and R. Watson. 2008. "A global map of human impact on marine ecosystems." *Science* 319: 948-952

PHOTOGRAPHS

PAGE 39, (UP LE) Kaz Mori/Getty Images; (UP RT) Chris Newbert /Minden Pictures/NationalGeographicStock.com; (CTR) Brandon Cole/Getty Images; (LO) Roger Coulam/Alamy

FRESH WATER pp. 40–41

CONSULTANTS

Nathan Eidem, Todd Jarvis, and Aaron Wolf
Oregon State University

GRAPHICS

WATER AVAILABILITY: Dobson, et al. LandScan 2000. Jerome E. Dobson, Edward A. Bright, Phillip R. Coleman, Richard C. Durfee, and Brian A. Worley. LandScan: A Global Population Database for Estimating Populations and Risk. *Photogrammetric Engineering & Remote Sensing*. Vol. 66 No. 7. July 2000, pp 849-57.

Vörösmarty, et al.: Vörösmarty, C.J., B. Fekete, and B.A. Tucker. 1998. River Discharge Database, Version 1.1 (RivDIS v1.0 supplement). Available through the Institute for the Study of Earth, Oceans, and Space / University of New Hampshire, Durham NH (USA) at http://pyramid.unh.edu/csrc/hydro/. Vörösmarty, C.J., B. Fekete, and B.A. Tucker. 1996. River Discharge Database, Version 1.0 (RivDIS v1.0), Volumes 0 through 6. A contribution to IHP-V Theme 1. Technical Documents in Hydrology Series. UNESCO, Paris.

Gleick, Peter. *The World's Water: 2006/2007*. The World's Water: The Biennial Report on Freshwater Resources, Peter H. Gleick (Island Press, Washington, D.C., 2006).

International Institute for Strategic Studies, *The 2008 Chart of Conflict*

WORLD AQUIFERS: Product of the Transboundary Freshwater Dispute Database, Department of Geosciences, Oregon State University. Additional information about the TFDD can be found at www.transboundarywaters.orst.edu.

PHOTOGRAPHS

PAGE 41, (UP LE) Bruno Morandi/Robert Harding/Getty Images; (UP RT) Mark Hanauer/CORBIS; (CTR) Bob Rowan; Progressive Image/CORBIS; (LO) Ed Kashi/CORBIS

CLIMATE pp. 42–45

CONSULTANTS

Edward Aguado
San Diego State University

William Burroughs

GRAPHICS

GLOBAL AIR TEMPERATURE CHANGES, 1850-2000: Reproduced by kind permission of the Climatic Research Unit

CLIMATE ZONES: Content from H.J. de Blij, P.O. Muller, and John Wiley & Sons, Inc.

SATELLITE IMAGES

Images originally created for the GLOBE program by NOAA's National Geophysical Data Center, Boulder, Colorado, U.S.A.

CLOUD COVER: International Satellite Cloud Climatology Project (ISCCP); National Aeronautics and Space Administration (NASA); Goddard Institute for Space Studies (GISS)

PRECIPITATION: Global Precipitation Climatology Project (GPCP); International Satellite Land Surface Climatology Project (ISLSCP)

SOLAR ENERGY: Earth Radiation Budget Experiment (ERBE); Greenhouse Effect Detection Experiment (GEDEX)

TEMPERATURE: National Center for Environmental Prediction (NCEP); National Center for Atmospheric Research (NCAR); National Weather Service (NWS)

PHOTOGRAPHS

PAGE 43, Gavin Hellier/Getty Images
PAGE 44 (LE), Oleg Nikishin/Getty Images; (RT), nagelestock.com/Alamy

CLIMATE CHANGE pp. 46–47

CONSULTANT

Michael Notaro
Center for Climatic Research, University of Wisconsin—Madison

GRAPHICS

AGES OF ICE AND HEAT: National Geographic Special Report: *Changing Climate*, 2008, p. 37

TEMPERATURE CHANGE: National Geographic Special Report: *Changing Climate*, 2008, pp. 36-37

SHRINKING ICE: NASA Goddard Space Flight Center

ETHICAL CONSIDERATIONS: Patz JA, Campbell-Lendrum D, Holloway T, Foley, JA. Impact of regional climate change on human health. *Nature* (cover) (2005); 438: 310-317.

PHOTOGRAPHS

PAGE 47, (LE) Manfred Mehlig/zefa/CORBIS; (RT) Dan Guravich/CORBIS

WEATHER EVENTS pp. 48–49

GRAPHICS

WEATHER: 2008 World Almanac; Encyclopedia Britannica Online (www.britannica.com); Dartmouth Flood Observatory (www.dartmouth.edu/~floods/); EM-DAT: Emergency Events Database (www.emdat.be); NASA (http://earthobservatory.nasa.gov); NOAA (www.spc.noaa.gov); Tornado Project (www.tornadoproject.com)

McGuire, Bill, Paul Burton, Christopher Kilburn, and Oliver Willetts. *World Atlas of Natural Hazards*. Arnold, Great Britain, 2004.

THUNDERSTORMS: Stuart Armstrong Illustration

LIGHTNING: NASA Marshall Space Flight Center Lightning Imaging Sensor (LIS) Instrument Team, Huntsville, Alabama

EL NIÑO: Blue Marble, NASA's Earth Observatory; NOAA; Encyclopedia Britannica Online (www.britannica.com)

PHOTOGRAPHS

PAGE 49, (UP) A & J Verkaik/CORBIS; (LO) Jim Reed/CORBIS

POPULATION pp. 50–53

CONSULTANTS

Carl Haub
Population Reference Bureau

Gregory Yetman
Center for International Earth Science Information Network (CIESIN), Columbia University

GENERAL REFERENCES

Center for International Earth Science Information Network (CIESIN), Columbia University: www.ciesin.org

World Migrant Stock: The 2005 Revision Population Database. United Nations Population Division

Population Reference Bureau: www.prb.org

United Nations World Population Prospects: The 2006 Revision Population Database: esa.un.org/unpp

World Urbanization Prospects: The 2007 Revision. United Nations Department of Economic and Social Affairs/Population Division. New York: United Nations, 2008.

GRAPHICS

POPULATION DENSITY: Center for International Earth Science Information Net work (CIESIN), Columbia University; and Centro Internacional de Agricultura Tropical (CIAT). 2005. Gridded Population of the World Version 3 (GPWv3). Palisades, NY: Socioeconomic Data and Applications Center (SEDAC), Columbia University. Available at http://sedac.ciesin.columbia.edu/gpw.

SATELLITE IMAGES

LIGHTS OF THE WORLD: Composite image: MODIS imagery; ETOPO-2 relief; NOAA/NGDC and DMSP lights at night data

PHOTOGRAPHS

PAGE 50, (LE) Gideon Mendel/CORBIS; (LE CTR) Owen Franken/CORBIS; (RT CTR) David R. Frazier/Danita Delimont.com; (LE) Ernst Haas/Getty Images

MEGACITIES pp. 54–55

GENERAL REFERENCES

United Nations, Department of Economic and Social Affairs, Population Division (2008). *World Urbanization Prospects: The 2007 Revision*. CD-ROM Edition—Data in digital form (POP/DB/WUP/Rev.2007)

PHOTOGRAPHS

PAGE 54, (LE) REUTERS/Darren Whiteside; (RT) REUTERS/Paulo Whitaker;
PAGE 55, (LE) Adrian Bradshaw/epa/CORBIS; (LE) Harald Sund/Getty Images

LANGUAGES pp. 56–57

CONSULTANT

M. Paul Lewis
SIL International

GRAPHICS

VOICES OF THE WORLD, HOW MANY SPEAK WHAT?, VANISHING LANGUAGES: Updated from *National Geographic Atlas of the World*, 8th ed., Washington, D.C.: The National Geographic Society, 2005.

EVOLUTION OF LANGUAGES: *National Geographic Almanac of Geography*, Washington, D.C.: The National Geographic Society, 2005.

LIVING LANGUAGES: Ethnologue: Languages of the World, www.ethnologue.com

PHOTOGRAPHS

PAGE 56, Patricio Estay/Nazca Pictures/drr.net

RELIGIONS pp. 58–59

CONSULTANTS

Frederic Kellogg
Religion Department, Emory & Henry College

Todd Johnson
Center for the Study of Global Christianity, Gordon-Conwell Theological Seminary

GENERAL REFERENCES

World Christian Database: Center for the Study of Global Christianity, Gordon-Conwell Theological Seminary www.worldchristiandatabase.org

CIA World Factbook: www.cia.gov/library/publications/the-world-factbook

GRAPHICS

MAJOR RELIGIONS: *National Geographic Atlas of the World*, 8th ed., Washington, D.C.: The National Geographic Society, 2005

RELIGIOSITY AND WEALTH: World Publics Welcome Global Trade — But Not Immigration, October 2007. Pew Global Attitudes Project, Pew Research Center.; And the Winner Is... *Atlantic Monthly*, March 2008

PHOTOGRAPHS

PAGE 59, (UP) National Geographic Photographer Jodi Cobb; (UP CTR) James L. Stanfield; (CTR) Tony Heiderer; (LO CTR) Thomas J. Abercrombie; (LO) Annie Griffiths Belt

HEALTH AND EDUCATION pp. 60–61

CONSULTANTS

Carlos Castillo-Salgado
Pan American Health Organization (PAHO)/ World Health Organization (WHO)

Ruth Levine
Center for Global Development

GENERAL REFERENCES

2006 Report on the Global AIDS Epidemic. World Health Organization and the Joint United Nations Programme on HIV/AIDS, 2006

Education Policy and Data Center: www.epdc.org

Global Burden of Disease Estimates. Geneva: World Health Organization, 2004

Human Development Report, 2007/2008. New York: United Nations Development Programme (UNDP), 2008

UN Millennium Development Goals: www.un.org/millenniumgoals

The State of the World's Children 2008. Table 5: Education. New York: UNICEF, 2008

The World Health Report 2006. Annex table 5. Selected national health accounts indicators. Geneva: World Health Organization, 2006

World Bank list of economies, 2008. Washington, D.C.: World Bank

World Health Organization: www.who.int

GRAPHICS

ACCESS TO IMPROVED SANITATION: Adapted from *WHO Water Supply and Sanitation Monitoring Mid-Term Report, 2004*.

DEVELOPING HUMAN CAPITAL: Adapted from Human Capital Projections developed by Education Policy and Data Center.

ECONOMY pp. 62–63

CONSULTANTS

Jamie Peck
University of Wisconsin—Madison

Richard R. Fix
World Bank

GENERAL REFERENCES

CIA World Factbook: www.cia.gov/library/publications/the-world-factbook

International Monetary Fund: www.imf.org

International Trade Statistics, 2007. Geneva, Switzerland: World Trade Organization

World Development Indicators, 2008, Washington, D.C.: World Bank

Note: GDP and GDP (PPP) data on this spread are from the IMF.

GRAPHICS

LABOR MIGRATION: *National Geographic Atlas of the World,* 8th ed., Washington, D.C.: The National Geographic Society, 2005

PHOTOGRAPHS

PAGE 63, Krafft Angerer/Getty Images

TRADE pp. 64–65

CONSULTANT

Daniel Griswold
Center for Trade Policy Studies, Cato Institute

GENERAL REFERENCES

International Monetary Fund: www.imf.org

International Trade Center (UNCTAD/WTO): www.intracen.org

International Trade Statistics, 2007, Geneva, Switzerland: World Trade Organization

United Nations Conference on Trade and Development: www.unctad.org

World Development Indicators, 2008, Washington, D.C.: World Bank

World Trade Organization: www.wto.org

GRAPHICS

GROWTH OF WORLD TRADE: World Trade Organization

GLOBALIZATION pp. 66–67

CONSULTANTS

Samantha King and Janet Pau
Global Business Policy Council, A.T. Kearney, Inc.

Shang-Jin Wei
Columbia Business School

GENERAL REFERENCES

Airports Council International: www.airports.org

Amiti, Mary, and Shang-Jin Wei, 2004, "Demystifying Outsourcing." *Finance & Development,* December 2004, pp. 36–39.

International Telecommunication Union: www.itu.int

World Investment Report, 2007. Geneva, Switzerland: United Nations Conference on Trade and Development.

GRAPHICS

TRANSNATIONAL CORPORATIONS: *World Investment Report, 2007.* Geneva, Switzerland: United Nations Conference on Trade and Development.

EXTREMES OF GLOBALIZATION: 2007 Globalization Index, A.T. Kearney, Inc.

GLOBALIZATION STATUS: 2007 Globalization Index, A.T. Kearney, Inc.
ECONOMIC INTEGRATION: UNCTAD FDI database, 2007; 2007 Globalization Index, A.T. Kearney, Inc.

PERSONAL CONTACT: International Telecommunications Union World Telecommunications Indicators, 2006; 2007 Globalization Index, A.T. Kearney, Inc.; Airports Council International: www.airports.org

TECHNOLOGICAL CONNECTIVITY: International Telecommunications Union World Telecommunications Indicators, 2006; 2007 Globalization Index, A.T. Kearney, Inc.

POLITICAL ENGAGEMENT: Balance of Payments CD-ROM, International Mondetary Fund, 2007; 2007 Globalization Index, A.T. Kearney, Inc.

IMPORTS IN BUSINESS SERVICES AS A SHARE OF GDP: Adapted and updated from Amiti, Mary, and Shang-Jin Wei, 2004, "Demystifying Outsourcing." *Finance & Development,* December 2004, pp. 36–39.

FOOD pp. 68–69

CONSULTANTS

Food and Agriculture Organization of the United Nations (FAO)

Kate Sebastian
The International Food Policy Research Institute (IFPRI)

Dirk Zeller
The Sea Around Us Project, University of British Columbia

GENERAL REFERENCES

Food and Agriculture Organization of the United Nations (FAO) Statistics Division: faostat.fao.org/faostat

GRAPHICS

MAIN MAP: IFPRI 2007 derived from cropland and pasture intensity data (Ramankutty 2002 & 2005) and FAO/IIASA (2000) climate data. Unpublished data.

GLOBAL CATCH FIGURES: Adapted and updated from Pauly, D., V. Christensen, S. Guénette, T. J. Pitcher, U. R. Sumaila, C. J. Walters, R. Watson, and D. Zeller. 2002. Towards sustainability in world fisheries. *Nature* 418:689-695.

LANDINGS: Data from The Sea Around Us Project, www.seaaroundus.org

WORLD CAPTURE FISHERIES AND AQUACULTURE PRODUCTION: Data from The Sea Around Us Project, www.seaaroundus.org

ENERGY pp. 70–71

CONSULTANT

Jean-Yves Garnier
International Energy Agency

GENERAL REFERENCES

American Wind Energy Association. *Global Wind Energy Market Report,* 2003

Bertani, Ruggero. World Geothermal Power Generation in the Period 2001–2005. *Geothermics,* Volume 34, Number 6, December 2005, pp. 651-690

http://pvresources.com

International Energy Agency (IEA) Statistics

Energy Information Administration, U.S. Department of Energy: www.eia.doe.gov

National Renewable Energy Laboratory: www.nrel.gov

Power Reactor Information System. International Atomic Energy Agency: www.iaea.org/programmes/a2/index.html

Survey of Energy Resources: Biomass. World Energy Council: www.worldenergy.org

The LNG industry. Groupe International des Importateurs de Gaz Naturel Liquefie, 2004

PHOTOGRAPHS

PAGE 70, (LE) Lester Lefkowitz/Getty Images; (LE CTR) Li Ga/CORBIS; (RT CTR) Shepard Sherbell/CORBIS; (RT) Farooq Khan/CORBIS
PAGE 71, (UP) David McGlynn/Getty Images; (LE) Courtesy National Renewable Energy Laboratory; (LE CTR) Mick Roessler/CORBIS; (RT CTR) Ryan Pyle/CORBIS; (RT) Bryan F. Peterson/CORBIS

MINERAL RESOURCES pp. 72–73

CONSULTANT

Philip Brown
University of Wisconsin—Madison

GENERAL REFERENCES

USGS Mineral Commodity Summaries, January 2008.

Mineral Fund Advisory, www.mineralprices.com

PHOTOGRAPHS

PAGE 73, (UP) Bohemian Nomad Picturemakers/CORBIS; (CTR) Peter Ginter/Getty Images; (LO) Claro Cortes IV/Reuters/CORBIS

MILITARY STRENGTH pp. 74–75

CONSULTANTS

Francis A. Galgano
Villanova University

H.R. McMaster, Bastian Giegerich, and Mark Fitzpatrick
International Institute for Strategic Studies

GENERAL REFERENCES

Hackett, James, ed., 2008. *The Military Balance 2008.* The International Institute for Strategic Studies, London: Arundel House, 2008.

GRAPHICS

MILITARY STRENGTH: Central Intelligence Agency, 2008. *The 2008 World Fact Book.*

Department of Defense (DoD), 2006. *The National Military Strategic Plan for the War on Terror.* Chairman of the Joint Chiefs of Staff. Washington, D.C.: U.S. Government Printing Office.

Galgano, F.A., 2007. A Geographic Analysis of Ungoverned Spaces. *The Pennsylvania Geographer.* 44(2): 67-90.

Keymer, Eleanor, ed., 2007. *Jane's World Armies.* 22nd ed., Surrey, UK: Jane's Information Group Limited.

Wertheim, Eric, 2006. *The Naval Institute Guide to Combat Fleets of the World.* Annapolis, Maryland: Naval Institute Press.

NUCLEAR POWERS MAP: Keymer, Eleanor, ed., 2007. *Jane's World Armies.* 22nd ed., Surrey, UK: Jane's Information Group Limited.

National Intelligence Council, 2007. *Iran: Nuclear Intentions and Capabilities.*

The Nuclear Information Project, http://www.fas.org/nuke/guide/summary.htm

Wertheim, Eric, 2006. *The Naval Institute Guide to Combat Fleets of the World.* Annapolis, Maryland: Naval Institute Press.

NATO MAP: Dorschner, J., and Radu Tudor, Questions remain after NATO summit. *Jane's Defense Weekly,* 16 April 2008, p. 18; *North Atlantic Treaty,* Washington D.C., 4 April 1949

PHOTOGRAPHS

PAGE 75, (UP) Check Six/Getty Images; (CTR) Check Six/Getty Images; (LO) Courtesy of Lockheed Martin

CONFLICT pp. 76–77

CONSULTANTS

Monty G. Marshall
Center for Systemic Peace and
Center for Global Policy, George Mason University

Christian Oxenboll and Henrik Pilgaard
United Nations High Commissioner for Refugees (UNHCR)

GENERAL REFERENCES

Center for Systemic Peace: www.systemicpeace.org

Globemaster U.S. Military Aviation Database: www.globemaster.de

Global Statistics. Internal Displacement Monitoring Centre (iDMC). 2007: www.internal-displacement.org

Marshall, Monty G., and Benjamin R. Cole. *Global Report on Conflict, Governance, and State Fragility 2008.* Foreign Policy Bulletin 18.1 (Winter 2008): 3-21. (Cambridge University Press Journals)

United Nations Peacekeeping: www.un.org/Depts/dpko

GRAPHICS

MILITARY DEPLOYMENTS AND BASES: GlobalSecurity.org

REFUGEES AND IDPs: The UN Refugee Agency (UNHCR): www.unhcr.org

WEAPONS POSSESSIONS: *Proliferation News and Resources.* Carnegie Endowment for International Peace. 2005: www.carnegieendowment.org/npp

TECHNOLOGY AND COMMUNICATION pp. 78–79

CONSULTANTS

Tim Kelly
Standardization Policy Division,
International Telecommunication Union

Sarah Parkes
Media Works Creative

GENERAL REFERENCES

International Telecommunication Union: www.itu.int

GRAPHICS

CENTERS OF TECHNOLOGICAL INNOVATION: *Human Development Report 2001,* United Nations Development Programme (source data updated by Human Development Report Office in 2006) and World Intellectual Property Organization.

MILESTONES IN TECHNOLOGY: Adapted from *Human Development Report 2001,* United Nations Development Programme.

THE DIGITAL DIVIDE: NG Maps. Source data provided by TeleGeography Research, a division of PriMetrica, Inc. (www.telegeography.com) and the International Telecommunication Union. The Fuller Projection map design is a trademark of the Buckminster Fuller Institute © 1938, 1967, and 1992. All rights reserved.

INTERNET pp. 80–81

CONSULTANTS

KC Claffy, Josh Polterock, and Brad Huffaker
Cooperative Association for Internet Data Analysis (CAIDA)

GENERAL REFERENCES

Cooperative Association for Internet Data Analysis (CAIDA): www.caida.org

International Telecommunication Union: www.itu.int

GRAPHICS

All images provided by the Cooperative Association for Internet Data Analysis (CAIDA), located at the San Diego Supercomputer Center (SDSC). CAIDA is a research unit of the University of California at San Diego (UCSD). URL: www.caida.org. Sponsors of this work include CAIDA Members, Cisco Systems, Department of Homeland Security (DHS, award NBCHC-070133) National Science Foundation (NSF, awards OCI-0137121, CNS-0433668, CNS-0311690, and CNS-0551542), and WIDE. Images © 2008 The Regents of the University of California.

MAPPING THE SPREAD OF A COMPUTER VIRUS: Cooperative Association for Internet Data Analysis (CAIDA) "Nyxem Virus Analysis." Copyright © 2006 The Regents of the University of California. All rights reserved. Used by permission.

GLOBAL INTERNET CONNECTIVITY: Cooperative Association for Internet Data Analysis (CAIDA) "Skitter" Internet Map, 2008. Copyright © 2008 The Regents of the University of California. All rights reserved. Used by permission.

WORLDWIDE DISTRIBUTION OF INTERNET RESOURCES: Adapted from Cooperative Association for Internet Data Analysis (CAIDA) "BGP Geopolitical Analysis Visualization." Copyright © 2006 The Regents of the University of California. All rights reserved. Used by permission.

ENVIRONMENTAL STRESSES pp. 82–83

CONSULTANT

Jane E. Barr
Associate, International Institute for Sustainable Development (IISD)

GENERAL REFERENCES

Acidification and eutrophication of developing country ecosystems. Swedish University of Agricultural Sciences (SLU), 2002

Centre of Documentation, Research and Experimentation on Accidental Water Pollution (Cedre): www.le-cedre.fr

EM-DAT: The OFDA/CRED International Disaster Database. Université Catholique de Louvain, Brussels, Belgium: www.em-dat.be

Energy Information Administration. U.S. Department of Energy: www.eia.doe.gov

Global Environment Outlook: Environment for Development (GEO-4). United Nations Environment Programme, 2007

Global Forest Resources Assessment. Forestry Department of the Food and Agriculture Organization of the United Nations, 2005

Natural Resources Conservation Service: www.nrcs.usda.gov

United Nations Environment Programme-World Conservation and Monitoring Program (UNEP-WCMC): www.unep-wcmc.org

GRAPHICS

CARBON EMISSIONS GRAPHS (MAIN MAP): *Carbon Dioxide Emissions - Total (UNFCCC-CDIAC), 2007.* United Nations Framework Convention on Climate Change and Carbon Dioxide Information Analysis Center (UNFCCC and CDIAC). GEO Data Portal, http://geodata.grid.unep.ch/

LAND DEGRADATION AND DESERTIFICATION: *The challenge of degraded land and its remediation,* Fig. 1.1 (after Oldeman et al. 1990, FAO-AGL 2000). Genske, Dieter, ETH-Zurich. Via www.contaminated-land.org

WATER SCARCITY: *Insights from the Comprehensive Assessment of Water Management in Agriculture,* International Water Management Institute (IWMI), Colombo, Sri Lanka, 2006.

CARBON EMISSIONS, BY REGION (SIDEBAR): *Global Environment Outlook: environment for development (GEO-4).* United Nations Environment Programme, 2007, p. 61. http://www.unep.org/geo/geo4/

CARBON EMISSIONS, BY SOURCE (SIDEBAR): National Geographic Special Report: *Changing Climate,* 2008, map insert.

SATELLITE IMAGES

DEPLETION OF THE OZONE LAYER: Ozone Processing Team at NASA/Goddard Space Flight Center

PHOTOGRAPHS

PAGE 83, (UP) Andy Caulfield/Getty Images; (LO) Yann Arthus-Bertrand/CORBIS

WILDLANDS pp. 84–85

CONSULTANTS

John Morrison
World Wildlife Fund (WWF)

GRAPHICS

ECOLOGICAL FOOTPRINT GRAPHS: *WWF Living Planet Report,* 2006, pp. 14–15.

HUMAN FOOTPRINT AND LAST OF THE WILD MAPS: Wildlife Conservation Society

PHOTOGRAPHS

PAGE 84, (UP) Tim Davis/CORBIS, (LO LE) Ron Sanford/CORBIS, (LO RT) Christopher Scott/Getty Images

BIODIVERSITY pp. 86–89

CONSULTANTS

Daniel Brito
Conservation International

John Morrison
World Wildlife Fund (WWF)

GENERAL REFERENCES

Conservation International: www.biodiversityhotspots.org

International Union for Conservation of Nature and Natural Resources (IUCN): www.iucnredlist.org

GRAPHICS

ECOREGIONS: Terrestrial Ecoregions of the World were developed by D.M. Olson, E. Dinerstein, E.D. Wikramanayake, N.D. Burgess, G.V.N. Powell, E.C. Underwood, J.A. D'Amico, I. Itoua, H.E. Strand, J.C. Morrison, C.J. Loucks, T.F. Allnutt, T.H. Ricketts, Y. Kura, J.F. Lamoreux, W.W. Wettengel, P. Hedao, K.R. Kassem, World Wildlife Fund. Marine Ecoregions of the World (MEOW) were developed by the MEOW Working Group, co-chaired by The Nature Conservancy and the World Wildlife Fund (Mark Spalding, Helen Fox, Gerald Allen, Nick Davidson, Zach

Ferdana, Max Finlayson, Ben Halpern, Miguel Jorge, Al Lombana, Sara Lourie, Kirsten Martin, Edmund McManus, Jennifer Molnar, Kate Newman, Cheri Recchia, James Robertson).

World Wildlife Fund (WWF) and the Nature Conservancy: www.worldwildlife.org/wildworld/

SPECIES DIVERSITY: Biodiversity. NG Maps for National Geographic Magazine, February 1999.

THE GLOBAL 200: A representation approach to conserving the Earth's most biologically valuable ecoregions. *Conservation Biology,* Volume 12: 502-515. Olson, D. M., Dinerstein, E. (1998).

PHOTOGRAPHS

PAGE 87, Tim Laman

PROTECTED AREAS pp. 90-91

GENERAL REFERENCES

Antarctic Protected Areas Information Archive: www.era.gs/apa

UNEP-WCMC, World Database on Protected Areas: www.unep-wcmc.org/wdpa/

United Nations Educational, Scientific and Cultural Organization (UNESCO) World Heritage Centre, Official Site: whc.unesco.org

PHOTOGRAPHS

PAGE 91, (UP) Skip Brown/ NationalGeographicStock.com; **(CTR)** Robert Francis/ Getty Images; **(LO)** Frans Lanting/CORBIS

WORLD HERITAGE SITES pp. 92-97

GENERAL REFERENCES

United Nations Educational, Scientific and Cultural Organization (UNESCO) World Heritage Centre, Official Site: whc.unesco.org
World Heritage, 2007-2008, NG Maps

PHOTOGRAPHS

PAGE 93, (UP) Frans Lanting/CORBIS; **(CTR)** Livio Sinibaldi/Getty Images; **(LO)** Mark Laricchia/CORBIS
PAGE 95, (UP) John Warburton-Lee/ DanitaDelimont.com/drr.net; **(LO)** Robert Harding Picture Library Ltd./Alamy;
PAGE 96, Pete Oxford/Minden Pictures/Getty Images
PAGES 96-97 Panoramic Images/Getty Images

ADDITIONAL CONTRIBUTORS, WORLD THEMATIC SECTION

Robert Aiken (Environmental Stresses)
Bill Buckingham (data processing)
Richard Connor (Environmental Stresses)
Chelsea Zillmer (Climate, Weather Events)

See also: contributing writers, page 416.

ANTARCTICA pp. 250-253

Antarctic Digital Database, British Antarctic Survey
www.add.scar.org

Jill E. Caldwell
National Geomagnetism Program, U.S. Geological Survey

National Geographic Maps

WORLD OCEANS pp. 254-269

ETOPO2 database
National Geophysical Data Center (NGDC)

Tibor G. Tóth
Map relief

LIMITS OF THE OCEANS AND SEAS

Adam J. Kerr
International Hydrographic Management Consulting

SPACE pp. 270-283

OVERALL CONSULTANT

Alexei V. Filippenko
Department of Astronomy, University of California, Berkeley

THE MOON pp. 272-275

Paul D. Spudis
Lunar and Planetary Institute, Houston, Texas

THE SOLAR SYSTEM pp. 276-277

Lucy McFadden
University of Maryland, College Park

THE PLANETS pp. 278-279

Henry Kline
NASA Jet Propulsion Laboratory (JPL)

MARS pp. 280-281

Damond Benningfield
StarDate radio series

THE UNIVERSE pp. 282-283

Todd J. Henry
Georgia State University

Edmund Bertschinger
Massachusetts Institute of Technology

Donald P. Schneider
Pennsylvania State University

Marc Postman
Space Telescope Science Institute (STScI)

Christopher D. Impey
University of Arizona

R. Brent Tully
University of Hawai'i

August E. Evrard
University of Michigan

FLAGS AND FACTS pp. 284-301

Carl Haub
Population Reference Bureau

Whitney Smith
Flag Research Center

For a detailed key to the Flags and Facts section, see page 301.

SPECIAL FLAGS pp. 302-303

Whitney Smith
Flag Research Center

GEOGRAPHIC COMPARISONS pp. 308-309

John Kammerer
National Geospatial-Intelligence Agency (NGA)

George Sharman
NOAA/NESDIS/NGDC

Peter H. Gleick
Pacific Institute for Studies in Development, Environment, and Security

R.L. Fisher
Scripps Institution of Oceanography

Philip Micklin
Western Michigan University

Physical and Political Maps

Bureau of the Census, U.S. Department of Commerce
Bureau of Land Management, U.S. Department of the Interior
Central Intelligence Agency (CIA)
National Geographic Maps
National Geospatial-Intelligence Agency (NGA)
National Park Service, U.S. Department of the Interior
Office of the Geographer, U.S. Department of State
U.S. Board on Geographic Names (BGN)
U.S. Geological Survey, U.S. Department of the Interior

Principal Reference Sources

REGIONAL SPREADS

PROTECTED AREAS AND WORLD HERITAGE SITES: UNEP-WCMC, World Database on Protected Areas: www.unep-wcmc.org/wdpa/; United Nations Educational, Scientific and Cultural Organization (UNESCO) World Heritage Centre, Official Site: whc.unesco.org

URBANIZATION AND LARGEST CITIES: Population Reference Bureau: www.prb.org; United Nations, Department of Economic and Social Affairs, Population Division (2008). *World Urbanization Prospects: The 2007 Revision.* CD-ROM Edition—Data in digital form (POP/DB/WUP/Rev.2007)

NATURAL LAND COVER DATA: Tom Patterson, US National Park Service: http://www.shadedrelief.com/natural/

GENERAL SOURCES

Columbia Gazetteer of the World Online
www.columbiagazetteer.org

Human Development Report, 2007/2008. New York: United Nations Development Programme (UNDP), Oxford University Press, 2007

International Trade Statistics, 2007. Geneva, Switzerland: World Trade Organization

McKnight, Tom L. *Physical Geography: A Landscape Appreciation.* 5th ed. Upper Saddle River, New Jersey: Prentice Hall, 1996

National Geographic Atlas of the World, 8th ed., Washington, D.C.: The National Geographic Society, 2005

National Geographic Collegiate Atlas of the World, Washington, D.C.: The National Geographic Society, 2006

National Geographic Family Reference Atlas, 2nd ed., Washington, D.C.: The National Geographic Society, 2007

Strahler, Alan and Arthur Strahler. *Physical Geography: Science and Systems of the Human Environment.* 2nd ed., John Wiley & Sons, Inc., 2002

Tarbuck, Edward J. and Frederick K. Lutgens. *Earth: An Introduction to Physical Geology.* 7th ed. Upper Saddle River, New Jersey: Prentice Hall, 2002

World Development Indicators, 2007. Washington, D.C.: World Bank

The World Factbook 2008. Washington, D.C.: Central Intelligence Agency, 2008

The World Health Report 2007. Geneva: World Health Organization, 2007

World Investment Report, 2007. New York and Geneva: United Nations Conference on Trade and Development, 2007

Central Intelligence Agency
www.cia.gov

CIESIN
www.ciesin.org

Conservation International
www.conservation.org

Energy Information Agency
www.eia.doe.gov

Food and Agriculture Organization of the UN
www.fao.org

International Monetary Fund
www.imf.org

National Aeronautics and Space Administration
www.nasa.gov

National Oceanic and Atmospheric Administration
www.noaa.gov

National Climatic Data Center
www.ncdc.noaa.gov

National Geophysical Data Center
www.ngdc.noaa.gov

National Park Service
www.nps.gov

National Renewable Energy Laboratory
www.nrel.gov

Population Reference Bureau
www.prb.org

United Nations
www.un.org

UN Conference on Trade and Development
www.unctad.org

UN Development Programme
www.undp.org

UN Educational, Cultural, and Scientific Organization
www.unesco.org

UNESCO Institute for Statistics
www.uis.unesco.org

UNEP-WCMC
www.unep-wcmc.org

UN Millennium Development Goals
www.un.org/millenniumgoals

UN Population Division
www.unpopulation.org

UN Refugee Agency
www.unhcr.org

UN Statistics Division
unstats.un.org

U.S. Board on Geographic Names
geonames.usgs.gov

U.S. Bureau of Economic Analysis
www.bea.gov

U.S. Census Bureau
www.census.gov

U.S. Geological Survey
www.usgs.gov

World Bank
www.worldbank.org

World Gazetteer
www.world-gazetteer.com

World Health Organization
www.who.int

World Trade Organization
www.wto.org

WWF
www.worldwildlife.org

UNESCO World Heritage Information

DONATIONS TO THE WORLD HERITAGE FUND The granting of international assistance from the World Heritage Fund to finance World Heritage conservation projects is an important tool established by the convention. If you would like to participate in conserving World Heritage, please send a contribution. Please indicate that the contribution is a donation to the World Heritage Fund.

Donations in USD should be made to:
UNESCO account: 949-1-191558
CHASE JP MORGAN BANK
International Money Transfer Division
4 Metrotech Center, Brooklyn
New York, NY 11245, USA
Swift code: CHASUS 33-ABA: 0210-0002-1

Donations in EUR should be made to:
UNESCO account: 30003-03301-00037291909-97
SOCIETE GENERALE
Paris Seine Amont
10 rue Thénard
75005 Paris, France
Swift code: SOGEFRPPAFS

UNESCO WORLD HERITAGE CENTRE The map of World Heritage properties is produced each year by the UNESCO World Heritage Centre. If you would like to receive more information about the World Heritage Convention and World Heritage conservation, please contact:

UNESCO World Heritage Centre
7, place de Fontenoy, 75352 Paris 07 SP, France
Telephone: + 33 (0)1 45 68 18 76
Fax: + 33 (0)1 45 68 55 70
E-mail: wh-info@unesco.org

Explore World Heritage sites on the Internet at
http://whc.unesco.org

World Heritage donations online:
http://whc.unesco.org/en/donation/

Photographs

TITLE PAGE
2, Melissa McManus/Getty Images
2-3, Pete Turner/Getty Images

TABLE OF CONTENTS
6, InterNetwork Media/Getty Images
7 (UP), Ty Allison/Getty Images
7 (CTR), Stephen Simpson/Getty Images
7 (LO), Murat Taner/Getty Images
8 (UP), Steve Allen/Getty Images
8 (LO), Keren Su/Getty Images
8-9, Panoramic Images/Getty Images
9, Doug Allan/Getty Images

GALLERY
10-11, Ron Watts/CORBIS
12-13, BL Images Ltd./Alamy
14-15, Ralph Lee Hopkins/NationalGeographicStock.com

WORLD: OPENER
21 (UP), Jean-Pierre Lescourret/CORBIS
21 (UP CTR), Frans Lanting/CORBIS
21 (LO CTR), Hans Strand/CORBIS
21 (LO), Jami Tarris/CORBIS
21 (RT), Bob Krist/CORBIS

WORLD: LANDFORMS
34 (LE), Diehm/Getty Images
34 (RT), Frank Krahmer/Getty Images
35 (LE), John W. Banagan/Getty Images
35 (CTR), Momatiuk - Eastcott/CORBIS
35 (RT), Jeremy Woodhouse/Getty Images

WORLD: LAND COVER
36 (UP LE), Tom and Pat Leeson/Photo Researchers, Inc.
36 (UP RT), Michael Nichols/NationalGeographicStock.com
36 (LO-A), Stephen J. Krasemann/Photo Researchers, Inc.
36 (LO-B), Rod Planck/Photo Researchers, Inc.
36 (LO-C), James Steinberg/Photo Researchers, Inc.
36 (LO-D), Matthew C. Hansen
36 (LO-E), Gregory G. Dimijian/Photo Researchers, Inc.
36 (LO-F), Dr. Sharon G. Johnson
36 (LO-G), Georg Gerster/Photo Researchers, Inc.
37 (A), Rod Planck/Photo Researchers, Inc.
37 (B), Jim Richardson
37 (C), George Steinmetz
37 (D), Steve McCurry
37 (E), B. and C. Alexander/Photo Researchers, Inc.
37 (F), Robert Estall/CORBIS
37 (G), James Randklev/Getty Images

WORLD: OCEANS
39 (UP LE), Kaz Mori/Getty Images
39 (UP RT), Chris Newbert/Minden Pictures/NationalGeographicStock.com
39 (CTR), Brandon Cole/Getty Images
39 (LO), Roger Coulam/Alamy

WORLD: FRESH WATER
41 (UP LE), Bruno Morandi/Robert Harding/Getty Images
41 (UP RT), Mark Hanauer/CORBIS
41 (CTR), Bob Rowan; Progressive Image/CORBIS
41 (LO), Ed Kashi/CORBIS

WORLD: CLIMATE
43, Gavin Hellier/Getty Images
44 (LE), Oleg Nikishin/Getty Images
44 (RT), nagelestock.com/Alamy

WORLD: CLIMATE CHANGE
47 (LE), Manfred Mehlig/zefa/CORBIS
47 (RT), Dan Guravich/CORBIS

WORLD: WEATHER EVENTS
49 (UP), A & J Verkaik/CORBIS
49 (LO), Jim Reed/CORBIS

WORLD: POPULATION
50 (LE), Gideon Mendel/CORBIS
50 (LE CTR), Owen Franken/CORBIS
50 (RT CTR), David R. Frazier/Danita Delimont.com
50 (RT), Ernst Haas/Getty Images

WORLD: MEGACITIES
54 (LE), REUTERS/Darren Whiteside
54 (RT), REUTERS/Paulo Whitaker
55 (LE), Adrian Bradshaw/epa/CORBIS
55 (RT), Harald Sund/Getty Images

WORLD: LANGUAGES
56, Patricio Estay/Nazca Pictures/drr.net

WORLD: RELIGIONS
59 (UP), National Geographic Photographer Jodi Cobb
59 (UP CTR), James L. Stanfield
59 (CTR), Tony Heiderer
59 (LO CTR), Thomas J. Abercrombie
59 (LO), Annie Griffiths Belt

WORLD: ECONOMY
63, Krafft Angerer/Getty Images

WORLD: ENERGY
70 (LE), Lester Lefkowitz/Getty Images
70 (LE CTR), Li Ga/CORBIS
70 (RT CTR), Shepard Sherbell/CORBIS
70 (RT), Farooq Khan/CORBIS
71 (UP), David McGlynn/Getty Images
71 (LE), Courtesy National Renewable Energy Laboratory
71 (LE CTR), Mick Roessler/CORBIS
71 (RT CTR), Ryan Pyle/CORBIS
71 (RT), Bryan F. Peterson/CORBIS

WORLD: MINERAL RESOURCES
73 (UP), Bohemian Nomad Picturemakers/CORBIS
73 (CTR), Peter Ginter/Getty Images
73 (LO), Claro Cortes IV/Reuters/CORBIS

WORLD: MILITARY STRENGTH
75 (UP), Check Six/Getty Images
75 (CTR), Check Six/Getty Images
75 (LO), Courtesy of Lockheed Martin

WORLD: ENVIRONMENTAL STRESSES
83 (UP), Andy Caulfield/Getty Images
83 (LO), Yann Arthus-Bertrand/CORBIS

WORLD: WILDLANDS
84 (UP), Tim Davis/CORBIS
84 (LO LE), Ron Sanford/CORBIS
84 (LO RT), Christopher Scott/Getty Images

WORLD: BIODIVERSITY
87, Tim Laman

WORLD: PROTECTED AREAS
91 (UP), Skip Brown/NationalGeographicStock.com
91 (CTR), Robert Francis/Getty Images
91 (LO), Frans Lanting/CORBIS

WORLD: WORLD HERITAGE SITES
93 (UP), Frans Lanting/CORBIS
93 (CTR), Livio Sinibaldi/Getty Images
93 (LO), Mark Laricchia/CORBIS
95 (UP), John Warburton-Lee/DanitaDelimont.com/drr.net
95 (LO), Robert Harding Picture Library Ltd./Alamy
96, Pete Oxford/Minden Pictures/Getty Images
96-97, Panoramic Images/Getty Images

NORTH AMERICA
99 (UP), George H.H. Huey/CORBIS
99 (UP CTR), Douglas Peebles/CORBIS
99 (LO CTR), Bob Krist/CORBIS
99 (LO), Frans Lanting/CORBIS
99 (RT), Panoramic Images/Getty Images
106 (UP), Hemis/Alamy
106 (LO LE), Galen Rowell/Mountain Light/Alamy
106 (LO RT), Richard T. Nowitz/CORBIS
107 (UP), Daryl Benson/Getty Images
107 (LO), Yves Marcoux/Getty Images
110, George Steinmetz/CORBIS
111 (UP), Richard Cummins/CORBIS
111 (CTR), David Muench/CORBIS
111 (LO), Kenneth Garrett/DanitaDelimont.com/drr.net
114, Macduff Everton/Getty Images
115 (UP), Ralph Lee Hopkins/NationalGeographicStock.com
115 (CTR), Walter Bibikow/Getty Images
115 (LO), Free Agents Limited/CORBIS
116 (UP), John Noble/CORBIS
116 (LO), Oyvind Martinsen/Alamy
117 (UP), Robert Fried/Alamy
117 (LO), Brandon Cole Marine Photography/Alamy
118 (UP), James L. Stanfield
118 (CTR), Steve Winter
118 (LO LE), Bob Krist/CORBIS
118 (LO RT), Peter Adams/Getty Images
119 (UP), Mark Lewis/Alamy
119 (CTR), James P. Blair
119 (LO), Jon Arnold Images Ltd./Alamy
120 (UP), Bob Krist/CORBIS
120 (CTR), George H.H. Huey/drr.net
120 (LO), Wolfgang Kaehler/CORBIS
121 (UP), Paul Thompson Images/Alamy
121 (LO), Neil Emmerson/Robert Harding World Imagery/CORBIS

SOUTH AMERICA
125 (UP), Laurie Chamberlain/CORBIS
125 (UP CTR), imagebroker/Alamy
125 (LO CTR), Paulo Fridman/CORBIS
125 (LO), Momatiuk - Eastcott/CORBIS
125 (RT), eStock Photo/Alamy
132 (UP), Pete Turner/Getty Images
132 (LO LE), Paolo Gasparini/Fundación Villanueva
132 (LO RT), O. Louis Mazzatenta
133 (UP), Robert Caputo/Aurora/Getty Images
133 (LO), Kevin Schafer/Getty Images
134 (UP LE), Tui De Roy/Minden Pictures Collection/Getty Images
134 (UP RT), L. Scott Shelton
134 (LO LE), David Noton/Getty Images
134 (LO RT), EVARISTO SA/AFP/Getty Images
136 (UP), Jeremy Woodhouse/Getty Images
136 (LO LE), Peter Adams/Getty Images
136 (LO RT), Hiroyuki Matsumoto/Getty Images
137 (UP), Angelo Cavalli/Getty Images
137 (LO), Paulo Fridman/CORBIS
138 (UP), James L. Amos/CORBIS
138 (CTR), Atlantide Phototravel/CORBIS
138 (LO), DEA/G. Kiner/drr.net
139 (UP LE), Cesare Gerolimetto/Grand Tour/CORBIS
139 (LO LE), Sebastien Burel/Shutterstock
139 (RT), Chad Ehlers/Alamy

EUROPE
141 (UP), Silwen Randebrock/Alamy
141 (UP CTR), Art Kowalsky/Alamy
141 (LO CTR), Kenneth Geiger, NGS
141 (LO), David Sanger Photography/Alamy
141 (RT), Dan Tucker/Getty Images
148 (UP LE), Aldo Pavan/Grand Tour/CORBIS
148 (UP RT), Hubert Stadler/CORBIS
148 (CTR), Jon Sparks/CORBIS
148 (LO LE), Altrendo Travel/Getty Images
148 (LO RT), Peter Adams/Getty Images
149, De Agostini/Getty Images
150 (UP LE), Sandro Vannini/CORBIS
150 (UP CTR), Atlantide Phototravel/CORBIS
150 (RT), Douglas Pearson/CORBIS
150 (LO LE), Richard Cummins/CORBIS
151, Guy Edwardes/Getty Images
152 (UP), Graeme Norways/Getty Images
152 (CTR), Joao Paulo/Getty Images
152 (LO LE), John W. Banagan/Getty Images
152 (LO RT), Alan Copson/JAI/CORBIS
153 (UP), Marco Simoni/Getty Images
153 (LO), Peter Adams/Getty Images
154 (UP LE), Tom Mackie/Getty Images
154 (UP RT), Bob Krist/CORBIS
154 (LO), Steven Vidler/Eurasian Press/CORBIS
155 (UP), Jose Fuste Raga/zefa/CORBIS
155 (LO), Edyta Pawlowska/iStockphoto.com
156 (UP LE), JTB/drr.net
156 (UP CTR), Jorg Greuel/Getty Images
156 (UP RT), DEA/C. Sappa/Getty Images
156 (LO LE), Panoramic Images/Getty Images
156 (LO RT), Jose Fuste Raga/zefa/CORBIS
157, Ingolf Pompe/Getty Images
158 (UP LE), Keren Su/CORBIS
158 (UP CTR), DEA/W. Buss/Getty Images
158 (UP RT), Raymond Gehman/CORBIS
158 (LO), Stanislav Bokach/Shutterstock
159, Renaud Visage/Getty Images
160 (UP LE), Robert Harding/Getty Images
160 (UP RT), Douglas Pearson/CORBIS
160 (LO LE), Iuri/Shutterstock
160 (LO RT), Joel W. Rogers/CORBIS
161, Herbert Spichtinger/zefa/CORBIS
162 (UP LE), Danin Tulic/Shutterstock
162 (UP RT), Danny Lehman/CORBIS
162 (CTR), Bojan Brecelj/CORBIS
162 (LO), Walter Bibikow/Getty Images
163 (UP), Gavin Hellier/JAI/CORBIS
163 (LO), Jose Fuste Raga/CORBIS
164 (UP LE), Photographer/Alamy
164 (UP RT), ML Sinibaldi/CORBIS
164 (LO), Maynard Owen Williams/National Geographic Collection/Getty Images
165 (LE), Atlantide Phototravel/CORBIS
165 (CTR), Robert Everts/Getty Images
165 (RT), Jean-Pierre Lescourret/CORBIS
166 (UP), Andreas Gebert/dpa/CORBIS
166 (CTR), Andrey Grinyov/iStockphoto.com
166 (LO), Peter Adams/Getty Images
167 (UP), Jean-Pierre Lescourret/CORBIS
167 (CTR), Harald Sund/Getty Images
167 (LO), Dmytro Korolov/Shutterstock
168 (UP LE), Gavin Hellier/Robert Harding World Imagery/CORBIS
168 (UP RT), Ellen Rooney/Getty Images
168 (LO LE), AFP/Getty Images
168 (LO RT), Vladimir Medvedev/Shutterstock
169 (UP), Goodshoot/CORBIS
169 (LO), David Turnley/CORBIS
170, Franz-Marc Frei/CORBIS
171 (LE), De Agostini/Getty Images
171 (RT), Chris Hellier/CORBIS

ASIA
173 (UP), Floris Leeuwenberg/CORBIS
173 (UP CTR), Hemis/CORBIS
173 (LO CTR), Hemis/CORBIS
173 (LO), Liu Liqun/CORBIS
173 (RT), Best View Stock/Alamy
180 (UP), Yusuf Anil Akduygu/iStockphoto.com
180 (LO LE), Yoray Liberman/Getty Images
180 (LO RT), David Turnley/CORBIS
181 (UP), Atlantide Phototravel/CORBIS
181 (LO LE), Caro/Alamy
181 (LO RT), Stephane Victor/Lonely Planet Images/Getty Images
182, GPO/Getty Images
183 (UP LE), Fred Friberg/Robert Harding World Imagery/Getty Images
183 (LO LE), Ivan Vdovin/JAI/CORBIS
183 (RT), CJPhoto/Shutterstock
184 (UP), Jens Buttner/dpa/CORBIS
184 (UP CTR), Mike Nelson/epa/CORBIS
184 (LO CTR), James L. Stanfield
184 (LO), Tor Eigeland/Alamy
185 (UP), Michele Falzone/JAI/CORBIS
185 (LO), Michele Falzone/JAI/CORBIS
186 (UP), Nico Tondini/Robert Harding/drr.net
186 (CTR), Nik Wheeler/CORBIS
186 (LO), Targa/age fotostock
187, Michael S. Yamashita/CORBIS
188 (UP), Ali Majdfar
188 (CTR), Kazuyoshi Nomachi/CORBIS
188 (LO), Jose Fuste Raga/CORBIS
189 (UP), Christina Gascoigne/Robert Harding World Imagery/Getty Images
189 (LO), George Steinmetz/CORBIS
190 (LE), Manca Juvan/CORBIS
190 (CTR), JTB/drr.net
190 (RT), Jane Sweeney/JAI/CORBIS
191, Robert Harding/drr.net
192 (UP), Ivan Vdovin/age fotostock
192 (LO LE), Michele Falzone/JAI/CORBIS
192 (LO RT), Michele Falzone/JAI/CORBIS
193 (LE), Therin-Weise/age fotostock
193 (RT), Jeremy Horner Images/drr.net
194 (UP LE), Win Initiative/Getty Images
194 (UP RT), Alan Kearney/Getty Images
194 (LO), David Sanger/Getty Images
195 (LE), Jon Hicks/CORBIS
195 (UP RT), xyno6/iStockphoto.com
195 (LO RT), Robert Harding World Imagery/CORBIS
196 (UP), Michel Renaudeau/age fotostock
196 (CTR), Guiziou Franck/age fotostock
196 (LO LE), Martin Beaulieu/drr.net
196 (LO RT), IMAGEMORE Co., Ltd./Getty Images
197, Christophe Boisvieux/CORBIS
199 (LE), Gavin Hellier/Getty Images
199 (CTR), Radius Images/Alamy
199 (UP RT), Li Liqun/CORBIS
199 (LO RT), Harald Sund/Getty Images
200 (UP), Alain Nogues/CORBIS
200 (LO), TongRo Image Stock/Inmagine
201 (UP), Kim Jae-Hwan/AFP/Getty Images
201 (LO), Christophe Boisvieux/CORBIS
202 (UP), PictureNet/CORBIS
202 (CTR), Free Agents Limited/CORBIS
202 (LO), Tibor Bognar/CORBIS
203 (LE), John Van Hasselt/CORBIS SYGMA
203 (RT), Akira Kaede/Getty Images
204 (UP LE), John Wang/Getty Images
204 (LO LE), Cory Langley/CORBIS
204 (RT), Carson Ganci/Design Pics/CORBIS
205 (LE), Angelo Cavalli/age fotostock
205 (RT), Paul Chesley/NationalGeographicStock.com
206 (LE), Robert Harding/Getty Images
206 (RT), PCL/Alamy
207 (UP LE), National Geographic Photographer Michael Nichols
207 (UP RT), Jerry Alexander/Getty Images
207 (LO), Theo Allofs/CORBIS

AFRICA
209 (UP), Martin Harvey/Alamy
209 (UP CTR), Kazuyoshi Nomachi/CORBIS
209 (LO CTR), blickwinkel/Alamy
209 (LO), Yann Arthus-Bertrand/CORBIS
209 (RT), AWPhoto/Alamy
216 (UP), David Sanger/Getty Images
216 (LO LE), Jean Du Boisberranger/Getty Images
216 (LO RT), Paul Hardy/CORBIS
217 (UP), Wolfgang Kaehler/CORBIS
217 (LO), Kazuyoshi Nomachi/CORBIS
218 (LE), Volker Kreinacke/iStockphoto.com
218 (RT), Aldo Pavan/Grand Tour/CORBIS
219 (LE), Martin Gray/NationalGeographicStock.com
219 (RT), Bettmann/CORBIS
220 (UP), Bruno Morandi/Getty Images
220 (CTR), Atlantide Phototravel/CORBIS
220 (LO LE), Gavin Hellier/Robert Harding World Imagery/Getty Images
220 (LO RT), Werner Forman/CORBIS
221, Christopher Herwig/Aurora/Getty Images
222 (UP), Jam.si/Shutterstock
222 (CTR), Paul Almasy/CORBIS
222 (LO), Franz Aberham/Getty Images
223 (UP), Atlantide Phototravel/CORBIS
223 (LO), Martin Harvey/CORBIS
224 (UP), National Geographic Photographer Michael Nichols
224 (CTR), Martin Harvey/Alamy
224 (LO LE), National Geographic Photographer Michael Nichols
224 (LO RT), Steve Bloom Images/Alamy
225 (UP), Konrad Wothe/Minden Pictures/Getty Images
225 (LO), Frans Lanting/CORBIS
226 (UP LE), Gavin Hellier/JAI/CORBIS
226 (LO LE), Ariadne Van Zandbergen/Lonely Planet Images/Getty Images
226 (RT), Hugh Sitton/zefa/CORBIS
227 (LE), Art Wolfe/Danita Delimont Agency/drr.net
227 (UP RT), Daryl Balfour/Getty Images
227 (LO RT), Tom and Pat Leeson/drr.net
228 (UP), Tibor Bognar/CORBIS
228 (CTR), Frans Lanting/CORBIS
228 (LO LE), Gallo Images/CORBIS
228 (LO RT), Christopher Scott/Getty Images
229 (UP), Frans Lanting/CORBIS
229 (LO), Frans Lanting/CORBIS
230, Justin Guariglia
231 (UP), Matt Lambert/Getty Images
231 (LO), Ralph Lee Hopkins/NationalGeographicStock.com

AUSTRALIA AND OCEANIA
233 (UP), David Wall/Alamy
233 (UP CTR), Chee-Onn Leong/Shutterstock
233 (LO CTR), Theo Allofs/CORBIS
233 (LO), Ron Watts/CORBIS
233 (RT), Horizon International Images Limited/Alamy
242 (UP), Yann Arthus-Bertrand/CORBIS
242 (LO LE), Frans Lanting/CORBIS
242 (LO RT), Barry Lewis/CORBIS
243 (UP), Dr. Paddy Ryan
243 (LO), Steven Vidler/Eurasia Press/CORBIS

ANTARCTICA
251 (UP), Maria Stenzel
251 (UP CTR), Momatiuk - Eastcott/CORBIS
251 (LO CTR), Gordon Wiltsie/NationalGeographicStock.com
251 (LO), Momatiuk - Eastcott/CORBIS
251 (RT), Frans Lanting/CORBIS

OCEANS
255 (UP), David Pu'u/CORBIS
255 (UP CTR), Richard Broadwell/Beateworks/CORBIS
255 (LO CTR), Henri Bureau/Sygma/CORBIS
255 (LO), Jeff Hunter/Getty Images
255 (RT), Bill Ross/CORBIS

SPACE
270-271, NASA, ESA, S. Beckwith (STScI), and The Hubble Heritage Team (STScI/AURA)
271 (UP), NASA
271 (UP CTR), NASA/ESA and E. Karkoschka (University of Arizona)
271 (LO CTR), NASA/JPL
271 (LO), NASA, ESA, M.J. Jee and H. Ford (Johns Hopkins University)
273, Clementine Topographic Map of the Moon: Courtesy of the Lunar and Planetary Institute, Houston, Texas
275, Clementine Topographic Map of the Moon: Courtesy of the Lunar and Planetary Institute, Houston, Texas
278-279, The Planets: Courtesy of NASA/JPL-Caltech
281, Vastitas Borealis impact crater: ESA/DLR/FU Berlin (G. Neukum)

FLAGS AND FACTS
286-287, Richard Laird/Getty Images

SLIPCASE
Daryl Benson/Getty Images

Satellite Image

PAGES 26-27, WorldSat International Inc. and National Geographic Maps

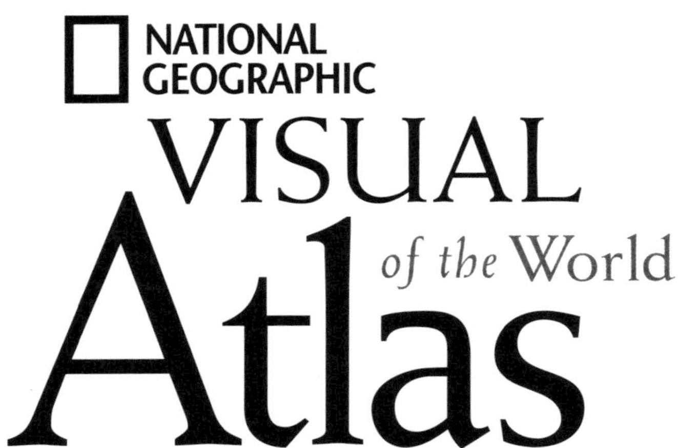
NATIONAL GEOGRAPHIC
VISUAL
Atlas
of the World

PUBLISHED BY THE
NATIONAL GEOGRAPHIC SOCIETY

John M. Fahey, Jr.
President and Chief Executive Officer

Gilbert M. Grosvenor
Chairman of the Board

Tim T. Kelly, President
Global Media Group

John Q. Griffin
President, Publishing

Nina D. Hoffman
Executive Vice President;
President, Book Publishing Group

PREPARED BY THE BOOK DIVISION

Kevin Mulroy
Senior Vice President and Publisher

Marianne R. Koszorus
Director of Design

STAFF FOR THIS ATLAS

Carl Mehler
Project Editor and Director of Maps

Nicholas P. Rosenbach
Supervisor of Map Editing

Laura Exner, Sven M. Dolling, Steven D. Gardner, Thomas L. Gray, and Scott A. Zillmer
Map Editors

Steven D. Gardner, Lee McAulliffe, Gregory Ugiansky, and XNR Productions
Map Researchers

Matt Chwastyk
Map Production Manager

Matt Chwastyk, *Principal;* **Sven M. Dolling, Steven D. Gardner, Michael McNey, Gregory Ugiansky, Martin S. Walz, and XNR Productions**
Map Production

Tibor G. Tóth
Map Relief

David B. Miller
Contributing Geographer

Kevin P. Allen, *Director of Map Services;* **Richard W. Bullington,** *Project Manager;* **Michael J. Horner,** *Manager, Database Editorial;* **Derek Azar and Theodore A. Sickly,** *GIS Analysts*
National Geographic Maps, GIS Support

Chris Carroll, Kevin G. Craig, Daniel Griswold, Matthew J. Jewell, K.M. Kostyal, Whitney Smith, and Robert Tilling
Contributing Writers

Victoria Garrett Jones, Judith Klein, and Jane Sunderland
Text Editors

Marty Ittner, *Principal;* **Nicole DiPatrizio**
Book Design

Meredith Wilcox
Administrative Director, Photography

Lee McAuliffe
Photography Editor

Jennifer A. Thornton
Managing Editor

R. Gary Colbert
Production Director

Michael Horenstein
Production Manager

MANUFACTURING AND QUALITY CONTROL

Christopher A. Liedel
Chief Financial Officer

Phillip L. Schlosser
Vice President

Chris Brown
Technical Director

Nicole Elliott and Rachel Faulise
Managers

Reproduction by Quad/Graphics, Alexandria, Virginia
Printed and Bound by Mondadori S.p.A., Verona, Italy

NATIONAL GEOGRAPHIC SOCIETY
INCORPORATED A.D. 1888

Founded in 1888, the National Geographic Society is one of the largest nonprofit scientific and educational organizations in the world. It reaches more than 285 million people worldwide each month through its official journal, *National Geographic*, and its four other magazines; the National Geographic Channel; television documentaries; radio programs; films; books; videos and DVDs; maps; and interactive media. National Geographic has funded more than 8,000 scientific research projects and supports an education program combating geographic illiteracy.

For more information, please call 1-800-NGS LINE (647-5463) or write to the following address:

National Geographic Society
1145 17th Street N.W.
Washington, D.C. 20036-4688 U.S.A.

Visit us online at
www.nationalgeographic.com/books

For information about special discounts for bulk purchases, please contact National Geographic Books Special Sales: **ngspecsales@ngs.org**

For rights or permissions inquiries, please contact National Geographic Books Subsidiary Rights: **ngbookrights@ngs.org**

For more information about all our award-winning National Geographic atlases, please visit **www.shopng.com/atlases**

Printed in Italy